MW00799450

To Survive and Excel

To Survive and Excel

by
William B. Jones

Southwestern University
Georgetown, Texas

First Edition, 2006

This book is made possible by a generous grant from The Brown Foundation, Inc., of Houston, Texas.

Library of Congress Cataloging-in-Publication Data

Jones, William B.

To survive and excel : the story of Southwestern University, 1840–2000 / by William B. Jones ; foreword by Jake B. Schrum.

p. cm.

Includes bibliographical references and index.

ISBN 0-9670912-4-1 (alk. paper)

1. Southwestern University (Georgetown, Tex.)—History. I. Title.

LD5143.J66 2006

378.764'289—DC22

2006043655

Endsheet: The University Building (Administration Building, Cullen Building) in 1904. Hyer operated as Regent out of his physics office adjacent to the physics lab on the first floor at the southeast corner of the building. During the Fleming years, it once again became the Office of the President. Southwestern University, Special Collections.

Frontispiece: The Main Building at Southwestern donated by the Georgetown College Trustees in 1873 to procure the University for the town. The third story was added in 1881. Williams Elementary School now occupies the site. From Mary Katherine Metcalfe Earney, ed., *For God and Texas: Autobiography of Francis Asbury Mood, 1830–1884*.

Jacket and text design by Tom Dawson

Printed in Singapore by CS Graphics PTE LTD

10 9 8 7 6 5 4 3 2 1

To Carol,
My Wife of 53 Years,
And My Four Children,
Rebeca, Débora, Judith, and Dean,
All Southwestern Graduates

Contents

Foreword

SINCE HIS ARRIVAL AT SOUTHWESTERN IN 1965, William B. Jones has spent a great part of his career discovering a way to put the University in perspective. In the modern era, no one is more familiar with the struggles and joys of Southwestern's journey than Bill Jones. Therefore, in 2000, when Roy B. Shilling, Jr., invited Bill to write a new history of Southwestern, he chose not only an extraordinary historian, but also a person who for most of the past half century has played a significant role in making that history.

To Survive and Excel: The Story of Southwestern University, 1840–2000 tells the compelling saga of how a struggling Methodist-related college on the Texas frontier became one of the top 100 liberal arts colleges in America. These pages are filled with facts and human figures weaving a story that is especially meaningful to all who love and admire Southwestern. Those who have heard somewhat mythical stories about the history of Texas' first University, chartered in 1840 by the Republic of Texas under the name Rutersville College, will now know the details of each carefully researched vignette.

The University's financial struggles, the beginning of its serious engagement with difficult societal issues, and its strategic decision to concentrate on undergraduate liberal arts education preceded the present era in which Larry Milas, former President of the F. W. Olin Foundation, New York City, said, "Southwestern's is a remarkable story and one that should be a required case study for all other colleges."

Finally, if one is interested in the history of private, church-related education in Texas, this book will serve as a constant reference point. However, if you already have some knowledge and care about Southwestern's rich and meaningful history in the development of quality higher education in Texas, please set aside a significant portion of time to read *To Survive and Excel: The Story of Southwestern University, 1840–2000* because when you begin, you will not want to put it down.

Upon completion of this new history, the Southwestern Board of Trustees chose to bestow the honorary title of University Historian on William B. Jones. It is a designation that is richly deserved. An official 1996 alumni survey asked respondents to identify the most "revered" and influential teacher/mentor impacting her or his Southwestern educational experience. Bill Jones was overwhelmingly identified as that person. As I visit alumni across the country, many inquire, "How is Dr. Jones?"

I join countless others who love Southwestern and want to know more about its place in history in applauding William B. Jones for this magnificent volume.

JAKE B. SCHRUM

14th President of Southwestern University

Introduction

... [Once] the historian [has] abandoned the false analogy with the natural sciences and admitted that history involves no special concepts or terminology, he will see that his task is to "explain" history in much the same way he explains events in ordinary life, and with much the same language.

Willie Morris, *North toward Home*, 1967, p. 393

THE TITLE OF THIS BOOK IS TAKEN FROM A COLLECT composed by Dr. Farley W. Snell, Southwestern University Chaplain, for the Inauguration of President Roy B. Shilling, Jr., in 1982. The same Collect was subsequently used at the Inauguration of President Jake B. Schrum in 2001. It begins: "We celebrate the heritage and the vision of Southwestern University, its determination *to survive and excel* . . ."

To Survive and Excel. That phrase, to my mind, sums up the history of Southwestern as well as any I have encountered. For its first hundred years, from 1840 to about 1949, its history is a story of survival. The University survives one crisis after another. Since 1949 the story has not been one of survival but rather of becoming an excellent institution of higher education, one that is known and respected at the national level. This latter "becoming" is in itself a kind of crisis as well, not the same kind of crisis as those that beset the school earlier, but a crisis nonetheless. The crisis now is that of defining how a Church-related institution with Texas roots can transform itself into a nationally known institution while remaining true to its heritage.

The five specific crises of Southwestern around which this book revolves are: (1) that of creating a vision for Methodist higher education in the new Republic of Texas; (2) that of taking the charters of four moribund frontier colleges and melding them into a central university for Texas Methodism; (3) that of losing its central university status in the newly emerging urban Texas just after the beginning of the twentieth century; (4) that of seeking a new sense of direction while surviving the threat of bankruptcy in the Great Depression of the 1930s; and (5) that of the definitive establishment of the liberal arts and sciences direction being followed today and sustained by a strong resource base.

As I studied these crises, I was more and more impressed by the fact that, in all of them, individuals rather than institutional or societal forces were the most important factors in their resolution. In the four crises of survival, devoted persons simply would not let the vision or the institution die. In the fifth crisis, that of determining the kind of excellence Southwestern is to display in the world of today, particular persons provided the resources and reworked the old vision that is propelling the institution forward into the twenty-first century.

With this in mind, I decided to use a different paradigm for the history of the University than that generally used when writing the history of a school. Rather than focusing on institutional elements, such as academic philosophy, curriculum, organizations, and presidential administrations, I focus on individuals and the human dimension. Institutional and social elements are important but secondary emphases. This focus leads to the subtitle of the book—*The Story of Southwestern University, 1840–2000.*

Writing the book in this fashion makes it more a story than an analytical history. It is the story of individuals whose service to the University made it possible for it to survive and excel when an objective assessment of its situation at given points might have prognosticated failure. It is not, however, simply the story of important individuals. Some presidents, for example, do not get as much space as teachers or trustees whose lives are not so well known. Some persons are included because their careers reflect a facet of the character of the institution that might not be revealed were the test of renown to be applied to them. Various teachers, alumni, and friends, who might not ordinarily have been featured, receive significant treatment because they were the burden bearers, carrying on the ordinary responsibilities of the University day after day without much subsequent recognition or applause. Other persons receive treatment not so much because they were important in and of themselves as because they represent a genre of persons whose collective contributions were essential to the institution.

This focus on Southwestern's past means that many things have been left out about which the reader might desire more information. The reader might also desire to study some of the facts used in the book from an angle other than that chosen by me. Fortunately for that reader, there is already a history covering the years up to 1961 written by Ralph Wood Jones, a professor at Southwestern for fifteen years beginning in 1946–1947. Published during the centennial year of Southwestern's establishment in Georgetown, it is entitled *Southwestern University, 1840–1961* (Austin: Jenkins Publishing Co., 1973). Originally written as a doctoral dissertation, it carries Southwestern's history through the Finch administration. Ralph Jones supplemented it with a short chapter covering the Fleming years up until the date of its publication. Written before the advent of computers, the Internet, and the splendid library resources available today, the history by Ralph Jones still needs to be consulted. I have referenced him in this book where the matter is one of significance and/or where it is necessary to avoid the possible charge of plagiarism.

I also want to note the fine contribution to the history of Southwestern University made by Dr. Judson S. Custer, Dr. Martha M. Allen, and Dr. Norman Spellmann. As Professor and Chair of the Education Department for forty years, from 1949–1950 through 1988–1989, Custer played an important role in preserving many University records that would have otherwise been lost. He was also instrumental in establishing the Mood-Heritage Museum that from the mid-1970s to the mid-'90s annually honored persons significant in the early history of the University by printing brief biographical tracts of their lives and work. I owe him a special debt of gratitude for the books he kindly furnished me from his own personal library gathered over the years. I shared with him some of the early chapters of this work before his death in 2003. Dr. Allen was my colleague in the History Department. Whereas Dr. Custer preserved many of the records from the long ago past, Dr. Allen was particularly instrumental in preserving records from the immediate past. She provided an incalculable service in writing up the story of the Negro Fine Arts School. Using the techniques of oral history, she also taped long interviews, later transcribed, with former Presidents Finch and Fleming in the early 1990s, thus providing us with an opportunity to hear them reflect on their own times. She also encouraged students in some of her classes to use the oral history technique to interview persons of lesser fame in Southwestern's history whose experiences and observations lend color to the story. The work of Dr. Norman Spellmann was very important. He provided information in his writings about the four root colleges and about the integration controversy of the 1950s and '60s. His biography of Bishop A. Frank Smith, covering the years from just before 1900 until the early 1960s, was of immense value.

Four other persons need to be recognized for their roles in making a full history of Southwestern possible. They are Francis Asbury Mood, Claude Carr Cody, Margaret Mood McKennon, and Pearl Alma Neas. All four of them kept meticulous scrapbooks covering Southwestern's history from the 1850s to about 1960. The plethora of letters, newspaper articles, and other printed material found in these materials provides written sources for almost every decade through 1960. The scrapbooks are kept today in the Special Collections section of the A. Frank Smith, Jr., Library Center. The custodians of those scrapbooks and many other valuable materials I consulted are Kathryn Stallard, Head, Special Collections, and Sheran Johle, Library Assistant, Special Collections. Without Kathryn's and Sheran's guidance to these and other resource materials, this book would have been seriously incomplete. They knew the materials available for the project and constantly shared that knowledge with me. I shared with them each chapter as it was written and had full confidence that I had dealt with all the material available in Special Collections if the chapters passed muster with them.

On one occasion, when I was lamenting to President Shilling the fact that there were no scrapbooks for modern times comparable to those of earlier times, he revealed that he had been keeping his own set of scrapbooks. He kindly lent them to me for use in composing this work. Francie Schroeder, Assistant to the President, also deserves special recognition with regard to sources. She made available the extraordinary index done by her of the presidential archives dating from about 1940 now kept in an Austin storage facility. She ordered the files sent up from storage, as they were needed.

A special word of thanks is due to Dr. T. Walter Herbert, Herman Brown Professor of English and University Scholar at Southwestern. He read every word of every chapter. Without trying to change the style of the book, he offered valuable suggestions for improving its argument at several significant points and its readability at many points. His interested, frank, yet gentle approach was a marvelous inducement for completing the project. Richard Anderson, Mary Ann Barbour, Douglas Benold, Ed Lansford, Jr., David Medley, Farley Snell, Clara Scarbrough, and Norman Spellmann also read sections of the manuscript where their knowledge was particularly relevant.

I also want to thank George Ann Ratchford for her work in turning my manuscript into a book. Her dedication to the project, management skills, and quiet suggestions over the course of almost a year were very important in guiding the enterprise to a successful conclusion.

President Schrum and President Emeritus Shilling read each chapter as it was produced. Their comments were never self-serving, and they never tried to quash the inclusion of any subject or event. At the age of ninety-four, President Finch read the five chapters related to his participation in the University. His precise recall of events was amazing, and his objectivity in appraising them was extraordinary. Harriett Vivion read the chapter covering the administration of her father, Dr. King Vivion. The task of reading the text regarding the administration of Dr. Durwood Fleming fell to his son, Dr. Jon Hugh Fleming.

The book would not have been written at all except for the suggestion of Dr. Roy B. Shilling, Jr. After overcoming my reluctance to do it, he broached the idea to the Board of Trustees, which in turn voted to support it. He then carried the idea to Mrs. Isabel Brown Wilson, daughter of George and Alice Brown, and herself a former trustee of the University. She graciously obtained a grant from The Brown Foundation, Inc., in 1999 that covered the expenses of composition. Subsequently, in 2006 The Brown Foundation, once again at her behest, agreed to complete the entire funding for the project. In conclusion, I must pay special thanks to President Jake Schrum for his interest in picking up the project after the retirement of Dr. Shilling. The handwritten notes and personal words of encouragement from the President, who once sat in my classroom as a student, have been heartwarming.

William B. Jones
Professor Emeritus of History
Executive Vice President Emeritus
Southwestern University
January 23, 2006

THE VISION

1840–1873

Martin Ruter's Vision for Texas

Missionaries for Texas

Methodist higher education in Texas was born in the missionary venture of Martin Ruter, who crossed the Sabine River into Texas on November 23, 1837. A few Methodists were to be found among the settlers in Texas as early as 1815, and a few circuit riders had already begun their rounds, ministering to small household congregations that met here and there, but until Ruter's mission the Methodist Episcopal Church in the United States had not officially sent ministers to Texas. Ruter's coming was the first such endeavor.

The reason for the effort at this juncture was the recent victory by Sam Houston and his little army over Santa Anna at San Jacinto a little more than a year earlier, resulting in the independence of Texas from Mexico and the formation of a new Republic. News of the victory of April 21, 1836, came to Cincinnati, Ohio, while the General Conference, the governing body of the Methodist Episcopal Church, was in session there. Caught up in the enthusiasm for Texas, Dr. Ruter, a delegate from the Pittsburgh Annual Conference, volunteered to go to Texas as a missionary. Writing later about his decision, Ruter said: "I offered myself as a missionary in Texas. . . . The Superintendents . . . believed that the unsettled condition of the country, in reference to its political relations, was not suitable for the immediate establishment of the mission, but that in all probability it might be within a few months. . . . I felt a strong desire to be useful in that distant land."[1]

Early in 1837 the Missionary Society of the Church felt that conditions had stabilized sufficiently for the establishment of a Texas Mission and asked Bishop Elijah Hedding to appoint several missionaries for it. Hedding, who knew Ruter well and remembered his earlier "offer," sent him a letter naming him Superintendent of the mission and appointed two other persons who had also volunteered to go with him. They were Littleton Fowler of the Tennessee Conference and Robert Alexander of the Mississippi Conference. Though Ruter's vision would inspire the formation of Rutersville College, the first college in Texas, Fowler would play an important role in the establishment of Methodism in Texas. Ruter and Fowler would die at relatively young ages, at fifty-three and forty-four, respectively. Alexander, the only one of the three to live beyond 1846, would link these first official missionaries to the establishment of Rutersville College in 1840 and to its successor, Southwestern University, in 1873. He served on the governing boards of both institutions.

Martin Ruter, superintendent of the first official Methodist Episcopal mission in Texas. He died after six months in the field. He established the vision of having a central Methodist institution of higher education for Texas. Southwestern University, Special Collections.

Conditions in Texas

In the spring of 1837, the same year the three missionaries entered Texas, an anonymous Southerner, currently then residing in Ohio, made a six-month trip through Texas, entering by ship at Galveston Bay and traveling by land to Houston, San Antonio, and places in between. His description of the country and its society is useful because it overlaps the entry of Ruter, Fowler, and Alexander. He passed by San Jacinto and described the battlefield within a year of the battle. He mentions particularly that travelers feared encountering scattered groups of Mexican soldiers still trying to return home and Indians who occasionally swooped down on isolated groups.[2] Ruter mentioned in one of his letters a few months later that while traveling near Bastrop he saw "six graves of persons whom the Indians had recently killed and robbed."[3]

The city of Houston, where a few months later Ruter would make the acquaintance of President Lamar and General Houston,[4] was in the process of being laid out. By late March "improvements consisted of a one story frame [building], two hundred feet or more in length, which had just been raised, intended by the enterprising proprietors for stores and public offices, several rough log cabins, two of which were occupied as taverns, a few linen tents which were used for groceries, together with three or four shanties made of poles set in the ground and covered and weather-boarded with rough split shingles." The four or five hundred people lived mostly in linen tents until houses could be built, "which gave to the city the appearance of a Methodist camp-ground."[5]

Dissipation, uncharacteristic of a Methodist camp-ground, was rampant, particularly as to the consumption of alcohol, which "was reduced to a system and had its own laws and regulations." Gambling was carried on to such an extent that Congress, during its spring session, prescribed severe penalties for those who engaged in it even though "those who passed the law were the most active in breaking it."[6]

In spite of the low state of public morals described by the anonymous traveler, early attempts were being made to improve them and to bring the practice of religion to the people. He heard, he says, "the first sermon that was ever preached in Houston." The announcement that a sermon was to be preached was a novelty and "excited general attention. All resolved to attend that they might at least have the satisfaction in after days of saying it was their lot to have heard the first Christian service that was ever performed in the new capital of Texas." Beneath the shade of some trees that grew on the edge of town, Zacariah N. Morrell, a Baptist elder with a colorful subsequent career, preached to the assembled crowd on March 26, 1837.[7] Martin Ruter would preach twice in Congress Hall on December 17 later that year.[8]

An Uncommon Circuit Rider

Though Methodist circuit riders were almost always better educated than the frontier people to whom they ministered, their level of culture was not appreciated by many people in more settled areas, particularly by the New England clergymen among whom Ruter, a native of Massachusetts, lived his early years. Even Bishop Asbury, an early circuit rider and the first Methodist bishop, was treated with studied contempt by the faculty and students of Yale College after a preaching service in New Haven.[9]

Ruter, however, was different. In spite of his lack of a college degree, due to the penurious circumstances of his family, his educational attainments resulting from private study were widely recognized, and some writers maintain that he was the best-educated Methodist of his day.[10] He became pastor of St. George's Church in Philadelphia, the largest structure in the Methodist Church, received two honorary degrees, an M.A. and a D.D., and became president of two colleges—Augusta College and Allegheny College. Augusta College was the first and for many years the only chartered Methodist school of collegiate rank in

St. George's Church, Philadelphia, Pennsylvania, where the first Methodist Annual Conference in America was held in 1773. Martin Ruter was one of its early pastors. From Olin W. Nail, ed., *Texas Methodist Centennial Yearbook 1834–1934*.

the world. During his administration, it graduated the first class of Bachelor of Arts students ever to be graduated from a Methodist college.

So far as is known, Ruter is the first American-born Methodist preacher to be awarded an honorary degree.[11] It is a commentary on the Church of the time that, after he received the D.D. degree from Transylvania University in Lexington, Kentucky, attempts were made at the 1832 General Conference to enact a rule prohibiting Methodist ministers from accepting honorary degrees. "But," comments one author, "as the debate on the memorials [to enact the rule] progressed, it was apparent that the preachers wanted more degrees, not fewer." Commenting on the degree himself, Ruter is reported to have said that "while the degree had not made him any wiser or better, the recognition had helped to allay the contempt often shown toward Methodists by some educated people."[12]

Books and Self-Education

Ruter followed a plan of self-education throughout his life. He read widely in English literature and the classics and was especially apt in languages. He acquired a working knowledge of Greek, Latin, Hebrew, Chaldee, and French. His French, which he spoke well, in which he read widely, and which he taught at Augusta College, was learned during a pastoral appointment to Montreal during his early years in the ministry. While at Augusta College he published a *A Conjugation of French Regular Verbs* for his classes.[13] He also studied Hebrew under a rabbi in Montreal and later wrote a Hebrew grammar for students, who, like himself, might not have the privilege of learning it in school.[14] While he was Book Agent in Cincinnati, his proficiency in Hebrew and Chaldee caused him to be offered the professorship of Oriental literature by Cincinnati College, but he was too devoted to the work of the Church to accept.[15]

The self-education forced upon Ruter by the circumstances of his life did not diminish his appreciation for higher learning. He was an advocate of theological education and one of the proponents of resolutions passed at the General Conferences of 1820 and 1824 saying that each of the Annual Conferences in Methodism should have "at least one literary institution."[16] American Methodists, who had no college graduates among their early members, were anxious to rectify this deficiency rapidly. Wilbur Fisk, who graduated from Brown University in 1818, is said to have been the first American Methodist preacher to receive an earned college degree from an American institution.[17] He was the principal founder of Wesleyan Academy and Wesleyan University in Connecticut.

Along the way to his presidency at Allegheny College, where the events of 1836 in Texas found him, Ruter had also served for eight years (1820–1828) as Book Agent for the Methodist Book Concern in Cincinnati. It was one of the most important positions in the Church of that day. The Cincinnati that Ruter knew was called the "Queen City of the West" and was the most important center in the West for book publishing and distribution, especially of textbooks. Ruter himself wrote and published several. In addition to his Hebrew grammar, he wrote an *Arithmetick*,[18] for which his publishers secured the recommendation, printed on the flyleaf, of William H. McGuffey, author of the popular series of school reading and spelling books known by his name. He also published two other textbooks—*The New American Primer* and *The New American Spelling Book.* Claude Carr Cody says that he also published "a collection of *Miscellaneous Pieces*, extracted from the best English authors, intended to cultivate a taste for reading among the young people of the Church."[19]

Ruter began his writing career, however, not with textbooks but with a series of religious tracts. The first was a little pamphlet in 1811. This was followed by a series of doctrinal tracts over Calvinism for the edification of Methodists faced with the necessity of defending Wesley's Arminianism against the formidable system of the French reformer. In 1814 he published a nineteen-page *Sketch of Calvin's Life and Doctrines.* This work, says Cody, caused a sensation in the community in which it was published.[20] It called forth a reply entitled *Defense of Calvin and Calvinism* from a certain Francis Brown, pastor of a church in North Yarmouth. The next year Ruter replied with a sixty-four-page *Letter addressed to Rev. Francis Brown . . . containing an Answer.* Brown responded again, whereon Ruter issued a sixty-two-page rejoinder entitled *Reply to Rev. Francis Brown, President of Dartmouth College, Containing Animadversions on his Second Publication in favor of Calvin and Calvinism.*[21] By now, however, the pastor with whom he had maintained the controversy had become President of Dartmouth College and was involved in a more famous controversy, the Dartmouth College case, being heard by the United States Supreme Court. Ruter had inadvertently touched the fringes of one of the most famous judicial cases in early American corporate law. In it Daniel Webster successfully argued for Dartmouth that Dartmouth was a private rather than a public entity and that the state of New Hampshire did not have regulatory power over it. The verdict had far-reaching consequences, since it limited the control a state government may have over a corporate charter. It is the occasion when Webster made his famous statement "It is, Sir, as I have said, a small college. And, yet there are those who love it!"[22] Brown, in his new position, with his heavy responsibilities, had little interest in pursuing the contest over the merits of Calvinism with his relatively little-known opponent. The tract writing ended.

Ruter's other religious writings were more positive. His first work, the small pamphlet of 1811 referred to above entitled the *Ninth Chapter of Romans*, was an attempt to help people understand Paul's rather dense argument on Israel's unbelief. His *History of Martyrs* was written to encourage them to emulate the faith of the Christian heroes of the past. His most often published and most widely distributed book was *A Concise History of the Christian Church*.[23] He states in the long title and in the preface that the book was a condensation of an earlier two-volume work by George Gregory published toward the end of the eighteenth century and that he had "extended and corrected" it in a number of ways, particularly by adding more emphasis on missionary work and by bringing it up to date.[24] It was printed at least three times (1834, 1840, 1845) and became the standard textbook of Christian history for Methodist preachers in America for nearly half a century.[25]

By 1836, the year he volunteered to go to Texas, Ruter was one of the most widely known and important men in the Methodist Episcopal Church. He was elected regularly by his colleagues to represent them at General Conferences; he had served as pastor of a major urban congregation; he was a fine preacher known for his powerful sermons that attracted large crowds; he had served as president of two colleges; he had been the principal leader of the Book Concern of the Church in the "West"; he was the author of books and tracts, both religious and secular; he was esteemed for his fine mind and learning, particularly in languages; and he was a major force in promoting Methodist education, particularly higher education, in all its forms. When he left Allegheny College in early 1837 for Texas, he was giving up all the emoluments from these recognitions and accomplishments for the uncertainties of a frontier life that would claim his life in little more than a year. Many tried to dissuade him from going, but he would not be deterred. He was determined to answer the call made by William Barret Travis for the Methodist Church to send some "educated and talented young preachers" to Texas.[26] He was a member of a generation that made the Methodist Episcopal Church a "militant evangelistic force."[27]

Ruter in Texas

Surrounded by the nervous enthusiasm of an assembled group of students and citizens of Meadville, Martin Ruter pushed off for Texas on a flatboat with his family and belongings on a July day in 1837. He poled the craft down French Creek to where it joined the Allegheny, which in turn emptied into the Ohio. Arriving at New Albany, Indiana, he remained for several months with two brothers who lived there. A yellow fever epidemic along the southern reaches of the Mississippi River made him postpone his departure until the early frost had broken it. He used this interval to visit local congregations, to attend Annual Conferences, and to supply himself for the mission. Leaving his wife and family in New Albany with the two brothers, he and David Ayres, a Methodist layman returning to Texas from the East, took a steamer down the Ohio and Mississippi Rivers. With all the delays, the trip from Pennsylvania to San Augustine, his first Texas destination, took a little over four months.

Robert Alexander, who had preceded Ruter to Texas, met him as he entered the Republic. Ironically, Alexander

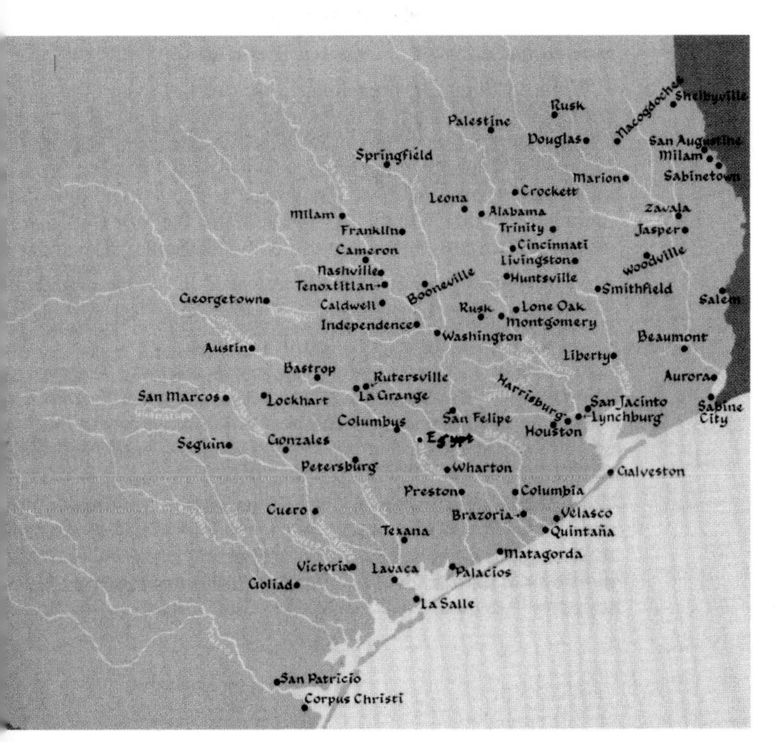

Map of early Texas towns. From Walter N. Vernon, et al., *The Methodist Excitement in Texas*. Used by permission of the Archives, Center for Methodist Studies at Bridwell Library, Perkins School of Theology, Southern Methodist University.

Robert Alexander served under Ruter as one of the three official missionaries from the Methodist Episcopal Church to the Republic of Texas. He was a trustee of Rutersville College, of Soule University, and of Southwestern University. From Walter N. Vernon, et al., *The Methodist Excitement in Texas*. Used by permission of the Archives, Center for Methodist Studies at Bridwell Library, Perkins School of Theology, Southern Methodist University.

was going east to Natchez to attend the Mississippi Conference, to which the work in Texas was adjoined, and had just crossed the Sabine River when he learned that he had missed Ruter going west to San Augustine. He turned back, and the two met at Gaines's Ferry on the Sabine.[28] Each proceeded in his original direction after spending almost the entire night discussing the work they were just beginning.[29]

Leaving San Augustine, Ruter carried on an active preaching and personal ministry, forming Sunday Schools and small congregations, while traveling through Nacogdoches, Washington, San Felipe, and Fort Bend on the way to Houston. Houston, the new capital of the Republic, was his destination. There he remained a week, where he "became acquainted," he says, "with the place, people, members of the Legislature, officers, etc." He met with President Lamar and General Houston and "got the promise of their cooperation for an educational institution for Texas youth."[30] He arrived on Friday, December 15, and met with Littleton Fowler, who had already been there for about a month. [31] On Sunday he preached morning and evening in Congress Hall. He preached before good congregations, among which were members of Congress and officers of the government.[32]

In spite of the apparent success of his first few days in Houston, one Methodist there was not sanguine about his long-term prospects. Henry Matthews, a former Ohio circuit rider now practicing as a physician in Texas, commented in his diary after a cordial meeting with Ruter and Fowler: "I do most deliberately look upon the religious prospects of this country as unpromising, peculiarly so, and I base my opinion upon near one year's close observation & experience, yet I will regard these servants of the Church in the light of superiors & be obedient."[33]

Ruter's Educational Vision for Texas

Preaching was not Ruter's only activity. Everywhere he went he imbued the people with a sense of urgency about the need for education. David Ayres says:

> Dr. Ruter did not confine his labors and thoughts to preaching and orgnizing [sic] societies. His enlightened and sagacious mind saw the importance of establishing educational facilities for the country. His grand plan was, to establish a good school, of the ordinary kind in every settlement, and to lay the foundation for one Central University for all Texas. His plan for the latter was, to establish an Academy, or High School, in a central location, and concentrate the attention and interest of the growing Methodist Church in Texas upon it, until it should be gradually developed into a College, and finally into a University in fact. *It is a remarkable fact, that the location he had chosen for this University for all Texas, after a careful and patient examination of the country, was only six miles south of the present site of Soule University, at Chappell Hill, Washington county* [italics in original]. He conversed frequently and long with the writer [Ayres] on this subject, and in the last conversation they ever had, it was arranged that a donation of a half league of land was to be made for the location of the institution. It is a mistake that he chose the present site of Ruterville; he never saw the place. He frequently said: "You need schools in every settlement, but you need but one University." He was the man who originated that suggestion.[34]

Lydia Ann McHenry, a teacher and prominent Methodist laywoman, who knew Ruter well, wrote a letter of condolence after his death to Mrs. S. R. Campbell, Ruter's daughter in Mississippi. In it she describes Ruter's success in winning the interest of leading Texans in establishing an institution of higher learning. She says that he

> was encouraged by many of the leading men of the country to establish such a seat of learning . . . [and that] . . . liberal offers were made by several large landholders, until some six or seven leagues [one square league = 4,428.4 acres] were pledged for the benefit of

> the institution, in the event of his removing to Texas. He went so far as to draw up several articles of a charter to be presented to the next Congress, styling the contemplated institution *Bastrop University* [italics in the original], intending to locate it at Bastrop.[35]

To show his good intentions, she says, Ruter purchased land and began to arrange his family affairs to move to Texas after a return to some Eastern and Northern cities to plead the cause of Texas. "With him," she continues, "originated the idea of establishing such an institution of learning in Texas as should qualify the youth of the country for filling stations of honor and usefulness, without their being compelled to go out of the country [the Republic of Texas] for education."[36]

The difference between McHenry and Ayres as to where Ruter intended to establish his institution of higher learning is puzzling. The two writers knew each other well. In fact, McHenry established her school in the home of David Ayres.[37] Yet the two locations for the school mentioned by them—Bastrop and just south of Chappell Hill—are about sixty-five miles apart. One wonders if perhaps Ayres, writing almost twenty years after the fact, at the time when the Methodist Conferences were pulling away from Rutersville, may not be "making a case" for the correctness of this move in favor of Soule University, which had just been established by the Church. His negative comment about Rutersville—"It is a mistake that he [Ruter] chose the present site of Ruterville; he never saw the place"—may be an instance of special pleading. Yet each writer makes his or her statement authoritatively. In a letter to his daughter on January 9, 1838, Ruter says that the areas around Independence and Bastrop "are the two places which I have thought might be kept in view, if we all come to Texas."[38] It is quite possible, since the letter shows that Ruter liked both the Independence/Chappell Hill and Bastrop areas, that either Ayres or McHenry might have remembered his or her conversation with Ruter about the location for the college as being more definitive than he intended it to be.

Using land donations to endow his new university was the technique used by Ruter to entice cash-poor Texans to establish the school. Writing to the Missionary Society in New York, he says:

> It has appeared to me that we ought, as soon as practicable, to establish in this Republic a well-endowed University and several subordinate schools of different gradations. In two or three places, subscriptions have been offered sufficient for buildings; and to provide permanent funds, we propose obtaining donations of land. Many of the citizens are extensive landholders, and would, while lands are cheap, make large subscriptions. But as lands are rising in value, a fund thus invested would in a short time be sufficient for the above purposes.[39]

Ruter's vision was not merely to establish a university but to establish schools at every level, whose crown would be an institution of higher learning. Writing from Washington, Texas, he says that the citizens of the town "have a charter for an academy, and are desirous of a female academy first." He describes in the same letter the purpose of his labors in Texas as being "directed for forming societies and circuits, establishing schools, and making arrangements for a college or university."[40] He remarks in another letter that after a trip to the North, he hopes to return "to try to get some churches built, some school-houses commenced, and have a foundation laid for a college."[41] With him originated, according to Ayres, the concept of "one Central [Methodist] university for all Texas." An attempt to actualize this concept would lead to the establishment of Southwestern University in Georgetown a quarter of a century later, but a controversy shortly after the beginning of the twentieth century stripped the Central university idea from Southwestern's mission.

Subsequent Travels and Death

Within two weeks of arriving in Texas, Ruter says he has traveled five or six hundred miles. He considers, he says, the whole Republic of Texas as his district, and he travels incessantly to cover as much of it as he can. He and his colleagues soon established four circuits—Houston, Washington, Trinity, and San Augustine—each with many preaching points, mostly in homes. He comments that the living circumstances of the people are terrible but that "Texas is well adapted for the industrious poor. . . . Indeed, the rich, the poor, the pious, and the impious, seem determined to making this their home."[42] By early winter he mentions that he has traveled 1,200 miles. By early March the number is 1,500, then 2,000, and, in probably his last report (April 26) to the Missionary Society, he says the total is 2,200 miles. That distance in five months since his arrival would be an average of almost 15 miles a day, every day—on horseback, in winter, rain or shine. Homer S. Thrall writes that "the

Doctor rode a large horse, and traveled wherever he went in a sweeping trot."[43]

In spite of the difficulties encountered while traveling during the winter—northers, rain, fording streams, sleeping on the ground—he still has the ability to find majesty in the Texas landscape. He writes to his daughter that Texas "is, in some respects, the most beautiful place I have ever seen. It consists of rolling prairies, and on some of them the prospect is very grand. I presume the horizon, in some directions, is from thirty to fifty miles, and very distant in every direction. It seems almost like the vast ocean. In the spring these rolling lands are not only green with grass, but covered with flowers, and are said to appear like enchanted grounds." Continuing his soliloquy concerning the prairies, he states that "as on the ocean, the horizon is formed by the union of the blue sky with the smooth surface; and when clothed with the verdure of spring, spangled with the richest flowers, and brightened with the sunbeams of heaven, it seems, indeed, a fit place for the assemblies of angels."[44]

By early April, however, shortly after his fifty-third birthday on April 3, he mentions "being afflicted with fever," and the next day is too ill to preach. He rides on but writes that he is still unwell. Almost every day thereafter he mentions the illness in his journal and letters. On the 19th he and a companion begin the projected trip home to his family in New Albany, Indiana. After several days he is too sick to journey on, and, encouraging his companion to go on alone, he turns around for the forty-five-mile ride back to Washington. He is feverish and mentions that the ailment is settling in his lungs. Writing twenty years later, his daughter calls it "typhoid pneumonia."[45] Though her diagnosis combines what today are commonly conceived of as two entirely separate diseases, the information at her disposal makes her diagnosis not unreasonable for the times. Confined to bed, Ruter writes that "his travels may have been too great for his strength."[46]

After arriving back in Washington, he lingers for twenty-four days, attended by two physicians who, with their wives, give him every attention. He takes considerable medicine, and they bleed him in an attempt to break the fever. But nothing seems to work. On learning of the illness, Robert Alexander visits him and finds him so ill that he stays a week. Forced to return home, he is himself attacked by a fever and is not well enough to return until after Ruter's death. During the same time, Fowler, in Houston, is also ill with chills and fevers. A letter to his future wife in Nacogdoches is a commentary on the health conditions of the times in the area. He calls Houston a "House of Death."[47]

In his last days Ruter tries to complete his affairs. He writes a final letter to his wife on April 23, telling her about his aborted attempt to return home, and tries to be candid about his condition without alarming her unduly. He makes plans with Alexander for the continuance of the work and on April 26 makes a frank report of his physical condition to the Missionary Society.

He dies on May 16 and is buried by his Texas friends in the little cemetery in Washington. Alexander writes to Fowler that "he has never had anything afflict him as much, not even the death of his own dear father." He says that he and Dr. Manley, a Methodist lay preacher and one of the attending physicians, are raising "money to pay his funeral expenses and to erect a decent monument or tomb over the grave." They intend to send to New Orleans for a fine marble slab.[48] They did, indeed, place such a slab over his grave with a beautiful inscription memorializing Ruter's life and accomplishments.[49] Littleton Fowler, visiting the grave with a friend about a year later, writes: "I never had such strange feelings of sorrow and affliction. Dr. Ruter was a great and good man. Texas has lost one of her best friends and our church one of the best ministers, in his strange and mysterious death."[50]

Ruter's Contribution

Ruter did not live to see the fruition of his educational vision, not even its commencement. At the time of his death he and his colleagues estimated that they had twenty societies, twelve local preachers, and 325 members.[51] They had built no schools of any sort. Yet the seed had been planted. Henceforward his name would be connected in the minds of those who followed him with the concept that the mission of the Church on the frontier includes education of the people. He was, in addition, an example of the kind of person Christian education could produce—learned, informed, high-minded, generous, committed, articulate, courageous. He dared to dream beyond the present to what might be and to act decisively to realize his dreams. He was a wise counselor and strong leader for his colleagues and an exemplar for those who succeeded him. Small wonder that when these colleagues and other pioneer Methodists a short time later decided to establish a college in a small town constructed for that purpose that they should name both the college and the town after him—Rutersville College in Rutersville, Texas.

Pursuing the Vision: Rutersville College

Robert Alexander Pursues Ruter's Vision

Though Martin Ruter represented the best the Methodist Episcopal Church had to offer in Eastern "literary" education, he was unable to establish it in concrete form on the Texas frontier. The challenges of nature defeated the ability of his body to endure, and the monument to him in Navasota today is more a memorial to his vision than to his success. Yet his vision did not die. Some of his colleagues and others who honored his memory had been imbued with it and established the first operational institution of higher education chartered by the Republic of Texas.[1]

Only five weeks after Ruter's death, ten persons met to form a mutual and joint stock company.[2] As owners of the company, they would be the Proprietors of a new town to be established six miles north of La Grange named Rutersville. Two of the ten, A. P. Manley and William P. Smith, were the minister-physicians who attended Ruter in his final illness. In a sorrowful letter, Manley had informed Mrs. Ruter of her husband's demise. Robert Alexander, one of the three original missionaries to Texas, had spent a week with him during that final illness and preached the memorial service about a month later. These three persons are the first Proprietors listed in the "Articles of Agreement and Constitution of the Rutersville Company" and were the principal instruments in carrying through the initiative to found a town and establish a college named after Ruter. The other seven Proprietors were active Methodist laymen whose names are found occupying one role or another in early Methodist records.

Alexander in particular, as Ralph Jones says, "kept the spark from dying." He took up Ruter's plans, organized a board of proprietors, that, under his chairmanship, raised funds, elected a president, obtained a charter for the school, and secured a generous grant of land from the Republic so that it could open in 1840.[3] Because he was primarily a preacher without a college degree and never made any pretense of being a schoolman, his role in the development of early Methodist higher education in Texas is easy to undervalue, but he was, in a self-effacing way, one of the important figures in its development. In the educational field, he is the actor who makes small but important appearances in a drama. He remains off stage until called on to play his part, after which he retires to the wings in favor of the lead actors. Alexander came on stage three times and played important roles on each occasion.

Alexander's physical appearance was striking. His six feet five inches brought him instant attention wherever he went, yet his reddish hair and blue eyes indicated a basically gentle nature. Early authors mention that nature, which drew people to him and made them trust his counsel, as much as they mention his height. Nevertheless, stories about him emphasize his courage as well. They may have been embellished in the retelling, but the fact that such stories gathered around him bespeaks his reputation. During his first years in Texas he lived in a rough society, and he coped with it in frontier terms. Washington on the Brazos was so rough that Alexander told a friend he never went there without his pistols.[4]

One of the stories most frequently cited has him holding a worship service on a Sunday morning in a hall above Hatfield's Saloon. He had sent word a few days ahead that he intended to preach there, but the gamblers who customarily met at that time to play cards sent word back that the space was taken. He repeated his announcement and was there Sunday morning as he said he would be. "He walked leisurely into the hall, spoke courteously to the men assembled, assuming that they were there to hear him, though he knew it was not so." When he made preparations to begin the service, a few of the assembled men started to rise and protest but for some reason did not. Twice before beginning the service, he asked those present who did not want to hear the gospel preached to leave, but none did. Once, during his "fire and brimstone sermon," he noticed a commotion. He quietly called for attention, and order was restored. When the service was over, the men came forward, shook his hand, thanked him, made up a purse for him, and told him that if he ever needed money to call on them.[5]

Alexander had been instrumental in precipitating the action that brought Rutersville College into being and had been named a Trustee in the legislative Act of February 5, 1840, chartering it. He also served as its financial agent for a time. When the first catalog was printed at the end of the first session, he was listed as one of the six honorary trustees rather than as one of the eleven regular trustees. His direct involvement in the institution became more occasional as he carried out his ministerial duties. At the point of Methodist severance with the school in 1856, he and the then president of Rutersville College, William Halsey, affiliated themselves with the new official Methodist school, Soule University, Halsey as president, Alexander as trustee.

When Francis Asbury Mood, who became President of Soule after the Civil War, determined that it was no longer viable and conceived his grand plan for a Central university for Texas Methodism, the first person he sought out for advice was Robert Alexander. He, in spite of his doubts about their being able, as he said, to unite five Methodist Conferences on anything, nevertheless became chairman of the Educational Convention of 1870 that formulated and approved the plan for the establishment of what, a few years later, became Southwestern University. Upon its successful conclusion, he took Dr. Mood to the back of the church, embraced him, and tearfully said, "I never expected to live to see this day."[6] In his mind the vision of Ruter for a Central Methodist university was now at the point of fulfillment. He, the only survivor among the first three official Methodist missionaries to Texas, felt that he had now, thirty-three years later, witnessed the realization of a dream.

Establishment of the Town and the Academies

In the summer of 1838 the future Proprietors purchased a league of land [4,428.4 sq. acres] for the new settlement and college. A few of them met on September 23 with the Rev. John Wesley Kenney, a minister-surveyor, who began to survey and lay off lots for the new village.[7] Kenney's Irish mother had been converted under John Wesley's preaching before crossing the Atlantic to America, and he was named after her spiritual mentor. His presence at Rutersville provides a direct link between the eighteenth-century evangelical movement in England and the nineteenth-century movement on the Texas frontier.

Kenney, who had known Martin Ruter in Ohio, moved to Texas with his family in 1833. His house had been burned in the flare-up the year before in Illinois and Wisconsin of Indians trying to avoid eviction from their lands. Though they failed in their bid to avoid resettlement, they were ably led by Black Hawk. The so-called Black Hawk War took his name. Kenney, who had served in it as captain, determined to move to Texas where liberal grants of land were being made to immigrants. By the time Ruter arrived in Texas, Kenney, a former member of the Ohio Conference, had already been preaching here and there. Colonel William Barret Travis attended a camp meeting held by him in 1835 and sent his little son to attend the school taught by Kenney's sister-in-law, Lydia Ann McHenry, in the home of David Ayres, Ruter's traveling companion when he came to Texas.[8] Though he had joined Houston's army during the momentous events of 1836, Kenney received a two-week furlough after the fall of the Alamo and the massacre at Goliad to find a place of safety for his family and did not get back to the army until the day after the Battle of San Jacinto, thus losing the opportunity of being a veteran of that victory.[9]

The prospective college site comprised fifty-two acres, and twenty-four were set aside for the Female Academy. The new town attracted residents immediately, and the educational enterprise got off to a good start. Alexander moved there in October and formed a Methodist circuit for the surrounding area.[10] A clause in property deeds prohibiting gambling and the sale of "ardent spirits" apparently did not deter development. A number of other civic units, including the state, had enacted similar prohibitions with regard to gambling in behalf of good order in the rough society.[11]

Alexander says that the educational plan from the beginning was to establish two academies before April 1839, letting one of them "grow into a college as soon as practical."[12] This plan was in accord with the best educational practice of the time. The academy movement in the United States first began in Philadelphia in 1751. The one established there later grew into the University of Pennsylvania. Academies, with their broader and more practical training, were more appropriate for the new frontier republic than the old Latin grammar schools, with their almost exclusive formal training in classical languages. Where girls were not admitted to instruction with boys, separate academies were established for them with studies calculated to meet their special needs, as people of the time understood them. Instruction at Rutersville in the Female and Preparatory [male] academies, later called departments in the catalogs, was begun in April as planned, with thirty students in attendance under the instruction of the Rev. D. N. V. Sullivan, a local Methodist preacher.[13]

President Chauncey Richardson and the Charter

Little time was lost in securing a leader for the nascent institution. Most surprising is that the school was able to enlist a New Englander who was already President of a Deep South institution in the venture. The reason for this success seems to have been a matter of personal connections.

Ann Catherine Haynie and her new husband, James, moved to La Grange, Texas, from Tuscumbia, Alabama, in 1835, shortly after their marriage. She was the sister of Martha Richardson, the wife of Chauncey Richardson, President of Tuscumbia Female College. James immediately became a successful businessman in La Grange, owning a building in town at what was known as "Haynie's Corner," where he operated a mercantile and produce factoring business.[14] Ann Catherine and James, fervent Methodists, became the link, either directly or by convincing Robert Alexander to be the intermediary, of conveying information about the start-up of Rutersville College to the Richardsons in Tuscumbia. Within a few months, in March 1839, Chauncey and Martha Richardson were on the scene in Rutersville where the trustees, in the words of Robert Alexander, "unanimously elected [him] President of Rutersville College and Academies, and his lady Associate Principal of the Female Academy."[15]

Richardson, born in 1802, had served pastorates in the New England Conference until 1832, when he was forced because of health problems to "locate," that is, in Methodist terminology, to give up the traveling ministry. He used the opportunity, says John H. McLean, to study at Wesleyan University, whose president, Wilbur Fisk, influenced him heavily. While at Middletown, he was elected President of Tuscumbia Female College. He held the position for six years before moving to Texas.[16]

When Richardson and his wife arrived at Rutersville, McLean says, the college "had only a prospective existence being without a charter, without a building, without apparatus and without patronage." Nevertheless, Richardson was enthusiastic about his call to its presidency. His enthusiasm is reflected in a letter written by him on April 26, on his way back to Alabama to prepare for his return. He calls the area a "rich and romantic country" and says that "the college site commands an extensive view of the richest landscape scenery in the world." He likes the town and its people and feels that it is an ideal site. "With commendable zeal and industry," he avers, "Rutersville College can be as richly endowed, even more so, than the oldest institutions in the United States now are. The friends of learning in Texas are numerous, and rich in land and are able to make large donations, in land, to this institution." Without any prompting except for his hopes and dreams, Richardson has already bought into the notion that was to prove so injurious to the school—that possession of land is equivalent to cash on hand and can substitute for a lack of tuition income from a penurious clientele. On one point, however, he was prophetic. At a time when the population of Texas had probably reached no more than 125,000 residents, he foresaw a time when, fully developed, it could "sustain a population of 70 millions of souls."[17]

On arriving permanently at Rutersville in early November, Richardson immediately prepared a charter for the school and went to Austin to help secure its approval. In Congress the idea of chartering a sectarian school was not popular. Nevertheless, it had a strong advocate in the person of Francis Moore, Jr., editor of the *Telegraph and Texas Register*, who represented Harris, Liberty, and Galveston Counties. Moore, as chairman of the committee on education, urged the chartering of Rutersville College and, furthering his particular interest in geology, proposed that geology be included in the school's curriculum.[18] The Act passed by Congress constituted Rutersville College as an institution with a self-perpetuating Board of Trustees in which "the students of all religious denominations shall enjoy equal advantages." It did not mention the word "Methodist."[19] Thus was introduced an element that would eventually weaken the institution. As the initial fervor for establishing the school waned, Methodists became increasingly loath to support an institution not officially connected with the Church that might at any given moment take actions inimical to Church interests or be taken away by a headstrong group of independent trustees.

The College Takes Shape

Classes under the new administration and charter began on February 1, 1840, four days before President Mirabeau B. Lamar officially signed the charter. Physical conditions that winter day were terrible. A norther had blown into Central Texas several days before, and the temperature had dropped in nearby San Felipe from 75° to 31°F in a matter of only twelve hours.[20] Two permanent college buildings were under way, but neither was ready for occupancy. Classes for the approximately twenty-five shivering students who had arrived were begun in one small building. Another was completed near the end of the session for the Female Department. "But both buildings were in a very rude and unfruitful condition."[21]

The number of departments listed in the first catalog, published in 1841 (covering 1840), was nine: Moral Science and Belles Lettres, Mathematics, Natural Science, Ancient Languages and Literature, Modern Languages, Preparatory, Female, Medical, and Law, all with their own individual courses. The number of teachers was three. They were Chauncey Richardson, A.M., President, Charles W. Thomas, A.B., Tutor, and Martha G. Richardson, Preceptress. The disparity between the number of courses to be taught and the number of teachers to teach is obvious. Julia Lee Sinks explains it by saying that "from the force of circumstances most of them [the students] would have to enter the Preparatory Department, and the requirements for entrance into the classical [college] course were set before them only as a mark of a higher calling."[22] No students were listed for the five departments offering classical or collegiate courses, while fifty-four were listed under the Preparatory Department and forty-nine under the Female Department. This number excludes the names of some parents, teachers, and trustees who were also listed under the two departments. Women took the same courses as men. In addition, they might "attend to Music on the Piano-forte, Drawing and Painting."

Elements listed for the Preparatory curriculum were the English Language, Davies' Arithmetic, Davies' Algebra as far as Quadratic Equations, Ancient and Modern Geography, Latin and Greek Grammar, Caesar's Commentaries, Cicero's Select Orations, the Georgics and Aeneid of Virgil, Jacob's Greek Reader, or St. John's Gospel in Greek. However much the term "academy" was used to describe the preparatory work of the school, its close relationship to the old Latin grammar school is evident.

Students with competency in all the preparatory fields were admitted to studies for the Bachelor of Arts degree. Persons obtaining that degree must pass a "thorough and satisfactory examination in the entire classical course." The examination could be taken whenever the student felt ready "without regard to the time he may have been in the college."[23] Of course, the Medical and Law Departments were only dreams in the eyes of the teachers and trustees. Their inclusion was so unrealistic that they were dropped from the second catalog published in 1842 (covering 1841). That catalog listed an increase from three to four faculty members and from 63 to 100 students, 59 males and 41 females.

There would be no catalog for 1843 or thereafter, but *The Telegraph*, published in San Felipe as the official organ of the Republic of Texas, prints an advertisement for the seventh session, on September 23 of that year, containing catalog-like material. It states that the collegiate year is divided into two terms of twenty-one weeks, the first beginning on the third Monday of January, and the second on the third Monday of July. Each term is followed by a five-week vacation, making a total of fifty-two weeks, forty-two weeks of classes, ten weeks of vacation.[24]

During the first several years, however, interruptions because of Indian attacks were a repeated problem, so much so that one student in later years said that the older boys "did little but hunt Indians." On one occasion two of the students, while hunting, were attacked by Indians. One of them, Henry Earthman, was killed. His brother, Fields, escaped to the school. His companions immediately searched for the body, which they found "dreadfully mutilated" about a mile away. Almost all the boys, ranging in age from fourteen to sixteen, joined in a pursuit of the Indians that lasted about three weeks.[25]

The first catalog states that in addition to the 17,776 acres given by the state and the 76 acres set aside in Rutersville for the college and Female Department campuses, the school had received donations of 24,237 acres of land from forty-six donors and twenty-four town lots of undetermined size from four donors. There is also a list of forty-two financial donors, followed by a list of ten persons who had donated a total of about a hundred books. Governor James K. Polk of Tennessee, soon-to-be President, under whom Texas would be admitted to the Union, had donated ten books. The list of donors is dropped from the second catalog.[26] Natalie Ornish, author of the book *Pioneer Jewish Texans*, has uncovered a land grant of 320 acres made on March 11, 1841, to the "President & Trustees of Rutersville College" by Dr. A. M. Levy, a hero of the Texas Revolution.[27]

Early Assessments of Its Progress

In spite of the difficulties and privations confronting the school when it opened, early assessments of its progress were generally positive. An example is that of Thomas O. Summers, later to become a prominent editor and theologian, who was appointed to Houston in 1840. He reported after a long tour of all the Methodist mission work in Texas that Rutersville College was doing well, principally because of the "persevering and indefatigable" work of Chauncey Richardson, "principal" of the institution. He attributes to Richardson "a Christian demeanor and gentlemanly deportment, combined with . . . industry." His statement that "the college proper is to go into operation . . . in September, 1842," is another indication that all the students enrolled to date had been engaged in preparatory work. [28]

His positive assessment of the school, however, is qualified by his mention of the suspicion in which many prospective supporters hold it because of its legal standing. He says that the action of the Congress in forcing Rutersville College to become an independent rather than a Methodist institution does not sit well with some of the ministers, and he hopes that Richardson, who has been elected Senate chaplain, will succeed in amending the charter to allow for Methodist control.[29] The charter was indeed amended in 1849 to allow the Methodist Conferences to fill vacancies on the Board, but by then so much negativism had

The Rutersville College bell. The original bell was procured by Southwestern in 1953 and is rung on special occasions. Southwestern University, Special Collections.

Rutersville College building. Nearing completion in late 1841, it passed into possession of the Texas Monumental and Military Institute in 1856, when that Institute was formed to replace Rutersville College. Southwestern University, Special Collections.

been generated that it only took one more unfortunate event shortly thereafter, the Applewhite affair, to diminish whatever confidence was left in the school among its constituency. In so doing, the affair became a major factor in Rutersville's closure. But that was almost a decade later.

Visiting Rutersville for a second time in 1841, Summers says that the school's progress has been notable, with students in both departments progressing rapidly. A two-story frame building, 52\' x 26\', he says, is under construction and should soon be completed.[30] When completed, it was crowned with a bell that was procured by Southwestern in 1953 and is rung on special occasions.[31] At the same time, a stone building for the Female Academy was being constructed on an adjoining hill, approximately 800 yards from the main building.

The Telegraph and Register of January 20, 1841, is full of praise for Rutersville College. It reports the completion of the main building and says that "already has the institution at Rutersville obtained a standing by the proficiency of its teachers, and by all other requisites for a good and thorough institution of learning, which renders a resort to the seminaries of the United States for the education of children, wholly superfluous and unnecessary."[32]

Unsteady Administration

Though early reports by outsiders unconnected with the school were generally favorable, trouble began to build up

Dormitory for young women at Rutersville College. Destroyed by fire in 1933, some of its stones were used in the patio of the house that replaced it. From Olin W. Nail, ed., *Texas Methodist Centennial Yearbook 1834–1934*.

from the outset with Richardson's administration. Part of the difficulty stemmed from the fact that early on he was given or sought responsibilities not germane to his main task or that kept him away for long periods of time. Though his name appears in the first catalog as a teacher, C. C. Cody, first Dean of Southwestern, says that the Trustees elected him as the financial agent of the college and that he spent his first year in that role. D. N. V. Sullivan, who had already begun instruction prior to the arrival of Richardson, filled his teaching place during the year.[33]

When Charles Wright arrived in May of 1845, he says that he found Homer Thrall teaching and successfully managing the school. Richardson, he says, is "nominal head" but does not instruct the students.[34] Little wonder. In addition to his presidential responsibilities, he was also Presiding Elder of the Rutersville District. In a report of August 7, 1844, Richardson states that he has made two tours of his circuit of churches comprising 1,500 miles of travel.[35] During his absences, things did not always go to his liking. Wright reports on July 30, 1845, that during the previous session a disagreement arose between the President and the principal teacher, resulting in the removal of the teacher, who took most of the students with him.[36] Charles Wright, writing privately to his sister in mid-1846, says that "I am by no means satisfied with the conduct of the President in his management of the affairs of the college. . . . Indeed he does every thing connected with the institution after the counsel of his own will insomuch that it has been said 'there is but one Trustee and he is President[,] Treasurer and all.'"[37]

Though Richardson's role as a teacher is uncertain and he was unsteady as an administrator, he was well respected by his fellow ministers. John McLean, future president of Southwestern University, who knew him, describes him as tall and muscular, with gray eyes and a dark complexion. He is described as modest, agreeable, and methodical. He was a well-known figure in the Church and on the state scene.

After leaving the presidency of Rutersville College in 1846, he was elected editor of the *Texas Wesleyan Banner*, the church paper of the Texas and East Texas Conferences, and served briefly, before his sudden, unexpected death in 1852, as Presiding Elder of the Galveston District. He was Chaplain to the Texas Republic during its existence and President of the first state Educational Convention held in Houston in 1846. He delivered an address before that body in Houston that was put in pamphlet form.[38] He gave the prayer opening the Convention that same year that voted to accede to annexation by the United States. He organized the Texas Library Institute and was its President. He was also President of the Texas Bible Society. He was, says McLean, an interesting speaker with a clear, solemn voice and a classically chaste style. Henry Matthews, a former Ohio Methodist preacher turned Texas physician, says in his diaries that he heard Richardson preach "most engagingly & splendidly" on the last Sunday in May 1840. "It would be impossible," he says, "to trace on paper any thing like the sublimity of this searching discourse."[39]

Notable Teachers—Ann Catherine Haynie

It may be too much to say that Ann Catherine (Goodwin) Haynie, Richardson's sister-in-law, was the first female faculty member in the state of Texas, but she was certainly among the first. She taught art, French, poetry, and "Good Manners." It is not clear whether she taught female students exclusively or whether she taught both genders.

Haynie was born in 1807 to a Boston family that traced its arrival in America to the *Little Anne*, the first ship to arrive after the *Mayflower*. She received a fine Eastern education and among her mementos was a book by John Flavel (ca. 1630–1691), popular Puritan theologian, presented to her in 1822. It was inscribed: "To my Pupil and Friend, as a gift from the Methodist educator, Wilbur Fisk, who established Wesleyan University in Middletown, Connecticut." Her interests were broad, and she kept a scrapbook of newspaper clippings from American and foreign newspapers. These consist mostly of poems and editorials, but items concerning new devices and processes also appear. Little more is known about her other than that she was, according to Sharon Duncan, who studied her life, "a well-educated, gentle, cultured woman of faith."[40]

Notable Teachers—Charles Wright

Judson S. Custer says at the beginning of his pamphlet on Charles Wright that "Pioneer colleges such as Rutersville . . . were sometimes graced with remarkable faculty and administrators who were themselves pioneers, adventurers, and, in the case of Charles Wright, scholars of note. These talented and unusual people spent a portion of their professional lives working in the interests of educating the youth in an evolving culture in a new land."[41]

Though born in Connecticut, Charles Wright had the kind of wanderlust that took him to faraway places. Soon after obtaining his Yale degree in 1835, he went south. His position immediately prior to coming to Texas was teaching in Natchez, Mississippi. He reached Texas in late 1837 or early 1838 and worked at various jobs until he reached Rutersville in the spring of 1845 to teach. Beginning in July, he taught one-and-a-half years, leaving in late December 1846. While at Yale he had become interested in botany, though he was not trained in it. At about the time he came to Rutersville he began to correspond with Asa Gray, the eminent Harvard botanist, developing a professional friendship and voluminous correspondence with him that lasted their entire lives.

Wright was aware of the academic limitations of Rutersville College, saying that in the "old states" it would rank somewhat lower than the common academy, but adding that its prospects were good if properly nurtured.[42] Since the price of tuition was only ten to twenty dollars for a twenty-one-week term, and the semiannual income of the college was only five to six hundred dollars, faculty members sometimes received their pay in grants of land. Wright speaks at one point of having to sell some "headrights" to buy a seventy-five-dollar horse. The cash-flow problem of the college as a whole became a problem for its faculty down the line. While at Rutersville, Wright joined the Methodist Church and participated in some prayer meetings and other religious activities.

His influence on students can be seen in the "Report on the Public Examination at Rutersville College" made by a Committee of Examination on July 11–12, 1845. The young ladies under Wright's instruction were complimented by the examiners for their herbariums and their "copy-books," which were said to give evidence of "respectable proficiency in penmanship and botany."[43] Within a year, however, after Richardson's departure and at the point of Halsey's coming, Wright left for Seguin and Austin, where he taught temporarily before following his real interest—botanical exploration and description.[44] He engaged in his first important expedition at Eagle Pass in 1847–1848. There, he says, he "botanized" both sides of the Rio Grande. During the next forty years of his life, he carried out many expeditions in different parts of the world, and the Smithsonian Institution published some of his writings. He completed his life working in the Gray Herbarium at Harvard, dying on his family farm in 1885.[45]

Thomas Bell at Rutersville

Haynie and Wright were high-minded, conscientious teachers operating in a restricted cultural environment to bring out the best in their students. Perhaps the person corresponding most closely to the image of Texans held by many people of the time—that they were adventurous, opportunistic, daring—was a tutor, Thomas Bell, employed by the school during its second and third years. Studying Bell's career at Rutersville makes it possible to learn something about the circumstances of the college from one who was a participant in its life but not temperamentally wedded to its mission. His is the only "inside" view we have from an outsider, i.e., one who did not have any initial religious or proprietary stake in the institution.

Bell came to Texas following the path traced by many others—moving ever southwest, in his case from North Carolina, where he was born, to Tennessee, to Mississippi, and finally to Texas. His move to Texas was precipitated by the failure of a venture in the hog business in Grenada, Mississippi. He, a cousin, and an uncle by marriage reached Austin, the new capital of Texas, on August 6, 1839. After trying his hand at carpentry in Austin, Bell eventually ended up almost a year later in Rutersville, after writing his family in Tennessee that "Teachers are much in quest [sic] here and I think I can make something at the business; certainly more than in Tenn."[46] By the middle of autumn he writes to his family that he is "entirely contented here [in Rutersville] while I can do as well as I am doing." He says that he thinks he can get a forty-acre lot that he can improve for a profit. He is very satisfied with the forty dollars per month he is now earning by his work as a carpenter and is thinking of teaching in the winter to increase his income.

On the last day of May 1841, Bell, now a tutor at the school, writes to his brother about his restlessness at being single and says he would get married if the right situation presented itself. The May Day celebration at the Female Academy may have served as one inducement to this feeling because he describes that event, saying that the young ladies of the Academy crowned a queen and that it was a splendid affair. It had speeches and concluded at Mr. King's, his uncle's, boardinghouse with a tea party. "The college is still improving," he says, "and gaining credit in different parts of the country and I think cannot fail to become one of the best institutions of the country. There is no other that anything like ranks with it at present."[47] He is concerned, however, about his pay, saying that making collections on his salary "is a very slow business." At the time he has nearly three hundred dollars owing him.[48] His comment speaks directly to the continual financial distress of the institution.

At the beginning of the second term at the end of July 1841, Bell says that the main building will be completed in a few months. There is no doubt, he writes, about the continuance of the school, and he intends to stay there for several years at least. Every day he works six hours for the school and studies six hours for his own improvement. "I do not now intend to quit study until I shall obtain at least a respectable standing in the literary world. I am satisfied this is the place it can be attained and I can do it and be paid at the same time for my services."[49] Nevertheless, the limited number of faculty members inhibited the work of the school. This became apparent in the fall when Bell says that the ill health of "the professor," possibly Chauncey Richardson, caused many to lose confidence in the school during the session. Toward the end of the second term, just as at the end of the first, he mentions his doubts about being paid his salary. "I do not know whether the teachers can be paid off at the end of this session which is within three weeks of a close, but if it fail for a time its final success is based on a firm foundation."[50]

In spite of the financial situation of the school, Bell's year of teaching leaves him in an optimistic mood. Much of his contentment arises from the fact that he has resolved his religious feelings and is sure that a change has been wrought in him through a "merciful Providence." Earlier he had asked his father for some advice about which church he should join, and a paragraph in this letter makes plain that neither he nor his family is Methodist. His preference is Presbyterian. He says: "Could I join the Presbyterian church I think I could enjoy this life better." But the reality is, he continues, that Methodists run Rutersville College and "it would seem from my present situation that it would be my interest in this world to unite with the methodist [sic] church. . . . When I speak of the college being conducted by methodist [sic] influence I do not mean that it is sectarian. It is far from this; but it has been started by persons of that denomination and [is] still under their patronage and supervision. There are not not [sic] expected to be any particular doctrines disseminated in the institution. The students of course are required to attend church on the sabbath, though not any particular church."

It is notable that in frontier Texas, where most denominations stressed doctrinal conformity, the first Methodist institution expressed the doctrinal amplitude of Methodism stemming from John Wesley and still characteristic of Southwestern University today. Later, on December 24, he writes that he has made a profession of faith and regrets that he has not done so long before.[51] It is clear that Methodist "influence" was strong at Rutersville College and that, however nonsectarian it might be, students and teachers, such as Charles Wright and Thomas Bell, felt it forcefully.

Bell Draws a White Bean

The year 1842 brought a completely unexpected turn of events for Bell that effectively ended his connection with Rutersville College and weakened the institution as well. On March 5, Rafael Vasquez captured San Antonio with his small contingent of Mexican troops and held it for a few days before withdrawing. Bell's uncle wrote to his parents in Tennessee that their son and "every student of the college that was 15 years of age took arms and hurried to the standard of the Lone Star" so that the male component of the college was decimated for a time. Even ten females left."[52] By the time they arrived in San Antonio, Vasquez, who was only making a show of force, was long gone. On Bell's return to Rutersville three weeks later, however, he was out of employment. He wrote his family that the citizens of the state were spoiling for revenge and that he knows no better employment than of "serving my adopted country [the Republic of Texas] although the service is hard and the pay nothing."[53]

Before leaving, Bell filed suit in the Fayette County District Court against the President and Trustees of Rutersville College for his back pay. He stated that the college owed him $600.00, of which only $145.09 had been paid. He petitioned to receive judgment for the remaining sum. His case was suspended when he and his attorney both left to join the Somervell and Mier expeditions. While he was gone, his aunt, Mrs. John A. King, took charge of the case, and a jury later decided in his favor.[54] Thus ended Bell's relationship with Rutersville College.

His story in Texas after this point is bound up with the Mier fiasco. Briefly told, he was one of the 261 who attacked Mier, Mexico, on Christmas Day 1842, under Colonel Fisher. Defeated and captured, he and the others were marched to Matamoros, then to Mexico City. Along the way they engineered a mass escape and tried to trek back to Texas, but the now reduced number of 176 were recaptured, only three evading capture and making it back to Texas. The punishment inflicted by the Mexicans was harsh and exact. Every tenth man was executed, having drawn one of the 17 black beans placed in a pitcher with 159 white beans. Bell drew a white bean. After twenty-one months in captivity in Mexico, Bell and the remaining prisoners were released. He subsequently wrote a book detailing his experiences entitled *A Narrative of the Capture and Subsequent Sufferings of the Mier Prisoners in Mexico, Captured in the Cause of Texas, Dec. 26th, 1842 and Liberated Sept. 16th, 1844.*

Contrasting Fates

One of the unusual elements in the Mier episode as far as Rutersville College is concerned was the contrasting fate of two of its students who participated in it. One of them, J. N. McD. Thompson, drew a black bean and was shot.[55] Another, John Christopher Columbus Hill, received from it what amounted to a new start in life.

Participating in the battle at the age of fourteen, Hill displayed such bravery and audacity that the opposing general, Pedro Ampudia, took notice. He was intrigued by the young man and sent him under special escort to President Antonio López de Santa Anna. A later Mier veteran characterized Hill as "a brave and handsome little fellow," and Waddy Thompson, the U.S. minister to Mexico, called him "a very shrewd and handsome boy." Santa Anna, Valentín Gómez Farías, and José María Tornel, three powers on the Mexican political scene, were so taken with him that they encouraged him to remain in Mexico. Though one would have thought that his bargaining position as a prisoner was weak, he agreed to stay only after they agreed to release his father and brother, who were also prisoners.

Living in the Tornel home in Mexico City, Hill entered the Colegio de Minería. He graduated with distinction in 1851. Soon he adopted the name Juan Cristóbal Gil, an almost literal translation of his English name, to smooth his way. His unusual ability to balance his Mexican and American sentiments was displayed when, during the American occupation of Mexico City, he pleased both sides by his careful interventions. His marriage to a Mexican woman in 1855 produced four children. He was successful during the Benito Juárez period, but it was in the regime of Porfirio Díaz, beginning in 1875, that he prospered most. His skills in mining and laying out railway lines agreed perfectly with the program of Díaz to modernize the country. Hill became one of *los científicos*, the technical experts whom he favored. In 1867 Hill procured the release of his old friend, General Ampudia, from a sentence of death for supposedly having sided with Maximilian in his hopeless project to become Emperor of Mexico.

During this time Hill regularly kept in touch with his Texas relatives and sent a son to Swarthmore. He made frequent trips back to the United States, finally returning to live in Austin permanently after the death of his wife in 1891. A few years later he married the sweetheart of his youth. He was made an honorary life member of the Texas State Historical Association in 1897, dying seven years later in Monterrey, where he was buried.[56]

Such were the contrasting destinies of two schoolboys who left Rutersville in 1842 to exact revenge on the Mexicans. Thompson's death, however, did not go unremembered. In 1845 he apparently received a posthumous A.B. degree from the college, since he is listed in Southwestern University records inherited from Rutersville as a graduate of that year.

Rebecca Gilleland Fisher was the most famous female student of Rutersville College. She was the only woman elected to the Texas Veteran Association, and her portrait was the first of a woman to be hung in the Senate Chamber. Painting by Royston Nave that hangs in the Legislative Reference Library at the Texas Capitol. Used by permission of the Texas Preservation Board.

Rebecca Jane Gilleland Fisher

Rutersville College produced other students whose lives were productive beyond what one might have predicted from the frontier circumstances in which they were schooled. Rebecca Jane Gilleland Fisher is one.

Born in Philadelphia in 1831, her family arrived in Texas in 1838, settling in Refugio County. Comanches attacked their home in 1840 and killed both parents. Rebecca and her brother, William, were captured. Remarkably, they were rescued within hours by a nearby detachment of soldiers led by Albert Sidney Johnston, of later Civil War fame. The pursuit by the soldiers was so immediate that the Gillelands' Indian kidnappers dropped them off rather than risk capture by keeping them. An aunt in Galveston subsequently reared them. Rebecca attended Rutersville College from 1846 to 1848, during the first two years of Halsey's administration.[57]

Describing many years later the conditions in which the female students lived and studied, Rebecca says that some of the girls, she among them, boarded with the President's family in the annex of the college. For classes, however, they had to walk "several blocks" each morning to the "primitive log school house which bore the dignified name 'academy.'" Only the males studied in the main college facilities. "But notwithstanding our rough and humble building—so unpretentious and unsightly—we were contented and happy." On winter nights, she says, all of them would collect in a large room "to while away the long and dreary hours by roasting eggs and potatoes in our bright and broad fireplace, enjoying those evening treats as only school girls could under such circumstances."[58]

Perhaps it was the opportunity to get away from those "long and dreary hours" of which she speaks that caused the seventeen-year-old Rebecca to accept the marriage proposal of Orceneth Fisher, an older widowed Methodist minister, when he visited Rutersville College in his rounds as editor of the *Texas Christian Advocate* in 1848. Seven years later they moved with their children to the Pacific coast, where he served as pastor in California and Oregon. They returned to Texas about 1871, establishing a home in Austin where he died in 1880.

Freed at the age of forty-nine to pursue her private interests, she became a prominent figure on the Texas scene.

She was a charter member of the Daughters of the Republic of Texas and served as its president for eighteen years. She delivered a speech at the unveiling of the Sam Houston monument in Huntsville and worked with the young Clara Driscoll in saving the Alamo from destruction. For several years she gave the opening prayer at the convening of the Texas Legislature. She was the only woman elected to the Texas Veteran Association and was its last surviving member. Southwestern students were enthralled by her story when she spoke to them at an assembly in May 1912 and could hardly cease clapping when she finished. Her portrait was the first of a woman to be hung in the Senate chamber of the Capitol. At her death in 1926, her body lay in state in the Senate chamber, where her funeral services were held. A resolution was adopted in her memory, and her portrait was draped in mourning cloth.[59]

Gradual Decline

Reading the report of the Public Examination of July 21, 1845, one would hardly suspect that the prospects of Rutersville College for the future were anything but excellent. The two outside examiners were very pleased with the performance of the students and with the meeting of the Board of Trustees, which they attended. The finances of the College were, they wrote, in "sound condition," though the cash flow left something to be desired. The location of the institution was excellent, the society in the village was good, and the buildings were "commodious and well arranged."[60] Enrollment for 1844–1845 was 194, the highest ever,[61] and the school was finally turning out college graduates, not just preparatory students. The first six had been graduated in 1844, with eight more in 1845.

Yet the appearance was deceptive. Within two years the President had resigned, enrollment was down to sixty-eight,[62] and the number of baccalaureate degrees awarded had declined precipitously. Of the thirty-two degrees awarded by the College during its existence, twenty-six were granted in the four years between 1844 and 1847 but only six in the final nine years between 1848 and 1856.[63]

As early as 1843 the Board of Trustees felt obligated to reply to the attacks of its "enemies" in its annual report to the Texas Annual Conference. It stated that "We are fully aware that the college has enemies, by whom it has been misrepresented and slandered, but these individuals have become enemies without any just provocation." It then proceeded to "disabuse" the public mind of the charges against it.[64]

One charge, however, was difficult to refute—the fact that the Board, though made up of Methodists, was legally independent of the Church. In spite of the fact that President Richardson preached regularly in Methodist pulpits and strove to cement his relations with his fellow ministers, he could not do enough to assuage the doubts of some that he operated the College according to his personal inclinations free from control by the Church. This sentiment is expressed crudely but succinctly in a letter written to Littleton Fowler by the Rev. Alford Caldwell in 1845. He says in part: "We are anxous [sic] to resuscitate, and give a fresh impetus to Ruthersville [sic] College. it [sic] has been under the management & control of our Mutual & worth[y] frd. Ch. Richardson until it is far below Zero—, and it appears that the members of conf. feel that it belongs to Bro. Richardson and that they have no right to interfere, or investigate the proceedings of this Institution. This is Wrong, and not as it should be." He then goes on to say that he and, of all people, Robert Alexander, who had employed Richardson six years earlier, have written to a member of the faculty at McKendree College to see if he would be available to take the presidency.[65]

The reappointment of Richardson to the presidency in 1845 was to be his last. The negotiations at McKendree referred to by Caldwell bore no fruit. Around the time of Richardson's resignation, likely in the spring of 1846, the *La Grange Intelligencer* printed an obituary of Rutersville College. It read: "Departed this life in the 2nd inst., at 5 o'clock, P.M., that young and interesting institution, Rutersville College. We had indulged the fond anticipation that she would one day become the 'Alma Mater' of many of the noble sons of Texas; but the fates have decreed otherwise."[66] Two teachers, first Homer Thrall,[67] then Charles Wright, held things together until the arrival of Dr. William Halsey as president in late 1846.[68] Halsey, a native of New York and a graduate of Wesleyan University in Connecticut, had come to Texas in 1845 as a teacher.[69] His academic title at Rutersville was Professor of Ancient and Modern Languages. Mrs. Halsey became head of the Female Department.[70]

In spite of his efforts, Halsey could do little to counteract the gradual decline of the institution. In addition to a decline in student numbers, the financial situation continued to weaken. By the time Halsey arrived it had deteriorated to such a point that the school, once "rich" in land, faced the prospect of having little. From the beginning, the Trustees had been forced to sell acreage to construct its buildings, purchase its equipment, and pay its professors. In a state where land was plentiful, prices were often low, and the school was forced to sell at a discount. Francis Asbury Mood later wrote that from the first year of its existence the College began to accumulate a debt that finally proved disastrous. "The lands donated by the State," he said, "were alienated at very low prices—some of it as low as a dime per acre—until its landed endowment was gone entirely."[71]

The Applewhite Affair

As if Rutersville College were not already afflicted enough, news of a sex scandal affecting it broke in early 1850, adding a salacious element to the mix. Macum Phelan, a historian of early Texas Methodism, says that Isaac Applewhite, a Methodist local preacher living in Rutersville and connected with the college, "came under serious charges of immorality and swindling," for which he was brought to trial by the Church.[72] The situation was heightened by the fact that the woman involved was Ann S. Richardson, daughter of the former President. None of the Church records of the trial exist today, and knowledge about the affair must be pieced together from other sources. They sustain the charge of "immorality" but say nothing about "swindling."

Rutersville College marker, with fence enclosing grave of Chauncey Richardson, its first president. His headstone shows above the top of the fence. Southwestern University, Special Collections.

Census records for 1850, collected at the height of the scandal, provide several pieces of useful information. Applewhite is listed as a thirty-eight-year-old "Meth Clergyman," born in Mississippi, who moved from Louisiana to Texas with his family sometime around 1840. At the time of the June 1 census collection date, he and his wife have eight children ranging in age from one month to thirteen years.

At the same time, Ann Richardson, Chauncey Richardson's daughter, is a sixteen-year-old girl living with her mother.[73] She and her mother live close to her aunt and uncle, the Haynies, who apparently moved from La Grange to Rutersville, probably to facilitate Ann Catherine's teaching in the Female Department when her sister, Martha, was Preceptress. The census taker, who lists his data in the order in which he visits homes, precedes his listing for the Richardsons with that of the Haynies, as if they live next door to one another. The Richardson household seems to have remained in Rutersville when Chauncey left the presidency. He probably performed his work as editor of *The Wesleyan Banner* in Houston, its headquarters, traveling back and forth as circumstances permitted. He is not listed in the Fayette County census. Ann attends classes at the college.

Ann appears to have been considered the aggrieved party in the affair and was exonerated in the public mind, or at least in the minds of those conducting the college, because on November 22, 1851, more than a year after the matter became known, she, as a student, made an original speech at the time of the examination and received a certificate of scholarship that was read to the audience by President Halsey.[74]

It is easy to understand why public opinion sided with her. In the mind of the people it was the case of a student in her mid-teens who had been taken advantage of by someone connected with her school, a man twenty-two years her senior, a local preacher, and a father of eight. This presumption of her innocence by the general public is buttressed by the fact that "Applewhite stood trial on September 27, 1852, before La Fayette Lodge No. 34 on the charges of unlawful and criminal intercourse," was convicted, and expelled from the order.[75]

During the course of these events, on April 11, 1852, Ann's father, former President Richardson, now Presiding Elder of the Galveston District, unexpectedly died in Fort Bend County west of Houston. His body was brought back to Rutersville and interred on the gentle hill topped by the main building of the College. His grave, with its tall marker, is one of the few remaining features of the site today where stood the first college in Texas, of which he was the first President.[76]

The negative effect of the affair on the circumstances of Rutersville College appears clearly in the correspondence of preachers. In a letter of May 18, 1850, J. E. Ferguson, a young minister in the Bastrop area, says:

> You wish to know something about the Applewhite case. To give you a history would require a weeks writing, but my private opinion is, that it is worse than we want it. . . . But this it has done, it has given the death blow to the Rutersville College. And I will say this to you if we can not move the College from that place I want the Conference to have no connection with it whatever; for I fear that the egg was laid wrong, and has never been hatched properly, and appears to be an ill star[r]ed thing. The citizens of Fayette county so far from fostering & patronising the College they have taken great delight in pulling it down.

Later, on July 24, he says:

> The Rutersville school is well ny dead. There is not a student from Travis or Bastrop Counties that has returned, and to name the matter to any parent is to insult them, and the reasons for all this I will not put on paper. Applewhite is up before the church for a new trial with some other charges of swindling & &.[77]

Phelan concludes his narration of these events by saying that he mentions the affair only to show that Rutersville College did not die a natural death.

Final Years

The College lingered on a few more years, but it graduated only one student with a bachelor's degree between 1850 and 1856. An attempt was made to "rehabilitate its sagging fortunes" by the Texas Annual Conference at its session on December 17, 1851, in the midst of the Applewhite affair, but nothing came of it.[78]

A perusal of the minutes of the Board of Trustees from 1853 to 1856, when the College ceased to exist, reveals one difficulty after another. In 1851–1852 the College authorized James Haynie to examine some of its land with a view to selling it. The Trustees claimed that after proclaiming it virtually worthless, Haynie, knowing it was in fact good land, purchased it for himself at a bargain price.[79] Consequently, the Trustees sued Haynie for restitution and won. In late 1856 Haynie countersued in late 1856, asking that the judgment be set aside.

This is the same James Haynie who, a few years earlier, had played a role with his wife Ann, Martha Richardson's sister, in bringing Chauncey Richardson to Rutersville as President. About the same time that the College sued James, one M. Z. Richardson [Martha?], as executor of Chauncey's estate, filed suit against the College in the District Court of Fayette County.[80] To such depths had fallen the fortunes of the College and its leaders.

The Trustees labored on, however, trying to shore up the College in one way or another. They sold land to repair buildings and began efforts to erect a new hall.[81] All to no avail. Parallel to their efforts, other events were transpiring that would remove Methodist influence from the College and force it to choose another direction.

Persons interested in placing Methodist influence elsewhere persuaded the state to amend the charter of the recently established Chappell Hill Male and Female Institute on February 11, 1854, to allow its control by a religious denomination. Since Philander S. Ruter, son of Martin Ruter, was President of the Institute, that denomination would surely be the Methodist.[82] The new Soule University, then in process of formation, would absorb the Male Department of the Institute and leave the Female Department intact to operate at a lower level. Within a few years it, too, would achieve collegiate status.

After Soule was officially chartered by the Legislature on February 2, 1856, the Board of Trustees of Rutersville College adopted a resolution (May 24, 1856) opening the way for its affiliation with the Texas Monumental Committee and the Texas Military Institute. In two futile gestures, it also exhibited its ill temper to the world by refusing the resignation of President Halsey, who had determined to cast his fortunes with Soule University as its president, and by removing Robert Alexander from the Board. The former had supposedly not offered his resignation in timely fashion, and the latter, whose real sin had been to participate in establishing Soule and becoming a Trustee thereof, ostensibly lived at too great a distance from Rutersville.[83]

The transfer of the physical assets of the College to the new Texas Monumental and Military Institute formed to replace it involves considerable irony. The original Trustees had founded Rutersville College to enshrine the pacific vision of Martin Ruter for a Church-related institution of higher education. The new institution was completely secular and military in nature. The Monumental Committee, as one element of the new Institute, had been incorporated by the state on January 19, 1850. Its object was to build a monument on the grounds of Rutersville College to commemorate the soldiers who suffered in the two military tragedies of 1842—the Mier prisoners and those slain at the Battle of Salado under Captain Nicholas Dawson, where the forces of Mexican General Adrian Woll killed thirty-eight of his fifty-three men. The monument was never built, but in 1856 the Committee made an agreement with the Texas Military Institute of Galveston under Colonel C. G. Forshey to lease the buildings and property of Rutersville College.[84]

By June 30, 1856, the date of the last meeting of the Rutersville Board, all arrangements had been made for the new Texas Monumental and Military Institute to occupy the premises of the college. Six members of the Rutersville Board were elected to the Board of the new institution, and Rutersville College ceased to exist except as a vacant charter.[85] Several Methodist ministers came to Austin between the meeting on June 30 and the enactment of the new charter on August 6 to exert pressure on the Legislature to nullify the proposal, but the effort failed.[86] The Institute moved there and began operation. The Texas Annual Conference still did not give up its efforts to recover its investment in the school. On January 10, 1858, it presented a Memorial to the Senate and House asking that the Rutersville College property or the value thereof be returned to the Conference, as it was the rightful owner of the institution.[87] This action met with no response.

Soon after the Civil War began, less than five years after the new charter enactment, the corps of the Texas Monumental and Military Institute petitioned the Superintendent to disband the school in order that the older members might join the services of the Confederacy. This he did on April 29, 1861.[88]

Competition in the Piney Woods: Wesleyan College

San Augustine—This Way to Texas

Frederick Law Olmsted, whose *Journey Through Texas* is probably the most interesting, thorough, and balanced travel book about Texas before the Civil War, says that "Texas has but two avenues of approach—the Gulf and Red River. Travelers for the Gulf counties and the West enter by the sea, for all other parts of Texas by the river." He and his brother entered by the river. For them this meant taking a boat to Natchitoches and, thence, making a "saddle-trip," as Olmsted called it, to San Augustine through the piney woods.[1] They crossed the boundary into Texas in 1855 over an "elastic pavement of pine leaves" just as Littleton Fowler, Robert Alexander, and Martin Ruter had done some years earlier. San Augustine, as a port of entry, had a customhouse that collected duties on imports from the United States. It was third in importance of the ports of entry under the Republic, with only Galveston and Matagorda ranking higher.[2] It maintained its importance as an entryway into Texas until annexation by the United States, when lands in the north and west opened up. At that point it ceased to be a port of entry, lost the customhouse, and became smaller and less important.

Because of its strategic location, San Augustine had attracted Methodist mission work from the beginning. Ruter preached his first Texas sermon there, and Littleton Fowler made it the center of his work. He had begun a subscription for building a church almost immediately after arriving in October 1837. He says that "in less time than two weeks a lot was deeded, $3500 were subscribed, trustees appointed, and building was under written[;] contract to be finished before the first of next September."[3] Appointed Presiding Elder of the Texas Mission District after Ruter's death, Fowler gathered his preachers in San Augustine to make plans for the future. By 1839 San Augustine had the largest church membership of any of the six Methodist preaching circuits in Texas. Its 246 members were more than twice as many as Rutersville's 102. The Texas Annual Conference, which had held its first session at the college in Rutersville in 1840, held its second the following year in San Augustine.[4] It returned there in 1845 and in 1847. San Augustine became a strong Methodist center. Three of its ministers had their homes there.[5]

Though there were strategic reasons why, if a Methodist college were to be placed anywhere in East Texas, it should be established in San Augustine, these reasons alone did not suffice to bring it about. As events turned out, the selection of San Augustine required a second compelling reason—denominational rivalry. Rutersville College had been founded in response to the humane vision of Martin Ruter for a frontier people lacking in almost all the accouterments of enlightenment. While still expressing Ruter's humane interests, the founders of Wesleyan College had another reason as well—the strategic and competitive interests of institutional Methodism.

The University of San Augustine

Once the battles for independence were concluded and the people of Texas were free to think about normal civic concerns, the citizens of various towns determined to establish adequate educational systems for their children and young people. In the first session of the new Congress of the Republic, charters were granted to three proposed institutions—Independence Academy in Independence, Washington College in Washington, and the University of San Augustine in San Augustine. The first two never materialized, and the third, the University of San Augustine, did not begin operation until late summer1842. Nevertheless, the mere possession of a charter gave the people a sense of imminent fulfillment. When Francis Wilson, the Methodist preacher who was later to play a prominent role in the establishment of Wesleyan College, arrived in late December

1839, he says that on Sunday he "preached in the University to a large assembly."[6] The building may have been the two-story building with basement in the eastern part of town received by the Trustees in exchange for a league of land.[7] Two-and-a-half years after the University had obtained a charter, two-and-a-half years before it became operational, without President, faculty, or students, Wilson joined himself to the expectant sentiment of the townspeople by saying that he "preached in the University." He did not come to establish another institution of higher education. He recognized the one already there, if only in prospect.

Apparently the fifteen Trustees listed in the Act of Incorporation had done little to secure a President for the school or had been unsuccessful in their efforts, because the procurement of that official in the late summer of 1842 appears to have been quite accidental. A traveler through town, the Rev. Marcus A. Montrose, spotted the structure constructed for the school and, upon inquiry, was told that the Trustees were looking for a President.[8] Born in 1808, Montrose, a Scotsman, was a graduate of the University of Edinburgh and an ordained Presbyterian clergyman who had come to the United States only two or three years before by way of Canada. He applied for the position and was hired by the Trustees.[9] All accounts say that he was an aggressive man, a good preacher, and a fluent writer. He also had a strong temper and was vigorous in defense of his views.

Montrose organized the school with a female academy and a grammar school for children under twelve. The Introductory Department was equivalent to the Preparatory Department at Rutersville. The curriculum for collegiate level students included theoretical mathematics courses as advanced as conic sections and differential calculus, science courses as abstruse as conchology (the study of shells) and oryctology (the study of fossils), language courses from the best Latin and Greek authors, and civics courses in the U.S. and Texas Constitutions and the Law of Nations. George L. Crocket says about the curriculum as a whole: "One is lost in wonderment at the thought of so much and such varied erudition displayed for the admiration and confusion of the youth of a frontier town."[10] The most directly useful courses were probably land surveying, use of globes, fortifications, and gunnery.

The Presbyterian Connection

With a Presbyterian minister serving as President, the local Presbyterian congregation became interested in the school. Until this point the operation had been secular, and the Board of Trustees was made up of persons of different denominations with various political persuasions. Whether the Presbytery or the Trustees broached the matter of Presbyterian support is unknown, but they came to an agreement resulting in Church support. When a new Presbytery was organized for Eastern Texas specifically to support the school, it agreed to cooperate with the Trustees, and a committee was formed to look for outside assistance. Both the General Assembly in Scotland and the General Assembly in the United States were approached. About 4,500 acres of land were donated as a result of the Presbyterian connection. From this point on the school can be said to be Presbyterian. Three Presbyterian ministers were generally on its teaching staff each term.[11]

From the beginning the school encountered the same difficulties already encountered by Rutersville College—insufficiency of income from tuition, an endowment constituted in land alone, lack of proper textbooks, and high teacher turnover due to low salaries. A difficulty not faced by Rutersville was its location in a town having a preponderance of persons from another denomination—the Methodist. When a Methodist clergyman newly arrived in town from Ohio preached on sanctification one Sunday in early 1843, Montrose preached one in reply. A challenge to debate the issue was offered by the Methodist minister and accepted by Montrose. The face-off drew the attendance of almost the entire population of the town. The two sources recounting the event are not clear as to the winner, but if it was anyone, one source conjectures, it was Montrose.[12] The effect of the debate, however, was detrimental to the Presbyterian cause he represented. It galvanized embryonic interest among Methodists in establishing a college of their own.

Daniel Poe and Wesleyan College

By the time these events took place, Methodist interest in establishing an educational institution in East Texas had already appeared, first in the mind of Daniel Poe. Poe had visited Texas in 1838 to wind up the affairs of a brother who had died in service as an officer in the Texas army during the War for Independence. Littleton Fowler, on a visit to the Ohio Conference in late September 1842, recruited Poe along with five other missionaries to come to Texas, and he now arrived in Texas just in time for the Annual Conference held in Bastrop on December 22, 1842. There he was given an appointment to the Soda Lake mission, not far from Marshall.[13]

Having brought his wife and three young children with him, Poe was impressed with the lack of schools and teachers in Texas, especially, says Macum Phelan, the historian of these events, because of the prospect of rearing his own children in that environment. He determined to take steps to improve those conditions. After receiving approval from Littleton Fowler, in whose District he served, he returned to Ohio and spent several months in his old Conference recruiting teachers for Texas. An announcement published in *The Red Lander* of San Augustine on July 13, 1843, reports him as being away for that purpose. That same announcement sets the beginning instruction date for a projected school as on or before November 1. Of special interest is the statement that tuition and boarding rates will be half of what is customary for such services "because of the pecuniary embarrassment of our country."[14] One wonders if the reduced prices were not as much an effort to cut into the clientele of the University of San Augustine as they were to meet the "pecuniary embarrassment" of the times. Also notable is the fact that in a short announcement of only about 250 words the proposed institution is spoken of indiscriminately as a university, a college, and a seminary. Fine distinctions as to the character of the institution were not seen as important, given the wide-ranging nature of the work to be done.

Upon his return, Poe "commenced laying the foundations of an institution of learning at San Augustine." The Texas Annual Conference of December 1843 resolved to adopt it and to give it their patronage. "This was the beginning," affirms Phelan, "of 'Wesleyan College.'"[15] Because of his interest in the new college, Poe was appointed as pastor for 1844 of the Methodist congregation in San Augustine.

The opening of the institution did not materialize as rapidly as its sponsors had hoped. Though the cornerstone for a two-story building had been laid on August 26, 1843, an announcement in *The Red Lander* of November 25 notified citizens that the opening had been delayed until the first Monday in December. Notice was given that the building and premises formerly occupied by Col. Campbell had been secured as the residence for the Principal and for the use of the Female Department. It is explicitly stated that the Female Department would be separate from the male and have only female instructors. This separation was apparently an important point in distinguishing its polity from that of the University of San Augustine, where boys and girls received some instruction together. The beginning half term was announced to be one of only eleven weeks, with a pro-rata reduction of charges. "The regular term," the announcement continued, "will consist of twenty-two weeks, and will commence the first of March next." The notice is signed by the Committee of Direction, D. Poe, Chairman.[16]

Before the end of the year 1843 the advocates of the new school reported in a Memorial to the Texas Congress petitioning for a charter that they had procured subscriptions for six thousand dollars in money and twenty thousand acres in land. They stated that they had already purchased a "commodious and elegant" house in San Augustine for the Female Department, including its grounds, and had "commenced and will soon have completed a spacious and commodious house three stories high beautifully situated upon a four acre lot" for the proposed "Wesleyan Male and Female College of San Augustine." They have also employed, so they say, some competent teachers of "exemplary character."[17] Forty-nine men, headed by Francis Wilson, signed the Memorial.

Congress granted the charter on January 16, 1844.[18] Fourteen Trustees were named, of whom three, Francis Wilson, Littleton Fowler, and Daniel Poe, were Methodist ministers. Poe, who possessed a master's degree, was also pressed into service as a faculty member for Pure and Applied Mathematics when the proposed teacher resigned. In addition, he was the local financial agent. Another Trustee was J. Pinckney Henderson, a lawyer, diplomat, and resident of San Augustine, soon to be elected first governor of the state of Texas after annexation by the United States.

Among those recruited by Poe in Ohio for the new college were Lester Janes, A.M., as President, and his wife, Mrs. S. H. Janes, as Principal of the Female Department. A faculty of nine was named and distributed between the Female and the Male Departments, with a number of overlapping appointments. It began its first session on the first Monday in March 1844.[19] As the main building had not been completed, accommodations were makeshift and finances were precarious. Francis Wilson, as Chairman of the Board of Trustees, set out to rectify this situation.

Francis Wilson—The Moving Spirit

Daniel Poe, the initiator of the Wesleyan College idea, was not destined to play a fuller role in the project. Hardly had he assumed his new position as pastor of the Methodist congregation in San Augustine when he and his wife became

Francis Wilson (1790–1867). The moving spirit of Wesleyan College, Wilson made extraordinary efforts to ensure its success but, ultimately, failed. From Francis Wilson, ed., *Memories of a Methodist Circuit Rider.*

ill and died of a "congestive fever." They died in adjoining rooms within forty minutes of each other and were buried in the same coffin. Poe was only thirty-three.[20] Francis Wilson immediately became the leading promoter of Wesleyan, so much so that Poe's important role in its initiation has often been ignored, and Wilson is given all the credit. George L. Crocket, the leading source on San Augustine history, says that Francis Wilson was "the moving spirit" in the decision to establish Wesleyan College.[21] John McLean, future Regent (President) of Southwestern University who knew him well, agrees.[22] Whatever the correct distribution of honors between Poe and Wilson, certainly no one else put as much time and effort into promoting its success as Wilson did.

Francis Wilson is one of the most colorful figures among the early frontier preachers in Texas. Born in 1790, he was reared in what is now West Virginia. His education was rudimentary, as is demonstrated by the distinctive spelling and punctuation one finds in his voluminous memoirs. He was also afflicted with a nervous condition something like palsy, which made traveling difficult. Nevertheless, his lack of education did not keep him from becoming a strong supporter of higher education, and his affliction did not hinder him from traveling widely.

After serving circuits in West Virginia and Ohio, he determined to go to Texas. He was opposed in this resolution by both his bishop and his family, especially his wife, who were shocked by the prospect of a man in his late forties and with a physical infirmity undertaking a venture such as he proposed on the Texas frontier. He solved his problem with the bishop by asking to be located, that is, not to be under appointment, so that he could go where he pleased. He solved the problem with his wife, whom he loved dearly, by saying that he would go alone and return from time to time when he could. She finally decided to go and worked with him faithfully in Texas. His tribute to her in his memoirs is touching.[23]

Crocket says that "Wilson was a pulpit orator of intense force and dramatic power."[24] His most famous sermon, one sometimes repeated by request, was the "Midnight Cry." It was first preached at a camp meeting near San Augustine in 1843. There a trumpet was blown at midnight after everyone had retired for the evening. When the people rushed out of their tents to discover the cause of the blast, they found Wilson in the pulpit, with hair disheveled, in long, flowing robe, Bible in hand. He then commenced to preach with great effect a fiery sermon on the last judgment.[25]

The Nature of Wilson's Support

In addition to his earlier trips throughout populated Texas to raise support for Wesleyan, Wilson made trips to the United States in 1844 and 1846. During both trips he lectured on the future of Texas and on Wesleyan College, soliciting financial aid and taking collections wherever he could. On the first trip he traveled through Ohio, the future West Virginia, and Maryland. On Wednesday, October 2, 1844, he went to Washington and on the 5th "went to see the President [John Tyler] and had a talk with him on Texas." He was strongly in favor of annexation, a view also espoused by Tyler, who ended his term by shepherding the Republic into the Union. Wilson then went to Virginia and South Carolina, down through Alabama to Mobile, finally taking a steamer to New Orleans, then up the Red River, across the Sabine, and to San Augustine. From there he returned home to Shelbyville.[26]

Wilson's basic speech in the North on behalf of Wesleyan College has been preserved. After giving facts and figures about the founding of the institution, he ends with an appeal. Cleverly, he begins with the women, only at the end obliquely referencing the men, assuming that by then the ladies are on his side helping him with their husbands. He says:

> You ladies sent help to the Texan Army when they needed help in a time when they were in a mighty

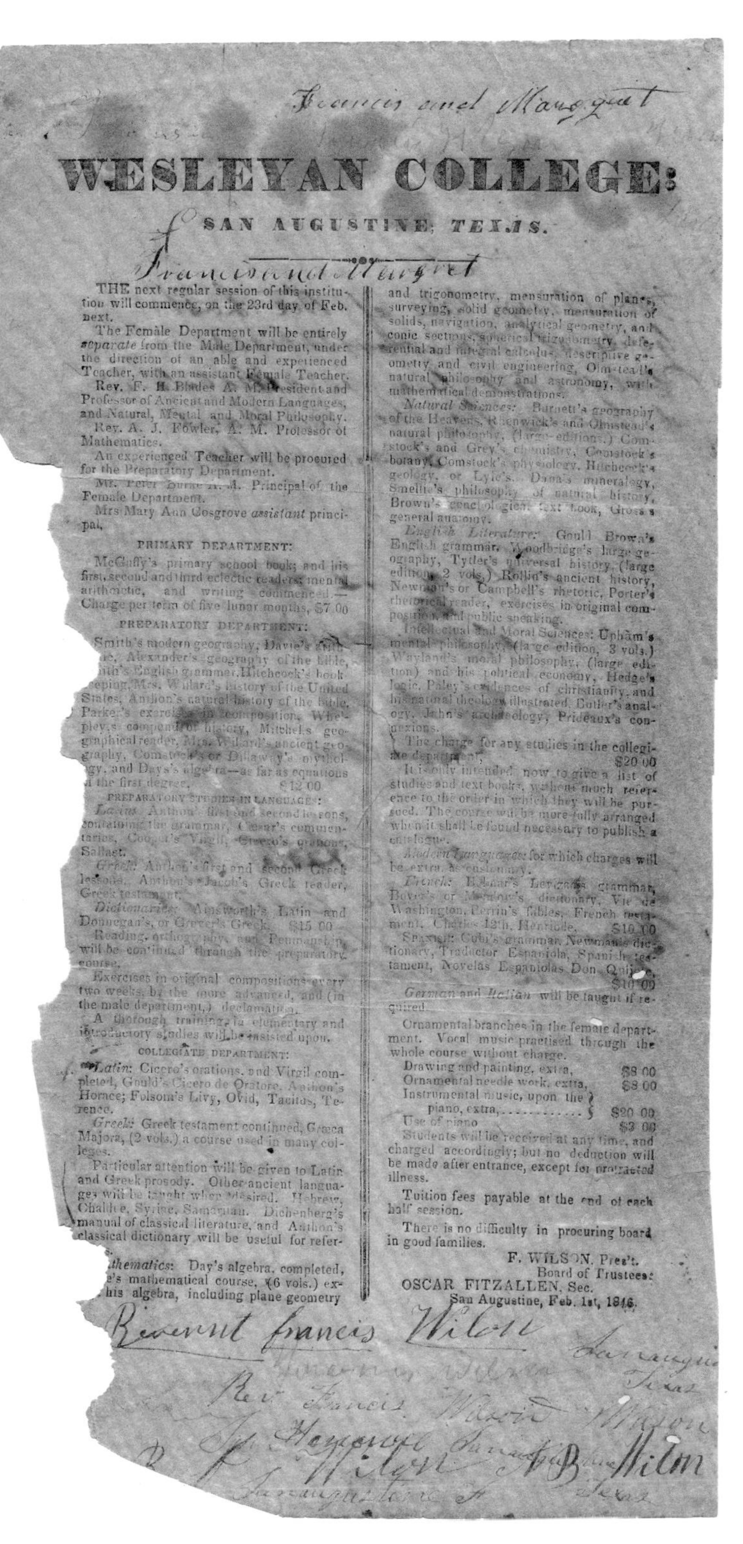

WESLEYAN COLLEGE:

SAN AUGUSTINE, TEXAS.

THE next regular session of this institution will commence, on the 23rd day of Feb. next.

The Female Department will be entirely *separate* from the Male Department, under the direction of an able and experienced Teacher, with an assistant Female Teacher.

Rev. F. H. Blades A. M. President and Professor of Ancient and Modern Languages, and Natural, Mental and Moral Philosophy.

Rev. A. J. Fowler, A. M. Professor of Mathematics.

An experienced Teacher will be procured for the Preparatory Department.

Mr. Peter Burke A. M. Principal of the Female Department.

Mrs Mary Ann Cosgrove *assistant* principal.

PRIMARY DEPARTMENT:

McGuffy's primary school book; and his first, second and third eclectic readers; mental arithmetic, and writing commenced.—Charge per term of five lunar months, $7 00

PREPARATORY DEPARTMENT:

Smith's modern geography, Davie's arithmetic, Alexander's geography of the Bible, Smith's English grammar, Hitchcock's book keeping, Mrs. Willard's history of the United States, Anthon's natural history of the bible, Parker's exercises in composition, Whelpley's compend of history, Mitchel's geographical reader, Mrs. Willard's ancient geography, Comstock's or Dillaway's mythology, and Days's algebra—as far as equations of the first degree, $12 00

PREPARATORY STUDIES IN LANGUAGES:

Latin: Anthon's first and second lessons, containing the grammar, Cæsar's commentaries, Cooper's Virgil, Cicero's orations, Sallust.

Greek: Anthon's first and second Greek lessons, Anthon's Jacob's Greek reader, Greek testament.

Dictionaries: Ainsworth's Latin and Donnegan's, or Grover's Greek, $15 00

Reading, orthography, and Penmanship, will be continued through the preparatory course.

Exercises in original compositions every two weeks, by the more advanced, and (in the male department,) declamation.

A thorough training in elementary and introductory studies will be insisted upon.

COLLEGIATE DEPARTMENT:

Latin: Cicero's orations, and Virgil completed, Gould's Cicero de Oratore, Anthon's Horace; Folsom's Livy, Ovid, Tacitus, Terence.

Greek: Greek testament continued, Græca Majora, (2 vols.) a course used in many colleges.

Particular attention will be given to Latin and Greek prosody. Other ancient languages will be taught when desired. Hebrew, Chaldee, Syriac, Samaritan. Dichenberg's manual of classical literature, and Anthon's classical dictionary will be useful for reference.

Mathematics: Day's algebra, completed, [illegible]e's mathematical course, (6 vols.) ex[illegible] his algebra, including plane geometry and trigonometry, mensuration of planes, surveying, solid geometry, mensuration of solids, navigation, analytical geometry, and conic sections, spherical trigonometry, differential and integral calculus, descriptive geometry and civil engineering, Olmstead's natural philosophy and astronomy, with mathematical demonstrations.

Natural Sciences: Burnett's geography of the Heavens, Renwick's and Olmstead's natural philosophy, (large editions.) Comstock's and Grey's chemistry, Comstock's botany, Comstock's physiology, Hitchcock's geology, or Lyle's. Dana's mineralogy, Smellie's philosophy of natural history, Brown's conchological text book, Gross's general anatomy.

English Literature: Gould Brown's English grammar, Woodbridge's large geography, Tytler's universal history, (large edition, 2 vols.) Rollin's ancient history, Newman's or Campbell's rhetoric, Porter's rhetorical reader, exercises in original composition, and public speaking.

Intellectual and Moral Sciences: Upham's mental philosophy, (large edition, 3 vols.) Wayland's moral philosophy, (large edition) and his political economy, Hedge's logic, Paley's evidences of christianity, and his natural theology illustrated, Butler's analogy, John's archæology, Prideaux's connexions.

The charge for any studies in the collegiate department, $20 00

It is only intended now to give a list of studies and text books, without much reference to the order in which they will be pursued. The course will be more fully arranged when it shall be found necessary to publish a catalogue.

Modern Languages: for which charges will be extra, as customary.

French: Bolmar's Levizac's grammar, Boyer's or Meadow's dictionary, Vie de Washington, Perrin's fables, French testament, Charles 12th, Henriade, $10 00

Spanish: Cubi's grammar, Newman's dictionary, Traductor Espaniola, Spanish testament, Novelas Espaniolas Don Quijote, $10 00

German and *Italian* will be taught if required.

Ornamental branches in the female department. Vocal music practised through the whole course without charge.

Drawing and painting, extra,	$8 00
Ornamental needle work, extra,	$8 00
Instrumental music, upon the piano, extra,	$20 00
Use of piano	$3 00

Students will be received at any time, and charged accordingly; but no deduction will be made after entrance, except for protracted illness.

Tuition fees payable at the end of each half session.

There is no difficulty in procuring board in good families.

F. WILSON, Pres't.
Board of Trustees:
OSCAR FITZALLEN, Sec.
San Augustine, Feb. 1st, 1846.

Wesleyan College flyer of February 1, 1846, printed over the signature of Francis Wilson, President of the Board of Trustees. Southwestern University, Special Collections.

struggle. . . . In their effort for liberty you kindly aided them, and they recollect you and bless you in their hearts. The Wesleyan is now in a mighty warfare against human ignorance even more fatal than Mexican cruelty and in their effort they have sent to you, fellow citizens, and ladies, for aid to rout this fiend of darkness. No new country has a greater desire to dedicate their children than Eastern Texas or the friends of the Wesleyan College. They have exerted all their powers and have made a trial which has proven to them that with a little assistance they can and will succeed. I am not pleading for a nation which you know not. We are your brothers, governed by the same form of government, worship the same God and are members of the same church; your children are with us. We are now before you asking your help.[27]

As a result of his efforts, a fund of about twenty thousand dollars was raised to pay for the main three-story building, about forty by eighty feet, being built on the nascent campus.[28]

Wilson took his job as Chairman of the Board of Trustees seriously. On February 28, 1845, he writes a letter to the *Western Christian Advocate* recounting briefly the history of the school and touting its prospects.[29] During the last week in July of that year, he notes in his journal that he is "arranging for college, setting time of scholarships and forming the ordinance."[30] The small catalog for 1846 is printed over his signature. It lists a Primary Department, a Preparatory Department, and a Collegiate Department, each with the appropriate studies.[31]

All in all, Wilson is the force behind the college. The Presidents are secondary figures. Janes for the first two years and Foster H. Blades for the last two made an impact as teachers and administrators but not as movers and shakers for the enterprise. Wilson is the unifying figure throughout its four-year history, pushing things forward. Nevertheless, his efforts were not enough. He was destined like Sisyphus to fail in his endeavor. One small town, with at most eight hundred to a thousand inhabitants, could not support two competing schools, and Wesleyan College was soon to face a disastrous event.

The Fateful Event

Montrose's innovative educational efforts at the University of San Augustine included using the Lancasterian plan, a major feature of which was instructing the older students, who then taught the younger. This method worked well for him, but he ran into intense opposition because of his manner of advertising. It was, in the mind of Oran M. Roberts, a young lawyer and farmer, bombastic and egotistical. Roberts, a graduate of the University of Alabama, had recently settled near San Augustine. His deep interest in education caused an acrimonious controversy to arise between the two men. As a result, Montrose resigned as President of the school in 1845, and Roberts was elected President of the Board of Trustees. While exercising this office, he taught a course in law at the University. Little could Montrose know at the time that he was jousting with a man who, as Frederick Eby says, "was destined a full generation later to play the most constructive role which any man has played in the educational progress of the state."[32] Elected governor in 1878, Roberts, during his two terms in office, set the system of public education on a firm financial basis and established the University of Texas.

Succeeding Montrose was the Rev. James Russell, who had been a teacher in the school. He was an accomplished man with a Master of Arts from the University of Edinburgh. He brought with him a selected library of five hundred books and a fine set of chemical and physical apparatus. He was a "trenchant" writer and a fine speaker. But he had, says Crocket, an "irascible, impetuous temperament and domineering personality, and was constantly in trouble one way or another. He was perfectly fearless and did not hesitate to meet an antagonist in a personal encounter. He possessed a biting tongue, and expressed his opinions regardless of possible consequences. It was this trait in the end that caused his death."[33]

When Russell succeeded Montrose as President, he also became editor of *The Red Lander*, one of the two town newspapers. Since the Rev. Foster H. Blades, the Wesleyan President replacing Janes, was editor of *The San Augustine Shield*, denominational rivalry was embedded in their periodicals. Blades, however, resigned his position as editor of the *Shield* on August 7, 1847, to be succeeded by Henry Kendal.[34] When Russell published a remark in *The Red Lander* about Kendal's sister, implying that she was a loose woman, Kendal decided to settle the affair in Western style. On August 9, each fired two shots at the other but missed. The following day Kendal caught Russell coming out of his office and killed him. Crocket says that Kendal fled to Mexico and lived there the rest of his life. He was never brought to trial.[35]

Though the immediate cause of the duel was Russell's remark about Kendal's sister, all sources agree that the underlying cause was the rivalry between the two institutions. This rivalry in the hands of intemperate partisans finally came to a head, resulting in the death of one man and the exile of the other. The effect of the event on the two schools was immediate. The doors of the University of San Augustine were closed, and Wesleyan College ceased to exist except as a shell ready for takeover.

Demise of the College

The end for both schools came quickly. They had barely been holding on, and the negative effects in the minds of the people caused by the duel removed any possibility of continuance. Both had reached their peak around 1845 and crumbled rapidly thereafter. The University of San Augustine declined from a student body of around 150 in that year to about a third of that number.[36] Wesleyan enrollment, which was 155 in its first year, was down to 85 in 1847. It ran a deficit budget every year, owing one thousand dollars by 1845, with the amount increasing annually. It graduated two students with baccalaureate degrees in 1846, but there were to be no more.[37] One of those two was Franklin Barlow Sexton, one of the most effective members of the Confederate Congress, later a judge on the state Supreme Court.[38] The University of San Augustine graduated none during its entire existence.

The events connected with the demise of the College involved much anguish and finger pointing. Late 1847 found Wilson winding up the affairs of the College. Because his health was bad, he had previously decided to "locate," i.e., not to take an appointment the following year, and to move with his family to some land he had purchased in Newton County. He had also determined not to attend the meeting of the Annual Conference two weeks hence, "for it seemed a death-like struggle for me to leave the work I had so long engaged in." Soon after informing the presiding officer of his intention, he was told that a certain minister had preferred charges against him for "unkindness and unchristian acts toward him under different specifications." As a result, on the advice of friends, he changed his mind and attended. He says that as part of a concerted effort against him, a committee was set up to examine the condition of Wesleyan College. The committee insisted that he account for the receipt and disbursement of all funds he had handled as the financial agent for the school and would not accept the report already issued by the Wesleyan Trustees that Wilson had "acted in all things highly honorable [sic] and right." He had to spend two days justifying his administration of the funds. Though the committee finally exonerated him and reported that all his business with the College was correct, the original charges leveled against him before the meeting of the Conference were brought up again, and on that complaint "they suspended him one year from preaching." Nevertheless, that same evening they reconsidered the vote and acquitted him by allowing him to locate in good standing.[39]

These dolorous happenings at the Annual Conference would seem to be inexplicable, given Wilson's previous standing in the Conference, were it not for the context in which they were set. Wilson says that he closed down Wesleyan College at some financial sacrifice to himself, leaving "$1,600, I had paid out of my own funds, for the trustees." The Trustees then voted to amalgamate the school with a new state institution that would also take over what was left of the University of San Augustine. This amalgamation was the action referred to by Bishop Capers at the Annual Conference on December 8 as a dreadful "blow-up" of Wesleyan College. It is clearly identified as such by the Rev. John W. Fields, Presiding Elder of the San Augustine District, whom Macum Phelan quotes: "Here . . . we had a dreadful 'blow-up' of the Wesleyan College. The Trustes [sic], through intrigue taking advantage of some legal defectability of the Charter, had amalgamated it with a [new] state University, over the head of the Conference."[40] This proposed state institution was to be called the University of Eastern Texas. An act was subsequently passed by the Legislature on March 8, 1848, incorporating it. It called for fifteen Trustees, with not more than three from any one religious denomination. The assets of the old University of San Augustine were transferred to it.[41] As it happened, the new institution did not materialize.

Francis Wilson was the chair of the Wesleyan College Board of Trustees during its entire existence. Available evidence does not allow a determination as to when, in the process of closing down the school and moving to Newton County, he stepped down from that office and ceased to act as a Trustee. Whether he was a part of the action of the Board of Trustees to amalgamate the institution with the proposed University of Eastern Texas, which the Conference would have opposed, is not known. What can be stated with assurance is that the members of the Annual Conference knew that they were losing the College and the Church's investment in it and that it had occurred on Wilson's watch. In their minds he was at least guilty of dereliction of duty for not preventing it whether or not he had actually played any role in it.

The three-story Wesleyan College building. After the demise of Wesleyan College, it passed into the hands of the Masonic Institute. It burned in 1868. Southwestern University, Special Collections.

The Masonic Institute

By 1850 the educational situation in San Augustine was bleak. Passing through the area in that year, Melinda Rankin, a mid-nineteenth-century educational observer, recounts some of the sad events relating to the rise and fall of the two denominational institutions. She says about the main building of Wesleyan College that "nothing now remains but a dilapidated edifice to show that there ever existed an institution for the cultivation of the arts and sciences." Her book, *Texas in 1850*, was written at just about the time the Masons tried to retrieve what they could by setting up the Masonic Institute.[42]

Since the University of Eastern Texas had failed to materialize, the two Masonic lodges in the area decided to take a hand in the matter. Masonry was strong in and around San

Augustine, and the two lodges there enjoyed the support of many prominent people. They decided to revive education for the youth of the community by setting up a new type of educational institution, to be neither a university nor a college, but an institute. Their Masonic Institute as constituted had two units, male and female, each maintained separately with its own corps of teachers. They used the vacant buildings of the now defunct Presbyterian and Methodist schools without ever gaining clear title for them. Modest tuition fees from the students and financial support from the lodges provided the economic resources necessary for the venture. They operated the school for about ten years until the Civil War put an end to the program.[43]

Though Crocket praises the success of the Masonic venture, saying that dissension disappeared and that instruction was appropriate to "the surroundings of a new country," Frederick Law Olmsted did not gain a very favorable impression of it about five years later. He says that "not far from the village stands an edifice [of the now defunct Wesleyan College], which, having three stories and sashed windows, at once attracted our attention." He then briefly recounts the story of the demise of the two denominational schools as a result of the duel. "After this," he continues, "both dwindled, and seeing death by starvation staring them in the face, they made an arrangement by which both were taken under charge of the *Fraternity of Masons.* The buildings are now used under the style of 'The Masonic Institute,' the one for boys, the other for girls. The boys occupy only their third story, and the two lower stories are falling to ludicrous decay—the boarding dropping off, and the windows on all sides dashed in."[44] The building burned down under mysterious circumstances during the session of the East Texas Annual Conference in San Augustine in December 1868.[45]

An Assessment

In 1851 the sixty-one-year-old Francis Wilson asked for an appointment in the Texas Conference and was given Bastrop and the Austin Colored Mission. He commented about the appointment that he "found a new field" and one he "was not acquainted with," but he visited the sick and preached in the houses of the poor. He especially admired some of the qualities he found in his African American flock. He was quite content with the appointment and with his labors of the year. His bad health, however, in addition to his lifelong physical infirmity, forced him to retire permanently the following year. He died in 1867, at the age of seventy-seven, about a year before his building, the main building of Wesleyan College, burned.

It is easy today to disparage the work of Wilson and his colleagues. They made many mistakes and were ultimately unsuccessful. The story of the failure of both the University of San Augustine and Wesleyan College is poignant testimony to the frailty of their efforts. Nevertheless, those who engaged in promoting and running those schools believed that what they were doing was for the welfare of the people they served and mattered deeply. They were full of ambition, hopes, and dreams. If in their hopes and dreams they were extravagant and if in their ambition they became too passionate, perhaps some margin may be granted them, because their efforts were the first of anyone to bring higher education to the piney woods country of East Texas.

Education and Plantation Economics: McKenzie College

McKenzie's Early Life

J. W. P. McKenzie and his wife, Matilda, operated the most successful college in Texas prior to the Civil War. The school closed after the war, and McKenzie supported Mood's establishment of Southwestern, serving briefly as Vice Regent. From Walter N. Vernon, et al., *The Methodist Excitement in Texas.* Used by permission of the Archives, Center for Methodist Studies at Bridwell Library, Perkins School of Theology, Southern Methodist University.

While plans were being made and charters secured for Rutersville and Wesleyan Colleges, a more modest educational effort was being made at the same time in North Texas. A Methodist minister, whose poor health caused him to give up the traveling ministry in favor of a less peripatetic form of service, started a little school on his farm. The fact that this school became, in the words of Frederick Eby, "on the whole, the most prosperous and vigorous institution in the Southwest, if not west of the Mississippi River, during the period up to the Civil War," is testimony to the success of the principles he used.[1] His name was John Witherspoon Pettigrew McKenzie.

McKenzie was born in Burke County, North Carolina, on April 26, 1806. His father was killed in a wagon accident while he was a youth, and his mother was the dominant force in the development of his character. As a youth of fourteen, she was converted under the preaching of Francis Asbury, the first Methodist bishop in America. As a result, her family shunned her. It had a Scottish Seceder background and was prejudiced against Methodists. Being forced by her father to renounce her faith or leave home, she chose the latter. Her parents finally relented, attended Methodist meetings, and became Methodists as well.[2] She transmitted her deep faith and strong will to McKenzie.

The educational path followed by McKenzie in developing his intellectual ability is uncertain. One source has him attending the University of North Carolina for two years before leaving for the University of Alabama at Athens, where he graduated.[3] Another says that he "started his collegiate career at the University of North Carolina but later moved to the University of Georgia, at that time called Franklin College."[4] Later family tradition places the Franklin College connection during the presidency of Moses Waddel (1819–1829). Records at the University of Georgia covering those years, however, do not put the young man there. Clearly the issue is confused. John D. Osburn, who has studied the matter carefully, surmises that the confusion may be due to the fact that Waddel was head of a "celebrated academy" at Willington, McCormick County, South Carolina, before he became President of Franklin and that McKenzie probably attended the academy rather than Franklin College. No other institution of higher education in the South existing at that time lists him as a student.[5]

Following his graduation, he served for a year as Principal of Georgia's Gainesville Academy.[6] He returned home in 1829 and married Matilda Hye Parks, ten years his junior. She was, says McLean, the perfect companion, furthering their common interests the rest of their lives. After their marriage, they moved to Maury County, Tennessee, where he taught for five years as head of his own school near Columbia.[7]

Missionary Work among the Choctaws and Texans

During his seven years of teaching, McKenzie had served somewhat irregularly as a local preacher. He finally determined to become a full-time minister and received appointment in 1836 as a missionary to the Choctaw Indians in the Indian Territory, now Oklahoma. The Indians among whom he worked had recently been transplanted from the Southeast on the "Trail of Tears," and gamblers and bootleggers victimized them, playing on their destitute condition. McKenzie took their part and warned the Indians strongly against the demoralizing influence of these men. His advocacy of the Indians was dangerous and brought him taunts and threats. Only his physical attributes and resolute attitude kept him from being harmed. Though short, only five feet six or seven, he had a deep chest and weighed a vigorous 180 pounds.[8]

After three years, the bishop moved him to a new missionary field in the Republic of Texas. He was appointed to the Sulphur Fork circuit of the Arkansas Conference with responsibilities almost as difficult as those he had left. His preaching round, which he covered every six weeks, consisted of thirty-two appointments in an area about 40 miles wide and 150 miles long, stretching from Rondo, Arkansas, to Preston Bend, near Denison, Texas.[9] He had great success. Preaching primarily in private homes, he received 609 persons into the Church within two years.[10]

The combination of McKenzie's inclination toward teaching and increasing health problems brought on by five years of constant service to his Indian and Texas congregations finally constrained him to retire from the traveling ministry. In 1841 he settled on 421 acres of land three miles southwest of Clarksville in Red River County. Appropriately, he named his residence "Itinerant Retreat."[11]

First Years at Itinerant Retreat

No sooner had he settled and begun to farm than he opened a school in his home with sixteen students. As the school grew, a separate one-room log house, about 16' x 20', was erected for it. A single log was left out of one wall, the vacant space becoming the window. The smooth side of a split log was placed before this opening and became the desk. When this building was outgrown, it was torn down and one twice its size was built. Shed rooms were added to the sides, and a long row of single cottages was built. These were presumably the residences of the male boarding students.[12]

Even at this point, at the beginning of McKenzie's educational enterprise in Texas, one recognizes some of the elements of his later success. He had a way of building for the future in measured incremental stages. He also had an uncanny knack for balancing the desirable with the possible. Through it all, he maintained an unshakable idealism in dealing with people while remaining a hardheaded businessman in the world of everyday affairs. Some of these characteristics are seen in his first major decision—to purchase a homestead. He did not just suddenly retire in 1841, buy some land, and start a school. He had bought his land in 1839 and given his school plan two years to mature before launching it. He did not then attempt to secure a charter or to outline elaborate programs toward academic degrees. He simply taught the students he gathered round him each year, formulating his tactics for the future on the basis of current experience. The school had no official standing until later. Accordingly, it did not bear a name other than that of his residence—Itinerant Retreat—until it received a charter in 1854.

Andrew Davis Finds a Home

A striking portrayal of his procedure comes from an autobiographical sketch written by Andrew Davis, later a prominent Methodist minister, who was one of McKenzie's first sixteen students in 1841.[13] A few years later, in 1844, he became the first student to receive an A.B. degree.

Davis, born in Red River County, was only nine or ten years old when Indian raiders killed his father. He lost contact with his stepmother, and his life was unsettled for the next few years. He became an expert hunter and once participated in an expedition against a band of Indian intruders. He lived where he could until older friends, recognizing the impending disintegration of his life, decided to send him, if possible, to live with McKenzie. Though McKenzie could not have been settled long at Itinerant Retreat, he was already recognized as a person who helped young people.

Communications were exchanged, and "Uncle Ab," John McKenzie's older brother and superintendent of "all the affairs of the home and farm," came in a buggy to get him.[14] They ended up, however, at a camp meeting, where McKenzie was preaching. Andrew could not imagine what a camp meeting was, since he had never seen any kind of religious service, nor had any person ever talked to him about religion. He grew fearful that it might have something to do with the military. He was sure from the white tents, wagons, horses, mules, and oxen that it foreboded trouble. What he saw when he got closer amazed him greatly. McKenzie was preaching "as though he stood on embers, running first to one end of the box and then to the other . . . , as though he wanted to get out of the box. He was talking loudly, and his gestures were the most violent in character." When things seemed to be approaching a crisis, it all ended, to Andrew's relief, without trouble.

After the service he was taken to meet John and Matilda McKenzie. "The manner in which J. W. P. McKenzie met me and talked to me," says Davis, "impressed me deeply and won my heart at the very first, and taking my hand he said, 'Come on with me up to the tent and see Mrs. McKenzie; you need a mother, and she will be a mother to you from this time on.' . . . I still had on my well glazed suit of buck-skin. I was greatly embarrassed. The children stood around and gazed at me as the wonder of the day. But Mrs. McKenzie met me with such an expression of love and sympathy that no mortal could keep from loving her. She led me away from the crowd, back into the cook room, and said to an old colored woman that seemed to have universal oversight of the cooking department, 'This, Aunt Dicey, is our adopted boy. I want you to spread him a good dinner here on this side table and see that he gets plenty to eat.' . . . Sister McKenzie sent a young man to Clarksville that afternoon after cloth to make me a suit of clothes. By 2 P.M. next day I laid aside my deer-skin suit of clothing and put the new suit on. . . . Late on the afternoon of this day my life began in my new home."

Many of the elements basic to McKenzie's method appear in Davis's narrative. The McKenzies look on everyone in their operation as part of one large family and bring the destitute young man into that family.[15] However strict the rules become as the school grows, its members are still a family, and the rules are there to promote good order. McKenzie looks on himself as a minister and during his career is father, teacher, and spiritual leader to his students. As he and Matilda became father and mother to Andrew, they serve in that capacity to many, if not most, of the other students as well. As a practical person, he divides the responsibilities of management among the family. He supervises the school, Matilda takes care of the students and manages the house, and his brother Abner runs the farm, soon to be large enough to be called a plantation. Aunt Dicey is the slave, soon to be joined by many others, who will produce the food needed for a dining table that will, at its peak, serve as many as 400 students. Just as Andrew, many of the approximately 3,300 students the school educated from 1841 to 1868 will attribute their success in later life to their "home" at McKenzie.

The School Begins to Grow

From 16 students in 1841, the number grew to 63 in 1846. In 1845 a "female department" and a "collegiate department" were added to the original "preparatory department." Soon after the inauguration of the collegiate program, degrees began to be awarded almost every year.[16] The reputation of the school grew rapidly, and a few years later Charles

Three of the four main buildings of McKenzie College. Southwestern University, Special Collections.

DeMorse, editor of the Clarksville *Northern Standard*, could write in an article that a "considerable number" of students had been refused admittance to McKenzie because of its inability to accommodate more.[17]

To remedy this situation, McKenzie began to supplant his earlier log cottages with more substantial buildings. Four large new frame structures were completed in 1853 at a cost of thirty thousand dollars. One, called the Chapel, had three floors, and contained the chapel auditorium, the President's office, the library, classrooms, the laboratory, and rooms for the school newspaper and the debating societies. A second two-story building was the President's home and the residence for girls. The two other buildings, called the Duke and Graft houses, named for their builders, were of two-and-a-half stories each and served as dormitories for the boys. There were eight rooms on each of the first two floors with two double beds in every room, accommodating four boys. Well lighted by day, the rooms were dark at night, and the boys had to study singly by the light of a flickering candle. The boy who studied last often slept during the earlier night hours.[18]

Located on a beautiful piece of land, McKenzie College ultimately provided facilities almost unrivaled among nineteenth-century schools in the South. The scientific laboratory was "modern," containing at least seven hundred dollars worth of equipment, including an old brass microscope still preserved. McKenzie was a lover of books and an incessant reader.[19] Consequently, the library was built up over the years and was extensive for the times. It eventually contained 2,000–3,000 volumes.[20] At the time Osburn made his study of the institution in 1960, it was still preserved by the McKenzie family at their old home, and consisted of about 1,500 volumes, many of which were Latin, Greek, or Hebrew texts, theological works, or volumes of history.[21]

State and Church

By 1854 McKenzie's "Itinerant Retreat" school had been in existence for thirteen years. It had survived its frontier origin and integrated itself into the dynamic structure of a rapidly developing antebellum Texas. It had built up an excellent reputation, had outstanding facilities, was solvent, and had fine prospects. Without having asked for or received a dollar to build or support the college, McKenzie had accomplished all this in little more than a decade. He relied, he said, solely on tuition, which was sufficient.[22] As the 1854 session began there were nine professors and tutors and over 300 students, most of whom boarded at the school.[23] It had one other attribute that year as well—a new state charter that officially designated it the McKenzie Institute.[24]

Until this point, John McKenzie had not found it necessary to ask anything for his school from either the former Republic or the present State. The Texas government did not concern itself, as it does today, in private educational matters, such as setting standards, and he could operate very much as he chose so long as he did not violate commonly received standards for community well-being in doing so. Other schools sought charters from the Republic or State to exempt themselves from taxes and to give their Boards of Trustees the legal right to act as corporations in handling finances and real estate. McKenzie did not seek tax exemption for the plantation of which his school was a part, and, as sole owner, he ran it without a Board of Trustees, obviating the need to set it up as a juridical person. But another reason began to make him consider seeking a charter—its long-term future. A charter tended to carry with it a certain cachet, suggesting recognition of its public welfare component, and implied a legal permanence that might be useful. Consequently he sought and received a charter.

The relationship of McKenzie's school to the Methodist Church is roughly analogous to its relationship with the State. It was Methodist in spirit but not in fact. McKenzie always looked on himself as a minister and a servant of the Church. He ran his school not simply to educate young people, but also to build character and to lead them to Christ. As he wrote in the *Catalogue of 1860–1861*, "The Bible is received as the only Book worthy of confidence and respect in morals, and is read daily by the students, and studied as part of the course, without which no one can be properly educated."[25] McKenzie felt that his institution, without being officially connected with the Church, was as much grounded in it as Rutersville College or Wesleyan College, which were sponsored directly by it.

As the years went by, he became more and more interested in establishing a formal Church relationship for the school. Looking into the future, without another person of his type on the horizon as his successor, he felt that the Church would be the best guarantor of its continuance. Consequently, in 1855 he deeded the Institute, as its new charter called it, to the East Texas Conference. He had been careful to include in his charter of the year before a section stipulating that its Trustees, of whom there were nine named by him, "shall have power to convey said institution entire, and all that in any wise appertains to it, to any branch of the Christian Church that they may see fit." The deed was valued at forty thousand dollars, including the immediate land on which the school stood but not the rest of the plantation. The Conference, however, could not fulfill the conditions of the gift, and the land was deeded back a few months later.[26]

He made another attempt to transfer the school five years later. At that time the ten acres of land on which the school stood was deeded once more to the Conference, and supervisory power over the school was vested in a twelve-person Board of Trustees appointed by it. A stipulation in the deed provided that the property, the ten acres, would revert to McKenzie or his heirs should the school cease to exist.[27]

The transfer made another state charter necessary to reflect the official Methodist affiliation and the new organizational structure of the institution. Though the enabling legislative act of January 31, 1860, called it the "McKinzie Male and Female College," McKenzie never used the new title, not even correcting the misspelling of his name. It didn't matter. The school was in his mind whatever it had become over the years, and the state charter was simply a validation of almost two decades of work, not an authorization. During the decade of the 1860s, all college records, diplomas, catalogs, and the like unofficially shortened the name to "M'Kenzie College."[28]

The new arrangement of McKenzie College as a Church institution failed to take hold. After a year the Board of Trustees ceased trying to manage it, and direction reverted to McKenzie, though the legal structure was not changed to reflect that. Ralph Jones surmises that McKenzie knew that his transfer of the school would not really affect his control and that what he was really doing was preparing for its continuance in the event of his own death.[29]

The Board of Trustees did have a hand in the management of the school for one year, but, with the coming of the Civil War, it gave up its limited efforts, and McKenzie ran it alone until 1868, when he, not the Board of Trustees, finally closed it. At that point he joined forces with Francis Asbury Mood and others to bring about the establishment of a Central university for Methodism in Georgetown.

The Curriculum during the Peak Years

The six years after 1854 mark the high point of McKenzie College. During that time it had over 300 boarding pupils per year from Texas, Louisiana, Arkansas, the Indian Territory, and Missouri. Maximum enrollment occurred in 1859–1860, with 405 students taught by nine faculty members.[30] Fortunately, the *Catalogue of M'Kenzie College, 1860–1861*, has been preserved and describes the curriculum when the College was at its peak. Each of the three divisions of McKenzie College, preparatory, collegiate, and female, had separate curricular requirements, though those of the female and collegiate departments were similar.[31]

The preparatory department had a lower primary level, in which students were taught the basics, such as spelling, geography, grammar, reading, arithmetic, and Spenserian penmanship. Subjects taught in the preparatory department were United States history, arithmetic and elementary algebra, grammar, astronomy, English composition, Latin, and Greek. Caesar was read in Latin while Xenophon's *Anabasis* and St. John's Gospel were studied in Greek. Mastery of these courses led to entrance into the collegiate department.

Mathematics courses in the collegiate department included algebra, geometry, plane and spherical trigonometry, analytical geometry, and differential and integral calculus. Latin began with Cicero and went through Virgil, Horace, Tacitus, and Livy. Greek began with Homer and the New Testament and included the history of Thucydides and the *Oedipus Tyrannus* by Sophocles. Butler's *Analogy* was taught to the seniors for religious edification. Other one-semester courses were logic, rhetoric, chemistry, "evidences of Christianity," mental philosophy, and "surveying and navigation." Original declamation was studied in the second semesters of the junior and senior years. Successful completion of these courses led to the A.B. degree. There was only one elective. One could substitute two modern languages for Greek.

The master's degree (A.M.) was conferred on bachelor of arts students "sustaining a good moral character," who, after three years devoted to literary pursuits, submitted an essay upon a scientific subject or delivered a written address approved by the faculty. Eighteen Master of Arts degrees were awarded from 1846 to 1872.

The curriculum for the female department was a hybrid program between the preparatory and the A.B. program that the men pursued. Both Latin and Greek were studied, as well as mathematics through trigonometry. Science, United States history, French, "evidences of Christianity," and "moral philosophy" were also parts of the program. One completing this four-year course was honored by graduation but without a degree.

The heaviest enrollment was always in the preparatory department and the lowest in the female department. Only a small number of young women attended annually.

Over the four-year period from 1857–1858 to 1860–1861, the time of maximum enrollment, only 72 young women attended, an average of 18 per year. The male ambience thus created does not appear to have been intentional. Part of the explanation for the low female enrollment seems to have been that there were excellent female seminaries in nearby Clarksville.[32]

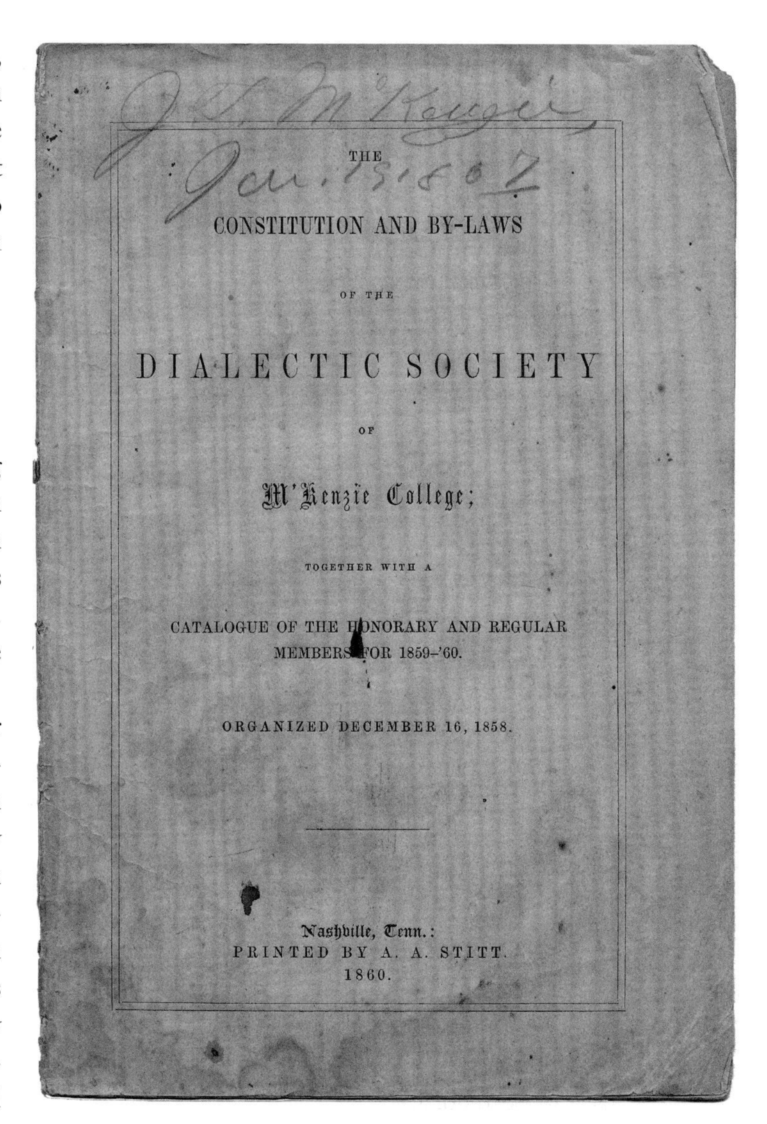

THE

CONSTITUTION AND BY-LAWS

OF THE

DIALECTIC SOCIETY

OF

M'Kenzie College;

TOGETHER WITH A

CATALOGUE OF THE HONORARY AND REGULAR MEMBERS FOR 1859–'60.

ORGANIZED DECEMBER 16, 1858.

Nashville, Tenn.:
PRINTED BY A. A. STITT.
1860.

Copy of *The Constitution and By-Laws of the Dialectic Society of M'Kenzie College*, 1860. Southwestern University, Special Collections.

Classroom Procedure

Class grading was done on a zero to nine basis, nine being the highest. An absence brought a zero. Each class began with a reading from the Bible by the professor, who then made a few remarks, followed by a prayer. Each class was supposed to begin with a review of the previous lecture. Grades were turned in each month and reported to the parents.

Boys and girls were taught in separate classes except for those of Dr. McKenzie. He permitted only women or married men to teach the girls. The girls sat by themselves in chapel, and "side glances" were discouraged. "Apparently some mild association was permitted, however, for Smith Ragsdale married the president's daughter, Patsy McKenzie, who was hardly fifteen years of age, while they both were students. Ragsdale eventually became McKenzie's partner at the college and later a regent of the University of Texas."[33] M. B. Lockett says that with all the restrictions placed on students about contact between males and females, the rule was often violated. Clandestine notes were passed during recitations or notes were given to a friend for delivery. "But woe to [the] fellow if found out!"[34]

The Literary Societies

Though the formal curriculum was the basis for classroom learning, the satisfactory completion of which was the standard for the procurement of degrees, an important vehicle for the training of the mind was declamation and debate. This form of learning has been so diminished in modern educational practice that it is difficult for persons living in the twenty-first century to appreciate the emphasis placed on it in former times. Not only was it a form of learning, but it was also tied up with the social system of the College, sometimes becoming the main form of social activity. The extracurricular organizations sponsoring these activities often became the equivalent of modern social clubs and fraternal societies, and students in after-years self-identified by the literary society to which they belonged in college. McKenzie College had a strong system of this type. John H. McLean said that he could think of nothing more useful to a student than participation in "high-class, well-conducted literary societies and school magazines. Throughout my public life I have felt myself to be a great debtor to my college debating society. One learns to think on his feet, acquires self-possession and becomes an ex tempore speaker."[35]

There were two such groups: the Philologian Society and the Dialectic Society. The first was older, but the second had a charter from the Legislature. They held weekly meetings at which the reading of essays and the holding of debates were central features. Members were expected to speak almost every week and were judged immediately.

Errors in style, content, and execution were called to their attention.[36] Debating topics included: "Is a lawyer justifiable in defending a bad cause?" "Is public opinion a standard of right?" "Is foreign emigration [immigration?] beneficial to a country?" "Whether a man be morally justifiable in obeying a civil law of which his conscience disapproves." "Whether personal interest in a subject of investigation be favorable to the discovery of truth." One of particular interest to young men was: "Is a bachelor in his isolated situation an object worthy of Commiseration?"[37]

The importance of the literary societies was reflected in the physical structure of the central building, the one used for chapel and recitation purposes, where the third story was dedicated to their use.[38] The kind of training received by students in the literary societies was especially useful at times of public examination and at graduation. The academic year, consisting of two terms, began on the first Monday in October and ended on or around July 4. Large crowds usually attended the final examinations at graduation time, which were public and oral.[39]

Daily Life of the Student

Students entering McKenzie could not say that they were not forewarned as to the rigor of life there. The catalog described succinctly the expectations of the school in that regard. "We wish," it says, "every student who comes here to have work to do, and plenty of it, to keep constantly at it, and to do it well." Then follows a series of laws, a virtual Ten Commandments for the school, governing academic procedure and regulating student conduct. The overall premise undergirding the whole is that the faculty, "as far as possible," will exercise "a parental government" and will endeavor to "substitute a moral power over the heart as a principle of order, in place of the fear of punishment."[40]

Nevertheless, recognizing that such general preachments were unlikely to provide much guidance for deterring specific instances of undesirable conduct, certain prohibitions were clearly specified. Prohibited were using profane or obscene language; playing at cards, billiards, or other unlawful games, or raffling; leaving the College grounds without permission; being out of room during study hours without permission, or being absent or tardy at prayers or recitation; being out of room at night, or engaging in any night-suppers, or other irregularities; smoking; keeping gunpowder, firearms, or deadly weapons of any kind, about the person, or in the room; allowing disorder in the room; attending any exhibition of an immoral tendency, or dancing-parties; using Keys or Translations; and other offenses not enumerated but obviously unacceptable. Students were also to repair or pay for any damage done to school property.[41] Apparently these rules had their effect. McLean states that he never heard an oath nor saw a bottle of whiskey or a deck of cards while there.[42]

In spite of the apparent strictness, student descriptions of everyday life dwell on their contentment rather than on their discontent. Sometimes students complained about "dull" weekends, especially the reduced diet for fasting purposes, but they found ways around these problems. The girls would make "midnight raids" on the College kitchen and make candy secretly in their fireplaces, being careful not to awaken Mrs. McKenzie. Boys and girls would also pull pranks on each other. One of the most memorable was the time when the girls, who published a little newspaper called the *Bee*, applied a heavy coat of white paint on a mule owned by the editor of the boys' newspaper, the *Owl*, with BEE painted in large block letters on the side of the mule. Everyone, it is said, enjoyed the joke, including the editor of the *Owl*, until he learned that the animal was his. Work and study were not the only aspects of the school day. McKenzie recognized the importance of play, and regular parts of the day were set aside for games.[43]

"Old Master"

> I can never forget my first night at the College when at a most inopportune hour—4 A.M.—the bell pealed out on the stillness of the night, calling us to the chapel for morning prayer. This exercise consisted of a scripture lesson, a lecture, song and prayer. It was in the dead of winter—crisp and cold—and yet "Old Master" was seen, candle in hand . . . wending his way to the Chapel, in his shirt sleeves and slippers, while the girls and boys were wrapped in shawls and blankets. His plea for this practice was, as a health measure, a morning air bath—it also served as a reproof to the boys and girls who sat shivering in their wraps, and also an excuse for no fire. Chapel service over, three successive tables were then served at breakfast, all by candlelight. Similar chapel services were held three times a day—4 A.M., 8 A.M., and at evening.[44]

Thus writes John McLean about his first night at McKenzie College. Later in life he was to say: "I have ever regarded my attendance upon McKenzie College at the turning point of life as a gracious providence."[45] He was not alone in remembering John McKenzie, the teacher, as an unusual, inspirational, and much-loved leader. Ralph Jones says that every personal account available to him "stresses the genius of the man's ability to inspire his young audience with intellectual and holy enthusiasm." He also says that all the testimonials to his memory emphasize his courage, wisdom, and humility as well.[46]

They also agree that McKenzie was a stern disciplinarian. He occasionally used a birch rod on malefactors, both male and female, which he called "riding Old Sawney." He also used embarrassment as a method of punishment. Boys who fought were sometimes forced to kiss each other to make up. Whatever the methods of discipline, he blended them with mercy, so much so that his pupils, as McLean above, affectionately called him "Old Master." The exact origin of the appellation is disputed, though all agree that he received it early in his career. His ability to identify with his students, yet maintain perfect order and authority, was remarkable. McLean says that he played with them on the playground as if he were a boy, but when the bell rang for books none disputed his supremacy.[47]

McKenzie's concern for his students was known and appreciated, though some of that concern was deemed eccentric, such as his early morning "air bath" and his insistence about the necessity for a weekly bath in the creek, at least for the male students.[48] He looked quite patriarchal in his old age because he wore a long, full beard, but the reason for it was not style. He grew it because he could never shave himself after being seriously burned in trying to rescue a schoolgirl on fire from an exploded lamp.[49]

As a preacher, McKenzie was, says McLean, a formidable pulpit orator. He says that he could hold an audience spellbound for two hours or more. M. B. Lockett, a student there in 1863–1864, is more restrained in his praise.[50] What with chapel services three times a day and four types of church meetings on Sunday, it was the rare student who could resist falling under his sway at some time or other during his or her academic career. McKenzie's books show that 2,250 of the aggregate 3,300 pupils were converted while attending.[51]

Yet, in spite of his overwhelming emphasis on things religious and on Methodist views, McKenzie was not narrow in a denominational sense. Differing views of Christian doctrine were apparently tolerated. B. F. Fuller, a lifelong Baptist, says that when he entered McKenzie he was worried about being permitted to retain his views. He found that no effort whatsoever was employed to change them. For a time, McKenzie employed a Baptist on his faculty, for which his bishop good-naturedly chided him.[52]

College Finances and the Plantation Economy

Though there were large numbers of students who could not pay tuition and board fees, McLean states that McKenzie never turned away a boy or girl, however poor.[53] Osburn agrees, saying that some indigent students were charged nothing.[54] The *Catalogue for 1860–61* exempts all students studying for the ministry from paying any tuition. Some students took out notes for their costs that they tried to repay. Meticulous steward that he was, McKenzie kept a record of these gifts, and at his death his books showed charities of $30,000 for educational purposes.[55]

One fee covered the basic expenses for the year at the College—tuition, board, lodging, and laundering. On average over the years it was about $130. Students were responsible for ordinary school and living necessities, but these were usually furnished by the school and billed to the parents. In 1848 the parents of one student, Malcolm Addison, were billed $48.67½ for books, paper, cash, several boxes of pills, shoes, ink, quills, candles, and postage.[56]

The faculty received good salaries for the times. One professor and his wife together received $2,000 for the school year. During his four years at McKenzie, John McLean incurred a debt of about $600. In order to pay it, he agreed after his graduation to teach for a year at the college. On the completion of the year, he settled his indebtedness, bought a mule, and left for his home near Marshall with $600 in his pocket.[57]

Certainly the financial situation at McKenzie differed from that found at Rutersville and Wesleyan. Whereas they were constantly struggling to stay afloat, the President of McKenzie College seemed to have the Midas touch. Not only did he contribute liberally to the education of poor students and pay his teachers well, but he also carried out all his land transactions in cash. The secret of his success was that he integrated the school into a plantation economy that was run with an eye to self-sufficiency. The entire farm and slaves were utilized for the College. No cotton was raised at all, not a single bale. The major crops were corn and wheat for bread. Hogs and cattle were raised in sufficient quantities to supply the school's needs for meat.[58]

Failure of the Plantation Economy

From the time of his original purchase of 421 acres in late 1839, McKenzie steadily built up over the next twenty-five years one of the most highly valued plantations in Red River County. He traded land frequently, hardly ever reporting one year the same acreage as the previous year. Between 1842 and 1855 he almost always farmed between 1,000 and 2,000 acres. From 1856 to 1864 he generally farmed between 2,000 and 3,000 acres. Only once during those nine years did he fall below 2,000 acres, and in 1858 he worked 3,641 acres. In addition, he had considerable holdings in other counties about which little is known. In 1860 he owned nine units of land comprising 4,556 acres in seven other counties that he reported for tax purposes on the Red River County roll.[59]

As McKenzie procured more and more land, he also procured more and more slaves to work it. Tax rolls report two slaves in 1843. He must have bought them shortly after settling at Itinerant Retreat. He reports one or two slaves each year until 1847, when he reports seven. The numbers then fluctuate between seven and nine through 1853. In 1854 he reports twelve. By 1859 it is eighteen. In 1860 it is twenty-five and a year later thirty-six. His large acquisitions for these last two years, seven for 1860 and eleven for 1861, suggest that he was probably taking advantage of cheaper prices for slaves caused by slave owners moving their slaves to Texas from the upper South to protect their investment in the face of the impending threat of war. In 1864 he reports a decline to twenty-nine. With the end of the Civil War, emancipation becomes effective in Texas, slavery is abolished, and he lists no slaves in 1865.

At the outbreak of the Civil War, slightly more than a third of Red River County's population of 8,535 were slaves. Only about one-quarter of the white families owned slaves, and only a quarter of those owned more than ten. By that criterion, McKenzie was a large slave owner. Though the end of slavery meant freedom for blacks, it meant the loss of capital for the slave owners. The 2,513 slaves listed on the tax roll in 1860 represented 49 percent of all taxable property in the county. McKenzie's tax valuation dropped from $35,998 that year to $12,010 in 1865. It dropped to half that the following year, and by 1868, the year he closed the school, it was only $950, though he still possessed 1,498 acres. The bottom had dropped out of land prices, and he seems to have quit farming except for immediate family needs.

In spite of the economic difficulties he faced, McKenzie tried to continue, but the school was never the same after the war that it was before. The 1860–1861 enrollment dropped to only 146, almost certainly because of the uncertain political climate just prior to the Civil War. One visitor to the campus at graduation time, July 25, 1861, comments that "only about 50 out of 150 pupils [were] left to witness the close."[60] In an attempt to accommodate to the war, McKenzie announced in the Clarksville *Northern Standard* (September 28, 1861) that "the services of a splendid drill master have been secured and military tactics will be taught to each student."[61] But nothing could reverse the decline in student numbers. It was largely a male institution, and those old enough to fight were away at war. Those too young to fight were kept at home to work in place of their elders who had left. Enrollment bottomed out in 1863 with 33 students. Times were hard after the war, and the College could count only 74 students in 1866–1867. There were no graduates from 1862 until its close in June 1868, when "at the final commencement, a solitary A. B. candidate received his degree."[62] He may have been William Johnson McDonald, who will figure later in the McKenzie story.

In the postwar years the financial problems of the parents of McKenzie's students plagued him persistently. Since parents often could not pay the tuition in cash, and he did not want to deny education to their children, he accepted promissory notes from them for it. He then endorsed the notes to the merchants in town for purchases. Sometimes the makers of the notes would refuse to honor them, and the Clarksville merchants would institute suits against both him and the parents. Some of the suits were settled out of court, but judgments for at least $10,697.86 were rendered against McKenzie and the other signers without any evidence that they were ever paid. The man who had paid cash for everything before the war now faced the ignominy of being a defaulter.[63] The tax rolls show no land held by him in other counties, and it is possible that he sold his property outside of Red River County to raise cash.

McKenzie College Students in the Civil War

The difficulties brought to John McKenzie and the College by the war were a consequence of the support of secession by him and by those who thought like him. They had not believed that a long war or defeat were realistic possibilities and went to war with enthusiasm. "Dr. McKenzie was a determined pro-slavery man and equally as determined a secessionist. He often entertained us at chapel service," says

M. B. Lockett, one of his students, "with his notions on these subjects. In his morning prayers or on Sundays he was as earnest in his petitions for the heavy hand of the Almighty to restrain and defeat the enemies of the Confederacy as the most violent politicians of the times."[64] Integrated as it was into the economic system of the Old South, McKenzie College furnished a large number of soldiers to the cause of the Confederacy. It must have been with considerable anguish that McKenzie heard the news of Confederate defeats and the deaths of students who had once sat before him in the classroom. Andrew Ragsdale, his son-in-law's brother, fell early in the war. Capt. Joe Dickson of McKinney and Rev. L. V. Brown were both killed at the Battle of Shiloh in April 1862. A few months later Col. John C. Burks of Clarksville was killed at the Battle of Murfreesboro, and Lt. W. J. Taylor, McLean's former roommate, died at the Battle of Raymond.[65] These are only representative of the total casualty list of McKenzie College students.

The most conspicuous soldier with McKenzie training in his background was Brigadier General William Hugh Young of San Antonio, who had obtained an A.M. in 1857. He was matriculating at the University of Virginia to further his education when the war broke out. As a Texan, he returned home and recruited a regiment of which he was elected Captain. He was promoted to the colonelcy after the Battle of Shiloh and to Brigadier General during the Atlanta campaign. Civil War historian Marcus J. Wright says that "few generals received more wounds or escaped death more often than did this thirty-year-old leader. He was wounded in the shoulder and had two horses shot from under him at Stone's River; at Jackson (May 14, 1863) he was wounded in the thigh; at Chickamauga, Young was wounded in the chest. He was shot both in the neck and the jaw at Kennesaw Mountain (June 27, 1863). At Allatoona his left foot was mangled [so badly that he ended up losing it], and his horse was killed beneath him." He was finally captured by Federal troops and ended the war as a prisoner. After the war, he returned to Texas and had a successful business career.[66]

The story before and after the war of another student is particularly intriguing and, in a sense, pathetic. Francis McMullan came to McKenzie College in 1858 at the age of twenty-three after having served in William Walker's unsuccessful 1857–1858 campaign to capture Nicaragua. After the war, during which he served the Confederacy in Mexico, he led a colony of 154 disgruntled Texans to Brazil rather than remain under a Reconstruction government. After considerable harassment in New Orleans, Galveston, and New York, they finally arrived in Brazil and settled south of Rio de Janeiro. Terminally ill with tuberculosis, McMullan died at Iguape, Brazil, on September 29, 1867, soon after arriving.[67] The colony successfully integrated itself into Brazilian life and, for its part, introduced useful American agricultural techniques and implements into the country.

McKenzie and Southwestern University

After a brief interlude at the plantation with no school to run, McKenzie became a participant in the effort of Francis Asbury Mood to construct a Central Methodist university. He went as an alternate delegate from the Trinity (later North Texas) Conference to the Educational Convention meeting in Galveston in April 1870. There, as the grand old man of Methodist education in Texas, he was nominated by the endowment committee as one of the two financial agents for the new university. When the second Convention met at Waxahachie a year later, he was elected as a delegate from the floor when the other delegates from the Trinity Conference failed to appear. He was also elected to preside in the absence of the bishop.[68] Soon thereafter he agreed to serve as the first President of the newly established Marvin College in Waxahachie. Waxahachie was a leading contender for the new Central Methodist university, and an expanded Marvin College might become that school. Some persons expected his fabled golden touch to bring it success. But it was not to be. He became entangled in debt problems connected with the recently completed college building and, in frustration, turned down the opportunity to serve another year.[69] He returned to Itinerant Retreat. From there he preached, held revivals, and worked in support of Mood's idea.

When the institutional structure of Southwestern University was set up in 1872, two boards were established to manage its affairs—a Board of Curators and a Board of Trustees. The former was made up of ministers and had charge of the educational and personnel affairs of the institution. The Board of Trustees was made up of laymen and had charge of all financial affairs. At the outset, each of the five sponsoring Conferences had one representative on the Board of Curators. At the meeting of the Curators on July 7, 1877, when the Board was expanded from five to thirty, the name of John W. P. McKenzie headed the list of new North Texas Conference representatives. The other three representatives of that Conference, J. H. McLean, M. H. Neeley, and J. C. Smith, were all graduates of McKenzie College. John Adams of the East Texas Conference and Andrew Davis of the Northwest Texas Conference were also McKenzie graduates, Davis being its first graduate. These six constituted 20 percent of the thirty members of the Board of Curators.[70] At the same meeting, McKenzie was elected to the largely honorific post of Vice Regent.[71]

Though he served in name as Curator for four years, McKenzie's ill health did not permit him to meet with the Board again. He died of cancer on June 20, 1881, in his seventy-sixth year. Matilda survived him about ten years.[72] They were buried side by side in the family graveyard near the College site.[73] McKenzie always considered Southwestern University to be the heir of his own institution,[74] and the Board of Curators adopted a memorial in his memory when it met the following year. "Coincidentally," says Ralph Jones, "this memorial appears on the same page of that dedicated to Robert Alexander. How fitting it is. These pioneer Methodist preachers who worked untiringly at distant points from each other in behalf of McKenzie College, Rutersville College, and Soule University, came together near the end of their lives to give what help they could to the institution whose charter effected a union with these three schools."[75]

McKenzie Alumni in the Professions

In the years after its closure, before the establishment of the large state universities, McKenzie College probably had the largest group of alumni of any school in the state. They were to be found in many places engaged in different professions. In his autobiography, entitled *Reminiscences*, John McLean lists several hundred of these former students. Under the categories of Soldiers, Teachers, Preachers, Physicians, and Lawyers and Statesmen, he mentions persons who became prominent in the state and made significant contributions to its development.

Some of them are known today for only one circumstance in their lives that makes them memorable. For example, Jasper C. Beckham was the physician who attended Jefferson Davis in his last illness. John Cochran, a Democrat, became Speaker of the Texas House, while his brother, Arch Cochran, a Republican, ran for governor in 1886 and lost. Smith Ragsdale, McKenzie's son-in-law, was a member of the Texas State Teachers Association group that memorialized the Legislature on founding the University of Texas. Before it opened, Governor Roberts appointed him to the Board of Regents. Another alumnus, John Ransom Parkes, opened a small school in Red River County in 1876 called Stonewall Seminary. The average attendance was about fifty. It became one of the "correlated" schools of Southwestern University when that program was initiated in 1887. It closed in 1892.

Three future cattle barons, James Monroe Daugherty, William Crow Wright, and George Thomas Reynolds, were also students at McKenzie College. Daugherty, who joined the Confederate army as an express rider at age fourteen, participated in the fabled long drive of the open-range cattle business at its inception. He made long cattle drives from 1867 to 1873 and was an important member of cattle associations for the rest of his life. Wright was the founder of the famous Chain Seven Ranch. He built up large landholdings in West Texas. Reynolds became one of the largest landholders and cattlemen in the state. The Reynolds Company acquired 232,000 acres in Jeff Davis County in 1895. It held ranchlands in eight counties and four states. At the time of his death his company had 330,000 acres in the Davis Mountains and 134,000 acres in other counties.

Many McKenzie students became lawyers and legislators and made a name for themselves. William Smith Herndon was elected to the U.S. Congress twice and was said by some to have been the finest orator of his day. William Jesse Swain was elected to the Texas House, to the Senate (twice), and in 1882, as State Comptroller. William Lyne Crawford was a member of the Constitutional Convention of 1875 and became a noted civil and criminal lawyer in Dallas. He tried cases of nationwide importance. James Price Hague and Thomas Jefferson Towles made their careers in West Texas, the former as the leading political figure working to connect El Paso by railroad to the rest of the state and the latter as the leading political figure in Van Zandt County. William E. Collard and George N. Aldredge had prominent careers as district judges. The biographies of all these persons appear in *The New Texas Handbook* of 1996.

Enough ministers have already been mentioned to illustrate the fact that McKenzie College was the leading training school for Methodist ministers in Texas until it was replaced by Southwestern University.

One of the most interesting alumni was William Johnson McDonald. Born in 1844, William and his two brothers were left as orphans when their parents died. John McKenzie became their guardian, and they, particularly William, received a thorough classical training in the McKenzie home and school. William developed a deep interest in astronomy, botany, zoology, and geology. His training was interrupted in 1864, when he became old enough to join the Confederate army, but it was completed after the war. He entered law and became recognized as one of the best civil lawyers of Northeast Texas. He moved from law into banking and opened banks in Clarksville, Paris, and Cooper. He moved to Paris, Texas, in 1887, where he lived thereafter. He worked hard, lived modestly, cared little for social life, and took no part in public affairs. He was not particularly religious but made unostentatious contributions to charity from time to time. He traveled to Europe and Mexico and studied botany in summer school at Harvard in 1895 and 1896. He never married and at his death in 1926 left the bulk of his estate to the University of Texas to establish an observatory. Distantly related heirs contested his will, but the University of Texas settled with them. It received $800,000 from the estate, a sizable figure for the time, and established the observatory. Today the University of Texas observatory at Mount Locke is named for him—McDonald Observatory.[76]

Final Assessment

McKenzie College prospered as long as the Old South economic structure that sustained it was maintained. It faltered, declined, and was finally closed when the Civil War destroyed that economy. The school was, says Osburn, in many ways a classic example of American higher education in the nineteenth century. It was a private institution, it developed around a great educator, and it did not outlast its founder.[77] McKenzie College was one of the remarkable early institutions in the development of Texas. It grew out of the life and aspirations of a person who, whatever his faults, and most of them were related to faults of the times, imbued over three thousand young people with a lofty vision and set before them high standards of accomplishment.

Occasion for Dismay: Soule University

It Was Not Supposed to Be This Way

At the end of their first day in Chappell Hill, November 20, 1868, Francis Asbury Mood, the new President of Soule University, showed Sue, his wife, the building where he would do his work. In spite of a heavy rain during the day, they walked to the site through the mud, "which clung like wax to our feet in such masses that they became a burden to lift."

> Entering the building[,] here was *occasion for dismay* [italics added] for the rain had poured through the leaky rood [sic; roof] & the water was dripping from dome to basement and the entire house [was] dank and musty. Of course, I did not intimate for a moment the real state of my feelings in the matter, but laughed heartily at our deplorable personal condition. . . . But my dear Sue could not make merry over the matter. Her common sense told her that *the whole aspect of matters* [italics added] was as unpromising as could be well imagined.[1]

Francis Asbury Mood, founder of Southwestern University. Southwestern University, Special Collections.

This "occasion for dismay," described by Mood, referred specifically to the condition of the University building, but both he and she, after only twenty-four hours in town, recognized that it pertained to "the whole aspect of matters." And they were right. After twelve years of existence, Soule University was in deplorable condition. It was ripe for dissolution.

How could it have come to this pass? It was not supposed to be this way. Dr. C. C. Cody, the longtime professor and dean of Southwestern University, writing about Soule more than forty years later, says:

> No educational enterprise of the church had been begun under more favorable conditions. Those who projected Soule University were not only familiar with the history of Texas Methodism from its beginning, but they [also] knew the causes for the failures of the several attempts of the Methodist church to found colleges in Texas. The plans were carefully laid to avoid every danger.[2]

Yet by 1868 the school was a failure. A second question follows the first. What kind of man was Francis Asbury Mood, who, beginning at this point, almost single-handedly took the remnants of four institutions, his own and the previous three already described, and out of them, in the face of overwhelming obstacles, established a "Central"

Methodist university? That question, to be dealt with first, is best answered by looking at the formation of his character and his behavior in various critical situations faced prior to his arrival at Chappell Hill.

Mood's Path to the Ministry

Mood's great-grandfather, Peter Muth, soon to be "Mood," immigrated to the United States from Germany in time to fight in Washington's army during the Revolutionary War and to lose his health therein. His son, another Peter Mood, moved to South Carolina after the war, where he married and became a silversmith. One of the couple's children was John Mood. He married Catherine Reader McFarland, whose antecedents were English. Nine children were born to the union, the sixth of whom was Francis Asbury, born on June 23, 1830.

Passing a Methodist Church one day, Mood's father, John, while still a youth, heard a sermon being preached in English, not the German to which he was accustomed. He went in and was delighted with the service. Though his father, Peter, initially forbade John to go to the church again, in time he relented, attended himself, and also joined the church. All the rest of the family followed him. John became a preacher and entered the South Carolina Conference in 1824. He located in 1830, resumed his jeweler's trade, and pursued it until his death. Francis Asbury was born the year his father located.[3] His mother's family was also Methodist, his grandfather McFarland having been the first local preacher in the Methodist Church in Charleston. In only two generations, that of his parents and of himself, his family on both sides produced seventeen Methodist preachers.

Mood reports his own conversion at the age of twelve at a camp meeting. It was no passing distraction. Thirty-three years later, while Regent at Southwestern, he wrote: "I thank God that I have never doubted the reality of the change of heart, experienced on that memorable Saturday night and I have never recalled the hour without deep emotions of thankfulness to My Heavenly Father."[4]

When two of his elder brothers graduated from Charleston College in 1845, one of them gave up his place teaching in a "little colored school," and Francis Asbury replaced him. He attended high school from 8:30 until 1:30 each day. From 2:00 until 5:30 he taught in the colored school. Reflecting on it in later years, he was satisfied with his efforts there. He said: "I think we did good and successful teaching and it is a great pleasure to me to know that by our labours in this neglected and at this time despised field of toil our family contributed so much to the intellectual and religious welfare of this race."[5] After graduating from Charleston College in 1850, he and his brother William, who was teaching with him, were able to change their hours at the colored school to mornings, and the attendance increased greatly. The income was so good that they were able to buy a buggy, harness, and good horses for themselves. They also lent their father $1,800, enabling him to buy a comfortable home and business stand. Temptation assailed him when the Trustees of the school, knowing that he intended to enter the ministry, besought him to continue, trying to persuade him by using arguments about the good he was doing. Recognizing that it was the income, however, not the good he was doing, that tempted him, Mood rejected the offer and continued on his path toward the ministry.

Rejection by the English Wesleyan Conference

Never robust, during his second year as pastor in Columbia, Francis's health deteriorated. This was the first instance in his adult life of what became a recurring pattern. He did not spare his body in pursuit of his work, and he periodically suffered the consequences. He was, for example, at this time, when he was working assiduously to establish himself as a young minister in his churches, also writing a weekly newspaper column about Methodism in Charleston. These articles were assembled into a two-hundred-page book entitled *Methodism in Charleston: a narrative of the chief events relating to the rise and progress of the Methodist Episcopal church in Charleston, S.C., with brief notices of the early ministers who labored in that city.*[6] The book was published at about the time his health broke. He became so feeble and emaciated that he could hardly stand. His uncle, Bishop Andrew, the famous bishop whose ownership of a slave had in 1845 caused the division of the Methodist Episcopal Church, advised him to rest a year and to travel abroad. With a thousand dollars he had saved from earlier years teaching in the colored school, he left in December 1856. After a cold and stormy voyage of twenty-five days, he landed in Liverpool. Following two months in England, he took the "grand tour." He crossed to France for two months before traveling on to Italy and Switzerland, returning to England via the Rhine and the North Sea.

Sue Logan Mood wearing widow's pin. Mood called her "the real founder of the institution" and said that after their death the "University should erect a monument" over her. Southwestern University, Special Collections.

Back in England among his fellow Methodists, he received a great shock. One senses in his plaintive self-justification written more than two decades later the distress it caused him. For two weeks Mood had regularly attended the open meetings of the Wesleyan Conference. Though he was encouraged by friends to request a ticket to the closed meetings, he was unanimously, by vote of the ministers, denied admittance. He says that the next day a Liverpool paper reported that

> although Mr. Mood was known to members of the body as an intelligent and amiable Christian Minister and gentleman, my connection with the Southern Methodist Church rendered my admission to the sessions of the body inexpedient. But my church did not and never had owned slaves. I had never nor did I then own slaves, so though "intelligent[,]" "amiable[,]" "Christian[,]" and a "minister[,]" having been guilty of the crime of being born in South Carolina where slavery was a political institution, I was voted unworthy to even look upon good men in Annual Conference session assembled. Such may be the madness and unreasonableness of good men![7]

In England the matter was reported in the *London Watchman*. The *Southern Christian Advocate* reported it in the United States in news items of September 10 and October 1, 1857.

Mrs. Mary Katherine Metcalfe Earney, a great-granddaughter of Francis Asbury Mood and editor of his *Autobiography*, provides information that sheds light on Mood's assertion. Whether or not he owned slaves himself, he came from a family in which three members, his mother, a sister, and a brother, owned slaves.[8] Though technically correct in what he wrote about his relationship to slavery, Mood was somewhat disingenuous. He was closer to "the peculiar institution" than he wanted to admit. In spite of the incident at the Wesleyan Conference, Mood recognized in later years that the trip abroad had been very important in changing many of his earlier views. He says that "While traveling[,] I found a thousand prejudices and bigotries of a national and social and religious character melting away. Some of them were quite dear to me . . . . [and] . . . I endeavoured in vain to try and maintain them; they passed away, and I have never been able to replace them."[9]

During the decade prior to the Civil War, Francis Asbury Mood became one of the leading Methodist ministers in South Carolina. His deep religious faith, personal integrity, steady resolve, keen intellect, and amiable disposition marked him as a leader at an early age. He was only thirty-one years old when the war began. By that time he had served several pastorates and was one of the Presiding Elders in the Conference. He had also published a book detailing the history of Methodism in his city of birth.

In addition he was a married man. Toward the end of December 1858, he had married Sue Logan, a young lady he had met in one of his earlier appointments. Though she had celebrated her fifteenth birthday only four months before the ceremony, they were otherwise perfectly matched, and their affection for each other was lifelong. Writing in later life to his children about her, he said:

> I here put on record the opinion that the alumni and friends of Southwestern University should [after our death] erect a monument over your dear Mama as the real founder of the institution. It is she who has borne the burden and heat of the day, who has had to plan day and night to make our limited means make us appear before the public with proper respectability and who by a thousand little methods known only to a devoted wife and a loving mother has sustained and encouraged Papa while she has ministered to your pleasure and

> comfort. How little did I anticipate in wedding my little blue-eyed Sue how much of heroism, of patient toil, of wise administration and of pious devotion would in her be thrown around my home.[10]

Secession and the Firing on Fort Sumter

Mood believed in the Southern cause and even journeyed from his residence just above the state line in North Carolina to Charleston in December 1860 to cast his vote as a South Carolinian for secession. Like McKenzie in Texas, he would soon come to mourn the day he first championed the cause of secession. He describes in his *Autobiography* the receipt by his family of news of the Battle of Manassas.

> I remember when the paper reached us containing the account of the battle, your Grandma, Aunt, Mama and cousins gathered round me to hear me read it. Going a little way into the bloody narrative[,] I felt horror struck and burst into tears and could not proceed, and there we sat in a circle all crying together, a comment on the horror of war.[11]

Such was their reaction to the carnage consequent upon a Southern victory. Southern defeats with even longer casualty lists were still to come.

But for the moment, at the beginning, with the firing on Fort Sumter, the war seemed more like a dramatic production than a real occurrence. Mood was there, and his description of the event is vivid. A servant awakened him at about 4:30 A.M., telling him that the firing had begun. Hastening down to the city, he found, except for the firing, a Sabbath-like stillness. The population had gathered in silence at the seafront, called the Battery, to watch the bombardment. "I shall never forget my mingled feelings of anxiety and distress when about midday Saturday [April 12] Fort Sumter flamed up like a volcano, the interior having caught fire and it seemed as if the men inside must either be consumed, or torn to pieces by the explosion of the magazines of powder, which was predicted on all hands [by everyone]." He spent the afternoon watching the actions leading up to the surrender. The next day he and two others in a small boat anchored about fifty yards from the fort to watch the official surrender ceremonies. Ironically, during a cannon salute, a man at one of the guns was killed by a premature discharge, the only loss of life during the whole affair. The seventy-eight Union soldiers marched out, having withstood thirty-four hours of bombardment.[12]

City Besieged and Running the Blockade

Mood was Presiding Elder at Orangeburg during 1861, and his presence at the firing on Fort Sumter was incidental to his normal living situation. His appointment as Presiding Elder of the Charleston District for 1862, however, brought him and his family to the center of the conflict. When the city was besieged and began to be bombarded regularly, he sent the family back to Orangeburg. Money from the Church was so little that he worked in his father's factory, "he being overrun with work for military equipment." They took a large Confederate government contract for making cavalry equipment, bits and spurs, and, as a consequence, lived comfortably for a time. Sorrow, however, was not far behind. While he was recovering from a bout of typhoid fever, his firstborn child, Frank, died from yellow fever. When the Confederate Congress passed a conscription bill that included ministers, he applied for and received appointment as chaplain of the hospital in Charleston. He shipped the last of the government work and closed down the factory. In early 1864 his father died, his mother following not long after.

His poor health caused the army to release him from duty, and, feeling that things were desperate, he placed the family in the care of one of his brothers so that he could "run the gauntlet of the blockading fleet to Nassau, in the West Indies" and transship from there to England. He hoped to be able to secure some help for the Church and his family there. In great hazard, his ship, on a "dark and stormy night," escaped the guns of the Union fleet and reached Nassau. A few days later he and his ministerial companion took passage on a small brig for Liverpool, which they reached after a turbulent voyage of thirty-five days. On reaching Liverpool, they learned "of continued disaster to the Confederate cause; the surrender of Charleston and the burning of the city of Columbia."[13]

Learning that Sue's house had been burned, he was for a time in great anguish as he imagined "ten thousand horrors as to their fate." He says that he could only await events. Within a few weeks he learned of the Southern surrender and received a letter from his wife. She said they had been burned out, were without food, and she begged him, if able, to come home. The next morning he went to London, saw the U.S. Minister, Charles Francis Adams, took the oath of allegiance to the United States, and started the day after for Boston.

Return to Charleston

In New York he was required to renew his oath of allegiance. Receiving assistance from his Uncle Peter Mood in New York and friends in Baltimore, he sailed for home with a large box of clothes and supplies for the family. On board a gentleman who had heard him preach before the war in Greenville, South Carolina, and who was returning to South Carolina as a U.S. Internal Revenue officer, offered him a job as Assistant at a salary of one hundred dollars per month. After consulting with the Confederate commissioned officers on board, he accepted the position.

Reunited with his family and working for a few months at his job, he was called on to take the "Iron Clad Oath" as a condition for receiving his pay. The Radical Republicans in Congress had enacted it to replace President Johnson's more lenient oath. Because he could not swear that he had "voluntarily given no aid, countenance, counsel, or encouragement to persons engaged in armed hostility" to the United States, he lost his job and the six hundred dollars owing him.

At the Annual Conference of the Church on November 1, 1865, he was appointed as Presiding Elder of the Charleston District. Reaching Charleston with his family, he found his parsonage and churches in the possession of the northern branch of the Methodist Church. Though the parsonage contained his library, private correspondence, and other personal items, the minister living in it refused to return it to him. "It seemed to me all the fierce passions of my nature rose in rebellion to reason, and grace & I confess to feelings of anger, contempt and hate of which I have since been heartily ashamed and for which I have implored God's forgiveness."[14]

The churches, parsonage, and personal possessions were returned to him through an unusual circumstance. On the boat trip down to Charleston he had been particularly attentive to the wife of General Rufus Saxton, the U.S. army general in charge of Charleston. Whereas other passengers at best ignored her, he attempted to make her trip pleasant through conversation and by providing small attentions. Later, back in Charleston, when he visited the office of General Saxton to enter a petition to the President for the return of the churches, General Saxton ushered him into his office immediately even though many earlier arrivals waited in the outer office. He thanked Mood for the courtesies he had extended to Mrs. Saxton on the voyage down from New York on board the *Arago*, endorsed the papers, and forwarded them to the proper authorities in Washington. In a few days the order came for the return of the Church property to the Southern Church.[15]

Postwar Activities in Charleston

By now Mood was one of the most respected citizens of Charleston. He was popular even among persons of other persuasions. When the vestry of the Unitarian Church asked him to preach regularly for them and offered a liberal compensation, he "wrote and advised Bishop Pierce, who told me by all means to serve them with the pure Gospel." In his interview with the vestrymen, they told him "they preferred Methodist doctrine from a South Carolinian to Unitarian doctrine from a New Englander." After the Unitarians secured their own pastor from England, a new request came to him from the Huguenot Church. He was installed there as pastor *pro tem.* He served them and received a comfortable support while they searched for a permanent pastor.[16]

With the help of a wealthy backer, he had begun a family newspaper in December 1865 called *The Weekly Record.* It did not do well and within a year had failed.[17] Its equipment was sold. He says that he was then "induced" to take a position in the state Normal School. He served as Vice Principal there for the first half of 1867.[18]

Within two years after the end of the Civil War, Mood, in addition to his Methodist responsibilities, had worked at five short-term jobs to make ends meet—as an assistant to a U.S. Internal Revenue officer, as editor of a newspaper, as a temporary minister to a Unitarian congregation, as a temporary minister to a Huguenot congregation, and as a teacher in a state teachers school. These commitments drained him so much both as to time and spirit that during 1867 he "resolved to let go everything but the work of the regular ministry."[19] He preached the annual sermon at the Conference in December 1867 and was appointed to Trinity Church, Charleston, the largest in the city. The work went well.

It is at this point that Mood first refers in his *Autobiography* to Soule University. He says that during 1867, while he was in "the S. C. State Normal School," Bishop H. N. McTyeire was in Texas trying to help Soule recover from the disasters of the war. As they were "anxious to open a Normal School Department," McTyeire recommended him for the position. He also received a request from Bishop Paine asking him to allow them to transfer him to New Orleans, Vicksburg, or Nashville. He declined both the Soule offer and the transfer request.[20] His refusal of the Soule offer, however, was not the end of the matter.

The Chappell Hill Male and Female Institute

About the time that Mood was beginning his ministry in South Carolina in the early 1850s, events were transpiring almost half a continent away in Texas that would bring about the establishment of the school over which he would be called to preside. These events had their genesis in the disaffection of many Methodists with a practically insolvent and semi-independent Rutersville College whose already unsteady reputation had recently been scarred by a sexual scandal. Letters were exchanged among ministers lamenting the condition of the school. Soon conversations among them and concerned laymen took the form of a quiet plan for abandoning Rutersville and placing Methodist resources behind another institution that would be firmly bound to the Church. Little in the record speaks directly to these efforts, but a pattern of actions with regard to Chappell Hill Male and Female Institute eventuating in the establishment of Soule University reveals the broad outlines of the picture.

The Chappell Hill Male and Female Institute was one of the many private schools, both independent and denominational, chartered by the State prior to the establishment of a public system of education. Though the exact date of its opening is uncertain, it was certainly in operation by 1850, the date when its first building was completed.[21] It appears that that it was originally called the Chappell Hill Male and Female Academy, that name appearing in a newspaper advertisement dated November 26, 1851.[22] It was probably one of the ninety-seven academies enumerated in Texas by the federal census of 1850.

Though Dean C. C. Cody states that it had a Methodist connection as early as that year, when a report to the Texas Conference affirms that it had five teachers, two male and three female, with an attendance of one hundred students,[23] any Methodist connection must have been unofficial, for its charter, granted on February 9, 1852, has a clause specifying that the school "shall never be under the control of any particular denomination of Christians or religious sect."[24] An official Methodist connection did not exist until two years later, when the charter was amended (February 11, 1854), allowing the Trustees of the school to transfer control to "any denomination of christians [sic] they think proper."[25]

Sometime in 1852 a second building was constructed "to keep the boys and girls apart." In October of the same year the election of Philander S. Ruter, son of Martin Ruter, to the presidency of "Chappell Hill College, heretofore Chappell Hill Male and Female Institute," was announced in the local newspaper. The article also announced Ruter's resignation from Transylvania University, where he was a professor, to accept the position. His sister, Charlotta, became head of the music department at the same time. Augustus W. Ruter, a third sibling, subsequently succeeded Philander as President. The two brothers served almost equal time over the period from 1852 to 1856 as Presidents of the school prior to the amalgamation of its male unit into Soule University.[26]

The presence of the children of Martin Ruter working at the Institute (or College, as the newspaper calls it, though the charter was never amended to reflect collegiate status) suggests that they had been enticed by an already present or prospective Methodist connection. This connection, mentioned by Cody, must have been the background for their coming even before the school became officially Methodist. It is hardly likely that they would have been known or invited except by Methodists knowledgeable of Martin Ruter's role in bringing Methodism to Texas or that they would have accepted positions at a struggling institution so far from their Indiana and Kentucky homes without knowing it was Methodist in spirit though independent by statute law.

The Establishment of Soule University

The movement to abandon support of Rutersville College in favor of the establishment of a "'central university' for Texas Methodism" became strong enough during 1854 that preliminary steps in that direction were settled quickly at the annual meeting of the Texas Conference at Chappell Hill on December 13. The Conference appointed a Board of Commissioners composed of nine persons to draw up the specifics of the plan, including the location of the school. This Board was a strong one and included persons, such as Robert Alexander and Homer S. Thrall, who had played prominent roles at Rutersville College, and others, such as Robert W. Kennon and W. H. Seat, who would later play prominent roles in the new university.[27]

News about the establishment of the institution excited the attention of aspiring communities, and, when the Board of Commissioners met at Galveston a few months later on April 3, it received location bids from Richmond, San Felipe, and Waco. In addition there was the expected bid from Chappell Hill. It won almost immediate approval. The other towns could hardly match the inducements presented by its representatives, R. J. Swearington and William Chappell, two Trustees of the Chappell Hill Male and Female Institute. They appeared before the Board with a promise of fifty thousand dollars, secured by notes and obligations, toward the founding of the new institution.

Given the circumstances, the decision was almost automatic. Not only was the promised financing attractive, but also the linkage afforded by a currently functioning Methodist Institute that would serve as the nucleus for the new university made the bid compelling. All in all, the selection of Chappell Hill was a formality. The process had been held to legitimize the process and to ward off any accusation later that the Board had acted prematurely without giving other communities an opportunity to make a better bid. After the decision had been made, the Board of Trustees of the Chappell Hill Male and Female Institute was asked to serve on an interim basis on behalf of the new institution until its own board could be appointed. Looking ahead, the Board of Commissioners appointed three of its members to select a site for the proposed university building and to engage an artist to depict it.[28] Meeting in Galveston on December 12, 1855, the Texas Annual Conference ratified the actions of the Board of Commissioners, appointed a sixteen-person Board of Trustees, and named the new institution Soule University.

The name Soule was in honor of the most venerated of the Southern bishops. Though born in Maine, Joshua Soule had presided over the Southern and Western Conferences of the Church during most of his episcopal career. From his election in 1824 until the separation of the Church into Northern and Southern branches in 1844, he had been the great conciliator, a Northern bishop presiding in the South. He was perhaps the outstanding bishop of the Church and, says his biographer Horace Du Bose, his word was usually accepted as "oracular."[29] As a young preacher, he was more than anyone the author in 1808 of the constitution of the Methodist Episcopal Church. When events at the General Conference of 1844 brought about a separation, he, though a New Englander, went with the Southern Church. He felt that, whatever the merits of the question at issue regarding slavery, the Church had broken its own law at the Conference in settling it. In all these events, says Du Bose, "the atavism so powerfully manifested in his character made him a Southerner by natural selection."[30] A year later, in 1845, he presided at the sessions of the Texas and East Texas Conferences and came to be known by Texas Methodists. By 1855, the year in which Soule University was named for him, he was seventy-four years old, a retired patriarch living at his adopted home in Nashville. "He had given up [his earlier] home and kindred and honors for the people of the South," says Du Bose. "They gave him in return—themselves."[31] In honoring him, the founders of Soule University were giving their institution the most revered name in Southern Methodism, next only to those of John Wesley and Francis Asbury.

First Classes and Charter

The new Board of Trustees met five weeks later (January 18–19) for the first time. It elected Thomas B. White as President of the Board, the Rev. William J. Sasnett as President, and John N. Kirby as Principal of the Preparatory Department. The Rev. James M. Follansbee, A.M., M.D., was elected President *pro tem* until the arrival of Sasnett. William Jeremiah Sasnett was a Georgian who graduated from Oglethorpe University in 1839. From 1850 until 1858 he was a faculty member of Emory College. "He probably achieved some prominence from his writings on higher education," says F. Edward Bentley, who discovered Sasnett's identity, "and from his discourses on the theory of female education. Thus, he must have had considerable reputation as an educator in Methodist circles."[32]

None of these appointments lasted more than a few years, that of Follansbee only half a year. Follansbee, however, merits special notice. Though a professor of Latin, Greek, and Modern Languages, he served as provisional leader during three critical periods—at the opening of the school in 1856, in the uncertainties connected with the departure of President Carter at the beginning of the Civil War in 1861, and at the start-up after the Civil War in 1865. At the end of the 1865–1866 session, he transferred to the Baltimore Conference.[33] After ten years of service, he appears to have finally given up on Soule.

For the moment, however, things looked bright. Follansbee and Kirby opened the University on February 1,

1856, by simply transferring the enrollment of the male students from the Chappell Hill Male and Female Institute to the Preparatory Department of Soule University. They met in one of the Institute's buildings. The next day the state legislature approved the charter of the new University.[34]

Nothing was left to doubt in the charter about who controlled it. The charter stipulated that the school "shall be under the control and supervision of the Texas Conference of the Methodist Episcopal Church South, and the Board of Trustees shall be re-elected from time to time, under the direction of said Texas Conference, and when elected, shall have the power to fill all vacancies that may occur therein, subject to ratification by the succeeding Conference." The Trustees were to make an annual report to the Conference "showing the exact condition of the University" in a number of carefully specified areas. It even blurred the distinction between Conference/Trustee control and executive operation by saying that the Conference could change the conduct of affairs, "transmit[ting] to the Board of Trustees such instruction for their observance as the prosperity of the University may demand."[35] Though four years earlier the Chappell Hill Male and Female Institute had been enjoined in its charter from ever falling under the control of a "particular denomination of Christians," its collegiate successor, Soule University, was specifically set up as Methodist.

At the time of the separation of the two units of the Chappell Hill Male and Female College, the male unit being incorporated into Soule University, the female unit was upgraded to collegiate status and given a separate charter (August 29, 1856). It became the Chappell Hill Female College. It became an institution parallel to Soule University, receiving consistent attention from the Church and townspeople. When Francis Asbury Mood was later transferred from the South Carolina Conference to the Texas Conference to become president of Soule, he found the Rev. W. G. Connor of South Carolina already there as President of the Female College. He gave the Mood family lodging in his home the first night after their arrival in Chappell Hill after the long train journey from the Palmetto State.[36] In spite of two fires and the yellow fever epidemics of 1867 and 1869, the Chappell Hill Female College persevered as a Methodist institution until 1912, when the changing character of the area and decreasing public support for girls' schools eroded its enrollment base and financial support. Nevertheless, during the 1890s the Texas Conference gave it more aid than it gave Southwestern University.[37]

Building Blocks for the Future

Because of the nonappearance of Sasnett by the time of the Commencement ceremonies on June 23, 1856, William Halsey was officially elected President. As already indicated in the chapter on Rutersville College, he was a native of New York who had come to Texas in 1845 as a teacher. He had become President of Rutersville College in late 1846, succeeding Richardson after Thrall and Wright had held it together briefly. His collaboration with Robert Alexander and others in the establishment of Soule University was an open secret, and the Board of Trustees of Rutersville College tried to embarrass him by refusing his resignation on the pretext that it had not been tendered in timely fashion. For their part, the instigators of Soule wanted Halsey to help legitimize the transfer of Methodist support from Rutersville to Soule. Apparently little blame attached to him for the general decline of Rutersville College during his eight or nine years there, especially for the unfortunate events that precipitated its demise at the end. His wife, who had been Preceptress of the Female Department at Rutersville, came as head of Chappell Hill Female College.[38] Classes began in September with ninety-five students enrolled, mostly in the Preparatory Department.[39]

The intent of the Texas Conference in starting Soule had not been to set up a school for itself alone but to establish an institution that both Methodist Conferences in the state could embrace.[40] To bring this about, R. W. Kennon, the Soule University financial agent, attended the East Texas Conference at Paris on November 6 to offer it the opportunity of participating in the endeavor. For its cooperation it would have the privilege of naming ten of the twenty-five Trustees allowed by the charter. The Conference accepted the offer and named its Trustees. This division of Trustees between the two Conferences became normative for the University, though it was never enacted into a charter change giving the East Texas Conference legal rights.[41] In essence, the Texas Conference had to elect as its own the ten trustees nominated by the East Texas Conference to make their participation valid. This arrangement apparently never posed a problem.

Big things were contemplated for Soule. On February 19, 1857, the Board of Trustees voted to establish a Medical Department, carrying through its action on November 25 by electing professors for both a Medical and a Legal Department.[42] These actions were followed by the establishment of two chairs. On November 25, 1857, the Uni-

Soule University Building, constructed 1858–1861. Because of the waxy soil, the foundation was unsafe and dangerous cracks developed in the walls. Southwestern University, Special Collections.

versity received the promise of two large gifts of twenty-five thousand dollars each. One was by Col. Jared Kirby to fund a Chair in Mathematics and Natural Philosophy. This Kirby Professorship was given to the Rev. W. G. Foote, A.M. The other was by the Hon. Gabriel Felder to endow a Chair in Languages, the Felder Professorship. The Rev. J. M. Follansbee was soon appointed to it.[43] Shortly thereafter, on January 29, 1858, Felder was elected President of the Board of Trustees, serving in that post for ten years until his death shortly before the arrival of Mood. Encouraged by the two gifts, the Board of Trustees on the same date formally established the Departments of Medicine and Law, for which it had already elected professors. Though the Department of Law never materialized, a Medical Department, to be dealt with more fully later, was set up soon after the Civil War, the first medical school to be established in Texas.[44]

By 1857–1858 an outside prognosticator might have predicted that Soule University was well on the way to success. In addition to the progress already mentioned, the number of students attending Soule was increasing annually. It rose from 95 the first year to 115 the second and to 166 the third.[45] Sixteen of the 166 students were of college grade, and a Mr. F. C. Foster would become the first graduate at the end of the academic year. The faculty consisted of three professors and two tutors.

Such progress demanded, so the Trustees felt, a university building other than that of the Chappell Hill Male and Female Institute building currently in use. Banking that their success to date would continue, they convinced themselves that they were in a position to initiate a building program. Consequently a cornerstone was laid on November 2, 1858, on ten acres of land earlier donated by Dr. R. J. Swearington.[46] Swearington, who had a son in school, was one of the old Institute Trustees now firmly committed to Soule. The building would be a three-story, 56\' x 84\' stone structure of approximately 14,000 square feet, eventually costing more than forty thousand dollars.[47] It would take about two-and-a-half years to build.

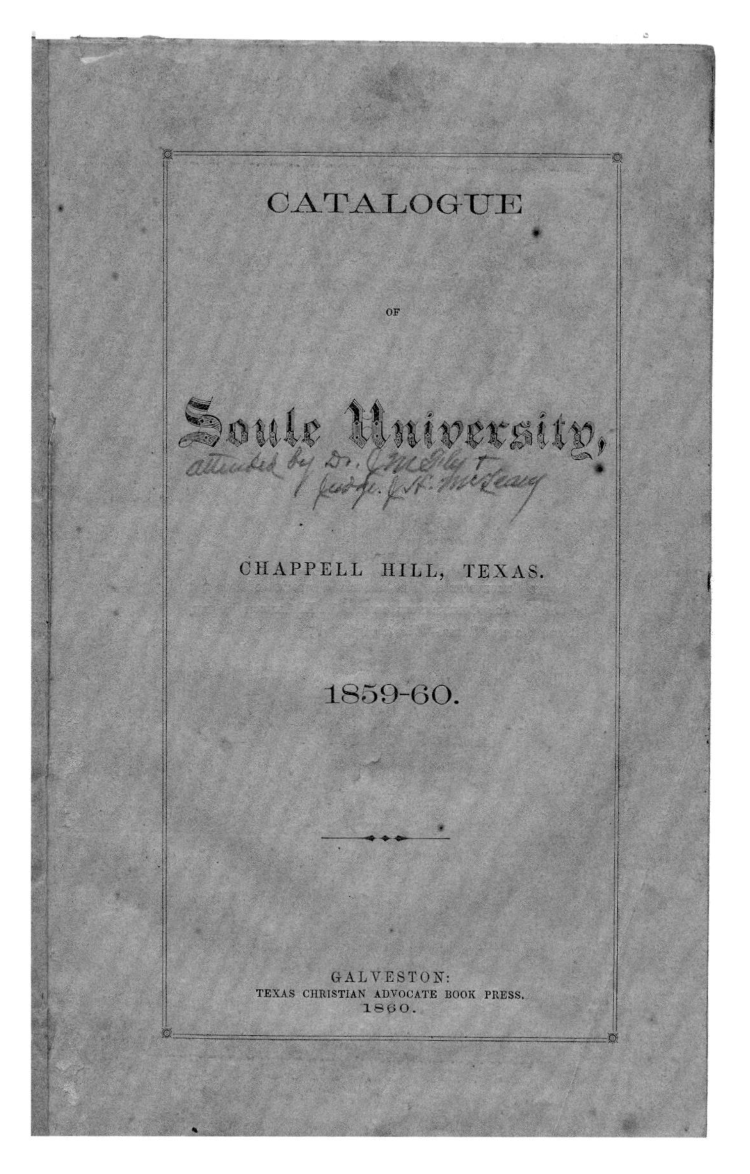
CATALOGUE

OF

Soule University,

CHAPPELL HILL, TEXAS.

1859-60.

GALVESTON:
TEXAS CHRISTIAN ADVOCATE BOOK PRESS.
1860.

Catalogue of Soule University, Chappell Hill, Texas, 1859–60. Southwestern University, Special Collections.

Curriculum and Student Body

The catalogs for 1858–1859 and 1859–1860 are extant and present a picture of the academic program as the University wanted it to be known to the general public. In addition to a historical sketch detailing the origin of the institution, they contain the names of the Board of Trustees and of two committees from the Texas Annual Conference—a Visiting Committee and an Examining Committee. They also list the faculty, the students, admission requirements, courses of study, items of expense, and some minor announcements. "The requisites for admission," says Cody, "adhered to the old Latin and Greek standards. The equivalent of two years' preparation in these ancient languages was necessary for entrance to the freshman class, and any student who did not study both Latin and Greek was 'irregular.' It was also necessary, for entrance, that a student be at least sixteen years old, be able to pass an approved examination in Georgraphy [sic], English Grammar, Arithmetic, Elementary Algebra, and the History of the United States."[48] The purpose of the Preparatory Department was to bring students up to the admission level.

The academic year was forty weeks long, "exclusive of an intermission of from one to two weeks at Christmas," and a vacation of ten weeks after Commencement, ending with the beginning of the next session the first Monday in September.[49] Four years of study were required for the baccalaureate degree, with a heavy emphasis on Latin and Greek. One course in French and a Spanish elective could be taken. Algebra, Geometry, Trigonometry, and Calculus were required, as were Mensuration and Navigation. The junior and senior years were heavy on oratory. Aside from Greek New Testament, the only specifically religious course, taken as a second-semester senior, was Evidences of Christianity. Natural and Mental Philosophy were senior year courses.[50]

Students not wishing to pursue the entire collegiate curriculum might opt for less. There were four types of certificates or degrees.

1. A Certificate of Proficiency could be given by any Professor for successful completion of an examination in a given subject.
2. Certificates of Graduation might be given by a Professor to all passing an approved examination on [all] the subjects of his department.
3. The Bachelor of Arts was conferred on those who presented Certificates of Graduation in all the departments except that of the Hebrew language and Biblical Studies.
4. The Master of Arts was conferred on those who, after pursuing three years of literary courses, submitted an essay on some scientific subject or delivered a written address approved by the Board.[51]

Annual expenses were $58.50 for undergraduates and $21.00, $31.00, or $41.00 for students studying Primary, English, or Classics and Mathematics respectively. In addition, students were advised that they could secure board with private families in Chappell Hill and vicinity, including washing and fuel, for $10.00 to $12.00 per month. Those preparing for the ministry and sons of ministers in the Texas Conference might attend without charge.

The catalog for 1859–1860 lists 167 students for the year, an increase of only one over the previous year but an increase in the number of regular undergraduate students from 16 to 42. The number of irregular students taking college-level courses is 45; the number of preparatory students is 79. One student is unaccounted for.[52] These figures show that in the four-and-a-half years of its existence, from the spring of 1856 to the spring of 1860, Soule University moved from being an institution with 100 percent of its students at the preparatory level to being an institution with more than 50 percent at the college level.

The Clouds of War: Leadership and Student Numbers

If the four-and-a-half-year period from the spring of 1856 through 1859–1860 was a period of progress for Soule University, the period from 1860–1861 through 1867–1868 was a period of precipitous decline. There were two interlocking problems during the period. The first was human—leadership and student numbers. The second was finances. Though both problems had existed before the war, they were exacerbated to an almost intolerable degree by it. Soule might have weathered them successfully in ordinary times, but the onset of that conflict dealt it an almost lethal blow.

Hardly had the new decade begun than President Halsey offered his resignation (January 23, 1860). Though we have no records for assessing his motives in resigning, he seems to have done so without prejudice to his reputation. He remained on the faculty and was elected President *pro tem* after his successor's departure the following year. The Trustees elected the Rev. George Washington Carter, D.D., of Virginia to fill the vacancy the same day as Halsey's resignation.[53] He was, however, teaching at the time at the University of Mississippi and could not assume the position until he had finished his obligation there in May.[54]

An excerpt from a letter of March 25, 1860, by an unnamed faculty member suggests that morale continued high at Soule through the change.

> The schools [Soule University and Chappell Hill Female College] are also prospering. . . . We are crowded in the University with students. Dr. Carter of [the University of] Mississippi has accepted the presidency and will be on here in May to organize the faculty anew. . . . We anticipate largely when the new order of arrangements shall have transpired.[55]

The academic year played itself out, and three young men graduated at the end of the session with the A.B. degree. One was R. M. Swearington, son of the donor of the land on which the main building stood, who afterwards studied medicine and became one of the most successful physicians in Texas.[56]

On his arrival "Dr. Carter entered upon the discharge of his duties, as president," says Cody, "with great zeal and ability," and an "advance movement was planned." Elements of it are to be found in the "Supplement, Circular for 1860–61" published as an addendum to the 1859–1860 catalog. In it new Departments of Metaphysics, Biblical Literature, and Law were added to the curriculum. Carter lists himself for Metaphysics.[57] This department included a conglomeration of courses, most unrelated to any definition of metaphysics today. They were political economy, constitutional law, international law, mental philosophy, ethics, logic, and history of philosophy. The Departments of Biblical Literature and Law were meant to be professional in nature. They were anticipatory, since neither was actually instituted at the time. Carter also made the departments more independent and changed some of the requirements for degrees.[58] The overall effect of these changes was to lessen the heretofore almost exclusive curricular attention given to math, language, and literature and, following Enlightenment principles, to move the instruction of students more specifically toward so-called "useful" studies. Carter was, for the times, a modern man. Ralph Jones says that these changes were in line with the Virginia model formulated by Thomas Jefferson. "Thomas Jefferson," he says, "rode to Chappell Hill on the coat-tails of George W. Carter, Virginian."[59]

The academic year 1860–1861 began with ominous forebodings in the minds of students and teachers as the crucial presidential election of November 1860 approached. Student enrollment was good, and Carter's educational reforms created a "halo" effect in the minds of students and faculty. Nevertheless, after the election of Lincoln, Southern states began to secede from the Union and secession sentiment grew in Texas. Governor Sam Houston, a Unionist, was able to slow down the movement for a while, but a secession convention was forced on him during the last days of January 1861, and a secession ordinance was approved on February 1.

Dr. Carter participated in the convention. Soon after his return from Austin to Chappell Hill, he requested leave for the duration of the war. Even before the firing on Fort Sumter on April 12, he felt that war was inevitable. A letter of William Halsey dated March 2 implies that Carter has already left for Virginia and that he, Halsey, is governing the school. The Board confirmed this status later by electing him President *pro tem* on June 26. A communication from Carter was also read to the Board on the same date suggesting a plan of operation for the University during the war. It contemplated a student body of about half the present size with a reduced faculty.[60]

In Virginia Carter received a Colonel's commission from the Confederate government, after which he returned to Texas, where he raised three regiments for the war, one of which he led personally.[61] Cody says that some of his recruits were former students whom he urged to enlist and follow him to the front. Following Halsey's return to his home in the North,[62] Follansbee, at the request of the Board on August 26, 1861, made an attempt to carry things on, but, Cody reports, "in spite of his best efforts, after a few months the halls of the university were deserted and silent. A few months later, under the urgent demands of the Confederate government, the building was converted into a military hospital."[63] Follansbee's name was carried in Methodist records as President of the University during the war. He appears as such in the records of the Texas Annual Conference for 1864.[64] James S. Giddings, nephew of J. D. Giddings, later so important in the establishment of Southwestern, was one of the few students there when the news of Lincoln's assassination reached the campus. He said that Dr. Follansbee "was much affected and shed tears. We boys thought it strange. He said that the South had lost its best friend, and I believe now [about 1910] that he was right."[65]

Carter never returned to Soule. His subsequent career as an officer in the Civil War, as a Reconstruction politician in Louisiana, and as minister resident to Venezuela was as controversial as later assessments of his short presidential tenure at Soule University. Wherever he went, his undoubted personal gifts won him immediate recognition. His need for attention, however, his prickly personality, and his penchant for immediate, decisive action created problems. He was married and divorced three times in an age when such was viewed with considerable disfavor, especially for a Methodist minister.[66]

Carter was undoubtedly a charismatic figure. John McLean, writing about him in later years, says that Soule University "was at its best, under the Presidency of that brilliant genius and peerless speaker and preacher, Rev. Geo. W. Carter, D. D." He admits that Carter "declined religiously, but [says that] late in life [he] came back to the church and ministry, in his native State, Virginia."[67] Cody, however, is not so charitable. He quotes the protest of President Jefferson Davis against Carter's enticing young men to leave college for the war because, by so doing, "we are grinding up our seed corn." Cody faults Carter for not following "this wise counsel."[68]

The Clouds of War: Financial Problems

The Board minutes of Soule University from 1856 through 1887 provide an abundance of numbers but do not help much in assessing the fiscal health of the institution from one year to the next.[69] Ambiguity surrounds almost everything. The reason for the ambiguity is not that those reporting intended to obfuscate so much as that almost everything they reported is in terms of uncertain worth—pledges, notes, obligations, and acres of land, items whose worth depended on the good faith and circumstances of donors or on market conditions. But it was clear that the financial situation of Soule University deteriorated from beginning to end.

Soule University had been attracted to Chappell Hill by a promise of $50,000 secured by notes and obligations. On June 26, 1857, almost two years after that promise, the endowment was reported as being about $40,000, with another thirty thousand acres in land. The addition of two endowed chairs shortly afterwards at $25,000 each, which should have raised the endowment to $90,000, resulted, however, in adding only $12,000 for each chair. Even that amount is deceptive. The gifts were in notes, not hard money. The Felder gift was only partially paid, and the Kirby gift was never paid. It was still on the books in 1872. On December 3, 1857, the Board reported about $56,000 "of available means." A year later it reported $74,005 in the tangible fund of the University. This amount "consisted of a bundle of notes." Part of the explanation for the slow growth of the endowment, even if the notes and obligations are counted, is the fact that the University was not taking in enough cash to meet its general operating expenses and had to begin almost from the outset to draw on the endowment to cover the deficit.[70]

The single greatest mistake in finances was the decision to construct a university building. It hung around the neck of the University thereafter like an albatross. The contract was let on June 28, 1859, for $29,500. When funds were insufficient to complete the building in November of the following year, the Board authorized the building committee to "hypothecate the whole personal and real estate of the University to some friend for the purpose of effecting a loan of money" to complete it. Problems dogged the construction project from the beginning. Writing about the building when he attended as a student in 1865, James S. Giddings says that it was built of rock. It was "three stories high on a level tract of land, which was black waxy soil, which cracks badly in dry seasons, and the foundation became unsafe. There were dangerous cracks in the walls when I went to school there."[71] Some of the students refused to attend classes in it and left the institution.[72] Its indebtedness and physical condition were contributing factors in Mood's later decision to vacate Soule University in 1869.

Wartime conditions worsened an already bad financial situation. The same unnamed teacher who a year before had written the positive letter quoted above about the morale at Soule, wrote another one a year later, on March 26, 1861, lamenting the conditions at the school. Says the writer:

> The crises, secession, the prospect of war, and the current famine of our land of Texas have produced their effects. . . . The want of all material aid from the College, the scarcity of money & provisions and a general destruction of all commerical [sic] faith shut up supplies to cash transactions. Add to all this, a general neglect and a bad management of University affairs, and you may readily imagine me in no plight to give you any good news, or a good account of matters & things, while an unwillingness to speak evil, led me to delay a reply. . . . It is true there are a goodly number of students here. But too many are beneficiaries, or have failed in payment of tuition fees to enable teachers to live. Besides, I think, the proceeds of too many scholarships have found their way either into the stone walls, or attendant expenses. . . . I look upon the Institution as in the woods at least for the present.[73]

This gentle complaint from one who hesitated to criticize because of "an unwillingness to speak evil" is as accurate an analysis from a contemporary as can be found about the situation of the University at the outset of the war.

In spite of these conditions, however, the school completed the spring term and graduated four students. Prior to the Civil War, Soule University had graduated only eight students—one in 1858, none in 1859, three in 1860, and four in 1861.[74] It had, however, built up a body of undergraduates and was at the point of graduating a small but steady flow annually when the war came. The eventual effect of the poor financial situation on the institution absent the war cannot be known. Nevertheless, poor finances alone brought down none of the other three institutions described in earlier chapters. They were amazingly resilient and found a way to operate on restricted resources. Southwestern University, as will be seen, did so later. In each case some other precipitating event, or combination of events, delivered the coup de grâce. In the case of Rutersville College it was a defective relationship with the Church and a sexual scandal. In the case of Wesleyan College it was an unseemly competition with another school and a homicide. In the case of McKenzie College it was the destruction of its socioeconomic base by the war.

A case can be made for believing that Soule University, under the leadership of George W. Carter, was on the point of achieving stability when the war destroyed its foundation. Even in its weakened condition after the war it emerged to begin a process of recovery. Just as it was getting underway it suffered another disaster—successive epidemics of yellow fever. These two epidemics finally destroyed any realistic prospect the school might have had. Mood recognized the inevitable and set a plan in motion to form another institution to replace it.

Resuscitation Endeavors: Securing a President

The redoubtable Dr. Follansbee opened classes in the fall of 1865 with a faculty of four, himself for Greek, Latin, and Modern Languages, and three others for English Literature, German, and Photography and Penmanship.[75] After serving as a hospital during the war, the university building had been left in shambles and had no equipment. The penurious condition of the institution can be inferred from an entry in the Board minutes of October 23, 1865, stating that the "faculty may get up a concert or fair or both, for the purpose of raising funds to purchase chairs and other furnature [sic] for the University."[76] While the faculty was trying to hold classes with the few students who matriculated, the Board of Trustees was trying to secure a new President.

For the next few years the Board cast around for a suitable replacement. On June 19, 1866, an M. Craven was "elected President of Soule University." A more precise identification of him in the minutes on October 11 lists him as "Dr. Cravens of Trinity College, N.C."[77] He never appeared on the scene, and there is no more mention of him.

On January 2, 1866, a person about whom little is known today, a certain O. H. McOmber, was offered and accepted the presidency. He served one-and-a-half years, leaving when the appearance of yellow fever caused the students to disperse. A faculty member, however, reports him to have had good scholarship, to have been a thorough disciplinarian, and to have been a hard worker under whom the school prospered.[78] A day after his resignation on June 23, 1867, a successor, the Rev. S. D. Akin, A.M., was elected. He, like Sasnett and Cravens, did not accept the position.

The desperation of the Board to find a strong President can be fathomed by noting the adoption of a radical plan to abandon the literary orientation of the school in favor of making it a military institute. At some point between 1865 and 1867, according to Ralph Jones, the Board invited General Alexander Peter Stewart to accept the presidency and convert the University into a self-sustaining military school.[79] The move was probably not so much based on educational principles as it was tailored to what the Board thought a man of his background and reputation might accept. Stewart, a native of Tennessee, was one of the foremost Southern generals during the war, and, like Robert E. Lee, found his reputation as a modest, reasonable person augmented by his lustrous military career. He ended the war as a Lieutenant General, having participated with distinction in many of the major battles. Prior to the war he had taught mathematics briefly at West Point before resigning from the army and returning to Tennessee. There he taught at Cumberland University and at the University of Nashville, where the beginning of the war found him. After the war he returned to Cumberland University, moving from there in 1868 to a professorship at the University of Mississippi. In 1874 he was elected chancellor of that institution, serving with success for twelve years.[80] Nothing came of Soule's invitation to him. Stewart was a military man by necessity, an academician by choice. A military school did not appeal to him. The Trustees had misread him. The University stumbled on without a President. The notion of changing Soule into a military institute was forgotten.

Resuscitation Endeavors: Establishing a Medical School

If the efforts of the Board of Trustees to secure a seasoned leader were fruitless, it succeeded almost effortlessly in another major academic endeavor. As early as November 25, 1857, the Board of Soule University had projected a medical department. A year later it appointed a committee to consider a medical school. The committee immediately got to work and presented a report several months later with concrete plans for establishing such a school. The Civil War and other obstacles postponed action until 1865, but the plan was not forgotten. On October 4, the Board appointed Dr. Jesse Boring and his son, Dr. Nicholas Boring, as professors in the Medical Department of Soule University.[81] On the 23rd of the same month it ordered immediate organization of the full department, stipulating that it must be self-sufficient. Inasmuch as the Medical School was to be located in Galveston and the treatment of patients would produce revenue, Soule University in Chappell Hill incurred no expense in setting up the enterprise. The school gradually took shape and gained status. In a private letter of July 25, 1867, to Mood in South Carolina, Dr. B. T. Kavanaugh, Professor of Biblical Literature, wrote: "We have a Medical Department in full operation in Galveston, which graduated a class of eighteen this past spring."[82]

The "Medical Department" became independent of Soule University during the events connected with the establishment of Southwestern University. Since the major efforts for that action took place in Galveston, where the medical school was located, the physicians of the city were well aware that Soule would soon lose the patronage of the Texas Conference. Consequently, the medical personnel of the school began to consider setting up the medical college as a separate corporate entity. Independent standing was gained on March 29, 1873, when the Texas Legislature passed two enactments establishing the Texas Medical College and the Hospital, thus terminating its relationship with Soule University.

Soule University ultimately left two successors—a medical unit, the University of Texas Medical Branch, Galveston, chartered in 1873, and a literary unit, Southwestern University, chartered in 1875. The medical department projected by the Soule Board in 1857, established by Board enactment in 1859, and opened in 1865, "was the first medical school in Texas. Furthermore, a lineage can be established between the medical department of Soule University and the present University of Texas Medical Branch, Galveston."[83]

The Peabody Fund and the Introduction of Mood to the University

On January 2, 1867, the Rev. B. T. Kavanaugh and his son Thomas H. Kavanaugh were elected to the Chairs of Biblical Literature and Natural Science, respectively. In

February after his election, the senior Kavanaugh learned about the establishment of the Peabody Fund, whose purpose was to aid education in the South. It was set up by George Peabody, a wealthy New England merchant and broker, who donated approximately two million dollars to assist education in the former Confederate states.[84] Acting with the knowledge of President McOmber, Kavanaugh formulated a proposal on behalf of Soule University to the Peabody Fund requesting support. He carried it to the Board of Trustees, which approved it. The proposal was then entrusted to the Rev. W. H. Seat, agent for Soule University, who was scheduled to go by Atlanta on a trip to New York.

In Atlanta, Seat met John Amos, agent for the Fund, who apprised him of the conditions for grant proposals. Kavanaugh's proposal at the time was little more than a sketch based on a newspaper report about the creation of the Fund. Seat learned that a two-thousand-dollar annual grant would be made to a selected school in each state submitting plans for a Normal School along with the name of the teacher who would occupy the chair. One of the emphases of the Peabody Fund was to help in the establishment of teacher training schools.[85] The most important of these later was George Peabody College in Nashville, Tennessee, now a part of Vanderbilt University.

Learning of these conditions, the Trustees at Soule immediately created a Normal Department on paper in order to qualify for the grant. In need of a teacher for the department, Kavanaugh wrote Bishop Holland N. McTyeire, who was scheduled to preside at the sessions of the five Texas Annual Conferences that year. He asked McTyeire to suggest a person for the position. Knowing that Francis Asbury Mood was then serving as Vice Principal of the State Normal School of South Carolina, McTyeire listed him as one of his three nominees. Mood, as already indicated, turned down the offer. The proposition to the Peabody Fund did not succeed, and the Normal School idea was dropped.[86] The grant proposal did not have much chance from the outset. Even if Soule had met all the stipulated conditions, the Peabody Board was not ready to act. It did not send a major representative to Texas until two years later, and the full Peabody program for Texas did not materialize until almost a decade later. The program eventually had great success in furthering the cause of Texas education, but it did little for Soule. That little, however, was very significant. The Soule attempt to secure a Peabody grant was the instrumentality for the introduction of Mood to the University.

Yellow Fever and the Invitation to Mood

Homer Thrall, preacher, teacher, and historian, says that "the year 1867 might, in Texas, be denominated the year of death."[87] The yellow fever in a malignant form appeared at Indianola in July and spread rapidly through the country to parts that had until then been considered exempt from its devastation. It was singularly fatal in Chappell Hill. Professor B. T. Kavanaugh describes its effects on both him and the University in a letter of December 24, after the epidemic had passed.

> Our University here has suffered severely with the Church and Country by reason of the Epidemic which was very distructive [sic] of life, and all our immediate prospects here. Our Halls were closed for nearly all the Summer or fall session—indeed it is closed still awaiting the beginning of the next session, on the 4th of Jan[uar]y. One of our professors fell a victim to the disease, Dr. T. H. Kavanaugh[,] Prof. of Natural Science—my only son. My only single daughter fell also, in 24 hours after her Bro. leaving me one child living, a married daughter. I had the disease, as did every teacher in both schools, and every person in our town with some 6 or 7 exceptions who kept themselves under strict exclusion. Some 6 or 8 of our advanced students also died, leaving the survivors, both teachers and students, under great depression of spirits.[88]

When January arrived, the Board of Trustees once against resorted to a general to lead the school, if only provisionally. It elected the forty-four-year-old Brigadier General John Creed Moore as President *pro tem* for the spring term.[89] Moore, like Stewart a native of Tennessee, had commanded the Second Texas Infantry during the Civil War. He had fought in many of its major engagements and moved to Texas to live after the war. But he, again like Stewart, had been a teacher before the war. He was basically a schoolman. He came to Soule and conducted its affairs until the close of the term in June 1868, afterwards moving on and teaching school elsewhere. He enjoyed a long career as a teacher and superintendent of public schools in various towns and cities in Texas.[90]

More significant for the future of the school than the past President, however, was the action of the Board of Trustees and its chair, the Rev. R. W. Kennon, to secure a new President. Kennon had been an important figure behind the scenes ever since the establishment of Soule. As the first agent for the institution, he successfully negotiated with the East Texas Conference in 1855, to bring it into cosponsorship of the school with the Texas Conference. Now he led the Trustees to reopen correspondence with Mood. On September 8, in the name of the Trustees, Kennon offered him the presidency. In doing so, he was quite honest about the situation being offered. He says that "we have been much set back; first by the war and its Results by which means we lost our endowment; second by the [yellow fever] epidemic from which we suffered last year; and third by the destruction of our cotton crops by the [droughts]." He avers that he cannot even promise Mood a fixed salary, "but can guarantee you patronage and the start for a support with a certainty of its increasing if the country is permitted to enjoy quiet."[91]

Mood received other letters, the most influential of which came from Bishop McTyeire and W. G. Connor. Both were fellow South Carolinians, and Mood felt that he could trust them. Writing on October 12, McTyeire makes a strong case for his accepting the situation. He says: "I wish you were in Texas—at Chapel [sic] Hill there. . . . You—or such a man as you—are in demand. . . . I hope you may see your way to be clear for the trip to Macedonia."[92] Connor, who is on the scene in Chappell Hill, is a bit more restrained, and, except for his description of the main building as being "the best edifice for school purposes in the state," says: "I will not advise you to accept the University, and still I am compelled to say in justice, I think there is a very fine field for the institution if properly managed."[93]

In late October Mood replies affirmatively to the offer of the presidency but states that he cannot be definite about coming because he does not have enough money to move his family to Texas. The pastor in Chappell Hill is so enthusiastic about the decision that he canvasses persons in the community who have an interest in the school to secure a loan to cover it. He raises $268.00, primarily from parents of potential students, giving each a receipt stating the object of the loan and promising that it will be repaid by Mood sometime in the future.[94] Since the only full-time teacher had just died, Kennon says that the school will suspend operations until Mood's arrival.[95]

A more wary person might have been deterred by the plethora of negative elements in the situation. Mood's comment in his *Autobiography* about his final decision, however, does not take these negative elements into consideration. He says: "After much correspondence, consultation with friends, anxious thought and earnest prayer, I determined to respond favourable to a call that seemed to come through the church from Him 'whose I am and whom I serve.'"[96] His decision to come to Texas, like that of Ruter, was ultimately based on religious principles, not considerations of utility.

Fulfillment of the Vision: Southwestern University (1868–1873)

"Undertaking to Resuscitate a Dead Institution"

Upon his election as President of Soule, Mood began to work immediately. Five days after arriving at Chappell Hill, he attended the annual meeting of the Texas Conference in nearby Brenham and was received by transfer into its membership. McLean says that he was a "Chesterfield in manners," and with his fluent and forceful speech, "he made a most favorable impression upon the conference."[1]

Bishop Doggett introduced him warmly to the ministers and gave him an opportunity to outline his plans for the University. Though they were adopted unanimously by the Conference, he later learned that his zeal was "a matter of great merriment to several of the body at the close of that day's session, so hopeless to them was the outlook."[2] Privately, Doggett told him "that in undertaking to resuscitate a dead institution, he was assuming a more difficult task, than if he were attempting to found a new one."[3] The Conference session was a disillusioning experience for Mood.

He was further disillusioned when he met with the Trustees during the session to deal with the question of the leaky roof of the University building. Recognizing that he could not conduct school in such conditions, he called a meeting of the Trustees and presented them with a tinner's estimate of $150 to repair it. They informed him that there was no money in the treasury. Not only was the University without funds, but it was also heavily in debt. He was, as he says, "horror stricken" to learn that a debt of $17,000, which he had been led to believe would be taken care of, was still outstanding. Only now did he realize the full extent of the University's indigence.[4]

On top of these revelations, the Rev. W. H. Seat, agent for the University, brought up for consideration at the Trustee meeting a trip to Europe he had planned. On the trip he proposed to help the school secure a library and other equipment and apparently asked for help in his venture. He had been planning the trip for some time and already possessed a letter of introduction from President Andrew Johnson to representatives of the United States government in Europe. Mood felt that the University could ill-afford the luxury of an agent in Europe when the immediate economy of the institution was in such an impoverished state. He opposed the expenditure.

The solution to these problems was that Mood secured a tinner's furnace and twenty pounds of solder from a friend, and, with help from a teacher, Bond E. Chrietzberg, just arrived from Wofford College in South Carolina, he repaired the roof.[5] The Board followed Mood's advice and made no contribution to Seat's four-year stay in Europe.[6] The debt problem went unsolved.

Back in Chappell Hill, Mood prepared advertisements and circulars announcing the opening of school on the first Monday in January 1869. The beginning was not auspicious. Gathered to hear his address, he says, were, besides the two other professors, "some four trustees, about ten citizens and some twenty six little urchins!. . . But why be downhearted, had we not a big building, a tight roof and twenty six little boys to begin with? We arranged our classes, got a good sleek strap, which I found out the first day we would need and started in to conduct a 'University.'"[7]

A Plan "Flashed into My Mind"

At the close of the school session in June, Mood traveled the countryside, as he said, "to stir up patronage." The result was an increase in student numbers for the fall. Some ten or twelve were of collegiate grade. But soon after the opening, yellow fever made its appearance in Galveston and Houston. To Mood's consternation, the Methodist preacher in Brenham hurried through Chappell Hill one day in his hack, informing people that the fever had spread as far as

Hempstead, only seven miles away. He advised them to flee. His announcement caused great alarm among the students and citizens. The terrible epidemic of two years earlier was imprinted vividly on their minds, and nothing that Mood could say or do could stem the panic.

In dismay he tried to sleep that night. With this "blackness and darkness" threatening, he says, he tossed in his bed, "thinking and praying," when "a perfectly clear and what seemed to me feasible plan . . . flashed into my mind." The next morning he prepared a paper and called the Board of Trustees together to hear it. On "a memorable night," October 4, 1869, he laid out his plan to them. "I suppose," he says, "if I ever reached the point of eloquence in my life, I was eloquent that night and[,] after long discussion, with [but] one dissenting vote, the paper was put on record as the sentiments of the Board."[8]

His paper was one of those brilliant pieces of writing that sometimes flow from the pen of an inspired author almost perfect from the outset. The plan it envisioned came fully formed into his mind. Though the East Texas Conference later made a few strategic changes in it, nothing essential was modified thereafter. Its directness, clarity, and cogency won assent for it everywhere. It became the basis for all the events of the next four years, resulting finally in the establishment of Southwestern University.

Mood introduced his subject by reminding his readers of all they agreed upon—that the Church needed a strong institution of learning to make education more affordable, that such did not now exist, that the absence of such an institution was causing the loss of young people to the State and Church, that the existence of such an institution required the support of the whole Church, that these ends were being only partially served by currently existing institutions, that the educational field was practically unoccupied, and that thirty thousand Texas Methodists should be able to establish an appropriate institution.

He then proceeded to outline seven propositions for adoption to remedy the situation. The several Annual Conferences should call a State Educational Convention. This Convention should arrange for "the organization, location, and endowment of a University for the South-West." Currently existing institutions should be invited to send delegations to present their claims. The delegates from each Conference should invite proposals for the most eligible sites within their bounds. The Bishop should appoint a financial agent to assist in raising the endowment. The Convention should arrange for a homogeneous system of preparatory schools to work with the proposed University. And each Conference should support the actions of the Convention without seeking to serve its own advantage. As if to reinforce the last point, the document concluded with words of encouragement to the entire Church throughout the state in undertaking the task before it. It also assured the Church that, though the Soule University Trustees presented the claims of their institution as the center around which everyone could unite, they would work to promote the common cause whatever the outcome for location might be.[9] Many of the Trustees who voted for this generous document later came to regret their generosity.

The irony of the situation is that within a few days "the news of the [yellow] fever being at Hempstead was contradicted, and the panic passed." Reflecting back on it later, Mood said that "there was never another day in which I could have succeeded with the Board as I did except the one on which action was taken—action which sealed the final doom of Soule University, but at the same time laid the foundation for its reappearance in more desirable and promising shape elsewhere."[10]

Securing Annual Conference Agreements

Though Mood knew in general the steps he would have to take to secure his goal, little could he have fathomed the tortuous path he would have to travel for four years to achieve it. He was like a mountain climber, who, upon cresting one summit, sees another, and another, and another opening up before him. If he did not know the turns and twists of the path, he was surefooted enough not to make any false steps and to take the right fork at every juncture in the road.

He finally succeeded because his plan was logical and appealed to the objective nature of thinking people. He succeeded because his interpersonal skills were remarkable and he could keep opponents from becoming enemies. He succeeded because his zeal was formidable and carried people who were less committed along with him. He succeeded because he appealed to the best instincts of people even when the action called for might run contrary to their currently perceived best interests. He succeeded because he believed he had a higher calling to his mission than personal self-interest and received consolation and strength in times of depression from that belief. He traveled thousands of miles, attended countless meetings, made numerous talks, and spent all his resources in the effort—all this from a man whose weak physical condition

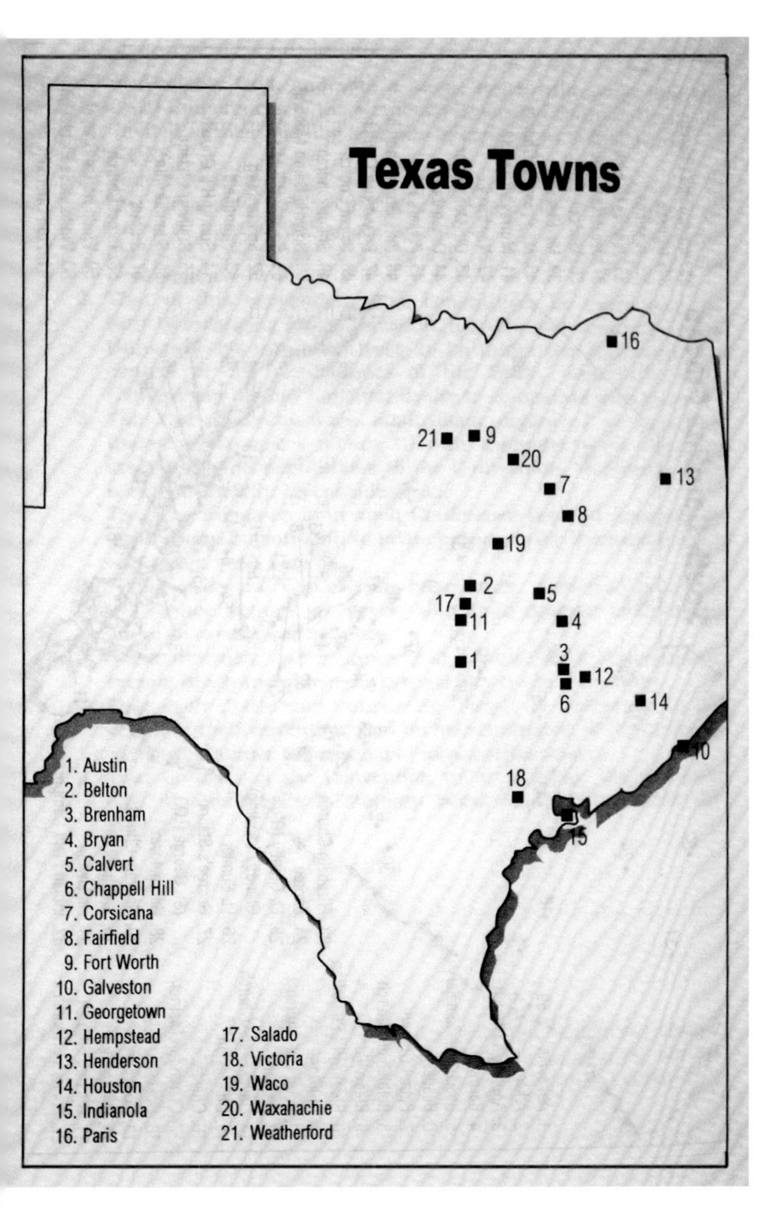

Towns mentioned in the contention surrounding the location of Southwestern University. From Mary Katherine Metcalfe Earney, ed., *For God and Texas: Autobiography of Francis Asbury Mood, 1830–1884.*

would bring him to his grave within scarcely a decade after he had succeeded in his mission.

His first effort, he knew, after securing approval from the Soule Board of Trustees, must be to gain the support of the person whose influence would be most helpful in the future. That person was Dr. Robert Alexander. He, as one of the three original missionaries to Texas and companion of Martin Ruter, was respected, almost venerated, everywhere. Consequently, Mood hastened next day to a camp meeting near Bryan where Alexander was preaching to win him for the cause. Though Alexander was negative as to the practicality of the plan, declaring it "an impossibility to unite the five Texas Conferences on anything," he was, nevertheless, excited by the idea.[11]

Mood's next step was to pick up the challenge referred to by Alexander—winning the support of the five Annual Conferences. He wrote Bishop Wightman about his plan and his desire to present it to the Conferences over which Wightman was to preside that fall. The Bishop's response was discouraging, but Mood took a stagecoach to Henderson, the site of the East Texas Conference meeting (October 20). On arrival, he followed proper procedure and sent his propositions to the Committee on Education, whose members "greeted me with the disagreeable statement that 'they would not touch it.' I replied confidently, because I felt certain of the result, why I cannot tell, 'Oh, yes you will' and proceeded at once to elaborate the plan and urge the matter. The committee became convinced, became enthusiastic; they reported favorably; the enthusiasm became infective and the scheme was heartily and unanimously adopted by the Conference. This fired the heart of the good Bishop[,] who followed the vote by one of his terse[,] earnest and eloquent appeals for zeal and unity in the movement."[12]

The Conference did make three changes in the document that became part of the document submitted to the other Conferences. It asked that the Educational Convention meet in Galveston on April 20, 1870, that the clerical delegates elected to the General Conference constitute the delegates to the Convention, and that the votes in the Convention on the matter of location be by Conference rather than by individual delegates.[13]

Mood then visited the Trinity (soon to be North Texas) Conference in Paris (November 3), where almost exactly the same thing occurred. The Conference acquiesced and the Bishop delivered another earnest speech. The same thing happened at the North West Texas Conference at Weatherford (November 17) and in turn at the West Texas Conference in Goliad (December 8) and the Texas Conference in La Grange (December 22). He was particularly encouraged because some people voluntarily, without his asking, gathered money and handed it to him to assist in defraying traveling expenses "so that I returned home without debt."[14]

While at the Texas Conference, he was appointed to Brenham as pastor. He was there for two years until moved by Bishop Marvin to Chappell Hill in December 1871. For the next three-and-a-half years he served as President at Soule during the week and as pastor on weekends. It caused a great deal of work but solved his immediate financial problems.[15]

The Educational Convention: Phase 1—Galveston

The proposed Educational Convention met at Galveston on April 20, 1870. Robert Alexander was elected President of the Convention and "Dr." Mood as secretary. He had the previous month been awarded an honorary Doctor of Divinity degree by his alma mater, Charleston College.[16]

Many of the delegates felt that the matters to be considered could be dealt with quickly, and a motion was made to proceed directly to the matter of location. Mood tried to head this off by proposing that a ten-person committee, composed of lay and clerical delegates from each Conference, study the matter and report back to the Convention. The Convention concurred, and he and J. D. Giddings of Brenham were appointed to the committee from the Texas Conference. To Mood's dismay, a majority report from the committee recommended that the University be located at Waxahachie and that a committee be appointed to work out a method of making arrangements with the recently established Marvin College to make it the nucleus for the University. Mood was forced to present a minority report as a substitute. That report listed reasons why adoption of the actions proposed in the majority report would be premature. The report and its substitute were both laid on the table. Then the Convention appointed two committees, one on organization and another on endowment, to report the next day. Mood was appointed to the former committee, Giddings to the latter. He and Giddings were recognized as key leaders; one or the other of them was always in a position to exert influence at the right place to secure their common goal.

Both committees reported as requested the following day. The organization committee made recommendations on Conference patronage, number of Trustees, method of their election, restrictions on Trustee action, the election of Board officers, and the responsibilities of an executive committee. It then made an extensive report, obviously written by Mood, on the departments of instruction of the proposed university. It is his most extensive statement of educational beliefs and later became the basis for the first academic program at Southwestern University.

The report—Mood—states that the universities of the Old World were established "with a view to the liberal education of a few." Something different, however, was needed for the New World. "Nearly fifty years ago the Trustees of the University of Virginia ventured to change this proc[r]ustean policy by the establishment of independent departments and schools[,] allowing each student to select and determine the particular branches of study to which he would devote his attention. The plan incorporated by the University of Virginia finds increasing favor over the Union each year."

The professions of law, medicine, and theology, "the original trinity," Mood continues, have now been supplemented by new "avocations—many of them worthy of being styled professions." The extent of knowledge is now so overwhelming that to try to cover it all results in giving the young person only a "superficial knowledge" of the whole. Mood abandons the Renaissance man concept, saying it is better, "by a judicious selection," to educate the young person "for the calling or profession he intends to follow." Therefore, "we unhesitatingly recommend the American University System." The academic program should "conform to that of the University of Virginia, the oldest and best organized institution in the United States."

The academic program should not be a single whole, says Mood, required of everyone. It should be composed of diverse disciplines, and a young person should be able to select the disciplines "that will best minister to his advantage in subsequent life." He later incorporated this principle into the first Southwestern University curriculum when it was established in 1873. The catalog for 1874 states that the course of study is at the discretion of the student, or his parents or guardians. Each student is required to take studies in four "schools," i.e., departments or disciplines (the terms were used almost interchangeably), one compulsory and three of his own choosing. The word "elective" is used for the choices.

In order to prepare students for the University, Mood persuaded the organization committee to recommend the calling of another convention at which the Conferences could discuss a system of "Homogeneous Preparatory Schools." This convention should be held in conjunction with the officers of the University to determine a uniform curriculum leading to university studies, including textbooks used. In this recommendation Mood echoes Martin Ruter, who had the same idea—one central university with feeder schools. "All schools & colleges concurring in the adoption of the course and enforcing the terms of scholarship thus agreed upon shall be regarded as associate schools and published as such in the catalogue of the University." In spite of the adoption of this paragraph, such a convention was never held. Nevertheless, at several points in its later career Southwestern University flirted with this concept, first in the late 1880s, with the "correlated schools" idea, and later in the 1930s and '40s, with the "University of Small Colleges" idea.

One feels in reading the committee report, from its thoroughness and cohesion, that Mood brought it with him to the Convention. He was not sure of the venue in which it would be presented, but he was determined that it should enter discussion at some point. This committee became that point, and it appears to have adopted Mood's draft with, perhaps, some minor revisions.

The other committee, the endowment committee, reported that a university such as the one proposed would need $500,000 to achieve its purpose. Of this amount, $100,000 should go for buildings and equipment, with $400,000 being set apart as a permanent endowment. It should "be held sacred for that purpose." Once agents appointed for raising the endowment have secured $100,000 of the permanent endowment and another $50,000 for buildings, then, and only then, should the University be organized and located. Each Conference should be requested to raise at least $5,000 annually until the latter two amounts have been achieved. The appointment of a committee of respected persons is recommended to manage the funds raised until the University shall be organized. Bishop Wightman is asked to appoint two agents, Rev. Orceneth Fisher and Rev. J. W. P. McKenzie, to take charge of raising the funds. Both were, like Alexander, patriarchs of the Church, whose names would lend weight to the movement. Wightman later appointed Rev. W. G. Veal of the North West Texas Conference, a strong supporter of Mood, as a third agent.

The rationale for the figures selected by the committee is not given. They were probably selected because some of the men on the committee, at least one, J. D. Giddings, a wealthy lawyer and banker, had experience with institutions of higher learning and knew the kind of money required to run one. As a Soule University Trustee and a member of Mood's church in Brenham, Giddings had contact with Mood in two different roles. He and Mood may have even conferred about the amount required, thus giving Mood input into both Convention committees. The statement that the endowment money should "be held sacred for that purpose" has the ring of Mood's own financial philosophy. At the end of his tenure at Southwestern, just before his death, one of the achievements of which he was most proud was that, in spite of its limited income, the University had progressed without building up any debt. In the last financial report of the University during Mood's administration, the chair of the Executive Committee of the Board of Trustees affirmed that "we are not in debt, and it is our settled policy to avoid this devouring maelstrom of colleges."[17] Whether or not Mood had any influence on that statement, it did reflect his point of view and the policy he followed as Regent.

The reports of both committees were adopted unanimously. Toward the end of the Convention, after a committee of three had been appointed to secure a charter, Mood proposed that the anticipated institution be known as the "South Western University." A majority of the delegates, however, moved by expansive pride, voted to call it "The Texas University." Even here Mood eventually won out. When the State later refused to charter the institution under that name, his name—South Western University—was chosen.

As a final act, the Convention appointed a committee to draft an address to the several Conferences setting forth its plans and the claims of its projected university to their interest, sympathy, and aid. As finally written, it outlined the accomplishments of the Convention, emphasized that the final decisions on all points were unanimous, and concluded with a parting exhortation.[18] It was after this Galveston Convention that Dr. Alexander took Mood to the back of the church in which the sessions were held "and embracing me said with his eyes filled with tears, 'I never expected to live to see this day.'"[19]

The Educational Convention: Phase 2—Waxahachie

Back at Soule as President and in Brenham as pastor, Mood had to work hard to keep up. He says that in some respects the year was "the darkest and most trying" in his life. By the winter of 1870 the three agents appointed at the Galveston meeting to secure means for the establishment of the new institution reported total failure to secure the necessary money. Few people wanted to pledge money to a proposed institution whose location had not yet been determined. The Conferences ordered the Convention to "reassemble" at Waxahachie on April 6, 1871. The directive to meet at Waxahachie put Mood in a delicate position. He would have to discuss the establishment of a Central university at a place with a budding movement to establish a college named after Bishop E. M. Marvin, who would also be conducting the meeting. Marvin was a deeply spiritual man, almost ascetic, and very popular with the people.[20]

In these less than ideal circumstances, the Convention

Second Educational Convention at Waxahachie, April 6, 1871. At the center of the photo is Bishop E. M. Marvin; clockwise from top are J. W. P. McKenzie, Buckner Harris, F. A. Mood, B. A. Philpott, W. G. Connor, R. W. Kennon, J. W. DeVilbiss, Thomas Stanford, H. H. Sneed, and W. G. Veal. Southwestern University, Special Collections.

met in the Methodist Church of Waxahachie over a period of three days. One of the important early decisions was whether this meeting was limited by the agenda and determinations of the first meeting in Galveston or whether it was free to act on its own and move beyond the previous meeting. On this issue, the chair, Bishop Marvin, decided that the proceedings of the Convention were *de novo*, i.e., that the meeting in Waxahachie was not a prorogation, not merely a suspension of the Galveston Convention, but autonomous in its own right.[21] Thus, it might properly be called a Second Convention, though everyone continued to refer to it as "the" Educational Convention. The ruling was helpful to Mood. The Convention could undertake independent action without being challenged that it was out of line with what the First Convention had done.

The first major action was a motion to move directly to the matter of location. Owensville, Hope, Fairfield, and Waxahachie had all come with written or verbal proposals seeking the University. Once again Mood was forced to oppose the attempt as premature, doing so, he felt, to the point of causing resentment against him. He was convinced that these and many other places were inappropriate for a university for such reasons as their having heavy debt obligations, being located in disease-prone areas, or, as he put it, exhibiting "immaturity of knowledge." He had to use all his powers to forestall location. His unwillingness to name his own candidate for location caused some delegates to feel that he was trying to secure it for Soule, the last thing he wanted. He not only used persuasion, but also resorted to parliamentary maneuvers to carry his position. He later wrote that of all the occasions of his life, this one was the most trying.[22]

He put the issue to rest by having everyone agree as to the limits within which the University should be located. The area consisted basically of the four central Texas counties of Bell, Burnet, Travis, and Williamson, in addition to some surrounding towns within carefully specified latitudinal and longitudinal boundaries. The limits excluded the entire Texas Conference, thereby excluding Chappell Hill.[23] By the terms of these boundaries, the new university was to be located astride the Balcones Fault, either slightly to the east in blackland country or slightly to the west in ranch country. No northern limits for the University were set, and, theoretically, it could have been established as far north as Dallas, Fort Worth, or Denton. Nevertheless, it is clear that Mood expected it to be in Central Texas. The lack of a northern boundary limit was probably in consideration of Waxahachie. It would have been impolitic for him to have excluded the town in which the Convention was meeting.

The Convention concluded its work by placing the matter of location into the hands of ten Commissioners of Location composed of two persons from each Conference, one lay and one clerical. They were instructed to "locate the University upon a large body of land accessible to Railroad" and to make a final report to the Convention to be held at the time and place of the next North West Texas Annual Conference. Mood and Giddings were appointed to the Commission from the Texas Conference. The commissioners began their work immediately after the conclusion of the Convention by authorizing publication in newspapers of announcements calling for donations of land and money and bids of location.[24]

Fending Off Attempts at Derailment

Back in Chappell Hill and Brenham, Mood met with indignation from some members of the two communities. They felt that the President of their school and pastor of their church had betrayed them. Recognizing the problem, Mood says, he taught his classes with such zeal and ministered to his congregation so earnestly that they came to respect the integrity of his efforts even though they disagreed with his policy. During the year he even managed to gather enough money to build a good parsonage at Brenham. The school did not do badly when compared with the previous year. It had fifteen or eighteen students of collegiate rank, two of whom, having entered as sophomores, graduated with the A.B. in 1872.[25] Nevertheless, the prospect of Mood's leaving was already having its effect. In late February of that year, a student wrote to J. D. Giddings that "if Dr. Mood gives up the college . . . it will operate very much against the school. So many speak of leaving. I never would have come here if I had thought he would have left."[26]

In spite of his best efforts, townspeople knew that, absent some unexpected occurrence, his leaving was just a matter of time. One group decided to do something about it. At some point during the year he was invited to the office of a prominent parishioner where an attractive financial proposition was offered him. His host stated that he represented certain parties who had purchased the debt of $17,000 on Soule University and that they proposed to foreclose on it and conduct it as a private enterprise. He stated that if Mood would agree to stay and become its leader, they would deed him one-half of the University and grounds. Mood was shocked and indignantly rejected the proposal, principally because of the injustice to the Church. His argument had its effect on the men involved, who were, he says, "intelligent Christian men," and they ceased to push their claims. He eventually induced them to cancel the debt, and, just before his final resignation the following year, was able to leave the school free of any liability.[27]

He also received letters from minister friends in different Conferences who warned him that the Central university plan was losing impetus, especially that it was losing the location fight. Marvin College in Waxahachie, they suggested, was slowly gaining support, and without a drastic change of events Waxahachie might win. They encouraged Mood to come up with "something tangible" to forestall this possibility. In the light of this warning, Mood began to correspond with interested laymen around the state, mostly in Galveston, and to devise a viable alternative. At the point of taking action, on September 13, he wrote J. D. Giddings.

We have already met Jabez Giddings at the Educational Conventions in Galveston and Waxahachie. Giddings was a devoted layman who had come to Texas in 1838 to settle the estate of a brother who had been killed at the Battle of San Jacinto. He remained and became acquainted with Martin Ruter on his trip to Texas. He became an early settler in Rutersville after his death. After the raids of Vasquez and Woll, he responded and joined Gen. Somervell's army until it was disbanded. Then he, with the great majority, returned home, thus escaping the slaughter at Mier.[28] After service with Somerville, he became a lawyer and entrepreneur in Brenham and made his first big money building the rail line from Hempstead to that city. He was one of the founders of the Methodist Church at Brenham and had Mood for his pastor during Mood's tenure there.[29] He had a talent for business and before the Civil War was one of the state's wealthiest men. He lost most of his money during the war, but by 1870 he had recovered it, the only Texan with a net worth of at least $100,000 in 1860 to do so. He and a brother founded one of the state's earliest banks. He acquired an oil "factory," as the records call it, and became a stockholder and member of the Board of Directors of the Houston and Texas Central Railway. The town of Giddings, Texas, was later named after him.[30]

In his letter Mood laid out his plans and asked for his friend's support.

> Dear Bro Giddings
>
> I have received several letters from the members of the other Conferences and all seem to despair of the University movement unless I will take hold of it and succeed in carrying up to the coming sessions of the Conferences something tangible wherewith to encourage them to hope for the success of the plan I have for two years urged upon the Church. If nothing is now done, the Conferences soon to meet will instruct their delegates to go to Corsicana and vote for Marvin College at Waxahatchie [sic]. This will commit irrevocably a majority of the delegates to that point and we will assemble there simply to ratify & perfect this predetermined action.
>
> I now propose to get the names of those who are willing to go into *a joint stock company to purchase the*

necessary land donating say half of the tract in alternate sections as a bonus for the location of the University upon it. This will remunerate the stockholders & at the same time confer a perpetual blessing on the Church of God in the State. I have spent much anxious thought, travelled much & offered ceaseless prayer to God that he would vouchsafe his blessing in some form upon this proposal to bless the future generations of the Church. My heart dies within me at the thought of its final failure.

I respectfully ask the use of your name with the amount you are willing to invest as a stockholder in such a scheme. I believe it will be of great advantage to me in my approaches to other gentlemen over the state with whom I have opened correspondence. What is done must now be done forthwith. Two or three weeks delay in my judgment fixes a failure beyond remedy. An immediate reply will greatly oblige.

Your brother in Christ
F.A. Mood[31]

Giddings must have replied positively, for he became a stockholder in the Texas University Company when it was formally organized three months later. Having won the support of Giddings, Mood began to elaborate his plan and by the time of the Corsicana Convention it was much more detailed.

The Educational Convention: Phase 3—Corsicana

The Convention met for its third and final time in Corsicana on November 1–3, 1871. The matter of location was now the principal item on the agenda, and proposals for location were heard from four cities including Salado, Waxahachie, and Milam County. The Rev. William Monk, Captain J. C. S. Morrow, and Dudley H. Snyder also presented a proposal from the stockholders of Georgetown College and citizens of Williamson County to place the University in Georgetown.[32]

After hearing the four proposals, the Convention took no action. It wanted to set up a process for making a decision that would ensure the consideration of every option. The previous Commissioners of Location were discharged, and a new slate of commissioners was selected. Like the previous committee, it was composed of ten persons, two from each Conference, but unlike that committee it was given full power to act without having to receive confirmation from another Convention session. It was merely to report what it had done. It was given authority to locate the institution, to act as Trustees for the property secured for it, and to arrange for its opening. A quorum of three of the Conferences would be required for action. Mood and Giddings were appointed from the Texas Conference.[33]

Meeting after the Convention had adjourned, the Commissioners of Location received a proposition to the Convention, which, "delayed in the mails, had arrived too late to be submitted to the Convention, from Messrs. Alford, McMahon, Norris et al of Galveston relating to the location and endowment of the proposed University [through means of a joint stock company]."[34] Mood, who had given them this idea, was appointed to investigate the proposition. The other Commissioners were appointed to investigate the proposals from Salado, Waxahachie, Milam County, and any others that might be presented in the future.

Reconciling Divergent Accounts of the Events

At this point we have some difficulty reconciling the description of events obtained from recorded minutes with Mood's later description of it. Writing a decade later about the actions leading to the establishment of Southwestern University, Mood presents an account somewhat at variance with that detailed in the minutes of the Corsicana Convention and of the Commissioners of Location appointed by it. He states that during the Convention, when the members were seething with impatience about the unsatisfactory report of the previous Commissioners of Location, "a proposition of an entirely novel character was submitted."

> A company of prosperous and active capitalists, members of the Church—a majority of them residing in the city of Galveston—proposed to *form a joint-stock company* with a capital of $100,000, of which they were willing to take $50,000, provided the Methodists of the State at large would take the other $50,000. With this money they assured the Convention *they could purchase an eligible body of land* containing nearly 20,000 acres, toward which an important line of railroad was then pushing. *The company from this purchase was to donate ample grounds for college buildings near the center, and every alternate lot and acre of the town to be laid out around the University, and every alternate section of 160 acres of the remaining land.* They promised, also, to erect plain

> buildings for the University and Faculty in which operations might begin and be comfortably accommodated for ten or fifteen years. These gentlemen limited the time of their offer to June 1, 1872, after which, if the Church at large had failed to respond to their proposition, it was to be considered null and void. The proposition was most favorably received by the Convention. The gentlemen originating the offer were appointed Commissioners of Location, with instructions that if the scheme failed, they were to select from the many places then claiming the location. In that event they were to become Trustees of the property accepted in behalf of the M. E. Church, South, and to make any and all arrangements for the opening of the University their wisdom should devise, and report their action to the several Conferences.[35] [Italics above added.]

An analysis of the proposition as narrated by Mood reveals a number of differences from the pattern of events derived from other sources. Obviously, the proposition is an expansion of the initiative mentioned by Mood in his letter of September 13 to Giddings. The details have been fleshed out beyond what is in the letter, but the basic premise is the same. He does not at any point, however, connect his name with the idea. Acting behind the scenes, he gives full credit to the Galveston businessmen.

He also fails to mention any meeting of the Commissioners of Location immediately after the Convention. He portrays events happening after the Convention as if they occurred during the Convention. Neither, as he alleges, were the gentlemen originating the offer appointed the Commissioners of Location. The Commissioners of Location were ten persons from the five Annual Conferences appointed during the Convention who met later and appointed Mood to investigate the offer. After the Texas University Company was formed, the Commissioners voluntarily relinquished much of their decision-making power to its directors, but the action was not by design of the Convention.

In writing a decade later about the matter, after it was all over and the tangle of details would be, he felt, of little interest to his intended readers, Mood telescoped events. He presents the eventual outcome accurately, but he does not feel a need to chronicle the minutiae. Neither is he interested in mentioning his own role in the matter. He is content that the University has been established, and he is grateful for the support he has received from the Galveston businessmen. His role as the originator of the idea would not have been discovered at all had not J. D. Giddings kept Mood's letter of September 13 and passed it on to descendants who would eventually donate it and other Giddings documents to Southwestern University.[36]

The Texas University Company

After the Convention, Mood carried out his committee assignment with dispatch. He went to Galveston to inform his friends about the decision of the Convention to place the matter of organizing, locating, and opening the University in the hands of the Commissioners of Location. Rather than waiting for the meeting of the Commissioners already scheduled for Salado in early February, he called them to a meeting in Galveston on December 9. Once having heard the results of Mood's discussions with the Galveston laymen, the Commissioners unanimously adopted a three-part resolution. The resolution said that they approved the plan of locating and endowing the University through the agency of a joint stock company, that they invited the formation of such a company by members and friends of the Church, and that they placed the financial control of the University in the hands of the company under terms mutually acceptable to both parties.[37] By vesting their financial powers in the new joint stock company, the Commissioners of Location appointed by the Convention became henceforth the conduit for reporting Texas University Company decisions and actions on those matters back to the five Annual Conferences rather than being the initiators of such.

Upon acceptance of the proposal, the meeting turned to the actual formation of the joint stock company. Basic to the enterprise was the establishment of an initial capital fund. This fund would be formed through subscriptions of stock. The Commissioners agreed that when $20,000 or more had been subscribed, the company would be organized and elect officers. The meeting was then opened to subscriptions, with shares valued at $500 each. Seventeen persons, fifteen of whom were laymen, with eleven from Galveston, immediately subscribed the required forty shares.[38] The Company proceeded to name a committee of three to bring back a plan of organization. It is interesting to observe that Mood took one share of stock and, thus, became not only a Commissioner of Location, but also a member of the Company. When the Company evolved into the Board of Trustees of Southwestern University, he was by right a Trustee on two counts—*ex officio* as Regent and by having been a member of the Company.[39]

The committee reported back, presenting "Articles of

Agreement" outlining the organizational structure of the company. They were accepted unanimously. The document describes the purpose of the Company as being to acquire at least $200,000 and not more than $500,000 for the development of a "University looking to the dissemination of knowledge and the principles of the Methodist Episcopal Church South." It will purchase "bodies of land in the immediate vicinity of the site of said University as will be enhanced in value by building up said institution." Profits realized by these transactions will be used "to assist in the completion and building up of said University." In conclusion, it adopts a name—"The Texas University Company."[40]

Modification of the Plan

The results of the meeting were immediately published in two articles printed in the *Texas Christian Advocate.* Their language is that of Mood, though he is not named as the author. After explaining the procedure for capitalization and the financial benefits that will likely accrue to the stockholders, he describes what he considers to be the benefits, other than financial, for the institution. It will engage the goodwill and actions of a thousand persons in working for the success of the new university. He writes:

> The plan inaugurated involves an advantage to the Institution that no previous offers could promise. Each stockholder is linked to the Institution, and committed to its success by the powerful motives both of love to the Church on the one hand, and hazards and profits of his investment on the other. With one thousand stockholders [at $500 each, yielding $500,000] scattered over the State, we will have one thousand agents, who will speak, write and labor for its prosperity and success.[41]

Much to Mood's disappointment the plan did not take hold. Outside investors were slow to purchase shares in the Company, and within two months the stockholders asked Mood to take responsibility for the progress of the enterprise as their agent. He was soon forced to go back to the earlier approach, i.e., to seek bids from already established towns. The most significant aspect of the endeavor was that when the six-month time limit for the offer passed on June 15, 1872, without the desired results and the Company was legally dissolved, the original stockholders continued their interest in the university project without murmur.[42] Though the plan had failed in its intention, it was, nevertheless, a success in another manner. It had put together a body of well-to-do Methodist laymen, centering largely in Galveston, who took specific responsibility henceforth for seeing to the establishment of the University.

There seems little doubt that the inspiration of the Galveston laymen for establishing a university came from Mood. Most of them had probably come to know him at the meeting of the Galveston Educational Convention in April 1870, and it was his vision they were following. Soon after the establishment of the stock company, they officially acknowledged this fact by employing him as their general agent for the state. Two years later they followed him to Southwestern as Trustees. By forming the Texas University Company, the Galveston laymen became the enabling agents for the formation of Southwestern University. Without them it might never have come to exist.

Mood as Agent of the Texas University Company

Mood recounts in his *Autobiography* the despair he felt, soon after the organization of the Texas University Company, at the seeming inaction of the Commissioners of Location. He heard nothing from them, he says, and "the whole project seemed to have disappeared with the final adjournment of the convention." He was tired, became ill, and was confined to bed with a slow fever. The illness was a long one, probably lasting well into the new year. He became very despondent.

In this condition, he received a letter from his Galveston friends. After sympathizing with him in his illness, the Directors of the Texas University Company asked him to come down for a meeting. The result of the meeting on February 5, 1872, was that they employed him as their principal agent for the state, agreeing to pay all his expenses for securing the means and a location for opening the University. Apparently the members of the Company had come to the conclusion that the only logical course of action was to empower the person who had led the university movement thus far to continue his work.

In poor health but with the prospect of considerable travel before him as agent of the Texas University Company, Mood told the Board of Trustees on February 15 that "his physicians had advised him to discontinue his services as Pres. Of Soule University in consequence of his declining health, and asked to be relieved of his responsibility as such." The Trustees heard him sympathetically and "cheerfully grant[ed] him permission to travel at pleasure for his improvement." He was granted freedom to "make such arrangements to supply his lack of service in the University as he may deem necessary." Less than a month later, on March 8, the Board met again for the purpose of trying devise ways of staunching a student exodus as a result of "Dr. Mood's inability to attend to his duties as Pres. Of the Faculty" and a "general dissatisfaction" among those remaining. Called upon to speak, he "spoke freely of the condition of the university, but had nothing to suggest as a present remedy." Three days later, the Trustees met again. Without a leader active in behalf of the University, it was rudderless. They elected Prof. McSwain to take the tiller as "Pres. Of Soule University for the remainder of the session." Mood was requested to announce the action in the *Advocate*.[43] Free of his responsibilities at Soule and after securing persons to fill his pulpit, Mood began to travel as he was able and visited the places contesting for the site of the new university. He mentions visits to Fairfield, Calvert, Fort Worth, Waco, Salado, Belton, Austin, and Georgetown.[44]

Georgetown and Georgetown College

Georgetown at the time of Mood's first visit was a relatively new town, having been established in 1848 specifically to serve as the county seat for the equally new Williamson County. A letter to his mother in Kentucky from a young lawyer, Thomas Proctor Hughes, beginning practice there in 1851, describes it as "a very prospering, healthy little village, the location of which is extremely sitely, intersperced [sic] with live oaks, and surrounded on one side with the a [sic] creek that is the clearest water I ever expect to see."[45] Hughes, later a strong Mood supporter, had a long career in Georgetown. The first newspaper in the county was established there in 1856.

Williamson County earned a unique distinction in 1861 when it became one of the few counties in Texas to vote against the secession ordinance, rejecting it by a vote of 480 to 349. Sam Houston visited Georgetown from time to time, and one of his daughters, Nancy Elizabeth Houston, wife of Captain J. C. S. Morrow, a prime mover in bringing the University to Georgetown, lived there with her family. Nancy, or "Nannie," as she was popularly known, states that her father often stayed at the Talbot home in Georgetown and that he met a representative of President Abraham Lincoln there shortly before the war broke out.[46]

The town counted 320 residents in the 1860 census and was incorporated in 1866. Several denominations had congregations there by 1870, and the present First Presbyterian Church was built in 1872–1873. There was as yet no Methodist congregation, and the fourteen Methodists there in 1873 were but one of twelve preaching points on a large circuit. An academy on the south bank of the San Gabriel River two blocks west of present Austin Avenue had been provided in 1850. The Georgetown Male and Female Academy Trustees purchased it in 1867.

Late in 1869 a group of men in town began talking about establishing a college. The Civil War had had a devastating effect on colleges in the state, their number dropping from twenty-five in 1860 to only thirteen in 1870, and many communities aspired to fill the void.[47] Colleges were not only economically beneficial to a community, but also gave it a certain status. They also provided preparatory schools for prospective applicants for degrees. These preparatory schools were valuable additions to whatever educational facilities the town already provided.

This interest in establishing a college in Georgetown materialized when, on January 29, 1870, a meeting was held at the courthouse to begin the effort by setting up a stock company. The participants approved a constitution for what they called Georgetown College and capitalized it through a stock offering. Stock, valued at $50 a share, was purchased by 112 people from whom a twelve-person Board of Trustees was elected. The large number of stockholders is remarkable given the small size of the town and indicates a total community, indeed countywide, interest in the venture. Captain J. C. S. Morrow was elected President of the Board. He would subsequently be reelected in 1871 and 1872.

At the same meeting, the Trustees selected as the site for the college building ten acres of land "immediately south east of Georgetown." Two days later a committee was appointed to draw up plans for a building to cost eight to ten thousand dollars.[48] The laying of the cornerstone on July 16, 1870, was a spectacular affair for the little town. After a ceremony at the building site, where a number of speakers expounded on the auspicious nature of the occasion, the crowd marched to the fairgrounds (the present San Gabriel Park). They crossed the river on a temporary bridge made by planks laid on stationary wagons standing in the riverbed.[49]

Thenceforward through the middle of 1873 the Board approved elements from time to time related to the con-

The Main Building at Southwestern donated by the Georgetown College Trustees in 1873 to procure the University for the town. The third story was added in 1881. Williams Elementary School now occupies the site. From Mary Katherine Metcalfe Earney, ed., *For God and Texas: Autobiography of Francis Asbury Mood, 1830–1884*.

struction. Construction costs were covered by calls issued to the stockholders on a regular basis to provide percentage portions of the value of their shares until they had paid 100 percent. By the time of the annual meeting in May 1872, over two hundred shares had been sold, representing a capitalization of more than ten thousand dollars. Nevertheless, the project began to run out of money. Some of the stockholders could not or did not live up to their commitments, and building costs ran beyond expectations. As a result, the Trustees were forced to resort to various expedients to meet the gap between revenues and expenditures. By the end of 1871, they were forced to secure loans. By the end of the project in early 1872, they were giving shares of stock in lieu of money in return for labor and supplies. Nevertheless, they could see the end of the effort and set May 1 as the date for occupancy. They let a contract for a stairway on April 13, 1872, to join the first and second floors of the two-story stone building. On May 1 they appointed a committee "to have the rubbish removed from [the] College Building." Apparently the stairway had been installed but the rubbish had not been removed when a committee from the Texas University Company visited Georgetown "about" April 25, 1872.[50]

Seeking a Methodist Connection

Georgetown College never held a college class, hired a teacher, or issued a diploma. Aside from the joint stock company, it was only a name without educational substance. So far as records go, the Trustees never discussed what they wanted in a college. Apparently, they proceeded on the assumption that possession of a structure would place them in a good position to bid for a college from among groups in the state interested in establishing one. Their tactic succeeded brilliantly. The Methodist Church, as one of those groups, was impressed enough with its proposal that it chose Georgetown over all the other applicants. Nevertheless, it was a touch and go process, and persons connected with the process were almost in despair before the relationship was finally established.

The Trustees apparently learned about the Methodist university movement from the pastor of the Georgetown circuit. The *Williamson County Sun* recounts how it occurred in a special edition published on January 26, 1923, celebrating the fiftieth anniversary of the establishment of Southwestern in Georgetown.

> After . . . a meeting of trustees in Waco, Reverend William Monk, minister in charge of the Georgetown circuit and a resident of Round Rock, was asked to look for a location [for the new university] in his district. On his way home from Waco, he stopped in Georgetown to talk with Colonel W[illiam]. C. Dalrymple "and suggested to him that Georgetown bid for the Methodist College and offer the Georgetown College building, then about finished, with its other property as a subsidy."[51]

Dalrymple, one of the original settlers of Georgetown and an important figure in Williamson County politics and other affairs for fifty years, reported the matter to the other Trustees immediately, and they acted quickly. They approved a resolution on August 18, 1871, after the Waxahachie Convention but before the Corsicana meeting, to the effect that "the Board of Trustees are willing to turn over the Georgetown College to the Methodists on condition of their establishing a first class University here." Several stockholders were appointed to "solicit subscriptions for locating the Methodist State University at Georgetown" in order to sweeten their offer. Once they got into action, the Trustees made the procurement of the University their primary goal. On October 7 they instituted a system for canvassing the entire county for subscriptions. Two weeks later they passed a more comprehensive resolution authorizing the officers to transfer Georgetown College to the Methodist Church and to "execute and deliver" all necessary documents once conditions were met. It then elected delegates "to represent our interests" at the forthcoming meeting of the Educational Convention in Corsicana on November 1.[52] At that meeting the Rev. William Monk, Captain J. C. S. Morrow, and Dudley Snyder appeared and presented a proposal from "the stockholders of Georgetown College and citizens of the county for the location of the University in Georgetown."[53]

Actions of the Texas University Company

As already indicated, soon after the adjournment of the Corsicana meeting, the Texas University Company was set up (December 11–12), and the university movement gained momentum. A few months later, in early February, Mood was appointed as general agent for the entire state. He visited all the communities that had indicated an interest in the location of the University and immediately lent his support for the Georgetown site. Quietly, but confidently, he urged Georgetown upon his fellow Conference commissioners "as the most eligible," and persuaded several of them to visit it. Their visits confirmed them, he says, in the appropriateness of his opinion. It came to be understood among them that "unless material changes came in the offers of other places, Georgetown would likely receive the prize."[54] Nevertheless, he and they recognized that the selection process must be honored, and they did not let their feelings be known.

The Corsicana meeting and visits by Mood and other commissioners to Georgetown acted as positive reinforcements to the Georgetown College Trustees. Hardly a meeting of the Trustees occurred during the winter without some action being taken to strengthen their position, especially in trying to acquire more land to go with what they already possessed. By early February they had agreed to state the worth of the almost completed building at $30,000 in their location bid. Captain Morrow asked to meet with the principal members of the Joint Stock Company of Galveston to "ascertain if any arrangements could be made with them advantageous to the Georgetown College."[55]

On April 23 he and Captain F. L. Price, representing "the citizens of Georgetown," met with the Directors of the Texas University Company in Galveston. There they submitted an augmented proposal in writing seeking the location of the Texas University "at or near Georgetown." It estimated the total value of the proposal at $70,000, which Morrow and Price indicated "would soon be increased to $100,000." As a result of the meeting, a committee of three directors was appointed to visit Georgetown to make a "personal inspection of the Buildings, lands etc proposed to be donated," with a report to be made at the next full meeting of the Directors.[56]

The Directors meeting occurred on September 20. There the committee made a verbal report on their visit of "about" April 25. They stated that they had examined critically the surroundings and conversed with all classes of people and found them "cordially enlisted in the enterprise." They were offered a "bonus equal to about $100.000.00 for the location of the University at Georgetown." In spite of the fact that Mood was present at the meeting and also made a verbal report recommending acceptance of the offer, the committee felt that it was not ready to make a corresponding recommendation.[57] Mood was on a different time schedule from the other Directors of the Company. They wanted to play out the process fully. He felt that it had been played out long enough.

During October the Directors of the Company heard offers from two other communities. A committee of two from Waxahachie made an offer to the Directors amounting in the aggregate to $100,000 to locate the University there. A committee of three from Fairfield made a proposition to the Company to locate the University there amounting to some $50,000. Propositions from other communities continued into the new year. In March propositions from Milam County and Calvert were gracefully declined as being from areas outside the demarcation limits set by the Educational Convention.

In May the Directors raised the ante. They stipulated that competing towns must offer $150,000 in bonds, lands, money, or solvent interest-bearing notes. They agreed that the following towns were still eligible and that the winner would come from among them: Corsicana, Waco, Fairfield, Georgetown, Waxahachie, Fort Worth. They further agreed that the winner would be chosen within ninety days, i.e., by August 21. A committee of three was empowered to assess all bids and to take such actions as it "may deem advisable to secure an immediate settlement of the question of location." Another committee, including Mood, was appointed to visit the most eligible areas to awaken public interest.[58] Though a terminal date had been set for the decision, the Directors continued to try to enhance the value of their university in the eyes of prospective locations.

Anxiety in Georgetown

With the visit of its representatives to Galveston and the encouragement they had received from Mood, the Trustees of Georgetown College felt that their chance of winning the new university was good. But as time went on, they became more and more anxious. By the middle of June they decided to force the issue. They adopted a resolution on the 20th stating that they would withdraw their "bid & subscription list" unless they heard by July 10 that a location decision had been made. Though nothing appears in the record about a response from the Texas University Company, it is likely that the Trustees received a hint from some source that their offer was still promising and that they should stay the course. Nothing appears in the minutes of Georgetown College from June 1872 to June 1873 about the Methodist university. They buttoned down and waited.

In the meantime, the Trustees had a new building on their hands and felt they must do something with it. They had already explored the possibility of leasing some of its rooms to the Superintendent of Public Schools of the State and continued to pursue this avenue during the delay of the university decision. They worked out an agreement to lease three rooms for three months ending July 1, 1872. The lease would not overlap any decision regarding their university proposal.

When no university location decision had been reached by July 10, the Trustees decided to explore the possibility of renting the building to the State for two terms, from September 1, 1872, to April 1, 1873, for a public free school. The Free School movement had come to Texas in 1870 with the Radical takeover of the old Democratic Party of the state. The Radicals pointed out that there was not a single State-supported school in Texas, and they determined to change the situation. To do so, they enacted a highly centralized school system in 1871. When the system was inaugurated, there were only one or two school buildings owned by the public in the entire state. Since buildings could not be constructed rapidly enough, the State was forced to rent them wherever it could. It was in this environment that the Trustees decided to rent their building to the State. Financial negotiations continued for two months until an agreement was reached. Within a month, however, the Trustees discovered that there was no guarantee of payment, and all contracts with the public free schools were cancelled.[59]

To replace the Free School, the Trustees decided to experiment with an independent school themselves until January 1. Prof. C. C. Robbins was employed as Principal and Lucy Harper as assistant. The school progressed well and its enrollment surpassed the fifty or sixty originally contemplated.[60] Consequently, the Board agreed to continue the school for six more months beginning January 1. A third teacher was also contracted. A decade later, after the establishment of the Young Ladies' School at Southwestern University, Lucy Harper was employed as Principal of the Elementary Department. She served from 1880 to 1890.

Two Governing Boards and a Regent

Though the slow pace of events must have taxed all of Mood's patience, he knew that developments were gradually moving toward the success of his university enterprise. Consequently, he began his round of Annual Conference meetings in the fall of 1872 with hope that the end was in view. Virtually unknown during his first round of Conferences three years earlier, he was now a well-known and respected figure. He had accomplishments to report and a plan of organization for his new university that he expected the Conferences to approve.

His plan had emerged after the formation of the Texas University Company. It was for the five Conferences to appoint a Board of Trustees with authority to locate Texas University and to assume its financial interests. The fifteen-member Board of Directors of the Company would become the Board of Trustees. Also a Board of Curators, composed of one clerical member from each Annual Conference, would appoint the Regent, confer degrees, and govern in all nonfinancial matters. This structure would maintain the stability inherent in the financial underpinning provided by substantial businessmen, while assuring the Church of control in matters essential to its interests, such as curriculum and employment of personnel. As expected, the Conferences adopted this structure, charged the Board of Curators to elect a Regent at its first meeting, and to prepare for opening the institution.[61] Use of the word "Regent" was Mood's way of emphasizing that "the office looked to the control of, in a large manner, the other connectional schools of lower grade in the Texas Conferences."[62]

While visiting the North West Texas Conference in Belton, the last Conference of the five to be visited, Bishop Keener, who had conducted all the Conferences, called Mood aside and told him that he wanted to transfer him as pastor to Waco. Mood presented his objections, but Keener held fast. When Mood said that he did not see how he could attend properly to the University matter while holding such a large church, Keener replied: "Go to Waco and let the University matter drop." Mood said that he would give him his answer in the morning. He was so disturbed by the conversation that he returned to his room, packed hurriedly, and left immediately by stagecoach. When morning came, he was forty-five miles away from Belton and without telegraphic communication. He had "left a note to be conveyed to the Bishop refusing under any circumstances to transfer." Keener did not hold it against him, and supported him strongly afterwards.[63]

Shortly after Christmas, on December 31, 1872, the new Board of Curators and Board of Trustees met jointly in Galveston. There Mood was elected Regent by unanimous vote and authorized to seek professors and tutors.[64] He returned to Chappell Hill, where he was pastor of the church and President of the school. He continued working normally until March 25, when he called the Trustees together and resigned his position as President of Soule.[65] He says that there was temporarily "considerable feeling" against him, but it dissipated with their realization that he had acted with integrity.[66]

Informing the Winner and the Losers

At this point Texas, soon to be Southwestern, University had a Regent, a Board of Curators, and a Board of Trustees but no location. Truth be told, no vote had yet been taken on the matter by the Trustees or the Curators, but they as well as Mood knew that everything was proceeding on the assumption that it would be Georgetown. Mood's task at this point was to devise a way of explaining the result to the other applicant cities without offending them and creating enemies for the new university at the outset. He did so by visiting each city. There he laid out the elements that would be necessary for a successful proposal in such a way that they began to withdraw one by one until only Georgetown remained. Learning that Georgetown had heard about what was happening elsewhere and was also thinking of withdrawing, he hurried there and gave its representatives to understand that they had a good chance of being chosen. The withdrawal of the others enhanced their chances. He told them that the decision would be made on August 21. By the 21st all the other places had withdrawn, and they could have no complaint when Georgetown, the only remaining applicant, was announced the winner.[67]

Mood must have visited Georgetown in late May or early June to keep the town in the contest, because on June 3 the Board of Trustees of Georgetown College met and discussed the Methodist university for the first time in a year. They had been told that their proposal for the Methodist university stood a good chance of acceptance and responded at the meeting by changing their constitution to allow the Board of Trustees to sell the college buildings and land "except that the Board of Trustees shall not have authority to convey said Buildings and Land for any purpose other than School purposes." They were still not quite sure of their situation, however, because when a committee of three was named to procure donations of land and money, the reason given was to obtain the location of the University at Georgetown "if possible."[68] As late as June 24, Corsicana had not given up the quest. On that date the Trustees in Galveston received a proposition from that city. The minutes record laconically that "it was not received favorably."

Though the Commissioners of Location by now were merely the means by which the Galveston laymen, former members of the original Texas University Company, communicated with the Annual Conferences, Mood attributes to them the responsibility of deciding in favor of Georgetown. Many years later J. C. S. Morrow refers to a visit to "Mood's" Board of Trustees in August 1873 in Galveston. On that occasion, he says, the claims for all the competing places were discussed. Then, by resolution unanimously adopted, Georgetown was declared the most eligible location.[69] There is, however, no record of such a meeting in Southwestern University or Georgetown College minutes that are otherwise complete. Writing thirty-seven years later, Morrow has possibly misdated in his own mind the visit to Galveston made a year earlier by him and Captain F. L. Price on April 23, 1872. Quite possibly the final choice of Georgetown was a consensus decision of everyone, the Trustees, Curators, and Commissioners. There may not have even been a specific meeting at which a final decision was made. Mood wrote in a news article a few days after the decision that "on Thursday evening of Aug. 21 last, at six o'clock, with entire unanimity and with joyful harmony, the papers were signed declaring the location at Georgetown."[70] For the minutes he wrote a description of the decision somewhat different from the normal style. There is no listing of those in attendance or of formal motions. He does not say that the Commissioners voted in favor of Georgetown but that they "declared" in favor of Georgetown.

> The Commissioners of Location having received favorable report from the Executive Committee through M. C. McLemore Esq Chairman relative to the subsidy, health, centrality and accessibility of Georgetown, Williamson County Texas, declared in favour of that place for the location of the Texas University. The Regent elect was requested by the Commissioners to proceed to Georgetown and as soon as practicable open a school of the best grade warranted under the circumstances and to call together the Curators as soon as convenient for the election of a Faculty and the early opening of the Literary Department of the University. F. A. Mood, Regent.[71]

It is interesting to note that the Board of Trustees of Georgetown College had, as already noted, passed a resolution on August 18, 1871, stating that "the Board of Trustees are willing to turn over the Georgetown College to the Methodists on condition of their establishing a first class University here." Now, faced with the actual necessity of opening the University, Mood recorded the mandate of the Commissioners in a more restrained manner. They called for him to "open a school of the best grade warranted under the circumstances."

The matter of location by this date was a foregone conclusion. It had already been so definitively decided in their minds that a meeting was not necessary. It was already official. Mood rounded it off by making a record in the minutes but that record is not so much of a meeting as of an agreement already reached.

"Not Enthusiastic" but "Hopeful"

"When the news . . . reached Georgetown the citizens 'expressed their great satisfaction by firing a hundred anvils.'"[72] At the final meeting of the Georgetown College Trustees on September 13, a motion was passed to transfer about ten-and-one-fifth acres of land with the buildings thereon valued at $35,000 to the new university, with the proviso that two encumbrances of one thousand and two thousand dollars in gold owed to J. J. Dimmit be paid by the Texas University Company, the first to be paid within two years, the second within three years. This proviso relieved the Georgetown College Trustees of those obligations, but they would come back later to worry the Southwestern University Trustees.[73]

Leaving his family in Chappell Hill to come later, Mood moved to Georgetown to begin his work. He had accomplished what many thought was impossible. Now he had to prepare for the first session of the University scheduled to begin on October 6. He comments about his situation that his "surroundings were no more comfortable or propitious now than at the memorable time we landed in Chappell Hill, [but] my feelings were very different. I was not enthusiastic by any means, but I was hopeful."[74]

THE CENTRAL UNIVERSITY

1873–1911

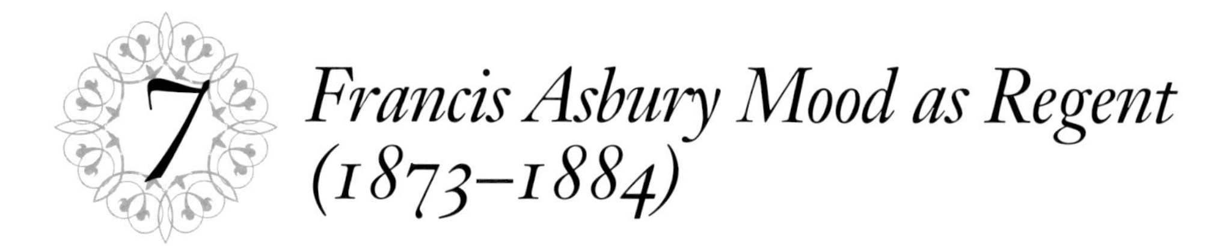

7 Francis Asbury Mood as Regent (1873–1884)

Preparing to Open the New University

Francis Asbury Mood had hurried to Georgetown soon after the location announcement of August 21, 1873. The opening of classes had been set for October 6, less than seven weeks away. But he had already begun to prepare while still at Chappell Hill. On March 29, even before the location decision, he had sent out a flyer announcing the imminent location and organization of Texas University. It was a simple one-page, 8½" x 11" sheet, printed front and back. It promised that the "FIRST ANNUAL ANNOUNCEMENT" would soon be published. The real object of the flyer was to make a direct appeal to "each friend of the Church" for help in securing a library, "apparatus," and funds for the endowment and support of the institution. It asked each recipient to make a gift of one dollar to be sent by mail according to specified directions. Though the flyer was addressed "To the Citizens of Texas," its specifically Methodist nature is indicated by the fact that each donor would be sent a steel plate engraving of any one of six listed Methodist bishops of his or her choice.[1] Only $139 came in from the solicitation.[2] Mood always thought that individual Methodists throughout the state would reciprocate his enthusiasm for the University, and he was always disappointed when the results of his solicitations proved otherwise.

Mailing out a flyer on March 29, 1873, however, was the crucial moment when Mood felt that he must shed his final role at Soule—that of Trustee. After having divested himself of presidential responsibility at Soule on February 15, 1872, he had continued as a Trustee. Bentley says that from the time he assumed the presidency on November 20, 1869, until his resignation from the Board on March 25, 1873, he was present at every Board meeting recorded except for March 5, 1873, a total of twenty Board meetings.[3] He now finally came to the point where he knew he must resign from Soule. It would be inappropriate for him as Trustee of one institution to send out an announcement in behalf of another institution even as Regent-elect.

Two months later, on May 20, he mailed out another flyer from Chappell Hill entitled "An Earnest Appeal," this time to the ministers in the five Texas Annual Conferences. In it he requested that each minister send him the names and addresses of the members and adult friends of his charge. He wanted the names so that he could contact them directly in behalf of Texas University without having to resort to newspaper advertising.

A final flyer from Chappell Hill, untitled but presumably the "FIRST ANNUAL ANNOUNCEMENT" promised earlier, was mailed in June 1873. It set October 6, 1873, as the opening date for the first session, outlined the curricular organization of the as yet unlocated institution, and provided certain other useful details. It stated that the University would be composed of eleven schools, to wit: Pure Mathematics; Applied Mathematics; Latin; Greek; Modern Languages; English Language and Literature; Mental and Moral Philosophy; History and Political Economy; Chemistry and Geology; Anatomy, Physiology, Hygiene and Vocal Culture; and Commercial. It said that students might attend any three schools of their choice, with the fourth, "Anatomy, Physiology, Hygiene and Vocal Culture," being obligatory for all. This curricular structure is basically the same, though expanded, as that sketched out earlier by Mood at the Educational Convention in Galveston. A Preparatory School would be open for those not ready for collegiate work. Rates are quoted as thirty dollars for one term of five months and fifty dollars for the Scholastic Year. Room and board with families could be secured for twelve to fifteen dollars per month. Rev. R. W. Kennon, an older minister who had been of great help to Mood at Soule, and W. B. Norris, a Galveston businessman, signed it as Presidents, respectively, of the Board of Curators and Board of Trustees. Mood signed the announcement as Regent.[4]

First Students and Teachers

Mood was pleased with the thirty-three students who matriculated the first day. He says that they were "young men appropriate for university studies, not child pupils." They averaged over seventeen years in age.[5] Three teachers were on hand to receive them. They were B. E. Chrietzberg, for Pure and Applied Mathematics, H. M. Reynolds, for Physiology, Hygiene and Vocal Culture, and Mood himself, for Mental and Moral Philosophy. Reynolds also taught Spanish, and Mood also taught History and Political Economy.[6] The Curators confirmed these three and two additional teachers on December 13. The two new teachers were Geo. F. Round, for Ancient Languages (Greek and Latin), and Albert Albrecht on a provisional basis for German.[7] Round later declined the position. Though all teachers filled in wherever possible to teach subjects other than those for which they were employed, not every field could be covered. In the first catalog published during the academic year, no one is listed for the School of Chemistry and Geology, for the Commercial School, or for the Preparatory School.[8] P. J. Malone is listed for English Language and Literature, though he had died in Austin en route to assume his position.[9]

The faculty as a whole handled the seventy "preparatory, elementary and primary pupils." No teacher was listed in the first catalog for them. Consequently, the Regent and faculty were authorized by the Curators to seek suitable teachers for the Preparatory School. They were instructed to employ none but male teachers in all departments.[10]

Chrietzberg came to Southwestern from his position at Soule. He was the professor who had helped Mood repair the roof of the university building there. Though he taught Greek and Latin at Soule, he taught mathematics at Texas University. He had been licensed to practice law in South Carolina before coming to Texas and returned to legal practice in Georgetown after only two years at Texas University. He eventually became the first Williamson County Attorney. Though he died in 1886, his wife lived to age 105 in 1957 and was celebrated in Georgetown as Mother Chrietzberg.[11]

H. M. Reynolds, M.D., was a graduate of the Jefferson Medical College in Philadelphia and had practiced in Pennsylvania. His role as Professor of Spanish came from having lived eleven years in South America. George F. Round was an ordained minister and a graduate of Wofford College, receiving his A.B. from there in 1861 and his A.M. three years later. Albrecht, often Anglicized in the records as Albright, was a native of Germany who had immigrated to America in 1853. Though his background in Germany was military, he entered the ministry of the Methodist Episcopal Church, South, in 1856.[12] None of these teachers taught for more than two years. The small but strong and committed faculty soon to become the backbone of South-

Cover of first catalog—*Texas University, 1874*. The motto—*Non Quis, Sed Quid*—still appears on the official University seal. Southwestern University, Special Collections.

western, especially after Mood's death, had not yet begun to form.

Sue Mood and the Move to Georgetown

Several weeks after Mood's arrival in Georgetown, Mrs. Mood brought the family to its new home. A description of her trip not only provides an insight into the social conditions of Central Texas, but also provides a graphic portrayal of the difficulties endured by the wife of the new Regent.

> Within a short time, Mrs. Mood had packed their possessions and, boarding a train for Austin with their young children, they left south Texas to join Dr. Mood. Margaret, about two years old, was quite ill with a fever when they arrived in Austin on a hot September afternoon. Richey, the son, was about five then. A driver and team had been sent to bring them back to Georgetown. All went well until the driver stopped at Cocklebur, a saloon south of Round Rock and a short distance from the Williamson County line. When the driver did not come back after what Mrs. Mood considered adequate time for a rest stop, she put Richey up on the driver's seat, took the reins loose from the hitching post, and put them in Richey's hands, telling him to hold tightly to them but to let the horses walk and that they would find their way home to Georgetown. Meanwhile, in Georgetown the Moods were expected. In late afternoon, when all business houses were closing, arrangements had to be made for their reception. Thirteen-year-old Temple Houston, youngest son of Sam Houston, who was living then in Georgetown with his sister, Mrs. J. C. S. Morrow, had been delegated to watch out for the Moods. Since the only place in town remaining open after dark was the local saloon, Temple was told to wait there for the guests. Far into the night when Mrs. Mood and the children finally reached town, the only lights they saw were at the saloon, so there they went and there were greeted by Temple Houston.[13]

So runs the story of Sue Mood's trip to Georgetown from Chappell Hill as recalled by two persons who got their information from Margaret Mood McKennon, the "Margaret" of the story and later head librarian at Southwestern for the forty-one years between 1903 and 1944. Elements of it must have dimmed over the years in the minds of the narrators, but the major features seem to be accurate. Austin was as far as Sue Mood could come by train. A railroad line was not extended to Round Rock until 1876 and to Georgetown until late 1878.[14] The five children traveling with her were Catherine (Kittie), aged eleven; Francis Asbury, Jr. (Asy), aged nine; Margaret (Maggie), aged six; John Richardson (Richie), aged four; and Susan (Susie), aged two. She was six months pregnant with another, Robert Gibbs.[15] Margaret, six, and Susie, two, are mixed up in the story. Whether it was Margaret or Susie who had fever is uncertain. The "about five" age for Richie is only a little off. He was actually four. It is likely, however, that Sue Mood put the reins into the hands of her nine-year-old son, Asy (Francis Asbury, Jr.), who is not mentioned in the story, rather than in those of four-year-old Richie. Temple Houston was indeed thirteen and living with his sister, Mrs. Morrow, in Georgetown. She had taken him in after the death of their mother when he was seven years old.

Mood states that he was in financial straits when they moved from Chappell Hill to Georgetown. Income from his church in Chappell Hill had diminished with the definitive announcement of his move, and he had spent money out of his own funds to carry through some of the preparations for opening the new university. Without sufficient means, he could not rent a house, and the family moved into the two south rooms of the university building. This home was a two-story 60\' x 75\' building containing six large rooms and a chapel. It seated four hundred people.[16] It had neither well nor cistern. The walls had not been plastered, and birds nested in the unfinished cracks in the stonework. It was, says Mood, "inconvenient in the extreme, but your dear Mama continued cheerful and bore all the inconveniences of our two years' life in the two rooms of the University with the greatest patience. The birth of your brothers Gibbes [sic] and Reader amid such exposed and noisy surroundings must have been an immense trial to your Mama, but as it was[,] I never discovered it from anything ever uttered by her."[17]

Francis Asbury Mood and his wife, Sue William Ann Richardson (Logan) Mood, did not complain about their difficulties, he about his continually worsening health or she about the conditions in which they were forced to live. They accepted their problems as a part of their mission. Sue Mood, wedded at age fifteen, was a remarkable person—a dutiful mother, a loving companion, and a tireless worker. Reared in comparative luxury, "she did not have to turn a hand at anything like housework" until the Civil War wiped away that life.[18] Her husband suffered grievously from their life in the university building. Mood states that "it was while living and teaching in the cold[,] unceiled rooms of the University in the early spring of 1875 that the disease, chronic bronchitis, which afterwards brought me so low[,] was developed."[19] He lived only nine more years, to age fifty-three. Sue Mood lived to age seventy-three.

Financial and Student Discipline

Texas University had the bad fortune to begin its work during the Panic of 1873. Though it might be traced to the failure of banking houses in New York, the Panic affected all parts of the country. Money was hard to come by in Texas, and the Trustees were determined not to allow the University to go into debt. At the meeting of the Board of Curators on December 13, W. B. Norris, Trustee President, appeared and spoke to the group, laying out some financial principles and presenting a schedule of professorial salaries. He stressed that the institution must live within its income each year and that failure of professors to receive their full salaries in any given year did not give them any claim upon the real estate or investments of the University. He stressed that they should impress upon the faculty that "all claims for annual salary ended at the close of each scholastic year and that there would be no claims for accumulated deficits, though the trustees would do all in their power to meet the promised salary." He also said that the Trustees would "put forth every effort" to increase revenues.[20]

As harsh as this message may have sounded to Curators and teachers, it was a dose of financial realism that helped promote the successful continuance of the University in the difficult years ahead. Neither the Regent nor the professors could undertake academic programs that involved deficit spending. For their part, they knew the rules, and no one entered University employment unaware of them. A group of sympathetic but hardheaded Trustees set the budget and kept expenditures from outpacing revenues. Salaries were paid from tuition revenues.

Students also received a dose of this strict regulation from the teachers and the Regent. Some of them were unruly and would not submit to discipline. Fights were frequent, often bloody. The faculty was disturbed and felt that something must be done. Confronting the problem directly, Mood conferred about the matter with the District Attorney, who had a son at the University, and asked for suggestions. He suggested that Mood turn the refractory students over to the civil authorities, holding that "students are as amenable to law as any other class." Mood determined to act on this advice. When the next major disturbance arose, he reported it to the officers of the law, resulting in the students being tried and fined. It happened that one of the two malefactors was the District Attorney's own son. On returning from an out-of-town visit and being apprised of what had occurred in his absence, he supported Mood's action completely. Cody remarks that when the students learned that "if they resorted to violence, they would be carried to the Court House, and dealt with by the officers of the law, and that public opinion sanctioned this course; it had a wonderfully soothing effect in allaying their dangerous passions."[21]

Other Trustee Actions

In addition to the current problems that compelled the Trustees to enforce budgetary discipline, the school had inherited some debts from Georgetown College that they wanted to clear as soon as possible. They also felt that they must improve the condition of the main building. Consequently, on February 10, 1875, they authorized the negotiation of a loan not to exceed five thousand dollars to improve the buildings and to erect new ones as needed. Supporters in Galveston were to be canvassed to pay off the debt, and Rev. William G. Veal, Southwestern's general agent, was authorized to collect money for these purposes. Erecting a dwelling for the Regent and constructing cisterns were mentioned as especially desirable objects of attention.[22]

Veal is an anomalous figure. He was a minister/businessman who helped Mood greatly in the early years of his efforts to establish Southwestern. He became moderately affluent through his business transactions and by 1870 had amassed a personal worth of fifty-five thousand dollars. He was an original member of the Texas University Company, the only minister other than Mood in the group. He supported Mood consistently, and Mood looked on him as a friend. In June of 1876, sixteen months after he was given the fund-raising task described above, he was charged with improper conduct toward a woman. A Church inquiry, however, vindicated him. Two years later he was arrested and charged with attempting to seduce a woman in Waxahachie. On this occasion the Church suspended him indefinitely. Though his wealth gave him sufficient means to live quite well, it could not protect him from the anger of persons he had wronged. Two months before his death, he received threats from someone warning him not to be seen in Dallas or he would be killed on the spot. He ignored the warning in order to attend a Confederate reunion at the State Fair of Texas. A gunman came by the door of his hotel room and shot him in the head, killing him instantly. His killer turned out to be the husband of a woman who reportedly had suffered advances from Veal ten years earlier. Though Mood was long dead by this time, he had included Veal in his 1882 list for posterity of those who had helped him most. Veal's actions had made it impossible for him to remain with the University, but when Mood made his list, he felt obligated to recognize the invaluable help he had received from his former colleague before his disgrace.[23]

Marvin College, which had once been a competitor with Texas University for the privilege of becoming the Central Methodist university, continued on its downward slide toward eventual extinction. One method of saving itself explored by its Trustees was to become a unit of Texas University. They made an offer to that effect with the proviso that it not be moved from Waxahachie and that the buildings be held and used for educational purposes. The Texas University Trustees in Galveston agreed to the offer provided the property was tendered with no encumbrances. Being heavily in debt, Marvin College could not meet this condition, and the transfer never materialized.[24] The mortgage on the College was foreclosed in 1879, and it ceased operation in 1884. It was finally taken over by the city of Waxahachie and made part of the public school system.[25]

A few years later the Southwestern Trustees "respectfully declined" an offer to take over Salado College. The property carried substantial debt, and a stipulation for maintaining the school could not be agreed to. Many small towns dreamed of having a college, but, unlike Georgetown, they could not find a substantial backer.[26]

With the establishment of Texas University in Georgetown, the number of Methodists in town began to grow, and they soon came to feel that they should form a regular congregation. Up until now there had been no Sunday School or worship services. They gathered to set up an organization for these purposes on January 11, 1874. The university chapel was secured from the Trustees for church activities, and regular preaching services, prayer meetings, and Sunday School began to be conducted weekly.[27]

Mood, Free Schools, and Reconstruction Politics

One of the elements in the thinking of Francis Asbury Mood that is discordant to the modern mind appears clearly in an incident that occurred in Calvert, Texas, on July 22–23, 1874. A Northwest Texas Conference Sunday School Convention met at Calvert on Wednesday, July 22.[28] Mood was there with two fellow ministers, R. W. Kennon and W. H. Scales, to attend the convention and to hold a meeting of the Board of Curators the next day. Since there was no quorum for the Curator meeting, business could not be conducted.[29] As it happened, Dr. Rufus C. Burleson, President of Waco College and state agent for the same Peabody Fund already referred to in Chapter V, was in town to speak to a gathering of citizens about the work of the Fund. He invited Mood and his colleagues to the meeting with such memorable results that he left a description of what occurred in his records.

> At Calvert my lecture was well received by a majority of the leading citizens, but I met open hostility from Dr. Mood, president of the Methodist University at Georgetown. I invited him and a number of the leading Methodist educators and preachers, who were in Calvert holding an educational convention, to hear me, hoping that they might be influenced to give me some aid in my arduous mission, and from courtesy I invited members of the convention to take part in the discussion. Whereupon, Dr. Mood, in an inflammatory address, appealed to the old prejudices of the South, and entered his protest against anything and everything [such as the Peabody Fund] originating in New England or the monarchies of the Old World. He especially objected to my position that the State had the right to tax the people of the country to educate the children of the improvident and the poor. Several of his brethren joined heartily in with him. I fear all the preachers and teachers of that church with any personal connection or interest in their church schools will throw every obstacle in the way of common schools.[30]

Burleson's account of the incident fits in with the political and social setting of the time. Dr. Barnas Sears, overall manager of the Fund, had visited Texas in 1869, within a year after its creation, to make a small grant as seed money for the future. Nevertheless, he found that conditions were too unfavorable to do so. Certainly Texas was ready from the standpoint of need. The National Bureau of Education reported in 1870 that Texas was "the darkest field educationally in the United States." It said that "after more than thirty years there was not a single state-supported school in Texas."[31] Seventeen percent of whites over ten years of age and 90 percent of African Americans were illiterate.

The unfavorable conditions that kept the Fund from beginning operations in Texas were political and social, not need-based, in nature. In 1869 a Radical government took control of affairs from the old Democratic Party of the state, allying itself with the Republican Party and the newly enfranchised African American population. As a part of its program, it determined to rectify the educational situation. It did so by writing a new constitution that provided for a highly centralized system of education. It required the organization of "a uniform system of public free schools for the gratuitous [sic] instruction of all the inhabitants between the ages of six and eighteen." School attendance was made compulsory for four months each year. Most of the income to support the system came from new taxes.[32]

Though a law was enacted in 1870 complying with the demands of the new constitution, it was generally ignored. This neglect angered the Radicals, who proceeded to enact a more drastic law in 1871. Its central provision was that a State Board of Education would act in place of the Legislature in school affairs. Its powers were comprehensive, from fixing teacher salaries to defining the course of study and selecting textbooks. Bitter opposition to this Radical system arose immediately. Many State officers resisted it passively, others actively. Taxpayers assembled in meetings all over the state to protest. A virtual school-tax war ensued.[33]

The real cause of the tax difficulty, however, was the opposition of the people to any tax for public education. "The policy of using force to compel one man to educate the children of another violated every sense of right and justice," says Frederick Eby, historian of Texas education. "It was regarded as nothing less than robbery and confiscation."[34] Compulsory attendance also violated another prejudice of the majority of Texas people. At this time only two states in the Union, Massachusetts and Vermont, compelled attendance. It was felt to be a violation of parental rights. The concept of education as an overarching social utility had not yet been established in the minds of most people. Many Texans suspected that the Radical program was a ploy to gain the support of African Americans.

The old political system was returned to power in 1873, and the destruction of the Radical system began. The result was a decline in school attendance from 57 percent in 1872–1873 to 38 percent in 1873–1874. The next year no reports of attendance were made at all. "The people reverted to private schools such as existed in *ante bellum* times. The public educational condition again had become completely chaotic."[35] No article was fought over more violently than that on education at the convention assembled to rewrite the constitution in 1875. The slogan used by opponents of the Radical system was: "Away with free schools; let every man educate his own child." Many of the partisans of sectarian schools wanted to perpetuate the old policy of State subsidies for private and denominational institutions.[36]

It was in this political climate that Rufus C. Burleson was employed as the state agent of the Peabody Fund for Texas. The managers of the Fund felt that they must employ a respected Texan to effect a change in public sentiment if they were to accomplish their desire of providing help for Texas education. He accepted the position reluctantly. His biographer says "he was appointed because he knew everybody, was not afraid of anybody, and was a friend of free schools."[37] In this capacity he visited every part of the state, speaking in favor of the free state school system.

It was Burleson's misfortune to encounter Mood in Calvert that day. His account reveals not only that Mood was in line with the attitude of the general public in Texas as to free schools, but also that he harbored strong Southern resentment against the North. His racial attitudes may have also been involved. In spite of the fact that he had taught in a black school during his pre-ordination years in South Carolina, he was patronizing in his attitude toward blacks. In 1881, when he went to London as an elected delegate to the Methodist Ecumenical Conference, he wrote a report back to an unnamed newspaper in the United States about an event there involving an African bishop. It was a minor incident but one that impressed itself on his mind. He wrote that "sentiment was pushed to an extreme" in the Conference and that it was presided over for one day "by a colored man." He says that "at no time during the day was anything like proper order in the ascendant" and that the poor man had to be helped by others to gain order in the assembly.[38]

Phelan reports that as late as 1879 public school sentiment had grown so little and that prejudice against it was so strong in certain quarters that Methodist educators refused to attend a state teachers' convention called by the governor in that year to advise the Legislature on educational policies. Methodist educators were not alone in this sentiment. John R. Allen, President of Marvin College and the only Methodist to attend the convention, states that nearly all denominational leaders in Texas held this position of opposition and that practically all of them stood aloof from the Austin convention.[39] After the failure of Marvin College in the early 1880s and after holding several pastorates, Allen came to Southwestern in 1892, where he became one of the respected members of the faculty teaching Mental and Moral Philosophy. He was chairman of the faculty and supervisor of the Annex during many of those years. He wrote *Man, Money, and the Bible* (1891) and *The Itinerant's Guide* (1897), both published by the Methodist Publishing House in Nashville.[40]

Though Mood and Burleson may have had their differences early on, those differences apparently did not keep them from developing amicable relations. Burleson visited him in his room when Mood attended the session of the Northwest Texas Annual Conference in November 1884 and invited him to address the students of Waco University. Mood accepted the invitation. He died a day or so later during the same Conference, and Dr. Burleson was chosen as one of the three persons to deliver tributes. The *Waco Examiner* printed an extensive extract of his address, in which it records that Burleson "referred especially to the moral grandeur of the man."[41]

Texas University Becomes South Western University

Within a short time after the Corsicana Convention had concluded its work and the Texas University Company had been set up, a charter for Texas University was drafted and presented to the Thirteenth Legislature (1872) for approval. Governor Edmund J. Davis, a Republican Reconstruction governor, vetoed it. He did not like the clause that exempted twenty thousand acres of University land from taxation and objected to its use of the name "Texas" for an institution other than one belonging to the state.[42] Mood's detailed letter to Davis from Chappell Hill dated June 5, 1873, defending the charter and asking Davis to reverse his veto had no success.[43] Davis's defeat in 1874 removed his opposition but resistance still remained in the legislative branch. In 1873, the charter lost in the Senate but passed in the House. They reversed roles the next year, with the charter passing in the Senate but failing in the House. Because of this stalemate, the name was changed to "South Western University" before it was presented for adoption again. With this change, the Fourteenth Legislature passed the charter on February 6, 1875.[44] The approval had required three years.

Finding itself deprived of the name it had been using for almost five years, the Board of Trustees immediately appointed W. G. Veal "to approach the Texas Legislature & endeavor to have the name of the University changed to the 'Texas University' and failing in that to the 'Texas & Southwestern University.'"[45] Nothing came of the effort, and the school began to use the name appearing in the charter.[46]

The University did achieve one of its principal aims in the charter—that of authenticating its lineage as a direct successor of the four root institutions. Section 7 of the charter states:

> That the right to confer degrees, regular and honorary in the arts and sciences, heretofore conveyed through the Legislature of the State of Texas in the charters of Rutersville College, Rutersville, Wesleyan College, San Augustine, Soule University, Chapel [sic] Hill and to McKenzie's [sic] College, Clarksville, Red River County, are hereby transferred and perpetuated and retained to said curators, and the graduates of said colleges and university shall be entitled to all the literary privileges and honors inuring to other graduates of the South Western University.[47]

One of the elements in the establishment of Southwestern University in the minds of Mood and of those who worked with him was to perpetuate the vision of Martin Ruter of establishing a Central university for Texas Methodism. Mood's plan brought that goal to fulfillment. Ruter had believed that Methodist evangelism on the Texas frontier involved helping to educate its citizens. The four previous institutions were a part of the endeavor of Texas Methodists to carry out that belief, finally culminating in the establishment of Southwestern University. The educational work done in those earlier institutions should, accordingly, be validated and accepted by the institution specifically established to perpetuate Ruter's goal and that inherited their charters. When Mood designed the seal of the University soon thereafter, he fashioned it to represent that conviction. It carries the names and dates of establishment of the four root institutions in intertwined circles overlaid with the shield and date of Southwestern University.[48] The level of seriousness with which the Trustees took their affiliation with Rutersville College is indicated by the fact that as late as June 22, 1880, they appointed a person "to investigate University claims to Rutersville lands and to take all proper steps for their recovery."[49] Of course, by this time such steps were hopeless.

At their meeting on July 17, 1875, the Curators adopted two resolutions related to these issues. One was to desist from any further argument with the State about the name of the University and to accept the charter action in that regard as final. The other had to do with the graduates of the four root institutions. The Curators requested that the Regent and faculty secure authenticated lists of the graduates and former students of those institutions. Their names were gathered over a period of several years, and the faculty was instructed to recognize them "as entitled to the regular degrees their literary attainments warrant."[50] Each catalog for several decades thereafter carried a list of the graduates, professors, and Presidents of the four root colleges.

Final Disposition of the Soule University Problem

No sooner did Southwestern achieve its charter than Mood began to receive letters from Captain John W. Neely, new President of Soule, objecting to the fact that in its charter it had usurped privileges belonging to Soule. These letters objected in particular to the statement that Southwestern was the successor of Soule and that Soule's authorization to confer degrees was transferred to Southwestern. They also objected to the fact that Soule's graduates should receive the privileges and honors of Southwestern graduates.

In response, the Board of Curators adopted a resolution stating that the objections were out of order. It declared that Soule was the property of the Texas Annual Conference and that the Conference had participated fully in setting up Southwestern. At a meeting in Austin on December 10, 1873, it had passed a series of resolutions completely merging Soule University with the new "Texas University." If Soule Trustees have a complaint, said the Curators, they should lay it before that Conference, "the only tribunal having authority to sit upon or decide the matters in question."[51] Apparently the Soule Board of Trustees did take up the matter with the Texas Conference, for that Conference soon transmitted a request from Soule to the Southwestern Trustees that "all reference to Soule be stricken from the Charter." The Trustees "agreed to act as soon as practicable" on the request.[52] Though a "practicable" time never arrived to change the charter, the Curators subsequently approved a motion "to omit all allusions to Soule University in any publications of Southwestern University."[53]

Soule University continued a fitful existence until 1887, receiving financial support from the local community, from student tuition, and intermittently from the Texas Conference. Well into the 1870s its leaders continued to put forward plans for rehabilitation. One of its financial agents visited Austin, Dallas, Waco, Houston, Galveston, and other points, seeking support to start a Law Department. He wrote J. D. Giddings in late 1877, trying to gain his backing for the effort.[54] The truth, however, was less appealing than the optimistic plans sketched out by the agent. Soule had lost any developmental impetus. Indicative of its loss of status was a name change less than a year later from Soule University to Soule College.

Attendance, never good, dropped from sixty-six students in 1886 to twenty-nine in 1887.[55] Though the last minutes of the Soule Board are dated June 18, 1887, its Trustees made one last effort after that to stay alive. They submitted to the previously unthinkable notion of making Soule a correlated school of Southwestern. The Curators denied the request. As a matter of principle, the Soule Trustees had refused to recede from any of their charter privileges of conferring regular and honorary degrees. By so doing, they prejudiced their own case. The correlated school concept was for schools of lesser grade to become feeder institutions to Southwestern, not for schools to join at the same level. Both the Trustees and the faculty endorsed the Curator action.[56] Soule quietly slipped into oblivion.

Summary of the First Two Years and Sense of Direction

After two years of existence, by the middle of 1875, Southwestern University had passed through the throes of initial organization. It was now set to become a major player on the Texas educational scene. The question now was not whether it would be established but what direction it would take. A small but important matter at this time presaged that direction. It was the matter of honorary degrees. Now that the University was established, the Curators received a number of requests to award honorary degrees to selected persons in the Church. The Board sidestepped the issue by stating that it would be inexpedient to confer any honorary degrees "in this the infancy of the University." But it also set a standard for the future. It established the principle that the Curators would not consider any recommendations for honorary degrees unless endorsed by the faculty.[57] By so doing they asserted their intention to maintain the integrity of the academic program by making the conferral of degrees a matter of professorial oversight rather than of administrative privilege.

Mood's Illness and the Insurance Imbroglio

Two years before his death, Mood traced back the prolonged illness that eventually killed him to the spring of 1875. He was never robust, and two winters in the drafty, uninsulated university building brought on a chronic cough that eventually weakened his lungs to the point that he knew his days were numbered. Those around him knew it, too. He lived in expectation of imminent death during the last nine years of his life.

As already mentioned, at their meeting in Galveston on February 10, 1875, the Trustees had taken out a five-thousand-dollar loan to make building renovations and to construct new buildings, if possible, on the Georgetown campus. Mentioned as desirable was the construction of a house for the Regent. With debts to pay and necessary repairs to make, the money did not go that far, and the idea languished.

A new minister, Horace Bishop, was appointed to the Georgetown Circuit in November and moved to the area soon afterwards. Characterizing Georgetown as "an old, dingy, unpromising place," he wondered why he had been sent there. He could not find a suitable place in town and had to find a residence for his family in Round Rock. It offered a better situation at a price he could afford. He comments that he soon learned why he had been chosen. It was because "a calamity" had occurred. "Dr. Mood, Regent of the University, had had a hemorrhage of the lungs and was not yet out of bed. Bishop Pierce informed me that he had put me there as a sacrifice to myself financially with the intention of my holding the school together in case of Mood's death until something could be done."[58] Mood was well enough by December 9 to attend the meeting of the Board of Trustees in Galveston held on that date.

At the meeting a life insurance scheme to raise money for the University was adopted by the Trustees. The South Western Life Insurance Company of Dallas proposed that the University lend its name to encourage people to take out policies on themselves made out to the University. Each policy would be paid in ten annual installments. One-quarter of each payment would be remitted immediately to the University over the decade until maturity was reached. The Company would lend the University 20 percent of each policy value at the legal rate of interest payable semi-annually should the University so desire. The Company would take full responsibility for securing the policies without cost to the University, while Southwestern would lend its "official, moral and personal influence" toward the success of the program by publicizing it to Methodists across the state. Persons purchasing policies would do so because of their desire to contribute the value of their policies at the time of their death to the University. The plan was designed as a relatively painless way for Methodists to build up the endowment of their Central University.[59]

The paperwork for the program was completed by the end of January 1876, and all that was needed were the Trustee signatures. Writing to Jabez Giddings in Brenham, Mood enclosed an original and a duplicate of the contract, asking Giddings to sign and forward. Giddings, who had not attended the meeting in Galveston, adamantly opposed the plan and wrote to Mood offering his resignation rather than to become a party to the action by signing the documents. Mood was dismayed. Giddings was one of his first friends in Texas and had helped him at every turn in working toward the establishment of Southwestern. He immediately replied, stating that the entire scheme had been arranged and signed by a majority of the Board before he even knew of its existence. Nevertheless, he felt that they were pursuing the best interest of the University as they understood it and were completely innocent of any untoward motive in approving the plan. He had hesitated to intercede because he had begged for a long time to be released from the anxiety of having to deal with money matters. He suggested to Giddings that they let the matter play itself out, since neither its success nor its failure would hurt the University.

His reply to Giddings on February 12 is perhaps the most plaintive of all his correspondence still in existence. The four-page letter begins by saying, "I write in great feebleness. The Drs forbid writing, speaking, or *thinking* [sic]. Your letter is too important to remain neglected and I venture to submit the following points . . ." After making his points, he returns toward the end of the letter to his physical condition and beseeches Giddings to remain on the Board. He says: "In asking you to remain on the Board I ask it for the institution, not for myself. I have now but a few years time to devote to this enterprise, but before I pass away I wish to leave the foundations far enough advanced that my absence will not be felt. I said a 'few years', it may be only a few months. On Feb. 1st a profuse hemorrhage [sic] from the lungs set in that continued at intervals for five days. I have been very low. Am now extremely feeble. The deep interest I feel in your continued attachment to the University is proven in my writing this long letter in the face of the absolute prohibitions of the Drs. May God bless[,] preserve & direct you."

Mood's letter must have affected Giddings deeply. Though we do not have his reply, its contents can be inferred from Mood's acknowledgment a week later. He says: "I have destroyed your [original] letter and it shall remain without mention."[60] Mood was right. Nothing came of the insurance scheme, and it was soon forgotten. Giddings, ironically, preceded Mood in death.

By spring, however, Giddings had returned to his original notion of resigning. On May 5, W. B. Norris, President of the Board of Trustees, wrote him a letter acknowledging his resignation from the Board and expressing a wish that he reconsider. Apparently, Giddings had a problem with the Board but not with Mood. The role he played in the procurement of a house for Mood reveals his ambivalence.

A House for the Regent

Having effected a reconciliation with Giddings, Mood wrote him a week later laying out his personal situation fully. He says that Judge Thomas P. Hughes gave him "an excellent lot" soon after his arrival in Georgetown and that, with a little additional money, he soon exchanged it with him for one nearer the University.[61] It was the northwest corner of the block on which the First Methodist Church is now situated. He "enclosed" it with his own hands but was unable to go any further. He had been forced to use all his resources, or, rather, he says, his wife's resources, amounting to some $1,600 or $1,800, in starting the University. If he were reimbursed this amount, he could build a house for himself. "I am anxious to leave my family in some sort of a house here where my children can be educated and where my wife by boarding students or something of that kind may make a support. I submitted the facts to the Trustees two years ago who examined my vouchers and ordered the money returned out of the first monies coming into the Treasury—No money has even been there. The curators last summer examined into the matter and had the resolutions passed at the late Conferences that each charge [contribute] $10—which to date however—after five months from the meeting of the first conference I have received [only] $36.50." He concludes by saying that he has no plan to suggest but submits the facts.[62]

In a letter of April 10, Captain J. C. S. Morrow writes Giddings, thanking him for his donation "to build a Residence for him [Mood] upon his own Block." He says that the amount is obviously only a start for the project and that he proposes to ask twenty prominent persons, all listed, to donate $100 each to fund it. He says he will write them, but, since he is unknown to some of the projected donors, he would appreciate it if Giddings would write some of them or suggest a better method.

Apparently nothing solid resulted from Morrow's effort, and toward the end of the year Mood, upon the urging of Morrow, wrote Giddings again. In the letter he rehearses his circumstances and states that by "advice of all parties I moved out [of the university building] into a small house of three rooms—but do not think [it] helped my condition. It is a small building—a box house only one plank thick and with seven children are so crowded we suffer great inconvenience." Getting to the point of the letter, he says that he has been encouraged to submit a proposal to him that Captain Morrow "thought if distinctly laid before you would enable me to adjust myself to my duties here & perhaps save my life—or at least prolong it." He asks to borrow $1,000, to which he can add $250. With this amount he thinks he can build a suitable dwelling on his lot. The house and property would be worth at least $1,500 or $1,600, and he would turn over the mortgage to Giddings for security. He would then repay Giddings $180 annually, the amount he is now paying to rent the small house he is in. He would also be willing to sign over his life insurance policy as additional security.[63]

The loan did not materialize, and Mood turned to the Board of Trustees. He asked it to lend him an amount of money sufficient to build a small residence, offering to repay the money with interest and to secure it by a mortgage. At about the same time "the masons & citizens of Georgetown" began an effort to help him secure a residence.[64]

It was finally, however, Jabez Giddings who took the decisive action to break the impasse. Giddings had, it seems, once again withdrawn his resignation and continued as a Trustee. His name was never removed from Trustee records. Learning of Mood's request for a Trustee loan and having little faith in further feeble attempts by other individuals and groups to solve the problem, he determined to settle the matter once and for all. His attendance at the Trustee meeting of December 21, 1877, is indicative of the fact that he came for a predetermined purpose. He did not customarily attend full Trustee or directors meetings in Galveston, this being only the second he had attended since the Educational Convention of April 1870. He had likely consulted with Mood about what he was going to do before the meeting.

In a later report to the Curators about what happened, Mood says that the Trustees refused to consider his request for a loan.[65] Five hundred acres of land had recently been sold for another purpose and Giddings moved "that whereas Dr. Mood was without a house & the University was indebted to him, that the Executive Committee be empowered to settle with him [and] that they use the money from the sale of the land for that purpose."[66] Since, he continued, the land had been donated for the endowment, he, as the donor of the land, would agree to have another tract of equal value transferred to the endowment from land not so designated.[67] The motion carried. Mood informs us that the actual amount paid him was not the $1,300 received for the land but $1,911 for itemized expenses he had incurred in establishing the University.[68] He built the house with his own money, not with that of the University.

Giddings died six months later, on June 25, 1878, from internal injuries sustained in a freak carriage accident. As he entered his carriage at home for a trip downtown, the horse bolted and ran out of control, throwing him from the carriage, causing the injuries that led to his death within a few days.[69] He had lived just long enough to lead the effort that provided the resources for Mood to build his house. The endeavor had required just over four years.

Even with this action, however, the Board of Trustees knew that Mood was in difficult financial circumstances. Consequently, a year later the treasurer was authorized to reimburse "to the relief of the Regent for money and labor expended by him in founding and establishing the University" up to the amount of $1,500 of any monies available and not appropriated for other purposes.[70] Everyone knew the privations he had undergone for the University. During his first two years, for example, he had received only $300 and $500, respectively, for his work. He insisted on paying the other professors what was due them first. His salary came from what was left.[71]

Everyone connected with the University was now trying to make the last days of its ailing Regent as pleasant as possible. They were under no illusions as to his condition. However slow his deterioration, his condition was terminal. Teachers taught his classes when necessary, and Trustees and Curators vied with each other to make up for the privations he had endured. Earlier, at the meeting of the Curators connected with the Commencement of 1877, feeling that he had but a few weeks to live, Mood had submitted his resignation.[72] It was refused, and he lived another seven-and-a-half years.

Changes in the Two Boards and the Georgetown Connection

The unique arrangement whereby Southwestern began its history with a Board of Curators, composed of five ministers, one from each of the supporting Annual Conferences, and a fifteen-person Board of Trustees, a majority of whom lived in Galveston, worked well at the outset. The Curators were persons who had sustained Mood when times were difficult and whom he could count on for support. The Trustees were laymen who had proved their loyalty to him and to the university cause in the complexities of its establishment. A sixth Curator was added in 1875 with the addition of a new sponsoring Annual Conference.[73]

As time moved on, however, and the institution became more and more secure, different qualities came to be needed in the two Boards other than those so important at the outset. With only six Curators, the University could appear to be the private preserve of a small group of persons rather than the property of all the Methodists of Texas. A larger Board of Curators would carry the Southwestern story to a wider audience. It would create greater confidence in the actions of the University and provide greater opportunities for fund-raising.

By now there were six supporting Annual Conferences. Consequently, in response to a request that four additional Curators be appointed from each Conference, the bishop appointed twenty-four persons as new Curators on July 7, 1877, bringing the Board of Curators up to thirty. The Bylaws of the Board were also revised. The election of a Vice Regent was specified, voting was to be by Conference on important matters, sessions of the Board were made private, and the rules for voting on degrees were tweaked.[74] The stability of the new Board over the years is remarkable. Of these thirty Curators, seventeen served at least eight years. Of the remaining thirteen, nine served at least four years. Only four served less than four years. J. W. P. McKenzie was elected Vice Regent at the first meeting of the new Board. The appointment was largely honorific. His health prevented him from ever attending again.

Two years later the Board of Trustees also underwent

change. Eleven of its members had been serving since the beginning, and it was becoming a heavier and heavier burden for them. The logistics of supervising an institution half a state away became more and more formidable as the institution grew and required closer attention. As a result, in 1879 the Executive Committee suggested that the working quorum be transferred to Austin.[75] The six Annual Conferences approved a new set of regulations. It called for five persons from Austin and two from Georgetown, Mood and Dudley H. Snyder, to manage institutional finances on a regular basis. Snyder was elected treasurer. The other eight Trustees were distributed more or less equally among the other Annual Conferences.[76] No one was appointed from Galveston. The Galveston epoch was over.

Four years later the Executive Committee in Austin asked to be relieved of further service in favor of having an Executive Committee "located in or near Georgetown." The Annual Conferences approved the recommendation in their fall 1883 meetings.[77] The first Georgetown Executive Committee consisted of Dudley H. Snyder and J. W. Hodges, who had already been elected as Trustees in 1878, Tom Snyder, D. S. Chessher, and Francis Asbury Mood.

Georgetown had bid for Southwestern University in 1872–1873 and won. Now some of its citizens wielded real power in the life of the institution. This turn of events is especially interesting in light of the fact that soon after moving to Georgetown, Mood was quite disillusioned with the support Georgetown had given the University. In a letter to Dudley Snyder of March 26, 1875, he voiced his disappointment. He says that at the time of location in Georgetown the University had been offered a subsidy of $154,000. Within the next few years one after another of the elements involved in making up that sum were not made good or were diminished in value to the point that the real value of the whole was not more than $55,000 or $60,000, with a debt of up to $5,000 as well. He begs Snyder to use his influence to wake up the citizens to their obligations.[78]

The $5,000 refers to the $3,000 debt, inherited from Georgetown College, that Southwestern owed to J. W. Dimmitt, with added interest over the years. Dimmitt tried to charge the University 3 percent interest per month on the debt. The Board of Trustees rejected Dimmitt's claim as exorbitant. The two sides went to court to resolve the matter. By that time the interest alone was supposedly $6,000. The University won and Snyder settled the entire claim for $4,216.68. Since the University did not have cash on hand to handle this amount, Dudley and his brother John covered $3,581.68 of the amount, and the University sold 260 acres of land to Dimmitt for the other $635.00 to finish off the obligation.[79] The University later reimbursed Snyder, but he deserves credit for urging denial of the claim and carrying the matter through to a successful conclusion. This action was only the first of his many contributions to the University over twenty-eight years as a Trustee.

There can be little doubt that Georgetown did not fulfill the financial promises made in its bid to bring Southwestern to the city. Nevertheless, Georgetown fulfilled its obligation on another front. What it failed to contribute in cash, it made up for by furnishing a number of strong supporters who harnessed themselves to its success. Captain J. C. S. Morrow, a primary mover in bringing Southwestern to the city, and Dudley H. Snyder, who probably did more than anyone in its early years to keep it solvent, were the first in a line of townspeople who over a century were as important to its success as some of its important teachers and administrators. Georgetown's fiscal contributions were not insignificant either when compared with what came in from the rest of the state. In summarizing the achievements of Southwestern two years before his death, Mood said that all of the success of the University had been achieved while the contributions to the school from outside Williamson County "have not aggregated four thousand dollars!"[80]

In spite of his criticism of Georgetown, on the one hand, for not fulfilling its contractual obligations with Southwestern and his praise of it, on the other, for providing more support than all the rest of Texas, Mood continued optimistic about it as a center for higher education. During the discussion by the Presbyterians in 1875–1876 about the removal of Austin College from Huntsville to a more advantageous location, Mood wanted it to be moved to Georgetown. He urged the authorities in Huntsville to do so. But, says Morrow, we had extended our resources "to the extent of our ability to pay" and could not do more. "All we could offer was the necessary grounds, so we lost the institution to Sherman."[81] Mood felt that two colleges in Georgetown would reinforce one another and would be beneficial to the city.

Religion in University Life

One of the major purposes of the University, in the minds of its faculty and sponsors, was to cultivate a Christian attitude in the life of students. This goal was as important as the cultivation of knowledge. Mood's major objection to secular, state-controlled education was that it did not include this component. The first of the eight principles listed by him for the operation of the University was that "the University, as an institution of the Church, is to use proper means to refine the manners, protect the morals, and improve the hearts of the young people, leading them, if possible, to Christ." In his yearly reports to the Curators and the Annual Conferences, he paid great attention to this principle. It had not, he felt, been served adequately the first year of operation but improved thereafter. Every year after 1873–1874, Mood makes a comment such as that "a fine religious feeling developed," or that "a number of students were brought to Christ," or that there was "a blessed baptism of the Holy Spirit," or some such expression. By 1878–1879 he could say that "each year has been signalized by a gracious religious influence among the students, resulting in many conversions and accessions to the Church." He felt that this fact was responsible for the "decided diminution of penalties, reproofs and dismissals [each year] for wrong conduct in proportion to the number in attendance."[82]

This religious goal of the University was not sought through course requirements in religion placed on the students, since there were none, at least none in terms of the understanding of such courses today, no School [Department] of Religion or Bible, theology, world religions, and other related courses. The most closely related School was that of Mental and Moral Philosophy, taught by Dr. Mood and later by his immediate successors in the regency. It was a standard offering in nineteenth-century colleges and universities and was included in the curricula of schools as widely divergent as the University of London, Yale, Princeton, Wellesley, and the University of Kansas. During the latter part of the nineteenth century it gradually began to disappear as elements within it moved into Psychology, Political Science, Philosophy, and Religion as those disciplines developed independent status.

The School of Mental and Moral Philosophy, for those pursuing its program, covered three years of work. It required four recitations a week during the sophomore year, three during the junior year, and two during the senior year. Books covered during the sophomore year were Rivers's *Moral Philosophy*, Watts's *On the Mind*, and Upham's *Mental Philosophy*. Those covered during the junior year were Hickok's *Science of the Mind*, Alexander's *Evidences of Christianity*, Hopkin's *Law of Love and Love as Law*, and Hickok's *Rational Psychology*. Hamilton's *Metaphysics*, Butler's *Analogy*, and Cousin's *History of Modern Philosophy* were covered during the senior year.[83] The purpose of the School was to help students come to an understanding of the mind, to develop a philosophy of life, and to sharpen the intellectual tools for ethical decision-making rather than to win them to the Church.

The influence of the Church in the lives of students came principally through professorial example and requirements in religious practice. All students were obligated to attend the church of their parents' or sponsor's choice each Sunday and to be present at morning and evening prayers during the week. Students from homes with no denominational affiliation were relieved of the church attendance requirement but did have to attend the prayer services each day. In addition to their religious function, these services were a time when general university announcements were made. All teachers looked on themselves as participants in achieving the religious goals of the University.

Mood also felt that the school should display its beliefs in the everyday management of the institution. His second principle for administration was that "the University should have a character of benevolence," such as making it possible for indigent students to secure education. During the first nine years, a total of ninety-two students, about ten per year, received free tuition. The number increased greatly during the 1880s. Seventy-seven students received free instruction in 1888–1889 alone.[84] According to his fifth principle, he allowed "no exaggerations, similes [sic], and extravagant claims to eminent superiority . . . in any publications." He was careful, according to his sixth principle, "not [to] antagonize any other institution, Church or secular." Following his eighth standard, he tried to run an institution where character ruled supreme, making "no effort in any way to acquire notoriety or to secure numbers."[85] His comprehension of Christian fellowship extended beyond the Methodist Church as well. Southwestern under his leadership offered the same tuition scholarships and discounts to children of ministers of other denominations that it did to those of Methodist ministers and offered free tuition to persons of other denominations studying for the ministry.

The "Young Ladies' School" and "Ladies Annex"

By the end of Commencement 1879, six years after its establishment, most people had come to feel that Southwestern was on its way to long-term success. Fifteen students had graduated with Bachelor of Arts degrees, and forty-four had graduated with proficiencies in a School, i.e., had covered successfully all the studies offered in what would today be called a department. By far the most popular such proficiency was bookkeeping, with thirty-one graduates. Second was Spanish, with five. Collegiate enrollment had increased each year, from 33 in 1873–1874 to 120 in 1878–1879. Except for the Dimmitt debt, which was at the time being solved, the University was free of debt. It had also reorganized its two governing boards for more efficient operation. Nevertheless, it was lacking in one area. It was not serving women.

Though coeducation was not the norm for institutions of higher education after the Civil War, most institutions did at least conduct separate female departments or units.[86] Rutersville, Wesleyan, McKenzie, and Soule had all maintained female educational units. The absence of such a unit at Southwestern was not thought to be a problem from the standpoint of educational philosophy or female rights, because "all-male" schools were quite acceptable, but Curators increasingly began to feel pressure to establish a female component.

First Woman's Building. Built in 1879, it was four blocks west of the old campus on a lot bordered today by Main St. and Austin Ave. on the east and west respectively, and by 11th St. and University Ave. on the north and south. Southwestern University, Special Collections.

Teachers, townspeople, and other constituents wanted their daughters educated, and they wanted them educated at Southwestern. Mood himself had three daughters who entered Southwestern immediately upon the formation of the Young Ladies' School in 1878, and the four girls from Round Rock that year were all progeny of the important Snyder clan. The correspondence of J. D. Giddings before the establishment of Southwestern manifests his lively interest in seeing to the education of his daughters in either Brenham or Chappell Hill.[87]

Perhaps pressure from Round Rock was part of the picture as well. Clara Scarbrough says that in late 1877, the Masonic Lodge there offered to donate to the Board of Trustees the first two floors of a three-story stone building in which the Masons had operated an institute or academy of their own since 1867.[88] Curator records describe a more generous offer "consisting of a large stone building with several acres of land." The offer was contingent upon Southwestern's maintaining a "young ladies seminary at that point." The Curators agreed to supervise the proposed seminary if the Trustees accepted the offer. From Galveston, they authorized Mood to deal with the issue provided it did not involve going into debt. The matter was still not settled sixteen months later, when the Trustees made their last reference to it.[89] By then, however, the Young Ladies' School was in operation at Southwestern, and the Round Rock plan never materialized. The prospect of a young ladies' seminary in Round Rock may have hastened the establishment of the Young Ladies' School in Georgetown to ward off competition.

Notwithstanding mounting pressure, Mood says that it was not until an announcement was made that a Female College would be opened by another unnamed denomination that teachers and Curators were galvanized into action.[90] Scarbrough says it was a rumor that circulated rather than a definite announcement, but both agree as to the immediate impact.[91] The Curators promptly authorized the faculty to open a Normal and Young Ladies Department as soon as it could be arranged.[92] The basement of the relatively new Presbyterian Church building was rented for its accommodation. Within a year a two-story frame building had been built for recitations four blocks west of the main campus on a lot bordered today by Main Street and Austin Avenue on the east and west, respectively, and by Eleventh Street and University Avenue on the north and south. It was close enough to be served by the University faculty but not so close as to risk much contact between male and female students during the course of a normal day. The new department opened on September 9, 1878. The catalog reports an attendance of fifty-four students for the year.

The Curators were quite specific that coeducation was not to be allowed. Cody calls the connection between the men's and women's units a "parallel" or "co-ordinate relationship."[93] The same teachers taught both groups, and both male and female students might enroll for preparatory or advanced studies, but the first catalog did not allow women to secure degrees. They would, however, "if they wish[ed] it . . . be furnished with a Diploma" testifying to their accomplishment.[94] This inequity was remedied a few years later, and in 1881–1882 women were accorded the full range of degree options given to men. There were five levels of completion: (1) Graduation in a School by taking the full range of courses in any one school; (2) Full Graduate by taking two years of specified work covering a range of schools; (3) Bachelor of Arts by taking four years of specified courses; (4) Bachelor of Science by taking a slightly modified B.A. program, particularly with regard to languages; and (5) Master of Arts by completing certain requirements beyond the Bachelor's level. The name of the "Young Ladies' School" was changed to "Ladies Annex—Southwestern University" in 1884 to emphasize its parallel relationship to the University.[95]

An analysis of the absolute enrollment numbers and the course enrollment patterns of the two genders at Southwestern in 1883–1884, Mood's last full year, reveals how the women accommodated to what had been set up a few years before as an all-male institution. Males outnumbered females significantly, 344 to 127, a ratio of 2.7 to 1. About 12 percent more men than women were also enrolled in the collegiate program. However, a larger percentage of the women taking collegiate studies were enrolled in full degree programs than men. Persons enrolled in full degree programs were normally enrolled in four schools. The average woman was enrolled in 2.7 schools as over against an average of 1.6 schools for men. A large percentage of the men at Southwestern during its first decade were enrolled in special programs, such as bookkeeping.

The women who entered Southwestern during the five years after they were first admitted took advantage of the full range of offerings except for accommodations related to the norms of the times. Music was one of the graces often present in a successful hostess, and women filled the music classes to help them with this likely role. Only a few men took music. Though women were deterred from enrolling in Greek, because they could not become ministers, and from Commerce, because they were not expected to engage in business, they did show their interest in numerical studies by enrolling in mathematics at a percentage rate twice as great as the males. They studied science in percentages equal to the males. Women took Latin in almost equal proportion to the men and replaced Greek with Modern Languages and English Language and Literature. They also expressed their interests more than did the men in the normative aspects of existence by taking Mental and Moral Philosophy in higher proportions than did they. Their underenrollment in total numbers by a ratio of almost one to three is indicative of the fact that, though society increasingly looked on education for males as being essential, for women it was still a decoration, an important decoration, but still not as important in a total sense as it was for men.

Since the Young Ladies' School had been begun so quickly, the administration was forced to arrange for female students' room and board with families or in approved boardinghouses. To allay the fears of their families for their safety, a statement in the catalog covering 1881–1882 said that "until the erection of the boarding-house, contemplated as a necessary addition to the Young Ladies' School, the Faculty will have personal supervision of the matter of the students' boarding, and will see them placed under the care only of those to whom they would feel willing to entrust their own daughters."[96] Faculty members rotated the responsibility of being in charge of the Y.L.S., as it came to be referred to in faculty minutes. They were so interested in the success of the program that they contributed in excess of $1,500 for the completion and furnishing of the first building.[97]

Another problem faced by the University in its rush to begin the education of women was a lack of rules to govern their conduct and that of the male students interested in them. Faculty members felt that they knew what the norm for such conduct should be, but none of it was written down. Since there were no separate student affairs administrators, all student conduct matters were settled in faculty meetings. Illustrative of its actions were several measures taken during the 1880–1881 and 1881–1882 academic years. On October 26, 1880, "it was agreed that the students of the Y. L. School be absolutely prohibited from attending balls and dancing parties." Four days later the faculty passed a resolution "that the students of Y. L. School are forbidden to receive the attention of young men unless they bring a written request from parent[s] or guardian[s] releasing them from control of [the] Faculty in that regard." On September 16 of the following year it passed a resolution stating that "young ladies [are] not allowed to receive attentions from young gentlemen or [to] attend places of amusements without [the] permission of [the] Faculty." This rule was amplified the following April to say that "the young ladies of the school, whether boarding or resident in town, shall receive no social visits nor other attentions from young men, except in connection with the public exercises of the school, in the presence and at the discretion of the faculty."[98]

The April Fool's Day Prank and Other Student Conduct Issues

After the early student problems that culminated in the arrest of the District Attorney's son, matters settled down and Mood could report good conduct on the part of students to the Curators in 1877. True, there had been a problem with saloonkeepers who had enticed some students into their establishments, but, after the dismissal of those students from the University and the closing of the saloons by the law, perfect order had been maintained.[99] This order, however, did not inhibit students from pulling pranks. Judge Walter Scott of San Antonio, undergraduate from 1878 to 1881, recounted one of them for the graduating class of 1937. He said that "one of the favorite stunts for our pranksters used to be to tie a yearling to the bell rope in the downstairs hall about 1 or 2 o'clock in the morning, thus rousing most of the population of the town."[100]

The cause célèbre in student conduct came a few years later as an April Fool's Day prank in 1880. At the ringing of the opening bell for the day, seventy students, by a previous written agreement, formed a procession and marched from the campus to the tapping of a drum.[101] They remained away from campus all day. Subsequent investigation determined that the matter had originated in a desire for fun, but the faculty did not interpret it so lightly. They viewed it as unbecoming and as an attempt to contravene their authority. They were particularly disturbed because they felt it had been prompted by several students who had transferred in from another institution and had introduced "a spirit of misrule" that, if not checked, might take root in a more intolerable fashion.

Consequently, they, in the person of Mood, presented a paper to the delinquent students for their signature. It read as follows: "The undersigned, connected with the transaction of April 1st, hereby express their regret thereat, disclaim intentional disrespect to the Faculty and will hereafter discountenance similar demonstrations in the institution." About twenty signed the declaration during the day, leaving about fifty recalcitrants. Claude Carr Cody, who was there as a new professor, describes the subsequent student versus Regent confrontation as follows:

> Dr. Mood, on the following evening saw each member of the faculty, and final action was decided upon. On the next morning the names of the students who yet appeared in the attitude of insubordination were called, and each one asked if the paper lying on the desk represented his sentiments. Upon answering no, his name was stricken from the roll, and each, in turn was required to retire from the building and the *campus* [italics in original], as no longer connected with the University. It was a very painful scene to the faculty, and the deepest excitement prevailed among the students, as one after another stood up in his place, answered in the negative, and walked from the chapel amid the intense silence of the occasion—for the eagle eye of Dr. Mood held them all in abeyance, so that there were no outbursts, nor a single disorderly word or act.[102]

The dismissal of such a large body of students, forty-four to be exact, caused a sensation in the community, some persons supporting, some denouncing, the faculty. One of them, an unnamed supporter of Mood, came to the campus seeking a resolution of the matter. After offering a number of theoretical arguments for more lenient treatment of the students, he concluded by recurring to expediency. The institution, he argued, depends on patronage. Expulsion of such a large number of students would create ill will and reduce income. It would prejudice the salary of the professors and possibly leave them without support. Mood replied that such questions could not be entertained. It all boiled down to a simple matter: "Shall the faculty or students rule?" This question, he felt, must be settled while the institution was still young.

Finding Mood inflexible, this supporter and several other persons went to the students. The matter was discussed, and the students agreed that an apology was due. The upshot of the matter was that three of Mood's supporters, some of the most prominent persons in town, Judge T. P. Hughes, Judge and future trustee D. S. Chessher, and businessman J. W. Hodges, called upon the faculty and presented a paper that had been voluntarily signed by the dismissed students: "We the undersigned, do hereby express our regret that our action on the first day of April has offended the Faculty of South-western University, and we do hereby promise, as gentlemen, to discountenance in [the] future any similar demonstrations, while we are connected with the institution." It was practically the same statement the faculty had sought previously. Other papers were presented "respectfully beseeching the leniency of the Faculty." In response, the faculty promptly agreed to restore the names of the dismissed students to the roll.[103]

The faculty took its student conduct role seriously. Faculty members monitored the Commencement speeches of students to make sure they did not veer into partisan politics and insisted on approving all invitations to student groups for intercollegiate athletic contests.[104] They prohibited students from participation at the skating rink and forbade them from leaving town without permission.[105]

Drunkenness was occasionally a reason for expulsion from the University. Two persons were brought before the faculty on that charge during Christmas week of 1883 and dismissed from school. About ten months later a beer-drinking incident at a bathing party on the river was dealt with. It involved consumption of a case of beer (twenty-four bottles). Six students who had participated were brought before the faculty, three of whom were dismissed from the University.[106]

By far the most common infraction of rules was contact between the sexes. In April of 1884 alone, twelve young ladies were given demerits for contact with male students. Four were given demerits for having corresponded with boys. Another received demerits for conversing with a young man at the exhibition of the graduating class. A sixth was penalized for conversing with a young man in the chapel, while two others were given demerits for walking with young men from the chapel. Two more were given demerits for simply walking with young men, and an additional two were penalized for appearing in public with young men. Only two young men received demerits for the same types of offenses.[107]

The most interesting of these April infractions, when one considers that only horses and buggies were in use, resulted in an assessment of demerits against a young lady for "reckless driving, it having appeared since last meeting that she had been previously admonished by one of the lady teachers." Clearly the female students were not always the demure creatures the faculty expected them to be and took risks knowingly, however innocent those actions may appear today. When one remembers that the Southwestern of the 1870s allowed "no vacation of any kind except the legal holidays," even at "Christmas or other special seasons on any plea whatever," one marvels that more infractions of the rules were not recorded.[108]

New Buildings

After eight years of operation, the main university building became too small for the university program that had developed. The move of the Mood family to its own home had earlier liberated two classrooms on the first floor for use, but the continued increase in students and faculty made things tight. Consequently, the Curators and Trustees determined to enlarge the building. A contract was let on July 2, 1881, to construct a third story with a mansard roof at a cost of $7,485. It was completed prior to the opening of school in the fall. Four large lecture rooms were added and the whole edifice renovated. Mood credits the successful and debt-free completion of the work "chiefly to D. H. Snyder, the Treasurer of the Board of Trustees, who, with his brothers, John and Thomas Snyder, contributed $2,500, and himself gave constant personal oversight of the matter."[109]

In April of the next year a contract was let for the construction of a chapel.[110] The chapel was not, however, so much a university project as that of the local Methodist church. The congregation had been meeting in the college chapel [auditorium] since its organization in 1874. Now an arrangement was worked out with the University to lease the southwestern corner of the campus where the church could construct its own building. Funds gave out after the completion of the first floor, and for more than a decade, until another building was erected diagonally across University Avenue, the "half-dugout" or "pancake"-like structure doubled as chapel for the University and as the Methodist church.[111]

With the completion of the third story on the men's building, some people, particularly Mood, became convinced that the women needed a larger building as well. Female enrollment and the future prospects of the Annex, he felt, demanded it. Though a new building would not be constructed for another four years, Cody reports that Mood began to push for it. It was, he says, the last great effort of his life. He began the campaign at an Educational Convention on November 2, 1883, during the session of the Northwest Texas Annual Conference held in Georgetown. Dr. R. A. Young of Nashville made "a great address" followed by Dr. H. A. Bourland, Financial Agent for Southwestern. They "made stirring appeals to the large audience congregated in the University Chapel. At this meeting $35,150 was subscribed toward the erection of a suitable building for the Ladies Annex," of which $21,000 was from the three Snyders.[112]

Though Mood's increasingly feeble health and death brought the campaign to a virtual halt, it would be restarted four years later by Dudley Snyder and his brother John, who stated to the other Trustees that, given the need of the Annex for improved facilities, they wanted to pay the pledge made during the campaign and offered a novel way of doing it. Their action would start the process of moving the University from its original campus to the site it occupies today.

Building a Strong Teaching Staff

On June 21, 1879, the faculty began to keep minutes of its meetings "for future reference." This simple action reflects a transition that occurred in other areas of the University as well—from the supervision of the institution by one man to a broader type of governance. As Cody says: "In the beginning, while the movement was yet small, Dr. Mood thought, planned, and acted for the Trustees, and Curators, directed every interest of the University, and shaped the policy of the Faculty. This was done with so much judgment, that nothing but harmony prevailed in all of the deliberations of these several boards."[113] Members of the original Board of Curators and Board of Trustees were close friends and supporters of Mood and were chosen for that very reason. In 1877 and 1879 the two Boards had been reconstructed with members chosen less often for reason of personal loyalty to Mood. He was still the dominant figure and remained so as long as he lived, but by the changes being made the institution was gradually moving to a position where, when he was gone, it could move ahead without him. This same phenomenon occurred in the faculty.

As has already been observed, none of the first faculty members remained more than a few years. Gradually, however, a group of five teachers was acquired who made their careers teaching at Southwestern. Four of them came to the institution as young men in their twenties. They came because of Mood, underwent tutelage under him, and carried on his ideals after his death. They were: Samuel G. Sanders, Latin and Greek, who came in 1875; Claude C. Cody, Mathematics, 1878; John H. McLean, Mental and Moral Science, 1879; Ryland F. Young, Modern Languages, 1879; and Robert S. Hyer, Physics, 1881. All five would teach together from 1881 through 1892, four would remain together through 1897, and three through 1911. Whoever else came and went, these teachers shaped the character of

Southwestern University faculty, 1880–81. Seated left to right: J. H. McLean, S. G. Sanders, F. A. Mood. Standing: R. S. Hyer, S. D. Sanders, C. C. Cody, R. F. Young, P. C. Bryce. Southwestern University, Special Collections.

the faculty for many years to come. They became known as "The Five." Two of them, Hyer and Cody, would take opposite sides in a struggle to redefine the University in the first decade of the twentieth century, namely, the removal controversy. The faculty as a body was ready, along with the Curators and Trustees, to assume new leadership roles in the University after Mood's death.

Their apprenticeship was hard. The Board of Trustees had accepted as a principle from the beginning that salaries came out of tuition and that the endowment of the University was not to be touched to meet the salary schedule. All salary claims against the institution ended with the closure of the fiscal year. When obligations exceeded income in 1878, the junior member of the faculty, Professor B. D. Dashiel, Jr., was asked to resign. He did so the same day he was asked, handing in a communication that read: "Gentlemen. I hereby most respectfully beg leave to tender my resignation as Professor in the Preparatory Department of [the] University. Very respectfully, B. D. Dashiel Jr."[114] He knew the rules when he came; he played by them as a gentleman when he left. Two years later the tuition income of $5,913.89 was "paid out to the Faculty in the proportions agreed upon between them."[115]

In the early 1880s a movement to regularize salaries and to recognize that unpaid salaries were a continuing obligation began to emerge. At the annual meeting of the Board of Trustees in 1883, authorization was granted "to pay several professors what is due them from the last year's salaries." The following year the treasurer was granted authorization "to pay the deficiency in the salaries now due the Professors of the University." At the same 1884 meeting, a salary schedule was outlined with "said amounts to be paid in monthly instalments *in advance*, beginning with the first month of the ensuing scholastic year." Mood was scheduled to receive $1,800 for the year; Sanders, Cody, McLean, and Young, $1,300; and Hyer and Burkhead, the two newest, $900. Miss Lucy Harper and Miss Kittie Mood were to receive $500 and $400, respectively.[116]

Though she taught longer than any other female teacher who entered during the Mood years, information on Lucy Harper is sketchy. She taught briefly in the short-lived preparatory school run by the Trustees of Georgetown College in 1872–1873 and began a period of ten years at Southwestern as teacher and Elementary Principal in the Annex Preparatory in 1880. In between she ran a private school, where one of the students was Willie Colbert (Daisy) Lane. Daisy became one of the first graduates of the Annex in 1883.[117] On June 7, 1889, Lucy Harper asked the Board of Trustees to authorize a scholarship for the preparatory department of the Annex "as is given to the Boys School." Two days later the request was denied.[118] She resigned the following year, though not as a result of the scholarship denial, and went into missionary work in Mexico. In the faculty report for 1890, she is called a "useful and godly woman" whose work was "faithful and painstaking."[119]

Nothing is known about Mrs. M. W. Ragsdale other than that she was the wife of the first Director of the School of Music at Southwestern, resigning in 1888, when he accepted a situation in Brownwood. She served as Assistant in Instrumental Music in the Annex for five years.

Catherine Mood, or Kittie, as she signed her name, was a new teacher, aged twenty, when she began teaching in 1882. She served for three years as Intermediate Principal in the Annex Preparatory. She was Mood's oldest daughter and married Professor Ryland F. Young on January 20, 1887. She died October 23, 1887, apparently in childbirth.

Of the other six female teachers employed during Mood's tenure, one served two years, while the other five served only one year. None of the women had a baccalaureate degree. The first woman to teach at Southwestern with a Bachelor of Arts was the twenty-one-year-old Carobel Villard Heidt, daughter of Mood's successor, who was briefly pressed into service as Intermediate Principal in the Annex Preparatory in 1886–1887.

Mood's Death

After requesting the resignation of one of the teachers in mid-1878 to relieve the pressing financial situation, the Curators approved a committee report that suggested asking the Trustees "to employ Dr. Mood as an agent to secure endowment and patronage." With Veal gone, they felt that someone in whom everyone had confidence was needed. In addition, the committee stated, it believed a change for Mood would provide relief from the confining duties of his office and might be of some advantage to his health. A system would be worked out to cover his classes while he was away.[120]

Appointed as a delegate to the First Ecumenical Methodist Conference at City Road Chapel, London, in September 1881, Mood made the trip in spite of his health. He used the occasion to visit for the last time the familiar scenes of his early years in South Carolina. He took an active role in the proceedings in London and delivered an invited address, but his health was too feeble to allow him to visit many places of interest. He did visit Oxford on his way south to London from Liverpool to see where Wesley had studied.[121]

By early 1884 Mood's condition had deteriorated to the point that his School of History and Political Economy was abolished as a separate unit. Its subjects were apportioned among the other schools. His other two schools, those of Mental and Moral Science and of English Language and Literature, were added to the responsibilities of Professors McLean and Jones, respectively. Toward the end of April he reported to the faculty on a visit he had made to Nashville to visit Vanderbilt University and Dr. Price's College for young ladies. In his report, he stressed the responsibility of the faculty for the spiritual side of the educational program. "He announced that the Faculty meeting hereafter would be opened with prayer, and then invited the Faculty to unite with him in prayer."[122] In all of his actions he appears to be preparing both himself and his colleagues for his departure.

On September 1, Mood brought some resolutions from the Curators to the faculty regarding procedural matters. They were procedures specifying clearly the rights of the faculty and of the Regent in handling disciplinary matters. Earlier such matters would have been left to his judgment, but, with the imminent prospect of his death, he wanted to clarify for his successor any ambiguities in governance that might remain unsettled. In addition, the Curators, at his urging, had determined that "in the event of the death or resignation of the Regent," the faculty should elect one of its number as soon as possible to administer affairs until the Curators should elect a Regent. Mood did not want to wait that long. He stated that he wished the faculty to elect a chairman at the next regular meeting. It did so, and Professor John H. McLean was unanimously elected.[123] Four days later the Executive Committee of the Board of Trustees met for the last time with him present. Due to his condition, it met in his residence.[124]

For some months before his death it was apparent that he could not hold out much longer. He was finally reduced to preaching to the students while seated. Though he was still suffering the ill effects of a recent journey to San Antonio, where he attended the West Texas Conference, he left Georgetown for Waco on November 5 for the annual meeting of the Northwest Texas Conference. In spite of his health, he would not be deterred from going. On Friday night he delivered the annual address on education. He seemed cheerful on Sunday morning to those who attended him in his room, but his lungs were full. His sufferings were extreme throughout the day until he died. Services were held for him in Waco the next morning and his remains escorted to Georgetown. Final funeral ceremonies were conducted in the University Chapel on the afternoon of November 14. Dr. McLean preached. He was buried on the College Campus, a few feet north of the Chapel. A Mood Monumental Association was organized to have a massive granite monument mark his resting place. It stands today in front of Mood-Bridwell Hall.[125] His death was recorded as an insert in the faculty minutes by a terse, one-sentence statement: "Nota. At the session of the Northwest Texas Conference, at Waco, Dr. F. A. Mood died, Nov. 12, 1884. Secretary."[126]

Mood's Legacy

Though Mood's greatest achievement was, certainly, the establishment of Southwestern University, that achievement must be understood in terms of its continuing implementation and not simply by the bare fact of the initial establishment itself. The two most important elements of this continuing implementation were the solvency of the institution and the building up of a cadre of teachers and supporters who carried the University forward after his death. Insistence on financial solvency kept the institution from falling victim to unsupportable visionary impulses. Building up a core of persons—faculty, Curators, and Trustees—who shared his vision was equally important. No single dominant figure arose to replace him after his death, but enough strong persons had become a part of the University idea under his leadership to carry on the tradition he established.

Some of the precedents and practices set during his administration have endured almost unchanged to the present, such as his concept that the school should be broadly ecumenical and not narrowly sectarian. Others preserve his intent, though they have been gradually modified with the passing of the years. One such is the continued emphasis on a broad-based, liberal arts education, though the curriculum that supports it has gradually evolved to look very different from what it did in earlier times. Others have been almost completely changed, reflecting the conditions, norms, and perceived needs of the twenty-first century rather than those of the nineteenth. Reflective of this change is a use, as part of the educational process, of modern technology that would have been completely foreign to Mood. Overall, it must be said that Francis Asbury Mood, building on the vision of Martin Ruter, is the overarching figure in the history of Southwestern University.

8 Townspeople, Trustees, and Teachers to the Fore (1884–1890)

Social and Economic Change in Central Texas

During the twelve years of Mood's regency, Georgetown and Central Texas underwent significant changes. Some of the changes in Georgetown were the result of Southwestern's presence in town. The existence of one of the major educational institutions in the state, with scores of students entering each session, increased the size of the community significantly each fall, with commensurate social effects and commercial spin-offs. It also made Georgetown a destination for many persons who would have otherwise never thought of visiting the town. Numerous families of students came each year to attend the Commencement ceremonies and other school events. It also gave the municipality a mark of distinction—the

William Oscar 'Patch' Stubblefield in front of the Williamson County courthouse built in 1877–78. At this time Georgetown was at the head of wagon navigation as the westernmost railroad town. There were cowboys in abundance with boots and spurs. Used by permission of the Williamson County Museum.

presence of a type of person formerly absent in the community: teachers who made their living in communication with books and the world of higher education rather than by the skills otherwise prevalent among the citizenry. The presence of Southwestern brought a unique element to the character of the town and made Georgetown somewhat different from other Central Texas municipalities.[1]

In other respects, Georgetown participated fully in the Central Texas ethos and experienced the changes that occurred as the frontier moved west. From a frontier community with more saloons than churches, it became after the Civil War a community whose economy was dominated by cattle raising and cattle drives. Many drives went directly through Georgetown, approaching it from the south coming down Rabbit Hill and going north along present Austin Avenue down "jail hill" and across the two Gabriels near the intersection of the two forks. On the first drive, made in 1867, about thirty-five thousand cattle were driven to Abilene, Kansas. When Claude Carr Cody arrived to teach mathematics in 1878, he says that "Georgetown was the head of wagon navigation, as it was the fartherest [sic] west railroad town. The stages got much mail here and the old 'prairie schooner' dragged frequently by a dozen oxen each, driven by men who called themselves 'freighters' trekked freight to and from much country west of us. To a new comer there were many things then about Georgetown that suggested the Far West. There were cowboys in abundance with boots and spurs [and] with cow ponies that always moved on the jump."[2]

These drives continued until the early 1880s, when barbed-wire fences doomed their continuance. At the same time, cotton farming developed in the eastern part of the county.[3] Williamson County changed from an economy dominated by cattle to one increasingly dependent on farming and commerce. Even after the day of the cattle drive, its residual effects continued to be felt. Writing in 1909 about those early years, D. H. Snyder said that cows and horses running at large in the streets were a nuisance and that the stiles crossing the fence of the original Southwestern campus, constructed to alleviate the effects of the loose animals, were "a discomfort to our visitors, a shame during the school year and a disgrace at Commencement."[4]

Symbolic of the change that had occurred in Georgetown during the two decades after the establishment of Southwestern in 1873 was the vote on prohibition in 1893. The presence of open saloons in town had been a problem for Southwestern since the beginning. Not only was total abstinence the official Methodist position, but the University also had problems with student use of alcohol. Beginning in 1878, University officials worked with like-minded residents to establish prohibition for the Georgetown precinct. At the election held on May 29, 1893, they were victorious. Over 60 percent of the almost 1,200 votes were in favor of banning the sale of alcohol. The saloons in Georgetown were ordered closed and the sale of liquor forbidden.[5] By 1893 the saloonkeepers could not compete with the ministers. M. B. Lockett says that "ministers were as thick in the town as Katydids in August, called here no doubt by the Southwestern University and the religious atmosphere of the community."[6]

Participants in many of these events were the Snyder brothers—prosperous cattlemen, leaders in the community, devoted supporters of Southwestern University, and prohibitionists.

The Snyders

Dudley H. Snyder, the oldest of three brothers, the others being John Wesley Snyder and Thomas Snyder, had learned trading by buying and selling apples on trips between Central Texas and Missouri. He and his brothers first rented, then bought, land between Round Rock and Georgetown. They soon ventured into horse trading and cattle raising. Recalling those times in later years, Dudley remarked: "In 1857 I walked from this county to San Antonio to purchase ponies on speculation. Of course you will wonder why I walked such a distance *in Texas*. It is almost a proverb that Texans never walk! But I answer, because we, my brother and I, had saved up our small earnings, and we found that we had only about $200 to invest. As I could buy so much cheaper in San Antonio than I could at home, I knew that I could make money walking."[7]

During the Civil War, they served the Confederate cause by moving cattle from Texas to Louisiana and Tennessee. Having lost their money invested in slaves as a result of the war, they reestablished themselves in the cattle business. Thomas lived at Liberty Hill, though he finally moved to New Mexico. Dudley and John lived first at Round Rock, then later at Georgetown.[8]

They made their first drive out of Georgetown in 1868, earning a good profit from the undertaking. Dudley and John became formal partners thereafter. Tom, though not a partner, worked closely with them. They regularly sent herds north and northwest until their last drive to Cheyenne, Wyoming, in 1885. They had been

The Snyder brothers. Left to right: Dudley, Tom, and John. All three served on the Board of Trustees for a total of 46 years. Dudley was treasurer of the Executive Committee for 22 years. Southwestern University, Special Collections.

the first cattlemen to drive a herd there fourteen years earlier. They delivered thousands of cattle, herds that often took one-and-one-half days to pass through Georgetown. They hired other persons to lead their drives, often riding trains themselves to intercept their herds along the way or to meet them at their destination. During his life, Dudley acquired large ranches in Cooke, Mitchell, Stonewall, Lamb, and Hartley Counties, one of which covered 130,000 acres. He was one of the builders of a link line from Granger to Austin that was purchased by the MKT Railway Company.[9]

In Colorado they regularly did business with another wealthy cattleman, J. W. Iliff. Both the Snyders and Iliff were strong Methodist laymen, and, after Iliff's death, his wife requested that they take charge of the entire cattle business of the estate. They did so for about ten years. Iliff's name today graces the Iliff [Methodist] Theological Seminary in Denver. The Snyders became strong patrons of Southwestern University.[10]

The three brothers translated their religious beliefs into their work ethic and had very strict rules for their trail drivers. They established three simple personal conduct rules for their cowhands. Dudley listed them as follows:

> First: You can't drink whiskey and work for us.
> Second: You can't play cards and gamble and work for us.
> Third: You can't curse and swear in our camps or our presence and work for us.[11]

Sunday was always a day of rest for the men and their herds, an unheard of practice among cattlemen. Finding that camp life and the open air were beneficial to his health, Dr. Mood occasionally accompanied the Snyder outfit in its trek to market. On these occasions, "Dr. Mood, at the request of the Snyders, had services in camp. Perhaps," writes John's granddaughter, "the problems confronting the fledgling University were discussed around the campfire."[12]

Dudley was one of the three persons from Georgetown who presented its case at the Corsicana Convention in 1872. All three of the brothers served at one time or another on the Board of Trustees, Dudley for twenty-seven years, John for fifteen years, and Tom for four years. Dudley's service as treasurer for twenty-two years is undoubtedly one of the reasons Southwestern was able to endure during its early years. He and his brothers made Southwestern an object of their particular interest and contributed time, talents, and money to its development. Dudley Snyder, who died in 1921, lived as an old man in a house on University Avenue close to the railroad tracks. He had lost most of his money by then and lived on a fairly restricted basis. President Finch says that on one occasion somebody asked him, "Mr. Snyder, don't you regret having made those gifts to Southwestern?" He replied, "No, that's the only money I've got, and I can see that investment every day as they [the students] pass me."[13]

The important role of the Snyders during the two decades following Mood's death is representative of one of the major developments during those years—the weakness of the first two Regents after Mood and the emergence of teachers, Trustees, and townspeople as leaders.

John Wesley Heidt Elected Regent

Inasmuch as the faculty at the instigation of the Curators and Dr. Mood had already elected Prof. John H. McLean to administer the affairs of the institution temporarily should the Regent die in office, McLean took over the administrative duties of the University when the news arrived from Waco of Mood's death.[14] The school had been operating for some years with the expectation of his imminent demise and continued to function normally when it occurred. Curators, Trustees, faculty, and students took up their responsibilities with special dedication as if by so doing they were honoring the spirit of their dead leader.

They continued in this mode from November 1884 until June 1885, when the Board of Curators met in annual session. During the interval, considerable background work had been done with reference to candidates for the regency. Mood had set such a standard of excellence in the minds of the Curators that, upon examination, they found no one at the University or among the ministers of the Annual Conferences equal to the job. The names of all Texas candidates were withdrawn at the annual meeting in 1885 in favor of one presented by a certain unnamed bishop or bishops—the Rev. John Wesley Heidt, D.D., of Georgia.[15] Heidt seemed to have every quality they could want. He was a prominent minister, an outstanding speaker, and President at the time of La Grange Female College in La Grange, Georgia.[16] Curator minutes state that he was elected unanimously because of his "ripe scholarship, administrative ability, large experience and Christian character, . . . endorsed by many of the leading men of our connection."[17]

Heidt was born on July 12, 1841, in Macon, Georgia. His early education came from private tutors and from the Springfield Academy. He entered the sophomore class of Emory College at Oxford, Georgia, at the age of fifteen, graduating three years later with distinction. After teaching a year, he entered the Law School of the University of Georgia and graduated in 1861 just in time to join the Confederate army for the war.[18] There he served in the Chatham Artillery until 1864, when, without having applied for the position, he was appointed by the governor to fill the unexpired term of the solicitor general of the Eastern circuit. He was afterwards appointed to a full term of four years.[19] About the time he was appointed solicitor general in 1864, he married Eliza Villard. Six children were born to them, each of whom was given "Villard" as a middle name.

In spite of his early successes as a lawyer, after the war (1867) he determined to enter the Methodist ministry. The immediate consequence was loss of his ample legal income. His annual salary on his first charge was $250. Later, while serving as pastor of Trinity Church in Atlanta that church became the largest in Southern Methodism. The Georgia Senate unanimously chose him as chaplain in 1881. In the same year he became President of La Grange College. He also received honorary degrees from the University of Georgia and from Trinity College, North Carolina.[20]

When the Curators selected the forty-four-year-old Heidt as Regent, there was every reason to believe that they

The four Regents of Southwestern University—F. A. Mood, J. W. Heidt, J. H. McLean, and R. S. Hyer. The term "Regent" had been chosen in the early 1870s to designate Southwestern's chief executive officer in anticipation of its being the Central Methodist University. Feeder schools would have presidents. The designation was changed to President in 1906. Southwestern University, Special Collections.

might be bringing another Francis Asbury Mood from the eastern seaboard. His selection by the Curators was unanimous, and his arrival was embraced with enthusiasm.

The Secret Societies

The initial enthusiasm, however, was marred by the early appearance of a student problem. The problem was not an open demonstration, with the tapping of a drum and the marching of students off campus, such as the one faced by Mood some years before, but a quiet, unobtrusive problem, that of the appearance of secret societies among the students. It surfaced less than a year after Heidt's arrival and placed him in a difficult position. Nothing that he could do positively for the University for a year or more was enough to overcome the fact that the burning issue for faculty, students, and Curators was that of the secret societies (fraternities). The problem would continue to fester until being settled definitively in mid-June 1887. Even after that it would continue to rankle in the minds of those who lost. Though other causes for Heidt's eventual resignation developed during his first two years, his handling of the secret society matter was an important ingredient in the mix of issues that eventually brought it about.

At the weekly meeting of the faculty on May 24, 1886, the Regent informed his colleagues that he had learned from a student of the existence of two secret societies in the University.[21] There were, in fact, three, and they had been organized for several years. The faculty was concerned and discussed the proper course of action to pursue. Secret societies had been forbidden since the publication of the third University catalog ten years earlier.

Now that faculty members knew of its existence, the Phi Delta Theta fraternity decided to steal a march on them by presenting its side of the matter directly to the Board of Curators at its impending June 5–8 meeting. It did so through a written statement. The statement did not achieve the result fraternity members desired. After conferring with the Regent and faculty about the matter, the Curators adopted a motion to leave the business of enforcing proper discipline wholly in the hands of the Regent and the faculty.[22]

The academic year 1886–1887 was filled with intense activity by the faculty working with the students. They felt that the existence of fraternities was a "menace" to their authority, since the catalog had repeatedly stated: "No secret societies are countenanced." Consequently, they voted unanimously to uphold the stipulation against their existence. At the beginning of the fall session, the various faculty members addressed the students giving the reasons for their action and asking the students to support it. The penalty was "to deny all college honors" to those connected with secret societies. Those elected to honors were called before the faculty and asked whether or not they were fraternity members. Those who admitted to membership were disqualified and their places taken by others. Since some had joined fraternities before announcement of the faculty action, the faculty agreed to exempt them from the penalty if they would forthwith withdraw from active membership.

After the spring elections, the same procedure was followed. Though the three fraternities declared that they had disbanded or that their members had withdrawn from membership, all the young men insisted that their actions applied only to the present and not to any future sessions. The faculty felt that they were resorting to an expedient in order to enjoy honors this session while resuming activity later on. It, therefore, constructed a tight statement indicating that withdrawal meant permanent cutting of ties. The young men refused to accept this interpretation and said that they preferred to lose their honors than to agree to it. "No doubt could then be entertained by us," reads the faculty report to the Curators in 1887, "that they valued their fraternities more than the awards of the University, and they intended to perpetuate the former even if they threw discredit on the latter."[23]

Unwilling to accept this definition, the Kappa Alpha fraternity reactivated its charter, and so-called "former" Phi Delta Thetas resumed their active membership. They appealed to friends in Georgetown and even to some Curators. In April the faculty demanded that the societies surrender their charters and dissolve their membership. They were given twelve hours to decide what they would do. Under this pressure, all the fraternities agreed to disband. "We are thus enabled to announce," says the Regent-Faculty report to the Curators for 1887, "in the presence of the assembled students that perhaps for the first time in years there is no secret society in the University."[24]

Once again, though supposedly not in existence, the secret societies—Phi Delta Theta, Kappa Alpha, and Kappa Sigma—appealed to the Board of Curators, this time for a hearing. The Curators set a time for the meeting, with the faculty to be present. After the meeting, the Curators went into executive session. A motion to rescind the rule against secret societies was made. Its proponents advanced the argument that there is a difference between things evil in themselves and things evil because they are forbidden. They stated that secret societies fell into the latter category. The rule should be rescinded, they said, because the experience of other universities has shown that they are very difficult to control. A substitute motion asked the faculty to prudently but firmly enforce the law against secret societies. It was laid on the table. Having failed to reach a satisfactory resolution of the matter themselves, the next day the Trustees threw the matter completely into the hands of the faculty. They adopted two resolutions:

> Resolved 1: that this Board is eminently satisfied with the action of the Faculty toward Secret Societies in the University during the scholastic year just closing, and that we continue to leave the whole treatment of the subject in their hands, with assurance of confidence and support whatever the treatment may be.
>
> Resolved 2: that we now invest the Faculty with Plenary powers in relation to the rule in regard to Secret Societies and they are hereby empowered to enforce, alter[,] suspend[,] or revoke the same in such manner as they may deem right and proper.[25]

Word of the Curator discussions and resolutions spread quickly. The Curators had not approved repeal of the prohibition against secret societies, but they had discussed it and a rationale had been offered for its repeal. Secret societies were not evil in themselves but only because they were forbidden. The three fraternities immediately sent a communication to the faculty, requesting that the faculty announce "tonight" how it would act on the matter "in fulfillment of what was virtually understood."

Though the faculty did not meet the requested deadline, it did assemble nine days later to take up the matter. A motion to refuse recognition of secret societies was lost by a vote of 5 to 4. Against recognition were McLean, Young, Hyer, and F. A. Mood, Jr. For recognition were Cody, Burkhead, Sanders, and Heidt. Faculty rules stipulated that in case of a tie vote, the Regent was entitled to cast a second vote. Therefore, the University's rule against secret societies was repealed by his double vote.[26] Within a year another fraternity, Sigma Alpha Epsilon, had joined the other three. In the report to the Curators in 1888, Heidt, writing for the faculty, reported that "the faculty sees both good and evil in them [the fraternities] without being able to agree whether the good or the evil predominates." The Curators approved the change in policy.[27]

It is clear that the imbroglio did Heidt no good. Whether right or wrong, the faculty had been unanimous in its actions until the final vote on June 16. At that point Heidt and three other faculty members voted to allow the fraternities a place on campus. The nature of the discussions held by the eight faculty members has not been recovered, but Heidt must have certainly wanted to carry the faculty with him. He had probably observed the deliberations of the Curators carefully, and, becoming convinced that they would be amenable to overturning the secret society prohibition, he had decided that continued resistance was a "no win" situation. Therefore, he changed his position and encouraged the others to join him. Nevertheless, he could persuade only three of the other seven to adopt his new position.

During the affair, Cody, who was already assuming a leading role in the faculty, seems to have developed some qualms about Heidt's leadership qualities. He wrote to a friend at Emory, in Oxford, asking him about Heidt. The friend replied positively, saying: "As to Dr. Heidt—He will do your work in Texas if [unintelligible] let him."[28] Cody followed Heidt and voted with him on the crucial faculty vote eight months later, but two future Regents, McLean and Hyer, and Francis Asbury Mood, Jr., who was now a faculty member, voted against him. This is the first known instance on an important issue where Cody and Hyer came out on opposite sides. It was a harbinger of their differences on the removal controversy twenty years later.

Heidt had been an outsider at the outset of his administration, and he did not win inclusion in the minds of his fellow faculty members during the secret society turmoil. Mood, in an equivalent student upheaval a few years earlier, had disdained any solution based on expediency. He always followed what he felt was the high moral ground, even when it bordered on being unreasonable. Those who voted against Heidt's position may have felt that he had abandoned the high moral ground in order to achieve peace. Later in his career, back in Georgia, Heidt was known as a peacemaker.[29] His attempt at peacemaking on the fraternity issue brought faculty dissension.

The Helping Hall (Giddings Hall) and Cottages

Though the excitement on campus during Heidt's first two years was about fraternities, a construction movement got underway soon after his arrival that continued through the McLean and Hyer administrations. It would ultimately fill up the old campus with new buildings and set in motion the creation of a new one.

University policy during the Mood administration for student board and lodging was to rely on private homes and boardinghouses approved by the University. The out-of-town students boarded with private families, who usually kept anywhere from two to eight or ten boys. These boarding places were usually designated by whatever might be the name of the host family, such as the Hodges Ranch or the Brooks Ranch, two of those actually in use.[30] Some students resided with faculty members. When Mood wrote Giddings about his desire to secure a place of his own in 1876, one of the reasons he gave was to enable him to board a few students to aid him in supporting his family.[31] Records of faculty participation in the room and board of students are plentiful until the University created on-campus housing arrangements for its students. In the period immediately before the completion of the new Annex building, female students roomed with "the Regent [Heidt], the Vice Regent [McLean], Prof. Young, and 'Sister Mood,' except where they have a Georgetown relative."[32] Even after campus housing facilities had been provided, faculty members were employed as supervisors and as managers of the boarding units. Faculty wives were sometimes employed as cooks.

Nevertheless, there was recognition that this policy limited the University and did not always operate in the best interests of students. Parents were often reluctant to place the welfare of their children into the hands of otherwise unknown families, the boardinghouses and hotel were not always as reliable as the University might hope, off-campus facilities were sometimes more expensive than students could afford, and students living off-campus were in many ways beyond University control and influence.

The first effective effort to change this housing policy came with a gift of $3,000 from Mrs. J. D. Giddings of Brenham in late 1885 soon after Heidt's arrival. It was designated to build a Helping Hall, soon to be called Giddings Hall, to provide lodging free of charge and board at cost for "young men studying for the ministry and others with limited means."[33] With additional small donations of approximately $1,100 for the project, the cornerstone of a two-story frame building was laid on the north end of the campus in late January 1886. It was ready for occupancy by the fall of the year for about forty boys.[34]

In spite of its stated function as a boys' facility, the two governing boards authorized the faculty to use Helping Hall temporarily as a boardinghouse for women. Concern for their welfare and safety was greater than the concern for strict adherence to the grant purpose. It is also probable that they consulted Mrs. Giddings about the change. Regent Heidt accepted responsibility for the management of Helping Hall.[35] In addition to other boarding arrangements for men, an off-campus house was secured for seventeen of them, who lived in a cooperative fashion during 1886–1887. The monthly cost per person was $6.93. By the end of the session the new women's building was so nearly ready that the Trustees turned the use of Helping Hall back to its original purpose—to house boys. It had, as the minutes phrase it, forty-nine "inmates" during 1888–1889 and fifty-nine in 1889–1890.

The Helping Hall concept was so successful that a plan was immediately implemented to build cottages on the east and west sides of the campus using the same cooperative idea. Each of the five Annual Conferences was encouraged to build a cottage for its students. Four had been completed by June 1890. The other followed soon thereafter. They provided accommodations for seventy students.

Mrs. Giddings, obviously pleased with the way her original gift had spawned an entire "Helping Hall system," donated another $670 in 1891–1892 to build a dining room adjacent to the Helping Hall. In turn, the residents requested that the Helping Hall be renamed for her, and it was done.[36]

The Annex Building and the Start of a New Campus

Mood's last major effort as Regent had been to conduct a financial campaign to erect a new Annex building that would include both classrooms and living quarters. The hastily constructed two-story frame structure four blocks west of the campus had become too small, and he felt the future prospects of the Annex demanded a more suitable facility. He translated his belief into action by leading a campaign to raise funds for a new building at an Educational Convention meeting in connection with the meeting of the Northwest Texas Annual Conference in Georgetown in late 1883. The participants there subscribed a total of $35,150 toward the project.

Mood was enthusiastic and apparently carried the notion of constructing the new ladies' building with him when he visited Nashville in the early spring of 1884. There he employed a Vanderbilt architect to draw up plans for the project. Ralph Jones states that plans for the building were delivered to him one week prior to his death.[37] He also says

that the Board of Trustees stated in its report for 1885 that the site of the building had been donated and that the plan envisioned a structure costing $56,000, of which $30,000 had been pledged.[38]

Heidt inherited Mood's plan, and two years after his arrival, at the 1887 annual meeting of the Board of Trustees, it was put into action. Dudley and John Snyder said that "in order to relieve the great and pressing demands for more and better facilities for the Young Ladies Annex" and to enable them to pay their 1883 pledge, they would sell to the school the J. W. Snyder residence situated in the Snyder addition to the city, with all its furniture and fixtures, for $17,000, and about thirty-seven acres of land worth $6,000, for a total of $23,000. The offer was immediately accepted.[39] Though the Snyders used the word "sell"

Painting of Dudley Snyder. No layman did more for Southwestern during its early years in Georgetown than Dudley Snyder. Among other things, he and his brother John gave the 32 acres to the west of the old campus that became the new campus. On loan "to the University he loved so much" by his daughter, Mrs. William H. Atwell. Southwestern University, Special Collections. Photograph by C. Smith.

The Ladies' Annex building, constructed in 1887–88. Dudley and John Snyder were responsible for seeing Mood's dream of a major woman's building completed after his death in 1884. It stands more or less where Brown-Cody Residence Hall is today. Another wing was later added. Southwestern University, Special Collections.

to describe their offer, it was not really a sale. No transfer of money was involved. The offer was simply credited against the outstanding Snyder pledge.

Though the offer would have been astonishing had it been made without forewarning, it was not a surprise to the Board of Trustees and the Board of Curators. They were ready for it and acted with alacrity. It had been in the air for at least two years, perhaps three. The Snyders likely discussed it with Mood after having made their pledge. Otherwise, one cannot imagine that Mood would have gone to Nashville and employed an architect to design a building for the old campus of the magnitude of the one specified in the plans. The old campus would have been inappropriate for it. He and the Snyders had likely already decided to build it on new land to the east. Mood had long recognized the need for more land in that direction. He tried to purchase about twenty more acres of land adjacent to the campus as soon as he moved to Georgetown. He says that he at once recognized the "comparatively limited character of the campus," when what was needed was thirty or forty acres. "What efforts I made to secure that land! How I went from one to another and tried to beg or borrow the money; I am almost ashamed to tell—but I failed."[40]

After agreeing to the Snyder offer, the Trustees immediately empowered the Executive Committee "to erect the building upon the grounds this day purchased from D. W. & J. W. Snyder." The Curators, for their part, stated at the same time that an architect from Vanderbilt University had already drawn up plans for a new Annex building, that the total cost would be $56,000, and that $30,000 had already been secured.[41]

In mid-July the plans that had hitherto been unofficial were officially accepted, and the Executive Committee of the Board of Trustees authorized advertisements for the rockwork. Work soon got underway on a plot of land eight blocks east of the old campus, on the highest eminence, slightly northeast of where the Fine Arts building stands today. In their fall report to the Annual Conferences, the Curators stated that the cornerstone of a "large, elegant stone building" to cost $50,000 when completed was laid on September 22, 1887, and that the first story was almost completed.[42] It was finished and dedicated in time for the beginning of the 1888–1889 school year. It was a lovely structure. Pictures show it as a three-story building of white limestone, with the darker-colored walls of a gable-type fourth story gracefully sloping upward and inward, everything surmounted on the west side by a shapely bell tower. The building was also graced by attractive wooden balconies. A final leg added in 1905 completed its footprint in the form of an "H."

The building contained sleeping apartments, parlors, recitation rooms, a chapel, and a 78\' x 38\' dining room. It also contained music and art rooms, society halls, a gymnasium, a library, and an infirmary. It was not, however, outfitted with central heating or modern bathroom facilities.[43] In 1897 the City of Georgetown agreed to connect the Ladies' Annex building, the proposed site for the new Main building, the old University building and grounds, and Giddings Hall with the city sewerage system. The City made the connection, free of all expenses for forty-seven years, for $2,000.[44] A smaller two-story building was added "at the Annex" the same year at a contract cost of $5,350.[45]

"Cannibalization of Endowment Funds"?

Ralph Jones states in his history of Southwestern that "cannibalization of endowment funds kept the university on a constant financial treadmill of increasing speed. The process was not halted and reversed until the middle 1930's."[46] It all began, he says, with the method used to build the Ladies' Annex building in 1887–1888.

Though Ralph Jones has studied the finances of Southwestern University carefully, his analysis is based on too narrow a focus. It is couched in a modern understanding of how established institutions of higher education in the twentieth and twenty-first centuries should conduct their finances and does not recognize what it took for a small, struggling institution without much in the way of resources to get ahead a century ago. Since "a pattern was set," he says, by the Ladies' Annex building for the construction of the Main building, for Mood Hall, and for the Williamson County Science Building, that "pattern" needs to be studied carefully to test his conclusion.

The first complete accounting of University assets and liabilities appears in a report of October 29, 1884, to the Annual Conferences. It lists only assets. There are no liabilities. The University has no debt. The total value of all assets, including buildings, campus, land holdings, and all other possessions is listed as $103,805.98. Of that amount, $44,889.33 is "Notes and cash donations" raised by the financial agent. In most subsequent reports this category is called "Notes for Endowment & outfit." More than half of the almost $45,000 in the account is the amount pledged by the Snyders and nine other major Georgetown donors in the capital campaign for the new Ladies' building in 1883.[47] The remaining $10,150 pledged by other persons would also be a part of the $45,000. Less than $10,000 of the $45,000 in the so-called "Notes for Endowment & outfit" fund was unrelated to the campaign for the new Ladies' Annex building. Thus, from the very outset, the so-called "Endowment & outfit" fund is more a capital building fund than a proper endowment fund. Various land holdings are listed separately and do not figure in the "Endowment & outfit" fund. Though some tracts were sold from time to time to cover small capital expense items, they were never enough to markedly affect the total pattern of University financial operations. Unlike the four root institutions, Southwestern was never land-rich.

The treasurer's report for 1885 shows that the total in the "Endowment & outfit" fund was $47,918.82. It is described, however, as "notes uncollected." Most of the notes, especially those related to the building campaign conducted by Mood in November 1883, are what would today be called "pledges." They might have moral status in the minds of the persons making them but did not have legal status. Modern-day accounting practices would not let them be placed on the books as assets.

By 1886 the new notes pledged and the amounts paid toward the pledges have reduced the notes uncollected to $46,912.34. In 1887 the amount is down to $45,112.34. In 1888 the "Endowment and Outfit Fund" is $45,212.34. Presumably, most of this amount would have been on hand to build the new Ladies' building could it have all been turned into cash.

In the treasurer's report for 1888 a category of "Liabilities" is included for the first time. Except for the Dimmit debt, inherited from Georgetown College and soon paid off, not until the fifteenth year of its existence does Southwestern report a debt on its books. It is important to know what would have caused a departure from the norm at this point.

The liabilities consist of four loans totaling $25,300.00 secured to complete the Ladies' Annex building. The loans were obtained because the money in the "Endowment and Outfit Fund" was in pledges, not cash. The Snyders paid off their pledge in 1887 by contributing thirty-two acres of land (instead of the original offer of "about 37") and J. W. Snyder's house (not a part of the original offer). The Snyder contribution, however, was not cash, and cash was what was needed to build the Annex building on the new campus. Therefore, loans amounting to $25,300.00 at the time of the report were secured to pay for the construction.

With the removal of the Snyder pledge and a few others, the "Endowment and Outfit Fund" by mid-1889 was down to $19,874.49. "Liabilities" were up to $28,893.45. Offsetting the liabilities were two assets—the value of the new Annex building itself at $40,000 and the remaining $19,874.49 of "Endowment and Outfit notes."

The original Ladies' building west of the old campus now became the Preparatory building. It and its grounds were valued at $5,000.00 on the books. During this same period, the Helping Hall was also built from a major donation by Mrs. J. D. Giddings and a few other small gifts. The Helping Hall was valued in 1889 at $6,000.00. A large farm valued at $14,000.00 had also been contributed to the University. Assets exceeded liabilities on University books by $128,249.79 in 1889, an increase of about $24,000 in five years.

During the five-year period from 1884 through 1889, the educational program of the University continued to pay for itself, mostly from tuition revenues. No tuition revenues were used for building purposes. An illustration of the solvency of the educational program is its report of a positive fund balance of $2,095.32 for the year 1892. The only outside funds used in the educational budget were the relatively small yearly contributions not designated for capital purposes made by the five Annual Conferences. The Trustees ran a tight ship, and the necessity of resorting to financing for capital purposes did not affect the pay-as-you-go philosophy that guided regular operations.

The Trustees, looking at their situation after the completion of the new Annex building in 1889, must have been quite satisfied with what they had done. They were obviously disappointed that cash revenues from the pledges were so meager, but they now had a major building on a new campus. In addition, the five Annual Conferences had made pledges, which they soon fulfilled, to build a series of three- and four-room cottages to house some of the male students from their Conferences.

In 1891 the Endowment and Outfit Fund was $15,643.00. Total University liabilities were $21,412.45. The Trustees went to work to pay down the debt further, and had liquidated all of it by 1899. They were now free to build an addition to the Annex building and to start the construction of the Main building.

In summary, to disparage what the Trustees did by stating that they "cannibalized" the endowment of the institution in erecting the Ladies' Annex building is to misunderstand the character of the "Endowment and Outfit Fund" and to place much too restricted a focus on the process in which they were engaged. They ran a balanced educational budget each year. As University-run room and board facilities came online, these, too, became a part of the balanced budget structure. The Trustees did not engage in land sales or use other unrestricted assets to pay for the University's regular program. This policy caused anguish at times, but it was adhered to strictly.

The Trustees also worked to secure funds for their major projects. They always employed a financial agent who was, for all intents and purposes, what today would be called the major development officer of the University. This person made every effort to secure funds for whatever project was under consideration. Most of the money he collected came in the form of small donations and from cash offerings. The fact that many of the larger pledges secured by him did not materialize in the amount pledged is probably more a result of well-meaning but overambitious intentions on the part of donors than lack of effort on his part or on that of the Trustees.

It is also true that there was not an endowment fund per se. As much as Mood believed in endowments and wanted to build one for Southwestern, the endowment concept was foreign to the practices of a penurious society. The Trustees carefully hedged their use of the term by calling it an "Endowment and Outfit Fund," with "outfit" being taken in the broadest sense. However much they might have desired a pure endowment fund, that possibility was unlikely given the economic situation of most University constituents and the narrow margin on which the Church as a whole operated.

The Church contributed ministers to the Southwestern cause but expected them to be paid out of University revenues, not its own coffers. Individual churches often helped support their students at the University, and Annual Conferences built relatively inexpensive cottages for their students, but the general Church expected the University to pay for itself much as local congregations did. It was not until 1894 that the General Conference mandated a small but regular assessment on local churches for their schools. Ralph Jones shows that the average yearly Conference donation for the twenty-five years between 1873 and 1898 was only $305.15.[48]

What Southwestern University did have was a cadre of persons—teachers, ministers, and laymen—who supported it faithfully. Though it did not have any persons of extraordinary wealth behind it, it did have a number of laymen whose dedication was strong enough and whose resources were ample enough to guarantee that it would not fail. Southwestern's real endowment was in the commitment of those people.

When the Trustees began the Ladies' Annex building, they planned carefully, acted boldly, and hoped for the best. When they were forced to borrow funds to complete it, they did so but immediately began an effort to pay it off, which they did before beginning the Main building. If they had not dared to act, nothing would have been done, and the likelihood of University success would have been compromised more by what they failed to do than by what they did.

When Southwestern faced difficult financial circumstances during Mood's early years, a number of people stepped forward and saved it. The people he especially mentions as having acted in this role are "Dudley, Thomas and John Snyder and, early in the history of the movement, Col. Geo. F. Alford, Rev. W. G. Veal, Capt. C. W. Hurley, W. B. Norris and Hon. J. D. Giddings."[49] Another who was especially conspicuous in the construction of the Ladies' Annex building was Heber Stone, son-in-law of J. D. Giddings. M. B. Lockett and others would soon be added to the list.

The Giddings Connection

The friendship of J. D. Giddings and Francis Asbury Mood was one of the foundation stones on which Southwestern was built. They worked together at the first Educational Convention in Galveston in 1870, and Giddings supported Mood afterwards in the various endeavors required to establish the University. He became a Trustee of the new institution and served until his death in 1878. His last act of importance was to make it possible for Mood to secure a house of his own in Georgetown.

His wife, Ann Giddings, continued her support of Southwestern after her husband's death. As described above, she donated $3,000 for the construction of Helping Hall and later financed the construction of a dining room adjacent to it. The name of Helping Hall was changed to Giddings Hall in her honor. The Mood family remained in contact with her for many years. One of them, perhaps Margaret Mood McKennon (the signature is missing), wrote her a letter of condolence in 1898 on the loss of a loved one who was her "friend and minister."[50]

Four years after Ann's donation to build Helping Hall, the Board of Trustees recommended her son-in-law, Heber Stone, for a position on the Board. A few months later

Regent Heidt notified them that the Texas Annual Conference had approved Stone as a Trustee.[51]

After the death of Col. Giddings, Ann Giddings had brought Heber and his wife, her daughter Mary Louise, to live with her in the Giddings mansion in Brenham.[52] There Heber joined fully the interest of his mother-in-law in Southwestern affairs. His participation was more than nominal. He remained as a Trustee for fifteen years, attended meetings on a fairly regular basis, served on committees, and helped the University in various ways from time to time. McLean wrote him a letter in 1895 expressing his appreciation for a proposed visit by Stone to Houston to raise funds for the contemplated Main building.[53] Two years later he made an address at Southwestern.[54] A lawyer wrote him from Austin the same year about arrangements for paying the $260 tuition of a young ministerial student studying at Southwestern.[55] Stone and Hyer became special friends. He called on Hyer for various favors related to Hyer's expertise in physics and chemistry, such as asking him on one occasion to assay some ores he had obtained in Mexico.[56] Hyer replied that he had done the assay and that Stone might have a very valuable property. He thanked Stone for a trip the two had taken together. "In every respect it was the most pleasant one that I have ever had," says Hyer, "and I am quite hopeful that you will never have any cause to regret having taken me with you."[57] During the late 1890s he was elected a state senator.

During these years, his son, Giddings Stone, was a student at Southwestern. Apparently he received no favors from the faculty for being the son of a Trustee and an important donor to the school. Faculty minutes record that on January 23, 1896, he was "allowed the alternative of taking a whipping or being expelled. He chose expulsion." He was back before the faculty five days later. The minutes of the meeting held on that occasion record that "Mr. Giddings Stone, having reconsidered, accepted the 1st alternative."[58] He took the whipping.

It was during the construction of the Annex building, a year after he came on the Board, that Heber Stone performed what his fellow Trustees regarded as his greatest service to the University. With the building fully underway and with money running out, the Board authorized the chair and secretary to borrow $10,000 to complete it. Stone agreed to make the loan at a rate of 10 percent.[59] As much as the loan, they appreciated his willingness to always allow payment according to the particular financial circumstance of the University at any given time. His was the last loan to be paid off. On May 26, 1899, a report was made that the Heber Stone debt had been paid during the year. A nice letter was sent him stating that "the Board of Trustees should be very grateful to brother Stone for his kindness in advancing the money at a time when we were in great need of it, and for his indulgence in extending time of payment of the note whenever requested to do so. Also for his generosity in remitting a part of the amount due on last payment."[60]

Correlation and Competition

From the outset Mood had looked on the founding of Southwestern University as only one part of a total Methodist educational program in the state. He envisioned Southwestern as the Central Methodist University at the apex of a pyramid of schools run by individual churches, districts, and Annual Conferences, all integrated by a common educational philosophy and bound by agreed-upon procedures. His use of the term "Regent" was in recognition of the fact that there would be educational units of lower grade in the system with their presidents, superintendents, and principals. All this was either clearly stipulated or implied in the document approved by the Educational Convention in Galveston in 1870.

Several things worked against the development of this structure after the establishment of Southwestern in 1873. One was the independent nature and shaky financial underpinning of the educational units already or soon to be organized by the Church. Preparatory schools, academies, high schools, and colleges were set up here and there, but most of them waned in the face of declining resources. They had no solid foundation and were established without much recourse to a larger educational picture. In addition to the many precollegiate schools that fell victim to this syndrome, at least two dozen Methodist institutions in Texas no longer in existence bore the title "college," however briefly, before World War I.[61]

Another group of Methodist schools of this genre, some already noted, attempted to affiliate with Southwestern in order to save themselves in their extremity. In 1888 Waco Female College offered its campus and facilities to the University if it would establish a Medical Department there. The offer was politely declined as being of too great a magnitude for acceptance without extensive consideration and planning. The Trustees of the college had made the offer verbally, not even reducing it to writing.[62]

Another factor working against the hierarchical plan envisioned by Mood was the gradual development of a system of public education in Texas from the primary to the graduate level. In spite of the early opposition in Texas to "free" schools already noted, the State began to join the rest of the nation in establishing a unified public school system in the 1880s. The change became marked during the administration of Governor Oran M. Roberts. His personal change is emblematic of the change that occurred in the thinking of many ordinary Texans. Originally a person strongly biased in favor of private schools, Roberts became a convert to public education. He now took a positive stand in favor of public education and guided the State in that direction.[63]

This change in the attitude of Texas citizens toward public education affected Southwestern at the collegiate level through the establishment of competitive state institutions with a low cost structure. It also affected Southwestern at the preparatory level. The public school system in Georgetown and elsewhere became competitors. In April 1886 the faculty discussed for the first time on record the possible effect on Southwestern of the adoption of a public school system by the city. Two years later there was a drop of fifty-six students in Preparatory School enrollment. Dr. Heidt may have been right in placing the blame on drought conditions, which forced many parents to send to public schools their children who might have otherwise attended Southwestern,[64] but a few years earlier there would have been no public schools to admit the children of those who were affected. The first notable direct effect of the new State system on Southwestern was the closure of the Primary Department of the Preparatory unit after the 1894–1895 school year.[65] Thereafter the Georgetown Public School system and Southwestern's Prep, or Fitting, School worked harmoniously. An agreement was reached in late 1897 that "no student [would] be admitted from one school into the other if said student be under discipline."[66]

In spite of the obstacles to setting up a Methodist system of education, Southwestern's leaders could not forget Mood's goal of providing for "a homogeneous system of advanced schools preparatory to the University." They pursued it fitfully. During 1886 they agreed that a new effort should be made to implement it by means of a system of correlation. To initiate it, they secured legislation at all five Annual Conferences meeting that fall to have their schools send representatives to meet with the Curators at their annual meeting in 1887. A small, unspecified number attended. At the meeting terms of correlation were adopted unanimously. They were as follows:

1. Correlation will be sought with first-class colleges and advanced schools.
2. A uniform system of textbooks should be agreed upon.
3. Students completing these schools should be admitted to Southwestern by recommendation of the Principal rather than by examination.
4. Eventually the University should not seek students for its Preparatory Department.
5. Honorary and other degrees by these schools should be limited or interdicted.
6. An annual scholarship should be awarded to each school.
7. Commencement at the correlated schools should not overlap Commencement at Southwestern.
8. All correlations should be reported to the Annual Conferences.[67]

Southwestern announced immediately that it would grant one scholarship to each school that correlated with the University.[68] The faculty was charged with validating the fulfillment of the stipulated terms by institutions seeking correlation.

Though this sounds like business, little of a concrete nature resulted from it. Only four schools sought and were accepted for correlation. They were Honey Grove High School of Honey Grove, Alexander Institute of Kilgore, Coronal Institute of San Marcos, and Central College of Sulphur Springs—one high school, two institutes, and one college. In a last dying gasp for life, Soule College sought correlation but was refused. It was unwilling to recede from any of what it considered its charter rights for the granting of regular and honorary degrees, though it did promise to be conservative in the exercise of those rights.[69]

All mention of correlation disappears after the 1888–1889 academic year until 1897–1898. Apparently legislation in that year by the General Conference designing a system of schools and appointing a secretary of education caused the University to revisit the matter. That same year the faculty acted favorably on a correlation request from the Peacock Military College of San Antonio.[70] The Curators also requested the faculty "to work toward a system of training schools for Texas."[71]

New Regent Robert Stewart Hyer, however, in a frank "Address to the Annual Conferences" in the fall of 1898, pronounced the correlation effort a failure. Southwestern, he said, is purported to be at the head of the Methodist system of education in the state. What the bond of kinship is, he continued, would be difficult to discover. "Several institutions are nominally correlated with it. In three years there have come to the University but three students from one of these, four from another, and not one from any other."[72] Hyer's negative judgment of the correlation effort in the first year of his regency may be the first evidence that he is already questioning Southwestern's ability to perform meaningfully its role as the Central University of Texas Methodism.

Complaints about Heidt and His Resignation

How much Heidt had to do with the activity that occurred during his administration, the building of Helping Hall and the cottages, the building of the Annex, maintenance of the Giddings connection, and the attempt to promote correlation, is unknown. Contemporary records speak more about the activities of townspeople, Trustees, and teachers than about him. In his last two years he was almost an absentee President. As a part of his responsibilities for the 1887–1888 academic year, he was commissioned to travel with Judge Rufus Y. King in the interest of the University to solicit aid. Though the extent of his travels is indeterminate, his attendance at faculty meetings dropped from the 85 percent of his first two years to 65 percent his third year. It dropped to less than 50 percent in the fourth year, when the Board of Trustees authorized him "to go East" as an agent for five months."[73] At its midyear meeting in 1889, the Board complained that he had not produced "any report as to what the Regent accomplished" on the trip. The Board also complained about his handling of the Snyder house. It said that "the J. W. Snyder property valued at $17,000.00 has never paid a cent of revenue, though it has been occupied for 2 years."[74] The occupant, of course, was Regent Heidt, whose family lived there and boarded young ladies from the Annex.

Heidt also had problems with the Curators that came to light in a curious manner. During the midyear meeting of the Curators in 1888, the faculty received a communication from the Curators asking whether or not, in view of the fact that Mr. Samuel Streetman had sent a paper to members of the Board of Curators attacking the "private and official character of Dr. Heidt," the faculty did not wish to reconsider its recommendations for degrees. Streetman was a graduating senior and valedictorian of his class. They decided it was indeed appropriate to reconsider their recommendation of Mr. Streetman for a degree.

Streetman was invited to a faculty meeting two days later and appeared before them. Heidt presided. Explaining the situation to the faculty, Streetman said that a member of the Board of Curators had asked him for his opinion with reference to Dr. Heidt. He had also been asked to collect the opinions of other members of his class and return them to the Curator. He did as requested and made five copies, which he sent to five Curators. He admitted that he was imprudent in doing so and that he should have sent the response only to the Curator who asked for it. He said that the Curator had suggested the points in which he had special interest. Streetman had promised not to reveal his name. He said he did not look on the request for information as unusual because he had been called before the Trustees the year before [1887] "to give his opinion as to Dr. Heidt's competency to manage the girls' boarding house." He said that the opinions of the faculty about Dr. Heidt were generally known in the school and that he may have talked with some of them on the point. He refused to go any further about any conversations with faculty members. In consideration of Streetman's testimony, the motion of the last meeting to withhold the recommendation of Streetman for a degree was withdrawn.[75]

As a result of the Streetman affair and other concerns, a suggestion was made in the next Curators' meeting to investigate the management of the institution. The matter was given to a committee for consideration. It reported back:

> Resolved. That it is the sense of this Committee that nothing can be gained to the institution by any further investigation of the management during the past year, but we most earnestly recommend that the Faculty co-operate with the Regent, and that the Regent give his full confidence to each one of the Faculty.[76]

A statement was also adopted by the full Board that said:

> Resolved. That we consider it for the best interests of the University that the Regent and Professors, except in cases of necessity should not be absent from their places, and that each officer and teacher confine himself as far as possible to his own appropriate work.[77]

Though Heidt could report to the Annual Conferences in the fall that Southwestern had opened the 1888–1889 academic year with the largest opening day enrollment in its history, he must have known that his situation was perilous. It had become even more so by the time of the next meetings of the Curators and Trustees. In addition to finding fault with him for not reporting on his five-month trip to the East and not producing revenue from the Snyder house, the Trustees stated that the balance for tuition for past years was still due and no effort had been made to collect it. Whether or not this was a direct slap at Heidt, since a faculty member, not he, collected the tuition income, it was at least an indirect reprimand. As Regent he was responsible for supervision of every area of University life, and they expected him to be vigilant.

The Board of Trustees also authorized the sale for $2,500 of the J. W. Snyder residence occupied by the Regent back to Snyder, adding that Snyder would assume the indebtedness ($6,256) now due on the property.[78] John Wesley Snyder's granddaughter, writing long after the event, says that the "mansion, with all of its furnishings," had been given to the University in the first place because of business reverses "that prevented the fulfillment of a monetary pledge given by the partnership, and John Snyder was as 'good as his word.' Later he was able to reclaim it."[79] Ralph Jones interprets this transaction as being heavily weighted in favor of Snyder.[80] Clara Scarbrough calls it a "sweetheart deal" for the University.[81] Whatever the economics of the issue, Heidt would be forced to move from the house.

The Curators attempted to go even further. Four of them introduced a resolution requesting the resignation of the Regent. It lost, but only barely—by a vote of 8 for and 11 against.[82] Heidt got the message. He tendered a letter of resignation on November 20. It is a model of affirmation and restraint at the same time. He asserts that during his more than four years of "anxiety and toil" the institution has been brought to a "prosperity, perhaps without parallel." He then lists the many accomplishments of his administration. Among other things, he says, the number of students and professors has increased, buildings have been renovated and built, the Helping Hall system has been organized, and the assets of the University have increased by $65,000. As a result, he feels that he can with a good conscience ask for release from his duties so that he can return to the pastorate in the North Georgia Conference. He asks that the resignation become effective on December 20. He concludes by expressing his love for the University and expresses the hope that God will guide the Board of Curators in the selection of his successor, whose work will be the beginning of a brighter future.[83] Heidt's letter of resignation evidences no bitterness. He believes he has served adequately and says so, yet he leaves with no word of recrimination against those who are forcing him out.

The Board accepted the resignation and placed the administration of the University in the hands of the faculty, led by Vice Regent McLean, for the remainder of the academic year.[84]

Assessment of Heidt

Whatever problems may have caused Heidt's resignation, the manner of his departure suggests a certain nobility of character also found in his subsequent career in Georgia. There he was known as a man of conviction and held some of the highest positions in his Conference. Six times he served as presiding elder [district superintendent]. He was a member of four General Conferences, a delegate to the International Sunday School Conference in Toronto, Canada, in 1881, and a delegate to the Ecumenical Conference in Washington, D.C., in 1891. He served as secretary of the North Georgia Conference for thirty-three years. At every General Conference he was chosen one of its secretaries. He was for two years associate editor and business manager of the *Georgia Wesleyan Christian Advocate*.[85]

Heidt's failure as Regent seems to have been that he was by temperament a pastor. He did well in public relations, especially where his excellent oratorical gifts could come into play, but he had difficulty making and staying with difficult decisions of the kind an administrator must make. He also seems not to have paid the kind of attention to details expected of him by the Trustees and Curators. Speaking well, writing well, and dealing with persons in a kindly, deferential manner were not enough. In their resolution to him on his departure, the faculty's strongest word of affirmation was their gratefulness for "the kindness and courtesy" he always exhibited toward them.[86] But, as a whole, they were not opposed to his departure. Professors Cody and Sanders, however, were special friends, and Cody kept their friendship alive over the years.

In an article in the *Texas Christian Advocate* shortly after Heidt's departure, Cody said: "We miss Dr. Heidt. We miss his counsel; we miss him socially. He is missed in our religious meetings."[87] Heidt and Cody, fellow Georgians, corresponded from time to time, and Cody visited his home on a trip back to Georgia in 1895. In a letter to Cody several months after his return to Georgia, Heidt said: "My hands are full of hard work and much responsibility [as pastor of Trinity Church in Atlanta] but I am happy and full of hope. . . . I miss you and other dear friends at Georgetown but how much sweeter is the life of a pastor." Several years later he expressed great shock on learning of the death of Professor Sanders. As late as 1896 he still owned fourteen acres of land in or near Georgetown, and when John McLean, his successor, proposed to buy it, Heidt consulted Cody to settle on a fair price.[88] He visited Georgetown in the summer of 1902, preached twice on Sunday in the First Methodist Church, and visited with friends.[89] Shortly after his death on January 23, 1909, his son wrote Professor Cody and sent clippings of the tributes paid him by various Georgia newspapers. He asked Cody to inform his father's friends, especially Mrs. Sanders.[90]

Especially notable is the fact that Southwestern did reasonably well during its first experience with a weak President. As mentioned earlier, this happy result was due to the buildup during Mood's administration of a cadre of teachers, Trustees, townspeople, and other supporters who stepped forward and filled the leadership gap.

9 *Leadership Problems and Campus Culture (1890–1898)*

Signs of Change

In 1893 a thirty-one-year-old instructor at the University of Wisconsin, Frederick Jackson Turner, astonished the American Historical Association with an epochal paper, "The Significance of the Frontier in American History." It has been called the single most influential paper ever delivered by an American historian. In it he called attention to the fact that the census bureau had failed for the first time to define an American frontier. The frontier no longer existed, at least in a geographical sense. He said that four centuries after the discovery of America and after a century of life under the Constitution, the frontier was gone. Its closing ended the first period of American history. The frontier environment, based on the premise of cheap or free land, which had given rise to a distinctive American character composed of nationalism, democracy, and individualism, had disappeared. Turner did not dwell on the consequences of this happening, but his paper was suffused with the foreboding that not all was well with the American Dream.[1]

Though Turner's perception of the American historical experience has been modified and altered by later historians, few will quarrel with the notion that he recognized a dimension of American development not before emphasized. That dimension is associated with the rapid industrialization of America, its great population growth with a consequent filling in of the interstices, its increasing urbanization, the growth of a vast transportation system, the development of instantaneous long-distance communication networks, and the resultant changing values and mores of the people. Before the end of two more decades, electricity, the automobile, the airplane, and the telephone would be, if not commonplace, at least on the horizon for the masses.

The events of Southwestern history during the last decade of the nineteenth and the first decade of the twentieth century took place in this environment. During these twenty years Southwestern's main struggle would be to maintain the Central university concept, envisioned by Ruter and put into place by Mood. The University's placement in a rural setting amidst a rapidly urbanizing Texas would bring about toward the end of the period an agonizing struggle between those who wanted to move it to a city and those who wanted to leave it where it was. Its two Regents, John H. McLean and Robert S. Hyer, would represent the contending forces, if not perfectly, at least closely enough to satisfy the model. McLean would represent the ideas, values, and social forces of the rural past; Hyer would represent those of the urban future. In a peculiar way, both forces would win but at a high cost. In the end, Southwestern University would remain alive but wounded, seeking a new raison d'être. Southern Methodist University would emerge as a new urban institution, but only after a difficult infancy slowing down its development. Passion would often override both reason and civility in the decision-making process.

A Disputed Election

By the time of the midyear meeting of the Board of Curators in 1890, John H. McLean had been handling the major administrative duties of the University for over half a year. It was his second experience in that role, having served an almost equal period of time as the provisional chief executive officer after the death of Mood. One might have thought that the fifty-two-year-old graduate of McKenzie College would have been elected easily. After all, he had been employed by Mood and served under him as Vice Regent. The Curators were ministers; he was a minister. They had just had a bad experience with an outsider; he was an insider. But it was not to be, at least at this point. With each of the Annual Conferences supposedly having one vote in the election, the total number of votes cast was six. They were, however, fractionated in some obscure way, and the Rev. E. B. Chappell of San Antonio emerged as the winner with three-and-one-twelfth votes as over against McLean's two-and-eleven-twelfths votes. Chappell had won support because of his known strength as a pastor and for his service as a Curator from 1885 through 1887.[2] A telegram was sent immediately informing him of his election to the regency by majority vote. He replied the same day: "Telegram just received. Let me pray over it till Monday. Help me."[3]

Chappell's request for a delay provided time over the weekend for some of the Curators to reconsider their action. By Monday the situation had changed. A resolution was offered that afternoon to the effect that the election on Saturday was illegal. The motion was ruled out of order by the chair. The maker then reworded it to say that the election was unconstitutional and was therefore null and void. His argument was that the German Mission and the Mexican Border Conferences had been given full votes, whereas, with only two Curators each rather than the normal complement of five, they should have each had only two-fifths of a vote. Also, the Curators had allowed a majority of the conferences present and voting to decide the election, whereas the bylaws state that election requires a majority of all the conferences, not simply those present and voting. The chair once again decided that the election was constitutional, but on appeal this decision was overruled by vote of the body. The election of E. B. Chappell was declared null and void. At that point A. H. Sutherland, a Chappell supporter, notified the Board that he would file a protest to be spread upon the record. It was accordingly filed with the signatures of seven Curators. Since the matter could not be resolved, McLean was authorized to act as Regent for the 1890–1891 school year. By the following year the procedural irregularities of the 1890 election had been settled. McLean was elected, receiving six-and-one-third of the seven conference votes. The office of Vice Regent was abolished.[4]

By the time of McLean's election in 1891, Southwestern had been in leadership turmoil for almost four years. The last two years of Heidt's administration had been clouded with dissatisfaction, and the more than a year-and-a-half of McLean's temporary oversight had been a time of uncertainty. Though McLean had finally been elected Regent, the manner of his election suggests that he did not have unqualified Curator support. It was not a good omen for the future.

McLean as a Person

The name of John Howell McLean has already appeared frequently in these pages, especially with regard to his education and teaching position at McKenzie College. Except for two years spent as a teacher at his alma mater following graduation and a short stint at the Paris Female Institute, of which he was elected President in 1869, he had continually served as an itinerant preacher under appointment by the bishop until he came to Southwestern. He was surprised, he says, when he received a letter from Mood in the spring of 1880 informing him that his name had been presented for a position at Southwestern. He wrote back asking to be excused from schoolwork, but Mood insisted on presenting his name, and he was elected. He says that he "entered heartily" upon his new assignment, and "on Christmas Eve, with my wife and seven children, I reached Georgetown in the snow, and stayed a week at the old Slaton Hotel, before I could rent a house for my family."[5] He traveled the state in behalf of the University during his first years.[6]

John Howell McLean. A graduate of McKenzie College, McLean was employed by Mood. More of an evangelist than an academician, he was virtually forced to resign by the curators. Nevertheless, he remained a staunch supporter of Southwestern during his entire life. Southwestern University, Special Collections.

The McLean presented by Ralph Jones is a one-dimensional figure. "All of his pictures show him," he says, "to be a spare, grim-visaged man, his bearded face claiming the conviction of John the Baptist. . . . He was a thorough-going fundamentalist. . . . To the original Mosaic zeal was added the emotional spirituality prompted by the act of conscious salvation. He was a frontier itinerant with the tongue of a classical scholar."[7] Herbert Gambrell, Historical Director of the Dallas Historical Society, amplifies this picture of him. Writing about him in 1974, Gambrell says that he saw McLean frequently as the grandfather of a classmate. He "was a familiar sight—bearded, frock-coated, with peremptory, stentorian voice."[8]

Along with this picture of McLean is a particularly graphic description by a female student of a chapel service featuring him.

> The students got the drift of the morning by the proverb selected and the manner of its rendition under Dr. McLean's long gesticulating fore-finger. Occasionally, Dr. Allen, sniffing the honor of the occasion, would deliver a sermonette of no importance, or Prof. Young would tonelessly read a Psalm, and offer a vacuous prayer, but Chapel was voted a total loss, when any other than Dr. McLean officiated. The talks centered around character and resisting temptation. He never intimated that these young men and women were just preparing for life. They were living it right then and there. And to be weighed in the balance and found wanting in youth was to be wanting for all time. He had a silly theory, so the students thought, that the best thing that could happen to any of them was to be caught and punished severely in their first minor transgressions. One of his choice subjects was the hell-daring sinfulness of low necks and short sleeves, addressed to the girls [sic] sections. Along with being a dynamic, swift-moving talker, he was a good actor as well, and he gave some rare exhibitions of his art. Sometimes his language was so forceful, it could hardly be restrained within the bounds of Victorian propriety. When it grew to such violence, he would turn to the female side of the chapel, and dismiss the young ladies, that his speech might have the freedom of utterance[,] which the presence of men alone assured.[9]

Granting the overall accuracy of the portrayal of McLean given above, there are other elements in his character that need to be considered. The depiction of him as a "fundamentalist" when he was at Southwestern is not accurate. Fundamentalism as a theological movement did not develop until the twentieth century and then not to describe persons such as McLean. He was an old-fashioned biblical literalist, as were most of the preachers and laymen with whom he associated. German literary criticism was only a shadow on the Texas theological scene during the nineteenth century, and he, along with most of his fellow ministers, knew only enough about it to be able to denounce some of what they had heard secondhand. He did not preach to advance or to oppose certain theological ideas so much as to exhort people to righteous living.

Also, McLean was not known in his own time as a mean and vindictive man. Students may have remembered his wagging finger, but they enjoyed hearing him even if only to parody him afterwards. He was interesting. They did not fear him. He had a sense of humor that moderated his severe mien.

He was also very popular among his fellow ministers. During his career he served as a presiding elder, as head of the Methodist Home (an orphanage), as a representative to the General Conference nine times (seven times as head of the delegation), as a member of the General Board of Education and of the General Board of Missions, and as a delegate to several ecumenical conferences. For seventeen years he was President of the Board of Publication of the *Texas Christian Advocate.*[10] He was not by nature spiteful or unkind and resumed his work in the pastoral ministry without complaint or recrimination after he was virtually forced to resign as Regent. M. B. Lockett, chair of the Executive Committee for twelve years during the McLean and Hyer administrations, says that "it never seemed to make the slightest difference in his loyalty to the University; he continued to send his children to the college until all had graduated" and supported the University in the removal controversy.[11]

The Race Question

One of the great voids in the records of Southwestern's history is a lack of material regarding its institutional policy on race and the racial views of its Curators, Trustees, faculty, and students. It is touched on so lightly that one might conclude that there was no racial problem. And, indeed, in a sense there was none. African Americans were not knowingly admitted to Southwestern until the mid-1960s, and that was that. There were no rules or regulations against their admission. It was just not done. Though Southwestern did not participate in the grosser forms of racial discrimination practiced throughout the South, its pattern of exclusion supported the prevailing ethos.

Apparently, however, the bar against African American admission was not perfect, and a few occasionally slipped through. One such who was detected was a Mr. H. C. Risner. Faculty records for May 17, 1886, state that "M. K. Bateman and S. B. Hawkins appeared and read statements from several persons acquainted with the family of H. C. Risner which asserted that he is of negro [sic] descent. On motion[,] the Regent [Heidt] was requested to advise Mr. Risner to withdraw from the University because of the above suspicion and of the discontent among the students."[12] Whether he was allowed to complete the academic year or not is uncertain, but early in the fall session the faculty approved a motion to have the secretary "write a certificate for Mr. H. C. Risner, testifying to his good conduct while in the University."[13] Several months later "Messrs. Bateman, Hawkins, I. Taylor, and J. P. Sessions appeared as a committee asking permission to organize a military company and to wear a uniform and drill on the campus. Action was deferred." The request died. Since Bateman and Hawkins were the two persons who turned in the complaint about Risner, one wonders about the connection between their racial views and their militaristic zeal.[14]

Faculty records also show that after the death of Jefferson Davis on December 6, 1889, a committee of students was excused from a late morning class three days later "that they might be permitted to march to the Court House and attend the memorial services in honor of Hon. Jefferson Davis."[15] The glorious cause had a place of honor in the minds of Southwestern students as surely as in the minds of their parents.

Given the paucity of information on the racial question, it is illuminating to find in the *Reminiscences* of John McLean, Regent during most of the 1890s, a full chapter about his views on the issue. He makes his observations from the background of having once been a slave owner himself.

Before the war he was, he says, "a slave-owner by heredity," inheriting fifteen and buying one. He did not traffic in slaves and only bought a "young negro man" so that he could be joined to his family, which he already owned. He says that "for his sake alone, I bought him. I never abused one, by corporal punishment or otherwise." McLean says that he and his mother, from whom he inherited the slaves, loved many of them and the love was reciprocated. She once traveled fifty miles to bring to her home an old servant so that she could nurse her in her last illness.[16]

McLean says that he feels the Southern states had a right to secession, but, once war was joined, he was glad the North won. "This doubtless was for the best." "It is," he continues, "a cause for congratulation that slavery, long a bone of contention between the North and the South, has been removed." The manner of its removal, however, without any compensation, was not just. It ruined the innocent as well as the guilty. "The traffic in slaves," he says, "was wrong, the buying and selling of human beings through mercenary motives—making mere chattels of them—was a sin against God and humanity. In the long run, however, a gracious providence overruled the wrong of slavery to the ultimate good of the slave."[17]

Toward the end of the war, he continues, with the Union army making steady gains, persons finding themselves in federal territory were required to take the oath of allegiance or go to prison. In this state of things, the Annual Conference passed a resolution "declaring it immoral under any circumstances to take the oath." He was, he avers, against the measure and was alone at the Conference in opposing it.[18]

Nevertheless, whites and blacks should not be considered equal. The whites are "a superior race," and any thought of "miscegenation is repulsive." For this reason, "precautions against association on terms of equality are wise and proper."

"Have negroes souls?" McLean asks.

"Frank [a Negro friend now dead] had a soul," he answers.

"Is the negro a beast?" he asks again.

"Frank was not beast, but a good Christian man, and I will enjoy heaven the more for meeting him there."[19]

Whatever rationale may be offered for the actions and attitudes of the Southwestern students, faculty, and Regent in these three isolated examples of racial feelings, it is clear that they participated in the general sentiment that excluded African Americans from enjoying the benefits accorded persons in white society. The exponents of the Jim Crow laws that were put into place throughout the South during the latter part of the nineteenth century had nothing to fear from the Southwestern community.

Student Enrollment

On the face of it, the enrollment growth of Southwestern from the time of its establishment in 1873 to 1898 was considerable, from 33 students reported in the first catalog to 393 in the latter year. This result, however, is deceptive and was not at all satisfactory to its leaders and supporters. The reason for the lack of satisfaction is that the enrollment pattern for the twenty-five years is not uniform. The pattern of the first part of the period was encouraging. That of the second part discouraging.

Overall, the total number of students of all types at Southwestern increased steadily from the original 33 in 1873–1874 to 416 in 1886–1887, a period of fourteen years. From that year on it fluctuated, rising to a high of 490 in 1893–1894 but dropping back by a hundred to 393 by 1897–1898. It increased during six of the last eleven years but decreased in the other five. The 393 in 1897–1898 was actually less than the enrollment of eleven years earlier. In effect, enrollment reached a plateau in the late 1880s and leveled off. It was a further matter of concern that 37 percent of the student body during those years was made up of preparatory students, and the number of collegiate students did not increase as a proportion of the total enrollment. During the last eleven years collegiate enrollment showed the same pattern as total enrollment. It fluctuated from year to year, rising in five and declining in six. Whereas the number of collegiate students was 229 in 1887–1888, it was 228 in 1897–1898.

This essentially static pattern caused a certain apprehension to develop in the minds of those who felt that Southwestern, during the Heidt and McLean administrations, was not making significant progress. It was, they reasoned, locking itself into a cocoon rather than breaking free and becoming, as was later asserted during the removal controversy, a real university.

Faculty Numbers and Gender Distribution

During this same quarter century, the number of persons listed in the catalog on the teaching staff increased from three to twenty. Of these twenty, nine were women and eleven were men. Of the nine women, one had an A.M. and one an A.B. Seven held no degrees. Most of them were music, elocution, and art teachers, who were employed more for their proficiency than for their academic credentials. Of the eleven men, two had Ph.D.'s, seven had A.M.'s, and two had A.B.'s. None was without degrees. Of the women, only three of the nine had four or more years of service. Of the men, ten of the eleven had four or more years of service.

The men were the core of the teaching staff. Though they outnumbered women only slightly, most of them held advanced degrees, their turnover was low, and they taught the fundamental subjects leading to degrees. The women did not attend faculty meetings. In fact, it was not until 1893 that male preparatory teachers were given that right. On September 25 of that year, the faculty passed a resolution inviting "to seats in the Faculty all gentlemen teaching in the University in whatever department." They were given the right to speak freely on all questions but could vote only on questions affecting their departments, "provided that all questions of degrees be settled by the Faculty of the University proper."[20]

Faculty Rights and Customary Procedure

Unlike today, where there are fairly clear demarcation lines between faculty members and administrative personnel, no such distinction existed in the early years of Southwestern. In addition to teaching, the faculty handled most of the administrative work of the University. Even the Regent taught his courses. Dr. Hyer accepted the regency at Southwestern in 1898 only on condition that he be allowed to continue teaching physics.[21] He taught regularly after he became President of Southern Methodist in 1911.[22] The faculty met once a week and decided on questions that would now be the responsibility of the academic dean, the head of student life, or the registrar.

The Regent, himself one of the faculty, normally wrote the annual report for meetings of the Curators, but he solicited suggestions from the faculty. The faculty was present at the Board meeting when he read the report, and each faculty member was given opportunity to speak to the matters of his department.[23] The entire faculty as a body or any faculty member who individually desired to bring a subject before the Board was invited to do so.[24] Faculty members did not, however, attend other portions of Board meetings.

At its meeting in 1885 the Curators elected two persons for honorary degrees and sent their names after the fact to the faculty for ratification. The faculty responded that it is "the universal custom" for the faculty to take the initiative in approving the names of persons to receive both academic and honorary degrees. They returned the names to the Curators.[25] Three years later the Curators replied in kind. Upon receiving the recommendation of the faculty for the conferral of honorary degrees upon two members of the Board of Curators, they reported back that they were opposed to conferring degrees upon their own members.[26]

From time to time the faculty used its report to do more than describe what was being done at the University. On one occasion it felt the need to make a statement as to why it claimed a right to participate in the direction of the University. It said:

> The University has been served in the several chairs by experienced and competent professors. Most of them have been long connected with the Institution, extending in terms of service from ten to fifteen years. We deem it no small consideration that those long identified with the history and prosperity of the University should be permitted to share in its service and in shaping its policy for the future. To them the conditions of success are well known. The principles of administration are largely the outgrowth of experience; and from long and familiar relations, they are better prepared to see eye to eye in the prosecution of the interest of the Institution.[27]

The Death of Professor Sanders

On September 30, 1892, Professor Samuel G. Sanders died of typhoid fever.[28] The death of Sanders affected the University community deeply, perhaps as no other death since that of Mood in 1884. Acclaim of him at his death was universal, both for what he did and what he was. He was the first of "The Five" core faculty members from Mood's time (see Chapter VII) to disappear from the scene.

Born in South Carolina in 1852, he graduated from Wofford College in 1871 at the head of his class. He came to Texas shortly after graduation to teach at Salado College. In 1874 he was brought to Southwestern as Professor of Modern Languages. After a year of postgraduate work at the University of Virginia, he returned to Southwestern. Four years later, in 1879, he took the chair of Latin and Greek, which he held to the end of his life. He served as secretary of the faculty from late 1881 to June 1890.

Cody describes his scholarship as broad and deep and says that Sanders "was the one man in the faculty in that day whose quiet influence directed the policy of the institution and placed it upon a sure foundation." He adds that his religion "was the secret of his life and power. He carried it into his home and into the recitation room. It gave direction to his daily walk and cast to his deepest thoughts." He loved to do church work and was superintendent of the Sunday School for eleven years at the Methodist Church. After his death its members placed a stained glass window in the church behind and to the left of the pulpit when viewed by the congregation. Persons who attend today may still read the inscription it bears as they hear the sermon:

> Our Beloved Superintendent
> Professor S. G. Sanders
> Erected by the
> Sunday School

Writing about Sanders twenty-seven years after his death, Cody says that had he lived, rather than dying at the age of forty, he would have undoubtedly become the head of Southwestern and "Texas Methodism would have escaped some disrupting incidents that can never be entirely lived down."[29] Cody could not help suggesting that had Sanders lived, he, rather than Hyer, would have become President and that things would have turned out differently. At the time of Southwestern's Golden Anniversary in 1923, a committee composed of Cody, John M. Barcus, and Laura Kuykendall summed up their estimate of Sanders in a brochure entitled *The Book of Southwestern.* They said: "No teacher in Southwestern ever made a deeper or more lasting impression for good."[30]

Though the loss of Sanders was a tremendous blow to the institution, his replacement, Wesley Carroll Vaden, became over time a beloved member of the faculty and the longest-serving classroom teacher in Southwestern's history, sharing that honor with Professor Ralph Whitmore in more recent times, both of whom served forty-four years. After completing his B.A. and M.A. in classical studies at Randolph-Macon College and teaching briefly, he came to Southwestern in 1893 to replace Sanders. Four years after moving to Texas, he wed Kate Lockett, the daughter of M. B. Lockett, the prominent Georgetown merchant who played an important role in Southwestern affairs for many years. Vaden did postgraduate studies at Cornell in 1901 and at Yale in 1905. In a piece written for the Golden Anniversary celebration in 1923, J. Frank Dobie referred appreciatively to Vaden as "that truly humanistic master." John C. Granbery, who wrote his obituary following his death in 1937, said in it: "It is difficult for us to understand how he dwelt not in the moment, but in the ages. A few of us are able to take a peep into the world of classic literature, but he dwelt there, feeling perfectly at home."[31]

Curriculum and Degrees

In 1898, at the end of its first twenty-five years, Southwestern offered four degrees. They were its traditional three—the Bachelor of Arts, the Bachelor of Science, and the Master of Arts—plus a new one added in 1894, the Bachelor of Philosophy. The B.A. was the model for all degrees. It required proficiency in seven schools (departments) through the junior year: Mental and Moral Philosophy, Latin, Greek, Mathematics, Natural Science, English Language and Literature, and any one Modern Language. The first students to receive it were James Campbell, B. Douglas Dashiell, Alfred S. John, and George H. Stovall in 1876.

The M.A. was an intensification of the B.A. It required completion through the senior year in all the seven fields required for the B.A. with the exception of English Language and Literature. The first students to receive it were Ryland F. Young, who became a member of the faculty in 1879–1880, the same year he received the degree, and John M. Barcus in 1882.

The B.S. modified the B.A. requirements by omitting Greek and English Language and Literature and by allowing students to take either Latin through the sophomore year or to complete one of the modern languages. It also required Natural Science through the senior year. The first student to receive it was John D. Hughes in 1880.

The Ph.B. modified the B.A. requirements by stressing Mental and Moral Philosophy and English Language and Literature. Studies in those schools must be completed through the senior year. It reduced the stress on the classical languages by allowing students to take either Latin or Greek rather than having to take both, but postulants still had to complete a modern language. They must also take elective studies equivalent to two hours per week for four years from the Schools of Theology, Mathematics, Science, Modern Languages, Latin or Greek.[32] J. W. Bergin, future President of Southwestern, was the first student to complete the Ph.B. in 1897.

During the quarter century from 1873 to 1898, the curriculum moved away from Mood's original model. It became more classical and less elective than his. His idea was that the curriculum should be oriented toward the professional direction one might take in later life. In 1873 the student was required to gain proficiency in four schools, only one of which was fixed. The other three might vary from student to student, who chose them from among the remaining ten schools. By 1898 the matter of choice was virtually restricted to choosing the degree one should take.

In 1898 the University consisted of seven academic schools and one professional school. They were the seven required by the baccalaureate structure and the Commercial School, whose courses were not included in any degree. Nevertheless, the Commercial School was so popular that in 1893 it was upgraded from a school to a college with three schools of its own—Penmanship, Business, and Shorthand and Typewriting. It was basically like a business school today, and the student could complete it with a diploma in about six months. It reverted back to a department in 1900–1901.

Between 1892 and 1898 the term "Preparatory School" began to be replaced by "Fitting School." The word "Preparatory" disappeared completely from the catalog for 1898–1899. The change does not seem to have betokened any immediate change in the curriculum or in the level of students admitted, and the term "Preparatory" continued to be used here and there, especially in popular parlance. Though the Trustees constructed a small Primary building in 1892,[33] the Primary Department was eliminated three years later.[34] Instruction at that level was too far removed from the central purpose of the Fitting School, which was to "fit" students for college. By 1898–1899 the Fitting School had in effect become a classical high school, offering as much as three years of Latin, Greek, English, history, and mathematics for students deficient in those areas for admission into collegiate studies. All lower levels of instruction were eliminated.

The first women to complete a course of studies in the Annex were called Full Graduates. In spite of the appellation, however, Full Graduate normally referred to one completing two years rather than four of specified work. The course was sometimes completed in one year, as in the case of its first two recipients—Catherine M. Mood and Mary Leavelle—in 1879. In 1887 the designation was changed to Mistress of Literature, and students having completed their work as Full Graduates in earlier years had their titles revalidated as Mistress of Literature.[35] Women were admitted to all degrees in 1880–1881. Lavinia Belle Henderson, Annie M. Mathis, and Virginia Moseley took the first Bachelor of Science degrees in 1883. Margaret Mood completed the first Bachelor of Arts in 1886. The first Master of Arts graduate was Willie Sampey in 1887. Music was offered in the Annex from the beginning. It was joined by Elocution in 1885 and by Art in 1888. Students received diplomas for completion of studies in those areas, normally taking two years. They were not a part of any regular degree structure.

During the first twenty-five years of its existence, Southwestern granted 296 degrees. Of these, 93 were the A.B. (6 to women, 87 to men), 125 were the B.S. (41 to women, 84 to men), 2 were the Ph.B. (both to men), and 76 were the M.A. (12 to women, 64 to men). In addition, 79 women received the Mistress of Literature certificate.

The Summer Normal School

In 1888 Dr. Cody established a summer normal school at Southwestern. It was for teachers in outlying areas who needed to take courses to qualify under the new State accreditation laws in order to teach. By 1890 the program was offered at twenty-six places in the state. Georgetown was listed that year in a published announcement as one of them, at a cost of $21 with C. C. Cody as conductor.[36] The normal school must have had a somewhat preprogrammed nature, since questions to be asked the students on their examinations were sent from State educational headquarters in Austin.[37] Persons holding Southwestern degrees did not need to attend. The State recognized Southwestern degrees without need for subsequent examination as sufficient guarantee for competency to teach in public schools.[38] Enrollment reached a high of 143 in 1904–1905, after which it gradually declined to only 22 in 1919–1920, the year the normal school ceased operation.

Literary Societies

An important element in the educational program of colleges and universities in the late nineteenth and early twentieth centuries was the existence of student-led literary societies. Nothing comparable exists in higher education today, and contemporary educators are constantly seeking ways of integrating the intellectual excitement of the classroom into the out-of-classroom experiences of the student. In the late nineteenth century, the literary society was the vehicle for this effort. For over half a century, from 1873, when literary societies at Southwestern were first instituted, until 1929, when they disappeared, most of the collegiate and many of the preparatory students were members of self-sustaining literary organizations. Students identified more closely with their literary societies than with any other institutional group.

Two literary societies sprang up almost immediately upon the opening of Southwestern. This development is not difficult to understand because the literary society was part of the nineteenth-century consensus of what constituted higher education throughout the country. Rutersville College had had its Young Men's Lyceum. McKenzie College had its Philologian and Dialectic Societies. And Soule University had its Alpha and Adelphi Societies.[39] The Alamo Society was founded sometime during 1873, though the date of March 6 ascribed to it, the anniversary of the fall of the Alamo, is more likely a backdating honoring that event than the real date of inception. Southwestern did not hold its first classes until October 6 of that year. In its self-description, the Alamo Society proclaimed itself to be a descendant of the Alpha Society of Soule University.[40] The San Jacinto Literary Society was organized on April 25, 1875. Though it began as a freshman debating society, it soon opened membership to all males.

Shortly after the Annex was established in 1878, the women organized the Alethean and Clio Literary Societies. The Alethean was originally founded as the Eutopian Literary Society on April 28, 1881. It was renamed because the "young gentlemen at college found the name hard to remember." The second female society was organized on February 22, 1885, as the Calliopean Literary Society. It was quickly renamed the Clio Literary Society after the males began referring to its members as "cantaloupes." Two societies, the Travis and the Sam Houston, were organized in the Fitting School in 1900. They merged in 1902. Several others, the Grady and the Helion, are mentioned in records of the mid-1890s as having been started, but they apparently did not last long.[41]

Both the men's and women's literary societies had a regular meeting place and a library. The University provided rooms in the Main building on the old campus for the two men's groups, and after the construction of the Main building on the new campus they occupied the large rooms on either side of the auditorium on the second floor. The women had similar space in the Ladies' Annex building.[42] On several occasions committees from the Alamo and San Jacinto Societies visited the Board of Curators during their annual sessions and invited its members to visit their rooms. The invitations were accepted, and the Board went in a body to visit them.[43]

Because Georgetown provided few activities for the student, student life revolved almost entirely around the University. This circumstance increased the importance of the societies. The activities of the literary societies, says

Randall Williams, "controlled the flow of the student for the average week." Meetings were held during the week, with intrasociety debates held on Fridays and Saturdays. During the 1890s they worked together and with the faculty to establish a lecture course that brought in speakers, humorists, musicians, poets, and singers. "The literary societies ran Southwestern at the student level."[44] The main event of the year was the annual intersociety Commencement debate between the Alamos and the San Jacs. It was named the "Champion Debate," renamed the "Brooks Prize Debate" in 1904 after Judge Richard Edward Brooks, A.M., class of 1884.[45]

As a whole, the success of the societies was based on four principles: esprit de corps, competition, relevance to the purpose of the University, and student responsibility. Both students and alumni identified themselves by the literary society to which they belonged and worked assiduously for its welfare. Enthusiasm was engendered by organizing many society activities in competitive terms, appealing to the natural instinct of wanting to be a winner. It was all done utilizing the educational elements being stressed in the classroom, such as writing essays and holding debates on meaningful topics. The students themselves, not the teachers, critiqued each other and kept meticulous records that can still be read.[46] J. Frank Dobie, class of 1910, received a backhanded compliment when his critic said: "We have known others to do much worse in their first attempt and finally come out on top." Another critic was somewhat sarcastic about Ernest L. Kurth, class of 1905, in one of his comments. He said: "Mr. Kurth showed himself to be equal to a great many of our modern politicians. For he spoke on both sides of the question."[47] In a day and age when most teachers taught to the book, the techniques used by the literary societies were remarkably successful at integrating the cognitive material of the classroom into the affective experiences of the students.

During the early 1900s, the influence of the societies began to wane. Readings, musical solos, and talks became more important as intrasocietal debates began to recede in importance. Entertainment replaced more intellectually rigorous pursuits. The societies came to be used more for social purposes than for academic enterprises. The two male societies engaged in an intersociety football game each year, and the women competed in a corresponding basketball game. Sometime in the late 1910s and '20s they began electing a May Fête king and queen.[48]

The declining influence of the societies is to be seen in the reorganizations that occurred in the last two decades of their existence. In October 1916 the Alethean and Clio Societies merged to form the Cody Literary Society. It, too, was dissolved three years later when the two male societies opened their membership to both sexes. The Alamo tried to refocus itself in 1928 but disappeared the next session. The San Jacinto Society lasted until October 1929, when its few remaining members voted to disband.[49]

An important part of the work of the societies was their sponsorship of the *Alamo and San Jacinto Monthly*. Born in 1881 under the aegis of Dr. Cody, it flourished brightly for several decades, when its role as a vehicle for student expression declined. Just as student interest in the two societies lessened, their interest in the *Monthly* lessened as well. It became the *Southwestern University Monthly* in 1895 and the *Southwestern University Magazine* in 1898. It began to receive competition from the annual yearbook, the *Sou'wester*, in 1904, and three years later a student newspaper, *The Megaphone*, began publication. The *Southwestern University Magazine* disappeared in 1916 but was revived by the Student Association in 1924 without any connection to the literary societies.[50] With slight name changes from time to time, it is published today as the *Southwestern Literary Magazine*, serving as a venue for student writing.

With the dissolution of the literary societies in 1929, an important chapter of Southwestern's life came to an end. Southwestern had passed from a pre–World War I social and pedagogical world into another. President Charles Bishop was lamenting the consequences of this change when, writing to Dean Cody prior to the opening of the 1914–1915 academic year, he said:

> One point at which we are open to criticism is this: Intellectual interests do not *dominate* the institution. There is no general intellectual ferment. The influence of the class-room does not go out to any great extent among the student body and determine their conversation with each other or affect their inchoate plans for life, or arouse new interests among them in the world in which they live or in the problems, special or general, of their times.[51]

Neither he nor any previous President would have made this statement in earlier years when the literary societies were strong. They provided a place for "intellectual ferment" and, to a large degree, did determine the conversation of students with each other.

First Intercollegiate Athletics and School Colors

Though students had participated in athletics among themselves from the beginning of the institution, they began to organize intercollegiate athletic teams in the 1880s and '90s. Teams were unofficial, and a Southwestern team for any given game was simply a group of the best players chosen by the students themselves. There was no faculty coach or anything like a regular schedule, and all games were by special invitation. Though the first baseball game with the University of Texas is celebrated as having been played in 1884, the first record of a game with Texas in the faculty minutes is dated April 2, 1885, where a statement reads: "On motion the Base-ball Club was allowed to accept a challenge from the Texas University Club."[52] All out-of-town games needed faculty approval, and the faculty did not hesitate to deny some of the requests. A request on May 5, 1890, by the "Base Ball nine" to go to Taylor to play a game at the fair was refused,[53] as were games during the next two years.[54] A football team was first mentioned in the minutes of November 19, 1895.[55]

With athletic teams in action, the faculty and students felt that school colors were called for. The faculty minutes of February 8, 1898, record that a committee to select school colors chose canary and black. They remained the colors until 1938, when they were changed to black and gold.[56]

Student Life and Discipline

Discipline for forbidden activities continued to be meted out to students during these years very much as in previous years, but all breaches of discipline were individual rather than corporate. There were no deliberate breaches of discipline by groups, such as had occurred once each during Mood's and Heidt's tenures. Students were punished, usually by giving them demerits. Typical offenses were attending a dancing party, going to the skating rink, attending a Hook and Ladder supper without permission, plagiarism, profanity, and cheating on examinations. Several ladies were disciplined for attending a circus in Austin without permission.[57] Two students who could not desist from the use of profanity were required to move out of Helping Hall.[58] Students could be expelled for other types of offenses as well, one of which was for lack of attention to academics. One student was compelled to withdraw from the University on grounds of "vicious worthlessness."[59]

Drinking alcohol persisted over the years, like a low-grade fever, as a violation of the rules. Every year the faculty was required to dispense the requisite justice to individuals or small groups of students for drinking or drunkenness. Whether the establishment of prohibition in the Georgetown precinct in mid-1893 is the reason or not, the Regent reported to the Curators two years later that for the first time in the history of Southwestern "we have not even had a suspicion of drunkenness among the students."[60]

In late 1887 the faculty became aware that some students had obtained keys to the recitation rooms and might be entering without permission. This surmise was validated shortly after the turn of the year when a young man appeared of his own accord and confessed to having entered the room of Prof. Sanders and inspected his examination grades, though he denied that he had changed the marks or altered the papers in any way. A week later two other boys confessed to the same transgression. They, too, said that they had not had any "evil motives" or altered any marks. One of them stated that "he had looked at his mark in Prof. Sanders' book, which other students held, and had looked at marks on Prof. Cody's examination papers." Another student said that he had never entered a room to look at marks except on one occasion when he had entered "to prevent others who were in the room from changing marks." Another confessed to having seen marks. The punishment for these transgressions was relatively mild. The faculty gave a general reprimand at chapel to those who had gained access to the professors' rooms and desks and used the occasion as a warning to others.[61]

Gender Relations

The seriousness with which Curators took their role of prohibiting social contact between the sexes can be seen in a statement adopted at their midyear meeting in 1886. They said: "Relative to the administration of discipline among the resident students, we would most heartily recommend that the Faculty rigidly enforce the law forbidding intercourse with the opposite [sex] and that they resort to expulsion—if need be—to secure an observance of the law."[62]

To the faculty, however, the matter presented complications, particularly with regard to "young ladies residing in Georgetown." As parents themselves of some of these young ladies, they recognized that parental rights came into play. Consequently, they requested that the Curators relieve them of responsibility for the conduct of young ladies residing in Georgetown out of school hours because they "recognize the right of parents to control their daughters in their own houses."[63] The Curators agreed with their request by changing the regulation.[64]

Nevertheless, this change still did not solve all their problems. Some of the teachers boarded young ladies who were not their daughters. What about them? The matter was settled by allowing these young ladies to receive company during the holidays so long as the professor with whom they resided consented. Nevertheless, a request from the boys that the entire rule forbidding young ladies to receive company during the holidays be suspended was refused.[65] The matter of how to deal with "town girls" must have continued to bother the faculty because in 1890 they requested the Curators to leave the government of the town girls entirely in their hands.[66]

Involved in the issue of faculty governance of town girls was that of whether or not campus girls could attend parties in the homes of town girls. The matter was more serious than it might appear because a number of prominent supporters had daughters studying at Southwestern, and these daughters wanted to entertain their friends. In light of this fact, the faculty allowed the graduating class of women in 1889 to attend a party at the house of one of its members provided a faculty member escorted the group to and from the party.[67] Privileges one year became precedents for next year until finally, on November 28, 1893, the faculty allowed the students to hold their first social. Another was allowed three weeks later. The Kappa Alpha's were shrewd enough to make Mrs. Mood a partner in sponsoring an event in 1896. Their request to have young ladies attend a social sponsored by them at Mrs. Mood's house was granted, provided the young ladies had a teacher escort.[68] Southwestern's version of the Gay '90s was definitely muted, but changes were beginning to occur.

Religious Practice

In the catalog for 1898–1899 Southwestern described itself as a Christian but not a sectarian institution. From the time of Mood on, the University understood its mission as being to promote Christian principles but not to proselytize its students into becoming Methodists. Some of the practices engaged in to promote this understanding were required student attendance at church on Sundays, required attendance at the daily chapel services, the opening of classes with prayer, and the encouragement of on-campus religious groups such as the Epworth League, student-led prayer meetings, and the Y.M.C.A. and Y.W.C.A. The school also sponsored a fall revival each year. According to the catalog, it measured its influence in the area of religion in terms of "the number of conversions and in the subsequent prominence in church work of its graduates."

The Regent/Faculty report to the Curators each year commented on many of these items. Heidt reported in 1886 that there were 100 conversions in the revival and that "the school room has become God's sanctuary for prayer and praise."[69] In 1891, 1892, 1895, and 1898 the number of students studying for the ministry was reported to be thirty-five, forty-six, fifty-seven, and fifty-four, respectively. A missionary society was organized in the Annex in 1886.

The faculty monitored attendance at required religious events. In 1885 they voted to conduct a roll call each Monday to ascertain the number of absences from church the preceding Sunday, assessing a penalty of five demerits for nonattendance without a good excuse.[70] A roll call was instituted several years later at the Annex for morning prayers.[71] One of the memorable sights for residents on University Avenue each Sunday was seeing Dr. and Mrs. John R. Allen marching the residents of the Annex double-file in their blue uniforms to services at the Methodist Church.[72] The young ladies had regular seat assignments there and received demerits for sitting out of place.[73]

Students came to Southwestern knowing what to expect, and most infractions in the area of religious observance were minor. There is little mention of discipline in the records on this point. One student, however, was brought before the faculty in 1887 for not rising for prayer in chapel when requested by Dr. McLean and for disrespectful language on the occasion.[74]

As the faculty grew larger and talent was not always to be found in Methodist ranks to fill the positions needed, a few Curators began to fear that the University might employ persons of other persuasions to fill those positions. At the annual meeting in 1888 a motion was made "that all teachers of the University and Annex shall be members of the M. E. Church South." It was laid on the table without a vote.[75] The following year the same resolution passed but with a time limit of one year's duration.[76] After the expiration of the time limit, the idea was never mentioned again.

M. B. Lockett Comes to Georgetown

One of the families that moved to Georgetown during these years because of the educational benefits provided by Southwestern was that of M. B. Lockett. Lockett was destined to be one of the important figures during the McLean and Hyer administrations and a leader in the momentous events surrounding the construction of the Main building and removal controversy. He was a Trustee for twenty-seven years and chair of the Executive Committee for almost half that time.

Born June 4, 1846, he entered the Confederate army at the outset of the war at the age of fifteen. While in the army he came down with typhoid fever. Though he almost died, he finally recovered. Even then, he was so emaciated and weak that he was unable to walk and was given a discharge in the summer of 1862. Upon the improvement of his health, his father took him to McKenzie Itinerant Retreat plantation and put him in McKenzie College. Students there were organized into companies and drilled daily. Lockett, because of his army experience, was made captain of a company. Though he remained at McKenzie for only ten months, from late summer 1863 through the spring of 1864, he ever thereafter held the figure of Dr. McKenzie in high esteem. With the war going badly for the South, conscription was instituted, and Lockett voluntarily joined the army again in mid-1864 to avoid it.[77]

After the war he became a mercantile businessman in Central Texas and was successful in almost everything he did. Though living in Bertram and doing well, he visited Georgetown in 1886 and, thinking about the future education of his children, attended the Commencement service at Southwestern. "The grounds and buildings did not impress me very favorabl[y]," he comments, "but the reputation of the school for mental and religious training was excellent." After several visits, he purchased a residence on University Avenue for $2,500. He moved to Georgetown in 1888. The Ladies' Annex building was being constructed on what was to become the new campus at the time. The population of the city was perhaps 1,500; certainly, he says, it did not exceed 2,000. He had been converted in Bertram in 1886 and joined the Methodist Church when he moved to Georgetown. Though he was a man of definite opinions, he was very temperate in manner. He wrote in his autobiography, "I do not now remember to have ever uttered an oath in my life."[78] Once again he was very successful in business, and the M. B. Lockett Building on the square today north of the courthouse bears his name.

Melville B. and Annie Johnson Lockett in 1872. Lockett fought in the Confederate Army, attended McKenzie College, was a fine businessman, moved to Georgetown to educate his five daughters at Southwestern, and became a major supporter and Trustee of the University. Southwestern University, Special Collections.

The children entered school the first fall after coming to Georgetown, his daughter, Kate, going to the Preparatory Department of Southwestern University, and two other girls, Pearl and Mellie, to the public schools. His other daughter, Elvie, only seven, did not start until the fall of 1889. Late that same year his fifth child, Gladys, was born. For twenty years they enjoyed the public schools and then the University. Three of the five daughters eventually married Southwestern professors. Kate married W. Carroll Vaden (Greek, Latin, French), Pearl married Albert Shipp Pegues (Latin, English, Dean in 1915), and Elvie married Claude A. Nichols (Assistant in Fitting School, Education). When he wrote his autobiography in 1916, Lockett says he was well pleased with their choices.[79] Little could he foresee the grief that one of those marriages would soon bring and how it would play a role in the reconciliation between him and his opponents in the removal controversy.

The New Methodist Church Building

Others shared Lockett's opinion about the unsightliness of the Southwestern University campus, particularly members of the local Methodist Church. Their earlier building, constructed a decade earlier on the southwest corner of the campus and used by the University for a chapel, was an eyesore. Lockett describes it in his autobiography as follows:

> The Methodist Church in Georgetown was an oddity in its way. It is not possible that any town in the history of the whole country ever had anything like. It was a one-story rock building with a flat roof, the intention originally being to add an upper story for an auditorium. It was an exceedingly unsightly structure. . . . Of course the building had to be abandoned and another erected. Sam Jones [the evangelist] who visited the Chautauqua as a lecturer made all sorts of fun of it. Once in his characteristic way he declared that if he owned the building he "would take a turning shovel and cover it up."[80]

Around 1890 the Snyders gave the church a lot on the northeast corner of the block where the church presently stands, diagonally across the street from the old church building on the southwest corner of the University campus.[81] A Mr. Price of Baltimore, general architect for the Methodist Episcopal Church, South, designed a building for the lot in a Gothic style with the sanctuary in the form of a Greek cross. The Belford Lumber Company constructed it under the supervision of Robert S. Hyer, Professor of Physics.[82] Professor Hyer made a three-foot scaled model prior to construction for the members of the church and for the stonecutters, Waterson & Sons of Austin, who hewed the limestone blocks by hand. Construction was begun in 1891 and completed in 1893.[83] A few years later Hyer and Waterson would cooperate again in approximately the same roles in the construction of the Main Building on the Southwestern University campus.

The New Main Building: Getting Started

In 1893 M. B. Lockett was elected to the Southwestern University Board of Trustees. He was made chairman of the Executive Committee at the same time, and took to the work with enthusiasm, holding the position, he reports, for twelve consecutive years until 1905. He says he became "absolutely familiar" with University finances and carried on a large correspondence in the interests of the University. He soon noted, however, that there was some friction between the Curators and the Trustees because the ministers felt they should have some say in financial matters. His own opinion, however, was that finances were best left to laymen, who were more in touch with the world of finance and less inclined to be moved by emotional considerations.[84]

First mention of a desire to build "a suitable building adequate to the necessity of the University" was made in Trustee records on June 6, 1891.[85] Because of the debt incurred in construction of the Annex building, the Board was unable to proceed further at the time, but the desire remained strong. Four years later the Curators reported to the Annual Conferences that there was a great need for larger and better buildings. "The present buildings," they said, "do not furnish the necessary accommodations for our work, whilst in appearance they disparage the work and worth of the institution."[86] The Board of Trustees took the matter in hand and secured the firm of Layton and Raymond to draw up plans for a new Main Building. By March 1896 the plans had been given to the faculty for study.[87]

In June the Board of Trustees gave the plans its approval. The Executive Committee was authorized to locate the new building near the Annex building but not too near. The Main Building was to be principally for males, the Annex exclusively for females. The project was to be commenced as soon as sufficient money was in hand to justify proceeding. The Committee was instructed to proceed in stages but not to begin a next stage if all the money for the present stage was not in hand.[88]

In spite of the enthusiasm, the project did not get off to a good financial start. A report by the Trustees to the Curators a year later stated that, counting only assets "as have been definitely given to aid in the erection of the new building," very little cash was in hand. Eleven land pieces were listed as having been donated, with a total value of $15,016. The Trustees were so dissatisfied with the efforts of the financial agent that they paid him off and contracted another, the Rev. F. B. Sinex. In effect, they began the financial campaign again.[89]

Sinex inaugurated a campaign with two separate objectives. One was to raise money for a so-called Guarantee Fund. The other was to raise contributions for a Cash Fund. The intention was to raise $50,000 in all. The Cash Fund would solicit small donations of $5 to $100 apportioned among 1,850 people so as to total $25,000. The Guarantee Fund would raise its $25,000 through graded subscriptions [pledges] from 203 people. Subscribers would not pay anything at the outset, but once the entire $25,000 had been pledged, they would pay a designated portion each month until their pledges had been met. Pledges would range from $50 to $1,000.[90]

Within a year Sinex reported success in raising the $25,000 for the Guarantee Fund, thus triggering the monthly donations. He also reported many small cash donations. In his report, he gave special thanks to J. W. Snyder and M. B. Lockett for "their unstinted efforts to make this work a success.[91] The Board was so pleased with his work that it would employ him later for another building campaign.

Prior to the forthcoming Board meeting, the Executive Committee authorized advertisements for bids for the new University building. It received three but rejected them all as being too high. After working with Flume & Waterson to reduce its bid from $54,985 to $50,095, the Committee accepted a contract that was approved by the full Board at its annual meeting in 1898.[92] The Curators reported to the Annual Conferences that fall that "the erection of a magnificent university building" was underway.[93] The construction firm, Flume & Waterson, was composed chiefly of the stonecutters from the British Isles who were imported especially for the Capitol job and who had cut the stone a few years earlier for the First Methodist Church.[94]

Monday, May 30, 1898, was a day of special celebration at Southwestern. After the Commencement ceremony, at 4:00 o'clock in the afternoon, the Rev. H. A. Boaz, A.M., class of 1894, addressed the Alumni Association. At 5:30 a groundbreaking ceremony for the foundation of the new building took place. That evening the graduation ceremony for the Ladies' Annex was held. Just before the close of the ceremony, it was announced that Professor Robert Stewart Hyer had been elected Regent and that he had reluctantly agreed to accept the office.[95] The cornerstone for the new Main Building was laid the following September 8.[96] It was presided over by Hyer. The one person not in attendance at these events was John H. McLean. He had resigned the regency under pressure a year before.

McLean's Resignation

As noted earlier, McLean's accession to the regency had not been without its problems. For although he was popular as a person and unwavering in his devotion to Southwestern University, many people did not think he fit the pattern of a university leader. He was too much an evangelist and too little a scholar. A straw in the wind may have been the procurement of John R. Allen in 1892 to teach Mental and Moral Philosophy, formerly taught by McLean.[97] McLean does not appear to have been conspicuous in the progress of the University. The names of others appear more often in relation to significant changes than does that of the Regent.

Shortly before the meeting of the Board of Curators in 1897, each of its members received a four-page typed letter from a certain W. A. Shaw of Dallas. It was a scorching indictment of John McLean, not only as a President, but also as a person. It also accused the Board of being guilty of gross mismanagement for making it possible for him to serve as Regent. The author alludes to himself as a loyal Methodist and as a journalist, having worked at one time for the *Advocate*, though not happy with its direction. McLean was President of the Board of Publication of the *Texas Christian Advocate* for seventeen years.

Shaw remarks that though Mood was kept in his position long after he was "both mentally and physically" unable to perform his functions, love for him and deep sympathy for his family justified the special treatment accorded him. The error in the selection of Dr. Heidt was natural, since it resulted "from following the bad advice of one or more good bishops." Those situations, however, pale into insignificance beside the one presently being endured.

> I affirm: Dr. McLean is in no sense fitted for the place, and you know it. He is not educated, and you know it. He has no repute as a scholar, and you know it. He is a weakness rather than a strength to the institution, and you know it. His influence is always repellant rather than attractive—whether in personal intercourse, from

> the rostrum or in the pulpit—and you know it. He is author of no book, article, paper or sermon that stamps him as of even medium mentality, and you know it.
>
> Then I submit whether it is right, just, wise, honest—or religious—to keep one of such calibre at the head of the gretest [sic] church enterprise in Texas, and whose career of greatness ought to be only at its inception [sic]. The question is correctly answered in the negative, and you know it. McLean's only merit, if it be a merit, is will-power rarely equaled, with exceptional shrewdness in compassing his individual ends, or ambitions as to place, and you know it. Hence it requires some nerve to oppose him.[98]

Shaw's letter, however intemperate, seems to have triggered determination in some of the Curators, who felt like him but had hesitated to express their sentiments. At a special evening session of the Curators on May 29, 1897, nine of them presented a petition asking for "consideration of the question of the Regency." Since McLean was not present, the Board took no action and invited him to appear. After he had joined them, "the chair call[ed] upon each member of the board to express his convictions concerning the necessity for a change and to give his reasons for the same. The secretary called the roll and each curator responded according to the aforesaid motion." After a statement by Dr. McLean, the Board adjourned. The next morning Dr. McLean made a statement relative to his position. He appears to have left the room at this point, allowing a friend, the Rev. S. P. Wright, "in behalf of Dr. J. H. McLean," to tender his resignation to take effect at once. A motion to accept the resignation was approved.[99] So ended McLean's seventeen years of service with Southwestern University.

M. B. Lockett's appraisal of the event is perhaps the most balanced contemporary assessment available. As a Trustee he did not participate in the Curator action.

> In 1897 Dr. McLean under pressure of some of his opponents on the Board of Curators tendered his resignation as President [read "Regent"] of the University. I had known Dr. McLean for many years and had always held him in the highest esteem. He was a man of unswerving character, honorable in all his dealings, a christian [sic] gentleman in every respect and was loved and honored by a host of friends and students in almost every community in the state. But some thought his scholarship was not sufficient for the advanced ideas of the present age and he had to go. His friends felt very sore at the manner in which he was treated; for it was felt that he should have had warning of his impending doom and should have been allowed to retire without the odium of compulsion.[100]

When the faculty learned of McLean's resignation, it called a meeting to elect a chairman who would lead the University until a new person could be chosen. Dr. J. R. Allen was elected on the first ballot. Dr. McLean, having been invited to join them, offered "a number of wise suggestions" about the work at hand and led them "in a touching prayer for Divine guidance and blessing."[101]

First Attempt to Elect a New Regent

In the afternoon after McLean's morning resignation, the Curators met to elect a new Regent. Two ballots were taken. Professor H. C. Pritchett was elected on the second, receiving fifteen of the twenty-two votes. A motion carried to make the election unanimous.[102]

H. C. Pritchett was at the time of his election Principal of the Sam Houston Normal School in Huntsville. He was a strong Methodist layman, and records exist of frequent contact between him and Claude Cody. Cody was a mathematician, as was Pritchett. He wrote Cody in 1890 asking him to use his influence to get Williamson County to vote for him, in the Democratic Convention, for State Superintendent of Public Instruction. He was duly elected to that post and wrote Cody the next year about the Summer Normal examinations. By 1894 he was Principal of the Sam Houston Normal School. His interest in Southwestern was manifested during the 1896–1897 academic year, when he made a "handsome donation" to the department of Natural Science, for which the Curators thanked him. As a strong Methodist educator with state connections, he was a natural choice for the regency. To the disappointment of the Curators, he sent a telegram the next morning declining the office.[103] Rather than try again to elect someone at this meeting, the Curators adjourned, to meet again in Waco on July 6.

Robert S. Hyer as a Scientist

Two special Curator committees on academic matters had been appointed at the meeting just completed (1897). One dealt with the library, the other with the Natural Science

Department. The purpose was to determine what might be done to enhance the work of each area. The library had been upgraded significantly in 1895 when the old chapel was refitted for library and reading room purposes. Homer S. Thrall, one of the most intellectual Methodist ministers in service, had also willed his library to the University. Two years later the Curators reported that the library contained 2,300 volumes."[104] The library committee made several suggestions duly adopted by the Curators about how to further develop the library.

Hyer demonstrating to the faculty in 1894 the sending and receiving of messages by wireless. According to some observers, this result anticipated that of Marconi by a year. He did not, however, publish his results or seek a patent. Southwestern University, Special Collections.

The other committee dealt with the Natural Science Department. Here its members came into contact with Robert S. Hyer, who, during the 1890s, had brought Southwestern into the world of international research in physics. In the summer of 1891, Hyer had gone to Harvard to attend a series of lectures on the latest developments in physics. The subject matter for the lectures was the work of James Clerk Maxwell (1831–1879) on electromagnetism at Cambridge, England, succeeded by that of Heinrich Rudolph Hertz (1857–1894) on radio waves at the University of Bonn, Germany. Returning home, Hyer repeated the experiments of Hertz. By adding a transmitter and a receiver to the Hertzian apparatus, he discovered he could send and receive messages by wireless. By 1894 he was sending messages from his laboratory on the old campus to the jail in Georgetown, a distance of over a mile. According to some observers, this result anticipated that of Marconi

Hyer's laboratory/classroom, with X-ray and telegraph machines. Southwestern University, Special Collections.

by a year. It is this machine that can be seen on the table in a well-known laboratory picture taken of him and the rest of the faculty. He did not, however, publish his results or seek a patent.[105]

By 1894–1895 physicists such as Wilhelm Konrad Röntgen (1845–1923), professor of physics at the Royal University of Würtzberg, Germany, were turning their attention to a new discovery called the X-ray. Hyer was quite excited by this research and worked on it diligently in his laboratory. He assembled an X-ray machine for himself by ordering parts from a scientific supply house. "He built a fluoroscope using heavy card board for the sides, lining the inside with black cotton flannel, whittling a handle from a cedar post."

Hyer learned that these rays would not penetrate bone or metal, leading to all sorts of possible uses for the machine. People in Georgetown and in neighboring towns became excited over the machine, and Hyer used it on several occasions to help physicians diagnose fractures and to locate foreign objects in the body. "For these pictures," says his daughter, "he would charge one dollar, the price of the plates." When Dr. A. C. Scott, of the Scott & White Sanitarium at Temple, got an X-ray machine in 1897, he invited Dr. Hyer to illustrate what he had learned about it from his own experiments. He finally wrote a monograph on "electric waves" that was published in *The Journal of the Texas Academy of Science*.[106]

Little wonder that the Curator committee gave a glowing description of his work when it reported back to the assembled Curators in full meeting. It said:

> Your committee is unanimous in the opinion that if Prof. Hyer had the facilities he ought to have, he could easily put our university in the very front rank on the lines of his special department. . . . The results of his patient study and careful investigation are sought for and complimentary notices are given both in England and America. This department needs apparatus. So much more could be done if it were well equipped.[107]

Second Attempt to Elect a New Regent

When the Curators assembled five weeks later in Waco to try for a second time to elect a Regent, their first ballot was inconclusive. The twenty-one votes were spread among six candidates. Obviously the Curators did not come with a predetermined plan to elect anyone in particular, and it was probably a surprise when Hyer emerged as the high man with five votes. Apparently without a campaign in behalf of anyone, the impression Hyer had made at the preceding session had caused five of them to ask the question, "Why cannot this unassuming, brilliant man—who has brought attention to the University and is also a dedicated churchman—be Regent?" Once the ice was broken, the result was immediate. The other Curators coalesced around Hyer, and he was elected. The secretary promptly notified Prof. Hyer in Georgetown of his election by telephone. They were disappointed, however, when he reported back that Hyer declined to accept.[108]

Hyer's negative decision was as immediate as that of his election. It seems to have been almost instinctive. Beginning with this refusal, one gets the impression throughout the rest of Hyer's career that he genuinely did not want to be a chief executive officer. He was by choice a teacher and researcher caught up in circumstances he did not devise and would have preferred to avoid.

Four further ballots were taken in an evening session without an election. No further action was taken with regard to the regency during the academic year 1897–1898, and Dr. Allen handled the Regent's responsibilities.

Hyer Reluctantly Accepts the Regency

The weakness of the Regent's office by mid-1898 is exemplified clearly in the pattern of events from 1889 to 1898. Beginning in the former year, one Regent, Heidt, is in effect invited to resign. The office is held for half a year by the faculty chair (McLean), only to have a disputed election at the end of that time, with the election of the principal candidate (Chappell) being nullified after one day. The faculty chair (McLean) serves the following year and is then elected without much enthusiasm on the part of the Curators. He, in turn, is summarily forced to resign in 1897, only to have the next person elected (Pritchett) refuse the position. A special meeting of the Curators, held a month later in Waco, elects a well-respected faculty member (Hyer), who refuses the office. The faculty chair (Allen) leads the institution again for another year. During these happenings, the largest construction project in the school's history is planned and put into execution by the Trustees with the cooperation and support of the Curators and faculty. The regency has little or no role in its implementation.

This background for the election in 1898 is necessary if one is to understand the pressure on Hyer to accept the verdict of the Curators when informed that he had once again been selected to lead the University. They had taken only two ballots to reach their result. The first had been 14 to 3 in his favor over Allen. Though this result would have ordinarily been sufficient to signify election, a second ballot was held, presumably to obtain unanimity. It was 16 to 1 in favor of Hyer. He was declared elected. He appeared in the afternoon and indicated his acceptance.[109]

On hearing of the election, the faculty met in called session "on the grounds of the New Building." It adopted a resolution stating that it had heard "with pleasure" of the election of Prof. Hyer to the regency and assured him of its "hearty support and cooperation."[110] Hyer's election, accepted "reluctantly," was announced that evening to the community at the graduation ceremony of the Ladies' Annex.

The first faculty meeting with Hyer in the chair met the next day. Thus began the thirteen-year tenure of Robert Stewart Hyer. It was to bring the greatest crisis in the history of the University to date, removing from it the Central university designation and leaving it searching for an appropriate mission to replace it.

10 Expansion during the Hyer Years (1898–1911)

Population Change and Southwestern's Future

According to the federal census of 1870, 1,573 people were being served by the Georgetown post office.[1] Clara Scarbrough states that probably fewer than 500 lived within the town itself. During the decade of the 1870s, the arrival of Southwestern, the integration of the city into the economics of the great cattle drives, and the establishment of a railroad connection with neighboring communities caused population to more than double in the town proper to 1,355 in 1880. Georgetown was also the connecting point of stagecoaches and mule trains going north and west. Though it appeared for a while that the town might be on the way to becoming a city of some size, the population surge slacked off around 1890, and the total hovered in the range of 2,400 to 2,900 for the next thirty years.[2]

The major reason for the loss of population momentum was that during those years the economic impetus of the county shifted east toward Taylor. Cotton replaced cattle as the dominant product of the area, and the main railroad lines went through Taylor, not Georgetown, to carry cotton and passengers to Houston, Dallas, and Austin. The Georgetown line was of secondary importance and did not connect directly with any major urban locale. The importance of Georgetown as a connecting point for stagecoaches and mule trains also vanished as railroads were built to cities farther north and west.

The leveling off in population growth over the thirty-year period created the impression in some minds that Georgetown was becoming a backwater community and that the future of the county lay with Taylor. Though in 1880 the federal census had not even differentiated the population of Taylor from its county precinct, which had a population of 2,543, by 1910 it had been recognized as a municipality with a population of 5,629. It had become the largest town in the county.

Meanwhile the population of Texas was increasing rapidly. It grew from 1,592,000 in 1880 to 3,897,000 in 1910, a population increase of 3.0 percent per year over the thirty-year period. Though much of the increase was rural, Texas cities were growing, and the state was developing some significant urban areas. In 1910 San Antonio, traditionally the largest city in Texas, was still the largest with 97,000, but not by much. Since 1880, Dallas had grown from 10,000 to 92,000, Houston from 17,000 to 79,000, and Fort Worth from 7,000 to 73,000. El Paso and Austin completed the lineup of largest cities with 39,000 and 30,000, respectively. If the future of the county seemed to lie with Taylor, the future of Texas seemed to lie with those urban areas. Georgetown was out of the main line of development. The static student enrollment pattern of Southwestern from about 1887 to 1898 roughly paralleled the static population pattern of Georgetown after 1890.

Hyer's Response to the Situation

As a man of facts, Regent Hyer was aware of these particulars when he assumed office—the population stasis of Georgetown in the face of the heavy population increase in Texas, the failure of Southwestern to increase its enrollment significantly, and the development of strong urban areas as the foci of forward movement in Texas. Indications do not suggest that his knowledge of these facts means that he entered his work with a concerted program to remedy the situation of Southwestern, but rather that, as a scientist accustomed to responding to objective evidence, he would be willing to entertain new options for the University not theretofore considered.

Hyer's modus operandi during his thirteen-year tenure was both that of taking personal initiative himself and of responding to the initiatives of others. In some instances he moved ahead resolutely, following his own sense of direction. He proposed new ideas and suggested changes in the customary practices of the University. As often as not, however, he reacted to ideas and developments that occurred independently of him, embracing them when he became convinced of their utility.

His years as Regent saw major accomplishments: the abandonment of "schools" for "departments" in the organization of the faculty and in the degree structure of the University; the use of "courses" to describe the curricular offerings; the broadening of the institution's instructional concept; the establishment of coeducation for male and female students; the initiation of an academic and administrative staff system; the professionalization of the library; the fashioning of the first real endowment campaign for the University; the implementation of a major building program to bring campus facilities into line with needs; the simplification of the Board structure by a revision of the charter; and the founding of a medical school in Dallas. His last effort was to try to move the entire University to Dallas.

Hyer experienced a remarkable degree of success in working through these issues until faced with the last one—the removal of the University to Dallas. He failed in that endeavor and, because of it, unintentionally helped destroy the Central University concept when he became the first President of a new Methodist university in that city. Of course, he had originally intended to strengthen the idea by moving Southwestern there, where he felt it could be successfully implemented. In his mind, it had already lost its real meaning in Georgetown.

Hyer's Personality and Character

Hyer was a many-sided person, a first-class scientist but also a dedicated churchman, friendly to everyone but also somewhat "aloof and reticent," a leader because of his natural talents but an unwilling one, a theoretical thinker who turned out beautiful woodcarvings with his hands. Like Mood, he was somewhat formal in his contacts with other people, though his careful attention to everyone in conversation and his unfailing desire to be helpful dispelled any notion that he was proud. When once asked why he listened to other people so intently, he replied: "No one can know all sides of a subject, and often you can learn something new by just listening to very simple people."[3] He was "a Southern gentleman of the 'old school,'" says his daughter, "dignified . . . in both manner of speech and dress." Nevertheless, he had a subtle but very keen sense of humor.[4] Though the students in private called him "King Bob," he was popular with them. When he and his wife returned home from the Ecumenical Conference in London in 1901, where he was a delegate, they gathered at the depot at 11:30 P.M. to shout, "Welcome home, King Bob!"[5]

In spite of the fact that Hyer was a skilled writer, he disliked writing letters and did not leave the wealth of intimate information about himself available today on Mood and Cody from their letters. One of the first things he did as Regent was to purchase a typewriter and to employ Alec Mood, Dr. Mood's youngest son, as secretary to use it. Thereafter he dictated most of his letters. He liked all of the new inventions except the telephone. He liked to talk to people face-to-face.[6]

His reserved manner was in part the result of a fractured upbringing, making him somewhat reticent to expose himself too quickly or too openly. Though he spent his early years at home with his family in Charleston, South Carolina, he had been born in Oxford, Georgia, the home of his mother, who returned there to give birth to her son. The daughter of a Methodist minister, Laura Stewart Hyer taught him early that the two most important things in life were religion and education.[7] He joined the two in his professional life. At Southwestern he would receive many offers to leave his ill-paid professor's position for one more lucrative elsewhere, twice being courted by the University of Texas. He refused both times, "his reason being that he believed his place in education was through the church—rather than the state."[8]

A major turning point in his life was the death of his mother on his fourteenth birthday, October 18, 1874. During her long illness, his grandmother Hyer in Atlanta cared for him and his sister. He received his elementary education while with her. After his mother's death, his father, a railroad engineer, apprenticed him to a watchmaker and engraver in Atlanta. He learned to engrave and to do lettering in gold and silver. His Uncle Joe, however, his mother's brother, felt that his intelligence called for him to be more than a tradesman and made it possible for him to leave the apprenticeship. He took him into his home at Oxford, where he was a professor at Emory College. Young Bob entered Emory and lived for five years with his uncle's family.[9]

At Emory he became an outstanding student. He graduated with first honors in the class of 1881. The records show that out of seventy grades, none was below 97, and forty-three were 100. He became an assistant in physics and received his master's degree in that field after two summer sessions. Though he and his father saw little of each other, William Hyer was proud of his son and gave him a railroad watch as a graduation present—closed face, yellow gold, very thick, with a gold chain. Bob was proud of the gift and carried it the rest of his life.

Though he had been reared under the strict religious influence of the Stewart family, he did not feel converted according to the Methodist understanding of his era until his senior year in college. He joined the Church one spring evening during "a protracted meeting." The text of the preacher on that occasion, "The harvest is past; the summer is ended and we are not saved," was one of his favorites for the rest of his life. He taught a Sunday School class most of his life and asked to teach two classes in Bible at SMU in addition to his physics classes after his resignation there as President.[10]

Hyer's Intellectual Formation

Hyer had decided long before he graduated from Emory that he would pursue a scientific career and followed a path leading to it in his studies. Nevertheless, he was unique in one particular. In a day when many Christians anathematized Darwin, he was a devoted Darwinist. Ray Hyer Brown says that she heard him remark several times that "he considered it *[Origin of Species]* the greatest scientific work in English." She quotes a passage from Dr. Herbert Gambrell, an SMU professor, about it.

> As a boy he [Hyer] had displayed unusual mechanical ability, but it was in college that he chanced upon the book that was to fix his determination. The book was Darwin's "Origin of Species," which was published in England some twenty years before. It had created a great furor in Great Britain, and it was destined to bring about terrific struggles between dogmatic theologians and scientists on both sides of the Atlantic. To young Hyer it was a door leading into another world. He read the book and re-read it. He once told me that there was a time when he could have substantially reproduced the entire work from memory. His mind was made up. He would be a professor of science. He would apply the method of Darwin to the teaching of science, but not in a great university. His life was to be spent among the people of the South, and in colleges of his own denomination.[11]

Mrs. Brown says that she has been told that while Regent McLean used to preach against evolution in chapel, Dr. Hyer would be explaining it in his geology classes. Some of the preachers over the state became agitated about his teaching of evolution, and, after his election as Regent, one of them circulated a petition to have him discharged from the University and from the Church on grounds of heresy. Whether or not it was ever presented is unknown, but the Board of Curators, taking note of the disturbance, addressed the issue at its midyear meeting in 1900. The following resolution was unanimously adopted.

> *Whereas* rumors have been circulated in certain sections of our state concerning instruction given in the department of Natural Science and
>
> *Whereas* we have heard the fullest and frankest statement on the part of the professor [Hyer] of that department concerning his methods and substance of teaching showing the harmony between God's two books, Nature and Revelation,
>
> *Therefore be it Resolved* that in the opinion of this Board of Curators the method of instruction in the department of Science is reverential towards the Bible as the revealed will and word of God and not in conflict with the fundamental teachings of our holy religion, and constantly recognizes the Scriptures as the only and sufficient rule of our faith and practice.[12]

One of his former students, says Mrs. Brown, told her that the greatest sermon she ever heard was one delivered by Hyer entitled "Why I as a Scientist, believe in God."[13]

Hyer Comes to Southwestern

Hyer was twenty-two when he came to Southwestern. Instrumental in bringing him there was Dr. Morgan Callaway, professor of English, first a teacher at Southwestern and later a distinguished professor of English at the University of Texas. Callaway had been a senior at Emory when Hyer was a freshman, and Oxford, Georgia, was his hometown as well. They had seen a lot of each other during summer vacations and became fast friends. They belonged to the same fraternity. Dr. C. C. Cody was also an Emory man, as was the Rev. Will Nelms, a Texas minister. Hyer and Nelms were also friends at Emory.[14]

Hyer was homesick and disappointed when he arrived

in Georgetown in 1882, for it "seemed such a barren little town—few trees, little houses and muddy streets when it rained." He missed the beautiful trees and flowers of Georgia more than anything else. He taught geology, chemistry, biology, and physics, in addition to carrying some classes in the Fitting School. He said that as a teacher he did not occupy a professorial "chair" so much as a "divan." In time, says his daughter, "he began to like the people in Georgetown and the people over the state that were interested in Southwestern, for he felt they were men with vision and he soon caught the same interest and enthusiasm."[15]

During his first summer vacation, he returned to Georgia, married an earlier acquaintance from Savannah, and returned to Georgetown. The following summer his wife returned to Savannah and gave birth to a baby. Both she and the baby died. He could not go to the funeral because he did not have the money to make the trip. "He had sent every cent he had saved to his wife's family for her expenses."[16]

In 1887 Hyer married again. He had come to know Maggie Lee Hudgins in a physics class two years earlier as the best student in his class. At the time of her graduation in 1886, she won the two medals offered to girls that year. Though they were very much in love and were congenial in most things, he was much stricter than she in social matters. Her parties and dancing stopped when she began to go out with him, and after their marriage she worked to change her thinking to conform to his views. They were married in Waco at the home of Dr. and Mrs. Horace Bishop. Mrs. Bishop was Maggie's aunt, making Bishop himself Hyer's uncle by marriage. This fact became important during the removal controversy, when Bishop, a recognized power among the preachers, supported Hyer's position on the issue.

Since Maggie was only nineteen when they married and Hyer was seven years older, he practically taught her, says his daughter, the arts of housekeeping. He had been brought up with girls and "knew how to do almost everything about a house."[17] Following old Southern custom, Maggie always called him Mr. Hyer. It is interesting to note that, whereas she was crushed when in the 1890s he refused the tempting offers from the University of Texas in Austin, she was opposed to leaving Southwestern in 1910–1911 for Dallas.

Hyer had little interest in personal encomiums or in financial gain. He and his family lived very frugally. When the University could not buy equipment he needed in physics, he would somehow buy it himself.[18] The Hyer family was one of the few in town with a bathtub with running water, but he had made it himself. He used his mechanical dexterity for the benefit of the University as well. During the first few years after the Main Building was completed, coal-burning stoves heated it. Finally, when there was enough money to put in steam heat, Hyer went to St. Louis to select the equipment. An expert engineer was sent to install the plant. He was paid by the day, with some local labor to help. Hyer followed the process carefully. He soon discovered that the engineer was making many mistakes that had to be torn out. The work was going slowly, and the money to complete it was diminishing. Finally, he could tolerate it no longer. He paid the engineer up to date and let him go. He retained the two laborers, put on overalls, and completed the installation himself. It was finished in time for the building to be cleaned up before school started.[19]

Little wonder that the bright, dedicated, unostentatious young scientist, conducting radio wave and X-ray experiments, soon came to the notice of Curators, Trustees, and educational leaders in the state. The Dudley Snyders invited him to spend a summer in Mexico at their gold mining camp high in the mountains not far from the West Coast in 1895. Two years later he made the trip to Mexico with Heber Stone already referred to in Chapter VIII. Of course, both Trustees wanted the benefit of his knowledge for their enterprises.[20]

The new thirty-eight-year-old Regent received his first honorary degree from Baylor University in 1898. Though in later years he received other honorary degrees, he always wore the yellow and green of Baylor on his hood.[21]

Constructing the Main Building

When Hyer became Regent, he found a challenging task awaiting him—to complete the Main Building just now underway. The final contract had been let at the same meeting where he was elected. As a faculty member, he had earlier been given the opportunity to review the plans presented in 1896. Now he became in effect the University supervisor of the work. Undoubtedly he and Lockett consulted regularly as they saw the building go up, for Lockett says that he visited the place daily to watch its progress.[22]

Hyer's hand can probably be seen in the distribution of the work space in the building. He may have been the one who suggested at the outset that physics needed to be on the first floor so that piers could be constructed for the instruments of precision, as was done. The first floor was

The University Building (Administration Building, Cullen Building) in 1904. Hyer operated as Regent out of his physics office adjacent to the physics lab on the first floor at the southeast corner of the building. During the Fleming years, it once again became the Office of the President. Southwestern University, Special Collections.

devoted almost wholly to the departments of physics and chemistry. Physics had a large lecture room on the east side measuring 999 sq. ft. and a laboratory of 1,809 sq. ft. In addition, it had a workshop and an engine and dynamo room. Chemistry on the east side had a lecture room of 1,350 sq. ft., a storeroom of 459 sq. ft., and an analytical laboratory of 999 sq. ft. It also had a balance room and an assay room. The only major effect on the floor plans of Hyer's becoming Regent was that the office of the physics professor now became the office of the Regent, who served in both capacities. It is still the office of the President today, though physics is elsewhere. The chapel/auditorium in the center of the second and third floors measured 86\' x 67\' and had society halls on each side, so arranged that they could be opened onto the chapel, giving it thereby a seating capacity of over 1,500. The third story had three rooms on the east side set apart for the library. In addition to the rooms already mentioned, there were fourteen large recitation rooms in the building.[23]

On the second floor were reception rooms in which female students could await the beginning of recitations under the care of matrons. They ascended to the upper floors on their own set of stairs on the west side, whose steps had a different rise and depth. Women's fashions supposedly demanded that their steps be not as tall and have a longer tread so that fourteen steps on the women's side equaled thirteen for the equivalent staircase on the men's side.[24] Though the interior of the building today is very different from what it was when it was constructed, the stairs today are just the same.

Built in the Romanesque style of southern France made popular by Henry Hobson Richardson (1838–1886), the building was a massive structure of native white limestone with two towers in front, a larger and taller square one with a steeple on the southwest corner and a smaller rounded one on the southeast corner. A square turret with lattices surmounted the center of the roof over the chapel, allowing the air in the attic to escape. The walls on the first floor supporting most of the weight of the building reached a width of three feet and were made of rubble. There was no structural steel or iron in the building. Large windows, wide halls, and 15-foot ceilings on the first floor and 13½-foot ceilings on the second and third accommodated the breezes in hot weather. The height of the auditorium ceiling was 34½ feet.

When completed the building was said to be the finest educational structure in the South. Though constructed on shifting soil that has been the bane of several subsequent campus buildings, it is still as solid today as when it was built. The Main Building, as it was called then, the Cullen Building today, transformed the image of Southwestern University in the minds of campus denizens and visitors. It was more than a building. It was a symbol for the University of quality, of serious purpose, and of stability. It was the anchor around which the new campus developed. Without it, the University probably would not have survived in Georgetown.

Financial Analysis of the Construction

In spite of the care with which the Trustees had addressed the financing of the building (see Chapter IX), the money needed to keep construction going was slow coming in. The Trustees had been very specific in insisting that the building be built in phases, with the next phase not to be initiated unless all the money was in hand to complete the one in progress. When they met in mid-1899, the first floor had been completed and all bills paid, but the next phase was problematical. Total remaining pledges amounted to $11,748.52, of which only $3,419.43 had been paid.[25]

When the Board met to consider how to carry on the work, it authorized borrowing up to $15,000 in $1,000 notes at 10 percent per annum. Most of the money, however, was not borrowed from banks or other lending agencies but from persons closely connected with the University—teachers, Trustees, and friends. They were mostly local people to whom the project was so important that they risked their savings to support it. Among the teachers purchasing bonds were Hyer, Cody, Young, and Pegues. Among the townspeople were M. B. Lockett, A. A. Booty, and five women, including Mary Sinex, the wife of the financial agent, and Mary Sanders, widow of Professor Sanders. Within the first two weeks of July they and other individuals bought bonds totaling $13,300 in amounts from ranging from $300 to $1,000. The two Georgetown banks purchased $3,000, overshooting the $15,000 for a total of $16,300.[26] Several other purchasers added to the amount in the next few months. Most of the individual bondholders were not wealthy people. They were ordinary people so committed to the building project that when it faltered financially in mid-course, they took it upon themselves to keep construction going. In addition to the sale of bonds, the Executive Committee sold off fourteen pieces of land or real estate for a total of $8,460.77 that was applied to the construction.[27]

By spring 1900, the building was nearing completion. Without funds for new classroom equipment, teachers brought their furniture from the old campus. Pews for the chapel, however, had to be purchased. Inasmuch as there was no cash on hand for the transaction, five persons, Hyer, Cody, Young, Moore, and Sinex, obligated themselves to a Grand Rapids, Michigan, firm to pay one of the three notes averaging $436.93 each should the Board of Trustees not subsequently take responsibility for the obligation.[28]

The Executive Committee met with Flume & Waterson at the building site on April 23, 1900. After inspecting the building, they adjourned to Lockett's store, where they agreed to receive the building and to pay the remaining $3,406.50 due within thirty days. At a meeting on May 26, 1900, they reported that the total cost of the building was $53,638.30. Indebtedness was $21,317.30. Against the indebtedness were listed subscriptions totaling $14,238.81, mostly from persons pledging to the Guarantee and the Cash Funds, and cash on hand of $1,962.21. Total indebtedness not covered by assets was $5,116.28.[29] This amount was less than that at the conclusion of the construction of the Annex building, twelve years earlier.

1902 as a Benchmark

The 1902 report of the Trustees, two years after the completion of the Main Building, is an important benchmark for understanding University construction and financial developments during the next decade. Soon after that meeting an unprecedented building movement began that would see the Annex almost doubled in size, a Medical Department with a new building established in Dallas, land purchased north of the Main Building for the construction of a new men's dormitory, the completion of that residence facility (Mood Hall), and planning for a new Memorial Administration and Library Building on a grander scale than anything theretofore contemplated.

Whereas up until then administrative officers, Curators, and Trustees had played their hand close to the vest and insisted on paying off prior obligations before accepting new ones, their policy changed. They decided that the slow, one-big-building-a-decade approach followed to this point was inadequate and that if Southwestern was ever to attain full university stature, it had to construct a campus worthy of the concept and build it quickly. The gains to be made by constructing a full university campus immediately outweighed the possible deleterious consequences of large-scale deficit spending. Both Hyer and Lockett were advocates of this policy and, apparently, did not have much trouble persuading the other decision-makers to embrace it as well. Hyer was moving from success to success in University accomplishments, and the accelerated building program, it was thought, would be a success as well.

Total Southwestern indebtedness when this new approach to construction began in 1902 was $12,404.34. All of it, except for a $30.00 annuity payment, had come as a result of the construction of the new building: $10,337.69 was owed on bonds, mostly to the individuals previously mentioned, $1,500.00 was owed to the Sanford Gibbs loan fund, and $536.65 to the Endowment fund.[30] The Trustees were realistic, and began a process of winnowing out pledges where persons asked to be relieved of their promises or where they were unlikely to pay. Following the normal pattern of the past, however, the Trustees would have found another way to cover the indebtedness in a few years. Certainly they could not have paid it out of endowment, for there was less than a thousand dollars in that fund, including the little note owed to it referenced above. John M. Moore was barely exaggerating when he wrote a letter to the *Texas Christian Advocate* on July 17, 1902, saying: "I must speak out for Southwestern. . . . What has Texas Methodism done for this institution in the thirty years of its existence? . . . There is not one cent of endowment."[31]

Hyer's Endowment Emphasis

While big plans were being made for buildings, Hyer was also emphasizing the need for Southwestern to acquire an endowment. In his first report to the Curators in 1899, he pointed out that collegiate work is much more expensive than preparatory work and demands a large endowment. A year later he added that "no school of college grade can exist without an endowment, and we hope this may be made a strong emphasis." A reduction in income from the Annual Conferences in 1901 brought forth from him a statement that Southwestern needs an endowment, the lack of which may sooner or later jeopardize its very existence. "Of the eight institutions of [Southern] Methodism ranked as colleges by the General Board of Education," he writes, "Southwestern University—while having the largest attendance, giving the largest amount of free tuition and educating the largest number of young preachers, is the only one of the list that has no endowment. . . . How much longer so many good bricks can be made with so little straw we will not attempt to answer."[32]

Apparently Hyer's campaign attracted attention, for ten articles or letters to the editor of the *Texas Christian Advocate* from the year 1902, pasted by Cody into one of his scrapbooks, contain the word "endowment" in titles referring to Southwestern. One of the letters by the Rev. J. E. Harrison, President of San Antonio Woman's College, said that "it is high time to endow Southwestern." All of the articles and letters took for granted that Southwestern had no endowment.[33]

As a result of Hyer's prodding and the interest manifested in the newspaper articles, a special session of the Board of Curators was called for October 1, 1902, to adopt a Plan for the Endowment of Southwestern University. Though the Curators labored all day, discussing and rejecting one solution after another for raising it, they came up with little more than asking the Annual Conferences to raise their contributions to Southwestern for operating expenses.[34]

Two years later Hyer came to both Boards with something he thought was more substantial. He reported that the J. I. Campbell family of Houston had made a gift of $25,000 to endow a Chair of History in memory of the late J. I. Campbell. He called it "the first gift towards endowment, and, if we mistake not, the largest gift ever made by any Methodist in the state for any cause of our Church." Unfortunately, he had to report the following year that the gift had been jeopardized by unfortunate circumstances having befallen the Campbell Lumber Company.[35]

But if the Campbell gift did not bear the fruit expected, another letter of J. E. Harrison did. He sent a letter to the *Texas Christian Advocate* in 1904 suggesting the endowment of a chair in physics named after Hyer. Hyer proposed a modification of the plan. He suggested setting up a series of student scholarships named after Francis Asbury Mood. His plan was that each District Conference in Texas would endow a $1,000 Mood Scholarship. He said that he had already received good support from the districts where he had presented the plan and hoped the others would fall in line. Harrison accepted the modification and said that he would undertake to secure the seven scholarships from the districts in his own Annual Conference. If all the Annual Conferences did likewise, it would produce forty scholarships.[36] The exact results of these efforts are not clearly specified in surviving records, but Mood Scholarships are mentioned from time to time.

Three years later, on February 7, 1907, Harrison made another proposal in the *Texas Christian Advocate.* He suggested the formation of a $100,000 Club, with 100 people contributing $1,000 each, of whom he would be the first, giving $200 per year in five installments. The issue caught fire, and the newspaper was able to report on August 1 that 50 persons had subscribed to it. Bishop Warren A. Candler, who had been appointed to hold the Annual Conferences in the fall, came early and worked industriously to complete the campaign. Eighty-two subscriptions were reported by October 17 and 88 a week later. William Wiess, a Beaumont Trustee, wrote to the *Advocate* in late 1907 saying that he had just talked with Candler and felt confident that within another week the entire amount would be subscribed. He called on wealthy Methodist laymen to step forward to finish it.[37] It had 114 subscribers when finally completed.[38]

Harrison's $100,000 Club campaign was the first carried out expressly for endowment. A marble tablet was placed on a wall just inside the southwest entry of the first floor of the Main Building with the names of the donors engraved on it in the order in which they fulfilled their pledges. It is still there today, and 35 names appear on it.

Building Up the Academic Program and the Library

Hyer believed in a strong academic program and moved immediately after his election to improve it where he could. His first effort was to bring the Southwestern catalog into line with those of other first-class colleges. He began by assembling the catalogs of other colleges and universities throughout the country. He checked their entrance requirements, credit hours for degrees, and how they described their work.[39] The result was a listing of Southwestern professors and offerings by departments, a description of degrees in terms of departmental requirements, and a listing of teaching matter by courses. Theretofore it had been principally by books to be studied. The thirteen departments were Mathematics; German; Spanish; French;

Margaret Mood McKennon. Employed by Hyer as Southwestern's first professional librarian in 1903, Mrs. McKennon served 41 years, retiring in 1944. From the 1933 *Sou'wester*.

Physics; Logic, Psychology, and Ethics; History and Political Economy; English; Latin; Greek; Chemistry; Geology; and Biology. Bible and Theology would have made fifteen departments, but they were listed with "courses arranged" rather than with a regular lineup of courses. Degrees were described as requiring from fifteen to nineteen hours of recitation time per week. The Master of Arts was made a postgraduate degree rather than simply an intensification of the A.B. degree, the Master of Science degree was instituted, and entrance requirements for new students were tightened up.[40]

Having served for a time as faculty supervisor of the library before the appointment of a professional librarian, Hyer was a great believer in the library as one of the important elements of a university. In several of his reports he states that a college without a library and laboratories is not really a college. He put his belief into practice in 1903 with the appointment of Margaret Mood McKennon as the first librarian contracted specifically for that job.

Mrs. McKennon, daughter of the founder, was an A.B. graduate of 1886 and afterwards a student at the University of Chicago, where she took some library work. Hyer states that she came "when re-arrangements and [a] new classification were necessary to bring our library methods in line with approved standards."[41] She immediately began to catalog the library books according to the Dewey Decimal System, still in use today, and Hyer could report in 1910 that Southwestern had nearly twenty thousand books. Over the years Mrs. McKennon became one of the most valuable and longest-serving faculty members in Southwestern history.

On the occasion of the meeting of the Southwestern 50+ Society in 2000, Mrs. Dorothy Shell Bunting, who attended Southwestern in the late 1920s, wrote that she worked for Mrs. McKennon in the library during her sophomore and junior years. She says that she "loved Mrs. McKennon. As my employer, she gave me a present, a vanity case. I treasured it so that even now with the case worn out, the jeweled top with the mirror inside has a place on a sunny window in my apartment in a retirement home. Her kindness to me is one of my precious memories." Mrs. McKennon served forty-one years, retiring in 1944.

Commenting in 1904 on his attempt to improve the quality of instruction during his first five years, Hyer said that the faculty had been enlarged by four new professors, the library had been created, the facilities in the physics and chemistry laboratories had more than doubled, the equipment of the Annex had been greatly improved, the entrance requirements had been advanced, and the courses of study had been broadened. In short, he said, "we have grown in all things that go to make up a College save in the attendance of students."[42]

In addition to the procurement of Mrs. McKennon for the library, Hyer employed two other persons who would have long careers at Southwestern. One was Randolph Wood Tinsley, who came in 1903. Though he came as a scientist with a B.S. from the University of Virginia, he gradually moved into administrative work and, before his retirement in 1936, he had served as Registrar for nine years, Bursar for six years, and Assistant to the President for eleven years. He served thirty-three years in all.

The other long-term faculty member who came under Hyer was Frederick C. A. Lehmberg, Professor of French and German. With a B.A. (1903) and an M.A. (1912) from Southwestern, he studied as a graduate student in various universities in the states and abroad, including the Universities of Texas, Chicago, and Colorado. In Europe he did graduate work at the Universities of Heidelberg and Munich. He taught twenty-six years.

Assessing academic advance after ten years, Hyer said:

[I]n ten years we have advanced the A.B. admission requirements from seven approved high school units, and the B.S. requirements from four, to the present requirement of fourteen. More than a full year of preparatory work has been added to the A.B. entrance requirements, and two full years have been added to the B.S. requirements. In the case of the latter degree there has been added not only these two years of preparatory work, but also a full year of College work beyond the requirements of 1898."[43]

The Summer Programs

Hyer's concern about enrollment was not simply to add numbers but to increase service. He felt that a university should offer a variety of educational opportunities in addition to regular courses. On this basis he and the faculty developed a substantial summer program that they put into operation just after the turn of the century. The Summer Normal School established in 1888 was already in operation and became a part of the program by default. It was a way of helping public school teachers. To this the faculty added a summer school program to help regularly enrolled students.

Though there is evidence that Cody began thinking about holding a summer school as early as 1894,[44] he did not carry the idea through at that time, and the first summer school, if it can be called such, was a student-run affair. On May 19, 1896, two students appeared before the faculty requesting permission to hold a summer school. Permission was granted, but it was limited to introductory classes and to freshmen. It seems to have been more a tutorial rather than a regular classroom program. Nevertheless, it was successful enough that when another student made the same request a year later permission was once again granted with the same restrictions.[45]

Now the faculty decided to begin a regular, University-run summer school.[46] Beginning with 32 students in 1903–1904, its enrollment increased regularly until 1910–1911, when 128 students attended. Its enrollment fluctuated thereafter, dipping as low as 67 in 1913–1914 and rising as high as 240 in 1923–1924. It would continue each summer until 1954 as a regular feature of the University program, when it was discontinued for lack of profitability in the retrenchment of the 1950s. It was reinstituted on a limited basis in 1969, with teacher pay being calibrated to the number of students taught.

Hyer's particular interest, however, was to add a permanent Summer Institute of Biblical and Theological

Study. This Institute, according to the plan approved by the Curators in 1901, should meet on campus each summer and enroll ministers in the course of study prescribed "for our undergraduate preachers" and such other subjects as may serve them best. It should be self-supporting and managed by a highly respected person.[47]

The first Institute program was held in 1902. Its leader was the Rev. Seth Ward, one of the stellar members of the clergy in Texas, soon to be elected bishop, and for whom a professorship in religion is still named at Southwestern. Outstanding speakers and teachers were brought to campus, and the average annual attendance for its first seven years was 220. Its name was soon changed to the Summer School of Theology and was headed by Dr. Edwin D. Mouzon in 1908–1909 and 1909–1910 just prior to his election as bishop. The events connected with the removal controversy reduced its average attendance to 154 for the next seven years. It continued until 1936–1937, when it was dropped. A summer Pastors' School, more a series of lectures than a course of study, replaced it, but its enrollment, unlike that of the Summer School of Theology, was not officially reported in University records.

Though the original and the revised charters offered the possibility of Southwestern's having a School of Theology, it does not appear that Hyer had this in mind even as an eventuality when he set up the Summer School of Theology. He explained his sentiments very clearly. He said that

> we do not believe in a "Theological School" if by such a term is meant either a distinctively technical school to which students are admitted without advanced standing, or a department of a university in which all ministerial students are segregated in class rooms and boarding halls. Any line of separation between those preparing for the ministry and other professions that is strongly drawn will be to the loss of both "Theologs" and "academics."[48]

Hyer had established a Department of Biblical Literature for undergraduates with six courses in 1900–1901, with a course in Bible required of students for all degrees. A few additional courses were added to the department over the years, but the degree requirement remained the same. The department was divided into two in 1906–1907—Biblical Literature and Practical Theology. The latter consisted of courses in homiletics and pastoral theology. They were obviously designed for preministerial students. These were combined in 1907–1908 into a single Department of Theology with additional courses and two professors. The department was further elaborated in 1908–1909, with John M. Barcus and Edwin D. Mouzon as professors. Nevertheless, the degree requirement in Bible was dropped, entirely for the B.S. and made an option for the A.B. With the election of Mouzon as bishop in 1910 and the resignation of Barcus, the department was scaled back in the number of courses offered in 1910–1911.

Hyer's design for Biblical Literature, Theology, or whatever other name the department was called during his tenure, was to offer or require some degree of biblical literacy for all students and to give the ministerial student enough courses in Bible, Methodism, Christian history, theology, and biblical languages that he—and it was definitely "he" in those years—might gain some of the tools needed for pastoral service. Hyer may have wanted a school of medicine, perhaps eventually one of law, but not of theology. He did not propose this even when such would have been helpful to his overall goal of building a real university.

The School of Fine Arts

The four academic units of the University when Hyer assumed control were the College, the Ladies' Annex, the Fitting School, and the Commercial School. The Commercial School was dropped in 1900–1901 and the School of Fine Arts added in 1902–1903. Theretofore the nomenclature of "school" and "department" had been used as being roughly equivalent to one another. From this point on, though not with immediate consistency, both the terms "school" and "college" would generally be used to denote one of the major academic units of the University. A "department" would be the disciplinary subunit offering majors.

Studies included in the School of Fine Arts at the outset were those arising mainly out of the addition of the Annex in 1878—music, elocution, and art. In those early years the courses were gender-specific, courses only for women, not looked on as academic but primarily as refinements for the cultured woman not pursuing a literary degree. Though by 1903–1904 the primary purpose of these courses was still said to be "the careful cultivation of the aesthetic nature," they were also said to be "an important part of a liberal education," and all candidates for degrees were allowed to include six credits in fine arts out of the total of sixty-four credits required for degrees.

By 1908–1909 students entering any course of study in fine arts were required to have the same fitting school or high school background as candidates for the "literary" degrees and to take two "literary" courses. Upon completion of their work they were known as "graduates" in their course of study—piano, voice, violin, expression, or art (painting)—but they did not receive degrees with titles.

Coeducation

The faculty and Curators had been very emphatic when the Ladies' Annex was established in 1878 that the presence of women at Southwestern did not mean coeducation. To protect them against any male student distraction, the first women's building had been constructed four blocks west of the main campus, and teachers had diligently walked there to hold classes. The second building a decade later had been constructed eight blocks east of the old campus. It combined classrooms with living space. The faculty adopted a resolution shortly after it was occupied stating that "it is the sense of the Faculty that no young man shall receive instruction at the Annex."[49]

Though women were not admitted to candidacy for degrees when first admitted in 1878, this deficiency was quickly remedied, and three women graduated with the B.S. degree in 1883 and one with an A.M. in 1887. Because some men began to desire courses taught only in the Annex, such as instrumental music, vocal music, elocution, and art, the catalog carried a statement for the first time in 1892–1893 that "young men may take these courses as well but do so separately."

The first actual coeducation occurred at the preparatory level. The increasing popularity of public schools created considerable competition for Southwestern, and the redundancy of having separate units for males and females at that level became more and more a financial burden. It was simply not cost-effective. Consequently, the two units were amalgamated in 1892.[50] This amalgamation must have been of the primary units only, for the Fitting School still held separate classes in 1898–1899. The primary unit of preparatory study was dropped in 1895.

The final yielding of university instructional practice to coeducation occurred gradually during Hyer's tenure, without fanfare and without a fiat on the subject. A small step was taken before his time when the catalogs of the College and of the Annex were combined in 1892–1893. After Hyer took over in 1898, his first catalog stated what had been a fact for some years, that though it was originally intended that young ladies should receive instruction in separate classes, instruction in the sciences, which he taught, made that intention difficult to carry out. The Annex did not have laboratories, and young ladies had, therefore, been admitted to laboratory work with males on a regular basis in the Main Building. Circumstances here and there caused exceptions to be made in other classes as well, especially in higher-level classes with their reduced enrollments, until it was agreed that separate classes would be the rule only for the first two years. Hyer assured the Curators in his report of 1899, almost apologetically it seems, that in spite of this development "all have cheerfully yielded to the restraints commonly enforced in young ladies' boarding schools."[51]

The separation-for-the-first-two-years rule was quietly removed two years later in the catalog for 1900–1901. Full coeducation came soon thereafter and was definitively established in the catalog for 1903–1904. It stated that "the present method is that of co-education in all departments."[52] For the first time that year current male and female students were listed together, and the alumni of the institution were not separated in the catalog by gender in the listing of earlier graduates as had been done until then. Males and females were listed together with the appropriate degree obtained by each person. The change included the Fitting School as well, for its male and female students were also listed together.

Two female faculty members, the only women with degrees, were listed as members of the theretofore all-male College faculty in 1905–1906. They were Cora Lee Smith, Ph.B., Instructor in Oratory, and Mrs. Margaret M. McKennon, A.B., Librarian. Smith taught for seven years. Since there was no longer thereafter any rationale for maintaining the Annex as a separate educational unit, all reference to it was dropped except as a housing facility in the catalog for 1907–1908.

Enlargement of the Annex Building

With the completion of the Main Building, Southwestern possessed two buildings on the new campus. Unlike the buildings on the old campus, both were impressive architectural specimens. By 1902 the Annex building was fourteen years old and in need of modernization. Furthermore, female enrollment had outgrown both the original building completed in 1888 and the smaller adjunct building added in 1898. The Trustees addressed both problems.

In 1902 they put in a steam heating system and a laundry. The cost of $4,828.51 did not add to the indebtedness

The Ladies' Annex after its enlargement in 1905–06 by the addition of the wing on the right. The women's gymnasium was on the fourth floor. From the 1940 *Sou'wester.*

of the institution, since the improvements were paid for over the next few years from the earnings of the Annex.[53] Two years later they put in an "electric light plant."[54] With these amenities completed, the Board next authorized a large addition to create more residential space. A contract of $18,300 for the work was signed with the Belford Lumber Company. The entire project was financed through loans. The Board of Trustees authorized the Executive Committee "to use any special funds that this board may now have on hand or that may come to hand to pay for the erection of the addition to the Annex, now under contract and to make a note or notes, in the name of the University, to the treasurer of the Board in trust for such fund, to bear 6% interest per annum."[55]

This action was the first instance of the financing of a large project through loans procured from University funds designated for other uses. Though everything was done in proper form by setting up a repayment schedule on the books with a reasonable rate of interest, the notion of adding more indebtedness to the institution before paying off earlier indebtedness was a new concept. The Trustees adopted this new policy because they felt that the welfare of the institution would be so enhanced by the Annex project that relaxation of the old standards was permissible. Everything seemed to be going so well under the Hyer administration that they were willing to take a risk that would not have earlier been acceptable.

The new addition, when completed, was aesthetically pleasing. Architecturally, it blended into the original design of the building. It added substantially to the housing facilities for women, with the expectation of increased housing revenues. By mid-1907, the Trustees reported that the indebtedness of the University from construction of the Main Building and the enlargement of the Annex was $9,771.58 and $19,230.75, respectively, for a total of $29,002.33.[56]

The Southwestern University Medical College

Though Hyer did not have a specific program in mind when he inherited the leadership of Southwestern, he did have a goal in mind: to make Southwestern the real uni-

Invocation by Rev. John R. Allen at the laying of the cornerstone of Southwestern University Medical College Building, Dallas, Texas, April 3, 1905. A special train of six coaches carrying 325 students from Georgetown attended the ceremony. Southwestern University, Special Collections.

versity in fact that its name betokened. Every step he took was an attempt to move it in that direction—his academic reforms, his stress on endowment, and his ambitious building program. One of his first responsibilities on assuming the regency in mid-1898 was to visit the sponsoring Annual Conferences in the fall. In each he was invited to make a statement. One of the primary sections in that statement was an analysis of the situation of Southwestern vis-à-vis the other institutions of higher learning in the state. Among the fifteen institutions whose data he referenced, Southwestern ranked third in number of collegiate students in 1895–1896. The University of Texas, Texas A&M, Southwestern, and Baylor were the top four, with 335, 320, 271, and 233 students, respectively.[57]

Relatively speaking, Southwestern appeared to be succeeding as a university in terms of numbers, but in most circles student enrollment was not the main criterion by which university status was judged. Before the day of regional accreditation agencies, the major educational agency with which Southwestern was affiliated was the General Board of Education of the Methodist Episcopal Church, South. It had begun to classify Southern Methodist educational institutions in 1898. As late as 1908 only Vanderbilt could be classified as a university, with several major units of professional character in addition to its undergraduate program. Criteria for colleges divided them into two categories. There were, in its ranking, ten Class A colleges, of which Southwestern was one, and five Class B colleges.[58]

Hyer took the problem of attaining university status seriously and began to address it. In 1903 the Board of Curators voted to set up Medical and Law Departments, beginning with medicine. The Board of Trustees did not immediately concur with this action and only agreed to participate in a joint committee to investigate the matter.[59]

A committee of six persons, of which Hyer was a member, was accordingly set up.[60]

According to Samuel Wood Geiser, in his pamphlet recounting the history of medical schools in Dallas during the first decade of the twentieth century, the joint committee approached the head of the University of Dallas medical school about the possibility of establishing an affiliation with it. The University of Dallas, however, was at the time completing an affiliation with Baylor University begun some time earlier. The affiliation was consummated in due time and resulted in the transfer of the University of Dallas medical school to Baylor, establishing the Baylor College of Medicine, which still exists. It moved to Houston in 1943, where it became the educational cornerstone of the Texas Medical Center. The relationship with Baylor University was severed in 1969, and it became an independent institution.

Having failed in its first approach, the joint committee then contacted persons connected with the projected Texas College of Physicians and Surgeons in Dallas. The negotiations were successful, and their school in due course became the medical department of Southwestern University.[61]

Lockett describes the decision to affiliate with the projected Texas College of Physicians and Surgeons in more personal terms. He says that the Rev. John R. Nelson, a prominent member of the Board of Curators, "got it into his head that Southwestern must have a medical school." He was a member of the joint committee and visited both Waco and Dallas to find an appropriate site. Lockett says that soon thereafter he received a telegram announcing that the Board of Trustees would meet in Dallas. He went and attended the meeting. A few doctors spoke to them all day [June 24], he says, about the need to act with dispatch and stated that they would "see the whole thing through without expense to the University, that it was a great opportunity and that we would be foolish not to make the effort." Nevertheless, Lockett was not convinced. He was one of three Trustees who in private discussions had doubts about the wisdom of establishing a medical school. He says that when he refused to vote for it, Nelson became very agitated and asked, "What is the matter with you, Lockett?," but, he continues, "This is one act of which I am very proud."[62]

Most of the Trustees, however, were convinced and voted for it at the end of the day. They approved the report of the joint committee to make the projected Texas College of Physicians and Surgeons of Dallas an organic part of Southwestern University. It became the Southwestern University Medical Department in Curator records but the Southwestern University Medical College to the outside world.[63]

The contract entered into by the University and the Medical College carefully protected Southwestern against liability for any debts the Medical College might accrue. This stipulation was one of the features that probably influenced Abraham Flexner in his 1909 report on medical education in the United States to refer to the Medical College as "nominally the medical department of Southwestern University."[64]

Background of the Medical College

In his report to the Board of Curators in mid-1904, Hyer included an undated (but surely early June 1903) letter from the leadership of the projected Texas College of Physicians and Surgeons to the joint committee explaining the origin of its school. It says that because of the existence of a number of medical schools in Dallas with which the "better element" of the medical profession in Dallas did not wish to have contact, a number of physicians finally decided to buy one of them and to run it themselves. In order not to multiply medical schools, they bought the Dallas Medical College, conducted by Dr. H. L. McNew. They dismissed all but two of the faculty and reorganized it completely, though keeping the name. The letter lists the Board of Directors and a long list of participating physicians. It states that they are a harmonious body, have spotless records, and "represent the best element of the profession." It boasts that they control practically all of the clinical facilities of the city. The College has a lease on a new brick structure that it will occupy until building a permanent one. It also has on its Board a large number of representative businessmen and important persons of the city. Sixteen are listed. "The institution as it now stands is practically a new school," says the letter, "with new Faculty and new funds, and new facilities, but we have felt that it was best to retain the name and charter of the Dallas Medical College, otherwise we would have increased the number of Medical Schools in Dallas."[65]

Thus, the projected name of the school, the Texas College of Physicians and Surgeons, was abandoned before the school was ever organized. It was organized under the charter of the school the physicians had recently purchased, the Dallas Medical College. Nevertheless, it never operated under that name because of its immediate affiliation with Southwestern University before any classes were held. Its letterhead carried the title by which it became known: Southwestern University Medical College.

First Two Years of Operation

Hyer's report on the new Medical College after one year of operation is very positive. He states that the Dean is Dr. John O. McReynolds, A.M., LL.D., M.D. He is, says Hyer, a noted eye specialist, originator of a special treatment being practiced in all the great hospitals. It is known in medical circles as the McReynolds operation.[66] McReynolds was indeed a reputable person. He graduated in 1891 from the College of Physicians and Surgeons of Baltimore and also studied in the Bellevue Hospital Medical College of New York. He had earlier obtained most of his education from the University of Kentucky, formerly known as Transylvania University. The LL.D. was conferred upon him by Transylvania.[67]

Hyer says that he has recently visited the school and talked with every medical student in the senior class. All of them, he says, have taken three years of work elsewhere before entering the Southwestern University Medical College for their fourth year and are very complimentary about the instruction they have received. Eleven of them graduated at the recent Commencement exercise in April. A piece of land has been secured, he continues, for a new building, and the Dean hopes to construct it during the forthcoming year. He will undertake a fund-raising campaign immediately to finance it.[68] That Dean, John O. McReynolds, would become a good friend of Hyer, staying often as a guest in his home in Georgetown and ultimately becoming one of the leading figures in persuading him to move Southwestern itself to Dallas.[69]

McReynolds was as good as his word. He donated a lot at the corner of Bryan and Hall Streets for the new building, the cornerstone for which was laid on April 3, 1905, at the time of the second annual Commencement.[70] The laying of the cornerstone became a festive event for Southwestern. A special train of six coaches brought 325 students and residents from Georgetown to Dallas. Five streetcars carried the students from the First Methodist Church, where they ate, to the place where the cornerstone was to be laid. The ceremony itself was under the direction of Dr. John R. Nelson, now pastor in Georgetown. Mayor Bryan T. Barry of Dallas delivered an address, and Bishop E. E. Hoss spoke for the Church. Dr. Hyer spoke briefly, expressing his pleasure in the event.[71]

At its meeting in mid-1905, the Board of Trustees approved an agent for the Medical Department to solicit funds for the building and equipment. It was careful, however, to instruct those responsible not to make the University liable for the construction in any way and enjoined the department from taking any action that would bring obligations or indebtedness on Southwestern.[72] The building was completed in a little over six months. Though Geiser says it was dedicated on October 3, the actual date may have been November 7, since faculty records at Southwestern in Georgetown show that the date for another student excursion to Dallas, originally set for October 3, was rescheduled for November 7.[73]

Curriculum and Student Body of the Medical College

The Medical College is described in elaborate terms in Southwestern University catalogs. It is also featured prominently in the annual issues of the *Sou'wester* from 1904 to 1911. Thirty-eight faculty members, headed by Hyer and McReynolds, are listed for 1904–1905. The primary clinical facility is Saint Paul Sanitarium, across the street from the new building, though a number of other hospitals are named as well. Twenty-five courses of instruction are listed for 1910–1911, ranging from specifically medical subjects such as obstetrics and diseases of the stomach and intestines, to practical subjects such as the practice of medicine and medical jurisprudence, to purely scientific subjects such as chemistry and bacteriology.

Yearly fees, which were $75 in 1904–1905, had been raised to $100 by 1910–1911. Students arriving with previous work in other medical colleges were given appropriate credit, and students presenting an A.B. or B.S. from a reputable college or university were given credit for one year of work. A College of Pharmacy with a two-year program was also a part of the system.

After the first year of operation, when its total enrollment was thirty-eight, the average enrollment of the Medical College for the remaining seven years of its connection with Southwestern was eighty-five, apportioned among students in the four years of study. The Southwestern catalog for 1906–1907 is the last one in which all previous graduates of the University are listed. In that catalog the Medical College is reported as having graduated eleven students in 1903–1904, fourteen in 1904–1905, and ten in 1905–1906.

Financial Problems

In spite of its many teachers, most of whom were private practitioners donating their time to gain the title of professor, and its elaborate lineup of courses, the College had budgetary difficulties that vitiated its program. John R. Nelson, now Commissioner of Education (the new name for Financial Agent) for Southwestern, reported in 1906 that the medical building was erected for $46,688. Its indebtedness was $24,900, with assets in notes and subscriptions of $8,751.75.[74] McReynolds himself was the major lender to the project. He held a note for $20,000. In mid-1910, the Medical College is listed as still owing him $11,500.[75]

The operational budget for 1907–1908 shows an institution trying to run its program on a shoestring. Total income for the year was about $5,900. A bank loan of another $1,000 had to be secured in order to meet expenditures of almost $6,900. The major problem was that slightly more than 30 percent of the operational expenditures went to paying down the building debt and making an interest payment.[76]

The Flexner report in 1910 criticized the Medical College for having an inadequate budget for a respectable medical program. It acknowledged that its new building was "externally attractive," but it added that it was "wretchedly kept." The College, the report continued, had little equipment. It had a reading room with nothing to read. The lecture rooms were bare, except for the chairs. The estimated fee income for the Medical College in 1910, said Flexner, was only $7,150, when $10,000 was needed.[77]

The Southwestern University Medical College Building at 1420 Hall Street, Dallas, Texas. Southwestern University, Special Collecitons.

Severance of the Medical College from Southwestern and Demise

The severance of the Medical College from Southwestern occurred without any major problems. A resolution with certain conditions was passed at the 1911 meeting of the Board of Trustees turning the Medical College over to the new Southern Methodist University. The principal condition was that Southern Methodist was to assume all debts and obligations that the Medical College might have accrued. It also committed itself to maintaining the College under the auspices of the Methodist Episcopal Church, South.[78] From 1911 to 1915 the Medical College operated as the Southern Methodist University Medical Department. Ironically, it was the only unit of SMU in operation during those years. However, before the rest of the University began classes in the fall of 1915, the Medical College had closed its doors (June 4, 1915). Southwestern received $2,036 on October 23, 1918, as its share of residual Medical College assets.[79]

In assessing the Southwestern University Medical College, it must be remembered that it existed in the premodern era of medical training. It was operating in the last days of basically unregulated medical training and was looked on differently in its own day than it appears today. By 1909 the State of Texas had put enough teeth into its regulations that it had driven the worst schools from the field, as the Flexner report acknowledged, but most medical education was still didactic, and scientific medical training was still on the horizon. The Flexner report itself would be one of the primary instrumentalities in bringing about that kind of education.

The Flexner report dealt with all the 155 medical schools in the country that had survived the first decade of the twentieth century. After his visit in November 1909 to the four medical schools in Texas, Abraham Flexner stated that only the Department of Medicine of the University of Texas in Galveston was "fit to continue in the work of training physicians." All three of the medical schools in North Texas—the Fort Worth School of Medicine, the Baylor College of Medicine, and the Southwestern University College of Medicine—came in for unsparing criticism in his report. He said that Texas was already "badly overcrowded with just the kind of doctor they are engaged in producing. Should the loopholes in the present state standard be stopped up, all three would quickly disappear."[80] The critique touched on a number of areas, but most important was that teaching was mainly didactic rather than clinical and experimental. This criticism was not unusual, for most of the schools across the country were harshly criticized on this point as well. Medical education everywhere slowly adapted to the new norms subsequently established. Baylor's school weathered the report and lived to thrive in modern times. The Southwestern/Southern Methodist school did not.[81]

Hyer's Attempts to Resign

One of the anomalous elements involved in the concatenation of events during Hyer's first seven years as Regent is his attempts to resign on two occasions. The attempts were not theatrical or contrived to serve a purpose but real expressions of his desire. They were not attempts to coerce the Curators in a particular direction nor were they the result of disappointments experienced by him. They were disclosures of the real inclination of a person who wanted to return to his primal commitment—to the classroom and the research laboratory. They are in line with his reluctance to accept the regency in the first place and help to clarify the motives that actuated him during his term of office. Because of his lack of desire to be an administrator, he was free during his tenure as Regent to act according to his best lights on any issue without fear that he might lose his position. He would have welcomed a return to the classroom.

On the first day of the Curator meeting in 1902, Hyer presented his resignation as Regent to the Board. It was not entirely unanticipated, because a brief newspaper notice had appeared on May 22, stating that "Regent Hyer will tender his resignation to the curators at their meeting tomorrow."[82] The Board responded to his action by saying that it had no prior knowledge of his intention until it was too late for them to take the necessary steps to secure someone capable of replacing him, and, consequently, asked him to remain in office for another year. If, at the end of that time, he was determined to resign, the Board would appreciate "timely notice of that fact." The motion to this effect was adopted by a rising vote. Hyer, who had not been in the room for the discussion, appeared when informed of the Board action. He finally relented and withdrew his resignation.[83] A few days later the newspaper reported that Dr. Hyer had withdrawn his resignation and would remain in office.[84]

Three years later, in mid-1905, he tried to resign again. Since he had advised each of the Curators of his intention by personal letter beforehand, they were forced to resort to some expedient other than the "lack of timely notice" argument they had used before in order to keep him. With him out of the room, they composed a resolution eulogizing his services and declining to accept his resignation. They earnestly encouraged him to remain in office. The chair reported back to them after Hyer had seen the resolution that he had the matter under advisement. Though the record does not contain his written response, he apparently set some conditions for continuing in office that the Trustees were unable to accept. The Board President "was appointed to notify the Regent that the conditions on which it had been stated he would accept continuance in the office of Regent do not exist." Having rejected his conditions, the Board appointed two Curators to confer with him "to learn further his wish respecting the regency." At this point he joined the Board meeting and told them that he really wanted to resign but that he was "in the hands of the Board." The Board then reaffirmed its former action declining to accept his resignation. The chair notified Hyer of this action and requested him to "send such recommendations to this Board as he may wish."[85]

By 1905 Hyer had become the indispensable man in the eyes of the Curators. The achievements of his administration to date had been such that they felt they could not afford to lose him. New educational programs had been instituted, buildings had been built, a medical school had been established, and student enrollment was up. In the year just completed University enrollment had increased more than a hundred to 541, not counting an additional 394 in summer programs. His conditions for continuance, which the Board regretfully refused, must have been of such a nature as not to have caused them to lose confidence in him, because, after he placed himself in their hands and they reaffirmed their decision to decline his resignation, they, in effect, gave him a blank check for anything he wanted except what he had earlier asked for. In his letter to them before the meeting, Hyer had said that he wanted to resign so that he could "devote all his time to physics." Though his natural gifts made him the kind of administrator the Curators felt was vital to the welfare of the University, his love was the classroom, not the Regent's office. His third attempt to resign in 1911, after the removal controversy, would be accepted.

The Texas Methodist Educational Convention

Hyer's work at Southwestern did not go unnoticed throughout the state, particularly in Methodist circles. What was happening in Georgetown (and Dallas) became a matter of conversation among ministers and laymen in churches and at the Annual Conferences. Many letters to the editor were printed in the *Texas Christian Advocate* about issues involving Southwestern. A dozen or more appeared in 1902 on the endowment question alone. The fact that something was happening in Georgetown raised the enthusiasm of alumni and attracted widespread attention among the general public.

Though there had been conversation from time to time about calling another educational convention to deal with educational issues, the Galveston Convention in 1870 being the model, the first printed call for one in the *Texas Christian Advocate* was in 1903. The writer says that there has been a great deal of talk of late, pro and con, concerning Southwestern University. Some of the suggestions have been good, others not so good. He suggests that "it would be wise to have a great educational convention, and in it decide upon some new plan by which a better educational system might be set on foot for the propagation of Christian education by the Methodist church of our entire state."[86] The idea gradually took root, and one was called to meet in Dallas on April 10–12, 1906.

Never in Texas Methodism had such an assembly of notables convened. About 1,200 delegates from all parts of the state were present representing their Annual and District Conferences. Many bishops, college presidents, and State and city officials attended. Selected speakers made thirty-one addresses of supposedly fifteen minutes each during the three days that were later compiled into a 226-page book.

The primary purpose of the Convention was declared to be educative. Its secondary purpose was to bring together the leaders of the church schools and other church leaders and to impress upon them the importance of working together. Particularly striking was the central role of Southwestern in the presentations and deliberations. Two of the presentations were about Southwestern itself. Persons connected with it made presentations on other topics. Among these were Hyer, Cody, and McReynolds as faculty members, and John M. Barcus, James Campbell, R. Gibbs Mood, J. Sam Barcus, and H. A. Boaz as alumni. All of them would figure prominently in the impending removal controversy, four on one side of the issue, four on the other. For the moment, however, all were together.

The significance of Southwestern as the Central university of Texas Methodism was mentioned time and again during the Convention, as well as the importance of building up its endowment. Nevertheless, Boaz, who was later to lead the movement to move Southwestern from Georgetown to Dallas, sounded a prescient note in his address. He stated that all the Methodist schools in the state should be part of a harmonious system under the charge of "our distinguished Regent of Southwestern University. . . . He should be released from all class-room work, and allowed to give his entire time to the work of supervising and building up the system."[87] Four years later he would add another element to that leadership role—that it should be exercised from a Southwestern located in either Fort Worth or Dallas, not Georgetown.

The Convention did adopt one action that was to have unexpected consequences in the removal controversy. It recommended the appointment of an Educational Commission in Texas to act as a supervisory board for Methodist schools in the state. It would have such powers as the Annual Conferences might grant it. A committee was accordingly appointed to prepare and present the rules and regulations of the Commission and to map out its duties.[88] The Commission, said an editorial in the *Texas Christian Advocate*, has great possibilities. It would do for the educational work of the state what the General Board of Education does for the entire Church. It could be the means for practical correlation among Methodist schools.[89] The Commission was to play an important role in the removal controversy leading to the continuance of Southwestern in Georgetown but also to the establishment of Southern Methodist University in Dallas.

Campus Life, Fraternities, and Sororities

Whatever was happening elsewhere, student life was proceeding normally. Coeducation made separation of the sexes in classes a thing of the past, and young men and women established more natural relations than in earlier years. Nevertheless, a degree of self-restraint was still expected in their contact with one another. Commenting later on relations between the sexes during his college days, J. Frank Dobie, who entered Southwestern in 1906, said that "association with womankind in our college was at this date about as limited as in any academy for men. Both sexes attended the classes and might greet each other, but it was against rules for them to converse in the halls or walk even up the stairs side by side." During his last year at Southwestern, the rules were relaxed to allow senior girls to date. "In my senior year I really fell in love with the girl [Bertha McKee] I later married, but had no opportunity surmountable by my timidity, to bring up the subject of love until we were out of college." Both he and Bertha graduated in 1910. They married in 1916.[90]

Sororities also made their appearance on campus. Fraternities had officially been on campus since 1887, but there were no sororities prior to 1903. At least one earlier attempt had been made at establishment in 1900, when Jessie Harriet Daniel (graduate of 1902) and another girl asked the faculty for the privilege of organizing the Pi Beta Phi sorority. Their request was refused.[91] Ray Hyer Brown reports that another student, Jennie Cornelia Wyse (graduate of 1906) went to Hyer three years later to ask him for permission to announce the organization of a sorority. Since he did not have authority to permit it, he took the matter to the Curators. They did not look on the plan with favor. There was much discussion for and against the idea. He settled the argument by saying that if the women were denied Greek letter organizations that he was in favor of abolishing the fraternities for men. They relented, and by Commencement of 1904 there were three local sororities at Southwestern.[92] Though the first sororities were locals, by 1909 they had all disappeared or been merged into four national sororities—Zeta Tau Alpha, Sigma Sigma Sigma, Alpha Delta Phi, and Phi Mu. In 1911 the Pi Kappa Alpha fraternity joined the previous three—Kappa Alpha, Phi Delta Theta, and Kappa Sigma—rounding out the four fraternities for men that would endure through the rest of the twentieth century.[93]

Whereas the literary societies had operated on the principle that everyone could become a member, the fraternities and sororities operated on a principle of selection, leaving out those whom they did not choose or who could not afford to join. This principle opened a breach between Greeks and Barbs (barbarians or independents) that was first manifested in University records in 1909. At the regular Trustee meeting in June, a group of Barbs met with a Trustee committee of five and brought complaints against the fraternities and sororities for social mistreatment. The grievances were such that certain alumni had taken their case directly to many preachers, Trustees, and patrons in a circular letter during the November just past outlining their situation. The Board approved the recommendation of the committee that the faculty "take this matter—and regulate all organizations existing among the student body to the end that such conflicts as this be reduced to a minimum."[94]

Athletics

Though some athletic contests had been engaged in during the late 1880s and '90s, they were entirely informal events with no University oversight other than to allow or disallow games with outside groups. In 1900 the students organized an Athletic Association with Dr. Hubert Anthony Shands, Professor of English Language and Literature, as president. Hyer reported to the Curators that the faculty had allowed a limited number of baseball games on an experimental basis but it did not agree with the petition to have intercollegiate games of football.[95]

Athletics became more and more a regular part of campus life, and within a few years the Athletic Association had become one of the more important organizations on campus. By 1905 it was responsible for five activities: baseball, track, football, the *Sou'wester*, and the University Glee Club. In that same year it was given permission to enclose the baseball grounds on campus with an eight-foot-high plank fence.[96] The baseball team, with faculty approval, also began to take a spring road trip of a week's duration each year. From an initial five games in 1900, the schedule moved to an average of twenty games per year from 1904 through 1910. In the eleven years from 1900 to 1910, the team won seventy-four games and lost ninety, with five ties. It played such teams as TCU, Trinity, Austin College, Texas A&M, St. Edward's, and the University of Texas.[97] In 1911 the team played Texas A&M two games at Brenham. Since the citizens of Brenham offered to pay the expense of the University band if it were allowed to attend the annual Homecoming at Brenham on May 11, the faculty voted to grant permission for the trip.[98] The band also led the parade of the Georgetown Rifles to the Katy depot adjacent to the campus on March 8, 1911, to meet former President Theodore Roosevelt.[99] A band of sixteen instruments is pictured for the first time in the *Sou'wester* for that year.

In spite of the popularity of baseball, the faculty had a problem with profanity on the athletic field. Its members discussed the issue at great length at a meeting in 1909 and asked President Hyer to call the squad together for a conversation on the subject. He told them that no man would be allowed to play on an athletic team who used profanity on the field and that every member of the team must obtain a card of eligibility from the faculty representative and submit it to the coach before being allowed to play in athletic contests.[100] In addition to validating the student as to the profanity rule, the card was an indication that the student was in good academic standing.

Women are mentioned as having tennis and basketball teams in 1903–1904, but no outside contests are indicated. The first mention of a game with another school appears on December 8, 1906, when the faculty gave permission to have a basketball game with the Coronal Institute team of San Antonio. The faculty followed up this permission the next month by allowing games with women's teams from a few colleges on a regular basis so long as all the games were played at the Annex. No games would be allowed away from the Annex except by faculty permission.[101] The *Sou'wester* reported two games in 1907–1908 and three in 1908–1909.

Though the faculty had not sanctioned intercollegiate football, students wanted it and had been playing it on an intramural basis since at least 1897. During World War II, when Southwestern became briefly a major football power due to the presence of a marine unit on campus, a member of the 1897 backfield shared his recollections, in an article in the *Austin Statesman*, of what that paper called "the first Pirate team."

> Houston, Nov. 5 [1943]—(AP)—The marine training program catapulted tiny Southwestern university of Georgetown to the nation's roster of 1943 grid giants, but back in 1897 the first Pirate team numbered exactly 12 men who romped through games clad in rattlesnake stockings and bike suits or knee pants.
>
> Among this untutored aggregation were Cong. Ewing Thomason of El Paso, Justice Harry Graves of the Texas court of criminal appeals and R. B. Creager of Brownsville, former republican national committeeman for Texas.
>
> The Pirate squad owned just three football suits and all belonged to one player, who brought them from another school.
>
> "Instead of helmets, we wore about a six-inch shock of hair," a member of that first Southwestern backfield, W. E. Thompson of the U. S. army engineers, recalled in an interview Friday. "A man with a GI haircut would have felt naked on the gridiron in those days."
>
> Keystone of the 1897 Southwestern attack was "Big Bill" Candler, a six feet four, 245-pound giant who spearheaded the flying wedge.
>
> Explaining the Pirate attack, Thompson said, "Picture a V composed of a ton and a half line formed far back of the line of scrimmage with a little quarterback tucked safely away behind the towering figure of the center.
>
> "Waiting for that charging battering ram down the field would have been good training for soldiers expected to stand a bayonet charge.
>
> "In the backfield played our head coach, line coach, backfield coach, captain and what have you all rolled into one. He was Gus Booty, a powerful 10 second man who had three football suits—the only ones on the team. The rest of us wore our old clothes."
>
> Since the Methodist church at that time refused to sanction intercollegiate competition, the pioneer Pirate team played what Thompson called "the unsung rookies in front of us at that time."
>
> "Ours," he recalled, "was strictly intramural football."[102]

In 1908 the Board of Trustees, on faculty recommendation, voted to reconsider its earlier action forbidding intercollegiate football. A special committee, established to formulate the rules under which it would be permitted, recommended that the University begin the sport. It said that a competent coach should be provided, that each player should stand a physical examination, that the same eligibility requirements should apply to the football team as to the baseball team, that the number of games should be limited to four, that not more than two games should be played away, and that training quarters should be provided. Other stipulations warned against excessively rough play.[103] Phil H. Arbuckle was employed as coach for 1908–1909. He also taught in the Fitting School. His team played five games, defeating Daniel Baker, St. Edward's, and the University of Texas, but losing to T.C.U. and Texas A&M. The next two years his team had three wins, eight losses, and three ties.[104]

Scholarship, the Council of Honor, and Enrollment

The level of scholarship at Southwestern was recognized on the state and national level by its furnishing three of the first five Rhodes Scholarship winners from the state during these years. T. Jeff Mosley, Albert G. Sanders, and

McDugald K. McLean earned the honor in 1905, 1907, and 1910, respectively.[105] Hyer reported proudly to the Curators after the election of the first two that their preeminence was so marked that the President of the University of Texas voted for them.

Though students were pledged to be on their honor from the beginning, no record of a specific written honor pledge exists until 1882. In that year an algebra exam from a young lady is signed at the bottom: "I received no assistance."[106] Nevertheless, cheating existed. For years the faculty tried to control it by giving demerits to those who were caught. The situation must have become bad enough by 1903 to require more stringent action, for the faculty adopted a rule in the spring to expel any student guilty of cheating. The first reference to a Council of Honor appears in University records of October 24, 1905, when a representative of the Council came before the faculty stating the purpose of the organization, which was to look into any charges of cheating on examinations. He reported that one student had been found guilty thus far and that the Council had recommended that he receive a one-year suspension. The guilty party, however, had the right of appeal to the faculty, as did all persons found guilty. After the report, the faculty voted "hearty approval" of the efforts of the Council of Honor.[107]

Beginning in 1904–1905, student enrollment grew rapidly. Counting only the enrollment in the three permanent Georgetown units, the College, the Fitting School, and the School of Fine Arts, the average enrollment for the first six years of Hyer's tenure was 437 students. Beginning in 1904–1905, total enrollment increased in these same units to 476, 461, 591, 633, 767, 730, and 882. These figures validated in the minds of Southwestern's leaders what they had done in making the addition to the Annex building and encouraged them to build soon an equivalent residence hall for boys.

Student and Alumni Morale

The morale of students was strong. The appearance of the *Sou'wester* in 1904 and *The Megaphone* in 1907 provided a permanent record of their years at Southwestern and became vehicles for their journalistic impulses. The Athletic Association published the *Sou'wester*, and *The Megaphone* emerged from *The Commencement Daily*, published by the

Homecoming Picnic in San Gabriel Park, 1909. This was the first homecoming celebration in Southwestern history. Former students raised funds, provided homes, prepared and served a barbecue supper, and decorated the town buildings. Members of the senior class waited tables. Southwestern University, Special Collections.

students during Commencement week of 1907. It became a weekly at the beginning of the next school year. J. Frank Dobie served as both business manager of *The Megaphone* and editor of the *Sou'wester* during his student years. A high level of student morale is indicated by the overwhelming response given by them when they learned of the proposed great Memorial Administration and Library Building in 1910. They subscribed $20,000 for it without any prompting.[108] The year before (1909) each member of the senior class had given the school a tree. The rest of the student body was given a half-day off to plant them.[109]

This positive campus morale also had a positive effect on the opinion held of the student body by townspeople. A letter to the editor from Thomas B. Stone, a new druggist in town during these years, commends student conduct in the highest terms.

> I came to Georgetown three months ago. . . . I was prejudiced against the University. Those prejudices are [now] gone, and my opinion of the school has been radically changed. . . . [T]he University is a marvel to me. Think of nearly half a thousand students in the town, creating no more stir or friction than if they were not here. Hard at work, . . . not loafing on the streets, and seen only when going for the mail, or to make necessary purchases at the stores. . . . Hen-roosts, calves, yard-gates and sign-boards are safe from disturbance, and there seems to be absolutely no friction between the citizens and the students.[110]

Student and alumni support for the University crystallized at the first Homecoming celebration held on April 21, 1909. The idea for it came from Mr. Allen K. Ragsdale, earlier a financial employee at Southwestern, who continued to support it after accepting a job with the Southland Life Insurance Company in San Antonio. He broached it to the faculty six weeks before the event took place. He suggested that it be held on San Jacinto Day and that all ex-students and former instructors be invited by letter.[111] Enthusiasm for the event ran high, and Georgetown residents, under the leadership of Col. W. K. Makemson, and former students raised funds, provided homes, prepared and served a barbecue supper, and decorated the town buildings. Members of the senior class waited tables. A faculty resolution following the event thanked all who helped to make it a success. The most unique vote of thanks went to the Artesian Manufacturing and Bottling Works of Waco for 1,200 bottles of Dr. Pepper.[112] Hyer stated in his report to the Trustees in 1909 that "the success of our athletic teams and our great Homecoming of April 21, have caused the great daily newspapers to devote more space to Southwestern affairs than they have ever done before."[113]

By 1910 Southwestern had been in existence long enough to produce a considerable number of alumni for many of the professions—clergymen, lawyers, doctors, housewives, teachers, businessmen, soldiers, government employees, accountants, and others. A few of them from these early years merit particular attention, both for what they did per se and because of what their lives and accomplishments reveal about Southwestern.

The Barcus Family

One of the major characteristics of Southwestern during its formative years was the establishment and persistence of family lineages among its students. Most students came from middle-class or relatively humble backgrounds, and Southwestern furnished them the means to rise in the world. Whether or not the applicant had money, the school seldom turned a student away if it had space. It had the highest percentage of tuition-free students of any college in the Methodist system, generally running from a quarter to a third of the student body.[114]

An illustration in point is that of the Barcus family.[115] Edward Rosman Barcus, originally from Ohio, married Mary Frances Smith on July 1, 1852. After teaching school at Marshall Institute in Mississippi near Memphis, he moved with her to Arkansas. There he entered the Methodist ministry. In 1874 they moved again to a farm near Waco, where he taught briefly in a Methodist school in town, served a small church, and farmed. Though he and his wife had thirteen children, eleven of whom survived childhood, they sent them successively over the years to Southwestern.[116]

The oldest male, John McFerrin Barcus, came with the family at the age of fourteen from Arkansas to Waco. Four years later at the age of eighteen he entered Southwestern University. He graduated with highest honors in 1882 with the second Master of Arts degree awarded by the institution. It is interesting to note that when he went to Georgetown he and his companions had to go by wagon, and, though it was only sixty-five miles, it required a week to send him there and bring the wagon back.

As a minister he served as secretary of the Central Texas Conference for twenty-one years and was elected to the General Conference six times. His thirty-two years as a

Trustee at Southwestern was broken only one time, when he served for the year 1911–1912 as President of Alexander Institute, now Lon Morris College. In 1893 the Northwest Texas Conference passed a resolution drafted by Barcus and two other ministers denouncing the holiness movement and urging their fellow clergymen to withhold their support.[117] He was awarded an honorary degree by Southwestern in 1905 and became one of the leaders in Georgetown, where he was serving as pastor at the time, against the removal of Southwestern from Georgetown.

His brother, James Samuel Barcus, graduated from Southwestern University in 1890 with an M.A. He served as Professor of Bible there from 1905 through 1909 and was President of the University from 1924 through 1928. His career will be dealt with more extensively in a subsequent chapter. His daughter, Annie Edward Barcus, took an A.B. degree from Southwestern and an M.A. degree at Columbia University. She married the Rev. Herbert Minga, taught for several years at Southwestern, and left an endowment for a speech contest held every year that still bears her name.

Overall, eight of the eleven children of the original Barcus couple that lived to adulthood attended Southwestern. Little wonder that they lined up solidly to keep it in Georgetown during the removal controversy. They were in the process when it occurred of sending their own children there. Thirty-eight children and grandchildren of the original Barcus couple attended in two generations.[118] The faculty adopted a resolution on April 4, 1922, lamenting the death of Mrs. Mary F. Barcus, "the progenitor" of a "large and influential family."[119]

Theological Directions and the Race Question

Little in the way of theological liberalism or the social gospel penetrated Southwestern University during the period prior to the removal debate. Those theological orientations were not significant on the Southwestern scene until the controversies surrounding the careers of Herbert Lee Gray, professor of Bible under various titles from 1910 to 1941, and of John Cowper Granbery, professor of history, economics, sociology, and education, who taught a range of courses in the social sciences from 1913 to 1925 and again from 1934 to 1938. But the race question was another matter. It was on everyone's mind. It was the great social issue.

A window on the race question at Southwestern comes from a particularly embarrassing incident reported by A. Frank Smith, later a Methodist bishop, that occurred during his sophomore year in 1909. Years afterward he remembered it vividly. A prominent United States senator from Mississippi came to the campus on a lecture tour to speak on the subject "Is the Negro a Human Being or an Animal?" Norman Spellmann, his biographer, records the incident in his biography of Smith.

> The conclusion of the lecture was that the Negro is an animal. Frank said that he was embarrassed at the time "because Turner Van Hoose, our colored janitor, was sitting down there by the stove, keeping the stove warm and hearing what was said. But nobody got up and walked out, and I never heard it mentioned in a classroom." Frank was amazed by the incident "because Georgetown was the center of as much culture as could be found anywhere in Texas at that time."[120]

Student Commencement orations often dealt with what could have been controversial questions. At the Commencement in 1903, for example, three of the topics were political—"The Death of Garfield," in which anarchism could have been discussed, "Chinese Gordon," in which British imperialism could have been critiqued, and "The Venezuelan Dispute," in which the U.S. Caribbean policy could have been questioned. Several were on social issues—"The Negro Question" and "Injustice to the Negro of the South," with their obvious ramifications for Texas society.[121] It is not likely, however, that the authors of those speeches advanced any arguments that would have disturbed the Georgetown community, because professors monitored them for content that might be offensive to the general public before they were given.

The senior class program for 1902 listed a presentation by Miss Jessie Harriett Daniel on "Aeschylus and Shakespeare—A Parallel."[122] Little could the audience present at her oration have surmised from that topic that she would become one of the foremost proponents of women's suffrage in Texas and that she would brand lynching as the greatest injustice still prevalent in the South. Lynching was, she said, not only an injustice, but also a perversion of the chivalric ideal that it supposedly upheld.

Jessie Daniel Ames

Born in Palestine, Texas, on November 2,1883, Jessie Daniel Ames was the third of four children of a railroad sta-

Jessie Daniel Ames. A graduate of 1902, Ames became national director of women's work of the Atlanta-based Commission on Interracial Cooperation and founded the Association of Southern Women for the Prevention of Lynching. She is buried in the I.O.O.F. Cemetery in Georgetown. Southwestern University, Special Collections.

tion agent and his wife. After a short move to Overton, the family moved to Georgetown in 1893 so that the children could enjoy the benefits of Southwestern University.[123] Jessie's familial circumstances created in her the independent disposition that characterized her later life. Though her mother had attended a Methodist school and became very active in the church in Georgetown, her father was an aggressive nonbeliever who taught his children that a God who willed such pain as existed in the world was "inhumanly cruel." The children were torn between the evangelical beliefs of their mother and the rationalism of their father. Nevertheless, much to the vexation of their father, they joined the church one summer during a revival.

In addition to the feeling of being caught between two contrasting views of life, Jessie also developed the feeling that she was an outsider looking in on other aspects of life as well. Her older sister received most of the attention of her father, and he placed little hope in Jessie's career. When she entered Southwestern, her father, she later wrote, "looked me coldly in the eye and said, 'Young lady, I am sending you to college because there is nothing else to do with you. But I want you to understand right now that . . . the first time that you fail in your classes . . . you come out of school and go to the kitchen. . . . I do not expect you to graduate.'"[124] Not only did she begin college with that burden, but her college years were also hedged about with severe restrictions on her social contacts levied by her father in addition to those already imposed by the Annex. This social deprivation created in her the stand-alone quality that she carried with her all her life. Ironically, the qualities of independence and a willingness to stand alone developed from her early experiences were helpful in making her successful as a social reformer.

Still dependent on her family after graduation, she moved with them to Laredo in 1904. There she met a handsome army surgeon, Roger Post Ames, whom she married a year later. The marriage endured but was not happy. He traveled here and there in the army pursuing the research made famous by Walter Reed. She traveled back and forth, living with him when she could and with her sister's family in Columbia, Tennessee, when necessary. When he died of blackwater fever in Guatemala in 1914, she moved back to Georgetown at age thirty-one with two children and pregnant with another.[125] In 1958 she was instrumental in achieving official government recognition for Roger's work, and he was posthumously awarded a Congressional medal for his work. Tragically, her youngest daughter, Lulu, developed poliomyelitis in 1920, and Jessie suffered the agony of having to stand by while watching Lulu undergo the long series of painful treatments recommended by the physicians.

Before her father's death in 1911, he had purchased the local Georgetown telephone company. Though her mother was the owner after his death, Jessie more and more emerged as the real manager and became a business force in Georgetown after her return in 1916. It was during these years that she began to exercise the latent independence that was the real backdrop for the life of social action that now began to emerge. As a businesswoman, she felt that she had the same right to vote on the issues affecting her business as did any businessman. She organized the Georgetown Equal Suffrage League to promote those rights soon after her return. She was elected its president and thus began her lifelong career as a leader for social reform. She also came to know faculty members and to become active in alumni affairs.

Two of those friends were John C. Granbery and his wife, Mary Anne Catt. Both were progressives and suffragists. Jessie's mother, Laura, as president of the local Methodist Woman's Missionary Society, "provided a forum for Granbery's early speeches on suffrage and other social issues" and contributed two thousand dollars to President Bishop's Campaign for a Greater Southwestern in 1914.[126] Jessie herself served as treasurer for Southwestern's Golden Jubilee Celebration in 1923, turning in a final report to the Executive Committee "stating the final condition of its finances" on October 11 of that year.[127] She spoke to the students at a chapel service the following year on the Constitution. They enjoyed it thoroughly.[128] She headed a committee of women that spoke to the Board of Trustees about the American Association of University Women at its midyear meeting in 1926.[129]

Ames became state treasurer of the Texas Equal Suffrage Association in 1918. When the state legislature passed a bill allowing women to vote in state primaries, she and her coworkers registered 3,800 women in Williamson County in seventeen days to vote in the next primary. After the ratification of the Nineteenth Amendment to the U.S. Constitution in 1919, she joined the League of Women Voters and conducted schools for the newly enfranchised voters. Her activities expanded successively to the Texas Joint Legislative Council, the Texas Committee on Prisons and Prison Labor, and the American Association of University Women.[130]

During these activities, Jessie Daniel Ames became more and more cognizant of the injustices being inflicted on African Americans in the South. She became chair of a women's committee of the Texas Interracial Commission, a branch of the Atlanta-based Commission on Interracial Cooperation. She soon became a field worker in the Southwest for the Commission. She moved to Atlanta in 1929, where she became its national director of women's work. On a return home from Atlanta that same year, she addressed the two "Y's" at Southwestern on "the negro problem." Her appearance brought a record attendance. The tables and the window ledges were all occupied. According to a *Megaphone* report of her speech, she said that "the negro does not want, as some whites would believe, social intermingling; but he does want and deserves social equality. This can be effected by a parallel—the whites and the blacks each equally educated, etc., but at the same time both recognizing the color line."[131] Though she would move beyond this position in later years, separate but equal was her position when she left Georgetown for Atlanta. A year later she founded the Association of Southern Women for the Prevention of Lynching. She spent the rest of her life battling that scourge.

By 1944 changing times and styles of leadership made her feel that her day had passed, and she retired. She moved to North Carolina, where she lived until 1968, when she returned to an Austin retirement home. She died at the age of eighty-eight in 1972 and was buried in the I.O.O.F. cemetery in Georgetown.[132] She spent a day on the Southwestern campus in May 1965 when she visited President Durwood Fleming and other persons in Georgetown, particularly persons connected with the American Association of University Women. Though during her retirement in Tryon, North Carolina, she willed her papers to the University of North Carolina at Chapel Hill,[133] she willed her personal library of more than 1,200 books in 1969 to Southwestern University in honor of her son, Frederick Daniel Ames, a Houston physician and 1926 graduate of Southwestern, who died in 1959.

Bohemian Students and Their Classmates

Certainly the most unique offerings in the curriculum from 1907 through 1912 were courses in the Bohemian language and culture.[134] Their presence in the curriculum came about through the Board of Missions of the Northwest Texas Conference, which employed the Rev. Vaclav Cejnar to carry on missionary work in Central Texas. Cejnar, born in 1862, was a native of Bohemia. He was converted and, after studies in Germany and Scotland, became a pastor in the Free Evangelical Church. He came to the United States in 1905 and engaged for two years in mission work among Slavic peoples in Pennsylvania and Chicago before being employed in 1907 by the Southern Methodist Board of Missions to work among Czech immigrants in Texas.[135] These immigrants had been coming to Texas since 1852, settling primarily in Fayette and adjoining counties. Fayetteville has been called the "cradle of Czech settlement." By 1900 there were fifteen thousand in the state.[136] Many settled in the area around Granger in Williamson County.

Cejnar joined the Northwest Texas Conference, and Hyer acceded to a proposal by its Board of Missions for him to teach Bohemian at Southwestern without cost to the University. Hyer told the Board of Trustees that there was little demand for Bohemian and that Cejnar was spending most of his time lecturing and preaching among his Bohemian brethren but that he felt American students who had volunteered for missionary work might study it with profit.[137] Catalogs from 1907–1908 through 1911–1912 list a Beginner's and an Intermediate grammar course, followed by advanced courses in Bohemian Literature and History by arrangement.

With this encouragement, Cejnar brought over six students from Bohemia. They were his own children, John A. and Frances Cejnar; a nephew and niece, Joseph and Marta Bartak, who were the brother and sister of his wife Anna; and two others, C. August Chval and Joseph Dobes. All of them enrolled in the Fitting School to prepare for college work. Several other persons came over to help in his ministry, but they are not listed in Southwestern records and apparently did not enroll as students. The six arrived at different times, but five were enrolled together for the years 1908–1909 and 1909–1910. Joseph Bartak came to America in 1907 without knowing a word of English. Joseph D. Thomas, writing in 1970 about his first year at Southwestern, says that he and his roommate occupied one room of a two-room cottage near Giddings Hall. In the other room were Joseph Bartak and August Chval. He says that they were "very studious and very smart."[138]

Bartak and Chval found themselves in the company of a group of Southwestern students who later had important careers. Oscar Benold of Maxwell and Otto W. Moerner of Fredericksburg, both of whom became prominent ministers and whose children attended Southwestern, were their fellow students in the Fitting School, as was Ruth Morgan, who as Ruth Morgan Ferguson became the beloved Dean of Women and Professor of English and History for thirty-seven years. In 1908 John D. Wheeler, who later served as chair of the Board of Trustees, was a senior, J. Frank Dobie, the famous Texas writer, and his future wife, Bertha McKee, were sophomores, and Hyder Rollins, later a famous Harvard professor, was two years away from graduation. Finis A. Crutchfield was a freshman, and A. Frank Smith had just entered the Fitting School. Both later became bishops. Smith found Bess Crutchfield, his future wife, along with her sister Hallie, in attendance as freshmen.[139] The Smith-Crutchfield union later produced A. Frank Smith, Jr., who became a well-known Houston lawyer, donor, and future chair of the Board of Trustees, and for whom the A. Frank Smith, Jr., Library Center is named.

J. Fred Rippy would be one of their colleagues as well. After graduating from Southwestern in 1913, the year he won the State Intercollegiate Oratorical Contest,[140] Rippy would earn an M.A. at Vanderbilt and a Ph.D. at the University of California. He became a professor at Duke in 1926, a Guggenheim Fellow in 1927, and a Carnegie Fellow in 1928. He would have a long and distinguished career as a Latin American historian, writing many books and articles.[141] On the golden anniversary of his entry into Southwestern in 1910, he would be awarded an honorary D.Litt. degree by his alma mater.[142]

All in all, the two young men of Czech extraction who entered in 1907 found themselves among a group of students, many of whom, they included, would distinguish themselves during their careers.

Subsequent Careers of the Bohemian Contingent

Cejnar had come to Central Texas and Southwestern with high hopes. He was a hard worker, and, in addition to preaching and teaching, he started a newspaper entitled *Buditel evangelicky methodisticky (The Evangelical Methodist Revival)* in 1908. Records of its existence are sketchy, and it apparently did not last long.[143] He became discouraged, and his name does not appear among the roll of ministers in the *Central Texas Conference Journal* of 1912. The reason for Cejnar's lack of success was due to the fact that he and others presumed that the Bohemian immigrants in Central Texas would be ripe for evangelization. In the United States, however, the two Churches the Czechs brought with them from their homelands became cultural rallying points. Most Czech immigrants to Texas were Roman Catholic. Of the ten to fifteen percent who were Protestant, most were United Brethren.[144] They were not interested in becoming Methodists. After leaving Georgetown, Cejnar entered service with the Presbyterians in the Midwest. Southwestern closed down the Bohemian program.

However Cejnar may have assessed his success or lack of it, most of his students led valuable lives after they left Southwestern. One Bohemian student from America who studied under him briefly in the Fitting School was Charles Knizek. Knizek, a student from 1909 to 1911, became a local preacher, obtained his undergraduate degree from Polytechnic in Fort Worth, and finally became a professor of Slavic languages at the University of Texas. There were other American Bohemians in the student body as well who probably took some of Cejnar's courses. Hyer reported in 1910 that there were nine Bohemians and twelve Germans preparing for the ministry.[145]

Two of the European Bohemian students, Josef Dobes and Joseph Paul Bartak, eventually returned to Czechoslovakia and had conspicuous careers as Church leaders.

Bartak took the full range of studies at Southwestern, from Fitting School to college, graduating in 1912 with an A.B. He subsequently secured Bachelor of Divinity and Master of Divinity degrees from Vanderbilt University and the University of Chicago, respectively. He served as a pastor in Chicago through the end of World War I.

After World War I, the Methodist Episcopal Church, South, undertook relief work in Czechoslovakia and provided soup kitchens, workshops, orphanages, and other types of assistance in that war-devastated country. Dobes and Bartak offered themselves for service and were sent back to direct the effort. The relief program ended after a few years, but the humanitarian work created an evangelistic urge in them that resulted in the establishment of permanent Methodist work in those countries. Bartak became pastor of the Vrsovice Church in Prague, for a time the largest local congregation in the Southern Church. In addition, he was a seminary professor and mission superintendent.[146]

During World War II the Church in Czechoslovakia experienced great suffering. Because the Czech Methodists before the war had been outspoken in their opposition to the Nazis, they were immediately attacked when the takeover occurred. Biblical materials that clashed with Nazi doctrines were forbidden and hymnals were censored. All the Methodist churches were closed in Slovakia.[147] Bartak, having become an American citizen, was not molested until Germany declared war on America, but on that same day he was arrested by the Gestapo and sent to an internment camp at Laufen, Germany. Later he was freed as part of an exchange for German prisoners in America.[148] He served as a pastor in Texas and traveled widely speaking about the Church under the Nazis. Two of his children, Marian Bartak (Malac) and Helen Bartak (Trimarchi) attended Southwestern briefly before returning with their parents to Prague after the war. Bartak continued his church work there until 1951, when the Communist government refused to let him continue to preach and serve. He and his wife then went to Vienna, where they continued working until 1958. He retired at the age of seventy. At his death on September 30, 1964, he left a donation to Southwestern.[149]

J. Frank Dobie and Hyder E. Rollins

Two students graduated in 1910, each of whom in his own way climbed to the pinnacle of literary success. They were J. Frank Dobie and Hyder E. Rollins. Dobie's name is by far better known today, for he remained in Texas and limned her people and prairies, producing a vast body of literature about the Southwest that brought its folklore to respectability and is still read today. He became internationally known, and his success finally took him from Texas to Cambridge for a special teaching appointment. There he succeeded Henry Steele Commager as professor of American history and received an honorary master's degree.

Rollins was the equal of Dobie in his own world, but that world was quite different from that of Dobie. It was the world of traditional scholarship at major Eastern universities, at Johns Hopkins, New York University, and Harvard, where he became a pioneer textual critic, producing authoritative editions of Elizabethan poetry. He eventually succeeded the famed George Lyman Kittredge as Gurney Professor of English at Harvard. Fastidious in appearance and meticulous in his research, Rollins was an apt contrast to Dobie, whose appearance was rumpled and much of whose material came from conversations with cowhands around a campfire.[150]

Neither Dobie nor Rollins, however, was devoid of an appreciation for the world of the other. Dobie could appreciate the classics, and Rollins never completely left the Texas of his birth. Recalling in 1957 his years at Southwestern, Dobie said, "I was my most essential self when I walked alone up the San Gabriel River with a volume of Wordsworth, reading him there as I imagined he had read and walked by 'sylvan Wye,' and making his lines an integral and abiding part of me."[151] Rollins, for his part, appreciated his native Texas. Between 1914 and 1916 he published thirteen articles on O. Henry and other Texas subjects.[152] Before his death he asked that his body be brought back to Texas and buried in his native Abilene.

Dobie came to Southwestern from the ranch country in South Texas. There he attended one-teacher schools until he entered high school in Alice, where he was salutatorian of his class. The most enduring impression of his first day at Southwestern was of a meeting with Dr. Hyer at registration. Hyer asked him if he liked to read. Dobie responded that he liked to read very much. Jeff Campbell, later professor of English at Southwestern (1962–1975), records Hyer's response as follows:

> Hyer then told the young man that he himself had long followed the practice or [sic: of] reading one book each week. Young Frank decided right then and there that he would do the same, and throughout his life he kept it up—without, he said, "being methodical." Dr. Hyer preached the following Sunday (as was his custom on the first Sunday of the college year), using as his text "I am

debtor both to the Greeks, and to the Barbarians; both to the wise, and to the unwise." This first sermon Dobie heard in Georgetown made a vivid impression on him. He remembered it all of his life, referring to it in one of his Sunday columns shortly before his death. That sermon, he said, elated me with ambition to know.[153]

Dobie attributed to his English professor, Albert Shipp Pegues, the responsibility for seriously turning him to literature. "His survey course in English poetry transmuted the world for me," Dobie wrote. On the lighter side, he was a member of The Frank Club, nine boys named Frank. A picture of them in the annual yearbook with their motto "Be Frank" included J. Frank Dobie and A. Frank Smith. His term as manager of the baseball team was also satirized in the annual yearbook. It said that he is coaching this year and that "last year he was manager of [the] Southwestern University [baseball team]. These are very important offices and the Alice High school is proud of her illustrious son."[154]

Dobie joined the faculty of the University of Texas in 1914 and retired in 1947. He was the self-styled "outlaw of the campus," speaking out on almost everything. Not counting newspaper writings, he had published over eight hundred articles, pamphlets, and books by the time of his death.[155] Five years after Dobie's retirement, on October 29, 1952, Southwestern set aside a day to honor him. He and Bertha gathered on campus along with a number of other Texas writers. The assembled group paid tribute to the Dobie influence on the literature of the Southwest, and some of the events of the day were broadcast on radio and television. Dobie said it was the happiest day of his life.[156]

The *Sou'wester* staff of 1910. J. Frank Dobie and Hyder E. Rollins, probably the two most distinguished literary figures in alumni history, are both shown as members of the staff. From the 1910 *Sou'wester*.

Hyder Edward Rollins was born in Abilene, Texas. He entered Southwestern at the age of fourteen in 1903. Taking some time off for teaching in country schools, he received his degree in 1910. He received an M.A. from the University of Texas and taught English there for two years. After attending Johns Hopkins for a year, he went to Harvard, where he received his Ph.D. in 1917. He served as a second lieutenant in the United States Army Signal Corps during World War I in France. In 1919 he went to Europe on a Harvard Sheldon Traveling Fellowship. He had turned it down earlier in order to enlist. Taking an assistant professorship at New York University in 1920, he became a full professor within four years. In 1926 he returned to Harvard and in 1939 succeeded Kittredge in the Gurney Professorship. He retired in 1956. He was the author of numerous books and articles and the editor or coeditor of some twenty volumes in the Harvard Studies in English, Harvard Studies and Notes in Philology and Literature, and *A New Variorum Shakespeare*. He had an international reputation for his scholarly work on the poet John Keats. He directed more than a hundred doctoral dissertations while at Harvard.[157]

In 1933 Rollins received an honorary LL.D. from Southwestern University. He died on July 25, 1958. Three months before his death, he wrote to the University, donating three letters to the library. He called them "voices from the past." They were letters of recommendation written for him in 1911 by Professors Mouzon, Moore, and Pegues. Pegues, his teacher in English literature, said about him: "In many ways, I regard him as the strongest, finest spirit I have touched in my class-room."[158]

Dobie followed him in death on September 18, 1964. The two young men, who had served together on the *Sou'wester* staff in 1909–1910, are perhaps the most outstanding literary figures produced by Southwestern.

11 The Removal Controversy: Hyer versus Cody (1907–1911)

New Charter and Board Consolidation

Several changes had occurred in the makeup of the Board of Curators and the Board of Trustees by the end of the Mood administration. The Board of Curators had been expanded in 1875 from five to six members with the addition of a new sponsoring Annual Conference. Two years later that Board had been expanded to thirty. In the same year, the old Board of Trustees, consisting of the fifteen members of the Texas University Company in Galveston, was changed to one that had a working quorum operating out of Austin. Four years later, in 1883, the Executive Committee of the Board of Trustees became a Georgetown group.

The arrangement of two separate boards, one of curators for educational and personnel matters, another of trustees for financial matters, became more and more cumbersome. Their annual meetings had to overlap so that actions important for both could be communicated immediately from one to the other, and the Regent was forced to keep in touch with both boards in between meetings. By 1889 a movement had originated to consolidate the two boards. The Curators adopted a motion in that year to appoint a joint committee with the Trustees to procure an amendment to the charter for that purpose. After some negotiation with the Trustees, a committee was set up and a subsequent motion was approved to prepare a new charter and to present it at the next annual session.[1] Because of the difficulty of making such an important operational change in the University while at the same time trying to elect a new Regent, the matter was quietly dropped and did not appear on the agenda for the meeting in 1890 at the time of the disputed Chappell-McLean election.

The matter came up six years later (1896) with the same result. A joint committee was set up to consider consolidation during the year prior to the next meeting. A motion at the subsequent meeting postponed the matter indefinitely.[2]

By the time of the 1906 meetings of the two Boards, Hyer had worked out the problems impeding consolidation. He reported that earlier action to combine the two Boards had been dropped for fear of losing the tax exemption privilege granted by the Legislature. He explained that the problem had now been worked out, and legal opinion held that they might draw up a new charter without losing their tax status provided the new charter established a balance between ministerial and lay members. This stipulation was apparently required to protect the current balance between the all-ministerial Board of Curators and the all-lay Board of Trustees. Hyer concluded by saying that he had taken the liberty of drawing up a proposed charter and that they had the result before them. It was the old charter with the minimum of changes required to effect the measures needed. Hyer had acted. There would be no committee or yearlong waiting period this time.

The two Boards met separately, then jointly, and approved the amended charter proposed by Regent Hyer. New Bylaws for the combined Board were adopted. The motion to approve asked Hyer to call a session of the new Board of Trustees once the Annual Conferences had approved the action.[3] In addition to the consolidation of the two Boards, the new charter would make Southwestern the official name of the University and change the title of the chief executive officer from Regent to President. The new charter also authorized the establishment of a school of law in addition to the already authorized schools of medicine and theology. Acting somewhat more than a year after the charter had become operative, the faculty decided that the official initials of Southwestern University should be "S.U." rather than "S.W.U."[4]

Not everyone was happy with the changes. Hyer and the ministers on the Board of Curators had pushed the issue. The Trustees had gone along reluctantly. Lockett says that the biggest change occurred in the makeup of the Executive Committee. It was changed from a group of independent

Georgetown laymen to a committee composed of one person from each Annual Conference, two Georgetown representatives, and two faculty members. The President of the University became its chair. Three of the members on the Executive Committee were now members of the faculty—Cody, Allen, and Hyer. The result was that the Conference members, living at a distance, often could not attend, while the faculty members could. Business, he says, came to be dominated by the faculty. This change had particular effect on the finances of the University. Lockett describes the new operation as follows:

> Before this the faculty had control of all money coming in for tuition, the fine arts, etc., but they could not touch a single cent coming in from any other course [read: source]—donation, sale of lands, etc. No money was ever drawn out by anyone except the treasurer, and then only on the order of the Executive Committee acting under the instruction of the Board of Trustees. But it was not long under the new rule before the faculty through the bursar received and paid out all moneys coming in. The result was that the Treasurer was a figurehead and knew nothing about the different sums paid out.[5]

Lockett's statement of dissatisfaction was followed by his resignation as treasurer of the Board in 1908. He had been elected treasurer on the retirement of D. H. Snyder from that post in 1906 and had been continued as treasurer in 1907 under the new structure. Nevertheless, he did not want to be "a figurehead" who "knew nothing about the different sums paid out" and resigned after one year. He would continue loyally until 1920 to serve on the Board, but he was critical of institutional management under the new system.

Lockett's successor as treasurer was Claude Carr Cody. The Curators had elected Cody unanimously as the first Dean of the University in 1907 when that office was created. Now a resolution was adopted that the treasurer need not be a member of the Board. It was obviously done so that Cody could be elected treasurer, as occurred immediately thereafter.[6] Cody was now both Academic Dean and University Treasurer. He was almost as strong as the President. Without knowing it, he had achieved this power just in time to become the foremost faculty opponent of President Hyer in his attempt to remove the University to Dallas.

Interestingly, Lockett's criticism of Southwestern officialdom after his resignation did not include Cody. Cody had lived in Georgetown for thirty years when he was elected treasurer. He had earlier become a part of the elite circle of Georgetown society when he married Mattie Hughes, the daughter of Judge Thomas Proctor Hughes, in 1883. His son, Hughes, had in turn married Lockett's daughter, Gladys, thus making Cody and Lockett the two grandfathers of their children.[7] Cody was a respected professor of mathematics, a meticulous accountant, and a person who seemed to be the friend of everyone. Rather than looking on Cody's election as an affront, Lockett probably looked on it as the best result possible. He, John Barcus, and Cody would become the leaders in Georgetown of the effort to maintain Southwestern where it was when the removal controversy arose two years later. He would be the town citizen leader, Barcus would be the Church leader, and Cody would be the faculty leader. The Trustee leader, siding with them and keeping in contact with them, would be William Wiess of Beaumont.

Claude Carr Cody

Cody, like Hyer, was a native Georgian and a graduate of Emory at Oxford. When he graduated in 1874, with an A.M. degree, a newspaper article said that he was "one of the brightest and most popular young men at Emory College."[8] All of his grade reports were excellent, with many marks of 99 and 100.[9] At the time of his election to the chair of mathematics at Southwestern in 1878, Atticus G. Haygood, President of Emory College, sent a warm letter of recommendation to Dr. Mood. In it he said that "Mr. Cody deserves what he receives from all who know him—respect, confidence, affection."[10] These were also his characteristics at Southwestern over the years. Though he himself extolled S. G. Sanders as the most beloved man in the early history of Southwestern, Cody had won that accolade in the minds of most people by the time he closed out his career. He became "The Grand Old Man" of Southwestern. Ralph Jones describes the meaning of the title as follows:

> His later sobriquet, The Grand Old Man of Southwestern, indicates his venerability and the esteem in which his many students held him. It was compounded from the nostalgic reminiscence of his good natured humor, kindly, encouraging friendship, and hopeful, stern counsel. It was tendered partly from their knowl-

Dean Claude Carr Cody. He came to Southwestern as professor of mathematics in 1878. He was named the first academic dean in 1907 and was one of the most beloved teachers in Southwestern history. He was the leader of the anti-removal forces in 1910–11. Southwestern University, Special Collections.

> edge of his open heart as a sympathetic teacher and his open house as an interested friend. It betrays his personal concern for them whether laughing with them, shedding tears over them, rebuking them, praying for them, leading their minds, filling their hearts, or shaping their characters. As a measure of these attributes, the title does him justice. It fails, however, to record his almost unbelievable range of interests and activities in church, state, community, and school.[11]

During his career, he was an active member of the Methodist Church, taught Sunday School for many years, was lay leader, attended church conferences, and held state offices in the Church. He was a leader in the Texas Chautauqua Assembly, held for a few years west of Georgetown, and was active in many civic affairs, being elected on one occasion as Clerk of the Superior Court. He was an officer in various state educational organizations and wrote several mathematics texts in collaboration with W. H. Bruce. He was an editor of *The Texas Methodist Historical Quarterly* and was one of the founders of the Texas Methodist Historical Association. He carried on an active correspondence with college presidents throughout the state on educational issues and with teachers on matters relating to the welfare of the profession.

Cody was born in Covington, Georgia, on November 5, 1854, the son of a prominent Georgia family. Its status is indicated by the fact that his father was a close friend of Alexander H. Stephens, a resident of nearby Crawfordville, who served as Vice President of the Confederacy during the Civil War. This friendship represented moderation on the part of the Codys, however, rather than strong support for the Confederate cause, because Stephens was the most reluctant of the Southern leaders to enter the fray. Three letters to Cody's father from Stephens before and during the war, bemoaning the radicalism of the Southern leaders, became a proud possession of Cody in Georgetown. They were resounding criticisms of the political strategy pursued by the South leading to the war. Cody gave at least one lecture on Stephens in Georgetown and published the three letters in the newspaper. A fourth letter from Stephens to Cody's father eight years after the end of the war said: "Do you remember the letter you wrote to me in the Fall of 1860 urging me to go to Warrenton to make a speech against secession? What sad, sad changes since then. I then thought we were in the Penumbra of the deep darkness which has come upon us since."[12]

After Mood's death it was the young Cody who was asked by the Mood family to do a biography of their father. Kittie wrote him a carefully phrased letter, saying that the family felt he was the most appropriate person to write the life of the Southwestern founder, but, she continued, they hesitated to ask him for fear he "might feel a delicacy in refusing" because of the press of duties.[13] He accepted the responsibility, and the family gave him access to all of Mood's papers and writings. His propensity for saving a record of everything that came his way resulted in the preservation of not only a great deal of Mood material, but also of much other information related to the early history of Southwestern University.

Cody, like Hyer, was well liked by Curators and Trustees. In August 1881, he is reported as having sent "a couple of beautiful fawns from San Antonio to Mrs. Harrell and to Capt. D. H. Snyder's little girls." He was later reported as spending the summer with Dudley Snyder at Renderbrook Springs, Snyder's summer home. The Snyders liked him personally but utilized his mathematical acumen as well. He was reported in one newspaper article as being absent for several weeks surveying lands for Dudley and Tom Snyder in Mitchell and adjoining counties.[14]

Students loved him. He was elected an honorary member of the Alethean Society of the Annex in 1883 and served for two years as the first editor-in-chief of the *Alamo and San Jacinto Monthly*. Edward Pilley, a spring 1895 graduate, chose him as the recipient in Georgetown of a report from Shanghai, China, about his initial experiences in China as a missionary. In his seventeen-page letter he calls himself Cody's "former student and friend." Ill health forced Cody to retire early at the age of sixty. His health did not improve over the next few years, and by 1922 everyone knew he could not last much longer. A magnificent celebration of his sixty-eighth birthday was held. Some of the speakers at the celebration were Dr. J. C. Granbery, Professor J. Frank Dobie, Miss Sue Mood, and Mrs. Margaret Mood McKennon. He received hundreds of letters and telegrams from former students, and his son, Dr. C. C. Cody, Jr., received many on the occasion of his death a year later.[15] He was buried in the I.O.O.F. Cemetery in Georgetown.

Cody took active leadership of the forces opposing removal in 1910, and his friendships all over the state with students, faculty, Trustees, and friends of the University were an important element in defeating the forces of removal. It is quite likely that, had he been on the other side of the removal question, Southwestern University would not have remained in Georgetown. The forces opposed to removal would not have had a central leader, and no one else could have called into play against the movement the hundreds of alumni and laymen who responded to him.

Construction of Mood Hall and Setting Up a Gymnasium

The need for a men's residence hall on the new campus equivalent to that of the women was voiced almost as soon as the Main Building was completed.[16] In 1904 Hyer made a plea for a campaign for $25,000 to construct a building to replace Helping Hall (Giddings Hall). The Curators responded by approving the construction of a new building to be called Epworth Hall.[17] No money was available, and two ministers proposed being responsible themselves for the project. The Board gladly accepted their offer and instructed the Executive Committee to cooperate with them and to designate a place on University grounds for it.[18] The offer was too good to be true, and nothing came of the proposed enterprise.

When the Commissioner of Education (Financial Agent), John R. Nelson, reported to the Executive Committee in 1906 that he had secured about $20,000 in subscriptions for the proposed "dormitory for boys," the Committee was ready to act. It authorized him to tell prospective donors that work on the building would begin at once. At a special called meeting of the full Board two months later, it followed through by authorizing the purchase of three blocks of land adjacent to the Main Building on the north as a site for the new building. At another called meeting on April 27, a construction bid from the Belford Lumber Company for $58,000 was accepted. By then subscriptions had reached $28,000.[19] The contract was let in May and the cornerstone was laid on June 2, 1906. The building was officially named Mood Hall.[20]

Construction proceeded rapidly—in fact, so rapidly that the public had to be disabused in July of the notion that it would be ready by fall.[21] The subscription drive did not make much progress, money already subscribed did not materialize in timely fashion, and construction had to be halted. At their midyear meeting in 1907, a year after the cornerstone had been laid, the Trustees were forced to report that the building would not be ready for occupancy in the fall due to lack of funds and "our present indebtedness."[22] With a beautiful building standing uncompleted, the Trustees were forced to take drastic action. They called another special meeting in December. There they voted to use endowment funds "as a loan" to pay indebtedness on the building up to $10,000, with an annual interest of 5 percent. The last $20,000 due on the building would be five notes of $4,000 each to the Belford Lumber Company, each note to be paid annually over a course of five years with 8 percent interest.[23]

With the financial situation temporarily taken care of, the building was completed rapidly and occupied in the fall of 1908. It was a beautiful building, constructed of the same type of stone used in the Main Building, with an architectural design complementing it. Mood Hall had eighty bedrooms, a dining room, a library, and parlors. It was the first building completed with steam heat and electric lights built in at the outset. It had bath and toilet rooms on every floor.[24] Its most unique feature was a patio opening to the sky in the center of the building, with veranda-type hallways overlooking it. This feature meant that most of the rooms

The Southwestern campus c. 1910 as seen across the railroad tracks looking from west to east. The three large buildings are the Ladies' Annex (1888, background), the Main Building (1900, right), and Mood Hall (1908, left). Southwestern University, Special Collections.

were, in effect, outside rooms, since they opened either on the exterior of the building or onto the interior patio.

At the same time that Mood Hall was being constructed, a gymnasium was carved into the Main Building. The idea of turning the old chapel, that is, the old Methodist Church, into a gymnasium was finally abandoned in 1906. With a new campus being constructed, it was deemed foolish to put money into the old campus for new projects. A plan was adopted to put the gymnasium on the main campus. To create a space for it, the physics laboratory on the first floor of the Main Building, underneath the east side of the auditorium, was moved to another room. The laboratory was turned into a gymnasium by lowering its floor eighteen inches.[25] Appropriate gym equipment was purchased, and pictures show young men in it using parallel bars, a punching bag, a vaulting horse, traveling rings, and other items. Hyer mentioned in one of his reports that it was as fine as that in any institution in the state. Nevertheless, the action was looked on as a temporary measure, with the idea of placing the gymnasium elsewhere in the future. With a gymnasium in place, Hyer reported that each young man in the freshman class was required to spend at least three hours per week there.[26]

Finances and Indebtedness

It was in the building-up of the new campus after the completion of the Main Building in 1900 that Curators and Trustees began to involve the University in substantial indebtedness to achieve their construction objectives. As mentioned earlier, as late as 1902 the total indebtedness of the University was only $12,404.34, with 83 percent of it owed to individuals in the form of small bonds. None of the debt had been incurred as a result of normal operational expenses. Very little of it was owed to special funds or to the endowment because there was so little of it. That situation changed, however, with the Harrison Fund Endowment campaign beginning in 1907 and the construction of Mood Hall in 1906–1908. By mid-1911 the Harrison Fund Endowment reported collections of $36,579.03 over a four-year period. Of that amount, $26,629.48 was invested to complete Mood Hall and $8,819.96 to make improvements in the Annex.[27] In other words, 97 percent of the Harrison Endowment money was used to complete those two building projects. The transaction was put on the books as a loan to be repaid with interest from the rent produced by the eighty rooms in Mood Hall.[28]

In 1907 the total indebtedness of the University was $35,641.60. By the following year it was "about $60,000."[29] Commenting on the amount of the debt at that time, the last year of his service as treasurer, M. B. Lockett said: "This was not a large debt considering that the University owned subscriptions [pledges] amounting to two-thirds of the amount, and besides owned several tracts of land in the state and had the good will of the Methodist church in Texas."[30] But the debt continued to grow. By midyear 1911, when Hyer left, it was $85,513.87, not counting the Medical College indebtedness of $11,500 to Dr. McReynolds for which the University in Georgetown was not responsible.

Financial Campaigns

During these years the University engaged in one fund-raising campaign after another. A general solicitation for $1,500,000, called the Twentieth Century Campaign and initiated by the General Conference of 1898 for all its educational institutions, was engaged in throughout the Southern states. Though by 1902 subscriptions totaling $2,031,948.17 had been obtained, only 20 percent of them ($411,511.86) had been paid in cash.[31] Ralph Jones estimates that Southwestern only received between $8,000 and $18,000 in cash. The historical importance of this small sum is that it was the first money ever received by Southwestern from the general Church.[32]

Another effort was a projected four-year $500,000 campaign initiated in 1907. Stimulated by the initial success of the Harrison Endowment Club campaign, this $500,000 campaign was renamed the Endowment Club of 500, sometimes called the "500 Club," in 1908. Initially without an endowment purpose, it was transformed in the same year into a more realistic campaign for $100,000 to sustain the Biblical Department. Donors were encouraged to purchase Biblical Bonds. Bishop Seth Ward, a supporter of Southwestern before his election to the episcopacy in 1906, worked zealously for the success of the project before his departure for Japan, where he died three years later. After his death, the campaign was renamed "The Ward Memorial Endowment Fund." Total subscriptions were $80,656.62, of which $31,669.44 was collected in cash. Almost half of it was expended for campaign expenses, leaving only $16,179.53 carried on the books in 1925. The Bishop Seth Ward Professorship of Bible and Religion was reported in 1978 as having a corpus of slightly over $40,000.[33]

Several other minor attempts to set up endowments occurred. One such was a small campaign to endow a German chair. A total of $10,095.89 was subscribed, but, after deduction for expenses, only $1,123.13 was carried on the books from it in 1925.[34]

Though none of these campaigns was more than partially successful, the fact that they were projected at all is an indication that Southwestern's leaders—administrators, Trustees, alumni, and students—had an expanded vision of its future. In fact, their ideas for enhancing its future came so fast that they seemed to trip over one another. These ideas did not, however, include changing the location of the University to an urban area.

Emergence of the Jesse Jones Friendship

Though the outcome of the Ward Memorial campaign was disappointing, it did result in the procurement of one friendship for the University that would have far-reaching consequences. During the year that Bishop Seth Ward died, 1909, Jesse H. Jones changed his religious affiliation from Baptist to Methodist and entered the history of Southwestern University for what would be a lifelong friendship. Though Jones does not say so directly, it is likely that his friendship with Ward was a part of the reason for his becoming a Methodist, for he says that he came to know Southwestern through the visit of a person whom Hyer had sent "concerning a contribution I had in mind for the creation of a Chair of Theology at Georgetown to my friend, Bishop Seth Ward."[35]

At the time Jones was thirty-five and on his way to becoming the most important businessman in Houston. Before long he became the largest developer in the city and was responsible for most of Houston's major prewar construction, owning nearly a hundred buildings in Houston. In 1908 he bought part of the *Houston Chronicle*, which he later purchased in its entirety. Between 1908 and 1918 he organized and became chairman of the Texas Trust Company and was active in most of the banking and real estate activities of the city.[36] Upon his death in 1956, the *Austin Statesman* said that "he built the skyline of the city [of Houston]."[37]

By 1912 Jones was president of the National Bank of Commerce, later the Texas Commerce Bank, whose president in 1947, A. D. Simpson, had been the emissary sent by Hyer in 1909 or 1910 to visit him about the Seth Ward Chair in Theology. Jones said that it was Simpson's general attitude and loyalty to Southwestern that had led to their friendship and of his offer of employment to Simpson. Though Jones would later receive twelve honorary degrees, Southwestern offered him his first in 1925, a fact he never forgot. He had quit school in the eighth grade to go to work. The state school that received his most consistent support was Texas A&M, which offered him an honorary degree in 1936.[38] A. Frank Smith became his pastor in the 1920s, leading to the close friendship that would be so important for Southwestern in the late 1930s and '40s.

Two of the gifts of Jesse Jones to Southwestern were among the most unusual in its history with regard to the method of payment. In a document to the Board of Trustees on April 24, 1937, Jones stated that on or about August 1, 1913, he had agreed to give Southwestern $25,000 payable at his convenience and to pay interest on it annually until it was paid, "which I have done." He designated this pledge as the Seth Ward Memorial Fund. On March 1, 1937, he agreed to give Southwestern a further donation of $7,500 for its Endowment Fund, payable, as in the case of his earlier pledge, at his convenience. He stated that "this indenture" of April 24, 1937, evidenced those two pledges and his intention to fulfill them either before his death or to have his executors do so after his death. In the meantime, he promised to pay the University 4 percent per annum on the $32,500. The agreement would end when he transferred to the University the $32,500.[39] Though by the terms of the agreement his Houston Endowment, Inc., was obligated to pay out the principal after his death on June 1, 1956, it overlooked the matter for fourteen years. On July 23, 1970, Mr. J. H. Creekmore, the President of the Endowment, acknowledged the mistake and sent a check for $25,666.67 for the Seth Ward Memorial Fund and $7,700.00 to the Endowment Fund.[40]

The Bishop Seth Ward Professorship in Religion in existence today originated with funds raised in 1909–1910. More than one-half of the amount secured was provided by Jesse Jones from his gift of 1913. The professorship is today supported by the Houston Endowment, Inc., which he created as the eleemosynary arm for distributing his fortune. A Jesse H. and Mary Gibbs Jones Professorship in Mathematics was established by the foundation in 1972, and the residence hall complex on the east side of the campus is also named for them. The Endowment contributed $5 million from 1982 through 1986 for the rehabilitation of campus residence halls and other facilities. The Fondren Science Building was renamed the Fondren-Jones Science Hall in 1981, when it was completely renovated and furnished with the latest in modern equipment with gifts from the Houston Endowment. A wide-ranging program of scholarships for minority students and other men and women was begun by Jesse Jones in 1948 and has been supported by the Houston Endowment since his death in 1956.

General Financial Assessment

A summary of the financial situation of Southwestern during Hyer's administration highlights several points. The slow pattern of building construction of earlier years was replaced by an attempt to build a new campus with first-class buildings. This construction was supposedly financed by subscriptions covering the building costs, but receipts from subscriptions were always considerably less than the amount pledged. In spite of this fact, subscriptions continued to be taken at face value rather than being discounted as assets on the University ledger.

A severe cash flow problem arose in the general operation of the University. This fact becomes apparent at times from actions taken by the Board. Faculty salaries were improved under Hyer, but obligations to the increased number of professors and staff outstripped the income from tuition, especially because of the large number of students, mostly ministerial students and children of ministers, over two hundred at one point, who paid no tuition at all. In 1907 the Trustees were forced to "apply the income of all available endowment funds to the payment of salaries of the faculty."[41] Finances were so pinched in 1910 that they authorized the Executive Committee "to meet any maturing indebtedness out of any fund having a cash balance to its credit."[42]

One should not, however, come to the conclusion that Trustees and administrative officers had forfeited good judgment and lost financial control. Psychological considerations must also be considered. During the decade, every aspect of University operation had seen tremendous advances. A new campus with three handsome buildings had been established. The faculty had been more than doubled, the educational program had been strengthened and expanded, the student body was larger than any other in Southern Methodism, a Medical College had been brought under the University's wings, and Rhodes scholars were being produced.

All of these happenings created an atmosphere of

excitement on campus. In the minds of those leading the institution the temporary financial stringency of the moment was the price to be paid in order to move the institution to full university status. The momentum of advance would soon bring the institution to the takeoff point where true university status would be reached and become self-sustaining. When this condition was achieved, financial solvency would be reestablished. Meanwhile, the momentum of advance must be maintained. This thought motivated University leaders to continue the pattern of advance. It was halted by a bombshell unexpectedly launched by one of its prominent alumni.

Proposed Memorial Hall. The proposal to build this Memorial Hall instigated the effort by President Boaz of Polytechnic in Fort Worth to remove Southwestern to that city. From the 1910 *Sou'wester*.

Plans for Memorial Hall

Musing on the past in his autobiography, some years after the removal controversy and without reference to it, former Regent John McLean describes a summer trip he made by pony in 1858. He says: "After a short ride of eight miles, [I] came upon the little village of Dallas sequestered on the east bank of the Trinity. Little then did I anticipate that the unpretentious village of a hundred or two people would in sixty years become the most attractive city of the State, with a population of 125,000."[43]

Just as Dallas was a vastly different city in the early twentieth century from the little village known by McLean prior to the Civil War, Texas was a vastly different state in 1910 than it had been in 1873, when Southwestern was established in Georgetown. Many people pondered on the significance of that difference for the Central University of Texas Methodism. As early as 1898 the highly respected judge, Asa Holt, who was either Vice President or President of the Board of Trustees for all but two years from 1878 to 1901, made a personal inquiry into the importance of an urban location for Church-related universities. In a newspaper article commenting on that inquiry, he wrote that he had corresponded with several prominent educators, particularly with the Presidents of Wesleyan University and of Emory College, about whether it was better to have a Church school in a rural or an urban setting. Their opinion, he stated, was that neither a rural, nor an urban, nor a suburban location was universally best. They felt that wherever it was located, the college should be the most important thing.[44]

Georgetown partisans occasionally felt it necessary to defend the Georgetown location, as did M. B. Lockett in an article of October 2, 1902, in the *Texas Christian Advocate.* He countered allegations against Georgetown printed in a previous issue by saying that Georgetown had contributed two or three times as much to Southwestern as the rest of the state put together.[45]

This doubt about a Georgetown location for Southwestern in an increasingly urban society surfaced as the fundamental reason for the removal controversy in 1910. The trigger of the controversy was a Board of Trustees proposal to construct another major building on campus. Frank Reedy, the University's first bursar, proposed it at a meeting of the Finance Committee of the Board of Trustees on January 31, 1910. Called Memorial Hall, it was to be "The Methodist Westminster Abbey" at Georgetown.[46] Students learned about it during a chapel service in early February 1910. They were so excited by what they heard that, without prompting, says Hyer, within an hour they subscribed $20,000 toward its erection. A subsequent meeting held in Dallas with representatives of the Alumni Association also elicited an enthusiastic response. They formed a committee to secure $100,000 toward the cost of the building. The Rev. F. B. Sinex of Phoenix, who had been so successful in securing funds for the Main Building ten years earlier, was employed to raise the remaining $130,000 necessary to complete it.[47]

The plans for the building, prepared by Fort Worth architects, were outlined in articles in the *Fort Worth Record* and the Dallas *News* on February 23. A sketch of the proposed building appeared in both those papers and in the *Sou'wester* of 1910. The building was to be a "three-story, domed structure purportedly modeled after the Congressional Library in Washington, D.C." It would feature a rotunda sixty-five feet in diameter. It would contain administrative offices, the library, a chapel seating 2,000, Y.M.C.A. and Y.W.C.A. meeting rooms, a gymnasium, and halls for literary societies. It would also contain parlors, reception rooms, a barber shop, bowling alleys, handball courts, a swimming pool, and a number of other halls and rooms.[48] It would be a magnificent structure.

Hiram Abiff Boaz and the Offer from Polytechnic

Then the bombshell struck. On March 7, 1910, Hiram Abiff Boaz, President of Polytechnic College in Fort Worth, a school connected with the Northwest Texas Conference, wrote a letter to President Hyer. In it he proposed the removal of Southwestern to Fort Worth and its merger with Polytechnic. The letter requested no publicity for the moment and asked for a meeting in Georgetown with Hyer and three representatives from Polytechnic, himself and two others.[49] The meeting was held and, contrary to the earlier request for no publicity, was reported immediately in *The News* of Dallas on March 15. The news article stated that Dr. H. A. Boaz, George W. Armstrong, and Sam Hay, Presiding Elder of the Fort Worth District, representatives of Polytechnic and Fort Worth, had just returned from Georgetown, where they presented a proposition to Southwestern. They proposed the removal of Southwestern to Fort Worth. The offer contained the provision that a first-class college would be maintained in Georgetown, with everything there now to be left there. They incorporated considerations valued at $525,000, including the entire Polytechnic plant, in their offer.[50]

The proffer by Polytechnic was not the first made to Southwestern by that institution. In 1899 the Trustees of the College had offered to transfer it to Southwestern under a specified set of terms. The Curators rejected the offer, thanking the Polytechnic Trustees for their tender

Cartoon from the 1910 *Sou'wester* showing Boaz carrying off the Administration Building to Ft. Worth in a wheelbarrow, with Hyer inside the building and Dean Cody tugging at his coattails to prevent it. John M. Barcus, the Georgetown pastor, is the little barking dog.

What Dr. Boaz proposed to do

but stating that "we can not accept the gift on their terms without doing violence to, or forfeiting the charter of the S. W. U."[51] The nature of their objections to the offer is unknown. Some years later, in 1905, the Southwestern faculty endorsed the action of its representative in voting against the admission of Polytechnic College to the College Council of Texas, for what reason is, once again, unknown.[52]

In 1908 an exchange of articles appeared in the *Texas Christian Advocate* between Dean R. A. Hearon of Polytechnic and chemistry Professor John H. Reedy of Southwestern. It involved Hearon's dissatisfaction with the Methodist General Board of Education's classification of Polytechnic as a Class C college, while Southwestern received a Class A rating. Their articles argued "over the relative merits of the entrance requirements of the two schools."[53] Letters to Dean Cody a year later from R. F. Milam, Attorney at Law in Fort Worth, speak to Milam's efforts to determine for Cody the ownership of the Polytechnic property. He indicates that his preliminary assessment is that "the property of Polytechnic College is the property of the corporation and not of the church."[54]

The upshot of these Southwestern-Polytechnic exchanges is that Polytechnic had usually been the seeker and Southwestern the sought-after in their contacts. The Boaz letter of March 7 was of the same nature—Polytechnic was again proposing something that Southwestern would be called upon to either accept or reject. This time, however, there were two differences. The first was that the Polytechnic agent, President Boaz, was not only a person of considerable promise and stature in the Church, but he was also one of the finest graduates Southwestern had produced, one who in time would become President of Southern Methodist University and later a bishop of the Church. The second was that the issue involved could not be particularized as a narrow educational matter of interest only to academic officialdom. It was an issue of interest to the whole Church.

Boaz had graduated with a B.S. from Southwestern in 1893 and an A.M., with first honors, the following year. He ascended the ladder of ecclesiastical preferment quickly and was invited back to Southwestern for the 1898 Commencement ceremony and the 1909 Homecoming celebration to give major addresses. In 1902 he was elected President of Polytechnic College (later Texas Wesleyan University), where he remained for nine years. After service as Vice President at Southern Methodist for a short time during its formation, he returned to Texas Woman's College as President from 1913 to 1918. Polytechnic had changed its mission and adopted that name after the establishment of Southern Methodist. He became Secretary of the Board of Church Extension in 1918, second President of SMU in 1920, and bishop in 1922. He retired in 1938.

During the years of the removal controversy, however, Boaz became the bête noire of those working to keep Southwestern in Georgetown. A humorous feature in the 1910 *Sou'wester* gives the following definition of Boaz:

> BOAZ (*Bos*, an ox), p. n. "An educational leader grossly ignorant of facts," who is president of an insignificant prep school; also special correspondent to the *Dallas News*. He is trampling on Georgetown's feelings by trying to move Georgetown—or rather the greater part of it, the University—to Ft. Worth. Synonym: "Poly."[55]

There is also a cartoon showing a giant Boaz with a wheelbarrow hauling off the Main Building. The legend reads: "What Dr. Boaz proposed to do."

Hyer's Reply and the Georgetown Anti-Removal Effort

Hyer replied officially to the Boaz letter on March 15. He began by accusing Boaz of bringing up the matter because Southwestern had announced its intention to build "a great Memorial Hall." It is the same question, he continues, that has arisen every time Southwestern has considered building a structure of this magnitude, namely, whether or not it is a good idea to do so without knowing the permanence of Southwestern in Georgetown. To the claim that the history of education shows that it is impossible to build a great university save in a great city, the answer is that whenever the Church has built an urban university it has sooner or later fallen out of the hands of the Church. Nevertheless Hyer admits that the question is one he has thought about for ten years without having come to a definitive conclusion in his own mind. He does know, he states, that if the Trustees decided to move, he would accept their decision without question.

The remainder of Hyer's letter is filled mostly with facts and figures showing that the Polytechnic offer, ostensibly generous, is in fact quite unacceptable. It does not come close to matching the resources that Southwestern already has in Georgetown. Looking today at the figures presented by both Boaz and Hyer, one is struck by their willingness to count subscriptions and certain other questionable assets as if they were real values. Hyer puts the total value of Southwestern at $1,100,000. The financial loss in accepting the Polytechnic offer, he says, would be at least $300,000. Furthermore, "at this particular time, any discussion of a change of the location of the University would [also] bring about such a state of suspense as would make difficult any forward movement for the great new building that we have planned. So far in these plans we have met with the most encouraging success, and it now appears that the raising of $250,000.00 for a Memorial Hall will be the easiest task that Southwestern University has ever undertaken."[56]

Hyer's letter pleased the faculty and members of the Georgetown community so much that they immediately concluded that he was a staunch opponent of removal. It is quite likely that much of the later opprobrium heaped on him, when he sided with those who wanted to move the University to Dallas, came from their feeling that he had deceived them.

The faculty met a week later and discussed the issue at length. "Resolutions were adopted assigning reasons why Georgetown is the desirable place for the University." During the week Dean Cody recast the resolutions into final form and read them at the next meeting. From that point on he became the behind-the-scenes faculty director of the anti-removal effort and probably the most influential anti-removal leader of any kind throughout the controversy.[57]

The Georgetown effort to retain Southwestern, regardless of whatever arguments might be used, was undergirded by one simple fact. Most citizens of the town felt that Southwestern and Georgetown were synonymous and that without Southwestern the city would wither away. Lockett expressed it clearly in his autobiography.

> The chief enterprise in Georgetown then as now was the Southwestern University. Without it Georgetown would have been a mere dot on the map or an ant hill, so to speak, and long since the county seat would have been moved to Taylor or some other place. . . . Because of the University the town enjoyed the reputation of having a high class of citizens, as well as being a fine place in which to rear and educate a family. On that account hundreds of people had moved to Georgetown from time to time to educate their children, and while many people remained here only temporarily, still they exerted a powerful influence throughout the state in favor of the University. And when they moved away other people took their places in the community.[58]

A few days after the Boaz letter became known, the people of Georgetown came together in a mass meeting at the City Hall to discuss the situation. A committee was appointed to lead the campaign against the proposition. Lockett was elected chairman. The ecclesiastical champion for Georgetown was its Methodist pastor, Rev. John M. Barcus. Lockett says that Barcus did most of the writing advocating the cause of Georgetown, or rather, of the University. He was in close contact with Cody. Some of his writings were replete with data obtained from Cody and use his arguments. When his time as pastor expired, the people of Georgetown presented him with a solid gold watch with his initials engraved on the case.[59]

Initial Sparring: Hyer, Boaz, and the Trustees

Hyer's letter to Boaz did not discourage him. A week later he penned another missive to Hyer giving a point-by-point response to his arguments. He admitted that the timing of the original letter "was to prevent the erection of the Memorial Hall in Georgetown." For him the case for moving Southwestern should not be impeded by the construction of a new building that might cement the connection of Georgetown and Southwestern forever. A North Texas location, he alleged, would immediately move Southwestern to a new level in terms of both population and financial resources far beyond what the successful completion of any building could. With this idea in mind, he had given the newspapers his correspondence with Dr. Hyer. In closing he said: "We love the Southwestern University, and are now seeking for it a wider field and a larger opportunity, and a more glorious future."[60] Hyer responded with another letter to Boaz on March 31, presenting a rationale for the funding policy of the University to date.[61]

With the matter out in the open, a number of Trustees began to correspond with Cody about it. William Wiess of Beaumont was particularly agitated. He had for some time been an active supporter of the University, though he was unable, because of the health of himself and his brother, to attend many Board meetings. He had become a Trustee in 1906 and served until 1913. He made contributions to the University from time to time, including at least two to the physics department mentioned in the Board minutes of 1904. During the financial exigencies of the latter Hyer years, he lent money to the University, $12,000 being owed him in 1910. He kept in contact with the Georgetown effort through his brother-in-law, C. S. Belford, and Dean Cody. Cody preserved ten letters from him written during the four months after March 23, 1910, and Wiess invited him to visit Belford and read their correspondence. In his letters to Cody, he comments on the controversy, suggests things for Cody and others to do, and relates what he is doing with other Trustees and friends of the University to combat the removal effort.

Meanwhile, the citizens of Georgetown began to take an active role in the controversy. John M. Barcus wrote a major article on April 4, signed by A. A. Booty, M. B. Lockett, and E. G. Gillett. It was subsequently printed as a sixteen-page booklet entitled *Southwestern University at Georgetown, Texas: Some Reasons why it Should not be Removed; Plain Statements by the Citizens of Georgetown.*[62] A major argument advanced in the article and booklet was that the presence of Southwestern in Georgetown was a binding contractual agreement made in 1873 that could not be legally breached. Cody secured several legal opinions supporting this argument.

Boaz answered the letter on April 9. In it he included many of the arguments that he would later incorporate in a letter of April 21 to Hyer. He says that there was nothing in the 1873 contract with Georgetown that insisted it would be any more permanent than the existence of Soule University in Chappell Hill. Having read this and other statements being made by Boaz about the intentions of their father, both of F. A. Mood's sons in the ministry issued refutations of his interpretation. John Richardson Mood wrote a long letter on April 12, followed by one from Robert Gibbs Mood on April 23. Both letters were printed. They implied that removing Southwestern from Georgetown would dishonor the intent of their father.[63]

Early in the controversy, Boaz tried to win over the Georgetown citizens to his plan. He complimented them by saying that Georgetown was no obscure village but a city of four thousand. At the same time, however, he mentioned that Fort Worth was a city of eighty thousand. He told them that they had misunderstood the proposal presented by Polytechnic. It did not propose to move the entire University to Fort Worth but "to leave a first-class college there [in Georgetown]."[64] Failing to convince them, he became exasperated with the Georgetown opposition and resorted to sarcasm. Commenting on a section of the booklet where the citizens talk about improvements in the city, Boaz remarks: "We are glad to learn that at last Georgetown has a few miles of cement sidewalks and graded streets. We refrain from comparisons on this point."[65]

Hyer Tips His Hand

On April 18 Hyer sent a questionnaire to the Trustees. With it he enclosed a letter in which he outlined a hypothetical plan "to have the University moved to Dallas instead of Ft. Worth." In it he refers to "the Dallas offer." Unfortunately, the first page of this letter is missing in the surviving copy, and details of the offer have to be teased out of a cryptic sentence on the second page. Hyer says in it that though the Boaz offer to move Southwestern to Fort Worth with the current Board of Trustees in control was rejected, such an arrangement might be worked out for a Dallas institution. "Southwestern," he says, still speaking hypothetically, "should not be moved just to gain $650,000, but to enter into a larger field of usefulness. This offer on the part of Dallas is made on condition that we build the Memorial Hall and raise $250,000.00 as a new endowment fund."[66]

Apparently an undesignated Dallas group had offered a subsidy of $650,000 to Southwestern if it would move to Dallas and build Memorial Hall there. In addition, Southwestern should raise an endowment of $250,000. The group making the offer was almost certainly a committee established by the Dallas Chamber of Commerce to look into the possibility of attracting a university to the city. This offer was the result of a Dallas interest in Southwestern that had been building for some time.

Hyer had shared the plans for the construction of Memorial Hall with the citizens of Fort Worth and Dallas from the beginning. He was trying to raise money for it there, and newspapers in the two cities had published pictures of the proposed building on February 23. After learning about the matter directly from Hyer, Dean McReynolds called J. R. Babcock, secretary of the Chamber of Commerce, and told him about it. He told him that the idea of a great Methodist university in one of the large cities of North Texas had circulated for some time and that he should talk to Dr. Hyer about it. On March 18, 1910, Babcock wrote Hyer asking about the possibilities of securing Southwestern for Dallas and what his own opinion was. Hyer replied that he would come to Dallas to talk about the matter. The first conference, involving Babcock, H. D. Lindsey, McReynolds, and Hyer, was held at the Southland Hotel a few days later. It lasted until after midnight.

On April 9, Babcock, McReynolds, and Mayor Hay visited Little Rock, where the trustees of the General Education Board of the Rockefeller Foundation were meeting. Dr. Wallace A. Buttrick, Secretary of the General Education Board, declared that "Dallas was the most inviting unoccupied educational field in the United States."[67]

Soon thereafter word spread in Dallas that the Chamber of Commerce might offer a subsidy to bring Southwestern there. McReynolds was likely the emissary of the committee to Hyer. Ray Hyer Brown says that "when Dr. McReynolds came to Southwestern with a definite plan and proposition to move Southwestern to Dallas, the plans were out in the open."[68] The six questions posed by Hyer to the Trustees in the questionnaire of April 18 ask them to express their preferences about the various options available. Nevertheless, he tries very specifically to obtain a dollar commitment from them for raising the Memorial Hall money, wherever it is to be built, and for obtaining a $250,000 endowment, exactly the amount specified in the Dallas proposal. He concludes the questionnaire by asking the Trustees to advise him if it would be wise to send out a like questionnaire to alumni, friends, and patrons.

On receiving Hyer's letter and questionnaire, the Executive Committee reacted immediately and unanimously. It sent a letter to the Board of Trustees stating that President Hyer had sent out a circular letter containing a "hypothetical proposition" on his own without consulting the faculty or the Executive Committee and that his letter did not represent either. It expressed the hope that "you will not commit yourself to this movement, until a full and fair discussion can be had." The letter cannot be taken as anything other than a resounding rebuke to Hyer and a declaration of war against a removal effort to either Fort Worth or Dallas.[69]

Hyer received one response that has been preserved. It came from B. D. Orgain of Bastrop. Orgain was a Trustee for thirty-four years, from 1883 to 1916. He was one of the most important members of the Board. He told Hyer that he was not prepared to answer the questions raised in the letter in detail but could not see the wisdom in writing it, especially coming from the head of the University. Whether or not Hyer believes in the removal of the University from Georgetown, Orgain alleges that the circular gives that impression. He says that as for himself, he "is opposed to the University being located in any large city."[70] Opponents of the removal effort would bring forward time and again the corrosive influence of urban society on public morals as an argument against it.

Analysis of Hyer's Position

Reflecting on Hyer's desire to move Southwestern, M. B. Lockett states that Hyer wanted to move the school from the beginning. After the Georgetown committee against removal, with him as chairman, was appointed, "it was arranged that the committee should meet with Dr. Hyer at his home the next night." The committee asked Hyer to visit Dallas at once to meet with Judge Brooks, President of the Board of Trustees. The committee little dreamed, he says, that "Dr. Hyer was as deeply involved in a plot to move Southwestern as Boaz or anyone else. . . . Imagine our surprise when a short time later we learned of the real attitude of Dr. Hyer."[71] Judge Brooks also ended up advocating removal to Dallas.

One can understand Lockett's sentiments about Hyer, but, in fairness to him, one must look at the matter from Hyer's perspective as well. Records abound regarding the Cody-Barcus-Lockett-Wiess position but few about that of Hyer. He was not a prolific producer of letters or a voluminous archivist like Cody. His personality was restrained rather than exuberant. He believed deeply but advanced his beliefs more by appeals to reason than to the emotions. He was at a disadvantage in situations where emotion was the dominant force, as it was in the removal controversy. In his frustration with Hyer, Lockett exaggerated, as he later admitted, the duplicitous elements in Hyer's actions.

As he tried to grow Southwestern to university status, Hyer had been reminded from time to time of the limitations placed on Southwestern by its location in Georgetown. Ray Hyer Brown says that he had once entertained great hopes that the Carnegie Foundation for the Advancement of Teaching would help Southwestern as it was helping many schools throughout the country. He made an application to the Foundation and traveled to New York to meet with its representative. Though the representative seemed interested, the application was turned down. The two reasons given for the rejection were that "Southwestern was located in too small a town" and that "too many students were receiving free tuition." The latter reason Hyer defended as necessary for a Church-related school, but the former he took seriously. Whenever he tried to raise money to enlarge the University's plant, he heard such statements as, "Georgetown is not the place for a big university," or, "If the Methodists want to build a real university, it will have to be in a large city." [72] At some point in the controversy, perhaps when the Dallas officials later contacted him on April 9, Dr. Wallace Buttrick of the Rockefeller Foundation indicated to Methodist officials that, located in a small town with a correspondingly small surrounding population and "under the very eaves of the State and Baptist University, Southwestern could not hope to properly fulfill its mission of becoming a great institution."[73]

A number of his friends, whose opinions he valued, were proponents of moving the University to a large city. On Hyer's trips to Dallas to visit the College of Medicine, Dean John O. McReynolds always shepherded him around, putting him in contact with the Dallas community. His uncle by marriage, Dr. Horace Bishop, was particularly influential. Ray Hyer Brown says that "every time Dr. Horace Bishop came to Georgetown he would say, 'Southwestern has outgrown Georgetown.'" Hyer valued his counsel. Bishop had been a friend of Dr. Mood and was a friend of the school.[74] These friendships and contacts with Dallas were frequent enough that Lockett claimed later that Hyer "had been one of a party for more than five years to move the University from Georgetown to Dallas."[75]

Lockett's five years correspond closely to the time element provided by a letter uncovered by Ralph Jones suggesting that Hyer had decided as early as 1906 to move the school to Dallas. Writing to Dr. Cody, a certain M. N. Graham, possibly from Dallas, said: "I think Prof. Hyer's decision that the S. W. U. be moved to Dallas a wise one from every standpoint, and hope that the plan can be consummated this summer. He should be able to devote his time to it; and, if the state continues in its present prosperous condition, he (and you, I hope) should be able to carry it out."[76] Graham was unaware, of course, that he was providing this information to the person who would become Hyer's foremost opponent in the removal controversy. Apparently, Cody did not reveal the contents of the letter to anyone at the time but brought it out four or five years later when Hyer tipped his hand and openly joined the forces for removal to Dallas. This longtime connection with Dallas must be the reason Hyer was so explicit in his rejection of the Fort Worth bid. He was not against removal. He was against removal to Fort Worth.

The question remains, "If Hyer wanted to move the school to Dallas as early as 1906, why did it not become an issue until 1910?" The reason, as suggested by a newspaper article of the time, is that there was no invitation from Dallas to do so.[77] Hyer knew the issue would have to be broached by some official group from Dallas. He, as the sitting President of Southwestern, trying to advance the school, could not risk initiating an effort to move it to a city that had not asked for it. He might lose both the advances being made in Georgetown and the removal effort as well. Lockett alleges that for some years prior to the controversy Hyer had been urging the Dallas people to come out openly for the University.[78] They did not, and he gave up on the possibility of moving the school. Cody kept his silence and did not mention his knowledge of Hyer's real views to anyone.

Hyer was as surprised as anyone by the proposal from Boaz in 1910, and he rejected it unequivocally, much to the pleasure of the Georgetown community. That offer, however, and the publicity associated with it were heard in Dallas and caused that city to join in the hunt. Though Hyer initially tried to finesse the issue and move it into the path of rational discussion, it became so volatile that he could not keep it within bounds. He had to expose his real feelings before having time to educate his constituency. A newspaper article reporting on the Board meeting in 1910 and substantiated by Lockett, who was present when it occurred, says that after the Board had turned down the Dallas proposal, Hyer expressed to the Trustees that it "had been a dream of his life."[79]

Boaz Begins to Change Course

A meeting of the Polytechnic's Board of Trustees on April 20 supported the Boaz position completely. By now Board members were aware that they were unlikely to win over the Georgetown contingent and the Southwestern alumni across the state, a large majority of whom, except for alumni in the ministry, were coming out against the proposal. Consequently, they introduced a new element into the controversy—that of going over the heads of the Southwestern Trustees.[80] They asked that their proposal be presented to the Annual Conferences at their next meeting regardless of whether or not the Southwestern Board of Trustees accepted it.[81]

Boaz, for his part, chided the Georgetown leaders on April 30 for the use of overblown rhetoric in support of their cause. Nevertheless, he himself was caught in a claim that was proved to be false. When Boaz stated that authorities connected with the General Education Board of the Rockefeller Foundation had given Dr. Hyer to understand that they would contribute $250,000 as an endowment if the University were moved to Dallas,[82] Cody, John M. Barcus, and J. R. Mood each contacted Wallace Buttrick, its Secretary. They received assurances from him that such was not the case. Barcus sent him newspaper clippings containing the Boaz statement. Buttrick replied that "the statements contained in the newspaper clippings inclosed [sic] with your letter are . . . without foundation in fact."[83]

Cody gently chided Boaz in another instance for misusing quotations from his biography of Dr. Mood in a newspaper article to make his case.[84] Responding to his "good friend and former student, Dr. H. A. Boaz," he says that "Dr. Boaz, in applying these quotations to the case in hand, puts an entirely different construction on the passages quoted to that intended by the writer." He then provides the correct interpretation.[85]

Notable in the Boaz article of April 30 is that he uses an argument helpful to a Dallas rather than to a Fort Worth location for Southwestern. He has obviously become aware of the recently launched Dallas effort to obtain the University, and he is signaling that he may be ready to switch. He will consummate the switch at the meeting of the General Conference in Asheville a few weeks later.

The Die is Cast: Actions at the Asheville General Conference

The quadrennial meeting of the General Conference of the Methodist Episcopal Church, South, met in Asheville, North Carolina, during the middle of May 1910. Present were all the bishops of the Church, the elected delegates from all the Annual Conferences, college presidents, and other important ecclesiastical figures. The Dallas *News* reported on its actions daily. It reported in its first article that Dallas would make a campaign at the ensuing Annual Conferences to bring Southwestern University to Dallas, adding that "a very large majority of the Texas delegates and visitors now here are in favor of Dallas."[86]

Hyer used the General Conference to advance his position. Sensing that most of the persons in the Texas entourage were persons whom he might count on for support, he immediately met with ten of his Trustees and something like fifty of the other influential Texas leaders. After the meeting, they exchanged letters and telegrams with persons in Dallas suggesting that if Dallas made "certain offers for the University they would certainly induce Southwestern to move from Georgetown to Dallas."[87]

Agreement came quickly, and Hyer announced on May 15 "that a tentative contract had been made for fifteen days, pending a meeting of the board of trustees of that institution [Southwestern] and the confirmation of the patronizing [sponsoring] Annual Conferences. He also stated that the agreement reached seemed to be satisfactory to the representatives of the Polytechnic college of Fort Worth."

The Dallas offer was for fifty acres of land and a subsidy of $400,000. A piece of the agreement was that Polytechnic would become a part of the institution but that it would continue in Fort Worth, probably becoming a women's college and conservatory. Boaz was quoted as saying that the Dallas offer was better than that of Fort Worth and should be acceded to in the interest of harmonious relations between the educational institutions. For its part, the agreement stipulated that the Methodist Church of Texas must provide $500,000 toward the enterprise. The fifteen days meant that Dallas had that period of time in which to raise the $400,000 or to propose an acceptable equivalent.[88]

The newspaper article reporting this agreement concluded by asking a prophetic question: "What authority have some of the officers of the Southwestern University to receive or accept a tender that can of right only be made to the board of trustees and the patronizing [sponsoring] conferences?" Hyer, the ten Trustees, and the fifty influential Texas leaders would, to their dismay, soon find out the answer to this question. They would learn that Cody and those who thought like him were not impressed by the tender or by the agreement. John M. Barcus, also a delegate to the Conference, informed Cody by letter of the actions taken at Asheville. He was not a part of them. He predicted to Cody what in fact turned out to be the Board action. He said: "I still feel confident that the Board will turn the whole thing down."[89]

One of the anomalous elements in the Asheville agreement was the complete capitulation by Boaz of his previous position and his coming out in favor of the Dallas offer. Various possibilities may be adduced to explain it, but one of them must have been a development related to Texas Christian University. On March 22, after only one exchange of letters between Boaz and Hyer, the main TCU building in Waco burned. Ralph Jones says that "before the walls had completely cooled, a bid was offered from interested Fort Worth citizens for the re-location of the school." With an offer out to TCU, one that presented a greater probability of success than that of Boaz to Southwestern, support for the Southwestern option must have diminished in Fort Worth. The citizens there might not have wanted to have a promise of two subsidies on the table. Within ten days after Hyer's announcement on May 15 from Asheville of a tentative agreement with Dallas, TCU finalized its decision to relocate in Fort Worth.[90]

The Dallas Effort and the Board Response

With the meeting of the Southwestern Board of Trustees scheduled for June 9–11, the Dallas proponents immediately set to work after the Asheville General Conference to raise the $400,000 subsidy, mobilizing the movers and shakers in the city and issuing regular reports detailing the progress of the drive. Dean John O. McReynolds claimed in one of them that "every bishop in Southern Methodism and the president of every Methodist college in the South is the champion of our cause."[91] Efforts were made by him and Hyer to secure written confirmation from Bishop Candler of his advocacy of the cause. Candler had earlier worked long and hard on behalf of the Harrison Endowment campaign.[92] He did issue a statement, but it was so ambiguous as to be of practically no use. A longtime friend of fellow Georgian Dean Cody, Candler wrote him explaining what he had done. He concluded his letter by saying that he had recently been to "Old Emory" with "old classmates" who thought of Cody, talked of him, and loved him.[93] Cody's friendships were invaluable to his cause. Cody also wrote an extensive letter to Bishop Hoss outlining the case for not removing Southwestern to Dallas.[94]

One bishop, however, the newly elected Edwin D. Mouzon, recently Professor of Theology at Southwestern, did come out strongly in favor of removal. Lockett says that at first it was thought by Georgetown people that Hyer had influenced him. They soon learned that the opposite was the case. Lockett calls Mouzon "the champion of that side on every occasion."[95]

Both sides tried to influence the citizenry of Dallas. The Dallas *News* reported on May 26 that a delegation of prominent citizens from Georgetown visited the city on behalf of the anti-removal effort. The party included R. E. Ward, Mayor, C. S. Belford, Vice President of the First National Bank, John D. Hughes of the Farmers State Bank, Lee J. Rountree, editor of the *Georgetown Commercial*, Hon. J. E. Cooper, Judge Cooper Sansom, and E. G. Gillett.[96] The citizen visit was responded to by a visit to the Dallas Chamber of Commerce by Judge M. M. Brooks, President of the Southwestern Board of Trustees, Board member J. M. Peterson, Presiding Elder of the Dallas District, and President Hyer. They invited the citizens of Dallas to present a proposition to the Board of Trustees in line with that formulated at the recent meeting of the General Conference in Asheville, stating that if they did so, they believed the Methodists of the state would contribute the $500,000 required of them and that they could go to the General Education Board of the Rockefeller Foundation in New York and secure $1,200,000.[97]

Both sides were pulling out all the stops to win their case. It was at this point that fifteen leading citizens of Georgetown suggested that if Dallas wanted a college, it should build one for itself rather than trying to secure one by moving Southwestern from Georgetown to Dallas.[98] It was too early yet for this idea to be taken seriously, since the leaders of both sides were as yet too committed to absolute victory to entertain other options, but an inability on the part of either to win a clear victory would eventually cause it to become the permanent outcome.

Meanwhile, the Dallas partisans continued their campaign to raise commitments for $400,000, while those from Georgetown tried to line up a majority of the Trustees against the removal effort. Both succeeded. The Dallas *News* reported on June 10 that the campaign goal had been secured the day before and that a committee from the Chamber of Commerce had left to present it to the Board of Trustees "today."[99] But the Georgetown supporters denied them a victory at the Board meeting. A majority of the Trustees voted against the proposal when it arrived.

A committee of three persons represented the Dallas Chamber of Commerce on the trip to Georgetown, one of whom was the Medical College Dean, Dr. John O. McReynolds. They were received courteously and given full attention by the Trustees when they presented their proposal. Their offer exceeded and was more flexible than what had been proposed in Asheville. It consisted of three parts. First, Dallas would provide a mutually acceptable site consisting of fifty acres of land. Secondly, $325,000 in bona fide subscriptions had already been secured and an additional fifty acres of land contiguous to the site would be provided, to be used or sold by the University at its pleasure. The total value of this item was stipulated as $400,000. Should the University not want the extra land, it could elect to receive an additional $50,000 promised by a group of citizens. Thirdly, on acceptance of the offer and its having cleared all legal hurdles, two gifts of $100,000 each would come from two persons and one of an unspecified but generous amount from another person, with other gifts from persons who had indicated that they were only waiting for a definitive decision to announce their gifts.[100]

After the Dallas offer had been presented, a long resolution to reject it was presented by its opponents on the Board. Its supporters countered by presenting a motion to have the offer transmitted directly to the several Annual Conferences for their decision rather than having the Board vote on it. It was rejected. The initial resolution to turn down the Dallas offer carried 20 to 13.[101] Three more Trustees, whose votes were not counted, wrote in against the offer. Twelve of the fourteen laymen present voted against it. Among those voting for the Dallas offer were Judge M. M. Brooks, President of the Board, the Rev. James Campbell, one of the first four graduates of the University, and Robert Stewart Hyer, President of the University. This voting breakdown exhibits the pattern of support and opposition that obtained for the entire controversy. Church leaders and a majority of the ministers, trying to establish an overall educational system in an increasingly urban society, tended to favor removal. Laymen and alumni, looking at the issue from a more historical, local, and experiential standpoint, tended to oppose removal.

The five-part resolution adopted by the Trustees stated that "Southwestern University has been and should permanently continue to be located at Georgetown, Williamson Co., Texas." It enjoined its personnel from taking any actions related to removal, saying that "all the officers of said University, the President, the Faculty, and the agents thereof are hereby instructed to hereafter discountenance and discourage the agitation of the removal of said University from Georgetown." In other words, Hyer was being told to cease and desist from any attempt to move the University. A motion was then approved to send the majority resolution to the Conferences. In spite of his actions to move the University and his expression of disappointment at the decision of the Board, Hyer agreed to abide by its mandate. For its part, the Board voted to include an expression of confidence in him in its transmittal of the majority resolution.

After approval of the majority resolution, twelve Trustees acting for the minority presented a paper dissenting from the action of the majority. Hyer was not one of them. He was following the instruction from the Board not to take any further action related to removal. The minority paper stated that the intent of the original founders was "to establish a real University," that it is impossible to do such a thing in Georgetown, that all units of the University should be in one place, that the offer of Dallas is magnificent, and that the interpretation that the school is forever bound to Georgetown is inaccurate. Consequently, the dissenters called on the sponsoring Conferences to invite the Oklahoma Conference to join the effort and to establish the institution in Dallas and undertake to raise $500,000 for its maintenance. The three Trustee officers of the Board elected for the following year, Brooks, Kilgore, and Weeks, as President, Vice President, and Secretary, all supported the minority position. C. C. Cody, the non-trustee treasurer, could not vote. Though the minority had lost the vote in the Board meeting, they were constructing a case for presentation to the Annual Conferences.

The Annual Conferences Adopt an Alternative Plan

Immediately after the Board meeting, J. M. Peterson, Presiding Elder of the Dallas District, phoned the Dallas *News* to put a positive spin on the action from a Dallas perspective. He let it be known that the vote by the Southwestern Board was only a provisional setback and that the real power to remove the University lay with the Annual Conferences. He emphasized that they would make the decision.[102] News of the Board action appeared in newspapers across the state, and a spate of letters to the editor appeared in the next issue of the *Texas Christian Advocate* commenting favorably or unfavorably on the vote.

Though Horace Bishop had been counseling Hyer for years to move Southwestern to an urban area, he had not participated openly in any of the events regarding removal to date. His entry into the debate at this point created considerable suspicion in the anti-removal camp. When the Dallas *News* printed a letter from him on June 17 favoring removal,[103] Robert A. John, Cody's legal counsel, drew from it the inference that Hyer was using him as a stalking horse to carry on the debate. The implication was that, being prohibited by the Board from participating further in the removal controversy, Hyer was using a kinsman, his uncle by marriage, to speak for him. John's letter reveals the fact that, in spite of the Board's unanimous vote of confidence in Hyer, some of his opponents did not trust his statement to the effect that "he recognized their [the Board's] right to instruct him in respect to the policy to be pursued in this matter."[104]

The debate continued throughout the summer in letters, in newspaper articles, and wherever ministers and alumni gathered. By mid-August Robert Gibbs Mood, Presiding Elder of the Greenville District, wrote Cody that he perceived a change in the strategy of the forces for removal. He stated that they were beginning now to plan for "a great Methodist University at Dallas without reference to

Southwestern."[105] He was probably reacting to news that a meeting had been held that included Bishop Atkins, some selected ministers, and a committee from the Chamber of Commerce discussing a proposition to build "a great central educational enterprise" without regard to Southwestern.[106] The Dallas *News* shortly thereafter reported that the Chamber of Commerce had adopted a proposition to build such a university.[107] In preparation for the Annual Conference meetings, about a hundred preachers and laymen committed to keeping Southwestern in Georgetown attended a rally in Waco. Resolutions opposing removal were adopted to be sent to all the Annual Conferences.[108]

The first Annual Conference to meet was the West Texas Conference in Austin. Actions there validated the earlier perception by R. G. Mood. The majority forces at the Conference supporting the Dallas offer had indeed changed their strategy. They were no longer pushing for the removal of Southwestern to Dallas but for the establishment of a new university. The seven-part resolution adopted by the Conference was prefaced by a statement that the development of the Church's educational needs in Texas was such that those needs could not be met by "the existing institutions with their present facilities." Consequently, the Dallas offer must be given "careful and painstaking consideration," with the object of establishing "a complete university" there. The Educational Commission stipulated by the Educational Convention of 1906, but not activated until now, was given the task of performing this consideration. The motion setting up the commission carried 104 to 46. Overwhelming majorities approved this same resolution at the other Conferences.

The commission as finally established consisted of two lay and two clerical members from each Conference. Called and chaired by the presiding bishop, the commission was empowered to accept or reject the Dallas proposal, to take other steps for the expansion of Methodist university education if this proved impractical, to determine the relationship of existing schools to the proposed university, and to act as a board of trust for any new university until other provisions for its governance could be made. The commission was to have a life of four years.[109] In order to explicitly protect Southwestern against the sweeping powers granted in the original resolution, a subsequent resolution, known as the Godbey resolution, stated that "we endorse the work which is being done in Southwestern University of Georgetown, and instruct said commissioners to make provision for its continuance with the present equipment, and as far as practicable provide for the enlargement of the same in the future."[110]

While Methodists in Texas struggled to resolve their problems in higher education, the General Education Board of the Rockefeller Foundation made a decision of its own. Whereas earlier Hyer, McReynolds, Cody, and others had argued pro and con about the effect that moving Southwestern would have on obtaining a grant from that body, failure to settle the controversy had apparently caused the General Education Board in New York to give up entirely on Southwestern. It announced on November 11, 1910, that it was making a $200,000 contribution to Baylor University.[111]

Decision for a New University and Southwestern's Response

The commission established by the Annual Conference sessions met twice, first in Austin on January 18, 1911, and two weeks later in Dallas. Cody and other persons associated with him went to Austin for the first meeting a day early to agree on a strategy.[112] Whatever their strategy, their efforts availed little, for the members of the commission had already decided what they were going to do. The commission members were almost without exception from the removal camp. They had decided, however, that a continued push for removal in the face of such unrelenting opposition as they had faced would be counterproductive. The consensus result of the meetings in Austin and Dallas was that a new university would indeed be established in Dallas and that no further effort should be made to move Southwestern.

After the Austin meeting, Cody, Barcus, and their friends no longer worried about the removal of Southwestern to Dallas but concerned themselves with what they should do in the face of the decision to establish the new university. John M. Barcus and his younger brother, J. Sam Barcus, outlined in letters to Cody soon after the Austin meeting what became in fact the program subsequently followed by Southwestern.

In spite of the fact that the elder Barcus had been moved from Georgetown to Weatherford in the fall of 1910, some said to punish him for his leadership in the Georgetown effort, he did not respond in kind or cease to speak out for the cause. He said that Southwestern's leaders should not "hurt or antagonize the New Complete University" but put on a campaign to build up Southwestern. They should do so in such a way as "to make it clear to those real estate boosters that what they are getting is not Southwestern with its history, prestige, Alumni and ex students, but an institution that will have to be built up *de novo* and depend for its success on an entirely new constituency." He felt that the alumni of the University should be reminded that "their allegiance as graduates is not to be transferred to the Complete University but is to remain with Southwestern at Georgetown." If they do this, the future of Southwestern will be assured "no matter what they build in North Texas."[113] His younger brother, J. Sam Barcus, wrote that Southwestern's "supply of nourishment [had been] partly cut off," but he offered with others "to lead a charge" in gaining recruits and building up resources for the school. "Our school has been crippled but she's worth saving." The Trustees should continue to do the job they were elected to do and act according to the rights granted them in the charter of the University.[114]

One of Southwestern's supporters, John H. Griffith, Vice President of the City National Bank of Taylor, wrote Cody that the "bone of contention" between Southwestern and the new university would be "which institution is entitled to be the Central University of Texas Methodism." He argued that if properly approached, Methodists would recognize that Southwestern is that institution. He was mistaken in his analysis. The notion of a Central university for Texas Methodism was now dead. Southwestern's leaders had enough common sense to recognize that such a claim would ring hollow, and the leaders of Southern Methodist University never claimed it for themselves. Hyer, who became the first President of SMU in 1911, refused to take any action in his position that would denigrate Southwestern. Afterwards its leaders had their eyes on a larger mission—becoming, along with Emory University in Atlanta, the two Methodist universities for the entirety of Southern Methodism, one for the Southeast, one for the Southwest.

Aside from an ill-advised attempt on the part of some of the Dallas supporters to wrest Southwestern's name away from it and to give it to the new university in Dallas, an attempt that was squelched by others of its own supporters, no issues of major importance arose after the commission meetings until the Southwestern Board meeting in 1911.[115] The main item of interest throughout the spring was who should succeed Hyer as President. Though Hyer remained in place at Southwestern until the end of the academic year, the group charged to set up Southern Methodist University elected him President of that institution on April 13.[116]

Board Meeting and Commencement 1911

The Board meeting and Commencement of 1911 were bittersweet events, outwardly correct, proper, and businesslike, inwardly poignant, sad, and emotional. Events followed one another in an almost scripted fashion. The first major action at the Board meeting was the presentation by Dr. Hyer of his resignation. It was accepted, effective at the close of the session. This action made it possible for him to present the diplomas to the graduating seniors. Dr. Charles M. Bishop, D.D., minister-scholar and pastor at the time in Wichita Falls, was unanimously elected President of the University. The Board secretary was instructed to inform Dr. Bishop and to request him to come to Georgetown at once. On arrival he was introduced and addressed the Board. Dean Cody was requested to attend the Annual Conference meetings in the fall with President Bishop.[117]

Reports and plans proceeded almost as if nothing unusual had happened during the year. Hyer reported that Southwestern had experienced the most successful year in the history of the institution. The increase in collegiate enrollment was the largest ever, from 331 to 443, some 34 percent. The total increase for the University in all its programs (excluding names counted twice) was from 1,002 to 1,123. This increase made it necessary to employ twenty-four student assistants to aid the sixty regular professors. Particularly notable was the growth of the Education Department. Thirty-six of the sixty-two graduating seniors were prospective teachers. In light of this strong report, six Trustees were appointed to cooperate with a committee of the Alumni Association in the program to increase the endowment, to erect a Library Building, and to join in promoting "all forward movements."[118]

But all was not normal and the uncertainties had to be addressed. Consequently, a statement was adopted to "forever set at rest all disquieting apprehensions" regarding the status of the University. The Trustees assured faculty, students, patrons, and the public that the high standard attained by the University would be upheld. Furthermore, the suggestion of the Educational Commission that the name be changed from Southwestern University to Southwestern College was rejected, as well as any thought that it would operate with other than a separate, freestanding Board of Trustees elected by the sponsoring Annual Conferences. Apart from these restrictions, the Trustees stated that they were ready to cooperate in a correlated system of schools as recommended by the Educational Commission when the details for such a system had been worked out.[119]

As to Hyer himself, the Board adopted a generous resolution. In view of his long connection with Southwestern, both as professor and President, and because of "his ripe scholarship, courteous bearing, executive ability, and Christian character," the Board expressed its "strong appreciation of the life-long self-sacrificing service which he has rendered the cause of Christian education." Furthermore, it assured him that its "best wishes and most earnest prayers shall follow him in his new field of labor."[120]

At the same time, the Board prepared for a new President of a different type. It directed that a new presidential office be created in the southwest corner of the Main Building, with the other rooms on the west side of the first floor being set up for business purposes. It also ordered the installation of a vault.[121] The President's office remained in this new location until the renovation of the Main Building in 1976, when it was returned to Hyer's old professorial office in the southeast corner of the first floor.

The Commencement ceremony was a moving event. Hyer presented diplomas for the last time to senior graduates of Southwestern, and the new President, Charles M. Bishop, was introduced to the audience. The climax, however, was the presentation of a gift by the student body to the President under whom they had studied for four years. A. Frank Smith, President of the student body, presented Hyer with a gold locket to be worn on his watch chain "in expression of the student-body's love and devotion."[122] Writing about it in a newspaper article years later, J. Frank Dobie described it as one of the momentous experiences of his life.

> Who shall describe Commencement Day—Monday? So long as a graduate, undergraduate, friend, or officer of Southwestern University who attended those exercises shall keep his memory and love for S.U., so long shall in his mind and heart remain a picture of the dignity, of the nobility, of the power, of the grandeur, and of the tenderness of Dr. Robert Stewart Hyer as he stood for the last time as President upon the old platform of an institution which owes, Gond [sic] only knows how much, to him. I have witnessed a few scenes of depth and sadness, I have read in the world's literature many accounts of partings sincere and great, but nothing thus far has ever so affected me as the presentation of a pure gold locket, set with a crytal [sic] diamond (all of it simple) to Dr. Hyer, in the name of the student body by Frank Smith. Accidentally Dr. Hyer dropped the jewel; then, picking it up, he said, quick as thought: "When Cortez landed in Mexico he is said to have stumbled to earth, kissed it and said, 'This is mine.' So do I say this is my home."[123]

Hyer's departure was particularly hard for his wife. The woman who had once encouraged him to take a position offered him at the University of Texas, had now tried but failed to dissuade him from going to Dallas. Their daughter, Ray Hyer Brown, says that the new President, Dr. Charles Bishop, and his family arrived in Georgetown before Mrs. Hyer left. A reception was given for Mrs. Bishop, and Mrs. Hyer felt it was her place to attend. "During the whole evening only one person spoke to Mother and that one was a newcomer whom she had known only slightly."[124]

Hyer at Southern Methodist University

Hyer's career at Southern Methodist was very different from his expectations. During his first four years there, he was occupied in raising buildings, establishing a curriculum, attracting a faculty, and recruiting a student body. The master teacher taught only sporadically, and he was forced to become more of a single-minded administrator than he had ever been at Southwestern. After classes began in September 1915, he was able to resume the mix of administration and teaching that had marked his career at Southwestern. His performance was not, however, satisfactory to the Board of Trustees and ended with his forced resignation in 1920.

In all that he did, asserts his daughter, her father went to great lengths to avoid hurting Southwestern. Before SMU opened in 1915, Hyer "gave emphatic instructions that no advertising or printed matter was to be sent to any one who was at that time attending Southwestern. There were a number of transfers from other colleges, including some students from Southwestern, but they came of their own accord. They were not solicited."[125]

She also avers that in recruiting faculty Hyer refused to entice teachers away from Southwestern.[126] Three of them, however, did end up on the faculty when the doors opened in 1915. John Reedy (Chemistry, SU 1905–1913), John McGinnis (English, SU 1907–1914), and Frank Seay (Hebrew and New Testament Greek, SU 1909–1915) had left Southwestern for postgraduate study. Hyer felt free to offer them positions, and they accepted. Three others came in 1918 and 1919 on their own initiative by making unsolicited applications for teaching positions. They were Dean Albert S. Pegues (English, SU 1893–1918), Prof. Stephen H. Moore (Latin, Greek, and History, SU 1894–1919), and Prof. Claude Nichols (Education, SU 1907–1919). However innocent Hyer may have been in employing these teachers (see Chapter XII), the fact that six former Southwestern faculty members were on the SMU faculty in 1919 led many at Southwestern to feel that he was raiding the faculty. In addition, Frank Reedy, Southwestern's first bursar, had gone with Hyer to Dallas as his right-hand man. To many in Georgetown these defections were not chance circumstances. They were a part of Hyer's plan and fitted into the pattern of duplicitous conduct already ascribed to him.

In 1920 Hyer resigned as President of Southern Methodist University. Ray Hyer Brown remembers learning about it as follows:

> I remember most vividly that cold, rainy afternoon when Mother and I were in the little garage house; Father came in with a strange look on his face, sat down, gripped the arms of the chair, and said in a strange voice: "I have been asked to resign the presidency." . . . It was a blow from which he never recovered. Mother and I were stunned. There was no warning, no premonition.[127]

Several reasons can be adduced for the Board action. Some of the members of the Board wanted to add a school of business administration to the University. Because of the school's difficult financial situation, Hyer felt it was a time for retrenchment, not expansion. Others wanted to sell some of SMU's land north of the school. Hyer felt that the land was a pledge to SMU's future and opposed the sale. Still others wanted to subsidize football. Hyer believed that the University should not compete for athletes except in terms of its academic program and that this was not right. Herbert Gambrell, later a professor at Southern Methodist, remembers the resignation letter vividly.

> Somehow I had got a copy of his letter of resignation and, as managing editor of the *Campus* student newspaper, printed it. I still recall its concluding aphorism, to this effect: "The president of a state school must be a politician; the head of a private school a financier; the president of a church school must be both. Since I am neither, I give you my resignation."[128]

As much as anything, however, it was probably the ambiguity in his own mind about his position as it was anything else that resulted in his forced resignation. He had never wanted to be a president in the first place and had only become resigned to it over time, developing a special style of leadership involving both administration and teaching. That style worked for him at Southwestern. It was small enough for a dedicated person to be both teacher and president. He had also grown into his position there and was surrounded by a host of longtime friends and colleagues who demanded no more of him than that he be himself. The advances Southwestern made while he was in office were so striking that no one questioned his modus operandi. He could not do the same at Southern Methodist. It was a school in a major city whose leaders had made heavy commitments to its success and where expectations were high. The Trustees were not interested in a president whose greatest love was teaching. They wanted a president, as Boaz had hinted in his speech to the Educational Convention of 1906, whose entire time was wrapped up in cultivating donors, dining with foundation chairmen, and cutting a figure on the state and national scene. When times got difficult shortly after World War I, the trustees decided to elevate Hyer to the status of President Emeritus and to put a promoter in his place. That man was Hiram Abiff Boaz.

Reconciliation

One of the persons from Southwestern employed by Hyer was Albert Shipp Pegues. He had joined the faculty in 1893 as a young teacher and had risen in the esteem of everyone over the years. He was the teacher who, according to J. Frank Dobie, opened his eyes to literature and his heart to the romantics. When Dean Cody's health problems forced him to retire in 1915, Pegues was selected to replace him. As a young professor, Pegues married Pearl Irene Lockett, second of the five daughters of M. B. Lockett, on June 6, 1899. They moved to Dallas in 1919, when Pegues resigned from Southwestern and accepted a position as Dean of the College of Liberal Arts at Southern Methodist University.

Shipp and Pearl had no children and, toward the end of June 1921, an affair involving him and a girl or young lady, both terms are used in the records, came to light. Some of the letters and telegrams between Pearl, her sister Mellie, and Mellie's husband, Franklin D. Love, a prominent lawyer in Georgetown, are extant. The exact details of the affair are obscure, because the letters presume that the reader already knows the facts. The guilt of Pegues is never a question of doubt in the correspondence. The young lady and her mother, particularly the mother, told Pearl about the affair, and Pearl had evidence that Pegues had destroyed some of his and Pearl's former letters that cast him in a bad light. Pegues tried to work out a settlement with her in which Pearl would promise that she would never do anything "in regard to his position" at Southern Methodist. But she refused, saying that the incident of the girl was such that she would never sign such an agreement. Still, Pearl was afraid that the authorities at SMU would not act in the absence of Boaz, who was away.[129] She need not have feared. The University fired him, and its Executive Committee even discussed the possibility of his serving jail time for abandoning his wife.[130] The incident ruined Pegues's career. Though *Who Was Who in America* carries a description of his career until 1921, the entry is blank from that year until his death in Dallas in 1960 at the age of eighty-eight.[131]

Though the incident was painful to M. B. Lockett, it ended up having a cathartic effect on his life. Because of it he found it necessary to revise his autobiography, the first draft of which he had completed in 1912, when he was sixty-six years old. Now, at the age of seventy-six, he apologizes for some of the severe criticisms of people mentioned in the original, particularly Bishop Mouzon, Dr. Hyer, and Dr. Boaz.

> Their attitude toward our daughter Pearl when she was overwhelmed by the tragedy which came into her life during the lastdays [sic] of June, 1921, will forever silence any criticisms against them, so far as our family is concerned. It is not necessary here to go into all the details of the cruel treatment and desertion of Pearl by her husband, as we all know them by heart. In the midst of Pearl's deep sorrow Bishop Mouzon visited her and consoled with her. Then Dr. Hyer and his wife have shown her every attention possible; they have visited her and advised with her, and have made every effort to assist her. And on top of that Dr. Hyer wrote me a beautiful letter, in which he expressed great sympathy for Pearl and with expressions of good will to myself and family. Now, how is it possible to still harbor ill will against him? Besides those mentioned Dr. Boaz wrote me a letter in which he strongly condemned the conduct of Pegues in his shameful treatment and desertion of his wife. And then what can be said against hundreds of people of Dallas, both men and women. The kind hearted people of Dallas have done everything possible, it seems to me, to comfort and cheer Pearl during her intense sufferings. The women have visited her by the dozens and showed her every attention possible. Nothing like it has ever been seen before. In the face of all these acts of kindness on the part of the good people of Dallas, I can not [sic] have it in my heart not to apologize for criticisms of them.[132]

Lockett still felt that a great wrong had been done to the people of Georgetown in the removal controversy, but he concluded by saying that two events had caused him to rethink earlier comments. One was the loss of Vanderbilt University to the Church. The other was the success of Southern Methodist University as a compensation for that loss. He says that Southern Methodist "is forging ahead with a large attendance of students and with fine prospects of success. . . . It is destined to be a great school in the future. . . . Now that the Church in Texas is firmly set on the school at Dallas, I shall cease my opposition to it."[133]

After his resignation, Hyer continued to teach his classes in physics, with two additional classes in Bible. He also gave daily Bible lessons on the radio.[134] Ray Hyer Brown says that however hard he took it, he consoled his wife, who took it harder than he did. He died of angina pectoris on May 29, 1929.[135] At its annual session in Georgetown five days later, the Board of Trustees of Southwestern University adopted a resolution recognizing Hyer's contributions to the University. Calling him "one of the foremost laymen of the M. E. Church South," "one of the foremost scientists in the South," and "one of the foremost educators in Methodism," it closed by expressing "our thanks to God for the life he lived among us" and by declaring "our appreciation of his character and work." One of the three authors of the resolution was A. Frank Smith, who, as president of the Southwestern student body in 1911, had presented him the gold locket from them at the Commencement ceremony that year.[136]

Though Lockett and Southwestern's Trustees became reconciled to Hyer, some people could never get over the bitterness surrounding the establishment of SMU Former President William C. Finch recounted a revealing anecdote to Dr. Martha M. Allen in 1992 and to this author in 2000 illustrating this fact. He said that when President Bergin employed him in 1941, Bergin called him into his office. In his direct way, he told Finch that he was a hot commodity on the teaching market. He said that Southwestern would do what it could to keep him, but he admitted that an offer might come along sometime that he couldn't refuse. If that should occur, Bergin continued, he would understand.[137] But he cautioned him against one thing: "Doctor, if you move out from Southwestern, I just don't want you to go to SMU."[138]

Finch respected President Bergin, but he did not feel bound by his continued hostility toward Southern Methodist University. Sixteen years later, as President himself, he accepted for the University a bust of Dr. Hyer done by his daughter, Mrs. Ray Hyer Brown, and presented at a special ceremony on October 18, 1955, the ninety-fifth anniversary of Hyer's birth.[139] The bust now resides in a glass case in the south entryway of the Fondren-Jones Science Hall. Finch also asked Mrs. Brown to write in detail some of her father's contributions to Southwestern. She included these in her book published two years later entitled *Robert Stewart Hyer: The Man That I Knew.*

SEARCHING FOR DIRECTION

1911–1949

12 A New Mission (1911–1922)

President Bishop and the Dynamic of Leadership

In spite of the positive statement of the Board of Trustees and others of like persuasion about Southwestern's future, there was considerable anxiety in the minds of even its most avid supporters about that future. The competition of a new Methodist university in Dallas, supported by bishops, ministers, and a great city, gave cause for concern. Its indebtedness and lack of endowment, which even in the best of circumstances would have been troublesome, now hung even more heavily around its neck. Much of the money that might have originally been expected to go to Southwestern would now go to Southern Methodist University. The loss of its status as the Central University of Texas Methodism robbed it of the mystique inherited from the vision of Martin Ruter and consummated in the work of Francis Asbury Mood.

The need for strong leadership was critical when Charles McTyeire Bishop assumed the role of chief executive in 1911. Though his stature in Southwestern history may not have the same magnitude as that of Mood and Hyer, he is nevertheless one of the pivotal figures in its history. His performance in the face of the obstacles he faced was remarkable. Failure on his part at this juncture in Southwestern's history would have been devastating. If at the time of his resignation in 1922 he did not leave a strong and vibrant institution that had surmounted all its most difficult problems, the fault was not due to lack of effort or ineptitude on his part but to forces beyond his control.

On his arrival from Wichita Falls to address the Trustees on June 12, 1911, Bishop brought to Southwestern a strong reputation already obtained as a result of his academic and professional accomplishments. He was a fine orator who almost always acquitted himself well before an audience. He knew his own mind, was confident in his leadership role, and was dedicated to the Church. He traveled widely in Church circles attending national meetings. He traveled extensively in Texas cultivating the constituency of the University. He was respected by his fellow college presidents, who elected him from time to time to chair their various committees and commissions. Southwestern could hardly have selected a stronger figure to begin the long process of constructing a new mission for itself and to give it instant credibility after the misfortune of the removal controversy.

Charles McTyeire Bishop: Background and Personality

Charles M. Bishop was born on February 2, 1862, in Ashe County, North Carolina. The son of a minister, he attended Emory and Henry College and graduated with the A.M. degree in 1884. After teaching Latin and Greek there for two years, he joined (1887) the Holston Conference, encompassing the valleys west of the Appalachians once traversed by Daniel Boone. He did not remain there long, however, as he was one of those ministers whose strength is such that he is transferred from Conference to Conference to serve the largest churches. After two years in Asheville, he went to the Southwest Missouri Conference, where he held churches in Kansas City and Lexington. His next assignments, after 1901, were in the Missouri Conference, where he first served St. Joseph, then Columbia. Finally, in 1910, he was transferred to the North Texas Conference to serve at Wichita Falls. He was there when he received the call from Southwestern in 1911. A contemporary news article describes him as "a profound student of the New Testament" and "one of the most scholarly ministers in our denomination."[1] One of the interesting sidelights of his coming to Southwestern is that he was the first cousin of Maggie Hyer, the wife of the man he replaced. Dr. Horace Bishop, the prominent minister who had supported Hyer in the removal controversy, was the uncle of both.[2] Uncle

President Charles McTyeire Bishop. Bishop was the first "modern" president of Southwestern. He was the leading college president in the South against lynching and organized colleges in both Texas and throughout the South to work against lynching. From the 1912 *Sou'wester*.

Horace worked intensively trying to dissuade his nephew from accepting the apparently suicidal job, to no avail.[3]

Bishop's service on national church boards, commissions, and councils was extensive. He was a member of the Inter-Church Conference in 1905, which originated the Federal Council of Protestant Churches of the United States, a member of the General Board of Missions of the Methodist Episcopal Church, South, and also a member of the commission that formulated the plan of union of the various missionary organizations of that Church. He was elected from his Annual Conference as a member of the General Conferences of 1906 and 1910 and was talked about for the episcopacy. The vigor and independence with which he championed progressive causes, however, stood in the way of his election.[4] At the time he came to Southwestern he was a member of the Federal Council of the Methodist Episcopal Church, South, and of the Commissions on Church Union of the Northern and Southern Methodist Churches.

He was in wide demand as a lecturer. He was President of the preachers' institute of the two Missouri Conferences from its beginning until he left, a lecturer on the poetical books of the Bible at Scarritt Bible School in Nashville, and a lecturer at the Summer School of Theology at Southwestern University. He was the first person other than a bishop to deliver the Cole Lectures at Vanderbilt University (1909). These lectures were later published as a book entitled *Jesus, the Worker*. His other book was *Characteristics of the Christian Life*. He received an honorary Doctor of Divinity degree from Central College in Missouri in 1899.

After leaving Southwestern in 1921 to reenter the pastorate, Bishop returned to the classroom five years later when he accepted an invitation to teach at Southern Methodist University. Over the years he had remained friends with certain professors there and was invited in 1925 to occupy a chair in New Testament in the theology school. Herbert Gambrell, a teacher at SMU, knew both Hyer and Bishop well. He says that Bishop once remarked to him "that Hyer was a sort of genius but that he made one great miscalculation in believing that Southwestern would fade away when he left to start SMU. 'I proved him wrong,' he said with emphasis." Gambrell says that he admired Bishop for his wit and "sometimes sardonic humor." In his later Dallas years, Bishop became known for that wit and humor. He was often refractory but always good-natured and interesting. Gambrell says that he was sometimes the hit of special occasions, where he mixed "a skillful blend of genuine appreciation [of others] and sly humor and non-caustic wit."[5] This was the man who became Southwestern University's fifth President.

Building Morale

Bishop strode onto the Southwestern stage with assurance and immediately set to work. Much of what he, Cody, and the others around him did during the first year was to engage in a program of morale boosting. Morale was low at the outset. Total enrollment was 149 students lower than the previous year. The College was down from 443 to 358, the School of Fine Arts from 199 to 187, and the Fitting School from 240 to 188. This decline had to be reversed.

Efforts to counteract the negativism took several avenues. J. Frank Dobie, who had spent the year following his graduation as Principal of the school in Alpine, was con-

Assemblage of automobiles with their owners in the public square adjacent to the courthouse on Friday morning, April 19, 1912, ready to take Southwestern Homecoming visitors on "a ride." Southwestern University, Special Collections.

The 1912 Homecoming barbecue was held on the grounds of the old campus behind the old Main Building that was at the time serving as the Prep School. Southwestern University, Special Collections.

tracted to act as the University correspondent for the daily papers.[6] He immediately began to turn out columns entitled "Southwestern Notes" almost once a week. He opened his first piece on September 28, 1911, with an exhibition of high-flown rhetoric. Describing the opening of school, his lead sentence read: "The book has again been opened; the scroll once more unrolled and ere the last line has been scanned the school session of 1911 and '12 will be history."[7] Dobie and Bishop got along well. They were both men who valued independent thinking, both loved playing with the English language, and both had a somewhat sardonic wit. During the spring, Dobie was invited to fill the newly created office of secretary to the President. He, Bishop, and Cody traveled together soon thereafter to a luncheon given

Alumni attending Southwestern University's 1912 Homecoming are pictured in front of the Main Building on the new campus. Southwestern University, Special Collections.

by ex-students in Houston.[8] Dobie's job as private secretary to the President also involved his serving as secretary of the ex-students association.

On September 4 Bishop presided for the first time at a faculty meeting. Soon thereafter the "ladies" of the faculty, including the instructors of the Fine Arts Department, were asked to sit with the faculty on all public occasions.[9] The women, who until now had been virtually invisible on public occasions, must have received this gesture very positively as an indication of the type of administration Bishop would lead. At a called session of the Board of Trustees on December 9 in connection with his inauguration, the name of the former Ladies' Annex building was changed to "The Woman's Building."[10] Dropping the word "annex" suggested that women's work at Southwestern was no longer an appendage, an add-on to the real business of educating men. Women were now an integral part of the real business.

Early in the semester he spoke to the students, trying to instill in them his faith for the future of the University. He told them that "Southwestern is still at Georgetown" and that "she will be here through the centuries to come. She is too well built, too deep rooted to ever fall or to ever be removed from her present beautiful site."[11]

Various speakers, activities, and entertainments were provided for the students during the year. Perhaps the most effective was the appearance of Mrs. Rebecca Gilleland Fisher as a chapel speaker in mid-May. Her story has already been told in Chapter II—saved from the Indians by Albert Sidney Johnston in childhood, a student for three years at Rutersville College, a colleague of Clara Driscoll, a charter member of the Daughters of the Republic of Texas and its president for eighteen years, the only woman elected to the Texas Veteran Association and its last surviving member, the first woman whose portrait was hung in the Texas Senate chamber, and one whose funeral was held in that chamber at her death in 1926. A description of her speech appeared in the *Georgetown Commercial.*

> In a tender appealing voice the lovable little lady carried them back to the beginning of Texas' history. . . . [S]he spoke with a conviction and convincing assurance, because she had been a factor and a personally concerned individual in those strenuous days. . . . She concluded her address by presenting the University with a large flag of Texas as a gift from the Travis Chapter of Austin, of which she is also president. She took her seat and then the student body gave vent to their pent up enthusiasm and appreciation of her words and gift to them and they clapped and clapped with a vim that left no doubt as to their hardiness.[12]

The main event of the year as far as the alumni were concerned was the Homecoming celebration of April 19, 1912. The first Homecoming, held in 1909, had been an outstanding success. Ordinarily others would have followed in 1910 and 1911, but the removal controversy of those years made it impossible. With Bishop providing strong leadership in 1912, the University determined to have the delayed Second Homecoming celebration. Its purpose was to move beyond the negativism of the past two years and to tie the alumni to their alma mater. The event seems to

have achieved its purpose. Attendance was conservatively estimated at a thousand people.

Illustrative of its spirit is a doggerel poem entitled "Dr. Cody Cannot Forget," written by an unknown alumnus for the occasion. Each stanza called up old memories of Cody, ending with the tag: "Dr. Cody cannot forget."[13] Professor of mathematics R. J. Eddy also composed a "Southwestern Song" of four stanzas sung to the tune of "Maryland, My Maryland." Its last four lines eulogize the new, hardly known President Bishop in unabashed manner.

All hail to those who offered most,
To Mood who counted not the cost,
Our Bishop now shall lead the host,
Bishop of Southwestern.[14]

A new constituency, hardly dreamed of a few years earlier, joined in the celebration. A "Notice to Automobile Owners" appeared in a newspaper advertisement on April 12, asking that "every automobile owner in Williamson County . . . assemble on the public square on Friday morning, April 19, at 9 o'clock, for the purpose of having a picture taken, form a county organization, and take the visitors to Homecoming on a ride."[15] The picture in the square of the numerous owners with their automobiles who responded to the advertisement is one of the famous photographs of the epoch.

Bishop Restates Southwestern's Mission

Bishop and the faculty must have been pleased with the results of their work during 1911–1912, for enrollment rose to normal the following year. The 848 students in the College, the School of Fine Arts, and the Fitting School was the second-best enrollment in school history, just under the level of 1909–1910.

But Bishop was not really a numbers person. The procurement of an adequate student body was necessary but what was done with them after they arrived was of more interest to him than the procurement process. Inheriting an institution that had had its original mission stripped away, Bishop described a new mission for the University. Over the years that mission came to be the controlling philosophy of the University. He outlined his views in a letter to Dean Cody prior to the opening of the 1914–1915 academic year, suggesting the direction in which the two of them should lead the faculty.

The role of Southwestern, he says, is as a college whose primary work is validating the "judgment that liberal culture is the very best preparation for life in the modern world." He says that "an eager intellectual spirit" ought to pervade the college community so that while here students will come to realize that they are "entering into their inheritance of human wisdom and achievement" and are "beginning to share in the forward push of society." This endeavor is not limited to a few special departments of the University. Every department "may share in the creation of this sort of atmosphere." "I want us to make Southwestern the very best college for young men and women in the great Southwest. We have the faculty that can do it I earnestly believe. But outside interests on the one hand, and narrow specialization on the other, can so interfere with our lively cooperative endeavor as to make impossible the realization of this ambition." His view, he says, is that "the ideals of liberal culture should be the controlling influence in the life of a college like ours."[16]

This new mission, however, would not be realized immediately. Some of Southwestern's supporters would hang on to the big university model from conviction until the 1950s and even later, continually trying to make it into what was not to be. During the 1940s some would try to preserve the university concept by introducing the "university of small colleges" idea. Some from time to time would try to move the school in the direction of professional specialization. During the financial exigencies of the Great Depression, the school moved in the direction of being all things to all people for the sake of attracting some. It carried weakened master's degree programs into the 1950s, and it offered nine bachelor's degree programs for fewer than a thousand students well into the time of my career at Southwestern.

Though a liberal arts and sciences orientation by and large underlay the educational structure through all these years, there was a lack of clarity in its realization. The trend toward clarification and simplification began with the Finch administration, continued through the Fleming period, and culminated during the Shilling epoch. The attainment of a Phi Beta Kappa chapter by Southwestern during the 1994–1995 academic year can be taken as the point, if one must be singled out, where Southwestern's mission was recognized on the national scene as having been established with clarity.

All of this was inherent in Bishop's philosophy of education, enunciated in a simple letter to his dean, written a few years after his inauguration. Two world wars, a great depression, and unwillingness on the part of Southwestern's public to depart from early tradition prevented its actualization earlier. After all, the name of the school was Southwestern *University*. It took more than three-quarters of a century after the removal controversy for Southwestern's administration, faculty, alumni, students, and friends to grow comfortable with the understanding that the "University" designation in its title is an historic artifact, valuable for what it evokes about Southwestern's long history but of little use as an operative educational concept for the school that exists today. Bishop's notion that "the ideals of liberal culture should be the controlling influence in the life of a college like ours" was easier to accept, but even its realization, through establishing a conducive curriculum and extracurricular program, has required and still requires much effort.

Financial Malaise

Though morale building was important, Bishop and those around him knew that forward movement must be built on more than enthusiasm. It required a solid underpinning of appropriate buildings, adequate equipment, and strong faculty members. All of this demanded substantial financial resources. Without a significant endowment base, Hyer had allowed a debt of well more than half the total annual operational income to build up on the assumption that, once the institution had achieved true university status, it would repay that debt. Now Bishop was faced with a larger problem than ever. Southern Methodist University was a competitor for funds, it had arrogated the great university designation to itself, and it had left a diminished Southwestern to cover the debts incurred earlier. Nevertheless, Bishop believed that through wise planning and careful management Southwestern could move forward.

His first effort was to bring the financial records up-to-date. An entirely new set of books was opened under the direction of an auditor with double entry bookkeeping.[17] When Isaac Joel McCook, the Business Manager employed in 1929, later tried to reconstruct endowment and other financial records prior to his time, he could go back no further than the beginning of the Bishop administration except by referring to Trustee Minutes. Precise records, such as ledgers, journals, etc., did not exist earlier than that.[18] Though the establishment of a new record system in itself was of little consequence for increasing resources, it did provide a modicum of comfort to those in charge of University finances. Auditors seldom failed during the Bishop years to compliment the University for its record-keeping system even when the record it portrayed was dismal.

Bishop's second effort was to ask the Annual Conferences to increase their assessments to $25,000 a year for Southwestern.[19] This amount would about double what they had given during the last several years. It was raised to $45,000 in 1918. Though they did not fully respond to these requests, they set new standards that were increasingly acknowledged. In 1913, after two years in office, Bishop could report that the University was "about $12,000 better off" than it had been the year before.[20]

Bishop's initial success, however, was not long-lasting. In mid-1914 he stated that the financial report was not as favorable as that of the previous year. Though income was greater, expenses had also increased, and more accounts than usual were uncollected. The Annex laundry had burned down the previous summer and had to be rebuilt and furnished out of operational monies.[21] A year later there was a net loss of about $10,000. Several Trustees immediately lent $5,000 to meet the most pressing needs of the moment, but more had to be borrowed during the summer.[22] In 1916 Bishop stated that it was almost impossible to conduct the affairs of the University with the present revenue flow and that he could not recommend viable ways of cutting expenses without careful study.[23] By May 1917 the situation had become critical, and he was ready with a programmatic retrenchment plan. The Executive Committee found it so unpalatable, however, that it refused to support it. When the Board met in June, it was faced with an operational deficit for the year of over $15,000 and no plan to solve it.

Without an overall solution at hand, various expediencies were resorted to. Since Georgetown banks already held part of the University endowment as security for previous overdrafts, lines of credit were opened elsewhere. Notes already held by them and others were extended. A number of Trustees, led by A. A. Booty, made special donations. Efforts were made to reduce the board expenses for the Mood dining hall by placing it in the care of a live-in widow with two children.[24] All male students, with a few exceptions, were required to live and board there.[25] Since these efforts were temporary palliatives and could not cover the deficit already incurred, an attempt was made to bring the Church into the picture. At a special called Board meeting in January 1918, it was announced that a campaign had been organized and endorsed by the Conferences to have them pay off the $58,000 indebtedness of the institution by districts.[26] The results of this effort are not clear, but in all likelihood it was not very successful, because talk soon turned toward taking out one large, all-encompassing loan at a lower rate to pay off the many small loans now held at higher rates. This solution was finally agreed to and a $50,000 issue of ten-year bonds at 7 percent interest, payable semiannually, was set in motion in October 1918.[27] The entire issue was sold to Major Littlefield of Austin in February 1919, the University having to discount the issue 1 percent, with $49,500 being received from the sale. All outstanding obligations up to the full amount of the proceeds were immediately liquidated.[28]

At the Board meeting in June 1919, President Bishop reported that the past year had been the most trying year of his presidency. It was made so, he reported, by the war, widespread droughts, and the "distressing financial effects" being felt by the people brought on by the inflation.[29] It was also made so by the "distressing financial effects" being felt by the faculty.

In the midst of the financial distress, Bishop reported to the Board of Trustees at its meeting in June 1918 that faculty salaries were so low "that one or two of our very valuable faculty members are living dangerously near the 'bread-line' of poverty considering the social position which they are compelled to maintain."[30] Consumer prices had remained relatively steady between 1911 and 1916, increasing at an average of only 1.7 percent annually, but they increased rapidly in 1917 and 1918 at a rate of 7.6 percent and 17.4 percent, respectively. By 1918 the purchasing power of the dollar had declined by 37.1 percent since 1911 without compensating increases in faculty salaries at Southwestern.[31] As a result of a plea by the faculty for a salary increase, the Board granted an overall 10 percent increase even in the financial crisis in which the University found itself. This outcome, however, came at the conclusion of another event—a complaint, to be dealt with later, by several faculty members at the 1918 Board meeting about Bishop's administrative style.[32]

Beginning of a $300,000 Building and Endowment Campaign

Though Bishop spent his first year at Southwestern boosting morale and learning about the institution, he was also gradually forming a plan. He knew that Southwestern had lost momentum from the now unfeasible campaign to build a great Memorial Building and felt that it had to regain that momentum some way. It must demonstrate promptly its ability to develop its facilities and resource base.

In late 1912 he worked out a plan with the Executive Committee to launch a major financial campaign. The money raised would be used to construct several buildings, first of all a music building costing about $40,000. The Executive Committee voted in December to have its commissioner (financial agent) solicit subscriptions (pledges) for the building and authorized Bishop to employ an architect to prepare plans and specifications for it.[33]

The next step was for him and Trustee E. G. Gillett to take a trip to New York in early 1913 to discuss with the Carnegie Foundation for the Advancement of Teaching the possibility of securing money for a library building. After the visit, he and Gillett reported to the Executive Committee that the visit was "entirely satisfactory." Dr. Henry S. Pritchett, the Carnegie representative, had given them to understand that he would take up the matter with Mr. Carnegie, and if the University would meet some very reasonable conditions the library building would be secured for the University.[34] Nothing ever resulted from the visit. A new library was not built until 1939.

At the Board meeting in June, Bishop presented a stirring call to action for Southwestern. He called for a movement enlisting the whole Church "to secure not less than $100,000 for new buildings and $200,000 for additional endowment." The Trustees approved his idea and authorized raising the $40,000 for a music building.[35] He immediately began to canvass the Annual Conferences and the Texas Methodist Board of Education. They all approved it. When the faculty discussed it they stressed that the University also needed science, Y.M.C.A., gymnasium, and fine arts buildings.[36]

Bishop announced the campaign to the students in chapel a few days later.[37] Early in the New Year the Executive Committee voted to recommend to the Board of Trustees that money be secured for three buildings—a science hall, a Y.M.C.A.-gymnasium building, and a fine arts building.[38] The Board of Trustees approved the plan at a called session on January 6, 1914. They also approved a motion to employ three commissioners to procure the money. They agreed that the music building should be built first, the science hall second, and the Y.M.C.A.-gymnasium building third. They also voted to secure a $10,000 loan to pay for the campaign until monies started to flow in.[39]

The campaign itself was launched in Georgetown on February 21, 1914, with a mass meeting held in the District Courtroom. After musical entertainment and some preliminary speeches by various persons, President Bishop made a strong appeal for a Greater Southwestern. Trustee E. G. Gillett explained the various parts of the $300,000 campaign, and Mayor Ward, the chair of the meeting, made the proposal. He said that it was his idea to have Georgetown and Williamson County responsible "for the erection of one splendid building for Southwestern University," a science building. By a unanimous rising vote, says the newspaper article reporting the event, the audience pledged $50,000 for the building from Georgetown and Williamson County.[40]

The First Campus Schematic Design

With the campaign proposal to construct several new buildings, a plan for their location had to be drawn up. A campus design by C. F. Ward, a Houston architect, appeared shortly thereafter in the *Southwestern Bulletin* of April 1914.[41] It shows the three current buildings—the Main Building, Mood Hall, and the Woman's Building—and situates the three proposed buildings in a rough semicircle with them, though the entire area is still platted in square blocks. The Williamson County Science Building is placed just in front of where the present chapel now stands. The Y.M.C.A.-Gymnasium Building stands to the west of it, while the Fine Arts Building stands at the end of the semicircle on the east. All the buildings were of stone in conformity with the other buildings and the scheme adopted for future buildings. One can see in the plan the earliest intimation of the semicircular drive that became the inner thoroughfare of the campus for many years and that was later transformed into the central pedestrian mall.

One problem was that the University needed to procure additional land to make the plan possible. The original thirty-two acres composing the new campus donated by the Snyders in 1887 began at the railroad tracks and generally extended east along what is now University Avenue. Its exact conformation is not known, but the Ladies' Annex building was constructed on it the next year in roughly the location now occupied by the Brown-Cody Residence Hall, with the J. W. Snyder house, the President's home through these years, a bit farther east closer to University Avenue. Additional land north of the Main Building had to be purchased for the construction of Mood Hall.

During the years in which plans were being made and the $300,000 campaign initiated, the Executive Committee began to buy up small parcels of land from time to time. One such was purchased on March 16, 1914, to procure "a strip of land 60 x 240 feet lying north of the J. W. Snyder

Letterhead used in the Building and Endowment Campaign of 1914 and later. It features the "Proposed Plan of Greater Southwestern University" and is the first campus master plan. Only the first, second, and fifth buildings had been built. The others were proposals. Southwestern University, Special Collections.

Building, to be signed by Mr. Snyder for the University."[42] It was the precise tract or one of the tracts of land "between the Woman's Building and Mood Hall" referred to in the next Board meeting upon which the new science building would be built. Waller & Co. of Fort Worth was proposed and later accepted as the architectural firm for the work.[43]

The Williamson County Science Building: Decision and Delay

At the meeting of the Trustees in June 1914, Bishop told them that "we are now at an epoch which is only second in importance to the founding of the University."[44] He reviewed all the steps that had been taken to date for the campaign and stated that he had worked out an agreement with the Educational Commission to prevent an overlap in solicitations in the different Annual Conferences by Southwestern and Southern Methodist, which was also engaged in its own campaign.

He said that to date $90,927.20 had been secured in the campaign, of which the citizens of Georgetown had subscribed $54,502 and members of the student body had subscribed $10,230. The students had designated their portion as a Campus and Grounds Fund. The total amount, he declared, was "not as large as we had hoped that it would be by this time, but . . . we have reason to be encouraged."[45]

Because of the strong response from Georgetown and Williamson County, the order of construction was changed. The science building was put first. It was "to be known as the Williamson County Science Building or by some such name in recognition of the fact that the whole amount was subscribed by citizens of Georgetown and Williamson County." The subscriptions were to be paid out by them over a period of five years. Operating from estimates by Waller & Co. that the "naked building" could be built for a sum not exceeding $40,000, Bishop urged the Board to secure financing for the building immediately. The building was needed now, and five years would be too long to wait. Consequently the Executive Committee was empowered to borrow money for the erection and completion of the proposed science building and the fine arts building.[46]

In spite of Bishop's exhortation and the Board's authorization to borrow funds in order to begin construction immediately, construction was not begun for almost two years. Too small a proportion of the funding commitments were in cash, and the Executive Committee was unwilling to proceed with a project requiring almost 100 percent financing.[47] Bishop reported to the Board in 1915 that "the disturbed financial conditions of the whole State" were such "that it was thought unwise to press the campaign as vigorously as it had been pressed." Consequently, two of the three commissioners discontinued their work and took appointments.[48] In this circumstance Bishop looked longingly at the outlay of funds from the operational budget being spent each year to pay the interest on $74,369.70 of endowment funds still invested in Mood Hall and the Woman's Building.[49] They were perhaps the warning that kept the Executive Committee from proceeding with the science building.

Construction and Endowment Considerations

Finally, in early 1916, the Executive Committee decided to go ahead with the construction of the building. With the cash already derived from earlier subscriptions and a recent gift from the Rev. T. F. Dimmitt, a retired minister who had just donated a 435-acre farm at San Saba, the Executive Committee felt that it had a basis for proceeding.[50] The Waller architectural firm of Fort Worth was contracted to proceed with the design and specifications for the building. Waller was given instructions to design a reinforced concrete and steel building not to cost over $35,000, not the original stone building contemplated by C. F. Ward in 1914. In the bidding by contractors, A. O. Harvey of Fort Worth was the lowest at $34,036.38. The contract was awarded to him. The building was to be completed by October 15 and, with the right conditions, to be ready for fall classes. With water, heat, light, ventilation, and fixtures, the building would cost about $50,000.[51] The Masonic Lodge was invited to officiate at the laying of the cornerstone on June 17 at the time of the Board meeting.[52]

The decision to proceed with the erection of the science building was partly the result of the decision at this time to close the Fitting School and to sell the original Main Building and grounds across the entire front of University Avenue to the city.[53] Though the transaction did not occur immediately, the prospect of its realization was considered to be as good as money in hand. When the $25,000 was received, it was directed to the Farmers State Bank to release the endowment funds being held there as a protection to accumulated overdraft expenses. This transaction made immediately available $25,000 of endowment that had theretofore been nonproductive.[54]

This transaction also helped cover another type of financial emergency that arose at this time. President Bishop informed the Board at the 1916 meeting that endowment funds needed to be increased by about $55,000 by August 15 for Southwestern to maintain its standing as an A-grade college. Since a minimum of $100,000 in income-yielding endowment was required, the University must have had only about $45,000 of income-yielding endowment at the time. An emergency endowment campaign was instituted to raise it.[55] Persons were delegated to visit nine major cities in the state in prosecution of the enterprise. Dr. Cody, only recently retired, was pressed back into service and made more visits than anyone else.[56] The exact result of the campaign is not ascertainable, except that by the time of the Board meeting in 1917 the income-yielding endowment had been increased to $124,000, an increase of $79,000 in one year.[57] Of that amount, $25,000 had come from the sale of old campus facilities to the city and $10,000 from the sale of the Dimmitt farm.[58]

Completion of the Science Building

There were many small problems connected with the completion of the building, the major one being heating. It was finally agreed to use the situation as an opportunity to connect it, the Woman's Building, and the Administration Building with the heating plant used for Mood Hall, thus creating a central heating plant. Heating fixtures had to be installed in the Administration Building, while the heating fixtures for Mood Hall and the Woman's Building were renovated. The report of this solution in Executive Committee minutes is the first occasion therein in which the Main Building is called the Administration Building, the name by which it was known until 1976 when it was renamed the Cullen Building.[59]

While the building was still under construction, the Executive Committee tried to restart the $300,000 campaign. Except for some money still coming in from early subscriptions, no progress had been made in some time to complete the total amount. The effort fell far short of the goal, and Bishop was forced to state to the Board in mid-1917 that during the three years of the campaign only $181,000 had been subscribed and much less, of course, had been collected. At that time $33,846.22 had been paid on the building, with $7,984.27 yet due, totaling $41,830.49. Though at the time of the Board meeting it had stood virtually finished for two or three months, no equipment had been purchased for lack of funds.[60]

With the imminence of the fall term, the old science equipment was moved from the Administration Building to the new hall. On September 17, only a week before the registration of students, President Bishop reported to the Executive Committee the immediate need of having sewerage and water connections made at the science building.[61] Though Dr. Cody reported in a newspaper article in mid-November that the building had been completed and equipped,[62] furniture for the classrooms and new equipment were still being purchased during the winter and spring terms of 1918.[63] Cement walks were laid on the grounds of the building sometime during the academic year under the direction of new chemistry Professor J. C. Godbey.[64] In order to finance the remainder of the academic year, bonds for $40,000 had to be issued in mid-March on the security of $45,000 in endowment notes and the buildings and grounds of the Woman's Building, Mood Hall, and the Administration Building.[65]

Though the Williamson County Science Building had required four years to build and was aesthetically out of keeping with the rest of the campus, it served the purposes of the University well for about two decades. In 1934 the visiting committee from the Southern Association of Colleges and Secondary Schools reported that it was "a good building, excellently lighted and with plenty of space."[66] Within the next few years, however, it developed significant problems. In his report to the Trustees in mid-1940, President Bergin stated that "within a few years at most the Science Building will become unsafe. The ground floor is cracking badly," he said, "and a large crack has appeared in the southwest wall."[67] The building was demolished in 1950. But for the moment it was the proud monument of what could be done in bad times.

Student Numbers, Admission, and Demise of the Fitting School

As already indicated, during the first year after Hyer's departure from Southwestern, enrollment in the College and in the School of Fine Arts dropped by 192 students, from 737 to 545. Bishop and the faculty managed to turn it around the next year and by 1913–1914 it was up to 695. From that high, it slipped annually for the next four years, reaching a low of 429 in 1917–1918. It rebounded the next year to 558 and was on the upswing during the last four years of Bishop's presidency, when it averaged 582.

Admission requirements were, on the whole, increased

during the Bishop era. Though the number of foreign language units necessary for entry was reduced from 3 to 2, the total number of units necessary for entry was increased from 14 to 15, and algebra units were raised from 1½ to 2. The category of Special students was dropped, and the requirements for Conditioned students rose. Persons who might have been accepted as Conditioned students with 10½ units in 1911–1912 were required to have 13 units in 1921–1922. The percentage of Conditioned students was twice as high under Bishop as under Hyer, but the general requirement for entrance (15 units) was higher, as well as the requirement for Conditioned entrance (13 units). These figures do not suggest that students entering under Bishop were any weaker than those entering under Hyer but that the criteria for entrance were more stringent. The faculty was jealous of its standards and even in the hard times of 1917–1918 maintained that it had not sacrificed them to expediency.[68]

During the decade of Bishop's administration, the State system of education made strong advances. High school work was regularized and made to meet known standards. Whereas Southwestern had felt compelled during Mood's time to set up a Preparatory School, later called the Fitting School, to prepare students to meet its college entrance requirements, this need diminished rapidly after the turn of the century. With the development of a system of secondary public education in almost every community, and with the rating of each school system published by the University of Texas each summer, colleges in the state came more and more to accept this objective appraisal by the State as a standard. The entire "Articles of Agreement among Texas Colleges concerning the Accrediting of High Schools" was copied into the Faculty Minutes of February 5, 1913. Southwestern got out of the business of making its own judgment of high school work.[69]

The number of "affiliated" schools, taken from the University of Texas listing and carried in Southwestern catalogs, increased from 136 in 1911–1912 to 535 in 1920–1921. The Methodist "correlated" school system in Texas fell into disuse except for a few schools remaining as vestigial remnants of a bygone era. This decline was in line with the decline in the number of secondary schools maintained by the Southern Methodist Church everywhere from ninety-five in 1902 to thirty-nine in 1908, thirty-one in 1914, twenty-four in 1926, and three in 1939.[70] Inasmuch as the Fitting School was a part of that feeder system, logic suggested that its time had passed. In its last few years students in the Education Department served under their professors as instructors there.[71] Bishop did not believe that the operation of a Fitting School accorded with the main purpose of the institution, and the University followed a calculated policy of phasing it out. Its enrollment declined rapidly from 238 students in 1912–1913 to 181, 89, and 79 students in its last three years. It no longer existed in 1916–1917.

Southwestern Joins SACS

Having adopted the standards of the University of Texas for accrediting high schools, Southwestern now moved to join the association rapidly becoming normative for the accreditation of Southern colleges. Receiving an invitation in 1912 from the Southern Association of Colleges and Secondary Schools to send a representative to meet with it at Wofford College on November 14–15 of that year, the faculty voted to accept the invitation.[72] Accordingly, someone representing the University attended and reported his findings to the group. A committee was appointed to review the standards for membership, and an application was duly submitted.[73] After a three-year process, Southwestern was admitted at the Association's annual meeting during the week of November 11, 1915.[74] Since 1915 the name of the Association has changed slightly from time to time. Today it is the Southern Association of Colleges and Schools, or SACS. That acronym is used throughout the book in referring to the Southern Association regardless of the timeframe.

Two years later a meeting of practically all the leading colleges and universities of the state was held in Waco to form the Association of Texas Colleges. Dr. Claude A. Nichols, Professor of Education at Southwestern, was elected its first president.[75]

The Passing of the Old Campus

After the construction of the Ladies' Annex and the Main Building on the new campus, the old campus had been dedicated to the work of the Fitting School, to athletic pursuits on Snyder Field, and to providing room and board for boys in Giddings Hall and the six cottages. With the construction of Mood Hall, the need for these housing units diminished. The cottages were sold one by one over a two-year period. The last one was reported at the Board meeting in mid-1915 as having been sold. With it passed the cottage system, in place for about thirty years. Operation of Giddings Hall was sporadic. Not much space outside of Mood

Hall was needed for boys. Finally, the University decided to get out of the rooming business there. It rented the building to a lady who used it as a boardinghouse. Ten or twelve preparatory students boarded with her during the last year of the Fitting School.

With the demise of the Fitting School after the 1915–1916 academic year, the old main building no longer served any University need. It and the land it occupied fronting University Avenue were sold to the city for a much-needed $25,000.[76] The Executive Committee, however, retained rights to the old college bell. Several years later it tried to sell the bell "for the best possible price" and to place the money in the Endowment Fund. After more than three months no one had inquired about it, and the committee had to pay the Georgetown school system for removing it.[77] It was then removed, first to the Methodist Church, then to the campus until the construction of the new Woman's Building in 1926, when it was placed on the roof atop the elevator shaft. One of Laura Kuykendall's pageants, *The Legend of the Bell*, written by Margaret Mood McKennon, was woven around it and performed on June 2, 1927. The conclusion of the pageant was the ringing out of the "old Chapel Bell," with "its rich tones, floating out upon the campus breezes . . . [as] a fitting benediction" to the pageant.[78] It resides today on a pedestal in the plaza fronting the Charline and Red McCombs Campus Center.

After its sale, Old Main served as the Georgetown high school for a few years. It was torn down in 1923 to make way for a new structure. Its stones were then used to build the six-room Carver High School for African Americans.[79] When the Carver High School was in turn torn down, the rock was sold to a number of area residents who used it for homes and walls. Southwestern students transported some of the remaining stones to the University for storage.[80]

Because Giddings Hall was now vacant, chemistry Professor J. C. Godbey proposed to tear it down and use its materials, along with new, to build a basketball court and a swimming pool, with rooms for storage, lockers, and a caretaker, where it once stood. Godbey planned a building 104\' x 80\', to be erected, he said, largely with student labor, out of student, faculty, and other donations. It was not to cost over $2,700. He was given permission to proceed at the Board meeting in 1919.[81] In the meantime, the freestanding dining room of Giddings Hall was sold.[82]

The quality of the new building is not known, but one observer attributed the success of the basketball team the following year to "the excellent indoor court in the new gymnasium."[83] It burned after little more than two years on December 2, 1921. The insurance on the old building was paid promptly, and Professor Godbey built a new gymnasium of corrugated iron within thirty days. It was said to be about as good as the old one.[84]

The story of the old campus came to an end in 1930, when Snyder Athletic Field, back of the old, now demolished, main building, was sold for $4,000 to the high school that had replaced the main building. A new athletic field for the University was constructed extending west from the Administration Building to the railroad tracks and north from University Avenue about halfway to the railroad depot. The Snyder Field name was transferred to it. President Vivion reported that it was equipped with a steel fence, steel bleachers, and Giant DeLuxe Mogul Floodlights. It was valued at $25,000.[85] The fence, lights, and bleachers were later removed. The field is still in use today, though the main athletic fields now lie on the northeast side of the campus.

Ryland Fletcher Young

Substantial attention has already been paid to four of "The Five" teachers who came to the University under Francis Asbury Mood and who became the core of the faculty for many years. They were Sanders, McLean, Hyer, and Cody. The fifth, Ryland Fletcher Young, retired from teaching in 1914 at the age of fifty-five after thirty-five years. With Cody's retirement the following year, no one on the faculty remained who had been employed by the founder of the University.[86]

Ryland Fletcher Young was the least conspicuous of "The Five," yet he rendered important service over the years. He began teaching in 1881 after becoming the first M.A. graduate of the University a year earlier. Over his teaching career, he taught Latin, Greek, German, French, and Spanish, with a year off along the way for advanced study at Heidelberg University. He was Professor of Romance Languages when he retired and manager of Giddings Hall before the construction of Mood Hall. He was also a dedicated churchman.

In addition to being a teacher, he was a fine businessman. He was a charter member of the Farmers State Bank and was one of the organizers of the Georgetown Cotton Mill. He moved to a farm on the San Gabriel River just north of the Southwestern University campus in 1901 and became a progressive dairy farmer after his retirement. Southwestern purchased the farm from his son in early

1943 to have its own dairy to furnish milk and butter for its student body, including a naval V-12 unit, during World War II. It is part of Southwestern's property today.[87]

The Reinterment of Francis Asbury Mood

At his death on November 12, 1884, Francis Asbury Mood was buried on the old campus west of the main building and north of the Methodist Church building, which was then on the southwest corner of the old campus. At the death of his wife, Susan Logan Mood, on November 13, 1916, the University offered a place for her burial on campus.[88] Her children, however, asked that she be buried "in the cemetery adjoining town." After the University sold the old campus, they asked that their father's body be moved to that cemetery and buried alongside his wife. "Therefore, the University, in selling the old school property, reserved for a time, the small plot of ground where Mood's body was buried with the monument thereon." At the meeting of the Board of Trustees on June 14–16, 1917, President Bishop asked its members to make plans to move his remains to the cemetery and to have the monument brought to the campus. He also asked them to erect a proper memorial to Mrs. Mood.[89] On Saturday, November 24, of that year, Mood's body was reinterred in the city cemetery. The article in the *Williamson County Sun* recounting the event is simple and compelling.

> When his wife died some months ago and was buried in the I. O. O. F. cemetery here, it was determined by her children to move their father's remains and place them by her side. It was also understood between all parties that the monument, which stands near the high school building, will be removed to the present campus of Southwestern University, where it will stand as a perpetual memorial of the great founder of this institution.
>
> This purpose to move Dr. Mood's remains was carried out last Saturday. Col. W. K. Makemson was requested by Mr. W. R. Mood to superintend the disinterment and reinterment of the body.
>
> On Saturday the new grave was dug. In the afternoon the body was disinterred and the old grave filled. At 7 o'clock P.M., Mr. Mood and Col. Makemson and a few invited friends, Dr. C. C. Cody, Prof. R. F. Young, Dr. John R. Allen, Prof. Rudolph Kleberg and Mr. John T. Coffee, gathered at the old grave to escort the honored remains to the new grave.
>
> When the coffin was raised it was found to be of copper, and except that the lid had been bent in by the weight upon it, it was in perfect condition. The coffin was not opened and the body was left undisturbed. It was reverently lifted and placed on a truck. The participants got into autos and, under the sheen of a beautiful moon, the solemn procession made its way to the cemetery and the new grave. Here the coffin was lowered, placed in a new box and the cover fastened down. As the little group gathered about the open grave, Col. Makemson asked Dr. Allen to lead in a word of prayer. Then, one by one, the friends gathered there cast a shovel full of dirt in the grave, which was then rapidly filled. Dr. Allen pronounced the benediction, and the little company dispersed, leaving the body of Dr. Francis Asbury Mood interred for the second time in the place by the side of his wife, where it will doubtless abide until the resurrection trumpet shall arouse it from its long sleep.[90]

The monument was not moved so easily. Though the Executive Committee, on motion of Dr. Cody, immediately determined to place the monument "just east of the Administration Building and just south of Mood Hall,"[91] its size, shape, and weight defied the attempts of several movers to carry out their wish. It still had not been moved by April 26, 1921, when Vice President Sessions reported that he had not been able to move the monument. It was finally moved to the campus sometime shortly after that.[92]

In addition to Mood, Presidents McLean, Bishop, Barcus, and Bergin are buried in the cemetery.

New Degrees, Correspondence Work, and Academic Distinctions

There was no change in the academic year, term structure, or system of major courses during the Bishop years. The academic year consisted of three terms, what would today be called the quarter system. Students took 3 "majors" each term. A major was defined as a course meeting five times a week for an entire term, Tuesday through Saturday. Some courses were "half-majors," meeting two-and-a-half times a week. Students normally completed 9 majors each academic year, adding a half-major somewhere along the way for the B.A. and B.S. degrees, which consisted of 36½ "major" units obtained over the four years of study.

The four traditional degrees, the B.A. (A.B.), B.S., M.A. (A.M.), and M.S., were tweaked somewhat but not changed significantly. Two others joined them in 1912–1913—the Bachelor of Science in Education and the Bachelor of Music. The Bachelor of Science in Medicine was added in 1921–1922. It was a "cooperative program" in which students received the degree after completing two years of specified liberal arts courses at Southwestern followed by two years of medical work at a Grade-A School of Medicine.

The B.S. in Education was different from the other degrees in that it pointed the student toward a particular profession and required 41 "majors" rather than the standard 36½. In addition to taking 21 majors of liberal arts work, the student was required to complete a further 20 majors consisting of 9½ majors of prescribed work in the Department of Education, 7½ majors in the first teaching field, and 3 majors in the second teaching field.

Though the School of Fine Arts was set up as one of the two units of the University in 1903, it did not have its own degree until 1913–1914. Its leader was not designated as a dean until Professor Arthur L. Manchester, Director of the Music Department since 1913, was given that title in 1916–1917. Though the five earlier Directors of Music were accomplished persons, Manchester was the first to bring a national reputation to the position. A graduate of the Philadelphia Musical Academy, he came to Southwestern in 1913 from Converse College in Spartanburg, South Carolina, where he was Dean of Music. He had previously been President of the National Music Teachers' Association, Editor of *Musician* (1896–1902), Associate Editor of *Étude* (1902–1906), and Director of the South Atlantic States Music Festival (1904–1913). He taught at Southwestern for five years.

After arriving, Manchester revised the Bachelor of Music degree that had been established the year before he came to Southwestern. He wrote that in 1914 it "was greatly enlarged" and "made to include more advanced work in academic subjects, while the specific musical work was very greatly increased. A total of twelve majors in academic work . . . and of sixteen majors of musical theory . . . are now required of candidates for the degree of Bachelor of Music in addition to the required work in the phase of practical music selected as a major. . . . This course is of the same scope and degree of difficulty and thoroughness as those offered in the largest and most influential institutions of the country."[93]

In addition to the new degrees introduced in 1912–1913, the University began to engage in correspondence work during the same year. In the fifteen months ending September 7, 1913, some 256 correspondence courses were given. Because of the increasing demand for such work, a separate University Extension Committee was set up to run it, with twenty-one regulations governing it. Not more than 25 percent of a student's work could be taken by correspondence, and each course had to be completed within six months. A correspondence bulletin and later a catalog listed some fifty courses; each professor had to furnish a syllabus for his or her courses, and grades had to be returned to the student as soon as possible. Meticulous records were kept in a central office of all transactions between teachers and students. Teachers received 80 percent of the tuition fees, the University 15 percent for overhead, and the overall supervisor 5 percent.[94] The peak years for correspondence work were the seven years between 1924–1925 and 1930–1931, when credit was given for between 200 and 250 courses each year. The program gradually diminished over the next eighteen years and was closed in 1949 with a final enrollment of only three students.

Degrees offering the distinctions of *cum laude*, *magna cum laude*, and *summa cum laude* were first offered at the Commencement exercises of 1914.[95] These stemmed from a desire on the part of President Bishop to emphasize the importance of distinguished work by students. In line with this desire, he took a leading hand in organizing a Scholarship Society in 1915. The faculty adopted a constitution of eighteen articles on April 7 and elected him and Professors McGhee (chemistry) and Eddy (German), all of whom had helped organize the society, as charter members. The following week the faculty elected the first fifteen student members to be inducted.[96] The organizational meeting was held in the President's home in Snyder Hall on April 24. The idea spread, and the Southwestern chapter became the nucleus for the Scholarship Societies of Texas. In time it assumed national status and was named Alpha Chi in 1934, with the Southwestern chapter being the Alpha chapter of Texas.[97]

Laura Kuykendall: "Efficiency and Devoted Energy"

If Samuel G. Sanders and Claude Carr Cody are generally considered to be the most beloved professors in the early history of Southwestern, Laura Kuykendall might stand next in the line of succession. Employed by Bishop in 1914 as a teacher of expression and named Dean of Women by him in 1918, she received an extraordinary tribute from him at the meeting of the Board of Trustees in 1921. He wrote in his report on that occasion that "Miss Kuykendall has been indefatigable in her work both as Dean of Women and Director of the Expression Department. The young women of the institution are, almost without exception, devoted to her. She is actually a genius in the management of girls. I do not know where we could find her equal in efficiency and devoted energy if we were compelled to seek another in her place."[98] Presidents Horn, Barcus, and Vivion expressed their feelings about her in strong terms as well.

Laura Kuykendall holds a special place in Southwestern history: she was felt to be indispensable during her period of service from 1914 to 1935. Her premature death on April 30 from a stroke at the age of fifty-one caused great mourning.[99] Laura Kuykendall came to Southwestern in 1914 as Instructor in Expression and Director of Girls' Gymnasium. She graduated from North Texas Female College in Expression and Gymnasium (physical education) with an A.B. degree in 1903. She fortified that degree with a year at Southwestern in Expression in 1903–1904, after which she taught at the Jefferson Academy, in the public schools of Moody, and at Coronal Institute in San Marcos. She came to Southwestern after one year at Trinity University, where she was Instructor in Physical Training. Her career blossomed almost from the beginning at Southwestern as if every experience in her previous thirty years had been a preparation for it.

The May Fête

The two homecoming events, that of 1909 and 1912, prior to the time of Laura Kuykendall, were probably the first grand occasions with a unique character in Southwestern's history. Commencement ceremonies and presidential inaugurations were always special in their own way, but they were looked on as regular affairs, not something as markedly different from what went on at other colleges. Some student carnivals seem to have predated the Homecoming events, but few records about them exist. Two of these are large printed posters advertising "Southwestern's Big Annual Carnival" to be held in connection with end-of-the-year events in 1913. One poster mentions "44 Attractions in which 1400 People Take Part." The event, it says, will have a parade two miles long, with sideshows, confetti, whips, balls, and balloons. The sideshows will involve clowns, minstrels, and actors.[100] Whether the carnivals lived up to their billings is doubtful, but the concept was grand. May festivals had also been "partially planned many times." The notion of holding grand campus events did not originate with Laura Kuykendall, but she was the person responsible for changing their focus and making them a regular part of Southwestern culture.

Seizing upon the idea of holding a May festival, Laura Kuykendall, still in her first year, attacked the project with vigor in the spring of 1915. She began to assign parts and announced that a May Queen would be selected by the teachers in the School of Fine Arts and a few other selected people.[101] When the event occurred a few months later, its impact on the campus was extraordinary. An article in *The Megaphone* stated that "never before has such a grand and magnificent pageant or anything similar to it taken place at Southwestern."[102] Dozens of cars and vehicles lined the area, while hundreds sat on chairs and on the ground around the Woman's Building. Both the Southwestern orchestra and the band furnished music for the occasion. It began at 4:30 P.M. with a Grand March that lasted forty-five minutes. One hundred sixty young women marched around and about forming various configurations. Nine drills followed one another in rapid succession, each involving from ten to fourteen girls. The royalty selected by the committee was introduced, and President Bishop crowned the queen, Miss Alma Barrett.[103] At the festival's conclusion, the royal party led a procession of all the participants through the campus. It ended at 8:00 P.M.

The May Fête became an annual occurrence. It soon expanded into a two-day event, with a Queen's banquet the first evening, the hanging of May baskets in the early morning of May 1, a ball game, and the pageant proper in the late afternoon. Soon the May Day pageants were developed according to themes appropriate to events of the time, such as the World War pageant (1918), the Victory pageant (1919), the Homecoming pageant (1921), and the Golden Anniversary pageant (1923) celebrating Southwestern's fiftieth year in Georgetown. The Victory pageant was "in honor of the successful winning of the war by the Allies and the peace that should follow." There was a great audience, including Governor and Mrs. Hobby. The Golden Anniversary pageant was shifted from May 1 to June 7 and became the main focus of the Golden Anni-

Women in the May Fête of 1921 forming the letters SU, with Miss Laura Kuykendall, director, at center front. Southwestern University, Special Collections.

versary celebration. As a result of the May Fête events, May 1 was made a school holiday in 1918, replacing April 21, San Jacinto Day.[104]

The Christmas Carol Service

Prior to the coming of Laura Kuykendall, Christmas at Southwestern was an event planned and sponsored by the local Methodist Church or by the University Sunday School, with a relatively traditional Christmas program followed by the distribution of small gifts.[105] It soon became something quite different. The success of the May Fête brought President Bishop's wife together with Laura Kuykendall to plan an elaborate celebration of the Christmas season, Mrs. Bishop as the director and Laura Kuykendall as the organizing force behind the scenes. The result was another type of pageant that, with gradual modifications, became traditional over the years. Like the May Fête, its center was the Woman's Building, the chief domain of Laura Kuykendall's sway. The first Christmas Carol Candlelight Service was held on Monday evening, December 6, 1915. A local newspaper called it "the most beautiful and elaborate pre-Christmas entertainment ever given at Southwestern."[106]

The guests for dinner included the faculty, members of the Board of Trustees residing in Georgetown, Methodist ministers and their wives, and a few other specially invited persons. President Bishop and his wife along with two junior members of the Music Department welcomed them in the lobby. They entered the dining room promptly at 6:00 and were handed programs by two Christmas spirits. "As the Southwestern University Orchestra played the inspiring music to 'Holy, Holy, Holy,' in the distance could be heard the chants of a hundred voices. Through the archway of green marched 125 girls each dressed in snowy white and carrying a lighted candle. As the lights were turned out and in the soft half light from the candles[,] the girls marched around the Christmas tree and formed two living chains while they sang the beautiful hymn." A prayer was offered by one of the pastors. "Then, clear and sweet, without the sound of musical instrument, every voice was lifted in that most beautiful Christmas Carol, 'Silent Night.'" This opening was followed by appropriate choral and instrumental music, by pantomimes, by readings, and by a buffet dinner. At 9:00 the young ladies of the Woman's Building received as their guests the entire student body and distributed favors to everyone.

The event was not planned as a one-time affair. Its organizers intended from the outset to make it a part of the Southwestern tradition. They stated to the reporters who covered it that it "would be made an annual event at Southwestern in the future." It was not held during 1925 and 1926 after the burning of the old Annex, but it was reinstituted in 1927 in the new Woman's Building. A major difference from the past in the event that year was that it involved both men and women.[107] It was held in the Woman's Building or in the chapel of the Administration Building until 1953, when it was moved to the new Lois Perkins Chapel.[108]

The Dinner of the Golden Bowl

The third major event originated by Laura Kuykendall was the Dinner of the Golden Bowl. Held early each fall, the script of the ceremony, "Service of the Golden Bowl," was written by Annie Edward Barcus Minga, class of 1922 and daughter of soon-to-be President J. Sam Barcus. Margaret Mood McKennon provided the Rainbow poem for it, and a brass service, symbolic of the pot of gold at the foot of the rainbow, was dedicated in 1929. The event was supposed to symbolize "the welding of friendships, interests and loyalty."[109] Jane Brown McCook, a speech, drama, and English teacher at Southwestern for twenty-nine years after 1947, describes it. She says that it was patterned after the Oxford Friendship Dinner and was held each October during the years 1925 to 1950.

> It symbolized, by various colors of the rainbow, the attributes of friendship and loyalty within the Southwestern "family." Each year a student was selected as the Rainbow Girl to represent Southwestern womanhood and to preside over the service. Special guests for the occasion were outstanding Texas women, Southwestern brides of the past year and mothers of senior girls.[110]

An Analysis of the Pageantry

Holding magnificent pageantry events was looked on in its time as one of the unique features of the Southwestern mystique. From the date of the first event in 1915, *Megaphone* articles covering the pageants consistently expressed the enthusiastic support of both male and female students for them. *The Book of Southwestern*, a thirty-two-page booklet published in honor of Southwestern's Golden Anniversary in 1923, has an article entitled "Pageantry in Southwestern University." Facing the article is a full-page picture of Laura Kuykendall. The article states that "Southwestern University was the first school in Texas to take up pageantry from an educational standpoint. The public schools of the state have been invited from year to year to send representatives, and large numbers have responded. Thus the pageantry of Southwestern has become so widely known that graduates and former students have been called upon to direct pageants in many of the public schools of the state."[111]

By the time of Laura Kuykendall's death in 1935, the pageantry that had once enchanted the student body and alumni was becoming largely a pro forma exercise. The Great Depression and events leading up to World War II and the war itself gradually changed the way it was viewed by the public, as more an out-of-date relic than a vibrant educational phenomenon. Pageantry became the property of the European dictators as they threatened Europe with another continent-wide war. The May Fête disappeared with the death of Laura Kuykendall in 1935 and was replaced by a May Day Festival that continued until 1950.[112] Though it was still occasionally called a May Fête, it was not that at all when compared with the Kuykendall spectacles. A Dinner of the Golden Bowl was held as part of the Centennial Celebration in 1940.[113] The ceremony disappeared completely after World War II. The only one of the three events to survive was the Christmas Carol Candlelight Service. Its connection with an enduring religious tradition and the more restrained nature it adopted once it had been transferred to the chapel guaranteed its continuance.

Kuykendall Attempts to Resign as Dean of Women

By the time Southwestern's Golden Anniversary celebration arrived in 1923, Laura Kuykendall had achieved outstanding success in the eyes of the Board of Trustees and of two Presidents, Bishop and Horn. The day before the great Festival in 1923, now postponed from May 1 to June 7 to coincide with Commencement and the Board meeting, a four-part resolution was passed by the Trustees. They resolved that, because of her "eminently satisfactory," "self-sacrificing," and "untiring" work as Dean of Women, and because of her "unceasing" labor in the May festivals, "her salary [will] be raised to that of a full professor, beginning with the next college year, plus room, board, and laundry."[114]

When President Barcus arrived in 1924, he learned to his dismay that Laura Kuykendall wanted to retire from the Dean's office and as Supervisor of the Woman's Building and to change her field of service. Reluctantly, he agreed to the change, stating that it would be "the going of a most remarkable Dean of Women." He said that though her place would be hard to fill, she had made it as easy as possible by agreeing to remain until a new Dean could be secured and installed.

It is difficult to know with certainty why she resigned, but it may have been that, after ten years of labor in teaching expression, in managing the Woman's Building, and in producing extravaganzas, she was simply tired. For the first time in ten years no May Fête was held in 1924.[115] It may have been that she wanted to gain the time for upgrading her academic credentials, for she shortly entered the master's program at Southwestern in the fields of sociology and economics. She completed it in 1926, with Professors M. L. Williams, W. P. Davidson, and Claud Howard as her thesis advisors. Though she may have resigned her administrative positions in order to gain time for this work, she in fact never left the job. She continued as Dean of Women until her death in 1935. Apparently she accepted the recommendation of a Board committee that she withdraw her resignation and continue employment under the direction of the President.[116] Since all major administrators, of which she was one, work under the direction of the President in any case, this last phrase was probably meant to encourage him to modify her workload in the light of her many responsibilities should that be helpful to her situation.

"Miss Kirk" on the Place of Women in Society

Because of Laura Kuykendall's success as an administrator and as a producer of extraordinary pageants, it is easy to overlook the social views of Laura Kuykendall, particularly her views on women's place in society. This topic is important because all sources suggest that her influence on her charges in the Woman's Building stemmed not from administrative finesse but from the love and respect the women had for her. To them she was "Miss Kuyk" (pronounced and often written as "Kirk") or Miss Laura. Certain passages in her master's thesis, entitled "The Dean of Women and Her Problems as Found on a Small University Campus," suggest why this was so.

Women, she felt, were as capable as men of doing a high grade of work. The authorities that state otherwise, she says, fail to realize that the selection of certain subjects by women has been forced on them by lack of opportunity rather than by lack of ability to master them. "The next generation of women seems fated to prove that women are the equal of men in intellect and achievements."[117]

One of the primary functions of the Dean of Women, she continues, is that of helping the girls with whom she works to find meaningful vocations. In addition to the traditional subjects, such as stenography, typewriting, and the various domestic science arts, she sees women in various lines of "manual training and shop work, including bench work, cabinet work, factory woodwork, wood turning and pattern making, forging, automobile mechanics, machine shop practice and printing, mechanical, architectural and engineering drawing."[118] Nothing is automatically foreclosed to them.

She hears much talk among older people "against the conduct of students of the present age," she says, but "in proportion to the number of boys and girls now on our

Picture of Laura Kuykendall in a Ford automobile, with legend certifying that she had completed the course of Ford Driving. Southwestern University, Special Collections.

campuses[,] many believe the morals are as good if not better than at any other period." She has a high view of the women with whom she works and says that "the Dean of Women who cannot see a beauty and charm in the new girl [of the 1920s] had better change her profession." The girl of the twentieth century "has come to claim the birth right that is her own. She will be led and guided, but it is my view that she will never again be dictated to." Previous women had only two avenues to realize their destiny—the way of marriage or "the other path of the spinster aunt. Either, except when chosen through preference, brought only dependence and heartache. But today a young girl has the choice of a profession as a third way out. Can a girl growing up with this third goal before her be the timid, dependent type of her predecessors? Never!"[119]

She says that one of the chief functions of the Dean of Women today is to help girls in college come "into a proper realization of the true significance of their spiritual welfare." This will not be done, however, as it was in the "good old days," through rigid religious discipline. "The girls were taken to and from church in a uniformed line; one chaperone walked in front, one behind, and two at either side. Such was the order of the day." That kind of religious training is unrealistic. "No community has all its members [as] church goers; not many homes can count each member a regular church attendant. So it may be expected that a college cannot expect each student to become a regular attendant upon religious services, but if the record of the boys and girls is followed after they leave college then one may see that the influences brought to bear upon them during their college days are bringing a rich harvest for good. We have spoken of religious life in the accepted form, but college gives to its students another lesson that is one of the greatest taught,—that is, the religion of service as taught through the Sociology, Education, Philosophy, Bible, and Theology Departments."[120]

"A Dean of Women," she concludes, "must not expect to be understood by a public that can and does see only one side of her work. She would indeed receive little encouragement if this were her source of appreciation, but she knows that her reward comes in the lives of the young women she sends into the world, year after year. Into these girls she has tried to put truthfulness, honesty, and straightforwardness. She has neither trained them exclusively for marriage nor an independent career, but she has trained them for whatever places in life they may find they are called upon to fill."[121]

The Fraternity-Barb Question Rises Again

As during President Heidt's term, the fraternity question became a major issue at the beginning of the Bishop administration. The faculty dealt with it quickly, however, and it had different consequences for him than it did for Heidt. It arose in late 1912 when a small, four-page, independent student publication, *The Barbarian*, was sent through the mails to every student and faculty member of the University. Underneath the title was the motto: "We recognize no aristocracy but that of work." Without listing its editors, it dealt with the fraternity question at colleges and universities and in no uncertain terms condemned the Greek letter organizations. It used specific illustrations to show that "fraternities are a menace [to] rather than an exponent of democracy."[122]

Shortly after the beginning of the winter term, the Barbs and Greeks engaged in a "gigantic street fight" on University Avenue. *The Megaphone* reported in its January 17, 1913, edition that they fought "until there wasn't a picket on the fences from the Main Building to town." This event seems to have galvanized the Barbs into action. Three of them appeared before the faculty even before *The Megaphone* report about the fight had been published, asking for the use of the auditorium for a free public discussion of the fraternity question. They said they represented directly thirty students but indirectly the majority of the student body at Southwestern.[123] Permission was granted, and a mass meeting was held on a Saturday evening toward the end of the month. About three hundred students attended and were treated to a number of speeches on such topics as "Fraternities and Religion," "The Aristocracy of Fraternities," "The Egotism of Fraternities," "What Is the Good and Evil of College Fraternities," and "Whether or Not College Fraternities are Democratic." A number of "barb" leaders from the University of Texas attended, expressed solidarity with the students, and spoke to their approval of the recently published paper.[124]

In the face of these events, the faculty appointed a committee to consider the tense situation. By late May it was ready with a five-part recommendation to rein in the fraternities and to set up strict procedures for fraternities on campus. It provided that no student could be initiated who had not completed two terms of work successfully, that no fraternity could run a house unless it had someone living in the house approved by the faculty and responsible to them, and that no freshman who had not passed two-thirds of his work in any term could live in a fraternity house. It also appointed a faculty member to be responsible for seeing that the rules were carried out.[125] Though some of the fraternities and sororities had difficulty coming into compliance with the new rules, President Bishop reported to the Board of Trustees a year later that since the enactment of the new regulations the faculty has had less trouble with fraternities than ever before.[126] The students complaining about the fraternities may not have gotten what they wanted, the complete elimination of the fraternity system, but they did cause the faculty to supervise the system much more closely than it had theretofore.

A Day in the Life of a Student

One of the difficulties in describing student life from available records is that they usually consist of the regulations governing student conduct and accounts of the disciplinary procedures taken against students breaking those rules. The life of the average student who keeps the rules is difficult to reconstruct. Fortunately, a collection of letters written by one student in the early years of the Bishop administration opens a window onto the world of normal student life.

Reba McMinn studied at Southwestern as a regular student for two years, 1913–1914 and 1914–1915. She also attended summer school in 1915. Though she loved Southwestern, she transferred to Southern Methodist University when it opened and graduated there as a member of the first graduating class in 1916. Georgetown was just too far away from Childress, her home in the Texas panhandle. She went to Columbia University in 1917 for graduate study. During her first year at Southwestern, she wrote back regularly to her best girlfriend at home, Mary Biggerstaff, a senior in high school. The collection of those letters consists of twenty-five written from Southwestern, three written from SMU, and one written from Columbia.[127] They are open, frank, and unadorned, providing an intimate view of daily student life.

Reba and her father arrived in Georgetown after a long train ride from Childress, a journey of well over four hundred miles with several train changes. Describing her first day at Southwestern to Mary, she says that she is "elated" by the prospect of college life, averring that she "has not cried a bit." One of her first-day friends is Fannie Dobie, sister of J. Frank Dobie. Observing everything carefully, she notices immediately the absence of any "lady teachers" in the first chapel service. She is very excited about the first meal, as she will continue to be about all the meals in the Woman's Building during the year. She feels that they are so good that she often lists the menu for the day in her letters. Music is played constantly in the building on a piano at the end of the hall. It is kept going all the time with "rags."[128]

Reba is particularly astounded at the number of girls driving automobiles. Some of them, she says, have "swell cars, and some have negro 'chiffoneers' too."[129] She, too, learns to drive in the spring when her parents visit her, and they take a motor trip to Beeville. After a month in school, she confirms her initial assessment of Southwestern. "O Kid! I just love this place. It seems like it is the finest spot in the world. A regular 'Garden of Eden.'"[130]

During the year Reba attended sporting events, church services, Y.W.C.A. prayer meetings, plays, musical events, and literary presentations. One of the outside speakers during the year was Jacob A. Riis, journalist, author, and social reformer. He was introduced by President Bishop, who told of Riis's work helping people in the slums of New York.[131] Performers and speakers of note in other years during Bishop's administration were Helen Keller, William Jennings Bryan, Alfred Noyes, John Masefield, Vachel Lindsey, William Butler Yeats, Rabinidrath Tagore, William Howard Taft, and artists connected with the New York Symphony Orchestra.

Reba was a good student and did well in her classes, particularly German. She was shy, however, and developed "a terrible case of stage fright" in Professor Wentz's class in May and forgot her declamation. Though it embarrassed her at the time, the grade she received was not her main concern. She was fearful that her weakness in speaking might keep her from making "suffragette stump speeches."[132]

Reba McMinn describes her year at Southwestern as a happy experience. She loves the "hen" parties in the Woman's Building, school picnics, and folk dancing in her gym class. Aside from the fact that the history class, in which she is a top student, is terribly dry, that she loses sleep from studying so much, and that the boys sometimes cut up in chapel, everything is fine.

Among the many positive aspects of student life during the Bishop era was the general good health of the student body. In fact, given the times, Southwestern was singularly fortunate during the entire first half century of its existence in this regard. During the first eight years of its history, there were no student deaths, either on or off campus. During the next twenty-two years, from 1881 to 1903, twelve died, ten men and two women, whether on campus or not is unknown, but it is known that there had never been a death in the Woman's Building during the more than twenty-five years of its existence when a report was made in 1914. From 1903 until 1914, there were no deaths at all.[133] Even during the influenza epidemic of late 1918, when half of the student body was affected, no one died.[134]

Student Conduct Problems

Most of the minor student conduct problems of earlier years, such as forbidden boy-girl associations and dancing, gradually lessened as concerns during the Bishop years, but certain new problems surfaced. Gambling was one of them. President Bishop was forced to report to the Board of Trustees in mid-1913 that there had been an unusually large number of serious discipline cases during the year. "Fourteen young men," he stated, "were publicly dismissed for grave disorder and violations of College regulations, including drinking and gambling; while several others were compelled quietly to leave school without honorable dismissal."[135] Drinking was an old issue, but gambling was new. It had only come to light recently, and the faculty was determined to stamp it out. Ten students were dismissed and ten were given heavy demerit penalties. These penalties were thought to be so harsh by some of the ladies in town, church ladies such as Mrs. W. K. Makemson and Mrs. J. M. Daniel (Jessie's mother), that they appealed to the faculty asking for the reinstatement of those recently dismissed. The appeal was denied.[136]

As the prohibition movement gained momentum in the country, a local student chapter was formed at Southwestern. Two student delegates were sent to a national meeting over the Christmas holidays of 1914.[137] Once national prohibition was enacted, however, some students who were cut off from their supply or who wanted to make a statement about their opposition to the new constitutional amendment, engaged in a daring act. They broke into the office of the chemistry department in February 1921, stole some alcohol, and got drunk. Eleven were eventually expelled, with another leaving voluntarily. As the faculty delved more deeply into the matter, it learned that the problem was more general than had first been believed. There were other students "present at the affair at the Science Building but who did nothing to prevent it." They were reprimanded publicly. A few of those expelled were later allowed to resume their studies.[138]

Some of the problems presented to the faculty came as a result of the freedom offered students by the proliferation of automobiles on campus. Two couples were called before the Discipline Committee in 1915 for "Joy Riding" and two others the following year "for auto riding without permission." They were given heavy penalties.[139] Because of restrictions regarding male-female association, students contrived ways to meet one another casually, sometimes surreptitiously. The matter came to such a pass that the faculty passed a rule in 1918 forbidding "loitering about the entrances, or corridors or sitting in cars, or in cozy corners."[140] Finally, in 1921, it prepared "strenuous resolutions concerning the possession of cars by members of the student body" and "decided to block the front entrance to the admission of vehicles."[141]

Student Church Attendance

Francis Asbury Mood had said that the main function of Southwestern University as an institution of the Church "is to use all proper means to refine the manners, protect the morals, and improve the hearts of the young people committed to its care and lead them to Christ." The chief way its Presidents provided proof that this function was being met over the years was by reporting the number of conversions among its young people. In 1914 President Bishop stated that in an "unbroken series of annual revivals running through forty years, not less than two thousand students have professed faith in Christ and been added to the Church." That test of success, he now suggests, is no longer a valid criterion. The primary work of the institution in this day and age is no longer that of evangelization while providing a first-class education but of instilling in the student the "ideals of liberal culture" as the Church understands them.

This view of the University's role caused Bishop to bring up the matter of "compulsory Church attendance" in a faculty meeting the following year (1915). After much discussion, the rule was abolished.[142] This action caused repercussions among the Trustees, who probably heard negative comments about it from their constituencies, and they reinstated the rule "requiring attendance of students at Church at least once on Sunday" (1917).[143]

Several years later Bishop felt compelled to speak to the Trustees about some recent criticism the school had received, namely because of the apparent failure of special revival efforts among the students as compared with other days when scores of them were converted and added to the

Church. He says the main reason is that of the 452 students enrolled in the college and in fine arts for 1919–1920, 436 were already members of the Church when they came. Of the remaining number, probably six or eight have joined while here. This proportion of Church members means that SU "seems now to be specially selected by parents and their children whose home and Sunday School training have been such as already to have brought our young collegians into the Church. The problems of the religious life in our Christian colleges therefore are those of Christian training and development of character rather than of 'evangelization' in the usual sense of the word."[144]

Reports have been received from various parts of the state, he continues, "to the effect that there was much worldliness among our students." If by worldliness is meant a concern "with other interests than those which are specifically Christian or which have to do with formal religious activities, then it is to be frankly said that there has been far too much of it; not a very great deal more than in former years, but it has amounted to a quite conspicuous eagerness in the pursuit of pleasure and also [to] the neglect of religious activity on the part of a great many, and some breaking down of reserve in the manners of young men and women in their relations to each other. These things have given us considerable distress of mind, and we have done what we could to correct them. But they do not constitute a problem which is peculiar to us; they are rather the breaking over into our more secluded and protected life of the waves of influence from a pleasure-loving and self-seeking and sensuous and distracted world."[145] In spite of his feeling that compulsory church attendance was no longer a helpful university directive, he continued to try to enforce it through the remainder of his tenure because the Board of Trustees insisted on it.[146]

"Prayers," the Y.M.C.A., and the Y.W.C.A.

In his letter to Dean Cody in the summer of 1914, the one in which he set forth the mission of the University, he also mentioned what had earlier been called chapel but which he called "our daily assembly" and was generally known among the students as "Prayers." He said that this service had almost broken down. He tried to rectify it by having the faculty put in new regulations governing both faculty and student participation. The Tuesday, Thursday, and Saturday services would thenceforth be devotional in nature. The Wednesday and Friday services would primarily follow a lecture format, with a very short devotional. The lecture "is to be made worth while, to the point, thought-out, appropriate, *alive*."[147] In 1916 the chapel period on Saturday was set aside as a "Conference Hour" for consultation with students. Chapel, thus, become a four-day rather than a five-day-a-week exercise.[148]

During the Bishop years, the main agency for campus religious activity became the Y.M.C.A. and the Y.W.C.A. Reba McMinn, as mentioned earlier, attended Y.W.C.A. prayer meetings during her two years at Southwestern. Professor J. C. Granbery became especially active in the work and reported to the faculty in 1917 that he had "never heard more genuine, wholesome, and virile expressions in testimony to the power of the gospel in the personal life than I have from our students in these meetings of this year. . . . A State Y. M. C. A. official is reported to have said that Southwestern has the best college Y. M. C. A. in Texas."[149] The two Associations were especially strong during the war, when the army Y.M.C.A. supplemented the regular campus program.

Bishop felt that "the largest realization of the spirit and aims of the gospel" in the lives of Southwestern students came through the work of the two "Y's." The "college pastor," he says, works through these organizations, and the faculty, through their representatives in the two cabinets of the Associations and in individual contact with students in them, "finds its best means of helping in the moulding and toning up of the religious life of the students."[150] The influence of the two organizations began to decline after the war.

Athletics

Regular excursions to athletic contests away from Georgetown were outlets from academics enjoyed by the students during these years. In 1911, for example, a group went to Austin for the Southwestern-Texas football game and to enjoy the United States Marine Band. A month later some went to Dallas for the Southwestern–Austin College game.[151] In the same year the baseball team played the Chicago White Sox, who were making a spring tour. The team made a respectable showing and played the White Sox again in Georgetown on at least two other occasions.[152]

Southwestern became a charter member of the Southwest Intercollegiate Conference when it was organized in 1914. Other members were the University of Texas, the

University of Oklahoma, Texas A&M, Oklahoma A&M, the University of Arkansas, and Baylor University. Since the maintenance of an athletic program competitive with these rapidly growing state institutions was impossible, membership was dropped after two years of play.[153]

Though athletics was curtailed during the war, one student from those years, Peter Willis Cawthon, became a famous coach on the state and national scene. Not only did he letter in football, basketball, and baseball during his freshman year (1917–1918), but he also coached the baseball team when the coach left for the war. He earned four letters and was an All-State halfback during his sophomore year, his last at Southwestern, before leaving to coach in high school and college. In 1923 he became coach at Austin College, where he had conspicuous success. While there he wrote back saying that he was "anxiously looking forward to returning for the 'Jubilee.' For despite the fact that I am now connected with Austin College, I am nevertheless still loyal to old Southwestern, and am interested in all her undertakings."[154]

He became one of the most successful coaches in the country during the 1930s at Texas Tech College and was the coach under whom the football team gained the nickname "Red Raiders." Sports writers across the nation began to call it that after he outfitted his high-scoring players in red satin uniforms. In all, he led the Raiders to seventy-nine wins, twenty-seven losses, and six ties. His team appeared in the Sun Bowl in 1938 and in the Cotton Bowl the next year after an undefeated season. He completed his career coaching and scouting in professional football and serving for two years as athletic director at the University of Alabama.[155]

Dean Pegues wrote about the baseball team of spring 1919 that it "was the despair of the Texas colleges, winning a large percentage of their games, thus giving it the championship of the T. I. A. A."[156] The first game between the current baseball team and alumni from previous years was played on Snyder Field in 1920. The 1919–1920 academic year was perhaps the best in the history of the school up to that point for all the athletic teams when taken together.[157] A report to the Board of Trustees in 1921 said that the baseball team of that year was perhaps the best team fielded to date.[158]

Faculty Matters

Except for some faculty dissension in 1917–1918 (to be discussed later), most of the matters involving the faculty during Bishop's tenure were relatively innocuous. At one point some one or more members of the faculty must have been discussing their actions with persons outside the faculty, for it felt the necessity of drawing up a series of regulations in 1913 clearly stating that faculty meetings were executive sessions and that as such their content should not be revealed to outsiders.[159]

In order to encourage good fellowship and to provide intellectual stimulation in the faculty, a Faculty Club "of a scientific, philosophical, and literary character" was established in 1914. It consisted of members of the faculty and "their wives," with membership and attendance voluntary.[160] It continued to meet with varying success for about seventy years, disappearing during the early 1980s. By then the concept of a homogeneous faculty where everyone could be presumed to share a common ethos was long gone. More and more faculty members began to live outside of the Georgetown area. Few of them were willing to make a second trip back to the campus in the evening for what had by then become more a social club than the academic club described when it was set up.

A resolution requiring caps and gowns to be worn by the faculty on Commencement occasions was passed early in 1915, only to be set aside for later action the following month and completely rescinded the following year. A motion was finally approved in March 1917 that Southwestern "adopt the custom of wearing academic costume on the annual Commencement morning, [but] that it be left to each member of the Faculty to furnish proper costume."[161]

Due to the fact that separate administrators apart from faculty members did not exist in the early history of the University, it became customary early on for what would later be called administrative matters to be cared for in faculty committees and in full faculty meetings. In the early years faculty meetings were held weekly. In 1913 they were changed to once a month, pushing back some faculty responsibilities onto committees. Even when administrators began to be appointed, such as the first academic dean in 1907, they were usually appointed from within the faculty and tended to continue teaching courses. The faculty as a whole well into the Bishop years made decisions that would today be made by the registrar and the dean for student development. Faculty members also managed and kept books for the residence halls. This manner of operation gradually changed, but one thing did not change—the presence of faculty committees.

Bishop inherited from Hyer a faculty with twenty committees. He left for Horn a faculty with thirty committees. Analyzing the committee structure for 1915–1916, close to the midpoint in his tenure, one finds twenty-five committees.[162] Listed in alphabetical order, they ranged from committees on Absences and Athletics to committees on Student Publications and the Y.M.C.A. and Y.W.C.A. There were two one-person committees, those of the Fraternity Adviser and Student Publications, and one, Registration, of nine persons. Most committees were composed of three or four persons. As far as the teachers were concerned, the workhorses were McGhee and Moore, with eight committees each, Pegues with seven, and Tinsley and Granbery with six. Wright and Nichols each had five. These seven faculty members, making up only 35 percent of the entire faculty, carried 57 percent of the committee load in terms of the number of committees on which they served.

World War I

Intimations of war had been in the air for some time before the United States entered. Writing on February 13, 1917, from New York after just having arrived at Columbia University, Reba McMinn said that there was a great deal of excitement about the war. Four German boats were interned in the port, and the fact that there were many Germans in the city gave cause for concern.[163] The prospect of the United States entering the war was also recognized in Georgetown before it was declared. The faculty adopted a resolution on March 31, which said that "believing in both the patriotism and wisdom of President Wilson we urge Congress to support him in the course that he shall recommend."[164] Four days after the April 6 declaration of war by Congress a "Grand Patriotic Rally" was held in the courthouse square with two thousand people in attendance.[165]

Southwestern felt the effects of the war immediately. Bishop reported to the Trustees in June that a considerable number of young men had left for the Officers' Training Camp at Leon Springs and others to enter military service. The faculty voted on May 8 to give credit for courses to students entering military service prior to the termination of the course if they had a passing average at the time of enlistment.[166] As a result of the loss of men, it was felt necessary to combine the boarding departments of the Woman's Building and Mood Hall. The Woman's Building took over the supplies of Mood Hall and provided meals for both young men and young women. Bishop says that as a matter of economy it was a wise arrangement, but it did introduce difficult problems of discipline at the Woman's Building.[167] The Trustees approved a motion instigated by President Bishop that all students who can meet necessary requisites be required to take "Military Training."[168]

Though Bishop's intentions might have been good in trying to help provide military training immediately for the 1917–1918 year, his desire was impossible to realize.[169] His effort to procure governmental commitments, instructors, and equipment ran up against a bureaucracy that was swamped. Government officials simply could not address in timely fashion the good intentions of schools like Southwestern and help them put into place the things they needed or wanted. It was not until the academic year 1918–1919 that Southwestern had an institutional programmatic response to the war with government support. Previous to that, during 1917–1918, most of the response was by individuals or groups.

Some members of the staff and faculty left immediately for military and other types of service. Economics and Sociology Professor John C. Granbery and his wife, May Catt Granbery, workers with the Y.M.C.A. and Y.W.C.A. on campus, were among the five hundred who sailed from New York on September 13 at the behest of General Pershing for the national Y.M.C.A. to send persons to work with the French army.[170] His year of service stretched into three, and he completed his service in Greece in 1920. A letter to his wife in mid-June of that year has him in Soufli, a city in Thrace on the border of Turkey, where he was wildly acclaimed by the people and awarded a medal, for what exploit is not mentioned except that he was an American of goodwill.[171]

Wilbur F. Wright, registrar and bursar, asked for and was granted an indefinite leave of absence in order to enter military service. He was granted a First Lieutenant's commission. His position as registrar was taken over by Randolph Wood Tinsley, Professor of Biology and Geology since 1903. Tinsley enjoyed a thirty-three year career at Southwestern in various positions, including assistant to the President. Pearl A. Neas was made assistant registrar, thus beginning her long forty-six-year career in the registration office.[172]

In addition to these persons, many other people joined the armed forces. Bishop reported in 1918 that 411 "sons of Southwestern" had enlisted. Out of the 137 men enrolled in college during 1917–1918, 38 had enlisted during or at the end of the academic year.[173] One of those "sons of Southwestern" was Dr. Claude C. Cody, Jr., son of the former dean and future chair of the Board of Trustees. Dean Emeritus Cody pasted seven articles in one of his scrapbooks about the work of his son's Ambulance Company #36 in France.[174] Those who could not join the army or go overseas tried to show their support for the war effort in other ways. The students left in school sacrificed the 1917–1918 yearbook, *The Sou'wester*, as a contribution to the War Work Fund of the national Y.M.C.A., an amount of about $2,500.[175]

The decrease in the size of the working staff as compared with former years was significant. In the faculty, sociology and economics, Romance languages, and physics went vacant. Physics was partially cared for by persons in other departments. Interest in German diminished considerably. Nevertheless, Bishop, according to his testimony, refused to engage in "ruthless reorganization of the faculty."[176]

By mid-1918 the University was ready to set up a military training program. The government had stated that it would furnish instructors and equipment to all A-class colleges having at least one hundred able-bodied men over the age of eighteen who were ready to receive military training. Though the University did not have that number during the previous spring, Bishop felt that having the promise of a military unit would enable it to recruit that many. He had worked with the government to set up "a special War Emergency Training School for training telegraphers and radio workers," but the program could not be instituted for lack of faculty qualified to do the work and the difficulty of obtaining instructors.[177]

In preparation for the military training in the fall, a contingent of six persons, one faculty member and five students, went to Fort Sheridan, Illinois, for a sixty-day training camp, from July 8 through September 16, 1918. The professor was John C. Godbey, and the five students were Paul Bruce Baker, Marcellus Powell Adams, Alonzo Lee Curtis, Paul Young, and Harold L. Egger. They were under temporary enlistment for sixty days, receiving housing, uniforms, subsistence, equipment, and military instruction at government expense. They received the pay of a private, thirty dollars per month and reimbursement to and from camp at 3½ cents per mile. They did not receive commissions but were issued certificates of qualifications as instructors.[178] A small staff of regular army personnel came to the campus when school opened and worked with these instructors to provide training in digging trenches, putting up barbed wire, bayoneting dummies, engaging in close order drill, and similar activities.

Hardly had Southwestern gotten into gear when the war ended and the need for military training evaporated. During its existence, however, 154 young men were enlisted in the Student Army Training Corps at Southwestern. The unit was organized on October 1, 1918, and disbanded on December 15. Several months after the dissolution of the unit, President Bishop attended a meeting of college presidents for a conference with army officers at Fort Sheridan, Illinois. The army was proposing the establishment of an R.O.T.C. unit on campus. Without going so far as to refuse it, Bishop "postponed" consideration of the matter.[179] The postponement continued indefinitely.

Bishop's "postponement" of a further connection with the army could hardly have been a surprise to anyone familiar with his appraisal of the venture. Speaking to the Board of Trustees in 1919, he provided a trenchant assessment of the "experiment."

> Whatever the explanation be, the fact remains that for the S. A. T. C. [Student Army Training Corps] the college was an army camp with but little of a college. Only the most determined members of the unit were able to make their courses and but a small number even attempted the final examinations, so greatly had their military duties encroached upon their college duties. And an army camp it was, also, in manners. Perhaps the least said on that score the better. Your Board ought to know, however, that the faculty was greatly disturbed over the reported profanity and gambling indulged in by members of the unit and made repeated and persistent protests both to the staff in command and to higher authorities.
>
> Two things, however, can and ought to be said entirely favorable to the experiment of the S. A. T. C.—first, that it provided a student-body for the college and made it possible for it to continue its work, for the probable effect of the Manpower Act of August 1918, reducing the draft age to eighteen, would have been to cut the attendance of men during the Fall Term to fifty, had the Government not established the S. A. T. C., and of not much over that number for the succeeding terms of the session; and, secondly, that the effect of the military training and care of the health of the men was a decided improvement in their physical conditions, which should be of great value to faculties in the further conduct of the athletic activities of their students.[180]

Just as the faculty had voted a resolution asking the Congress to support President Wilson prior to the war, it also sent a petition to the United States Senate in early 1920. It did so after receiving a request for that action from the New York–based League to Enforce Peace. The resolution was in the form of a petition asking "for action on the Peace Treaty and League of Nations" that has been prepared, signed, and sent to our representative.[181]

Rehabilitation of the Honor System

In the fall of 1918, the faculty felt that something had to be done to stop the climate of disrespect toward the rules and regulations of the University. Its remedy was to institute an Honor Pledge and to require every student enrolling for the winter term in January 1919 to sign it.[182] The action was taken at this time because of the perceived loss of control over student conduct stemming from the presence of the Student Army Training Corps on campus during the war. The Honor Pledge accomplished two things. It took care of the lax conduct that had supposedly become common during the S. A. T. C. days, and it put into place the final piece in the newly reconstituted Honor System.

Formally established around 1905 during the Hyer years, the honor system gradually lost strength over the next decade. A survey made by the faculty in early 1917 revealed that practically all the students felt that it had failed. Most of them felt that it applied only to examinations and that the faculty had failed to support it. The faculty committee appointed to study the system recommended that it be reestablished and that it cover every phase of college activity.[183]

Almost a year later the committee reported that an old copy of the constitution of the Council of Honor had come to light. The constitution had been lost for a number of years, and no one at the University knew for sure its rules and regulations. The committee felt that it was all that could be desired in a constitution and recommended that it be reinstated. Two of the most pertinent sections were sections 5 and 8, as follows:

> Sec. 5. This council of honor shall deal with all questions of cheating on examination and other conduct which it shall deem dishonorable.
>
> Sec. 8. It shall be the duty of every student of the University to report to some member of the "Council of Honor" any and all cases of cheating on examination, and other disorderly conduct of which he may be aware.[184]

The constitution was presented to the students at a chapel service with the understanding that the reconstituted Council would let "by-gones be by-gones," but it issued a warning that it would enforce the constitution from that moment forward.

In its own deliberations, the faculty agreed that it must cooperate with the Honor Council for the system to be effective and must not be more lax than the Council in dealing with cases that might come before it in the future. It reminded itself of the bad precedents set by its laxity in "dealing with the Reeves case last year and the stealing of the Pullman blankets by our foot ball team this year."[185]

As indicated above, an Honor Pledge was established in January 1919. All students entering for the winter term had to sign it. It read as follows:

> On my honor, I pledge my word to refrain from all such practices as those above forbidden, and to cooperate with the Student Self-Government and Honor Council and the Faculty in enforcing the regulations and maintaining the ideals of Southwestern University.[186]

Among the "practices above forbidden" were hazing, gambling, cheating upon examinations or on assignment, disorder or unnecessary noise, any disrespectful attitude or conduct in chapel or in the classroom, profane language, or any indecent or improper speech. This Honor Pledge became the basis for the one used by Southwestern students today. With the Council of Honor and the Honor Pledge in place, President Bishop was able to report to the Board of Trustees in June 1919 that "the Honor Council had almost no cases of dishonesty during the year."[187]

Bishop's National and State Activities

During the years of great financial difficulty for the University before the war, Bishop traveled widely on both the national and the Texas scenes. His address at a meeting in Evanston, Illinois, entitled "The Comparative Values of Federation and Organic Union," was hailed back in Texas as "a capital one" that the *Texas Christian Advocate* said it would print in its entirety in the near future.[188] A few weeks later he preached at First Methodist and at St. Paul's Methodist Churches in Houston. Reporting on the sermons, the *Georgetown Commercial* stated that "Dr. Bishop has taken his place as one of the foremost educators of the country since he became president of Southwestern several years ago, and he has done a wonderful work for Southwestern. He is putting its interests to the front in such a way that its future as an institution of learning is assured. The old students all have confidence in him as a leader and in Houston are thoroughly loyal and are giving Dr. Bishop and Southwestern unqualified support."[189]

A year later, in mid-1917, Bishop worked with the Southwestern faculty in supporting President Robert E. Vinson of the University of Texas against the attempt of Governor James E. Ferguson to dismiss him and, failing that, to curtail Texas University funds. It sent him a letter signed by Bishop supporting his stand "against political domination of the University of Texas." It assured him of its support in his "fight for the maintenance of proper academic freedom and fair dealings for members of the Faculty."[190]

President Bishop and the Anti-Mob Movement

Of all the issues that engaged Bishop's attention during these years before the war, that closest to his heart was the anti-mob (anti-lynching) movement. He played a prominent role in it on campus, in the state, and in the South. Though he had undoubtedly expressed his convictions on the matter in earlier years, his role as a leader in the movement began toward the end of 1915 when he helped organize and attended an Anti-Mob Convention of college presidents in Waco. He was elected its presiding officer. Back in Georgetown he encouraged the student body to organize a student Anti-Mob Association. It elected Angie Smith of Taylor, later to become a Methodist bishop, as its president. A news article reporting the organization of the group stated that Dr. Bishop addressed the meeting and that more than five hundred students enrolled. The article concluded by saying that this organization was the first anti-mob association formed among students in the United States.[191]

The October 25, 1915, meeting of college presidents in Waco had met "for the purpose of considering mob lawlessness and lynching in the South." With Bishop as its presiding officer, it issued a long statement, probably written by Bishop, to the people of Texas. It said that in addition to the people who have committed these deeds, "many other thousands have stood by and gazed upon these cruel deeds approvingly, and with a sense of satisfaction of the spirit of vengeance and race-hatred. Most of the rest of us have regarded this series of lawless crimes simply as the shocking incidents growing out of unfortunate conditions which we could not control, and have dismissed them from our minds as we laid aside the newspaper which contained their gruesome story. Officers of the law have connived at these proceedings and even our best citizens have passed them by with only a few words of sorrow or denunciation. . . . The whole South has suffered in the judgment of the civilized world, and our social and moral life is threatened with permanent degradation. . . . The peculiar conditions obtaining in the South explain but do not justify the crime or paliate [sic] the sin and shame of it."[192]

Bishop's next move was to write an article for the *Texas Christian Advocate.* In it he recounted the founding of the Anti-Mob Association by the Texas Church college presidents in Waco the previous fall. He now congratulates the "tax supported institutions" for following suit. He says that the movement began six or eight months ago and has now been endorsed by all the Methodist Conferences and the Baptist Convention. He concludes with strong words.

> Of course the passing of resolutions by Church bodies and the meeting of college men and others are only a beginning, and perhaps the work before them will be accomplished slowly. . . . But the cause is worth all the trouble and other expense that it will cost. The deep disgrace which our country suffers from this horrible, outrageous enlisting of whole communities in brutal crimes must be extinguished forever. The anarchy which is exhibited in these multitudinous murders is not theoretical but actual. It threatens the stability of the State and the very life of civilization and religion. . . . My own belief is that the only possible radical cure for a social disease like this is to be found in a great religious awakening and quickening. This trouble lies too deep for mere tinkerers.[193]

From Waco and Georgetown, Bishop went on to Birmingham and New Orleans. In Birmingham he helped form the Association of Southern Church Colleges, of which he was elected the first president. Its first action, so a newspaper article reports, would be to interest Southern colleges in anti-mob work. Eighteen colleges, embracing practically every state in the South, were represented at the meeting, with some twenty-two others lending the meeting their "sympathetic support."[194]

From Birmingham Bishop went to New Orleans, where he was one of the featured speakers at the Southern Sociological Congress. There he spoke on the three "c's," the cause, the consequences, and the cure of mob violence. In his speech he referred to lynchings as "the great American sport." He stated, however, that "lynchings are in reality criminal orgies, and, like all orgies, they coarsen the moral fiber." It is "savagery" in a supposedly civilized society. Its eradication, he continued, would be achieved through "the effort of the press, pulpit, and schools by a campaign of education to direct public sentiment against lynchings and in support of law and order." The Southern Sociological Association, he stated, "can make no better use of its energies than to devote them to the task of creating a public sentiment that will put down the practice of lynching."[195]

During late 1914, at the time Bishop began to assume a leadership role among colleges in the anti-lynching movement, Roger Ames, the husband of Jessie Daniel Ames, died of blackwater fever in Guatemala. Though Jesse Daniel Ames had lived in Columbia, Tennessee, with her sister and brother-in-law during the times when she and Roger were not together, she now moved back to Georgetown. As a businesswoman managing with her mother the local telephone company, she organized the Georgetown Equal Suffrage League in 1916, the year of Bishop's greatest anti-mob activity. Though we have no direct evidence connecting her to Charles M. Bishop, she participated actively in alumni activities after her move back to Georgetown and probably followed with interest his actions. They were reported fully in the two Georgetown newspapers. Her friendship with the Granberys was natural, especially given John Granbery's active opposition to the Ku Klux Klan in the early 1920s.

It appears that Georgetown in 1916 was becoming one of the centers of the anti-lynching movement in the state and that three persons connected with Southwestern were leading it. President Bishop, John C. Granbery, and Jessie Daniel Ames were all currently or would eventually become involved in it. Jessie may have gained some of her early awareness of the issue from Bishop. Certainly it was he who provided the platform from which Granbery launched his forty-year career in Texas.

Professor John Cowper Granbery, Jr. Probably the most controversial long-time teacher in the history of the University, Granbery was at Southwestern from 1913–1925 and from 1934–1938. From the 1922 *Sou'wester.*

John Cowper Granbery, Jr.

John C. Granbery, Jr., is probably the most controversial long-term teacher ever employed by Southwestern. He came in 1913 and continued until 1925, when he went to the Texas College of Technology, as the present Texas Tech University was then called. He was employed by Southwestern again in 1934 and continued until 1938, when his contract was not renewed. In spite of his controversial nature, four Presidents, Bishop, Horn, Barcus, and Vivion, supported him. He left voluntarily as a result of increasing pressure from outsiders and the need to improve his financial situation in 1925, but Vivion hired him back after he was later terminated at Texas Tech. Bergin and the Board of Trustees eventually let him go in what became a cause célèbre, to be discussed later.

Granbery was popular with his fellow Southwestern faculty members and was regularly placed by them in positions of trust. His brilliance as a thinker was undoubted, his dedication to the gospel as he understood it was absolute, his faith in rational discourse was unusual, his selflessness was exemplary, and his fearlessness was legendary. His wife, Mary Anne Catt, generally called May, was the perfect companion. They never had children and seldom had money beyond that required for immediate needs, sometimes not even that. If this description of the Granberys today seems implausible, it must be said that they also confounded people in their own day. J. Frank Dobie said of him, "I haven't known many nonconformists who remained so serene and reasonable."[196]

John Cowper Granbery, Jr., was born in Richmond, Virginia, on June 15, 1874. The family moved to Nashville when his father was appointed a professor of philosophy and theology at Vanderbilt.[197] Though his father was elected a bishop in 1882, John was more influenced by his father's social views than by his status. The senior Granbery was a pacifist and opposed the Civil War, though he served in it as a chaplain and lost the sight in his right eye as the result of a battle wound. Later as bishop he supervised the Methodist Church in Brazil and authorized the founding of a boys school in the state of Minas Gerais that eventually became Granbery College.[198] John Granbery, Jr., would go to Brazil in the early 1930s after he lost his job at Texas Tech and spend several years there. He had a gift for languages and learned Portuguese during that time. His father's opposition to slavery, his pacifism, and his devotion to missionary work prepared John, Jr., for his ready acceptance of the social gospel.

After graduating from Randolph-Macon College in 1895, he was ordained to the ministry. Four years later he received his B.D. from the Vanderbilt University theology school. "He alternated work as a minister in Virginia, West Virginia, and Kentucky with attendance at the University of Chicago from 1899 until 1909, when he obtained his Ph.D." At Chicago he "received a full training in the social gospel" and came to know such pioneer reformers as Florence Kelley and Jane Addams. Though he studied sociology, he realized that at a deeper level he must satisfy his interests in theology and philosophy. It was the age of Schweitzer and the quest for the historical Jesus, and he focused his attention on Jesus. He read everything he could from the original sources in Hebrew and Greek, as well as theological works in German, French, and English. He was particularly attracted to Adolph Harnack, in his attempt to determine "the essence of Christianity," and to Walter Rauschenbusch, who attempted to describe Christian theology in social terms. His Ph.D. dissertation, *Outline of New Testament Christology: A Study of Genetic Relationships within the Christology of the New Testament Period*, was published in 1909.

Though he had a doctorate and could have well become a seminary teacher, he chose to go out as a minister in the countryside. While serving two small churches in West Virginia, he realized that the social gospel he had studied was for urban areas, not the rural countryside. He had been trained to solve the problems of large cities. Consequently, he wrote an essay characterizing what he had learned. It was that "the static character of small towns, their mediocrity and common-place nature, the absence of inspiration and the presence of 'town-loafers' made them even worse than cities." At the same time, the strong conservatism and individualism of country people represented a strong barrier to any attempt to alleviate social evil.

Setting out to alleviate some of those evils himself, he fell afoul of the forces he had identified. His work on a child labor committee, as a public defender of women's rights, as a supporter of Woodrow Wilson, and as a prohibitionist brought him into collision with prominent persons. He lost his church in Virginia in 1906, and when he denounced the "foul bossism" of two important local leaders in West Virginia, they managed to have him transferred to Kentucky. There he accepted the presidency of a small rural seminary but came to feel that he was really a teacher rather than an administrator. He gladly accepted an invitation from Charles M. Bishop to serve as acting professor of Education and assistant professor of History and Economics for one year at Southwestern University during the absence of the regular teacher, who was away for a year studying at Columbia. The following year Bishop made him Head of the Department of Sociology and Economics.

Granbery's First Major Controversy

In addition to teaching his classes, Granbery immediately became popular as a speaker to groups in Georgetown and surrounding communities. Soon after the fall term began, he gave a talk to a combined meeting of the Review Club and the Art Club. His topic was "The Soul's Revolt, or the Protest of Individualism against Over-Socialization." The newspaper article reporting it stated that he "gave a splendid address," adding that "Dr. Granbery is a thinker, an earnest and forceful speaker, and he gave his hearers a real message." The speech was so impressive that it was printed in full on another page.[199] Granbery wrote out his major speeches, a practice that sharpened his rhetoric and occasionally protected him against false attributions by persons who cited graphic phrases from him out of context.

Elected chairman of the Methodist Social Service Commission in Texas, a creature of the seven Annual Conferences, he addressed it on April 9, 1914. In the speech he stated that "the world needed a better distribution of the wealth. The prevailing system should be replaced by a cooperative one, in which no leisure class would exist. The two keys to the transformation of the social order were the schools and the churches. He believed that unfortunately the churches were not fulfilling their duty." This kind of talk was new in Texas, at least in Methodist circles, and began to draw careful scrutiny from the editor of the *Texas Christian Advocate.*[200]

In late 1914 Granbery delivered an address before the State Conference of Charities and Corrections in San Antonio. Though the title of the talk was "Social Service in the South," the next day it was excerpted in the *San Antonio Express* under the headline: "Dr. Granbery Predicts Great Labor War." In the address he stated that the current war in Europe was only an "exhibition, compared with the greater conflict that we are about to confront in the United States." The war in Europe "is proof that Christianity has failed. . . . Already we have passed into industrial strife, and it threatens to be far worse than the terrible war in Europe. . . . We are dealing with the surface of things. All we know is that this is a good day, that we have our faces toward the light and are moving toward our divine home." Nevertheless, while we are here we should be intensely interested in trying to make the world a better place in which to live. The Church is not living up to that obligation. "I have tried to interest churches in the child labor movement and I have obtained more support from the labor unions for the cause than I have ever been able to get from religious denominations. Religion should be more socialized. Social welfare deserves a place in the life of the church worker."[201]

Two weeks after the speech the *Advocate* printed a critical editorial condemning it. Granbery complained about the quotations ascribed to him by the newspapers and provided the *Advocate* with a full text of the address. He asked that it be printed in full so that everything he said might be looked at from the standpoint of the context in which it was uttered. The *Advocate* printed the entire address. The editor stated, however, that the speech as written verbatim does not show that the reporters originally made mistakes in quoting him other than that they, as is usually done, used the most quotable parts of his address. The editor stated, furthermore, that the *Advocate* had received letters about it, some of whose authors said that they already knew that Granbery favored socialism and indoctrinated his students at Southwestern with it. There were several other exchanges between the two parties, but none did more than advance already established points, i.e., by Granbery that the reporters had misconstrued his speech by taking much of it out of context, which made it sound revolutionary, and by the *Advocate* that he had no one to blame but himself if he was not careful enough to speak in such a way that he would be understood and too careless to correct misstatements in the press if he detected them.[202]

Toward the end of December John H. Griffith wrote Dean Cody from Bertram. He remarked that he had followed closely the controversy involving "our friend Dr. Jno. C. Granberry [sic]" in the *Advocate.* He said that a controversy such as this would not ordinarily concern him, "but when it affects Southwestern University as I fear this controversy will, as it represents the viewpoint of one of our instructors I feel that the Institution will suffer from such visionary and socialistic views if permitted to continue. Our friend used poor taste and poorer judgment in appearing before a secular body at San Antonio and criticized the Church for what it is doing or is not doing to help 'child labor laws' or any other laws or programs. Nor is it necessary for a man to be a member of a labor union in order to be a Christian; these questions have no part in Church regulations. . . . In the controversy with Dr. Rankin our friend Granberry [sic] will lose out and so revolutionary are his views and attitudes that his usefulness as an instructor is gone and the sooner his successor is selected and installed the better for the institution. Southwestern cannot afford to endorse his position. Personally I like Dr. Granberry [sic] but he has proven himself unsafe to fill the position which he now holds."[203]

Griffith may have written Dean Cody about Granbery because he knew Cody and not Bishop, but it is likely that Bishop received his share of such letters over the years as well. Griffith must have weathered his feelings about Granbery with some degree of grace. He was elected a Trustee in 1919 and served four years. As for George Clark Rankin, the editor of the *Advocate* mentioned by Griffith, he died unexpectedly on March 5, 1915. With his death, the issue evaporated.

Granbery's Causes

Granbery continued to speak widely. One speech was entitled "Social Problems of Interest to Women." He began it by asking: "What social questions are there in which women should *not* be interested?"[204] He began to tire of being called a socialist and averred that his belief in a cooperative society was not socialism. But he did feel that there was, objectively speaking, a "tendency . . . toward common ownership and management of the instruments of production."[205] Though he continued to receive sporadic criticism for some of his positions, he was almost always popular with local audiences. The newspaper report of a baccalaureate sermon given by him in Thorndale states that his "splendid sermon was well received and highly appreciated."[206] He spoke four times to different groups in Bryan celebrating Labor Day 1915, lectured to the Austin Presbytery on the subject of "Over-Churching and Federation," discussed elsewhere the practices of good citizenship, and called at various times for prohibition. Newspapers covered all of these addresses. One of his addresses in Bryan was to a meeting of Italians.[207] Most of his talks were on social issues.

By mid-1916 Granbery was beginning to engage directly in political struggles. *The Megaphone* reported on his attendance as a delegate to the Democratic convention in San Antonio in May, stating that he had the "courage" to oppose former Senator Bailey on the floor of the convention and "returned with no noticeable scars." He recounted his convention experiences in class and said that he learned many things with which he was previously unfamiliar. He gave another overview of the convention in the evening to an audience of citizens at the town hall.[208] He let it be known regarding the 1916 gubernatorial election that he was against Governor Ferguson because he supported the liquor traffic.[209]

In the fall of 1916, Granbery addressed the opening of Baylor University. President S. P. Brooks introduced him by saying that he had heard him deliver a "splendid address" in 1914 at a meeting of the Southern Sociological Congress and had determined to have him address a Baylor and Waco audience. He told about Granbery's interest in both religious and political affairs and how during his vacation during the past summer he had used his time speaking and preaching to the men stationed on the Texas border. Granbery's topic was "Some Aspects of Texas Civilization." He spoke of factors in the state's development and of the ways in which the human race can be improved. The *Waco Morning News* reported that it "was one of the most informal [addresses] that has ever been delivered in Carroll chapel on a like occasion and the audience was impressed by its unique character. There was no hint of the conventional about it, and his hearers enjoyed very much the intimate and effective way in which he discussed his subject. Dr. Granbery impressed everyone as a man with a message, which he wished to deliver to the people face to face and heart to heart. His dry humor drew several hearty responses from the audience throughout the speech, but never did it detract from the fundamental seriousness of his plea for a better Texas."[210]

Back at Southwestern Granbery weighed in on the tobacco question. He read to the faculty a letter he had received from B. A. Graham, who wrote concerning the appearance of tobacco advertisements in *The Megaphone*. He then submitted a paper calling on the faculty to express its regret for "the appearance of these advertisements in *The Megaphone*" and suggested that, when the present contracts cease, "there be no further advertisement of tobacco in any Southwestern University publication." The faculty referred to matter to the President.[211]

Though he was still lecturing widely in early 1917, he now became engaged more directly in the woman's suffrage movement than earlier. He and a small group of like-minded persons met to organize a Woman's Suffrage League among the men of Georgetown. He was elected chair, Dr. W. H. Moses vice president, and Professor W. P. Davidson (Philosophy) secretary. Twenty-nine members joined. The stated objective of the group was "the enfranchisement of Texas women, and of American women, at the earliest date possible."[212]

Bishop's Unsuccessful Resignation

Several months later Granbery dropped a bombshell. Toward the end of a meeting of the faculty on June 5, he "presented a paper dealing with certain Faculty matters signed by three members of the Faculty and after reading moved that same be referred to the Board of Trustees as a statement from the Faculty. On division of the house the motion was lost."[213]

Though the contents of the paper are not given, subsequent developments suggest that it was composed of complaints against Bishop's administrative management. In spite of the vote by the faculty as a whole not to endorse the paper, it resulted in the matter's being brought up before the Board of Trustees at its meeting a week and a half later, on June 14–16. At that meeting, anyone having a charge to make about the management of the institution, "or of President Bishop's administration," was invited to present them.[214]

After studying the matter, the Board committee appointed to investigate it presented a report with six proposed resolutions, all of which were adopted. Though the resolutions as a whole supported Bishop strongly, they did recognize that there were differences between him and some of the members of the faculty. It said that "much of the unrest among Faculty and students has been brought about by too much talking, and peddling of irresponsible gossip. The acts of Faculty meetings have been disclosed in a way and to an extent that has been hurtful to the maintenance of the proper Esprit de Corps of the College." He and the faculty were called upon to compose whatever differences divided them and to work together. Some of the issues in the original paper of complaint may have been criticisms of Bishop's financial management, because he was asked to take special measures to bring expenditures into line with revenues. The Board closed the issue by expressing its confidence in President Bishop and rejoicing "in his splendid work on the platform and in the pulpit in behalf of Southwestern University." It ordered that the six resolutions be sent to the faculty.[215]

Six months later Bishop reported to the Executive Committee that he had been appointed as pastor of the Austin Avenue Church in Waco.[216] Obviously he had been disappointed by the complaints against him at the June Board meeting and had consulted with Bishop Mouzon, the presiding bishop, about it. Mouzon appointed him to a new position. A special session of the Board was called for January 18, at which time he formally presented his resignation. He retired from the room, and the Board took his resignation under advisement. Meeting in executive session, the secretary read "a communication from the students stating that it was their unanimous request that Dr. Bishop be retained as president of the University." In addition to the student "communication," a letter from fourteen faculty members was introduced.

> We have been impressed [, it said,] by his [Bishop's] great personal charm, his splendid character, and the lofty ideals which he has ever held up before the Faculty and Student Body of Southwestern. The principles which guided his administration have been our principles; his aims have been our aims; those principles and aims which, in our judgement, must be ever involved in the successful building of a great, strong, Christian, American, modern college. . . . We have reason to believe that there are certain conditions upon which Dr. Bishop could be retained. We desire that those conditions should be openly and frankly placed before you, and that they be considered in the light of the needs and the best interests of the Institution; and that, should it be deemed advisable to you, these conditions should be met and our beloved president retained for the noble work of carrying forward the Southwestern we love and cherish.[217]

After the letter had been read, Dr. Bishop was requested to come before the Board, where the Board president stated to him that it was their unanimous desire that he remain as President of the University. Furthermore, in the event that he should remain, the Board pledged to him its "heartiest co-operation and support." A motion was formally adopted to this effect, and, after a "full and frank" discussion with them, Bishop gave the Trustees to understand that he would remain if released from the bishop's appointment. The Board asked that Bishop Mouzon be notified of this action and that he release Dr. Bishop from the appointment to Austin Avenue Church in Waco. Bishop's salary was raised to $3,600.[218]

Analysis and Aftermath

Several questions remain about the resignation incident that extant records do not answer. What exactly were the issues that caused the three dissidents to formulate the paper brought before the faculty? Who were the three persons who signed the paper? What is the meaning of John C. Granbery's role in formulating it?

As to the issues, one of the Trustee resolutions suggests that they had to do with Bishop's management style and his handling of financial affairs. This is not surprising, since the incident occurred around the time when Bishop had to report that faculty salaries were so low "that one or two of our very valuable faculty members are living dangerously near the 'bread-line' of poverty, considering the social position which they are compelled to maintain." It was also the time when frustrations connected with the completion of the Williamson County Science Building were running high, wartime conditions threatened student enrollment, and a major bond issue had to be obtained to cover operational expenses.

Though the identity of the three dissidents who signed the paper presented to the faculty on June 5 cannot be known with certainty, there is reason to believe that they were three of the following four persons—Pegues, Moore, Nichols, and Granbery. The first three left soon after for faculty positions at SMU. Granbery, who presented the letter for action at the faculty meeting, soon left for France to do war work, though he returned in 1920. The fourteen faculty members who signed the letter supporting Bishop, presented at the specially called Board of Trustees meeting on January 18, 1918, can be eliminated, as well as those who were not present at the faculty meeting on June 5, 1917. They would have been there to vote if they had signed the paper. The other five persons present at the faculty meeting who did not sign the dissident paper do not seem to be very likely candidates. There are various reasons for eliminating each of them.

Trying to determine which three of the four listed above were the signers of the complaint against Bishop is problematical. Of the three who soon resigned and went to SMU, nothing is known about the departure of Claude Nichols (Education), who had taught at Southwestern thirteen years when he left. Nichols had a distinguished career at SMU and received many honors. He was also a strong church worker.[219]

Herbert Gambrell provides a little information about Stephen Moore (History), a twenty-five-year veteran of Southwestern. When former President Charles M. Bishop taught in the theology school at SMU in the late 1920s, Gambrell asked him why Moore had left Southwestern. Bishop replied: "Because I fired him, that's why. He didn't know enough history to teach it."[220]

By the time of the June Board meeting in 1918, Pegues had informed Bishop that he was going to SMU at the end of the ensuing academic year (1918–1919) as Dean of the College of Liberal Arts. At that meeting, Bishop made one last effort to retain him. He moved that "this Board request Dean Pegues not to accept a position with any other institution, and convey to him our high appreciation of his services to the University through the years." The motion carried.[221]

Granbery's Role in the Affair, Service in Europe, and Return

Granbery's role in the affair is difficult to resolve. Though he had only been at Southwestern four years when it occurred, he was the one that presented the paper signed by the three instigators of the issue. During the summer following the June meeting, he was invited by the international Y.M.C.A. to work for it in France and Greece. He left in August and was on leave of absence when Bishop offered his resignation to the Board in January 1918. Both Granbery's departure for Europe and his return to Southwestern, however, were with the blessing of President Bishop.

Writing to Cody from Greece on July 25, 1919, Granbery talks about the Southwestern faculty with affection. He says that he cherishes its members in his heart. He mentions a feeling of sadness at the departure of Moore, Nichols, and Pegues. He also deplores the departure of Lehmberg (Latin, Greek, and German), who had left Southwestern to become President of Cherokee College. Lehmberg was apparently disillusioned by the experience there and returned to Southwestern the following year. He continued to teach until his retirement in 1935.

Granbery continues in his letter stating that he feels the choice of Wunder (Mathematics) as the new dean is a good one that will serve the University well. He excuses himself for not being back at Southwestern for the fall term of 1919 but says he cannot as yet extricate himself from his work. He states that he wrote and cabled Dr. Bishop about his situation before Commencement and resigned his chair. "I suppose he did not present my resignation [to the Board of Trustees in June 1919]. I did not think it would be fair to the school to ask him to hold my chair longer for me."[222]

In the letter Granbery seems to count Bishop as a friend, whom he tries to help by resigning his position rather than asking him to hold it open any longer. Bishop does not take Granbery's voluntary resignation as an opportunity get rid of him but rather holds it open for another year pending his return. Granbery did return to the faculty a year later in the fall of 1920, while Bishop was still President. After Bishop's resignation on December 1, 1921, he was one of the three persons elected by the faculty to serve on the committee to handle presidential affairs until a new President could be elected. It may be that Granbery's personality was so transparent that he mistakenly saw nothing threatening in the paper for Bishop and offered it purely for what seemed to him the worthy purpose of helping to straighten out some of the affairs of the University. When Bishop returned to Georgetown for the Centennial Celebration in 1940, Mrs. Granbery, who was also in Georgetown at the time, entertained him for a special breakfast. He wrote her a letter of thanks in which he referred to the Granberys as "daily intimates" who helped give to his life "so much of its substance—and of its better flavors."[223] Whatever his role in the attempted resignation, Granbery's motives in the incident are obscure.

What evidence we have suggests that Granbery, Pegues, and Nichols are the most likely signers of the paper of complaint presented by Granbery to the faculty on June 5, 1917. For his part, Bishop did not retaliate against them. He preserved Granbery's position during the three years he was in Europe and proposed the motion approved by the Board encouraging Pegues to stay at Southwestern. There is no evidence about Nichols one way or another. The only person feeling the President's heavy hand was Moore, who, if we take Bishop's later statement to Gambrell at face value, was fired for incompetence, not for signing the paper of complaint.

Granbery and the Fraternity Question

Once the honor code and pledge were in place, student conduct returned to the normalcy that existed prior to the war. On the part of fraternities, however, that normalcy involved constant attempts to thwart some of the University rules and regulations. Minor problems continued to arise from time to time that had to be dealt with by the faculty. The most constant problem during and immediately following the war was hazing. Though hazing had long been forbidden, it broke out from time to time. In the fall of 1920 fourteen young men were expelled for hazing, though their sentence was suspended when the other young men of the student body pledged to refrain from hazing in the future.[224] Nevertheless, two had to be expelled the following fall.[225] As a result of the fact that another four young men had to be dismissed for breaking the pledge not to engage in hazing during 1921–1922, the Board of Trustees adopted a motion at its midyear meeting stating that "no hazing in any form should be tolerated" and that "the faculty are hereby directed to take steps to strictly enforce this resolution."[226]

Once back from Greece, Granbery entered fully into the life of the University. He was temperamentally opposed to elite organizations, which he considered the fraternities to be, and moved to challenge the system. He offered a motion in a faculty meeting during the first term after his return asking the faculty Fraternity Committee to investigate whether the time had come to take steps toward eliminating them. Professor Gray seconded his motion. The action taken by the faculty on the question is not recorded, but Granbery was on record as having taken a first step.[227]

While Granbery was away in Europe, the University had changed its regulations and now allowed pledging from the first day of entrance into college.[228] His next step was to try to overturn this rule. In May of 1921 he offered a motion that no fraternity or sorority be permitted to rush, pledge, or initiate freshmen students. Professor Ullrich, the new professor of education, seconded the motion.[229] Though the motion did not carry, Granbery was building up support among some strong future leaders. In June the faculty passed a regulation for sororities not allowing them to rush during the fall term, and the following December sororities and fraternities were not allowed to offer bids until after registration in January of each year.[230] The fraternities in particular and the sororities to a lesser extent did not help themselves with the faculty during this postwar period. At roughly half of the faculty meetings there was some Greek issue that had to be dealt with, either a discipline problem, an initiation problem, a petition to change a certain rule, or petitions to make exceptions.

At some point along the way the Fraternity Committee was charged to do what Granbery had originally tried to get it to do, that is, to study the system as a whole. In March 1922 it presented a majority and a minority report. The majority report was pretty much a restatement of the current policies with a few changes. It carried the signatures of Wunder, Vaden, Kuykendall, and Gray. John C. Granbery made a long, three-page, single-spaced minority report in two parts. The first and longest part was philosophical. The second concerned enactment. The whole minority report was based on a great deal of research and offered reasons why fraternities and sororities should not exist at Southwestern. It presented in clear language a view that was almost certain *not* to be adopted by the faculty.

On March 9 the matter was brought up again. Ullrich moved and Davidson seconded a motion to adopt the minority report. It was defeated. In an attempt to save most of it, its supporters allowed it to be amended by omitting the section stating that fraternities and sororities should not exist at Southwestern. It still failed. After the majority report was finally adopted, Granbery offered a motion to send a resolution to the General Conference asking it "to inquire into the [fraternity/sorority] situation" and to set up "a definite and uniform policy [for the Church] on the subject." Davidson seconded it, and it was adopted. Granbery's persistence had caused a faculty discussion on the propriety of Greek organizations on the Southwestern campus to be carried to the highest body in the Methodist Church.[231] Granbery was hopeful that carrying the controversy to a higher Church body would be helpful to the anti-fraternity cause. He had earlier been buoyed up by the fact that the West Texas Conference, on October 22, 1921, had adopted a motion calling for Methodist colleges and universities to eliminate fraternities and sororities.[232] Nothing, however, came out of the General Conference on the issue.

Improvement in Institutional Finances

At the nadir of the financial situation in 1918, at the Board meeting that considered Bishop's unsuccessful resignation, the Rev. Tom F. Sessions was elected Vice President and Financial Commissioner.[233] His selection by Bishop was one of the happy personnel choices made by him during his tenure. Sessions was indefatigable in his work and was commended several times by both President Bishop and the Board of Trustees for his work during his four years of service.[234]

One of the projects initiated by him was the creation of a League of a Thousand Friends. It was supposed to consist of persons who would contribute a specified annual sum to the institution.[235] It drew only a little more than $4,000 in subscriptions and petered out quickly.

A more formless campaign in its effect on Southwestern was the General Education Campaign of the Church authorized by the General Conference of the Methodist Episcopal Church, South, in 1918. Its goal was to raise $33,000,000 to be distributed among its educational institutions. It was supposed to result in each "A-grade" college receiving $500,000.[236] The campaign ran between 1920 and 1927. The schools themselves paid campaign expenses, Southwestern's share of the expenses being $12,500. Because Bishop was a leader in the movement and because it could not afford to miss the prospective payout, Southwestern borrowed money to pay the assessments. By March 13, 1927, three months after the formal close of the campaign, only $17,554,077, slightly more than half of the goal, had been pledged, and only $7,591,663 had been paid, slightly less than a quarter of the goal.[237] Southwestern's share of it will be discussed in Chapter XIII.

One of the successes achieved by Sessions was to complete the establishment of the Lois Perkins Aid Fund for Young Women. Mr. J. J. Perkins of Wichita Falls set it up in honor of his wife, Lois Craddock Perkins, a Southwestern student for three years, from 1908 to 1911. He had written a letter during the fall of 1919 indicating his desire to set up the fund with a gift of $5,000.[238] It was to be lent out to deserving young women "without interest or donated at the discretion of the Board of Control."[239]

Sessions was responsible for making the first attempt to bring some order into the subscriptions made during the many financial campaigns dating as far back as the Hyer administration. After tracking the subscriptions related to the 2,262 items in the account, representing $215,045.30 on the books, he recommended the realistic policy of writing many of them off.[240] A few were written off, but the more important consequence of his work was that it served as a basis for keeping a careful track on an annual basis of the payment of subscriptions during the next few years. One of the major accomplishments of the Barcus and Vivion administrations would be to follow up his work with careful audits and to make some hard decisions on the issue.

The faculty once again complained about salaries at the Board meeting in 1921. They said that teacher salaries did not meet their living needs and should be increased. They stated that whereas the cost of living in the last few years had increased about 81 percent, salaries had increased, on average, only a little over 25 percent. They then presented a table of salaries for all ranks of professors at Baylor, the University of Texas, Texas A&M, Southern Methodist, Millsaps, Hendrix, and Southwestern. Southwestern was the lowest of the schools in every category. Nineteen persons signed the request for an increase.[241] Indeed they had a right to complain. Modern figures show that the cost of living rose 17.4 percent in 1919, 14.9 percent in 1920, and 15.8 percent in 1921, a total increase in the consumer price index of 115.0 percent since 1911. In recognition of their complaint, the Board of Trustees voted an increase of 20 percent for 1921–1922.[242]

At the time Bishop left the presidency in mid-1922, he put great emphasis on the fact that the financial condition of the University had improved. And, indeed, it had from the standpoint of the operational budget. The year 1921–1922 showed receipts of $190,395.33, with disbursements of only $177,424.67, for a positive balance of $12,970.66. He said that "our financial showing for the year may be put in one sentence. We started the year with a deficit of $14,000 and we are closing the year with a credit of $6,000."[243] Discounting inflation, it was the best performance since 1912–1913, when he reported that Southwestern was "about $12,000 better off" than it had been the year before. Given the forces he had to contend with during the eleven years of his presidency, he must be given credit for his performance. It would be thirty-nine years and five Presidents before another President would assume office who would serve as many years as he did.

President Bishop Leaves Southwestern

Bishop announced his resignation at the Board of Trustees meeting in June 1921. He felt he had done all he could, and he wanted to return to the pastorate. Nevertheless, in order not to harm the institution and to give it time to seek another President, he made his resignation effective at the end of the next academic year.[244]

Though he apparently intended to serve out the entire

academic year, he decided during the course of the fall term to leave earlier when the opportunity to become pastor of St. Paul's Methodist Church in Houston presented itself.[245] He announced formally to the faculty that he would be leaving on December 1 to accept that position. He spoke "feelingly" of the loyalty of the faculty members and of the high esteem in which he held each individual member. He then suggested that the faculty choose a committee of three to act in official matters and that a presiding officer be elected. In accordance with his suggestion, three persons were elected by ballot and without nomination. They were Tinsley, Granbery, and Gray. Dean Wunder was elected to preside at meetings.[246]

The next day he met with the Executive Committee and asked it to act on his request for a leave of absence. It voted to grant the leave from December 1 until the Board meeting in June 1922. It acknowledged the election of Tinsley, Gray, and Granbery to act for the faculty in all matters usually referred to the President.[247] They did so in harmony for the remainder of the academic year without the development of any major problems. Bishop must have kept in contact with them from time to time. He attended and made a final report at the Board meeting in June 1922 but deferred to them to make faculty recommendations for the next year.

He returned to Southwestern a number of times while at SMU. He spoke to the Faculty Club on May 25, 1926, his wife, Phoebe, attended the Christmas Carol Candlelight Service in December 1927, and he preached the baccalaureate sermon for the graduating seniors in 1928.[248] He also delivered the eulogy for Laura Kuykendall at her funeral in 1935. He retired from SMU at the mandatory age limit and moved to Long Beach, California, because of Mrs. Bishop's health.[249] He also spoke at the celebration of the twenty-fifth anniversary of the founding of the Southwestern Scholarship Society (later Alpha Chi) on April 12–13, 1940, and attended other events connected with the Centennial Celebration in that year.[250] He moved back to Georgetown within the year. He died on November 30, 1949, at the age of eighty-seven. Both he and his wife, who survived him by nine years, are buried in Georgetown.

13 "Crippled . . . But Worth Saving" (1922–1928)

Two Decades of Presidential Leadership: An Overview

The first five Presidents of Southwestern, Mood, Heidt, McLean, Hyer, and Bishop, served from 1872 to 1922, a total of fifty years, an average of ten years each. The next four, Horn, Barcus, Vivion, and Bergin, served from 1922 to 1942, a total of twenty years, an average of five years each. The most recent four, Score, Finch, Fleming, and Shilling, served from 1942 to 2000, a total of fifty-eight years, an average of fourteen-and-a-half years each.

Looking at the strength of leadership exhibited by them, one is struck by the difference between the second group and the other two. Mood, Hyer, and Bishop stand out as strong leaders in the first group. They dominated the Southwestern scene and were known at both the state and national levels. None of the Presidents in the second group can be said to have achieved that dominance or those recognitions. All of the Presidents in the third group did so.

Paul Whitfield Horn, the first of the four Presidents in the second group, probably had the greatest possibility of achieving major stature, but he stayed at Southwestern only a year and a half. Though he was an experienced leader and a recognized educational figure when he assumed the presidency, he had hardly begun to live up to the expectations created by his forward-looking inaugural speech when he left to become the first President of the new Texas College of Technology, the future Texas Tech University.

Horn's successor, James Samuel Barcus, was a strong minister and a loyal alumnus. He had been a teacher at Southwestern for four years during Hyer's tenure and was in his eighth year of service as a Trustee when the search for a President to replace Horn bogged down. His credentials and standing were sufficiently strong that the Board turned to him to fill the vacancy. During his first year, he initiated a well-conceived fund-raising program, only to have it dashed at the outset by the burning of the Woman's Building and the necessity of diverting the campaign toward the construction of a new residence hall to replace it. His development program never got on track again after the catastrophe. He served four-and-a-half years.

The next President was Joseph King Vivion, an outstanding young minister in Galveston. Inaugurated at the age of thirty-two, he was universally accepted because of his positive attitude, his vigor, his oratorical skills, and his ability to work well with others. His administration was blindsided after only a year, however, by the onset of the Great Depression, and his efforts thereafter became a struggle to keep the institution afloat. He felt that he had done all he could after seven years and returned to the pastorate. John William Bergin succeeded him.

Bergin was probably the least presidential in demeanor of any of the chief executive officers in the history of the University. His election occurred after the first choice of the Board turned down the invitation. On the scene as chairman of the Executive Committee and as Presiding Elder of the Georgetown District, he agreed to take over the derelict fortunes of his alma mater. The youngest President ever to assume the presidency, Vivion, only thirty-two when elected, was succeeded by the oldest person to do so, the sixty-three-year-old Bergin. In spite of his problems as an administrative leader, Bergin was the President under whom the fortunes of the University began to turn around. During his presidency, Southwestern got out of debt and received a significant endowment grant from the widow of a former Trustee, William Wiess, so important in keeping Southwestern in Georgetown during the removal controversy of 1910–1911. That grant became the foundation of the Southwestern endowment of today. In spite of this notable achievement, Bergin's style of leadership was so exasperating that he was virtually pushed out of office after six-and-a-half years by the Trustees.

The period of twenty years beginning with Horn and ending with Bergin is the most painful in the history of the

University as far as day-to-day operations are concerned. It is one of almost unrelieved penury and of receiving one setback after another. Each President inherited a debt whose weight impeded his doing much toward building up the campus and the educational program. Yet during this period one finds the educational work of the University being carried on in an amazing way. There was a core of devoted teachers and administrators who continued to perform their duties, always underpaid and sometimes not paid at all. The stories of some of those teachers and administrators are remarkable. Students were also graduated who, in later life, looked back on their student years with great appreciation and declared that the lessons they learned during those impoverished times were of inestimable value.

The Presidents of this period might not have possessed the commanding stature of those who came earlier or of those who came later, but they had several commendable characteristics in common. Each gave the office his best effort and exhibited character, courage, and determination. As a group, they battled their times and conditions to a draw and left an institution after them that still had the resilience to recover and move forward when other times and circumstances made progress possible.

President Paul W. Horn. His influence on Southwestern was greater than his short tenure would suggest. He left Southwestern to become the first president of what became Texas Tech University. Southwestern University, Special Collections.

President Paul W. Horn

Everyone felt that in Paul Whitfield Horn Southwestern had found a worthy successor to President Bishop. He was perhaps the best-known public school educator in the state, having served as Principal and Superintendent of Schools in both Sherman (1895–1904) and Houston (1904–1921). He left Houston in 1921 to head the American School Foundation in Mexico City. He was elected president of the Texas State Teachers Association in 1910 and vice president of the National Education Association a few years later. During the summers he taught at the University of Texas, Tulane University, Peabody College, Boston University, and the University of Oregon. He was the author of many articles and several books, including *Our Schools Today* (1908), a series of readers, and *Best Things in Our Schools* (1914). He was coauthor of the *New Century Spelling Book* (1908) and *School Room Essentials* (1911).[1]

Among his accomplishments in Houston was the introduction of junior high schools. The introduction of the junior high school idea was, says his biographer, his outstanding contribution as an educator. His success as a leader in Houston was such that the citizens of the city gave him a dinner at the Rice Hotel on November 18, 1916, hosted by the president of the school board, with four hundred persons, including the mayor, in attendance. A resolution was presented Horn that was signed by every African American teacher in the city schools. The previous Saturday afternoon they had presented him with a "magnificent chest of silver."[2] It must have been the Houston dinner that prompted three colleges to confer the honorary degree of Doctor of Laws on him the following spring. They were his alma mater, Central College in Fayette, Missouri, Baylor University in Waco, and Southwestern University in Georgetown. He delivered the Commencement speech at Southwestern at the time his degree was conferred.

Horn was born into a Methodist parsonage family on April 30, 1870, in Booneville, Missouri. His father died when he was fourteen and his mother five years later. He began teaching immediately after completing his college degree in 1888 and married in 1890. The family moved to Texas in 1893, where he taught in several small schools before becoming a public school administrator.[3] He was a devoted member of the Methodist Church wherever he went and always taught a Sunday School class. He taught a large Sunday School class of college students at Southwestern. *The Megaphone* reported on December 12, 1922, that all previous attendance records were broken the previous Sunday when 229 students attended, 117 girls and 112 boys.[4] He had a class of over 200 young businessmen in Lubbock. While at Southwestern in January 1923, he began a series of lesson notes, *The Lesson in Every Day Life*, that he continued to write for the *Adult Student* until his death in 1932.[5] Over 250,000 copies of each issue were printed. Though he believed in the divine origin of the Bible, he also accepted many of the findings of higher criticism and was not interested in debating the fine points of theology. He was intent on the practical aspect of Christian living.[6]

Horn was in Mexico City when he received the invitation to become President of Southwestern University. Though he went to Southwestern in 1922, his inauguration as President formally opened the Golden Jubilee Celebration of 1923. In his inauguration address, he said: "The value of a curriculum is not in the textbook studies, but in those things into which the knowledge gleaned from the textbooks can be transmuted. It is the translation of education into terms of human service, into Christian service that counts."[7]

Horn believed deeply in democracy and in opportunity for every person. He had little patience with elitism in any form. One of the reasons he accepted the presidency of Texas Tech was to take the opportunity it gave him to establish rules for the new institution consonant with this belief. He announced before the opening of the College that no Greek letter fraternities would be permitted and that no hazing would be allowed. His idea was equality of opportunity for all.[8] While at Southwestern he published a widely read article in the *School Review* (Chicago) entitled "Bad College Risk." In it he criticized those institutions of higher learning that admitted only the top 10 percent of high school graduates. He said that our democracy was built upon the bad risk. Good soldiers, good businessmen, and good doctors were good precisely because they often took what might be called bad risks and succeeded. He pointed to a long line of eminent dullards that bear witness to the fact that it pays to take a bad risk—Abraham Lincoln, Ulysses S. Grant, Thomas A. Edison, and Henry Ford. "It is a matter of common knowledge," he said, "that the plodder who has deep determination is more likely to make good than the brilliant man who lacks determination."[9]

Horn exerted a commanding influence on those around him wherever he went. He did so not by the exercise of executive power but by his quiet but strong personality. He "dominated the governing board and faculty at Texas Tech," says his biographer, by his "moral force and inflexible will. He knew what he wanted; he had definite policies; he stood by his contracts and his teaching force. Dr. Horn would permit no injustice to be done to anyone for whom he was responsible."[10]

After leaving Southwestern, Horn frequently expressed his appreciation for it and came back several times. In February 1924, less than three months after his departure, he made a quick visit to Georgetown to attend one service of a revival preached by Reverend, soon to be bishop, Arthur Moore. He had tried to get Moore for services while he was President but could not do so. On the night he attended he spoke to the students before the service began.[11] Seven years after his departure memories of him in Georgetown were still deep and positive. A long article published about him in 1930 in the *Southwestern Magazine* described the man people remembered. It said that Horn never heard a poor sermon. He always found something good in the discourse. He would never leave a sermon, a picture show, or a ball game until the benediction, the finale, or the end of the game. He enjoyed watching baseball and football. He was fond of music, especially the violin, and thought that Fritz Kreisler's rendition of *Caprice Viennois* the most perfect music he ever heard. He thought all college students were good and usually referred to them as "angels." On one occasion someone summoned him to the phone by saying: "The chief of police is on the telephone to say that one of your angels is in jail."[12] Soon after assuming the presidency in 1922, he asked the faculty to begin thinking over the penalty generally called expulsion, "suggesting that this probably should be used only in extreme cases."[13]

The Golden Anniversary Celebration

The inauguration of Horn dovetailed nicely with plans already in the works for the Golden Anniversary Celebration. At the same session of the Board that elected him in June 1922, the Trustees appointed officers and committees to prepare for the "Golden Jubilee" of the school to take place at the 1923 Commencement.[14] The delayed inauguration became a major feature of the event. Also featured was the conferral of honorary degrees on ten persons related to the school. Among them were C. M. Bishop, President Emeritus, J. Sam Barcus, alumnus and next President, A. Frank

Smith, alumnus and future bishop, and Josef Dobes, alumnus now serving as a pastor in the new Czechoslovakia.[15]

In preparation for the occasion, J. Frank Dobie wrote a long, touching tribute to the school of his youth. Though the whole of it merits reproduction, a few paragraphs only will have to do.

> "But still will keep
> A bower quiet for us, and a sleep
> Full of sweet dreams, and health,
> And quiet breathing."—Endymion.

> When I try to summon up the best of Southwestern that has persisted in the best of myself down the years that have vanished since I left her quiet ways, those lines from Keats inevitably come to mind. When I reflect that I am no longer sentimental, but rather cynical, I am the more convinced that this "bower" was the finest thing that Southwestern had to give.
>
> . . . How quiet and healthy and wholesome it was!
>
> . . . I need not say to one who remembers the beauty and passion of poetry from the years of which I am speaking, whose voice it was that taught me to love those and a thousand other divine lines. "Happy," says Matthew Arnold, "the man in that susceptible season of youth [that] hears such voices! They are a possession to him forever." I think of that voice and in a moment I am sitting in a room on the third floor of the Main building looking out over the fields and hills to the east: . . . As I sit there looking over those hills and dreaming of others beyond, I hear Professor Pegues reading Wordsworth and teaching Emerson—and I pass from hills into the "Delectable Mountains."
>
> . . . It was an easy time, a smooth time, a time . . . in which the soul had invitation to grow ample and lay up store against the fever and narrowness and stridency of a gibbering world. It was a place not so much teaching dexterities of getting along in the world as practicing the art of living.
>
> . . . From negligence and worse that I shall never cease regretting, I never accomplished much under that truly humanistic master, Professor Vaden, but somewhere I have culled a quotation from the language he loves. The words carved on a Venetian sundial: "*Horas non numero nisi serenas*" ("I number only the hours that are serene"). So numbered for me Southwestern her hours, and I could wish for all collegians such a numeration.[16]

A committee of three persons, composed of C. C. Cody, John M. Barcus, and Laura Kuykendall, were designated to plan the celebration. Their names graced *The Book of Southwestern*, a thirty-two-page pictorial and narrative portrayal of the history of Southwestern and description of the pageant accompanying the event. Cody and Barcus, faculty member and graduate, respectively, had been more responsible than any other persons from the groups they represented for preserving Southwestern in Georgetown during the removal controversy. They were now, however, more honorary than actual leaders. Cody's health was such that he died within a month after the celebration, and Barcus lived at a distance. Laura Kuykendall was the dynamo behind the event. Working with her were many campus and town leaders. Among them were Etelka Evans, Dean of Music, who was in charge of the music, Pearl A. Neas, Assistant Registrar, who was in charge of the three hundred public school children participating in it, public school superintendent Lee, who was in charge of the persons masquerading as Indian warriors, and Coach Gardner, who was in charge of the University warriors.

The pageant was entitled *Spirit of Southwestern*. Written by an alumna, it was preceded by the entrance of the royal party of 1923, followed by the Kings and Queens of former years. The highlight was the crowning of Her Royal Majesty, Sue of the House of Mood, granddaughter of Francis Asbury and Sue Logan Mood, for whom she was named. The pageant proper began with the arrival of Time, with winds sweeping over the plains and bluebonnets springing up on the prairies. Segments depicting the coming of the Indians, the French, the Spaniards, and the Mexicans followed this "Awakening of Texas" and the Anglo pioneers. Herds of sheep and cattle, and two or three yoke of oxen, wagons and teams, as well as other things representative of early Texas history, were included.[17] Education then called for the founding of schools, to which the Church responded by the establishment of the four root colleges. Their charters were joined in 1873 to form Southwestern. Until 1912 the school enjoyed a period of steady and peaceful growth, but the Spirit of Discord entered. It was vanquished, however, through the combined efforts of Loyalty and Truth, and the Southwestern of the present emerged triumphant.[18]

The message of the pageant was to frame the central

question posed in *The Book of Southwestern*—"What of the Future?" It stated that Southwestern has a proud past, but "no worthy institution can afford to live on the laurels of its yesterdays. . . . She confidently looks to her children to supply the necessary funds to enable her to enter the gates of opportunity that are now open."[19] The Golden Anniversary Celebration was meant to be the first act in a major advancement campaign.

Horn's Financial and Facilities Activities

As a seasoned administrator, Horn had spent the year after coming to Southwestern studying the situation of the school. The Board had been forced at the meeting that elected him to borrow $35,000 and a year later $40,000 for operational expenses and repairs. The Committee on Finance reported in mid-1923 that the indebtedness of the University was $69,017, of which $50,000 was represented by bonded indebtedness.[20] In addition, the General Conference of the Methodist Church, South, had recently placed more stringent financial rules into effect for its colleges. It now stipulated that a college must have a permanent productive endowment of $250,000 or a productive endowment of $150,000 and an assured annual income of $15,000, exclusive of all tuition and after all debts had been paid.[21] Though Southwestern could not meet these conditions, the new rules did not go into effect for several years, in which time the school could undertake to measure up.

In his report to the Board of Trustees in 1923, Horn provided the conclusions of his yearlong study regarding the financial situation of the University and described his beliefs about educating post–World War I students in a Church-related institution. He presented a bleak picture of the former and a reformed picture of the latter.

In it he says that the current physical plant is not adequate for the needs of the present. A million dollars needs to be spent on facilities and endowment to make them adequate, half for new buildings and equipment and half for endowment. He then goes into a description of the building and equipment needs. He says he found, on taking charge at Southwestern, that the nominally active endowment amounted to only $105,000. Of this amount, however, $35,000, or one-third of the entire amount, was lying in the bank uninvested and idle. He mentions the large amount of uncollected notes and subscriptions and says that every effort should be made to collect them. He then lays out ten recommendations for making the operation of the University more efficient. Several of them are ways for knowing the exact financial status of the institution every month rather than once a year and for investing institutional money to better advantage.[22]

During his short tenure at Southwestern, Horn did not make much progress with these problems beyond identifying them, but some things were accomplished. Immediately after the Board meeting the Executive Committee began to use the term "budget" for the first time. "It was decided," say its minutes, "to adopt the $40,000.00 budget as compiled by Dr. Horn."[23] Necessary repairs were also made on the Science Hall, Mood Hall, and the Woman's Building. They were paid for with $40,195.81 collected by the Educational Campaign inaugurated during the latter part of the Bishop years and a $21,000 loan from the Farmers State Bank.

Only two months before his resignation, Horn reported the largest single gift made to the institution up to that time.[24] As finally worked out in 1924 after he had left, it resulted in an annuity bequest of $100,000 from R. A. (Uncle Lon) Morris, with the University agreeing to pay him $1,750 per quarter as long as he should live.[25] Morris, a banker and local preacher, also made gifts to Southern Methodist University and to Alexander Institute in Jacksonville. As a result of his gift of $100,000 to endow Alexander Institute, its name was changed to Lon Morris College. The quarterly payments were made, presumably twenty-six of them amounting to $45,000, producing a net gain of $55,000 for Southwestern.[26] The real value of the gift, however, was not in the ultimate gain. It was in the fact that the gift was unrestricted and came six-and-a-half years before the death of Morris on January 6, 1931. It was used to pay off the most onerous obligations of the University immediately. Nevertheless, the Trustees issued notes to the Morris Fund for the amount used to pay the debts, expressing their intention to eventually repay them and to use the Morris gift for endowment.[27]

Vice President Sessions, so successful as financial agent under President Bishop, found his wings clipped under Horn. He seems to have intruded himself so forcefully into University affairs that the Board of Trustees stipulated at its meeting in 1923 that he restrict his duties to that of financial agent "under the direction of the President and that his duties not extend to any internal affairs of the University, except on recommendation of the President."[28] He left the staff to take a pastoral appointment in the fall.

Horn on Educating the Students of the 1920s

Horn dedicated the longest section of his report of 1923 not to finances but to outlining the kind of education a Church-related school should give its students. The central idea of a Church school, he said, must be that of "the old gospel," but with its message adapted to the new needs of the day. "No such school can be successful if it ignores either the old gospel or the new needs." By implication, Horn is saying the same thing that Bishop had already emphasized—that the day of using the institution overtly to convert students is over. He mentions the occurrence of the annual spring revival but limits his report of its effect on the students to the statement that "undoubtedly much good was done." All this, he suggests, does not mean that the school is less interested in the religious life of its students than earlier but that times have changed and Christian education must change with them. Horn says that this is the most important topic with which a President has to deal but that it cannot be dealt with successfully by using strategies appropriate for a bygone age.[29]

> The first thing that should be borne in mind by one who would successfully administer the affairs of a modern school is that we are living today in an absolutely new world. The good year 1914 is already a full hundred years behind us. We have a new world in politics, in international relations, in industry, in literature. The State, the Church, the School and the Family must all recognize the changed conditions.
>
> In this new world youth has changed fully as much as has maturity. Does anyone doubt it? If so, let him look at his own sons, at his own daughters; at the sons and daughters of his neighbors. Are they of the same type as the young people he used to know? Do you deal with your own sons and daughters as your parents dealt with you?
>
> Whether we like it or not, it is an inescapable fact that the world of 1923 is different from that of 1914 and that youth has changed as the rest of the world has changed.
>
> . . . As a matter of actual fact, we have had within the student body of Southwestern University this year practically all those questions to deal with which have affected the State of Texas and particularly the Methodist church during the same time. These include amongst others, the problems of the Fundamentalists, the Ku Klux, the right relationship between the sexes, relation between privileges and responsibilities in citizenship. This is exactly as it should be. No one desires that the school be an institution absolutely apart from life.
>
> . . . Character forming should be recognized as the chief function of a modern college. Scholarship is at best merely a valuable by-product.[30]

Though President Bishop was an ordained minister and President Horn a layman, they agreed on the function of a Church-related school in the post–World War I epoch.

Granbery and the Social Issues of the 1920s

Horn's mention of the Ku Klux Klan and of Fundamentalism as issues in the life of the University was not simply the idle plucking of illustrations from society at large to adorn his report but using issues that had in fact invaded the campus. The first, that of the Ku Klux Klan, had already allied him with Professor John C. Granbery, who fought the Klan with determination. The second would soon ally his successor, J. Sam Barcus, with Professor Herbert L. Gray in resisting fundamentalist elements within the Methodist Church that tried to have Gray expelled from his position at Southwestern.

On coming back to America after service with the Y.M.C.A. abroad during and after World War I, Granbery felt that he had come back to an America that was headed in the wrong direction. Writing about it he said: "Upon my return to America from three years abroad, I found a reaction had set in at home, far surpassing anything I had imagined while abroad. This recrudescence of obscurantism, dogmatism, literalism, bigotry and narrowness in the Church, is but a part of what has taken place in other phases of our national life."[31] To counteract these forces, he resumed his role as campus gadfly. He battled the Greek system, tobacco advertising in University publications, and other campus evils as he perceived them whenever he had the opportunity.

In spite of this fact, his integrity, candor, and selflessness made him popular with both faculty and students. He was chosen to speak for the faculty at the sixty-eighth birthday anniversary celebration for Dr. Cody on November 5, 1922. *The Megaphone* carried the student point of view. It said that Granbery "had distinguished himself both as an educator and sociologist, being considered by many as the leading sociologist of the South."[32] Granbery soon carried one of his campaigns, that against alcoholism, onto the international stage. In the summer of 1923 he did survey work in Havana, Vigo (Spain), Madrid, Morocco, Algeria, Tunis, Tripoli, Greece, Albania, Serbia, Bulgaria, Rumania, Russia, and Latvia for the World League Against Alcoholism.[33]

Granbery and the Ku Klux Klan

Though Granbery made his influence felt on many different social issues in the early 1920s, his overriding cause was opposition to the Ku Klux Klan. At its height in 1923 the Klan had perhaps as many as 150,000 members in Texas. It was stronger in Texas than in any other state. Robed in white sheets and wearing conical hats, its members paraded in public to show their numerical strength and engaged in cross-burnings to show their power. It used its united voting block to elect state legislators, sheriffs, judges, and other local and state officials. It came to control the city governments of Dallas, Fort Worth, and Wichita Falls.[34]

Granbery's opposition to the Klan was manifested at the 1922 session of the West Texas Annual Conference meeting at Lampasas. When he, as chairman of the Committee on Temperance and Social Service, was unable to secure enough votes in his committee to approve a report to the floor condemning "bigotry, sectarianism, prejudice of race and nationality," he brought it to the floor of the conference as a minority report. In the final report as adopted by the conference, an overt provision against the practices of the Klan, such as that proposed by Granbery, was replaced by one the Klan could live with. It stated: "That we heart[i]ly cooperate with every organization having for its object the orderly enforcement of our laws."[35] Either to express their appreciation for the action of the conference or simply to publicize their support for "spiritual" endeavors, about fifty Klansmen came into the church at the close of the last night's preaching service and gave the church a gift of money.[36]

The Klan even invaded the Golden Anniversary Celebration at Southwestern. The local K.K.K. chapter in Georgetown ran an advertisement in the Jubilee Edition of *The Megaphone* on June 5, 1923, directed to the attendees, as follows:

BIG KLAN
Barbecue
Thursday Night
at the
Klan Hall
Directly After Jubilee Pageant
All Visiting Klansmen Are Cordially Invited to Attend
Transportation Will Be Provided For All Klansmen.
Look for Cars with Klan Placards.
Several Distinguished Klansmen will make Addresses.
Georgetown Ku Klux Klan No. 178.[37]

No record exists as to whether or not the Klan barbecue attracted anyone, but it may well have done so. Soon after the beginning of the next fall term, an advertisement in *The Megaphone* testifies to the existence, however brief, of a Klan chapter among the students. It read: "There will be an important meeting of the University Klansmen tonight at seven-thirty in Seldom Inn, Mood Hall. All members are urged to be present, as some important matters are to be discussed."[38]

The two advertisements were not irrational gestures on the part of the invisible empire. They came soon after the election of a Southwestern alumnus, Earl B. Mayfield (graduate of 1901), the dominant Democratic politician in the state, as United States senator. Though not a Klansman himself, he won with Klan support. It was during that election that John Granbery entered the political struggle against the K.K.K. Many persons, particularly Church people, supported Mayfield because he was a prohibitionist. Granbery, also a prohibitionist, went to the Democratic Convention in San Antonio to oppose him. He felt that Mayfield's stance on prohibition was a smoke screen. He and others like him supported George E. B. Peddy, assistant district attorney of Harris County. Both the majority of ministers and the Anti-Saloon League of Texas supported Mayfield. They, unlike Granbery, were more interested in supporting prohibition than in opposing the Klan. Granbery was disillusioned, because Peddy was also a prohibitionist, though he did not make such an issue of it. Granbery felt that Mayfield's victory signified how completely he dominated the Democratic Party in Texas, how he had "about captured the Baptist Church, and almost has the Methodist Church." The *Texas Christian Advocate* stated that Mayfield "had always championed the right side of every moral issue in Texas," as if the Klan problem were not a moral issue.[39]

The gubernatorial election of 1924 became almost a Klan and anti-Klan referendum. This time Miriam Ferguson represented the anti-Klan forces against Felix D. Robertson in the Democratic primary. In spite of her husband's unsavory record as governor, having been removed in 1917 for appropriating State funds for his personal use, Granbery endorsed Miriam in the anti-Klan effort. He gave a speech in support of her that received widespread publicity over the state. He was attacked vigorously for supposedly defending "Fergusonism." The *Texas Christian Advocate* and the Anti-Saloon League of Texas once again supported the Klan candidate for what they felt was the higher moral imperative of prohibition and the fear that "Ma" Ferguson's election would taint the integrity of the governor's office. Granbery felt that the Klan issue trumped all others.[40]

For his anti-Klan position, Granbery was threatened by Klansmen who used "terroristic tactics" against him. His wife, May Catt, describes one incident as follows: "Threatened with a tarring and feathering because of his opposition to the Klan which had taken over the Democratic Party in the State, lock, stock and barrel, the Professor [Granbery] found at his door one evening a young six-footer armed with a gun who offered to sleep on the front porch as a protection. I was thoroughly sold on the idea, but the Professor would have none of it. Rocking our house and breaking our kitchen window satisfied the Klan's spirit of violence for the time being."[41]

Letters were sent to President J. Sam Barcus demanding Granbery's dismissal. The most concrete attack on him came from the Woman's Missionary Society of the Methodist Church of Taylor, Texas, which declared to *The Taylor Daily Democrat* that he was "most willfully maligning the ministry of Texas." Granbery replied that certain "Methodist and Baptist churches had desecrated their churches by admitting members of the Klan in regalia during their services." Shortly thereafter he announced to the President that because his presence was "'obnoxious' to the Taylor ladies, he would hand in his resignation to the University Board of Trustees, at its regular meeting in June." Though he was not pressed to leave Southwestern, he did so.[42]

It is interesting to recognize that Granbery's anti-K.K.K. actions at Southwestern overlapped those of the dynamic young county attorney of Williamson County, Daniel J. Moody, Jr. From county attorney with offices in Georgetown (1920–1922), Dan Moody became, successively, district attorney of the Twenty-sixth Judicial District (1922–1925), attorney general of Texas (1925–1927), and governor of Texas for two terms (1927–1931). It was his successful prosecution as district attorney of a group connected with the Klan for criminal activities, sending some of them to prison, that gained a statewide reputation for him. It was his later successful prosecution of cases to set aside "unconscionable" high contracts during Ma Ferguson's first term that led to his running against her in her unsuccessful attempt to win a second term.[43]

There is no evidence connecting Granbery and Moody, but they likely knew each other. Persons fighting for the same cause in a community as small as Georgetown would have known one another. Charles Bishop, Paul Horn, Jessie Daniel Ames, John Granbery, and Dan Moody formed a strong coterie of reformers in Georgetown from about 1915 to 1925. All of them would leave Georgetown to pursue their activities on a more conspicuous stage—Bishop as pastor of a prominent church in Houston and as a professor at Southern Methodist University, Horn as first president of what became Texas Tech University, Ames in Atlanta as National Director of Women's Work for the Commission on Interracial Cooperation and founder of the Association of Southern Women for the Prevention of Lynching, Granbery as first head of the Department of History at Texas Tech, and Moody as governor of Texas.

Granbery Goes to Texas Tech

At the time that news of his resignation was made public, Granbery released to *The Megaphone* the text of his letter of resignation to President Barcus. It read in part as follows:

> We are now in the midst of a splendid [Greater Southwestern] campaign for buildings and endowment, and it is painful to me to think that my relation to the school stands in the way of the most hearty support of the movement on the part of some friends of Southwestern who do not approve my course in certain matters of public interest and policy.
>
> . . . You gave me to read a letter from one such who said that the movement for a Greater Southwestern was doomed before it started if I were retained on the Faculty, and he assumed to speak for a group. You said that was a sample of about two dozen such letters. Judging from my own correspondence, the action of the Woman's Missionary Society of our church at Taylor, and other signs, I had no reason to be surprised.
>
> . . . In a matter of this kind my personal interests are secondary, but it happens that I find myself unable to make ends meet financially under existing circumstances. When one cannot meet promptly his obli-

> gations, he ceases to be an asset to a community and becomes a liability. It is essential that I make some kind of a change.
>
> . . . Permit me, Dr. Barcus, to express the high regard in which I hold you, the pleasure that I have found in association with you in the work of Southwestern, and the hope and prayer that you, yours, and the grand old school may march on together to ever greater prosperity and achievement in the service of the Kingdom.[44]

Granbery gives two reasons for his resignation. He recognizes that he has become a liability to the institution in its fund-raising efforts. He wants to remove himself as an impediment. He also mentions that he is financially strapped and that it is essential for him to make a change to improve his economic circumstances. Whether or not he had already discussed a position at Texas Tech with President Horn before offering the letter of resignation is unknown. But whatever the timing in that regard, he and Horn were fast friends. They had become so during Horn's short tenure at Southwestern. Horn offered him a position as first Head of the History Department at Texas Tech so that he was there to teach classes when the first school session opened in the fall of 1925. Before leaving Southwestern, Granbery introduced his successor, Professor M. L. Williams, to the Southwestern community in a short article in *The Megaphone*.[45] He kept in contact with Southwestern and made at least one recorded trip back in 1928. He had been invited by students and friends and preached at an evening church service on that occasion.[46]

The John C. Granbery who went to Texas Tech was the same person as the one who had taught at Southwestern, and he promptly developed a reputation there that made his life difficult. It involved attacks by fundamentalist churches, led by J. Frank Norris of Fort Worth and the pastor of the First Baptist Church of Lubbock, against the supposed liberalism of Granbery and others on the faculty like him. Norris and his supporters also attacked the so-called socialistic and communistic teaching espoused by various teachers inimical to some of the members of the Board of Directors of Texas Tech.[47] Norris had been an open supporter of the Ku Klux Klan during its heyday in the early 1920s. In addition to fundamentalism and the Ku Klux Klan as issues during the 1920s, the Red Scare was a third. Granbery's economic views led some to feel that he was at least a socialist, perhaps a crypto-communist, though he denied both designations vigorously.

As long as Horn was alive Granbery had a protector. This protection ended when Horn died suddenly on April 13, 1932. His funeral services were held under the cloisters of the administration building on the campus of Texas Tech with an attendance of about five thousand people. Granbery was one of the officiating ministers.[48] Within a year the governing board failed to renew his contract and those of several other professors. He suddenly found himself without a job in the middle of the Great Depression. In this circumstance, President King Vivion offered him an opportunity to return to Southwestern. This invitation and its results will be discussed in Chapter XIV.

James Samuel Barcus Becomes President of Southwestern

President Horn presented his resignation to the Executive Committee on November 26, 1923. In it he stated that he had been elected to the presidency of the new Texas College of Technology to be established in Lubbock. His resignation was to become effective on January 1, 1924. In his letter of resignation he said: "I do not feel that during the year and a half of my presidency here I have accomplished as much as I should. Certainly I have not accomplished as much for the University in a financial way as I had hoped to accomplish. I have, however, done the very best I could. I feel that I am leaving the institution in better condition that [sic] I found it, and I sincerely trust that its future will be one of continuous success." The Executive Committee accepted his resignation.[49] *The Megaphone* informed the campus the next day, and the faculty adopted a generous resolution honoring him at its regular December meeting.[50]

The Executive Committee and/or the Nominating Committee, both are mentioned in the minutes as participating in the process, did not wait long to contact a prospect to replace him. He was forty-two-year-old Professor Thomas Hall Shelby, director of the extension service at the University of Texas. Shelby had received his B.A. from the University of Texas in 1907, following which he pursued teaching and administrative service in Texas public schools. From 1913 to 1916 he taught education at Sam Houston Normal School. He served as president of the Texas State Teachers Association in 1919, assumed his job at the University of Texas in 1920, and earned the M.A. degree from the University of Chicago in 1921.[51] As a Methodist he knew about Southwestern and had probably come to know persons from Southwestern at church meetings or on visits

President J. Sam Barcus. Thirty-eight children and grandchildren of Mr. and Mrs. Edward Rosman Barcus (Waco) attended Southwestern during the two generations after they sent their first son, John M. Barcus, there in 1878. Southwestern University, Special Collections.

to the campus. A committee from Southwestern seems to have contacted him and to have invited him to allow the Board to consider him for President. At a special Christmas Day meeting of the Executive Committee, Dr. Barcus read a letter from Shelby in which he declined to be considered.[52] Shelby subsequently served at the University of Texas as one of its deans until his retirement in 1951.

At the regular meeting of the Southwestern faculty in January 1924, its members voted to set up a committee of three, with Dean Wunder as chairman, "to ascertain the preference of the faculty as to a possible president of Southwestern, so that the Faculty, if called upon by the Nominating Committee, would be prepared to give expression of its preference." Professors Tinsley, Granbery, and Lehmberg were elected.[53]

When the Executive Committee received Dr. Horn's resignation, it had asked him to "remain nominally as president, without salary until his successor should be elected." Now, in mid-January, in view of the fact that its first choice had declined to be considered, it appeared that a new President would not be elected for some time. As a result, the committee rescinded its motion asking Horn to "remain nominally as president" and accepted his resignation as being effective immediately. Because finances were in bad shape, Tinsley, as chairman of the faculty, was given authority to cut expenses wherever possible.[54] After failing for two-and-a-half months to come up with another candidate, the committee called a meeting of the Board of Trustees for March 26 and recommended the election of Dr. J. Sam Barcus as President. He was elected unanimously.[55]

Barcus, the Man

There were many things about Barcus that made him an appropriate selection for the position. He had attended Southwestern for five years as a student, from 1885 to 1890, receiving both the A.B. and A.M. degrees, and he had attended the Vanderbilt School of Theology for two years before receiving his first pastoral appointment in 1892. The Doctor of Divinity degree had been bestowed on him by Southwestern during the Golden Anniversary Celebration in 1923 without any thought that the award might be going to its next President. He had taught Biblical Literature at Southwestern for four years beginning in 1905 and been a stalwart supporter of retaining the school in Georgetown during the removal controversy. He was a part of the Barcus lineage that had sent almost forty of its sons and daughters to Southwestern in two generations. All this meant that he was well acquainted with the traditions and alumni of the institution.

Barcus was currently serving as pastor in Marshall and had held pastorates in four of the Annual Conferences in the state. He was widely known and respected by both ministers and laymen. He would bring these connections with him to the presidency. He had gained considerable financial and executive experience in his conference committee work, as a presiding elder, and in his brief service as President of two small Methodist colleges, Clarendon College in Clarendon (in the Panhandle southeast of Amarillo, 1901–1904) and Seth Ward College in Plainview (in the Panhandle south of Amarillo, 1911). If not of the calibre of President Bishop as an orator and scholar, he was still a good speaker and had a good mind. He was in his eighth year on the Board of Trustees and came to the presidency with full knowledge of the situation at Southwestern. He would not have to learn about it on the job. He was fifty-eight years old at the time, "with a strong physical constitution and with a capacity for hard work."[56]

Barcus was personally a modest man and enjoyed pastoral work. With Horn supposedly in place at Southwestern for a long tenure, to return to Southwestern and become President himself had not been on his agenda. Nevertheless, he accepted the call without hesitation. He seems to have done it much in the vein of the comment he had made in a letter to Cody during the removal controversy: "Our school has been crippled, but she's worth saving."[57] He had known personally all the Presidents from Mood to Horn. He said in later years: "I heard the first president, Dr. F. A. Mood, deliver his last educational address. I heard his successor, Dr. J. W. Heidt, deliver his inaugural address. I sat in the classroom of Dr. J. H. McLean, the third president. During the incumbency of Dr. R. H. Hyer, I was a teacher in the institution. During the presidency of Dr. C. M. Bishop, who was next in office, I was a trustee and a patron. As a member of the board, I cast a ballot for Dr. P. W. Horn, who preceded me as president."[58] Now it was his turn. He came to Georgetown in April 1924 to try his hand at it. When he arrived at the depot, a band met him and escorted him with music to the Woman's Building.[59] After his resignation in 1928, he returned to the pastorate. He retired in 1941 and lived in Georgetown until his death on March 18, 1948, at the age of eighty-two. He is buried in the I.O.O.F. Cemetery along with four other Presidents.

Beginning of the Greater Southwestern Campaign

At the June meeting of the Board of Trustees soon after the arrival of Barcus, the Executive Committee of the Alumni Association and the Executive Committee of the Board of Trustees presented a joint report calling for a $1,000,000 campaign. At least half of it would go for endowment, while the other half would be used in a building campaign to include a library, a gymnasium, and a stadium.[60] How much Barcus had to do with the origin of the campaign is unclear. A later newspaper report using information supplied by the campaign director stresses that the movement was actually launched two years earlier in June 1923 at the Golden Jubilee Celebration, and that the first gift ($10,000) to the movement was from Judge W. L. Dean of Huntsville, President of the Board of Trustees.[61] If that date is accepted, it must be said that the movement had languished until Barcus brought it to life a year later, in June 1924. The plan was perfected at a special meeting of the Executive Committee on October 1 to which a number of prominent Methodists from across the state had been invited. An agreement was reached to call the effort the Greater Southwestern Movement and Campaign. The amount to be secured was scaled back to a more realistic $500,000, with $300,000 going to endowment and $200,000 for buildings. Subscriptions (pledges) were to be taken with the understanding that if the whole amount had not been subscribed by the next Commencement, any subscription could be rightfully canceled by the person making it. A motion was also approved to allow the borrowing of enough money to pay the expenses of the campaign.[62]

The campaign was ambitious and, given the track record of the past, had little chance of success at the contemplated level. This time, however, one factor was different. The Reverend Glenn Flinn was hired in September to conduct it, and outside professional help, a person from the National System Company of Minneapolis, was secured to assist him.[63] Flinn directed the campaign with insight, efficiency, and tact. As a Southwestern graduate of 1900 and with a Vanderbilt B.D., he served both as president of the Ex-Students' Association and as Secretary of the Greater Southwestern Movement. Though he had previously served several churches, he enjoyed student work. He was the founder of the Texas Methodist Student Federation. Flinn, who had become a member of the Board of Trustees in 1923, would continue to serve in that capacity until 1939. He would serve on the Executive Committee for eight of those years. When he left the campaign after three years, with the campaign 80 percent completed, no one like him would come along to finish it. President Barcus tried to do so himself, but he had so many responsibilities that he was unable to devote the time needed to do it.[64] In spite of Flinn's departure, the campaign was the most successful to date in Southwestern history.

The title of the campaign is of interest. So far as is known, President Hyer first used the term "greater Southwestern." In his questionnaire to the Trustees during the removal controversy on April 18, 1910, he closed by saying, "Yours for a greater Southwestern *at the place of your choice* [italics added]."[65] Supporters of removal to Dallas picked up the term and used it when referring to their desire not to destroy Southwestern but to build a greater Southwestern in Dallas. After the controversy was settled, President Bishop retrieved the term for Southwestern in Georgetown by using it occasionally, as in the opening of the financial campaign in 1914. A Georgetown newspaper reported on the occasion of the mass meeting in the courthouse that "a strong appeal for a Greater Southwestern was made by President Bishop."[66] The term remained in the air over the years and was used in a *Megaphone* article in 1922 when referring to John C. Granbery. It said: "He is a man who believes that Southwestern has a future and he is one of the biggest boosters that we have for a 'Greater Southwestern.'"[67] But it was J. Sam Barcus who appropriated it most effectively for Southwestern. His answer to Hyer's option of locating it "at the place of your choice" was that the place of his choice for a Greater Southwestern was Georgetown.

"Annex Swept Away by Fire"

Though the campaign got off to a good start on January 1, it was knocked off balance a week later by the greatest physical tragedy that has happened in the history of Southwestern. In the early Thursday morning hours of January 8, 1925, the Annex, now renamed the Woman's Building, burned to the ground. By morning only a few bare walls were left standing. The fire began in one of the sorority rooms on the fourth floor, probably due to faulty electrical wiring. It spread rapidly through the woodwork over the floor of the gymnasium and had a good start before it was discovered. It was fortunate that the building caught on fire at the top and burned toward the ground, because it gave the girls an opportunity to escape before the stairways caught fire. At the sound of the siren the boys of Mood Hall got up and rushed to the Annex. There they began helping the firemen. Some helped with the fire hoses. Others circled the building and entered wherever possible to save the effects inside. The pianos in the practice rooms were saved, as well as much in the kitchen and storerooms. The fire escapes on the north side were also entered, and the property in several rooms was completely saved. The furniture, rugs, and curtains in the parlors and halls were also saved. The boys were finally forced to abandon their efforts and to watch the building go down in ashes. "The stones of the old structure were alternately red and white with the heat. Presently the walls began to crumble, and as the huge stones hurtled into the holocaust, a great shower of sparks ascended and scattered about the campus."[68]

Meanwhile the girls were standing outside in the "brisk" winter night air "with nothing more to wear than pajamas and possibly a kimona and a pair of shoes." Everyone marveled at the fact that not a single life was lost.

The burned-out shell of the Woman's Building with the women standing in front after the fire of January 8, 1925. Southwestern University, Special Collections.

There was general agreement that much of the reason for this "miracle" was the work of Laura Kuykendall. Living in the building herself, she immediately took charge with her customary "composure and calmness" and had all the girls go down to the parlors and await instructions. "She was very skillful," says one report, "in preventing any excitement among the girls, and possibly a panic. Very cleverly and skillfully she got all the girls out and over to Snyder Hall where she gave further instructions. It is easy to see what could have happened with two hundred girls in a four-story dormitory, and it ablaze. . . . She has proven herself every inch a queen." One observer later said that the thing he remembered about "Miss Kuykendall was that she had a towel draped about her head, and that orders flew thick and fast from her mouth." Credit was also given to Sallie Belle Matthews, a first-year piano and voice teacher, who directed the boys in saving all the pianos and much in the kitchen and storerooms. "The boys were somewhat surprised to see that she could grab a box of tomatoes and carry them as far as anybody."

While the firemen were still fighting the flames, the townspeople began opening their homes for the girls. Temporary places were soon found for all of them until a more permanent arrangement could be worked out. "The next morning at chapel," says one account, "there was a feeling of deep emotion in the heart of every student. The President, with tears in his eyes, said that Southwestern would carry on." Miss Kuykendall was called on to speak and stated that all the girls would stay. She urged no one to go home. "A great spirit was manifested when, with tears in their eyes over their loss, they said they were going to stay by old S.U." After Miss Kuykendall, Mr. Hereford, manager of Mood Hall, "arose and offered the Hall to the girls. . . . And then the boys all stood up as a sign that they were turning their home over to the girls. And everybody was happy, even in the midst of the great tragedy. That afternoon the boys vacated the hall and didn't come back for a year and a half." Places were then found for the boys. "Some [of the boys] rented rooms and suites, while others bunched up and rented a house. All the fraternity houses filled up to the last twelve inches of cover, while other refuges consist[ed] of garages and old class rooms." At the conclusion of the chapel service, everyone stood and sang "The Southwestern Song." Trustee James Marion West immediately sent workers to help the University so that Mood Hall could be fitted out for girls.[69]

One of the ancillary consequences of the fire is that President and Mrs. Barcus moved out of the first-floor portion of Snyder Hall where they had been living so that girls could live there. Renting in town, however, was not satisfactory, and arrangements were made during the construction of the new Woman's Building to procure a house on campus. Consequently the Claude Griffith home was purchased with this in view. Since it was located where the Fine Arts Building now stands, it was moved from its position there to a place farther south and east on University Avenue when that building was built. It was described at the time as a large home, consisting of four bedrooms, baths, living rooms, breakfast room, kitchen and dining room, besides spacious halls and porches.[70] It served as the President's residence for almost forty years, by which time it had become inadequate.

The fire set the growing reputation of Laura Kuykendall in concrete. Theretofore she had been the indispensable person. She now became the campus icon. An article written in *The Megaphone* a year after the fire by its regular humorist, whose pen name was Charley, is intentionally humorous. It is, also intentionally, adulatory.

> The Dean of women folks in Southwestern is Laura Kuykendall. Miss Kirk ort to be dean of doplowmats too, for she is so diplowmatic that she can prove a girl was not at the picture show when you saw her yourself. Whatever she wants she gets—sometimes. Whatever she don't want turns to what she does when she gets it. That is diplowmassy. Consequently she has her ups and downs, and round and arounds.
>
> . . . Iffen she had been bornt a man fifty years ago in this country she would have been a excellent bull puncher. She can drive.
>
> . . . Miss Kirk is so full of pep when things is goin right to suit her that it runs over and everybody else around has got it. Then when everything goes wrong it jest makes her plum sick. She is well when she is happy and when she is miserable she is sick.
>
> . . . Like the Indians she paints her face. She aint no moss back in any way. The only way in which she will ever be sot in her ways is that she will never be sot in her ways.
>
> . . . And how she does like good lookin close! I bet she spends a lot of hard earned cash buyin close.
>
> . . . Miss Kirk is tolerant. She is kind—in her way. She aint ever intenshunally unkind either, so far as I have heared. She can fight tho, when she is jumped on and can you blame her. That is jest spirit. And when dissasster comes like when the Annex burned, well,

> Miss Kirk is just plum grate for a fact. She corralled them stampeding girls like a ole cow man might, and altho she lost a lot of her own possesshuns she didn't think about that only about getting them girls well sity-ouated in proper homes and then getting Mood Hall cleaned up and reddy for em.
>
> . . . She has got style, that is the word, style all the while.
>
> . . . She is a institushun herself.[71]

The New Woman's Building

The response of Georgetown to the disaster at Southwestern was overwhelming. Once again, as in the case of President Bishop's campaign of 1914, it responded magnificently. Not only did it open its houses to the young women and men who had lost their habitation, but its citizens also opened their pocketbooks to the Greater Southwestern Campaign. Within three weeks their subscriptions were approaching $40,000.[72] The town and the campus eventually subscribed over $60,000, $8,000 of which came from students. Their generosity, however, was predicated upon the implicit understanding that the priorities of the Greater Southwestern Campaign would be changed and that the reconstruction of the Woman's Building would become its principal object. This understanding was ratified at a specially called Board meeting on February 11. The Board also approved a suggestion by Barcus that now was the time to procure all the remaining land between the Administration Building and the old Annex so that plans could be made for future buildings. The Executive Committee immediately purchased five pieces of property.[73] By the time of the Board meeting in June over $300,000 had been subscribed, of which more than $168,000 came from Houston.[74] The Board voted special thanks to three of these Houston donors—James M. West, J. W. Reynolds, and Jesse H. Jones.[75]

The building committee met with the Houston architect C. B. Schopple on April 11 to review and adopt the plans. A decision was made to construct the building on the exact location of the old Annex. The building would be 360\' in length and joined to the dining room by an arcade 75\' to 80\' long.[76] Subscriptions on the books, however, were not money in hand, and cash was needed immediately to proceed with the construction of the new building. Though the Board considered the issuance of $350,000 in bonds to finance it and to pay off existing obligations, it finally decided to borrow $300,000 from the Missouri State Life Insurance Company in St. Louis.[77] Construction bids were opened on June 1, and the contract was let to the Johnson Construction Company of Waco for $183,000, not including furnishings, plumbing, wiring, and heating, which were bid separately. The total cost was projected to exceed $230,000.[78] The contract with the Missouri State Life Insurance Company was completed on September 28, and work on the building began. Drawings of the new building appeared in the newspapers. It was touted "to Be [the] Finest in [the] South."[79] Barcus reported at the June Board meeting in 1926 that it was approaching completion. It would be practically fireproof, with modern conveniences, and, with 102 rooms, would have capacity for something over two hundred girls. He said it would be a center for the social life of the University. "Its porch, terraces, reception rooms, arcade, assembly hall, roof garden, and dining room will make it a special place."[80]

Indeed it did become a special place for several generations of students until its demolition in 1996–1997 to make way for more modern facilities. Facing south, it was a building three stories high, consisting of a center with side wings, like a rectangle with one of the long sides removed. An attractive arcade connected it on the west with a large kitchen and dining hall that served the entire campus. Space for the fine arts was provided over the dining hall. The building was constructed of brick and steel-reinforced concrete. It was out of keeping with the stone construction of the Administration Building and Mood Hall, but the design was pleasing. Not a plain rectangular brick building like the Williamson County Science Building, the other brick structure, it had elements of iron filigree around the entrance. Early in the period of construction, Mr. C. S. Belford took over the work of local supervising architect and put into the building the painstaking care that he lavished on all his projects.[81] In the concluding stages of its construction, Laura Kuykendall retrieved the bell that had been brought to campus from the Main Building of the earlier campus and had it placed atop the elevator shaft.[82] A year later she wove a pageant around it called the "Legend of the Bell." *The Megaphone* reported that eight thousand persons were expected to witness it.[83]

The Financial Position of the University

The annual statements of Presidents Horn and Barcus on finances in their Board reports from 1923 through 1928 were uniformly gloomy. In 1923 Horn reported that when he took charge he found that the "nominally active endowment amounted to practically $105,000," a pittance with respect to needs.[84] The report for 1924 said that "the financial showing for the year is poor." That for 1925 referred to "one of the largest deficits in running expenses we have ever had." The one for 1926 said that "the one dark feature of this report is the financial showing." In 1927 Barcus referred to "these stringent times." By 1928 an Advisory Committee found that the University had a total indebtedness of $310,000 in round numbers, over $80,000 of which was due within the next six months.[85] The debt situation was not new, only the amount was. The $300,000 loan secured to rebuild the Woman's Building had changed the dimension of the debt from the normal $50,000 to $60,000 of the past to five or six times those amounts. Of course, the loan had been secured on the basis of repaying it from the successful completion of the Greater Southwestern Campaign, but the proceeds from the five-year campaign did not match the needs.

Every year different measures were taken to produce more income and to reduce expenses. Many small measures were taken. Several teaching slots were eliminated, and thirteen more students were taught in 1924–1925, compared to the previous year, for $4,013 less.[86] Income from correspondence work began to be treated as tuition income to be applied to twelve-month teacher salaries rather than as teacher income from which the institution deducted a small percentage.[87] Barcus suggested the formation of a Loyalty League "made up of those who are willing to make an annual contribution for maintenance till such time as the necessary endowment can be secured."[88]

Several measures of greater consequence were taken. The Board voted to set up a standing committee on finance composed of carefully selected businessmen to raise and invest funds rather than to depend on the local committee "composed mostly of men inexperienced in financial investments and largely engaged in other interests."[89] Though it was appointed during the next year, it would be almost a decade before it actually began to function.[90]

Unrealized income from the past was also looked at. As part of a contract with Ernst & Ernst to audit the books and to make whatever changes in the bookkeeping system it deemed necessary, the firm produced a listing of unfinished subscriptions from previous campaigns.[91] Its audit showed $192,974.10 in uncompleted subscriptions from seven campaigns dating back to 1907. Though still carried on the books as assets, most of the subscriptions were out-of-date, some for more than twenty years. Flinn worked them vigorously with small effect. Given power to close out those he thought it necessary or wise to abandon, he was forced by mid-1927 to cancel subscriptions totaling $134,931 on account of death, removal, or repudiation. Subscriptions worth $41,364 were retained for further investigation. Only $16,679 were retained as good.[92]

More or less the same result came from the conclusion of the General Education Campaign of the Church. It had been established in 1918, with President Bishop as one of its main promoters, to raise $33,000,000 between 1920 and 1927 to be distributed among all the educational institutions of the Church, with those such as Southwestern expected to receive about $500,000 each. Though Southwestern had received some money during the course of the campaign, Glenn Flinn reported at the end of the campaign in 1927 that Southwestern received $226,339 as its share of the unpaid pledges. "Prodigious efforts" were made to collect them, reports Flinn, but many people requested cancellation and discounts because of financial reverses. Only $6,581 was collected in cash; $28,000 was renewed, $45,000 was discounted and cancelled, and $146,000 remained at the time of the report to be adjusted.[93]

The Greater Southwestern Campaign was another matter. Designed and run by Flinn, it produced results. It raised a total of $395,976.72 during his three years of leadership, of which $274,786.88 was for the Woman's Building, $66,820.34 was for the projected Cody Memorial Library, $42,650.00 was for endowment and scholarships, and $11,719.50 was for Woman's Building furnishings. The amazing thing about the campaign, however, was not the total amount. It was the fact that $189,113.31 was in cash (47.8 percent), $119,000.00 was in interest-bearing notes (30.1 percent), and only $87,863.41 in subscriptions (22.2 percent).[94] Flinn and/or his counselor from the National System Company of Minneapolis conducted the campaign on an up-front, hard money basis as much as possible. They had learned the lesson of past campaigns that it is easy to promise in the enthusiasm of the moment. It is equally easy to renege with the passing of time. They took subscriptions only as a last resort.

Unfortunately, even a successful campaign barely enabled the University to keep its head above water. The payment of accumulated debts from past years and additional expenses connected with the construction of the new building used all the money. At the time he turned in his final report in June 1928, Glenn Flinn calculated that the University owed a little over $300,000. Against it was $100,000 in interest-bearing notes and pledges, leaving the University $200,000 to raise beyond operational expenses over the span of eight years for repayment.[95]

Though only three of the five years of the campaign had elapsed, Flinn felt that he had brought the campaign close enough to its goal that he could go back to the pastorate and leave its conclusion to other persons. Only $104,000 more needed to be raised to complete the $500,000 goal in the two years left. Before leaving, he penned some observations for the Trustees, of which he was one, for their consideration. He had visited all parts of the state and talked with ministers and laymen everywhere. He felt that he had his finger on the pulse of public sentiment.

First of all, he called for a strong finance committee. Secondly, he felt that the University needed "to commit itself definitely to the policy of safeguarding all funds for the benefit of the specific object for which they were given. The diverting of funds from their original object *either directly or by the method of a loan by the University to itself* [italics added] except when absolutely protected by the assignment of perfectly good securities, has in the past and will continue in the future to bring dissatisfaction and final disaffection of many of the University's best friends." Thirdly, he said that the University needs "a board of trustees whose interest and whose sense of responsibility for its welfare cannot be easily satisfied." Finally, the University needs to recognize that there is "at this time a considerable breaking down of morale among her ex-students and friends" that needs to be remedied. The reason for this breakdown of morale, he asserts, is that many people think the University is practically bankrupt and the recent agitation for Southwestern's removal has been hurtful.[96]

All of these recommendations would eventually become a part of the University's normal handling of financial operations, the foundation stones on which a strong, solvent institution with a substantial endowment would be built. But for now the most immediate task was to tackle the morale breakdown. Little could be done at the moment about the feeling on the part of many people that the University was almost bankrupt. Only time and the infusion of a substantial endowment gift in the mid-1930s would do that. But some steps could be taken immediately to allay the recently engendered fear that Southwestern might move to another city.

Continuing Removal Agitation

The idea of moving a college or university from one place to another seems unusual today, but such was not the case in the late nineteenth and early twentieth centuries. Most Texas colleges in the 1920s had been established in small towns. They had bid for colleges as cities now bid for industries. As Texas grew, however, new urban areas such as Dallas, Fort Worth, Houston, and Austin developed beyond the expectations of even their strongest proponents. Some of the towns with colleges, such as Georgetown, Independence, Tehuacana, and Waxahachie did not grow, at least not significantly. The developing urban areas, seeking to develop their economies, looked on colleges and universities as potential economic engines, desirable not only for their immediate economic impact, but also for producing a long-term educated work force. It was much easier for them to jump-start the process of acquiring an institution of higher education by enticing one already established than to try to start one from scratch. Colleges, for their part, needed both the revenue and student potential that cities offered. The result was that for a generation or so another round of bidding for private colleges ensued, only this time it was cities trying to attract already established institutions from smaller towns or cities. Several of these efforts have already figured in this narrative. Only as a last resort, as in the case of Dallas with Southern Methodist, did they establish new ones.

The idea of moving Southwestern did not die completely in the minds of some people with the establishment of Southern Methodist in 1911. Toward mid-February 1920, an article was printed in the *Dallas Times-Herald* and reprinted in the *Fort Worth Star Telegram* and the *S. M. U. Campus* saying that SMU and Southwestern were to be merged. It said that the merger would come as part of the effort then underway to unify the Northern and Southern branches of Methodism. Since all sectional names would have to be banned, the name of Southern Methodist would be changed, necessitating the adoption of a new name. The article said that the solution was to merge Southwestern and SMU and for SMU to receive the Southwestern name. A small college at Georgetown called Southwestern College would be created.

President Bishop immediately labeled the article as preposterous. He said that his membership in the principal unification commissions made him privy to what was being discussed and that nothing at all had been said on this subject. While rebutting the article, he took a swipe at Southern Methodist by alluding to the fact that while SMU's debt was four hundred thousand dollars, that of Southwestern was only fifty thousand. He added that SMU had been drawing "students, teachers, cooks, janitors, chaperones, professors, even a president from Southwestern." Making a tongue-in-cheek reference, he said that this showed the perspicacity of Southern Methodist. Southwestern personnel were indeed of a kind that other schools would want.[97]

Having tried its hand without success at attracting Southwestern, Dallas tried to attract Baylor to join Southern Methodist University as a second major private institution for the city in 1928. During the winter and spring of 1927–1928, an educational commission, appointed by the Baptist General Assembly, met to consider the removal of Baylor to Dallas. Dallas, through its Chamber of Commerce, had offered $1,500,000 in money and a campus of one thousand acres if Baylor would move there from Waco. The commission voted 14 to 1 to recommend acceptance of the offer to the General Convention. Though longtime President S. P. Brooks was amenable to the idea, former Governor Pat Neff, chairman of the Baylor Board, opposed it, and the Convention turned it down.[98] As might be imagined from a town that had itself experienced a removal controversy, the First Baptist Church in Georgetown rejected the idea "almost unanimously."[99]

It was in this atmosphere of flux for small, Church-related institutions that the idea of moving Southwestern was broached again by several of its graduates. Their idea, however, was to move Southwestern to San Antonio. San Antonio had no large Protestant educational institution and was ripe, they felt, for the entry of one. In early May 1927 they wrote an article in the *Texas Christian Advocate* proposing such a course of action. A later news item from San Antonio was published in a number of papers that officials of Southwestern had held a conference with the San Antonio Chamber of Commerce about it. Upon investigation of the matter, it was found that the only basis for the report was that the same person who had written the article went to the Chamber accompanied by another graduate and the President of Westmoorland College. Authorities at Southwestern obtained letters from the President of Westmoorland and from the Chamber "disclaiming any part in arranging for the conference or [of] giving publicity to the informal discussion." The Chamber affirmed that it was not going to make any effort to remove Southwestern from Georgetown and had so informed the parties who presented the matter.[100]

Once again, as in 1920, the agitation for removal had no substance, but it caused considerable anxiety in Georgetown. The unknown alumnus, joined by two other students, wrote letters "to numerous alumni endeavoring to create sentiment in favor of the removal," but was unable to awaken any interest in it. For its part, the Executive Committee had immediately prepared a statement for the press. It "declared that there is absolutely no truth in reports circulated in some of the newspapers of the state that it is contemplated to move Southwestern University to San Antonio. . . . No such proposition has been made by any responsible person, and would not be considered if made."[101] Dean Ullrich appeared in chapel and told the students that "there is just about as much chance of moving Southwestern to San Antonio as there is of moving Texas University to El Paso and using the buildings occupied at Austin for a penitentiary."[102] Barcus quoted the president of the San Antonio Chamber as saying that he thought Southwestern was located where it ought to be—Georgetown. "This rumor was started by a former student of this school whose reason for doing it is still in the dark."[103]

Almost the last thing the Executive Committee asked of Barcus before he stepped down as President was to draw up a paper on "removal." This he did and presented it to the Committee on August 14, 1928. In it he briefly outlined the support of the 1870 and 1906 Educational Conventions for Southwestern. He mentioned how support of Southwestern was part of the 1910 report adopted by the Conferences setting up Southern Methodist University. He now asked the educational convention called to meet in Dallas on September 4, 1928, and the Annual Conferences meeting later that fall to execute plans that would free Southwestern from debt and provide it a substantial endowment.[104]

His mention of an impending educational convention reveals the reason the authorities at Southwestern took so seriously the removal proposal generated by several alumni but with little substantial backing. It could not have come at a worse time. Fundamental decisions were to be made at that convention, and the minor removal flap cast the University in an unfavorable light, as if its alumni were asking for changes to be made. Committees of the forthcoming convention had been meeting during the past year studying reports from all the Methodist institutions of higher education. The time was now arriving when the convention itself would meet and determine whether or not to approve their recommendations. The final recommendations of the convention would then be passed on to the Annual Conferences of the Church for consideration. The actions of the convention, of the Annual Conferences, and subsequent developments regarding removal over the next five years will be treated in Chapter XIV.

Rebuilding the Core Faculty

One of the most important reasons Southwestern survived the Great Depression was that it was able to replace the faculty members who had carried it through the first half century with a core of persons who would in turn carry it through the economic calamity of the 1930s. The first-generation stalwarts who had served the University from the time of Mood began to leave the scene in the 1890s. They were Sanders, McLean, Hyer, Young, and Cody, listed in order of their departure. By 1915 they had all died or retired. Their departure overlapped the acquisition of a second generation of persons, Vaden, McKennon, Tinsley, Lehmberg, and Gray, who would retire together after a paid retirement program was initiated in 1935. John Robert Allen, who was forty when employed in 1892, knew Mood and is more properly considered a first-generation person. He retired within its 1915 time frame. He returned from Dallas at the age of eighty-one as a special honoree for the Commencement of 1933, dying on February 6, 1937.[105]

Pegues, Moore, Nichols, and Granbery, employed from 1893 to 1913, were second-generation acquisitions, but they dispersed to Southern Methodist and Texas Tech. The total list of long-tenured persons in the second and third generations, all employed before the Great Depression, is as follows:

Persons Serving at Least Fifteen Years

Year Hired	Name	Field	Total Years
1892	John Robert Allen	Mental and Moral Philosophy; Dir. Annex	22
1893	Albert Shipp Pegues	English and Latin	25
1893	Wesley Carroll Vaden	Greek, Latin, French	44
1894	Stephen Halcutt Moore	Principal; Latin, Greek, History	25
1903	Randolph W. Tinsley	Biology, Geology	33
1903	Margaret McKennon	Head Librarian	41
1909	F. C. A. Lehmberg	French and German	26
1911	Herbert Lee Gray	English Bible and Biblical Theology	29
1913	John C. Granbery	History, Economics, Sociology, Education	16
1914	Laura Kuykendall	Expression, Dean of Women	21
1915	William P. Davidson	Philosophy	17
1917	John C. Godbey	Chemistry	35
1917	Pearl A. Neas	Registrar, Dir. Publicity, Dir. Correspondence	46
1919	Claud Howard	English	39
1920	Oscar A. Ullrich	Education, Academic Dean	38
1923	Ruth M. Ferguson	English, Dean of Women	37
1925	George C. Hester	History, Political Science	40
1925	Myron L. Williams	Sociology, Economics	33
1925	C. M. ("Lefty") Edens	Athletic Director, Coach	15
1926	Henry Edwin Meyer	Music, Dean of School of Fine Arts	35
1926	Albert Russell Wapple	Mathematics	16
1928	Luther J. Waggoner	Religious Education	31
1929	Isaac Joel McCook	Business Manager, Vice President Finance	39
1929	Lucy Belle Morgan	Spanish	19

Looked at as a whole, the second generation of faculty persons did not make a contribution to its task equivalent to that made by those of the first generation. Not only did several of its members leave the institution before retirement, but it also did not establish a cohesive faculty personality known later for its achievements. The third generation of faculty members and senior staff, however, established a distinctive character that merits recognition. Laura Kuykendall, John C. Godbey, Claud Howard, George C. Hester, Lefty Edens, and others of the third generation left an indelible imprint on both the University and its students.

George C. Hester

Many years after graduating in 1929, Dorothy Shell Bunting wrote about some of those teachers. Dorothy was a Georgetown girl, living just a few blocks away from the old depot that stood next to the railroad just south of the juncture of Maple and East Seventh Streets. She and her sister walked down the railroad tracks to Southwestern not far away. Writing about her "great teachers," she mentions Hester, Ferguson, Howard, Tarver, Paul Young, and McKennon. In writing about Dr. Hester, she inadvertently opens a window onto the circumstances of how a pair of sisters coped with their difficult financial circumstances.

> Now I must tell you what a good history teacher Mr. Hester was. For his class my sister and I could not afford a text book. My Mother said, "We are so sorry, girls, but we just can't spare the money. Your three little brothers all need shoes." She continued: "Just listen carefully, take notes of everything Dr. Hester says, and use your notes to review." We never told any one we did not have a book. We did just what Mother said. We passed our tests with good grades, and in doing this we learned to appreciate and love history for the first time and for *all* time.[106]

Hester was an outstanding lecturer and a well-known author in the field of Texas government and history. He was joint author with two others of *State and Local Government in Texas*, a college textbook published in 1940. It went through at least five editions. He also published *Fiscal Policies of the State of Texas* in 1941 and a public school textbook on Texas history in 1954. He was elected to the state House of Representatives and was a member of the Federal Power Commission in Washington, D.C., during the early New Deal period. He took a leave of absence for the spring semester of 1933 for the work in Austin and the entire academic year 1934–1935 for that in Washington. Following his return, he declined the presidency of Texas A&I College in Kingsville to remain at Southwestern.[107] He was elected mayor of Georgetown on a write-in vote in 1946 in spite of not campaigning for the job.[108] He was chosen to occupy the first endowed chair at Southwestern from money provided in 1952 by Herman and Margarett Brown. It was named the Lucy King Brown Chair in History in honor of the mother of Herman and George. Hester loved archaeology and participated in many digs for Indian artifacts. He was a consummate gentleman, who, without putting himself forward, was frequently called upon for advice by various political leaders during his years as a professor. He became the confidant of one of his students, John Goodwin Tower, who was elected the first Republican senator from Texas in 1961. Hester retired in 1965 and died in 1978 at the age of 81.[109]

Claud Howard

Perhaps the teacher most recognized for his erudition and classroom presence from the 1920s through the 1940s was Claud Howard, Professor of English and later chairman of the Division of Humanities. Born in 1888, he held a B. Lit. (1906) and an A.B. degree (1907) from East Texas Normal College, two M.A.'s, one from the University of North Carolina (1909) and the other from Harvard (1911), and a Ph.D. from the University of Chicago (1922). His first book, *The Dramatic Monologue: Its Origin and Development*, was published in 1910, a year before he went to Jacksonville (Alabama) Teachers College as Head of the Department of English. He came to Southwestern in 1919 to replace Pegues. Five years after his arrival he published the work for which he is best known, *Coleridge's Idealism: A Study of Its Relationship to Kant and to the Cambridge Platonists.* It was touted in *The Megaphone* as the first systematic treatment of Coleridge's philosophy.[110] Ellsworth Peterson, Professor of Music and holder of the Margarett Root Brown Chair for thirty-seven years (1965–2002), describes Howard as the most outstanding teacher under whom he studied at Southwestern.

Howard was not, however, all erudition. He was an avid golfer and made a hole-in-one at the new Country Club golf course in 1928. By the end of 1935 he had five holes-in-one, the last one coming on the new Southwestern links.[111] When the Texas Conference added golf as a major sport soon thereafter, *The Megaphone* opined that Southwestern might be low on known golf talent but that its team would have one advantage. It would be the only team in the state coached by a Ph.D., Dr. Howard, head of the English Department.[112] A nine-hole campus golf course was built under his leadership and is listed for the first time in the catalog for 1933. It ended at the back of the Administration Building, so that, says John Score, "you just walked right out of the back door of the Administration Building and you were on the golf course."[113] Howard died in 1958 at the age of sixty-nine.

John C. Godbey

Perhaps the most versatile person on the faculty was John Campbell Godbey. Employed by President Bishop in 1917 to teach chemistry, he has already been mentioned as the person who laid the "cement" sidewalks on the grounds of the Williamson County Science Building, as one of the fourteen who signed the letter to the Board of Trustees in 1918 supporting the retention of Bishop as President, as the faculty member selected to receive training at Fort Sheridan, Illinois, for leadership in the World War I campus Student Army Training corps, and as the builder of two gymnasiums on the old campus. Using his year at the Music Conservatory at Howard Payne as background, he also directed the band for about four years after 1917.[114]

In 1926 Godbey was appointed assistant physical plant director with a small stipend to recognize his constant concern for the improvement of the plant. He was one of those who in that same year sold his house and property between the Main Building and the old Annex to the school to facilitate campus cohesion and expansion.[115] He was the main force behind the organization of a system of intramural athletics in 1927–1928 and was the regular faculty representative on committees dealing with intercollegiate athletics from his earliest days on campus. He also served as an officer of the Texas Athletic Conference. A *Megaphone* article in 1929 calls him the "daddy of athletics." In addition, he got up early every Sunday morning to teach a men's Sunday School class at the Methodist Church and sang bass in the choir. His civic activities involved his serving as a water and light commissioner for Georgetown from 1919 to 1942, as mayor *pro tem* of Georgetown from 1922 to 1942, and as a member of the Advisory Council of the Boy Scouts of America.[116]

These "extracurricular activities" of Godbey were in addition to his academic interests. In 1932 he and Dean Ullrich were the first persons mentioned from Southwestern as being members of Scholia, an organization of selected professors of what is now Texas State University, the University of Texas at Austin, and of Southwestern that met monthly for dinner and to hear invited speakers. By 1936 the members were Ullrich, Godbey, Meyer, and Granbery. Only one officer, known as the Factotum, presided at meetings, arranged the programs, and attended the business of the club.[117] Scholia lasted as an organization for sixty or seventy years and included many later Southwestern professors. In 1934–1935 Godbey held several positions in educational associations at the state level. He was chair in that year of the Visual Instruction Section of the Texas State Teachers Association and president of the Texas Academy of Sciences.[118] He was a member of other national scientific organizations as well.

Born into a parsonage family in 1882, he received his B.A. and M.A. degrees from Central College in Fayetteville, Missouri, in 1904 and 1905, respectively. Following three years of high school teaching and a summer at the University of Missouri, he became a Fellow in Chemistry at Vanderbilt in 1908. Leaving there in 1910, he became a member of the faculty at Central College for three years. While there, he married and took a year of further study during 1911–1912 in Leipzig, Germany. Somewhere in this background is the legend of the man who told a *Megaphone* reporter that "most of my youth was spent in the West." He went there, he says, before the Indians had been driven onto reservations. After going to Sheridan, Wyoming, where he staked out a claim, he went up into Montana. During that time, he remarks, he went skating with the thermometer at thirty-six below zero.[119] At whatever point these youthful adventures fit into Godbey's early life, they are in line with the heroic mold of him that was held in the minds of many of his students. He received an honorary Doctor of Science degree from McMurry College in 1943, retired in 1952, and died in 1970.

Women in the Faculty

The disparity in academic preparation and faculty turnover between men and women continued during the thirty-one years from 1911–1912 through 1941–1942. Though the number of women employed was only slightly less than the number of men, their turnover rate was much higher, so that their proportion on the faculty at any one time was generally about a third of the total. Whereas only 8 of the

102 women employed during those years served ten years or more, 25 of the 111 men did so. Only 24 percent of the women possessed a master's degree or higher, while 58 percent of the men did. Two of them, Velma Tisdale and Katherine F. Tarver, were important not so much for length of service as for the disciplines they taught. Velma Tisdale was employed in 1922 as Assistant Professor of Mathematics, the first woman to be employed in what is presently the Division of Natural Sciences. With a B.A. from Southwestern and an M.A. from Columbia, she taught eleven years, from 1922–1923 through 1926–1927, 1933–1934 through 1935–1936, and the single years of 1943–1944, 1945–1946, and 1947–1948. Katherine Tarver taught nine years, from 1924–1925 through 1932–1933. With a B.A. and an M.A. from Southwestern, she was employed as Assistant Professor of English and Mathematics. She received further advanced work as a special student at five universities—Chicago, Wisconsin, California, Tennessee, and Mexico—and as a graduate student at the Universities of Chicago and Texas in the summers of 1927 and 1930.

Deans and Other Senior Staff Leaders

Two persons who would play important administrative roles in the future were both named deans within a year of each other. President Barcus appointed Oscar A. Ullrich, Professor of Education and later head of the Psychology Department, as Dean of the Faculty on the resignation of Dean Wunder in the summer of 1926. Having come to Southwestern in 1920, Ullrich would serve in that role for thirty-two years until 1958. President Vivion, who inherited him as dean when he became President, wrote in his Board report two years later that "we record our humble judgment that Dean O. A. Ullrich, dean of our faculty, is without a superior in the southwest."[120]

The other academic dean was Henry E. Meyer. The year that Ullrich was made Dean of the Faculty, Meyer came to the University and was made Dean of the Department of Music. An organist, pianist, and vocalist, Meyer held both a teacher's and an artist's diploma from the Ithaca Conservatory of Music (1910) and had done a graduate course for supervisors of public school music at Cornell University in 1912. He had studied as an organ, voice, and piano student under several important figures and had taught at the University of Minnesota, Howard Payne College, and Daniel Baker College before coming to Southwestern. The Southern School of Fine Arts in Houston honored him with a doctor's degree in music in 1942. He became Dean of the School of Fine Arts when it was activated in its current form in 1947. He conducted an annual conference for church musicians at Southwestern during the spring of each year beginning in 1929 and regularly took his choir around the state to hold concerts in churches and schools.

With Ullrich and Meyer as the deans of the two academic units, Pearl A. Neas as Registrar, Laura Kuykendall followed by Ruth Ferguson as Dean of Women, Margaret Mood McKennon as Librarian, and I. J. McCook, employed by President Vivion in 1929 as Business Manager, Southwestern had a group of senior staff persons that would tie together the administrations of five Presidents. They were all together at Southwestern when the Great Depression began and served into the administration of President Score and several even beyond.

Enrollment and Changes in the Degree Structure

Though fluctuations in regular enrollment, with a low of 554 in 1922–1923 and a high of 676 in 1924–1925, caused concern, the average enrollment for the Horn and Barcus years was 614, an increase of 16 over the average for the Bishop years. Barcus proudly remarked that in his last year 104 students graduated, the largest in proportion to enrollment of any college in the state. The days when teachers were paid to travel during the summer to stimulate enrollment gradually gave way to more organized approaches to student recruitment, such as bringing prospects to the campus for visits. Two hundred seniors from neighboring high schools came as guests to the University during the Easter weekend of 1928, with good fall enrollment results.[121]

The 1920s saw the first significant impact of the social sciences on the degree structure of the University, as psychology and political science requirements were added to the Bachelor of Arts. They were added by reducing the foreign language requirement from 15 percent of the degree total to 8 percent, while mathematics was eliminated entirely. The number of required courses was also dropped from 56 percent to 50 percent of the degree. A part of the reason for reducing the total number of requirements for the degree was to provide additional room for music. In 1927 music courses were recognized as a valid part of a liberal education rather than as only an art or a vocational study by allowing them to form a significant part of the Bachelor of Arts degree. By counting them as electives, as many as one-third of a student's B.A. degree could now be taken in music. This change was described in the catalog "as a new departure in the history of music education in Texas."

Though the Bachelor of Music degree did not change much, it did follow the other baccalaureate degrees in adding some social science courses as requirements, in this case, psychology and education. History was dropped to make way for them. Most music students went into public school teaching, and the education requirement was added to provide background for them. At the same time, the Bachelor of Science in Education degree was dropped entirely in 1924. This change, however, did not betoken a lessened interest on the part of the University in turning out students for public school teaching, but rather a feeling that students should prepare for that vocation within the structure of the Bachelor of Arts. Both four-year and six-year levels of elementary certification continued to be offered, as well as two-year, four-year, six-year, and permanent levels of high school certification. Overall, the concept of the Bachelor of Arts gradually moved away from its original classical orientation and expanded to include music, education, and the new social sciences.

The Bachelor of Science degree received a substantial makeover. It assumed a character of its own rather than, as in the past, looking like a Bachelor of Arts with strength in the sciences. Eliminated entirely as requirements were history, public speaking, and German, though as much language as ever was required, since the previous requirement in French was doubled to take over the courses vacated by German. Requirements in English, Bible, and mathematics were all reduced. Philosophy absorbed the space lost by Bible, and political science was introduced. The concept of a major disciplinary field, called "the principal subject," and a minor disciplinary field, called "the secondary subject," was established for the first time. This concept replaced the earlier requirement that basically required a specific number of science courses to be spread among the four sciences—physics, chemistry, biology, and mathematics. Now the student declared a major and a minor field of study.

The Bachelor of Science in Medicine, the Master of Arts, and the Master of Science continued to be offered with no substantial changes. After 1925, no more conditional admissions were allowed to the University.

The Library

Soon after Dr. Cody's death in 1923, community sentiment coalesced around the idea that his contribution to

Pamphlet describing "The Greater Southwestern Movement" in 1925. Two of its goals were to build a Cody Memorial Library and to rebuild the Woman's Building. Southwestern University, Special Collections.

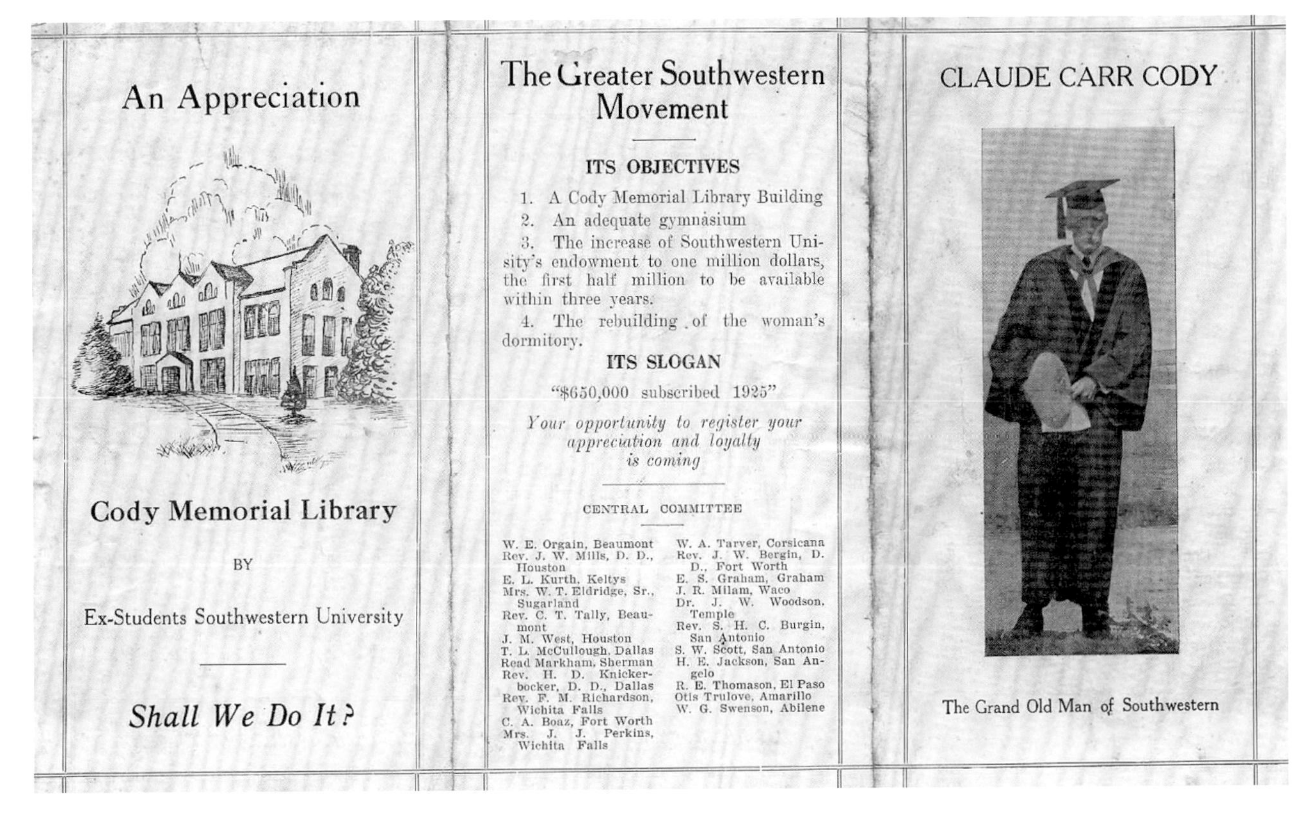

An Appreciation

Cody Memorial Library

BY

Ex-Students Southwestern University

Shall We Do It?

The Greater Southwestern Movement

ITS OBJECTIVES

1. A Cody Memorial Library Building
2. An adequate gymnasium
3. The increase of Southwestern University's endowment to one million dollars, the first half million to be available within three years.
4. The rebuilding of the woman's dormitory.

ITS SLOGAN

"$650,000 subscribed 1925"

Your opportunity to register your appreciation and loyalty is coming

CENTRAL COMMITTEE

W. E. Orgain, Beaumont
Rev. J. W. Mills, D. D., Houston
E. L. Kurth, Keltys
Mrs. W. T. Eldridge, Sr., Sugarland
Rev. C. T. Tally, Beaumont
J. M. West, Houston
T. L. McCullough, Dallas
Read Markham, Sherman
Rev. H. D. Knickerbocker, D. D., Dallas
Rev. F. M. Richardson, Wichita Falls
C. A. Boaz, Fort Worth
Mrs. J. J. Perkins, Wichita Falls
W. A. Tarver, Corsicana
Rev. J. W. Bergin, D. D., Fort Worth
E. S. Graham, Graham
J. R. Milam, Waco
Dr. J. W. Woodson, Temple
Rev. S. H. C. Burgin, San Antonio
S. W. Scott, San Antonio
H. E. Jackson, San Angelo
R. E. Thomason, El Paso
Otis Trulove, Amarillo
W. G. Swenson, Abilene

CLAUDE CARR CODY

The Grand Old Man of Southwestern

the University should be honored through the construction of a library building named for him. Both the senior class and the Faculty Club made such a request to the Board of Trustees in 1924.[122] *The Megaphone* picked up on the matter and made it the principal topic for an issue soon thereafter.[123] With campus sentiment at a high pitch for a new library named after Dean Cody, it is quite likely that it would have been built fairly soon as a result of the Greater Southwestern Campaign had not the burning of the Annex changed the nature of building priorities. As it was, even in the face of the disaster, talk continued from year to year about building a new library. The money that was raised for it during the Greater Southwestern Campaign, though not enough, was looked upon as inviolate. Though it cannot be said with certainty that it was never used for other purposes, it was always repaid quickly. Though Vivion made a great effort to build it in the early 1930s, the Cody Memorial Library would not be built until 1939, fifteen years after the idea was broached. It and the Jim West Gymnasium, built at about the same time, were the first new buildings since the Woman's Building in 1926.

In the meantime, Mrs. McKennon as librarian did what she could. In her report for 1927, she listed library holdings of 22,881 volumes on the third floor. This number did not include about half the library holdings, which consisted of books stored on the first floor. Their weight precluded their being kept with the others on the third floor. Space was at such a premium that some of the government books had to be returned rather than kept. Using the students assigned to her for work, Mrs. McKennon ran a bindery that bound 315 magazine volumes and books during the year, about one a day. The following year she listed 23,373 volumes (excluding government documents), 7,000 government volumes, 5,000 bound magazines, and 6,000 pamphlets. The average number of daily loans was 47.[124]

Accreditation Warning

The problems felt by the library extended to the entire academic program. Dean Ullrich informed the Board of Trustees in 1928 that the Southern Association of Colleges and Universities had informed Southwestern that it was delinquent in meeting certain standards, the chief of which "is that of endowment or yearly income." He said that all of these problems could be met with sufficient annual income but that without it Southwestern's standing would be in danger, perhaps even becoming a fatality.[125] The mention by Ullrich of a looming problem with the Southern Association at this juncture is particularly important. It is the first mention of what would become a decade-long struggle to maintain Southern Association accreditation.

Whereas the Church alone had accredited Southwestern until it joined the Southern Association in 1915, the Church got out of the business of accrediting its colleges entirely in 1926 and began to rely on the standing they achieved as a member of the Southern Association. Its removal from the picture of accreditation, however, does not mean that Southwestern's fate was turned over to a hostile agency. The standards of the Church and those of the Southern Association in 1926 were quite similar, and the influence of Methodist institutions within the Association was very strong during the worst years of the Great Depression. Of the twenty-four members of the main accrediting commission of the Association in 1935, five were representatives of Southern Methodist colleges. The important position of secretary-treasurer was held by a representative of one of the Church's colleges for thirty-four out of the forty-four years from its inception to 1939. In addition, the first Executive Secretary of the Association, who served from 1929 through the decade of the 1930s, was a professor from Birmingham-Southern College, a Methodist institution.[126]

Special Events and Compulsory Attendance

Given the financial difficulties of the school, the number of artistic events, nationally known speakers, and special programs is remarkable. The first opera ever performed in Georgetown was *Carmen*. The San Carlo Grand Opera Company presented it on January 7, 1926. The Típica Orchestra of Mexico gave a concert that same spring, and the campus Glee Club and girls' Choral Club put on a performance of *The Mikado*. The Double Quartette of the San Antonio Oratoria Society performed the *Stabat Mater* during Music Week in May. The Mask and Wig Players, a self-supporting student dramatic group dating from 1922, performed regularly under the direction of Professor Dwight Wentz, and a Southwestern Little Symphony Orchestra performed in both Georgetown and elsewhere under the direction of Edward P. Onstot.[127] Lighter fare was also provided. Dean Ullrich announced at the beginning of the fall term in 1927 that weekly picture shows would be given in the auditorium.[128]

Among the many lecturers during the Horn-Barcus

years were Robert Frost (poet), Lorado Taft (sculptor), Josephus Daniels (former secretary of the navy), Wilfred T. Grenfell (medical doctor in the Arctic), Grace Noll Crowell (poet), Charles Paddock (world's fastest human), and Will Durant (writer, historian). All spoke on campus between 1922 and 1928. The Durant lecture, entitled "Is Progress an Illusion?," caused the *Daily Texan* to condemn the Southwestern student body for the "rude reception" it accorded the speaker. Its reporter states that "it actually became necessary for him [Durant] to interrupt his splendid lecture several times, in order to ask his listeners to quiet their excessive coughing, to call attention to their drowsy inattention, and finally to order one husky but ill-mannered young man out of the room. . . . The entire student body at Southwestern should bow down to him in humble penitence, for they have proven unworthy of his presence."[129]

The dissatisfaction of Southwestern students with daily required chapel or assembly, as the nonreligious gatherings came to be called, is a constant theme in faculty reports to the Board of Trustees over the years. Ullrich called it "the ever-recurring problem." "Many students," he said, "think that they would prefer to attend if they were not compelled to do so."[130] Apparently, as the Durant lecture suggests, this dissatisfaction did not focus so much on the content of the programs as on the fact that, as Ullrich alleges, attendance was required. Unable to obtain modification of the requirement, he used various techniques over the years to make it palatable. He practiced one such technique three years after the Durant incident. In its May 13, 1930, issue, a *Megaphone* article entitled "Dean O. A. Ullrich Rudely Interrupted" reported the occurrence of another incident.

> Thursday morning, Dean O. A. Ullrich had just begun to read a selection from one of the great writers when someone out in the audience, in the Sophomore section, laughed out loud. Instantly everything was still. A pall was over the student body. Who could be so rude? In a stern voice the dean continued. Again the laugh sounded, this time from the Freshman section. Such defiance! Where had the respect for authority gone? Twice more he was rudely interrupted, once by each of the other classes.
>
> This was more than even a good-natured dean could stand. He called on a member of the sturent [sic] body to come to the platform and explain the meaning of such a show of rudeness. The feeling was tense! With shaking nerve the student made her way to the front and in unfaltering tones said, "I was laughing about the Barn Party Monday night."
>
> Whew! So the whole thing was a frameup [sic] on the part of certain students and the dean. The psychology which had been used had worked to perfection, and the announcement, together with a few scenes from the show, to use a slang expression, "got over big."[131]

The problem of compulsory attendance would continue to exercise student sentiment for another forty years. By 1966–1967 only one required chapel service and one required assembly were held each week. The assembly requirement was dropped for the 1967–1968 academic year, followed by the elimination of required chapel for 1968–1969.

Student Life—Conduct, Grades, and Athletics

The picture of student conduct in the 1920s depends on how one assesses the evidence emanating from that decade. On the one hand there is ample indication of seriousness of intent. The Scholarship Society formed by President Bishop became the mother chapter of the Scholarship Societies of Texas, soon to become the Alpha Chi national organization, and a new leadership society for men, Blue Key, was also organized.[132] Both are still in existence today. Many other manifestations of student seriousness exist. *The Megaphone* was an interesting, worthwhile piece of literature for students and is a useful historical source today. The yearbooks were well done, and the *Southwestern Magazine*, though irregular in its publication schedule, had substance.

On the other hand, incidents of another sort suggest something quite different. Student drinking continued to be a problem, and fraternity misconduct, to be dealt with in the next section, rose to significant proportions. From a perusal of the entire record, however, one emerges with the feeling that most student attempts to relieve the stress of academic life were of the more frivolous variety. April Fool's Day was turned into senior day, when absences from classes were not recorded against seniors, and "merrymaking" took place on a picnic ground on the San Gabriel.[133] Dancing was engaged in on the sly, much to the discomfiture of the more serious. Professor Tinsley said about it: "This Charleston has a grip on this country and if it isn't stopped I don't know what is to become of us."[134]

Putting on his psychologist's hat, Dean Ullrich observed a curious phenomenon in 1928 with regard to the grade averages of men and women. He noticed that the boys showed a higher level of ability as measured on the University of Texas Freshman Psychological Examination than the girls, the median being 41.00 and 37.11, respectively, but he also pointed out what had become common knowledge on campus since coeducation had been introduced some twenty years earlier, that "our girls on the whole make better grades than do our boys." He attributed it to the still too prevalent "notion that it is effeminate for boys to make good grades."[135]

With the appointment of Charles Messervie Edens in 1925 as Director of Athletics and Coach, Southwestern obtained the man who was to become the outstanding figure in Southwestern athletics prior to World War II and one of the greats in its entire history. Graduating from Southwestern in 1920 as a three-letter man, Edens came back from the North Texas Agricultural College in the fall of 1925 to assume direction of the athletic program.[136] A rare combination of personality and performance characteristics made him at once popular and successful. In his first year at Southwestern his football team won the Texas Intercollegiate Athletic Association championship. This success continued in the next few years, with championships in basketball, baseball, and tennis. During his career, he achieved as much as could be expected in his program considering the talent at his disposal and the conditions of the times. The death of "Lefty" Edens on July 29, 1939, from drowning on a fishing trip on the Colorado River cast the campus into utmost gloom.[137] It was the second death in five years of a beloved figure—first Kuykendall, then Edens.

"Fraternityism"—A "Problem in and of Itself"

If the fraternities thought that with the departure of Granbery they had gained the freedom to operate as they chose, they soon discovered differently. Major problems began to arise during the 1927–1928 academic year, and the faculty responded by bringing the matter to the Board of Trustees for action. Ullrich reported to the Board that men from the four legitimate fraternities had organized "an outlaw fraternity . . . to further drinking on the campus." He said that he was able to get rid of it after he made it known to everyone that he had secured a list of its members. At that point each student involved sought him out to avoid discipline by giving his word of honor that he would have nothing more to do with it. Eighteen boys were complicit in the effort, all but one of whom were fraternity members. Seven did not finish out the year, there was insufficient evidence to convict another seven, and four were allowed by the Honor Council to remain in school on probation on condition that they reveal their sources of supply. They did so, and the information secured was given to the County Attorney. The result was that one bootlegger was sentenced to two years in the penitentiary, two left for parts unknown, and another was still under confinement at the time of the report. Ullrich said that he had reliable information that drinking on campus had now practically ceased.[138]

Another issue arose late in the 1927–1928 academic year when the Pi Kappa Alphas received girls into the fraternity house in the absence of the housemother. On being confronted, "they confessed their dereliction, promised not to do so again, and asked to have their right to receive girls restored." The privilege was restored after all the actives and pledges signed the confession of guilt and promised once more, this time individually, not to do it again.[139]

Ullrich concluded his presentation by telling the Trustees that "fraternityism" had become the problem in and of itself. He said that the faculty and the dean feel "that the days of secret societies in Southwestern has passed unless fraternities change radically, so as to become assets rather than remain liabilities. For disciplinary reasons it became necessary this year to place fraternities on probation, and a number of fraternity men are expecting abolition." He said that even though the resolution passed in 1926 referring the whole matter "to the faculty for such action as they might see fit" gave them the authority to abolish the system, the faculty hesitated to resort to such an extreme remedy without conferring with the Board. With that, he placed the matter in their hands.[140]

The Board of Trustees for its part was equally unwilling to impose such an extreme remedy. Rather, it stated that the fraternities "should be required religiously to observe all of the rules and regulations prescribed by the faculty and suggest[ed] that the whole matter be left up to the faculty for discipline whenever necessary." This occasion in 1928 and its follow-up in 1929 are the only times the Board has been called upon to make an up or down decision on the existence of the fraternity system per se since it was first recognized in 1887. Interestingly, nothing was said at all about the sororities during the fracas, and it is not known whether or not they would have been included in a prohibition had one been enacted.[141]

The Threat to Academic Freedom

Though Southwestern was a strongly religious school from the time of its foundation, religious sentiment there was not dogmatic and had moved, during the administrations of Presidents Bishop and Horn, away from the notion that evangelizing its students was a part of its role. Nevertheless, its teachers were expected to uphold the Christian mission of the school. That mission might be interpreted differently than when it was first established by Mood, but it was still part of the intellectual underpinning of the University. Many of its instructors, such as Professors Howard and Godbey, were prominent Sunday School teachers. J. C. Godbey taught his Sunday School class more than a quarter of a century. Having been established in 1920, the class celebrated its twenty-seventh birthday at the First Methodist Church on March 10, 1947.[142] Southwestern's five ministerial Presidents and two lay Presidents were dedicated churchmen. President Barcus could say about his tenure in 1925 that "no teacher has been employed who is not a professed Christian and a member of the church." Neither Barcus nor Ullrich, however, operated on the basis of narrow doctrinal principles. Ullrich proudly reported to the Trustees at their 1927 meeting that the Faculty Club "had the pleasure of listening to Rabbi Lefkowitz of [the Temple Emanu-El of] Dallas on the subject: 'Where and How Can Liberal Jews and Liberal Christians Meet.'"[143]

Though Southwestern operated on the premise that to be distinctively Christian did not necessitate the denigration of other groups, argument within the Methodist Church in Texas was lively during the 1920s with respect to its own beliefs. The issue of precise doctrinal definition had seldom arisen within the Methodist Church as a whole prior to the twentieth century, but the rise of modern science, particularly the theory of evolution, the development of higher textual criticism, and the application of the historical approach to the Bible brought about a redefinition of some traditional doctrinal affirmations. These changes troubled certain segments of the Church and made them ready to sympathize with the fundamentalist movement that arose outside the Methodist Church shortly after the turn of the century. Fundamentalism insisted on a biblical literalism different from the conservative orthodoxy of the past. It singled out five main points as a kind of credo. They were: the literal infallible Bible, the Virgin Birth, the physical Resurrection of Christ, his Substitutionary Atonement, and the imminence of the Second Coming.[144] The movement's day in the national limelight against modernism was in the summer of 1925 at the Scopes trial in Dayton, Tennessee, where William Jennings Bryan won a Pyrrhic victory over Clarence Darrow.

Fundamentalism resonated differently in every denomination according to previous doctrinal standards and historical experience. It was not strong in the Methodist Church as a whole, but pockets of it could be found here and there. It also resonated differently in terms of the focus of activity in which the Church was involved. In terms of Church schools, the possibility of conflict with the principle of academic freedom was very real and extended beyond the area of theology. The breakdown of academic freedom in the teaching of religion in a college could very well lead to its demise in other areas as well. The risk run by religious groups in having colleges at all, at least colleges that were intellectually respectable, was the risk of allowing them to extend academic freedom into the area of religion as a teaching field. This risk was not deemed to be high prior to the intellectual and scientific developments just mentioned beginning around the middle of the nineteenth century, but came to be seen more and more clearly as a considerable risk by the beginning of the twentieth century. Some groups tried to lessen the risk by insisting that faculty members sign statements of faith.

Institutions of the Southern Methodist Church fared well as a whole in the struggle for academic freedom. Robert Glenn Massengale states that in his cursory examination of all the issues of the *Bulletin of the American Association of University Professors* from 1915 to 1939, not a single case is to be found of an institution of the Southern Methodist Church being investigated for a violation of the principles of academic freedom. The American Civil Liberties Union stated in 1940 that of the more than fifty instances of reported interference with freedom of expression in American colleges from 1926 to 1940, only one involved a Southern Methodist institution. It concluded that privately supported colleges "with a tradition of liberalism and a strong and tolerant president were the freest from censorship."[145]

An incident not fitting the criteria of either the A.A.U.P. *Bulletin* or the A.C.L.U. pamphlet, however, did occur at Southern Methodist University in 1921. One of its theology school professors, Dr. John A. Rice, received severe criticism for statements in his book *The Old Testament in the Life of Today*. The *Texas Christian Advocate* received so many letters condemning Dr. Rice that its editor finally announced that he would print no more of them. In its issue of November 1921, it printed a terse news item stating that

Dr. Rice had resigned as a member of the School of Theology a few weeks earlier and that he had been appointed to a church in the East Oklahoma Conference.[146]

As far as State educational institutions were concerned, academic freedom came to be considered especially precious as state governments came to be seen as possible and, in many cases, actual oppressors of academic freedom. As indicated earlier, the University of Texas experienced such a controversy during the time of President Bishop. Bishop led the Southwestern faculty on that occasion in adopting a resolution (1917) supporting President Vinson at Texas in his stand for academic freedom against overweening State forces. By early 1936 twenty-two states and the District of Columbia had some form of teachers' oaths.[147]

It was the fate of Southwestern during the Barcus administration to become involved in one of the academic freedom controversies that arose in Texas colleges during the decade. Its successful effort to prevent one of its sponsoring Annual Conferences from requesting the removal of a professor would set a precedent for the future of Southwestern and do more to establish the character of President Barcus in the minds of future generations than any other act taken during his administration. It also generated a reaction in the Church against prosecuting teachers who expressed unpopular ideas and prevented other such cases from developing. The controversy involved for Southwestern three persons—an inconspicuous recent graduate, Thomas Henry Gibbs, a longtime professor of religion, Herbert L. Gray, and its President, J. Sam Barcus.

How the Issue Arose

During the regular meeting of the West Texas Annual Conference in Austin on October 30, 1925, Gibbs, a former student of Professor Gray and later a student at SMU, presented himself for admission on trial into the conference. His application was debated on the floor by a number of ministers who spoke both for and against it. He was finally allowed to speak in his own behalf and made "a dramatic and eloquent appeal, during which tears flowed from many eyes." He indicated that he was willing to pour out his life for the Methodist Church, if it would let him. Addressing the central point to which his opponents objected, his unwillingness to state his belief in the Virgin Birth, he said: "You have asked me to answer the question 'yes' or 'no' about the conception and birth of Christ—and that I cannot do. I know that He was Holy and blessed by the breath of God and was absolutely divine, but whether there was a physical contact, I do not know." He was denied admission.[148]

This action by the West Texas Conference was the culmination of an increasing preoccupation by the Church at large with doctrine in the face of the increasing fundamentalist surge. The General Conference meeting in the spring of 1922 had adopted a series of resolutions affirming the "time-honored and universally accepted doctrines of our Church." It had requested that "all persons occupying seats of power work for the prevention of heretical teaching."[149] In the fall of the same year, following the adoption of a resolution asking for a committee "to investigate rumors of unorthodox teachings in some of our schools," the Texas Conference sent a visitation committee to Southwestern and elsewhere to investigate the teaching in its institutions of higher learning.[150] After conferring with President Horn, faculty members, and students at Southwestern, it issued a favorable report on it and the other schools under investigation.

The following year the Northwest Texas Conference passed a series of resolutions commending the Presidents of Southern Methodist University, Clarendon College, and McMurry College, "whose faculty members had signed a paper asserting their allegiance to the articles on doctrine." Conspicuous by its absence was the name of President Barcus of Southwestern, who, "apparently for reasons of conscience," along with Professor Gray, had refused to sign the document.[151] The document was in line with one of the standing rules of the Conference that read as follows:

> Before this Conference will consider making an appropriation to any institution of learning there must be placed in the hand of the conference secretary and the Chairman of the Board of Education the following statement signed by the president of the institution, the dean of each department, and all teachers of science . . . [that] . . . "there is no teacher in our school, within my knowledge, who believes or teaches that man had his origin in a lower form of animal life. All the teachers of our institution, within my knowledge, believe without mental reservation, equivocation, or without interpretation other than that of the accepted standards of our Methodist church in the inspiration of both Old and New Testaments and in every statement of the Apostles' Creed."[152]

Following its denial of admission on trial to Gibbs, the West Texas Conference voted to investigate Southwestern and Southern Methodist, the two schools attended by Gibbs. A five-person committee was named to conduct the investigation. It visited the campus and spoke with both Gray and Barcus. Its report in the fall of 1926 to the Conference exonerated Southern Methodist because its nine theological school professors all signed the "Statement Regarding Doctrinal Standards" prepared by the bishops. It was chastised, however, for knowingly having sent out some students whose views were "not in harmony with the teachings of Methodism." About Southwestern it simply remarked: "We are very sorry to say that Dr. H. L. Gray of Southwestern University was unwilling to sign the above statement regarding doctrinal standards."[153] As a result of Gray's failure to sign the document, a resolution was introduced at the Conference that he be asked to resign from Southwestern. A member of the committee stated that Gray did not believe in the Virgin Birth of Jesus Christ and that he felt it was not an essential belief. Gray was invited to speak on his own behalf and did so.

Professor Herbert Lee Gray, who was the subject of the academic freedom controversy of 1926–27. Southwestern University, Special Collections.

Herbert L. Gray—Character and Beliefs

At the momentous Board meeting in 1911 that saw the departure of President Hyer and the election of President Bishop, the Reverend Herbert Lee Gray was elected Professor of English Bible and Biblical Theology at Southwestern. A native of Georgia, he received an A.B. degree from Emory College in 1887, after which he served as a missionary to China for seven years. Upon his return he studied in the Theological Department of Vanderbilt and did ministerial work in Georgia. He once again entered missionary work and served in Mexico and Cuba until 1906, following which he taught at the Training School in Nashville, from which place he came to Georgetown. He spent the summer of 1909 at the University of Chicago.[154] Coming to Southwestern at the age of forty-two after fifteen years of missionary service in China, Mexico, and Cuba, he was in his mid-fifties when the controversy surrounding him broke in the 1920s, a mature man with most of his career already behind him. He retired in 1935 but continued to teach part-time until shortly before his death in 1943.

Except for his brief brush with fame in the controversy over his refusal to sign the statements of faith, Gray's career at Southwestern was unexceptional. He was not a major leader, but he was a well-loved and highly respected figure. He is reported in the newspaper as having addressed the Equal Suffrage League in Georgetown in 1916, where he criticized it for its support of Hughes as over against Wilson in the presidential election of that year.[155] He was one of the fourteen signers of the faculty resolution to the Board of Trustees in 1918 supporting the continuance of President Bishop.[156] He generally sided with Granbery in his attempts to curb or eliminate the fraternities[157] and was elected to serve with Granbery and Tinsley as one of the three professors to perform the presidential functions during Bishop's six-month leave of absence prior to his departure.[158]

Mrs. Annie Ethel Gray, his wife, had bad health and was not expected to live long. The faculty gave her and her husband a surprise party on their twenty-fifth wedding anniversary in 1924.[159] Soon thereafter she went to Canada for her health. In December 1926 the students took up a collection to send Dr. Gray to Canada to see her. *The Megaphone* reported that without their help, "Dr. Gray would not have been able to see his wife this year." They raised close to six hundred dollars for the trip.[160] The Grays sent them a letter of appreciation from Detroit dated January 1, 1927.[161] She died within the year and was buried in the Georgetown cemetery. He was laid to rest beside her sixteen years later.

Gray was a quiet, unostentatious man, but one who was secure in his convictions. Bishop John M. Moore, who presided at the session of the West Texas Conference that debated his case, felt strongly about him. He called him "a very devout man" and let it be known clearly that he stood for the academic freedom of the faculties of Methodist schools. Nevertheless, he could only preside with fairness as the proceedings of the Conference unrolled and had no power to interfere.[162]

Gray attempted to assuage whatever doubts may have been raised about him during the controversy by publishing his own 1,200-word creed, "A Statement of Personal Faith," in the *Southwestern Magazine* of November 1926. Using language from the traditional creeds and from scripture, he attempted to express what he felt was the received faith of the Church in a form that was not antithetical to historical accuracy and modern scientific knowledge. It was organized around ten "I believe" statements, a ten commandments of belief.

> I believe in God, the God and Father of our Lord Jesus Christ. . . .
>
> I believe that God's nature and man's nature are not separate and unlike; but that man is God's child made in the image and likeness of God, and that God is the indwelling Ground and Source of all human life. . . .
>
> I believe in the Holy Spirit of the Christlike God, energizing unceasingly in the heart, mind, and will of men,—all men, but especially of those who love and obey God. . . .
>
> I believe that "God was in Christ reconciling the world unto Himself," bearing our burdens and our sins. . . .
>
> I believe in the communion of saints, the church universal composed of all loving hearts everywhere. . . .
>
> I believe in the immortality of the soul, the preservation of our personal identity and the conservation of the eternal values of personality. . . .
>
> I believe in the progressive revelation of the mind and heart of God through the ages, mediated to us through the experience of men and of nations, and especially through the divinely endowed souls of the Hebrew prophets, poets, and apostles, culminating in the person and life and teachings of Jesus Christ. . . .
>
> I believe that human selfishness is the root of all the moral evils of the world. . . .
>
> I believe that the forces of nature are the forces of God and the processes of nature are God's methods of working, so that there is no nature without God and there is no chasm between nature and the supernatural. . . . Nevertheless, the God who is immanent in nature is also transcendent. . . .
>
> I believe that a man's creed must be vital, the expression of life and producing life. . . .
>
> Therefore, the things above stated are the things I live by and by the grace of God shall die by; and they are the things I can give to my students and to my children after me in the hope that these things will grip their minds and hearts as they have mine.[163]

After his retirement, shortly before his death in 1943, Professor Gray presented to the Southwestern University library five manuscripts of material dear to him. All are in typescript and range in length from 59 to 135 pages. The manuscript entitled "The God Within" is the most complete and polished statement of his beliefs and probably comes closer to addressing the issues involved in the controversy than any other. In one of its key passages, Gray touches on progressive revelation and the concept of inerrancy. He says:

> The natural extension of the historical study of the individual books of the Bible is the study of the development of specific ideas from period to period, from thinker to thinker, under the pressure of great crises of history and by the inspiration of great movements of of [sic] thought among various nations. The thought of the progressive development of conceptions of God, of man, of human rights and duties, of sin and salvation, of the future life and of other fundamental moral and religious ideas may be repugnant to the minds of those who believe in an inerrant revelation, given to man in the beginning of human life

> upon earth; but such a thought is quite in harmony with the facts of the psychological development of the individual. . . . Men may be truly inspired without being infallible.[164]

Outcome of the Controversy

Gray's statement on the Conference floor did not satisfy those who were partial to the fundamentalist approach, but Gray had a number of elements working in his favor. His long service in the Church and on the mission field, the significant number of ministers serving in the Conference who had studied under him, his exemplary personal life and piety, and the personal support of the presiding bishop were helpful. He was no recently minted student asking for admission into the Conference but a seasoned and respected veteran who had fought in the trenches over the years. Of greatest help was the fact that his President, J. Sam Barcus, stood firmly with him on the issue.

Before the vote was taken on the resolution asking for the resignation of Gray, Barcus was asked to address the Conference. He had expected that he might be given this opportunity and was ready when called upon. Reading a previously prepared paper to the assembly, he offered a strong defense of Gray and of academic freedom. In it he took the offensive and painted their opponents rather than themselves as standing outside of the Methodist tradition. He mentioned how the signing of the paper by the professors at SMU had settled nothing. Only two of the committee members were present when they signed it, and one of these admitted that the act of signing did not satisfy him. The members of the committee, he suggested, were after something deeper than the mere signing of a paper. If they were not prepared to accept the signatures of those professors as satisfactory, what was it they were really seeking? The document, he suggested, was really a cover for something more fundamental. They wanted him and Gray to agree to an underlying theological position with which neither of them and, by implication, the Methodist Church were in accord. They did not and would not sign a paper to get rid of an issue if by so doing they might be implying that they agreed with that deeper position.

Then Barcus focused on what he said were the weaknesses in the paper itself. In its introductory statement it alleged that "there can be no doubt as to what we as Methodists believe and what our preachers should proclaim." He then pointed out instance after instance where this claim to unanimity of belief broke down, from the issue of human depravity to the ritual of baptism, from trying to describe the punishment of the wicked to the doctrine of holiness.

He also pointed out the very unfairness of the document. Why should professors in colleges alone be required to sign it? Why were bishops, presiding elders, pastors, and Sunday School teachers not required to sign it? Did they not have responsibilities as important as those of college teachers? And if people who have never been trained in colleges have a better knowledge of science and philosophy than those who have attended, why build colleges at all? Is it wise for popular bodies, such as Conferences, to pass on questions of scientific and biblical accuracy? Is it prudent for committees appointed by these bodies to write questionnaires that must be answered only in terms that they can approve? "Is it not better to commit the whole matter of teacher qualification to the trustees of the institution?" Barcus flooded the assembled ministers and laymen with so many questions that they lost track of where Gray fitted into the argument in an effort to answer these questions in their own minds. They became, so Barcus implied, more culpable than Gray if they condemned him while being unsure themselves on these points.

Barcus then reversed the argument. He ended his address by stating that the very thing they were questioning—not putting restrictions on its members to seek after truth—was the glory of Methodism.

> In the Roman Catholic Church the very form of doctrinal teaching is regarded as infallible. It has never been so regarded by Methodists. True, we have an official form of doctrine, but any member has the privilege of suggesting a better form. In this respect Southwestern is a Methodist institution. She never asks a president, when elected to office, to confine his thinking and speaking to certain schools of thought. She never attempts to tell her teachers what they must regard as true and what as false. She has always sought to select men of scholarship and Christian character and set them free to find and teach the truth. The result has been highly satisfactory to the Church. With very rare exceptions, the preachers and teachers whom she has sent forth have adorned the Church by upright living and faithful service.[165]

The resolution to ask for Gray's resignation was turned down by a margin of 128 to 79, 62 percent to 38 percent.

Effect of the Barcus Stand

The controversy involving Gibbs, Gray, and Barcus has sometimes been portrayed as a heresy trial. It was not that at all. None of the three men was ever accused of heresy, and there was no trial. The question of heresy may have hovered in the air around the issue, but it was finally a question of an Annual Conference deciding for itself whether or not, in the case of Gibbs, a postulant satisfied its standards for membership. These standards were set in terms of doctrine, personal morals, and professional training. Whether or not the Conference acted correctly in denying admission to Gibbs is another matter. But it had the right to make the choice.

The extension of its action on Gibbs to involve Gray, however, brought it into conflict with the principle of academic freedom. The question with regard to him was not of admission into an Annual Conference. Gray was already a member in good standing. The issue was that if the Conference voted affirmatively to request his resignation on the basis of his classroom teaching, it would be curtailing his academic freedom. It was the successful countereffort by Barcus to dissuade the Conference from making such a request that was important. It marked the end of such efforts on the part of the Texas Annual Conferences to seek signed statements of faith and the like.

Within a week after the conclusion of the controversy in the West Texas Conference, the Northwest Texas Conference struck its earlier standing rule that had required Presidents, deans, and teachers of Bible, sociology, and science to sign a statement in order for their institutions to receive Conference allotments. In its place it formally gave to the Trustees of Methodist institutions of learning the responsibility for attending to the character of its faculty members.[166]

Dean Ullrich exulted in the outcome of the controversy. He wrote in his Board report for 1927 that

> the greatest single event of the year was the vindication of the right of Southwestern teachers to a sane freedom of thought and of teaching, subject to the best of its working in the life of the individual and of the institution. One of the faculty, Professor H. L. Gray, head of the department of Bible and Religion, who is completing seventeen years of service to the college, became an object of attack in the West Texas Conference. In the fight he was compelled to make, he received the hearty support of the President and of an almost unanimous faculty and student body, as well as of his old students who are now members of the West Texas Conference; and the final result was a very gratifying expression of the Conference's faith in Southwestern University and in the trustworthiness of its faculty and administrative officers to be entrusted with our high responsibilities. We ask for freedom only to do our highest and best work for a Christlike God and for humanity; and we rejoice that this has not been withheld from us.[167]

The Barcus Resignation and Election of a New President

After serving only four-and-a-half years, J. Sam Barcus handed in his resignation, to become effective August 15. His was one of the most tumultuous tenures of any President on record. For a man whose first love was the pastorate, he had performed in remarkable fashion. At the faculty meeting on July 27, with Barcus presiding, the faculty, without nomination, elected Professor Tinsley as Acting President by a vote of 9 to 7 over Dean Ullrich.[168] On September 20, 1928, the Board of Trustees unanimously elected Joseph King Vivion as its next President.[169] He appeared before the Board and was immediately installed.[170]

Holding On during the Great Depression (1928–1935)

The Place of King Vivion in Southwestern's History

During the administrations of Presidents Bishop, Horn, and Barcus, from 1911 to 1928, Southwestern acquired a set of teachers and administrators whose contributions in riding out the storm of the Great Depression fully matched the efforts of the first generation of leaders in making its establishment successful. The perseverance of administrators such as Ullrich, Meyer, Neas, Kuykendall, Ferguson, and McCook, accompanied by the loyalty of teachers such as Godbey, Howard, Hester, Williams, and Edens, brought Southwestern through perhaps the most critical financial period in its history. Yet little recognition has been given to the person who led them through that storm—Joseph King Vivion. It might be too much to say that without him the effort would not have been successful, but it is certainly true to say that a better person could hardly have been found.

Almost as important, Vivion was at the helm when the institution weathered the last two attempts to move it from Georgetown. His consistent and astute leadership was a major reason the conference educational commission handed down its decision in February 1934 that Southwestern would not be moved. That decision finally put an end to almost twenty-five years of discussion about moving the University. Because Vivion did not serve long years at Southwestern and because his effort was basically one of preservation, of keeping the institution from "going under" rather than of leaving some more innovative or tangible legacy, his name has not been generally accorded the attention he deserves. But he was truly an important figure in Southwestern history.

President Joseph King Vivion. Vivion was at the helm when Southwestern weathered the last two attempts to move it from Georgetown. Southwestern University, Special Collections.

Joseph King Vivion—The Man

In many respects King Vivion was an unlikely candidate to lead Southwestern through the Great Depression and a major set of removal controversies. He was only a thirty-two-year-old minister when elected and did not, unlike Barcus, have much experience or a previous Southwestern connection. He was a Missourian and his three degrees came from other institutions, two of them from Southern Methodist University. He knew President Hyer there but such knowledge was not necessarily a positive recommendation for him in the eyes of some persons when his name was first proposed as a candidate for the presidency of Southwestern.

Toward the middle of his first year as President, Vivion recounted for a *Megaphone* reporter an early contact with

Dr. Hyer. He was a nineteen-year-old theology school student at SMU in his first year when it occurred. Hyer caught him one day "trying vainly," he puts it, "to anchor some victim's trunk at half mast to the university flag pole." In his struggle to get the steamer trunk into place, he failed to note Hyer's approach. Hyer asked him, "Won't you ever grow up?" Vivion responded, "I don't know, Dr. Hyer. It doesn't look that way, does it[?]" When asked by Hyer if he could see him in his office the next morning at eight, Vivion responded promptly, "Yes, sir."[1]

The venturesome spirit revealed in this episode, coupled with a personality both self-deprecatory and cautiously witty, made him popular with people wherever he went. Later, in a time of depression, they enjoyed his positive spirit. Harriet Winton Vivion, his wife, referred to his humorous side in an article about him in the *Southwestern Magazine* shortly after their arrival at Southwestern. She said that "being a Scotchman, King likes his Scotch jokes."[2] In the middle 1940s, when I, as a teenager, knew him as my pastor at McKendree Methodist Church in Nashville, Tennessee, Vivion was a vibrant, medium-height person with a mane of white hair who walked rapidly with his head slightly bent down as if in thought or out of deference to anyone he might encounter. He spoke with a pronounced Scottish burr and paid anyone a penny that told him a Scottish joke he could use from the pulpit.[3]

Vivion was born during a meeting of a Quarterly Conference held at his father's church on February 16, 1896, in Southwest City, Missouri. Because the Rev. Joseph King was preaching a revival at his father's church at the time, the baby was given the name Joseph King Vivion. He used his regal name, King, to advantage the rest of his life. To encourage scholarship among the males at Southwestern, he personally purchased a house back of Mood Hall where ten worthy boys could live and, by making "A" grades, pay no rent. It was called "King's Palace." The Board of Trustees bought it from him at the time of his resignation in 1935, though full payment for it had still not been completed in 1943.[4]

One year after his graduation from high school in 1913, his mother died. He was licensed to preach the same year. At Drury College, where he graduated with a B.A. in 1916, he was good at Greek and won a prize for it. After one semester at Emory, he transferred to the new Southern Methodist University. While there he joined a dramatic club. There was a dramatic flair about Vivion during his entire life that he exhibited in some of the things he did at Southwestern and in his pastorates. At his big downtown church in Nashville after leaving Southwestern, he conducted Sunday evening services during the summer on the front lawn of the church in the heart of the city. Passersby on the main street often stopped to hear the fine music from the choir and the sermon of the big-chested man with the booming voice.

During World War I he was commissioned as a Second Lieutenant of Infantry and was assigned to duty as a Company Commander in the Student Army Training Corps at Rice Institute. Upon his discharge, he returned to SMU, where he completed Bachelor of Divinity and Master of Arts degrees in 1919. After graduation he worked with one of his brothers as a guide in Yellowstone Park. He also held religious services nearly every Sunday for the tourists. His first appointment as a minister was to Bryan, Texas, in the fall of 1919, where he was sent to organize a church for Texas A&M. He was appointed to College Station the next year. Because there was no church building, he established Sunday night services in the Electrical Engineering building. Having met and married his wife while there, he built a house for his family and helped build a wooden structure for church services. During his time at College Station, his fellow ministers recognized him as a "comer," and he was sent in the fall of 1924 to Jacksonville, Texas. Two years later he went to First Church, Galveston, where he was stationed when Southwestern called him to the presidency two years later. By that time he had earned three academic degrees and had done work three summers at the University of Chicago toward a Ph.D. In later years he was awarded the D.D. and L.L.D. degrees.

Vivion's name was not initially among those being considered for the presidency. A newspaper report of mid-July mentions as candidates Dr. W. J. Johnson, a prominent pastor in Wichita Falls, Dr. Frank Onderdonk, an alumnus whose career as a minister and worker among the Spanish-speaking population will be discussed later, and the Rev. W. Angie Smith, an alumnus serving as pastor in El Paso.[5] Smith was later elected a bishop. Vivion's rise to prominence in Texas, however, was so pronounced that when Bishop Hay presented it to the Board, he was elected unanimously. That he was well known beyond Texas is proved by the fact that he had already been offered but had declined the pastorate of McKendree Church, Nashville, Tennessee, regarded as the mother church of Southern Methodism.[6] He did go to McKendree in 1935 after his seven years at Southwestern. Following a long pastorate there of seventeen years, he subsequently served several prominent churches in Kentucky and Georgia.

Vivion was one of the three ex-presidents who returned to Southwestern for the dedication of the Cody Memorial Library and the Centennial Celebration in 1940. Upon his retirement he returned to Springfield, Missouri, close to where he was born. He died there on January 27, 1969, at the age of seventy-two.[7] Vivion was in much demand as a speaker during his career. He preached regularly throughout the state while at Southwestern. Illustrative of his popularity as a speaker is the summer of 1933, when he preached Commencement sermons at three colleges—Centenary, Blinn Memorial, and Baylor.[8]

When Vivion was announced as the new President of Southwestern, Judge W. L. Dean of Huntsville, President of the Board of Trustees, said that the Board was guided in its selection by Vivion's "common sense, youth, energy, enthusiasm, high ideals, and religious life."[9] Though he was installed as President within a week after his election, the inauguration occurred a year later, on June 3, 1929. The faculty and delegates donned their academic regalia at the Woman's Building. Then, headed by the Southwestern band, they marched to the Main Building, where the inauguration was held. Governor Dan Moody gave a greeting, and President Emeritus Charles M. Bishop gave the opening prayer and benediction.[10]

A Quarter Century of Removal Controversies

The removal controversy of 1910–1911 was so fraught with emotion and surprising consequences that it has been common to think of it as a two-year disturbance that Southwestern, though weaker as a result of the outcome, soon put behind it. It was, in fact, the beginning of a series of removal attempts that lasted almost twenty-five years, from 1910 to 1934. The possibility of removal persisted in some circles like a low-grade fever, with rumors of removal surfacing from time to time, such as the one already mentioned in 1920 during the Bishop administration. The question of removal arose again in early 1928 just before the departure of Barcus, more serious this time than in 1920. Vivion inherited it from Barcus when he assumed office. By the end of October 1929, he and those who thought like him had beaten it down. Three years later, in October 1932, it arose again, this time more serious than at any time since 1910–1911. After a year and a half of struggle, they beat it down once more. Whether or not the controversy would have arisen yet again had not the University freed itself from debt is a hypothetical question without an assured answer, but the fact is that within two years it did free itself from debt. The issue never arose again.

There were, however, some major differences between the later struggles and the earlier one. In 1910–1911, the Southwestern community was divided on the issue. The President, the chair of the Board, and a majority of ministers were for removal. The dean, most Trustees, and most alumni were against it. In the struggles of 1928–1929 and 1932–1934, the Southwestern community was united against removal and was led by the President in a campaign to defeat it. In the earlier attempt, the issue arose from an interchange between two schools, Polytechnic and Southwestern, and only involved the Church at large as the issue developed. In the latter attempts, the issue arose from the Church at large and involved not one or two schools but all the Methodist institutions of higher learning in Texas. The former struggle was waged in relatively good times, and the primary force promoting change was the desire of Fort Worth and Dallas to enhance their economic development by attracting Southwestern to move to those cities. The motive force in the latter two struggles was the desire of the Church itself to rationalize its educational enterprise in harsh economic times. In the first removal attempt, the issue assumed highly emotional overtones and resulted in broken friendships and recriminations. In the last two removal attempts, emotional overtones were largely kept in check even in the face of high tension. The possibility of Southwestern's removal from Georgetown was the one constant in all the controversies, but, beyond that, each controversy was unique.

Decline in the Number of Small Colleges

The decade of the 1920s was not kind to small, Church-related colleges. Located mostly in small towns, they could not compete with the attractions provided by institutions located in cities. The emergence of State institutions also provided a comparatively cheap alternative to private education. Southern Methodist University opened in 1915 with several hundred more collegiate-level students than Southwestern had after forty-two years of existence. By the early 1920s, SMU had several thousand students, while Southwestern was only just holding its own in enrollment.

Even Baylor, as discussed earlier, had a removal controversy in 1928, and barely missed being moved to Dallas. The proposed change for Baylor was part of a general shakeup in Southern Baptist higher education. In the thirteen months prior to 1928 the Southern Baptists had lost thirteen institutions across the South and had been compelled to reduce ten others to the rank of junior colleges. In ten years thirty-six of its institutions had been closed, and five others were at the point of closing by the end of the 1928 session.[11]

The decline in the number of small Methodist colleges in the 1920s was not a new trend. In the history of Methodist education in Texas more than seventy colleges had existed for various periods of time. Only nine or ten, depending on one's definition of a college, still existed in Texas in 1929.

Background of the New Removal Controversy

Though the individual Annual Conferences owned the different Methodist colleges and operated them through autonomous boards of trustees, the Church as a whole attempted to weld them into a Church-wide system through the General Board of Education, located in Nashville. Meetings of the college presidents from the entire Church were held under its auspices from time to time. The Board supplied other services as well. Each college provided a basic statistical report each year to the Board. These data were compiled and distributed to the member colleges and to the boards of education of the Annual Conferences. The College Section of the General Board elected a president each year. President Vivion of Southwestern was the elected head of that unit in 1935.[12]

Through this information sharing and planning mechanism, each Annual Conference not only learned about its own college, but also about how it fared in relation to the entire system of colleges. Because of the worsening situation of most colleges during the late 1920s and early '30s, the General Board conducted detailed surveys of all Methodist colleges in cooperation with the Annual Conferences from 1928 through 1934. Dr. B. Warren Brown conducted the earlier surveys, while the later ones were by Boyd M. McKeown.[13]

While the surveys were being conducted, the five Texas Annual Conferences were taking steps of their own to unify their enterprise in higher education. At three meetings in 1928, and after approval by the conferences, an Educational Commission was set up and basic ground rules adopted for Texas Methodist colleges. One of those rules was that no college could be conducted as a Grade A college unless it had an endowment of $500,000 by January 1, 1933.[14] The Commission consisted of members appointed for four years: the resident bishops, the presidents of the colleges in the system, the presidents of the conference boards of education, and a minister and layman from each conference. The charge of the Commission was to carry out the wishes of the conferences as to correlation, finances, buildings, and other items.[15] Chaired by Bishop John M. Moore and with President King Vivion as a member, the newly constituted Commission met in late December 1928 to undertake its work. There was an implicit understanding at the outset that the most important part of its work was to study the consolidation and/or elimination of existing institutions.[16] For this purpose, it invited Dr. Brown to come to Texas and to formulate his assessment of the situation.

Effect of an Erroneous News Report

News of Brown's impending arrival in Dallas and of the supposed contents of the report he would issue appeared in an Associated Press dispatch printed in the *Dallas News* on January 12, 1929, two days before he came. Other newspapers throughout the state immediately picked it up and published it. On January 14, the day Brown arrived in Dallas, the *Austin American* was already publishing the reaction of Georgetown people to the supposed contents of a report that had not yet been issued.[17] The actual status of Brown's survey and whether or not he even had a report when he arrived are unknown. He had already issued detailed survey instruments to the nine Methodist colleges participating in the study and had presumably received their data. When Bishop Moore later referred to Brown's work in a newspaper article of January 25, he said that Brown was now in Texas assembling his data.

The supposed plan as described by the Associated Press was to join Southwestern with Southern Methodist and to rename it Southwestern. It would head the Methodist schools in the state. Coming to Dallas would be the name, the fifty-six-year history, and the $400,000 indebtedness of the Georgetown institution. Its indebtedness, said the supposed report, has become "a thorn in the side of Methodism. . . . It is recommended that the buildings there [in Georgetown] be used as an industrial school or a school for women."[18] The source of this scenario as portrayed in the newspaper article was not identified.

Fearing the harm that the fallacious news in the article could do to Southwestern, President Vivion immediately refuted it. He called a meeting of the faculty, so the secretary records, "and begged that we 'keep cool' and stated that he believed everything would come out all right."[19] He then joined with Dean Ullrich to put out a joint statement to the *Dallas News* and *The Megaphone*.[20] In it they stated that the Educational Commission had met only one time, in December. At that meeting it had set up three committees to study future action but had not discussed a plan. Whatever plan might eventually come out of the Commission would have to be approved by the five Annual Conferences in any case. Vivion charged that the press dispatches presuming to prognosticate the future action of the Commission were erroneous. "There is every reason to expect," he concluded, "that Southwestern is permanently located at Georgetown and will grow and develop as a coeducational college of the highest rank, with limited enrollments."[21] In his statement Vivion laid down for the general public, and, by extension, for the Educational Commission, the line he would adhere to through the entire controversy. He would not support any Commission report that contemplated the transfer of Southwestern to any other city.

Vivion took one further step to assuage the turmoil caused in Georgetown. He invited Warren Brown to come to Southwestern to make a chapel talk. In that talk, Brown explained the purpose and work of the Educational Commission. "He [also] warned students not to believe false newspaper reports in regard to moving church schools. He stated that 'no definite move would be made for a few years.'"[22] Even as late as early June, however, Dean Ullrich stated in his annual report that there has been a "general restlessness caused by repeated rumors that the school would not remain permanently at Georgetown."[23]

Southwestern officials were not the only ones displeased with the erroneous newspaper report of January 12. Officials at Southern Methodist were now eighteen years removed from a desire to take the Southwestern name, and President Selecman issued a statement saying that the article in the *Dallas Morning News* was without foundation.[24]

Bishop John M. Moore, chair of the Educational Commission, felt compelled to protect the future work of the Commission by making a long, comprehensive statement about the erroneous news report. His purpose was to inform the constituency of the Church fully about the work of the Commission and what it was attempting to do. He discussed the invitation extended by the Commission to Dr. B. Warren Brown, "the expert survey secretary of the general board," and denied that there was a predetermined outcome to his work. About the reporter who wrote the Associated Press article, he asked: "Why did he not say that Southwestern would be moved to San Antonio where an A grade college is greatly needed? There is as much chance of it going there as to Dallas. But there is a greater chance that it will not be moved at all. Georgetown is an excellent location for such a college as Southwestern is and has been." He said, however, that the indebtedness question is very real for Southwestern wherever it is. "If its entire indebtedness can be paid and then its endowment increased by $750,000 to $1,000,000, Southwestern will almost certainly, not be moved from Georgetown."[25]

In his statement Moore touches on what he conceives to be the nub of the question. It is a question of finances, not of location per se. If it were not for its indebtedness and lack of endowment, there would be no thought of moving Southwestern. Eight years later his conditions would be met, and there has, indeed, been no thought of moving Southwestern since that time. For the moment, however, even before Southwestern had achieved these conditions, one senses that Moore is unwilling to consider moving Southwestern absent compelling circumstances. With Vivion, a new, energetic president who has, before the onset of the economic depression, temporarily improved the financial situation of Southwestern, Moore appears to be saying that the reasons for moving Southwestern must be based on more than the theoretical possibility of improvement.

Outcome of the Controversy

After the inauspicious beginning of Brown's work and Moore's attempt to put the work of the Educational Commission back on track, records are silent as to occurrences during the next three months. Something must have been happening, however, because Vivion felt compelled by the end of April to assemble a group of supporters to establish a program for maintaining Southwestern in Georgetown. A newspaper report states that about forty persons met in Georgetown on April 20 and "made a compact to preserve and perpetuate the institution." The event was highly publicized, and articles appeared in most major newspapers about it. One newspaper put the number of attendees at thirty-five, another at thirty-seven.

The businessmen, educators, ministers, and politicians who formed the group were carefully chosen alumni and friends who had achieved status in their fields and whose names would be recognized at the state level. One article affirms that the leaders of the Democratic and Republican Parties put aside their differences for the moment and joined in the cause. They were D. W. Wilcox, the state Democratic chairman, and R. B. Creager, State Republican national executive committeeman, both ex-students of Southwestern. The group adopted a declaration for the "17,000 ex-students" stating that Southwestern "must and shall be preserved as a class A college in Georgetown." In light of Bishop Moore's statement that there would be no thought of moving Southwestern except for its financial situation, the group determined to remedy that situation. It stated that the debts of the University must be paid and an adequate endowment established. A committee of seven was chosen to formulate plans. They were J. M. West, Sr., of Houston, E. L. Kurth of Keltys, J. W. Reynolds of Houston, W. A. Tarver of Corsicana, R. B. Creager of Brownsville, E. L. Crain of Houston, and Julius Germany of Dallas.[26] All except for West had been students at Southwestern, and West had adopted the school for his own, as illustrated by his many benefactions to it over the years. A year later the committee promulgated its plan for a major financial campaign.

With a dynamic young president in place and a strong committee at work planning a major financial campaign, any previous sentiment within the state for moving Southwestern appears to have evaporated. The formation of an alumni committee of well-known names was as much as to say that Southwestern alumni would not stand by quietly if an attempt should be made to move the University. Removal talk disappeared, and things remained quiet until a final meeting of the Educational Commission in Dallas on October 22. A newspaper article reporting the meeting said that "it was evident that no recommendation would be made for the consolidation of any of the major schools of the State, if, indeed, there would be any consolidation at all."

Bishop Moore referred to the possibility that the Presbyterians would "build a big Protestant school" in San Antonio.[27] Moore had obviously been in contact with Presbyterian leaders who were discussing the transfer to San Antonio of Trinity, a Presbyterian school in Waxahachie, long before it did move in 1942. In that year the Southwest Texas Conference voted to donate the University of San Antonio, the former Westmoorland College, to the Presbyterians. It became part of the new Trinity University there. The predisposition of Bishop Moore that Southwestern should remain in Georgetown and the almost unanimous alumni sentiment led by a determined president for that position killed any possibility that the Educational Commission would recommend its transfer to another city. The Commission died a quiet death.

One of the puzzling matters for the investigator today is the presence of a Brown report from these years in the records of the Methodist Board of Education in Nashville, where Robert Glenn Massengale found it while pursuing his doctoral work in 1950. That report was never, so far as is known, presented to any Texas Church leader or group. Both Ralph Jones, the author of the first major history of Southwestern, and I learned about the Brown report from Massengale. Ralph Jones, however, *assumed* that the Brown recommendations contained in the report became known in Texas and that the actions of the 1929 participants in the controversy were based on that knowledge.[28] Nevertheless, neither the report nor its contents are ever mentioned in any of the Texas records, and the actions of the participants, especially that of Bishop Moore, do not seem to be based on knowledge of its contents.[29]

Temporary Deferment of Depression Woes

Only two days after the last meeting of the Educational Commission, Black Thursday initiated the stock market crash of October 29, 1929. Southwestern, however, was not immediately affected. Few of its assets were tied up in Wall Street stocks, and the ripple effect that eventually affected everything was not felt strongly until the second half of 1930. The financial report for mid-1929 was, if anything, a little better than that of the previous year, though the school was further behind in payments of principal to the Missouri State Life Insurance Company for the note on the Woman's Building.

Vivion stated at the midyear meeting of the Board before the crash that the first priority of the University should be to pay off its indebtedness, after which it needed "a minimum of two million dollars for endowment."[30] This figure had been set by the committee of seven prominent alumni that had been put in place in April of the previous year during the removal controversy. The plan was to raise $100,000 a year, presumably for twenty years.[31] It was considered to be an extension of the Greater Southwestern Campaign of Barcus and was called by that name.[32] The campaign was independent of a parallel attempt to eliminate the indebtedness of somewhat more than $500,000.[33] In this regard, a concerted effort was begun to repay the money owed by the University to itself. Before 1935 it had redeemed its own notes for funds advanced to build Mood Hall and the East Wing of the Annex a quarter of a century earlier.[34]

All in all, if looked at from the standpoint of indebtedness, the financial situation of the University improved during the first year and a half of the Vivion administration. An audit conducted at its beginning compared with one conducted nineteen months later reveals the following change:[35]

Indebtedness Category	8/31/1928	3/31/1930	Improvement
Owed insurance companies and banks for plant	$286,095.55	$263,539.41	+$22,556.14
Owed insurance companies and banks for operations	28,169.86	15,257.23	+ 12,912.63
Due to other University funds for plant	60,156.15	68,274.21	- 8,118.06
Due to other University funds for operations	70,603.01	58,744.81	+ 11,858.20
Other operational debts	815.00	4,683.67	- 3,868.67
Deficit to Surplus	108,110.92	76,373.47	+ 31,737.45
TOTAL	$554,950.49	$486,872.80	+$68,077.69

Taking the "Deficit to Surplus" category as being a bookkeeping rather than a real improvement, the finance committee congratulated "the President and his co-workers for reducing the indebtedness of the University by something like $35,000, actually $36,340.24, during the year." Vivion, however, recognized that the improvement was small compared with the need. He said that when the debt was subtracted from the endowment, "we have practically nothing."[36] In addition, payments of $50,000 to the Missouri State Life Insurance Company, $27,500 to banks, and $7,700 to annuity interest loomed on the immediate horizon. Nevertheless, in comparison with some earlier years and the economic situation of the country, the University had performed reasonably well.

I. J. McCook, business manager. The Southern Association's report of 1934 said that he was "a wide-awake, intelligent officer with a splendid conception of his duties and efficient in the exercise of them." From the 1933 *Sou'wester.*

Isaac Joel McCook—Dedication and Quiet Competence in Finance

Probably the most important appointment made by Vivion during his tenure as President was that of Isaac Joel McCook, who became business manager on September 1, 1929. A native of Louisiana, I. J. McCook was educated at Louisiana State University. Though his later honorary Doctor of Commercial Science degree received from Daniel Baker College in 1946 was not in itself a strong honor, having been received the same year that Daniel Baker became a part of the Southwestern University system, McCook's personal demeanor and stature at Southwestern was such that no one questioned the appropriateness of calling him "Doctor Mac."

McCook had been with one of Kurth's lumber companies in Pineland for eight years when, according to Grogan Lord, Kurth sent him to the University "on a salvage operation."[37] Contracted only two months before Black Thursday, McCook served the University thirty-nine years, retiring in 1968 as Vice President, Finance. Working under five Presidents, he became the man behind the scenes who managed institutional funds on a day-to-day basis and quietly worked with them and the Trustees to develop the courses of action best calculated to further the financial interests of the University. They trusted him because they knew of his unswerving dedication to the interests of the school, because of his unassuming manner, and because he knew about the past and present intricacies of Southwestern finance better than any other person. One of his first acts as business manager was to study carefully its financial records as far back as adequate documentation allowed, to the beginning of the Bishop administration in 1911.

McCook became a nonvoting member of the Executive Committee in 1935 and served as secretary of that body for most of the time until his retirement. He also attended meetings of the Board of Trustees and kept its records in meticulous fashion. His appointment coincided with placing the finances of the University on a strictly cash basis and reorganizing the financial system. He maintained a strict budget each year and administered it with scrupulous integrity and attention to detail. A senior skit at a chapel program on April 9, 1932, attributed McCook's nonappearance in the skit to the fact "that somebody dropped a nickel behind the piano just before he was scheduled to go on the stage and he spent the rest of the hour hunting for it."[38]

In spite of the lampooning of his thrifty practices by the students, McCook was in fact a warm and modest man. He and his wife, Maymie, entertained the faculty at Christmastime every year with a reception at their home. They were also responsive to the needs of faculty members in distress. After John Granbery was dismissed from the University in 1938, he and May continued to live in Georgetown for several years before moving to San Antonio. During that time what income they received was sporadic, and their financial situation was shaky. Writing from Georgetown in mid-1939 to John, who was away on a speaking trip, May said: "Mrs. McCook comes around each morning to see if I want to do any errands."[39] Shortly before McCook's retirement in 1968, Mrs. Alma Thomas, one of Southwestern's most generous patrons, wrote him saying that she had felt closer to him than to anyone else on the Executive Committee or the Board of Trustees. "It has always been easy for me to talk to you," she said. ". . . I can't imagine Southwestern University without you. When you retire that really will be a sad day."[40]

McCook was respected by Trustees and outside observers. The Southern Association report of 1934 said that he was "a wide-awake, intelligent officer with a splendid conception of his duties and efficient in the exercise of them. . . . The Committee considers Mr. McCook one of the most capable business officers it has seen in its several studies this year."[41] A great deal of Southwestern's success in emerging from indebtedness and remaining solvent thereafter was due to him. He it was who drove from Georgetown to Houston on the last Sunday evening in February 1937 to deliver the next day, March 1, 1937, the deadline date, the final documentation attesting to Southwestern's having met all the conditions for receiving the Wiess gift that changed the fortunes of the University.

Critical Changes in Financial Operations

When asked by Ralph Jones in the late 1950s to characterize the financial situation of the University when he arrived, McCook wrote as follows:

> When I reported in the Summer of 1929 to assume the duties of Business Manager, I had the opportunity of gaining an immediate insight into the financial condition of the institution by assisting the Independent Auditors with the annual audit. It was a shocking experience to discover that of the total Endowment of \$313,397, \$41,420 had been used for plant construction without much prospect of repayment of principal and no interest; that of the total Annuity Funds of \$110,000, \$75,618 had been used by Current Funds to cover debts created by prior years' deficits amounting to \$107,116; that the Current General Fund owed banks and other creditors \$32,825 with assets of only \$1,279; that the entire plant was mortgaged to an Insurance Co. for \$279,039. Thus, indebtedness, exclusive of interfund transactions, was only \$1,533 less than the total endowment. At that time, investments were handled exclusively by the Treasurer of the Board with superficial oversight by the Executive Committee, composed almost entirely of local business men in addition to the President and the Dean of the College.[4]

Though McCook cannot be credited with all the business reforms instigated during the Vivion administration to help correct these matters, his support for and implementation of them were very important. Ralph Jones suggests that there were four such reforms. They were: (1) the initiation of a budget system for operations; (2) the transference of investment responsibility from the treasurer of the Board of Trustees to the finance committee; (3) the inviolability of endowment funds; and (4) a shift in the membership of the Executive Committee.[43]

Most of these reforms were not new ideas. Some of them had been suggested at one time or another during the previous decade. (1) President Horn had established a budget for the year he was in charge, but the idea did not persist. (2) The creation of a finance committee to replace local responsibility for investment had been called for during the Barcus administration but had not been implemented. (3) Glenn Flinn had advocated a policy calling for the inviolability of endowment funds when he left the Greater Southwestern Campaign in 1928. Inviolability had technically always been the policy of the University, but he added a new stipulation. The University should not touch endowment funds either directly *or indirectly*, such as by making a loan to itself. (4) On recommendation of the SACS visiting team of 1934, the nature of the Executive Committee was changed from one dominated by faculty-Georgetown persons to persons representing the entire state. The President of the University, the academic dean, and the faculty representative were removed. Only one member was required to be a person from Georgetown. The new committee was made up of the president (chairman) and treasurer of the Board, one member from each annual conference, and four other members elected by the Board.[44] The faculty and Georgetown, which had dominated the Executive Committee since 1906, now lost that dominance. In order to always have a quorum available on short notice, the Executive Committee over the years had been composed mostly of persons in one city, first Galveston, then Austin, then Georgetown. Now it did not reside in any particular city. It became statewide. As a matter of fact, the Board continued to elect more than one Georgetown member for some years, but membership was not a matter of right. The number of Georgetown members on the committee would diminish over the years. J. W. Bergin, chairman of the Executive Committee when elected President of the University, lost his membership for 1937–38 and 1938–1939 by virtue of being elected President. The Board elected him as a member for 1939–1940.

A fifth reform was the diversification of the investment policy. By 1936 the portfolio balance of the University looked quite different from that of 1929. When McCook took over in 1929, investments were almost equally divided among Real Estate Mortgages, Real Estate, and Interfund Advancements.[45] Holdings in Stocks and Bonds were insignificant. By 1936 Real Estate Mortgages had been reduced to less than 6 percent. Real Estate holdings had increased to 60 percent. This increase was due to the enforced takeover of real estate where the holders could not meet interest payments. Stocks and Bonds, almost nothing in 1929, were at 21 percent seven years later. Interfund Advancements had been reduced by more than half to only 14 percent.[46]

Category	1929	1936
Real Estate Mortgages	32.1%	5.7%
Real Estate	35.6%	59.6%
Stocks and Bonds	0.7%	20.9%
Interfund Advancements	31.7%	13.7%

A sixth reform was the establishment of coordinated planning and review in the financial process. The business manager, finance committee, and Executive Committee consulted regularly. The finance committee had general oversight of investments, but the Executive Committee reviewed each item in the portfolio every year. The business manager served as the nexus maintaining communication with them and acting as the implementation officer.

The major direction of all the changes when taken as a whole was to move the operation of the Executive Committee more in the direction of the model used in the corporate world. This six-point set of reforms acted to brace the institution during the perilous times of the Depression by placing the responsibility for financial affairs in the hands of professionals and business leaders with broad experience.[47] It removed faculty influence and reduced that of persons from Georgetown. Faculty resistance to this reduction in faculty input will be dealt with later.

Merger with Blinn Memorial College—Background

Methodist work among Germans in Texas began in 1846. The German Methodists were on the whole anti-slavery, and, when they organized after the Civil War, they affiliated with the Northern branch of the Methodist Church. The immigrants around Brenham established a small institute there for their children in 1876 but could not maintain it, and it soon disappeared. Six years later the Southern German Conference of the Northern Methodist Church, of which they were a part, made a second effort. It purchased the partly deserted property of Rutersville College for less than a thousand dollars with the intention of starting a school there for the children of its members. It, too, soon vanished for lack of support.

A third effort to establish an educational institution began on March 28, 1883, when instruction commenced in Brenham with three students in what was called Mission Institute. It grew slowly. A breakthrough occurred when the school leader received a letter from the Rev. Christian Blinn of the East German Conference in New York. Subsequent correspondence ensued, and Blinn and his wife visited Brenham in March 1887. They offered to aid the work by erecting a two-story building. Blinn remained long enough to supervise the construction of the building and to see it dedicated. In 1888, the same year the Institute became coeducational, he sent ten thousand dollars, the interest from which was to support teachers. The following year Mission Institute was renamed Blinn Memorial College. Though Blinn died in 1891, Mrs. Blinn maintained interest in the work and came to Texas several times. She also gave another three thousand dollars to the school.[48]

Charles Frank Schmidt, teacher, registrar, dean, and President of Blinn during his career there from 1913 to 1947, says that Blinn, though called a college, was actually a school of academy rank, offering in addition some twenty accredited college entrance courses. Total regular-term enrollment of all students from 1893–1994 to 1927 ranged from 99 to 177 each year, the high coming in 1907–1908. By 1923–1924 it was 119. Just as in the case of Southwestern, which abandoned its Fitting School in 1916, competition from public high schools became so strong that an academy-type institution could no longer be maintained. Consequently, measures were taken in 1926–1927 to organize the institution as a junior college. Its first session as a junior college was 1927–1928. Its financial situation, however, did not improve. Arthur August Grusendorf, its President, sought a merger with another institution as a way out and approached leaders of various colleges with that possibility. Vivion and other Southwestern University leaders responded favorably to his contact and began conversations about a merger.[49]

Merger with Blinn Memorial College—Completion

Though there is no record as to the names of the other colleges contacted by Grusendorf, his interest in Southwestern was natural. Both Blinn and Southwestern were Methodist schools, and Southwestern was not much more than a hundred miles away. Both Presidents were young and had been recently installed, Vivion in 1928, Grusendorf in 1929. Grusendorf felt that the association of Blinn with Southwestern would help the institution by linking its two-year curriculum to that of a senior college with a well-known name, a long history, and a strong alumni base. The two Presidents knew that neither school could extend direct financial help to the other, and, in fact, the subsequent agreement carefully protected each unit against the mingling of funds, but they did presume that some efficiencies of scale would occur as a result of the merger. For Southwestern's part, it would be able to use Blinn as a feeder school. The curriculum of Blinn would be tailored somewhat to make it conform to that of Southwestern's first two years. Its graduates would then be able to enter Southwestern seamlessly for their junior and senior years. The prospect of appearing to enlarge its radius of action would also provide a psychological lift for Southwestern to counter the negative impact associated with its recent removal controversy.

Merger conversations proceeded rapidly. A group of Blinn College Trustees visited Southwestern in August 1930. The following month they appointed a committee to pursue the merger arrangement. That committee met with representatives of Southwestern, and a tentative agreement was reached. The Blinn Board of Trustees approved it unanimously. The Southwestern Executive Committee then passed it on to the Southwestern Board with the suggestion that "it should be studied seriously."[50]

The Southern Conference of the Northern Methodist Church, owner of Blinn, then met in Georgetown on December 5 and unanimously ratified a twelve-point "Merger Agreement." It stipulated that the merged institution would have the name of Southwestern University, with the unit in Brenham having some such name as Southwestern University Blinn College. The President of Southwestern would become the President of the merged institution, and the President of Blinn College would become dean of that branch. Brenham would be the site of a local executive committee for Blinn, and all monies from the Methodist Episcopal Church would continue to be directed to the Blinn College unit at Brenham. The Southern Conference of the Methodist Episcopal Church would become a sponsoring conference of Southwestern and would have representation on the Board of Trustees equal to that of the larger conferences. All the records of Blinn Memorial College would be transferred to the main office of Southwestern, and Blinn's ex-students would become ex-students of Southwestern. A brief history of Blinn Memorial College would be written and incorporated into the history of Southwestern University. The merger would be declared effective when the two Presidents exchanged papers declaring that the necessary deeds had been passed and negotiations completed. Presuming that the unit at Brenham could be successfully continued, Blinn would become a feeder to Southwestern. Should continuance at Brenham be deemed impracticable in the future, the assets would be reduced to an endowment fund to be known as "The Blinn College Endowment Fund" and become a part of the Southwestern University endowment.[51]

Meeting at a special called session on January 8, 1931, the Southwestern University Board of Trustees approved the merger and authorized the Executive Committee to take the necessary steps to comply with civil and Church law.[52] Evidence of the haste associated with the merger is the fact that President King Vivion was inaugurated as President of Blinn College at a banquet at the Blinn dining hall only two weeks later, January 22, just after the beginning of the new term there.[53] With his inauguration, Grusendorf became dean and Schmidt became assistant dean.

Due to the fact that the merger process had begun after the meeting of the five Texas Annual Conferences in 1930, the steps leading to the merger through the fall of 1931 had been taken without their approval. This matter, however, was largely technical, since Vivion and all the parties concerned had kept in touch with the conferences through their representatives on the Southwestern Board and the conference boards of education. By the middle of December the *Williamson County Sun* could report that formal approval from all the conferences had been secured.[54] The final step as far as the Church was concerned was approval by the General Board of Christian Education in Nashville. Its approval was not needed to ratify the actual merger, which was the responsibility of the Annual Conferences, but to accept the combined Southwestern-Blinn institution as a recognized part of the overall Southern Methodist educational system. Dr. Vivion met with that body in Nashville on January 1, 1932, and secured its assent to the merger.[55]

Faculty, Executive Committee, and Board minutes, as well as newspaper articles during 1932, regularly record the steps being taken to meet the stipulations required by civil law to consummate the merger. In spite of the best efforts of Southwestern and Blinn leaders, finality in those matters continued to elude them. After having already worked together for a year and a half, they had to report to the Board of Trustees on June 2, 1933, that "all the legal papers completing the Blinn merger" have "not been passed" but that "everything will soon be completed."[56] They had hardly been completed when a movement leading to dissolution of the merger began.

Merger with Blinn Memorial College—Dissolution

Grusendorf and Vivion conferred from time to time, and Dean Grusendorf attended meetings of the Southwestern University Board of Trustees on a regular basis. At the April meeting in 1932 he presented a report covering enrollment, faculty, improvements, curriculum, extracurricular activities, and finances. Though there had been a slight enrollment increase in the college division during the "Long Session" over the previous year from 163 to 176, there was a decrease in the non-college division that portended, he suggested, its discontinuance sometime in the near future. The budget had run a deficit of $1,146.66 during the year, and $1,064.00 in notes were coming up for payment. He recommended a total staff and faculty, including the dean, of fifteen for 1932–1933. He concluded by asking the Board of Trustees to help the school to meet its current obligations for the remainder of the year and requested further help in raising $50,000 during Blinn's fiftieth anniversary session in 1933.[57]

A year later, in June 1933, Grusendorf reported the unhappy news that $15,000 in notes issued by the Blinn Memorial College Trustees on February 18, 1924, would become due on the anniversary date in 1934, only eight-and-a-half months away. To cover them, the Southwestern Board authorized the issuance of thirty notes of $500 each dated February 18, 1934, maturing on February 18, 1944. The notes would bear 6 percent interest.[58] At about the same time, the five Texas Annual Conferences of the Methodist Church, South, fearing that all of its schools were facing disaster, set up a Joint Commission on Methodist Educational Work. A basic operating premise underlying its work was the notion of concentrating resources. Some schools were sure to be eliminated. Grusendorf, recognizing that Blinn would certainly be one of those schools, began to discuss separation from Southwestern with Vivion. He had already held discussions with officials in Washington County and "certain contiguous counties" and felt that the Blinn College plant could be used to establish a "joint-county junior college" in Brenham. Both Southwestern and Blinn officials now felt that it was in the best interest of each school to separate and to give each freedom of action.

The Executive Committee of Blinn College met with the members of the Southwestern Board from its own annual conference and prepared resolutions that were brought to a special called session of the Board of Trustees on October 24, 1933. The resolution finally adopted by the Board offered the Blinn Junior College plant to a joint-county junior college district composed of Austin and Washington Counties, to be formed upon its assumption of the bonded indebtedness of the institution for a total of $65,000. A $25,000 bond issue was authorized. It was to be secured by the income from the present Blinn Memorial College Endowment Fund, the use of which would be to retire "the entire indebtedness" of Blinn Memorial College, with any residual amount to be used for the benefit of Southwestern University "in accordance with the merger agreements effecting the merger between Blinn Memorial College and Southwestern University."[59]

The separation movement proceeded just as rapidly as the merger agreement that had preceded it three years before. In full harmony, the Executive Committees of both schools met on February 8, 1934, and unanimously agreed that Blinn College at Brenham would not be operated by Southwestern University after June 4, 1934. They further declared their intention to "discharge any and all indebtedness of whatever nature against Blinn College" using Blinn's assets. A committee composed of Vivion, McCook, and Grusendorf was appointed to carry out the resolution.[60]

Grusendorf's plan, however, did not proceed smoothly. Some citizens of Austin County halted the creation of a joint-county junior college district for Washington and Austin Counties by securing an injunction against it. In order to keep the school in operation, the citizens of Brenham leased the main building from Southwestern and chartered Blinn as a private, nonsectarian institution with a new name: Blinn College. On Founders' Day, March 28, 1934, the transition from the old institution to the new was observed. Dean O. A. Ullrich represented Southwestern. Old Blinn Memorial College as an institution sponsored by any branch of the Methodist Church was closed.[61]

Legally, however, the Blinn College property still belonged to the Southwestern University Board of Trustees, now containing the ten Trustees from the Northern Methodist Church, the original owner of Blinn. President Vivion explained that because of the more than fifty-year Methodist sponsorship of Blinn Memorial College, its records as a Methodist institution would be kept in the archives of Southwestern University for historical purposes. He further stated that the ex-students of Blinn Memorial College would be considered as ex-students of Southwestern and expressed the hope that their affection would be transferred from Blinn to Southwestern.[62] Without any knowledge of what the future held for the new Blinn, he hoped to perpetuate the heritage of the old Blinn Memorial College in an institution with the same church heritage.

The Southern Conference of the Northern Methodist Church continued to furnish members to the Southwestern Board of Trustees until a Church union in 1939, when the Northern and Southern branches of the Church, along with the Methodist Protestant Church, united into one nationwide Methodist Church and that conference was amalgamated into the new structure. In 2003, after almost seventy years, the considerations deemed important in 1935 regarding records had become moot, and all the records of Blinn Memorial College were returned by Southwestern so that, under whatever auspices, they might become a part of the present-day Blinn College and its heritage of providing education for the young people of Brenham and south-central Texas since 1883. It is today the oldest county-owned junior college in Texas and underpins one of the largest college districts in the state.

Dr. Grusendorf attended a meeting of the Southwestern Executive Committee on July 26, 1935, and presented a new plan to complete the severance of the two institutions. He said that a new charter had been secured for the college vesting authority in the administrative officers of the institution. He explained that the new college wished to acquire the Blinn properties from Southwestern and presented a resolution for action. The resolution authorizing the sale of the property was approved with the sale price being $22,500 in cash or its equivalent. Apparently that sum, a paltry figure in comparison with those that had previously been used for its value, was calculated at an amount that would be possible for Grusendorf and his new sponsors to pay, while at the same time allowing Southwestern to cover the school's indebtedness without obtaining any substantial gain for itself. The president of the Southwestern Board of Trustees was authorized to enact a deed of conveyance.[63] After all the debts had been paid off, $2,500 was set up on the Southwestern books as the Blinn Memorial College Endowment Fund.[64]

Southwestern and the German Mission Conference

Another fund based on Methodist work among German immigrants was also established during these years. The German Mission Conference had come into existence during the second half of the nineteenth century and had furnished Trustees to Southwestern from 1884 through 1917. When it was absorbed into the regular English-speaking conferences in 1925, its educational fund continued to be administered by a specially designated committee of ministers from the former conference. After conversations with Vivion, it agreed to turn over its corpus of about $3,500 to Southwestern to perpetuate the German Mission Conference name. This money would be allowed to accumulate until it reached the amount of $10,000, at which time it would become a perpetual revolving fund to sponsor lectureships.[65]

Alfredo Náñez. A graduate of 1930, Alfredo Náñez had a long and distinguished career in the Church. In his books he became the chronicler of Methodist work among persons of Mexican background in Texas. He concluded his career as a professor at SMU. From the 1929 *Sou'wester.*

Hispanic Students and Missionary Work

In 1930 Alfredo Náñez graduated from Southwestern University with a Bachelor of Arts degree. He was the second person of Mexican background to do so, the first being Vicente Ramos in 1908. Little is known about Ramos except that he had entered the Fitting School seven years earlier and proceeded in regular fashion to complete his preparatory studies and undergraduate classes in orderly sequence, receiving his Bachelor of Science degree in due course. Náñez, however, was to have a long and distinguished career in the Church and to become the chronicler of Methodist work among persons of Mexican background in Texas.

The plans of Náñez, who was born in Monclova, Coahuila, in 1902, to attend the university in Mexico City were upset by the Mexican Revolution, and he went to Eagle Pass. There he joined the Methodist Church and decided to enter the ministry. After attending Wesleyan Institute in San Antonio, he entered Southwestern in 1927. Though his uncertain educational background made it necessary for him to be admitted on individual approval, his natural aptitude catapulted him forward, and he graduated three years later.

Náñez held many prominent positions in the Church at both state and national levels during his career as a minister. He was at one time President of Lydia Patterson Institute in El Paso and concluded his career as professor of practical theology and lecturer in Mexican-American Studies at Perkins School of Theology, 1970–1973. He edited the first *Himnario Metodista* in 1955 and the *Ritual Metodista* in 1965. He was the historian of Methodist Spanish-speaking work in Texas, writing the section about Texas Methodism in the book *One in the Lord* (1977) and the comprehensive *History of the Rio Grande Conference of the United Methodist Church* in 1980. That conference is one of the sponsoring Annual Conferences of Southwestern today.[66]

The first students of Mexican background entered Southwestern in 1885. They were Crescencio and Joaquín Rodríguez. Their presence at Southwestern came about after the University affiliated with the Mexican Border Mission Conference when it was organized in 1885. The two ministers appointed by the conference to represent it on the Board of Curators were the Rev. Alexander H. Sutherland of San Antonio and Crescencio Rodríguez, the father of the two boys. Sutherland had earlier become a Curator in 1877 as a member of the West Texas Conference, but his work among the Spanish-speaking population of San Antonio and points farther south predisposed him to join the new conference when it was organized. Earlier, on one of his journeys along the San Antonio and Medina Rivers, preaching and distributing Bibles and religious tracts, he made a convert, one Crescencio Rodríguez. Rodríguez joined the ministry and became a colleague of Sutherland on the Board of Curators. Sutherland served until 1890.[67]

Though Crescencio Rodríguez, senior, served as a Curator until 1901, sixteen years in all, his two sons stayed at Southwestern only two years. This was the pattern followed by most of the other Mexican American students who entered until the Fitting School was closed in 1916. All fourteen students who enrolled during those forty-three years entered the Fitting School. Four advanced to become undergraduates in the College. One, Ramos, mentioned above, graduated.

After the closure of the Fitting School until the graduation of Náñez in 1930, a period of fourteen years, another eleven students with Spanish surnames attended Southwestern. Eight of the eleven entered the undergraduate program, while three attended only summer school and a special program. One of them, Náñez, graduated with a degree.

Interest by Southwestern faculty members and students in Hispanic mission work was strong from the outset. Several teachers who went to Mexico as missionaries have already been mentioned. Lucy Harper, Elementary Principal in the Annex Preparatory from 1880 to 1890, resigned to go to Mexico in the latter year. Margaret Mood McKennon taught in several mission schools in Mexico from 1895 to 1900 before becoming head librarian at Southwestern in 1903. Herbert L. Gray, who did missionary work for sixteen years, spent six of those years (1895–1900) in Mexico before taking his teaching position at Southwestern in 1911. Paul W. Horn left Houston in 1921 to head the American School Foundation in Mexico City, where he was working when called to the presidency of Southwestern. Dean Cody wrote in a newspaper article in 1907 that more than twenty students "are now or have worked as missionaries in Mexico."[68]

The most conspicuous of these missionaries was Frank S. Onderdonk. Born in the Valley, he was sent by his parents to Southwestern at the age of seventeen. There he had a deep spiritual experience at a revival meeting conducted by Sutherland, the Curator from the Mexican Border Mission Conference mentioned above. So convicted was Onderdonk that when he returned to school, he was sure that he had been called to work in Mexico. He said about it: "I returned belonging to the Mexican people. I love[d] them so much that I felt one in spirit with them and it was then that I resolved to give my life to them." Sources differ as to whether or not he finished his degree. If he did, it is not recorded in University records. They indicate that he did one year of preparatory work and two years of undergraduate work. The University remedied his degree status when it awarded him an honorary Doctor of Divinity degree during its Golden Anniversary Celebration in 1923. Onderdonk left Southwestern in 1892 and spent the rest of his life working on both sides of the border among the Mexican people. Both Mexicans and Americans held him in great esteem. He died in 1936.[69]

Academics during the Vivion Years

At the end of Vivion's administration in 1935 none would have guessed that his tenure would mark the low point in Southwestern's struggle for existence and that the University would begin almost immediately thereafter a slow ascent to the position it holds today. Nevertheless, many elements of the financial operation and academic program that facilitated that ascent were put into place under Vivion and have, in the main, endured. Just as it is true to say that the basic policies undergirding the financial system today were put into place during the Vivion years by I. J. McCook and those associated with him, it is also true to say that the academic program established by Dean Ullrich and his colleagues at the same time is the first which would be completely familiar to a current faculty member and student today.

One of the first changes made by the faculty was to establish a senior examination in the major field covering all the courses in that field. Its purpose was to determine whether or not the candidate possessed "a unified view of and a general acquaintance with the selected field of study." It was to be taken at least two weeks before the end of the term on a date mutually satisfactory to the department head and the student. The examination was chaired by the department head, who was assisted by the other members of the department. At least one instructor from an unrelated department was also required to attend.[70] Though this requirement was established at a faculty meeting on March 12, 1929, it was still almost exactly the same thirty-six years later when I began teaching at Southwestern in 1965, at which time it was called the comprehensive examination or the oral final. Though it has been gradually changed over succeeding years to respond to the unique elements associated with each discipline, a senior examination or its equivalent of some sort is still required in all departments. "A non-credit course in orientation for freshmen" was also introduced at about the same time. Its purpose was "to introduce the student to the various fields of knowledge and to aid the student in getting his bearing in college life."[71] Orientation courses have been offered ever since, some of them quite elaborate.

President Vivion himself was quite interested in improving the quality of the student body by limiting enrollment. The Board approved limiting freshman enrollment to two hundred students beginning in September 1929. Students were to be "selected on the basis of scholarship and fitness." Vivion's talks on the subject became so well known to the students that the senior takeoff on the faculty at a chapel program in the spring of 1932 began with a skit about it. *The Megaphone* reported that "Benjamin Bohmfalk opened the program with his famous impersonation of Doctor King Vivion in his well-known discourse on 'The Selectivity of Students in our Southwestern Family.'"[72] The difficulty with Vivion's emphasis on selectivity was that it overlapped a general decline in student numbers occasioned by the economic depression, and it is difficult to determine how effective it could have been in those circumstances. Nevertheless, the fact that Vivion was continuing to stress it three years into the Great Depression indicates how important he considered it.

Paired with the emphasis on selectivity was an interest in providing a program for students with unusual ability. A departmental honors program was established in 1931 in which a student could obtain honors by taking three or more advanced courses in a department as an honors student. Students obtaining honors received certain privileges such as optional attendance at chapel and more relaxed class attendance regulations. Students gaining honors had that fact indicated on their permanent records.[73] Given the student resistance to required chapel already noted, relaxation of this requirement for honors students was certainly a valuable award in their eyes for academic performance.

The following year the faculty finally abandoned the "major-minor," or quarter system, described in earlier chapters, for the semester system. Two eighteen-week semesters now replaced the three twelve-week terms. All courses were recalibrated to the new system, some meeting on Monday, Wednesday, and Friday and others on Tuesday, Thursday, and Saturday rather than every day for five days. The requirement for a B.A. degree was established at 124 semester hours, with 4 of those hours being in Physical Education. The general education program was composed of 66 hours, and requirements were established for the major and minor fields.[74] These requirements had changed hardly at all when I came to Southwestern in 1965, including morning classes on Saturday. Saturday classes were abandoned a few years later.

A further move away from the classical norm for the bachelor's degree occurred with the addition of elective courses in stenography and typewriting. They were placed under the head of the Department of Economics. Offerings were also increased in the Department of Physical Education and Health Education to allow a minor in this field.[75]

Ex-Students and Summary of Degrees Awarded 1876–1935

Because the Vivion administration marks the end of Southwestern's long struggle for solvency and permanency in Georgetown, it is a useful point for making an overview of the 2,316 degrees and diplomas awarded in the sixty years from 1876 to 1935. Of these degrees, men had taken 1,297 and women 1,019. A table of the distribution among types of degrees reveals the following:[76]

Degree	Number	Percentage	First Granted	Last Granted
B.A.	1,786	77.1%	1876	Still granted in '35
B.S.	197	8.5%	1880	Still granted in '35
M.A.	166	7.2%	1880	Still granted in '35
Mistress of Literature	81	3.5%	1879	1900*
Ph.B.	37	1.6%	1897	1909*
B.M.	32	1.4%	1915	1935*
B.F.A. in Music	5	0.2%	1935	Still granted in '35

continued on following page

continued from preceding page

Degree	Number	Percentage	First Granted	Last Granted
B.S. in Ed.	5	0.2%	1914	1924*
M.S.	4	0.2%	1900	1922**
B.S. in Med.	3	0.1%	1927	1931**
Total	**2,316**	**100.0%**		

*Degree terminated.
**Still listed in the catalog as offered for 1935–1936 but none granted after the years indicated.

The above figures include only those who took degrees or diplomas. Persons who studied in the Preparatory/Fitting School or who were Graduates in a school (department) or were Full Graduates (completed two years) do not figure in the count.

The committee of seven prominent alumni set up in 1929 during the removal controversy spoke of 17,000 ex-students, that is, of 17,000 different persons who had enrolled at Southwestern at one time or another, however briefly. There is good reason to believe that this figure is roughly accurate when considered in relation to year-by-year enrollment figures. Total enrollment of all students in whatever academic unit in regular annual sessions from 1873–1874 to 1934–1935 (duplicates included) was 29,913. There were an additional 12,268 enrollments (duplicates included) in the Summer Session, the Summer School of Theology, the Summer Normal, and in correspondence work. The total for all these enrollments is 42,181. Reducing this figure by a factor of 2½, a reasonable figure to eliminate duplicates, produces a count of 16,872, roughly the 17,000 ex-students mentioned in 1929. Our ability today to work from precise enrollment figures and other numbers associated with the academic work of the university for more than forty years is due to the remarkable work of Pearl A. Neas, the registrar or assistant registrar from 1917 to 1962. She is probably the person who supplied the number of about 17,000 ex-students.

Pearl Alma Neas—Registrar Extraordinary

When she died after a short illness in the summer of 1962, Pearl Alma Neas had served the University fifty years, longer than any other person in its history before or since. Employed as a stenographer in 1913, she soon became the person to whom President Bishop dictated his personal correspondence. When Wilbur F. Wright left his registrar's position to join the army in the fall of 1917, Neas was appointed assistant registrar to help Randolph W. Tinsley, the new acting registrar, in his work. Tinsley, professor of biology and geology, came more and more to depend upon his efficient assistant registrar to handle most of the work.

Within a short time Neas had mastered the intricacies of the registrar's office to the point that she became the de facto head of the office and managed a staff of eight or nine persons. She was so vital to the operation that, when she became seriously ill in the spring of 1921, President Bishop felt it necessary to call it to the attention of the Trustees. He said that "Miss Neas, our efficient and obliging Assistant Registrar, who has practically grown up from girlhood in our office, has been threatened with a serious break-down of health and is, at present, unable to attend to her work. She is one of the most efficient workers and managers in a college office to be found in any of our institutions and is as loyal to Southwestern as a child to her mother. We are greatly hindered in our office now by her necessary absence from her post."[77] Paul W. Horn discussed with her a position as his personal secretary at Texas Tech soon after he left Southwestern to assume the presidency there and wrote her a letter of recommendation in which he stated that "had I remained there [at Southwestern], it was my intention to recommend her for the registrar's position."[78] Within a few weeks, however, Barcus did appoint her registrar, a position she held until her death on July 3, 1962.[79]

Bishop's reference to her as having "practically grown up from girlhood in our office" was almost literally true. Reared on a farm near Weir, a few miles northeast of Georgetown, she was listed as a sixteen-year-old young woman in the census of 1910. She was the second daughter in a family of six children. The four girls were born before the two boys, and she grew up having to do farm work. She and her older sister

Pearl A. Neas, registrar. "The registrar seems to have real executive ability. She understands her duties and performs them admirably." From a report of the Visiting team of the Southern Association, 1934. Photo from the 1933 *Sou'wester.*

are listed in the census as "farm laborers," specified as working both in the "house" and on the "farm."[80] Her family was strongly attached to the Methodist Church, and her father was a Sunday School Superintendent for fifteen years. He died in 1919 at the age of fifty-two, following his wife's death four years earlier at the age of forty-six. Both are buried in the cemetery at Weir.[81] Though Neas had attended the Summer Normal program at Southwestern during the summer of 1910 to prepare as a teacher, she did not complete her preparation and went to Tyler Business College, from whence she graduated.[82] The difficult circumstances of her family and the loss of both parents with teenage children still at home must have contributed to her not attending college. She had a good voice and took occasional voice courses in the School of Fine Arts during her career at Southwestern, but she never took a degree. She began as a stenographer at Southwestern at the age of nineteen when other girls her age were studying for degrees.

Pearl Neas's talents were soon discovered. These were supplemented by her winning personality and maturity. Wilbur Wright, the registrar who had first employed her, wrote in a recommendation for her in 1918 that she "is a young woman with an old head; she is quiet, level-headed and possessed of splendid judgement. She is a capable young office executive, one of the most efficient I have ever known."[83] R. W. Tinsley, the Acting Registrar under whom she worked following Wright's departure, said about her: "I consider her the sum total of efficiency when it comes to office work. In addition to this she has a most pleasing personality and an unlimited capacity for work."[84] Students liked her as well. An article about her in *The Megaphone* said: "Most freshmen hear from her before they enter Southwestern, they meet her when they matriculate, and from that moment they count her as a true friend. She is always pleasant and agreeable and is willing to stop her own work to help the students at any time. She has won the friendship and love of every student in Southwestern."[85] Charles Bishop, the President who was most instrumental in promoting her career and with whom she maintained a lifelong friendship, said that she was "gracious in manner, helpful in spirit, willing to spend all her strength upon her task, modest in her bearing toward all other officials and Christian in all her principles."[86]

In spite of her lack of academic credentials, she won her way to the top in her profession. She was one of the three founders of the Texas branch of the American Association of Collegiate Registrars in 1921.[87] She served at least one term, perhaps more, as its president and was elected its vice president for six successive years.[88] She delivered an annual address before that body and also served on the Membership Committee of the National Association of Registrars. She was asked twice to deliver a lecture at the national meeting. Though her lack of academic credentials did not hinder her in her work as registrar, the Southern Association of Colleges and Secondary Schools criticized Southwestern for using her as a part-time teacher, probably in her role as head of correspondence work for sixteen years.[89]

In addition to her official duties, Pearl Neas was "a tower of strength" for Laura Kuykendall in arranging and carrying out May Fêtes. She also made student recruitment trips for the University. Examples are trips in the fall of 1932, visiting high schools in the lower Rio Grande Valley,[90] and in the spring of 1933 through North Texas, visiting Corsicana, Waxahachie, Dallas, Fort Worth, Weatherford, Cleburne, Hillsboro, and Temple.[91] During the mid-1930s, with Depression budget stringencies in effect, she assumed responsibility for University publicity and the ex-students organization for four years. She also took over the correspondence course operation, which she managed for sixteen years until its demise following World War II. The visiting team of the Southern Association commended her highly in its special study in 1934. It said that "the registrar seems to have real executive ability. She understands her duties and performs them admirably. Her assistants are well trained."[92] The Business Women's League of Georgetown named her "Woman of the Year" in 1956.[93]

The work of Pearl Neas was so efficient during her thirty-two years working with Dean O. A. Ullrich, her immediate superior, that he virtually turned over to her some of the decision-making responsibilities associated with the registrar's office normally handled by the dean. Since she died during the summer of 1962, while students were away, a special memorial service was held for her in the chapel on Friday, February 22, 1963.[94] The Alumni Association of Southwestern currently offers a Pearl A. Neas Award to an outstanding staff member each year at Homecoming.

Student Performances and Special Events

Student performance groups were very active during the early 1930s. The Mask and Wig Players presented plays such as *A Doll's House*, by Henrik Ibsen. The choir, formed in 1929 and directed by Dean Henry Meyer, made many trips to various parts of Texas. In 1934–1935 the debating team won forty-three decisions out of fifty-two debates.[95] Activities in athletics, literature, and music were also a part of the picture. A twelve-piece orchestra called "The Versatile Vikings," with, Ralph Jones says, "instrumentation suspiciously like that of a dance band," performed both on and away from campus. The band "became buccaneers in appearance" by outfitting itself in a uniform consisting of a "red bandana handkerchief as a head-piece, a yellow vest over a black shirt, black pants, black boots with a yellow turn down cuff, and a brass ear-ring."[96] The election of a Miss Southwestern each year, begun in 1926 to raise money for the *Sou'wester*, had become an annual event by the 1930s and was an object of considerable student interest.

Budgetary difficulties forced the curtailing of the lyceum program during the Depression years, and fewer speakers of the quality of those in the past came to the campus. Nevertheless, Norman Thomas, the socialist leader and presidential candidate did appear on campus in 1929. Carl Sandburg also read his poetry to a Southwestern audience in 1935.[97]

Though a news article in 1931 states that Founders' Day ceremonies have been a custom for many years, the printed "Founders' Day Program" a year later had to explain that the event was held on April 20 because "it was on this date in the year 1870 that representatives from the four Methodist Colleges of the State met in Galveston and officially established the one institution belonging to the whole M. E. Church South of Texas."[98] Founders' Day was a muted event through the years at Southwestern even when it was celebrated.

Student Religious and Political Affiliations

Southwestern continued to be heavily Methodist in its student enrollment. Out of its 316 full-time students in the fall of 1934, 207 were Methodist. Of the other ten denominations, the Baptists ranked second with 35 and the Presbyterians third with 18. Only 2 Catholics were enrolled. Seventeen reported no religious affiliation.[99] The local Methodist pastor, the Rev. Edmund Heinsohn, was so popular that the students signed a petition in 1931 requesting his return for a fifth year and supposedly turned out "almost one hundred per cent to church services" on the first Sunday after his return.[100] The popularity of the local Methodist pastor, however, did not change student attitudes about required daily chapel and assembly attendance, and University officials worked assiduously to make those events palatable. Though chapel and assembly in 1934 met six days a week, only two days were given over to "devotional services." Of the other four days, two days were given to student organizations, one day to class meetings, and one day to programs of an academic or musical nature.[101] The Y.M.C.A. and the Y.W.C.A., organizations that had been such important parts of campus life several decades before, were gone by 1935, as was also the last of the literary societies.

In a straw poll taken before the presidential election in 1928, Southwestern students followed many Southerners by favoring Herbert Hoover, the Quaker Republican, over Al Smith, the Catholic Democrat, by a vote of 167 to 126.[102] Four years later the Democratic candidate, Roosevelt, outpolled President Hoover by a substantial margin, 120 to 33.[103] This latter result was undoubtedly related to the dire economic circumstances being faced by the students. To help them, a student labor director on campus helped boys secure work in town, where about twenty-five students were employed. He also provided work for about one hundred on campus.[104] In early 1934, Southwestern began receiving federal aid for working students. Twenty-eight students received aid, eighteen boys and ten girls. Of that number, 25 percent had to be new students. They were paid thirty cents per hour for not less than ten or more than twenty hours of work.[105]

Pirate Tavern

Pirate Tavern, a privately owned student hangout on the corner across University Avenue from the Administration Building, was opened on February 11, 1930. Prior to that a little store and post office had existed there, but a new, one-story building designed in a Spanish architectural style, finished in pink stucco and trimmed in blue, replaced it. Almost the entire inside length of the west side was taken up by a soda fountain and counter equipped with leather-cushioned stools. Showcases occupied the east side, with shelves holding lines of toilet articles, school equipment, and confections. Cars could park "headed in" on the gravel parking lot on the west side.[106] Though not a part of Southwestern itself, over the years the Pirate Tavern became a fond memory in the mind of every student who sipped a soda there. The University bought the building during World War II and now owns it. Though its function as a hangout has long since been replaced by on-campus facilities for the same purpose, it is still used, but for other purposes.

The Pirate Tavern inside and outside as seen from the Administration Building. Opened in 1930, it was the student hangout for more than 25 years. It closed in 1957 with the opening of the Bishops' Memorial Union Building. From the 1957 *Sou'wester.*

The Megaphone

Student newspapers in all colleges have their ups and downs. They are sometimes surprisingly good one year, only to be incredibly bad the next. In most cases, as in that of Southwestern, the administration and/or faculty has a publications committee or something equivalent that tries to nudge the newspaper toward an equilibrium encompassing freedom of speech, journalistic responsibility, and institutional well-being. An issue testing this balance occurred during the winter and spring terms of 1931.

In February freshman, sophomore, and junior class editions of *The Megaphone* were published at weekly intervals. Each had an issue editor. Kermit Gibbons was the editor of the senior edition. Its publication on May 19 ignited a firestorm. In addition to his editorial criticizing mercilessly the regular *Megaphone*, the *Southwestern Magazine*, and the *Sou'wester*, Gibbons printed a front-page retrospective column about his four years at Southwestern. It was extensive and well written but also cynical and condescending. In it he lampooned the "positive Christian atmosphere" mentioned in Southwestern's promotional literature and said that he had not been on campus thirty minutes before he realized that the statement was either a misprint or "cheap, enticing, not to say mendacious, advertising." He satirized the classroom teaching as teaching for "the Great God Examination." He found the professors to be "not one scintilla above the students," the students to have no intellectual interests beyond the minimum necessary to sustain life in "the great and crass American mode," and the citizens of the town to be "local Babbitts."[107] However poor he alleges his education to have been at Southwestern, someone must have introduced him to Sinclair Lewis somewhere along the way.

The tone of his article was very much in the style of H. L. Mencken, to whom, after the controversy, he addressed a letter that somehow ended up in the hands of Dean Ullrich. Though the edition in question was delivered successfully on campus, Ullrich managed to confiscate the copies to be sent by mail. The publications committee and various faculty members interviewed Gibbons and proffered "vague charges" against him, he says, but nothing was done to punish him. He graduated two weeks later. The senior class, however, was not so lenient. It met and, by a 21 to 18 margin, voted to apologize to the student body for the senior edition.[108]

The following year *The Megaphone* was almost as provocative but less supercilious. It survived faculty review untouched, publishing fifteen special editions devoted to different topics. The topics were entitled Football, Library, Music, Conference, Heinsohn, Collegiate, Greek Letter, Fumer, Christmas, Prosperity, Dedication, FISH [freshmen], Sophomore, Junior, and Senior. Each edition covered its topic with some degree of thoroughness, usually in both a serious and a humorous way. The "Fumer" issue of December 8, 1931, featured articles having to do with student problems and complaints. One of its articles was entitled "Mud from Mood Hall." The "Prosperity" edition of January 26, 1932, had a cartoon featuring Professor Tinsley, saying , "TIME—HELL! What's time to a setting hen!!" A note from the editor underneath the cartoon said: "Due to the fact that *The Megaphone* is a member of this sedate and religious organization—we wish to say that the undesirable word seen above was part of a joke told by 'Doc' and also a typographical error."

Disciplinary Problems and Fraternities

The normal quota of familiar student problems from the past, such as drunkenness, hazing, cheating, petting, necking, and dancing, was dealt with by the Honor Council and the faculty Discipline Committee. Once Ullrich became dean in 1926, he began to have the results of student Honor Council and faculty Discipline Committee meetings regularly copied into the faculty minutes. The greater number of cases thus reported does not necessarily mean that student conduct was worse than earlier, only that it was more carefully recorded. In fact, Ullrich reported to the Board of Trustees in mid-1933 that student conduct was the best since 1926–1927.[109] A first, however, was the punishment of girls for drunkenness. Faculty minutes in 1932 show that on one occasion, when five students were given heavy penalties, three of them were girls who "acknowledged being drunk in the Woman's Bldg."[110]

Dean Ullrich and the faculty had tried to rid the campus of fraternities in 1928 by expressing to the Board of Trustees their sentiment against the fraternity system in strong terms. The Trustees, however, had tossed the ball back to them by stating that the faculty should compel the fraternities to obey campus rules "religiously," exercising whatever discipline was needed. A year later the faculty brought the issue to the Trustees once again. This time they specifically included sororities in their condemnation. The report, written by Dean Ullrich, began by saying that "Fraternityism is our cross." It then outlined six indictments against the system. Fraternityism, so it said, is "inimical to the ideals of scholarship," is "inimical to democracy" and promotes "snobbery," is a "barrier to the development of Christianity at Southwestern University," is "expensive and promotes extravagance," causes "serious disciplinary problems," and is "inimical to the aims of a college education." It then went on to state that of the thirty-nine cases of student misconduct convicted during the year, thirty-three, or about 84 percent, were for offenses committed by twenty-six students who were members of fraternities and sororities. The remaining six convictions were for offenses committed by five nonfraternity students. These figures, it continued, were even more significant when one considers that there are only 157 Greeks and 260 Barbs. Therefore, 84.6 percent of the trouble has been perpetrated by only 37.6 percent of the student body.

On the basis of these facts, Ullrich said, the faculty suggested that "the Board of Trustees either abolish fraternities and sororities at Southwestern or else delegate the authority to the faculty to dispose of the problem as it may think best for the interests of Southwestern. The former course would in our judgment be the preferable one, since it would remove from the faculty considerable embarrassment."[111] Once again the Trustees ducked the issue and accepted an alternative proposal made by Ullrich when he saw that the "preferable" faculty suggestion had no chance. They approved a motion to require that all fraternity groups attain the scholastic average of the whole student body. Those chapters that did not do so would not be permitted to initiate during the following term.[112]

Even with these new initiation requirements, Ullrich soon came to feel that the fraternities and sororities did not have the will to "work themselves out of their current situation." "Hell-Weeks" were reported in *The Megaphone*, with "pajama parades" and "Slime" initiations. One of the fraternities lived in a big house on the corner diagonally across the street from the Administration Building. The person who lived next to it on the west had the railroad tracks on the other side. Commenting about it, he said that he lived "between hell and the railroad tracks." Working from feelings such as this, Ullrich told the Trustees that it would eventually be necessary to require fraternities to move on campus.[113] Fraternities, which had always maintained their houses off campus, were now threatened with having to move onto the campus so the faculty could maintain better control. When grades were tabulated, all but one of the sororities met the scholastic average but none of the fraternities did. They were not permitted to initiate. Because the grade average against which they were being measured was unusually high that year, they felt that the faculty was using the grade requirement as a "subtle method of abolishing them." To avoid this criticism, the faculty set an arbitrary average of 81 for the spring term. This action enabled all the fraternities and sororities to initiate pledges.[114]

After the faculty attempts in 1928 and 1929 to get the Trustees to eliminate the Greek system from the campus, the faculty and the fraternities settled down to a nervous coexistence. At one point the fraternities overplayed their hand and paid the price for it. In April 1932 they asked that a special dispensation be allowed and that an average of 79 be set as the grade average for initiation. The faculty agreed to allow it for the spring term but not for the winter. Later the fraternity representative appeared again and asked that the average be lowered all the way to 70. Feeling that it was being toyed with, the Executive Committee set a permanent average of 80 for both boys and girls.[115]

Enrollment Decline and Alumni in the Professions

A simple table illustrates the enrollment crisis that affected Southwestern during the Depression years. Comparing fall semester enrollments for the first six years, enrollment declined from 426 in 1930 to 286 in 1935, a total decline of 32.9 percent. The decline was reversed in 1936, and a slow ascent to pre-Depression levels began to occur, until the threat of World War II caused enrollment to decline once again in 1941 and 1942.

Fall of Year	Enrollment	% Change
1930	426	
1931	377	-11.5
1932	309	-18.0
1933	284	-8.1
1934	320	+12.7
1935	286	-10.6
1936	380	+32.9
1937	417	+9.7
1938	403	-0.3
1939	402	-0.0
1940	440	+9.5
1941	390	-11.6
1942	376	-3.6

The 12.7 percent increase for 1934 may have been due to the decrease in student charges established for that year. The decrease was announced in the newspaper as a "big slash in tuition," and Vivion stated that "we are correcting the long established fallacy that costs at Southwestern are more expensive than at some other places."[116] The previous annual tuition charge of $160 did not include additional room, board, registration, science labs, medical costs, student publications, and athletic fees. The new "flat charge" system for 1934–1935 included everything. Increases the following year of 7.6 percent for men and 5.3 percent for women resulted in a decrease of 10.6 percent in enrollment for fall 1936. Increases and decreases in student charges may not explain everything related to enrollment changes, but they certainly were a prominent factor.

Meanwhile, Pearl A. Neas was keeping up with graduates in her usual meticulous manner. In 1932 she reported their distribution by professions since 1876 as follows:[117]

Professions of Graduates	Number	Percentage
Housewives	503	25.3
Business of all types	445	22.3
Public/private school teachers, officials	436	21.9
Ministers and other religious workers	220	11.0
College professors, coaches, officials	136	6.8
Doctors, surgeons, dentists	84	4.2
Farmers and ranchmen	35	1.8
Lawyers, judges, congressmen, senators	23	1.2
Bankers and financiers	22	1.1
Chemists	9	0.5
Unaccounted for	79	4.0
TOTAL	**1,992**	**100.1**

The largest single category was "housewives." "Business of all types" and "public/private school teachers, officials" followed in second and third place, respectively. Most women were found in the first and third categories. They had not yet broken into the other professions in significant numbers.

Vivion, the Academic Program, and the Faculty

King Vivion assumed the presidency of Southwestern with high aspirations for improving the academic program. His emphasis on student selectivity, the setting up of "King's Palace" for ten needy boys making an "A" average, the replacement of the quarter system by the semester system, the introduction of a senior examination in the major field of study, and the development of a departmental honors program have already been mentioned. Dean Ullrich was certainly the person who led the last three efforts, but he was encouraged in them by the knowledge that Vivion supported him. Vivion's statement to the Trustees in 1930, as already noted, that Ullrich was "without a superior in the southwest" indicates the level of presidential support he received.

Vivion was also interested in stimulating the faculty to higher performance. One way in which he attempted to do so was to announce a system in 1929 that would recognize faculty merit. Recognition would be based on four points—vital Christian influence, scholarship, teaching effectiveness, and general usefulness to the school. He also set a target date of 1934, by which time every department head would have a Ph.D. or its equivalent.[118] Neither the awards program nor the Ph.D. goal was reached. Just as the student selectivity program was torpedoed by the decline in student enrollment, the two faculty programs were never instituted because of the precipitous economic downturn. Awards in a period of salary stasis were impossible. Nevertheless, Vivion's relations with the faculty were good throughout his tenure. He took the same 25 percent cut in salary that they did in 1932 and called annually on the Board of Trustees to set up a retirement program. The first retirement program for the faculty was enacted in his last Board meeting in 1935, the one thing he was able to salvage out of the ambitious faculty program he had set out to accomplish at the beginning. Retirement pay was $50 a month for those having attained age sixty-five with thirty years of service. A prorated amount would be given to those having served less than thirty years but more than fifteen.[119] It is not surprising that all five of those who retired in 1935 continued to teach part-time to supplement their $600 a year retirement pay.

In 1933, with the faculty laboring under a 25 percent reduction in salaries and with those reduced salaries behind in payment, Vivion became discouraged and contemplated resignation. At the Board meeting on October 24, Bishop

Sam R. Hay was asked to make "a statement concerning certain rumors involving the resignation of President Vivion." After his statement, the Board adopted a motion requesting Dr. Vivion "to refrain from entertaining any thought of resignation at this time."[120] He labored on for another two years.

Personnel Changes

One of the effects of the semester plan as compared to the earlier system was its greater efficiency in utilizing teaching resources. A report to the Board of Trustees in mid-1933 after one year's experience with the new system says that it "enabled the administration to distribute the work in such a manner that the services of a number of faculty members could be dispensed with without serious hurt to the efficiency of the college."[121] Nevertheless, the report implies that no one was dismissed. The six teachers who departed after the 1931–1932 year left "for other fields" and were not, it seems, the victims of a studied plan of retrenchment. Most of them probably left to improve their economic circumstances. They were simply not replaced.

The most senior of them, William Paul Davidson (Philosophy and Psychology) was employed by the Civilian Conservation Corps in early 1934. A seventeen-year veteran who had rendered strong service to the University, Davidson went with the C.C.C. to do educational work under the direction of Mr. Leon W. Rodgers, former State Superintendent of Education and a Southwestern graduate.[122] Davidson's daughter, Dorothy, a student at Southwestern at the time, was later the State Superintendent of Education herself and received an honorary degree from the University in 1978. In 1934 Alpha Chi presented her a dictionary for having the highest freshman average.[123] She was a state finalist in tennis and one of the two *magna cum laude* seniors in 1937.[124]

Annie Edward Barcus (English), author of the script accompanying the Dinner of the Golden Bowl and a B.A. graduate of Southwestern with an M.A. from Columbia, married the Rev. T. Herbert Minga at the end of the spring semester in 1932 and left her teaching post in English to become a minister's wife. Both she and her husband later rendered significant service to the University. Similar stories could probably be written about the other four teachers who left without further record.

The first class of teachers to take advantage of the new retirement program in 1935 was composed of five persons—Vaden (forty-four years), McKennon (forty-one years), Tinsley (thirty-three years), Gray (thirty years), and Lehmberg (twenty-six years). Though Tinsley, like the others, has been mentioned previously in this narrative, his career was eclectic and merits summarizing. Possessed only of a B.S. degree (1898) from the University of Virginia, Tinsley came to the University in 1903. He taught biology, geology, chemistry, and physics at one time or another during his career. He was Acting Registrar (1917–1926), Director of Summer School (1919), Bursar (1923–1929), and Assistant to the President (1924–1935), all the while handling a class or two on the side. On three occasions, after the presidencies of Bishop, Horn, and Barcus, he served either as Acting President or was part of the faculty team that held executive responsibility pending the arrival of the new President. He was a perennial member of the Athletic Committee after 1904 and one of the organizers of the Texas Intercollegiate Athletic Association. He was its president for seven years.[125] The yearbook of 1935, which was dedicated to him, said that "his humor was delicious" and that "he always kept his audiences in a roar of laughter." Toward the end of his career, Pearl A. Neas replaced him as registrar, I. J. McCook replaced him as bursar (business manager), and SACS questioned his competency for teaching biology. Yet his reputation for rendering selfless service to the University in his many capacities and his "splendid contact with the student body" were such that he was awarded an honorary Doctor of Laws degree by McMurry College in 1933.[126]

Luther J. Waggoner (thirty-one years, Religious Education and Church History), Lucy Belle Morgan (nineteen years, Spanish), Sherman D. Lesesne (twenty-six years, chemistry), and Iola Bowden Chambers (thirty-three years, piano) began their long careers at Southwestern during these years. Waggoner and Chambers would figure prominently in events connected with later administrations.

Rodney J. Kidd, employed in 1929 to supervise physical education for men, experienced a meteoric rise in the faculty during the 1930s. An A.B. graduate of 1925, he had lettered in three sports. On completing Southwestern, he became a successful coach and principal at Georgetown High School within four years.[127] Acquisition of "Captain Kidd," as he was called, brought a second person to the coaching staff at Southwestern for the first time. He assisted Edens in the major sports and directed intramural athletics. By 1934 he had been elected president of the Texas Physical Education Association. The high regard in which he was held by the administration is indicated by the fact that he was the only faculty member whose salary improved between

1932–1933 and 1935–1936, rising 30 percent during those three years. He left Southwestern on February 1, 1938, to accept a position with the Equitable Life Insurance Company.[128] Three weeks later he was named Director of Athletics of the Interscholastic League.[129] He remained a loyal supporter of Southwestern during the rest of his life.

John C. Granbery Returns to Southwestern

The most important faculty acquisition having implications for the next administration was that of John C. Granbery. Toward the end of August 1934, President Vivion announced the return of Professor Granbery as Acting Professor of Philosophy and Political Science for the 1934–1935 session. A résumé of his career was sketched out in the newspaper item announcing the appointment, though Granbery's release from Texas Tech was not mentioned. The article simply says that he held his position there until 1932 and that he had spent the last two years in Brazil.[130] Immediately after Granbery's dismissal from Texas Tech, Vivion had offered him a teaching position.[131] Given Granbery's turbulent history at Southwestern before going to Texas Tech in 1924 and his similarly turbulent history there, one might wonder why Vivion, with all the problems confronting him from the Great Depression, would be interested in Granbery's return. The reason, however, is not hard to determine. Granbery had always been popular on campus at Southwestern—with all the Presidents under whom he had served, with his fellow faculty members, and with students. Whatever his difficulties with the general public because of his supposedly advanced views, the people closest to him appreciated his modest demeanor, believed in his integrity, and appreciated his dedication to principle.

He had also recently confirmed their opinion of him by opposing strongly the removal forces in mid-1928. In a letter written from Lubbock published in the *Williamson County Sun*, he said that after an absence of three years, he was still attached to Southwestern. "It was in this spirit that I left, with good will toward all, and as far as I knew, from all, and not a moment has my affection for Southwestern grown dim. . . . In passing I may be permitted to mention the beauty and quiet of Georgetown—the ideal town for a home and a school. . . . We all know what a problem is created in our colleges by intercollegiate athletics. At Southwestern, I understand, the record is kept clean. Players are real college students who are making their work and whose athletic activities are subordinate to academic interests. Scholarship is emphasized at Southwestern. Methodists of Texas have reason to be proud of Southwestern. . . . Should Southwestern ever pass, which God forbid, then something fine and priceless will have gone from us."[132]

A year later he broadened his perspective in an article on Church-related education published in the *Texas Christian Advocate*. Reflecting on the pressure Church schools increasingly face, he holds up the glory of their supporting teachers, toiling on low salaries, who do not hesitate to express their views on religious, political, or social questions. Though they are underfunded, Church schools provide something a State school cannot provide. Granbery builds a case for their seeking out teachers who will express their views on vital issues rather than "fill[ing] up our colleges with colorless mediocrities, while stronger men go elsewhere. What a school of brilliant personalities," he muses, "could be established if we might secure the services of those who have left some one institution, often under pressure!"[133] One can imagine the approving nods that must have come from the heads of Gray, Ullrich, and the other faculty members at Southwestern as they perused this article with the recent academic freedom controversy through which they had just passed in mind.

It is notable that Southwestern, where he had taught for twelve years and which knew him better than any other institution, still wanted Granbery after his dismissal from Texas Tech. It speaks volumes to the character of the persons who supported him through the years—the four Presidents, Bishop, Horn, Barcus, and Vivion, and his colleagues on the faculty. Among them he was a moral leader. Though Vivion offered him a permanent twelve-month position in 1934, Granbery preferred to leave his future open and accepted a nine-month contract instead.

The faculty received him and May Catt warmly. In October 1934, a few months after their arrival, Dean Kuykendall honored her by naming May Catt guest of honor at the annual Dinner of the Golden Bowl.[134] Ever the popular speaker in Georgetown, John began to respond to a round of invitations. He and Mrs. McKennon were on the program of the Faculty Club in November, at which time he spoke on "Latin American Culture."[135] He spoke formally to the faculty at its January meeting on "The Church College and Its Function."[136] He was offered and accepted another nine-month contract as Professor of Philosophy for 1935–1936.

After Laura Kuykendall died on April 30, the Dean of Women's position was left vacant pending an appointment to that position by the new President who would replace Vivion. With the delay involved in the process, Bergin did not make the appointment, his first, until August 31, when May was named supervisor of women. Her education at Wesleyan Institute, Mary Baldwin College, and the University of Chicago was mentioned in the announcement. Her wartime experience in France and Greece with the Y.W.C.A. and her editorship for six years of *The New Citizen*, the official publication of the Texas League of Women Voters, were also mentioned.[137] The Executive Committee approved her appointment on October 22, 1935, at a salary of $100 per month, plus room and board for her and John.[138] With room, board, and a combined salary of $2,340, she and John were better off financially than at any time in years.

Southern Association Accreditation Problems

Dean Ullrich had alerted the Board of Trustees in 1928 to the possibility of trouble with Southwestern's regional accreditation body, the Southern Association of Colleges and Secondary Schools. He said that Southwestern was delinquent in meeting certain standards and that unless something was done the problem might even become fatal. The delinquencies, he added, were all connected to finances. With an adequate endowment and annual income, they could all be met.

Though the endowment problem was not resolved, Vivion announced on January 9, 1930, that Southwestern's accreditation had been renewed for another three-year period. That accreditation, however, was tainted by the fact that the University was still on probationary status, a status it had occupied ever since it had become associated with SACS. The main problem was, as it had always been, endowment. Vivion said that the school had been warned about its endowment being far short of the $500,000 required for a Class A college. He explained that SACS calculates endowment by subtracting the total indebtedness from the productive endowment and counts only the net balance. Calculating in that manner, Southwestern, he said, has a net balance of only $50,000. Since SACS allows Church schools to count as endowment the amount that would be required on a 5 percent basis to produce what they receive from the churches, Southwestern can add an additional $200,000 to its net endowment of $50,000, making a total of $250,000. Therefore, Southwestern must raise an additional $250,000, he concluded, if it wishes to keep its standing as a Class A college.[139]

The 1934 SACS assessment included a team visit to the campus on March 2–3. Its report criticized the school for lack of endowment, low teacher salaries, liberal grading by the faculty, and weakness in the teaching of biology/geology and French.[140] It requested that certain supplementary materials be supplied after the visit. The dean organized the faculty to provide them.[141] The materials must have been satisfactory, because President Vivion, reporting in mid-December on his recent attendance at the annual meeting of the Southern Association in Atlanta, said that "the examining committee . . . made a very favorable report on S.U." Nevertheless, the school was still retained on probation because of its endowment,[142] and SACS requested further information from the faculty "on their training in Education."[143]

The part of the SACS report most troubling to the faculty was the section having to do with faculty credentials and grading "too liberally." They could do little about endowment and low teacher salaries, but they were directly responsible for their own training and grading. The SACS review team had even sent examination papers and other materials to a University of Florida Reviewing Committee for study.[144] The faculty was apparently galvanized into action on this issue, because Vivion reported in mid-1935 that "this fault will be remedied. There is already a lower scholastic average this year."[145]

Practically Bankrupt

Whatever else the other problems during these years, there was no doubt in the minds of those in charge that the fundamental problem of the University was finances. There are so many data from the Vivion years covering the continuing financial decline that it is not very helpful to detail them. With much or little data, the result is the same. By 1935 Southwestern was, for all intents and purposes, practically bankrupt. The saving grace was that none of its creditors wanted to pull the plug, and many persons dedicated themselves to holding the school together long enough to receive the hoped-for reprieve that did in fact occur in 1937.

The number of outstanding debts coming up for payment toward the end of 1931 became critical. In order to solve the problem, the Board of Trustees set up a special committee to examine the endowment to determine whether or not some of it could be used to meet debt payments to banks. On December 22, it received the report of that committee. The report stated that nine of the University's accounts consisted of funds not specifically designated for endowment by the donors and that they might be used to pay debts or for any other legitimate purpose. It was what accountants call "quasi-endowment." Accordingly, the Trustees authorized that those accounts, totaling $51,851.49, be moved from the Endowment section of the books to the Current section. Another $53,135.03 carried in Unrestricted Endowment was transferred to the Current section, making a total of $104,986.52. The Trustees considered the short-term emergency to be so grave that they were willing to sacrifice the long-term interest of the school in order to solve it.[146]

Having engaged in this one-time fix, Vivion and the Trustees commenced a campaign to raise $100,000 to meet other outstanding obligations. It was inaugurated on campus at the annual Founders' Day observance on April 20, 1932, with two bishops, members of the Board of Trustees, and five hundred ministers and laymen present.[147] Many pledges were made on-site, and Vivion began a round of visits across the state to promote it. A month later he returned with little to show for the effort. Interviewing him on his return, a reporter from the *Williamson County Sun* said that he found Vivion "fatigued and worn from the strenuous campaign." Vivion admitted that the response had "not been as large as it should have been, nor as generally participated in among the Methodists of Texas as hoped for by any means." Nevertheless, he said, a few men and women can be found here and there who are meeting the challenge.[148] Illustrations of gifts from these "few men and women" were gifts made by the Tapp Estate in 1932 and the Harrell family in 1933. Dying at the age of seventy-four, Miss Jennie Tapp included Southwestern as a beneficiary of her estate.[149] About $125,000 was received from it. The Harrells were a Corpus Christi couple that had lost their son, Kenneth, a Southwestern student, in a railroad accident.[150] They made a gift of $30,000 to the University in his honor. By mid-1935 it was carried in the audit at $43,413.[151] These gifts brought the endowment back to where it had been before the nine accounts and the Unrestricted Endowment had been touched.

The "Great White Whale" for Southwestern was its debt to the Missouri State Life Insurance Company of St. Louis. By mid-1935 no payment had been made to it for three-and-a-half years on the loan originally taken out to build the Woman's Building in 1925.[152] Year after year interest on the unpaid principal due at the time was added to the debt until by 1935 the total debt was $363,452.52. During these years, efforts were made by the Trustees to work out a payment arrangement with the company that, in Depression times, might be reasonable for a poor, almost bankrupt institution. One or another of the Trustees or the President made trips to St. Louis on an almost annual basis for discussions with the company. These discussions were always amiable, and the emissary generally returned with a new offer for the resumption of payments or a settlement.

Vivion reported to the faculty in early 1933 that on his recent visit the company had agreed to "re-write the loan, fixing it so that for twenty-four months we will not be required to pay them anything; also, that for the following twenty-four months only interest will be required. They will reduce the interest rate from six to five and one-half percent."[153] Yet the Trustees did not accept the offer. A school that could barely meet operating expenses each year could not guarantee payment on even the most generous terms. Each year the offer became more generous. By 1935 the company had gone out of business, and its paper was taken over by the Great American Life Insurance Company.[154] The final disposition of the debt was a part of the "miracle" in 1937.

The Faculty: Unwillingly Buying an Interest in the Corporation

The first indication of a potential problem paying faculty salaries occurred at a January meeting of the Board of Trustees in 1931. After listing the "current obligations now past due," a committee report listed those that would soon become due. Among the items listed was $9,000 needed for the faculty payroll.[155] By September the financial situation of the University had become so bad that "a 10% salary cut was discussed at length." Nevertheless, no action was taken, and no 10 percent salary cut was made.[156] The actual cut would be even worse seven months later—25 percent. At an open meeting of the Board on April 20, 1932, the financial situation of the University was discussed. In addition to the twenty-six Trustees, many others attended, including faculty members.

The report of the faculty, written by Dean Ullrich, presented a bleak picture of the faculty situation. It reported that the University was five months behind in its salary obligations. After listing some of the difficulties faculty members were undergoing, it ended up on a positive note. It stated its appreciation for the merchants in town

Psychology Professor O. A. Ullrich, who served continuously as academic dean for 32 years from 1926–1958 and for one additional year in 1961–62. President Vivion extolled him as being "without a superior in the southwest." Southwestern University, Special Collections.

who "have been gracious enough to carry the accounts of faculty members," expressed its recognition that President Vivion "is bending every energy to find relief," and said that the "faculty as a whole has worked as harmoniously and as cheerfully as the conditions would permit."

> Southwestern University has been and is now fighting for its existence, and the near future will determine whether your college will live. While we realize that the Board of Trustees has heard this plaintive note before, it is not this time a mischievous cry of "Wolf", "Wolf". The wolf is really at our door. The faculty is still wistfully hoping for some five months of its salary. The faculty is still heavily indebted to the merchants of Georgetown, who, because of their faith in the moral integrity of the Church, have been gracious enough to carry the accounts of faculty members. However, the limit of the credit that can be extended has been reached, and some faculty members have been compelled to drop some of their partially paid up insurance which was their only protection against old age. . . . However, realizing that the depression is nation-wide, even world-wide, and not confined to Southwestern only, and realizing furthermore that President Vivion is bending every energy to find relief, the faculty as a whole has worked as harmoniously and as cheerfully as the conditions would permit. The fine spirit of the faculty in the face of all the difficulties has been the marvel of business men in Georgetown and elsewhere.[157]

Four teachers, Williams, Hester, Kuykendall, and Ullrich, proved the truth of "the fine spirit of the faculty" when they stated in the meeting that the faculty would be cooperative in whatever developed. This statement was especially strong given the fact that a motion had already recommended "that the salary schedule be reduced by twenty-five percent, retroactive to January 1, 1932." As finally adopted, the motion reduced salaries by that amount for "at least" twenty months, from January 1, 1932, until September 1, 1933. The reduction in fact was still in place for 1935–1936.[158]

In October 1932 the Executive Committee tried to ameliorate some of the anguish of the faculty and staff by adopting a motion to pay 6 percent interest to them on salary amounts due previously on September 1.[159] This action was immediately counterbalanced, however, by an announcement that reduced the amount each instructor received for supervising correspondence courses. Hereafter, the usual fee for correspondence work would be collected only after thirty-three semester hours had been completed. Fees for the first thirty-three hours would go to the University.[160]

The details of some of the actions taken are difficult to fathom except for the common thread uniting them—that the faculty is being asked to make another contribution of some kind. In early 1933 President Vivion approached the faculty about an undescribed challenge grant made by Mr. Jim West. He said that enough money had already been raised that the conditions of the grant could be met if the staff would agree to contribute to it one month's salary from the accrued unpaid salary account. "Mr. Williams moved that beginning in the morning, each member of the faculty who will agree to give one month's salary will call at the Business Manager's office and indicate that fact. Mr. Kidd seconded the motion. The motion prevailed."[161]

By mid-1933 the school was some $35,000 in arrears on faculty salaries, and instructors were carrying an increased teaching load as a result of the nonreplacement of the teachers that had left.[162] They were soon forced to accept the notes of students for salary. These notes, received by the business office in payment of tuition and other student expenses, were used to pay the merchants in town who were willing to accept them. At a faculty meeting immediately after the Executive Committee had thanked the faculty for its cooperation in accepting student notes, President Vivion tried to regularize the transaction. He suggested that each regular faculty member take two months' salary in student notes. The action taken as a result of his suggestion is not indicated.[163] The visiting team from the Southern Association of Colleges and Secondary Schools reported in March 1934 that several of the faculty voiced to the Committee their objection to receiving student notes in lieu of cash from the University. They said that this procedure placed the responsibility of collection upon them.[164]

McCook reported to the Executive Committee in July that he had been unable to pay the last two months on the salaries of those on the twelve-month scale and the last month of those on the nine-month scale. He proposed to give faculty members full payment by transferring amounts covering those salaries to accounts in their name at the University that could be used to pay for University services, such as eating in the dining hall.[165] By using this and other like methods, the amount of faculty salaries payable had not increased from June, 1933, to January 31, 1934, when $34,557.02 was reported on the financial sheet as due.[166]

The faculty report to the Board of Trustees in 1934 had a different tone from that of 1933. It came after a nine-month period, from September 1, 1933 to May 31, 1934, when the faculty had been paid only four-and-one-fifth months' salaries, that is, just less than half of what was due them. Nearly all of the faculty had been eating in the dining hall during that time.[167] Though it was written after the Educational Commission had issued its ruling that Southwestern would be maintained permanently in Georgetown, the faculty report questioned whether that could be done without a radical change in the financial circumstances of the University. It expressed appreciation for the efforts of the Executive Committee and the administration for what they had done during the year to ameliorate the situation of the faculty, but it questioned the continued viability of Southwestern in Georgetown without a fundamental change in circumstance. It said that "since the faculty has unwillingly bought an interest in the corporation," it should also be given a larger share in determining the financial policies of the university. The irony of the request is that only a year later, as already mentioned, the Executive Committee was reorganized and the two faculty representatives were removed from it.

> As for the first question . . . [y]our faculty cannot be expected to continue under the disheartening conditions to which it has been subjected. . . . To compel the faculty to submit to a retroactive reduction in salary, while very questionable in method, was on the whole cheerfully accepted as an absolutely necessary move on the part of the Board to save Southwestern University. But to allow the conditions to arise that forced the faculty into the position of having to choose either a further reduction in salary or else to accept student notes and accounts in part payment of their salaries, and to allow the situation so to shape itself that the faculty had to serve as a banking institution by extending enforced loans in the form of delinquent salary payments while the hired help received its pay regularly, are factors in the total situation that have caused the faculty to doubt whether the Board of Trustees, the alumni, and the Methodist Church in Texas are interested in Southwestern University vitally enough to come to its rescue.
>
> The Executive Committee and the Administration have done everything within their power to give relief. When the merchants of Georgetown could extend credit no longer, the faculty members and their families were permitted to board in the University Dining Hall, and to pay their board bills with a portion of the salaries due them. In other respects, such as serious illness, the Administration, in individual cases, advanced money to tide over emergencies. These measures the faculty endorses whole-heartedly. It has been by such drastic means that the institution has been able to keep its doors open. These emergency measures have not, of course, and could not be far-reaching enough to save the faculty from the annoyance of creditors and from the necessity of sacrificing insurance policies, their only life's savings. . . . As for the second question; namely, to what extent shall the faculty be privileged to shape the future policies of your college, the faculty is of the opinion that since it is in fact helping to finance the institution in the form of enforced loans, it should have a larger share in determining the future financial policies of the school. Since the faculty has unwillingly bought an interest in the corporation, it might not be amiss to make the members of the faculty stockholders in the enterprise.
>
> The faculty has always been, and is now, ready

to do its part in saving Southwestern University; but to make further sacrifices either in money or in continuing to accept an excessive teaching load without an adequate guarantee of its permanency is out of the question. . . . If Southwestern University can be financed at Georgetown, let us do so all together and cheerfully; if it cannot be financed here any longer, let us face that reality bravely, and act accordingly.[168]

Vivion was as forthright as Ullrich in explaining the necessity of the action taken by the University giving rise to such faculty anguish. He said that the reason the University did what it did was "that banks forced us to repay loans, and there was no other way to take money than from the current treasury. This meant forcing a loan from the faculty to pay the bankers. Since last August, the University as such has not been indebted to any bank for a penny, whereas two years ago we owed to banks more than $50,000.00." He pled with the Board now to come to the relief of the faculty, especially for it to set up a retirement program for them, something he had brought to their attention now for three years.[169] Nothing substantial was done, and the University discontinued group life insurance for employees in December. It did continue, however, to cooperate with individuals in their payments.[170]

Ten days before the meeting of the Board of Trustees in May 1935, Dean Ullrich typed a three-page letter to the President. It was endorsed by five of the oldest and most respected members of the faculty—Tinsley, Gray, Godbey, Williams, and Vaden. The salutation is to "My dear President Vivion."

Southwestern University is insolvent. Everyone acquainted with the affairs of the University knows that to be a fact. Repeatedly the statement has been made that the faculty cannot carry on much longer. Because the doors of the institution have not been closed, some may be disposed to conclude that the cries of distress were and are false alarms.

For evidence of the fact that Southwestern University cannot carry on as an a-grade college of liberal arts, your attention is called to the following facts: . . .

Then Ullrich calls attention to the situation of four teachers who have had to resign to accept either full-time or temporary situations elsewhere. He says that other members of the faculty will do the same as soon as they can find suitable employment. A feeling of restlessness pervades the entire faculty, he says, and this feeling of restlessness does not make for a high grade of college work. He states that the "paramount" problem is

settlement of the indebtedness of the University. It matters little else what is done unless this problem is solved. If that could be done, a budget, though stringent, could be worked out to run the school on even keel. A pension program giving faculty members enough to meet the necessities of life is extremely important. If this is done, a guarantee has to be given that the monthly pensions will be paid promptly. If such a guarantee cannot be given, the plan should not be inaugurated.[171]

When the Board and the Executive Committee met on May 23–24, 1935, they took two actions. They instituted a retirement plan and reinstituted the group life insurance policy for all employees.[172] Two months later the Executive Committee set up a thirty-day sick leave plan at full pay each year for all administrative and faculty officers. It hedged the plan by stipulating that should there be a deficit at the end of the year, the amount of the deficit would be prorated back to the salary schedule for the year. At the same session, the five professors already mentioned were declared to be on the retired list, not, however, because of their having signed the letter to President Vivion, but because they were all eligible to retire and were the first beneficiaries of the new retirement plan.[173] All of them taught part-time after their retirement.

The Last Removal Effort: Details of the Plan

Just as Isaac Joel McCook was the standard-bearer, so to speak, of the Trustees in managing the University through its financial crisis, and Oscar Alvin Ullrich was the champion of the faculty in highlighting its interests in the salary crisis, Joseph King Vivion was the leader of Trustees, faculty, alumni, and students in bringing the University through the final removal crisis in 1933 and 1934. A box bordered in black in *The Megaphone* on February 27, 1934, recognized that fact.[174] It reads as follows:

> The recent decision of the educational commission to retain Southwestern at Georgetown rewards the untiring efforts of President King Vivion, who has lead [sic] the fight against moving the institution ever since the old commission's unfavorable report.

Just as in the case of the previous removal effort, it would be improper to label the attempt of the five Annual Conferences to rationalize their work in higher education from 1932 through 1934 as a removal effort per se. It was seen as a removal effort from the standpoint of Southwestern observers, because, for Southwestern, that is what it amounted to. But from the standpoint of the Church at large, it came about to protect its schools from what was thought to be imminent financial disaster. Three years deep into the Depression, and before the election of Roosevelt, Church leaders had little faith that a political change would rescue them.

The effort of the conferences to study the situation of their colleges and universities began with the creation of another Joint Educational Commission in late 1932. Composed of twenty persons, two ministers and two laymen from each conference, it was charged to survey conference schools and to design a unified program.[175] To ensure the objectivity of the commission, none of its members could be an employee or board member of any of the Church schools.[176] Vivion, who had been a member of the commission in 1929, was not a member this time. The new commission was charged to present a plan for action at the regular sessions of the Annual Conferences in 1933. The essence of the plan would be to create a program for a unified educational system and a way of financing it.[177]

In contrast to the commission in 1928–1929, the new commission utilized heavily the survey work of Boyd McKeown, the emissary from the Board of Christian Education in Nashville. The final report was a product of the entire commission, and it is unclear how much McKeown had to do with making the recommendations. Its chair was C. N. Montgomery, a Southwestern alumnus and a professor at the University of Texas. As issued in late September 1933, it proposed radical changes for Southwestern. Southwestern would be merged with Westmoorland in San Antonio and take with it both its booked assets of $303,260 and its obligations of $432,414.[178] The new school would be called Southwestern University, and a women's junior college would be set up in Georgetown.[179] The plan would, in effect, reverse the roles of Westmoorland and Southwestern. Both Westmoorland and its predecessor institution, San Antonio Female College, had been women's junior colleges until 1933, when Westmoorland became coeducational. Now the women's work in which they had traditionally engaged would come to Georgetown, and the four-year coeducational institution would go to San Antonio.

In addition, all the Methodist schools in Texas except for Southern Methodist would become part of "The Southwestern university system," which would be incorporated and jointly owned, operated, and controlled by the five Methodist conferences in Texas. The Southwestern system would consist of coeducational colleges located at Abilene, San Antonio, and Jacksonville, and possibly a women's college at Fort Worth.[180] It would have a joint board of trustees for all the schools, to succeed the individual boards now existing. The debts of each school would remain charged against it, and individual endowments and gifts would be recognized and maintained.[181] The plan was novel, rational, and straightforward. There would be two Methodist university systems—that of Southern Methodist in Dallas and that of Southwestern operating out of San Antonio. The former would consist of one large university. The latter would be composed of a system of small colleges, with Southwestern undoubtedly growing larger over the years by being located in a large city.

The rest of the plan, however, was quite speculative. Inasmuch as the new Southwestern in San Antonio would bring with it obligations as well as assets, these obligations would have to be liquidated immediately if the University was to have a better chance in San Antonio than in Georgetown. To make this possible, San Antonio would be asked to provide sufficient inducements to trigger the move. San Antonio would in effect be invited to make the kind of offer to the Southwestern of 1934 that Dallas had made almost twenty-five years before to the Southwestern of 1910. The deadline for San Antonio to make its offer would be May 1934, approximately six months after the last Annual Conference had approved the plan. Failing the procurement of adequate inducements from San Antonio by May, the five Annual Conferences should permit the Trustees of Southern Methodist University to negotiate for acquisition of the name and all the other assets of Southwestern, provided, of course, that it assumed its obligations as well. If neither the San Antonio nor the SMU proposals should work out, the report recommended that Southwestern be closed.[182]

Defeat of the Removal Plan

When asked to comment on the recommendation to move Southwestern, President Vivion said that he was unperturbed. "The idea of moving Southwestern University is not to be thought of and will not be [done] by the conferences," he said.[183] His view of the financial situation of the University was very different from that outlined by the commission. He said that the school was completing negotiations at the time with the Jennie Tapp estate that would probably bring between $100,000 and $125,000 to the institution. Another gift of $15,000 would soon be announced. In addition, all endowment funds were intact and drawing interest, including $30,000 for the Cody Memorial Library. The only truly heavy obligation was $250,000—he did not include the accrued interest—to the Missouri Life Insurance Company and, he added, "I am confident the company will deal generously with us."[184] A few days later he assured Southwestern students in a *Megaphone* article that they had nothing to fear. He said that Southwestern is in Georgetown permanently.[185]

During the month between the issuance of the report and the meeting of the first Annual Conference, Vivion set to work and called a meeting of the Board of Trustees for October 24. It went on record unanimously "as being unalterably opposed to the removal of Southwestern University from Georgetown" and charged a committee already formed to see that the report of the Educational Commission be amended by the Annual Conferences. It also published a seven-part resolution detailing the contributions and strengths of Southwestern.[186]

Any action taken by the Southwestern committee to try to alter the report of the Educational Commission was not effective in the West Texas Conference when it met in San Antonio three days later. That conference adopted the commission report as written. The North Texas Conference, however, meeting simultaneously in Denison, was a different matter. Led by Vivion, the Southwestern proponents succeeded in convincing the delegates there that a new commission was needed. An amendment calling for the dismissal of the current commission in favor of a new, more diverse, and larger one was approved. The new commission would consist of thirty persons, three ministers and three laymen from each of the five conferences. The restriction limiting membership in the last commission to persons free of involvement with any of the educational institutions being considered was dropped. The commission would also have the power to act definitively rather than having to report back to the conferences the following year. The two Texas bishops would appoint its members chosen from a pool of persons nominated by the boards of education of each conference.[187] Once the North Texas plan was adopted, it was immediately sent to the West Texas Conference, still in session, for its consideration. It, in turn, approved the North Texas plan rather than stick by its previous action. The other three conferences approved it as well within the next two weeks. The report of the previous commission was referred to the new commission for action.[188]

The action of the North Texas Conference was looked on everywhere as a victory for Southwestern, and the *Williamson County Sun* headlined it as such in reporting on it.[189] Vivion received great praise for his work from Southwestern's supporters. *The Megaphone* reported him as being actively engaged in representing Southwestern at the meetings of the different conferences and said that it was through his influence and efforts that a new commission was appointed.[190] The astuteness and efficacy of his work would soon bear the desired results.

Meanwhile, efforts were being made in San Antonio to raise funds to meet that city's financial obligation to effect the transfer. Dr. Joseph Mayer, Washington, D.C., executive secretary and treasurer of the American Association of University Professors, consultant in sociology in the Library of Congress, and an alumnus of Southwestern, was brought to the city for the purpose of launching a drive to raise the necessary funds.[191] He need not have come. By the time the new commission convened at Waco on February 20, 1934, Vivion's work was in place. By having the two bishops, Hiram A. Boaz and Sam R. Hay, both Southwestern alumni, appoint the members of the commission from among persons nominated by the conference boards of education, he had assured himself of a friendly commission. Boaz, who had initiated the removal effort in 1910, reversed himself in the 1934 controversy. The bishops named a commission with a majority now as predisposed to support the maintenance of Southwestern in Georgetown as the earlier commission had been to move it. At least half of the approximately twenty-five delegates in attendance, including the bishops, were either Trustees or alumni of Southwestern. Though the number of college presidents in attendance is not known and they were without a vote, at least some of them who had worked with Vivion in his efforts to undo the work of the earlier commission were there. With this commission makeup, it would have been surprising if any other result had been obtained from the meeting than the one desired by Southwestern.

A morning, afternoon, and evening session were held. The morning session was devoted to reports from the committees designated to visit the respective colleges. A motion to make a consideration of Southwestern the order of the day for the afternoon session was approved. The importance of this action was that it made possible an independent discussion of Southwestern rather than having it presented in the context of the earlier commission report, which would have otherwise been the order of the day. During the discussion of Southwestern, President Vivion was asked to make a statement about the condition of the school and to give his own opinion as to its future. He expressed confidence in the ability of Southwestern to carry on provided the commission would cooperate and make a positive statement to the public. During his presentation, while he held the floor, Bishop Boaz, Bishop Hay, and four other committee members spoke by his permission in favor of his position. After a short executive session, the following motion was then presented:

> Whereas it seems urgent that our people know the mind of this Commission respecting Southwestern University at Georgetown, therefore be it resolved:
>
> FIRST, that it is our judgment and conviction that Southwestern University shall continue at Georgetown, Texas.
>
> SECOND, that we pledge our support to every effort toward the solution of the problems of this institution.
>
> THIRD, that we authorize the President, the administration and the trustees to inaugurate immediately a campaign to liquidate its indebtedness, increase its endowment, and enlarge its usefulness.
>
> Signed: J. W. Mills, O. P. Clark, W. M. Pearce, L. N. Lipscomb, E. E. White[192]

Though the chairman of the earlier commission, C. N. Montgomery, tried to head off the vote on the resolution by offering as a substitute that the commission consider the report of the earlier commission before voting, his motion was ruled out of order because the matter under discussion was the order of the day. Further discussion ensued, and Bishops Hay and Boaz once again "spoke in the interest of Southwestern." Though the vote on the actual motion is not recorded, the vote on a closely associated matter was 14 to 8. That vote probably indicates the actual division of opinion on the resolution itself. A follow-up motion suggested by Bishop Boaz was approved that a campaign for Southwestern be executed and completed by June 1935. Not only had Southwestern maintained its place in Georgetown, but it had also gained an endorsement for a new financial campaign. The campaign, however, never took place.

The commission completed its work at an evening session by patching up the earlier commission report with actions regarding Southern Methodist University, McMurry College, Kidd-Key, Wesley College, Weatherford College, Blinn Memorial College, Westmoorland College, and Texas Woman's College. Those actions were perfunctory. The real object of the meeting had been the disposition of the Southwestern question. The Educational Commission continued its work into 1935, perfecting the makeup of a Southwestern System of Colleges from a Southwestern in Georgetown. That system, like the financial campaign, never materialized.[193]

Assessing the reasons for Vivion's success in the two removal campaigns during his administration, one is struck by several things. First was his success in working with his built-in constituency, the students, faculty, and alumni. He always exuded confidence before them, and, except for a few people, they backed him strongly all the way. The report of the visiting SACS team in 1934 said that Vivion was "an affable gentleman, with a vigorous and compelling personality." It also credited him with not trying to dominate his faculty "as do some of the less striking executives observed."[194] *The Megaphone* became essentially that for him—a megaphone touting his accomplishments. A second thing was his success in working with the delegates to the Annual Conferences. Starting with the base of Southwestern alumni in those bodies, he impressed the others by his commitment to a cause in which he had no personal stake other than that of securing the welfare of the University. Consequently, they gave him the benefit of the doubt even when his arguments were sometimes less than cogent, as in his arguments for setting up a new commission. Finally, he had a remarkable way of corralling episcopal support. When one examines the two controversies, he is struck by the fact that Bishop Moore in the first controversy and Bishops Hay and Boaz in the second were on his side and, though without votes in the matter themselves, conducted proceedings, made appointments, and offered quiet statements from time to time favorable to the Southwestern position. All of this translates into one major reason for Vivion's success. King Vivion had remarkable people skills.

Conflict in Laura Kuykendall's Career and Her Death

The role of Laura Kuykendall in establishing the May Fête (1915), the Christmas Carol Service (1915), and the Dinner of the Golden Bowl (1925), along with her position as Dean of Women (1918), established her as a primary force on campus. Her magnificent leadership in managing the escape of the women in the fire that destroyed the Annex (1925) solidified her position to almost iconic status. All the Presidents under whom she served praised her and felt that her work was indispensable. Bishop said about her in 1921 that "the young women of the institution are, almost without exception, devoted to her. She is actually a genius in the management of girls."

In spite of her accomplishments in all these areas, there was a slight undercurrent of doubt about her in the minds of some people. Though her flamboyance and flair for the dramatic brought her attention wherever she went, these characteristics at times became too much for some people and put them off. Her outspoken, early feminist point of view expressed in her master's thesis (1926) did not endear her to those who identified that position with the cigarette-smoking "flappers" of the 1920s. In addition, rumor had it that her point of view was not merely theoretical but that she surreptitiously acted out some of the more dubious aspects of it in her personal life. Godbey and Gray are mentioned in student letters as having information detrimental to her character. Though she attended church regularly on Sunday morning, she took little part in any other religious activity except for her own dramatic Christmas Carol Service.

These doubts surfaced in January 1932 in two petitions and a group of letters condemning her sent by thirty-seven students to President Vivion and Dean Ullrich. They requested that conditions be changed in the Woman's Building or that she be removed as Dean of Women. The two petitions, one signed primarily by the twenty women involved in the protest and the other by the seventeen men, arrived in the offices of Vivion and Ullrich during the last ten days of January. The women's petition stated that "we have no intention of returning to this dormitory to live next long session unless either the present condition [in the Woman's Building] is corrected or the present authority is replaced." The men's petition stated that if the present condition is not corrected or the present authority replaced, "we will not only refuse to encourage any students to come to Southwestern but will rather discourage such action."[195]

In addition to the two petitions, fifteen women, most of them already having signed the women's petition, wrote personal letters detailing the conditions that demanded redress. Widespread indoor smoking, swearing loudly in the hallways, occasional drunkenness without punishment, and outrageous petting and necking in the lobby of the Woman's Building were singled out as the major offenses. In addressing Miss Kuykendall's personal faults, they were careful to distinguish between those things they knew from personal experience and those things that were hearsay. Though each letter has its own particular emphasis, the one that demands the most attention is that written by Lillian Gorzycki, a student employee who worked under the Dean.

At the time of the letter, Lillian was a senior who had worked as the night supervisor in the Woman's Building for more than two years. In her highly detailed letter of about 3,500 words, she says that Miss Kuykendall is unfitted for the position she holds because of her personal life, because she is often untruthful, because she belittles students who do not share her opinions, because she is "opposed to definite active Christianity," because of her inability to control her temper, because she protects girls who break the rules and regulations of the University, because of the way she conducts herself around men, because she tries to keep the administration from knowing what goes on in the Woman's Building, and because she "fails to act on things she should act on."

Lillian illustrates these faults copiously from her personal work experience. Illustrating the Dean's use of profanity, she says that "when she turned over a basket of decorations in the lobby, her exclamation was, 'God damn it!' Then upon calling to the janitor she said, 'You'll have to clean up this God-damned mess.'" Illustrating the Dean's antipathy to persons of a religious temperament, she says that Dean Kuykendall called actively religious girls "strange," "amusing," "peculiar." Her temper was exposed one night, says Lillian, when during her round of duties "I surprised her by walking in on her nursing a group of drunk girls. She so lost her temper that with her fist she knocked me through two swinging doors and up against the wall." About her inappropriate conduct with men, Lillian Gorzycki says: "I remember distinctly coming down into the lobby after finishing my work after 11:00 o'clock one night and finding Miss Kuykendall and a married man there talking and acting in a manner entirely unsuited to any married man or the dean of women." They then went outside. The night watchman told her later that the two acted "contrary to the way they should have been acting." Because she was a Life Service student, says Lillian, Miss Kuykendall tried to swear her to secrecy regarding actions taken by her of which Lillian disapproved. The employee, said Miss Kirk, should always support the employer. Lillian said she would always tell the truth.

Laura Kuykendall was, in the way she carried out her responsibilities, an advocate of a different kind of experiential education for girls than that officially promoted by

Southwestern. Her way advocated freedom for women from many of the traditional restraints and accepted different norms of conduct than those advocated by Church and University leaders. The students in their letters contrast her with Dean Ullrich, the academic dean and chair of the Discipline Committee, of whose standards they approved. Laura recognized this conflict between the two, saying that Dean Ullrich interfered with her work, and tried to win Lillian Gorzycki to her side. Failing in this attempt, she threatened Lillian with the loss of her job if she revealed to him what she knew. Rather than firing her, she sadly confessed her real sentiments to Lillian. She told Lillian that she would not try to stop dancing by the girls and that she reprimanded them for smoking and dancing only "to hold my job." The insecurity revealed by Laura Kuykendall in this incident is a touching indicator of her conflicted relationship with the institution she served, sometimes wanting to do one thing but being forced to do another to hold her job.

Whatever the full story, Laura Kuykendall continued in her position for three more years until her death at the age of fifty-one from a stroke on April 30, 1935. Her funeral service was held in the main lobby of the Woman's Building, and Dr. C. M. Bishop, President Emeritus, who had hired her two decades earlier, gave the funeral address. A royal red carpet was spread from the door of the lobby to the hearse, with hundreds of boys and girls lined up on each side of the carpet. The girls, holding bouquets of flowers, were attired in dresses of pastel shades, and the boys wore dark suits. Her beautiful silver casket was borne by ten male students down the line of honor. She was buried in Moody, where she was born in 1883. The magnificence of her funeral was in keeping with the pageants she had inaugurated and produced for two decades.

The reaction of President Vivion to the petitions and letters of the students is not recorded. He probably handled the matter discreetly, arriving at some accommodation among the three parties—himself, Dean Kuykendall, and the students—that ameliorated the situation. At the time of his departure from Southwestern only a few months after Laura's death, Vivion took with him only a few items of particular interest from the presidential files. One of them was the file related to the student protest against Dean Kuykendall. This file passed into the hands of his daughter, Harriet, after his death and was among the Vivion papers returned by her in 2005 for placement in the Southwestern University library. With Laura Kuykendall dead, King Vivion wanted to close the book on judgments of her character and did not want to leave the file with its cache of letters for others to assess and possibly misuse.

Whether President Bergin knew about the student protest or what their letters said about Laura is unknown. He proposed renaming the Woman's Building, her home after 1926, in her honor in his report to the Board on June 7, 1937. The proposal was formally adopted in 1940, and the building appeared as Laura Kuykendall Hall for the first time in the catalog announcement for 1941–1942.[196] With that building having been replaced by the Brown-Cody hall for women in 1997, Laura Kuykendall's memory has now been dimmed to a few shelves in the lobby of that building holding memorabilia associated with her. But Laura Kuykendall was a strong and influential woman, perhaps the most influential woman in her two decades of service of any woman in Southwestern's history.

The Vivion Resignation

By mid-1935 Vivion felt that he had done all he could at Southwestern. When asked who he was, he had always said he was a pastor. He offered his resignation to the Executive Committee on July 26 to resume that role. In his letter of resignation he said that he had worked for Southwestern to the "very limit" of his ability. He expressed his continuing love for the school and indicated a willingness to remain for a reasonable time to help with the transition to a new person. The committee regretfully accepted his resignation.[197] A special committee of three composed of Dr. Claude C. Cody, Jr., chair, Judge Tom McCullough, and Dr. J. W. Bergin was appointed to consider the matter and to discuss it with the Board. A terminal date of September 1 for his leaving was agreed on.[198]

Vivion's decision probably did not come as a surprise. As indicated earlier, he had contemplated resignation two years before only to be dissuaded by the Trustees. A newspaper report in Georgetown had publicized beforehand his recent visit to Nashville to preside over the executive committee of the college section of the Board of Christian Education, of which he was president. It had further stated that while there he would preach at McKendree Methodist Church, "the famous old Methodist church" to which he had been invited as pastor before accepting the presidency of Southwestern.[199] Grady Timmons, a Southwestern graduate of 1919, was pastor at McKendree. Somewhere along the way an arrangement was worked out whereby Timmons would return to Texas to take Travis Park Methodist Church in San Antonio, while Vivion would replace him at McKendree.[200] Now Vivion left to become pastor there. Timmons preached the baccalaureate sermon at Southwestern the following year.[201]

Refusal of Russell Score and Election of John W. Bergin as President

At a meeting of the Executive Committee on Saturday, August 17, Dr. C. C. Cody, Jr., chair of the Nominating Committee, presented the name of Dr. J. N. R. Score, pastor of the First Methodist Church in Fort Worth, for election as President. Apparently Dr. Score had listed several stipulations to the committee that would have to be met if he was to consider the position, for two of the persons present mentioned them. One was a "stipulation relative to debt settlement" and another had to do with the "athletic program." Dr. Vivion, for his part, endorsed the Score nomination and said that he had known him since the early days of his ministry. The committee took a vote by ballot, resulting in a unanimous 8-0 vote in Score's favor. It then approved an annual salary of six thousand dollars for Score, plus house rent and travel account, and elected Dr. John W. Bergin, chair of the Executive Committee, to serve as Acting President from September 1 until Dr. Score assumed office.[202] The nomination was immediately taken to the Board of Trustees, which was meeting on the same day, where another unanimous vote of 20-0 in favor of Score was secured. The chair was asked to notify Dr. Score, and Dr. Cody was thanked for "his untiring and efficient work" for the University, particularly with reference to securing a new President.[203]

Score's election was announced immediately to the public. Dr. Cody told the *Dallas Morning News* that he was confidant Dr. Score would accept. It was also stated that between September 1, the date of Vivion's departure, and September 16, the date Dr. Score was being asked to assume the presidency, the Rev. J. W. Bergin would serve as Acting President. Appointment of a new Dean of Women would be left to the new President.[204]

The following Tuesday evening, August 20th, the Board of Stewards at Score's church in Fort Worth adopted a resolution asking him to decline the offer. The next day he visited Georgetown to talk with University officials. From Georgetown he went to Houston to talk with Dr. Cody.[205] A week later, on the 29th, he refused the position, announcing his decision from Colorado Springs, where he was on vacation. He said that he had talked to members of his church board by phone. They did not want him to leave, and he "would not leave without their sanction."[206]

Having been turned down by Score, Southwestern began the new academic year of 1935–1936 with Dr. Bergin serving as Acting President. There is no record of the Nominating Committee's making an attempt to locate another candidate, and the Executive Committee presented Bergin's name to the Board on October 22 as its nominee for President. Dean Ullrich, speaking for the faculty, urged his election. He was elected unanimously. His salary was set at five thousand dollars, plus the normal housing and travel arrangements. Cody then made a statement about his correspondence with J. N. R. Score, discussing all his earlier communications with Dr. Score regarding his possible election, his actual election, and his "declination."[207] Cody had apparently come away from his contacts with Score believing that Score would accept the offer. His rejection of the Southwestern offer bothered Cody. Score did not completely clear his name with him until sometime after his assumption of office when he was again elected in 1942.[208]

A week later a "Welcome Day" was celebrated for the newly elected President. Hundreds of students, faculty, and citizens of Georgetown and nearby towns gathered in the University auditorium to pledge "unwavering support to that energetic little leader, who has already endeared himself to those with whom he had come in contact." The Pirate band played, and the mayor, the dean, the president of the Ex-Students' Association, and others pledged their support.[209]

15 Toward Financial Stability (1935–1942)

John William Bergin—"The Moving Force!"

Until Bergin's two months as Acting President, he was not a candidate for the presidency itself. He was the Presiding Elder of the Georgetown District of the Methodist Church, a resident of Georgetown, and a loyal alumnus. The intention behind his selection as Acting President was for him to serve as a caretaker who would guide the University until the President-elect, Dr. J. N. R. Score, could get loose from his pastorate in Fort Worth to assume the reins of the institution. The news that Score had refused the position caused consternation on campus, where bad news was already a staple of its diet. For Bergin, however, it unleashed a striking pattern of activity. Temperamentally a positive thinker, he now took charge of the institution with vigor. He pleased the students and faculty by immediately appointing Mrs. May Catt Granbery as Supervisor of Women, using that title so as to leave the permanent appointment of a new Dean of Women to the new President when he should be elected. He worked in the same decisive but judicious manner with Dean Ullrich to fill the remaining faculty appointments by reappointing the recently retired faculty members for another year so as, once again, not to usurp the place of the new President by making permanent appointments.[1] His chapel talks were buoyant, and his speeches in town to various groups were optimistic.

Don Scarbrough, a soon-to-be graduate and later long-time editor of the *Williamson County Sun*, describes Bergin in those days as "a small man, slim, bald except for a fringe of grey hairs in the vicinity of the ears, and [with] blue eyes that sparkled with unbounding energy." He says that Bergin was "all over the place those first few days," but his favorite spot was on the athletic field, where Coach "Lefty" Edens was training the Pirates for their opening game. His exuberant, ever-ready "hot ziggity dog!" whenever a good play was made put life into the team. "Before many weeks had passed, the whole student body was for the new 'Prexy'—one hundred per cent. Whenever talk was made of a permanent president they had one man in view—John W. Bergin. Thus," continues Scarbrough, "on the flood of enthusiasm generated by the united student body, was the 'acting' president made permanent." The "small man" with "unbounding energy" was elected permanent President on October 22, 1935, with the enthusiastic support of Trustees, faculty, and students. Scarbrough says that Bergin did not cause the turnaround of the institution by himself, but he did supply "the steam that kept the wheels spinning; he was the moving force!"[2]

Bergin's Path to the Presidency

Four years after his election, Bergin recounted his life story to a reporter for the *Houston Post*. The interview reminded him that his first business venture was as a newsboy of seven, selling papers for the same newspaper now interviewing him. A year later, his mother, a widow, moved to Robertson County, near Calvert. Her great gift to him, he says, was that she had him do memory work in scripture and general literature, the effects of which, he said, had lasted a lifetime. At seventeen he left home to make his own way. For two years he lived with a farmer, doing chores for his board and keep, and riding or walking about two miles to school every day. During this time he made the acquaintance of a philanthropist in Calvert, who took an interest in him. He invited the young Bergin to move into his home, thus enabling Bergin to graduate from Calvert High School. This same friend provided him funds to attend Southwestern University. When the friend asked him what he intended to do with his life and learned that Bergin was studying for the ministry, he laughingly told him to forget the loan because he would never make enough money to repay it.

Bergin finished his studies in 1898 with one of the few

Bachelor of Philosophy degrees given by the University and was ordained to the ministry. He served pastorates in Marlin, Longview, Marshall, Corsicana, Fort Worth, and other Texas towns. He believed in making use of modern technology, and, as pastor of the First Methodist Church in Fort Worth, he was one of the first ministers to make use of radio, over WBAP. He served as presiding elder of the Waxahachie, Georgetown, and Waco Districts and was elected five times as a delegate to the General Conference. He twice served as the Conference Secretary of Education. Southwestern honored him with the Doctor of Divinity degree in 1919.

Though there is no record of it, he states that, while pastor of the First Methodist Church in Fort Worth (late November 1921 until late November 1925), he was asked to take the presidency of Southwestern. He must have been referring to the period after Horn's resignation at the end of 1923 and the refusal on Christmas Day of the Board's first nominee to replace him. Southwestern was without a President until another alumnus, J. Sam Barcus, was elected on March 26, 1924. Bergin was probably approached during this interval about the possibility of his becoming a candidate for the presidential position. It is not likely, however, that he was offered the position outright. An actual offer would have appeared in the record. Though elected permanent President in October 1935, Bergin acknowledged in his interview that he was not an academician. Referring to his initial appointment as Acting President, he described himself as a "pinch hitter." The dominant impression of Bergin on the reporter at the end of the interview was that he was constantly "on the go." Though born sixty-six years previously, he was said to be "as energetic as a young man of 40."[3]

Bergin's Program of Renewal for Southwestern

Immediately upon his election, Bergin announced a six-point program for his administration: to celebrate Southwestern's centennial in 1940; to build the Cody Memorial Library; to liquidate all financial obligations; to secure a million-dollar endowment; to enroll seven hundred students; and to put on Snyder Field the best football team in the Texas Conference.[4] He added a seventh goal a few days later—to build an adequate gymnasium. Even though during the year he reduced the number to five by omitting the centennial and the football objectives as not being in keeping with the other five,[5] these were amazing goals during the Depression for a man taking over an almost bankrupt institution as the second choice of its Board. More amazing is that he came close to fulfilling them during his tenure. A careful study of his success reveals that much of it was due to factors largely independent of him, including good fortune, but he must be given credit for what he did do in the amazing transformation of the University. His success was partly due to recognition on the part of others that he had accepted what seemed to be a hopeless task, to his vision in setting out specific goals in clear terms, and to his ability to convince others that they could be achieved. His personal dedication to the task was unquestionable. Who could not but be impressed by the picture of a President who slept in his car on recruiting trips to save money?[6]

When questioned about the audacity of his goals a few days after his election, he said: "A stupendous task? No, just worthy objectives[.] What do we care about difficulties?" He added: "And when we observe the Centennial, the one hundredth year of Christian Education by Southwestern University, and our 700 students have gathered . . . [and] . . . our million dollar endowment is secured, I should be glad to lay down my life, and to have no other monument than a modest tablet on the walls of the Cody Memorial Library saying I came to Southwestern in an hour of need."[7]

New Directions in Public Relations—Mme. Slaviansky and the Russian Chorus

By the mid-1930s Southwestern had developed a strong tradition of impressive ceremonial events. Of these events, the May Fête, the Christmas Carol Service, and the Dinners of the Golden Bowl were the most outstanding. By the mid-1930s, however, they had lost some of their luster and had become more formal observances, unlike the exciting events they had been under Laura Kuykendall. With her death, the May Fête had been changed to a more modest May Day observance without the pageantry of the original. In the mind of Bergin the Christmas Carol Service, the Dinner of the Golden Bowl, and the May Day observance failed to reach the general public. They were in-house events without significant public relations value. Students on campus and persons who came to the campus to witness or participate in them were highly impressed, but the events had little effect

The Southwestern Chorus, led for four years by Russian émigré Mme. Margarita Agreneva-Slaviansky, brought considerable notoriety to the University. Southwestern University, Special Collections.

beyond Georgetown. Their slow pace and dependence on what were, in the minds of many, prosaic themes did not accord well with an age of action and novel public shows. During his first year Bergin instituted two programs that did display these characteristics. Though his new events were not pageants in the technical sense, they were pageant-like. They were the addition of a colorful Southwestern Chorus directed by a talented Russian "gentlewoman" and the only college Swing Band in Texas.

Wandering the country during the Great Depression were Russian émigrés set adrift by the Communist revolution of 1917–1918. A small group of these émigrés was the Slaviansky Chorus, directed by Mme. Margarita Agreneva-Slaviansky. Arriving in America around 1927, the Chorus gave a performance at Southwestern four years later.[8] It presented hundreds of other performances between 1931 and 1936. A newspaper report of the group's 1933 performance at a teachers' college in Stevens Point, Wisconsin, describes what must have been a typical program and the audience reaction:

> Exotic, even bizarre in quality was the program presented. . . . The audience felt that something different and something really good was coming from the first appearance of the chorus, which consisted of five women, five men and a young boy, with their colorful native costumes and their inscrutable Russian faces.
>
> The Director, Madame Slaviansky, was a regal, imposing figure with her gown and headdress bedecked with jewels and her graceful hands, with which she conducted her chorus, sparkling with rings. Her pink and white face was expressionless except when her daughter, Mlle. Mara Slaviansky was enthusiastically applauded after her first solo numbers. The director and her daughter alternated as accompanists.
>
> The entire program was in Russian, with the exception of two songs, but the explanatory notes on the program and the dramatic quality of the voices helped in the understanding of the type of song. All types were included, such as the folk song, love song, dance song, religious song and patriotic song. Mlle. Slaviansky was a favorite with the audience, and she used her sparkling dark eyes as effectively as she did her clear soprano voice. The American numbers were interesting. A tall tenor with an ascetic face sang "Going Home" and the entire company joined in an

amusing college song, "Massachusetts." It seemed a bit incongruous to see a stalwart Russian bass with a black mustache boom out collegiate absurdities in an amazingly deep voice, but it was fun for the audience, and the singers didn't seem to mind. As a variation to the musical program strenuous Cossack dances were performed by the small boy and two of the men singers, all of whom were vigorously applauded. Lighting effects synchronized with the music increased the color appeal of the program.[9]

Though the details of Mme. Slaviansky's employment by Southwestern in March 1936 are not known, the *Williamson County Sun* reported three days before the campus concert on March 30 that she had already worked out an arrangement with Dean Meyer to become a voice teacher in the School of Music and director of the Southwestern University Chorus. Though the Russian chorus performed the concert, the Southwestern Chorus concluded the concert with two pieces under her direction.[10] Dean Meyer turned the Chorus over to her on a full-time basis, and she immediately began to give it a new flavor by supplementing the student voices with members of her Russian chorus.[11] She was featured two months later in the *Bulletin of Southwestern University*, which said that she was "a graduate of music conservatories of Paris, Milan, and Berlin. . . . Mme. Slaviansky's father," it continued, "the famous exponent of Russian folk songs, founded the [choral] organization in Russia in 1858, and conducted it until she succeeded him in 1908."[12]

Both Dean Ullrich and President Bergin praised her in the Board report of 1936. Ullrich said that the University Chorus "reached unusual heights this year" and "did excellent service in advertising Southwestern University in different parts of the State." Bergin called her "a cultured and experienced gentlewoman" who had made "a profound impression" wherever she carried the chorus and had won "the admiration of the entire student body."[13] She was paid a basic salary, which, when supplemented by private voice lessons, was calculated by him to be a respectable Depression salary.

Under her direction, the Southwestern University Chorus traveled widely over the state and to different parts of the country. The Chorus is pictured in a University view book in 1937 with fifteen women in striking costumes seated in chairs, thirteen men also in costumes standing behind them, and two ladies—Mme. Slaviansky and her daughter—posed in gorgeous costumes in the center as the primary objects of attention. A boy or young college student holding a tambourine is reclining in front of them on the floor.[14]

The Megaphone reported in mid-May 1937 that "Madame Slaviansky, six Russians, eighteen Southwestern University choristers and three discouraged Packards returned to Southwestern Thursday from a five thousand mile trip that carried the organization to the sandy shores of Lake Michigan."[15] Bergin stated in his next Board report that, "exclusive of concerts given on campus, the chorus gave 27 performances to a total of approximately 26,600 people. Six of the performances were given in other states. Three radio performances were given, one over WFAA, two over KNOW."[16] Perhaps the most ambitious trip of the group was taken two years later to Baltimore by bus. Invited to sing at the Biennial Convention of the National Federation of Music Clubs, the Southwestern University Chorus gave twenty concerts in ten states. Approximately thirty-five people made the trip.[17]

The Chorus was used at practically every event of any importance during the four years of Mme. Slaviansky's tenure. It participated in the grand Texas Centennial celebration in Georgetown in 1936, it presented a "Christmas in Old Russia" program at a Christmas Carol Service in 1937, it performed in the Hogg Auditorium in Austin in 1938, it sang the "Hallelujah Chorus" at the dedication of the Cody Memorial Library in 1939, and it participated in the University's own Centennial Celebration in 1940. It also participated on an annual basis in the baccalaureate and Commencement ceremonies. These travels and performances were in addition to the regular student and faculty recital programs connected with Mme. Slaviansky's academic work in the School of Music. The Vocal Department gave its summer program in 1939 on the lawn of the Swedish, now St. John's, Methodist Church. On that occasion the students, Mlle. Mara Slaviansky, and the Chorus joined in presenting sixteen musical pieces.[18] Soon thereafter a newspaper article announced that beginning on Sunday, September 15, 1939, Mme. Slaviansky would direct the choir at the First Methodist Church, with Miss Iola Bowden as pianist, and with Mara Slaviansky as soloist.[19] The two Slavianskys were listed as hostesses for a Faculty Club meeting in the spring of 1940.[20]

By 1940 it seemed that the two Slavianskys, exotic though they might be to Central Texas residents, had become integrated into the University and into Georgetown society. Mme. Slaviansky's basic salary had been almost doubled, and her work was so satisfactory that

President Bergin recommended giving her for 1940–1941 any excess in fees above a given level generated by her for individual lessons. By then her daughter, Mara Slaviansky, had also been taken on as an instructor in Voice.[21] However, just before the opening of the fall semester, she reported to President Bergin that she would be unable to teach because of illness.[22] The University was forced to employ someone quickly to replace her.

Though she was perhaps indeed ill, it may also be the case that over time the world of Georgetown had grown too small for Mme. Slaviansky. For four years it had been a haven for her during the worst days of the Depression. By 1940, however, she was ready to exercise her talents once again on a wider stage. She, her daughter, and Edward Gross went north to establish a place on the Chicago scene. Edward Gross was a young protégé first hired by the Russian chorus as a baggage boy. He had acquired an M.A. in Music under her while at Southwestern. A few months later Mara and Edward were presented in concert in Kimball Hall.[23] Mme. Slaviansky herself became director of a seventy-five-voice choir and in March directed a massed chorus of five hundred voices at the Slavic-American festival held at the Civic Opera House in Chicago.[24] The *Musical News* of April 3, 1941, showed a picture of Mme. Slaviansky with her Russian chorus of seventy-five to eighty voices in full costume. The article praises her two performances in the Civic Opera House on March 16 to "large and appreciative audiences." She is called a "suave and accomplished director who has trained her charges so well that in public performances she needs only to resort to the slightest gesture to obtain the effects she desires."[25]

In an article recounting these later accomplishments of the Slavianskys, the *Williamson County Sun* makes the following comment: "Georgetown will long remember the many occasions on which these gracious and accomplished artists gave their time and talents, and will continue to be grateful to them and regret that they are no longer among us."[26] The Slaviansky-Southwestern connection seems to have been one in which both parties received full value from the relationship while it lasted. Bergin was not disappointed. He believed that extraordinary actions needed to be employed to shake Southwestern out of its doldrums. The Slaviansky episode was indeed extraordinary.

New Directions in Public Relations—Tom Johnson and the Swing Band

A second effort by Bergin to make an impact on Southwestern and the general public was by the employment of a new band director to introduce a new kind of musical program. When the previous director could not complete the year because of illness in the spring of 1936, Bergin immediately employed Tom Johnson, the most famous, though controversial, band director in the Southwest.[27]

Johnson came to Southwestern with an already established reputation. As director of the Southern Methodist Mustang Band, he had taken it to some of the leading

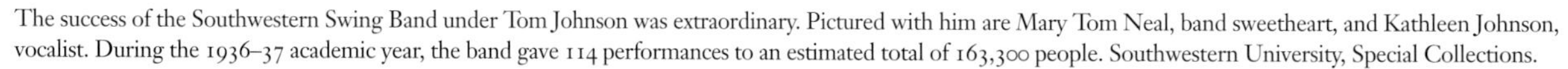
The success of the Southwestern Swing Band under Tom Johnson was extraordinary. Pictured with him are Mary Tom Neal, band sweetheart, and Kathleen Johnson, vocalist. During the 1936–37 academic year, the band gave 114 performances to an estimated total of 163,300 people. Southwestern University, Special Collections.

theaters in the North and East. Immediately prior to his coming to Southwestern he had taken the band to the Rose Bowl (January 1, 1936), where it played for the Stanford-SMU game. During the week preceding the game the band had played at the Paramount Theatre in Los Angeles.[28] Following the Rose Bowl game, he toured California, making bookings for the band without permission from SMU authorities. This procedure was not considered to be academic or proper, and he was asked to leave SMU. He was released at precisely the point where the Southwestern band director could not complete the year.[29] Bergin took advantage of the situation and hired Johnson to come to Southwestern.[30]

Apparently the swing style posed no problem for Bergin. He had no objection to using the "big band" style of music to publicize Southwestern on the stage and on the football field. Newspaper articles publicized Southwestern's Swing Band, and the *Williamson County Sun* said that "the Mustang Band is marching—right down to Southwestern University, another Methodist institution." It said that Johnson had been given a free hand by the President "to select his musicians and they have been instructed to swing out. When they strut on the field at Georgetown for the first grid game, Johnson won't be the only ex-Mustang jazzician on the field. Most of the star performers of Johnson's SMU Band will be wearing the colors of Southwestern, too. . . . Fred Stulee, former Mustang bandsman now with Tom[my] Dorsey's orchestra, is doing arrangements for Johnson's Southwestern show band."[31] Nevertheless, the SMU musicians would only form the nucleus of the band in its transitional stage. Bergin granted Johnson twenty band scholarships to attract to Southwestern capable musicians who would become the nucleus for the future.[32] A picture of the University band in the 1937 view book shows twenty-four members in new uniforms provided by the Lions Club, with three girls standing in evening dresses left, right, and center.[33] The city was so enthusiastic about the band that the Chamber of Commerce provided it with a new International bus.[34]

Over his six-year career at Southwestern, Johnson became a strong promoter of the University. In the summer of 1936, before he had ever marched a band onto the football field or met a class, he took a two-week trip into the Rio Grande Valley with Captain Kidd in "an active drive for students."[35] The three promoters, Bergin, Slaviansky, and Johnson, participated together in the second "annual" Pirate Pageant on April 3, 1937. The pageant had a strong student recruitment component. Invitations were sent to all the high school principals within a one-hundred-mile radius inviting them to choose a senior boy and girl to represent them at the pageant. The event began with a reception, banquet, and musical program led by Mme. Slaviansky. It then moved to Snyder Field, where Bergin crowned "the Sweetheart and the captain of the Pirate fleet." Following the coronation, seventy-five members of the physical training classes presented a dance drama featuring the customs and habits of foreign countries. Tom Johnson and the swing band provided incidental music throughout the program, concluding with Tchaikovsky's "1812 Overture," using simulated cannon fire and real smoke.[36]

Bergin reported to the Board in 1937 that the success of the Southwestern Swing Band had been so great that "echoes of its performances are returning from all parts of the State. Since last September, it has given 114 performances to an estimated total of 163,300 people."[37] Illustrative of its trips was one to Kingsville to play at the Southwestern–Texas A&I football game. On the way to its destination, the band stopped for a fifteen-minute program at the Lockhart high school followed by lunch in Cuero. While there it "gathered around a turning post in the middle of main street and did some swinging for the over-joyed [sic] populace. After performing at the football game, they gave shows at the Plaza and Nueces Hotels."[38] Probably at no point in Southwestern's history have two student groups traveled as much and performed before as many different audiences as did the University Chorus and the University Swing Band in 1936–1937.

In spite of Bergin's quick acceptance of the swing style for the band in 1936, his decision caused disquiet in some quarters. Two years later the Board Committee on the Student Body had received enough complaints that it issued a carefully worded report bringing the issue to the fore. It asked the question: "'Does a Swing Band make its appeal to those prospective students who will likely acquiesce in the attitude of our church and your Board of Trustees toward modern dancing?' There is, in the minds of many Methodists, the question 'Does such a band, and the music in which it specializes, properly represent the spirit of Methodism before the public?'"[39] These questions were apparently enough to cause Bergin and Ullrich to engage Johnson in rethinking the band program and to come up with an alternative approach. Describing the new approach to the Board of Trustees in a written statement, Johnson displayed no discomfort with the change. He said that "while our present Band is a popular advertising feature[,] I feel that a concert unit would better represent the finer things for which a University stands."[40] He suggested two major changes. First, he proposed to make band a major field of study in the Bachelor of Arts degree program, and, secondly, he suggested that the Swing Band become a concert band. His program was adopted. Though in succeeding years the swing style was de-emphasized, it was not eliminated.[41]

The transformation to a "concert" band was hardly noticed by the general public. During the first fall after arriving in Georgetown, Johnson had produced a Pigskin Revue that became a staple of band performance. Bringing the idea with him from SMU, it was not so much a concert as "a collegiate show with the band serving as a back ground [sic] with special solos and acts by talented musicians, singers, and dancers of not only the band but also the whole student body." Johnson had begun his career as a child magician, and magic acts were included in some of the band programs.[42] The musical numbers ranged from the latest tunes of the season to the "1812 Overture."[43] Even after it became a "concert" band, it carried much the same program on the road as before. By this time it was the only college band in the Southwest that made extensive annual tours. In the spring of 1941 it visited Hearne, Lufkin, Port Arthur, Beaumont, Longview, Palestine, Nacogdoches, Henderson, and Troup. Though it still carried a student comedian, Jimmy Hotchkiss, for relief between acts, its music was much the same as earlier, ranging from its staple "1812 Overture" to a patriotic potpourri entitled "American Youth Salutes America." The climax of the show was a special arrangement of Gershwin's *Rhapsody in Blue*, with its haunting clarinet riff at the beginning. One of the two female vocalists with the band was Johnson's wife, Kathleen.[44]

Johnson's unique band program ended with the war, when he was inducted into the army in late 1942. Never again would the band play as strong a role in the total life of the institution as it did between 1936 and 1942, when it helped Bergin publicize the University to tens of thousands of people in Texas.

Connections and Enablers

Though the transformation of Southwestern from a debt-ridden institution with little productive endowment to a debt-free institution with over half a million dollars in productive endowment on March 1, 1937, has been referred to as a "miracle," the miracle has a more natural explanation. That explanation centers around one word—connections. Southwestern was able in 1937 to tap into its connection with one family of wealth whose gift changed the financial situation of the University completely. The success of the University in meeting the conditions of the Wiess grant in that year validated it in the eyes of others in the philanthropic community who were encouraged thereby to include Southwestern in their programs of gift giving.

By the 1930s there was considerable wealth in the hands of certain Methodist families and their friends in Texas. Many of them were connected to Southwestern through family members who attended as students or who were connected by friendship with other persons who had. Some of the prominent family names in this category were Wiess, Root, Brown, Jones, Perkins, McManis, Fondren, Thomas, West, Kurth, Cullen, and Germany. The reason they are familiar to those who know the history of Southwestern is that all made significant gifts and/or contributions of time in soliciting major gifts in the forty years between the Wiess grant in 1937 and The Brown Foundation challenge grant forty years later in 1976. The gifts that were the product of this period eventually changed the face of the campus and transformed Southwestern from an institution that had to scratch and claw for existence into one that today has the opportunity of defining the level and type of excellence it shall have.

This phenomenon did not occur automatically. It occurred because of the connections these families had with Southwestern and with each other and because they were assisted by a group of enablers—certain Presidents and Trustees—to translate their philanthropy into endowments and buildings. The overriding importance of the Wiess grant in 1937 was that its success triggered the rest. It changed the image of Southwestern from being a dubious enterprise with an uncertain future to one that was not only likely to survive, but also had the possibility of surviving with some degree of quality attached to its name. The school with the oldest charter heritage in Texas suddenly became one that might burnish that legacy in the future. Bishop A. Frank Smith, the first of the great modern enablers, played a significant role in the effort.

A. Frank Smith as Enabler

A key figure in the change of fortune experienced by Southwestern from the mid-1930s to the mid-'60s was A. Frank Smith. First as a pastor and then as bishop over several Texas Annual Conferences, he was a member of the Board of Trustees for thirty years. As pastor of Houston's First

Methodist Church, he brought to the Board his friendship with a number of members who had already or who would soon play prominent roles in Southwestern history. They were such persons as S. F. Carter, Mr. and Mrs. Walter Fondren, Jesse H. Jones, E. L. Crain, R. E. ("Bob") Smith, and Eddy Scurlock. His membership on the Board as bishop overlapped almost exactly the tenure of Dr. Claude C. Cody, Jr., also of Houston, who served as President of the Board and Chair of the Executive Committee during most of that time. The connections of these two men with the Houston community solidified the Southwestern relationship to Houston that had already been established.

Frank Smith served on the boards of trustees of six different colleges and universities during his career. His service as chairman of the Board at Southern Methodist University from 1938 until his retirement was crucial for that institution. He was largely responsible for securing the magnificent gift from Joe and Lois Perkins that undergirds its Perkins School of Theology today. He was also instrumental in working through successfully the racial integration of the Theology school in 1952. In a less able person his service at SMU might have diminished his contribution to Southwestern, but, to the contrary, it enhanced it. He encouraged some of the same people who gave to Southern Methodist also to make contributions to Southwestern, his alma mater. Writing to President Finch in 1953, he commented about his relationship to the two institutions. He said: "As you well know and as I have often said to you, . . . [Southwestern] . . . is where my heart is even though my activities have been, in largest part, with another institution."[45] Dr. J. N. R. Score, Bergin's successor at Southwestern, was a close friend. Smith helped make him President in 1942. Smith's last significant act for Southwestern was to convince others that Durwood Fleming should succeed Finch as President in 1961. After the inauguration ceremony, he wrote to Fleming: "Incidentally, I have participated in the Induction of your five immediate predecessors in that office [Barcus, Vivion, Bergin, Score, Finch]."[46] Never, however, did he intrude into the administrative affairs of the University. He always worked with the President as an enabler.

The Smith-Wiess Connection

In mid-April 1936 President Bergin and Dr. J. N. R. Score, pastor of the First Methodist Church in Fort Worth and a Trustee of Southwestern University, visited Harry C. Wiess, president of the Humble Oil and Refining Company of Houston. Score accompanied Bergin on the visit because he had been the pastor of Mrs. Wiess for eight years while at St. Paul's. They made the visit as part of a financial campaign to raise $65,000 to help the University meet its many obligations during the first year of Bergin's presidency. They were merely seeking a gift of $5,000 or $10,000.[47] When the outcome of the visit eventually resulted in the $110,000 "conditional" grant that pulled Southwestern out of debt, Smith gave Score credit for placing the idea in the mind of Wiess.[48] However preeminent may have been the role of Score in initiating the idea, Smith was the person who more than any other brought the idea to fruition.

Wiess must have mentioned the idea of a large gift soon thereafter to his cousin, Dr. Ed Hodges, a prominent physician and surgeon in Houston, because Hodges suggested to Smith that he call on Wiess. This suggestion by Hodges to Smith was not unusual, because Harry Carothers Wiess and A. Frank Smith had been boys together, and both lived in Houston. Their mothers, Louisa Elizabeth Carothers and Mary Elizabeth Marrs, had gone to school together in Georgetown before Louisa married Captain William Wiess and before Mary married William Angie Smith. Accordingly, Smith went to visit Wiess not as a dignified bishop visiting an oil magnate but as one childhood friend visiting another. Wiess told him that his mother, soon to be eighty, wanted to make a gift to Southwestern but said that he didn't know if the school was secure or not. "I don't want her to give it to a school that is going to go under."[49]

Smith immediately went to work. He called W. E. Orgain, who was also a friend of Wiess. Orgain was a Southwestern Trustee from 1915 to 1947, president of the Board in 1933 and 1935, and chairman of the Finance Committee in 1936. Smith suggested that the two of them visit Wiess. Their purpose on the visit was to provide some assurance that Southwestern would not go under. They determined that the way to do it was to propose that the Wiess gift be contingent upon Southwestern's paying off its indebtedness. Wiess liked the idea and telephoned the family attorney, Frank Andrews, for advice. Andrews, the son of a Baptist preacher, had gone to Southwestern with Frank's father and mother in the early 1880s and "stood up with them, as they said in those days, when they were married."[50] Andrews was very enthusiastic about the gift. Andrews told him that "Southwestern University has sent more men of distinction out of Texas than any other school, not excluding the State University." That statement, said Wiess, was enough for him. He then asked them how they were going to proceed. The two men told him they would get out and raise the money to pay off the indebtedness. Mrs. Wiess "joyfully acquiesced," and "on June 26, 1936, . . . [she] . . . conveyed to Mr. Andrews, as trustee, one thousand shares of Humble Oil and Refining Company stock, one thousand shares of Montgomery Ward and Company stock, and one hundred shares of Air Reduction Company stock—a total value of approximately $110,000." He was to hold it pending the successful completion of the campaign.[51]

Mrs. Wiess died two weeks later, on July 7.[52] Andrews died five months later, on December 7.[53] Harry Wiess himself died scarcely more than a decade later of inoperable cancer. President Score wrote about Harry Wiess at the time that he was "a good man. I was his mother's pastor for eight years and have known him for more than twenty. He is but sixty-one."[54]

William Wiess and Louisa Carothers Wiess

The Wiess connection with Southwestern stemmed from the girlhood of Louisa Carothers Wiess in Georgetown. She had moved to Georgetown with her family in 1871, two years before Southwestern was established there. Having been born on March 27, 1856, she was twenty-two when she entered the Young Ladies' School as a member of the first class in 1878. Through some unknown instrumentality she met William Wiess, fourteen years her senior. He had been born at Wiess Bluff, Jasper County, Texas, on October 23, 1842. They married in 1880, with Francis Asbury Mood performing the ceremony. Wiess at the time was a widower. One of the children born to the first union was Mrs. W. A. Priddie. She cooperated with Harry, a product of the second union, in facilitating the gift to Southwestern in 1936–1937.[55]

After their marriage, William and Louisa moved to Beaumont, where he made his fortune in the lumber, mercantile, and oil business. He also ran a line of steamboats on the Neches River. An account of his life published in *The Southwestern Advocate* says that he was very interested in public affairs and was primarily responsible for the law banning gambling on horse racing. "He did not," it continued, "wait to see upon which side the majority stood before choosing and making known his own stand, thereafter laboring with all his might for the right as he saw it." He was a staunch supporter of the Methodist Church and was largely responsible for the erection of First Church, Beaumont. His support of worthy causes was not limited to finances. He always gave personal assistance and encouragement to those causes in which he had an interest.[56] He served as a Trustee of Southwestern from 1906 until his death on June 12, 1914. He both lent and gave money to the University prior to the removal controversy of 1910–1911 and was a strong supporter of Cody and John M. Barcus in their efforts to retain it in Georgetown. Though he was already in poor health at the time of the controversy, he kept in close touch with Dean Cody by correspondence.

Meeting the Specifications of the Wiess "Conditional Gift"

Wiess, Smith, Andrews, Orgain, and Bergin worked out the specific terms of the "conditional gift," and the Finance Committee began a quiet campaign to meet the five conditions agreed upon. They were: (1) that the debt with the General American Life Insurance Company and other debts be satisfied; (2) that an additional $40,000 in cash or marketable securities be raised; (3) that no present asset of the University be used in payment of the debts; (4) that there be no public campaign; and (5) that all the conditions of the agreement be accomplished by March 1, 1937.[57] The Board had approximately eight months to complete the task.

The crucial issue for success in the campaign was settlement of the big debt with the General American Life Insurance Company of St. Louis. General American had earlier taken over the paper on the Woman's Building from the now bankrupt Missouri State Life Insurance Company. Though that debt by mid-1935 had technically reached $363,452.52, General American had taken over the debt at a discounted rate, and both sides knew at the outset that the settlement would be much less than that amount. At a meeting held in Houston between the Finance Committee and a representative of the insurance company, the Committee offered $75,000 in cash as an adjustment. This amount was only about 21 percent of the total debt carried on the books, and the insurance company countered with a request for $100,000, or about 28 percent. No agreement was reached, and Cody called a special Board meeting for January 19, 1937, to inform the Trustees of the situation and to determine what should be done. Over six months had elapsed, and the March 1 deadline was looming closer and closer. At the meeting the Board was adamant in its position and determined "to wire an offer of $75,000.00 to the insurance company, the money to be paid in cash by or before March 1, 1937." A further resolution was adopted that if the offer was accepted the Finance Committee would be "authorized to organize and prosecute a campaign for adjusting and paying all indebtedness of the University and [for raising] the sum required for the securing of the Wiess gift."[58]

An agreement acceptable to both sides was quickly reached, and a concentrated effort to liquidate the rest of the indebtedness and to raise the necessary matching funds began soon thereafter. Both Georgetown and the faculty responded magnificently. Bergin had earlier received an agreement from the city that it would raise $30,000, half of the local indebtedness of the school. By late February some $34,000 had been raised, most of it from business leaders who relinquished their claims on the University. When it was learned at the last minute that the Houston group had failed to meet its quota by some $16,000 and that the success or failure of the entire campaign hinged upon raising that amount of money within a few days, twenty-four faculty members met with eighteen members of the Chamber of Commerce in an evening meeting on February 27. After a discussion of the problem, the faculty adjourned to meet separately. Though it had earlier pledged a smaller amount to the campaign, it now pledged the entire amount needed to complete it by "releasing back salaries and all amounts owed them by the University with the understanding that five months' salary of each faculty member be payable to the University for this purpose."[59] The total amount raised by Georgetown, including the faculty contribution, was about $51,000.[60] The final list of all contributors to the campaign comprised less than two hundred individuals, all of them employees, former students, patrons, or close friends of the University.[61]

After the campaign was over, Dr. Cody wrote a letter to Dean Ullrich expressing his appreciation for the faculty contribution. Dean Ullrich thanked him for the remembrance but mentioned a problem they were having. He said that they were "wrestling" with the problem of equalizing the load borne by them in relinquishing their claims on the University. "The institution owed nothing to some [faculty] members, a small sum to others, and a large sum to others. The reason for this discrepancy," he said, "is the fact that some faculty members took over large blocks of student notes in order that the University might be helped."[62]

Though the notarized document from Southwestern signed by Bergin and McCook testifying to the completion of the conditions of the campaign is dated March 3, 1937, McCook probably drove from Georgetown to Houston on Sunday night, February 28, to inform the appropriate persons there by the March 1 deadline that the conditions of the Wiess trust had been met. Southwestern lore has called this "the midnight ride" or "the wild ride."[63] Since McCook likely had to prepare papers on Sunday after the Saturday night faculty meeting showing that the conditions of the Wiess proposal had been met, he made his trip to Houston late the next day so as to be there by the deadline of Monday, March 1. Informed there about the kind of documentation needed to satisfy legally the completion of the grant, he returned to Georgetown, where he and Dr. Bergin prepared the appropriate document dated March 3. Miss Neas certified it as the notary public. It was then transmitted back to Houston.[64]

The South Texas Commercial Bank of Houston delivered the funds from the Wiess grant to Southwestern on March 13. During the nine-month interval between the time when the stocks had been turned over to Andrews until the time when the bank sold them, the stocks had increased in value from about $110,000 to $162,325. Newspapers throughout the state announced simultaneously on March 15 that Southwestern was free of debt, with a freestanding endowment of about $600,000. At the Board meeting in June, Bergin thanked the Finance Committee along with Dr. Cody, Bishop Smith, and Bishop Moore, who, he says, negotiated the debt payment and endowment addition. He also included the people of Georgetown among those to whom the University was grateful.[65]

A table constructed from various sources of the money raised to satisfy the conditions of the Wiess grant follows:

Financial Campaign for Wiess Grant
Concluding March 1, 1937

Cash raised	$88,217.14
Credit on debts	$316,398.98
Notes and pledges	$44,004.23
Dividends	$5,475.00
Total	**$454,095.35**

When the Wiess gift of $162,325.00 is added to the $454,095.35, the total monetary benefit realized from the campaign by removing debits and adding credits was $616,420.35, or about $7,400,000 in 2000 dollars adjusted for inflation.[66]

Emergence of Faculty Problems in 1937

The academic year 1936–1937, the second of Bergin's almost seven years as President, was the high watermark of his administration as far as the satisfaction of his constituency was concerned. During that year two musical groups toured the state and brought great attention to Southwestern. A campaign was completed that not only eliminated the debt that had crippled the University for thirty years, but also established a modest productive endowment. The academic year 1936–1937 was the most exhilarating year since 1908–1909, when Mood Hall was completed and the first Homecoming event was celebrated. Bergin was commended by the Finance Committee at the Board meeting in mid-1937 for building up the endowment and "discharging the indebtedness of the University."[67] The students, too, were caught up in his success. When some people in Georgetown began to talk about Bergin for bishop, Don Scarbrough, the editor of *The Megaphone*, wrote that they should "call it off, for we cannot spare him!"[68]

There would be other successes during Bergin's years, such as the construction of the Cody Memorial Library and the West Gymnasium, and major events, such as the Centennial Celebration in 1940, but his last five years would be marked by almost continuing controversy. The exhilaration that pervaded the campus in mid-1937 was short-lived. It was followed by a series of events that eventually left the President in disfavor with many faculty members, students, and Trustees. It led to his reluctant resignation in late 1941. Since information regarding these events is limited, making it difficult to draw definite conclusions about them, one must be content with a simple narration of what occurred as best it can be unraveled.

Faculty problems manifested themselves in the first Board meeting after the conclusion of the financial campaign. On that occasion three faculty members were called before the Board to be "thoroughly reviewed." They were Albert Russell Wapple, Lucy Belle Morgan, and Luther Jacob Waggoner, in Mathematics, Spanish, and Religious Education, respectively.[69] Wapple had been employed in 1926, Morgan in 1929, and Waggoner in 1929. Wapple, chair of his department, was called before the Board "because his teaching . . . [had] . . . not been strong" and for his unwillingness to try to improve it by seeking further education in his field. In a letter to the Board, Ullrich explained that the University had kept him to this point because "it seemed heartless to discharge him" during the Depression when he was making sacrifices, along with others, in salary.[70] After being heard by the Board, he was continued in his position. The problems of Lucy Belle Morgan were poor teaching and lack of respect by students. A committee of the Southern Association of Schools and Colleges had also recently criticized Spanish, her field.[71] Nevertheless, after being heard, she, too, was continued in her position.[72]

Waggoner was a maverick, a person with an idiosyncratic teaching style who did things his own way. With a B.A. and a B.D. from Southern Methodist University and an M.A. from Columbia, he never completed his doctorate, though he came to Southwestern in 1929 with one year and seven summers of work toward it from the Chicago and Union Theological Seminaries.[73] A *Megaphone* article recounting the senior spoof of the faculty held in 1932 says that a student named Bill Conerly stopped the show when he appeared on stage as Mr. Waggoner with umbrella, briefcase, and blackboard. The student body hilariously received Conerly's speech about "Us Nordics," his anecdotes about the young East Texas preacher, and his beautiful and symbolic drawing in many-colored chalk.[74] Waggoner was on leave of absence during the academic year 1936–1937. Commenting on Waggoner's absence from the classroom, a *Megaphone* reporter said that "he is a man without an enemy. His generous, kindly manner and friendliness with all make it difficult for any individual to look upon him otherwise." He has one other characteristic, says the reporter, "his unfailing and untiring loyalty to Southwestern University. He has deliberately kept out of anything calculated to injure the school in any way, and has always been ready to help."[75]

However friendly Waggoner was as a person, Ullrich was negative about his teaching ability, putting him "at the lower end of the scale in teaching efficiency." He was also dubious about Waggoner's loyalty to the institution. He felt that Waggoner had tried to manipulate the administration during the recent financial campaign to liquidate indebtedness. "He did not sign over to the school the amounts owing him when the others did so . . . and made his contributions contingent upon his being retained."[76] Though he was continued in his position in 1937, his case was brought up once more in 1938. Again he was continued. In an article honoring Waggoner on his birthday in 1941, Granbery said that "it is . . . refreshing to find in a college faculty such a man as Luther J. Waggoner. Altho [sic] never disposed to defy authority, he has his own way of seeing and doing things, and he leads his own life. He wears no man's collar. His reading is extensive, but it is on lines of his own choosing. He does his own thinking."[77] It was Bergin and Ullrich, however, not Granbery, who made salary assignments each year, and they kept Waggoner at the very bottom of the salary scale for full-time teachers during his entire career.

What is unusual about these three cases—of Wapple, Morgan, and Waggoner—is that they were brought before the Board at all. Heretofore the President had simply brought his recommendations for faculty continuance or noncontinuance to the Board for approval, often unobtrusively in the salary schedule. Never had faculty members been required to go face-to-face before the Board to justify their continuance. The same phenomenon occurred again in 1938, when three faculty members, Granbery, Thrift, and Waggoner, were brought before the Board.

What appears to be the case is that in 1937, after his conspicuous success in other areas, Bergin determined to rid the faculty of persons who had been kept on from year to year even though they were, in his view, liabilities to the institution. Though there were no tenure rules at this point to impede him, the Southern Association took the matter of faculty treatment seriously. Bergin was careful to state to the Board in 1938 that he had consulted with a SACS representative about the three persons being recommended in that year for dismissal. Also, Wapple and Waggoner were "permanent" rather than "temporary" members of the faculty. Though we do not have a copy of the "Rules and Regulations of the Board" in use prior to 1939 defining those terms, a new set of regulations was adopted in that year. In it the term "permanent" applied to a Professor or Associate Professor with three years of satisfactory service. Such a person was "to continue during efficient performance of duties and good behavior; unless specifically stated in advance to the contrary."[78] As it turned out, Bergin did not succeed in obtaining Board approval in 1937 for the dismissal of any of the three persons concerned. The Board heard the faculty members in question and opted to retain them. Wapple retired in 1942, Morgan in 1948, and Waggoner in 1959. Bergin's lack of success in this effort was not a good omen for his future.

Granbery before the Executive Committee

The first intimation of a rift between John C. Granbery and President Bergin appears in a letter to Granbery from his sister, Ella Granbery Tucker, written on January 27, 1937, from Brazil. She was serving there as a missionary with her husband. In it she alludes to a previous letter from him in which he must have said something about his or the faculty's difficulty with Bergin. She replies: "I hope that things are moving smoothly at Southwestern as far as the President is concerned."[79]

At the time, May Catt was serving as Supervisor of Women, and the couple was living in the Woman's Building. She had already, however, announced her resignation from that position, to be effective at the end of summer school.[80] Pearl Neas published a lovely tribute to her after her announcement, commenting especially on the loss felt by the girls. They felt, she says, that Mrs. Granbery "trusted and loved them." May Catt, Pearl continues, is "gallant and gay, a delicate and sensitive spirit without the temperament and irritableness that so often accompany these attributes." Neas says that upon May Catt's resignation President Bergin expressed his appreciation for the "cultural and efficient service rendered by this charming gentlewoman," whom he had made his first appointment two years previously.[81] This rendering of May Catt's departure conflicts with a statement by Rosemond Stanford, Granbery's later trustee counsel, who said in a letter to Dr. Cody after Granbery's dismissal: "I understand the fight on Dr. Granbery started when Mrs. Granbery was discharged from the Woman's Building."[82]

By late 1937 Bergin's position with regard to John Granbery had hardened into unremitting opposition. In December he informed Granbery by letter that he would not be recommended for continuance.[83] Granbery took steps to defend himself and sent letters to the Trustees.[84] When the Executive Committee met on February 11, it took up the matter and asked Granbery to appear before it. He did so and "discussed his relationship with the University as he understood it from [the] date of his reemployment to the present." He then answered questions from various members of the committee. After he left, the committee "authorized" the President "to insert the name of Dr. John C. Granbery in the catalogue on the same basis as he is listed in the 1935–36 catalogue."[85] Granbery had survived the first round.[86]

Claude Carr Cody, Jr., and the Ullrich Letter

Before the Board meeting in May, however, Cody wrote Ullrich asking him to share with all the Trustees his own analysis of the faculty persons to be considered for dismissal. This request from the chair of the Board directly to the dean, thereby bypassing the President, is the first such direct request on record. Though the dean was accustomed to making appraisals of each faculty member for purposes of setting salaries, in this case he was being asked to comment on faculty members whom the President was seeking to dismiss.[87] For his part, Cody wanted to get the opinion of the well-respected dean for the Board members before the meeting took place.

At the time he wrote the letter Claude Carr Cody, Jr., was one of the most respected men in the medical profession in Texas. Both his familial and his professional connections were remarkable. Son of Dean Cody, his mother was a member of the well-respected Hughes family in Georgetown. His wife, Florra—whose younger sister, Margarett, married Herman Brown—came from the Root family, also of Georgetown. He and Herman sat on the Board together for twelve years. After obtaining a B.A. and an M.A. from Southwestern in 1904 and 1905, he studied at Johns Hopkins University in Baltimore, where he received his M.D. in 1910. He attended the University of Pennsylvania Graduate Medical School in 1920–1921 and took further training in Vienna in 1931. He led an ambulance corps in France during World War I.

In 1913 he set up practice in Houston, where he lived the rest of his life. He worked in various Houston hospitals. In 1926 Cody became consulting otolaryngologist at Methodist Hospital of Houston and was appointed professor and head of the Department of Otolaryngology at Baylor University College of Medicine in 1943. He served in these last two positions until his retirement in 1955. He published numerous articles in his field, as well as writings on medical education and medical economics. He was a life fellow of both the American Academy of Ophthalmology and Otolaryngology and the American College of Surgeons. He was president of the State Medical Association of Texas in 1946–1947, as well as of many other professional associations from time to time. Cody was a Trustee of Southwestern University from 1934 to 1959. In addition, he helped found the Houston Eye, Ear, and Throat Hospital, served as director of the Houston Chamber of Commerce in 1946, and was a steward of St. Paul's Methodist Church.[88]

Cody was a kindly but authoritative man respected by everyone. Except for his first year, he served as President/Chair of the Board and Executive Committee for twenty-five of his twenty-six years as a Trustee. Even taking into account the fact that the Board and Executive Committee were much more directly involved in the procurement and dismissal of officers and faculty members through the first century of Southwestern history than they are today, Cody's direct interposition at this point suggests that he is already on the way to becoming Bergin's most formidable opponent on the Board. The request placed the dean in a difficult situation.

Ullrich complied with Cody's request and wrote the Trustees. He began his letter by alluding to the "tough spot" he was in. Nevertheless, he continued, "a Dean must be loyal to the President. . . . My duty in this case has been clear to me. The President has had and has now my full support." The reason for his support, he said, is that Bergin "undertook what to many seemed a hopeless task, a lost cause. . . . He did change the psychology [of the University] from one of defeatism to one of optimism." Much has been accomplished during his administration and his five objectives may well be met by 1940. While some may say, continued Ullrich, that Bergin is not really responsible for liquidating the indebtedness, it did happen during his term of office.

Ullrich admits that Bergin has his shortcomings. "He has his faults, even as you and I. Moreover, he has had crosses to bear." Those who have worked closely with him understand them and have learned to cooperate and support his program. He has tried to do what was best for the University and to support the Board's wishes. "In some respects he did not follow academic practices, but then he is not an academician, as he will readily admit. Moreover, when the school was rapidly going under, there was no time for us to quibble over methods of procedure." Ullrich concludes by providing some facts about the cases of the four professors—Thrift, Wapple, Waggoner, and Granbery—to be presented for dismissal at the forthcoming May 1938 Board meeting.[89] As it turned out, only three names were presented. Wapple's name was excluded from the list. Ullrich says that "the case of Dr. G. is the chief problem. The issue here is positively not one of academic freedom or liberalism. The issue is noncooperation. The President has stood up for him on all questions of freedom of speech."[90] The nature of the "noncooperation" was not specified.

Granbery before the Board of Trustees

At the Board meeting on May 19, Bergin did not list for continuance the names of John C. Granbery, Charles T. Thrift, and Luther J. Waggoner in the 1938–1939 faculty salary schedule. He stated that he had presented all three cases to "the visiting representative of the Southern Association of Colleges and Secondary Schools before Southwestern was given full membership in the Association" and that, in addition, he had received the "expressed approval of the Advisory Council of Southwestern University which consists of the heads of five departments."[91]

Acting as a Committee of the Whole, the Board investigated the issue. Bergin was given an opportunity to make his case and did so in a "lengthy" statement. Trustee Rosemond Stanford, appointed on the morning of the second day to act as counselor to the three teachers, did not feel that Bergin was particularly harsh on Granbery. Writing to Cody ten days after the meeting, he says that he considered the feeling of the President against Waggoner and Thrift to be "much stronger than the feeling between the President and Dr. Granbery. The only argument the President made against Dr. Granbery was that he would have more influence on the campus than the president."[92] Other than that, he continued, the matter was presented primarily as a financial necessity.

Though not appearing in Board minutes, Bergin's "lengthy" statement is probably the three-and-a-half-page, single-spaced document dated March 5, 1938, addressed to the Board found in the Ullrich files. Its style suggests that it was meant to be read aloud.[93] Ullrich probably came to have it because Bergin shared a copy of it with him before the dean responded to Dr. Cody with his letter to the Trustees on March 10. If such is the case, Ullrich's statement in the letter that he supported the President was made with knowledge of what he knew Bergin would say at the forthcoming Board meeting.

After reviewing his five goals for the University and the progress to date in achieving them, Bergin enters into a discussion of the Granbery affair. He says that "several obstacles, *one in particular have loomed up in my path which make it impossible for me to continue unless you remove them* [italics added]. . . . I cannot go on and put my soul into the work when I have some one here engaging in subversive activities against the administration amounting to a conspiracy. . . . I recommend] . . . that you decide now not to renew the contract with Dr. John C. Granbery." In this statement Bergin makes the Granbery case an issue of confidence or no confidence in him as President. If the Board does not support him, he will leave. That he is deadly serious about the matter is revealed in the fact that he concludes his presentation by saying: "*If you should decide that I continue* [italics added], I am prepared to make recommendations for the election of faculty members for next year."

In making his case against Granbery, Bergin alleges that the issue is "not one of academic freedom, ultra liberalism, or freedom of speech." Members of the Finance Committee can testify to that fact. At a meeting of that committee held before March 1, 1937, someone showed him, he says, a clipping from the *Daily Texan*, "quoting a statement from Dr. Granbery [saying] 'God damn War,'" after which a member of the committee asked him, "If we put this campaign over, will you 'Fire' Dr. Granbery? I answered, No, I am not going to 'fire' Dr. Granbery. If the Board wants to do that, it is their business. I won't do it."

Having disposed, he feels, of the freedom of speech issue, Bergin describes various incidents involving the Granberys that have proved to him that they are "subversive" and engaged in a "conspiracy" against him. He describes an incident when Mrs. Granbery as Supervisor of Women took the part of a girl against his wife in the lobby of the Woman's Building and said in the presence of others that if Mrs. Bergin "does that again I'll slap her face." He alleges that on other occasions May Catt has stated in substance, "Have you heard the latest about the Bergins?" He says that prior to February 11, the date of the last Executive Committee meeting, Granbery's "activities were not in the open but undercover and insideous [sic]. His method of attack was through others, especially through students. Dr. Granbery is too skillful in his tactics to be caught in an overt act. By a hint here, a suggestion there, a leading question at another time, usually in the presence of students and some faculty members, a feeling of unrest was engendered." Bergin says that Granbery has been especially skillful in spreading the notion "that the President had begun a Purge" of the faculty.

Bergin then mentions Granbery's relations with the dean. Dean Ullrich, "who, as all of you know, has been one of the best friends of Dr. Granbery and who championed his cause continually and consistently," as late as February 11 "recommended that Dr. Granbery be given the status of other department heads with a salary appropriate for such a rank." Shortly thereafter, he regretted his action and "handed me" the following note:

> Mr. President: On Feb. 11 last, as you will recall, I recommended to the Executive Committee, then in session, in the presence of Dr. John C. Granbery that he be given the status of other heads of departments with a salary in line with such a rank. Prior to that date, rumors and bits of gossip had come to my ears, but I dismissed them as idle, trivial, and of no consequence.

> Since that time . . . evidence has come into my possession convincing me that adverse activities have been going on of so grave a nature that the usefulness of Dr. Granbery to Southwestern University has come to an end. With heavy heart, I feel it my duty to withdraw the recommendation I made to the Executive Committee Feb. 11, 1938. Faithfully yours, Oscar A. Ullrich.

Bergin concludes by saying: "Now if I am to steer the ship to the five objectives, I must have complete cooperation and harmony here. Only you can secure that. *If it is your wish to take the helm from my hands and entrust it to another* [italics added], I shall return to the pastorate happy in the thought that we have out-ridden the heaviest gale."[94]

The three faculty members being considered, Waggoner, Thrift, and Granbery, were called one by one before the Committee of the Whole. Waggoner appeared first at the end of the first day. He made a statement and answered the questions put to him by the committee. The committee recessed until the next morning, when Thrift was called. He made his statement and answered the questions put to him. Granbery was then called before the committee. A motion to limit the time of his hearing to thirty minutes was laid on the table. After he had apparently finished his statement, Judge McCullough, who was presiding, asked him if he wished to make any further statement. Both Granbery and Stanford replied in the negative. Remarking about the procedure in his letter to Stanford, Cody said that he "detected not the slightest desire, much less effort, to limit or to hurry either you or Dr. Granbery by the Committee."[95]

The Board of Trustees, having completed its work as a Committee of the Whole, then proceeded to vote on the three persons one by one. The issue was whether to add the names of the three faculty members to the list of persons recommended by the President for continuance. The vote taken by secret ballot was as follows: Granbery, 13 yes, 15 no; Waggoner, 16 yes, 11 no; Thrift, 17 yes; 11 no.[96] After Granbery learned that he was not to be reemployed, he sent a "communication" to the Board. It was "read, and ordered filed with the Secretary."[97] That "communication" has not subsequently come to light.

Aftermath

The next day, Saturday, the Southwestern University community awoke to find that during the night some students had hung "a black flag with a white swastika emblazoned in the center" between two front windows on the second floor of the Administration Building. A picture of the scene appeared in the Sunday edition of the *Austin American-Statesman* with five boys giving the flag a "straight-right arm salute." All had their right legs in the air as if goose-stepping. Three of the boys were identified as Don Scarbrough, editor of *The Megaphone*, Norman Stafford, business manager of the *Southwestern Magazine*, and Doc Mann, president of the student body. The article said that "students and officials saw the swastika as a veiled charge against the board and Dr. John W. Bergin that they were being dictatorial in ousting Dr. Granberry [sic], who has become associated with liberal thinking in the university and who was instrumental in bringing Norman Thomas, socialist, to speak at the school."[98] *The Megaphone* did not report the incident.

About a month later some of Granbery's friends and advocates of his causes decided to take action. They published in Austin a newspaper announcement addressed "TO FRIENDS OF CIVIL LIBERTY AND INTELLECTUAL FREEDOM." It invited them to a meeting to be held the next Sunday afternoon, June 26, at two o'clock at the University Y.M.C.A. Stating that with "the dismissal of Dr. John Granbery from the faculty of Southwestern University there sounded the death knell of one of the few remaining centers where intellectual integrity was respected and independent thought [was] encouraged," the signers announced that they would take steps to challenge the "unfair and dictatorial dismissal of Dr. Granbery" by Dr. John William Bergin. If the dismissal of one who "has fearlessly and consistently espoused the cause of the underprivileged, is not challenged, where are we to look for another such champion for the defenseless, where such another spokesman for the inarticulate, long-suffering masses? . . . In the name of your devotion to the cause of preserving the Southwestern University as we have known it and in the name of ordinary justice to a great leader and teacher we are asking you to meet with us and help us enlist the help of other thousands in this cause." The announcement was signed by the Presiding Elder of the Austin District of the Methodist Church, by a representative of the Austin Trades Council, by a representative of the American Federation of Teachers, by an Instructor at Weatherford College, by the Principal of Mann School, and by a representative of the Wesley Foundation at the University of Texas.[99]

Though little came of the efforts of students and friends to help him, Granbery was remembered by an ally of years past—the French. In July 1938 he received honorary cor-

Students protesting the Granbury ouster by hoisting a homemade swastika on the front of the Administration Building in 1938. Their action was reported in an Austin newspaper "as a veiled charge against the board and Dr. John W. Bergin that they were being dictatorial" in removing him. From the *Austin American-Statesman*, May 22, 1938.

responding membership in the Conseil Historique et Heraldique de France (the Historical and Heraldic Council of France). In fulfillment of the requirement that he submit an article to the Council for publication, he sent a speech he had delivered amidst "the rumbling of cannon" in a "theater of the front" on July 4, 1918, at Dieue-sur-Meuse. On that day he had spoken in French to a house crowded with French soldiers and officers, with a few Americans present.[100]

An Analysis of the Dismissal

It is quite possible that Bergin did not read his document of March 5 at the Board meeting on May 19 exactly as it appears in the surviving copy. Considered reflection during the interval between the writing and the delivery may have caused him to excise some of its more harsh statements. Undoubted, however, is the fact that he did make a "lengthy" statement of some sort. Stanford agrees that in it Bergin at least said that if Granbery were not terminated "he would have more influence on the campus than the president." He probably meant that a failure in his attempt to oust Granbery from his position would be taken on campus as a victory for the latter, inasmuch as the Board had supported him rather than the President. It is hard to imagine that Bergin would have made such a statement unless he were suggesting that such a result would be untenable for his own continuance. That Bergin waged a high-stakes fight in the Board meeting to have Granbery dismissed is undeniable, perhaps, even probably, putting his own job on the line to secure that result. Stanford claims that at the last minute before the vote Bergin even "attempted to introduce new charges."[101]

The most remarkable thing about Granbery's dismissal is the deep division it reveals in the Board of Trustees about Bergin. Even though the President considered the issue a vote of confidence in him, thirteen of the twenty-eight Trustees present voted to retain Granbery. If the votes for retention of the three faculty members whom Bergin had recommended for dismissal are tallied as anti-Bergin votes, there were at least thirteen anti-Bergin votes on all three ballots. If the votes to sustain Bergin's recommendations are tallied as pro-Bergin votes, there were only eleven pro-Bergin votes on all three ballots. Given that there were twenty-eight votes in all, this means that there were four crossover votes. The four who crossed over to vote against Granbery brought about his dismissal. Bergin's threat to resign, either explicit or implied, was likely a strong reason for their change. However much they may have disagreed with Bergin and voted against him on the Waggoner and Thrift recommendations, they were unwilling to face Bergin's threat to resign if not supported on the Granbery question. They did not want to face the prospect of having to seek a new President after the difficulty of securing one only two years earlier.

This leaves the question unanswered, however, of how much Granbery's economic and political views influenced the vote against him. Stanford says that though Granbery's views were not questioned at the time of his dismissal, there was "a strong prejudice against him [in the meeting] on this account."[102] As far as Ullrich is concerned, one must take his disclaimer on this point at face value. He supported Granbery until the last minute, when, as he says, he finally came into possession of some evidence that forced him to change his mind. One is similarly inclined to accept Bergin's disclaimer as well, given his refusal at a Finance Committee meeting to fire Granbery after hearing that he had said "God damn the war" in a speech. Bergin had personal reasons for wanting to dismiss Granbery apart from having to use what he said in the speech. He felt Granbery was conspiring against him. As he said in introducing the matter to the Board, "I cannot go on and put my soul into the work when I have some one here engaging in subversive activities against the administration amounting to a conspiracy."[103] Bergin's use of the words "subversive" and "conspiracy" in describing Granbery's actions suggests that an element of paranoia may have motivated his actions.

Granbery's economic and political views and his speech in Austin undoubtedly worked against him in the estimation of some Trustees. His strong declarations against capitalism and imperialism in addition to his Austin speech made it easier for those four Trustees who had stood against Bergin with regard to Waggoner and Thrift to join their other eleven colleagues and vote with them against Granbery.

Granbery was very active in the peace movement on the Southwestern campus during the mid-1930s. As counselor for the campus chapter of the American Student Union, he encouraged it to participate in a late April national student strike in three successive years, in 1936, 1937, and 1938. Student groups across the nation chose April because that was the month when the United States had entered most of its wars. Actually, at Southwestern the so-called strikes involved more a varied series of actions by a limited number of students than real strikes. During the three strikes, guest speakers declaimed against war in the auditorium, discussion groups debated war and peace issues, some students engaged in a one-day fast, and the small assembly of those interested adopted resolutions for peace.[104] It was in a speech by Granbery at the University of Texas in April, 1936, as a participant in an equivalent student peace rally that he began his address by repeating three times successively, "God Damn the War," quoting from Harry Emerson Fosdick and Walt Whitman. Not a man who used profanity, he felt that he, like they, were using the expression properly, not as common cursing.[105]

These peace rallies were held on campuses in both the United States and Great Britain. The most famous was held at Oxford University in 1933. In that year the Oxford Student Union conducted a debate over whether it was moral for Britons to fight for king and country. In that debate the leading intellects of that university reviewed the many ways in which British colonialism exploited and oppressed the world. They cited the ways in which vengeful demands made of Germany in the wake of World War I had helped to kindle nationalism and fascism. They saw no moral difference between Western colonialism and world fascism. The Oxford Union ended its debate with the famous proclamation: "Resolved, that we will in no circumstances fight for king and country." When Southwestern students were encouraged to pass a similar resolution in 1936, they modified it. They changed the resolution proposed by the American Student Union that read "I will not support this government in any war it may undertake" to "I will not support this government in any *foreign* [italics added] war it may undertake."[106]

Granbery included more than peace issues in his work as a counselor to the Southwestern chapter of the American Student Union. At its meeting in September 1937, he "suggested that the club closely watch bills to be proposed in the State legislature relating to taxes particularly. He also proposed that Maury Maverick be invited to address the student association under the auspices of the A.S.U." At the same meeting Ed Stanford, a student, was elected president of the organization.[107] It was his father, Rosemond Stanford, a Fort Worth pastor and a Trustee of the University, who was appointed to represent Granbery, Waggoner, and Thrift at their hearing before the Board. His representation of the three men, though imposed on him at the last minute and not ultimately successful for Granbery, was quite strong. It was a matter of conscience for him, and he felt that an "injustice" had been done to Granbery.

The split in the Board regarding the dismissal of the three faculty members represented more than a vote on the narrow issues concerned, which were somewhat different in the case of each man. The thirteen Trustees who voted against Bergin's position did so because they thought of Southwestern, as did Presidents Bishop, Horn, Barcus, and Vivion, as a place where faculty members should not be penalized for being different. Those who supported Bergin's position were those members of the Board who felt, at best, that professors should not embarrass the University by discussing unorthodox matters in public and, at worst, that they were aiding and abetting social and political reforms that were opposed to the American way. Granbery had strong supporters on the Board just as he had strong opponents. The dismissal by two votes was a narrow thing and was a harbinger of further divisiveness soon to come.

Granbery's Last Years

Though Granbery's career with Southwestern ended technically with his dismissal in 1938, he had been such a prominent part of it for twenty-five years that it seems only right to round it off. Without a job at the age of sixty-three, he and May Catt continued living in Georgetown until the summer of 1941, when they moved to San Antonio. There W. W. Jackson helped him get some part-time courses to teach at the University of San Antonio. Without work in Georgetown, the couple had initiated publication of *The Emancipator*, a political and social monthly that promoted liberal democracy. It lasted until the year of his death, 1953. In spite of its eminent mailing list, it ran on a shoestring. It appeared first in September of 1938, the year Chamberlain met Hitler in Munich. Granbery "despised Hitler but was more worried about Hitlerism at home," about the fascist, anti-Semitic tendencies he saw in the United States and in "our own hearts."[108]

In the United States, many conservative Democrats turned against the New Deal, liberal Congressman Maury Maverick of San Antonio lost his office, Martin Dies, of Texas' Second Congressional District, became chairman of the House Committee on Un-American Activities, and Texans elected W. Lee O'Daniel as their governor.[109] Granbery's magazine supported Maverick and worked against Dies and O'Daniel. Granbery had a radio program on WOAI, "defended Methodist welfare organizations from charges of communism, and was branded a 'subversive' by the Houston chapter of the Minute Women of the USA."[110]

John Cowper Granbery lived life on the edge, always in the service of ideals rather than of compromises. "My favorite explanation of my own philosophy," he said, "is . . . the word radical. . . . I am not a reformer . . . I want to go the whole way. Half-way measures, superficial remedies, compromises, do not appeal to me. This position is forced upon me by acceptance of Christian philosophy. Now is the axe laid at the root of the tree. Ye must be born again. Seek ye first the Kingdom of God. No man can serve two masters. . . . Here are absolutes. There are no compromises, no qualifications, no exceptions." Granbery did not believe radicalism necessarily signified a position to the political left or right. He pleased neither side. Those on the right disliked his interest in Social Security and other social reform matters, while leftists complained "because we," said Granbery, "believe in religion as a vital power in individual and social life, and because we do not utterly condemn the church."[111]

As much as he was appreciated as a speaker, Granbery was not an orator. He "spoke jerkily as he searched for words, spoke without passion, but spoke emphatically."[112] In his talks he always enjoyed the complete attention of his audiences. They became absorbed in what he was saying because his talks were rational, logical, and cogent, and his conviction always came through. He died on May 5, 1953, at the age of seventy-eight at his home in San Antonio.

Cody Challenges Bergin: The Case of Charles T. Thrift—1938

Though the case of Charles T. Thrift was completely different from those of Waggoner and Granbery, it soon became a major element in the growing rift between Cody and Bergin. Thrift, with three degrees from Duke and a Ph.D. in religion from the University of Chicago, came to the Southwestern faculty in 1936 through the instrumentality of Dr. Kenneth Pope, the popular pastor of the local First Methodist Church, who wanted someone to establish a Campus-Church Religious Activities Program for 1936–1937.[113] Even with funds from the General Board of Christian Education in Nashville, the local congregation did not have sufficient resources to finance the program. To make it possible, the college "acquiesced," says Ullrich, by creating two courses in religion for Thrift to teach in spite of the fact that it did not need them. The major part of his job was to serve as Director of Religious Activities, coordinating this role with the local church. Since no summer teaching was needed in 1937, Bergin employed Thrift as a field representative engaged principally in securing students. Because funds from other sources to support him were even shorter the following fall, Ullrich created one more course for him.[114] Consequently, in 1937–1938 he was teaching three-fifths of a regular load. Bergin and Ullrich acceded to this arrangement because Thrift was doing good work in his religious activities program. Ullrich commended him in his Board report in 1937 for the "unusually high order" of chapel programs he produced.[115]

By 1938, however, Bergin and Ullrich felt that they could no longer afford to carry the financial burden that Thrift's position required. Since in their eyes he was a temporary rather than a continuing faculty member, they proposed to release him. The Board, however, felt differently when it met in May. The Committee on the Student Body reported that it had been impressed with "the splendid work" he had done and "was highly pleased" with the type of service he had rendered. It said that the kind of work he was doing was "vitally essential to the development of Christian character" and urged the faculty and student body to cooperate with him.[116] Consequently, the Board overrode the President's recommendation and ordered Thrift's reemployment on the same basis as the previous year.[117]

A week after the Board meeting, Thrift reported to Cody on two unsatisfactory interviews with Ullrich and Bergin concerning his work for 1938–1939. He said that when he went to them for an assignment he was told that there was "no work" for him. President Bergin told him that the catalog was already made up, the courses fixed and published, and teachers assigned to all courses. The conversation became animated, with Bergin finally asking, "Who do you think is running this University any way [sic]?" The upshot of the matter was that the Executive Committee handed Bergin another defeat when Cody reported Thrift's complaint. It directed, in accordance with the Board resolution ordering the continuation of Thrift and Waggoner on the same basis as the year before, that they should be reinstated in the faculty exactly as they were listed in 1937–1938. In addition, they should receive any salary increases or decreases that might subsequently be given to the rest of the faculty.[118]

Cody Issues Direct Charges against Bergin—1939

As a result of the previous issues involving Bergin, Dr. Cody became convinced that the President was running the University according to his own determinations rather than following Board directives. Bergin, for his part, felt that what he was doing was in line with the intent of the Board even when he did not follow the letter of its provisions. He felt that above all the Board wanted him to present a balanced budget. To do so required that he bring the number of faculty members into line with the actual needs of the University. He continued to press his case to drop Thrift. At the Executive Committee meeting on February 21, 1939, he stated that because the Board had returned Waggoner to the faculty, the school had one more teacher than was needed. Consequently, he said that he was not going to nominate Thrift for a faculty position in 1939–1940. Cody felt that this action was the last straw and that Bergin needed to be confronted directly about what he was doing.[119] Shortly before the Board meeting in May, he wrote Bergin a letter leveling two charges against him and three charges against Professor M. L. Williams that related indirectly to him. He asked Bergin to respond to each of the charges. Bergin did so in a long document that covers four-and-a-half single-spaced, legal-sized pages in Board minutes.[120]

The first charge was that the Board of Trustees at its last meeting had asked the President to present a revised budget to the Executive Committee with estimated expenditures to be some five thousand dollars less than the estimated income. Cody alleged that Bergin did not do so but, rather, presented the same budget to the Committee that he had previously presented to the Board. Bergin defended himself by showing that the Board did not ask exactly what the charge specified and that he worked carefully with the Executive Committee in settling on a budget that in fact contained deep cuts.

The second charge was that at a meeting of the Finance Committee on August 18, 1938, the President agreed to conduct a campaign over the state to secure additional money for the library, and Mr. E. L. Crain was to raise more money in Houston. "It is reported," said Cody, "that later the President of the University in a telephone conversation with Mr. Crain declined to co-operate in attempting to collect additional money over the State for the Library." Bergin responded to the charge by showing exactly how the library was funded and by pointing out that the total project was successful. "How much more would the President have had to do," he says, "before receiving your approval rather than being summoned to appear before you and explain in writing why I have not done more?"

The charges against Professor M. L. Williams involved his participation in efforts to have Dr. Thrift dismissed from his role in the local church. He did so by writing the General Board of Christian Education in Nashville, which was paying part of Thrift's salary, by refusing to cooperate with him, and by consulting with Bishop Smith on the matter. Bergin responded that whatever Williams did, he was acting as superintendent of the Sunday School and as a steward in the local Methodist Church, not as a functionary of the University. These actions necessarily involved an overlap with his role at Southwestern, since both he and Thrift worked in both places. The truth is, he says, that the minister and the church people did not want Dr. Thrift to continue his relations with the church another year. Williams was working in their behalf, not in behalf of the University, in his dealings with Thrift.

Bergin concluded by objecting to Cody's use of the term "It is reported," which he used six times in his letter. He objects to the chairman's receiving "reports" independently and then having him or various members of the faculty summoned "to appear before some tribunal" to explain what is in the reports.

Bergin's paper was referred to a committee of five that reported on the validity of the charges. It agreed that technically Bergin did not comply with the recommendation of the Board in presenting his budget, but it stated that "he did not intentionally contravene the action of the Board of Trustees." On the second charge, the committee said that given the fact that the library is now being built and will be completed free of debt, there is no need for action. It also rejected items one and three in the charges against Williams as pertaining to local church, not to Southwestern, matters. It sustained item two, in which Williams asked for a written resignation from Thrift, thus contravening "in spirit the action of the Board of Trustees relative to the status of Dr. Thrift." In spite of the committee's exoneration of Bergin except for a mild slap on the wrist, Cody moved that the name of Thrift be added to the Faculty Committee report as a professor for 1939–1940. This time, however, as opposed to the year before, the motion lost.[121] Bergin had finally won in his attempt to remove Thrift from the University, but he had done so at the expense of weakening an already shaky working relationship with the chair of the Board. Ironically, in 1940, in the midst of these events, the University conferred the honorary degree of Doctor of Science on Claude Carr Cody, Jr.

At the next meeting of the Executive Committee, held on June 13, Dr. Charles T. Thrift tendered his resignation, effective September 1. Though he made it contingent upon the satisfactory resolution of three financial considerations, the Trustees accepted it without hesitation. Thrift had served three years as Director of Religious Activities. Though the money for the position was supposed to have come from outside sources, the amount was not sufficient to fund the post. The University made the position possible by creating courses for him. When it tried to withdraw from its commitment, Thrift became a pawn in the chess game being played between the Board chairman and the university President over presidential freedom to interpret Board decrees in the light of their intent rather than literally in terms of their exact words. Thrift went to Florida Southern College as Professor of Religion in 1940, was made Vice President in 1946, and became President in 1957. He received an honorary degree from Southwestern in 1965.[122]

Construction of the Cody Memorial Library Building

While the drama between the President and the Board chairman was slowly being played out with the end not yet in sight, three events of importance for the life of the University occurred—the construction of the Cody Memorial Library, the building of the West Gymnasium, and the Centennial Celebration.

As pointed out earlier, the idea of constructing a library in honor of Dean Cody had been broached soon after his death. President Barcus would have probably built it had not the old Annex burned, forcing him to redirect his efforts to constructing a new Woman's Building. The seriousness of the project in the minds of University leaders is shown by the fact that the corpus raised for it by 1930, roughly $30,000–$35,000, was guarded very carefully even during the worst years of the Great Depression. President Vivion made the library his construction priority in 1930 but had to abandon his attempts to raise additional funds for it a year later in the face of the country's worsening economic condition.[123] The idea hovered in the air, however, and everyone in the Southwestern community expected that the next building, whenever one should be built, would be the Cody Memorial Library.

In August 1938, a year after the University had cleared its indebtedness and during which it had operated with a balanced budget, the Finance Committee held a special meeting in Houston. It met in the office of J. M. West, with Bergin, Cody, and other members present. Bergin announced to the group that the purpose of the meeting was to consider the advisability of constructing a library and a gymnasium. The Georgetown city council would sponsor the building of the former, to be called the Cody Memorial Library, through a Public Works Administration grant and the latter through a Works Progress Administration grant. Bergin and others, probably including Dr. Godbey, who was an alderman, had already worked out with the city council that a library could be built for Georgetown at Southwestern if the school would deed a plot of ground on the campus to the city. The committee unanimously approved the library project, with the project presented for the P.W.A. grant not to exceed $100,000. The president of the Board, Dr. Cody, was empowered to deed the required plot of ground. Another resolution was also approved unanimously to deed a similar plot to the City of Georgetown for the erection of a gymnasium.

At the meeting the ethics of the matter was discussed thoroughly. The members "decided that no subterfuge had been employed in requesting the City Council to sponsor the P.W.A. grant, that the officials of the P.W.A. were informed and were cognizant with the details of the arrangement, that the title to the property would be held by the City of Georgetown, and that the University would take a lease on the property for 99 years with the right of renewal at an annual rental mutually agreeable to the Board of Trustees of Southwestern University and the Council of the City of Georgetown, Texas."[124]

The grant application submitted to the state headquarters of the P.W.A. in Fort Worth called for a building to cost $80,000. The P.W.A. would fund 45 percent of the project, amounting to $36,000. The University would provide $44,000–$45,000. Since the library fund at the time was almost $33,000, some $11,000–$12,000 in additional cash would be required. By the time of the Executive Committee meeting on October 14, the President had raised $7,000 in cash, and another $4,000 had been raised in Houston. Only $1,000 more was needed. With the entire amount so nearly in hand, the Executive Committee authorized the construction of the library but once again emphasized "that no subterfuge had been employed in requesting the City Council to sponsor the P.W.A. grant, that the officials of the P.W.A. were informed and were cognizant with the details of the arrangement." A proper document was signed authorizing Dr. Cody to deliver "all of Block No. 12 [the so-called Gillett block], of the Snyder Addition to the City of Georgetown."[125]

The Bishop Goes to Washington

At this point the action switched to Washington, where the decision approving the grant would be made. Someone was needed who knew the person—Jesse Holman Jones—who would be making the decision on the grant. That person was Bishop A. Frank Smith. Smith and Jones were friends. Smith had been his pastor in Houston before President Roosevelt appointed Jones as chairman of the Reconstruction Finance Corporation in 1933. During Roosevelt's first two terms, Jones was one of the most powerful men in America. He had received his first honorary degree (1925) from Southwestern. He had given $7,500 to the Wiess campaign when Smith had gone to see him in Washington at the time. Now was the time to see him again. The friendship of Jones and Smith was of a special kind. When President Score went to Washington to see him in 1945 about Southwestern's Navy unit, Score reported back to Smith "that he [Jones] had received a lovely letter from you [Smith], and with a kind of catch in his voice he said, 'Brother Score, the Bishop will never know how I appreciated it.'" Smith describes his visit to Jones about the library as follows:

> I went up to Washington to talk with Mr. Jesse Jones, who at that time was head of the Reconstruction Finance Corporation. I sat by his desk and he called Mr. Ickes and told him he would like to get this appropriation granted. And Ickes told him he wouldn't do it. I could not hear Ickes, but I could hear Jones. He and Mr. Ickes had no love for one another, absolutely none. And Jones said, "Mr. Secretary, I have never asked you for anything before, but things are constantly coming across my desk that you are asking for. I have a request from you right now on my desk asking the RFC for a million dollars or more. If you do not give me this, I will not give you what you are asking for." And he hung up. He turned to me and said: "Go on back to your hotel and wait. We'll let it stew for a while."
>
> Well, I went back to the Dodge Hotel where I always stayed, up close to the capitol. My train was to leave about 6 o'clock. About 4 the phone rang, and Mr. Jones said, "You can catch your train. We have squared it." So I came back in jubilation and told the folks about it, and we all jubilated together.[126]

Smith says that about a week later he learned that the deal was off and that the application would be denied. The Houston Trustees beseeched him to return to Washington to see what had gone wrong. He decided, however, to visit Senator Morris Sheppard, whom he knew, who was home in Texarkana at the time. On arrival in Texarkana he saw Sheppard and his wife boarding his own train for Washington. Smith quickly reboarded without being noticed by

Sheppard. They met each other on the train, and the three enjoyed the long trip to Washington together. Smith, of course, had ample opportunity to acquaint the senator with the library grant application. Sheppard gave him the name of a man to see. The conclusion of the story is better told in his own words.

> Well, when we got into Washington the next morning, I went over to the man's office. He was a Philadelphia lawyer, literally, one of those young fellows and a "New Dealer." And he said very positively and dogmatically, "Bishop, we are not going to grant this." And I said, "Why not?" And he waved a newspaper clipping and said, "It is our definite policy not to make grants to church institutions. This clipping says the grant has been made to Southwestern University, and a Baptist college over in North Carolina has sent us a protest. Anyway, your name is Smith and the Mayor of Georgetown is named Smith. Is there any connection there?" "None whatsoever," I said, "except back to the time of Adam." And he said, "Well, I'm sorry, but we have rescinded the grant." Right at that moment the door popped open and in came Senator Sheppard. This fellow jumped up—nearly turned over his chair—"How are you, Senator?" Then Sheppard turned to me and said: "Bishop, I thought I'd better come by here on the way over to my committee meeting." And this fellow said, "What can I do for you, Senator?" "I just came by here to tell you to give my good friend Bishop Smith anything he wants." And he walked out the door saying, "Let me know, Bishop."
>
> Well, this fellow said, "All right, Bishop, we'll sign the papers." And I said, "Why, you just said you couldn't do that." "Oh," he said, "Mr. Ickes says that Senator Sheppard is the most honest man he has ever known in public life, and for us to grant every request he makes without any investigation or question. Since the Senator has said to give you what you want, we'll sign the papers." And that's the way we got the library at Southwestern.[127]

Bishop Smith immediately sent a telegram to Mayor M. F. Smith in Georgetown, saying: "Allotment just granted. Matter closed. Secretary Ickes is notifying Fort Worth today." Mayor Smith also received telegrams from Lyndon B. Johnson, in whose congressional district Georgetown was located, from Senators Morris Sheppard and Tom Connally, and from the regional director of the P.W.A.[128] Bishop Smith made another trip to Washington in late February 1939 to consult with the General Counsel of the P.W.A. in behalf of the City of Georgetown and Southwestern University.[129] Inasmuch as P.W.A. rules required that the construction should begin before January 1, 1939, city and Southwestern officials gathered on Saturday, December 31, 1938, on the site of the proposed building and with shovels in hand turned the first earth for the foundation.[130]

The library was formally opened on Sunday, November 26, 1939. Various persons, including Congressman Lyndon B. Johnson and Bishop A. Frank Smith, participated in the ceremony.[131] A formal resolution by the Board thanking the persons most responsible for it mentioned Dr. Jesse H. Jones, Senator Morris Sheppard, Bishop A. Frank Smith, Mr. E. L. Crain, and Mr. J. M. West.[132] Less than a year later Jesse Jones delivered one of the main addresses at the Centennial Celebration.[133] The Houston Foundation, established by him in 1937, has been a substantial benefactor of Southwestern through the years (see Chapter XI).

The library architect, Cameron Fairchild of Houston, provided a lovely modified Gothic style design for the building. Facing University Avenue, it was well built and continues to serve the University community. Though it has become part of a much larger library complex by being joined on its north side into two subsequent library enlargements, it is still distinctive when looked at from University Avenue as originally intended. Today it constitutes a part of the A. Frank Smith, Jr., Library Center.

Though the City of Georgetown originally opted to carry library income and expenditures, including the payment of library salaries, on its books and Southwestern had to issue vouchers to the city to cover expenses as they occurred, the system of dual, or bifurcated, control became onerous to both parties almost from the outset.[134] On May 13, 1941, the city relinquished control back to Southwestern, and the University purchased the deed to the property.[135] Citizens of Georgetown still have full library privileges today.

Construction of the West Gymnasium

With the sale of the northern half of the old campus to the city in 1930, Southwestern was left without the gymnasium that stood there. Part of the deal with the city was that it would share use of the gymnasium with Southwestern. For ten years, from 1930 to 1940, Southwestern students and teams had to trek across the railroad tracks to the old

Godbey gym, now owned by the city, to practice basketball. In exchange, the city high school played its football games on Snyder Field. For Southwestern, as for the city, the construction of a new gymnasium on campus was a high priority. In fact, for the city it was a higher priority than the library. Originally, Bergin had mentioned both projects simultaneously to the Executive Committee, and it had authorized the deeding of plots of campus land to the city to get federal help in building both the library and the gymnasium. The city wanted to build the gymnasium first. Because Dr. Cody preferred the library, Bergin says that the city council "reluctantly changed the project from that of a gymnasium to that of a Library."[136] Though losing its priority place in the construction process, the gymnasium project was not dropped, and steps were initiated to build it not long after library construction got underway. The idea of asking for government help to do it, however, was dropped. The gymnasium would be built without federal help.

Still hoping to enlist the aid of the city in the project, Bergin and McCook approached the Chamber of Commerce, the retail merchants group, and the Lions Club to gain their support in having the city pay $5,000 toward the project. They said that Southwestern would provide $15,000 and that interested persons in Houston would provide $20,000 to complete the $40,000 project.[137] The $5,000 from the city did not materialize, and shortly thereafter the amount promised "from certain individuals in Houston" was raised to $25,000 if Southwestern would raise its previously agreed-upon $15,000. At its meeting in mid-1939, the Board of Trustees accepted the challenge to raise $15,000 to meet the Houston offer.[138]

Because the $25,000 "from certain individuals in Houston" was really the pledge of one person, Jim West, the University had little difficulty securing the remaining $15,000 needed. Gifts from everyone else in the state, including persons from Houston, would be counted toward its quota. After the completion of the Cody Memorial Library, its architect, Cameron Fairchild, was chosen to design the gymnasium. He completed the task quickly, and the plans were placed out for bids. The Executive Committee rejected all of them in late December as not falling within the $40,000 cap.[139] After some design changes by Fairchild, the project was rebid. The construction company of R. H. Folmer was awarded the contract with a bid of $39,038.55.[140]

The gymnasium, built of native stone, was located between the Science Building and the Woman's Building. The Olin Building occupies that location today. It faced the Administration Building across the long, open space between them at a forty-five-degree angle. A house that stood on the site at the time was moved to a place adjacent to Snyder Field, where it was renovated to become a field house.[141] The gymnasium had offices for both the physical training and athletic departments. It had permanent bleachers on the long, north side of the gym floor seating eight hundred people. The men's and women's dressing rooms were underneath and behind the bleachers. The exterior design of the building was pleasing and made a handsome addition to the campus. Foundational problems caused a delay in the construction and eventually added $4,000 to the cost. Some of the elements originally called for in the plan were removed to compensate for the cost of the unexpected foundation work. An outdoor swimming pool was built later back of the gymnasium. The West Gymnasium served the University for more than fifty years, from 1940 until the 1994–1995 academic year, when it was demolished. In the meantime, larger and more modern athletic facilities had been built.

The formal opening of the West Gymnasium took place at Homecoming on October 5, 1940.[142] The building was named for J. Marion West, Sr., the man who had furnished 60 percent of the funds for the building and had been a Trustee of Southwestern since 1923. How he originally came to favor the University is not indicated in the records, but somehow he became as loyal a supporter of Southwestern as any alumnus. He sent workmen to Georgetown to help the University outfit Mood Hall for Women in 1925 after the fire that demolished the Woman's Building and responded to almost every appeal made by the school. A. Frank Smith speaks of "corralling" him for $32,500 in the Wiess campaign in 1937.[143] In 1938 he established the West Foundation, the funds of which were to be devoted to religious, charitable, educational, literary, and scientific purposes. The following year he sold 30,000 acres of land in southern Harris County to the Humble Oil and Refining Company for $8 million in cash and royalties estimated to have an eventual worth of $30 to $40 million. He owned a 120,000-acre ranch, a hardwood manufacturing company, and an oil company.[144] He bought several newspapers late in life to fight what he perceived to be the "collectivism of the Roosevelt administration."[145] He died less than a year after the completion of the gymnasium, and his portrait was hung there in his memory.[146]

Both West's wife and sons continued his largesse to the University during the Score and Finch administrations. Both of his sons had attended Southwestern, and Jim West, Jr., had graduated with a B.A. in 1927. Mrs. West, who had been an intimate friend of Laura Kuykendall, gave $25,000 in 1947 to establish a loan fund for students at low rates of interest. At the end of fifty years, the fund was to revert to the Trustees to be used however they chose. She died in 1953.

Conspicuous are the gifts from the West Foundation between 1951 and 1954, the first years of Finch's tenure, when the postwar enrollment decline was bottoming out and the institution was in such financial straits that it abandoned intercollegiate football. During those years the West Foundation gave five undesignated gifts totaling $190,000 to the University. Jim West, Jr., who largely ran the Foundation and who was a member of the Board of Trustees, died in 1957 at the age of fifty-five. The *Dallas Morning News* headed its announcement of his death as follows: "Eccentric Millionaire, Silver Dollar West, Dies." It spoke of how he loved to play cops and robbers in some of his forty Cadillacs. Peace officers were among his best friends, and many of his cars were equipped with riot guns and pistols. He gained his nickname "Silver Dollar" from carrying pockets full of silver dollars for tipping.[147]

Plaza established on the south side of the Cody Memorial Library after the Centennial Celebration of 1940. The round table is the grinding stone from McKenzie College. The bench rests on stones taken from Rutersville College, Wesleyan College, Soule University, and the burned-out Woman's Building. Southwestern University, Special Collections.

The Centennial Celebration

When the centennial of the charter granted by the Republic of Texas to Rutersville College rolled around in 1940, marking one hundred years of charter lineage for Southwestern, there was much to celebrate. Within the last ten years the school had weathered a national economic depression, had liquidated its huge indebtedness, had established a modest endowment, had constructed a new library, and had built a new gymnasium. At the time of his election, Bergin had targeted the centennial as the point at which he hoped to have achieved all five of his goals. He may not have quite reached his desired endowment figure or the number of students he aspired to have, but the other three goals were in hand.

The Centennial proper took place over a three-day span of time, April 12–14. Alpha Chis from past years gathered and celebrated the twenty-fifth anniversary of the founding of the local chapter. All three living ex-Presidents—Charles M. Bishop, J. Sam Barcus, and King Vivion—returned and participated in different events. Governor W. Lee O'Daniel and Judge Ralph Yarborough spoke for the political contingent, while President Homer Price Rainey of the University of Texas and President Umphrey Lee of Southern Methodist represented academe. Bishops John M. Moore, Hiram Abiff Boaz, A. Frank Smith, Ivan Lee Holt, and Claude Selecman represented the Church. Jesse Jones presented a message "From the Nation's Capitol." Various soloists, Mme. Slaviansky's chorus, and Tom Johnson's band rendered music by Handel, Mozart, and Tchaikovsky. A special Service of the Golden Bowl was celebrated with Mrs. T. Herbert Minga, the author of the service, in attendance.

Looked at in comparison with the Golden Anniversary Celebration of 1923, the Centennial Celebration of 1940 was restrained and formal, not at all like the magnificent pageant with thousands of people in attendance in 1923. In spite of the efforts of the musicians, the lecture format predominated. After the Centennial Celebration honoring the foundation of Rutersville College in 1840, a desire developed to create a permanent memorial honoring all the root institutions from which Southwestern emerged. Consequently, in 1941–1942 a small plaza was established on the lawn between the Cody Memorial Library and University Avenue. It consisted of a circular stone platform with a pedestal in the center topped with the grinding stone from the gristmill at McKenzie College and a concrete bench on the west side resting on stones from Rutersville College, Wesleyan College, Soule University, and the Ladies' Annex at Southwestern.[148]

Campus Development

One of the main features of the celebration in 1940 was the announcement that Mrs. Rosa Dimmitt Hughes of Georgetown had stated her intention to give the University eight-and-a-half acres of land just north of Snyder Field, a promise she fulfilled shortly thereafter. It extended the campus north from the playing field to the Katy depot.[149] The Snyder donation of land across the railroad tracks from the old campus in 1887 that began the development of the new campus consisted of about thirty-two acres of land. Beginning at the railroad, it ran east along University Avenue to a point where it turned northward, allowing it to encompass the site of the Annex and its successor, Laura Kuykendall Hall. Three blocks of land north of the Main, or Administration, Building had to be purchased in 1906 to provide a site for Mood Hall when it was built. Additional plots of land were purchased for the construction of the Williamson County Science Building.

The C. F. Ward campus design of 1914 shows the developed land on campus platted into blocks with short streets separating them. The land beyond was mostly open field. Streets were both opened and closed as the campus grew. Private houses, which dotted the area here and there, were bought up when need and opportunity coincided. Another campus design plan around 1933 by Hare & Hare shows an elaboration of the 1914 plan. The present interior U-shaped pedestrian mall, originally a roadway, appears fully developed in it. A second U-shaped roadway outside the inner one, corresponding to the sidewalk that now begins at the Science Building and runs north by the west side of Mood Hall and the McCombs Center and around back of the chapel, is also a major feature. A future chapel is situated at the apex of the interior semicircle with buildings on either side corresponding to the present location of the McCombs Campus Center and the Olin Building. Along University Avenue stretching east on a line with the Administration, or Cullen, Building are three buildings corresponding to the present Fondren-Jones Science Hall, the A. Frank Smith, Jr., Library Center, and the Fine Arts Building. The new Woman's Building on the east has replaced the old Annex. Back on an angle to the northwest of the proposed chapel are residence halls and fraternity houses. The old Williamson County Science Building occupies the space immediately in front of the present chapel. The Hare & Hare design is an elaboration of the 1914 design much as the present campus design is an elaboration of that sketched out in 1933.

Six or eight rather handsome houses once lined the north side of University Avenue from about 1900 to 1990 in what would today be the 1100, 1200, and 1300 blocks. The University gradually bought them for use or campus expansion, eventually removing them one by one. The John Snyder house in the 1300 block was the first one purchased. In addition to serving as the President's home when needed, it also served as a residence hall for both men and women, especially after 1926 when the Griffith house just west of Snyder Hall was bought to serve as the President's home. Snyder Hall was taken out of service around 1955. The Roots, whose daughter Margarett married into the Brown family with fortuitous results for the University, lived next to the John Snyders.

An airplane view in 1937 shows Snyder Field immediately adjacent to the Administration Building, with no street in between. A wide track encircles the playing field, with the long eastern side of the track running more or less where Maple Street is today.[150] By the time Bergin took over in 1935, the campus consisted of about sixty acres.[151] The Hughes gift brought campus acreage up to almost seventy acres.

One of the most exciting things accomplished by the liquidation of the indebtedness and the procurement of a modest endowment in 1937 was the impetus it created for the construction of new campus buildings. The Cody Memorial Library and the West Gymnasium were the first results of that impulse. E. L. Crain, who as a Trustee played an important role in these events from 1937 to 1950, employed a landscape engineer at his own expense to study the grounds, arrangement of buildings, and other matters connected with the physical plant of the University. He brought the resulting plans and blueprints for a beautiful and harmonious campus with him to the midyear meeting of the Trustees in 1939.[152]

Ullrich's Plan for the Future

The person who over the years wrote the most thorough and thought-provoking reports about the future of the University was Dean O. A. Ullrich. Almost from the day he took over the deanship, his Board reports display a mind that is both analytical and creative. After the University escaped insolvency in 1937, he formulated at the invitation of the

Trustees a vision for the future. He began with Southwestern's mission. He said that if Mood's aim for the University were to be recast in terms of "present-day thought patterns," it might well be: "It is the function of Southwestern University to use all proper means to develop critical thinkers, to build strong personalities, and to cultivate Christian idealists." In this reformulation of Mood's aim can be seen for the first time the "critical thinker" phrase used in many later Southwestern statements. His organizational plan for the University divided the work of administration under the President into four units, each headed by its own officer. The units were Finances, Academics, Student Life, and Public Relations. All the current functions of the University would be placed under one or another of them. Though this structure may not appear novel today, it was novel at the time because of the explicit description for the first time of the cabinet or senior staff system still in use today. In the same report he presented a carefully formulated twelve-point program to take advantage of the new freedom that escape from indebtedness had presented the University.[153]

In 1940 he presented at the behest of the Executive Committee another master plan for the future. In it he called for an endowment of $4 million; presented an ideal percentage operational expenditure pattern by major categories; called for the creation of three academic divisions, to wit, Humanities, Natural Sciences, and Social Sciences, with Fine Arts and Music being included in the Humanities; and called for a student body of 600 with an upper limit of 700, to be taught by a faculty of forty. In addition, he outlined a building construction plan. It would include an additional residence hall for boys accommodating 150 ($200,000); a new science building for biology, chemistry, physics, and geology ($200,000); a chapel seating 1,000, with a pipe organ ($250,000); a Student Activities Building ($125,000); and a new central heating plant ($100,000). Current buildings would be remodeled on modern lines, and several small buildings would be built for other purposes. The entire package totaled $1,100,000.[154] The Buildings and Grounds Committee of the Board of Trustees was so impressed with the plan that it adopted it without change.[155] The construction part of the plan was pretty much fulfilled over the next two-and-a-half decades as outlined. The academic division structure was also set up, except for the suggestion to fold the music and fine arts programs into the division of humanities. Fine Arts was eventually set up as a School of Fine Arts rather than as a Department of Fine Arts within Humanities (see Chapter XVII).[156]

Revision of the Bylaws and Other Operational Documents

A number of factors from 1937 to 1939 led the Trustees to feel that a restructuring of the Board and a revision of the Bylaws were necessary. One factor was the very unwieldiness of a Board with sixty-one members. Another was the fact that the union of the three major bodies of Methodism, the Methodist Episcopal Church, the Methodist Episcopal Church, South, and the Methodist Protestant Church, was on the horizon. It occurred in 1939, and the old Southern Conference of the Northern Church was folded into the regular Texas Conferences of the new, unified Methodist Church. Since that Conference had furnished ten Trustees to the Board, its disappearance automatically changed the makeup of the Board. A third was the fact that ex-students of Southwestern had been so important in helping the University eliminate its debt that it was felt they deserved to be represented on the Board as a required category of persons. Bergin expressed this sentiment in mid-1937.[157] Finally, during the course of the dispute between Cody and Bergin in mid-1938, the inadequacy of the Bylaws with reference to some of the issues raised was recognized. As a result, a committee of five persons, composed of Cody (chair), Bergin, Wilcox, Ullrich, and McCook, was appointed to revise the major procedural regulations of the University.[158] The outcome was a comprehensive reformulation of those documents between 1938 and 1940.

The result of their work was the revision of two documents—the Bylaws and the Rules and Regulations of the Faculty—and the writing of two new documents—the Regulations of the Business Manager and the Regulations of the Registrar. The Bylaws contained eight chapters covering authority, membership, officers, committees, concurrence, finances, and faculty. The number of elected Board members was reduced from sixty-one to twenty-five. Each of the four big Conferences would furnish four members, while the two smaller ones would furnish a total of three. A new category of six At-Large members was added to flesh out the total of twenty-five.[159] A certain number of them had to be ex-students. In addition, the President of the University and the bishops of the sponsoring Annual Conferences were included as *ex officio* members. The first meeting of the Board with this new structure was the midyear meeting in 1941.[160]

The financial base of the University received special attention in the Bylaws. The use of donations for purposes other than those for which they were specifically given was categorically forbidden. Undesignated money placed in the endowment was also protected. A donation of any sort once credited to the endowment could not be diverted to any other purpose without the unanimous consent of the Trustees present and voting.

The faculty was defined as consisting of the President, the deans, the librarian, teachers with the rank of instructor and higher, the business manager, the registrar, and the athletic director. Either the President or other faculty members could refer a disagreement between them to the full Board or to the Executive Committee for a final decision. The President was confirmed in his right to veto any action of the faculty involving the general welfare of the University, but he was required to state in writing his reasons for doing so. That veto, however, could be appealed to the Board or to the Executive Committee by a two-thirds vote of the faculty. Individual faculty members had their rights as well. Any member was to "be heard forthwith at his request on any matter pertaining to his status, duties or privileges at a meeting of the Executive Committee or of the Board of Trustees." The faculty as a whole was confirmed in its traditional privilege of being the only source of nominating candidates for academic and honorary degrees. Particularly interesting was the reinforcement written into the Bylaws about the responsibility of faculty members to support chapel services. It said that they were "expected to attend Chapel services" and "to encourage by example the attendance of the students upon public worship."[161]

SACS Removes Southwestern from Probation

The main stumbling block over the years for the removal of Southwestern from probationary status by the Southern Association of Colleges and Secondary Schools had been its poor financial condition. As Dean Ullrich had said in 1928, all of Southwestern's other problems could be solved if that could be taken care of. President Vivion echoed this sentiment in 1930. The escape from indebtedness in 1937 with the establishment of a freestanding endowment created a new situation for the University. It began to live within its income each year. By 1942 the Finance Committee of the Board of Trustees could congratulate the administration for completing its sixth consecutive year without a deficit.[162]

SACS continued Southwestern on probation until March 1938. At that time it took notice of the great change in university finances and removed it from probation.[163] The removal, however, was based on Southwestern's promise to do three things: (1) to discontinue offering work leading to the master's degree until the annual per student income for instructional purposes reached $250; (2) to spend at least $3 per student in 1938–1939 on the library for books and magazines, with the amount increasing to $5; and (3) to increase the faculty salary scale to meet the minimum set by the Association. Of the three conditions, Ullrich said that the first was most drastic. In discussing it with the Trustees, he presented an analysis of what the forty-seven students who had obtained master's degrees since 1922 were doing. A little over one-third of them were teaching in institutions of higher learning. He did not call on Southwestern to renege on the promise to discontinue offering the master's degree, but he did affirm the necessity of reentering the field after vacating it for a few years. He stated that the other two conditions could be met easily.[164] In order to meet the salary levels demanded by SACS for heads of departments, Bergin announced that Southwestern would combine some departments. Philosophy, for example, would be combined with Religion to make a Department of Religion and Philosophy.[165]

During the winter, the Executive Committee asked Bergin to take up with SACS its right to offer the master's degree, especially since Southwestern "is not the only institution on the approved list not meeting the requirements fully."[166] It was not at the point of the master's degree, however, that failure to meet the three promised conditions caused SACS to place Southwestern once again on probation in the spring of 1939. SACS reported that the school was deficient in its annual per student expenditure and that the faculty salary scale was still below the required standard.[167]

In order to remove these impediments, the University carried through its intention in 1939–1940 to reduce the number of academic departments from sixteen to ten. A curious feature of a maneuver the previous year to satisfy the SACS standard on faculty salaries had been to reduce the rank of several faculty members to bring their rank into line with the salary they were being paid. Since the school was now back on probation, Ullrich proposed to the Executive Committee that the school restore them to their previous ranks. Bergin opposed Ullrich on this point, stating that it would "destroy the work accomplished during the past two years." The individuals concerned had by now, he said, accepted the reduction in rank, and restoration to their previous rank would disturb a now settled situation.[168] A resolution of this issue was postponed to the next Board meeting. Before it could be settled, however, word came from SACS that Southwestern had been removed from probationary status once again. This achievement had been prompted by Bergin's unqualified promise that Southwestern's salary scale for 1940–1941 would meet SACS standards.[169] Never again would Southwestern's status with its regional accreditation organization be a matter of major concern.

Degrees, Enrollment Patterns, and Teaching Loads

Even before Southwestern was removed from probation the Executive Committee had voted to resume graduate work.[170] Five of the nine students admitted for the master's program in 1939–1940 completed their degrees.[171] At the time of Bergin's departure from Southwestern in mid-1942, the University offered six bachelor's and one master's degree. They were the B.A., the B.B.A., the B.F.A. in Music, the B.S., the B.S. in Education, the B.S. in Medicine, and the M.A. During Bergin's tenure, the B.B.A. had been introduced, the B.S. in Education had been restored, and the M.S. had been dropped.

Student enrollment increased dramatically during Bergin's first two years. This increase was due partly to the country's gradual emergence from the Depression and partly to the strong public relations effort put forth by the new President that included Madame Straviansky's chorus and Tom Johnson's Swing Band. From a student body that numbered only 286 in the fall of 1935 when he took over, numbers improved to 417 within two years and to 440 by the fall of 1940. The conditions prior to the outbreak of World War II, including a peacetime draft of young men, caused a decline of 64 students, or 14.5 percent, by the fall of 1942. Even at its best, however, student enrollment during the Bergin years was significantly lower than it had been during the 1920s.

The structure of the student body had not changed substantially by 1937 from its makeup in the past. In that year over half of the student body had relatives who had preceded them as students, almost 10 percent were from parsonage homes, and two-thirds were Methodists (66.7 percent).[172] The next largest denominational representations were Baptists (10.8 percent) and Presbyterians (5.3 percent). There were only three Catholic students in attendance. Some 7.5 percent of the student body had no religious affiliation.[173] In 1940 most of the students came from a distance of more than a hundred miles (63 percent). Only a little more than a third (37 percent) came from within a radius of a hundred miles.[174] One of the major problems of the University over the years was that of retaining the students who entered. One of the reasons why the size of the student body did not increase more than it did was that student attrition was very high. Over a twenty-three year period from 1915 to 1938 about one-half (49.4 percent) of the freshmen entering did not return for the second year.[175] Placement of graduates, however, was good. Ullrich reported in 1941 that for a period of about twenty years almost 100 percent of the graduates had been placed by the following September, about half of whom entered the teaching profession each year.[176]

Thirty-nine teachers taught these students in 1939. Fourteen of them taught a full load of from four to six courses, averaging 16.6 hours per week. The other twenty-five taught from one to nine hours, averaging 5.1 hours per week. The Social Sciences had the largest number of students with 655, Languages (including English and Speech) had 596, the Natural Sciences had 453, Fine Arts (Art and Music) had 295, Physical Training had 289, and Religion and Philosophy had 163. Excluding Fine Arts and Physical Training, where the instruction was not of the regular classroom type, the average class size was as follows: Religion and Philosophy, 23.3; Social Sciences, 20.9; Natural Sciences, 16.8; and Languages, 18.6.[177]

New Appointments—Ferguson, Finch, Wolcott, and Medley

After the resignation of May Catt Granbery as Supervisor of Women, Mrs. Ruth Morgan Ferguson was named Dean of Women. Though a very different kind of person from Laura Kuykendall, she also became revered over time for her general culture, social graces, and gentle way with the women she supervised. She and her husband, soon deceased, were both graduates of Georgetown High School and Southwestern. Graduating with a B.A. in 1914, she began teaching English as a faculty member in 1923.[178] She was at the time in the graduate program and received her M.A. in 1924. In announcing her appointment as Dean of Women, *The Megaphone* said that she had "excelled as a teacher of creative literature and is one of the most popular teachers that ever occupied a chair in Southwestern University. Her poems and short stories have appeared in various magazines."[179]

After the death of Dean Kuykendall, the big pageant idea of the May Fête was abandoned by Dean Ferguson in favor of more modest May Day celebrations, sometimes still called May Fêtes, but without the grand pageants of the past.[180] Girls from the sororities would go around town early in the morning on May 1 to deliver baskets of spring flowers to the homes of faculty members, some staff persons, and local alumni. A May Day celebration was also held with young ladies dancing in frilly dresses around a May Pole. May Day celebrations, or May Fêtes, were abandoned completely as an annual exercise in 1950.[181]

Mrs. Ferguson continued as Dean of Women until 1955 but returned for two years from 1958 to 1960. Nell Barnes Benold recounts as one of her memories while living in Laura Kuykendall Hall how Dean Ferguson would give the girls late-hour talks on how to behave and dress properly as they sat in their pajamas and rolled their hair. The girls called them "G and L" talks, from the admonition to be "Gracious and Lovely" that fell often from her lips.[182] That tradition, too, of the mature gentlewoman imparting her distilled wisdom to her receptive charges, would end with her retirement. The notion itself of a separate dean for women would end in 1972. Laura Kuykendall and Ruth Morgan Ferguson occupied the office of Dean of Women for thirty-eight of the fifty-eight years it existed, from 1917 until it was terminated in 1972.

While one student life position, that of the Dean of Women, was on the way to being phased out, that of the Dean of Students was on the way to being phased in. Dean Ullrich first mentioned it as a possibility in his administrative organization plan of 1937.[183] In it he called for a Student Personnel Officer, Dean of Student Life, or College Provost, different names for the same function. President Bergin instituted it in late 1941 when he appointed Dr. William Carrington Finch as Dean of Student Life.[184]

Finch had just arrived on the Southwestern scene. Though he came as the long-term replacement for Dr. Herbert Lee Gray, head of the Department of Bible and Religion, his appointment was as head of a newly renamed Department of Religion and Philosophy. Though only thirty-two years old, he brought outstanding credentials to the position. A native of Virginia, he had an A.B. from Hampton-Sydney College, an S.T.B. from New York Theological Seminary, a Th.M. from Union Theological Seminary in Richmond, Virginia, and a Ph.D. from Drew University. He had also studied at Oxford and Zurich. Though he had served five years as a pastor, he was an Assistant Professor of Religion and Philosophy and Dean of Student Life at Oklahoma City University when he came to Southwestern. He was uniquely qualified to step in as the first Dean of Student Life when Bergin nominated him. Finch would have an outstanding career at Southwestern, eventually becoming President.[185]

Two other teachers were secured during Bergin's years who would have considerable impact on the institution. Employed in 1937, Gordon C. Wolcott was an accomplished biologist with a B.S., M.S., and Ph.D. from the University of Virginia. He taught at Woods Hole and James Madison University before coming to Southwestern. His presence at Southwestern immediately brought the heretofore rather weak Department of Biology and Geology to a respectable level. In the fall of 1939, he, as a one-person department, taught eighteen semester hours of classroom work to accommodate the 143 students who enrolled for biology. The Board made him head of the department and voted him "continuous service," the nearest equivalent to present-day tenure, in 1940. Though he left in 1947 to conduct research on sleeping sickness and malaria with the Bureau of Public Health, he came back in 1958 and served until his death in 1967.[186]

The other person secured who would have long service at Southwestern was Randolph M. Medley. Medley came in the summer of 1939 to replace the recently deceased "Lefty" Edens. He was a graduate of Missouri Wesleyan College in 1922, where he lettered in football, track, baseball, and basketball. As coach at McMurry, beginning with the establishment of the school in 1923, he led teams winning approximately 75 percent of their basketball and football games. He was the son of a Methodist minister and was selected from among forty applicants for the job at Southwestern.[187] He came to Southwestern just in time to coach the football team, composed mostly of men in the Naval V-12 unit, during World War II. After two remarkable seasons, the team received Sun Bowl invitations on New Year's Day 1944 and 1945. Southwestern won both games. He asked to be relieved of his coaching responsibilities in 1948 for health reasons, at which time he became Head of the Department of Physical Education, Director of Athletics, and the person responsible for intramural athletics.[188] Medley retired in 1969 after thirty years as athletic director and coach.[189]

Student Life during the Bergin Era

Though student life was affected by the great national events of the time such as the Great Depression and the drift toward war, in many respects it continued to pose many of the same problems for the administration as in earlier years. Dean Ullrich and the faculty continued to feel that "fraternityism" was one of the major "stumbling blocks" for the University program and carried recommendations from time to time to the Board of Trustees suggesting that the fraternities be abolished or placed under more stringent regulation.[190] The remedy proposed to the Trustees in 1940 was to force the fraternities to operate their houses on campus and for them to have house managers employed and paid by the business office from funds collected from members for that purpose.[191] The Trustees took no action, and the faculty was left to deal with the problem as best it could.

Compulsory attendance at chapel continued to be a sore point for the students. Dean Ullrich told the Board of Trustees that "the compulsory rule without the possibility of enforcing it through expulsion is futile." Personally, he felt that "a prayer or a scripture reading in a strained atmosphere, not to say a hostile one, is of little benefit. It may even," he said, "do a great deal of harm."[192]

Though the Student Association was able to change a few things, such as having the school colors changed from black and canary to black and gold, it made slow progress in abolishing the rule against dancing.[193] Though he did not use the word "dancing," Ullrich used a code phrase for it in 1936 when he pleaded with the Trustees to leave "all forms of social entertainments" to the discretion of the faculty.[194] Two years later Bergin made a case for relaxing the rules against dancing, saying that the current rule forced young people to hold their "Formals" away from the school, sometimes in Austin, making them more dangerous because of the travel involved.[195] The first approved all-school, on-campus dance on record was sponsored by the band in the West Gymnasium in December 1940. A group of band members formed a ten-piece combo that played for the occasion.[196]

A major problem for the administration from time to time was the independence displayed by the *Southwestern Magazine* and *The Megaphone.* The Board committee responsible for student body affairs was quite disturbed by an article published in the January 1940 edition of the magazine entitled "The Man Who Wouldn't Sin." It called all the parties involved before it—the President of the University, the Faculty Advisor, the editor of the magazine, and the author of the article. The committee received from them "expressions of regret and assurances that no other such contributions would be published."[197] As a result of the incident the Board of Student Publications was reorganized. It now came to be made up of five faculty members and two senior students. The two seniors were Grady Anderson, who would eventually become Associate Vice President for Admissions, and Joe Sneed, who would become a distinguished federal judge. This action, however, did not deter the editor of *The Megaphone* from saying what he felt. On February 1, 1941, he published an editorial critical of the rules and regulations at Laura Kuykendall Hall. It was deemed serious enough by the Executive Committee that the chairman read it aloud to the other members. After lengthy discussion, no action was taken.[198] At the Board meeting in May, the Board Committee on the Student Body stated that their action with regard to student publications had "yielded wonderful results." *The Megaphone* had been selected by the Associated Collegiate Press for the highest honor received by any college paper in the five-hundred-student division in Texas.[199]

Though the drowning death of Coach "Lefty" Edens in the summer of 1939 had shocked the campus, the death of a student a year and a half later shocked it perhaps even more because of the horrible nature of the event. It occurred after a picnic held by four Southwestern students celebrating the forthcoming birthday of one of them, an eighteen-year-old junior named Gloria Hawker. Following the picnic they were returning on the Katy railroad bridge north of the campus when they were trapped by the sudden onrush of a southbound train. Though the others escaped, she was hit and killed instantly. They had felt safe in crossing the bridge because they had observed the northbound train pass a short time before and knew it would be an hour until the southbound train came. However, the northbound train had been off schedule, and the southbound train came much sooner than they had anticipated. Gloria Hawker was a popular and accomplished person, a sorority member, a member of Mask and Wig, on the staff of *The Megaphone*, and coeditor of the previous week's issue. She was killed on Sunday evening. Her birthday would have been the next day.[200] A contingent of persons from Southwestern attended the funeral in her hometown. Dr. Bergin was the officiating minister.

In spite of fraternity shenanigans, required chapel, fractious student editors, and occasional tragedies, one student from those years reports that "student life was mostly a lot of fun until World War II. We were generally incredibly innocent and quite carefree," she says. "It was a much better and far safer time for being young. Some lifetime friendships were made during those years in addition to the lessons that were learned in and out of the classroom."[201] World War II brought an end to that innocence.

War Warnings: Godbey, Bartak, and Knickerbocker

The campus peace movement engaged in by the Student Association in 1936, 1937, and 1938 under the auspices of John Granbery died away as the clouds of war gathered. In a chapel talk in the fall of 1937, Dr. Godbey alluded directly to a coming war in Europe, a greater war than that of twenty years before. He said: "The great war in Europe [in 1914–1918] was not a war to end war but only a war to make conditions ready for another greater one; it only served to instill in the hearts of the peoples of Europe a more intense hatred, a deeper distrust, for each other."[202]

When Dr. Joseph Paul Bartak, alumnus of 1912, visited his alma mater from Prague in April 1939 on his way to attend the uniting conference of the Methodist Church in Kansas City, he spoke at the First Methodist Church in Georgetown. Though his talk did not deal with the political situation in Czechoslovakia, he answered directly when asked pointed questions about it. First, he was asked as to the effect upon the work of the Methodist Church of the capitulation of Chamberlain and Daladier with regard to Czechoslovakia at Munich the year before. He said that the churches in the Sudeten area had been ruined by the flight of members. Then he was asked whether Hitler interfered with religion or was interested simply in the political aspects of power. He replied that totalitarianism took everything, including religion. He was asked whether the Church could adapt itself to the Nazi regime. He answered that in his judgment it could not, for it would violate the First Commandment. He was asked whether there was any semblance of liberty left in Czechoslovakia. He said there was not, that letters going and coming were censored and that the newspapers had big blank spaces where material had been excised. A minister preaching, he said, might on account of a single reference be sent to a concentration camp.[203]

Two years later another famous Southwestern alumnus spoke on campus about the prospect of war. He was Hubert Renfro Knickerbocker, son of a Methodist minister and a graduate of 1917. At the time he visited Southwestern, he was one of, if not the, leading newspaper journalist of European events. He covered Europe from 1920 to 1928 for the New York *Sun* and the New York *Evening Post*. He became chief Berlin correspondent for the *Evening Post* and the Philadelphia *Public Ledger* from 1928 until 1941. He was a witness to the Beer Hall Putsch of Adolph Hitler in 1923. From 1925 to 1927 he divided his time between Berlin and Moscow, where he reported for the International News Service. His critical views on Soviet economic and foreign affairs were generally well received in Germany, making it possible for him to travel in the highest social and political circles there. In 1931 Knickerbocker won the Pulitzer Prize for his articles analyzing the Soviet Five-Year Plan, which he called a menace.[204]

By the time he was deported from Germany in 1933 after Hitler came to power, Knickerbocker had published six books in German detailing his understanding of events. He was strongly opposed to the Nazi movement. After being deported, he made an extensive research tour of Europe in which he interviewed hundreds of public figures and many heads of state. From these interviews he wrote a book in 1934 forecasting a general European war. He covered the Italo-Abyssinian War in 1935–1936, the Spanish Civil War in 1936–1937, the early phases of the Sino-Japanese War in 1937, the *Anschluss* in Austria, the Czech crisis in 1938, the defeat of France in 1940, and the Battle of Britain in 1940. He was a correspondent in North Africa, the Far East, and the South Pacific after the United States entered the war. He was killed with other journalists in a plane crash in Southeast Asia in 1949.[205]

Knickerbocker spoke at Southwestern on a lecture tour during late April 1940. There, unlike at Southern Methodist University, where students opposed to his point of view engaged him in a heated exchange, he received a warm welcome from students and old friends. The reporter for the *Austin American* said that Knickerbocker was "obviously moved by the memories recalled by the auditorium where he had attended chapel for three years before receiving his bachelor of arts degree and leaving for the army." Speaking to the student body he touched on appeasement, saying that the appeasement policy of Senator Wheeler and Charles Lindbergh would "only increase the contempt Hitler had for Democracies in general." He urged support of the Lend-Lease program and other efforts in behalf of the enemies of Hitler because "before long you boys are going to be in the army" fighting them. His speech was a recital of the events that had led to the war, such as the fatal mistake by the United States after World War I in allowing "a few willful men" to keep the United States out of the League of Nations and the appeasement efforts of Chamberlain at Munich. He said that Britain should now be supported with all possible aid.[206]

As a result of warnings such as these by Godbey, Bartak, Knickerbocker, and other sources, the Southwestern community had become very supportive of Roosevelt's foreign policy in favor of Great Britain and against Germany by the time of Pearl Harbor.

The Draft and the Civilian Pilot Training Program

In August 1940 the Executive Committee discussed the question of whether it should offer the facilities of Southwestern to the U.S. Army. Though it postponed a decision on the matter for the Board meeting, it did not do so because of any doubt about U.S. government policy. It authorized the University leadership to cooperate with the federal government in promoting national defense.[207] Shortly thereafter, on September 6, 1940, the U.S. Congress passed a conscription law setting up the first peacetime draft in American history. It made provision for training 1,200,000 troops and 800,000 reserves each year.

The draft brought negative enrollment consequences for the University. In his report to the Board in mid-1941, Ullrich mentioned that it and the other prewar measures taken by the government had caused a restlessness to develop among young people. He said that many young men were thinking about volunteering for the armed forces, while those past twenty-one were being given one year to complete their educational work before being drafted.[208] At the last Board meeting before Pearl Harbor, held on November 25, 1941, Ullrich reported accurately that there had been a decline in student numbers of about 12 percent. It was caused, he said, by the draft, by the transfer of some young people into national defense work, and by the effects of birthrate decline in the early Depression.[209]

In the same month as the beginning of the draft, Southwestern signed an agreement with the Civil Aeronautics Administration to institute a Civilian Pilot Training Program. It was one of a number of prewar programs set up by the federal government to train persons in skills that might become vital in a wartime situation. The government would pay most of the expenses connected with the program. Students would pay only $35 each. As it worked out, Southwestern made a slight profit from its participation in the program.[210]

To institute the program, Southwestern entered into an agreement with two flight contractors, Mr. Frank Bryant and Mr. Virgil Reynolds. They were responsible for leasing the necessary acreage for an airport, erecting a hangar, and constructing runways. Mr. Robert N. Sexton was the flight instructor.[211] The airport they built was located on the old fairgrounds property and on land owned by W. W. Edwards, north of the city and just west of present Interstate Highway 35. It would eventually become the Georgetown airport in existence today. A hangar with concrete floors, offices, a classroom, and other facilities was erected. The overall length of the field was 6,000 feet, with a width of 2,800 feet.[212] By mid-October 1941 it had become a $400,000 construction project.[213]

Two-thirds of the ground flight instruction for students was done by Southwestern University. A physics teacher, Professor Burgin Dunn, handled it for the University, teaching meteorology and related material. The two operators, Bryant and Reynolds, handled the other third, which included Civil Air Regulations, parachuting, and aerodynamics. Ground school instruction covered a total of seventy-two hours in the classroom. Flight training covered a minimum of thirty-five hours of flying time. Students received private pilot's licenses upon successful completion

President Bergin in an airplane used during the Civilian Pilot Training Program run by Southwestern during 1940 and 1941. Southwestern University, Special Collections.

of the course. Further provisions provided ways for students to go elsewhere for training to become instructors and to receive commercial licenses.[214]

Since the students who received pilot's training were taking a course rather than working toward a degree, their names were not listed in the catalog. Consequently, the total number who took training is uncertain. A newspaper article reports a class beginning in early October 1940, and another reports the following February that nineteen men and one woman received their pilot's licenses.[215] The original plan had been to begin new classes about every three or four months. Another newspaper article in mid-May reports the successful completion of another course, with the expectation that the course will be broadened in the near future to train one hundred.[216]

Everyone was pleased with the results. The program was exciting to students, it had a patriotic flavor, it produced a small profit for the University, and Georgetown received a new airport without cost to itself. Southwestern announced in September that it planned to develop it further. It would be expanded by establishing new provisions that would allow students to become cadets with thirty hours of work.[217] In the midst of this planning, however, shortly before Pearl Harbor, the federal government discontinued funding the program, and Southwestern was forced to drop it.[218]

Events Leading to Bergin's Resignation

At the Board meeting on May 8, 1941, the Committee on the Faculty brought in a report recommending that Dr. Bergin, sixty-nine years old at the time, retire on the date of the opening session of the Central Texas Conference. The reason given for this action was that the retirement rules of the University required that its officers and teachers retire at the age of seventy, and Dr. Bergin would reach that age in April 1942. Since the retirement age for ministers was seventy-two, retiring at the date of the opening session of his Annual Conference in November 1941 would allow him to take a pastorate or other position if he so desired without any loss of work time. The Board did not approve the recommendation.[219]

This failure to force Bergin to retire was apparently unacceptable to Cody. He had been at odds with Bergin since at least 1938, perhaps earlier, and he chose at this point to put pressure on the Board to let him go. At the close of the meeting, when Cody was nominated as President of the Board and as a member of the Executive Committee for another year, he requested that his name be withdrawn from the list of nominations. Rather than force the issue, the Board recessed without electing any new officers.[220] A "recess" rather than "adjournment" was necessary, since a recess would continue Cody in his current position as chair until the next session.

The recessed session of the Board resumed its deliberations two months later, on July 10, 1941. Although there were a few items of business to be attended to, the real item was the unfinished election of officers from the last meeting. The Nominating Committee took a different tack from its action at the previous meeting. It said that before it could make a report "a ballot should be taken on whether a change in the Presidency [of the University] should be made." Considerable discussion ensued. When the ballot was taken, the vote was: Yes, 16; No, 8. The issue was so momentous that the Board voted to go into executive session to discuss it. When Dr. Bergin was given "the courtesy of a word," he spoke of the personal problems that such a course of action by the Board would involve for him. After long discussion in the executive session, the full Board resumed its regular meeting and a new ballot was taken. It reversed the previous ballot by one vote: Yes, 10; No, 11. Various options were presented but no consensus could be reached. As a result, Cody ruled that there was nothing before the house.

Once again the Nominating Committee presented the slate of Board officers it had presented originally. Once again Cody requested that his name be withdrawn from the recommendation. Ignoring the request, E. B. Germany moved adoption of the original Nominations Committee report, with Cody's name on its list, and it was so ordered. Cody was urged to reconsider his intention to resign. Without indicating exactly what he said, Board minutes record that he "was gracious in his closing words to the group." By now E. L. Crain had also become very frustrated. He tendered his resignation to the Board. It was not accepted. Apparently Cody and Crain received some signals that their continuance would not go unrewarded, for they were present at the next meeting in November.[221]

By the time of the November meeting, Bergin recognized that he must give way. He did so by presenting a plan for his "contingent retirement." He prefaced it by justifying his continuance to this point. He stated that during his tenure, members of SACS had declared that no institution in the Association was making progress as rapid as that of Southwestern University. He was told by one of its commissions that "a college president should be elected for life" and that Southwestern changed Presidents too frequently to have consistent membership in the Association. He then referred to the actions of Dr. Cody. He said that "on two occasions during the calendar year, the chairman of the Board . . . [had] . . . declined to be re-elected to his post if the President of the institution were retained. This," he continued, "has become current over the State and beyond and with its resultant effects is becoming hurtful to Southwestern." The chairman has indicated, he stated, that $3 to $4 million in endowment money is in prospect within the next three to five years and has implied that it cannot be raised by the incumbent president. Bergin said that such an amount is unrealistic, but of one thing he is sure. He is sure that the million-dollar endowment he set out to procure when he was elected could have been achieved "if we could have had the wholehearted cooperation we had in 1936 when all indebtedness was liquidated and $210,000.00 [was] added to the endowment." Having laid out his case against Cody, Bergin offered his plan of "contingent retirement."

> Having had a District Superintendency in my conference at the time of coming to Southwestern, I feel that it is but just, all things considered, that I receive that kind of an appointment by our Church, before relinquishing my position in the college from which Mrs. Bergin and I graduated, which every child of our home has attended, and to which I have contributed rather liberally of my meager means, and for which I have given without any kind of time out for rest, relaxation, or pleasure, the last six years of my life.
>
> I am, therefore, offering to retire contingent on receiving the kind of an appointment I relinquished on accepting the Presidency of Southwestern University to be effective when such appointment is made by our bishops.[222]

After long discussion, the Board accepted the plan. A committee of six, three laymen and three ministers, was appointed to nominate a new President. The laymen were Judge T. L. McCullough, Dallas, Dr. Jesse R. Milam, Waco, and Dr. Claude C. Cody, Houston. The ministers were Dr. Paul Quillian, Houston, Dr. J. N. R. Score, Fort Worth, and Dr. Edmund Heinsohn, Austin.[223]

The Election of Dr. J. N. R. Score as President

Abandoning his reticent attitude of seven years before, Dr. J. N. R. Score was now definitely interested in the job. When he was first approached for the presidency in 1935, he was just beginning as pastor of one of the premier Methodist churches in the nation, and the situation at Southwestern was very poor. Both conditions had now changed. After a long tenure in Fort Worth, Score was ready for a change, and, seven years later, Southwestern was a good opportunity. He knew, however, that Dr. Cody had not appreciated his refusal in 1935 and did not support his election. Cody had put considerable effort into recruiting him at that time and even felt that he had received Score's tacit agreement to accept the position. His refusal had left Cody disenchanted. Though Score knew that his faithful service on the Southwestern Board of Trustees during subsequent years had won him the support of many of the Trustees, he realized that he needed Cody's support. He wrote Bishop A. Frank Smith, his close friend, about the problem. Smith replied that he would see Cody at once.[224] He was unsuccessful in his effort and wrote in his diary that Cody was "not particularly enthusiastic." Two more visits produced the same result. He finally called Score and told him that he should take the position anyway if elected and that Cody would "fall in line" after he took office.

One more obstacle now presented itself. During the jockeying with Cody, Central College in Fayette, Missouri, had talked with Score about becoming its President. Score called Smith after returning from a meeting with the Trustees there and told him that they wanted him to take the job and that he was very much interested. The mutual interest of Score and Central College is not hard to understand. He was an alumnus of the school by virtue of the amalgamation of his old alma mater, Scarritt-Morrisville College in Morrisville, Missouri, with several other Methodist schools in the state to form Central College in 1924.

In response to the overture by Central College, Smith went to visit Judge Tom L. McCullough in Dallas and Dr. Paul Quillian, pastor of the First Methodist Church in Houston. Both were members of the Nominations Committee. McCullough was one of the most respected persons on the Board of Trustees. A member since 1910, he had served three years as chair of the Board and as a member of the Executive Committee since 1922. Quillian was pastor of the largest church in the Texas Conference. His procurement of their support for Score virtually guaranteed that the Nominations Committee would present his name for election.[225]

Score's name was duly presented when the Board met on February 11, 1942. Though Score had, of course, absented himself from the committee whenever his name was discussed, he knew where he stood before the meeting began. He wanted the position, but he wanted the Board to commit itself to setting up a situation conducive to success. He did not want to accept the situation without securing some changes. Consequently, he presented five conditions to the Board for acceptance before he would consent to serve as President. They were:

1. That he have the whole-hearted cooperation of the Board of Trustees in raising sufficient funds by September 1, 1942 to place the physical properties of the University in first-class condition, this work to include the Administration Building, Mood Hall, Science Building and Laura Kuykendall Hall.
2. That the President's residence be placed in first-class condition before he moved into it.
3. That he receive a salary of $7,500.00 per year in addition to the President's home rent free.
4. That he could not assume the actual administration until June 1, 1942.
5. That a general progressive policy for the University be worked out in conjunction with the Board of Trustees and the Faculty.[226]

The conditions were accepted, and Score was elected with only one dissenting vote. The dissenting vote was not that of Dr. Cody, since the unanimous recommendation from the Nominations Committee presumes a favorable vote from him. The person casting the negative vote "explained that his vote was a protest against the set-up rather than in opposition to Dr. Score. He pledged continued loyalty to the institution and administration, both as an ex-student and member of the Board."[227]

The situation with Cody worked out just as Smith had predicted. He quickly became a strong supporter of Score. Smith wrote Score from time to time assuring him of that fact. In one of his communications, he told Score that during his last conversation with Cody, the chairman had said: "Score is doing a swell job."[228] The three of them, Score, Smith, and Cody, virtually became an administrative team during Score's tenure as President, though Score was uncomfortable at times regarding Cody's tendency, as Board chair, to usurp the President's role in speaking for the University. Nevertheless, he knew that, as he said, "no one loves Southwestern as he [Cody] loves it," and he was "devoted" to him.[229] After Cody's death in early 1960, his funeral was held in the Lois Perkins Chapel. Finch wrote Mrs. Lois Perkins that they "felt it most fitting and appropriate that his final services should be held in the Perkins Chapel at the heart of the institution to which he had given so much of his life and thought."[230] Dr. C. C. Cody, Jr., and his wife are both buried in the Georgetown cemetery in the same plot with his parents, Dean and Mrs. Cody.

Passing the Baton

After the Board elected Score, but with knowledge that he would not assume the position for almost four months, it passed a flurry of legislation covering that period. Bergin was asked to continue fulfilling the office of the presidency so long as he remained on campus. Score, for his part, was requested to attend meetings of the Executive Committee during that time with the right to vote. Score then had the Board authorize him "to appoint an acting President" on or after February 25. This legislation seems to have been a fail-safe mechanism in case Bergin should leave prior to Score's coming on June 1. Score then secured from the Board authorization to "negotiate with the Trustees of Westminster College to take over [the] assets of that college without obligation [on the part] of Southwestern University and [to] report to the Board of Trustees." Because of the recent entry of the country into war, the Board also requested Score "to contact the proper authorities of all [the] armed forces to ascertain if an officers' training corps of some branch of the service may be instituted at Southwestern University."

The President-elect concluded the meeting by submitting a long, previously prepared statement about Southwestern's rich heritage, his appreciation of Bergin's leaving the institution "in perhaps the best condition in the history of the school," his recognition of the honor associated with the job, his agreement with the steps now being taken to modernize the curriculum, his vision of Southwestern's prospects, and his understanding of its role as a part of the total educational structure of the Methodist Church. He referred to his desire to establish an Institute of Pan-American Affairs and quoted with approval a comment by Dr.

Cody that "the first building we must build at Southwestern is a great Chapel in the very center of our campus."[231]

With the successful resolution of the presidential question, everyone seems to have taken special care to create as harmonious a situation as possible. The students, for their part, had mixed feelings about Bergin. In spite of their openly manifested discontent with his action in dismissing Granbery in 1938, he had secured for them the right to hold all-campus dances in the fall of 1940, and he was an avid supporter of the football team. When the student body tried to carry the football players off the field on their shoulders after the team defeated Austin College in November 1941, the players refused the honor. "Instead, they carried President Bergin off the field and presented him with the football used in the game."[232] Bergin never seems to have resented Score at any point, and he presented the President-elect to the faculty at its regular meeting on February 25, 1942.[233] The note of conciliation was especially evident at the last meeting of the Board of Trustees of Bergin's administration on May 8, 1942.

In his concluding report to the Board, Bergin thanked the Church authorities for their assurance that he would be given a position equivalent to that he held before becoming President. Then, with a touch of humility, he stated that "in a mystical sense . . . possibly I have never been other than an acting President. . . . The fortunes of the University were so low, or faith in my ability to negotiate the situation so doubtful that I was never given a formal inauguration." He complimented his replacement, saying that if he had been allowed to choose his own successor, "it would have been no other than the Rev. J. N. R. Score." At the same time, his humility did not keep him from staking out his place in Southwestern history. He placed his administration among those of the great figures in its century of existence. He said that he would make no résumé of his accomplishments but that "if posterity or history should allow my presidency to rank with that of Martin Ruter, Francis Asbury Mood, Robert Stewart Hyer, and Charles McTyeire Bishop, it would be gratifying."[234] He was proud of what had been accomplished during his tenure and was unmoved by the negative elements surrounding his departure. He felt that history would vindicate him.

The faculty for its part voted unanimously to recommend that the University confer an honorary LL.D. on its retiring President, an action the Trustees endorsed by an 18 to 1 vote. President-elect Score suggested that Dr. Bergin be invited to preach the Commencement sermon. Inasmuch as Bergin would be absent much of the time until Commencement, a motion was approved to appoint Score as Acting President until his assumption of full-time duties, the only time in Southwestern's long history that a President-elect has been appointed Acting President before assuming the office in full.

Bergin did not leave Southwestern a defeated man. To the very end he continued to draw succor from the vast reservoir of self-confidence that had allowed him to shed criticism without injury to his psyche during the years of his service. In spite of his enforced departure, he felt that time would be his friend. History would recognize his administration as having brought about one of the major turning points in Southwestern history. In that assessment he was right. The question of his role in bringing it about, however, will be long debated. One thing is undeniable. He stood in the breach when no one else was found to do so.

16 World War II Expansion (1942–1945)

The Personality of the New President

If John Nelson Russell Score were to be characterized by one word, that word would be dynamic. He dominated by the sheer brilliance of his agile mind, facile tongue, and vibrant personality almost every occasion, circumstance, and person he encountered. Few who knew him would quarrel with the description of him penned by Ralph Jones, whom he employed in 1946 to teach music in the School of Fine Arts.

> A scholar himself, he [Score] insisted on the academic proficiency of his faculty. He was a skilled politician, having learned the art in one of the better schools, church politics. As a preacher, Score was a spell-binder and an artist with the English language, although, if the occasion called for it, he could use stronger language. Abandoning for the moment his inveterate cigar when he approached the pulpit, he became a consummate liturgist and sought to bring a comparable beauty and dignity to the academic life of the university.
>
> Score possessed a keen, legalistic mind. He was articulate in the realm of the abstract as well as the practical world of college administration. His wit was sharp and sometimes Rabelaisian.
>
> This president drove himself and sought to drive everyone else. He was a powerful, dominating personality and automatically seemed to command situations and people also, if he could, and often he was able.
>
> More than anything else, Score brought a type of positiveness to the position for which the school was aching. He immediately attained the universal respect of all the elements connected with the university but, as is characteristic of men of this type, not universal love.[1]

Some of the people with whom he dealt were put off by his manner. One such was Mr. J. J. Perkins in the process of negotiations about the construction of the Lois Perkins Chapel. At one point, when a seeming impasse had been reached between the two men, Perkins complained to Bishop Smith, their mutual friend. He said that "somehow or other I cannot hit it off too well with Dr. Score. I presume I am more to blame than he is." Smith knew both men to be strong-minded and sought to keep them working together. He wrote back to Perkins that he had been closely associated with Score for twenty-five years and "long ago came to a definite conclusion about him."

> He is as capable a man, as brainy and as versatile a man as I have ever known. He has an indomitable will and determination. . . . Score is a brilliant fellow, and a very demanding person. . . . I listen to what he has to say, but I do my own thinking. When one says "yes" or "no" to him, that ends it. The things he wants done are worthy; he is a remarkable administrator and deeply consecrated.[2]

Score's Plans and Accomplishments

Ralph Jones ranks Score above any of his predecessors, "with the possible exception of Mood[,]" for shaping the events of the University and for "impel[ing] it toward new goals and aspirations."[3] But if one measures the record of Score's accomplishments against the statements he made from time to time as to what he wanted to accomplish, that assessment seems excessive. Score's "University of Small Colleges" was in the process of dissolution even before his death, his vision for campus construction was little more than Ullrich's earlier plan, his effort to carry on a major fund-raising campaign never got off the ground, and his desire to establish a Pan-American program and a Graduate School of Social Service never even got to the planning stage.

The listing of what he did not achieve, however, should not be taken as a disparagement of what he did accomplish. One gets the feeling that his announcement of the objectives listed above was not what he was really after anyway. They were announced haphazardly and sporadically, not as the result of a carefully thought out plan for the future. Score's real design for the University was to make it a first-class institution. His plan is to be found in a statement made to a reporter for the *Fort Worth Star-Telegram* a day after his election as President. He said: "We have no desire to make Southwestern a big university, but we believe that there is a place for this institution as a small, Church-owned college, *than which there shall be none better* [italics added]. . . . This is the overwhelming challenge of Southwestern University to me, and the only reason why I could leave one of the greatest pulpits of Methodism to become its president."[4] Achievement of this goal would not be tied to a grand design produced by the staff, faculty, or Trustees, but would spring from the efforts of everyone *led by him* to improve the University at all points—staff, curriculum, caliber of the student body, facilities, endowment, and efficiency of operation. He was confident in his own ability to control events so as to bring this about.

In trying to accomplish this goal he took the University successfully through World War II, when many other schools of Southwestern's type were experiencing severe trauma. In doing so, he changed completely the prevalent image of presidential leadership from one of contention and drift to one of affirmation and strength. His strong personality, possibly a liability with some, resonated positively with other strong leaders with whom he worked in Austin, Houston, Nashville, New York, and Washington. They knew that in him Southwestern had a leader of consequence and tended to measure the school by the man and not by the numbers. Some of the numbers are very strong. Under him the campus expanded from about seventy acres to almost six hundred, providing an incalculable benefit to the University for the long-term future. He was very popular with the Board of Trustees and with other Church and educational officials. In the Texas Methodist system of higher education, he became the linchpin for establishing a pattern of cooperation rather than competition among its colleges and universities. Southern Methodist awarded him an LL.D. in 1945. He paid special attention to faculty procurement, and some of his faculty hires were notable. Of the teachers employed during his tenure, sixteen served twenty years or longer, forming a new core faculty. Three of those who became permanent members of the faculty were German refugees who, scattered by the Nazi terror, brought the benefits of their fine European training to Southwestern. All three of the men had doctorates, as did two of their three spouses. His failure to complete successfully a major financial campaign was compensated for by his phenomenal success in bringing in big money through the Perkins, Fondren, and McManis families. Finally, before integration became a major federal effort in the United States, he created an environment at Southwestern in which a few dedicated teachers and students felt free to develop a Negro Fine Arts School that would, under a future president, produce the first African American student to enter the regular baccalaureate program at Southwestern.

Score's Work Habits

Score's major problem was that he tried to do too much. He spread himself too thin and made up for it by his intensity and by working inordinate hours. In a letter to Professor Frederick W. Lenz of July 26, 1948, after the heart problem that finally felled him had already become a major threat to his life, he apologized for not being able to see him. He said that during the last two weeks he had been to Houston, Chicago, Fort Worth, and Dallas and would be leaving within the next fifteen minutes for Houston again. "While I have been at home, I have been 'snowed under.' I dictated yesterday from 8:30 in the morning, taking time off for necessary conferences and for lunch and dinner, until 11:30 last night." He commanded his body to be subject to his will just as he did people. It finally rebelled.

During his tenure, Score brought three small colleges under the Southwestern umbrella, at least temporarily, thus increasing the responsibility he already bore as a chief executive officer. He served as the main point of contact with officials of the federal government during the war, participated regularly at the national level in major endeavors carried on by the Methodist Church, one of which was to produce the *Book of Worship*, visited alumni groups throughout the state, engaged in an active preaching schedule, and spent as much time fund-raising as he could schedule. Added to this agenda were the tasks that he had difficulty handing off to other persons if he could possibly do them himself. Because he could not bear to see things done badly, he kept his finger on as many pulses as he could to keep a close watch on what was being done by others.

An example of the intensity of his work pattern is his relationship to the Foreign Language Department. Because he was unwilling to entrust the department to any of the currently employed faculty members when he arrived at Southwestern in 1942, he took it over himself, continuing as Head of that department throughout his entire tenure as President. He taught New Testament Greek to regular classes during his first few years, reporting diligently to the Dean the absences of his students from class.[5] He continued to teach a few seniors each semester even after Professor F. W. Lenz came to the University in 1945 and kept in close contact with the department. There are dozens of memos and letters in the presidential files between Score and Lenz dealing with departmental matters in detail. His son, John, reports that he began each day at home by reading the New Testament in Greek. Each night he would take a short nap around eleven, then get up and study and listen to the shortwave radio until two or three A.M.[6]

Score tried to see everyone who wanted to talk to him and to answer every letter. There are 79 memos and letters in the files addressed to Dean Ullrich and 127 to the Business Manager, Dr. McCook, during the nine months before his death in 1949 when he was most ill. He also sent dozens of memos to other University officials during the same period. He succumbed to his heart ailment at the age of fifty-three. Fortunately for the University, by then he had associated with him a very capable and scholarly presidential assistant, Dr. William C. Finch, completely different in style, who was able to pick up the reins of the University with grace, ability, and aplomb and become the next President.

Approachability and Sense of Humor

Though Score had a strong personality, he had a ready laugh, was not difficult to approach, and mixed easily with students. Yvonne Cain (Mrs. J. Q. Vardaman) expresses the freedom she felt working as a student in his office in recounting how she informed him about the dropping of the atomic bomb in 1945.

> Dr. Score was one of the most dynamic ministers in the pulpit I have ever heard. In addition, he was a really impressive and fascinating man. When I was a senior I worked in the little anteroom of his office. . . . I went rejoicing into his office to say that when I had gone down the hall for a drink of water, two sailors had told me about a "huge bomb we dropped on the Japs" that might end the war. Dr. Score grabbed his radio and he, Jean Culberson [his secretary], and I listened to a news broadcast about the dropping of our first atomic bomb together. Several days later, still thinking only of the war ending and my fiancé coming home, I discussed with Dr. Score the entrance of Russia into the war against Japan. He said it was a tragedy, and then he proceeded to tell me why. I think subsequent events have proved him right.[7]

About no other President do official records preserve as many instances of intimate conversation and humor as do those pertaining to Score. This characteristic breaks through repeatedly in his communications with major staff members. In letters written from the field, Howard Knox, the much younger Public Relations director, addressed Score as a friend in a charmingly free, intimate style. As will be seen, he had an especially close relationship with Bill Finch. His humor is very evident in the memos exchanged with Dean Ullrich in 1943 and 1944. The humor might not have always been of the highest quality, but it was often quite clever. Knowledge of its existence softens the depiction of his personality. Score was able to tease and to be teased.

On changing his mind about an issue that he and Ullrich had been discussing, he began a memo to the Dean explaining the change as follows: "Through the centuries women have had the privilege of changing their minds. Occasionally it has become necessary for their fathers, husbands, brothers, sweethearts, slaves, or what have you, to do likewise."[8] Ullrich replied in a similarly humorous vein. After a meeting between the two in the President's office when Ullrich had left his pipe behind, Score, the cigar smoker, returned it to its owner, attaching a derisive memo about that "instrument of torture." The Dean replied with an elaborate four-stanza poem on smoking. Shortly thereafter, writing Ullrich about a minor issue, Score concluded his rather long memo by saying that no reply was needed, but he was sure he would receive one anyway.[9] President and Dean had an easy relationship. From the time of Mood through that of Vivion, the President of the University had always presided at faculty meetings. Bergin did not feel comfortable in that role and had turned it over to Dean Ullrich. Ullrich, for his part, felt equally uncomfortable doing it. Soon after Score's election he asked the President-elect to reassume that role, which he did.[10]

The Score Family—Russell, Ruth, and John

The new President was born into a parsonage family on April 21, 1896. He earned his A.B. degree from Scarritt-Morrisville College in Morrisville, Missouri, in 1914. He received his B.D. degree from Emory University in 1916. After serving as chaplain in the United States Army in 1918–1919, he did further graduate study at New College and the University of Edinburgh in 1919. Returning to America, he served two small pastorates in Arkansas, one at Parkin and the other at Wynne, before going to Epworth University Church in Berkeley, California. While there he obtained a Th.D. degree (1924) from the Pacific School of Religion. Upon his return to Texas, he was appointed to St. Paul's in Houston, one of the great churches of American Methodism, which he served from 1926 to 1934. He led the church in constructing an $800,000 edifice. His service at St. Paul's was followed by eight years at First Methodist in Fort Worth until 1942. He was a delegate to every General Conference from 1934 to 1948 and to the Uniting Conference in 1939. He was a member of the Board of Education of the former Methodist Episcopal Church, South, and president of the Board of Education of the Methodist Church after union. His trusteeships, memberships, and offices in other groups were numerous.[11]

Score married Margaret Ruth Smith on January 12, 1921. They had one son, John Nelson Russell Score II, called John in distinction from his father, who was called Russell by his friends. John Score, the son, was a high school senior in Fort Worth when his father, Russell, was named to Southwestern. He enrolled immediately in Southwestern for the fall of 1942. Graduating in 1945, he obtained a B.D. from Garrett Biblical Institute in 1948. After teaching at Southwestern during his father's final year in 1948–1949, he did graduate work before joining the faculty permanently in 1955 in the Department of Religion and Philosophy. He obtained a Ph.D. from Duke University in 1964. Russell was proud of John and wrote letters in 1943 to Lyndon Johnson, Bishop A. Frank Smith, and others seeking their help in the effort to have John approved for the V-12 prechaplain corps program at Southwestern during the war. He wrote Johnson that he should have heard John's "Comanche yell" on getting the news that his application had been approved.[12]

John Score carried on the Score name in the faculty until his death in 1995, serving a total of forty-one years. He was a provocative teacher. Under his gruff veneer, he cared deeply about his students, friends, and colleagues. And he was loved equally in return. Students knew that he was not afraid to direct the same critical ability against administrators as he did against them when he felt it was needed. Stanley Hauerwas (B.A., 1962), the eminent Duke University theologian and Southwestern graduate, attributes his intellectual awakening as a student to John Score. Never married, John left his entire estate of about $1 million to Southwestern at his death.

All three Scores were cremated. Though the ashes of Russell Score were placed in the altar of the newly finished Lois Perkins Chapel in 1950, they were removed to a niche in the northwest corner of the original Fondren Science Hall at the behest of John when the chapel altar was replaced in the early 1990s. There they rest behind a bronze plaque, engraved with a tribute to him and a list of his accomplishments provided by the Fondren Foundation. Mrs. W. W. Fondren had admired and respected Score and was responsible for the funds making possible the chapel's construction. Another box holding the ashes of Ruth lies alongside his.

John Score was a great supporter of the theater. He attended most productions, and Angus Springer, chair of the Department of Speech and Drama, said that the laugh of Jane Brown McCook, together with that of Dr. John Score, was "more to be prized at the performance of good comedies than any laugh-track yet recorded!"[13] After John's death, Dr. Farley Snell, University chaplain, sprinkled his ashes in the chapel garden. John loved the chapel, attended its services regularly, and made gifts to it for such things as altar and pulpit paraments. Though John was like his father in appreciating the finer elements of liturgy, he felt that sermons should be short and to the point. He chided persons who preached too long.

Getting Started

Though Russell Score had stated at the time of his election on February 11, 1942, that he could not take office until June 1, he began to make his presence felt in University life almost immediately. He attended an Executive Committee meeting in late February, a faculty meeting in March, and spoke at a campus banquet in early April. He launched a banquet tour of twelve cities between April 20 and May 8, meeting alumni across the state.[14] Enthusiasm for the new President pervaded every meeting.

Chairman of the Board, Dr. C. C. Cody, Jr., presents to Dr. J. N. R. Score the instrument for impressing the seal of the University on official papers as a part of the inauguration ceremony in 1942. Southwestern University, Special Collections.

The opportunistic nature of Score's approach to University development efforts became apparent early on. It is illustrated in an effort engaged in by him and Bishop A. Frank Smith in the spring and summer of 1942, when the two men spent many hours trying to persuade Dr. Charles H. Harris of Fort Worth to establish his proposed Harris College of Nursing at Southwestern. The school would be supported by the Harris Foundation and would involve the transfer of the already established Harris Dormitory for Nurses to the campus in Georgetown.[15]

Though the effort was ultimately fruitless, it had an entirely plausible rationale. The full impact of the war on Southwestern had not yet been felt, but one thing was clear. It was going to create a campus populated mostly by girls, with the few boys being those too young, too old, or physically unfit for service. None of the major programs for on-campus training of army, navy, or marine units had yet been announced. The training of nurses would certainly fit into the war effort in some way, and a nursing school on what might become a predominantly female campus was a logical action.

The Westminster College Merger

Score's first action as President-elect was taken at the same meeting where he was elected, almost four months before he assumed office. At that time he asked the Board to authorize him to conduct negotiations with the Trustees of Westminster College to take over its assets and, in effect, to take responsibility for running the college, with no financial obligation to Southwestern. Without any recorded discussion, the Board approved.[16]

The timing of Score's request is important for understanding his motive in attaching Westminster College (1942), Weatherford College (1944), and Daniel Baker College (1946) to Southwestern during his administration. Ralph Jones is correct when he characterizes the merging of these colleges into Southwestern as an attempt to save dying enterprises.[17] Score attached them to Southwestern not as part of a concerted plan to expand Southwestern, but individually, as occasion provided, in an effort to save them. He believed in small, Church-related colleges, and he used Southwestern University as an umbrella to keep them alive. The rationale he offers for what he has done in his 1947 brochure, entitled "A University of Small Colleges," is not philosophical or expansionistic. He explains his action as being a practical way of helping *the small college idea* to persevere in an age when economic and financial problems in running small colleges are enormous and when the gigantism of State institutions appears poised to overwhelm them.[18] He hopes to give prestige to the three small colleges in question by making them a part of the Southwestern tradition, to use the Southwestern structure to relieve them of major administrative costs, and to achieve economies of scale in other areas by absorbing them into a larger, but still small, college structure.

Score came to the Board meeting when he was elected President of Southwestern knowing that Westminster College was in bad shape and a candidate for early demise. Formerly an institution of the Methodist Protestant Church, it had become a part of the new, unified Methodist system when that Church joined the two other major branches of Methodism at the time of Church union in 1939. Score's desire as President-elect to join Westminster to Southwestern was not designed so much to help Southwestern as to help this particular junior college survive. Though he was ultimately unsuccessful in saving it, he was determined not to walk away from it without trying. One might have thought that the earlier experience of President Vivion with Blinn Memorial College from 1930 through 1934 (see Chapter XIV) would have been a warning, if not to him, at least to the Trustees who remembered it, against making such an attempt, but the positive attitude of the new President was so compelling that everyone acquiesced to his desire to try again.

Westminster College, located in Tehuacana, slightly more than thirty miles northeast of Waco, was chartered in 1895 as a preparatory school to train ministers for the Methodist Protestant Church. It later became a junior college, with one major building serving both administrative and classroom purposes.[19] Score reported to the Executive Committee that the College now owed the General Board of Education of the Methodist Church some $16,000, which was secured by $13,000 of bonds and stock. There was no mortgage on the property, and the school owned some land. Its total assets were approximately $110,900. As a result of these facts and successful negotiations with the Westminster Trustees, a merger was voted by the Executive Committee and entered into by the end of the year. Sixty-seven freshmen and sophomore students matriculated for the 1942–1943 academic year, with thirty taking additional extension courses from Southwestern. It closed the year successfully without a deficit.[20] The year 1943–1944 was not as successful. Without military students to make up for the loss of men away in the armed forces, enrollment dropped to forty-two, and the school ran a deficit of $1,500. Score reported that the citizens of Tehuacana were endeavoring to cover it.[21]

By this time Score and his Southwestern advisors had come to feel that the school, with only seven teachers in 1942–1943 and six in 1943–1944, would not be viable as a literary institution in the future and began thinking about dedicating it to vocational training, especially for disabled veterans. Dairy work, bookbinding, printing, woodworking, and metal work were being considered as areas of instruction.[22] Clearly, long-term prospects for Westminster were not promising and had not improved during the first two years of Southwestern's stewardship.

The Greater Southwestern Program

At the same time Southwestern was taking over Westminster Junior College, Score recommended to the Board in November 1942 that the school launch a "long-time" development program. Familiar with the campaigns of Bishop, Barcus, and Vivion, the committee of three (he, Ullrich, and McCook) that designed the program called it by the term those three Presidents had used—the Greater Southwestern Program. They used Ullrich's earlier work previously adopted by the Buildings and Grounds Committee (see Chapter XV) as the basis for the program.

As endorsed by the Board, the program recommended that the College of Arts and Sciences be set up with four divisions: Humanities, Social Sciences, Natural Sciences, and Fine Arts. Also, a Department of Home Economics should be added in the Division of Social Sciences. Six departments would be formed by reorganization and addition. They would be Religious Education, Sociology, Physical Education and Training, Mathematics and Astronomy, Physics and Aeronautics, and Geology. Looking to the future, the program called for a student body of 735 to 833 students with a complement of 49 teachers. Teachers would be procured incrementally as student numbers increased. A "fortified" master's degree would offer majors in nine areas: English, Religion, Education, History and Government, Psychology, Sociology, Biology, Chemistry, and Mathematics-Physics-Astronomy. This academic organization part of the Greater Southwestern plan, calling for the four major units listed above, was achieved during the Score years. At his death in 1949, there were three divisions and a School of Fine Arts, the organizational structure that has continued to exist until the present.

Modernization of buildings and equipment plus the procurement of new equipment would cost about $1,050,000. This amount is about the same as that in the earlier Ullrich report for the buildings he recommended. It would be part of a total program of $3,500,000 to $5,000,000 to be raised for buildings, equipment, and endowment during the campaign. The Board voted to "endorse [the program] in principle."[23]

When Mr. and Mrs. J. J. Perkins announced in 1943 that they had decided to provide sufficient money to build a chapel, Score stated that the gift "means the beginning of the Greater Southwestern Program which has been under discussion for so many months."[24] Of course, its construction would have to wait until after the war.

In the interval between November 1942, when the plan was adopted, and the Executive Committee meeting of late March 1944, Score engaged in an effort to set up a joint financial campaign with Southern Methodist University to raise $8 to $10 million.[25] The Executive Committee expressed support for this effort but warned that Southwestern must raise at least $3.5 million for itself during the next three years whatever might be the fate of the joint campaign. It felt that Southwestern should begin immediately the preparation of a prospect list for either a cooperative or a separate effort. At that point, almost a year and a half after the Greater Southwestern Program had been adopted, no prospect list of any sort existed.[26]

Apparently this warning acted as a stimulant for Score, because shortly thereafter the *Williamson County*

Sun announced that a campaign for expansion with a $3.5 million goal would be pursued during the next two years.[27] Though the procedure to be used in the financial campaign was outlined in the next Executive Committee meeting in September 1944, nothing concrete had been done by the time of the midyear Board meeting in 1945. The Trustees at that time reaffirmed "their commitments to the final goals and plans heretofore approved" and obligated themselves to such special efforts in the next six months as might be needed. The administration was also authorized to employ such help in public relations as might be needed.[28]

Score announced to the faculty that the Greater Southwestern Campaign would begin with a banquet on Founders' Day, February 5, 1946.[29] In April a booklet entitled *The Southwestern Story* was mailed to the Trustees and other special persons. Score told the Trustees at their spring meeting that he believed Georgetown would give more than $60,000, that more than $25,000 had been pledged by the faculty, that a banquet had been held in Houston, and that campaigns were already planned for eighteen cities, with others to be held in the Rio Grande Valley. He acknowledged that some Trustees might have grown impatient with the background work, but he was convinced that it was "best to have adequate preparation rather than to rush in."[30] These events, the banquets, the booklet's publication, and the plans for events in other cities, made it appear that at last the campaign was underway. But more than a year later, on May 19, 1947, Score wrote to Mrs. Perkins that campaign organizers would be initiating solicitation by cities immediately after the Annual Conferences in the fall, six months away. Fall 1947 would be almost two years after the original dinner in Georgetown. He assured her that the campaign was going well and that they had secured "a number of verbal promises."[31]

Though a citywide campaign was held in Houston soon after the turn of the year, Score had to report to the Trustees in April 1948 that the campaign had been halted in its tracks. It had been handicapped, he said, because of a sickness that had kept him in bed for more than a month. It was his first reference to the heart problem, though he did not know it as such at the time, that would increasingly trouble him until his death a year and a half later.

> As I make my personal report to you, it is with a sense of chagrin that I tell you that because of sickness I have not been able to carry on as I had hoped and expected. This has had its effects on the total work of the University and especially on our financial campaign. We spent a great deal of time before Christmas [1947] and immediately after and quite some money in getting ready for the Houston Campaign. We had a splendid dinner meeting there at the beginning of our campaign and the following week I had to go to bed and for more than a month was totally incapacitated. This has meant that many of the projects that I would have been carrying on have had to be postponed and we are just now getting back into the swing of our work. As you receive this report we are at work in Houston on the campaign.[32]

A week later Score explained to the Executive Committee the work that was being done with various foundations on the Greater Southwestern Campaign.[33] Another hiatus ensued. It was not until a year and a half later, after Score's death in late September 1949, that another reference would be made to it. At that time Acting President Finch reported that the Greater Southwestern Campaign was being continued with two persons in the field.[34] He mentioned it again in his tribute to Score at the Board meeting on November 15, 1949, stating that the new chapel then being constructed was the "first building of the greater Southwestern campus plan."[35] Realistically, however, the campaign died with Score. There is no mention of it anywhere afterwards. It simply disappeared.

Assessment of the Greater Southwestern Campaign

A careful assessment of the Greater Southwestern Campaign suggests not that it failed but that it failed to materialize. Voted into existence by the Board in late 1942, it went out of existence in late 1949 without ever having become a real campaign. There was a great deal of rhetoric and preparation but little substantial action during the seven years it was supposedly in effect. The program had no bearing on the action of the J. J. Perkins family in providing the money for the Lois Perkins Chapel or of Mrs. W. W. Fondren in providing the money for the Fondren Science Building. Their gifts came as a result of personal predilection, not as a result of campaign publicity or solicitation. When McManis made his remarkable gift, he was giving to the man he had come to admire as pastor of St. Paul's in Houston between 1926 and 1934, not to a favorite institution or as a result of a campaign solicitation.

The campaign's inability to get off the ground was

caused by a number of factors. As President, Score rationed his time as best he could among the many tasks he set for himself. During the war, his top priority was procurement and maintenance of the Naval V-12 Unit. Without that unit to supply students, Southwestern would have had great difficulty. Score spent much of his time ensuring the success of that enterprise. In an April 1944 letter to Congressman Lyndon B. Johnson, who had been so instrumental in securing the program, Score wrote: "Of course you know that since the Naval unit came here we have done practically nothing but sleep, dream, and think Navy and Marine Programs."[36] Neither did he employ a Glenn Flinn, as Barcus had in the late 1920s (see Chapter XIII), to take the burden off his back, even though that model had resulted in the most efficient, long-term financial campaign to date. The other administrative officers were competent, but their days were filled with their own responsibilities.

Though it is unfair to fault Score today for the priorities he adopted during the war that prevented his bringing the Greater Southwestern Campaign to a successful conclusion, he can perhaps be faulted for presenting diffuse signals to potential contributors. Unlike Bergin, who set out five simple, clear goals for his administration at the outset of his administration and maintained them throughout, Score's rich mind continually found new objects to support and new directions to pursue. Already mentioned have been his mergers with a new college every other year, his attempt to establish a joint financial campaign with SMU, and his occasional efforts to interest people in the establishment of a Graduate School of Social Service.

Another program proposed to the Perkins family in 1947 was for them to endow the Departments of Bible, Religious Education, Religion and Church History, Philosophy, and Church Music—in effect, to use Score's words, to set up an Undergraduate School of Religion. Money for Rural Sociology, for the library, and for fellowships was also included. The endowment needed to sustain the program would be between $540,000 and $840,000. This Undergraduate School of Religion would take care of the 150 to 200 ministerial and life service students enrolled in the four units of Southwestern. It would act as a feeder to the Theology School at Southern Methodist University, which had already been funded by the Perkins family.

The problem was that Joe and Lois Perkins had already committed themselves in 1943 to building a chapel for Southwestern after the war and that Score had only recently proposed to them the funding of a Graduate School of Social Service. When he proposed the establishment of an endowment for an Undergraduate School of Religion, J. J. Perkins became frustrated and virtually threw up his hands. He liked to do one thing at a time. Mrs. Perkins rejected the new proposal graciously, writing Score that "he would not be a good president if he did not 'dream dreams and see visions,'" and that sometime her husband might "become interested in helping Southwestern secure such a school. But as you know he is not one to spread his interests."[37] She and most other persons of her kind appreciated Score even when he exasperated them. He was exciting and stimulating, not boring and sycophantic. Using the technique of Bishop Smith, the Perkinses listened to what Score had to say but did their own thinking. When they said "no," that ended it. No more was said about the Undergraduate School of Religion.

Ultimately, Score played to his strengths and to the necessities of the moment, as he perceived them, not to formal plans. He set up the Greater Southwestern Program because a big campaign was de rigueur for financial development. His strength, however, was in dealing with big donors and with big ecclesiastical, political, and business people on a personal basis. In this he was very successful, even, as in the case of McManis, when he did not really cultivate them. His self-assurance, decisive manner, verbal skills, and personal magnetism drew their support. The Lois Perkins Chapel, the Fondren Science Hall, and the W-K-M endowment gift from Fred McManis are his legacies, as is his procurement of the Naval V-12 Unit, which fed Southwestern's need for students during the war and created the atmosphere of a successful educational institution.

While attempting to attract the Harris College of Nursing to the Southwestern campus, promoting a merger with Westminster College, and initiating the Greater Southwestern Campaign, all of which were unsuccessful or of doubtful advantage to the University, President Score was engaged in another endeavor that was very successful—attracting a military unit to the campus. Lyndon Baines Johnson, congressman from the Tenth District, in which Southwestern was located, was the person primarily responsible from the Washington end for Southwestern's success in this venture. The story of Johnson's rise to political power in Texas and his interest in Southwestern is unusual. The former has been well chronicled in a number of biographies. What he did for Southwestern and why he did it are less well known. Johnson used unstintingly his presence in Washington during World War II to assure the continuance of Southwestern as a viable institution. Without him, Southwestern would have faced a bleak future.

The Rise to Power of Lyndon Baines Johnson

After graduation from Southwest Texas State Teachers College in San Marcos in 1930, Lyndon Johnson taught school for a year and worked for other persons in several political campaigns. From the beginning of his work in politics, he was recognized as a "wonder kid."[38] In late 1931 he became the secretary of Congressman Richard M. Kleberg in Washington. In this role he galvanized a moribund organization of congressional secretaries, sometimes called "The Little Congress," and became its leader. Some called him "The Boss of the Little Congress." Everyone soon recognized him for his adroitness in the political maneuvering that brought him to and maintained him in that position. In addition, he was very successful in implementing New Deal programs for Kleberg back in Texas. He became friends with Sam Rayburn, also from Texas and Speaker of the House. In 1934 Rayburn secured agreement from the White House to the appointment of the twenty-six-year-old Johnson as first director of the National Youth Administration for Texas.

Johnson succeeded just as skillfully as head of the Texas N.Y.A. as he had in Washington. He put into place a system of roadside parks using young Texans as workers, introducing, at the same time, the participation of African Americans in some N.Y.A. programs. He had already become mindful of the destitution of Hispanic students during his year of teaching in Cotulla before completing his degree at San Marcos. Years later, in 1965, as President, he would sign the landmark Voting Rights Act that ensured the full participation of these two groups in the political process.

The political opening for which Johnson had been searching came in 1937, when James P. Buchanan, congressman from the Tenth District, died. His seat, which included Austin and Georgetown, would be filled in a winner-take-all election called by Governor James V Allred. Though he was hardly known in the Tenth District, Johnson was one of the seven candidates that filed for election. His single theme in the campaign was all-out support of Franklin D. Roosevelt and the New Deal.[39] Johnson was a tireless campaigner. Ed Clark, an important, politically connected Austin lawyer, ex-Southwestern student, and future fund-raiser for Southwestern, said about the campaign: "I never saw anyone campaign as hard as that. . . . I never thought it was possible for anyone to work that hard." From his student days in San Marcos Johnson had operated on the principle that "if you did *everything*, you would win."[40] He would later work for Southwestern in Washington with almost the same intensity.

Johnson's election on a 100 percent Roosevelt platform caught the President's attention. Johnson had been elected during the hullabaloo surrounding the Supreme Court packing controversy, when tension was at its height. Though the Texas Legislature denounced Roosevelt's court reform plan, Johnson supported it. Before the newly elected congressman went to Washington, he received an invitation from Roosevelt to meet him at Galveston when he landed on return from a fishing vacation in the Gulf of Mexico. Roosevelt was so impressed with him there that he invited Johnson to accompany him on his train trip through Texas to Fort Worth. On the trip Roosevelt informed Johnson that the Agriculture Committee was his if he wanted it, but he suggested the Naval Affairs Committee instead. Naval Affairs was powerful, and, the President said, world trends portended that it might be more powerful still. Johnson accepted.[41] His acceptance of a seat on Naval Affairs in 1937 would have portentous consequences for Southwestern in 1943. He would be in a strong position to maneuver a Naval V-12 and Marine Unit to Southwestern. When his time came during World War II to join the military, he joined the navy as a lieutenant commander.

Lyndon Johnson and the Brown Connection

Johnson also engaged in one other activity during his first few months in Washington that would ultimately redound to the benefit of Southwestern. It was his all-important role in getting through Congress the appropriation of funds for the construction of the Marshall Ford Dam, later renamed the Buchanan Dam. Construction of the dam had already been awarded to the Brown & Root construction company, and it was well along in its work when a defect was found in the title for the land on which the dam was being built. Federal regulations stipulated that such a project could only be built on federal land. The land on which the dam was being built was not federal property. The government had acquired ownership of all public lands in the West as the territories accepted statehood, except for Texas. Being a republic when it came into the union, it had retained its ownership of public lands.[42] The funding for the project was likely to be annulled.

The finding of this defect threatened Brown & Root with financial disaster if some way were not found to remedy it. Brown & Root by this time in its development had become an important regional construction firm, but the dam was its first project of national magnitude. It had already committed millions to the project and might not be reimbursed for what it had done. Though he had not supported Lyndon Johnson in the just completed congressional election, Herman Brown turned to his new congressman for help. Johnson responded to the Brown & Root problem immediately. The headquarters of Brown & Root had been in Georgetown for a number of years before moving to Austin, both cities were in the Tenth Congressional District, and the dam was in Johnson's district as well. In response, he steered a private bill through Congress that was signed by the President authorizing funding for the Marshall Ford Dam. The Marshall Ford project was the breakthrough for Brown & Root for large projects. It led to other big projects during the war, such as the building of other large dams, the construction of the Corpus Christi Naval Base, and the entry of the company into the shipbuilding business. With the successful completion of the dam, Brown & Root was on the way to becoming one of the great construction firms in the world.

Success in resolving the financing problem associated with the Marshall Ford project established a permanent relationship between Johnson and the two Brown brothers. Herman Brown believed in repaying his debts. He wrote Johnson: "Remember that I am for you, right or wrong and it makes no difference whether I think you are right or wrong. If you want it, I am for it 100%." Johnson and the Browns became friends for the rest of their lives, and the two brothers supported Johnson's political ambitions generously. This friendship, initiated on the basis of expedience, came over time to have a deeper basis. The men developed respect for the prowess for each other, and their wives became friends. Margarett, Herman's wife from Georgetown, Alice, George's wife from Temple, and Lady Bird, from Karnack (near Marshall), genuinely enjoyed each other. Margarett and Alice were Southwestern alumnae. Both loved Southwestern and would later repay that love. Lyndon Johnson surely knew their feeling for the school. The men liked each other as well. George Brown said that Johnson seemed to enjoy matching wits with Herman, sixteen years older, and neither man ever pulled punches in his arguments. "Lyndon and Herman would have some knock-down, drag-outs, but they would always get back together because they all appreciated each other as a worthy opponent."[43]

Lyndon would eventually secure the Naval V-12 Unit for Southwestern, Herman would become Vice Chair of the Southwestern Board of Trustees, and The Brown Foundation would make the single most generous grant to Southwestern in its history, a grant whose results provided the financial base for its transformation from a regionally recognized institution to a nationally recognized institution. But all of this was in the future. In 1942 none of it had yet materialized.

Pearl Neas and Lyndon Baines Johnson

Once Johnson had been elected, he began to solidify his political base. He had been elected in a special election in 1937 and was faced with the prospect of running again in 1938 for a regular term. He had lost Williamson County in 1937 to Sam Stone, a native son of Georgetown, and was fearful that Stone might run again in 1938. He courted Stone, as he did his other earlier opponents, encouraging them by subtle displays of friendship not to run against him. His tactics worked, and he ran unopposed in 1938. Before that election, Pearl A. Neas, Registrar at Southwestern, sent him a letter pledging her support. He replied a few days later, thanking her for her "thoughtful letter of March 30 and for your generous offer to cooperate with me." Thus began a long friendship and correspondence between Lyndon Johnson and Pearl Neas that lasted from 1938 until at least 1949, when the records go silent. She contributed her voluminous correspondence with Johnson covering the Score years to the Southwestern University library for preservation. There are more than two hundred communications between them in the collection.[44]

When Pearl Neas came to know Lyndon Johnson is unknown, but it was at least by the time of her letter to him of March 30, 1938. She would have known Margarett Root and Alice Pratt when they were Southwestern students through her work as secretary to the President from the middle 1910s, as registrar from the 1920s, and as director of alumni work during the 1930s. She had probably known Margarett from childhood, since Margarett had grown up in the Root house on land that later became a part of the Southwestern campus. As her scrapbooks show, Pearl followed the news carefully and was probably aware of Johnson's efforts in behalf of Margarett's husband, Herman, in funding Marshall Ford Dam. She may have come to know Herman during the time when the headquarters of Brown & Root was in Georgetown, where he courted Margarett, a schoolteacher at the time. Apart from any other reasons that might have led her to support Lyndon Johnson, Pearl

Neas may have determined to help the man who was helping her acquaintances.

Having established epistolary contact with Lyndon in 1938, she perhaps talked to him during the dedication of the Cody Memorial Library in 1939, which he attended. She was never bashful about initiating conversations with important persons. She seems to have corresponded with him between the time of her initial letter on March 30, 1938, and the next letter on record written on January 1, 1942, for that letter seems to be picking up on an already established pattern of contact. She did not include in the collection later given to Southwestern any of her correspondence with LBJ before that date or after October 7, 1949, a week and a half after Score's death. The inclusion of the solitary 1938 letter in the collection was either a fortunate accident or her way of saying, "Here is where it all began."

The relationship of Pearl Neas to Lyndon Johnson is difficult to characterize. He would have been thirty-four in 1942, she forty-eight. She calls him "Lyndon" or "Dear Lyndon" from the first, while he calls her "Miss Pearl." It later years it becomes "My Dear Pearl." In a letter of January 1, 1943, she addresses him as "Dear Friend." Then she goes on to explain it.

> If I could make this salutation any stronger, I would. But "dear" means "precious" and a friend is the richest possession one can have. The many evidences of your fine friendship have meant much to me. Brilliant, gallant and gay, your presence at once makes a place such as one would desire to be in. Many great personalities have crossed my path leaving gracious memories that augment life's beauty, but you have a special place in my affections. No distance of place or lapse of time has lessened my friendship. I wish for you and Mrs. Johnson peace and happiness in the New Year. Faithfully.[45]

While Johnson was serving in the navy during 1942, with a brief tour of duty in the South Pacific, Lady Bird ran his office in Washington, and some of Pearl's correspondence was with her. On the birth of Lynda Johnson in 1944, she sent a package to the couple containing gifts for the baby. Lady Bird wrote back a handwritten thank-you note in which she stated that she and Lyndon had fun together opening the packages and "examining the dainty jacket and the cute little duck blanket-holder."[46] In a follow-up letter to Lyndon, she expressed the hope that "Lynda will someday become one of our fair coeds on the Southwestern campus. Of course, I will probably be in a wheel chair by that time, but I hope she will come by and let me learn to love her as much as I love her parents."[47] After the Johnsons purchased radio station KLBJ in Austin, Lady Bird gave Southwestern a series of half-hour programs. The first originated from the Southwestern campus on August 20, 1943. The theme of the broadcasts, aired from the auditorium of the Administration Building, was "Southwestern Builds Americans."[48]

Pearl also paid attention to Lyndon's mother. She wrote him on May 1, 1943, that she had recently had a "pleasant visit" with his mother by telephone. "I shall accept her invitation," Pearl said, "to come by and get better acquainted, the first time I am in Austin with a bit of time on my hands."[49] Four years later she described a visit to his mother during her hospital convalescence. She said that Rebekah was in a wheelchair at the time but that she expected to walk around her room the next day. Johnson responded that his mother had already told him about the visit.[50] Rebekah Johnson sent her a note a few days later thanking her for her visit and flowers. She asked her to come by again.[51]

From early in the correspondence Pearl began to act as an unofficial political consultant to Johnson, telling him both good and bad, supporting him in every endeavor, while at the same time using his services to help Southwestern and her friends. She recommended persons whom she felt worthy for such positions as postmaster in Georgetown and students for appointment to Annapolis and West Point. He went to great lengths to honor her requests, and most times he was able to do so. Typical is a letter to him of March 27, 1945, in which she tells him about the criticism he is receiving over delay in the construction of the Georgetown airport, but, she says, she knows he is not to blame. The next day a telegram arrived saying that the airport suspension order previously issued would be canceled.[52] When a Mr. Buck Taylor ran for Johnson's seat in the 1944 election, she wrote him, saying that LBJ had spent nine months in foreign service and was awarded the Silver Star. Then she asked him, "What is your war record?," knowing he had none. Johnson had joined the navy on December 11, 1941, the first congressman to do so. He returned to Capitol Hill in July 1942 when Roosevelt recalled members of Congress from active duty. Though she exaggerated slightly Lyndon's time in service, she had made her point.

She definitely had influence on Johnson and was recognized, if not as a major player, at least as a loyal, respected person in the LBJ entourage. She had free access to Ed Clark in Austin and recounts parts of several conversations with him in her letters. She received special invitations to all the big Johnson events in Austin, and Clark made sure she received a special invitation to the celebration in Austin honoring Admiral Nimitz after the war.[53] Johnson frequently expressed his esteem for her. On finding a letter from her on his desk in Austin after returning from an out-of-state trip in 1944, he replied: "I know of no woman whose judgment I admire more."[54] He had reason to admire it. It was constant in its admiration of him.

She and Score communicated frequently with each other on their contacts with Johnson, and, in contrast to his problem with Cody's writing letters to persons with whom the President was negotiating, Score encouraged Pearl Neas in her correspondence with Johnson. The congressman for his part wanted to make sure that Score did not inhibit her. On October 23, 1943, he wrote Score saying that he hoped he would not keep Pearl so busy that she could not report to him "ever so often." "She writes me," he said, "such interesting and newsy letters." Johnson seldom did anything significant for Southwestern without telling both Neas and Score at almost the same time what he had done. Neas was so devoted to the causes of both men, exercised such good judgment in what she did, and was so open in her relations with them that when dealing with her they put aside the normal protocol of not allowing persons in lower-echelon positions to act independently in important matters. When, in 1945, Johnson received some accusations from friends of Southwestern about "his double talk," he complained about it in a letter to Score, with a copy to Neas. Notable is the fact that he addresses them as equals in discussing the matter.

> Each and every time I have talked to you and Pearl or written you, I have tried to speak frankly and honestly with you. Apparently some folks who are friends of Southwestern are not friends of mine. . . . Perhaps I shouldn't be so irritated about the situation, but I do think that if these self-appointed critics had spent as many hours working for Southwestern as I have, it wouldn't be so necessary now that they occupy a major part of my time each day [reading and answering their letters]. . . . When I see you and Pearl I will be glad to tell you everything that has transpired. . . . Needless to say, I am on your team and will do what I can.[55]

Neither Johnson nor Score ever had reason to regret his trust in her. Neas was devoted to Dr. Score. In a letter to Lyndon in late 1947, she said, "Off the record, there is much talk about the possible election of our president to the bishopric when General Conference rolls around next spring. I can have a cold chill just thinking about the possibility!"[56]

About Lyndon Johnson she remained euphoric to the point where our evidence ends in 1949. He was equally enthusiastic about her. She made a five-minute radio talk on his behalf in his 1948 senatorial campaign and a speech at an LBJ rally at the Austin Hotel, the election he won by eighty-seven votes.[57] After his victory in the primary, she wrote him that she had given up her vacation so that she could spend more time in the campaign. "Why did I do this? Because I was convinced that you could, if elected, serve the whole state as effectively as you have served our Tenth District. . . . I am glad that I belong to the Johnson organization which has never had a legitimate defeat." She says that she is proud to be working with a man "whose sincere desire is to serve all mankind, including the 'little people,' from whom there can be no hope of reward, except gratitude."[58] After her New Year's Day greeting to Johnson in 1948, Johnson replied:

> Dear Pearl, In looking back over my years in public life, I realize that I am indebted to many people; however, I can't think of anyone who has been more consistent and more conscientious in making my progress possible than you. I don't even know how to express my gratitude.[59]

Though she lived to see Johnson's election as Vice President in 1960, she died two years later, a year before he became President after the assassination of John Kennedy.

Score and Johnson

As dedicated as Pearl Neas was to Lyndon Johnson, Russell Score was almost if not equally committed to him. The expressions of her dedication were more effusive and spontaneous than his, but his were sincere and deep. If her frequent use of the word "beloved" in her letters to Lyndon is dismissed as the product of her animated personality, one must recognize that use of that word and other terms of affection by Score, a man noted for his tough exterior, cannot be explained that way.[60] In his correspondence, Score was warmest in his expressions of regard to three persons—A. Frank Smith, Bill Finch, and Lyndon Johnson. Russell Score was not the only person in his household that supported Johnson. He wrote Johnson that his wife, Ruth, in the 1944 congressional race was "taking the floor in every meeting" telling people "that she had never seen a congressman who did as much for his District as a young man named Lyndon Johnson, and that he has done more for Georgetown in the last two years than anyone has ever done before."[61]

The relationship of Score to Johnson, though slightly tinged in his correspondence with elements of emotion, was more like that of Herman Brown to Johnson than of Neas to Johnson. Johnson and Score were 100 percent committed to each other but could still disagree on the level of equality and friendship. When, at a crucial juncture in the Cold War, Truman advocated universal military training and selective service at the same time, the former to build up the reserves, the latter to build up the armed forces immediately, LBJ supported him. Score disagreed with LBJ's support of universal military training. In a letter to him, he expressed that disagreement but said that his letter was not a "request that he vote except in any way he ought to vote. . . . If I had not thought you were competent, I would not have worked for you and voted for you. So this is not a pressure letter."[62]

Though Score had never committed himself to a candidate politically before he began to support Johnson, he did so fully in light of Johnson's services to Southwestern.[63] After Johnson announced his intention to run for senator in 1948, Score wrote him reinforcing his earlier pledges of support. "I think you know without my saying," he writes, "to where I stand on the matter; but if you do not, you are to take this letter, I hope, as a renewal of the statement I have made to you in the past."[64] He wrote a two-and-a-half-page campaign document for Johnson that he broadcast over a statewide network on July 23.[65] One paragraph of it is as follows:

> My business with him has been transacted in his office in Washington, in his office in Austin, in my office, and in my home. In these contacts, I have found that no question related to any part of the institution or personal life of his district is insignificant in his eyes. Our correspondence has been voluminous. I have discussed everything with him; questions that were facing the House of Representatives; I have discussed these with him as a citizen. He has taken the time to answer them. We have not always agreed. Frequently he has had information I did not possess. Sometimes there has been an honest difference of opinion, and out of it I have come to regard him as a man willing to listen to the other man's viewpoint, and equally ready to make the necessary study to be sure of his position. He is careful of his promises, and more careful to fulfill, to the best of his ability, the promises he makes.[66]

After Johnson won the primary, Score wrote him that he would continue his support in "the run-off campaign, and on down the line." Following his victory in the general election, Johnson sent a letter thanking Score for his radio speech. "Frankly, if we could have had you on the air a few more times I think our final lead would have been much larger."[67] Score responded a few days later in a letter addressed to "Senator Johnson" but signed "Your friend, Russell," the first time he had signed himself by his given name through all their years of exchanging dozens and dozens of letters. Johnson, the younger man by twelve years, had always used "Lyndon" as his signature. Score concluded the letter by saying he would be on hand for the reelection "in six years."[68] He was unable to fulfill that commitment. He would be dead within a year.

Procurement of the Naval V-12 and Marine Unit

Though available records show that President Score and Johnson first established epistolary contact on September 3, 1942, it was not until three months later that Score met him for the first time in what was booked as a ten-minute appointment. His purpose was to acquaint him with Southwestern's proposal to procure a military unit. The school had been approved since the previous April to offer the navy V-1 program, but that program did little more than keep some presently enrolled students on campus. It was designed to educate freshmen and sophomores who were enlisted as Apprentice Seamen in the United States Naval Reserve. They paid their own expenses. At the end of two years, those who aspired to become naval aviators would be taken into Class V-5. If successful in this training they would be commissioned as ensigns in the Naval Reserve. Those who were candidates for deck or engineer training would continue in college until graduation, after which they would be put in Class V-7 and trained as deck and engineering officers.[69] In practice, the program would be completed in a maximum of three years, not four, since the educational calendar would be speeded up. John Score, the President's son, enrolled in the V-1 program toward the end of his first semester in late 1942 as a freshman at the age of seventeen.[70]

Southwestern, however, needed more than a program that would keep a limited number of men on campus at their own expense. It needed a program that would bring to campus replacements for those men who, because they were being drafted, never entered college, and those who were being drafted while in school. Such a program was announced nationally around December 1, 1942. Score says that it was announced at the time he and the staff were preparing a book entitled "A Presentation of the Facilities of Southwestern University, Georgetown, Texas." Copies of it were sent to the proper authorities.[71]

Looking back a year later, in December 1943, on his first recorded meeting with Johnson, Score remarked in a letter to him:

> It is just a little over a year since you so graciously gave me ten minutes of your time in Austin—ten minutes that somehow, through your interest and courtesy, grew to about two hours and a half. I shall always remember that first conference with you, the subsequent trip to Houston, and all of the other things you have done for Southwestern and for me. It seems so little to say, "Thank you," and yet I don't know how to make it any bigger; and I think you know how sincere is my personal appreciation and the appreciation of us all.[72]

Apparently the two men hit it off immediately, for the ten-minute meeting turned into "two hours and a half," with a "subsequent trip [presumably together] to Houston." Score probably had with him the seventy-three-page "Presentation" prepared by the staff. Divided into nine sections, it presents a campus plat, describes the University and its President, and depicts the physical plant, dormitory facilities, and service facilities in detail, with photographs. It outlines the curricular offerings, the services now being provided with the present staff and equipment, and the services that could be rendered with additional staff and equipment. It concludes by describing the kinds of training it feels the University is currently best prepared to render. "While we feel we can adequately care for one of the proposed units of 600 men, we would prefer one of the units in the field of Army or Naval Aviation sent here for a specific training in Mathematics and the Sciences or a unit in the Basic Meteorological Training." Mood Hall and West Gymnasium were designated to serve as the housing facilities for the servicemen, the latter equipped as a dormitory.[73]

Johnson suggested that Southwestern should target a Navy College Training Unit in its application.[74] Score accepted the suggestion and went to Washington, where he met with Frank Knox, Secretary of the Navy, Jesse H. Jones, Secretary of Commerce, Sam Rayburn, Speaker of the House of Representatives, and other persons to promote it. Jones was a close friend of A. Frank Smith; Rayburn was a close friend of Johnson. Score returned home and left Johnson in charge of shepherding the proposal through the labyrinth of navy officialdom.[75]

Johnson began immediately to seek approval for it. Score on several occasions requested Johnson by telegram to phone him, and Johnson always did so. On January 8, 1943, for example, Score sent him a telegram at 10:20 A.M. saying: "Need to talk to you today, if at all possible. Please call me collect, Georgetown 230, day or night at your convenience. J. N. R. Score."[76] The following day Score wrote him a letter, thanking him for the good telephone talk "last night and for the interest that he was taking in Southwestern's request." At the end of the two-and-a-half-page letter he says, "Since talking with you, I have talked with Bishop Smith, and when you feel it is advisable for us to come to Washington, we stand ready to come."[77] In response, Johnson told him that nothing more could be done from Southwestern's end, but "the Southwestern project is the first one on Lyndon Johnson's list and no stone is going to be unturned." Score replied a few days later. He said resignedly: "We shall possess our souls in patience until we hear from you."[78] During the waiting, Pearl Neas was writing Johnson as well, displaying her anxiety about the outcome of the proposal. On February 18, 1943, Johnson wrote her: "Be patient with me just a little longer and I believe that Southwestern University will have a Naval Training Unit established there."[79]

Finally the good news came to the campus. A telegram from Johnson to Score late in the afternoon of February 27 read as follows: "Happy to advise definite selection selection [sic] of Southwestern University for utilization by Navy for establishment of basic training unit. Negotiations for contracts with college will follow shortly. This is for release Sunday February twenty eighth. Lyndon B Johnson."[80]

Pearl Neas either received a separate telegram from Johnson conveying the news or was informed immediately by Score. In a letter to Johnson two days later she said:

> When your telegram arrived, I simply sat down and wept for joy! How happy we are over the consummation of the task to which you have given so much of your valuable time. I hope you will get your reward in heaven, because there is nothing earthly good enough for you! . . . We called a special convocation this morning and Dr. Score outlined the process through which the Unit was finally obtained, and he paid you glowing tribute for your unselfish efforts in behalf of your No. 1 program.[81]

Johnson replied: "I do not need to wait until I get to Heaven for a reward—the gratitude expressed by you and Dr. Score is enough for me."[82] Two years later he said about his two Southwestern friends, "If every University in the nation had people like you and Dr. Score to plan for its future, I would have no fears for their success."[83] Johnson never had reason to doubt the rightness of what he had done for Southwestern.

At the end of the second year of the program, Johnson wrote Pearl: "Comparatively speaking, I doubt that any institution has received more consideration, attention and sympathy upon the part of all concerned including Yours Truly, as Southwestern. . . . The Navy believes, I feel, that such obligations as they may have felt to our little school and to your little Congressman have been fully met and justified."[84]

President Score presenting Congressman Lyndon Baines Johnson the LL.D. degree on May 31, 1943. Johnson was instrumental in procuring the Naval V-12 Unit for Southwestern. The flag in the background has a star for every Southwestern alumnus in the armed forces. Southwestern University, Special Collections.

At the meeting of the Executive Committee on March 5, Score explained the basic shape of the expected program. It contemplated a curriculum, he said, based in general on English, history, mathematics, and the physical and engineering sciences. He felt it would fit in well with plans already made for the enlargement of the Division of Sciences. Southwestern would receive about one thousand dollars per year per student, an amount later adjusted to accord with the standard rate for civilian students.[85] The academic calendar would be divided into three semesters (or tri-semesters) of sixteen weeks during the year. He warned the committee that the University would run a deficit for the current year, the first year since 1936–1937, but "it was felt best to do so than to risk not receiving the Unit by retrenching." He praised the Trustees for their work. He said that practically every one of them had written one or more people in Washington during the procurement process.[86] The Executive Committee for its part thanked Score and McCook for their excellent work in securing the Navy Unit. McCook was likely the person responsible for supervising the preparation of the proposal, with its detailed facts and figures.[87]

Subsequent Negotiations and Expression of Thanks to Johnson

During March a navy inspection group came to the campus and, according to a Johnson letter, determined that Mood Hall would not serve as a residence hall for the Unit because it was not fireproof. Nevertheless, the navy would send as many boys as Southwestern could house and feed.[88] A week later Johnson told Score that the number would be 400. Score replied that 350 would be about right.[89] The number enrolled for the first tri-semester beginning July 1, 1943, was actually 391. Once this number was factored into current budget equations, it became the "quota" sought by Southwestern authorities in each of the nine tri-semesters during the next three years.[90] Attention immediately turned to the preparation of Kuykendall Hall and the floor over the dining hall used by Fine Arts as residence facilities for the men.

Though physical preparations began immediately for reception of the seamen and marines, Score felt that one more thing needed to be done. Lyndon Johnson had to be thanked appropriately for what he had done for Southwestern. Score said to the assembled Trustees, "I wish to say to you . . . what I have said to many of you as individuals, namely, that if ever a University had 'a friend at court,' we have had one in the Honorable Lyndon B. Johnson, Congressman from this District."[91] The most appropriate honor, he felt, would be the conferral on him of an honorary Doctor of Laws degree. Score offered one to him, knowing that the faculty would validate his action. Johnson demurred, feeling that it might smack too much of a deal or a quid pro quo. Score replied, saying that he would not want to confer a degree if it would be impolitic or embarrassing to him, but the school could elect him to a degree, with the actual conferral to come later.[92] Within a few weeks he wrote Johnson again, emphasizing the respect he felt for him, both because of his work for the school and for "your patience and kindness to me."[93] With this expression from Score, Johnson acquiesced, accepted the degree, and gave the Commencement speech on May 31. It was broadcast by radio.[94] By the time of the speech Johnson had played a role, along with Rayburn and other persons of influence, in securing for Texas and the Southwest various naval installations, including the nation's largest Naval Air training base at Corpus Christi, the ship-building yards at Orange and Houston, and the Naval R.O.T.C. at the University of Texas.[95] The Naval V-12 Unit at Southwestern, however, was the first V-12 Unit anywhere in the Southwest.[96]

Score spent the week of May 10 in Washington and New York. In Washington he conferred with appropriate naval offices and in New York attended a meeting at Columbia University of the heads of all colleges and universities selected for navy V-12 training to discuss the details of the program.[97]

Initial Preparations for Wartime Operation

Southwestern operated for almost exactly a year between the time of Score's election (February 11, 1942) and reception of the welcome news that it would receive a Naval V-12 Unit (February 27, 1943). During that uncertain time, it prepared for wartime operation as best it could. The enrollment prospects were dismal. Its approval to participate in the V-1 program hardly staunched the outflow of male students, and the failure to attract the Harris College of Nursing did not bode well for making Southwestern more attractive to females. To counteract the student drain, Southwestern made an application to the U. S. Army to establish an R.O.T.C. Unit, offered the facilities of the University for the training of interpreters, and sought to have the Civilian Pilot Training Program reestablished by the Civil Aeronautics Administration, all without success.[98] During the fall semester of the academic years 1940–1941, 1941–1942, and 1942–1943, student enrollment dropped from 440, to 390, to 376, respectively.

Inasmuch as Dr. Score had set as one of the conditions for his acceptance of the presidency that the Board would put the major buildings on campus into first-class condition, it set out to fulfill its pledge to do so. By mid-1942, however, the Buildings and Grounds Committee of the Board had to report that "even if the money were available, a thoroughgoing renovation of the Administration Building, Mood Hall, and The Science Building would not be desirable until the war . . . [was] . . . over."[99]

Score failed in another one of his efforts as well. It had to do with the admission of Japanese American students to the University in the year after Pearl Harbor when their families were being interned. Score brought the matter up before the Executive Committee in April 1942, while still President-elect. His request to admit them was denied.[100] In late July he brought the matter up again before the Executive Committee. He stated that he had received a request from the American Friends Service Committee, working in behalf of the government and the students, to admit certain Japanese American students. With that subsequent development, he resubmitted the matter to the executive committee for its consideration.[101] This time the matter was tabled. When the final list of schools approved to receive Japanese American students was published in early 1943, Southwestern was not on the list.[102]

From the beginning of the war, the business manager, I. J. McCook, had, in view of shortages and rising prices, begun buying provisions in extraordinary bulk quantities as a hedge against scarcity and inflation. The Executive Committee commended him for his "masterly management" leading to a balanced budget for 1941–1942.[103] At its November meeting, the Board approved using land owned by Southwestern in or near Georgetown for the raising of staple commodities or other agricultural products as might be advisable during the war.[104]

One of the effects of this approval was the purchase of the Young Dairy farm. Walter Young, son of Professor Ryland F. Young, one of "The Five," had indicated in late 1942 that he would be willing to sell his farm and dairy herd to the school. The Executive Committee unanimously approved the offer by mail ballot. The farm consisted of 35 registered Jersey cows and a farm of 273 acres adjoining the campus on the north, with all equipment. In final negotiations, Young included 5 registered heifers, and the school purchased an additional 15 heifers. A portion of the farm was leased to a gravel company, the income from which, along with the profit made from selling excess milk in Georgetown, made it possible to pay out the total investment of $29,150 within a few years.[105] A problem arose, however, when, in the spring of 1944, the navy required that all milk fed to its seamen be pasteurized. To meet this requirement, truck drivers had to haul the milk into Austin to be pasteurized until a pasteurizing plant could be built on the farm in early 1945.[106] By then the farm had 125 producing Jersey cows.[107] As late as the fall of 1953, the dairy continued to run a profit, but its operation became less profitable and out of keeping with the image of the institution.[108] In 1956 the herd was reduced to 55 milk cows.[109] Dr. McCook was given a free hand with the dairy and presumably sold the remaining herd and equipment, since mention of the dairy disappears from the record.[110]

Though it sold the dairy equipment, Southwestern kept the Young farm and added other tracts after March 1944, when the President and business manager were authorized to negotiate for property adjacent to presently owned campus property on the north and east.[111] The last substantial purchase was 50 acres in 1947 from Mr. and Mrs. Bolton Gilleland. With that purchase the school owned almost 600 acres of land in one piece.[112] A few parcels were purchased or sold here and there between 1947 and 2000 to smooth out the holdings, but the changes in acreage were minor. The Southwestern campus was substantially completed during the Score administration with the addition of slightly more than 500 acres of land. President Schrum has purchased additional land to protect the campus from undesirable development on the eastern edge of its property bringing the total to about 700 acres. Southwestern has not, like so many colleges, become landlocked, even with the expansion of metropolitan Austin in the latter part of the twentieth century to encompass the Georgetown area.

Curricular Changes

Shortly after the beginning of the war, the faculty began to enact regulations pertaining to students joining the armed forces. The administration enacted its recommendation that all students called for war service before mid-semester should have their tuition returned on a proportional basis and that those being called after that time should be given credit for all courses in which they were passing with no return of tuition money.[113]

The faculty also instituted a new curricular concept, the so-called "National Defense" courses, labeled as such in the catalog. These courses were either new or already instituted courses in regular departments that were deemed especially relevant to the wartime situation. Examples of such courses were: Research in Camouflage, First Aid Training, Home Nursing, and the Psychology of Morale. A Special Physical Training paragraph in the catalog stated that "combative sports and elementary marching techniques" would be a daily part of the program.

During the fall of 1942, some "war courses" were added to the regular curriculum, such as the Three-Language Interpreter Course, the Five-Language Interpreter Course, Colloquial Japanese, Elementary Portuguese, a Reading Course in Russian, General Linguistics, Intermediate Linguistics, World Population Tensions and War, four meteorology courses, and two aeronautics courses. All civilian students, both men and women, were required to take five days of physical training each week. The men's course was called the "Commando" Physical Training Program. The women's course was called Physical Fitness for Women, though they, too, called it "Commando" just as the men did. It consisted of wall scaling, boxing, cross-country running, wrestling, jujitsu, sitting-up exercises, combative sports, and elementary marching techniques.

The faculty discussed various expedients about ways to save money. Early in 1942, it asked a committee to study possible savings that could be made in athletics. Dr. Finch reported for the committee that it did not appear that savings would be very significant. In addition, he stated that the President-elect had asked that "no drastic change of policy" be instituted before he arrived.[114] The faculty did adopt the daylight saving schedule of the government by moving clocks up one hour and moving the class schedule back one hour, thus saving fuel and electricity.[115]

Getting the Campus into Shape for the V-12 Unit

The original Southwestern proposal to the navy for housing the V-12 Unit had been to put it in Mood Hall and West Gymnasium, equipping the latter as a dormitory.

Naval V-12 personnel marching in front of the Administration Building. From the 1945 *Sou'wester.*

When navy authorities rejected this option because the two building were not fireproof, the school was forced to use Kuykendall Hall. It had been built to replace a previous building that had burned, and special care had been taken when it was constructed in 1926 to make it as fireproof as possible. The navy agreed to the change. The women's residence hall and the Fine Arts space over the dining hall were designated for navy men. Women would be moved to Mood Hall. Other buildings had to be reconditioned as well, particularly the Administration Building. The Executive Committee authorized the procurement of a loan of $150,000 for that purpose, using the government contract as its guarantee for repayment.[116]

Since school was in session and Commencement was not until May 31, 1942, only the month of June was available to equip the two main residence halls and refurbish the rest of the campus before the arrival of the V-12 Unit. Rooms in Laura Kuykendall Hall that had been built to house two women in each were now equipped for four men in double bunk beds. Laura Kuykendall Hall and the Fine Arts space eventually housed almost 400 young men. During their occupancy of the building, it was called both the "U.S.S. Kuykendall" and "The Ship."[117] Score reports that "superhuman efforts" were required to make the U.S.S. Kuykendall ready for the arrival of the navy men on June 28.[118]

Mood Hall was also reconditioned to prepare it for women. Originally designed to house 100 to 125 men, it housed more than 200 women during the war. The rooms were painted in pastel shades, white tile showers and baths were installed, the patio, formerly open, was enclosed, and a hardwood floor was laid.[119] It, along with other elements of the all-campus reconditioning program, was not ready on July 1. Some projects were still being worked on several months into the summer tri-semester. The opening of classes was postponed a week to allow everyone to settle down into the new accommodations and to take care of the orientation and scheduling connected with the beginning of any new school year. If Southwestern had to play catch-up after classes began, so did the V-12 Unit. The enlisted students had to drill in civilian clothes for about two weeks until uniforms came in.[120]

Other space had to be secured as well. With the Fine Arts space taken for men's housing, another teaching location had to be secured for the School of Fine Arts. For this purpose, an arrangement was entered into with the First Methodist Church to use its Education Building for the duration of the war. Students dutifully walked the half-mile between the campus and that site for their fine arts classes during the war.[121]

In order to house civilian men, the University purchased the Sherman Hotel for $25,000. Renamed Southwestern House, it was a frame building near the campus with one apartment and twenty-five bedrooms. A faculty member and the members of one of the fraternities lived there. Since the Kappa Sigmas and the Phi Delts had rented their houses to the University for the duration of the war, one of them may have been that fraternity.[122] The building was sold back to private owners after two years of use.[123] The Kappa Sigma house was used to house more than 20 young women. The other houses were used for civilian men. The Kappa Alphas bought the house of the recently deceased Professor Gray on University Avenue, located approximately where the Episcopal Church is today.[124] Housing space was so tight that some men were given permission to seek their own rooms in town.[125]

Because of a lack of classroom space, the Sneed House, across University Avenue from the library, was purchased. Fifteen classes met there on July 6, the first day of the summer tri-semester. Even with the Sneed House, some classes still had to meet in the homes of faculty members when classes began.[126] Sneed House served as classroom space until enough was found on campus, at which time it was converted into a dormitory for women.[127] Both Sneed House and Snyder Hall housed over 30 young women during the war. Sneed House was still in use as an honor residence hall for women when it burned in 1978.[128]

In order to fulfill a stipulation in the navy contract that the University have a store to accommodate the needs of its seamen, it purchased the Pirate Tavern across from the Administration Building, along with its merchandise and fixtures, to serve that purpose. After buying the lease from Mr. J. Leroy Peterson and hiring him to run the newly renamed University Store, it eventually purchased the building, which it still owns.[129]

Alumni in the Service and Killed in Action

Shortly after the V-12 Unit came to Southwestern, Mr. & Mrs. I. J. McCook received news that their son, First Lieutenant Charles Woodruff McCook, or "Woodie," was missing in the Asiatic war zone. Woodie had graduated from Southwestern in June 1941, joining the Army Air Corps immediately thereafter. He was commissioned in February 1942. After commissioning he was assigned to China overseas duty. He was reported missing after a bombing flight over Burma. His last letter to his parents was dated July 23.[130] Though he was not the first Southwestern graduate to die in the war, he was the first closely connected to the faculty and staff of the University. Sympathy for the McCook family was overwhelming. The most conspicuous gesture was that of former President King Vivion, at the time a pastor in Nashville, who, with his wife, donated their equity in the King's Palace (see Chapter XIV), back of Mood Hall, to be used as a university infirmary named for Lt. McCook.[131] When completed and put into service around September 1, 1944, it had living quarters for nurses, three bedrooms, a diet kitchen, and storage space for supplies. Theretofore infirmaries had been maintained at Mood and Snyder Halls, making it necessary for the nurse to divide her time.[132]

The first former Southwestern student to receive fame in the war was Lt. Ross Wilder of Taylor. Commissioned in 1941, he was one of the thirteen men decorated by the War Department for the part he played in the bombing of Japan on April 18, 1942. He was one of the pilots in Brigadier General Doolittle's squadron that attacked Japan from "Shangri La," as Roosevelt called the secret place of plane departure.[133]

The highest-ranking female graduate of Southwestern in the military during World War II was Lt. Col. Anne Marie Doering. Born near Haiphong, in what was then French Indochina, of a German mother and a French father, she lived her first fourteen years there, where her father was an official of the French government. Coming to America at the age of fifteen, she became an American citizen when her mother married an American, Mr. B. E. Solomon of Georgetown. She took her B.A. from Southwestern in the early 1930s, after which she worked for nine years in New York. She joined the Woman's Auxiliary Army Corps in February, 1943, and served in the Far East during the war.[134] She completed her service in General MacArthur's headquarters in Manila.[135] In a letter of October 30, 1981, to President Shilling, she expressed her delight at having just attended her fiftieth class reunion. She established a Gertrude Solomon Award for Excellence in French in honor of her mother.[136]

Sixteen alumni had died in the war by the time of the first V-12 assembly in July 1943.[137] They were represented on the huge Service Flag by sixteen gold stars. By late 1944 the number was thirty. By the end of the war it was thirty-six.[138]

The Relationship of Southwestern and the V-12 Unit

The first military person to arrive on campus was navy Lieutenant Fred C. Blanchard. He was an academic, with a B.A., an M.A., and an M.S. earned from the University of Washington and the University of Idaho. He also possessed a Ph.D. from New York University. In addition to having taught at those schools where he had studied, he had also taught at the University of Omaha and Chicago City College.[139] Toward the end of the month Pearl Neas wrote Lyndon Johnson that all of the office personnel for the Navy Unit were on hand and "we are delighted with all of them. Lieutenant Blanchard, who came on June 1, has endeared himself to all of us. Commander [Martin A.] Heffernan [USNR] arrived a few days ago and has already made us know how lucky we are to have him."[140] Heffernan's coming was necessitated by a change of plans that brought a marine detachment of one hundred men as a part of the almost four-hundred-man V-12 contingent. The change demanded a person of higher rank to be in charge.

By the end of the Unit's first year on campus, Heffernan was Commanding Officer, Blanchard was Executive Officer, Lieutenant Charles R. Goodwin, M.D., was Medical Officer, Lieutenant H. R. Giles, A.B., A.M., was Physical Fitness Officer, and First Lieutenant J. J. Fitzgerald, B.S., was Officer-in-Charge of the marine detachment. Fitzgerald was later transferred to the Pacific theater, where he was killed on Iwo Jima.[141] Score was very pleased with them. He told the Executive Committee that they "have been most friendly and on the highest plane of Navy tradition.... Commander Heffernan has spoken for us in Chapel, as has Lieutenant Blanchard."[142] On that occasion, Heffernan was introduced and Blanchard spoke. A newspaper report of his comments states that he placed the Unit in clear perspective vis-à-vis the University program:

> "We are not here to take over the University. This is a college program, and it is our belief that men can go from here to officer training better than if they were called immediately from civilian life." He stated that, for the most part, [the] trainee's relationship to the university will be the same as the civilian's except for military discipline. He noted with satisfaction that some men in uniform were in the chapel choir, and that others are interested in journalism, as well as in sports.... Lt. Blanchard spoke in appreciation of the splendid job the university and administration has done in preparing for the Unit.[143]

President Score and Jack Dempsey shaking hands. The world's former heavyweight boxing champion came to the campus as part of an entourage of notables in the service, including Robert Taylor, Nancy Gates, and heroes from "over there." Southwestern University, Special Collections.

The initial spirit of mutual, friendly accommodation between the V-12 Unit and Southwestern University continued throughout the entire period of the Unit's three-year stay on campus. The V-12 students participated in all normal university activities, their individual pictures were included in the university yearbook, and two of them were pictured as the student body president and vice president in the *Sou'wester* for 1945. No disciplinary problems of any consequence are reported in the record, and the program worked out almost faultlessly for the navy and for Southwestern. Score reported to the Trustees in May 1944 that "the men we have received are of very high caliber" and the school enjoys very happy relations with the officers. "They have been uniformly courteous and cooperative," he says, "and have carried on their work in a spirit which has led us to believe that they have felt themselves actually a part of Southwestern University. They have supported every area of the University life and have made a distinct contribution not only to our University community but [also] to the town of Georgetown." A marine colonel, he added, had said "he considered the work of our Unit the best of any of the Marine sections in the Eighth Naval District, and off the record these gentlemen all spoke of our work in most flattering terms."[144] Commenting in a letter to Lyndon Johnson on the visit of a top-ranking navy chaplain to the campus to review the prechaplain group in the V-12 program, Score wrote that "he had just come from certain other colleges and he was pleased beyond measure to see the spirit on this campus and that this was the only campus where he had been where he thought the relationship between the Navy Unit and the college authorities was that which the Navy hoped it might be."[145]

The Southwestern navy V-12 program received national attention when Cedric Foster, a nationally known radio commentator, featured it on one of his radio broadcasts. Score wrote to Lyndon Johnson that "it was almost all Southwestern."[146] A ten-thousand-ton freighter named the SS *Southwestern Victory* was launched by the California Shipbuilding Corporation on April 30, 1945, in honor of Southwestern University.[147]

The relationship established between regular navy men, marines, and officers with Southwestern was in many cases quite deep. A case in point is the experience of L. D. (Jack) Jones, Jr., of Wichita Falls, Texas. He was a senior at Baylor in his last semester when, as a member of the Marine Corps Reserves, he was ordered to report to Southwestern on July 1, 1943. He remained at Southwestern only one session before completing his baccalaureate work and being ordered to service elsewhere. He transferred enough academic hours of course work from Southwestern back to Baylor to receive his B.B.A. there at the end of 1943. In a letter written in 2004 to a Southwestern friend, he included portions of a manuscript detailing his wartime experience. In it, he says:

> I have some very fond memories of Southwestern. I have supported it regularly for many years.... Southwestern has become one of the outstanding small universities in the nation. Southwestern was unique in my experience.
>
> Up until that time, and maybe later at some institutions, there was a very close rapport between the students and faculty. At Southwestern there were ten or twelve two story Victorian houses across the street from the campus.... There was no air conditioning in those days. These houses all had large front porches with swings and rocking chairs. Every evening after supper, several of these professors, different ones on different evenings, would sit out on the porch and "Hold Court." Anyone was welcome to drop by, sit down and visit. The subject was anything anyone wanted to talk about. The conversation would usually gravitate to the field that was the professor's specialty. On other occasions they would make pertinent observations about anything else—world affairs, the war, other professors, etc....
>
> There wasn't much exciting around Southwestern except the excellent football team. One event that merits mention was an inspection that we had. Jack Dempsey, former world heavyweight Boxing champion was a Lt. Commander in the Navy. He mainly had to do with public relations and physical training. Robert Taylor, the matinee idol actor, was a Navy Lieutenant. They came to Southwestern along with some pilots who were already war heroes for shooting down enemy planes. They inspected our group. In the course of the inspection, I was about 18 inches from each of them, face to face. I can truthfully say that I have never seen a man as handsome as Robert Taylor. In addition, he seemed to be a very nice guy as did all the rest of their group. Incidentally, they were accompanied by an ambitious young congressman named Lyndon Johnson.
>
> After the inspection the university had a chapel program. Each of the dignitaries was asked to make remarks. Dempsey got to the podium and declared, "I'll wrestle any woman in the house!"[148]

Though to Jack Jones the appearance of Johnson was secondary to that of the other celebrities, the event was played up in Georgetown differently. In announcing the event for August 27, 1943, the *Williamson County Sun* stated that Johnson would inspect the Naval Unit and address a special school assembly at ten o'clock. It then mentioned the screen and military celebrities as accompanying him. He was identified as a member of the House Naval Affairs Committee.[149]

Score's appreciation for the last navy commander, George F. Howe, is revealed poignantly in his attempt to help him after Howe developed a heart problem following his retirement. Howe had replaced Heffernan as commander for the 1945–1946 year. He, too, as Pearl Neas says, soon "endeared himself to everyone on the campus."[150] When he suffered a coronary occlusion several weeks after his retirement in late 1947, he was denied full navy coverage for it because his final navy medical examination had not detected any symptoms of a heart ailment. Consequently, his illness was not deemed to be service-related. In dejection, he wrote Score "a very pitiful letter" in early 1947 telling him about it. In response, Score wrote Johnson's office in Washington to see if anything could be done to help Howe. He followed it up with another letter to Johnson about three weeks later. Since the regulations were clear about service-related and non-service-related health benefits, nothing could be done unless something could be found that would place the start of Howe's problem during the time of his military service. Though it was almost a year before Johnson could report anything satisfactory, he wrote Score on March 1, 1948, telling him that they had found a navy doctor who had treated Howe for heart disease in February 1946 prior to his leaving the service. "It was not, however, entered in his record. The entire matter is now being reconsidered," said Johnson.[151] Score, for his part, followed up on Johnson's information by informing him that Dr. Martin, a local Georgetown doctor, had treated Commander Howe when he "had a little flare-up here, and either Commander Bracken or Commander Hollander of the Medical Corp [sic] knew about his condition and treated him for it."[152] This last letter to Johnson in behalf of Howe came after Score himself had already suffered the first major signs of his heart problem, though it had not been recognized as such at the time. He died within a year and a half from the same problem that troubled Howe.

Merger of Weatherford College with Southwestern

In the middle of the war, two years after the merger with Westminster, Southwestern brought another junior college into its system. Score presented to the Board a case for action at a winter meeting in early 1944, and it voted to accept Weatherford. Score listed five reasons for the merger: (1) the assets of the University would be increased by at least a quarter of a million dollars; (2) Weatherford would become a "feeder" rather than a competing institution; (3) the merger would make possible the operation of the college without a deficit; (4) it would strengthen Southwestern in a section of the state where it had been weak; and (5) it would make Weatherford a church college rather than a municipal school. As to any possible dangers connected with the action, these would be prevented by premerger agreements. These would exempt Southwestern from responsibility for any of Weatherford's indebtedness, and Weatherford would be responsible for raising its own capital and operating funds. There would be no commingling of funds, and Weatherford would take away from any subsequent separation from Southwestern everything it had procured for itself during the period of the union. Should separation become necessary, the school would be returned to the City of Weatherford to become a municipal junior college. Southwestern would guarantee that it had no desire to take over Weatherford for the purpose of liquidating its assets and make a good faith effort to operate it successfully.[153]

Weatherford was the oldest junior college in the state. The Phoenix Lodge of the Masonic Order had founded it in 1869 after it received a charter from the state to establish a school named the Masonic Institute. Classes began a few years later. In 1884 its name was changed to Cleveland College in honor of Grover Cleveland, the first Democratic President elected since the Civil War. In 1889 the Central Texas Conference of the Methodist Episcopal Church, South, moved Granbury College to Weatherford and combined the two institutions as Weatherford College. For the rest of the nineteenth century, it offered classes from grade school through the senior year in college, with an average attendance of about 300 students. Its President resigned in 1902, and from 1903 to 1921 the school operated intermittently, even serving briefly as an academy. It was reorganized as a junior college in 1921, was accredited by the Texas Association of Colleges, and acquired a sound financial basis through grants from two estates of prominent Weatherford persons.[154] Through all these circumstances it had maintained its Methodist connection, and its President in 1943 was Dr. C. A. Sutton, an ordained Methodist minister.[155]

Though there is no evidence as to what initiated conversations between Score and Sutton, it was probably the fact that Weatherford's enrollment had dropped to 68 students in 1943–1944. It was threatened with either closure or being taken over by the municipality. A takeover by Southwestern was the only way to prevent either of these alternatives. Sutton, acquainted with Score, knew of the Southwestern action with regard to Westminster. Score wanted to keep the school alive as a part of the Methodist system of higher education.

The takeover of Weatherford College occurred in

stages. The Board of Trustees authorized President Score to employ faculty and staff for both it and Westminster on September 19, 1944,[156] the ex-students of both schools were recognized as "ex-students of the Southwestern system" on May 16, 1945,[157] and the final papers for the merger were signed sometime in the fall.[158]

The enrollment at Weatherford in its regular program and in its School of Fine Arts grew to 151 in 1944–1945 and to 228 in 1945–1946. It also had a summer school of 39 and 50 students, respectively, during those two years. Score reported that it ran a balanced budget in 1945–1946 if claims against the Veterans' Bureau were considered as cash in hand. Some seven thousand dollars of its income had come from money raised in Weatherford, and the citizens of the town seemed to want to support it.[159] Unlike Westminster's, the program of Weatherford seemed to be making progress.

At Westminster, however, there seemed to be no progress at all. From an enrollment of 42 in 1943–1944, it dropped to 27 in 1944–1945 and increased to only 46 in 1945–1946. Score felt that a minimum of 100 students was needed.[160] Consequently, he decided to concentrate on turning Westminster into a unique school where special training would be provided for those who planned to specialize in town and country work. To that end, he secured the gifts of several farms by elderly residents to support that ministerial training program.[161]

Southwestern as a Football Powerhouse

With the coming of the marines, Southwestern became a football powerhouse for a short time. When Coach Medley assembled his players for the first time in the summer of 1943, he found that he had more than thirty men who had one or more years of college football experience in addition to about seventy-five with impressive high school records. There was also a good sprinkling of top-notch athletes in other sports, such as golf, wrestling, track, baseball, and basketball.[162] Because for three seasons the football program was so dominant, these other sports are sometimes overlooked, but they were played and, at times, thrilled a campus that became wedded to football during these years.

During the same 1943–1944 academic year in which the football team did so well, the basketball and the baseball teams also did well. The basketball team won twelve out of sixteen games, splitting two games with the University of Texas and defeating Baylor and Rice in single games. The baseball team began its season in late March by splitting a two-game series with the Longhorns. The Bucs won the first game on Friday by a score of 14-4. David Switzer, future chaplain at Southwestern for eight years from the mid-1950s to the mid-'60s, pitched for the Bucs and allowed only six hits. The team was not so fortunate in its rematch next day. It lost by a score of 14-1. Bobby Layne, the future football star, pitched for the Longhorns and allowed only three hits. G. H. Berry, petty officer in the V-12 unit, coached Southwestern in both games. He also did the catching.[163]

A sports article covering the future prospects of the Southwestern football team before the 1943 season opened was entitled: "Lucky Southwestern! Football Stars Drop Right Into Her Lap."[164] The article was right on target. It was as if Medley had been given the opportunity to raid other major football schools in the Southwest and to select some of their best players for his team. Among these players were seven members of the University of Texas team that the previous year had won the Southwest Conference and Cotton Bowl championships. Baylor furnished nine players, SMU provided six, TCU four, the University of New Mexico three, and the University of Arkansas one. Other lesser football powers also contributed good players. When Southwestern defeated the University of Texas on the first Saturday in October, the *Austin American-Statesman* entitled its article covering the game: "U.T. Exes Take Bucs to 14-7 Victory Over Former Clubmates."[165] Some of those Longhorn exes playing for the Pirates were Jackie Field, Ken Matthews, Spot Collins, and Harold Fischer.

The truth was that Coach Medley's greatest problems were not the quality of his players. His major problems were welding the players together, the limited time available for practice, V-12 restrictions, scheduling, and personnel turnover. Though the officers in charge of the V-12 Unit were very cooperative, they had to follow a rigid program for their men in which classroom and training took precedence over athletics.

Coming from different schools, the players brought with them familiarity with the particular system used where they had played. Without the luxury of time to meld them all into one system, Medley had to piece the different systems together as best he could to take advantage of the talents of each player. Since the student was playing for Southwestern and not for the navy, he could not practice on V-12 time. Each student had only two absolutely free hours each day, from four to six p.m., and practice was cur-

With a record of 9-1, the Southwestern football team defeated the New Mexico Lobos in the Sun Bowl game in El Paso on January 1, 1944. The SU players were mostly a contingent of sailors and Marines sent to the school from other colleges as a part of the V-12 program. From the 1944 *Sou'wester.*

tailed during heavy assignment and examination periods. Medley estimated that he got only forty-five good minutes of practice during the two free hours each day, for a total of only seventeen hours before his first game on September 18, 1943.[166] All football games had to be played from Saturday noon to Sunday night during the time each trainee was excused from duty, thirty-six hours at the most. The fact that special permission was required for the student to be absent from campus for as long as forty-eight hours ruled out long trips.[167] Some of these regulations were occasionally stretched, but not by much.

Trips were usually made in an old yellow bus. There are many stories about it.[168] One told to this writer directly by I. J. McCook is that returning from a game late one night the lights in the bus went dead and could not be repaired. In order to get the boys back to campus, McCook drove ahead of the bus in his car at a slow speed so that it could use his headlights to illuminate the road.

Especially troubling for the coach was the regular transfer of his players in and out of Southwestern. Each trainee remained at Southwestern only as long as was needed to complete his particular program. In some cases it was only one tri-semester, as in the case of thirteen players at the end of the fall 1943 football season. They were immediately transferred to marine boot camp and could not play in the Sun Bowl game.[169] Coach Medley had to remake his team constantly in light of the turnover of trainees in the V-12 Unit.

In spite of these problems, both the 1943 and 1944 football seasons were remarkable. Playing big-time football, the 1943 team lost only one game, to Southwestern Louisiana Institute, and tied one, with the University of Tulsa. S.L.I. was another team like Southwestern, not a major football school. Its team was also made up of football players taken from larger institutions, in its case mainly from Rice University. It was led by Alvin Dark, later a great baseball player and manager. In the final Williamson national football rankings of the regular season, S.L.I. ranked eighth, Tulsa ranked tenth, Southwestern ranked eleventh, the University of Texas ranked twelfth, and Arkansas A&M ranked seventeenth. Southwestern lost to S.L.I., tied Tulsa, and defeated both Texas and Arkansas A&M during the season.

The Southwestern University Pirates had the best record of any team in the state, nine wins, one loss, and one tie.

As a result of its winning season, Southwestern was invited to play the New Mexico Lobos in the Sun Bowl on January 1, 1944. Perhaps as remarkable as the game itself, won 7-0 by Southwestern, was the fact that the team had to sandwich its Sun Bowl appearance within the navy regulation imposing a forty-eight-hour time limit for being away from the campus.[170] Though Southwestern dominated the game, gaining 231 more yards on offense than did the Lobos, the team did not score until the final three minutes of the game.[171] The standout performers for Southwestern were Harold "Spot" Collins and R. W. MacGruder.[172] Spot Collins came back as coach of the football team in 1948 for two years when Coach Medley, after twenty-five years in that role at McMurry and Southwestern, restricted his coaching to basketball, to several of the minor sports as occasion demanded, and to directing intramural athletics for the remainder of his career.

So as not to appear to be taking advantage of marine and naval trainees for its own purposes beyond the navy contract, the University contributed most of the $20,031.18 it made from football beyond expenses during 1943–1944 to four wartime charities—Navy Relief, the National War Chest Fund, the Navy Mothers Relief Society, and the Brown Shipbuilding Yard Naval Escort Welfare Association. In addition, the proceeds of three games played in army or navy posts or for service personnel went to their service funds.[173]

The success of the football team was not as striking during 1944–1945 as it had been a year earlier, and the team finished with a record of six wins and five losses. Nevertheless, it was invited once again to the Sun Bowl to play the University of Mexico Pumas on New Year's Day 1945. Frank Means and Fred Brechtel, known for their passing, and Bobbie McDonald, known for his broken field running and punting, were Southwestern's chief offensive threats. This second Sun Bowl game was not close like the first one. The Pumas, lighter by eighteen pounds per man, were outclassed, and Southwestern won 35-0. The Pirates gained 408 yards on offense, the Pumas only 39.[174]

During the 1945–1946 season, the last year of the navy at Southwestern, the football program started the downhill slide that eventually brought about its demise in 1951. Though it was ranked 49th in the Williamson early season national ranking of 113 college football teams, the strength of its starting players was nearly wiped out when the navy transferred five of them to the University of Texas just after mid-season.[175] "And so," said a newspaper article, "Southwestern returns the complement [of players] that Texas extended back in 1943 when seven starters off the championship 1942 team were sent to the Georgetown school by the marine program."[176] The 1945–1946 basketball team did win the Texas Conference championship. Most of the players were in the Naval V-5 and V-12 Unit. Coach Medley was the basketball coach and his son, David Medley, who was in the V-5 Unit, played on the team.

Wartime Changes in the Campus Equation

When the Navy V-12 Unit came to Southwestern in 1943, it radically changed the equation that had previously operated with regard to campus housing, number of teachers, the curriculum, and budgeting. On-campus housing during the prewar years had been built to accommodate up to 400 persons, with another 75–125 expected to live off-campus in fraternity houses and other places. The faculty that taught these students numbered around thirty. The curriculum was fairly stable, and most of the teachers were permanent or nearly so. By 1943, Southwestern had overcome its indebtedness and had operated for six years with a balanced budget. Budget formation was a fairly straightforward process of estimating the expected numbers for the line items that were very much the same from year to year.

The coming of the V-12 Unit changed the parameters of all these categories of operation. The 391 seamen and marines that entered in July 1943 were more numerous by themselves than the total enrollment of all students in the fall semesters of 1941 and 1942. Including civilian students, the total enrollment for the first tri-semester of the V-12 Unit on campus in July 1943 was 673, or 79 percent more than in fall 1942. In July 1945, the beginning of the last year of the V-12 program, the total enrollment of all students was 783, or 108 percent more than in fall 1942.

In addition to the increase in numbers was the increase in student mobility, the number of students who entered without staying long. Before the war, students entering in the fall generally stayed at least for the spring semester. A few entered in the spring to take the place of those who failed out or who left for some other reason. During 1941–1942, only 425 different students attended Southwestern during the two semesters of the academic year, just 9 percent more than the original 390 entering in the fall. During 1943–1944, 1,166 different students studied during the academic year, some 73 percent more than the July enrollment of 673. Of course, the fact that the latter year had three tri-semesters while the former had only two semesters means that the percentage turnover might be expected to be higher, but not by that much. The navy followed its own judgment of what was best for the service rather than adhering to traditional academic prescriptions for continuous study. For example, whereas no second-semester senior, on the brink of graduation at his or her own school, might have been expected to transfer into Southwestern during ordinary times, there were a good number of such V-12 transfers when the program began.

The curriculum also grew rapidly during the war years. Not counting physical education activity courses and private instrumental lessons in Music, the number of one-semester standard courses increased from 393 in 1941 to 693 in 1945, an increase of 76 percent. These were taught by sixty-two teachers, not including naval personnel, an increase of 100 percent over 1941. Not included in these totals are five specifically V-12 courses—Naval Organization (I and II), Naval History, Seamanship and Communications, and Engineering and Damage Control—taught by V-12 personnel rather than by Southwestern teachers.[177]

Particularly notable among the curricular changes were the following: the setting up of Journalism as a separate major with 24 courses within the English Department; the addition of 30 Japanese, Portuguese, Russian, Sanskrit, Linguistics, and Interpreter courses; the expansion of religion courses from 24 to more than twice that number; the introduction of a Home Economics Department, with 42 courses; the establishment of a Department of Astronomy and Meteorology, with 16 courses; the setting up of a separate Geology and Mineralogy Department, also including geography, with 12 courses; and the establishment of a Department of General Engineering, with 15 courses. All of the courses required or allowed for V-12 students were designated as such in the catalog.

The budget implications of all of these changes were significant. The difficulties associated with managing a dairy, purchasing about 500 acres of land, reconditioning current facilities, buying and leasing additional housing, doubling the faculty payroll, keeping up with the other colleges in the Southwestern system, and dealing with the other multifarious day-to-day problems posed a formidable challenge for those in charge of the budget process. A final settlement with the navy in Washington for what it owed the University was not accomplished until two months after Score's death, when the Board reluctantly voted to settle for $17,644.77.[178]

17 From War to Peace (1945–1949)

Transitioning Away from the V-12 Unit

Though everyone knew that the war would not continue forever and recognized that a time would come when Southwestern would have to return to normal operations, the actual process was fraught with as many problems and almost as much anxiety as the establishment of the wartime system in the first place. The main difference was that, aside from being a process of retrenchment rather than one of expansion, the retrenchment occurred over a longer period of time than the process of expansion. Whereas the expansion was sudden, the retrenchment was gradual. The retrenchment was postponed immediately after the war by the influx of military veterans returning for degrees under the G.I. Bill of Rights, when student numbers even increased temporarily, but with their disappearance, decline became inexorable until 1951. In that year the student body reached its nadir with a fall semester enrollment of 414, almost the same number with which Bergin had begun his third year in 1937 fourteen years earlier. By 1951–1952, the third year of Finch's presidency, one is able to detect several new trends in institutional life. Southwestern would hesitantly but consistently become more focused as a liberal arts institution, and student numbers would increase slowly but regularly.

Actual fall semester enrollment figures over the wartime and immediate postwar period appear in the following table.

Fall of Year	Enrollment	% Change
1942	376	
1943	673	+79.0
1944	569	-15.5
1945	783	+37.6
1946	808	+3.2
1947	870	+7.7
1948	790	-9.2
1949	678	-14.2
1950	581	-14.3
1951	414	-28.7

No sooner had the V-12 Unit come to the campus than hints of reduction in numbers began to be heard. Score and Johnson wrote back and forth to each other about Score's concern that the number of trainees would be reduced. Through the first year Johnson could reassure him that the number would stay the same, but he could not do so as the war progressed and conditions changed.[1] Score reported to the Board in mid-1944 that he expected the full complement of 391 navy students for the summer tri-semester but, with the certain prospect of eventual force reduction, he had written the navy requesting that Southwestern be included in any naval postwar program, "either for a Unit of the Naval ROTC or some postwar V-12 Program." He felt good about Southwestern's chances of inclusion in such a program. Representative R. Ewing Thomason, a Southwestern alumnus, was chairman of the special committee designated to study the matter, and Lyndon B. Johnson was a ranking member of the committee. "These two gentlemen have assured us," he continued, "that if and when a plan is devised, they will keep Southwestern's interests in mind." Nevertheless, because he knew that the V-12 had adopted a program of reducing the number of general personnel for the next year [1945–1946], Southwestern would engage in a "vigorous program of student recruitment."[2] In the spring of 1945, Johnson wrote Pearl Neas that "we aren't going to get the ROTC. More than 15 states won't even have one unit."[3]

In mid-July 1945, Score went to Washington to meet with Johnson and the Navy Department about the possibility of continuing the Navy Unit. He returned to Georgetown feeling that there would be some sort of unit for the fall. Then came the sudden end of the war in August, with the immediate announcement that all V-12 Units would be discontinued. Having accepted this prospect, Score was greatly encouraged when the navy notified him in late September that it had decided to stay at Southwestern. This change of plans, however, put the school in a bind. It had recruited 330 young women whom it had slated to live

Freshmen collect wood for the bonfire at the Homecoming pep rally in 1944. Veterans' Village appears in the background. From the 1949 *Sou'wester.*

in Laura Kuykendall Hall. Now that the navy would be retaining its place there, the number of young civilian men and women Southwestern could take would be reduced. Recruitment of new students had been good, and fifty or more prospects that might have otherwise been approved were denied admission. Ironically, this action allowed the University to recruit a "better" class. Only students in the top three-quarters of their high school graduating class were admitted. Practically everyone that required housing had to accept arrangements different from what they had been led to expect. With the 318 navy men and the 465 civilians that finally matriculated, the total enrollment for the fall of 1945 was 783, the largest in the history of the school to date.[4] With the disappearance of the V-12 Unit in 1946, Southwestern did retain a V-5 program, but most of the currently enrolled students dropped out of the program.[5]

Because of the housing pressure caused by the sudden influx of veterans whose expenses were covered by the federal government under the G.I. Bill of Rights, the administration applied for surplus housing in which to place some of them. The result was the construction of Veterans' Village, a group of temporary buildings provided by the federal government. Sixteen apartments of three and four rooms were provided for married veterans, and dormitory rooms were made available for 180 single veterans. The project was completed by the end of 1946 and was located north of the McCook Infirmary and Odds and Ends Hall, a bit northwest of Mood Hall.[6] Odds and Ends Hall had been built in 1944–1945 by joining the former Art House and Band House and veneering the result with stone. It accommodated Home Economics, Physical Education for Women, Art, and Band. Odds and Ends Hall endured into the Fleming years, when it was removed. In addition, two other buildings were secured from the federal government in 1947. The government paid the cost of demolition and transportation of the buildings from their previous locations elsewhere, as well as the costs for all equipment and reerection on campus. One became a shop building, housing a new print shop, several offices, and Art and Band, which were moved from Odds and Ends Hall. The second building housed the university Bookstore and the Student Center.[7]

Faculty Acquisitions during the Score Years

Those teachers mentioned by V-12 student Jack Jones (see Chapter XVI) as holding late afternoon court on the front porches of their old "Victorian houses" across University Avenue from the campus were older faculty members such as Claud Howard and M. L. Williams. New teachers employed by Score joined them during and immediately following the war. Most of them came after the war. A listing of those with the longest terms of service at Southwestern is as follows:

Name	Title/Subject	Year	Years
Brown, Bob Marion	Physics (1942–47, 1953–61, 1967–81)	1942	27
Lundblad, Elizabeth Riley	Business Administration and Economics	1943	32
Springer, Roland Angus	Speech and Drama	1943	35
Fox, Mary Elizabeth	History, Journalism, Speech	1944	32
Luksa, Frank E.	Sociology	1944	31
Whitmore, Ralph Martin	Physics, Mathematics	1944	44
Lenz, Frederick W.	Foreign Languages	1945	13
Lenz, Mali G.	Foreign Languages	1945	14
Berglund, John V.	Religion and Church History	1946	24
Gaupp, Frederick	History and Government	1946	22
Jones, Ralph Wood	Woodwinds, Music Ed, Band, Orchestra	1946	15
Richards, John D.	Music Education and Choruses	1946	29
Steelman, Edmund H.	Bible	1946	32
Watts, Harvey D.	Religion	1946	31
Douglass, Thomas Claire	Violin and Stringed Instruments	1947	36
McCook, Jane Brown	Speech, Drama, English	1947	29
Score, John N. R. (son)	Religion and Philosophy	1948, 1955	41
Deupree, Irene Whiteside	Home Economics	1948	23
Osborn, Wendell Lincoln	Voice, Psychology	1948	29
Custer, Judson S.	Education	1949	40
Merzbach, Ludwig Herman	Business Administration and Economics	1950	18*

*He also taught four years (1946–50) at Daniel Baker, part of the Southwestern system.

Only nine teachers or administrators have served forty years or more at Southwestern University during the time span covered by this book. They are Wesley Carroll Vaden (1893, forty-four years), Margaret Mood McKennon (1903, forty-one years), Pearl Alma Neas (1913, forty-nine years), Oscar A. Ullrich (1920, forty-two years), George C. Hester (1925, forty years), Ralph M. Whitmore (1944, forty-four years), Judson S. Custer (1949, forty years), John N. R. Score II, (1948, 1955, forty-one years), and William Douglas Hooker (1961, forty-three years). Score, Whitmore, and Custer began during the tenure of President Russell Score.

John Score's career has already been discussed (see Chapter XVI). Ralph Martin Whitmore (B.A., University of San Antonio, M.A. and Ph.D., University of Texas) ended his career at Southwestern as Professor and Chairman of the Department of Mathematics and Computer Science and holder of the Jesse H. and Mary Gibbs Jones Professorship in Mathematics. He joined the faculty on September 1, 1944, as a teacher who had recently completed an Army Electronic

Training Course at the University of Texas. At Southwestern he taught mathematics to members of the Naval and Marine V-12 Unit who were pursuing their education at the University at that time. He continued at the University after the war, receiving a furlough in 1953 to do atomic research work with the Sandia Corporation and to study at the University of New Mexico.[8] He was very well liked, and his colleagues in the Division of Natural Science regularly elected him chairman of that division after the position was made elective rather than appointive. He was the person most trusted by the faculty over the years for dealing with the administration regarding important faculty matters, such as health insurance and retirement benefits. Faculty members and administrators alike appreciated the knowledgeable, unassuming manner displayed by him that almost always brought positive results. He was also a leader in the local chapter of the American Association of University Professors when that organization was at its strongest during the Fleming years.

Judson Samuel Custer was Professor and Chairman of the Department of Education and holder of the Will W. Jackson Professorship in Education during the latter part of his career at Southwestern. Score buttonholed him at his wedding reception in Georgetown on June 22, 1946, and offered him a position while his bride, Louise Edwards, daughter of the Georgetown District Superintendent, was forced to wait for him to finish talking to her groom. At the time, Custer was a graduate student at the University of Texas and was not ready to accept Score's offer. He accepted after he completed his Ed.D. in 1949. Custer served as a consultant to the State Board of Education and as a member of various committees connected with that agency from time to time. As the University moved more and more in the direction of emphasizing the liberal arts and sciences during the Finch, Fleming, and Shilling administrations, Custer emphasized the necessary relationship between higher education and the vocations. He was more responsible than anyone else for the appearance of that emphasis in the Aims of the University adopted by the faculty and Board of Trustees in 1972, not modified until 2000. His interest in preserving the history of Southwestern University has been acknowledged in the Introduction to this book.

Angus Springer and the Department of Speech and Drama

Angus Springer was employed for one year by President Score during the fall of 1943 to cover a wartime leave of absence by the then head of the Department of Speech and Drama, Professor Thomas Hodgin Marsh. He brought with him an M.A. from Northwestern University, which was later supplemented by a Ph.D. from New York University in 1956. Springer stayed until retirement thirty-five years later, becoming the one who, more than any other person, is responsible for the development of the Department of Theatre that exists today.

Speech and Drama, as the department was called when Springer arrived, was a part of the Humanities Division. It remained there until 1956, when, upon the construction of the Alma Thomas Fine Arts Center, it moved into the School of Fine Arts. It was renamed the Department of Theatre and Speech in 1971 and the Department of Theatre and Speech Communication in 1980. By 1988 the "Speech" had been dropped, and it was renamed the Department of Theatre and Communication. In 1999 the two disciplines were divided into separate departments, with that of Communication, though basically interdisciplinary in nature, going into the Social Sciences Division.

Springer and his predecessors owed the establishment of their craft at Southwestern to Professor William Dwight Wentz, who came to Southwestern in 1913 as Professor of Public Speaking and English. He continued for fourteen years. Wentz introduced drama courses into the curriculum in 1918 and formed the Mask and Wig Club the same year. The first play produced by the club and Wentz's Dramatic Literature class was Shakespeare's *Merchant of Venice* in the spring of 1919. Lewis A. Harding succeeded Wentz for one year, followed by Ernest R. Hardin, who had been one of Wentz's students. He stayed four years. Hardin required every member of his Dramatic Literature class to write a play, cast it, and direct it. Marsh succeeded Hardin for ten years and was followed in turn by Springer. Even though Marsh was forced to trim the curriculum of his Department during the Great Depression, he and his associates produced plays on a regular basis.[9]

When Springer arrived, he found the facilities for his work to be woefully inadequate. The contractor who was hired to put the buildings into shape for the arrival of the navy and marine trainees in the V-12 program had dismantled all the flats and other scenic units and used the lumber in the renovation project. The stage for theatrical productions was that of the Administration Building. It was designed for chapel worship and assemblies, not theatrical productions. The acting area was only nine feet, ten inches deep, and the off-stage spaces right and left were ten feet wide. Score gave Springer permission to knock a large opening in the back upstage wall for a door to be used as an entrance from the wide second-floor hall. The lighting system was composed of six porcelain sockets on one circuit, mounted behind the proscenium and controlled by an open knife switch. Springer used these and other contrived production spaces for thirteen years until the Alma Thomas Fine Arts Center was completed in 1956.[10]

One of Springer's most memorable productions came on V.J. Day, August 14, 1945. A mystery courtroom drama, *The Night of January 16th*, had been scheduled for that date to be played outdoors on a stage built on the east side of the Administration Building. Springer narrates the event as follows:

> Late in the afternoon came the announcement of V.J. Day. In anticipation, a celebration had been scheduled in the city park, the block where the Wesleyan [Retirement] Home now stands. Dr. Score, always a strong supporter of the theatre program was the principal speaker. At the conclusion of his speech he announced the play and suggested that his listeners continue celebrating by seeing it. At 8:30, so-called "curtain time," there were three people present. Thirty minutes later the box office was swamped, ticket sellers overrun, and the crowd (as well as the actors and director) enjoyed the show, most of them for free![11]

Springer's closest friend at Southwestern and afterward was navy Lieutenant Fred C. Blanchard, the erudite professor who had been the first person sent by the navy to the Southwestern campus. The two men arrived on campus within six months of each other. Blanchard supported Springer strongly during the two years they were on campus together and sponsored his Ph.D. program after the war at New York University.[12]

The most memorable production by the Theatre Department seen by this author during Springer's tenure was *The Hackberry Cavalier*, produced by Drexel Riley on April 21–22, 1966. *Saturday Evening Post* writer George Sessions Perry had composed the play from a book of stories. Perry attended Southwestern University briefly in 1928. Though he did not receive a college degree from Southwestern or anywhere else, he returned from traveling abroad in 1931 to marry his future wife, Claire Hodges, whom he had met at Southwestern. They moved back to his hometown of Rockdale. Rockdale and the surrounding area furnished the setting for nearly all of his fiction, including his novel *Hold Autumn in Your Hand*.[13]

Three Professors from Germany: Frederick Walter Lenz

President Score was a man of deep human sympathy, displaying his concern for putative enemies as well as persons close by. This side of his personality was illustrated in his failed attempt to have Japanese American students admitted to the University in 1942. It was illustrated again by his employment of three displaced German professors immediately after the war. They were Frederick Walter Lenz (Ph.D., University of Berlin), Ludwig Herman Merzbach (Ph.D., University of Berlin), and Frederick Ernest Gaupp (Ph.D., University of Breslau). Each had a talented and effective wife whose independent contributions to the University magnified the work of their husbands. They were Amalie (Mali) Goldmann Lenz (Ph.D., University of Hamburg), Margaret Kober Merzbach (Ph.D., University of Berlin), and Mrs. Ilse Pártos Gaupp. Ilse Gaupp was the only non-German among them. She was Hungarian. Each man remained with the University until retirement. Two of the couples fled Nazi Germany during the 1930s, and the other suffered in a German concentration camp.

As a chaplain in World War I, Score had experienced frontline duty. He was proud of his service and took his family back to Europe in 1936, the year of the Olympics in Germany, to visit the old battlefields he knew. While there, he found out that the Germans were killing the Jews. When he came back, he could not keep silent. He talked about it and preached about it from his pulpit in Fort Worth. The F.B.I. put a tap on his phone line, says John, "because Daddy was talking about the way the Germans were killing the Jews."[14] From that time on Score took the oppression of the Jews to heart. Thus, when he learned after the war that some of the German academics that had escaped the Holocaust were seeking employment, he was disposed to help them. Though several whom he employed only stayed at Southwestern briefly, three of them had long tenures and made a strong impact on the school.

Dr. Score first learned about the Lenzes in a letter from Roland H. Bainton, the eminent professor at the Yale University Divinity School. He informed Score that a Dr. Frederick W. Lenz had been forced to leave Germany in 1933 and that he had lived in Italy for six years before coming to America in 1939. He had been given courses to teach at Yale and Beecher College, not because there were genuine vacancies but from a desire of persons there to help him. "He was paid by neither institution," said Bainton, "but was supported by refugee committees." Neither school retained him because of the lack of an opening. "In Germany," continued Bainton, "they both belonged to the Lutheran Church, for despite Jewish blood they come from one of the ancient families long since assimilated to German culture and Christian faith. In this country Mrs. Lenz has joined the Congregational Church. Mr. Lenz has waited because he found no church affiliation which quite took the place of the Lutheran."[15] Though Score had no vacancy for Lenz at the time of Bainton's letter, he sent Lenz an urgent day letter a year later asking him if he was interested in a foreign language position at Southwestern. Lenz replied affirmatively, was offered a position, and arrived in Georgetown with his wife Mali on October 30.[16] She was given a part-time job in the department as well and came to love Southwestern.

Frederick Lenz was perhaps the most widely recognized scholar in his field of any person ever to teach at Southwestern. He was the world's greatest living authority on Ovid, and his research was wide-ranging on ancient and medieval subjects.[17] He seemed to have a knack for locating previously unknown ancient manuscripts. His articles in scholarly journals in various languages were numerous, and various publishing houses in Europe vied for the right to publish his editions of ancient authors. Because the war completely destroyed his volumes done in Italy, he rewrote them for publication after arriving in the United States.[18]

Lenz did his best to accommodate his finely honed scholarly approach to the academic needs of an undergraduate institution, but he never entirely succeeded. His formal approach to student-faculty relations, derived from his European background, prevented him from becoming the friendly counselor often expected by his students, and his colleagues were somewhat intimidated by his erudition. He was also a proud man, in whom decades of repression had created a tendency to see slights where they did not necessarily exist. He and President Score, a proud man himself, exchanged some testy letters over supposed slights detected by Lenz. Because of these characteristics, Score never felt that he could turn over the department to Lenz, and he continued to serve as chair of the Department of Foreign Languages. Though Lenz did most of the departmental work, he was forced to seek Score's approval before making decisions of any importance. It was not until shortly after the death of Score that his status was changed.

One of the first actions of Finch as new President was to name Lenz Acting Head of the department.[19] Finch handled him with care and consideration. His correspondence with Lenz over the years was very respectful. He gave Lenz a full year's leave of absence to serve as Visiting Professor in the Department of Classical Languages and Literatures at the University of Texas when Lenz requested one for 1953–1954.[20] The following year Lenz was elected to tenure at Southwestern and made Associate Professor.[21] He was subsequently granted a leave of absence for 1954–1955 to study in Europe in the fields of ancient and medieval Latin poetry, with the purpose of publishing several books and papers.[22] By now his eyes, which had been giving him trouble for a long time, were deteriorating rapidly, and he had to limit his teaching to two courses. Mali took the courses he vacated and was made a full-time teacher at the University.[23] In 1957 she was elected to tenure as Associate Professor and Chairman of the Department of Foreign Languages.[24] Lenz finally asked for retirement in the spring of 1958 on account of his eyes.[25] A year later, having already retired, he was promoted to Full Professor and listed as Head of the Department of Foreign Languages.[26]

On retirement the Lenzes moved to Austin, and Frederick entered into a part-time relationship with the University of Texas as Research Professor of Classics. In that environment he performed, to the extent that his eyes permitted, the kind of scholarship he enjoyed, with professors around him who appreciated his work. At the time of his death, a Friedrich Lenz Memorial Committee of his Texas University colleagues penned a fulsome tribute to him and appended a bibliography of the amazing literary output he had created during his lifetime.[27]

After Frederick's death on November 17, 1969, Mali continued living in Austin. Members of the Southwestern community remembered her with visits and letters. She sent small checks to President Fleming as contributions to various fund-raising activities from time to time. In a handwritten letter to him on March 5, 1975, she sent a $25 check for the Program for Progress. She remarked in her letter accompanying it: "Often I think back to the 15 years I taught there with great satisfaction." She died in 1979 at the age of eighty, ten years after Frederick's death at the age of seventy-three. The Lenzes had two sons, one of whom married a daughter of Professor Howard. One became a naval officer, the other an official with American Airlines.

Three Professors from Germany: Frederick Ernest Gaupp

Though both were Germans, Fred Gaupp was quite different from Frederick Lenz. Whereas the latter could be characterized as a rationalist, Gaupp was a romantic. Whereas Lenz parsed the written word, Gaupp painted portraits with the spoken word. Whereas Lenz was most at home in the world of the sober Romans, Gaupp was most at home with the exuberant figures of the Renaissance. And whereas Lenz was caught in the crucible of being exiled because of a Jewish past he no longer felt, Gaupp, a gentile, chose to identify himself with the fate of his Jewish wife, whose Jewish present was ever with them. Both men had fled from Hitler's Germany, but Gaupp's loathing of the Nazi regime hovered around him the rest of his life in a way that Lenz's own did not. In a lecture entitled "Twenty Years Ago" delivered by Gaupp on campus in November 1959, he said:

> It is extremely difficult for us—in particular your history teachers—to teach a class in twentieth century history, because we are speaking about our own lives. How can we be objective; how can we speak without hatred, without being stirred up again and again in our innermost feelings and memories which are so fresh, as if all this had happened a few weeks and not twenty years ago? It is much easier for me to lecture about the American Revolution or the persecution of Christians in Rome at the time of Nero than about Hitler's war or the German concentration camps. It still hurts. It will continue to hurt us and poison our memories and sometimes our dreams as long as we live.[28]

Though both the Lenzes and the Merzbachs enjoyed traveling back to Germany after the war, Fred and Ilse Gaupp never returned. He told me he could not do so. He might without knowing it sit down beside a Nazi on a trolley car.

Though these characteristics might make it appear that Fred Gaupp was hate-driven, such was not the case. His was more a case of revulsion than of hate. He and Ilse were in fact gentle people, beloved by Southwestern students and faculty. They opened their home every Thursday evening to anyone who wanted to drop by for conversation and refreshments. Many students and faculty did so. Every test paper turned in by a student was graded with meticulous care, first by Ilse, who made her comments about it to Fred, then by Fred, who finally gave it a grade.[29] The students elected Gaupp to receive the Best Teacher Award in 1957.[30] He also served as the faculty sponsor for Invitation to Learning for many years. The Invitation to Learning was a once a month evening for teachers and students in the Faculty Lounge of the Bishops' Memorial Union, where one of the teachers delivered a lecture on a topic of his or her choice. It was the most interesting and pleasant lecture series experienced by me during my many years at Southwestern.

Gaupp completed his doctorate in 1922 during the terrible decade in Germany after World War I. During the thirteen years between then and his flight from Germany in 1935, he made his living as a dramaturge and stage manager of theaters. He also wrote a number of essays and short stories, five novels, and two histories, in addition to working as an editor for publishing houses. He commented on those times to me in various conversations. He said that inflation was so bad that the actors demanded their pay on a daily basis. Their wives, Ilse among them, would line up to receive it each day before noon. They would immediately go out and spend it the same afternoon before it lost value. At Southwestern Gaupp sometimes reverted back to his days as an actor and played supporting roles in productions of Mask and Wig. He also played violin in the Sinfonietta.

After leaving Germany, Gaupp stayed in Italy for four years, spending most of the time in Florence as a free-lance writer. It was in Florence, he later said, that he became a historian. While there he studied the early Italian Renaissance, which became his field of concentration, his great "love." Because of the deterioration of the political situation in Europe, the state of affairs of German immigrants in Italy became intolerable. With the help of the Quakers, the Gaupps were able to send their two sons to England in July 1939, where they lived with the eminent British historian George Peabody Gooch. The Gaupps managed to cross the border from Italy into Switzerland on the last train. There, as refugees, they were supported by the Swiss Protestant Church. Working for money was forbidden. They found hope, he said, listening to broadcasts by President Roosevelt over shortwave radio.

Though the details of their coming to Southwestern are not entirely clear, there is a letter of September 24, 1946, to Score from Fred Gaupp in Ascona, Switzerland. In it he refers to letters previously received from both Score and Lenz about the possibility of his coming to the United States. He encloses a curriculum vitae and a photograph of Ilse and himself. Fred and Ilse arrived in the United States on November 22, 1946. A week later President Score presented him to the faculty as a new member.[31] He then sent a memo to Dean Ullrich covering the hire and stating that he had also employed Mrs. Ilse Gaupp as Director of the Bindery at the Cody Memorial Library.[32] The following spring Score assisted the Gaupps in bringing their two sons, Dieter, age twenty-two, and Peter, age eighteen, from England to Georgetown.[33] The boys both subsequently received baccalaureate degrees from Southwestern and master's degrees from the University of Texas.

Three Professors from Germany: Ludwig Herman Merzbach

Ludwig Merzbach and Fred Gaupp, born within four months of each other in late 1896 and early 1897, arrived in the United States during the same year (1946), and retired from Southwestern in the same year (1968). They were both avid stamp collectors and had fabulous stamp collections. The first purchase of any substance made by Merzbach upon arriving in New York from Europe with his family in the summer of his arrival was of some stamps from a philatelist to start a new collection. An incident involving him and his love of stamps occurring on the day of his death twenty-seven years later reveals something about the man. Describing it in his eulogy of Merzbach, Dean Clifford said:

> I am told, as Dr. Merzbach was being wheeled into the intensive care section of the hospital, he drew from his pocket a brief note which indicated that there was a small account still to be cleared for some stamps he was buying. . . . His life came to its conclusion well-ordered, consistent, just, how demonstrably right![34]

Merzbach followed a very different course of action with regard to the Nazi danger than that followed by Lenz and Gaupp. Whereas they fled Germany for Italy in 1933 and 1935, respectively, Merzbach held a very important business position, and his employers tried to protect him against the rising tide of Nazi anti-Semitism. Officials at the Allgemeine Electricitäts-Gesellschaft (General Electric Company) wrote a letter in his behalf on May 17, 1938, explaining the importance of his work for them. They said that his "versatile ability" made it possible to entrust to his care important work of a diversified character.

> Thus he has been at times in control of several of our subsidiaries, comprising branch factories devoted to the manufacture of electrotechnical products and industrial porcelain, likewise paper mills, foundries, and our printing establishment. Within the general management of our main business Dr. Merzbach has acted as permanent administrator of the above mentioned affiliates, some of which were partly organized and/or reorganized by him. For a number of years he has managed the real estate, housing, and settlement companies of our concern.[35]

Nevertheless, his thirteen-year position with that firm ended in 1938, and his biographical account states that he was the comptroller, accountant, and advisor of the Association of Jews in Germany until 1943. What that position actually meant for him and his family is unknown. It at least meant that he, his wife, and his daughter were not sent to a concentration camp until 1943. Theresienstadt, the Austrian fortress or prison northwest of Prague near the Elbe where Gavrilo Princeps had been held after his assassination of Franz Ferdinand in 1914, was the camp where important detainees were sent. During the imprisonment of the Merzbachs there, it was the so-called Nazi model camp, used on occasion to fool Red Cross inspection teams. It was the grotesque alibi of the Nazis. Actually, 140,000 persons were brought there in three-and-a-half years. Of these, 33,000 died, 90,000 were transported elsewhere, of whom only 3,000 returned, and 17,000 survived. The Merzbachs were three of the survivors. The camp was liberated by the Soviets on May 8, 1945.

Remarkably, the same personality and organizational talents that had served him so well in the business world served him well in the camp. Immediately after his arrival, he was appointed to the management of the self-administration of the free camp as controller of organization and accountancy. In March 1944 he became assistant manager and in October departmental chief, in which role he continued to serve until liberation in May 1945. On August 14, 1945, at the time of his departure from the camp, he was given a "Certificate" testifying to his work in behalf of the inmates.

> In times of the severest oppression and under the most difficult conditions he succeeded in finding ways and means out of every precarious situation to attain an alleviation in the fate of his fellow sufferers, just as well as after the liberation his professional knowledge, combined with his human qualities, met with the entire approval of all those who had to work with him, especially of the Czech and Russian authorities. Moreover, it is, to a remarkable extent, due to Dr. Merzbach's efforts that the repatriation of the non-Czechoslovak ex-internees of the camp, to whose interests he never

ceased to attend energetically and consciously, was effected in an irreproachably smooth way.[36]

After leaving camp, he was managing director of the Bavarian Relief Organization in Munich for a brief time before coming to the United States. He arrived in New York on May 24, 1946. How he came into contact with Southwestern is not known, but he and Margaret were appointed to teach at Weatherford College during 1946–1947 and at Daniel Baker College from 1947 through 1950. He taught there as Assistant Professor and Acting Head of the Department of Business Administration and Economics. Margaret served as Assistant Professor and Acting Head of the Department of Foreign Languages. When Southwestern relinquished its role in the administration of Daniel Baker, the Merzbachs were brought back to Georgetown, where he became an Assistant Professor in the University. He was promoted to Associate Professor in 1956, to Head of the Department of Economics and Business Administration in 1958, and to full Professor in 1962.

Merzbach became a leader in the Southwestern faculty because of his quiet, friendly temperament and the effective use of the people skills that had so successfully enabled him to weather every storm in the past. He became almost the paterfamilias of the local chapter of the American Association of University Professors. Its executive committee met monthly in his home, and that organization honored him after his death with a bronze memorial plaque extolling his contributions. It is now found in the faculty lounge, called the Merzbach room, of the Red and Charline McCombs Campus Center.

Merzbach was a proponent of peace and reconciliation in human affairs. In spite of the treatment he had received during the war, he never abandoned his faith in humankind and the necessity of exercising rationality in human affairs. If he was passionate about anything, it was about democracy. Though he and Margaret joined the local Methodist Church, one feels that they did so without giving up the core of the Jewish heritage. They were simply not ideologues in a religious, political, or economic sense. They believed in participating actively in every situation in which they found themselves in order to bring the best out of it for themselves and to help others do the same. Their daughter, Uta C. Merzbach, who spent her teenage years in a concentration camp, at Brownwood, and in Georgetown, became an important educator in her own right. She received a Ph.D. in mathematics from Harvard University in 1965, became the mathematics curator at the Smithsonian Institution in Washington, D.C., and taught at Johns Hopkins University. Specializing in the work of Leibniz, Gauss, and Scheutz, she is particularly well known for her collaboration with Carl C. Boyer in their history of mathematics volumes.

Daniel Baker College Joins the Southwestern System

The Daniel Baker College in Brownwood, to which the Merzbachs were sent in 1947 and where they taught for three years, had just become a part of the Southwestern system when the Merzbachs went there. Daniel Baker was an old school named for a preeminent Presbyterian preacher-educator in pre–Civil War times. Baker was the founder and first President of Austin College in 1849. Daniel Baker College was organized as a Presbyterian college in 1888. Though enrollment was usually less than a hundred each year, it continued operation and managed eventually to build a physical plant consisting of a main building, a women's dormitory, a chapel, and a gymnasium. Financial difficulties plagued the college, and in 1929 the Presbyterian Church relinquished control. The school continued operation, however, as an independent Presbyterian college.[37]

Though Score in his presentation of the Daniel Baker case to the Southwestern Trustees in August 1946 did not indicate its enrollment, he did say a year later that it had lost 60 percent of its students during the war.[38] It must have been this sharp enrollment decline that caused the Daniel Baker Trustees to approach him with an offer to turn over the school with all its assets to Southwestern. Surprisingly, the condition of the school, apart from its lack of students, was remarkably good. It had no indebtedness and had a fund balance of eleven thousand dollars in addition to income from a small endowment fund.[39] Its immediate problem was the dearth of students occasioned by the war.

By now the procedure for adding a small college to the Southwestern system was well known, and a document was prepared more or less similar to the agreements already entered into with Westminster and Weatherford. It stipulated the responsibilities of both Southwestern and Daniel Baker and protected Southwestern from financial loss in running the school. The document was ratified by the Trustees of Daniel Baker, and Score reported to the Southwestern Trustees on November 20, 1946, that the merger had been completed, the deed filed, and all funds and securities transferred to Southwestern.[40]

Score immediately went to work to rejuvenate the college. In December, after the merger, all its requirements of admission, curriculum, equipment, and library were revised to help it meet the standards of the Southern Association of Colleges and Secondary Schools. The salary of every faculty member was raised to the SACS minimum, which meant the doubling of a number of salaries and an overall increase of approximately 50 percent.[41]

The School of Fine Arts as a Part of the Southwestern University System

One of the incidental achievements of Score's University of Small Colleges idea was the definitive establishment of the School of Fine Arts at Southwestern as a separate academic unit with its own dean. From the inception of fine arts courses as a part of the Ladies' Annex curriculum in 1878, the status of the fine arts as an organizational unit at Southwestern gradually changed as fine arts courses became a regular part of the Southwestern curriculum.

A School of Fine Arts was first set up as one of the two units of the University in 1903, though it did not have its own degree or a dean at the time. It gained its first degree in 1913 and its first dean in 1916–1917, when Arthur L. Manchester was granted that title. Though his successor, Frederick Kraft, was given the title in 1918, Etelka Evans, Kraft's successor in 1920, was designated Dean of Music, not of Fine Arts. Soon thereafter she was awarded the Doctor of Music degree, the first woman at Southwestern to receive an honorary doctorate. Her leaving brought a short period when no one carried the dean's title. When Henry E. Meyer came in 1926, he was again given the title of Dean of Music. The notion of a School of Fine Arts disappeared, and by 1940–1941 the catalog carried it as the Department of Fine Arts with Meyer as Dean of Music. The catalog for 1941–1942 restored the title to School of Fine Arts, with Meyer as "Dean" of the School. Though the catalog for 1944–1945 continued to carry the Fine Arts title for the academic unit, Meyer was once again listed as Dean of Music. This listing continued until 1947–1948, when his title was listed as "Acting Dean." The following year Meyer was described as Dean of the School of Fine Arts. That listing of a School of Fine Arts with its own Dean of Fine Arts has been followed from 1948–1949 until the present.

This description of the nomenclature since 1903 of both the School of Fine Arts and of its dean suggests an ambiguity in the thinking of successive Presidents and Boards of Trustees about the school until the definitive establishment of both titles in 1948–1949. That Score intended to end this ambiguity is clearly stated by him in Board minutes for 1947. In the spring meeting of that year he explained his plan of reorganizing the School of Fine Arts as a separate "College" of the University.[42] At the fall meeting he stated that his report covered "the first semester of our operation of the School of Fine Arts as a separate college."[43] The following spring he reported that Ernest L. Kurth had given ten thousand dollars in an endowed scholarship for the School of Fine Arts, in addition to stimulating another thirty thousand dollars in gifts. Included in these gifts was the purchase of a new electronic pipe organ.[44] Score probably encouraged Kurth to make the gift to the School of Fine Arts as a way of highlighting its new status.

Score's action in establishing the School of Fine Arts in 1947 as a separate college was not done merely to rectify what he felt was a longtime organizational ambiguity. It was done as a part of the publication of his rationale for "A University of Small Colleges." The rationale was published the same year that the School of Fine Arts was definitively established, and he specifically included it as one of the colleges of Southwestern University. In the brochure he describes the Southwestern system as being made up of five colleges—the College of Arts and Sciences (Georgetown), the School of Fine Arts (Georgetown), Westminster College (Tehuacana), Weatherford College (Weatherford), and Daniel Baker College (Brownwood).[45]

Score's curricular vision of a University of Small Colleges was described the following year in the most elaborate catalog ever published by Southwestern University. Printed in June 1948, it was composed of seven sections with 414 numbered pages and 20 additional unnumbered pages of pictures. In the opening pages of Section I, covering General Information about the University as a whole, the catalog states that "Southwestern University is composed of five colleges." Then separate sections are devoted to each college in order of its chronological attachment to the Southwestern system. The concluding section covers "Aviation." It announces that Flight Training is to be offered under the regulations of the Civil Aeronautics Administration and the Veterans Administration. It states that this program, though not yet established, will be available for students of all the colleges. In spite of an elaborate nine-page description of the proposed program, nothing was ever set up. The catalog also announces the imminent establishment of a Graduate School of Social Service and an International Institute. Neither was ever created.

Disassociation of Southwestern from the Three Colleges

Five years of intense work by President Score, with ever expanding responsibilities, became too much even for him, and by late 1946 he determined to do something to alleviate his situation. He talked about it with Dr. William C. Finch, Professor of Religion, and asked him to become Administrative Assistant to the President. Finch would be relieved of his teaching load and become a member of the administrative staff of the University. Though Finch was reluctant to do so, he accepted the appointment for nine months, that is, until just before the beginning of the next academic year. They agreed that he might return to his chair in Religion at that time if it seemed advisable from either his or Score's standpoint.[46] Score was eminently satisfied with the new arrangement, and a few months later the Board of Trustees approved a motion at Score's behest to promote Finch to full professor with tenure.[47]

The major reason for Score's appointment of Finch was to have him take over administrative supervision of Westminster, Weatherford, and Daniel Baker. That work had become so time-consuming for him that he could not handle it properly. Finch was the main Southwestern contact with the three schools from early 1947 until their disassociation from Southwestern in 1949 and 1950.[48] He spent a major portion of his time in travel and correspondence with them. Score was very pleased with his work and told the Trustees at the fall 1947 Board meeting that Dr. Finch was "the right man in the right place."[49]

At first it seemed that the situations at Weatherford, Daniel Baker, and Westminster might be remedied. The influx of students under the G.I. Bill of Rights after the war brought hitherto unheard of enrollments for them. In 1946–1947 the enrollments of Daniel Baker, Weatherford, and Westminster were 495, 243, and 135, respectively. Thereafter, enrollment dropped off every year as the students completed their programs and left. Two years later Score reported to the Executive Committee that most of the veterans had left and that enrollment was at dangerously low levels in each school.[50] Score and Finch tried to encourage the citizens in Brownwood, Tehuacana, and Weatherford to support their institutions by means of financial campaigns, but the results were poor, except in the case of Daniel Baker, where the citizen push came too late.

By early 1949 a combination of introducing higher standards to meet SACS requirements, particularly at Daniel Baker, of the loss of the veterans without compensating replacements, and of the failure of the three communities to take timely responsibility for their institutions caused Score, Finch, and the Trustees to consider the prospect of their disassociation from Southwestern. Since all three colleges were badly in the red and Southwestern could not cover their deficits,[51] their supporters were warned that unless sufficient funds were raised immediately to maintain them properly, Southwestern would be compelled to discontinue its operation of their schools.[52]

In exasperation with the fact that the citizens of Weatherford had progressively withdrawn their support from the college there, Score said: "We feel there is no more reason for our operating a junior college [at our expense] for the citizens of Weatherford than for any other city in Texas."[53] When the mayor of Weatherford sent a letter advising him that the citizens of the city seemed to want to operate Weatherford as a municipal college, the Executive Committee drew up a document of separation in conformity with the merger agreement.[54] At the first Board meeting after Score's death, the Trustees granted Finch and McCook full power to act on the matter of Weatherford College as they saw fit, and they completed the separation.[55]

After the separation, interested parties in Weatherford successfully carried on a campaign to establish a countywide college district, and the school officially became Weatherford College of the Parker County Junior College District. In 1966 the college district purchased ninety acres of land and built a new campus. In 1998 it had 436 faculty members, with 2,585 students for the fall term. By 2001 it had added a new Education Center at Mineral Wells and eleven extension centers in nearby communities.[56]

A final attempt was made to stabilize the budget at Westminster by obtaining income from work programs where products made by students in training would be sold, but it failed when the company that was to purchase the goods was prevented from doing so by its union contract.[57] When it seemed that all efforts over the years to introduce a viable educational program at Westminster had failed, the Board voted to discontinue operations at the end of the 1949–1950 academic year.[58] The junior college was closed in 1950, and its property was sold to the Congregational Methodist Church, which opened another junior college there in 1953 by bringing its Bible College from Dallas. The school was renamed the Westminster Junior College and Bible Institute. It operated at a low enrollment and financial level but managed to stay open until 1971, when 35 students and seven teachers moved from Tehuacana to a forty-acre campus at Florence, Mississippi, near Jackson, a location more central to the majority of Congregational Methodist members.[59]

Because the supporters of Daniel Baker College took the warning of the Southwestern Trustees to heart and raised between $65,000 and $75,000 in cash and subscriptions, the Board of Trustees voted to operate the school for one more year while trying to help it find other connections.[60] In 1950 the college and its assets were transferred back to the original Trustees, who made an agreement with the Dallas Diocese of the Episcopal Church to operate it.[61] Though it had temporary success, once again the school failed financially. It closed in 1953, and its campus was taken over by what is now Howard Payne University. Under its auspices, the main building of what was Daniel Baker College now houses the Douglas MacArthur Academy of Freedom.[62]

In an assessment in November 1952 of the financial effects on Southwestern of the associated colleges endeavor, President Finch concluded that the assets gained from those schools by the University in the separation process had been $127,774 to date. Another $7,500 from Weatherford and $4,300 from Daniel Baker brought the total to $139,574 in early 1953. He did not state a figure for Southwestern's expenses, but he concluded that "although the associated college program did not prove a successful venture, . . . it at least has not hurt the University to the extent once feared."[63]

Score and the Texas Methodist College Association

If Score ultimately had little success with his University of Small Colleges, except, perhaps, in helping Westminster and Daniel Baker survive a bit longer than they otherwise would have and keeping Weatherford alive long enough for it to become established as a strong municipal junior college, and in causing the definitive establishment of the School of Fine Arts at Southwestern as a separate college, he had more success in being one of the principal architects of the Texas Methodist College Association.

Though various attempts had been made to coordinate the work of Methodist higher education in the state over the years, the divisive effects of the removal controversy of 1910–1911 and the economic effects of the Great Depression prevented any enduring coordinated effort from developing. When Score became President of Southwestern in 1942, he brought with him a deep belief that this should be done, and, partly due to his influence, an organization was set up to bring it about.

Bishop A. Frank Smith, chair of the Board of Trustees at SMU and an alumnus and member of the Board of Trustees at Southwestern, was the episcopal leader in the effort. It was largely due to Smith's belief that the two schools should not compete in the field of Methodist giving that Score joined in a discussion with SMU and McMurry in 1943 about cooperating in a statewide campaign.[64] That campaign did not materialize, but Score tried to help McMurry College by launching its $1,750,000 endowment campaign "with a plea to the citizens of West Texas and New Mexico at the annual meeting of the Northwest Texas Conference in Lubbock" on November 10, 1943.[65] In 1946 Texas Wesleyan College and Southwestern University made a joint appeal to the Central Texas Conference and agreed to divide the receipts equally.[66]

These and similar efforts caused the Presidents of Lon Morris College, McMurry College, Texas Wesleyan College, Southern Methodist University, and Southwestern University to appoint in the fall of 1946 an Inter-Conference Commission to study how to encourage further cooperative endeavor. The result was the formation of the Texas Methodist College Association, which held its first meeting on March 9, 1948, at the Methodist Publishing House in Dallas. Bishop A. Frank Smith presided, and the organization was incorporated.[67] According to Ralph Jones, the immediate success of the Association was phenomenal. He says: "During the decade from 1949 to 1959, disbursement to the participating institutions increased from less than $50,000 to $322,067.07. In 1958–59, S.U.'s 20% share was $58,000."[68]

Faculty Tenure and Salary during and after the War

The first effect of the war on faculty rights and privileges was a communication authorized by the Board and read to the faculty by President Bergin at its meeting on January 6, 1942, its first meeting after Pearl Harbor. It informed the faculty officially that "the services of all teachers not in continuous employment will be dependent upon the conditions during the war period."[69] This warning to the nontenured faculty was followed up in May by a Board announcement that for the duration of the emergency the Bylaws relating to eligibility for continuous tenure would be suspended.[70]

Though consideration about revoking the suspension of

tenure began immediately after the war, it was not achieved until April 21, 1948. During the three years before that date, the Board, the administration, and the faculty engaged in a discussion regarding changes that should perhaps be made in the old regulations. When all was said and done, the regulation finally put into effect was virtually the same as that before the war. It stated that "the connection with the University of a professor or associate professor after three years of satisfactory service shall continue during efficient performance of duties and good behavior, unless specifically stated in advance to the contrary." It further provided that salaries might be changed as conditions demanded.

The most interesting piece of the three-part regulation was section "c." It stated that "the Board of Trustees shall not waive its responsibility to the University by failure to dismiss any member of the faculty, officer or employee when in the Board's judgment it is to the best interest of the institution to do so." This unusual provision was obviously a *post hoc* chastisement for the Board's failure a decade earlier to support Bergin in the dismissal of several professors brought up by the President for release. Score dealt with one of the teachers that survived that controversy when he first arrived by offering him service at Westminster College. He refused to take it and was dismissed. The new provision was Score's way of preventing a repeat of the earlier action when Bergin was forced to keep some ineffective teachers because an internal dispute between him and some members of the Board kept it from considering the continuance of the faculty members in question on the basis of actual performance rather than on the basis of the issues involved in the dispute.[71]

Before the arrival of the Naval V-12 Unit in 1943, with the consequent substitution of the tri-semester system, faculty members were employed on a nine-month basis but were paid on a twelve-month basis. Members were required to teach summer school if needed. After the reestablishment of the regular two-semester system in the fall of 1946, all faculty members were employed on a twelve-month basis. A summer leave might be granted one summer in three for professional advancement. Teaching two semesters and summer school left the faculty member with six-and-a-half to seven weeks each year as vacation.[72]

Inflation remained flat during the five years from 1935–1936 through 1939–1940. The cost of living rose only 0.7 percent during those years. Southwestern salaries remained flat as well. Though inflation rose slowly during the five years from 1941 through 1945, it rose rapidly during 1946 and 1947 with the removal of price controls. Since faculty salaries had been frozen during the war, they were already behind when the inflationary surge of 1946 and 1947 occurred. At that point they were adjusted upward. Score remarked to the Board in late 1947 that "the nationwide agitation for increase in the stipends of teachers and the so-called 'minimum salary law' passed by the last legislature has created the most difficult situation I have faced during my tenure at the University."[73] In spite of the difficulty, he did relatively well. Whereas inflation rose 51.7 percent from 1941 through 1947, the average increase in faculty salaries by rank for those years for continuing teachers was: Instructors, 40 percent; Assistant Professors, 70 percent; Associate Professors, 49 percent; and Professors, 58 percent. With these increases, the salary scale for the spring of 1948 for a twelve-month contract was as follows in 1948 and 2000 dollars, the latter in parentheses: Instructors, \$1,600 to \$2,500 (\$11,919 to \$18,624); Assistant Professors, \$2,400 to \$3,500 (\$17,879 to \$26,073); Associate Professors, \$3,000 to \$4,000 (\$22,348 to \$29,798); Professors, \$3,600 to \$5,000 (\$26,818 to \$37,247).

Commenting in 2005 on the contributions of President Score to the University, former President Finch remarked that as a young faculty member he appreciated greatly Score's upgrade of the retirement system. When Finch came in 1941, he had no retirement program. The program instituted at Southwestern in 1935 was minuscule (see Chapter XIV) and did not offer much to look forward to. In 1945, says Finch, "Score installed, with trustee approval, a modern, if limited, retirement program." The individual teacher paid 5 percent of his/her salary, which was matched by another 5 percent by the University.[74] This system continued until July 1, 1959, when Finch, as President, was trying to improve faculty salaries. He did so by having the Trustees approve a measure authorizing the payment of the entire 10 percent by the University. The beauty of the plan was that it effectively improved faculty salaries by a nontaxable 5 percent.[75] Though the University placed its faculty retirement program with the Teachers Insurance Annuity Association in 1937, it opted in and out of the system several times, using various insurance companies as the carriers from time to time. It finally settled on the T.I.A.A. system permanently in 1968.

The Honor System and Grade Inflation

Soon after the arrival of the V-12 Unit, Ullrich sent a note to the faculty that a considerable amount of cheating was occurring on tests, particularly in the larger classes, and that proctors would be used for final examinations.[76] Though this abandonment of the honor system was felt necessary during the war, with the constant arrival and departure of students making it difficult to acquaint them with University traditions, the process of reestablishing the system began soon after the V-12 Unit left. Just as with the tenure system, the reactivation of the honor system was taken as an opportunity to study it carefully. The Board approved the proposed new regulations except for one section and asked that that section be referred to the Student Senate and the faculty for study and agreement. The matter was ironed out without difficulty, and the revised code was introduced to the students in the fall of 1948 by a letter from Dean Ullrich.[77]

After receiving a report from the Registrar in April 1947 about the grades being given by teachers, Score sent Ullrich a memo about grade inflation. He said that in the Registrar's report between 20 percent and 25 percent of all grades were above 90. Only 9 percent were failing. He asked Ullrich to conduct an official investigation. "Evidently some teachers still grade a bit generously," he said. "We might say, more generously than they tend to pay the Preacher on Sunday." A few days later Ullrich replied with a careful analysis of the grade situation by department and by section. Though in it he showed that Home Economics was the worst offender, Score's Department of Foreign Languages was also an offender. Score replied: "I make no apology—it is part of the general situation to which I referred in the previous memo. Things have grown during the war."[78] On a happier note, Berglund requested approval from him on November 24, 1947, for establishing the "Blue Key" and "Cardinal Key" men's and women's honorary societies. Score approved the request.[79]

Student Life and Truman's Visit

Forces related to the war largely governed student life and discipline during the war. The excitement caused by having almost four hundred seamen and marines on campus was always present to some degree. The regular marching drills of the men in uniform were spectacles worth watching, and the athletic teams largely dominated by them exhilarated the campus with their winning ways. The military men caused no major disciplinary problems because they were kept busy, and their officers monitored their discipline more effectively than any college administrator would have dared. The civilian students were also restrained by the fact that gasoline rationing kept them from straying far in the few cars on campus. That having been said, the campus carried on normally. In addition to war bond rallies, dances were held, romances blossomed, and a normal quotient of student cynicism existed. For example, some of the civilian students who had already completed the physical education requirement for their degrees complained about having to engage in the additional five-day-a-week physical training regimen required of all students.

One of the unique organizations on campus was "The Glamazons." It was a "Tall Girls' Club" founded in 1946. The group, originally called Basileis, had twenty-six charter members, who had to be at least 5 feet 7 inches tall. The Dean of Women, Mrs. Ruth M. Ferguson, described the club's members as "representing a cross-section of the six social organizations on the campus." The charter members chose the white calla lily as the organization's flower, and the phrase "divinely tall, divinely fair" as their motto. According to the constitution, the purpose of the organization was "to promote pride in height, grace, poise, and dignity among its members, and to form closer bonds of friendship and maintain high cultural standards." The group lasted almost exactly a decade, voting to disband on May 25, 1956.[80]

One of the memorable events for many students after the war was the visit of President Truman's train to Georgetown on September 27, 1948, during his campaign for a

Students listening to President Truman speak from the rear platform of his campaign train in 1948. President Score rearranged the morning class schedule so that they could walk the short distance across Snyder Field to the railroad station to hear him. From the 1949 *Sou'wester*.

second term. In anticipation of the event, Score had memos posted on every bulletin board of the University to the effect that 8:00 classes would be dismissed at 8:30 to make possible the attendance of anyone who wanted to meet the President's train. Classes scheduled to begin at 9:10 were delayed until 9:40.[81] Since the train stopped on the tracks immediately adjacent to the campus on the west, students were able to attend and return within the allotted hour and ten minutes.

The 1942 Mission Statement

One of Score's first acts as President was to drop from the catalog the mission statement of the University provided by Francis Asbury Mood. That statement read: "It is the function of the University as an institution of the Church to use all proper means to refine the manners, protect the morals, improve the hearts of the young people, and lead them to Christ." Though it said nothing about academics and the Board of Trustees had never formally voted on it, it had appeared regularly in catalogs and been treated as an official statement. President Bishop had stated in 1914 what in fact over the decades unofficially became the mission of the University (see Chapter XII), but no one at the time recognized it as such. It remained for later generations to give it credit for what it was. When Score dropped Mood's statement, he was not so much rejecting a living mission statement that animated the actions of University faculty and other leaders as recognizing it as an artifact of the past that was honored more because of its source rather than because of its content.

Score replaced it with a "Purpose" statement that appeared in the catalog for 1943–1944. That statement appeared in every catalog for the next ten years, when a new one appeared in the catalog for 1953–1954 during the Finch administration. Since then the prevailing mission statement of the University has been modified from time to time and brought into conformity with the history of the school, its current self-perception, and its contemplated future direction. Some elements in them have remained relatively constant over the years, but others have changed. Mission statements subsequent to that of 1953 were adopted in 1962, 1972, and 2001. SACS now requires that each institution study its mission statement carefully in preparation for its decennial accreditation visit. Whether this requirement was a factor in the issuance of Score's "Purpose" statement in 1942 is unknown.

"Southwestern's Purpose," as Score called his statement, had three parts, emphasizing Christian culture and character, the scholarly life among undergraduates, and the vocational callings that students might later pursue. It read as follows:

> For more than a hundred years Southwestern has had as its ideal the development of men and women of Christian culture and character. Our purpose is to train men and women for the high responsibilities of service to the Church and the State.
>
> Southwestern seeks to enhance scholarly life among undergraduates and has maintained a reputation in thorough scholarship, rather than in large numbers.
>
> It is the purpose of Southwestern to do a high grade of work, thus preparing graduates for special achievement in whatever later callings may be chosen. While Southwestern emphasizes the values of broad, general training as preliminary to real achievement in any field of life, it seeks also to offer such variety of courses as to provide definite adequate preparation for later professional training in such special fields as engineering, law, medicine, the ministry, religious and social service for laymen, scientific research, teaching, and other fields.

Score's composition of a new purpose statement for the University did not mean that he was less committed to the Church than other Presidents had been. In fact, though he was a pragmatist in action, he was one of the most ecclesiastical Presidents in Southwestern's history. During the decade of his presidency, religious concerns expressed themselves quite strongly in spite of the war.

The Postwar Religious Scene at Southwestern

In the midst of the war, two persons close to Southwestern were elected bishops. They were W. Angie Smith, pastor of First Methodist Church in Dallas and Paul E. Martin, pastor of First Methodist Church in Wichita Falls.[82] Angie Smith was the brother of Bishop A. Frank Smith. He had been a student during the Charles Bishop years and was the person elected by his fellow students to head the student anti-lynching organization in 1916. Martin was the pastor of the Perkins family in Wichita Falls, who had recently announced their intention to build a new chapel on campus.

After the war Southwestern served as the site for many conferences and Methodist Church meetings. Some of them were the annual Pastors' School, sessions of the Woman's Society of Christian Service, meetings of the Methodist Youth Fellowship of the Central Texas Conference, and a regional Town and Country Conference.[83] These meetings were in addition to regular lectureships, mostly of a religious nature, offered at various times during the year. Mr. and Mrs. J. M. Willson of Floydada established the Willson lectureship in 1947. He was a graduate and she a former student at Southwestern.

The war had a number of effects on young people throughout the country. On the one hand, particularly in the case of many who had served in the armed forces, it created a sense of disengagement from the forms of organized religion. The cruelty and violence of the war destroyed the innocence of their upbringing and produced in them a kind of religious skepticism. On the other hand, the experience of cruelty and violence produced in other persons a deeper religious sensibility and the kind of idealism that comes from having supported a "righteous cause"—the destruction of fascism. This idealism made them determined to help create a better world. Religious enthusiasm ran high in schools across the country. Colleges after the war had more ministerial students than they had ever had before.

Southwestern felt this latter effect strongly, and religious enthusiasm was high. Score reported in late 1947 that the University had over 125 ministerial students in the fall and would run between 150 and 160 in all for the academic year. Southwestern, he said, had more ministerial students that any other Methodist college in the country.[84] One of the categories of student records kept by the Registrar during these years was of those students that intended to enter the Life Service professions. They were ministerial students, Christian Education students, and those students interested in missions or the helping professions. The percentage of the student body in that category in the fall of 1946 was 6.5 percent. By the fall of 1947 it was 12.5 percent and by the fall of 1954 it was 25.2 percent.[85]

Ellsworth Peterson, later Professor of Music and holder of the Margarett Root Brown Chair, states that vesper services were held in the old library auditorium every Wednesday evening, and morning Watch Services were held two mornings every week at seven o'clock. Out of the student body of about 425 when he was in school in the early 1950s, about 50 or 75 people attended these services. The Methodist Student Movement at the First Methodist Church would have perhaps a hundred people or so on Sunday mornings. The Student Christian Association also sponsored outreach programs in the community. Peterson remembers that it would often have game nights at Carver School and take food to particularly needy black families throughout Christmas.[86]

Inspiration for the Negro Fine Arts School

This religious idealism among students, as Peterson indicates, was not limited to preaching services. It was felt in the area of human relations and social service as well. It caused a dedicated piano teacher and some committed students in the Student Christian Association to begin a program in 1946 that for twenty years improved the educational opportunities of African American students in Georgetown. Professor Martha Mitten Allen has beautifully told its story in her book *The Gracious Gift: The Negro Fine Arts School 1946–66.* Most of the following material comes from her book.

One day in a Religious Education class, Professor B. F. Jackson was talking about the need to do something to improve race relations. After class, a student, Dana Green, came up and asked: "What is Southwestern, or you, or anybody doing about race relations?" He thought it looked like "a lot of talking and very little acting."

Jackson, the teacher of the class, was a Southwestern graduate of 1929. He later attended Yale Divinity School, where he majored in social ethics, with a minor in Christian ethics under Richard Niebuhr. For a time in the 1930s he and his wife Elsie were the directors of an American Friends work camp in Mississippi, an unsegregated, cooperative farm with African American and white sharecroppers. During World War II, while working as Director of Education at First Methodist Church in Fort Worth under Dr. J. N. R. Score, he registered as a conscientious objector. He remembers that Score "backed him to the limit." Score brought him to Southwestern in 1945–1946 to work at Westminster College. He came to the main campus at Georgetown in 1946–1947.[87]

The next day Jackson told his class about his conversation with Green. It acted as a stimulant to action. Several students came up after class and said that they were piano majors looking for students to teach. They said that they might "go over to the Ridge [the section where most African Americans lived] and start some piano classes." The three students who did so were Nettie Ruth Brucks, Elmina Bell Krieg, and Barbara Leon Scheef. They were studying at the time with

Iola Bowden, who was training them in her new concept of teaching class piano. It was how to teach students in a group rather than using the traditional one-on-one method.[88]

Brucks was the daughter of a Methodist clergyman. She and her family had once lived in Goldthwaite, a town northwest of Austin with a sign on the edge of town that said, "If your skin is black, don't let the sun set on you in our town." In spite of this experience, she had been an integrationist from her early days. At Southwestern she was accompanist for the Navy Chorus and toured the state with that group. In her senior year, she was named Miss Southwestern and later married Morris Bratton, a ministerial student and football player.[89]

That anything as wildly out of character with the South of 1946 as a Negro Fine Arts School could be carried off successfully might have seemed very unlikely to an outside observer. After all, Georgetown was a city where an ordinance in 1936, only ten years earlier, had made it illegal for a white person to live within the "Negro residential zone" and vice versa.[90] Both Southwestern and the Methodist Church in the South were segregated. Martha Allen describes that segregation as follows:

> Southwestern University was as strictly segregated as the rest of Georgetown. Ellsworth Peterson remember[s] an incident when a campus group invited the Huston-Tillotson College choir to perform at Southwestern and then found out that they could not host them in the dining hall. Nettie Ruth Brucks Bratton told about inviting a black man to speak, under the auspices of the Student Christian Association, and discovering that they would not be able to have him join them for dinner in the dining hall. The SCA "asked the [local] Methodist Church [probably the minister, Billy Morgan] if we could have a pot-luck dinner down at the church, so we . . . went down there and cooked up things and ate down there with him. . . . That's how segregated the University was." No black person could have joined the First Methodist Church, applied to Southwestern, or attended Georgetown High School. Not that there were always rules to that effect: "that's just the way it was. It was very accepted."[91]

Iola Bowden Chambers

Iola Bowden—married at the age of fifty-one and only then becoming Mrs. Chambers—is one of those persons who labors for a lifetime in rather inconspicuous positions and is not fully recognized until after her death as having made a remarkable contribution to the welfare of her fellow citizens. Born in May, Texas, in 1904, she began to study music at an early age. She finished high school at Daniel Baker Academy in Brownwood in 1921 and attended Daniel Baker College from 1921 to 1923, receiving a diploma in piano. While at the Academy she studied under Henry E. Meyer, a teacher in the college, who eventually as dean at Southwestern would bring her to Georgetown. She studied Advanced Piano and Harmony at the Washington Conservatory of Music and received a graduate diploma in piano in 1926. Returning to Brownwood, she gave private lessons and opened a studio. She next went to Baylor University. There, in addition to practicing three to five hours a day, she taught elementary and junior high school students in exchange for her tuition. She overextended herself and developed an ulcer in 1929. She was so ill that she stayed in bed eighteen months while being treated at home by her father, a physician. Her illness was a time for reflection, and, on her recovery, she rededicated her life to Christianity. She felt that she had been selfish and wanted to work for others. On her recovery she began once again to teach private lessons.[92]

Her invitation in 1933 from Dean Meyer to come to Southwestern to study and to teach college students, faculty children, and town children set her on a new path. Though a piano teacher herself, she became a regular student in University classes, completing a B.F.A. degree in 1935 and a B.A. in 1936. She began a master's program at the Cincinnati Conservatory of Music in 1938, completing it three years later by devoting most of her summers to it. During these years, she continued the spiritual journey that had begun with her illness, writing on one occasion, "I had a strange sense that there was something I must do." While at the Cincinnati Conservatory, she was greatly impressed by a "Negro Folk Song Festival," writing afterward: "My style spiritual [sic]." At the same time, she developed a strong classical style while studying under the Finnish-born pianist Madame Karin Dayas. She was quite versatile as a pianist, and on one occasion accompanied Paul Miller's Swing Band at the local U.S.O. during the war. In Georgetown she served as organist at the First Methodist Church. At Southwestern she was head of the junior music department and advanced over the years from Instructor to Associate Professor. She was a member of many state and national music organizations. As a person, she exhibited strong social skills, including a quiet sense of humor, and valued good taste, performance, and etiquette. She tried to inculcate these qualities in her students in the Negro Fine Arts School.[93]

Operation of the Negro Fine Arts School

Iola Bowden took to the idea of teaching piano to black students with alacrity. She was already teaching one black student whom she had met through her next-door neighbors, the Petersons, who employed the student's mother. From this student she learned of other students in the black community that were either studying piano or were interested in it. In order to establish a piano program, however, she would have to secure a place for the instruction, get permission from the University to use its students as teachers, and secure transportation for the children.[94]

The place she obtained was the First Methodist Church. The pastor there was the Rev. James William Morgan, familiarly known as Billy. He became a crucial ingredient in the process. The selection of the First Methodist Church was logical, since Southwestern University had rented its educational building from the middle of 1943 through the middle of 1946 to serve as classrooms for its School of Fine Arts. The School had just moved back on campus into a new frame building, and the church classrooms would be free for a Negro Fine Arts School. The presence in the church of another Fine Arts School run by Southwestern personnel could be seen as a sign of continuity rather than of radical innovation for those that needed that type of validation. When Martha Allen asked Morgan in 1992

Iola Bowden (Chambers) instructing E. J. and Margie Nell Johnson in the Negro Fine Arts School. Southwestern University, Special Collections.

if he had ever asked the Church Board for permission to have the Negro Fine Arts School in the church building, Morgan replied, "No, and I was bragging about it from the pulpit all the time. I think they established a kind of pride, that it was happening. I don't remember any resistance, and that is surprising, because there were plenty of prejudiced people sitting out there."[95]

Bowden's easiest task was to get permission from the University to use the students in the program. Score was known as a friend of disadvantaged persons. "In the summer of 1946," says Allen, "he was appointed to the state Negro School Planning Board to help advance higher education opportunities for African Americans in Texas." B. F. Jackson, who knew Score well, said that if there had ever been "trouble" over the Negro Fine Arts School, "Dr. Score would have fought like a tiger to defend it."[96]

The third problem was to secure transportation for the children. During the first year of the program, the students were taken from Carver School to the Church by private car for their lessons. During the second year, the Board of Education voted that "the music education program conducted by the Student Christian Association of Southwestern University be classified as released time for musical activity for the Carver School students and that a school bus be made available twice a week to transfer the music pupils from Carver School to and from the First Methodist Church and that the cost of the driver be born[e] by the S.C.A. group." At the time of this approval, Bill Finch, soon to be appointed as Assistant to the President at Southwestern, had just been elected as one of the seven persons comprising the Georgetown Independent School District Board of Education, and he had a hand in passage of the motion. The same motion was approved the next year, with him making the motion. In the fall of 1949 the Board voted to absorb the cost of the driver's expense itself.[97]

The Negro Fine Arts School began operation in the fall of 1946 with Miss Bowden and the three student teachers. Bowden went to the Carver School, and the teachers there invited any students who might be interested to take piano lessons. The Southwestern student teachers walked to the Methodist Church twice each week to teach. They reported to Miss Bowden's pedagogy class about how things were going with their students. Allen describes the method used in the first year as follows:

> The first year, there were three teachers, Nettie Ruth Brucks, Elmina Bell, and Barbara Leon. Each of them had a class of four students. They taught harmony, improvisation, and rhythm. Each student had a practice keyboard that teachers had made out of cardboard or wood. One student would be at the piano and the others would play on their cardboard keyboards on their desks. After the student had played, the whole class would discuss how it sounded and whether or not the rhythm was right. Then another student would take a turn at the piano. As the students improved, one teacher would teach harmony and rhythm to the class and another teacher would take the students one at a time to another practice room to listen to them play their longer pieces and help them individually.[98]

The big feature the first year and each subsequent year was the Piano Recital. Notices were printed in the newspaper, and a formal program was printed for the persons in attendance. By 1950 the School had added an art class. The printed program for that year listed thirty piano students and seven art students. A newspaper article also from that year lists an Executive Committee for the School. It was composed of Dr. W. C. Finch, the Rev. J. W. Morgan, Dr. B. F. Jackson, and Miss Iola Bowden. A $100 scholarship was given that year for the first time. The scholarship part of the program grew more important over the years and helped a number of students who would not have gone to college. In a note from Iola Bowden to President Finch in April 1950, thanking him for an increase in salary, she said:

> I am deeply grateful to you for your efforts in my behalf. This and other word received on yesterday made the day a high point in my life. I was greatly moved by the King's Daughters' scholarship because it came, as it seemed to me, as an answer to a colored woman's prayers that the Lord would "open the way", in her words, for her daughter to go to college.[99]

End of the Negro Fine Arts School

The Negro Fine Arts School continued for twenty years until segregated public school facilities finally gave way in Georgetown to comply with the 1954 *Brown v. Board of Education of Topeka* decision and the School was no longer needed. In the spring of 1963, the Negro Fine Arts School announced a change in its procedures. It announced that in light of the probable integration of the Georgetown schools, it would become something different. "It would be ironical," the announcement continued, "if, now that the

Georgetown schools are to be integrated, the Negro Fine Arts School was the only segregated school in town." Students would now be on their own to come to the church after school rather than being excused from study hall. The lessons would be aimed at "quality individual instruction." The article announcing the spring recital that year informed its readers that over "150 Negroes have been students . . . some earning degrees, some now following music as a profession, some becoming teachers, several having earned music degrees." The number of students served over the years was reported as "approximately 200" in a 1965 article. By that year the School had moved out of the Methodist Church and was teaching on a one-to-one basis in the Fine Arts Building at Southwestern University. It now attracted its students from the community rather than from Carver School, which had closed in 1964.[100]

Where Presidents and Trustees were unable or unwilling to break the chains of segregation at Southwestern before 1965, some teachers and students worked for twenty years in a humble but persistent fashion to subtly break those chains. The effect of their work on both themselves and on Southwestern is incalculable. Martha Allen describes that final effect as follows:

> In terms of Southwestern University, the program had come full circle, in another way. Ernest Clark, one of the star students in the Negro Fine Arts School in the 1960s, was the first African American student to be admitted to Southwestern University. . . . It all fit together. The Negro Fine Arts School had filled a need for twenty years for students from the segregated Carver School and for students at Southwestern University. Many people benefited, many were proud of the program, and ultimately, it became the means by which Southwestern could take a first step to integrate the student body. Southwestern integrated in the fall of 1965, Mrs. Chambers retired in the spring of 1966 after the twentieth Negro Fine Arts School recital, the Georgetown School system desegregated in 1966, and the Negro Fine Arts School was no more. It lived on, however, in the memories of its participants. Its legacy can be seen in the lives of the generations of students who were influenced by it.[101]

Ernest Clark was the nephew of Addie Wilson, one of the first students in the program. She had gone on to a career in music. He was the grandson of Ernest Wilson, a well-beloved custodian at one of the dormitories at Southwestern University long before and during most of the years of the program.[102] A very handsome, full-page picture of Ernest Clark at his 1969 graduation recital, dressed in a tuxedo and seated at a piano, appeared in the 1970–1971 University catalog.[103] He later became a versatile, effective, and respected band director in the Dallas Independent School District.

Ernest Clark preparing to perform at his senior recital in 1969. Clark, a product of the Negro Fine Arts School, was the first African-American student to earn a degree from Southwestern. From the 1970–71 Southwestern University Catalog, p. 109.

Mrs. Fondren's Gift for a New Science Building

In early 1946 Mrs. Ella Fondren of Houston announced the gift of a science building to Southern Methodist University. On learning of it, President Score immediately wrote Bishop A. Frank Smith, chairman of the SMU Board. He said: "I rejoice with you, Umphrey Lee and with Southern Methodist University in Mrs. Fondren's gift. If you will help me now with Mrs. Fondren, I feel that we have an excellent chance to get her to duplicate her gift here."[104] Score immediately went to work and almost three years later was indeed able to have her duplicate her SMU gift with a gift to Southwestern for the same purpose.

Though he sought Smith's help, Score already had a solid connection with Mrs. Fondren. She and her husband had been members of St. Paul's Church when he was pastor there from 1926 to 1934, and they had given major financial support for the construction of its new $800,000 building in 1929. Score knew them well. In 1938 they donated nearly half a million dollars to SMU to build the Fondren Library. When Score went to Southwestern in 1942, he began to cultivate her interest in his new school. At the same time that each of the Perkinses received Doctor of Humane Letters degrees after announcing their gift for the chapel in 1943, Score conferred one on Mrs. Fondren in anticipation of the largesse he hoped to receive from her.[105] Thereafter, she occasionally came to Georgetown, where the Scores entertained her. Mary Ann Barbour, daughter of Dean Ullrich, who was a Southwestern student in the early Score years, says that "the Scores really courted Mrs. Fondren." Faculty members were invited to play 84, a favorite domino game of hers, where they were always instructed to let her win.[106] By early 1945 she had been won to the Southwestern cause as well. These attentions had their effect, and she sent "a nice block of Humble Oil stock" to the University and indicated that it was the beginning of an annual contribution.[107] Score hailed the gift as "the establishment of the Fondren Foundation of Southwestern University."[108]

The gift of Humble stock was natural in her case. Her late husband, Walter William Fondren, had made his fortune as an oilman and in 1911 was one of the founders of the Humble Oil Company. Many years later it became Exxon. Walter and Ella married in 1904. She worked with him zealously and invested money independently in a firm that over time became Texaco, Incorporated. That investment was eventually worth millions. He retired in 1933 and founded the Fondren Oil Company. The following year he accepted the post of district director of the Houston office of the Federal Housing Administration. In addition to funding the Fondren Library at SMU, they funded the Fondren Lectures in Religious Thought. He served on many Methodist boards and committees, and together they contributed liberally to Methodist causes. On his death in early 1939, she carried on his philanthropic interests and assumed some of his directorial posts. She replaced him at Southern Methodist University, thereby becoming the first woman to serve on SMU's Board of Trustees and Governors. She was also elected a delegate to several Methodist General and Jurisdictional Conferences. She founded the Fondren Foundation in 1948. The foundation supports agencies for education, health, and human services. She died in 1982 at the age of 102.[109]

In late 1948 she made what was perhaps the most unusual proposal to Southwestern that had been made to that point in its history. Acting anonymously, the "person or foundation," as the write-up of the transaction puts it, offered to lend the University securities in the amount of $1,000,000 to serve as backing for obtaining a bank loan of $500,000, the proceeds of which would be used in turn to purchase stock in a certain corporation that was expected to double in value in the next two or three years. The "certain corporation" was the Transcontinental Pipeline Corporation. The unidentified "person or foundation" lending the securities would pay the annual interest of $15,000 on the loan, said advances to be charged to the increment on the investment when it was finally completed. Southwestern would not be held responsible in any way for the securities. The Board immediately accepted the offer, and the President was "requested to convey to the principal and relatives, the grateful thanks of the Board of Trustees, for the proposal."[110] Though there was general knowledge at the time of who the unidentified person was, Bishop A. Frank Smith identifies her clearly as Mrs. Fondren in an annotation made in his daily journal on November 8, 1948, only three days after the Board meeting. He writes: "Talked to Mrs. Fondren. She has made [a] $500,000 gift to Southwestern for a Science Building."[111]

Unfortunately, President Score died within a year, and it would become the responsibility of his successor to consummate the venture and build the science building. The story of the outcome of the financial undertaking and the construction of the building will be told in Chapter XVIII.

The McManis Gift

If the features of the Fondren gift of late 1948 were the most unusual in Southwestern's history up to that time, another gift given in mid-1949 immediately superseded it in unusual features. It would, when completed in 1955, almost triple the endowment of the University and, in a sense, set the University on the road to its endowment of today. Score was responsible for it, but, as in the case of the Fondren gift, he did not live to see its results. These would in large part accrue to the University after his death.

Ralph Jones says that Fred McManis, of Houston, president of the W-K-M Company, contacted Score on May 23, 1949, about selling his company to five institutions of higher education, of which Southwestern was one.[112] The contact with Score about the gift may have come even earlier than Ralph Jones indicates. Though the McManis gift appeared to come out of the blue to the Executive Committee when Score announced it at a meeting on May 30, it may have been a subject of discussion between him and McManis for several months.[113]

Score received anonymous gifts from time to time, which he duly reported without ever revealing the name of the donor, even to his friend A. Frank Smith.[114] He kept his confidences inviolate. A week before his death, Score sent a tantalizing letter to Smith in which he seems to be musing on this attribute. He says that when he and "a new friend in Houston . . . wound up the matters which are to be signed and sealed this week," the new friend remarked: "I want nothing said about this and do not wish to appear in it at all." About six weeks later, Score continued, "Bill Finch preached at St. Paul's and this brother invited Bill to have dinner with him, whereupon he told Bill the whole story and seemed to be surprised that I hadn't told Bill, and sort of left the impression with Bill that he was just waiting for us to make some big splurge of announcement about it."[115] The "new friend" of Southwestern who was a member of "St. Paul's" was, so says Finch, Fred McManis, who was a member of the Board of Stewards there, and the "matters" under discussion were the terms of the forthcoming gift to Southwestern that was, indeed, "signed and sealed this week," the week of the letter.

Whatever the path of its origin, the nature of the gift was unusual. At the time it was made, Fred McManis was the sixty-nine-year-old president of the W-K-M Company, primarily a maker of valves for the oil industry.[116] He and two partners, Clint Williams and Lee Koen, started the firm in 1918, the initials of their last names giving the firm its name. The most popular early product of the company was a rotary tubing slip. The ones manufactured by W-K-M were such an improvement over all the others that for about ten years W-K-M had about 95 percent of the market.[117] In 1949 McManis was the sole remaining original partner. Though Fred McManis and his wife Carolyn had a son, a daughter, and five grandchildren when he died in April 1952, the couple had no interest in perpetuating their ownership of the $5 million firm or in leaving its proceeds to a foundation to distribute after his death. Consequently, he and his wife devised a plan in 1949 whereby they might receive a competence for themselves while alive, which would eventually be divided among his heirs. The transaction at the same time would benefit five selected institutions of higher education. They would sell their company to the five institutions on very favorable terms.

Each participating institution would only have to put up a minimal sum to become fully invested as an owner. The value of the W-K-M stock would be set at $250 per share, with twenty thousand shares being issued for $5 million. The institutions would pay only $1 per share at the outset, at which point all the company stock would be distributed among them. The other $249 of the share value would be paid to the McManis couple over the years out of the earnings of the company, now under the ownership of the participating institutions. Seventy percent of the annual earnings would be paid on the stock purchases, 20 percent would be carried to the operating reserve, and 10 percent would be paid out to the new owners *pro rata* until the stock was paid out. McManis would at the outset remain as active manager of the company. Once the stock had been entirely paid up, the owners might determine whatever distribution they desired or sell their stock. Southwestern accepted the offer "with appreciation, subject to negotiations."[118]

The negotiations referred to had to do with the tax implications of the transaction. Some of the institutions determined that the offer might be a tax evasion scheme and did not accept. Bishop Smith himself was fearful of the same thing, but Southwestern officials consulted with the Bureau of Internal Revenue and were assured of the complete legality of the matter.[119] In the end, three of the original five colleges to which the offer was tendered refused to participate. Finally, only two colleges were left—Southwestern and Wheaton College in Illinois. The transaction was completed and the papers signed by Score on behalf of Southwestern on September 22, four days before his death.[120]

Because Southwestern did not have the $10,000 in cash necessary at the moment to purchase its allotment of ten thousand shares, McManis advanced the money, to be repaid out of the University's first earnings from the company.[121] Southwestern's annual share of earnings from the company increased from $4,877.24 to $147,053.49 over the five years it was half-owner of the company, a total of $384,743.29, a regular outside income the like of which the school had never before experienced. The story of the sale of its W-K-M stock in 1955, with the resultant addition of $3,055,378.15 to the endowment, will be told in Chapter XVIII.[122]

Lois Craddock and Joe Perkins

On the occasion of receiving the Ex-Students' Outstanding Alumna Award in 1970, Mrs. Lois Craddock Perkins, at the age of eighty-three, penned some comments that were read to the audience by her daughter, Elizabeth Prothro. In them she described why she had maintained a lifelong interest in Southwestern. She said:

> I want to thank all of you for this honor. I am not sure why I am receiving it, unless it is for my loyalty to one of the finest universities in the world. I have felt honored that I was privileged to be a student here [1908–1911], and that I was able to sit in the classes of such eminent scholars as Dr. Cody, Dr. Allen, Dr. Mouzon, Dr. Amos Tinsley, Dr. Sam Barcus, Dr. McGinnis, and dear Miss Howern. I had Bible under Dr. Barcus and Church History under Dr. Mouzon. They gave me a love for my church and for the Bible which has never left me. Few are so fortunate. Of course this dates me, but I want to pay tribute to all who molded my life at Southwestern.
>
> I was here when Dr. Hyer left us and went to Dallas. We couldn't understand why, for we felt that Southwestern was meeting the needs of a Methodist university in Texas. But Dr. Hyer was far-sighted; and look what we have in Dallas! And look what progress we have made here at Southwestern University. We have had some fine, ambitious presidents. . . .
>
> I have always been sorry that I did not return to Southwestern and receive my degree. But after two illnesses, I felt I should teach school and pay off some debts. It was while teaching in Wichita Falls that I met my husband, and teaching and degrees were laid aside. This award means as much to me as a degree, and I am grateful to the Ex-Students Association for adding one more valued tie to my relationship with Southwestern.[123]

The husband she found in Wichita Falls was Joe J. Perkins. Starting out in the mercantile business, he was later involved in business ventures such as coal mining, oil, ranching, and banking. He and Lois were married in 1918. Though they made many gifts to the Wichita Falls General Hospital, Boy Scouts, Camp Fire Girls, Y.M.C.A., Y.W.C.A., Red Cross, Community Chest, Salvation Army, and U.S.O., most of their substantial giving went to Methodist causes in the state. They donated millions of dollars for the endowment and new buildings of the Perkins School of Theology at Southern Methodist University, which, as a result, was named after them. Many of the other major Methodist efforts in the state received their attention as well. They were especially attentive to causes involving women and children, both here and abroad. In addition to money, they gave their time as well. Both of them served in the Church at local, national, and international levels. Their son-in-law, Charles Prothro, who married Elizabeth, served on the Board of Trustees at Southwestern for thirty years (1952–1981), eleven of them as chair, and their grandson, Joe Prothro, served on the Board for seventeen years (1982–1998).

On November 19, 1966, Lois wrote her family a letter that was sealed until her death and read at her funeral service on November 22, 1983. Joe had preceded her in death in 1960. Its text, giving thanks to God, "who has blessed me far beyond my merit," and to her husband, family, and friends for their love and support, now appears on a bronze plaque in the vestibule of the chapel bearing her name.

The Lois Perkins Chapel Project

The origin of the chapel project is connected with an unnamed occasion at Southwestern in which Bishop A. Frank Smith participated. All indications suggest that it was the inauguration of President Russell Score on October 6, 1942. Smith had driven to Georgetown with Bess, his wife, that morning from Austin.[124] Lois Craddock Perkins and Bess Crutchfield Smith, former schoolmates at Southwestern, sat together during the ceremony in the chapel—that is, in the Administration Building auditorium, as it came to be called after the construction of the Perkins Chapel in 1950. Though Lois remarked in an interview thirty years later that Frank was preaching, he actually presided at the inauguration ceremony and was probably making comments about the program and introductory remarks about the distinguished guests. Governor Stevenson and Bishops Holt, Selecman, and Boaz were present. Lois related her chapel conversation with Bess to Joe during the journey home to Wichita Falls. Joe took it to heart and phoned Score that evening. He, in turn, commented on it to Frank Smith in a letter of October 28, only three weeks after the ceremony.[125] Lois remembered the event as follows:

> Frank was up preaching in the old chapel, and Bess and I were sitting together. We got to laughing because the

Joe and Lois Perkins (1944) view an artist's rendering of the proposed chapel built by them in 1950. From the 1944 *Sou'wester.*

old pew shook every time we moved. It would go like this and then like that. We really couldn't move, and we said, "This seat is going to fall down with us before Frank gets through preaching!" Well, when my husband and I were coming home, I told him about the old seats and how it needed to be done over. Then I said, "Joe, I wish they had a nice chapel at Southwestern. It's a shame they don't have a place to have these meetings." Now my husband was a man of very few words, and he didn't say anything. But that night when we got home, he called Dr. Score and said, "Dr. Score, what do you need more than anything else down there?" And Dr. Score said, "We need a chapel, Mr. Perkins." And my husband said, "Well, get an architect who knows his business, and we will give you the money." Just like that! That's the way my husband did things.[126]

In a letter of November 24, 1942, Perkins formally told Southwestern University officials that he and Mrs. Perkins had decided to set aside $75,000 to build and furnish a chapel in honor of Mrs. Perkins. The gift was announced to the public at a meeting of ex-students in Georgetown on April 13, 1943, with the Perkins couple in attendance. Score secured Cameron Fairchild, the architect for both the Cody Memorial Library and the West Gymnasium, as the architect for the chapel.[127] From the beginning, Joe Perkins stated that the chapel would be named in honor of his wife. The project was her idea, and she had attended Southwestern. When, seven years later, before the dedication, she tried to change the name to something else, even to the point of having the Executive Committee vote to change the name to St. Paul's, he would hear none of it. The Board of Trustees rescinded the name-change action already taken by the Executive Committee and restored the name he had chosen.[128]

After the telephone conversation with Perkins, Score immediately began to angle for a larger and more expensive building than $75,000 would allow. He had built four churches, and his idea of a proper chapel for Southwestern far outstripped what Perkins had in mind. He and Score parried from time to time about it. From the outset Score felt that $125,000 to $150,000 would be needed, including the price for an organ. Though he mentioned that figure to Perkins early on, he did not push the matter.[129] The building could not be built during the war in any case.

By the time that Score and Perkins began to think the proper time had arrived to build the chapel in early 1948, wartime inflation made Perkins realize that his initial gift figure would be insufficient, and he added another $75,000 to it. Score called the architect, Cameron Fairchild, and instructed him to get to work on the plans.[130] The Perkins couple were enthusiastic about what he submitted.[131]

They had reason to be. Fairchild had designed a chapel that would cost much in excess of the amount designated for it. The lowest original bid of $346,000 was so far beyond the $150,000 gift that Score did not even relay the figure to Joe Perkins until Perkins pointedly asked for it.[132] Second and third rounds of bidding were still unsatisfactory and frustrated Score completely. He felt at this point that the contractors might be in collusion and that they were rigging the bidding.[133] Privately, he faulted the architect for not being able to design a building close to the amount in hand for it.[134]

Fairchild's final design changed the cruciform plan of the chapel by eliminating the transept that crossed the length between the nave and the apse, by reducing the length of the nave by 20 feet, and by reducing the height of the tower by 16 feet.[135] In the final blueprint, the nave still remained 175 feet long and 47 feet wide, with the main tower rising 92 feet above ground level. The low figure in the fourth round of bids was by Mr. William A. Tarver, Jr., of Austin, Texas, for $189,821.[136] Score was by now convinced that neither the architect nor the contractor could do any better without changing completely to another plan and wrote Joe Perkins on September 8 that the bid had been accepted. Perkins, having followed the bidding process carefully, immediately replied that he would add another $39,000 to the gift.[137] Score responded: "You will never know how deeply I appreciate this latest gift and what a joy it will be as I go along my way to recovery to have the process hastened by the construction of the Chapel."[138]

On September 20, Score sent a long memo to McCook about the contract for the chapel. He said that he had read it carefully and that it was satisfactory with certain exceptions. He then wrote three paragraphs to be inserted about those matters. He concluded: "I trust this contract may be drawn in time for it to be signed Wednesday or Thursday of this week."[139] The final contract was ready the next day. Score, ill and alone in his bedroom except perhaps for someone left to attend him, wrote Joe Perkins his final letter while the first chapel services of the new academic year were being conducted. In it he said: "We signed the contract yesterday [September 21] in due and ancient form, the architect, the University attorney, Dr. McCook the Business Manager, and the contractor coming to my bedroom. We had present two-thirds of the Building Committee, and having agreed upon the contract, the papers were signed. . . . Tell Mrs. Perkins that they are meeting in the Chapel she remembers so well and will march in a body to the site and have the ceremony and that we will send pictures in a little book that I am preparing for you."[140] While he was writing the letter to Perkins, Ruth Score was representing her husband at the groundbreaking ceremonies held in connection with the chapel service. At the conclusion of the service, the audience walked to the site of the new chapel and Mrs. Score turned the first spadeful of dirt.[141]

Score's Illness and Death

The first indications of Score's illness appeared in January 1948. In his report to the Board of Trustees in April, he says that a week after a splendid dinner meeting in Houston at the beginning of the financial campaign, he had to go to bed and was "totally incapacitated" for more than a month.[142] In spite of various, seemingly small ailments that continued to bother him from time to time, he followed his normal vigorous pattern of activities for the remainder of the year and into early 1949, traveling widely throughout the state and nation. On May 26, he wrote Lyndon Johnson that for the past several days he had had "a bout with a strange sort of bug that has laid me low."[143] A few days later his condition was such that the Executive Committee ordered him to take a three-week vacation, encouraging him to take the time off by allotting him $20 per day in addition to his regular salary for vacation expenses, "subject only to the advice of his physicians concerning his vacation plans."[144]

Apparently he did not take the vacation, because on June 16 he wrote Joe Perkins about a recent visit to Wichita Falls, where he preached. He says: "You will recall that I had a coughing fit during the sermon at First Church, Wichita Falls. After leaving your house, Ruth and I started home, and on the way, the most violent sinus infection I have had in fifteen years hit me. The only day I have put in a full day of work since then was Commencement day. I have just come back from Houston from a stay in the Methodist Hospital."[145]

Though, because of the timing, it is tempting to mark down the sinus attack as a misreading of his heart condition, it probably was sinus. Score suffered with sinus problems throughout his career, and he would not have confused it with angina. As a chaplain in World War I, he was gassed and had chronic sinus problems ever after.[146] The coughing fit could have well been problems with his lungs exacerbated by his cigar smoking over the years. Throughout his career, Score's dominant personality and voracious appetite for work made those around him overlook his health problems. He never complained about them. During his

Mrs. Score turns a shovel of dirt for the beginning of work on the chapel in 1949 as I. J. McCook looks on. From the 1950 *Sou'wester.*

pastorate in Houston in 1929 or 1930 he suffered a bout of poliomyelitis that kept him out of the pulpit for three or four months. "Afterward," says John, "he always had trouble with his legs. His legs always hurt."[147] The pain in his legs, his sinus problems, his constant cigar smoking, and the stress from constant overwork apparently caught up with him in 1948 and 1949 and brought him low.

Score's hospitalization for examination in Houston seems to have taken place in connection with the ordination service of John in June of 1949. Before the service, how long before is unknown, he entered the hospital quietly so as not to attract visitors. He was surprised when Durwood Fleming, the pastor of St. Luke's Methodist Church, who had probably learned about the hospitalization from Smith, visited him there. He says he found Score in bed surrounded by books and papers.[148] Writing to Smith after his return to Georgetown, Score says: "May I thank you again for your courtesies to me at Houston. I was not sure I could get through the ordination service but I knew you did not know what condition I was in and, of course, John and I shall both always remember that hour. . . . I have followed the doctor's orders strictly since returning. I hope to be allowed to go down stairs tomorrow and to the office for an hour a day beginning Monday."[149]

At the beginning of the Executive Committee meeting on Friday, July 1, Dr. Cody, the chairman, reminded those in attendance of the effect on Dr. Score of the long meeting on May 30. He indicated that he had no desire to keep anyone from talking but suggested that a time limit be placed on discussion so that action might be expedited. Discussion on each issue, therefore, was limited to ten minutes.[150] The next week Score went to a clinic in Fort Worth for another examination. On the 13th he wrote to Trustee Eugene B. Germany that he felt the doctors had now discovered his difficulty and that before too long he would be returned to circulation.[151]

Score's ailment gradually became a matter for conversation among his fellow ministers. Bishop Smith wrote him on July 29 that he was sorry to hear he was back in bed. He also told him that "several brethren" had told him a couple of weeks ago that he intended to resign. "I told them they were rather premature." On receiving Smith's letter, insecurity took momentary possession of Score. He wrote back that his resignation "was wishful thinking on the part of the brethren for I have not mentioned it to a soul." He must have meant that he had not mentioned it to anyone individually outside of a core group of Trustees because he had indeed offered his resignation two weeks earlier, to whom or what group, he does not say, but, he says, "it was not accepted." "Of course," he continues, "I feel I am too young to retire and I know I haven't money enough to retire, and hope I shall not have to. At least I am making no plans in that direction."[152] His reasoning in the letter is somewhat conflicted.

Smith wrote back the following day, August 2, and assured Score that the men who had mentioned his resignation were not indulging in "wishful thinking" but were "greatly distressed to think that your resignation could be even a possibility. No one of them mentioned a heart involvement, either." Smith says that even he has just learned from Dr. Cody that he might have a slight angina. "Your word," he continues, "is the first I had heard of your proposing to the Executive Committee, or whoever it was, that you resign. Don't you think of such a thing! If you can't arrange your affairs there so as to get the rest you need, take a year's leave of absence, which the university will gladly give you on full pay, and go wherever you think it best to for recuperation. But dismiss the possibility, even, of your leaving Southwestern. That cannot and must not be. Dr. Cody is of the opinion that your heart involvement is not of a serious nature. I do hope and pray so. Take care of yourself. That's something you have never done in your life, but the odds are too great now for you to run any unnecessary risks. Please keep me informed. No person will be more concerned than I."[153]

Soon the doctors told Score that his heart condition was permanent but not serious and would probably not be fatal. By now, however, he was beginning to have doubts about such medical encouragements, if they can be called such. He wrote Smith that he had had "four attacks of angina; two of them mild and two not so mild. In fact, I had one while at the clinic in Fort Worth a month ago[,] which lasted almost two hours, and which I thought was going to kill me. Of course, now I have the nitroglycerin[,] which seems to be good. I feel I have made considerable progress during the past week, but I am still in bed or upstairs only and have been ordered not to think about going back to the office until the middle of September."[154]

By mid-September he began to feel that the encouraging words of Ruth and John about his condition were wishful thinking. Aside from them, Frank Smith was his closest confidant, the one person to whom he completely unburdened himself. He told him everything. He said in one letter: "Ruth and John think I am improving. I don't, which seems to be a difference in opinion, but I know how I feel. I have had four spells of angina since coming home and as John remarked this morning, they seem to come in cycles, two at a time, and in fact they have been coming that way for two months. I had two at a time, skipping a day, three times before going to Houston. In the hospital in Houston, I had two within twenty-four hours. I had another pair Monday and Tuesday of this past week and the latest pair Saturday and Sunday. I am anxious to talk to Ghent Graves and to see what the next cardiograph will show."[155] Smith replied the next day, concluding his letter with these words: "And you know a lot of us are knocking daily at the door of that Great Physician, if so be we can help Him to help you."[156]

Score answered two days later. He said: "The last paragraph of your letter means more to me than you will ever know. I have had days of very real discouragement because I think whatever it is that is wrong with me has not followed the normal pattern, and I am having more discomfort and more pain now than I had four weeks ago and certainly more than I had eight weeks ago. How much of this is psychological, I don't know. A good part of it may be psychoneurosis, but it is still pain, and as long as I think it is there, Mrs. Eddy was right, it is there."[157]

During all this time, Score kept up with University affairs as best he could. His secretary brought or sent what was considered to be absolutely essential mail to his bedroom. He dictated replies as he was able. John came to be of considerable help as well. He would occasionally answer memos or letters, prefacing his replies with "Daddy says," or "Daddy asked me to acknowledge your letter," or something similar. Finch was recognized on campus more and more as the person to talk to. He carried reports on the President's condition to the faculty. Score's last efforts were expended in formally accepting the McManis gift for Southwestern and in signing the chapel construction contract.

At last, at 12:40 p.m., Monday, September 26, 1949, he died. A. Frank Smith's grief at Score's death was profound. He wrote in his daily journal: "He was my dearest friend."[158] John Score says that Bishop A. Frank Smith and his father were great friends and that while serving in Houston together they talked every night, just at bedtime. His mother said that sometimes her husband would get so quiet listening to Frank Smith that she would get up to see if he had gone to sleep talking.[159]

Diagnosis of Score's Ailment

Attempting to learn more about Score's heart ailment, I consulted two Georgetown physicians who knew President Score. One was Dr. Hal Gaddy, now retired. Gaddy and his wife, Peggy, came to Georgetown in 1948. She became Score's secretary soon after arriving, and Gaddy, the new doctor, was called to his bedside once when Score had a flare-up. He says he found Score in bed at home in an upstairs room. Score told him at the outset that he was using a Houston doctor, almost certainly Dr. C. C. Cody, Jr., as his primary physician. Though that doctor had told him to quit smoking cigars, he was sitting in bed at the time with a cigar. The visit must have been before June 20, 1949, because Score wrote Smith on that date that he was following the doctor's orders strictly. He was suffering, says Gaddy, from a coronary artery condition. There was not much, he said, that could be done for him.[160]

The other physician was Dr. Douglas Benold. Benold was a student at Southwestern when Dr. Score was President and later studied under Dr. C. C. Cody, Jr., at the Baylor School of Medicine in Houston. After reading the material available on Score's condition, he wrote: "I have just read over the multiple quotations [you provided] by various writers concerning Dr. Score's final illness. These letters tell a clear but sad story. From what I read, I agree with Dr. Gaddy that Dr. Score almost assuredly died of a myocardial infarction (or "coronary thrombosis" or "heart attack" in common language). Unfortunately, in 1949 there was no good treatment available for coronary artery disease."[161]

Afterwards

Simple but appropriate services were held for President Score the day after his death in the First Methodist Church of Georgetown. Bishops Martin and Smith and the Reverends Neal D. Cannon and J. William Morgan officiated.[162] The University held a memorial service on campus on October 6, the eighth anniversary of Score's inauguration as President. Because, likely at his request, his body had been cremated, the Executive Committee voted to allow the altar in the soon to be built chapel to be used as a repository for his ashes.[163] Mrs. Score thanked them and Mrs. Perkins for allowing it. Writing for herself and John, she said: "We are so appreciative of you[r] allowing the remains of his earthly body to be placed here on the campus where his love and interests were centered. I think under the Chapel altar will be the appropriate place and Mrs. Perkins, like you, has graciously consented to this."[164]

The Board included a long tribute to Score in the min utes of its November meeting. Its statement summarized Score's contribution to Southwestern in simple but strong language. It said in part: "In the administration of the affairs of Southwestern University during the period covered by Dr. Score's presidency, something more was needed. An unshakable inner courage and a great daring in the making of decisions were indispensable. Wrong decisions or no decisions would have proved fatal. Dr. Score had the ability to read the signs of the times, and the courage to act with precision."[165]

Immediately after Score's funeral, the Trustees met in the same sanctuary where the service had been held to appoint someone in his place.[166] There they authorized Dr. William C. Finch to assume executive responsibility as Acting President "with full powers and authority to act on behalf of Southwestern University."[167] At a meeting of the Executive Committee two weeks later, he spoke of the honor the Trustees had accorded him, but he encouraged them to select a new President as soon as possible so that the President might set his policies for the new year. At that point, the chair, Dr. Cody, stated that the Committee had full confidence in Finch's establishing such policies and that he should do whatever he felt was right and proper, a sentiment immediately endorsed by the full Committee.[168] Though the full Board approved a presidential nominating committee on November 15, it noted with approval the recent statement of the Executive Committee voicing its confidence in Finch and endorsed its action of having him "make recommendations for establishment of policy."[169] It was apparent from these actions that Finch would be given every opportunity to prove himself worthy of being selected as permanent President.

Mrs. Score was given every consideration as well. On the day after Russell Score's death, she was told that there was no hurry for her to vacate the President's home and that his salary would be paid to her until the next Board meeting in November.[170] When that time arrived, the Board offered her occupancy of the home until the end of the current school year if she wished. She would be paid $300 per month, rather than the President's regular salary, until May 31, 1950. On Finch's recommendation, the Board also agreed to appoint her as a field representative for the school. This position would pay her an additional $300 per month.[171] At the end of the stipulated time, she moved to Dallas, where she occupied a position with the Texas Methodist College Association, the association that her husband had been so instrumental in forming a few years earlier.[172]

MISSION DEFINED

1949–2000

18 Emergence of a New Campus (1949–1961)

Finch's Reputation and Score's Support

Seldom has an institution been as fortunate in a leadership transition in otherwise unfortunate circumstances as Southwestern was in 1949. Having lost a dynamic President, it had on hand a man with outstanding credentials who knew the institution well and had been working with the former President for several years in a major leadership role. His reputation was such that other colleges in search of a new President were looking at him as a candidate for their vacancy.

In his last year, President Score found himself in the unusual situation of writing letters of recommendation for Finch for those positions and counseling with him about them. One of the schools interested in Finch was Score's alma mater, Central College in Missouri. Score himself had been considered for the presidency there before he came to Southwestern in 1942. A memo from Score to Finch on May 23 suggests that Finch met a committee from Central on April 23, 1949, but was put off by what he conceived to be the negative attitude of Bishop Holt, who was on the committee.[1] Though in the memo Score tries to persuade Finch "not to close the door" to his thinking about Central because of Holt, he provides other thoughts he hopes Finch will consider. Because Finch has recently exercised his option of returning to the classroom at Southwestern for the fall semester, Score tells him that he does not think he will ever be as happy as he "ought to be back teaching Bible at Southwestern." He suggests that faculty affairs would soon "become a new set of irritations" for him as a teacher, presumably equal to those he is experiencing as an administrator. Anyway, says Score, the situation at Daniel Baker will probably require his presence through the next fiscal year, and he hopes, without trying to bind him, that Finch will be open to continue in his present role that long.[2]

In September Score received a letter from the Acting President of Southwestern College in Winfield, Kansas, another Methodist college, informing him that it was considering Finch for the presidency there and asking him to "evaluate this man's ability."[3] Whether Finch knew that he was being considered is not known. Though he was in his last month of life and suffering from severe angina attacks, Score felt compelled to respond. He replied: "Dr. Finch is tall, has an almost commanding presence, makes an exceptionally good appearance. He is married to a splendid and attractive woman and they have two fine boys. Their home life is happy. For the past two and a half years, Dr. Finch has served the University as Administrative Assistant with particular responsibility for the colleges located away from Georgetown. . . . Because of my illness for the past three months, he has had to neglect the work at Daniel Baker in order to carry my work as well as his own. He gets along well with men and I think would make a great college president. I personally shall not stand in his way but I should hate very much to lose him."[4] Finch was thirty-nine years old at the time.

Development of the Score-Finch Friendship

Score's friendship with Finch seems to have developed almost instantaneously from the time of their first contact. In the same week that he was elected President of Southwestern, Score invited Finch to Fort Worth to teach in a training school at his church and to preach for him at an evening service.[5] Finch accepted, and the friendship developed rapidly. In the summer of 1943, Finch took a two-week Naval Indoctrination course at Columbia University. The course was designed to give him knowledge of the various branches of the navy and marine corps to prepare him for his role as Director of Student Life at Southwestern with a V-12 Unit on campus. This was followed by about ten days at the Marine Officers Candidate School at Quantico, Virginia.[6] In the fall after Finch's return, Score invited himself to a wrestling match that Finch planned to attend by means of a humorous memo, suggesting that, as chaplain, he should not attend his "customary wrestling orgy" unless "you will include me in your party."[7] The young thirty-three-year-old Professor of Religion must have felt complimented by this attention from his President.

Soon Finch felt that he must play an active part in the war effort and volunteered for the navy chaplaincy. In mid-January 1944, on the same day that the Board of Trustees granted him a Leave of Absence for the duration of the war and six months thereafter, Score wrote a letter of recommendation for him to the navy.[8] He said that the loss of Finch would be "a blow to the school" but that Finch felt it was his duty to serve the navy. "Only under these circumstances," continued Score, "would we consider releasing him at all."[9] As Finch was preparing to leave about two weeks later, Score sent him a memo to accompany the book he was contributing to Finch's "professional library as a Navy Chaplain." It was entitled *Fifteen Years in Hell.*[10] Score had served for a year in World War I as a chaplain.

Once Finch had been posted to active service, the two men wrote to each other frequently. The letters were long and full of information about their activities. Score responded to a letter from Finch on December 2, saying: "It was so good to hear from you. In fact, I wonder if you know how very much I have missed you. So on my return from New York, to find your letter brought me real pleasure indeed." He remarked that he was sorry to hear that Finch would soon get sea duty because it might delay his return to Southwestern.[11] Before his ship was commissioned, Finch made a brief return to Georgetown, where he visited his wife and sons and saw the Scores. Toward the end of January 1945, he said that his ship, the U.S.S. *Bingham*, was busy with commissioning, shakedown, and amphibious training. He said he liked his new assignment very much.[12]

Writing later to Score from his ship somewhere in the South Pacific, Finch reflected on the effects of war on the sailors around him. He said: "It is extremely difficult for a young and immature person to retain his sense of values when the conditions about him are so generally destructive of such." He added that they had had some interesting experiences, "none particularly dangerous or exciting, except one mildly so. I suspect that many of the things would recall old memories to you, convoy travel, crowded ships, troops all over the ship, and awkward and handicapped services on the open deck with the addenda of worship at a minimum but the attendance and enthusiasm of the men higher than I'd expected."[13]

In June Finch wrote Score that his ship had been "swinging at anchor in one of the lovely but lonely Pacific atolls for more than a week. I am able to write you now that we were in Saipan and Eniwetok about a month ago. I was ashore briefly in both places." There was lots of evidence of bitter fighting in both places, he said, and some Japanese were still in the hills. "It is nevertheless, an inspiring thing to see two or more hundred men stand quietly in field dress around a rough hatch, with only the sketchiest of worship centers and aides available, to receive communion."[14] Score replied not long afterwards: "I think that you have sensed through the months that somehow you have been pretty close to me, and I have gotten the picture of a good and growing man."[15]

The war ended quickly, and Finch wrote Score from Pearl Harbor on October 10, saying that his ship would be back in San Francisco on the 17th.[16] With the tri-semester system still in effect, Score told him that the new term would begin November 5.[17] Finch wrote back, authorizing Score to arrange his courses as needed.[18] He returned and resumed his regular activities as teacher and chaplain. Score appointed him Administrative Assistant almost exactly a year later.[19]

Transition and Agenda of the New President

By the time of Score's death, Finch had been working closely with him for almost three years in an administrative capacity. Because of Score's appreciation for his work, Finch was well acquainted with almost everything undertaken by the University during those years. In addition, he had handled most of the routine matters of the President's office during the last three months of Score's life. He was well known by faculty and students and was respected by the Trustees. In addition to Finch's natural aptitude for working easily with people, the Trustees accepted Score's estimate of him as their own. Their appointment of him only as Acting President on September 27, 1949, was more a matter of protocol than an indication of lack of trust in him. The normal nomination process would be followed, with due time for deliberation. That time, in this case, was short. At the next Board meeting on April 14, 1950, less than six months later, the Nominating Committee presented Finch's name for President. Nothing appears in the record about any other person being considered. The roll-call vote of the Trustees voting by Annual Conferences was unanimous in favor of him.[20]

There were four pressing items on the agenda left by Score. They were: (1) the final disassociation of Southwestern from Westminster, Weatherford, and Daniel Baker Colleges; (2) the construction of the Lois Perkins Chapel; (3) the consummation of the W-K-M transaction; and (4) the construction of the Fondren Science Hall.

The first of these matters, that of the affiliated colleges, was so far advanced when Score died that, as described in Chapter XVII, it was addressed and disposed of within a year except for residual details, mostly involving relatively small financial settlements and land disposition, that hung on as late as 1956.[21]

There would be no Southwestern University system. There would be a Southwestern University in Georgetown that over the next half century would gradually restructure itself into an institution devoted exclusively to preparing students in the liberal arts and sciences and to giving them appropriate pre-professional preparation at the undergraduate level.

With this action of disassociating Southwestern from the three off-campus colleges, Finch had taken the first step toward one of the defining characteristics of his administration—the clearing away of the underbrush of almost forty years of operating as a baccalaureate institution while trying at the same time to maintain some of the characteristics of a major university. This action of relinquishing control of the non-Georgetown colleges began a retrenchment process that would also include dropping the football program, abandoning the graduate program, giving up summer school, and reducing the size of the faculty to fit a scaled-down academic program.[22]

On the more positive side, Finch's administration would see the successful completion of three projects initiated by Score—the construction of the Lois Perkins Chapel (1950) and the Fondren Science Hall (1954), with the establishment of a $5 million endowment, principally from the W-K-M venture (1954). The Finch administration would also develop its own projects. They would be the construction of the McCook-Crain Clinic (1953), the Martin Ruter Dormitory (1955), the Brown Swimming Pool (1955), the Kyle E. White Religious Activities Center (1956), the Alma Thomas Fine Arts Center (1956), and the Bishops' Memorial Union (1958). Finch would also leave the Ernest L. Kurth Hall under construction to be completed by his successor. Old cross streets would be removed from the interior of the campus, and new streets and parking lots would be put in place, creating basically the present-day configuration of the center of the campus. A landscaping program would also be instigated, involving the construction of a golf course and the installation of a major campus irrigation system. All of this would be done while maintaining a balanced operational budget every year. It would not be done, however, as part of a long-range planning process. As Finch commented many years later, "We were running for one year at a time, or one day or one week at a time."[23]

Though Finch, unlike Bergin, did not mention a set of clearly specified objectives when he assumed the presidency, he did have a "clear vision" of what he was doing and what he wanted to achieve. In a report less than two years after becoming President, he described that vision to the Trustees.

> The war situation, following the completion of the Veterans' Program has necessitated a contracting in the place of an expanding program. *This has been undertaken with care to conserve every essential feature of our academic program* [italics added]. The University presently stands at a high peak in its reputation and prestige. In the national study of good first-class small independent colleges made by "Good Housekeeping" magazine and appearing in the February [1951] issue, of the four Texas colleges listed, two were Catholic womens' colleges and the two Protestant institutions were Rice and Southwestern. This is the classification we desire, deserve and must maintain. There is no other first-class liberal arts college in the Southwest presenting as effectively the high type of education offered by Southwestern. There is every reason to believe that the Christian liberal arts education embodied in the University's program will increasingly be recognized and will increasingly serve a unique area in the educational system in the Southwest. . . . With the completion of the Science Building, we shall have seven of the ten permanent buildings called for in the future campus program. . . . *The Trustees and the Administration working jointly[,] with a clear vision of the University we desire[,] can build during these days[,] despite the necessary retrenchment, a physical plant, permanent endowment, and an educational program which will make Southwestern the most outstanding college of liberal arts and pre-professional work in this entire area* [italics added].[24]

Retrenchment: Reducing Faculty Numbers

Finch's mention of retrenchment as a necessity was based on what everyone knew. Enrollment was declining, and Southwestern had to accommodate its program to that fact. In the fall of 1951, its fall semester enrollment bottomed out at 414. Just as the school had added faculty and staff members to handle its large enrollments during and immediately after the war, with a peak of 870 in 1947, it must now gear down to its present level. Finch and McCook took this into account when preparing the budget for 1951–1952 and presented one to the Board calling for severe faculty cuts. In addition to the voluntary departure of two persons, Dr. B. F. Jackson in Religious Education and Audio-Visuals and the Reverend Mr. Howard Knox in Publicity, both of whom resigned to accept other positions with the Church, he announced that he had notified seven faculty members that their services would no longer be needed. He said that very few salary adjustments had been made, though he recognized the hardship this posed for University personnel with inflation on the increase. To indicate the good faith of the administration, he proposed that all faculty members and persons in the offices of the President and business manager making less than four thousand dollars per year be given token increases of one hundred dollars as evidence of the University's desire to do everything possible.[25]

In the final budget for 1951–1952, the total salary for all institutional personnel was 19.4 percent lower than that for the preceding year, four-fifths of the decrease coming from the reduction in faculty numbers.[26] Some persons in the faculty resisted the radical decrease. After a teacher complained in his report that the loss of a colleague in his department had caused a "loss of faith" in the administration's desire to maintain an adequate department in his area, the Board chastised him, saying that it took "exception to the concluding paragraph in his report to the President . . . , that his remarks were not well taken and that he must be more courteous and considerate in future comments on official actions."[27] Reporting on the reduction of institutional personnel in April 1952, Finch said that since 1949 the number of faculty members had been reduced from fifty-three to thirty-seven and the administrative staff, including secretaries, matrons, and health service personnel, had been reduced from twenty-three to fourteen, a reduction of 38 percent and 30 percent, respectively.[28]

Retrenchment: Dropping the Football Program

In addition to approving a major decrease in faculty numbers, the Board also approved the elimination of football. The intercollegiate football program that had begun in 1908 was dropped. Finch told the Trustees that even after having made severe cuts in the number of institutional personnel, he and Dr. McCook could not present a balanced budget without making significant programmatic cuts as well. Inasmuch as the total deficit for athletics over the previous twelve-year period had been $207,336.10, with the largest annual deficit of $35,579.00 having been recorded in the year past, they felt that it was the logical program on which to focus. Athletics had run a balanced budget only one year since 1939–1940, the magic year of 1943–1944, when the Southwestern team loaded with V-12 football players had gone to the Sun Bowl and won the trophy. In addition, because of the Korean War, now being fought, Coach "Spot" Collins had just been recalled to the marines.[29] A number of colleges had abandoned football, he said, and done very well. In spite of these elements, he was very reluctant to do so. He commented to the Trustees about his football recommendation as follows:

> I, personally, would like to see it retained if we could afford it. Under the present circumstances it is difficult for me to see how we can afford to include this item in the budget which is already heavily strained. Our academic and physical needs are so great and our resources so limited, that it has seemed imperative to us, recognizing the possible danger involved in student discontent and ex-student dissatisfaction, nevertheless, to recommend the budget without the inclusion of football. We are including [outside the budget] the additional figure for football and if the Board sees fit to underwrite and attempt the program we would be most happy and pleased to see it continued.[30]

Finch was telling the Trustees, in effect, that if they wanted to balance the budget without giving up football, they would have to find the way to do it themselves. They reluctantly approved the budget as presented. Nevertheless, perhaps to assuage the old alums mentioned by Finch in his statement, they passed a motion of regret at having to do so.[31] When looked at over five-year intervals from 1935-36 to the end of Finch's tenure in 1960-61, the percentage of athletic expenditures as a portion of the total Educational and General Expenditures of Southwestern was as follows:[32]

Year	Total Intercollegiate Athletic Expenditures*	Total other Educational and General Expenditures	Total Athletic and Other E&G Expenditures	Percentage Athletic Expenditures of Total
1935–36	15,551	98,789	114,340	13.6
1940–41	14,342	127,539	141,881	10.1
1945–46	45,236	241,225	286,461	15.8
1950–51	50,956	320,565	371,521	13.7
1955–56	15,168	455,531	470,699	3.2
1960–61	29,018	784,816	813,834	3.6

*Includes athletic grants in aid.

The percentage of the annual Educational and General budget devoted to athletics during the Fleming and Shilling years thereafter ranged from 2.4 percent to 4.1 percent at each five-year interval.

Retrenchment: Abandoning the Graduate Program

The graduate program, though a victim of the general retrenchment begun in 1949, would hold on for another five years. Annual enrollment in the graduate program during Finch's early years averaged between ten and twenty students each year, with about five persons receiving degrees annually. There were nine students in the program when the Trustees voted to abandon it in 1955.

During the 1953–1954 academic year, the regional accreditation agency of Southwestern placed it in an uncomfortable position when it issued new regulations for accredited graduate programs. The most difficult new rule was that one-third of the courses in the student's major field must be limited to graduate students only. Since Southwestern could not meet this criterion in most fields in which it offered the master's degree, the Board voted to restrict the entry of new persons for the degree to the field of education.[33]

During the ensuing year, representatives of the Southern Association recommended that Southwestern either drastically refinance its graduate work or discontinue it.[34] In coping with this recommendation, the faculty Graduate Committee considered the option of enlarging the program and setting it up as a separate unit adequately staffed and financed. Its report stated that such a program should have at least fifty students and four full-time graduate professors. In addition, an infusion of funds would be needed to defray the needed library acquisitions, to set up special laboratory facilities, and to offer scholarships to students. This expanded program was calculated to cost fifty thousand to seventy-five thousand dollars annually.[35] Since the Committee felt that the prospect of finding that kind of money was unrealistic, it strongly recommended that the graduate program be discontinued and that the University's efforts be concentrated on its undergraduate program. Finch concurred in this recommendation and said that "the University's efforts [should] be concentrated on developing the finest and strongest undergraduate college in the South."[36] Though some of the Trustees, particularly Dr. C. C. Cody, Jr., opposed dropping the graduate program and felt that a stronger effort should be made to resist the demands of the Southern Association, they could not overcome the essential fact that Southwestern could not afford the program any longer.[37]

Thus ended Southwestern's graduate program eighty-five years after the first master's degree had been given to Ryland Fletcher Young in 1880. The program was appropriate for Southwestern when it began work in Georgetown. Southwestern had been established by Mood to be a full-fledged university, not only in name but also in fact. By 1955 it had lost that possibility. Also, the master's degree in Southwestern's early years was really an intensification of the bachelor's degree, with no clear line separating undergraduate from graduate courses. The same faculty that taught undergraduate courses could offer a master's degree. By 1955 the master's degree had become more narrowly focused in American higher education and emphasized specialization and a modicum of research. It required teachers with higher degrees emphasizing those same qualities to offer it. When faced with the reality presented by the new accreditation standards, Southwestern accommodated the inevitable and dropped the program.

Retrenchment: Giving Up Summer School

Southwestern began to hold a regular summer school in 1903–1904. Beginning with 32 students, its summer school enrollment increased regularly until 1910–1911, when 128 students attended. Enrollment numbers fluctuated thereafter, dipping as low as 67 in 1913–1914 but running as high as the 240s and 250s for four consecutive years in the mid-1920s. Though holding up pretty well during the decade of the 1930s, with an average of about 160 students each summer, enrollment declined to an average of about 125 for the four summers prior to the arrival of the V-12 Unit in 1943. With the arrival of the V-12 Unit in that year, the University did away with its normal system of two eighteen-week semesters each year and inaugurated a system of three sixteen-week semesters (tri-semesters), leaving only one month without classes. Summer school was dropped and was not instituted again until the restoration of the old two-semester calendar for the 1946–1947 academic year.

Summer enrollment never picked up again after the war to prewar levels. It was 114 in 1952, 86 in 1953, and 66 in 1954. Because of this postwar decline, a faculty committee studied the matter and in 1953 recommended that summer school be discontinued. Finch held the recommendation in abeyance for a year, but, when enrollment dropped another 20 students in 1954, he added his voice to the faculty recommendation. He said that "it is uneconomic in time and personnel to tie up 30 faculty members for 66 students." Nevertheless, he stated that this recommendation should not affect faculty salary. The faculty would now be paid the same for the new nine-month schedule as for the present eleven months.[38] Also, all the salaries of kitchen employees, janitors, and similar jobs would be maintained. They would be given other responsibilities to complete their time.[39]

Effect of the Retrenchment Program

By eliminating summer school teaching from the regular obligation of faculty members, Finch began a faculty revitalization program that expanded to include elements not foreseen at the time, including the reduction of course loads from fifteen to twelve semester hours for most teachers, the sharing by the University in the expense of the faculty hospitalization and insurance program, the inclusion of Social Security coverage for the faculty and staff, the addition of a summer study grant program, the setting up of a paid sabbatical leave program very much the same as that in effect today, and a salary augmentation program.[40] The salary augmentation program was aided by a Ford Foundation grant of $171,000 specifying that the grant money must be kept in the endowment for ten years.[41] Finch reported that the faculty salary schedules for 1956–1957 included increases averaging approximately twice the minimum set by the terms of the Ford grant.[42] The first step in this faculty revitalization program was to give back to the faculty the two summer months it had been forced to cede to the University during more penurious times.

Though it might have been prognosticated otherwise, the retrenchment actions taken by Finch strengthened rather than weakened him with the Trustees. After he took the step of reducing faculty numbers, he received a commendation from the Board congratulating him for his action. In spite of the opposition of some of its members to some of his actions, the Board as a whole appreciated his decisiveness in meeting the financial difficulties encountered by the University during the postwar years. Working with Dr. McCook, with whom he formed a strong alliance, he ran a balanced budget every year. A little more than two years after Finch had taken over from Score, Bishop A. Frank Smith praised him profusely for his work. He said: "You have made a big place for yourself in your present position. I have not known a President of Southwestern who had the united and enthusiastic support of the Methodists of Texas that you have. Dr. Cody and Mrs. Perkins never fail to sing your praises upon every occasion, as does Mr. Perkins."[43]

This approval came because at the same time that Finch was reducing the exposure of Southwestern on some fronts, he was advancing its interests on other fronts. His actions, though taken without a formal plan, without campaigns and without the help of a development office, gradually assumed the nature of a plan over the years.[44] Apart from Finch's retrenchment program, some of his positive actions were: continual progress in a building program; the "move from an ill defined campus to a well developed and carefully planned campus with form and design"; success in bringing new donors into the fold; the gradual building up of student numbers; the establishment of a harmonious working relationship with the Board; and the promotion of "a philosophy of liberal education and selected enrollment" that was continued by his successors in the presidential office.[45]

Though by early 1952 the retrenchment program had not been concluded and the construction program had barely begun, Finch already saw the outlines of what Southwestern could become. Musing privately in a letter to Bishop Smith, he said: "The peculiar purpose of Southwestern now is to operate a first class liberal arts undergraduate college. There is no other institution in Texas with this as its goal in quite the sense that it is here. I want the University to become in time the equivalent to the institutions back East which have made such contributions in this area, namely, Amherst, Swarthmore, Haverford,

Randolph-Macon, etc. This we are already doing and could do in even greater fashion if our plant facilities . . . [were] . . . enhanced and our endowment increased."[46] The construction of plant facilities and an increase in endowment would be his next major objectives.

Construction of the Lois Perkins Chapel

Construction of the Lois Perkins Chapel, begun during the last week of President Score's life, proceeded rapidly and was the first project completed under Finch. Because the chapel was built immediately after Score's death, his life and contribution to its construction were celebrated in several ways. His ashes were placed in the altar, and three grand memorial stained-glass windows were placed in the apse in his memory. They were installed in time for the dedication on November 13, 1950. The altar was the gift of Mrs. Score and John Score II. When Mrs. Perkins heard about what they were doing, she said she thought it was a "lovely" gesture in behalf of their loved one."[47] The three windows were the gifts of the faculty, staff, and Trustees.[48] Many small gifts covered the cost of furnishings for the apse, chancel, and nave.[49]

Since the new building had been placed directly behind the now condemned Williamson County Science Building, that structure was removed forthwith. The Physics and Chemistry Departments moved into the now vacant veterans' barracks.[50] The dedication of the chapel was part of a two-day celebration, concluded on November 14 with the formal inauguration of President Finch.[51]

Though the chapel had been dedicated, it was still without three essential items—stained-glass windows for the sides and front, a pipe organ, and a carillon for the tower. The problem of funding for the stained-glass windows was solved when Mr. and Mrs. Charles Prothro, daughter and son-in-law of Mr. and Mrs. Perkins, indicated that they wanted to contribute them in honor of her parents. The firm chosen for the work was the Jacoby Art Glass Company of St. Louis, Missouri. The windows were designed and executed by Mr. Joe Mayer, a German stained-glass specialist, from ideas conceived by President Finch himself.[52] The most impressive window is that above the front entrance representing Christ ministering to the needs of all people.[53] The tall clerestory windows lining the east side

Construction of the Chapel, 1950. It was built immediately behind the old, dilapidated Williamson County Science Building (shown in photo) that was torn down once the chapel was completed. Southwestern University, Special Collections.

depict important persons in the history of Methodism, and those on the west side depict outstanding reformers and educators in Protestant history. The aisle windows beneath each clerestory window feature the seal of the University associated with each person in the window above.[54] The windows were completed and installed during the spring of 1952 at a cost of $36,000.[55] They were exquisitely done and would be irreplaceable today. That same spring the Trustees elected Charles Prothro as a member-at-large of the Board.[56] He served for thirty years, eleven of them as chair.

The organ, intended by Joe Perkins to be covered by his original gifts, had been omitted because of the higher than expected cost of the building. Recognizing the need to complete the building properly, he now responded by funding the organ with another gift. After a careful search by the University for the right instrument, Perkins authorized the purchase of an Aeolian-Skinner organ at a cost of $30,000.[57] Mr. Donald Harrison, the president of the Aeolian-Skinner company, installed and "finished" it himself in late 1953.[58] A set of Schulmerich Carillonic Bells was purchased and installed in the chapel tower.[59] Mrs. Herman Brown added a special touch to the grounds by commissioning Fred Umlauf, of Austin, to prepare a sculpture of the Madonna and Child for the lawn in front of the chapel.[60] It was installed on September 1, 1953.

The design and placement of the Lois Perkins Chapel immediately made it the central piece in the campus building design. Its semi-Gothic stone exterior, with a simple, Trappist-like interior, attracted favorable attention from everyone. Alumnus J. Frank Dobie said about it: "The new chapel at Southwestern is the most beautiful college chapel I have ever seen on the western side of the Atlantic Ocean."[61]

However much the chapel was praised for its beauty, it was not as serviceable as it was beautiful. Problems with acoustics arose immediately. Sound waves reverberated off the hard walls so much that a person sitting anywhere but in the very front could hardly understand what the speaker said. Within a year after the dedication, Finch announced plans for installing carpet in the aisles and altar area to replace the asphalt tile and to put acoustical tile in other places.[62] Some of the same problems associated with the chapel later arose in the new Alma Thomas Fine Arts Center, and Finch used the example of how the University had resolved problems in the chapel to convince Mrs. Thomas that the same could be done with her building. He said that the heating system of the chapel was not adequate and that they had been forced to cancel some regular chapel services because of an inability to heat the building sufficiently. There was also occasional leakage in the stained-glass windows caused by the expansion of the graphite caulking compound in the summer heat letting water into the building in a driving rain. He admitted that the acoustical problem was still an issue even though $3,000 to $4,000 had been spent trying to cure it. Nevertheless, he felt that they had corrected the window and sound problems and kept the chapel in good shape. "[T]he same," he said, "can be done with proper engineering advice and time for your lovely building."[63]

Though the problems described by Finch were eventually corrected, the acoustical problem persisted until it was addressed again in the renovation of the chapel in 1981. In that year the Prothros funded a major renovation. A new altar was installed, wood paneling was provided in the apse and outer aisles, a protective clear plastic weatherproof window was installed over each stained glass window to shield it from hail, the vestibule was renovated, entirely new heating and air-conditioning systems were installed, and an improved sound and light system was provided. New parquet floors, new carpeting, refinished pews with cushions, new roofing, and a new treatment of the main door were also provided. In addition, a small chapel lounge building in the same style as the main building was added on the east side of the front. It was built to open onto a new chapel garden encompassed by a wall in which Umlauf's Madonna and Child statue was now placed to serve as the focal point.[64]

Herman Brown Takes a Hand in the Work

Margarett Brown's commissioning of a sculpture to adorn the chapel grounds indicates the special attention she and her husband began to take in the University after he was named to the Board of Trustees in November 1948. This developing interest by Herman in Margarett's old school in the 1940s parallels the corresponding development of George Brown's interest in Rice University during the same period.[65] Margarett's older sister, Florra, was married to Dr. Claude C. Cody, Jr., Chair of the Board of Trustees, and the two sisters, both alumni of Southwestern from the 1920s and both living in Houston, likely kept one another informed about events transpiring at Southwestern.

Herman was very aware of the special interest his close political ally, Lyndon Johnson, was taking in the school. Cody wrote Herman a letter in the summer of 1939, asking him to discuss with Johnson "the present financial distress of Southwestern University and other denominational colleges and a proposal for their relief. If you will recall," he said, "I have discussed this with you a number of times in the past several years." After describing his own attempts to gain some help from Washington, he asked Herman if he would take up his proposal with Johnson.[66] There is no record as to the nature of the proposal or the results of the letter.[67] When Lyndon brought a bevy of important persons to Southwestern four years later to inspect the recently arrived Naval V-12 Unit, he brought Herman with him from Austin and introduced him to the audience "as one of Texas' leading citizens."[68]

Three years later Score wrote directly to Herman to enlist his support for the University. In his efforts to develop the Greater Southwestern campaign in 1946, Score wrote him that he had been selected as a member of the permanent committee being established in Houston to manage the campaign. The purpose of the committee, he said, was not only to solicit funds, but also to give advice, counsel, and assistance for the total University program.[69] Though there is no record of a response from Brown, he was invited to attend a luncheon meeting of the committee on December 12, 1947, that was held at the Rice Hotel. He and Margarett were also invited to attend the kickoff dinner held at St. Paul's Church in Houston on January 26, 1948.[70] The invitation to serve in the financial campaign was a preliminary to Herman's being invited later to accept an even more important position as a member of the Board of Trustees. He was elected as an at-large member on November 5, 1948.[71] He responded affirmatively to his election in a gracious letter, expressing "pleasant surprise" at his election and stating that "I, of course, have always had considerable interest in Southwestern on account of my wife and her family and Dr. Cody."[72]

From the day of his election until the day of his death, Herman Brown was a staunch supporter of Southwestern and a key figure in its success during the fifteen years he served on the Board. Elected treasurer in his third year, he served in that capacity for six years before being elected vice chairman for his remaining seven years. Though in bad health during the last decade of his life due to his demanding work pattern and failure to take proper care of his body during his early years, he attended Board meetings regularly and performed significant services for the University. Writing to President Finch about his last Board meeting before his retirement as dean in 1958, Dean Ullrich reflected on the participation of Herman Brown on the Board as he had known it since 1949. He said:

> My esteem and high regard for Herman Brown has risen progressively to higher and higher levels as I have noted his understanding of and sound judgment expressed on matters dealing with higher education. It is significant that such a busy man shows such great interest in the cause of liberal education. He is modest, even appears humble. He uses words sparingly; but when he speaks one is impressed by the keenness of his mind and the pertinence of his remarks. His advice always deserves careful consideration.[73]

Joseph Pratt and Christopher Castaneda state that on the last day of his life, November 15, 1962, Herman flew from Houston to Austin and drove to Georgetown for a meeting.[74] He returned later in the day to Houston, dying at 6:35 P.M. that evening from an aneurysm. The funeral took place two days later at St. Paul's Methodist Church, with its pastor, Dr. Alfred Freeman, and the new President of Southwestern University, Durwood Fleming, formerly pastor of St. Luke's in Houston, officiating.[75] At the time of his death, there was an outpouring of gifts to Southwestern in honor of him, some of which were $25,000 from the Calder Foundation for an exchange student program with Latin America, $16,000 from Mr. and Mrs. John Lynch, $10,000 from the directors of Brown & Root to be matched by a similar gift from the company, $6,000 from the Houston Endowment, and $5,000 from the Texas Eastern Corporation.[76] A Herman Brown Chair in English was established by The Brown Foundation in 1963, and a Herman Brown residence hall for men was completed in 1966 by a matching grant from The Brown Foundation, Inc.

Margarett Brown's Campus Projects

Margarett and Herman combined their efforts at Southwestern, she to beautify it, he to help it prosper. During the years he was at work promoting the financial interests of the University, she was at work promoting its beautification and contributing to its cultural improvement. Both she and Alice, George's wife, gave rare books to the Cody Memorial Library from time to time.[77] Among those contributed by Margarett were some of William Blake's works, including a set of engravings from the Book of Job. At the time this gift made Southwestern the owner of the largest collection of original Blake works in the Southwest.[78] Another unique gift was Margarett's contribution in 1951 of a limited facsimile edition of the *Book of Kells*.[79] A decade later she and

Herman contributed facsimile editions of the Gutenberg Bible and the Lindisfarne Gospels.[80] An inventory of books contributed by her to Southwestern through September 1957 lists 118 titles, not counting the UNESCO World Art Series of eight volumes. Twenty-two of the titles are Bibles, dating from the 1514 New Testament Greek version of Erasmus and a 1522 edition of Luther's New Testament to early-twentieth-century Bibles.[81]

After the opening of the new Alma Thomas Fine Arts Center, she highlighted the new gallery by sponsoring a series of exhibitions in the spring of 1957, ranging from contemporary to classic and traditional art. The following fall she provided a series of six shows from the American Federation of Art.[82] The gallery had been planned to have rotating art shows so that students could hardly fail to look at the exhibits as they came to compulsory assembly in the auditorium once a week, and Margarett Brown furnished them with high-quality art to initiate the system.[83]

Margarett's interest in the aesthetic side of life manifested itself both outdoors and indoors. In 1952 she had Herman send a Brown & Root work crew to the campus to plant sycamore, laurel, and redbud trees and install a water line at no cost to the University.[84] At the same time she had Finch employ the first full-time campus gardener to maintain them.[85] Not satisfied with a casual approach to campus planning, Margarett and Herman authorized the University to have a topographical survey of the campus done at their expense. Hare & Hare of Kansas City developed a general plan for the campus on the basis of which a planting program was prepared.[86]

Margarett was particularly interested in funding the attendance of foreign students at Southwestern. Her scholarships for these students began in 1950 and continued until her death in January 1963. She and Finch exchanged a number of letters each year on the subject of her scholarships. In her last handwritten letter to Dr. Fleming on April 12, 1962, she discussed the system used by her and Dr. Finch to select five or six foreign students each year for awards. There were two stipulations: the student had to speak adequate English in order to participate effectively in classes and had to return to his or her own country on graduation. Unusual cases would be considered separately on their individual merits. "Mr. Brown and I want to give these young men and young women some idea of life in a small, conservative American town," she said in explaining the purpose of her scholarships.[87] Not all of Margarett's aid was for academic purposes. Miss Lucy Song was given a white formal dress in 1954, probably for use in a recital by her.[88]

Two foreign students who came to Southwestern in the early 1950s and graduated together in 1954 (whether funded by Margarett Brown is unknown) were the present Samia Nasir Khoury and her cousin, Diana Nasir Langley, Arab Christians from Jordan. They have remained in contact with Southwestern over the years and have returned several times. At the Homecoming celebration in 1998, Samia Khoury delivered an address entitled "Palestine Today." She lives in Jerusalem, where she is an educator and an official or member of the board of various beneficent organizations.

Margarett always signed her letters to Finch "Margaret Root Brown," with one *t*, though her secretary always typed her signature as "Margarett Root Brown," with two *t*'s. One finds this ambiguity in the spelling of her name constantly in surviving records.

It is interesting to note that on the occasion of Dr. John C. Granbery's death in 1953, she and Herman sent a $100 check to the Cody Memorial Library in his honor.[89] She would have known him from her growing up days in Georgetown and even, perhaps, had some classes under him.

Herman Brown Builds a Swimming Pool

Ever since World War II, when the navy placed the San Gabriel River off-limits for swimming by its V-12 Unit, Southwestern had aspired to having a swimming pool on campus. Since there were so many other pressing needs, the project kept being put off. Score's first thought about how Herman Brown could help the University after he became a Board member was to ask him to build a pool. Knowing that his own acquaintance with Brown was not close enough to make him want to broach it directly, he wrote Lyndon Johnson, asking him to make the request to Herman for a pool. He said to Johnson, "I am writing you all this because I know that you have more influence with Herman Brown than all the rest of his friends put together." Johnson replied immediately but begged off from dealing with anything as detailed and specific as a swimming pool, which was more personal than political in nature. Score responded a few days later, apologizing for trying to use him "as a solicitor" for Southwestern.[90]

The swimming pool idea, however, did not go away. It was mentioned in Board meetings from time to time, and estimates for building a pool were secured.[91] Finally, the Board agreed to build one in the spring of 1954, but it was smaller (60' x 35') than Herman felt it should be and would use construction money that could be better spent on the proposed Student Union Building.[92] At the close of the Board meeting that authorized the pool, he offered to build one at his own expense, returning the $20,000 gift from the West Foundation allocated for its construction to the Student Union Fund.[93] He then had his engineers draw up plans for the kind of pool he wanted, one that was 50 percent larger, measuring 75' x 42', the size of the pool at Rice Institute. Construction of the pool behind West Gymnasium began in the fall and was completed the following year. Brown's engineers said that the pool as built would have cost $50,000 if it had been bid out professionally, about twice the cost of the pool Southwestern had intended to build.[94] One of the get-acquainted rituals for new teachers after 1955 as they moved to Georgetown each summer was meeting their new colleagues around the Brown Swimming Pool. It was eventually removed as new physical education facilities were developed, and an indoor pool was included in the new Sid W. Richardson Physical Education Center in 1976.

Herman Brown's Influence on the Board of Trustees

Herman's presence on the Board of Trustees began to be felt immediately after his arrival. He brought into play the same skills, primarily commitment, daring, and shrewdness, he had used in building up Brown & Root into one of the great construction companies in the nation. At a meeting of the Trustees in late 1950, he spoke of enlarging the vision of the University by setting a goal of $5 million for the endowment.[95] Of course, he was not alone among the Trustees in knowing about the potential gain likely to come in a few years from the McManis gift, but he was the first to suggest that the Board formally adopt the $5 million figure as a goal rather than to talk about it as a hope. That figure was attained in 1956, when the Ford Foundation grant to augment faculty salaries finally pushed the endowment to that level. In twenty years, from 1937 to 1956, the endowment of the University increased from about $600,000 to about $5 million, an increase of 833 percent.

Brown's influence on the Board proceeded as much from his commitment as from his money. Everyone could see the Brown commitment by the hands-on approach he and Margarett took toward the institution. They had a sculpture created for the new chapel, donated valuable books to the library, brought art exhibitions to the new gallery, landscaped the campus, and built a swimming pool. Their contributions, large and small, in unexpected places and at unexpected times, built up the morale of everyone because they seemed to be doing it from real affection for the institution rather than out of a sense of obligation. Sometimes things had to be done, and they just did them. An example of this characteristic was Herman's handling of a trip by President Finch to England in the summer of 1951.

At the spring meeting of the Executive Committee, Finch mentioned that he had been named by the Bishop to go as a delegate to the Ecumenical Conference of the Methodist Church in Oxford. Because Southwestern was at the time at the low point of its postwar enrollment, he was uncertain whether he should go. He asked the Committee for its advice. It told him to use his own judgment. Brown and John D. Wheeler went further. They gave him encouragement to go by having the Committee approve a motion that if he did go, his expenses would be paid by Southwestern.[96] The next day at the Board meeting, Brown went even further. He agreed personally to raise the funds necessary to cover Finch's expenses.[97] In the end, he did not end up soliciting money but gave it himself. On Finch's return from England, he expressed thanks for "Mr. Herman Brown's gift to current operational expense [that] more than adequately took care of my travel expenses."[98]

But Brown did solicit money for Southwestern on other occasions. President Finch mentioned in his report for the spring of 1957 a "splendid" $10,000 gift from the Armco Foundation [now of Zanesville, Ohio], "made entirely because of the interest of Mr. Herman Brown in Southwestern."[99] Speaking in 1992 about that gift, Finch said that Herman had told him to write the Armco management and "tell them that he had urged me to make application for a grant, and he would speak to the man. . . . We got the grant simply because he was on that Board. Herman was the owner of the second largest construction company in the United States, and they wanted to keep him happy, so they made a gift to the little college where he was a trustee."[100]

The Texas Eastern Transaction

Two years after joining the Board, Herman made his first big "gift," if it can be called such, to the University. It was really advice and a guarantee, but it was very generous and benefited the University handsomely. His proposal was similar to the gift made by Ella Fondren a few years earlier to finance a new science building. He may have taken the idea from her. He proposed to guarantee a loan for Southwestern sufficient to make it possible for it to buy 20,000 shares of Texas Eastern Transmission Corporation stock. He said he expected the stock to appreciate significantly in value and that it should be held until it might be sold at a price satisfactory to Southwestern. To back up his belief, he agreed to pay the interest on the loan as long as it was carried and to be repaid out of the profit made on the stock. In addition, he agreed to absorb any loss that might occur for any reason.[101] He said that he expected the transaction to make $75,000 to $85,000 for the University. The Trustees accepted the offer gladly.[102] A year and a half later he enabled the school to buy an additional 1,625 shares of Texas Eastern stock.[103] Rather than selling the stock, Southwestern made it a permanent part of its investment portfolio, trading a little of the stock in and out over the years. At the last Board meeting during Finch's tenure on April 14, 1961, the 18,131 shares of Texas Eastern stock had a book value of $387,626.44 and a market value of $670,847.00.

If it is difficult to calculate the exact amount Southwestern gained from the Texas Eastern venture, it is not difficult to understand Brown's confidence in the stock. The story of the purchase of the Big Inch and Little Big Inch pipelines after World War II by a group led by George and Herman Brown that led to the formation of the Texas Eastern Corporation is a classic story of business enterprise. Pratt and Castaneda in their biography of the two brothers state that "these [pipe]lines were the single most valuable properties in the government's entire surplus inventory after World War II.[104] The lines had been built during the war to ship Texas oil to Eastern markets by land to avoid the threat of German submarines to carrying it by sea. A conglomerate headed by George Brown acquired the two lines in competitive bidding in 1947 and turned them into pipelines that carried natural gas from the Southwest to Eastern markets, thus furnishing a new source of energy for heating the homes and running the factories being built there during the postwar boom. Just as Herman predicted, everyone holding Texas Eastern stock during the early 1950s experienced its meteoric rise. This kind of rise made Brown & Root the largest engineering and construction firm in the United States in 1969.[105]

The Brown Foundation and the Lucy King Brown Chair in History

On July 2, 1951, Herman and George formed The Brown Foundation to serve as the vehicle for their philanthropic giving. The officers of the five-person Board of Trustees were Herman, president, George, vice president, and Herbert Frensley, secretary-treasurer. Margarett and Alice were the other two Trustees. Herbert Frensley, Brown & Root's longtime financial officer, had joined the company during World War II in its shipbuilding operation, of which he became president in 1963. He would subsequently play an important role in the Foundation.

The history of the Foundation falls into four periods—from its inception until 1962, from 1962 until 1976, from 1976 until 1996, and from then until the present. During the first period, the Foundation operated on the basis of a limited endowment. It distributed about $700,000 in grants, an average of about $70,000 per year. Pratt and Castaneda state that Southwestern University was "the most frequent recipient of its grants, which included numerous small gifts targeted for specific needs of the university and other organizations." The second period began on June 30, 1962, when the brothers donated to the foundation their Brown & Root stock. This stock represented 95 percent of the company's value. During this period, as the Browns continued to make significant contributions to the endowment of the Foundation, it began to distribute an impressive array of grants to educational, cultural, and medical institutions. Southwestern was one of the recipients of these grants. The third period dates from 1976 to 1996, when the Foundation focused the major part of its giving for twenty years on three institutions—Rice University, the Houston Museum of Fine Arts, and Southwestern University. Its matching gifts program changed the three institutions significantly, Southwestern most of all.[106] The Foundation has broadened its program of giving during the fourth period while continuing to manifest its interest in Southwestern.

The first act of the Foundation after its formation was to set up the Lucy King Brown Chair in History at Southwestern. Dr. Claude C. Cody, Jr., Herman's brother-in-law and Chairman of the Board, announced the gift to the Executive Committee on February 20, 1952.[107] The distribution of securities to finance the Chair had to wait six months until the IRS certified the tax-exempt charitable and educational status of the foundation on August 28. The value of the securities when received was $152,295.38, and the endowment for the chair was set up at that figure.[108] The Foundation contributed another $98,000 in 1963 to bring it up to the $250,000 level of the other three chairs it established in that year.

Though the endowment for a Lucy King Brown Chair in History was mentioned in each successive catalog from 1952 until 1960, it was not until the 1960 catalog that Dr. George C. Hester was listed as the holder of the Lucy King Brown Chair in History. Because President Finch made a reference in a 1955 document to the "Lucy King Brown Department of History," it may be presumed that proceeds from the endowment were used to finance the entire Department of History and Government prior to the specific appointment of Dr. Hester to the chair.[109] Whatever was done, it was done with the full knowledge of Herman, who was treasurer and vice chairman of the Board during that time.

Beginning in 1951, The Brown Foundation, largely, as indicated earlier, because of the interest of Margarett, provided scholarships to worthy students, particularly foreign students, many of them Asian. It increased its gift amount each year. From a total of $1,370 given for that purpose in the fall of 1952, its gift reached $5,436 in the fall semester of 1962.

Within two years of his becoming a member of the Board of Trustees, Herman Brown's total contribution to the University to date and the expectation of his continuing generosity were such that the Board of Trustees, on recommendation of the faculty, voted him the honorary degree of Doctor of Laws.[110]

W-K-M Tax Matters

Potential income from the W-K-M stock on which Southwestern was counting so heavily was diminished by the U.S. Internal Revenue Act of 1951, which resulted in new tax regulations regarding such relationships as that held by Southwestern and Wheaton College to business enterprises. Though neither of the schools objected to the future impact of the legislation, they did object to its retroactive aspects and the failure of the Act to take into account their payments of debentures for the purchase of W-K-M stock. The amount to be paid to Fred McManis each year from company earnings to cover the balance of the money owed him for the stock had been covered by debentures, a portion of which Southwestern and Wheaton paid down each year.

The two schools immediately began to seek relief from Congress on these issues. Dr. Cody conceived, promoted, and directed the campaign for Southwestern and was more responsible for its success than anyone else.[111] The retroactive aspect of the final law exempted from taxation "feeder" corporations such as W-K-M for educational institutions for the fiscal years beginning before January 1, 1951.[112] The law further stipulated that income from W-K-M was taxable except that portion applied specifically toward the settlement of outstanding debentures. Strong supporters of Southwestern in Congress from Texas tailored the law carefully to the interests of Southwestern and Wheaton. They saw that those two institutions got exactly what they needed. These supporters were identified by Herman Brown at the next Board meeting, where the Board approved his motion that the following persons be thanked for "this favorable result": Tom Connally, Lyndon B. Johnson, C. Rhea Starnes, Sam Rayburn, and D. W. Wilcox.[113] By next spring the Executive Committee could record in its minutes that "all problems associated with the tax issues related to the W-K-M Company have now been resolved very favorably."[114]

With the tax matter settled, the Trustees began to look forward to the future with some optimism. In view of the "hit" taken by faculty members in the 1951–1952 budget, the Trustees voted that the first available cash received from the improved financial prospect "be used for the general increase of salaries" and that "increase in salaries take precedence over any building program to be financed out of [the] Current General Fund and that announcement of the adoption of this policy be authorized to be made to [the College and Fine Arts] faculties and staff."[115] The announcement of this policy must have been welcome news to a faculty whose morale had been decimated by the recent severe faculty cuts. During the interval between receipt of the stock in 1949 and its sale in 1954, W-K-M income was used to pay down the loan secured to purchase the Texas Eastern stock. Until that loan was taken care of, said Finch, the W-K-M income could not be used to increase regular budgetary expenditures.[116]

Sale of the W-K-M Stock

The actual transfer of W-K-M stock to Southwestern and Wheaton had originally been consummated on November 26, 1949. At that time 20,401 Income Debentures were issued, aggregating $5,079,849.00. It was thought that twelve years would be required to retire the debentures out of the profits of the Company. However, as of March 1, 1954, only $51,003.50 worth of the debentures was still outstanding. It was apparent that the whole issue would be retired by September 1, 1954, the next payment date.[117]

Southwestern and Wheaton did not wait. They moved immediately to sell the company and appointed a joint committee for that purpose. Cody, Brown, and Kurth served on the committee for Southwestern.[118] The sale attracted a number of offers, the best of which was for $7,000,000 by the American Car and Foundry Company of Houston. A Memorandum of Agreement was signed between the two proprietors and the buyer on April 10, 1954. It called for a retroactive closing date of December 31, 1953. Southwestern and Wheaton as technical owners would still run the company "in full cooperation and with oversight by the [American Car and Foundry] Company" until final consummation of the agreement sometime in 1954.[119] When the transaction was completed, Southwestern received $3,565,433.87, of which, after deducting many commitments, $3,055,378.15 was transmitted to the endowment.[120] The "many commitments" were all of Southwestern's outstanding debts and obligations at that point, such as its share of the payments for the remaining debentures, the income taxes due on a year's operation of the W-K-M Company, money due to the Fondren Science Hall Fund, the establishment of a Business Office Working Fund, and the like. The Southwestern Executive Committee approved the report made by Herman Brown for the proprietary joint committee on May 31, 1954.[121] The $3,055,378.15 that was added to the endowment adjusted for inflation alone would be worth $19,000,000 in the year 2000.

Continuing W-K-M Influence

Though Herman Brown was quite satisfied with the sale, he was not satisfied with the treatment the W-K-M Company had received from the IRS on the matter of income taxes before the sale.[122] His problem was not with paying taxes per se but with the fact that he felt the District Director of Internal Revenue had not granted W-K-M the same depreciation for patents held by W-K-M as the IRS granted other corporations. Consequently, two years after the sale, Brown convinced the Executive Committee to file suit for recovery of the disputed amount for the fiscal years ending August 31, 1952, 1953, and 1954. He was so convinced of the rightness of the suit that he used the staff of Brown & Root, Inc., to prepare and file the suit on behalf of Southwestern without cost to the University.[123] Though the IRS contested the suit, it lingered in the courts until October 17, 1963, a year after Herman's death, when both parties agreed to a settlement. The IRS returned $78,700.00 to the University.[124]

Even the reimbursement from the IRS of some W-K-M income taxes nine years after the sale did not end the flow of funds Southwestern received from the Fred McManis gift. After McManis had sold the company to Southwestern in 1949, he set up a trust for his wife with some of his own money. Three trustees managed it. Two months after the death of Mrs. McManis on October 6, 1968, the trustees notified Southwestern of their intent to fund a Carolyn and Fred McManis Professorship (or Chair) by the establishment of a fund of $250,000, payable in installments over seven years.[125] When the twenty-five-year time limit for the trust expired in 1975, the trustees liquidated it and distributed its assets among three beneficiaries. Southwestern's one-third, amounting to $280,000, was received a few days after the final payment on the earlier $250,000 pledge setting up the Chair.[126] The Carolyn and Fred McManis Chair in Philosophy was inaugurated in the fall of 1978.[127]

Though Fred McManis never visited the campus, Mrs. McManis came on several occasions and took special interest in a number of students. She provided a scholarship program through the establishment of a McManis Mission Fund. In response to one invitation to attend a special campus event, she asked if she should bring Mrs. Fondren with her.[128] She corresponded frequently with Finch, who visited her from time to time in Houston. After the sale of the company in 1954, he wrote her: "It is the most significant thing that has ever happened to Southwestern, and we are deeply grateful to your husband for his wisdom and his generosity in making this possible for these two schools. Our present endowment is $1,750,000 and this additional endowment from the sale of the Company will bring us to approximately $5,000,000, which will rank Southwestern sixth among all the senior Methodist colleges and will give us the security and stability that the University has always needed and never had."[129] She was very fond of Finch and included admonitions to him in her letters about taking care of himself. Soon after he informed her of the completion of the W-K-M sale, she wrote: "I am three million dollars worth interested in you and I think you are a prince in the household of God. . . . Please don't answer this. . . . I hope you are somewhere resting. There is more said about resting than about working in the Bible & university presidents have a magnificently big job." Though she praised him, she also teased him. She said on one occasion that an intestinal virus had been the cause of her not "writing to your Royal Highness."[130]

Financing the Fondren Science Hall

Everyone thought in 1948 that the completion of the Fondren Science Hall would not be far behind that of the Chapel. Two problems, however, slowed down the construction process so that it was not completed until 1954. They were the difficulty encountered in selling the Transcontinental stock at a price sufficient to finance the building and the procurement of an agreement with Mrs. Fondren on an acceptable building design.

Like the W-K-M and the Texas Eastern stock, the Transcontinental stock purchased at Mrs. Fondren's behest and with her backing to finance the science building appreciated rapidly in value. By spring 1951, half of it was sold for well over $500,000 to repay the loan secured to buy it. The remaining 25,000 shares were held for future sale to finance the construction of the Fondren Science building itself.[131] By that time the architect, Cameron Fairchild, was well into development of the plans and hoped to finish them by midsummer. Finch hoped to sell the remainder of the stock at a favorable price and to begin construction in the fall. This timing did not work out, because the value of Transcontinental stock went down enough to cause its sale to be postponed. In early 1952 Finch instructed Cameron Fairchild to stop work on the plans due to the uncertainty of the date of the stock sale. Herman Brown and C. C. Cody, Jr., were authorized to sell the stock whenever the proceeds might be enough to pay for the project.[132] They did so in the fall of 1952.[133]

Though Mrs. Fondren had been kept informed of everything and had approved the preliminary plans for a three-story building with a lecture hall extending out toward University Avenue from the southwest corner of the building, she did not approve the final plans when President Finch and Dr. Cody later presented them to her. The reason for her disapproval was that an old friend had convinced her that the placement of the lecture hall made the building unattractive. Consequently, Mrs. Fondren asked that it be removed and incorporated into a new design. The project was so far along at this point that such a change would have been very expensive, running the cost beyond available resources. Finch and Cody said they would be happy to make the change if she would bear the extra cost. Since she was unwilling to assume it, they told her that they had no option but to construct the building according to the original plan.[134]

Construction of the McCook-Crain Clinic and the Fondren Science Hall

At the same time that the Fondren Science Hall was ready to be built, another new building had reached the final planning stages. It was the McCook-Crain Clinic. By the early 1950s the McCook Infirmary, an old house remodeled during World War II, was no longer deemed suitable for the kind of campus being developed at Southwestern. The opportunity to build a new one arose when ex-student and long-time Trustee Edward L. Crain died in 1950 and left a $25,000 bequest to the University. The Trustees decided to use the money to build a new clinic that would be named the McCook-Crain Clinic.[135] Consequently, Cameron Fairchild drew up plans for a one-story colonial style building of Austin stone to be constructed on the east side of the campus north of Laura Kuykendall Hall.[136] The Clinic would have two general wards, two isolation wards, a nurse's quarters, a doctor's examination room, and a treatment room.[137] Both it and the Fondren Science building were let under the same contract to the John Broad Construction Company of Austin for $438,926.00 on April 17, 1953.[138] Furniture, equipment, and other added costs would bring the price to $549,778.46. The Clinic was completed quickly and was ready for occupancy by the fall semester.[139]

The financing, design, and construction of the science building had been long and tedious. Mrs. Fondren was less than enthusiastic at the end. When Bishop A. Frank Smith saw her in late April, she told him that she was uncertain as to whether she would attend the dedication on May 17th. Smith told her that "it would be an outrage if she were not there & that she had to come." Apparently she took his comment seriously and later suggested that she would be there by telling him to arrange the event with Finch. Smith wrote Finch that they would "proceed upon that assumption & go ahead with the program, whether she is there or not."[140] Soon thereafter Finch followed up with a telephone call to Mrs. Fondren as he passed through Houston on a trip. He wrote Smith about it, saying that he had "had a very pleasant visit with her over the phone, the most pleasant in years."[141] Mrs. Fondren did attend the dedication ceremony, and two days later Bishop Smith wrote Finch that she "was highly pleased, with the building, the program, and the

Dedication of Fondren Science Hall. Standing left to right: President Finch, Dr. C. C. Cody, Jr., and Mrs. Fondren. Seated: Bishop William C. Martin. Southwestern University, Special Collections.

attention that was paid to her. The transformation that has been wrought at Southwestern under your leadership," said Smith, "is no surprise to us who know you, but is nonetheless a source of continuing joy and pride to us all."[142]

The dedication ceremony celebrated two people—President J. N. R. Score and Bishop A. Frank Smith. The west wing of the building was dedicated to the memory of Score and the east wing in honor of Smith and his wife, Bess. Chemistry Professor Sherman Lesesne played the strongest faculty role in the design.[143] The most noteworthy educational characteristic of the building was its use of a consolidated laboratory plan adapted from the "modern" trend in commercial laboratory techniques.[144] The most notable architectural feature was the disputed lecture hall. Its unique characteristics broke the lines of the otherwise rectangular Georgian design of the building. One of those features was a set of three concrete panels on the slightly curved face of the lecture hall on the outside facing south. The names of many of the great scientists of the past were incised prominently on them. For whatever reason, the name of Charles Darwin, so important to President Hyer (see Chapter X), was not among them.

Summary of Accomplishments through mid-1955

By the midpoint of his administration in 1955, President Finch had accomplished a number of important things. One of the most important was carrying through a retrenchment program that eliminated four major financial pressures on the University. This cutback was done while maintaining a balanced budget, building up Trustee morale, and increasing student numbers each year. He had also successfully carried through the unfinished business inherited from the Score administration, entailing the construction of the Lois Perkins Chapel and the Fondren Science Hall, along with the establishment of Southwestern's first substantial freestanding endowment as a result of the W-K-M transaction.

While taking care of these issues, Finch had also undertaken a number of other initiatives. A new McCook-Crain Clinic and a new power plant had been built,[145] and especially close contacts had been developed with Mrs. Alma Thomas and with three Texas Annual Conferences, both of which would soon result in the construction of new buildings—the Alma Thomas Theater and Fine Arts Center and the Martin Ruter Dormitory for men.

Mrs. Alma Thomas

Less than three months after having been appointed Acting President, Finch began the long correspondence with Mrs. Alma Thomas that during his presidency and that of Durwood Fleming would mount to dozens and dozens of letters, theirs typed, hers always handwritten, until just before her death at the age of ninety-two. Though Southwestern has had many loyal Trustees during its existence, she must be reckoned as one of the most devoted from the date of her election in 1950 until her death in 1977.

Her pastor, the Reverend Ted I. Richardson, former student of Finch and pastor of Tarrytown Methodist Church in Austin, was the person responsible for introducing Finch to Mrs. Thomas in late 1949. Several months later Finch wrote Bishop A. Frank Smith telling him about the budding relationship. He said that at the time Mrs. Thomas had already been on campus twice, once to speak to the International Relations Club and again to have dinner in the President's home. Knowing of the respect Mrs. Thomas had for Smith, Finch wondered if the two of them could arrange a luncheon to discuss Southwestern with her.[146] Smith responded with enthusiasm to the idea of their

President Finch with Mrs. Alma Thomas at the presentation of her portrait in the Alma Thomas Fine Arts Center. The painting fell to the floor with a heavy crash. "I remember telling them," she later remarked, "that I now belonged to the big class of fallen women." Southwestern University, Special Collections.

working with her but felt that they should proceed a little further individually before seeing her together.[147]

From this beginning, the Finch-Thomas relationship developed rapidly, and she was Finch's first nominee for a place on the Board of Trustees in 1950, the second woman to serve as a Trustee. She became very fond of Dr. Finch and bought an elegant academic gown for him in 1954.[148] After her election as a Trustee, she endowed five annual scholarships at Southwestern for graduates of the Methodist Home in Waco, one of the objects of her largesse. A lover of the arts and a patron of the Austin Symphony, she set up the Alma Thomas Foundation at Southwestern, effective January 1, 1951, to endow the School of Fine Arts and promote its music section. She funded it by transferring to the University some mineral interests in Ector County that produced an income from twenty thousand to twenty-four thousand dollars a year at the time.[149]

Born in Texas, Alma Thomas moved with her family in early childhood to Indian Territory in Oklahoma, where she lived until after she was married. The family, now including two sons, moved to a ranch near Midland in 1915. Alma took to ranch life and often rode herd at roundup time along with the cowpunchers. In 1923 her husband fell from a windmill and died shortly afterwards. This accident left it to her and her two teenage sons to keep the ranch going. Though times were bad, they were successful through their combined efforts in keeping the ranch holdings together. Alma taught school, one son went off to work, and the other remained to run the ranch. The discovery of oil on their land changed their fortunes completely.

Moving with her two sons to Austin in the late 1920s, the three of them enrolled in the University of Texas. She graduated with a B.S. in Education in 1930 and with an M.S. in Economics in 1931. One son graduated with her in each of those two years with his own degree. After graduation, she returned to Midland, where she became an elementary school principal with thirteen teachers. She stayed there eight years before moving to Austin permanently.[150]

An inveterate traveler, Mrs. Thomas had visited 127 countries by 1971, gone around the world twice, visited South America five times, and made three visits to the Soviet Union. She traveled to Europe frequently and to Africa occasionally. A picture in the *Austin Statesman* on March 2, 1955, shows Alma Thomas with four other women traveling with her in front of the Taj Mahal. When the photo was taken, they had already visited Hawaii, the Fiji Islands, New Zealand, Australia, Indonesia, Thailand, China, the Philippines, and Japan.[151] On returning from the Soviet Union in 1958, she remarked in a talk to the students at Southwestern that "all peoples but not all governments want to be friends."[152] One of her trips was to the North Pole, where she had to land in a helicopter.[153] Her attendance at a meeting of the National Education Association in Japan was noted at the time she was voted an honorary Doctor of Laws degree by the Southwestern Trustees in 1951 (conferred in 1953).[154]

Alma Thomas was a strong, yet tender, woman, unaffected and without pretense. When her full-length portrait by Wayman Adams was hung in the gallery of the new Alma Thomas Theater and Fine Arts Center after a piano performance,[155] it fell to the floor with a heavy crash. "I remember telling them," she later remarked, "that I now belonged to the big class of fallen women."[156]

This woman, who exhibited so much devotion for Southwestern, resigned from the Board of Trustees at the age of eighty-two in 1967. On learning that she had been elected as a permanent honorary Trustee, she wrote her thanks to Dr. McCook, who was retiring at the same time. "Southwestern University has been so kind and generous to me in conveying so much honor on me (and how little I deserved it) and now this last [honor] really melts me all inside."[157] Three years later she donated a copy of Dobie's book *Coronado's Children* to the library. On the dedication page is an inscription written by Dobie, penned by him for her when she was completing her M.A. at the University of Texas. It reads: "Inscribed with genuine appreciation to Mrs. Alma Thomas—a salt-of-the-earth woman who belongs to the winds and plains of Texas. J. Frank Dobie. Austin, Texas, June 6, 1931."[158] On February 16, 1972, at the age of eighty-seven, she attended the Arthur Rubenstein piano recital in the Alma Thomas Theater with another Texas doyenne, Miss Ima Hogg.[159]

Her last appearance on campus came at the age of ninety-one to make a special donation of figurines to the University. When she had attended the coronation of Queen Elizabeth II in London in 1952, she had purchased a collection of Royal Doulton figurines, eight famous "Great Ladies" of England. She had enjoyed them in her home in Austin until the last. Now, knowing that her end could be near, she wanted to donate them to Southwestern to be kept in her building on campus as their final home. She wrote her last letter to President Fleming in connection with that project on July 3, 1976. She came to the campus for the last time and made a special presentation of them on September 21, 1976. She died about eight months later on May 3, 1977.[160]

The Alma Thomas Theater and Fine Arts Center

Though there is no record of when Mrs. Thomas first discussed the possibility with President Finch of her funding the construction of a Fine Arts building, he sent her a receipt on February 25, 1954, for a $25,000 contribution to the Fine Arts Building Fund. With the contribution she had apparently sent a letter committing herself to the project because Finch thanks her for her proposal concerning future funding. He states that it will make possible the early construction of the Fine Arts building and exclaims that it "is exciting beyond words."[161]

It must have been exciting. Never before had such an offer been made to a Southwestern President. The Perkins family had committed itself to financing the chapel, but the financial constraints set for the building, though generous in intent, were so tight in terms of post–World War II prices that Score and Finch were always wondering whether everything would work out. Mrs. Thomas said, in effect, build the Fine Arts building you need within reason, and I will deed certain mineral, oil, and gas royalties to pay for it. Two weeks later Finch wrote Mrs. Thomas that he had authorized Cameron Fairchild to prepare preliminary plans for the proposed building and that the faculty had submitted its list of needs.[162] In his interview with Dr. Martha Allen in 1992, Finch said that the gift by Mrs. Thomas to build the Fine Arts Center was sacrificial. She cut her income by one-third in doing it.[163]

In spite of the apparent open-endedness of the offer, there were several practical constraints that in fact limited what could be done. Since the money came in from oil royalties over time, a loan had to be procured to furnish the immediate building funds. A consulting engineer evaluated the mineral, oil, and gas interests conveyed by Mrs. Thomas to Southwestern, and the amount set up on the books for them was $429,639.[164] Because a bank loan would be expensive and because the guarantee from the oil income was secure, the Trustees decided to borrow approximately $400,000 from the W-K-M endowment to finance the construction, to be repaid with 4 percent interest over time.[165] By now interfund borrowing was used from time to time for major plant fund projects, but, in distinction from half a century earlier, when the payback of such money was a dubious enterprise, payback now with interest was always certain and covered by impeccable collateral. Interfund borrowing had also been used to build the Fondren Science Hall and would later be used for the construction of the Bishops' Memorial Union and Kurth Hall. Cameron Fairchild was asked to design a fine arts structure that could be built for the projected amount.

The Martin Ruter Dormitory

While funding for a new Fine Arts building was materializing, funding for a new men's residence hall ("dormitory," in the parlance of the records) was also being put into place. About a year after becoming President, Dr. Finch wrote Bishop Smith about the inadequacy of men's housing at Southwestern. Though when built in 1908 Mood Hall had been called the finest men's dormitory west of the Mississippi River, forty years later it had become a problem. "We are losing students each year at Southwestern because our dormitory facilities are not attractive enough," Finch wrote Smith. Unable to persuade prospective donors to give a men's dormitory, he sought the bishop's support in asking the Annual Conferences of Texas Methodism to launch a million-dollar program whose proceeds would be shared by the Methodist colleges and Wesley Foundations in the state.[166]

Though Smith's response is not on record, Finch began working quietly soon afterwards with ex-students and various church groups in the three Annual Conferences most closely connected with Southwestern to promote a revised plan. The revised plan was for the Central Texas, Texas, and Southwest Texas Conferences to unite in a joint campaign to raise money for a dormitory for Southwestern. It is quite possible that Smith advised him to restrict his request and suggested that he ask the conferences to fund a building for Southwestern alone. He then supported Finch in persuading the Annual Conferences to support it. Whether this was exactly the scenario, it is unlikely that Finch would have approached the conferences without having obtained some episcopal support. Telling the conferences that Mood Hall was no longer adequate as a modern dormitory, Finch proposed that they unite in raising $250,000 for one unit of a proposed boys' dormitory quadrangle.[167] They accepted the proposal and over a period of three years raised enough money to build the Martin Ruter Dormitory.[168]

With Mrs. Alma Thomas having committed herself to the funding of the new Fine Arts building and the three Annual Conferences having agreed to fund the new men's dormitory, the Executive Committee decided to bid the two buildings jointly.[169] Cameron Fairchild now drew plans for a one-hundred-bed men's dormitory using a Georgian style with straight lines and a hip roof.[170] Just before Christmas Finch wrote Bishop Smith that contracts for both buildings would soon be signed for approximately $750,000, the largest figure in the history of the University.[171] In early 1955 the Executive Committee voted to award the joint contract to the Rex D. Kitchens Construction Company of Austin for $713,807.[172] It began to work immediately, and the Martin Ruter Dormitory was completed in time for new students seven months later.[173]

The Fine Arts Center: The Generosity of a Remarkable Woman

The Fine Arts building was completed in the spring of 1957 and dedicated at the time of the Board meeting on April 14.[174] It was described in the brochure printed for the occasion as "a handsome limestone building containing an ultra-modern theatre seating 750 persons, with green room, dressing rooms, costume storage, and workshops; a recital hall; 11 studios, 27 air conditioned practice rooms; an art department with facilities for lithography, clay modeling, and painting; classrooms; a listening room and small library; a band and orchestra rehearsal room, with storage and workshops; and a handsome art gallery."[175] During the time the building was under construction, the School of Fine Arts was given full membership in the National Association of Schools of Music. Finch wrote Mrs. Thomas, who was on a trip "around the Pacific" at the time, that her "endowment of the School of Fine Arts, and now the gift of the building, ha[d] made this recognition possible."[176]

Mrs. Thomas did not forget Southwestern during her trip "around the Pacific." On the day after Finch penned his letter to her from Georgetown, she penned one to him from the Far East. In it she said that since money had to be borrowed from other University funds to complete the Fine Arts building, she wanted the oil and gas money from her to continue until the loan had been repaid to the appropriate fund. Her intention was that her oil and gas money should completely pay for the building.[177]

The Fine Arts Center, originally talked about as a project in the $400,000 range, ended up costing $544,215.13, including preliminary costs, contractor, architect, utilities, and landscaping.[178] Far from complaining, Mrs. Thomas simply accepted the additional expense as a part of her obligation. In addition, she made a very substantial gift for furnishings and equipment completely apart from the cost of the building itself. The final payment was for $17,000 in late 1958.[179] During the twenty years between spring 1954, when she made her commitment to the building, and spring 1974, Southwestern maintained a trust made up of mineral, oil, and gas interests deeded by her to cover the expenses of the scholarships that she donated each year and covering regular reimbursement payments, with interest, to the W-K-M endowment fund. Finally, Basil Phillips, Vice President for Fiscal Affairs, reported to President Fleming on March 29, 1974, that the income in the trust to retire the debt had covered the debt and that income from the oil royalties would cease.[180] The elements making up the trust were returned to her.

Even while the trust was systematically performing its annual function of paying down the W-K-M loan, Mrs. Thomas continued to make other contributions to the University. Among those of record are gifts of $8,000, $6,000, and $20,000 to the Advancement Fund in 1965, 1966, and 1967, a $25,000 gift to the Challenge Campaign in 1968, and a $10,000 gift to the Program for Progress in 1972.[181] She also made gifts to the endowment in honor of Pearl A. Neas, Herman Brown, and Bishop A. Frank Smith on their deaths in 1962. She also, as if she were a University functionary, wrote letters in her own hand to George Brown, Roy Cullen, Mrs. Corbin J. Robertson, Isaac Arnold, Douglas B. Marshall, and A. Frank Smith, Jr., thanking them for their wonderful gifts to Southwestern in 1968.[182]

The Fine Arts Center: Problems with the Dream

Hardly had the Fine Arts building, dreamed about since the times of President Bishop forty years earlier, been completed than problems arose with it. Water problems under the building caused the floors in the gallery and elsewhere to buckle and the walls to crack. Chairman John D. Wheeler stated that the condition of the building, marring its beautiful interior, was one of the bitterest experiences he had to face in his career.[183] After the spring 1957 Board meeting in which the problem was discussed, Finch wrote Mrs. Thomas: "I do want you to know that I hope I will not ever have to attend a Board meeting at which the circumstances are as unhappy as they were at this one."[184] Mrs. Thomas expressed her shock at the development in a plaintive letter back to the President in which her ultimate regret was for the financial burden it created for the University.

> [F]or me it was entirely a shock that I was wholly unprepared for. The crack in the foyer seemed a minor thing, but as trouble spot after trouble spot was revealed I felt worse and worse. And now after making some adjustment to the situation that we have, I find myself blaming Mr. Fairchild for much of the trouble. He should have known what was going on. I'm sorry I feel this way toward him, and it is not that I am seeking someone to place the blame on, but an honest conviction that he was neglectful. With all the sacrifice and money that went into the building I can't get much satisfaction from "structurally right" outside walls when there is so much that is wrong inside of them. I didn't know how proud I was of it until this came up. The few moments that I have had in thinking that perhaps the repairs will be satisfactory are soon lost in thinking of the terrible financial burden this creates for the University, and one which it is so little able to carry. This is my keenest devastating disappointment now.[185]

Corrective measures were begun immediately to take care of the problem. Consultants were brought in and engineers were employed to come up with a solution. Within a year a subsurface drainage system for the Alma Thomas Fine Arts Center, which took care of the problem, was completed at a cost of $29,503.61. Sump pumps were installed and checked daily. After heavy rains following completion of the remedial measures, there was no evidence of water under the building.[186] Fortunately, the information that had been communicated to Mrs. Thomas, that the outside walls were "structurally right" and that the problems were on the inside, was correct.

In 1979 the Hoblitzelle Foundation made possible the refurbishing, air-conditioning, and reconditioning of the entire building with a $500,000 grant.[187] The construction in 1993 of a thrust stage theater facility on the north side was made possible by a grant from the Houston Endowment Inc. A major addition on the east side in 1999 to house the study of music and the visual arts was funded by a gift from Mr. Fayez Sarofim of Houston. A makeover of the main building, also funded by Mr. Sarofim, is now being designed. After half a century of use and with several additions, the building still serves the University community.

The problem at the Fine Arts Center arose from the fact that a fault line runs generally north and south through the campus and that the Fine Arts building was built astride the fault. The engineers, says Finch, failed the institution in not dealing with the issue. The land on one side of the fault line "was gumbo, which was like a sponge absorbing water with pressure building up and lifting the building," while the land on the other side had a less absorbent character. Finch says he had at least learned enough to force the builders to lay all the utility lines for the building around the outside rather than in the floors that lay directly on the soil. Therefore, they did not break when the floors buckled. He and McCook would plaster and paint the cracks before every Board meeting or any function so that they wouldn't show. Specialists from San Antonio "literally bored holes in a great reaming out under the entire Fine Arts building from one end to the other, and laid some pumps in to draw the water off. . . . Finally, in Durwood's time," Finch continues, "the floor was leveled off and recast to be square across and not buckled."[188]

The Kyle E. White Religious Activities Center

Before the Fine Arts Center was finished, another building, the Kyle E. White Religious Activities Center, was initiated. Mrs. Kyle E. White of Anahuac had committed herself in February 1956 to contributing $50,000 toward its construction in honor of her deceased husband.[189] The building would be placed next to the chapel so that an observer, standing in front of the chapel and looking toward it, would see it to the right and slightly behind the chapel. It was a one-story limestone-covered edifice designed by Cameron Fairchild very much like the McCook-Crain Clinic.[190] It was moved to another location during the Shilling administration and is now behind the President's home, where it serves the Department of Religion and Philosophy. It was completed quickly and was ready by September for use during the fall semester.[191] The final cost of the building was $58,437.72, of which the Current Fund paid the last $8,437.72 beyond the $50,000 grant.[192]

Because it was built before the lesson of the Fine Arts Center had been learned, the same water condition, though not as bad, was encountered in it as in the larger building. Consequently, a subsurface drainage system was also put in it two years later to solve the problem.[193] From that time on, all buildings being put up, at least those where the least possibility of unsettled foundation conditions exists, have had the ground tested with deep holes previous to construction.[194]

McCook Tries to Change the Use of the General Fund Surplus

One of the financial policies adopted by the Board of Trustees when the University emerged from debt in 1937 was to regard the endowment as inviolate. The Bylaws enacted in 1940 protected undesignated money placed in the endowment and stated that a donation of any sort once credited to the endowment could not be diverted to any other purpose without the unanimous consent of the Trustees present and voting (see Chapter XV).

No such rule, however, controlled the use of any surplus that might develop in the Current General Fund, the fund related to the general operational budget. A surplus could be used for whatever purpose might be most in need with little regard as to whether it was for an unmet budgetary item or for a capital expenditure. The amount of money reported by I. J. McCook as having been spent out of Surplus for capital items from the time of his first report in 1930 through 1955 was $151,019.16. Historically, then, Current Fund surpluses could and had been used for both operational and capital purposes as far back as McCook had been employed at Southwestern. He seems never to have been happy with this practice, and his careful recording of the amounts involved year by year was a way of holding it up for examination by the Trustees. Beginning in 1956, however, and continuing through 1961, he began to express his ideas "vigorously" both verbally and in his written reports to the Board.

The trigger for the objections he voiced at this time appear to have been related to the payment of the more than $8,000 from the Current Fund for the completion of the Kyle E. White Religious Activities Center, large expenditures from the General Fund for a program of street paving, parking, and curbing improvements, and a consideration of the best way to finance the prospective Student Union Building. At the meeting of the Board in the fall of 1956 McCook "protested vigorously" a suggestion made that some of the securities out of the investment portfolio be sold and that the gain be used for building purposes.[195] From this attempt to draw from the endowment for capital purposes, he moved on to a consideration of the Current Fund surplus. He had come to believe that any surplus in the General Current Fund should be plowed back into use by the operational budget just as endowment gains should be plowed back into endowment capital. This view was contrary to the long-term practice of both the Board and the President. Though Finch agreed with the use of the surplus for special purposes related to plant improvement that could not be funded otherwise, the Trustees did not consider him extravagant. The Trustees looked on him as being fiscally responsible and had great faith in his recommendations. When Dr. Edmund Heinsohn retired from the Board in 1959, he mentioned that Finch always presented understatements so that results were much better than expected.[196]

When McCook "protested vigorously" the use of surplus funds for capital purposes at the meeting in the fall of 1956, he was at the height of his influence on the

Board. Just two years earlier his devoted service of twenty-five years had resulted in his title being changed from that of Business Manager to Vice President, Finance, "a well deserved recognition for his outstanding services" in President Finch's words.[197] He was disturbed, however, that $247,919.09 of the surplus had been used for plant expansion from 1954 through 1957, and he determined to use his influence to end or modify the practice if possible.[198] His protest seems to have had little effect, and he continued to comment on the matter in subsequent Board reports. In 1959 he said: "We have been disturbed for some years at the large amount expended from the General Fund for plant improvements, as we have pointed out in previous written reports. On several occasions, we expressed our conviction that these funds would be better employed in granting salary raises as, otherwise, it might be found that the faculty and staff were actually bearing these costs."[199] He pointed out that if this surplus had been invested, it would now be yielding a substantial sum to support educational aims and objectives.[200]

McCook continued to make his case through the end of the Finch administration in 1961. In his last report under Finch, he wrote: "In a number of reports in prior years, we have pointed out the fact that actually the faculty and staff pay for these capital outlays, since funds are used which otherwise would be available for salary increases not granted because of lack of resources to cover the cost. The majority of these expenditures, it is true, fall within categories for which it would be very difficult to secure gifts, such as streets, parking lots, extension of utility services, etc. Nevertheless, the effect remains the same in any case."[201]

Finch, for his part, did not deny the cogency of McCook's observations. In his last report before he left for Vanderbilt, he remarked that there had been only one deficit in all his years as President, a small one of $2,500 in the budget inherited from the previous administration. "It would be," he continued, "a matter of greater pride if this sound fiscal record could have been achieved without such high cost to faculty salaries in the earlier days of the fifties. It is gratifying that since the addition of the WKM endowment funds, salaries have begun to move forward with encouraging regularity, while at the same time plant maintenance and improvement has also been steadily undertaken."[202]

While accepting McCook's analysis, Finch justified his decisions with regard to the use of the surplus on the basis that it was not simply a matter of adopting one course of action completely to the exclusion of another. A university, he held, has to be moved forward on many fronts at the same time. He had tried to answer the need for the advancement of faculty salaries while at the same time taking care of twenty years of maintenance deferred because of an official budget that generally accorded its more prosaic items much less than was needed and sometimes nothing at all.[203]

His was in some senses a Hobson's choice that his successors would also be called upon to make. For them, however, it was probably easier to make after 1976, when the influx of additional resources from The Brown Foundation betokened a new day in financial administration.

The Bishops' Memorial Union

The movement for a major building to provide a center for student activities began in November 1943, some four months after the arrival of the Naval V-12 Unit on campus. The large number of students on campus occasioned by their arrival gave impetus to what had been recognized as a major institutional need since Hyer had proposed the construction of the grand Memorial Hall for student services in 1910. That proposal had served as the trigger for the beginning of the momentous removal effort of that era (see Chapter XI). Just as in 1910, the alumni in 1943 took charge of the effort. A meeting of ex-students on November 6, 1943, joined the desire to construct a student center with wartime patriotism by proposing that 2,500 alumni purchase a Series F or G bond each to be contributed to the effort.[204] The drive initiated for this purpose got off to a good start in the spring but petered out shortly thereafter in spite of a picture of the proposed building in the University catalog. As late as the board meeting in the spring of 1949, however, Score was still displaying sketches of a proposed Student Union Building to the Trustees.[205]

Because of his agreement on the need for a student activities building and because the funds contributed for it during the Score administration were still in hand, Finch made it one of his building priorities. He reported to the Trustees in 1953 that $150,000 was already in hand for what would probably be a $250,000, two-story building of 20,000 square feet. The Trustees voted to name a building committee to further the project.[206] The campaign continued through the next three years.

In 1956 Finch presented schematic drawings by Cameron Fairchild of the new Union Building, with the cost now projected at $400,000.[207] By the time of the fall Board meeting, with $254,900 in hand, the Board voted to go ahead and let the contract.[208] It was awarded to R. B. Butler, Inc., of Bryan, Texas, for $395,292, with 6 percent for the architect.[209] Final contributions by The Brown Foundation, Inc. ($75,000), the Houston Endowment, Inc. ($75,000), and E. L. Kurth ($45,000) brought funds in hand to well over $400,000.[210] Kurth made four donations in all totaling $90,000. About twenty persons or foundations contributed from $1,000 to $90,000 each toward the building, with many ex-students and faculty contributing smaller amounts.

During the construction, the Trustees decided to put in a new steam distribution plant to take care of the new building and other campus facilities. Two new boilers were placed in the Mood Hall boiler plant, which, with other expenditures connected to it, cost $124,740.[211] Since no one was likely to make a donation for such an unromantic project as boilers and because some of the pledges toward the Union were still not completed, the Board voted to borrow $200,000 to cover its cost and the $75,000 still due on the Union.[212]

The Bishops' Memorial Union was completed in early 1958, an Open House was held for the citizens of Georgetown on April 13, and the building was dedicated at Homecoming on April 26.[213] The dedication ceremony was a fitting tribute to Bishop A. Frank Smith for what he had done for Southwestern over the years. Though the Trustees had voted to name the building the Bishops' Memorial Union in honor of the six Methodist bishops who had been associated with Southwestern (Sam R. Hay, 1889; H. A. Boaz, 1907; A. Frank Smith, 1912; W. Angie Smith, 1917; H. Bascom Watts, 1913; Edwin D. Mouzon, theology teacher, 1908–1910), the soon-to-be official name, the Bishops' Memorial Union, had been kept secret from Smith until the last moment. Whereas usually the donor presents the building to the Board chairman, on this occasion the chairman, Mr. John D. Wheeler, presented it to Bishop A. Frank Smith.[214]

Though the Bishops' Memorial Union gave way to the Red and Charline McCombs Campus Center in 1998, it served thousands of students for forty years. It was an elegant building for its time. It was built of the same limestone that by this time had become the building material of choice for Southwestern. Its five large windows facing east in the main lounge covered about half the front of the entire building and covered the entire height of the two-story building, similar in design to the Baths of Caracalla in Rome. The lower part of each window contained double doors by which one could exit onto a large raised terrazzo plaza. The lounge, with its expansive parquet floor, served from time to time as the site for large all-campus dances made popular earlier during the Big Band era or for large banquets where several hundred people could be served. The north end contained a faculty lounge and storage, while the south end contained a music room, a post office, a snack bar, and a bookstore. The basement contained recreational space, including bowling alleys.

A Campus Not Only in Name but Also in Appearance

When Finch took over as President of Southwestern in 1949, there were six substantial stone buildings on campus. They were the Administration Building (1900), Mood Hall (1908), the Williamson County Science Building (1917), Laura Kuykendall Hall (1926), the Women's Commons, or dining hall (1926), the Cody Memorial Library (1939), and the West Gymnasium (1940). Snyder Hall, the Sneed House, the McCook Infirmary, and the President's home were dated wooden structures. The Field House, Home Economics Hall, Arts-Shops Building, Student Center, and Veterans' Village were temporary buildings. Most of them had been secured from the federal government after the war and fitted out for purposes other than those for which they had been originally built. An aerial view of the campus would have shown a crosshatch of streets very similar to those found in the rest of Georgetown. The placement of the major buildings had been done so that possibilities existed for the emergence of a unique campus design, but these possibilities were far from realization.

When Finch left Southwestern in 1961, five of the six stone buildings were still in use. The Fondren Science Hall, however, had replaced the dilapidated Williamson County Science Building. In addition, the McCook-Crain Clinic, the Alma Thomas Theater and Fine Arts Center, the Martin Ruter Dormitory, the Kyle E. White Religious Activities Center, and the Bishops' Memorial Union had been built, all of limestone. All the temporary buildings had been removed except the Field House and the Home Economics Hall, which were both now faced with limestone. The Sneed House and the President's home were all that remained of the old wooden structures. The Brown Swimming Pool, the Kurth Golf Course, and the Kurth Tennis Courts had also been built. The change in the number of buildings and the character of campus structures was remarkable.

Though the construction of the buildings was significant, perhaps the most notable change in the campus during these years is that it was tied together physically as a unified cam-

Veterans' Village building being moved off campus, 1954 or 1955. Southwestern University, Special Collections.

1954 aerial view of the campus immediately after completion of the Fondren Science Hall. Shortly thereafter, Veterans' Village (not pictured) and cross-hatch streets were removed, Maple Street was constructed west of the Administration Building, and the crescent drive was put in place. From the 1955 *Sou'wester.*

pus for the first time. It became a campus not only in name but also in appearance and assumed many of the characteristics still familiar today. This change came about through the opening and closing of streets, the construction of parking lots, the construction of a crescent drive, landscaping, and the installation of a sprinkler system, most of it according to a campus plan designed by Hare & Hare of Kansas City and paid for by the Browns. Finch presented the plan to the Board of Trustees at their fall meeting in 1954.[215]

The Hare & Hare plan envisaged the closing of all through streets on the campus, extending Maple Street from where it ended at University Avenue along the side of the campus just west of the Administration Building to the Katy Station, and building a street around the back of the campus giving access to the buildings on the perimeter.[216] Speaking at the Board meeting in the fall of 1955 in favor of the project was Herman Brown, who argued that it would be more economical to do all the work at once rather than piecemeal. It should be done all together rather than in segments, and it should be done, he said, even if it created an operating deficit.[217] The biggest design transformation would be the construction of a "crescent drive centering at the Lois Perkins Chapel."[218]

Brown's financing of the Hare & Hare study, his experience in road building, and his support in the Board meeting carried the day. It was sufficient to cause the Trustees to approve the project even though it had to be paid out of general funds. In the discussion they mentioned that eventually the utility lines must be placed underground and that the University would have to consider a sprinkling system.[219] Work got underway and was soon completed. Finch could report in 1956 that "new streets, parking areas, curbing and sidewalks have given shape and orderliness to the campus."[220]

Until 1956 fraternities maintained their houses off campus. Dean Ullrich had used the threat of forcing them to move on campus in 1930 to exact better conduct from them (see Chapter XIV). Times were now different. The fraternities had been forced to change houses so many times in the last two decades that they saw an advantage to having permanent houses on campus in spite of the fact that it would bring about closer supervision. The first fraternity to set up an on-campus arrangement was Phi Delta Theta. It worked out an arrangement with the University to lend it "not more than $17,500" to complete construction of a house to cost approximately $40,000, with a lease for ninety-nine years.[221] Houses built by the Kappa Sigmas, the Kappa Alphas, and the Pi Kappa Alphas soon joined the Phi Delta Theta house completed in 1958. The four houses, built just west of the new Bishops' Memorial Union, constituted a fraternity row.[222]

In order to give access to the new Bishops' Memorial Union then on the drawing board and to the new fraternity houses soon to be constructed, the city agreed to close a through street running through the site of the proposed Union Building if the University would open another running north and south just west of the Administration Building, as proposed by Hare & Hare. As an extension of Maple Street, it would require moving the football field twenty feet west. As compensation, it would permit the center of the campus to be closed to through traffic.[223] Parking lots for the Administration Building and the proposed Union Building, with a street running behind the Administration Building and Fondren Science Hall, were also constructed. The entire street project was completed by fall 1957, in time for the new Union Building and the Phi Delta Theta house.[224]

Golf Course, Tennis Courts, and Sprinkler System

Though a nine-hole golf course had been built under the supervision of Dr. Howard in 1933 and listed in the catalog for that year, it gave way to Depression and wartime exigencies and was not listed in the catalog by the time Finch took over as President. With all the land procured by Southwestern during the war, golf was a natural activity for its constituents and pressure built up for a course. Mr. E. L. Kurth, a regular donor to the University, gave $11,000 in late 1953, and permitted $5,000 of it to be used to build a nine-hole golf course, which was subsequently named after him. The course was laid out during the summer on the eastern edge of the campus and was officially opened for play in the fall of 1955.[225] Some tennis courts were later placed near the new Martin Ruter Hall and were also named after him.[226]

When questioned about the construction of the golf course forty years later, both Ellsworth Peterson, a student at the time, and former President Finch remembered well the day that the land designated for the golf course was cleared of rock. Someone conceived the idea of using student help by designating the day for clearing rocks as an all-school holiday. Everyone was invited to come and help in the endeavor. Great lines of students and teachers picked up rocks and piled them in heaps. Others hauled them off.

All the rocks were cleaned up in one afternoon, and a picnic supper was served to the two or three hundred people involved in the effort.[227]

The installation of a campus sprinkler system might not seem to be a big thing when compared with the construction of buildings and the establishment of an endowment, but, like the creation of the golf course, the circumstances surrounding the sprinkler system have caused it to be remembered in a special way.

Central Texas has long been subject to large floods and long dry spells. The great flood of 1921 and the great drought of the early 1950s are particular instances. The campus irrigation system was put in just at the end of the drought of the '50s. While the Alma Thomas Fine Arts Center and other buildings were being constructed, says Finch, "the land was so dry there were cracks on campus into which you could almost put your entire foot."[228] Many trees and shrubs died, and flowers withered away. The drought was followed in 1957 by excessive rain. Writing at this time to a friend about the phenomenon, Finch said: "We had a stemwinder of a flood in Georgetown and all across this area; and it has not ended apparently, for the weather reports indicate further rain. When Texas breaks its Texas-style drought, it does it in a Texas-style way. The [San] Gabriel [River] got up higher than it has been since the famous flood of 1921 and literally washed out the park and did considerable damage across the county. The estimated damage is three million dollars."[229]

About this time Finch learned of a wealthy alumnus in Dallas who was born in Georgetown and who had graduated in 1912 with Bishop A. Frank Smith.[230] His name was Neely G. Landrum, president of First Federal Savings and Loan Association of Dallas. He was a member of the Highland Park Methodist Church in Dallas and president of the Lighthouse of the Blind. As a result of Finch's contact with him, he became interested in doing something for his alma mater.

In early 1958, toward the end of the drought, Landrum proposed building a sprinkler system for the campus. He employed Forrest and Cotton, water engineers of Dallas, for the project.[231] They divided about fifty acres of the campus into eighteen sections for irrigation, with a centrally located underground pumping station.[232] With the help of Grogan Lord, who had just come on the Board, beginning his long service in that capacity, the water was purchased from the City of Georgetown, which drew it from deep springs in San Gabriel Park. The system was completed at a cost of $64,975.04, and Landrum transferred to Southwestern cash and stocks in the amount of $73,527 to pay for it.[233] The Neely G. Landrum Campus Sprinkler System was formally dedicated on October 15, 1959.[234] One of the ironies of the dedication was that a heavy rain accompanied it, so that the day became popularly known, says *The Megaphone*, as "the day that the rains came down."[235] Landrum provided a gift of $28,000 two years later to establish a sprinkler system for the golf course.[236]

Neely Landrum continued to give money from time to time for specific outdoor landscaping improvements, one of which was sprigging the campus with carpet grass. His last major landscaping gift was of $67,500 in 1963 to build a memorial fountain honoring his deceased daughter, Mrs. Marguerite Landrum Williams. It was dedicated on April 18, 1964.[237] Though a newer fountain has since replaced it, his fountain established the notion of a large fountain near University Avenue opposite the Lois Perkins Chapel across the long, open mall around which the campus centers.

19 *Emergence of a New Institutional Model (1949–1961)*

"Exciting, Almost Revolutionary Progress"

In late 1956 the Committee on Faculty Personnel produced an elaborate twenty-four-page report on data it had requested from forty-four colleges and universities. Of the forty-two schools in its endowment study, the top five endowments were those of Harvard ($442.0 million), Cornell University ($50.2 million), Rice Institute ($41.5 million), Dartmouth ($34.0 million), and Duke ($26.9 million). Southwestern was in seventeenth place with an endowment of $4.8 million. The five schools immediately above it were Wake Forest, Southern Methodist, Davidson, De Pauw, and the University of Alabama. The five below it were the University of the South, Denison, Wheaton (Illinois), Wabash, and the University of the Redlands.[1] Looked at as a part of the Methodist system of colleges and universities, Southwestern trailed only Wesleyan (Connecticut), DePauw, Ohio Wesleyan, and Albion in endowment at the time.[2]

This interest in endowment comparison came from the fact that Southwestern had just received the McManis money and, for the first time in its history, had an endowment it was willing to compare with other institutions. Now that Southwestern was an upwardly mobile institution, this kind of comparison would henceforth become a regular feature of its publicity.

During his tenure, Finch was able almost every year to point out some mark of distinction achieved by the University. In 1950 and 1951 he reported the appearance of Southwestern in the *Good Housekeeping* magazine's annual study of superior first-class smaller colleges.[3] In 1954 the editors of *Who's Who in America* notified the University that six new alumni were listed in the current volume, which when added to the alumni already in the volume, gave it first rank in Texas and twenty-fourth in the nation among privately controlled institutions in the listing of alumni in relationship to enrollment.[4] In 1956 a survey revealed that Southwestern ranked in the upper 25 percent of the institutions in the United States in the Baccalaureate Origins of Doctorates granted in Arts, Humanities, and Social Sciences.[5] The following year a study prepared for the National Academy of Sciences reported that fifty-five graduates of Southwestern had received their Ph.D.'s from American universities in the last twenty years, an enviable record for a school with as small a graduating class each year as that of Southwestern.[6] In the same year a National Merit Scholar enrolled for the first time.[7]

The Traxler Report in 1958 entitled "An Appraisal of American Colleges on the Basis of Men Graduates Listed in *Who's Who in America*" studied 489 colleges. An index figure was established for each college. Those with an index of less than 100 were deemed excellent. Only 67 of the 489 colleges in the study were in that category. Only three schools from the South were among them—George Peabody College with an index of 56, Southwestern with a 60, and Rice University with a 76.[8]

Requesting a grant from the Armco Steel Company Foundation in 1957, Finch wrote that during the last ten years Southwestern had had among its alumni:

5 Bishops of the Church;
2 Federal Judges;
1 Chief Justice, U.S. Court of Claims;
2 Justices of the Supreme Court of Texas;
1 Justice, Court of Criminal Appeals;
7 College Presidents;
The President of the Texas Medical Association;
The President of the Texas State Teachers Association;
The Man of the Year of the South, 1949;
The winner of Pulitzer Prize Award in Journalism, 1954;
The Texas Doctor of the Year, 1955;
The Chief Counsel of the Gulf Oil Corporation; and
The President-Elect of the Texas Medical Association, 1958.[9]

In 1959 Southwestern seniors received two Danforth Fellowships, a Woodrow Wilson Fellowship, and a Southern Foundation Fellowship.[10] A study in 1960 of the baccalaureate sources of college and university faculties in the United States ranked Southwestern in the upper 20 percent of all colleges studied in the number of its graduates teaching in colleges and universities.[11] Having observed the academic change at Southwestern as a teacher and President over two decades, Finch said toward the end of his tenure: "Southwestern in the past twenty years has made exciting, almost revolutionary progress."[12]

Reemphasis on the Liberal Arts

Finch's interest, however, was not simply in helping Southwestern to become a better institution. It was in helping it to become a really good *liberal arts* institution of the kind envisioned by President Bishop. In 1914 Bishop had stated that the role of Southwestern was as a college whose primary work was validating the "judgment that liberal culture is the very best preparation for life in the modern world." (See Chapter XII.) In 1955 Finch suggested that Southwestern had strayed from that goal in the ensuing years. He said that Southwestern's curriculum, its degree program, and, to some extent, its major purpose had been "greatly modified by the exigencies of the depression, the war and postwar expansion." It had followed the "all-too-common tendency . . . to drift toward courses that are technical, professional, methodological rather than to maintain the central emphasis on the broad general courses traditionally classified as the 'Liberal Arts.' This trend or drift," he continued, "has been evident across the nation and has been resisted by only a few very vigorous liberal arts colleges."

Some of this change, he allowed, was not bad. It was the "correct adaptation of the traditional liberal arts to the needs of the current age. In no sense could Business Administration, Home Economics, and the Department of Education be strictly considered 'liberal arts,' but few at Southwestern would wish the University to withdraw entirely from these fields." The problem of how best to present the liberal arts in the modern world, stated Finch, is now under study. The result of that study is not something fixed that will be achieved once and for all in a matter of weeks or months but will require continual study and modification. It "will produce a growing sense of the importance of and a re-interpretation of the liberal arts and the liberal arts college, and the peculiar, vital service it can offer its students, its supporting Church, and the society it serves."[13]

This reemphasis on the liberal arts, he felt, should strengthen the relationship of Southwestern and the Church.

> [I]t appears that the University [Southwestern] has one of the best, if not the best, chances of being one of the colleges which may and should emerge from the classification of "good" to become recognized as one of the "really significant liberal arts colleges," which has not lost, but actually strengthened its relationship to its Church, both in service and sense of total relatedness. *There is no real reason why a college should not be academically among the best and at the same time represent the highest and best in its church-relatedness. This juncture of two major purposes, it appears, should be the central goal and chief purpose of Southwestern* [italics added]. . . . Liberal learning pursued in this spirit can contribute much to the days ahead, and Southwestern should chart its course so that the future will find it among the leading collegiate institutions because it has striven toward the highest standards of learning and of faith.[14]

The Board of Trustees was so pleased by the three-page statement of "principles and policies" containing these ideas that it voted immediately to have it printed and to use it as "the guide for the administration and faculty in formulating and developing the work of the University in future years."[15] Rather than being printed exactly as Finch wrote it, the "principles and policies" document was apparently turned over to a faculty committee that reworked it. It was then adopted by the faculty and the Board and printed as a brochure entitled "A Sense of Direction."[16]

This declaration is the clearest description by Finch of what he conceived to be the educational mission of Southwestern. It fleshed out his "vision" statement of 1951 with clear expressions of the complementarity of the liberal arts and the Church-related underpinnings of the University. It was made at a time when everything seemed to be working together for the institution and provided guiding principles for the future. Unproductive programs were being jettisoned, buildings were being built, enrollment was increasing, and endowment was being created. The budget was balanced each year, and the University had no debt. Though certainly not among the top liberal arts institutions in the country, Southwestern was at least among the top half dozen Methodist senior colleges in resources, and a momentum of advance had taken hold of the Board of Trustees. Finch's statement of "principles and policies" at this point was an important initiative. It provided a sense of direction for the long-term future. Its goal, however, was not something that would be realized immediately. He recognized, he said, that institution-building is not an instantaneous matter. Nevertheless, Southwestern's becoming a "significant liberal arts college" in the next quarter century was not an impossible dream.

In his interview with Dr. Martha Allen in 1992, Finch said that when he took the helm at Southwestern in 1949 it could have almost been classified as a teacher training school, one with a strong liberal arts component, but, nevertheless, one where the curriculum "was almost a duplicate of the teacher training program at the University of Texas."[17] This emphasis had been established during the Depression, when teaching and the ministry were the most marketable jobs available to liberal arts graduates. "I take some pride," he confessed, "in moving Southwestern away from [being] a teacher training institution" and moving it more in the direction of being a liberal arts institution. His successors followed him in that direction.[18]

Gradual Transformation of the Faculty

The faculty and senior staff inherited by Finch in 1950 were mostly made up of persons who had joined the University during World War II and the immediate postwar years. Only eleven persons had experienced the entirety of the Great Depression at Southwestern. Six of them—Godbey, Howard, Ferguson, Williams, Meyer, and Waggoner—would retire during the Finch years. The other five—Neas, Ullrich, Hester, Bowden, and McCook—would either retire or die soon afterwards during the early Fleming years. McCook was the last. He would retire in 1968. The hardships of the 1920s and '30s were gradually transmuted into fading memories as the Southwestern of those years was transformed into an institution on the rise rather than one in decline. A few occurrences reminiscent of that past occurred from time to time, such as the suspension of the tenure rule during the Korean War, but it was reinstated immediately following the war and has remained in force ever since.[19]

One of the major changes that occurred was in the socialization of faculty members among themselves. President Finch remarked that when he came in 1940 there was a Faculty Club.

> Every institution had a very formal faculty club. Men wore whatever formal clothes they had or their equivalent. I can remember Dean Meyer being dressed in tails and white tie, which he probably had worn for his piano concerts and what have you. And the women were wearing their evening dresses, and it was all very formal. Somebody read a paper, and it was just a traditional University club, which I think died within two or three years, probably after or during the war. It just disappeared.[20]

At the faculty meeting on September 15, 1956, Angus Springer reviewed the activities of the Faculty Club since its inception in 1930. A motion was approved to abolish the club and to have the Faculty Committee on Receptions take responsibility for arranging the annual faculty dinner in the yard of President Finch.[21] The difference was that the faculty members pretty much ran the old Faculty Club themselves, whereas socialization under the aegis of a faculty committee became more an institutional function.

A new activity instituted during the Score years that became more formalized during the Finch years was the faculty retreat. The retreats began as a result of Score's desire to assemble all the faculty members of the Southwestern system so that they would feel that they were truly one university. Since the institution did not have enough money to go off campus, the faculty members of Westminster, Weatherford, and Daniel Baker came to Georgetown, where a structured series of studies and lectures was held.[22] From this beginning emerged the annual faculty retreat where the faculty went for a day to some other location. By 1954 the faculty retreat had become a regular feature initiating the academic year. In 1958 a family picnic supper was held at the home of Board chairman John D. Wheeler in San Antonio.[23] The retreats were still being held there during the first several years of my career at Southwestern in 1965 and 1966. Various persons were brought in each year to lead the faculty in the discussion of some relevant topic or book. In 1959 the focus of the retreat was Dr. Elton Trueblood's new book, *The Idea of a College.*[24]

Faculty procurement had been entirely a function of the President from the time of Mood through the appointment of the first dean under Hyer. Beginning at that time, the President usually but not always consulted the dean before making a new hire. The appointment of faculty members was his unique responsibility, from making the initial contact to writing the final contract. Though Score usually conferred with Dean Ullrich in making appointments, he would sometimes inform him by means of a memorandum of someone he had already procured for a particular position. With the advent of the School of Fine Arts and the other three divisions under Score, the President began to appoint divisional heads. They were always mature members of the faculty and held their positions for long periods of time, sometimes until retirement. They met on a regular basis with the dean between faculty meetings to consider academic and other relevant matters. They were sometimes but not always consulted about faculty appointments. Candidates for positions, says Finch, were interviewed by "me and the Dean and that was it. Occasionally I guess, well, I know more than occasionally, we would involve the heads of the Division."[25]

Faculty Salary

The President also made salary determinations. He relied more heavily on the dean for recommendations in this matter than for initial appointments, but he always operated from the base of a previous budget determination made by him and the Business Manager as to how much money was available. As a result of the successful completion of the W-K-M transaction in late 1954, more than $3 million was added to the endowment, giving Southwestern a significant working endowment for the first time. In response, Finch's first action was to provide an across-the-board salary increase for all faculty members. Those with fifteen or more years of service received $1,000, while those with less than fifteen received $500.[26] When the Board also tried to reward him and Dr. McCook with substantial raises, he refused to accept them, saying that he did not want "to allow the Board to tip the salary scale further in behalf of the president and vice president."[27] The salary scale at the time provided that the President, Vice President, and Dean of Arts and Sciences should receive, respectively, a salary of 1.5, 1.375, and 1.25 times that of a full professor.[28] A year later the Board approved Social Security coverage for Southwestern faculty and staff.[29]

By 1957, however, Finch voiced frustration in his efforts to raise the salary scale. He reported to the Trustees that in spite of devoting 59 percent of the budget to instructional salaries, Southwestern's salaries still compared unfavorably with "really quality" institutions.[30] Unable to provide further significant salary increases, the Board awarded faculty and staff employees Christmas bonuses for the next three years. More important than the bonuses, however, were improvements in the fringe benefits package. In 1959 the Executive Committee voted to authorize the payment by Southwestern of the entire cost of the retirement plan.[31]

In Finch's last full year, the average salary for full-time teachers was $6,177. In addition, the faculty member received 15 percent in fringe benefits, including 10 percent in retirement payments, 3 percent in Social Security payments, and 2 percent in supplementary payments for hospitalization and life insurance. All of this together amounted to $7,105.85.[32] Adjusted into 2000 dollars to account for inflation, these amounts would be $35,246.10 in cash income and $5,300.03 in benefits, for a total of $40,546.13. Finch reported that this salary level placed Southwestern at the median when compared with private colleges in the West and Southwest with an enrollment of 500–999, but distinctly under that of publicly supported colleges of the same size.[33] Southwestern would retain roughly this same position among colleges of the same size and type during the next twenty years until faculty salary enhancement became a major priority during the early years of the Shilling administration.

Long-term Faculty Procurements

The following faculty members began their service at the invitation of President Finch and had long careers at Southwestern.

Name	Title/Subject	Year	Years
Girvin, Eb Carl	Biology	1953	35
Beaver, Elizabeth Platt	Latin	1954	23
McCook, Jane Brown	Drama, English	1956	29
Gervasi, Mildred Quillin	Head Librarian	1957	18
Penick, R. Cochrane	Music (Organ)	1957	22
Clifford, Frederick Burr	English, Classics	1958	23

continued on following page

continued from preceding page

Name	Title/Subject	Year	Years
Nelson, George E.	Music (Band)	1958	33
Lancaster, Robert L.	Sculpture	1959	16
Allen, Martha Mitten	Dean of Women, History	1960	37
Spellmann, Norman Woods	Religion	1960	39
Hooker, William Douglas	Psychology	1961	44*
Huffmaster, Drusilla	Music (Piano)	1961	27

*Retired in 2004.

Eb Girvin became, in the Biology Department, the rock around which it developed in the thirty-five years of his tenure. He was especially important in securing and defining the space needed by biology in the renovation of the Fondren-Jones Science Hall in 1980–1981. He was also an active advocate for the integration of the Georgetown public school system. Millie Gervasi performed the same function for the library. She was the person who shepherded through from the academic side the major addition to the library in 1966.

Elizabeth Platt Beaver and Jane Brown McCook represent perfectly the special contributions made by part-time teachers to Southwestern throughout its history. Both were so respected by their fellow teachers and popular with students that the other faculty members treated them as if they were full-time.

The School of Fine Arts employed four faculty members who became a core faculty for many years. These were Cochrane Penick, George Nelson, Bob Lancaster, and Drusilla Huffmaster. Penick was an excellent organist and the first to be employed as such by the School of Fine Arts. Nelson, the long-tenured band director who replaced Ralph Jones when he moved into history after procuring his Ed.D. in 1960, gave the band and other instrumental groups directed by him the expertise and stability they needed. Lancaster was an outstanding sculptor, trained by Fred Umlauf. His works were displayed widely and were sold commercially throughout the Southwest.

The procurement of Drusilla Huffmaster, pianist, in 1961 as Artist-in-Residence was the first such "artist" appointment made at the University. She had studied with an eminent Viennese pianist and at the Juilliard School of Music. In addition, she had appeared at Town Hall in New York, in London, Amsterdam, The Hague, Copenhagen, Hamburg, Munich, Zurich, Milan, and in numerous cities throughout the United States before she came to Southwestern. She divided her time between teaching and performing at Southwestern.[34]

Martha Mitten Allen and Norman Woods Spellmann were fine teachers in their respective fields. Each was also noted for speaking candidly in faculty meetings and standing up for student rights. To their teaching each brought an interest in preserving the history of Southwestern through the use of oral history techniques in addition to the careful perusal of written records. Allen's most important publication about the history of Southwestern was *The Gracious Gift: The Negro Fine Arts School 1946–66* (1998, 2003). Spellmann's was the excellent biography of Bishop A. Frank Smith, entitled *Growing a Soul: The Story of A. Frank Smith* (1979).

Douglas Hooker was a popular psychology teacher who developed an internship program for his students that was widely respected by clinics, hospitals, and other educational institutions. Many of his students received graduate degrees after completing their work at Southwestern, a larger number perhaps than that produced by any other teacher in Southwestern history. He authored or coauthored several books emphasizing the humanistic psychology he taught. The one closest to his central interest was *The Healthy Personality and the Christian Life* (1977), a study of the insights gained from Barthian theology for the development of a healthy personality.

Hooker also brought to the classroom the benefit of his experiences received in England and in World War II. Born in Michigan of British parents, who moved back to England when he was a child, he was educated in English schools until he joined the Royal Navy during World War II. He served on a destroyer that did the Arctic-Murmansk run and participated in the sinking of the battleship *Scharnhorst*, the D-Day landings, and the sinking of the Japanese cruiser *Haguro* in the Indian Ocean. After the war he received degrees from Wofford College, Wayne State University, and the University of Texas before coming to Southwestern.

One of the characteristics of the faculty that became very notable during the Score and Finch years was the increasing number of persons with doctorates. In 1941 there were only five such persons. In 1957–1958 there were eighteen, with five others only lacking the completion of their dissertations.[35] Soon the doctorate rather than the master's would become the basic requirement for all teaching positions in fields where a doctorate could be obtained.

Balanced Budgets and the Pattern of Expenditures

From 1937 through 1961 Southwestern experienced only two budgets that ended with deficits, both due to unusual circumstances. The first was permitted to develop purposely in 1942–1943 while seeking the Naval V-12 Unit so as avoid the appearance of retrenchment. The second was a small deficit that occurred in 1949, the year President Score died. A balanced budget was an article of faith in the operation of the University, and great care was taken to achieve it each year. That care was exercised primarily by Dr. I. J. McCook, to whom, said Finch, the excellent financial management of the University was due.[36] When the budget passed $1 million for the first time in 1959, Finch said that it was a matter of pride to be able to do so while still maintaining a balanced budget.[37]

The income pattern for the University in 1958–1959 was: from endowment 39.5 percent, from student fees 37.7 percent, from gifts 19.6 percent, and from other sources 3.2 percent.[38] Though everyone recognized that the weakness in this pattern was the low percentage of income from student fees, everyone was also afraid of raising tuition significantly for fear of losing students. Because everyone believed that a significant increase in tuition would have a significant impact on student numbers, tuition increases were held to a minimum and made as seldom as possible. Nevertheless, Finch felt that Southwestern was so far behind on this point by the time of his departure in 1961 that he left as a parting word for Fleming that tuition must be raised for the following year.[39]

Particularly interesting is the fact that the same pattern continued through the Fleming and into the Shilling administrations even when they tried to raise the percentage of income from tuition by raising the student tuition charge significantly. The rapid increase in endowment funds occasioned by the success of the Brown Challenge and the rise in the stock market in the 1980s and '90s outstripped any ability to raise tuition by commensurate percentages. The low level of tuition maintained by the State schools also forced private schools to charge lower rates than they might have preferred in order to stay competitive.

Enrollment Pattern

In spite of the draft during the Korean War, which took students away from college, Southwestern experienced a healthy growth in enrollment during the decade of the 1950s. From its low fall semester enrollment of 414 in 1951, it grew by an average rate of 5.2 percent per year to 653 in the fall of 1960, Finch's last year. When it appeared in 1959 that the earlier enrollment limit of 750 set by the Board in 1943 might be achieved within a few more years, Finch suggested that it be modified.[40] The goal should be, he said, to have 700 residential students—400 men, 300 women—and 150 commuting students, for a total of 850.[41] His proposal was discussed, but no action was taken. One of the reasons for the hesitation of the Board to approve the change is that 400 male and 300 female residential students could only be handled by building more housing accommodations for both men and women.[42]

Only a few of the students were from outside of Texas. In 1954 fifteen students were from other countries and nineteen from other states. In 1961 thirteen were from other countries and eighteen from other states. These proportions were about the same every year during the decade. Practically all the foreign students required extensive scholarship aid to attend, and the President worked hard to secure scholarships to make that possible.[43]

The most popular major field at Southwestern in 1961 was Education, with 15.3 percent of all majors. It was followed by Economics and Business Administration with 15.0 percent. The other social sciences enrolled 20.3 percent of the majors. The Division of Social Sciences, including Education and Economics/Business Administration, enrolled 50.6 percent of all majors. The Division of Natural Sciences and Mathematics followed with 22.3 percent, the Humanities Division with 16.1 percent, and the School of Fine Arts with 11.0 percent.[44]

Fraternity and sorority influence continued to be very important through the 1950s and into the 1960s. Slightly more than three out of every five students were members of

Greek letter organizations. These organizations were also getting their share of the better students. Whereas today it is almost a truism that non-Greek students have a consistently better grade average than Greeks, the same was not true in 1961. In that year both Greek men and Greek women had a slightly better grade average than non-Greek men and women.[45]

Religious Orientation of Students and the Chaplaincy

Ever since its founding, most of Southwestern's administration, faculty, and students had been Methodist. Though statistics were not kept on the denominational affiliation of students until the 1930s, a respectable minority attending during its first half century were not members of any denomination and received their first consistent contact with the Church during their college years. The Presidents used the number of conversions achieved among these and irresolute church members in their reports to the Trustees to prove that Southwestern was fulfilling its role as a Church-related institution. President Bishop abandoned the practice after he assumed office in 1911. He said that practically all the entering students were already church members. Pearl A. Neas, in her meticulous way, began to track the number of students by denomination in the early 1930s. She reported that 65.5 percent were Methodists in 1934 and 66.7 percent in 1937.

One of the significant changes that occurred during and immediately after World War II was the increasing percentage of students who were both church members and Methodists when they entered. By 1954, 71.7 percent were Methodist, a percentage that had increased to 82.2 percent by 1957. Southwestern can be said to have been a Methodist school in terms of student church membership during Finch's administration probably more than at any other time in its history. A good number of these students planned to enter the ministry or some other form of professional religious service. The number of ministerial students fluctuated between fifty and sixty-one each year during the 1950s and between forty-four and sixty-three for Life Service students. Between 15 percent and 20 percent of the student body at any one time planned to enter some form of religious service.

The basic nonacademic religious requirement for students was attendance at chapel services each week. They were also encouraged to attend some of the voluntary events. Principal among them was Morning Watch, held twice each week, and Vesper Services, conducted in the chapel each Friday night. A more formal voluntary occasion was the fall Preaching Mission each year, conducted by a prominent visiting minister. The Preaching Mission services during these years were held at eleven on Tuesday, Wednesday, and Thursday. The Tuesday and Thursday hours were the normal assembly and chapel hours. Whether or not the faculty dismissed its normal eleven o'clock Wednesday classes each year to allow students to attend on that day is an unresolved point, but it at least did so in 1957. The Preaching Missions brought in outstanding preachers such as Chess Lovern and Kenneth Pope, both of whom later became bishops. The Danforth Foundation sponsored a series of formal lectures in 1959, 1960, and 1961 that featured three of the leading theologians in the country. They were George A. Buttrick, H. Richard Niebuhr, and Carlyle Marney.

Prior to 1956 members of the administration and faculty ran the religious program of the University in close connection with the First Methodist Church of Georgetown. The chaplaincy was not a full-time position, and either the minister of the church or a member of the Religion Department was the chaplain. In that year the University employed its first full-time chaplain. He was David Switzer, a member of the Naval V-12 Unit at Southwestern during World War II, an honor student, president of the student body, and a letterman in baseball. After graduating from Southwestern, he earned a Bachelor of Divinity degree from Emory University. He gave his entire time to the supervision of the religious programs on campus, conducting the chapel services, and serving as a counselor. He was popular with both students and faculty and served for nine years.[46]

Intercollegiate Athletics and Cultural Productions

Though the intercollegiate football program was dropped in 1951, the University continued to participate in basketball, baseball, track, tennis, and golf as a member of the Big State Athletic Conference. Neither the teams nor student support for them was strong in comparison with earlier years. By 1961 women's athletics had been restricted almost entirely to intramural events. In that year the Board of Trustees voted "to permit women students to participate in intercollegiate sports on a tournament basis only, to be sponsored as part of the program of Physical Training for Women, and not to be or become a part of an inter-collegiate athletic program for women in manner, shape or form."[47]

Cultural productions became stronger during the decade, especially after 1957, when the Alma Thomas Fine Arts Center was built. In that year Margarett Brown sponsored exhibits in the new gallery, the Mask and Wig Players presented a fine bill of fare, and the Artists Concert Series was very good. It included the Pamplona Choir, the San Antonio Symphony, the Dublin Players, and other artists of ability. The Southwestern A'Cappella Choir under Dean Richards was invited to sing the Bach *Magnificat* and to furnish the choral group for *Amahl and the Night Visitors* for the Christmas concert of the San Antonio Symphony on December 15 in San Antonio after having done it on campus two days earlier.[48]

Student Life

The 1950s was a quiet decade relatively speaking, as to student behavior. A return to normalcy was in the air, and students took their cue from the returned veterans, who wanted to get on with life, not with student shenanigans. Not even the Korean War disturbed the trend for long. The grand ballroom of the new Bishops' Memorial Union was a perfect setting for the all-campus dances. The Honor System went through one of its periodic revisions in 1953, and a long set of "Regulations Governing Student Organizations" was promulgated in 1956.[49]

With the impending retirement of Dean Ullrich in 1956, one of his fondest aspirations was achieved. Chairmanship of the Discipline Committee was turned over to another person. Ullrich, who had served as chair of that committee since his assumption of the deanship in 1926, had tried several times to have it moved into other hands, all to no avail. He dealt strongly but equitably with students over the years, and the Board refused to let him give it up.[50] Now in light of his impending retirement it was given to the Dean of Men, John Berglund.[51]

Berglund, however, was not challenged in the job the way Ullrich had been in some of his earlier years. The Report of the Discipline Committee for 1955–1956 showed that of the fifty-one cases handled, only nine were for infractions of college rules. The others were for excessive absences, appeals, and other kinds of committee housekeeping rules.[52] In 1959 the worst cases handled by the Discipline Committee were theft, entering an office for the purpose of stealing an examination, carrying a prohibited weapon and drinking in a public place, entering an off-limits area of the Union, and two cases of entering the dormitory while under the influence of intoxicants.[53] In 1960 the Dean of Men reported that the Discipline Committee had not had any cases in the fall and only two cases involving infraction of dormitory regulations in the spring. He said that a very fine group of housemothers was in place for the fraternities and of directors for the dormitories. There were no serious problems, he concluded, and "the situation is good."[54]

Trustee and Senior Staff Turnover

Just as most of the faculty that served through the Depression gave way to a faculty with a postwar mentality during the 1950s, the same occurred with the Board of Trustees and the senior staff. Finch was fortunate with the Board of Trustees inherited from Score, one of the strongest in the state of Texas, as he later said.[55] At his last Board meeting in 1961, he credited members of the Board of Trustees with personally having contributed $1,850,000 to the University in the last decade for its building and endowment program.[56] Working together with the President, the Board tripled the endowment and constructed buildings one after another for almost a decade. Its members knew each other well, and they almost vied with one another to help the University.

In 1955 Dr. Cody's health did not allow him to stand for reelection as Board chair.[57] Though he remained as a member of the Board until 1958, he was sometimes not able to attend and died the following year. Thus was lost the last connection by a member of the Board with the beginnings of the University through a parent, his father, Dean Cody. The event was, in a sense, memorialized by the family's presentation in 1955 of the Dean's library and extensive collection of Southwestern materials, so valuable for the composition of this work, to the Cody Memorial Library.[58]

John D. Wheeler, a prominent San Antonio lawyer, was elected to take Cody's place as chair.[59] Wheeler, who came on the Board in 1942 when Score was elected President, served as a member twenty-seven years until 1968. Finch held Wheeler in high esteem and said that he was a remarkable man, a person with strong Christian convictions but objective in his appraisals and flexible in his methods.

The Board lost, in addition to Cody, two others of its oldest Trustees by death in 1959. They were Dr. C. P. Yea-

The Board of Trustees, 1954. Left to right, first row: W. H. Atwell, C. C. Cody, Jr., Alma Thomas, E. B. Germany, A. F. Smith; second row: Walter Willis, Herman Brown, E. A. Hunter, R. H. Nichols, E. L. Kurth; third row: Charles Heyne, G. F. Jones, C. N. Prothro, C. P. Yeager, H. B. Lloyd, C. H. Sisserson; fourth row: Edmund Heinsohn, O. A. Ullrich, I. J. McCook, W. C. Finch, H. L. Egger. From the 1954 *Sou'wester.*

ger and E. L. Kurth. The three together had given approximately one hundred years of service to Southwestern, each serving through the crisis days of the Depression and the pressure of the war and postwar years.[60] Among the ministers who left the Board were Dr. Edmund Heinsohn and Dr. L. U. Spellman. It was fitting that Heinsohn, often the voice of conscience on the Board, should be succeeded by James William Morgan, pastor of University Methodist Church in Austin.[61] As pastor in Georgetown from 1946 to 1951, Morgan made it possible for the Negro Fine Arts School to meet in the First Methodist Church. He would later become the spokesman for the pro-integration forces on the Board of Trustees during the Fleming administration. Spellman was active in helping Southwestern through the crisis years of the 1930s. A resolution of appreciation was given him at the time of his retirement in 1958 for his long and "unflagging" zeal in promoting the interests of the University.[62]

Though the Board lost a number of stalwart members, it also gained new members who expressed the same loyalty to the institution that had animated those who were lost. Mrs. Alma Thomas and Charles N. Prothro have already been mentioned. Another was W. Grogan Lord. Lord was the last person elected explicitly as a Georgetown representative. Beginning his service in 1958, Lord continued as an active member until 1998, when he was elected an honorary member. His son, Griffin, replaced him on the Board. Once elected, Grogan Lord immediately went to work and procured an arrangement with the city council to make untreated water from a well in San Gabriel Park available for the campus sprinkler system just being completed.[63] He provided many services and benefactions to the University over the years, among them providing the resources for the Lord Chair in Computer Science and the Grogan and Betty Lord Residential Center. The residential center is an apartment complex for two hundred students located on the northwest corner of the campus. It was dedicated in 1995.

New Deans and a Vice President

The Board approved a requirement in 1952 that administrative personnel who were also teaching must give up their administrative positions at the age of sixty-five. This rule changed the time frame for the retirement of the persons in the three traditional deans' positions.[64] Under this rule both Ferguson and Meyer would have to retire from their deanships in 1955 and Ullrich in 1956.[65] When the time arrived for Ferguson and Meyer three years later, they retired and were given the title of Dean Emeritus.[66] They did, however, continue teaching for five more years until reaching the mandatory retirement age of seventy for teachers.

Meyer's replacement, John D. Richards, was already on hand. He had been on the faculty since 1946 and was Head of the Department of Music Education and Director of the Southwestern University Choruses. He held B.F.A. and M.Mus.Ed. degrees from the University of Oklahoma. In recommending him to the Board, Finch said about Richards that he was in tune with "the threefold emphasis in Fine Arts; the preparation of musicians and artists in their own right, the development of an outstanding program of Church Music at Southwestern, and the continuation and enrichment of the present program of preparing music teachers."[67] He retired in 1975 after twenty-nine years of service.

Mrs. Joan Smith, with B.S. and M.S. degrees in Home Economics from the University of Texas, became Dean of

Women and was named Assistant Professor in the Department of Home Economics. Upon her resignation after three years, Mrs. Ferguson agreed to return for a one-year appointment that lengthened into two before Martha Mitten assumed the deanship in 1960. She held the position for seven years and taught part-time in the Department of History and Government. A Phi Beta Kappa graduate from Southern Methodist University, she was encouraged by her colleagues in history to complete her doctorate and become a full-time history teacher. Consequently, she gave up her position as Dean of Women, entered the University of Texas, secured a Ph.D. in American history in 1972, and completed her career at Southwestern as a highly respected history teacher in 1997.

In addition to the deans, a new administrative office was created to oversee the financial development of the University. Financial development, traditionally a function of the President, would continue to be so in the overall sense, but until 1958 the President had never had a permanent staff in that area to work with him on a full-time basis. He even had to use his own car or other transportation until the University purchased its first car for him. In that year President Finch recommended the establishment of a Development Office with a Director of Development.[68] The Board of Trustees approved that idea and furnished him a university car as well with all expenses paid.[69]

Procurement of a person of the type needed was difficult, and it was not until the title was changed to Vice President, Development and Public Relations that a person was secured. He was William Graves Blanton, Director of Development at Baylor.[70] Various fund-raising initiatives were begun, such as the Southwestern Associates and the Living Endowment programs. These programs raised some money but did not have a significant impact on the University. Finch's analysis of the new Development Office program during the three years of its operation under him determined that it was not very effective.[71] Blanton remained with the University until 1968.

New Dean of the College of Arts and Sciences

A crucial administrative replacement in the eyes of everyone was that of Dean Ullrich. Appointed dean in 1926 as a young man, he, like Dean Cody some years before, came to represent what the deanship meant in the eyes of most people. He had served over a period of thirty years, from the days of the flapper doing the Charleston in the pre-Depression 1920s to the bobby soxer doing the jitterbug in the 1940s of the World War II period and into the 1950s with Elvis Presley and rock and roll. Ullrich would become sixty-five in 1956 and must relinquish his place to someone else.

Recognizing the importance of the appointment, Finch began his search a year early. Having decided to bring in someone from the outside, he consulted with other persons in the field of higher education and at the Methodist Board of Education in Nashville. As a result of these consultations, his attention was drawn to Dr. Howard S. Greenlee, Associate Professor and Head of the Social Sciences Division and Associate Dean of Simpson College at Indianola, Iowa. Though he was only thirty-six years old, he had an outstanding résumé. He held an A.B., M.A., and Ph.D. from the University of Chicago and was on the staff at Simpson College, a Methodist liberal arts college of approximately six hundred students. He had been a Visiting Scholar at Union Theological Seminary, where he studied under Paul Tillich, Reinhold Niebuhr, and Wilhelm Pauck, on a faculty fellowship granted by the Ford Foundation. He had also traveled in Europe.[72]

After visiting him at Indianola and in Des Moines, Finch invited him to visit the campus for a weekend, where he was interviewed by most of the staff. He was subsequently nominated at the spring Board meeting for the position of Associate Dean for a period of one year, with the understanding that upon its "mutually satisfactory conclusion," he would be nominated to succeed Dean Ullrich.[73] The Board approved Finch's recommendation, and Greenlee assumed his responsibilities at Southwestern in the fall of 1955.[74]

Surprisingly, for a man who had been so thoroughly vetted, Greenlee did not satisfy the expectations people had for him. Though he was an exemplary history teacher and his administrative performance was very good, he revealed traits that led Finch and others to feel that they needed a steadier hand at the helm of the academic enterprise than he might provide. Though he was a Presbyterian when he came, he church-shopped upon arrival in Georgetown and gave other evidences of "an unwillingness to come to terms with the total situation in which he found himself at Southwestern." He and his wife had been reared in Chicago, and Finch felt that he and his family were unable "to accept completely life in a little town." There was "a note of inflexibility" in his approach, and he did not show the reliability expected of a dean.[75] Consequently, Finch informed Greenlee fairly soon after the beginning of the new year that he would be happy for him to remain as a teacher on the faculty but could not recommend him as dean.[76] The two men discussed the problem in a professional manner, but neither was willing to modify his position sufficiently to bridge the gap between their understandings of what must be done to correct the situation.

Having come to Southwestern to be dean, Greenlee was unsatisfied to remain in any other capacity. Therefore, he sought a position elsewhere, which he had no difficulty securing. Greenlee left Southwestern amicably, and he and Finch remained friends. The two men and their wives corresponded with each other from time to time at least through 1961, when Finch left Southwestern and the files run dry.

Given the unexpected turn of events with Greenlee, Dean Ullrich was asked to defer his retirement another year. One year turned into two, and Finch was not ready with his replacement until the spring of 1958. When Ullrich finally retired, he wrote a gracious tribute to the President in his Board report.

> To you, President Finch, I wish to state that working with you has been relaxing and, therefore, a pleasure. Your training both for the church and for higher education has equipped you in a unique way for administering the affairs of a church related college. Moreover, your personality is such that I never felt the need of being on guard when discussing matters relating to our common task. As I look back, I am amazed to note how often we were of one mind. When we differed, you yielded to my judgment so often that I must testify that you are a good president.[77]

The Finch-Wicke Friendship

Soon after becoming Acting President, Finch secured the services of Dr. Myron Wicke to lead a Conference on Vocation in the Church at Southwestern during the first week in January 1950.[78] At the time Wicke was on the Board of Education of the Methodist Church in Nashville as Secretary of the Department of Higher Education. A native of Cleveland, Ohio, he had secured a B.A. from Baldwin-Wallace College and an M.A. and Ph.D. from Western Reserve University. He had done graduate work at Columbia, the University of Chicago, and Oberlin College. Prior to going to Nashville, he had returned to Baldwin-Wallace, where he served first as Dean of Men, then as Dean of the College. Possessed of a pleasant and efficient disposition and in contact with many colleges and universities across the country, he was an ideal person to act as a counselor for a new college president.

After he was elected permanent President, Finch invited Wicke to return to Southwestern to make an assessment of the institution. He spent five days on campus visiting classes, attending meetings, and talking with students and faculty members. His visit overlapped Dobie Day on October 29, 1952. At the conclusion of his visit he shared with the faculty some of the observations he had made during his time on campus and stated what he felt to be the imperatives of college education.[79] About a month later he sent back a twenty-eight-page paper detailing his impressions. It was very well done—thorough, moderate in its recommendations, and modern in its understanding of educational methodology. Some of its recommendations

J. Frank and Bertha Dobie on Dobie Day, October 29, 1952, riding in a hack from the era when they were college sweethearts. A number of prominent writers gathered at Southwestern to honor Dobie's influence on Southwest literature. Dobie said it was the happiest day of his life. From the 1953 *Sou'wester*.

are worth noting for what they have to say about Southwestern education in 1952 as seen through the eyes of a knowledgeable outside observer. Overall, Wicke says that "the instructional program ranges from poor to brilliant." Some of his particular observations are as follows:

- There is too much lecturing.
- There are too many courses.
- The honor system seems to be working quite well.
- A vigorous annual faculty planning conference would be very helpful.
- A course syllabus should be a "must" for every course.
- Faculty rating scales would be helpful.
- More seminars would be useful.
- The college bulletin would profit from drastic revision.
- Southwestern graduate work is "the most vulnerable part of the entire program, and the most likely sooner or later to bring serious criticism."
- The use of a high school "absence system" is both expensive and educationally indefensible. "It is wasteful to record every absence."
- Students are not happy with the present chapel arrangements, featuring the same speaker regularly. "It is my opinion that the chaplain would be better liked if he did not speak so often."
- "The desperate need for a student union is understood by everyone."
- A college dean would find it profitable to meet occasionally with student leaders in groups in an informal and relaxed situation.[80]

About a month later Finch shared the contents of the report with the faculty, which placed it in the hands of the Committee on the Improvement of Instruction for further study.[81] How much attention it received from the committee is unknown, but some of its recommendations had already been attended to by the time Wicke became dean six years later. The number of courses had been reduced, the graduate program had been eliminated, a full-time chaplain who did not preach at every service had been secured, and a student union had been built. Wicke would undertake some of the other recommendations as dean. One of them, that the college bulletin would profit from drastic revision, would come back to haunt him.

Over the next few years the exchange of letters between Finch and Wicke became more and more cordial, and Wicke invited Finch from time to time to become a part of survey teams that visited other colleges. On one trip he and Wicke visited Iowa Wesleyan College, Morningside College, Simpson College, and Cornell College.[82] Finch in turn received many helpful suggestions from Wicke about things that might be done at Southwestern. In 1956 Finch invited him to be the principal speaker at the faculty retreat that year. When Wicke fell ill and could not attend, Finch invited him again for September 1957. He also announced that Wicke had informed him that Southwestern's request for a two-thousand-dollar grant from the Board of Education had been favorably acted upon and that a Committee on Faculty Summer Study would be activated to study its use. The grant required a one-thousand-dollar match from the University.[83] In the spring Wicke visited SMU, Texas Wesleyan College, McMurry, Lon Morris, and Southwestern, in that order.[84]

Wicke Appointed Dean

With Greenlee's candidacy for the deanship having failed, Finch consulted with Wicke by correspondence about other candidates. They likely discussed it as well when they were together. Wicke stayed in Finch's home in September 1957 during the faculty retreat that was held at Rockledge on Lake Austin.[85] His topic at the retreat was "The Teacher and the Academic Community."[86] It was perhaps something taken from or related to the material in his sixty-seven-page manuscript entitled "The Teacher in the Christian College," which he had recently sent to Finch.[87]

At the fall Board meeting, Finch presented to the Trustees two candidates for the deanship. One was the Head of the Department of Romance Languages at Duke University. The other was Dr. Myron F. Wicke. Given the frequent contacts of Wicke with Southwestern during the last eight years, it is not surprising that he was the overwhelming choice.[88] Finch issued the formal invitation by letter. Wicke asked for several weeks to think it over but indicated that his present inclination was to accept the position. His one question was whether the members of Finch's staff who knew of the offer were "friendly to the idea" of his coming.[89] He phoned Finch in early December accepting the offer, and Finch sent a memorandum to the faculty in mid-January announcing Wicke's appointment as Professor of English and Dean of the College of Arts and Sciences, effective September 1, 1958.[90] Wicke visited the campus in March on a trip to Texas already scheduled for another purpose.[91]

Wicke's Immediate Influence

Finch immediately began to inform Wicke about campus events and decisions being made. The most interesting of those decisions was with reference to the vacant position in English, where one of the candidates was Frederick Burr Clifford. Considering the fact that Clifford became his replacement as permanent dean in 1961, Wicke's role in bringing him to Southwestern means that he, unknowingly, had a hand in selecting his successor.

In his first letter written as dean-elect to Finch about a Southwestern matter, Wicke wrote: "I hope you look closely at Clifford."[92] Finch wrote back that he had received a nice reply from Clifford and "he is anxious to be considered." Claud Howard and Dean Ullrich, however, were bothered by the fact that his training was primarily in Comparative Literature and in Classics rather than in English. Finch said that since Wicke knew Clifford personally, he would waive the necessity of a personal interview before bringing him to the campus. "We like him very much with this exception."[93] Wicke wrote him back detailing his knowledge of Clifford. "My acquaintance with Clifford began at Adrian when he was teaching a most unusual course in freshman literature. We helped to place him at Emory where he had contact with such men as Ernest Colwell in what is in many respects a unique program. I have felt him to be an excellent teacher with original ideas. His classical background always seemed to me a great strength, and the University of Michigan a top-flight graduate school to have represented on a college faculty." Nevertheless, he emphasized that he was not carrying the torch for Clifford and that those presently responsible at Southwestern should make the decision.[94]

Clifford was selected for the position, and Finch presented his name to the Board of Trustees, which duly confirmed his choice. He described Clifford as a person with a Ph.D. from the University of Michigan and a B.D. from the Oberlin Graduate School of Theology. He was a member Phi Beta Kappa, a member of the Detroit Conference, the son of a minister, and had been an active pastor for nine years. In addition, he had taught at Adrian College and was presently Associate Professor of Humanities and Chairman of the Curriculum Committee at Emory at Oxford. "At 44 years of age," said Finch, "he is a seasoned teacher with ability."[95]

Within two years of Clifford's coming to Southwestern, Finch said that he had undertaken major responsibility for the new curriculum in English and that an exciting program was being developed in that department. He nominated him to the rank of full professor and to become head of the English Department.[96] The following year he was given tenure.[97]

All parties concerned looked upon the appointment of Wicke as a coup for Southwestern. The President had secured a congenial person with whom he had already worked for almost a decade, the faculty looked on him as an experienced person with whom they were familiar, and student reaction to his coming began on a positive note. After providing a brief résumé of his career, an article in *The Megaphone* said that he was "a charming, amusing, and witty man."[98]

Reaction to Wicke's appointment in higher education circles was basically astonishment, astonishment that a person as prominent as he in the circles of Methodist higher education would give up a major position to accept the deanship of a college that had not theretofore distinguished itself. Most educators knew that Southwestern had come a long way but not far enough to attract a person of Wicke's caliber. In addition to his academic and administrative credentials and his position with the Methodist Board of Education, Wicke was a Trustee of Alaska University, a member of the Executive Committee of the American Council on Education, and the author of many publications. One of them was his *Handbook for Trustees.* Another would be his soon to be published *Handbook for Faculty.*[99] It seems that a major reason for Wicke's coming to Southwestern was his desire to translate what he had learned and written about over the years into practice at a school on the rise where he and the President had similar goals. He delivered the Commencement address as dean-elect in June 1958. His topic was "Choose Something Like a Star."[100]

The Race Issue at Southwestern through 1951

The Negro School of Fine Arts, begun in 1946 by Iola Bowden Chambers, had been in operation eight years when the *Brown v. Board of Education of Topeka* decision was handed down in 1954. By then it had carved out its niche in community practice and understanding so that it continued through the next decade unaffected by the turbulence that developed around the question of race in the country and in Georgetown. Professor Bill Finch had been a member of the city school board that had arrived at an accommodation allowing some public school resources to be used in behalf of the Negro Fine Arts School at the First Methodist Church and had been one of the Executive Committee for the School itself.

President Score supported the venture and did not allow it to become an issue for Miss Bowden or for her students who worked in the School. Nevertheless, his support for the Negro Fine Arts School off campus did not lead him to support racially integrated activities on campus. In a letter addressed to Mary Elizabeth Fox, Director of Publicity, in 1963, ex-student Walter J. Ligon referred to an issue involving Score that arose in that regard.

> During my sophomore year at SU, in 1947–48, I was one of the officers of the student group that met at First Methodist Church. We had invited as the speaker for one of our programs a distinguished Negro educator from another Texas college. He was to be with us over the weekend and our plans included showing him the campus and having him eat a meal with us in the student dining room, which was then Mood Hall. Permission to offer him school facilities for a meal was denied us, however, and although I took it up with Dr. Score personally, he remained adamant.[101]

In 1946 integration became a major issue in Texas public education when Heman Marion Sweatt applied for admission into the University of Texas Law School. His application was denied, but the case lingered on. Though the State of Texas established a temporary law school just for him and any other blacks that might apply, its effort to circumvent integration failed. Sweatt was duly admitted to the University of Texas Law School in 1950.[102]

In the same year that Sweatt entered the University of Texas Law School, Southwestern was in the process of trying to obtain an R.O.T.C. unit to bolster its lagging enrollment. Finch reported to the Trustees in the spring of 1951 that the school had received strong help from Senator Johnson, Congressman Thornberry, and Judge Marvin Jones, and particularly fine help and assistance from Admiral W. L. Mann in its effort.

By the time of the Board meeting Southwestern had also been inspected by officers of the air force in connection with a contract program for the training of secretary-office personnel for the Department of the Air Force as well. Finch felt that there was an excellent possibility for securing such a contract. "We were told by the inspection officer on April 4th," he says, "that we were one of the two schools in Texas ready to receive a contract, pending the Air Force Department's decision concerning segregation and our own bid. Under the present non-segregation policy of the Air Force, it was necessary for me to withdraw our application, but they have requested that it be renewed, pending the clarification of their segregation policy. The application as finally submitted to them clearly indicates that under present circumstances, we are not submitting an application for a non-segregated unit."[103]

The ambiguity in the statement by air force personnel to Finch proceeded from the fact that although President Harry S. Truman had issued an executive order wiping out segregation in the armed forces on July 31, 1948, the process of desegregating the military was proceeding slowly. Whatever his own thoughts on the issue, the new President at Southwestern was unwilling to recommend an application that would bring to Southwestern an integrated air force program that he knew the Board of Trustees would almost certainly oppose.

Finch's Race Policy during the 1950s

Quietly, on his own, Finch began to take steps that would prepare the campus for the integration that must surely come. On November 24 and 25, 1953, Negro college administrators were welcomed as guests of Southwestern University for meals in the University Commons. On April 26, 1954, "Negro baseball players from the Gary Air Force Base enjoyed their noon and evening meals in the University Commons."[104] When Finch was accused in 1959 of having broken the unwritten but nevertheless actual policy of segregation by allowing Southwestern to play integrated teams, he replied that "we have been playing integrated teams for more than ten years." He also said that the Big State Conference, of which Southwestern had become a member in 1951–1952, had three integrated schools that fielded integrated teams. Though Huston-Tillotson College was not a member of the Big State Conference, Southwestern had also been playing it for two years.[105]

In addition to athletic events, Southwestern began to sponsor Church conferences and other like meetings on campus on a nonracial basis around 1953 or 1954. Writing in 1959 about these events, Finch said: "For more than five years [since before 1954] Southwestern, as a Methodist Church–related college, has been sponsoring church conferences on our campus, which are held on a non-racial basis. These have ranged from audio-visual conferences to the Texas Methodist Student Movement conference, which is held annually on various college campuses. This conference met on our campus in the fall of 1957 and will meet again during the Thanksgiving holidays this coming fall on our campus."[106]

Writing to a friend in Nashville in 1960 about integration, Finch outlined the policy he had been trying to follow for the last decade. He said:

> From many people's point of view our progress here in Georgetown and at Southwestern would be lamentably slow. We are making some progress with integrated conferences held on our campus and with participation on the part of Central [Negro] Jurisdiction delegates in our Pastors School and with bringing Negro speakers and guest artists to the campus. By this means, we are trying to acquaint our student body and the general town with the major facets of the problem and begin to acquaint our college students with men and women of very real character and ability from the opposite races. We hope that this will be a part of the continuing process which will enable us eventually to do the thing that a Christian college should do as far as admission without race discrimination is concerned.[107]

Students and Alumni Begin to Express Themselves: 1954–1955

Announcement of the *Brown v. Board of Education of Topeka* decision by the Supreme Court on May 17, 1954, galvanized a significant number of Southwestern students into action. They wrote a long document signed by 124 persons saying that "the doors of Southwestern University should be open to all qualified students, regardless of [their] race."

> We, the undersigned students of Southwestern University, would like for this document to be taken as an expression of our sentiment on the very important issue of segregation in the public schools, as it affects this institution. . . .
>
> We wish to leave no doubt in the minds of the policy makers of Southwestern University as to where we, the undersigned students of Southwestern University, stand. We, as students, as part of the Church, as those who would have direct contact with Negro students, believe that the Church must take the leading role in this issue. We, who would have them in our classes, in our groups, and in our dormitories, believe that in harmony with our professed Christian beliefs, the doors of Southwestern University should be open to all qualified students, regardless of their race.[108]

Though the document was filed away and its object would not be achieved for another decade, it would be one of the two documents on integration specifically passed on by Finch to his successor, Durwood Fleming, who would accomplish integration.

Honorary degrees through the time of the Fleming administration were ways of recognizing distinguished persons who had benefited society, of rewarding donors, of cultivating potential donors, and of gaining the goodwill of people of influence. They were badges of honor. They are seldom granted now at Southwestern, and their use has fallen out of favor by a faculty reluctant to grant them. The granting of one of them in 1955 fell out of favor with one of Southwestern's most distinguished alumni, J. Frank Dobie, the moment he learned about it.

The faculty and Trustees elected three persons to receive honorary degrees in 1955. They were Hyman J. Schachtel, R. E. (Bob) Smith, and John Ben Shepperd.[109] Dobie had no problem with the awards to Schachtel and Smith. Schachtel, rabbi at the Congregation Beth Israel in Houston, had come several times to Georgetown, where he had delivered stimulating lectures to the pleasure of everyone. Smith was one of the wealthiest men in the state and had used much of his wealth for eleemosynary purposes, including gifts to Southwestern. But Dobie was incensed about the award to Shepperd, Attorney General of Texas. He wrote Finch about his objections. He said: "I absolutely know that his word is not to be relied upon. I know that he is a self-seeking, small-natured man without intellectual integrity and with no conception of civilization or enlightened intellect."[110] In a follow-up exchange of correspondence with Finch, he explained the reason for his antipathy to Shepperd. It centered on Shepperd's attempt to defend the record of Texas before the Supreme Court with regard to the education of African Americans. He said:

> I don't have to know John Ben Shepperd personally to know that he lied outright in arguing before the Supreme Court of the United States that the school

facilities for Negroes in Texas are equal to those for whites. I know that if the Negroes had as many votes as whites, Shepperd would never have made such an argument.[111]

The Race Issue Comes to a Boil: 1958

The race issue at Southwestern came to a boil in 1958 and stayed hot through 1962, when it simmered down, awaiting the admission of the first African American student in 1965. It was fought on several different levels, on that of student idealism, of faculty activism, of alumni action and reaction, and Trustee division.

The issue broke into the open on campus when Joe Wilson, president of the Student Senate, reported to that body in early November 1958 about the stand taken on "the Segregation Issue" by the National Student Association Conference in August. *The Megaphone* reported that the Association had taken a definite stand of firm opposition to segregation and demanded complete desegregation in conjunction with the Supreme Court ruling of 1954. Representatives from fifty colleges in nine Southern states voted unanimously in the summer conference to support the move. This decision, including Wilson's vote at the conference, was discussed and affirmed by the Student Senate.[112] Later, as a Methodist minister, Wilson was elected a bishop. Upon his retirement he moved to Georgetown and came to Southwestern in 2004 as its first Bishop in Residence.

The following March the Student Senate conducted a poll involving a cross section of one hundred students. On the first question, "Are you in favor of the total integration of the United States?," 78 percent answered "Yes." To the second question, "Would you go to an integrated Southwestern University," 94 percent replied "Of course" or "Certainly." To the third question, "Would you be in favor of the Administration of the United States pushing integration by a stiff legal program? Would you sign a petition requesting legislative action?," only 18 percent replied affirmatively.[113] Most of the sample agreed with integration but did not feel that it should be imposed by coercive measures.

Concern over Desegregation by Two Trustees

The poll taken by the Student Senate was a matter of concern for one of Southwestern's most devoted Trustees, Mr. Ernest L. Kurth. Kurth, a 1905 graduate of Southwestern, was an East Texas lumberman. He was a modern man in the forestry business, supporting reforestation and the establishment of the Texas State Department of Forestry. His greatest business venture was his decision to manufacture quality newsprint from southern yellow pine, a process that had never before been attempted commercially. He turned his company into a great complex of enterprises throughout the South, one of them being the Southland Paper Company. Because of his success in helping rejuvenate the economy of East Texas, he was honored by many organizations.[114]

Elected a Trustee of Southwestern University in 1929, he served as a Board member until his death. Southwestern was one of his most cherished interests, and he and his wife, whom he met at Southwestern, gave regularly to the institution. Among other things, their gifts made possible the tennis course, the golf course, and Christmas bonuses for Southwestern employees. They gave generously to the construction of the Bishops' Memorial Union and provided a large endowment fund bearing Mrs. Kurth's name for the School of Fine Arts. They provided scholarships to more than two hundred students at Southwestern. Finch said that Kurth, at the time of his death, had given more than "$250,000 across the past years."[115]

Kurth opposed the policy being followed by Finch and wrote him about it. Finch tried to assuage him with a long conciliatory letter in which he discussed his own Virginia background and his course of action with regard to the desegregation controversy. He closed by assuring Kurth of his respect for him and his awareness of his concern for his fellow human beings, "which is evident in all I see whenever I am in Lufkin and elsewhere."[116]

From left: Herman Brown, President Finch, Margarett Brown, E. L. Kurth, and Florra Root Cody. From the 1959 *Sou'wester.*

Finch sent copies of both Kurth's letter to him and his reply to Chairman John D. Wheeler. Wheeler felt that in the interest of friendship and candor, he must write Kurth about his own views. The result was a remarkable letter, showing that for him the desegregation issue was not a matter to be decided on principles of expediency but on principles emanating from the New Testament.

> I do not assume any air of piety, but there is no fundamental principle which runs more consistently through Christ's teachings, Paul's letters and other books of the New Testament, than the fact that God is no respecter of persons and that racial prejudice is contrary to the cardinal teachings of the Master. . . .
>
> [Here he inserts resolutions passed by the General Conferences of 1952 and 1956 that "There must be no place in the Methodist Church for racial discrimination or enforced segregation."] . . .
>
> As stated above, I would certainly welcome the matter going along as it has gone along in the past, but Southwestern being a Christian institution, owned and controlled by the Methodist Church and the policy of the Methodist Church being clear and definite as set out in the above quotations, if a negro student applied for admission to Southwestern University and this negro student possessed all of the requisite qualifications, culturally, educationally and spiritually, I would have no option except to cast my vote as a member of the Board of Trustees in favor of his admission just the same as I would be in favor of admitting members of all of the other races of the world if they possessed the requisite qualifications. . . .
>
> I have tried to tell you on many occasions the great admiration that I have for you and we having been for so many years such very close friends, and you apparently feeling so strongly on this subject, I feel that it is only fair that I advise you frankly of my attitude.[117]

Further developments on campus and in the Methodist Church continued to disturb Kurth, and he wrote his fellow Trustee Eugene B. Germany a year later about his concerns. Germany, class of 1914, was a fellow East Texas businessman. He, too, was a faithful alumnus of the University who was elected to the Board in 1940. Though he was known as the tough, shrewd president of the Lone Star Steel Company, he was active in many beneficent organizations. He was a member of the Board of Trustees of the Dallas Methodist Hospital, the Dallas Scottish Rite Crippled Children's Hospital, the Dallas Y.M.C.A., the Texas Safety Commission, the National Rivers and Harbors Committee, and the Texas Academy of Sciences and other organizations. He was also vice president of the Texas Law Enforcement Foundation and Regional Director of the Boy Scouts of America. He was mayor of Highland Park from 1934 until 1942, when he stepped down to form the Lone Star Steel Company.

Germany helped Southwestern in many ways over the years, notably in helping it secure the favorable tax bill regarding the McManis business in 1954. He was chosen as the recipient of the Algernon Sydney Sullivan Award by Southwestern in 1959. The award was named after the first president of the New York Southern Society and was intended to recognize and encourage in others the principles of love for and service to mankind. As late as November 3, 1970, Germany sent a contribution of five thousand dollars to the Challenge Campaign. He died on July 12, 1971.[118] His daughter, Annette Germany Wilkes, succeeded him on the Board in 1973 and served until 1990.

Both Kurth and Germany were representatives of a generation of Texas businessmen that were conservative in their politics, believers in relatively unrestricted free enterprise, and strong supporters of church and community. A number of them served on the Southwestern Board of Trustees over the years and supported it strongly. Now they were faced with the question of governmentally sponsored desegregation in public education and the pressure it placed on the private institution they supported to do the same. Most of them came to recognize the inevitability of the process and accommodated to it, but some tried to evade it or hold it back as long as they could.

On receiving Kurth's letter, Germany replied with one of his own. He said: "I am spending considerable money for a man of my means, and also I am having my company support to an unusual degree a college [Jarvis Christian College] at Hawkins, Texas. I have also given some support to the Negro school [Wylie College] at Marshall. Through the years I have known and given my personal support to the various presidents of the Negro Jarvis Christian College, ever since the discovery of oil at Hawkins. . . . If our [Methodist] Church is going in the direction that you have indicated[,] it will destroy all of this good we have tried to do in the uplifting of these splendid colored people."[119] Germany was personally very committed to helping African Americans where they were, but not to integrating them into Southern society.

On sending his response to Kurth, Germany had sent

a copy of his letter to Finch, who responded immediately, saying that no change in Southwestern's racial policy was in the works and that no student would be accepted without Board approval.[120] Finch wrote to Wheeler on the same date, saying that if "either my program or my personal principles" should cause any serious division among the Trustees or Southwestern's constituency, he would be "more than anxious" to offer his resignation and to eliminate himself from the picture.[121]

Kurth continued to resist the President's policy and tried to influence the Board to take steps to reverse certain aspects of it. He sent a letter to Finch that Finch received on March 30, 1960, one day before the meeting of the Executive Committee. In the letter Kurth proposed that Southwestern cease scheduling integrated athletic teams. Finch gave the letter to Wheeler, who did not bring it up before the Executive Committee. Instead, he mentioned the matter toward the end of the Trustees' meeting the next day, April 1. They referred it for consideration to the November meeting. Wheeler wrote Kurth and was forthright in telling him what he had done. He then outlined Southwestern's policy in the matter, using material taken from the "Current Policy Concerning Integration Statement," largely formulated by Finch, that was passed at the meeting. He said that he knew of no athletic conference in the state of Texas in which all of the teams were all-white teams, "and unless Southwestern University withdrew from all athletic contests [our athletes] would necessarily be playing against teams upon which there were Negro members."[122]

Kurth sent Finch a letter on October 6, 1960, discussing his concerns about a *Megaphone* editorial of September 30 referred to him by his son. Finch replied a week later on October 13. In his reply he agreed that they differed about the correct policy of the University on desegregation but that what the school was doing was the policy of the Church, and "it is a position with which I personally concur." He also stated that it would be difficult for him and a number of others to continue at Southwestern if it should adopt a segregationist position.

> I know that the matter of admitting Negro students at Southwestern creates sharply divided feelings among many Southwestern alumni. I am aware of your own feelings concerning this and respect them as sincerely held and deserving of serious consideration, especially because of your great love for and service to Southwestern. I think that Mr. Wheeler in his letter of June 25 [actually, June 23], 1959, set forth very clearly the Methodist Church's position on this matter. It is a position with which I personally concur. (A number of us on the faculty and in the administration would find it difficult to remain permanently with Southwestern if the University adopted officially a segregationist position.) Nonetheless, this is the responsibility not of any individual but of the Board of Trustees; and, as I assured you a year ago, Southwestern will not admit students of the Negro race until this has been approved by the Board of Trustees and adopted as an official University policy.
>
> Southwestern students now come from conferences and churches—and some from educational institutions—where integration has been effected without serious dislocation. They find Negro students accepted in the state university next door, sharing in church services, etc. The lack of this they find difficult to reconcile with Southwestern's position and purpose as a church college. Within a week of the Supreme Court's decision a group of students filed a petition requesting Southwestern to admit Negro students on the same basis as white students. I requested their permission to hold this petition, and this they granted; but it is doubtful that such a request from the students themselves can be permanently delayed.
>
> I have felt that the interim steps we have taken, some of which have been of concern to you, have been the best resolution of this until the University was ready to take official action on this matter. I still feel it would be better for the University to proceed as we are, without taking official action until we have received a bona fide application from a qualified Negro student.[123]

Ernest L. Kurth died on October 26, 1960. In the Board meeting of November 10, his friend Eugene B. Germany "spoke very feelingly and graciously of his affection and admiration for Ernest L. Kurth," says the trustee record. "He mentioned particularly, the late Mr. Kurth's great love for negroes [sic] and of their undying affection for him." It is easy now to play down Germany's statement as a late-hour attempt to salvage Kurth's reputation on the race issue, but there is ample evidence during his career that Kurth really did care for blacks. Finch states that on a visit to Lufkin with the Southwestern choir, Kurth showed him the hospital he and his company had built for the town. It had a segregated wing for blacks, but it was "precisely and meticulously equal in every detail to the white wing.

He practised," says Finch, "'separate but equal,' which in all too many cases education in both north and south did not do."[124] Up until the last Kurth was planning to attend the meeting of the Board that occurred two weeks after his death. "In his last conversation," says Eugene B. Germany, "Mr. Kurth stressed his great love for Southwestern University, and his very keen desire to see it continue to make progress."[125]

A Reactionary Alumni Protest

While Ernest Kurth and Eugene Germany were protesting the dangers of desegregation in strong but measured terms, several alumni were doing the same in much more aggressive language. Pete Cawthon of Tuscaloosa, Alabama, sent a letter dated April 18, 1959, to Pearl Neas stating that he was "disturbed over some reports of Southwestern stooping to the low level of playing negro [sic] baseball teams recently. I can hardly believe it," he said, "but it comes from responsible people, all of whom are upset as we are." He then asked Miss Neas to authenticate the facts for him. "If its' [sic] true, then we don't want to be on the exes [ex-students] list and never plan to claim any connection with the ole school." He signed it: "Kindest wishes to you personally. I am sure you had nothing to do with such an idea anyway."[126]

Neas gave the letter to Finch, who then replied to Cawthon, explaining his policy and how it had been executed over the last ten years with regard to athletic, cultural, and religious events.[127] He sent a copy of Cawthon's original letter with his own response to Grogan Lord and John Wheeler. With his copies to them, he included some small cards distributed on campus by some unknown person, of which ten or twelve were picked up that very morning, April 23. The cards were printed on both sides with the same picture of a black figure caricatured so as to resemble both an ape and a Negro. On one side the picture was labeled "The Ape." On the other side it was labeled "The Negro." The same twenty offensive characteristics ("ape groove in skull," "animal smell," "syphilis carrier," "dolichocephalic mellon shaped head," etc.) were pointed out on each side of the card as belonging to the labeled figure. The purpose of the card was to illustrate that there was supposedly no difference between an ape and a Negro.[128]

In his cover letter to Lord and Wheeler, Finch attributed the disturbance caused by Cawthon to Lil Dimmitt, a Georgetown person with whom he had recently held a discussion on University policy. He immediately wrote Dimmitt saying that he had received a letter from "your friend and our alumnus, Mr. Pete Cawthon" along the lines of the recent conversation he and Dimmitt had held. Consequently, he furnished Dimmitt with a copy of his letter of response to Cawthon. In his letter to Dimmitt he says: "It has been reported by a number of people in town that I have given direction to the Athletic Department to seek a Negro student for an athletic scholarship and to be enrolled as a student at Southwestern. This is not the case.... [T]he policy of the University is formulated by the Board of Trustees, and no change in admissions policy could be made without their authorization." He concluded by saying that he would be willing to discuss this matter with him and any other alumni who might be concerned at the forthcoming Homecoming celebration.[129]

Cawthon responded to Finch's letter a few days later. He rejected Finch's reasoning and reiterated his point of view. He said that "it was a white Southwestern I knew, not one that played on its' [sic] own campus against Negroes, or who had them live in the boys dormitory and be served by white Southwestern boys. None of this can I go for. It cuts my heart out to see this institution drop to such a level." He included with his letter to Finch a copy of one sent to his niece and her husband in Houston. They had a daughter who was interested in attending Southwestern, and his letter to them was one in which he discouraged that interest. He listed for them the objectionable things he had heard about Southwestern and concluded: "Considering these things I am sure you will not want your daughter to enroll under such terrible conditions."[130]

His niece's family ended up coming to Southwestern to see things for themselves. Finch wrote them a long letter after the visit explaining the current policy of having certain mixed athletic, cultural, and religious events. He concluded: "This will continue to be Southwestern's program as a Methodist institution. It is our feeling that these experiences, conducted under the most advantageous circumstances, provide valid opportunities for students and adults to develop effective relationships which will be useful to them in their later experiences.... This note is simply to assure you that in no way would your daughter be embarrassed or forced into contacts in which she herself would not wish to participate."[131] A few days later the niece responded with a handwritten letter. She expressed appreciation for Finch's "kind letter" and stated that "since no negro is actually enrolled as a student... Southwestern will still meet our requirements and standards for a College....

I am writing my uncle about our views on the subject." The Alma Thomas Fine Arts Center had recently been completed, and his niece said that the facilities for music students were wonderful for students, like her daughter, who wished to major in Sacred Music.[132]

While Cawthon's niece was considering whether or not to send her daughter to Southwestern, President Finch sent a terse directive to Coach Medley. The two men had recently had a conference about the matter of athletic scheduling, and his brief note was to confirm the decisions they had made. He said: "Confirming our conference, it is my request and direction that Huston-Tillotson College continue to be included in Southwestern's athletic schedule for basketball and baseball for the year 1959–60. Southwestern University's policy decisions must not be made under threat of duress of any kind. The correct and cordial athletic relationships which now exist between sister Methodist institutions should be continued. Please notify me when you have been able to schedule Huston-Tillotson."[133]

Dr. Cody, still a member but not chair of the Executive Committee, had been kept in the information loop on the Cawthon matter. He seems to have realized for the first time during the exchange of letters that Southwestern was regularly scheduling athletic contests with Negro colleges. He felt that this indeed did mark a change of policy. Finch rehearsed his now familiar explanation about how the school had been scheduling integrated athletic, cultural, and religious events for many years and that it was no change in policy. The Executive Committee accepted his explanation without comment, and the matter was dropped.[134]

Student Activity Regarding Integration

The original opinion survey on segregation conducted by the Student Senate was a sample of one hundred students. Now a second survey was conducted. It was written by two students at the request of the Student Senate and brought to Dr. Finch for approval prior to a proposed presentation to the student body at a regular Assembly.[135] He approved it, and it was distributed to the students on May 12, 1959.

The three questions with the highest approval rating, with between 359 and 374 students responding to each question, were: "Would you be willing to eat with Negro students at your table in the Commons?"—Yes, 63.4 percent. "Would you be in favor of admitting Negro students to Southwestern University if they meet admissions standards?"—Yes, 61.3 percent. "Do you approve of the Supreme Court's decision of 1954 which called for the abolishment of the segregated public school?"—Yes, 54.7 percent.

The students were almost equally split on the question "Do you think your parents would oppose an integrated Southwestern?" Out of 359 responses, 179 answered "Yes" and 180 answered "No."

Both men and women, with 205 and 158 answering, respectively, said that they would be opposed to having a Negro for their roommate. The "No" votes were 62.4 percent for men and 63.3 percent for women.

Slightly more than three out of every five Southwestern students in the spring of 1959 were in favor of integrating Southwestern, they were almost equally split as to whether their parents would approve such a move, and slightly more than three out of every five said that they would be opposed to rooming with a Negro.[136]

In a meeting with student leaders only a few months before his departure from Southwestern, Finch told them that Southwestern had been moving to a more liberal position towards the integration question for the past ten years but that he "would personally oppose the move until we can fully accept integration with no reservations attached."[137]

Summary of Finch's Integration Policy

The best summary of where Southwestern stood on the question of integration at the end of the Finch administration is provided in a letter Finch wrote to President S. Walter Martin at Emory University shortly before he left for Vanderbilt. He said:

> On the whole, the reaction of the faculty and students has been quite good. We have had student petitions for immediate integration, and I would think the bulk of our faculty would be ready for integration, although fearful of the economic implications. The reaction of the alumni has been very mixed, with some vehement objections to the scheduling of events with Negro colleges. This has been in the minority—but, alas, a vocal minority. Two out of the twenty-eight Trustees have been seriously concerned over what they considered to be a change of the policy of the institution. The rest of the Trustees have felt that this was a matter of the administration's day by day operation of

the college and have not raised any question concerning it. . . .

The University has flatly refused to accept any gifts that were racially restricted, and the Chairman of our Board, a dedicated Christian lawyer, has clearly stated that he believes it is both the position of the Methodist Church and the position of Christian faith to admit students on a non-racial basis. This, of course, has provided much help to my administration.

I do not personally feel that the entire student body and the constituency of our University, both alumni and parents, and the town in which we live, for that matter, are quite ready for the admission of Negro students on the campus at Southwestern; but *if we received a bona fide application and one that we could clearly determine was not just a test case, I would bring this application immediately to the Board of Trustees with the recommendation that the student be admitted* [italics added]. I would not be honest if I did not say that I hope such an application would be deferred for several years; but, at the same time, I would hope that Southwestern University would not be the last institution to open its doors on a non-racial basis.[138]

By the end of the Finch administration, Southwestern had no regulation limiting its student body on a racial basis, but by common consent the pattern of Southern white student admission continued to be practiced.[139] Finch's first goal during his administration had been to keep the Board of Trustees from hardening its Southern white position and possibly legislating a segregation policy. His second goal had been to move the policy and Southwestern's constituency gradually toward the acceptance of full integration without discord and division. He felt that Southwestern was not quite ready for full integration, but the time would not be far off when it would come. Some people felt he was moving too slowly; others felt he was moving too quickly. No formal application by a black student had been received, but none had been sought, either. Both Finch and the chairman of the Board of Trustees had indicated, however, that if a "*bona fide*" application were received, they would carry it to the Board and personally vote to approve it. For them it was not a question of whether but of when. When full integration would have occurred if Finch had remained at Southwestern is a moot point. It would be left to the next administration to complete the process of bringing it about.

The Construction of Kurth Hall

The death of E. L. Kurth affected the Board strongly. Though most of the Trustees felt that he was on the wrong side of the integration question, he had been a Trustee of the University for so long and had done so much for it that they looked on his passing as the loss of a mighty oak. He and Will E. Orgain of Beaumont were two of the persons most responsible for saving Southwestern in 1937 by underwriting "the sum still necessary to pay all creditors."[140]

Finch reported to the Board in the fall of 1959 that Southwestern had reached its maximum enrollment with 634 students. One hundred fully qualified women were turned away for lack of space.[141] Students filled every bed the following year, and a waiting list for women was established. The need for additional dormitory space was evident.[142] In light of these facts, the Executive Committee authorized Finch to draw up plans for a new dormitory for women. He did so and brought Mr. George Page of Page, Southerland and Page, architects, of Austin to the Board meeting in the fall of 1960 to present the initial overall plans. The Board authorized the Building Committee to proceed with the planning for construction.[143]

The building would be named the Ernest L. Kurth Hall. It would be the Board's way of honoring Kurth for his many benefactions over a period of thirty-one years that helped make it possible for the institution to survive. The Trustees felt, so say the Board minutes, that it would be unseemly to solicit the Kurth family for funds to cover the cost and decided to raise the funds themselves. The administration was given authority to secure a temporary loan so as to be able to begin construction as soon as possible. A tentative budget of $350,000, including architects' fees and furnishings, was set up for the project, of which $185,000 was already in hand or pledged. When bid on February 1, 1961, the cost was $352,720, including a waiting room for the food service. When completed it ended up costing nearly $400,000.[144]

Kurth Hall was designed as a separate three-story structure of Texas limestone, located east of Laura Kuykendall Hall, to house ninety-two women. With its completion, the women's dormitory complex would have a capacity of three hundred resident women.[145] Construction did not proceed as rapidly as expected. Progress was slow due to the extra precautions necessary to ensure sound footings in order to avoid a repeat of the Alma Thomas Theater experience.[146] Though it had originally been hoped that the dorm would be ready for occupancy on September 1, 1961, for the beginning of the fall semester, it was delayed until the beginning of the spring semester. This delay provided an immediate student housing and budgetary problem for the new Fleming administration when it arrived on the scene. It was a budgetary problem because the housing income in the budget for 1961–1962 had been predicated on the greater revenue that occupancy of Kurth Hall would have brought from students rather than the reduced income brought about by the reduced fees that came from the doubling up of women in Laura Kuykendall Hall.

Kurth's wife, Isla Kinsolving Kurth, attended the dedication of Kurth Hall in 1962. Ernest, Jr., replaced him on the Board of Trustees in the year of his father's death and served twenty-three years. He and his mother made a nice donation to the Program for Progress shortly before her death in 1970.[147]

Mary Moody Northen and the Moody Foundation

Just as President Fleming inherited the completion of integration and the completion of Kurth Hall from President Finch, he also inherited completion of Finch's extensive cultivation of Mrs. Mary Moody Northen of Galveston to secure a grant from the Moody Foundation. Mrs. Northen was the chairperson of the Moody Foundation, one of the wealthiest foundations in the United States at the time with assets reputed to be in the range of $400 million.[148] Finch first contacted her by letter in mid-1958. He said in it that he had before him as he wrote an old catalog of the University. He was pleased to find in it, he said, that her grandfather, John Shearn, graduated in the second class of Rutersville College in 1845. Rutersville was, he continues, the oldest predecessor institution that merged into Southwestern when it was established in Georgetown in 1873. Shearn was listed at the head of his class at Rutersville with an A.B. degree.

All the catalogs of Southwestern into the first decade of the twentieth century carried the list of all graduates of prior years granted by itself and by its predecessor institutions. Finch must have had one of them in front of him as he was writing Mrs. Northen. The catalog for 1903 has a listing of six Rutersville College graduates in 1844 and eight in 1845, among whom is "John Shearn, A.B." Finch says that he is pleased to know of the connection of her family with Southwestern's history.[149]

In November he writes her asking that the Moody Foundation consider placing a dormitory on the Southwestern campus bearing the name John Shearn Hall. It is to be the second of three dormitories in a quadrangle that already has one of the buildings, Martin Ruter Hall.[150] She replies that the present obligations of the Foundation will probably prevent the Foundation from being able to make a grant at this time but that it will keep the application on file.[151]

In mid-February Finch writes Mrs. Northen that two other interesting references to her grandfather have been found, which they are having photographed. He says he would like to bring them to her sometime in the spring at her convenience.[152] He is later forced to write her that the second catalog of Rutersville College is in such fragile condition that they have been delayed in having photostatic copies made. When the task is completed, he says, a copy will be sent her.[153]

Sometime in the fall he sends her the story of how her grandfather saved his father's life, an event covered in detail in Homer Thrall's *A Brief History of Methodism in Texas.* She replies that she is "indeed grateful to you for sending me this data and the many other records also and greatly appreciate your kindness."[154] Toward the end of October he says he has found that Southwestern has a copy of Thrall, which he would like to have the pleasure of presenting to her on a visit to Galveston in early November.[155] She replies: "I am so delighted that you have been able to locate a copy of Thrall's *History of Methodism in Texas* and can hardly wait to see it."[156] Though he is unable to go to Galveston in November, he writes her that he will be preaching there for her pastor on December 13 and will see her then.[157] He does so and presents her with a copy of Thrall inscribed: "Presented by Southwestern University."[158] She later writes him expressing appreciation for the book and for the time she, the Rileys [her pastor and his wife], and Finch spent together. The time went so quickly, she says, that she was astonished on returning home to discover the lateness of the hour. She says she is thrilled to have Thrall's book and has found two other places in the book where there is more about Charles Shearn, her grandfather.[159]

In commenting in 1992 on his contacts with Mrs. Northen, Finch says: "She showed me her father's desk like the day he died, newspapers, letters unsigned, I mean unanswered and all on the desk just as he left it—a temple and memento of her father."[160]

Before his trip to Galveston, Finch informed the Board of Trustees about his contacts with Mrs. Northen and about the possibility of securing support from the Moody Foundation through her. He spoke of asking for two men's dormitories, naming one John Shearn Hall and the other Moody Hall. He reported that his plan was to ask for $500,000. "Herman Brown asserted vigorously that the asking should range from $1,000,000 to $1,500,000 and this amount was agreed on as an objective."[161] On December 12, 1959, just before his trip to Galveston, Finch wrote Mrs. Northen a letter requesting a grant of $1,000,000 from the Moody Foundation for the construction of two dormitories to be named John Shearn Hall and William Lewis Moody, Jr. Hall.[162] Once again the Foundation informed him that it had already obligated itself so that it would not be able to make any additional sizable grants for some time.[163] Finch had already learned about the turndown, however, directly from Mrs. Northern. She told him some of the factors involved in the Moody Foundation's program for the immediate future. She did offer him hope. She said: "We hope that when the Foundation begins to make assignments other than the commitments they already have, Southwestern University will receive favorable consideration for a grant."[164]

At this point Finch resigned himself to the fact that the Foundation was not going to abandon its already scheduled gift program to accommodate his proposal and that Southwestern would just have to wait. He did, however, continue to correspond with Mrs. Northen from time to time and in the fall of 1960 sent her another book she wanted that he had purchased in New York.[165] On the last day of May 1961, he informed her that he was leaving Southwestern and going to Vanderbilt but would like to visit her before leaving.[166] He took Durwood Fleming with him to Galveston to meet Mrs. Northen.[167] After the visit, Fleming wrote her about how much he enjoyed the meeting. In the meantime, Finch had sent her something else he had found for her. Consequently, she wrote him on June 30, saying how "pleased [she was] with the advertisement of her grandfather's company from March 29, 1873" that Finch had sent her and that she enjoyed meeting Dr. Fleming.[168]

When Finch turned over the reins of Southwestern on July 1, he left his careful cultivation of Mrs. Northen in the hands of his successor, who brought it to a successful conclusion in 1966, when the Foundation provided funds for the construction of Moody-Shearn Hall.

Dean Wicke's First Two Years at Southwestern

Wicke's first year at Southwestern was uneventful, and he was generally accorded good marks for his performance. Marjorie Beech, the President's secretary, wrote him in mid-November after hearing him preach in chapel that he was "accorded rare and complete attention" by the students. She said that during the sermon she had sat in the rear section of the chapel, where there was generally "an undercurrent of whispering," and found none.[169] At the behest of the Committee on the Improvement of Instruction, Wicke gathered representative rating scales for measuring the classroom performance of teachers, but he made clear that no one was being urged to use them and that, if used, the information would be for the faculty member only.[170] Early in the year the President created an Academic Policies Committee. With Wicke as chairman, it was designed to serve as a guide to the two deans and faculty in the study of the University program.[171] From this time on over the years, under whatever name it might be called, this committee or council would be one of the major bodies the University. Its unique characteristic was that it made academic decision-making more representative by circumventing the old system where the dean and the four division heads made most of the academic decisions. At its summer meeting the Executive Committee voted to approve the participation of Southwestern in a cooperative television program with other institutions in the area, amending the 1959–1960 budget to include it.[172]

The faculty was very surprised when at the beginning of the 1959–1960 academic year it received an "Information Bulletin" of fifty-four pages. It was a very well designed brief catalog with a dark green cover. On the inside it carried eight full-page photographs of campus buildings and other scenes in addition to the text. By now the constituents of the University were used to receiving catalogs covering two years at a time. The last three catalogs were for 1954–1956, 1956–1958, and 1958–1960. The "Information Bulletin" was a supplement to the 1958–1960 catalog and included the most necessary material for 1959–1960. The fact of the "Information Bulletin" did not become an issue, but its title soon did. The cover bore the title: *Southwestern of Texas.* The second line read: "*Information Bulletin 1959–1960.*" The first inside page carried on three separate lines the text: "Southwestern University, Texas's Oldest University, 1959–1960." The idea of putting "Southwestern of Texas" on the cover and "Southwestern University" on the second page drew considerable discussion and negative comment from the faculty but no concerted opposition. The issue of the title might have disappeared had not a second similar publication appeared the following year.

During the first two years of Wicke's tenure, he and

Finch had a series of faculty retreats in which they studied and worked on ways of emphasizing the liberal arts. The dean or associate dean of Duke, as Finch remembers it, came in on one occasion to lead the discussion. He was a purist, says Finch, on the question of the liberal arts, and we "learned later that he made Mrs. [Irene] Deupree, who was in the Home Economics Department, weep. Of course, she thought he was really attacking her. And, no one, least of all I, had certainly intended to hurt her feelings." But Finch was happy, he declares, when home economics, shorthand, and typing were removed from the liberal arts emphasis. Typing and shorthand were demoted by no longer according them college grades.[173] Home Economics was de-emphasized by eliminating the Bachelor of Science in Home Economics degree in the fall of 1959.[174] Home Economics was continued as a major field until 1971, when, with the retirement of Mrs. Deupree, it was eliminated entirely as a teaching field. Finch took "no small satisfaction," he says, from initiating "the thrust towards [the] liberal arts."[175]

In addition to these initiatives reported by the President, Wicke could report to the Board in the spring of 1960 that some "interesting experiments in instructional methods" were underway. Seminars were being taught in science, philosophy, American history, sociology, and psychology.[176] The department heads had approved advanced standing credit in ten fields.[177] The budget for next year also included funds for the initial stage of an electronics laboratory for the Foreign Languages Department.[178] Funds for the lab, however, did not have to come out of the budget. By the following fall, the Piper Foundation had funded a new language laboratory.[179]

The academic thrust that excited Wicke most was that being made in the English Department. "I am happy to record," he wrote in his report to the Trustees, "the university's deep indebtedness to Dr. F. Burr Clifford for his extraordinarily creative work in planning . . . two courses."[180] The two courses were entitled Major Literary Works. In them the students read some of the best works of Homer, the Greek dramatists, Virgil, Chaucer, Shakespeare, Dante, Goethe, Wordsworth, Melville, Murasake, Dostoievsky, and one modern work.[181] As a result of all these academic changes, Wicke said, "the institution [was] on the verge of becoming the best college within 1000 miles of Georgetown."[182]

In spite of these advances, Wicke felt that there were some significant weaknesses still to be remedied. The library was not adequate for the kind of academic program Southwestern was developing, the honor system was not working as it should, though it would be difficult to isolate its weaknesses, and present retention rates were weak. "Our present retention rates from freshman admission to graduation," he said, "of roughly 50 per cent must as rapidly as possible be raised to at least 75 or 80 per cent. This is not impossible of achievement within the next five years."[183] Wicke was an optimist, since those percentages are still fairly difficult to attain.

While Wicke was pursuing these initiatives, he was keeping up an active schedule of seminars, workshops, and committee meetings on the national level. During the summer of 1960, he attended the meeting of the Executive Committee of the American Council on Education in Washington, a Danforth Seminar on "The Improvement of Instruction" at the University of Texas, a three-day workshop sponsored by the Southern Regional Educational Board in Tallahassee, a committee meeting of the National Education Association, and the annual meeting of the Institute on Higher Education in Nashville sponsored by the Board of Education of the Methodist Church, at which he presided.[184] He also went to Alaska from time to time to attend the annual meeting of the Board of Trustees of Alaska Methodist University. The academic dean at Southwestern was a well-known national figure in higher education.

Faculty Dissatisfaction and Wicke's Resignation

The grumbling of the faculty about the use of the title "Southwestern of Texas" on the cover of the "Information Bulletin 1959–1960" was muted until its members learned in the spring of 1960 that it might be used on the forthcoming issue of the catalog for 1960–1962. The matter was brought up at the faculty meeting of May 12, 1960, for discussion. A motion stating "that the Administration be requested to use the official name of the Institution, Southwestern University, on the front cover of the catalogue" passed unanimously, 29 to 0.[185] When the catalog appeared in September, the wording on the green cover read: "*Southwestern University of Texas*, Bulletin of Southwestern University 1960–1962." The term "Southwestern University" was there as requested, but it was modified by "of Texas." Most of the faculty felt that the intent of its motion had been ignored, since it had specifically in its motion referred to the official title as "Southwestern University" without the modifier.

At the November faculty meeting, "Dr. [Bob] Brown moved, and was seconded by Dr. [Ralph] Jones, that a list of all catalog changes made by the Academic Policies Committee and not brought to the faculty be prepared so that the faculty might have the opportunity to make these changes official. The motion carried."[186] What the motion suggests is that Wicke took the matter of what was to appear on the cover of the catalog to the Academic Policy Committee, headed by him, which then approved it. What is clear is that the later Brown-Jones motion implied that the faculty, in light of what had occurred, did not trust what appeared in the rest of the catalog and wanted an accounting. There might be other material in the catalog that it had not approved as well. Their motion's broader implication was that the faculty did not trust the academic dean.

Six days later Dean Wicke sent a "Memorandum" to the faculty responding to its request. He said: "You will recall that at the November faculty meeting I was requested to prepare a report on any and all curricular revisions which had been made by the Committee on Academic Policy without reference to the faculty. I have examined the committee minutes with care and find not a single instance in which curricular changes have been made except by faculty action."[187] Though Wicke had technically covered his bases by taking all his actions through the Academic Policy Committee, both as to the cover of the catalog and as to its content, the faculty felt that he had used the Committee as a cover for what he had determined should occur.

In early January, less than two months later, Finch announced Wicke's resignation, effective July 1, 1961. He said that Wicke had already intimated to him the previous September the possibility of his returning to the Board of Education. This possibility was confirmed when Dr. John O. Gross, head of its Division of Higher Education, had visited the campus in October. On January 6, 1961, Dr. Wicke was elected to occupy a newly created position as the No. 2 administrative officer of the Division.[188] Three years after his departure from Southwestern, he became General Secretary of the Division on the retirement of Dr. Gross.[189]

In commenting about the catalog affair in later years, President Finch says that it "nearly tripped Myron [Wicke] up, and me too, because I had approved it, and Myron and I had done it together." There were "half a dozen other Southwesterns—Southwestern of Missouri, Southwestern of Kansas, and what have you." He and Wicke had lived where Southwestern principally referred to Southwestern at Memphis, now Rhodes College. They were trying to undo the confusion and make Southwestern University distinctive. Finally, "Myron talked with me about it and I said let's do it that way." The problem was, "everybody, including Marjorie Beech and some of the faculty, on up and down, became highly indignant that we were diminishing Southwestern University's status as a separate institution. . . . All we were trying to do was identify Southwestern."[190] Though Finch and Wicke thought they were adhering to the faculty resolution when they got the Academic Policy Committee's approval for the title that appeared on the cover of the 1960–1962 catalog, they underestimated the suspicion the matter had generated in the faculty from the previous year. Fortunately for Wicke, his contretemps at Southwestern was looked upon as a minor matter in wider circles, and he moved on at the end of the 1960–1961 academic year to a successful career in his new position in Nashville.

Wicke's Last Year and Appointment of Ullrich for Another Year

Once the catalog affair had been resolved in the mind of the faculty by Wicke's resignation, it settled down and worked harmoniously with him for the remainder of his time on campus. In his final report to the Board in April, he could point to a number of accomplishments during the year.

The Academic Policy Committee required for the first time that a portion of the faculty have its students fill out rating scales for each class. So as not to offend seasoned faculty members, the requirement was put in place only for new faculty members.[191] Wicke also announced that in the fall of 1961 a closed circuit television program, the first of its kind, involving eleven institutions from Georgetown to San Antonio and financed by grants from the Department of Health, Education and Welfare and from the Ford Foundation, would begin. Southwestern had elected to use three courses from its lineup during the fall semester, courses in history, German, and math, with the possibility that others might be added. The most notable course would be the "Great Plains," taught by Dr. Walter Prescott Webb of the University of Texas.[192]

Wicke's most important contribution was the completion of the decennial Self-Study required by the Southern Association of Colleges and Secondary Schools. The faculty had been working on it under his direction since the fall of 1959. He told the Board in his last report that it would be completed and bound by August.[193] Both he and Finch agreed to be present for the SACS visit if the new President desired it. After his arrival, Fleming found the Self-Study to be invaluable in orienting him into the situation of the institution and wrote Wicke at the beginning of the new semester that the faculty and staff of Southwestern at its recent Faculty Conference had voted unanimously that he should convey to him their deep and sincere appreciation for his wisdom and industry in producing the Self-Study Report. "The report," said Fleming, "is an extraordinary one—clear, comprehensive and challenging, and it will furnish the real direction and motivation for the future.[194] In 1993, thirty-two years after his departure from Southwestern, Wicke wrote a short letter to President Shilling thanking him for the "pleasant note" recently received from him. He expressed appreciation for Shilling's "kind words" and said that he kept in touch with Southwestern through Bill Finch and the Cliffords. He was, he said, "greatly delighted" by what he heard. "SU is a great place."[195] Prior to Wicke's departure, Finch appointed Dr. Oscar A. Ullrich to serve as academic dean for the year 1961–1962.[196]

Resignation of President William C. Finch

Sometime during the fall semester of 1960, Bishop A. Frank Smith mentioned to Finch the vacancy in the deanship of the Vanderbilt University Divinity School. How Finch's candidacy progressed after that conversation is unknown, but Smith wrote him at the beginning of February saying that Chancellor "Harvie Branscombe called me from Nashville some weeks ago and told me that he was very favorably disposed toward inviting you to become the Dean. . . . I told him that he could look the church over and not find a better man for the place than you are. . . . I say this with full knowledge of the loss we all will suffer here in Texas. You have done a magnificent job and you have advanced Southwestern from a struggling small college up to a place of preeminence in Methodism and in the academic world."[197]

By February 3 he had accepted the invitation from Vanderbilt, and a public announcement was made.[198] Finch met with the faculty on February 8 and explained "the procedure of electing a new president as provided by the Constitution and By-Laws of the University. He stated that he would recommend to the Executive Committee of the Board that it consult with a faculty committee, acting in an advisory capacity, in selection of a president. Furthermore, he would recommend that the Academic Policy Committee act as an advisory committee to the Board." The faculty accepted a resolution offered by Dean Ullrich expressing the hope that the Board would confer with representatives from the faculty in selecting a successor.[199] Finch relayed to the Board the faculty request for "participation in an advisory capacity," and the Trustees approved it, appointing the Academic Policy Committee as the appropriate group.[200] The committee consisted of the two Deans, the three Division Chairs, three faculty members, and Dean Ullrich. As it worked out, Grogan Lord, a member of the Nominating Committee and the Trustee from Georgetown, met with this faculty committee and reported its suggestions and recommendations to the Nominating Committee.[201]

Though Finch went through some trying circumstances in his last year at Southwestern that, according to Dean Berglund, resulted in "negative criticism," he turned the tide during the fall semester by conducting a series of meetings with various groups in the University community.[202] Later, in his formal letter of resignation to Mr. John D. Wheeler, it was not to "negative criticism" that Finch attributed his departure. He had overcome the effect of the criticism by talking it out openly with students and faculty. He explained his reasons for going to Vanderbilt as the taking up of something he had always hoped to do. He said: "I have always hoped ultimately to return to teaching, and the opportunity at Vanderbilt to work with the preparation of young ministers, to serve in academic administration, and ultimately to teach in my own field was an opportunity I could not turn down." The Board minutes reporting the occasion say that "he spoke feelingly of the difficult time he had experienced in deciding to accept" the Vanderbilt offer.[203]

Election of Durwood Fleming as President

Upon receiving Finch's resignation the Executive Committee immediately appointed a Nominating Committee of fourteen persons. It began to work with a list of potential candidates informally discussed by the Executive Committee at its meeting just concluded. The list was composed of nine persons, all of them professors or administrators at other colleges or universities. In sending the list to Wheeler, Finch said that Bishop Smith had called him and suggested that they add the name of Dr. Durwood Fleming, pastor of St. Luke's Methodist Church in Houston. Either just before or just after his call, Smith wrote Finch about Fleming. "Durwood and Lurline [Lurlyn]," he said, "have social graces of extraordinary capacity. He has done a magnificent job here, both as pastor, preacher and administrator. No Methodist preacher in this city has greater influence than he has, and his contacts with men and women of means is phenomenal. He is in his fifteenth year at St. Luke's Church and insofar as I am able to judge, he could stay another fifteen years. But . . . I have a feeling he would welcome an opportunity to go to Southwestern."[204]

Smith was sure of his "feeling" that Fleming would welcome an opportunity to go to Southwestern because he had already spoken to him about it. In a later interview with Norman Spellmann in 1973, Fleming recounted the first time he learned that he was being considered for the position at Southwestern.

> On the first Friday of February, 1961 [Feb. 3], Bishop Smith and I had a funeral service together [in Houston]. When I got into the car, he said: "Did you know that Bill Finch is leaving Southwestern?" "Well," I replied, "I have just read it." "Yes," Bishop Smith continued, "and I think you ought to go." And all the way out to the cemetery, which was a long distance, he was talking and I was listening. I couldn't believe what I was hearing, but I could tell that he had done a lot of talking. That's the way he was: he'd just start with an idea and start talking to people. He set these things into motion and they just carried you on. He didn't press me about it. He simply said to me: "Don't talk about it to anybody; just let it happen."[205]

At the regular spring meeting of the Board on April 14, 1961, Bishop Paul V. Galloway presented the report of the Nominating Committee. He said that the committee had devoted "quite a bit of time in considering a large number of men, having conducted several personal interviews." He then placed the name of Dr. Durwood Fleming in nomination for the presidency. There were no nominations from the floor. "A few expressed the opinion that the Executive Committee had been rather hasty in forming a Nominating Committee and recommending the election of a president at this session of the Board, since it was the first session since the resignation of Dr. Finch." But "[t]he rules were suspended and Dr. Fleming was elected President of Southwestern University by acclamation." Wheeler requested Bishop Paul E. Martin to telephone Fleming to inform him of his election and to secure his acceptance or rejection. He returned soon and said that he had indicated that he would accept the presidency.[206]

As a parting gift to Finch, the Board of Trustees voted to give him the University car he was driving.[207] For his part, he kept up with Southwestern over the years, returning from time to time to attend special events at the invitation of his successors, Presidents Fleming, Shilling, and Schrum. He was awarded the D.Litt. honorary degree in 1966 during the Fleming administration. The President Emeritus status did not come until 1998 during the Shilling years. It came late, because the honor is usually awarded upon the retirement of a President from the institution. Since Finch, rather than retiring, went successively to Vanderbilt University and to Emory and Henry College as dean and President, respectively, the emeritus status had never been granted. [208] Feeling that the omission should be rectified, President Shilling and the Board of Trustees awarded him the President Emeritus status in 1998. Three years later the lovely William Carrington Finch Plaza north of the chapel was dedicated in his honor under President Schrum. The plaza provides easy access to the chapel and is named for Southwestern's eleventh President.

Finch's recommendation of me to Fleming in 1963 resulted two years later in my accepting a position at Southwestern. At the time, Finch was Dean of the Vanderbilt University Divinity School, and I was completing my doctoral studies at Vanderbilt. In 1979–1980 Finch's wife and two sons, Lucy, Dr. William Tyree Finch, and Dr. Richard Carrington Finch, made a gift to the endowment to establish the William Carrington Finch Award. The award, consisting of a cash grant, is perhaps the most coveted faculty award at Southwestern. It is given every other year to a full-time faculty member for conspicuous accomplishment in furthering the aims of the University.

Southwestern during an Age of Social Unrest (1961–1981)

Two Decades of Change and Controversy

In earthquake-prone Chile, there is a saying that runs: *"A cada presidente toca su terremoto,"* or, in English, "Every president has his earthquake." This saying seems to apply to Southwestern University Presidents as well. During the tenure of almost every President, one or more events have occurred that have disturbed severely the stability of his administration. One of the reasons for the continued existence of Southwestern since its founding is that its Presidents have generally responded well to those devastating events.

The administration of Durwood Fleming is no exception. In fact, national and international problems during his tenure were especially tumultuous. His twenty years were some of the most turbulent in the history of the country. In those years the United States was locked in a Cold War with the Soviet Union, the most critical event of which was the Cuban missile crisis in 1962. Leadership at the national level was shaky, with six presidents holding office. One President, John F. Kennedy, was assassinated, and his alleged assailant was killed at point-blank range while in police custody. President Lyndon B. Johnson declined to run for a second term because of the ever-deepening Vietnam conflict. Senator Robert F. Kennedy was assassinated when he ran as a candidate to replace Johnson. President Richard M. Nixon resigned in disgrace as a result of the Watergate controversy. Vice President Spiro Agnew resigned in dishonor for having accepted bribes earlier as governor of Maryland. Governor George C. Wallace was shot and turned into a

Student and faculty marchers who opposed the Vietnam War crossing the railroad tracks on Moratorium Day, October 15, 1969, on their way to town. The Administration Building is in the background. From the 1970 *Sou'wester.*

paraplegic while campaigning as a presidential candidate. Three leaders of the black movement, Medgar Evers, Martin Luther King, Jr., and Malcolm X, were assassinated.

In 1965 U.S. troops, previously in Vietnam only as military advisors, were authorized to enter combat for the first time. The buildup of troops proceeded rapidly and by early 1969 more than half a million U.S. soldiers were stationed there. By that time more than thirty thousand troops had been killed in the fighting, with the end not yet in sight. Resistance to the war on the home front grew rapidly, and huge gatherings in Washington in both October and November of 1969 pulled as many persons in protest of the war on each occasion as the number of U.S. troops fighting in Vietnam.

These and other events influenced the development of the hippie movement in the late 1960s and early 1970s. Best representative of the style of music associated with it were Bob Dylan and Janis Joplin. During 1964, Dylan introduced the Beatles to marijuana. Seventy-four million people watched that same year when they first appeared on the *Ed Sullivan*. It was the largest audience in the history of television up to that time. Timothy Leary went further and began sponsoring LSD sessions. A prominent theme in the hippie subculture was opposition to the war with the famous slogan of "Make love, not war." The Woodstock gathering of August 1969 in upstate New York, with its three days of continuous music, brought together a mélange of causes being espoused by youth across the country. Prominent among these causes was resistance to authority.

All of this took place while the black freedom movement, with its pacifistic lunch-counter sit-ins and freedom rides, was occurring. Other persons in the movement, such as the Black Muslims and Black Panthers, were anything but pacifistic. In response to the abduction and killing of three freedom workers near Philadelphia, Mississippi, the cruelty displayed in breaking up peaceful black demonstrations in Birmingham and Selma, and other such atrocities, violent uprisings occurred in black ghettoes in large Northern and Western cities, particularly in the Watts community of Los Angeles and in Detroit.

These movements found expression on college campuses. Students for a Democratic Society took over five buildings at Columbia University in April 1968, and three hundred black students occupied the administration building at Boston University. The following year students seized buildings at Howard University and Penn State. Thousands rampaged through nine buildings at the University of Wisconsin, Madison, over black enrollments. Three hundred students at Harvard seized University Hall and evicted eight deans. In 1970 National Guard troops shot and killed four students at Kent State University. The following year Congress voted to lower the voting age to eighteen in hopes of channeling youth energy into more legitimate avenues of expression.

The fact that Southwestern largely escaped incidents of this sort is undoubtedly due to a number of factors other than measures taken by the administration and faculty, but some of the credit must go to them. Other institutions of Southwestern's kind did experience sit-ins and violence. By 1973 a Vietnam ceasefire agreement was signed, and the nation gradually turned its attention away from the war and focused on the developing Watergate scandal, which, together with the previous Gulf of Tonkin resolution, created a climate of distrust in the leadership of the federal government.

All of these events resonated at Southwestern and help to account for the student activism, the rapid pace of student life changes, and the many curricular developments during the 1960s and '70s. Though the administration developed its own contingency plan for "any overt rebellion," stating that disruption of the normal processes of the institution would not be tolerated, it was never forced to use it.[1] The most conspicuous event that occurred was a student march from the campus through the downtown area of Georgetown that took place peacefully, with city and campus policemen accompanying the marchers to prevent any trouble.

The President as Pastor

The current President of Southwestern, Jake B. Schrum, then a student, was moping over having lost an election when he met Fleming on the sidewalk. He had just experienced a disappointment and mentioned it. The resulting interaction was so helpful that he said to himself at the time that he wanted to become like Fleming and to help other students in the same way. Thus the vision was implanted in his mind that led to the position that he holds today.

This incident illustrates one of the major characteristics of Fleming as President. Though he had enormous strength of mind that was sensitive to the academic conversation, he also approached his job as a pastor. Illustrations of this characteristic are numerous.

On one occasion shortly before Christmas, when I was

serving under him in the late 1970s, Fleming suggested that we drive together to Jacob's general store in Andice northwest of Georgetown to buy some sausage.

> He said we would talk business on the way and we did. When we got there, he picked up the large package of link-loop sausage that he had earlier asked the vendors, Ben and Gus Jacob, to prepare. He told me that he had a custom of taking little presents to some special persons in Houston each year. He and Lurlyn would divide the sausage into smaller packages and take them around to the houses of these friends. His son, Jon, who accompanied him on many of these trips, says that, among others, they visited the Scurlocks, Blantons, Wests, Browns, Rockwells, and Smiths. These visits to friends of St. Luke and Southwestern, says Jon, "became somewhat legendary in Houston." The fact that he and Lurlyn had packaged the sausage with their own hands turned a very unexciting gift that could have been bought in any grocery store into a gift that brought with it a personal touch that money couldn't buy. This and similar incidents made me understand, though I never really knew whether to believe it completely or not, when he told me he had never asked a person for money. He simply presented the need, he said, and let the person respond.[2]

On another occasion, probably in 1974, President Fleming visited Mrs. Virginia L. O'Hara in Dallas. She was the daughter of Robert Sherman Lazenby, the person most responsible for bringing Dr Pepper to popularity as a soft drink. She was the widow of J. B. O'Hara, who was Lazenby's younger partner. Mrs. O'Hara, who had not long to live, said to Fleming when he entered the room, "Durwood, you needn't visit me. I'm not going to give you any money." He answered, "Mrs. O'Hara, I didn't come for money. I just came to visit and to renew acquaintances." They talked pleasantly for about half an hour, never mentioning money. He came back to Georgetown and forgot about it. Less than a year later she died. Much to his surprise, her will contained a generous gift for Southwestern. Two Southwestern representatives were soon thereafter invited along with other beneficiaries of the estate to attend a meeting with executives of the Dr. Pepper Company. The result was the receipt of stock that by 1981 amounted to $1,544,091 on the books. It was used primarily to endow a Robert Sherman Lazenby Chair in Physics.[3]

Fleming and the Ames Family

Another poignant illustration of Fleming as pastor during his presidency was his almost serendipitous contact with the Ames family—Jessie Daniel Ames and two of her three children, Frederick D. Ames and Lulu D. Ames. The career of Jessie Daniel Ames, graduate of 1902, was dealt with in Chapter X.

During World War II, Dr. Frederick Ames, Jessie's son and an ex-student of Southwestern, served in the navy medical branch. During the Guadalcanal campaign he suffered serious wounds from which he never entirely recovered. After the war, he returned to Houston and became, with his family, a member of the new St. Luke's Church, of which Fleming was pastor. This contact began, says Fleming, "a long and special friendship between them and the Flemings." Dr. Ames was the family physician of the three Fleming children. Fleming came to know Jessie Daniel Ames and Lulu D. Ames during the last illness of Dr. Ames in the late 1950s. He conducted Frederick's funeral service in 1959.

In her retirement in Tryon, North Carolina, Jessie began to weed out her books. In 1964, at the age of eighty, she sent to the library five bound volumes of the *Southwestern University Magazine* covering the years 1898 through 1902, when she was a student at Southwestern. Fleming wrote her back, thanking her for the gift but also using the occasion to reflect on the turn of events that brought him as President to her alma mater and where Frederick had attended school. He wrote:

> It is rather uncanny—is it not?—that once I was pastor of the church in which your late, beloved son and my dear friend, Frederick, was an active and devoted member; and now I have come to Southwestern University, your beloved alma mater and where Frederick himself was in school, to be its president. His memory continues to be a source of great inspiration to me, and the strength of it will remain with the entire Fleming family throughout life.[4]

Jessie replied:

> You speak of Frederick in terms that tend to weaken my self control. Even now I rarely speak of him for I cannot with out [sic] breaking. When Frederick died, something, a sense of desolation, came over me.

I shall never recover completely from his loss. It was something like losing his father again and my son too. He was much like his father, both [in] his weaknesses and [in] his strength.

You and his doctor, Dr. Lewis, were closer to him than any one else outside the family. I am sure you made his end one of strength and hope and peace.

Some day I hope to see you again and the beautiful home you have there.[5]

She visited the Flemings and other old friends in Georgetown on the campus in 1965 (see Chapter X). She and Durwood continued to correspond occasionally. Jessie wrote him in June 1967 expressing her delight in the honorary degree conferred by Southwestern on her nephew, Dr. James Hardy, another Southwestern product. She said: "Though I do not know you so well, nevertheless you have a special place in my mind because of the close friendship between you and my son Frederick."[6] They exchanged other letters during the year.

In 1969, a year after moving to a retirement home in Austin where her daughter, Lulu, an Austin businesswoman, could tend her, Jessie donated her personal library to the University (see Chapter X).[7] From this point on she declined rapidly, and all subsequent correspondence is between Lulu and Durwood. They were contemporaries and called each other by their first names. She had attended Fleming's inaugural in 1962 as a representative of Agnes Scott College.[8] In late October 1969 she invited "Durwood and Lurlyn" to her mother's birthday party in the retirement home and asked if Southwestern could provide the flowers for the table holding her birthday cake.[9]

A year in advance of her mother's death, Lulu prepared an order of worship for Jessie's funeral, using the *Methodist Hymnal* and the *Book of Worship*. She told him that "whatever you choose to say in your statement will be right and appropriate, as your statements always are." Her mother was still alive, she said, but was on the "verge of death." The person of her mother, however, was not there, she continued, even though she "opens her eyes a little." There is "nothing in them," she said. She was particularly hurt because of the estrangement between certain members of the family but felt they could overcome it for the funeral. One final favor she asked was for Durwood and Lurlyn to let their home in Georgetown "be the place where we gather after Mother dies."[10]

Jessie Daniel Ames lived almost another eight months after the letter, dying on February 21, 1972, at the age of eighty-eight. Durwood Fleming delivered the principal eulogy at her funeral at the First Methodist Church in Georgetown on February 24, 1972.[11] She was buried in the Ames plot in the I.O.O.F. Cemetery.

Fleming blended the role of pastor and President at Southwestern as much as or more than any other of its Presidents, most of whom also came from the pastoral ministry.

"If I Could be President, I Could Do It at This School"

Born in Sulphur Springs, a little less than halfway between Dallas and Texarkana on what is now IH 30, Fleming spent his boyhood in the east Texas farm country. His father, originally a farmer, received a call to the ministry when Durwood was six years old. After graduating from Cooper high school just north of Sulphur Springs, Durwood entered East Texas State University. He earned a high school teacher's certificate after one year and a summer. Then, teaching for two years at Pecan Gap and with two more summers at East Texas State, he earned a four-year certificate.[12] He transferred to SMU in 1935 and completed his A.B. in 1937. In spite of his small-town, northeast Texas background, he was a conspicuous success as a campus leader at SMU. Though not a member of a fraternity himself, he met and married Lurlyn January, member of a prominent national sorority and well integrated into the social structure of the campus. However different their backgrounds, they became partners in ministry for the rest of their active careers. Though his first three pastorates were in small churches much like those in which he had been reared, his opportunity for bigger things came when a delegation of laymen selected him as the founding pastor of the new church they were establishing in Houston. Bishop Smith had given them the freedom to nominate whomever they wanted, and, after a delegation from Houston appeared at his church one Sunday and heard him preach, they decided on him. Starting off in a school building, Fleming had built St. Luke's into a major congregation with a membership of four thousand persons housed in a magnificent building by the time he left to come to Southwestern fifteen years later. Among its members were some of the most important people in the city.[13]

Fleming's nomination for Southwestern by Bishop Smith came as a great surprise to him. He had once turned down the position as pastor of University Methodist Church in Austin because he didn't relish the prospect of preaching regularly to university professors. Though he habitually preached to important people in Houston, he wasn't sure he wanted to serve a church with a large proportion of professional intellectuals. He said: "That's not who I am."[14] Unlike Score and Finch, who had earned doctorates, Fleming's doctorate was an honorary D.D. from McMurry College in 1957. He never pretended to be an expert in curricular or other academic matters. It was this fact, one that he recognized, which made his selection of a dean for the College of Arts and Sciences in his first year at Southwestern so important.[15] The leadership of that dean would largely determine, he felt, the direction of the academic enterprise during his administration. Fleming understood his role as being that of making the major management decisions, selecting the principal officers and teachers, leading the financial development effort, and setting the tone of the University as a Church-related institution.

As President, Fleming sometimes made his decisions almost instinctively, developing his rationale for them after the fact. This does not mean that he did not generally appraise issues on a rational basis. He spent much time in reflection, balancing one course of action against another. When I once asked him why he always drove to Houston, when he could save time by flying from Austin and renting a car on arrival, he replied that he used the driving time to reflect on the issues facing the University.

Perhaps surprisingly, Fleming was not particularly knowledgeable about Southwestern when he arrived. It was simply another institution of the Church that he supported as any pastor might. Most of what he knew about it had come from his friends in the ministry, such as Bishop Smith and J. Sam Barcus, who had been associated with it. He did not have any significant personal experience on which to draw.

In addition, the presidential selection process had not been particularly helpful to him in learning about it. Illustrative of this fact is a crucial meeting with key members of the Board of Trustees that occurred on April 1, 1961, at Apartment 8F of the Lamar Hotel in Houston. This location was the famous downtown apartment of the Brown brothers, where many important Texas political decisions were made. The meeting was presided over by John Wheeler, chairman of the Board. Also present, among others, was Herman Brown, vice chair of the Board. Fleming answered their questions as best he could, but, when he asked if he could see the books, they said that that was up to Dr. Finch.[16] Fleming says he left the apartment knowing little more about the school than he did when he entered, "but," he continues, "I did know this: if I could be [a] president [at all], I could do it at this school."[17] Wheeler formally called him on April 13 and offered him the position.

The First Year at Southwestern

Once the Fleming family arrived on campus, it took up residence in Sneed House, across University Avenue from Fondren Science Hall, until the Finch family left for Nashville. They hardly unpacked. "It was like we were camping," says Fleming.[18] A wealthy benefactor, Mrs. Percy Turner, announced at a going away party for the Flemings in Houston that she was setting up a fund to build a new President's home. Little time was wasted in starting the project. Mr. Turner, who had made his millions in the lumber and construction business, came to Georgetown to visit the site. Designed by her own Houston architect, the house was Georgian Colonial, with 5,200 square feet. Mrs. Turner completed the project by setting up a $500,000 endowment for future upkeep.[19]

A number of problems confronted Fleming during his first year. Labor problems delayed construction of the new E. L. Kurth Residence Hall, and it was not ready when school opened in September. Not only was the residence hall behind schedule, forcing students to double up for the fall semester, but also a newly appointed professor was in trouble with the law. Fleming's first significant personnel action was to request termination of his contract so as not to hurt the institution.[20] On top of these inconveniences, at about the same time, September 3, 1961, Hurricane Carla battered the upper Texas coast. Some students lost their homes, and the Perkins Chapel lost its roof. "It was a community-building time," says Fleming. "Mother nature had forced us together, and the students were really beautiful about it."[21] Though slightly beyond his first year by the calendar, Fleming lost early on two of the persons who had been most influential in his life and in the development of Southwestern. Bishop A. Frank Smith died on October 5, 1962, followed by Herman Brown on November 15. Little could he have foreseen in the unhappiness of the moment that the son of Frank, Frank, Jr., and the brother of Herman, George, though already well known to him, would pick up the mantle of their kin so completely and prove to be of incalculable benefit to the University for the next twenty years.

The major academic challenge facing the new administration was the choice of a permanent dean. The choice would signal the academic direction the University would

A new dean, Professor F. Burr Clifford, replaced Dean Ullrich in 1962. Clifford, trained in English and Classics, was President Fleming's first major administrative appointment. He served as dean until 1977. Southwestern University, Special Collections.

take. The two persons most favored by the faculty were Dr. Judson S. Custer, head of the Education Department, a twelve-year veteran of the University who had come in 1949, and Dr. F. Burr Clifford, head of the English Department, who had only come to the University in 1958. Custer represented the university idea associated with an emphasis on the professions. Clifford, a classicist, represented the more purely liberal arts emphasis. Fleming announced his choice of Clifford in the spring of 1962. His selection of Clifford reinforced the Finch-Wicke liberal arts emphasis and was fundamental for the curricular direction of the University during Fleming's tenure. The two men worked together as a team for fifteen years. Fleming trusted Clifford completely, even though he wished Clifford were a bit more "aggressive."[22] Fleming later expressed his appreciation for Custer by appointing him Vice President for Educational Services, a position he held from 1969 to 1983, when he resigned to return entirely to teaching.[23] In his role as Vice President for Educational Services, Custer carried out special educational projects.

The inauguration of the new President occurred at a convocation attended by many distinguished persons on May 4, 1962. Bishop Paul Martin represented the Church and Governor John Connally represented the State. Finally, after a frenetic but "glorious day," President Fleming and family went to bed at about eleven P.M. Much to their dismay, their day was not over. At about two in the morning the students decided to have their own celebration—a panty raid. "It wasn't even in vogue then," Fleming remembers, "and I didn't know what to do." He got dressed and went out at a determined pace. As he approached, says Fleming, "the men whispered, 'here he comes,' and slowly fell back. None forced a confrontation, which was good because I don't know what I would have done."[24] The incident ended uneventfully. Fleming's success on that occasion was a harbinger of future relations with the students.

Fleming's Relations with Students

Fleming was one of the most student-oriented Presidents in Southwestern's history. He granted them some of the privileges they had been seeking for many years and some new ones that came into being in the 1960s and '70s. During his administration, compulsory chapel and assembly were discontinued, all dress codes were removed, a Student Liaison Committee was set up to talk with Trustees at the time of each regular Board meeting, a modern student life program was inaugurated, and student housing was improved. The regular and ad hoc meetings Fleming held with assorted groups of students were one reason the University never faced a student disturbance during the worst of the Vietnam years.

Musing in later years about how he dealt with students, Fleming said:

> I'll never forget the students coming to me on a few occasions over everybody's head. They wanted this or they wanted that. I tried to always hold my fire. Just to listen. Just listen until they got it out, and then try to use the process of reasoning and matching it up with

> this side and that side. Then we'd get a consensus. After the clash, we'd get a consensus, and usually that's a good way to go.[25]

His search for a consensus, however, does not mean that one was reached on every issue. Six weeks before Commencement during one of the years in the early 1970s, a group of graduating senior leaders came to tell him that the senior class was not going to wear the traditional academic robes for the ceremony. Without saying "No," he examined with them for more than an hour the possible consequences of such an action. He told them that, from having read in newspapers about what happened on other campuses where this had been done, he felt that the forthcoming graduation ceremony would be turned into a farce. Were they ready for that? Would this mean that some might attend in shirtsleeves or wear cutoffs? Would they support the right of an individual "weirdo" to upset the ceremony? After an hour and a half, he told them that he was not going to approve their request because it was the University's ceremony to organize, not theirs. It was a time when the University conferred its degree on them. Nevertheless, he agreed that the gowns used were of the "throw away" type and not very elegant. They might be different next year. The senior representatives reluctantly accepted his verdict, he heard no more about the issue, and the ceremony was held without incident. By the following year the episode had been forgotten, and there was no mention of not wearing robes.[26]

Megaphone Problems

Some student problems, however, were more difficult to solve than that of proper Commencement attire and could not be worked out by a conversation leading to consensus. The erratic career of the campus newspaper, *The Megaphone*, during the decade between 1966 and 1976 illustrates this difficulty. Because of a widely perceived ambiguity in the role of students, faculty, and administrators in relation to the newspaper, an ad hoc committee composed of professors Hummel (French), Osborn (Music), Campbell (English), and Fox (Publicity) was created "to consider the role and operation of *The Megaphone*." The committee produced a long report that was published in the paper on February 24, 1967. It became the operative institutional document for the newspaper during the decade. It established an editorial board made up of the editor, three students not connected with the newspaper elected by the Student Senate, two faculty members (one elected by the faculty, one appointed by the President), and the Vice President for Fiscal Affairs or his representative.

Even with editors chosen by this seemingly strong and representative group, the newspaper displayed little stability during the decade. Between 1966 and 1968 the editor of the paper adopted an editorial position highly critical of U.S. foreign policy. To some students, alumni, and faculty, his editorial position was deemed naïve at best and antipatriotic at worst. An editorial published in November 1967 suggested that "we Americans should look upon the anniversary of the Russian Revolution as a celebrated event." It drew a trenchant rejoinder from a recently graduated student and former *Megaphone* reporter, who wrote in response that "the history of Communism is one of the worst frauds ever witnessed by mankind," one that left "in its wake . . . widespread death and destruction."

The next two editors (1968–1969 and 1969–1970) followed a management and editorial policy that satisfied both students and the administration and are generally recognized as having run a strong operation. The next editor (1970–1971) was a bright but unconventional young man who made the newspaper a reflection of his personality. He was finally removed from the paper by the editorial board. His management is at best characterized as "eccentric." His letterhead pictured a Texas Horny Toad waving both a Texas and a U.S. flag with the motto "Sock it to me," with the legend: "The Texas Horny Toad Party of the U.S.A." In a letter to "Southwestern University Administrators" dated January 30, 1971, he said that he had been "terminated as Chief Cook & Bottle Washer of *The Megaphone* as of this week."

In commenting to the President about the newspaper situation on March 29, 1973, Basil Phillips said that the difficulties of *The Megaphone* stemmed from "a lack of editorial candidates, lack of a faculty sponsor because the editors didn't want a sponsor and the faculty didn't insist on one, negative journalism through editorials, front page articles that should have been on the editorial page, and photography which is at best in poor taste and reflects poor editorial judgment." His analysis was proved apt when the October 22, 1973, issue of *The Megaphone* featured the picture of a male nude and an article entitled "What's the Ugliest Part of Your Body?" It drew considerable negative response.

After these and many other incidents, the furor over *The Megaphone* subsided. In 1976 the paper adopted a code of ethics adapted from the United States Student Press

Association Code of Ethics.[27] In spite of the chaotic career of *The Megaphone* during the decade from 1966 to 1976, the administration, in contrast to its predecessors, never censored any articles or confiscated any issues.

The Student and Faculty Liaison Committees

Fleming attributed much of his success in dealing with student and faculty discontent to one of the innovations he instituted in administrative procedures—the Liaison Committee.[28] He instituted the concept as soon as he came to Southwestern and maintained it, though modified from time to time, through his entire twenty years as President. Originally it involved two students and two teachers, elected by their peers, who met with designated Trustees at the time of each Trustee meeting. No administrators were present at their meetings. The student, faculty, and Trustee members of the committee set the agenda in the meeting itself. The Trustees later reported on the meeting to the full Board. Their reports show that they enjoyed the meetings and felt that they gained from them an unfiltered insight into student and faculty concerns.

By the early 1970s, the one Liaison Committee had become two, one for the faculty and one for the students, and later four. At that point Fleming felt that the system might be fragmenting into sessions where trivia rather than matters of substance were being discussed, and he began to meet with all four committees at the beginning of their meetings to help them establish an agenda. He then absented himself from the actual discussion of the agenda items carried on by the committee members. The Liaison Committees were formalized into the Board structure in 1976 when the original names were dropped and the committee members were placed on two Board Committees, called Academic Affairs and Student and Religious Life.[29] By 1980–1981 the Board Committee idea had been dropped, and two committees once again had been set up, a Faculty Liaison Committee and a Student Liaison Committee. The former was composed of four Trustees and eight faculty members, while the latter was composed of five Trustees and eight students.[30]

Fleming's ability to work successfully with students and faculty is somewhat surprising in one sense because he was quite magisterial in manner and appearance and did not try to create a "chummy" atmosphere in meetings. Always impeccably dressed on the job, he exuded the aura of a person in command. Dr. Farley Snell, who was employed as chaplain in 1972 and served twenty-seven years until his retirement in 1999, complained to Dean Clifford on one occasion soon after his arrival about Fleming's use of the phrase "My chaplain," when referring to Snell. He says that Clifford gave him good advice when he said, "Just be glad he isn't calling you something else."[31]

Fleming's Background for the Integration Controversy

The most important problem left to Fleming by the previous administration was the integration controversy. Fleming was not a stranger to controversy, and one of the marks in his favor in the minds of some Trustees when he was elected President was that he had been conspicuously successful in dealing with controversy during his career. In addition, from the time of his college and seminary years at SMU, he had shown strong qualities of leadership and held social views that were fairly progressive. The Trustees believed that these qualities would serve him well in dealing with the integration question.

His leadership qualities are evident during his four years as an undergraduate at SMU, where he was a prominent campus leader. He was president of the campus Y.M.C.A., regional director of Blue Key (honorary and scholastic fraternity), member of and student advisor to the Student Council of Religious Activities, winner of the Saner Oratorical Contest, and a member of Alpha Phi Omega. In seminary he was president of the student body.[32] He was also an assistant to Dr. L. F. Sensabaugh as director of Methodist students and a student assistant at Highland Park Methodist Church during this time.

His social consciousness was displayed when he, as president of the North Texas Conference Youth in 1937, along with Dean Walter N. Vernon of SMU, sponsored "one of the pioneer interracial events" in Texas Methodism at the Conference Youth Assembly held on the SMU campus in June. They invited Mr. L. V. Williams, principal of Booker T. Washington High School of Dallas, to give an address at the conference. The event also featured the choral singing of Negro spirituals led by Mrs. Carrye Mae Morgan of Boll Street Methodist Church, a black church.[33] This occurrence, which would draw no notice today, broke new ground for the time.

Fleming's Experience in the "Pink Fringe" Controversy

The major controversy in Fleming's pastoral career was his participation in the "Pink Fringe" issue that erupted in Houston Methodism soon after his arrival there as the founding minister of St. Luke's Methodist Church in 1946. On the national political scene that controversy was tied to the dubious activities of the House Committee on Un-American Activities, which issued a pamphlet in 1948 entitled *100 Things You Ought to Know about Communism and Religion*, and the Army-McCarthy Hearings of 1954.

The issue of socialist and/or communist influence in the Methodist Church broke out in Houston on December 26, 1947, when the *Houston Press* carried an article about the forthcoming annual meeting of the Methodist Federation for Social Action in Kansas City. The article stated that "the prestige of the Methodist Church" would be used in Kansas City "to furnish a national sounding board for Communists and fellow travelers to expound the gospel of the Communist line."[34] From that point on the issue of Methodist leaders and Church literature as being infected by socialist and communist sentiments was a prominent subject for debate among a segment of influential Methodist laymen in Houston. Bishop A. Frank Smith had some success in dealing with it during the next two years and calmed the issue by assuring them that the Methodist Federation for Social Action was a purely private organization with no official standing within the structure of the Methodist Church, though its title included the name Methodist.

The issue exploded again in February 1950 when Stanley High attacked the Methodist Federation for Social Action as "Methodism's Pink Fringe" in an article in the *Reader's Digest.* The article appeared the same month that Senator Joseph McCarthy made his famous Wheeling speech about communists in the State Department. The confluence of the article and the speech caused great concern among Houston's Methodist community, which included such persons as Jesse H. Jones, former Secretary of Commerce, and Hines Baker, president of the Humble Oil Company. Baker was a member of Fleming's church. Forty-two of these persons created the Committee for the Preservation of Methodism in December 1950. Their express goals were to stop "the spread of Socialistic and Communistic theories in our church" and to remove the Methodist Federation for Social Action from any connection with the Church at all, including its name. In 1951 the Committee for Preservation published fifty thousand copies of a thirty-five-page booklet entitled *Is There a Pink Fringe in the Methodist Church?* Thirty-three conservative Methodists from several states met in Chicago in October 1951 and formed the Circuit Riders to combat radicalism in the Church. Its vice president was a prominent Houston layman who was a member of the Committee for the Preservation of Methodism.[35]

The climax of the controversy for the Methodist Church came in 1952, when the General Conference repudiated the Methodist Federation for Social Action. It stated that only the General Conference could speak for the Church, that the Methodist Church could not approve of many of the statements and policies of the Federation, and that the organization did not speak for the Church. It also asked the Federation to remove the word "Methodist" from its title, which it refused to do. It was forced, however, to move out of the Methodist Building in Washington and to seek new headquarters.[36]

Bishop A. Frank Smith continued to be the principal person who tried to stem the tide of lay disaffection within the Church in Houston. One of his tactics was to advise and support his pastors who fought to keep the Church from losing members. One of the most important and conspicuous of these pastors was Durwood Fleming, the young pastor of St. Luke's, who was becoming a major player in the city. His St. Luke's Church was one of the dynamic churches in the city and included many prominent persons. Fleming supported Bishop Smith strongly and tried to educate his members as to the spurious nature of the "Pink Fringe" matter. Through his efforts, he kept it from becoming a divisive issue in his congregation.

Fleming came out of the decade-long controversy having gained the respect of his bishop, who later nominated him for the presidency of Southwestern, and the support of his congregation that, as late as fifteen years after he had left, established a Durwood and Lurlyn Fleming Scholar in Residence in Religion Fund at Southwestern totaling one hundred thousand dollars. One of his St. Luke's members built and endowed a new President's home for him on the campus at Georgetown soon after his arrival. Another member, the bishop's son and namesake, already an influential Houston lawyer, joined the Southwestern Board of Trustees as a member and later became its respected chair. When Bishop Smith informed A. Frank, Jr., that Southwestern was offering the presidency to Fleming, he told him: "I want you to go on the Board and help Durwood." Frank, Jr., then phoned Durwood and told him: "For whatever good it is, I want you to count on me; I'll be there for you."[37]

When Fleming came to Southwestern he was not only experienced in dealing with controversy, but he was also adept in emerging unscathed from it. His general approach, one he later employed at Southwestern, was to give everyone an opportunity to talk, to listen carefully, and to act only when he felt he could intervene in such a way that a majority decision could be reached or that a majority would support a decision made by him. His faculty meetings were long and freewheeling, not bound by any necessity of ratifying a predetermined decision but with a result arrived at through the give-and-take of discussion. It was inefficient in its use of time, since it involved accepting the many turns and twists by the faculty as it hammered out from year to year the curricular and student life issues of the day, but it left the faculty feeling that it was genuinely participating in the development of the University. Fleming also employed this technique with the Board of Trustees when confronted with the integration question.

Integration of the Georgetown Independent School District

Though the issue of integration faced at Southwestern was different in many respects from that of the public schools in Georgetown, they were thought of as two sides of the same coin by many people who suspected, with reason, that a significant number of Southwestern faculty members were opponents of segregation in the public schools. The establishment of the Negro School of Fine Arts, in which a Southwestern faculty member and some of her students taught piano and the arts to African American children at the First Methodist Church (see Chapter XVII), finessed the matter for a time, but eventually the question of integration in the public schools of Georgetown rose to the surface with the active participation of a number of faculty members.

The onset occurred when a faculty member wrote a letter to the president of the Georgetown school board expressing disappointment about reports published in the *Williamson County Sun* that the board was contemplating the construction of a new school for the Negro children of the district. The letter read as follows:

> While I am in full agreement that the present facilities for those children are both inadequate and unsafe, I believe that we should rather recognize this as an opportune time to integrate fully our public school system. An integrated system would save us considerable funds in teachers' salaries, new construction, and maintenance. These savings could make possible a number of educational advantages in the area of foreign languages and science, for example, that our students are presently denied.[38]

The president of the school board, Frank Luksa, chairman of the University's department of sociology, wrote a reply on Southwestern letterhead stating that the board was considering "all possible alternatives" and would inform the public of its findings in due time.[39] Luksa was responding to majority board sentiments, not necessarily his own.

In the spring of 1962 it became clear that the school board was going to call for a bond issue to build a junior high school in the white area of Georgetown and a new twelve-grade school on the west side of town in the predominantly black residential area for African American students. Consequently, on May 4, a group of citizens met in the home of Dr. Eb Girvin, Professor of Biology, to discuss strategy for opposing the school board's program of continuing segregation. It proposed the organization of a Committee for Better Schools. Two days later the first slate of proposed officers met at the First Methodist Church to perfect the agenda and to revise the slate of nominees for the organization. On the 18th the first general meeting of the Better Schools Committee was held in the basement of the church. The pastor, Rev. Richard Smith, acted as temporary chair. Father Joseph Pawlicki of St. Helen's Catholic Church spoke on the moral and religious perspectives on integration, and Mr. Gilbert Conoley, the County Superintendent of Schools, discussed educational goals and the detrimental aspects of segregation. Mr. Harvey Miller, a local African American citizen, made some personal observations.

Though a number of prominent community persons were there, including a banker, a lawyer, a physician, a former president of the Chamber of Commerce, and persons engaged in other professions, Norman Spellmann states that Miller was the most important. He was the "most important person in the entire movement, because we already knew that he was willing to put his name and that of his daughter on the federal suit to integrate the Georgetown school system. . . . [A]t that time, he was one of if not the head chef at the Wesleyan Homes. This is a vital fact, because the Wesleyan belonged to the Central Texas Conference of The Methodist Church. There was no way that the powers of segregation in Georgetown would be able to deprive him of his job!"[40]

The group approved a motion by Professor Wendell Osborn (Voice) that it organize a Committee for Better Schools but turned down the suggestion that it contact the N.A.A.C.P. They wanted the people of Georgetown to win the battle without outside help. All funds subsequently used in the campaign came from local voluntary donations. Professor George Nelson (Music) was elected permanent chair and Betty Spellmann was elected secretary. The group's first action was to authorize the executive committee to hire legal counsel to bring suit in behalf of the Committee for Better Schools to stop the school board from buying land or building schools until a satisfactory plan of integration should "be shown to satisfy a federal judge."[41]

At the time these actions were taken there was one school for blacks, Carver School, located on "The Ridge" between the downtown business district and the south fork of the San Gabriel River. In 1963 there were approximately 150 black children enrolled—74 in grades 1–6 and 76 in grades 7–12, with only four seniors. These students were taught by a total of seven teachers in an overcrowded and unsafe building that had been condemned by the State Education Agency. There were two schools for white and Hispanic students. They were the new Southside Elementary School (presently Annie Purl School) and the junior high–high school diagonally across from the First Methodist Church (presently the Williams Elementary School). Both schools together enrolled about 950 students.[42]

The attorney chosen by the Committee for Better Schools was Mr. Price Ashton, a well-known Austin attorney with experience in school desegregation cases. He laid out a plan of: (1) stopping the building of a twelve-grade school for blacks only as being illegal; (2) obtaining a ruling from the state attorney general overturning the state law that prohibited school boards from integrating public schools without an election; and (3) bringing suit in federal court to desegregate the Georgetown public schools. The white taxpayers could bring the first two suits but one or more Negro families would be required for the federal suit. Hispanics were interested in the suit because, though they had been integrated into the white schools a few years earlier, they had heard the threat that they would be sent to the new black school. "This threat was later confirmed," says Norman Spellmann, "in sworn testimony in the state court case in the Williamson County Courthouse."[43]

On May 24, 1962, the *Williamson County Sun* carried a striking statement supporting the ends sought by the Better Schools Committee prepared by seven local ministers. They were the ministers of St. John's Methodist, First Methodist, St. Helen's Catholic, First Presbyterian, Christ Lutheran, Crestview Baptist, and the District Superintendent of the Georgetown District of the Methodist Church.[44]

In spite of this support, the school board's bond issue of $525,000 to construct the two schools passed in early July 1962 by a four-to-one margin (387 votes for and 92 against). Since $142,000 would go for the construction of a new but still segregated Carver school, nineteen persons signed a petition to the state court seeking an injunction to prevent the building of any segregated schools. Of these nineteen, nine were from Southwestern (Eb and Ginger Girvin, Wendell and Alice Osborn, George E. Nelson, Norman and Betty Spellmann, Gordon and Elizabeth Wolcott). The injunction was denied on the basis that all administrative remedies had not been exhausted. When twenty-nine Negro students sought to enroll at the all-white schools at the beginning of the fall semester, the Trustees denied them entry on September 3, holding that facilities were overcrowded and alleging that there were other valid reasons.[45]

From this point on most of the action was in state and federal courts, with half a dozen suits and appeals lasting until early 1964.[46] Though in the midst of the controversy (April 1963) Georgetown voters had shown their support for racially segregated schools by giving the two school board candidates that publicly declared for segregation more than 60 percent of the vote, the cause of segregation per se was now lost. Once it had to defend itself in the federal courts, the school board was forced to submit a plan for integration. The question then became not whether it would occur but how speedily it would occur. The school board submitted a grade-a-year plan to the courts that would require twelve years, while the Committee for Better Schools submitted a three-year plan. The courts finally approved the board plan in February 1964, with one slight modification. Integration according to the approved plan began the following September.[47] In the meantime, earlier court decisions had allowed the board to construct its two schools with the bond money already voted in 1963. The new Carver school, originally intended to serve African American students for all twelve grades, became a part of the integrated Georgetown school system and within a few years served all students.

The Better Schools Committee lists forty-four persons in its minutes as having participated in its actions. Of these, thirty-two were townspeople not connected with Southwestern and twelve were persons connected with

Southwestern. In addition to the Southwestern persons already named, Graves Blanton (Development), Jud Custer (Education), and Mrs. Helen Switzer (wife of the chaplain) are other Southwestern persons mentioned in the minutes. Once the African American community became convinced that the Committee for Better Schools was serious in its endeavor, it furnished a number of persons who lent their names to the legal suits. They also sent their children in the fall of 1962 to try to integrate the Georgetown school system before it had been ordered to do so.

One of the important elements for faculty members in the struggle was the attitude that their new President, Durwood Fleming, might take toward them and what they were doing. Norman Spellmann says that after the conflict was over, he learned that "someone asked President Fleming to put pressure" on him because of his stand on the integration matter. "Though he [Fleming] never said anything about it to me, which is part of what I appreciate," says Spellmann, "I learned later on good authority that he refused to do so and said that his faculty members were citizens like anyone else who had a right to express their points of view."[48] All of this was occurring at the same time, principally in 1962, that Fleming, unknown to them, was making an agreement with the Trustees that would finally integrate Southwestern.

Students Forewarn Fleming of Their Integration Plans

When Fleming arrived a Southwestern, he found a letter awaiting him from a student Committee on Integration. In it the students rehearsed what they had heard from President Finch. They said that they were told by the administration that if a Negro ever applied and if he was qualified that the Board of Trustees would accept him. But, at the same time, they were told that Southwestern was not ready for integration. "There are," said the letter, "shades of incompatibility in these two pronouncements." Because of this, the committee members decided to take it upon themselves to secure the application of a qualified Negro. They contacted two outstanding Negro high school seniors about applying. At this point the committee talked to Dr. Finch about what it had done. He told its members that he felt it would be a mistake to present the new President "with so tremendous a problem" before he had established rapport with the Board and become acquainted with the academic community. The letter concludes as follows:

> The committee is disappointed with the delay that seems inevitable with this change in administration, but it intends to continue work toward integration in the coming year with the aim of having a Negro applicant in the spring of '62 when the campus community is still intact. The committee wanted to tell you of the coming plans, so that you would know its concern and conviction on this problem. The committee will be in contact with you next year, hoping that the committee can work with you in anticipating the forth coming [sic] application and preparing for that event. There will be some letter writing to trustees and organization work this summer, but the bulk of the work will begin in September. The committee looks forward to your administration and to your cooperation. Sincerely. The Committee.[49]

Though the letter sounds as if the committee is prepared to work hard during the fall of 1961 to secure a black applicant, its members did not pursue the matter. The likely explanation is that the writer of the letter for the committee was Buddy Renick, who graduated in May 1961 and entered Union Theological Seminary in the fall. Renick was the head of the Student Christian Association during 1960–1961, and the committee letter has a tone similar to that found in Renick's subsequent correspondence with Board chairman Wheeler and President Fleming during the summer and fall of 1961.

The correspondence consists of five letters from him to them and two from them to him in reply. Renick's letters are the well-written outpourings of a student who is completely committed to his cause. He says that "only in the last year [of my college career] did I realize that in the love of God I had to work to erase this injustice."[50] He states that the students are ready for integration, the town is ready, and that only the Trustees are unready. The issue is one of Board hypocrisy. "Are we afraid," he continues, "of losing endowment? Has the dollar sign become the conscience of the church-related institution?" His reference to the Trustees as having their eyes on money rather than on conscience was too much for Wheeler. Wheeler replied that Renick should not impugn the integrity of the Board. Only recently, he says, it lost $350,000 in a will because it would not adopt a segregationist position for Southwestern.[51] Fleming responded to Renick in strong but measured terms, pointing out some of the complexities of the situation and asking him how he would balance them all. Renick replies, saying: "Now we are getting somewhere." He feels that he is finally not being talked down to but is being heard. He ends the correspondence by thanking Fleming for his frankness and for giving him "the opportunity to say these things."[52]

The Trustees Agree on a Course of Action

While faculty members had been participating in an attempt to integrate the Georgetown public school system and some students had been prodding the administration to become more resolute in bringing about integration, the Southwest Texas Conference put additional pressure on the Trustees by asking them to make a report to it of its "integration policy and plans." Its resolution urged all Methodist institutions to provide "complete access for all qualified persons without regard to race or national origin" at no later date than 1966 and to report their progress at the 1962 annual session.[53]

When the Board at its spring meeting in 1962 began to discuss the nature of the report it would make, Trustee J. William Morgan preempted the discussion by stating that at the fall Board meeting he would present a resolution for adoption stating that: "When and if an applicant of a race not now on the campus appears for admission, the candidate will be considered on qualifications of character and academic standing alone." His purpose in forewarning the Trustees of what he was going to do at the next meeting was to let them know that further delaying tactics were unacceptable and that they would be called on to adopt a definitive course of action on integration in the fall if they did not do so at the present meeting.

Following Morgan's statement, the Board considered a proposed report from the Executive Committee to the Southwest Texas Conference drafted by Chairman Wheeler. After stressing that the Board and not the Conference is charged with the responsibility of acting on this issue, the proposed report nevertheless expressed appreciation for the interest of the Conference in the issue. It concluded by stating that Southwestern University was making satisfactory progress and that the Board would study the matter further at its next meeting. Morgan said that he felt acceptance of this report "would be no more than an evasion." He was supported by Dr. Edmund Heinsohn, who "characterized the position of the University as being [that of] the occupant on the top of a powder keg, since the student body is very much in favor of integration." Morgan agreed. Even

Playing important roles in the solution of the integration question at Southwestern were, from left, Dr. C. C. Cody, Jr., John D. Wheeler, Herman Brown, and Charles N. Prothro, all of whom served as chair or vice-chair of the Board of Trustees at one time or another. Southwestern University, Special Collections.

though some Trustees disagreed that such was the case, the statements of Morgan and Heinsohn carried weight. They were not outsiders. Both had been popular pastors of the First Methodist Church in Georgetown before going on to occupy the pulpit of the University Methodist Church in Austin, where Morgan was the current pastor. Both had received honorary degrees from Southwestern, Heinsohn in 1931, Morgan in 1960. Morgan also had a daughter at Southwestern who was active in the student Committee on Integration.

Though he had not expressed an opinion until this time, Fleming spoke up and said that he was uneasy with the proposed Executive Committee draft report to the Annual Conference. After continued discussion, the Board agreed that the chairman should appoint a special committee to consider this matter and report to the Board of Trustees.[54] Because a committee of three students representing the Methodist Student Movement had requested that Fleming let them know after the meeting what the Board had decided on the integration matter, Fleming wrote them a letter. He said that the Board was in the process of working out the issue and that no statement could be made on it until the proper time.[55] When the North Texas Conference adopted a resolution in late May calling for all Methodist educational institutions to adopt integration "as rapidly as possible," the *Austin American* tried to get statements from both Wheeler and Fleming. Wheeler responded somewhat testily that he wouldn't answer any question of any kind.[56] Fleming replied that "there is no racial segregation policy" at Southwestern and that no application has ever been received from a Negro student for admission.[57]

The special committee that met on June 29 to decide on what to say in the report to the Board consisted of seven persons. They were Herman Brown, Durwood Fleming, Grogan Lord, Brown Loyd, J. William Morgan, Charles Prothro, and J. D. Wheeler. I. J. McCook attended as secretary. It is because of him that we have today the remarkable account of the committee discussion in eleven double-spaced pages. The meeting consisted of a wide-ranging consideration of all aspects of the integration question as it affected Southwestern. J. W. Morgan was the proponent of immediate integration, while Grogan Lord was the proponent of further delay. Because the matter was being discussed at the same time that the Committee for Better Schools was seeking to integrate the public school system in Georgetown, that issue came up, particularly the action of faculty members participating in it.

When it appeared that no consensus would be reached, J. D. Wheeler suggested that they consider the procedure that had been adopted by Trinity University in San Antonio. He explained that "the matter was discussed thoroughly in the meeting of the Board at Trinity, and that, without any official action, the discussion resulted in a consensus of opinion [sic] that the matter be left entirely to the discretion of the president and other administrative officers. There was no formal resolution and no publicity of any sort." Fleming reinforced the idea by saying that when he had been interviewed for the presidency he had discussed the subject of integration with many Board members. It was his opinion, he said, that the Board was so divided that there was little possibility of unanimity. As a result, "he had concluded that the president must, therefore, bear the burden." He stated that if the Board of Trustees would give him "absolute authority," he would accept the responsibility. He further stated that he would "not accept responsibility" if he must seek advice from individual Trustees, faculty members, or students. He felt, he continued, that "the problem is imminent" but could be handled objectively as an administrative matter.

Herman Brown agreed. He stated that the Board of Trustees is ultimately responsible for the school, but he felt that the less commotion there was about the matter the better off the University would be. He expressed the opinion that it would be easier for the President and for the other administrative officers to handle the issue at the time an application was received from a Negro than it would be to have to submit the question to a regular or a called meeting of the Board at that time for judgment. Morgan agreed and said that he would cooperate fully in the future if the plan for granting the administration full authority to act was approved by the Board, informally or otherwise.[58]

Once the committee agreed on what it would report to the Board, Board approval in the fall was a foregone conclusion. A committee, carefully constructed of strong Trustees who represented difference shades of opinion, had held a wide-ranging discussion. Everyone was now ready to put the matter to rest. The agreement was a compromise. Neither the proponents nor the opponents of integration had won a complete victory, but neither side felt that it could do any better. The opponents had known for some time that integration must come, but they had won some significant concessions. The proponents finally had a Board resolution specifically committing the University to integration that they felt would not be long in coming. The major concession by both groups that made the agreement possible is that the final decision was moved out of the full Board into the hands of the President. Even though five provisions attached to the agreement would limit the President, he would not have to recur to anyone else in making the decision. Those limitations were as follows:

1. That no individual or group actively seek a qualified Negro applicant.
2. That a Negro applicant meet in every respect all requirements placed upon any other applicant.
3. That the admission of a Negro applicant be conducted in an orderly manner.
4. That the application for admission of a Negro student be considered only when such application of admission is entirely free from pressure brought about by any individual or group.
5. That no public announcement or publicity of any type surround the application for admission of a Negro student.[59]

In order to ensure that the five-point agreement was fully understood, Fleming restated it in a document written in his own language that explained how he would apply it. There was nothing new in it except his agreement to abide by the five points in both letter and spirit without any attempt at evasion. "While it may be a year or ten years before a Negro student or students apply for admission to Southwestern University," he said, "it is my understanding that if and when one does and meets all the requirements mentioned above, he will be accepted and enrolled with the full privileges offered to any and all other students. We shall be deliberate and cautious but shall not employ delaying tactics."[60]

Implementation

The entry of the first black student, Ernest Clark, into Southwestern did not occur until 1965 (see Chapter XVII), three years after the Board of Trustees decision. Not only did the five provisions specified by the Board delay it, but it was also delayed because no one but Board members and a few administrative officers knew that a decision had even been made on the matter. The Board had adopted a statement that "no written policy or statement of whatever action the Board of Trustees may take be included in the official records of the University and that no announcement of any sort be made of the Board's consideration of this matter." Most of the records on the matter were kept in a special file in the President's office that was made available to me.

Following the Board decision, Fleming was very cautious about how he referred to integration. When former student Walter J. Ligon read that the Georgetown public schools would have to integrate, he wondered about his alma mater. He wrote on September 17, 1963, inquiring about Southwestern's policy. Fleming replied tersely: "With regard to your inquiry regarding the policy on race, I can say that Southwestern is open to any qualified student, regardless of race."[61] About a month later he received a letter about integration from a student in Canyon, Texas. She was a member of the Methodist Student Movement and had been charged with conducting a survey of each Methodist institution in the state about its policy on integration. Fleming cautiously replied: "Southwestern University has never had a policy regulating admission with regard to race. We accept applications of all students on the basis of credentials and character." He issued a caveat about the use of his statement, saying that it was for use in the survey and could not be quoted or identified without "our explicit permission."[62]

Students were unaware of the new institutional policy on integration. When Fleming learned in late January 1964 that students might be planning a meeting to discuss integration, he wrote the two leading instigators connected with it that "if a meeting with students is contemplated to discuss their interest in integration, it is essential that I be present." Whether he knew at the time that Ernest Clark would apply to enter in the fall of 1965 is unknown. His request to talk to the students was not unusual, since he often met with students in informal groups.[63] In reporting about his meeting with the Liaison Committee at the spring meeting of the Board in 1964, Trustee Preston Doughty said that the two things the students were most interested in were integration and compulsory chapel.[64]

Teachers and library personnel were likewise unaware of the change in policy. When Mrs. Mary S. Bailey and Mrs. Willie E. Hall, two prominent black women, came into the library in the summer of 1964 to buy library cards, as all citizens of Georgetown had the right to do, they were told that "none were [sic] available at this time."[65] The Mary Bailey Head Start Center was later named for the former because of her lifetime of contributions to the community.

Only one black person inquired as to the possibility of attending Southwestern prior to the admission of Ernest Clark. Late in August 1964, before the beginning of the fall semester, the Reverend Wilburt Bledsoe, minister of the St. Paul Methodist Church, came to visit Dr. Fleming. He and his family had recently moved from Marlin, where he had been pastor for four years. He was thirty-six years old, with a wife and five children. His prior education was spotty. He finished the tenth grade at Rosebud, when he left school and joined the army. On his release, he returned to Rosebud, where he was allowed to take an examination that permitted him to skip the eleventh grade. He took one more year and finished high school. He later took one semester at Paul Quinn College in Waco. With these credentials he came to discuss the possibility of entering Southwestern. He said his other option would be Huston-Tillotson. After Mr. Bledsoe left, Fleming wrote Dean Clifford about the interview. He said he spent considerable time with him and discussed the situation carefully, telling him that the matter seemed to turn on the point of the accreditation of Paul Quinn College, which he felt might be unaccredited. "He seemed to appreciate the situation and understood it," wrote Fleming. "Neither on the other hand, did I close a door. I told him that I felt he should have a conference with you."[66] There are no further records about him, and

Bledsoe probably took the interview with Fleming as being essentially negative and did not follow up on it.

When Ernest Clark entered Southwestern as a first-year student in the fall of 1965, his enrollment was quiet and uneventful. Fleming simply noted it by one line in his report to the Board of Trustees on October 18: "We enrolled our first full-time Negro student this Fall."[67] Clark's presence on campus as a student in the School of Fine Arts was so inconspicuous that I, coming to Southwestern the same year, did not notice it for some months. No public announcement was made regarding it. When an alumna wrote Fleming in the spring of 1966 asking when Southwestern would be integrated, he replied that "we have one Negro student enrolled full time this year, and he's doing splendidly in his work. We have also had a workshop in the area of the new math in which Negro teachers have participated. They have indeed been enrolled, inasmuch as there was tuition cost attached to the course. While we are not actively recruiting Negro students for Southwestern, we will be more than glad to consider any application from any one of them at any time."[68] Though Southwestern was integrated technically in 1965, several years would ensue before it actively recruited blacks.

In January 1969 Southwestern underwent its first Civil Rights Compliance Review. At the time Southwestern had eleven black students. In the review the school had to show that it treated Negroes the same as whites in recruitment, in student-teacher training, in dissemination of information, in the recruitment of faculty members, and in other ways. The review went well, and Fleming emphasized in his reply to the Deputy Regional Director in Dallas that Southwestern was completely integrated by desire and not merely to satisfy legal requirements. He said that "the institution has never segregated minority groups in the residence halls. There is no discrimination practiced in the assignment of rooms and will not be. Negro and foreign students are assigned together only when they request it. The resident [sic] halls' directors encourage these students to room with white students, in fact. We do not wish segregation practiced on the part of either the white or black students." In addition, he said that the institution had secured letters from the national Greek-letter organizations that they do not discriminate and letters from the locals as to how they practice their policy at Southwestern. He is willing, he says, to turn over all the correspondence on this issue. By 1969 there was no equivocation on the issue of integration.[69] Dean Bill Swift, who had come to Southwestern the same year Clark entered, was managing the issue of compliance for Southwestern, and he was strongly committed to full integration.

Enrollment Patterns and Affirmative Action

Student body enrollment grew slowly during the Fleming years, from the 691 he inherited from Finch in 1961 to the 1,000 he turned over to Shilling in 1981. The annual average increase in the number of students each year was just over 15, a compounded annual rate of increase of 1.9 percent. After a fairly good rate of increase in the early 1960s, Fleming spoke to the Trustees in 1970 about increasing the student body to 1,100 or 1,200, only to have the number of students immediately drop by 41 to 819 in the next two years. In 1972 the Trustees approved his recommendation to move the enrollment to 900. When the enrollment increased by 81 students the very next year to top out at exactly 900, he again began to talk about 1,200 as the desired enrollment.[70]

In truth, the real culprit in the student numbers situation was not recruitment per se so much as it was the poor average retention to graduation figure of 50 to 55 percent that made it necessary to conduct a special effort in student recruitment each year to make up for the number of students that transferred out. The major reasons given by students for going elsewhere were rising costs, lifestyle issues, desire for a "marketable degree," and desire for a larger university, with cost being the primary factor. Fleming said in the spring of 1972 that requests for transfers had reached an all-time high. "It is our belief," he said, "that each time we announce raises in student costs, this 'triggers' an increase in the number of transfers. The cost of attending Southwestern is not the real reason; but, psychologically, the announcement of the next round of raises apparently 'sets off' the latent consideration 'to go to a cheaper school.'"[71]

Because of the difficulty in raising student body numbers, five recent graduates were employed in 1974 as admissions counselors. They contacted more than three hundred high schools in Texas, New Mexico, Oklahoma, and Louisiana in their first year on the job.[72] With the addition of permanent admissions counselors and with Dean Swift in charge of admissions after 1978, student numbers improved. Enrollment went over a thousand for the first time in the fall of 1979 and stayed above that number.

In the mid-1970s, Swift produced an affirmative action program for the University that was submitted to the proper authorities in Dallas. He also completed a Self-Evaluation for the Title IX equality in women's athletics requirement and worked with the Registrar's office to implement procedures that gave eighteen-year-olds the rights accorded them by recent federal legislation. Since each eighteen-year-old was now considered legally to be an adult, the Registrar's office could no longer send out grade reports automatically to parents without the permission of the student even when the parent paid all the expenses. The explanation of this change in procedure was very difficult to make clear to parents.[73] Though their disagreement should have properly been with the federal legislation that occasioned their indignation, their contact with Southwestern authorities in the process of its implementation meant that some of the persons in the Registrar's office received blistering phone calls about it. Federal legislation regarding the treatment of handicapped persons also brought necessary changes. Swift told the Trustees in 1976 that the school must begin taking steps to implement legislation prohibiting discrimination against persons who were physically or mentally handicapped.[74] This implementation involved making curb cuts, constructing access ramps for all buildings, securing readers for blind students, and other such requirements.

Effect of the Increase in Student Diversity

Not only was the Southwestern student body changing because of the slow but steady increase in numbers, but it was also changing because of the increasing diversity of students being attracted to the University. Moving away from the homogeneous student body of earlier years, Southwestern began to attract a new mix of students. As Affirmative Action officer, Dean Swift was more aware of this change in student body composition than any other person. He described it and its consequences as follows:

> For generations Southwestern was populated primarily by students from [the] upper middle class and middle class socioeconomic strata. We had what would be called a homogeneous student body. Having similar backgrounds, the students shared a common set of values. Ten years ago [1965] the situation began to change when we introduced our first minority race students. We now have nearly 70 students who are members of minority races and this factor has had its impact on changing the composition of the campus. . . . At the same time [that] we began to bring in students from minority races and therefore from different cultures, we also began to recruit, through the use of increased financial aid funds, students from the Caucasian race who were also economically and socially disadvantaged. By bringing in minorities and Caucasian students from a different socioeconomic background, we actually changed the campus population to such an extent that the culture has been altered significantly. . . . One of the results of this change is the fact that we will never have the kind of "community" to which we all hark back so frequently. Those days are gone. Community is always based on a commonality of values. We no longer have such a sharing of values among our student body.[75]

In terms of religious affiliation, the increasing diversity of the student body was noticeable in the declining percentage of Methodists over the years. Whereas during the 1930s approximately two-thirds of the student body identified themselves as Methodists, a number that increased to more than three-fourths during the Finch years, that fraction had declined to just more than half by 1976. The decline was not so much in the slightly smaller number of Methodist students as in the percentage they formed of the growing student body. Many of the additional new students being attracted to the University were students that in earlier years would not have chosen Southwestern. Now, with diversity being emphasized by federal affirmative action initiatives, with substantial financial aid being offered, and with an increasing academic reputation, Southwestern began to attract a new type of student. For example, whereas in 1954 there had been only four Roman Catholic students on campus, in 1976 there were forty-three.[76] They formed the fifth-largest religious group on campus, following the Methodist, Episcopal, Baptist, and Presbyterian in that order. During the Shilling years, Roman Catholics would become the second-largest group on campus. The major reason for this increase in the number of Catholic students was the increasing number of Hispanics in the student population. The number of Hispanics would gradually rise to slightly more than 15 percent during the Shilling years.

The End of Required Chapel

The lack of a commonality of values in the student body spoken of by Dean Swift was eventually the chief reason for the abandonment of required chapel. Though students at

Southwestern had complained about required chapel almost since its inception, their complaints were fairly easy to ignore in earlier years in an almost uniformly Caucasian, Methodist, and, where not Methodist, Protestant student body and faculty. This uniformity diminished during the Fleming years not only in practice but also in theory. With electronic communications breaking down the walls between peoples and cultures at the international level and with the ending of racial segregation as the effect of this at the national level, the concept of diversity itself began to become a major value on college campuses across the country.

Chaplain Joe Foor (1965–1968) voiced the possibility of looking at the required-chapel concept in terms of this new ethos in the spring of 1967. He said in his report to the Trustees:

> The Chapel service this year has been a worship service. That is, we have presupposed a commitment on behalf of the students. However, I believe this to be a false assumption. Therefore, I cannot see how our worship in the Chapel service has much integrity. It seems to me that the primary purpose of Christian worship is not conversion, or apologetics, but [rather] worship is the result of conversion. Because our Chapel contains such a mixed congregation, and justifiably so since we are striving to be a university, worship is extremely difficult as the Body of Christ. Therefore, I suggest that we begin some experimentation with worship which is not compulsory.[77]

Foor was not unaware when he made his report that Fleming had been voicing problems with required chapel for some time. He had mentioned his concern to Chaplain Switzer soon after he first came, saying that he couldn't live with a situation where "newspapers went up" whenever a speaker in chapel began to talk. Fleming said that he "was in revolt inwardly" against it at SMU as a student, though he never spoke up against it. The job of the college, he felt, was to provide students with "exposure" to chapel and give them an opportunity to attend. "Whether they take it . . . , well, that's finally their decision and their right. We hope they all will come, but I rather doubt it." He recognized the reality of the situation and warned Foor about what would happen when chapel was made voluntary. Soon the chapel would be empty. It would then be up to the chaplain to try to fill it.[78]

Fleming never mentioned his unease with the required chapel attendance regulation to the faculty and even announced to them at a faculty meeting on February 16, 1965, that he would speak at the student assembly two days hence on "The Philosophical Foundations for Required Chapel Attendance."[79] Consequently, there was considerable surprise when two years later he announced that the requirement had been abolished. He was wrong in only one of his predictions. Students were so pleased with the abolition of the required attendance policy that they attended in record numbers when school reassembled again in the fall of 1967. The chaplain reported that about 475 students, faculty, and staff had attended during the first month.[80] In the long run, however, he was right. Chapel attendance eventually dropped to about 50 before doing a rebound to around 100.

A Reappraisal of What Church-relatedness Means

Fleming's willingness to abandon the requirement for chapel attendance does not mean that with it he was weakening, to his way of thinking, the concept of Church-relatedness. It only meant that times had changed, and Southwestern had to develop a new approach to helping students develop a meaningful religious direction for their lives. Consequently, he took steps to help develop this new approach. In 1970 he called for a President's Committee on Religion and Religious Life to study the issue. It did so and identified the principal issue as being an "identity crisis" in the life of the University. This crisis had arisen, the committee report stated, from a Southwestern that in earlier years had defined itself in "doctrinal and pietistic terms" on the basis of "a monolithic society where students, faculty, and trustees [had] come from the same general religious, economic, and ethnic background." New forces at work during the last twenty-five years, however, had reshaped the character of society. The monolithic social structure was being replaced by a pluralistic structure. The question of the moment was "to determine what type of community is possible in a pluralistic society." The problem of the Church-related college was not, said the committee, in any sense a question of the validity of its task but one of replacing outmoded methods for performing that task with methods appropriate to the times. Southwestern should turn away from "unity based on identity and . . . turn to a unity which embraces diversity." Such a unity can be built on a model of committed action presupposing the free response of the individual. This model should encompass "the great ground swell among the young" of affirmation for committed action.[81] The kind of commitment being exhibited by young people in their opposition to war and in their support for integration should be turned during their college years toward participation in everything serving the common good.

On the basis of this model, the committee addressed three areas—the academic religion requirement, community life at Southwestern, and the chapel program. Recommendations were made for each area. Many of these recommendations were adopted, the most novel of which was the establishment of a social internship program to fulfill three hours of the six-hour religion requirement. Benjamin T. Jordan and Paul Blanton served successively as directors of the program after it was instituted in 1971.[82]

Without required chapel services, a new appraisal of the meaning of the University's Church-relatedness became a matter of discussion. Dr. Farley Snell, chair of the Department of Religion and Philosophy and chaplain from 1972 to 1999, voiced his view of it in one of his reports (1976) to the Trustees. He said:

> Religious values are at the heart of what Southwestern University seeks to achieve and are the continuing basis on which we evaluate our success and failure: the manner in which teaching and learning are done, the way we treat human beings, and the kind of larger questions that are raised. The Aims of the University are expressed in this way; the President in his philosophy of education and administrative priorities bespeaks this commitment; the manner in which governance planning and programming are pursued indicate this perspective. This is not rhetoric. The attempt is ceaseless. The disagreement on particulars is present. The failures are real. But the focus is clear.[83]

In line with the approach outlined above, the Department of Religion and Philosophy restructured its program in 1977. Whereas up to that time it had been run on the "little seminary" model, teaching almost exclusively subjects related to Christianity, Methodism, professional studies such as Christian education, and traditional philosophy courses, it now described its approaches to religion and philosophy as encompassing: (1) phenomenological studies; (2) historical studies; (3) constructive studies; (4) methodological studies; and (5) value studies.[84] Under this program the department added a study of comparative religions, the great, non-Western religious traditions, and value questions in relation to contemporary issues and professional career objectives.[85]

The Fleming Building Program: Phase I (1961–1967)

All three of the Presidents that served Southwestern after 1949 were builders. Each left the campus a very different place from the one he inherited. Fleming had been a builder at his church in Houston, and one of the few negative elements mentioned by him regarding his move to Georgetown was his reluctance to leave the magnificent new sanctuary at St. Luke's that had recently been completed. He preached in it for only a little more than a year before coming to Southwestern. Nevertheless, he brought his carpenter's apron with him and for the next twenty years continued as a builder at Southwestern. He was seldom without a building project underway and never completed one project before beginning to talk about the next. By the time he finally left the University, every building of any consequence on campus was either new or had undergone a significant renovation.

This building activity, for the purpose of description, falls conveniently into two phases. Phase I includes the years 1961 through 1967. It consisted of the following projects:

- Kurth Residence Hall (new; begun by Finch; completed 1962)
- President's home (new; completed 1962)
- Old President's home (converted into Guest House; 1962)
- Sneed House (converted into a women's honor residence hall; 1962)
- Herman Brown Hall (new; completed 1966)
- Moody-Shearn Hall (new; completed 1966)
- University Commons (new; completed 1966)
- Library Addition (new; completed 1966)
- Laura Kuykendall Hall (renovation; completed 1967)
- Air-conditioning of chapel and all residence halls except Ruter (includes construction of a chilling plant; completed 1967)

The story of the first two new facilities, Kurth Residence Hall and the President's home, now called the Turner-Fleming House, has already been told. Their completion in his first year at Southwestern made possible the immediate conversion of the Sneed House into a women's honor residence hall and the old President's home into a Guest House.

The Herman Brown and Moody-Shearn Residence Halls

Soon after the death of Herman Brown, the Board discussed the possibility of raising $300,000 to $350,000 to endow a Herman Brown Department of Economics and Business Administration.[86] This idea was abandoned, however, when The Brown Foundation shortly thereafter made a matching grant proposal for permanent improvements that included the establishment of three professorships, one of which would be a Herman Brown Professorship in English. Since the heart of the proposal was for the Foundation to contribute $500,000 "for permanent improvements" conditioned upon the raising of $1,000,000 by the University, the University decided to use the $500,000 to build a Herman Brown residence hall.[87] Gifts from some of Herman Brown's friends were also added to this amount. The Brown grant was soon matched by a gift from the Moody Foundation for a Moody-Shearn residence hall. The two gifts in equal amounts made it possible for the University to construct two similar buildings.

Following up on the contacts carefully initiated by President Finch with Mrs. Mary Moody Northen of Galveston, Fleming wrote her from time to time. A surprise visit by her to Southwestern in February 1963 indicated that she had a real interest in doing something for Southwestern in honor of her grandfather, John Shearn, who had graduated in the second class at Rutersville College in 1845, and her father, William Lewis Moody, Jr., founder of the family fortune.[88] Though a proposal submitted to the Moody Foundation requested a grant for two men's dormitories, one named for each man, Fleming was pleased to receive a telephone call from Mrs. Northen on April 14, 1964, advising him that the Foundation had granted $500,000 to build a memorial dormitory to be named in honor of both her father and grandfather.[89] She subsequently attended a banquet at the fall meeting of the Board of Trustees as guest of honor.[90] At a chance meeting with Mrs. Northen when both he and she were on vacation in Scotland in the summer of 1966, Fleming got a commitment from her to attend the dedication of her new building along with the other three to be dedicated at the same time on October 25, 1966.[91] The Moody Foundation supplemented the building with a grant of $400,000 for a John Shearn Chair in Business Administration in honor of her grandfather in 1974.

The earlier proposal by Southwestern to the Moody Foundation for two men's "dormitories" was predicated upon a plan from the Finch era that Martin Ruter Hall would be one of three men's dormitories forming a quadrangle with an open side facing south. By the time the Brown and Moody gifts came through, however, University officials had become convinced that the former plan was inadequate. Ruter was an old-style dormitory, with single rooms and gang showers and other bathroom facilities shared in common on each floor. The idea now was to build "residence halls" in a more apartment-like style. Consequently, two virtually identical buildings were constructed on what was then the northwest corner of the campus adjacent to Maple Street. Holding one hundred men each, the two buildings formed a complex of two- and three-story units with exterior corridors and courtyards. A bath was provided for each four-student apartment, and each student was provided with a study carrel.

The University Commons and the Library Addition

At the same time that architect George Page was commissioned on October 29, 1964, to proceed with plans and specifications for the two residence halls, he was also instructed to do the same for a new University Commons and an addition to the library.[92] Fleming had been appalled by the food service in the Laura Kuykendall Annex when he first came and had proposed at the first regular meeting of the Board after his coming that a new food service facility be built in connection with the Bishops' Memorial Union.[93] The proposal was postponed at the time but was acted on three years later, only now the new facility would be a freestanding building located in back of the chapel on the south side of Southwestern Boulevard.

When completed, the new University Commons was the most stunning building on campus. Except for the type of stone used in it, it had few carryover design elements from any other campus building. The use of a copper-sheet covering for the exterior of a prominent circular skylight that jutted out above the roof over the center of the dining area highlighted its exterior appearance. The dining area itself was circular, with a diameter of approximately one hundred feet, giving the building, except the kitchen area on the east side, a round shape. The roof tapered down from the skylight and overhung the exterior walls by about eight feet, covering a concrete walkway around the entire outside of the building. The dining area inside was connected to a scatter serving area. Faculty, student, and Trustee dining rooms on the second floor above the rectangular kitchen on the first floor could be operated either as three independent rooms or joined into one large room by folding back the flexible partitions separating the three units.

Though the building was aesthetically pleasing, it was out of harmony with the style of other buildings on campus. Also, over the years, as the student body grew in size, lines of students waiting to be served developed that clogged the interior serving area and snaked out through the revolving entry doors. Function had been sacrificed to form to such an extent that the building was eventually razed after the Red and Charline McCombs Campus Center was constructed in 1998. The place where it stood is a bit east of but adjacent to the present William Carrington Finch Plaza.

The new addition to the library was also modern in design and unlike any other building on campus. Built in the International style of concrete, smooth limestone, and panel walls, it was connected to the original three-story building constructed in 1939. Given their different styles, the joining of the two was not harmonious. The old building had a high, steeply tapered roofline, while the new building had a flat roof. The entrance to the old building facing University Avenue was closed, and the library as a whole was turned toward the interior of the campus by opening a new front entrance on the north through the addition. The north side of the addition, completely faced with glass, became the main part of the library. Though the functional aspects of the design were serviceable on the interior, the appearance of the exterior, like that of the new Commons, was out of keeping with rest of the campus. When the library was enlarged once again in 1988, the glass exterior of the 1966 addition was removed in favor of a design more in keeping with the rest of the campus. Both the new University Commons and the new library addition of 1966 were mostly financed by the Brown "permanent improvements" challenge campaign of 1963.

Completion of Phase I of the Building Program

Following the completion of the four new buildings, architect George Page was asked to set out a remodeling program for the Laura Kuykendall Annex (old Commons area) and for the air-conditioning of all the residence halls with the exception of Ruter.[94] The L.K. Annex project resulted in the creation of twenty new rooms for students. It was completed within ninety days prior to the opening of the fall semester in 1967. Dr. McCook proclaimed that it resulted in a complete metamorphosis of the Annex with a magnificent result.[95] The chapel was also air-conditioned at this time.[96]

Though most of these projects had Moody and Brown money underwriting them in addition to surplus funds from the operational budget, the final cost of all capital improvements from 1962 through 1967 was $4,252,309. This amount was considerably more than the amount on hand. Justifying these expenditures, Fleming said that the buildings put up were absolutely necessary constructions. Without them Southwestern would have been uncompetitive.[97] Available funds covered only about 60 percent of the cost. When an Advancement Fund Campaign from 1965 to 1967 failed to raise the balance as anticipated, the University was forced to borrow $1,700,000 from the Southwestern Life Insurance Company to pay it off. This loan, payable over ten years in quarterly installments of $54,900, became a millstone hanging around the neck of the University until it was finally paid off in 1975.[98]

The United Capital Funds Campaign

In a conversation during the late 1970s, Durwood Fleming remarked to me that if he could do it over again, he would do one thing differently in the area of financial development than he did when he came. He would have put on a big financial campaign immediately upon assuming the presidency rather than waiting to do it. On the face of it, one can agree with him. Yet, at the same time, one can understand why he waited three years to do it and why, at that point, it was not very successful. He felt blocked by the United Capital Funds Campaign.

When he assumed the presidency in 1961, a United Capital Funds Campaign for Methodist higher education in Texas run by the Annual Conferences had just gotten underway. It would supposedly raise $32,000,000 to be distributed as follows: 29 percent to SMU and the Perkins School of Theology; 15 percent each to McMurry, TWC, and Southwestern; 15 percent to the Wesley Foundations; and 11 percent to Lon Morris College. The campaign had begun on December 1, 1960, seven months before Fleming assumed the presidency. It was supposed to last for two years.[99] High hopes were held by the Trustees for using the $4,800,000 that would accrue to Southwestern from a successful completion of the campaign to "liquidate the debt on the heating plant, wipe out the balance due on Kurth Hall, and provide funds for the two remaining men's dormitories."[100]

Fleming, as the new President of Southwestern, naturally supported the campaign when he came to Georgetown. As the end of the two-year campaign approached, some of the members of the Board of Trustees recognized that it was seriously behind schedule and would fall short of its objective.[101] The statewide leaders of the campaign, however, were reluctant to accept this verdict and the campaign was extended. By spring 1963, Fleming knew that the campaign would be a failure and suggested that Southwestern pursue a "broad, bold development program" for itself. In spite of the fact that a number of Trustees felt such a program would be difficult to pursue as long as the United Capital Funds program was still technically in operation, the Board adopted a motion authorizing the administrative officers to proceed with the organization of a strong and aggressive development program.[102]

The Advancement Campaign

As a consequence of the perceived failure of the United Capital Funds Campaign, Fleming began to develop an Advancement Fund Campaign for Southwestern. By the time of its final report of April 29, 1967, it, too, had failed to achieve its objective. How much of that failure was due to its overlap with the continuation of the United Capital Funds Campaign throughout the state is an unresolved problem, but some of it is certainly attributable to that effort. The United Capital Funds Campaign continued until a statewide Victory Dinner was held in Houston on December 16, 1966. At that dinner, Fleming reported for Southwestern, while others reported for the general state leadership and for other institutions. What they did in fact at the meeting was to call the campaign a victory and retire from the field.

Fleming's report at the campaign dinner is probably representative of the type made by the other leaders. He reported that Southwestern had oversubscribed its part in reaching the overall goal of $32 million. He reported an endowment increase of $2,207,108, a plant fund increase of $1,754,567, a buildings improvements increase of $2,736,966, and total gifts of $3,120,809 over the six years of the campaign. The grand total was $9,819,450.[103] Of course, most or all of this money had come to Southwestern because of what it had done for itself during this period rather than because of the United Capital Funds Campaign. The almost $10 million figure reported by Fleming was reached by counting the total endowment increase regardless of how it came about, by including the Moody and the Brown gifts, and by including other gifts, grants, and surplus operational funds that went into the totals of the four categories listed above. No overall report was ever made, so far as I know, of funds that came to the University exclusively because of its participation in the United Capital Funds Campaign.

The proposed Advancement Fund Campaign did not get underway until the spring of 1965. During the two-year interval between the time it was first broached and when it was initiated, a ten-year fund-raising program was developed that included all the projects that were voted in 1964 and completed during 1966 and 1967. Since the Development staff consisted only of Mr. Graves Blanton, who had been employed by President Finch in 1959, and Mr. James A. Reid, who was employed as Director of Alumni Relations in 1964, Fleming sought a professional firm to conduct the campaign. The Patrick Organization of Fort Worth was employed to raise the projected $12 million. Of that amount, $7 million would be for endowment, and $5 million would be for capital improvements. Five million dollars would be raised in the first three years, with the remainder being raised in the following seven years. R. E. (Bob) Smith became the General Chairman of the campaign.[104]

The campaign began with a Big Gifts and Special Gifts convocation, in which a "Committee of 125" friends and supporters of the University came to the campus on October 25, 1966, to hear Governor Connally and to attend a banquet.[105] Six months later the campaign reported a total of only $469,167.68 raised.[106] The only segment of the campaign that reached its goal was the Georgetown segment, where the goal of $100,000 was superseded. Feeling that the Patrick Organization "had failed rather dismally to furnish the kind of leadership needed" in the Advancement Campaign, the Board put the firm on ninety-day notice.[107] Fleming also penned a report for the Trustees that went beyond placing the entire blame on the fund-raising organization. He analyzed quite objectively the faults of the administrative and Trustee leadership of the University, starting with himself.[108] Though Fleming announced that the Vice President for Development and Public Relations, Mr. Graves Blanton, would take charge of the campaign and that he as President would redouble his efforts, the campaign was soon abandoned. Blanton resigned within a few months and took a U.S. State Department Agency for International Development job as an educational consultant with the Catholic University of Rio de Janeiro.[109]

In place of the Advancement Campaign, Fleming was soon able to announce a Challenge Grant by The Brown Foundation, together with gifts of $100,000 per year for three years by the Foundation to support the budgetary operations of the institution. He was also able to express appreciation for a Cullen Foundation gift of $450,000 to establish an endowed Chair in Economics memorializing the late Mr. and Mrs. Hugh Roy Cullen. He paid special tribute to A. Frank Smith, Jr., who worked hard securing the gift.[110] The University secured the $1,700,000 loan from the Southwestern Life Insurance Company already mentioned to cover the capital expenditures that had been approved with the understanding that any excess would be covered by income from the now defunct Advancement Fund Campaign,.[111]

The Fleming Building Program: Phase II (1972–1981)

After a hiatus of five years, the building program resumed and continued from 1972 through 1981. It includes the construction and/or renovation of the following buildings and the establishment of the Mood-Heritage Museum.

Sid W. Richardson Physical Education Center
Jim West Gymnasium
Rockwell Field
Administration Building
Mood Hall
Mood-Heritage Museum
Alma Thomas Fine Arts Center
McCullough Hall
Fondren-Jones Science Hall
Lois Perkins Chapel
Ruter Hall

Athletic Facilities: Richardson P. E. Center, West Gym, and Rockwell Field

Even in the midst of the earlier building cycle, Fleming had his eyes on what should be done next. He mentioned to the Trustees in 1964 what was obvious to everyone—that the Administration Building, Mood Hall, and Laura Kuykendall Hall needed to be renovated.[112] Before those projects came on line, however, the Sid W. Richardson Foundation of Fort Worth announced in December 1973 that it had voted a $1 million grant to build a physical education center on campus. Fleming had been negotiating with the Foundation for the grant since 1968. The new center would cost more than the $1 million from the Foundation, but, it was hoped, it would not exceed the grant by much. When the final plans were completed, however, George Page, the architect, estimated that it would cost $1,741,000. Even this estimate was negated by the ravages of the inflation of the mid- to late 1970s. By the time the final bid was accepted on February 25, 1974, the cost had escalated to $1,950,000 and finally topped out at $2,027,000 when the building was completed. The $1,027,000 beyond the Richardson gift was taken from the W-K-M Endowment. The W-K-M Endowment fund was a "quasi-endowment fund," or "fund functioning as endowment"—in other words, unrestricted funds recorded in the endowment at the discretion of the Board of Trustees and thus available for the Board of Trustees to use for this purpose. With this financing, the Center was built, dedicated, and formally opened on September 25, 1976.[113]

With the completion of the Richardson Center, the University now had two buildings for athletic competition—the Richardson Physical Education Center and the Jim West Gymnasium. The West Gymnasium, erected in 1941, had been completely renovated by the Jim West Foundation in 1974.[114] The possession of two gymnasiums now made it possible for the University to face without difficulty the federal Title IX requirement to provide adequate facilities for women's athletics. Both men and women would use both facilities, but the old facility was particularly suited for women's volleyball.

Another project related to the athletic program was the construction of the Henry M. Rockwell baseball field on the east side of the campus. Through the many years of its history, the baseball team had never had a really good field. At various periods it practiced and played its games on the city baseball field in San Gabriel Park across the river. This situation changed after James L. Mallon came to the University in 1970 and became one of the leading college baseball coaches in America. During his career at Southwestern, he won over a thousand games and attracted better players than his scholarship program would have brought in without his name. A new, adequate baseball field was built for him and his winning teams in 1978, though, in truth, Mallon himself put in a great deal of the labor. It was named Rockwell Field in honor of Henry M. Rockwell, who paid for it and who had supported Southwestern athletics for many years.

"Foots" Rockwell graduated from Southwestern in 1922 with a degree in economics. He followed his father in the family lumber business and became the president of the Rockwell Trust after his father's death. When the West Gymnasium was completed in 1941, he led the other ex-lettermen in putting a concrete sidewalk around it.[115] He and his brother set up endowed scholarships in 1958 in honor of their parents and made generous donations from time to time for the various projects of the University. He was very supportive of Durwood Fleming, whom he considered a fellow Houstonian, and donated a discretionary fund outside the regular University budget to be used by the President for special purposes. The Rockwell Fund made a $100,000 donation to the ill-starred Advancement Fund Campaign in 1966. Rockwell was given the Distinguished Alumnus Award in 1967 and had the Doctor of Humane Letters degree conferred on him in 1969. He was ever the athlete, and his heart was in baseball. He attended the game played at the field named for him when the field was opened fifty-six years after his graduation. The Henry M. Rockwell Historical Rotunda in the McCombs Campus Center was later named in his memory.

Renovation of the Administration Building

In early 1975 Fleming announced the receipt of two large gifts, one for $1 million from the Cullen Foundation for the renovation of the Administration Building and the other for $500,000 for the renovation of Mood Hall. Roy Cullen and A. Frank Smith, Jr., were thanked for their work with the Cullen Foundation. Charles Prothro was thanked for his influence with the Bridwell Foundation.[116]

By 1975 the Administration Building was in poor shape. The auditorium was in such disrepair that it had been taken out of use, and its doors were boarded over to keep anyone from entering. The old gymnasium on the first floor, with its dropped floor, had been fitted out as a rabbit warren of small faculty offices. Bats often invaded offices and classrooms on the third floor. The building was extremely hot in the summer because it was not air-conditioned, and it was heated in winter by big metal radiators that banged away as they were warmed up by heat from the central plant. The electrical wiring was primitive.[117]

Mood Hall was not any better. It was completely taken out of use after the construction of Herman Brown and Moody-Shearn Halls but was put back into limited use for a few offices in 1971–1972. It received limited remodeling in 1975 to make it possible for the offices and classrooms in the Administration Building to be moved there for about eighteen months while the Administration Building was remodeled in 1976 and early 1977.[118]

The Administration Building was formally reopened and rededicated as the Roy and Lillie Cullen Building on October 14, 1977.[119] The cost of the remodeling was $1,323,000, with the additional cost beyond the original Cullen grant of $1 million being borne by that Foundation as well.[120] The building was air-conditioned and the remodeling beautifully done, especially the woodwork, except for the old window frames that would await a future renovation project. The main floor of the auditorium was restored and, with its new Italian student-style chairs with fold-down writing arms, became a locale for handling two-hundred-plus persons for lectures and performances. The balcony could hold up to one hundred more.

Mood Hall and the Mood-Heritage Museum

Like other building projects of the mid-1970s, the remodeling of Mood Hall was affected severely by inflation. The project also encountered design problems. Unlike the Cullen Building, which was supported by strong rubble walls throughout, Mood Hall was constructed in a "balloon" style, that is, with strong exterior but with minimal interior support walls. The interior "hung" from the outside support structure. As a result, large steel beams had to be brought in to support some of the new design elements called for in changing the building from a residence hall to a classroom and office building.

Though the original estimate for remodeling is unknown, by the time the project was started the cost was $1,150,000.[121] The Board authorized the funding of the $650,000 beyond the $500,000 from the Bridwell Foundation by selling some of its own real estate, the Lil Hall ranch in Burnet County and the Young Dairy Farm, from the Current Fund, where their assets were held, to the Endowment Fund. The gain of $834,000 occasioned by the sale was used to complete the Mood Hall project and to fund several other small projects.[122] Since the J. E. and L. E. Mabee Foundation of Tulsa, Oklahoma, had earlier said that it would provide the last $100,000 for the completion of the building if Southwestern raised $300,000, it judged that Southwestern had met its challenge and provided the final $100,000 for the building.[123] When completed in 1978, the building was renamed Mood-Bridwell Hall. It provided offices for forty faculty and eight staff members in addition to ten classroom and seminar rooms. A space for the telephone operators, a faculty conference room, the computer center, a storage area, and a space for the Mood-Heritage Museum were also created.[124]

The remodeling plans for Mood Hall had been drawn up with the intention of providing space for a Mood-Heritage Museum sponsored by volunteers from Southwestern and the Georgetown Heritage Society. Its purpose was to preserve records and artifacts related to the history of Southwestern University and the local area, though it came to house a few other special items. The organization raised its own operational funds, and its members donated their time to the project. Though it was not included in the University budget, its obvious primary interest was the University, and the organization was given several rooms in the southwest corner of the first floor of the new Mood-Bridwell Hall when the building was completed. Dr. Judson S. Custer headed the museum movement, and Dr. Edmund H. Steelman (retired) served as curator.[125] The museum was successful in assembling an impressive array of important historical objects that would not have otherwise come to the University. Some of the permanent exhibits of the museum were located in the atrium of the building. In 1980 it established a Gallery of Honor, recognizing in annual ceremonies important historical personages in Southwestern and Georgetown history and publishing information about them in attractive brochures.[126] The Museum was discontinued when the space it occupied was needed for other purposes. Its holdings were inventoried and are today stored in the library, where they are maintained as a part of Special Collections.

Alma Thomas Fine Arts Center, Sneed House, and McCullough Hall

The renovation of the Alma Thomas Fine Arts Center by the Hoblitzelle Foundation of Dallas has already been treated in the chapter covering construction of that facility (Chapter XVIII). By the spring of 1978 that renovation was nearing completion. A year later President Fleming stated that the building was "one of the most beautiful centers for the arts in the Southwest."[127]

At 3:30 A.M. on October 30, 1978, the second major fire in Southwestern's history at a women's residence hall occurred when the Sneed House burned.[128] Though the house was full of sleeping students, the smoke alarms sounded and awakened the women, who marched from the house in their bedclothes and robes and stood outside while the house burned. Television and newspaper reporters from Austin converged on the scene. Fortunately, the University had installed the smoke alarms within the past year, and the media focused attention on its good judgment in having done so rather than on the dangers inherent in housing students in frame buildings, as had been mentioned by the SACS Visiting Committee in 1971 in response to the Self-Study Report of that year.[129] At the next meeting of the Executive Committee about two weeks later, additional expenditures of $135,000 were voted to further the fire safety program of the University.[130] After the fire, Mr. Kirk Treible, Vice President for Fiscal Affairs, arranged with Mr. Harry Gold to let the girls that had lost their belongings in the fire to outfit themselves temporarily at Gold's Department Store at University expense so as to be able to continue school without interruption. The University also offered interest-free loans of up to $1,500 to make replacement purchases until insurance settlements could be made.[131]

The complete remodeling of the Laura Kuykendall Annex in 1979 soon made up for the loss of the twenty-six women's spaces in the Sneed House fire. The remodeling job in 1967 that created twenty rooms had left a great deal of storage space. This space was now converted into residence rooms and sorority rooms. The conversion was largely funded by a gift of $250,000 from Mr. and Mrs. Marvin McCullough of Wichita Falls. The remainder of the $325,000 project came from the insurance settlement of $85,000 for the loss of the Sneed House.[132] When completed in 1979, the old Annex, which housed for many years the dining hall on the first floor and the School of Fine Arts on the second floor, was renamed McCullough Hall in honor of the parents of the donors. Three of their four parents had attended Southwestern.[133]

Fondren Science Hall Becomes Fondren-Jones Science Hall

Fondren Science Hall, which had been a state-of-the art science building when it was built in 1954, was badly in need of renovation twenty-five years later. The building itself was still sturdy and without major construction flaws in need of remedy, but it was not air-conditioned and was extremely uncomfortable during the hot days of late spring, summer, and early autumn. The laboratory equipment was old, and the building was only minimally provided with the kind of special labs necessary for high-level undergraduate scientific research. Southwestern simply could not continue to compete in the area of science with other first-rate undergraduate institutions unless it upgraded its scientific teaching facilities. This fact was so obvious that the President and the Board of Trustees began to present proposals for the renovation of the building to various foundations in late 1978.[134] Ambassador Ed Clark and A. Frank Smith, Jr., presented one of those proposals to the Houston Endowment, Inc., in the spring of 1980. The trustees of the Endowment received them cordially, and soon thereafter awarded the University a $1 million gift for the project. The building would be renamed the Fondren-Jones Science Hall in honor of Jesse Jones, the longtime friend of Southwestern in earlier years, who had founded the Houston Endowment.

Because of the pressure of time, the Board of Trustees voted to go ahead immediately with the renovation even though it was estimated to cost up to $2.5 million. For that purpose it authorized the temporary borrowing of the balance needed to complete the project from the Capital National Bank of Austin.[135] A contract for $2,354,913 was let.[136]

The prosecution of the project involved the complete displacement of science classes and the use of innovative methods of teaching science for the year 1980–1981. With work underway, Dean G. Benjamin Oliver reported the handling of the academic work in science as follows:

> Southwestern's science facilities are now scattered around Georgetown and as far south as Austin! Faculty offices for Biology and Chemistry are temporarily located in Mood-Bridwell Hall; the chemical research facilities are housed in part of the McCook-Crain Clinic; Biology laboratories are in the building on University Avenue which used to house the Georgetown Hospital; Physics labs and classrooms are in the Odds and Ends Hall; and students enrolled in Chemistry laboratories for the fall semester ride a bus to Austin every Thursday to meet those classes at The University of Texas.[137]

Most of the renovation was done on the interior of the building. The large attic was transformed into a fourth story, with private research laboratories for chemistry, biology, and physics. The building was air-conditioned, and new equipment was purchased. Though the Trustees had intended to raise funds to cover the loan procured from the bank, nothing came in to cover the portion of the cost not covered by the Houston Endowment gift. Consequently, the Trustees voted at the spring 1981 Board meeting to transfer $1,500,000 from the W-K-M Endowment to the Plant Fund to cover the remaining balance.[138] Once again, as in the case of the Mood Hall renovation, the University took the gain that accrued from selling some of its holdings from one fund to another in order to pay for a project. This method was perfectly legitimate in terms of fund accounting as normally practiced by institutions of higher education. The gain could have been recorded as an asset gain, thus raising the book value of the endowment, but the Board would have had to find another way to pay the unfunded costs for the renovation of Fondren-Jones Science Hall.

Lois Perkins Chapel and Ruter Hall

Three projects attributable to the Fleming administration were completed during the year he retired and President Shilling took over. They were the renovation of the Fondren-Jones Science Hall, the Lois Perkins Chapel, and Ruter Hall. The renovation of Lois Perkins Chapel was paid for entirely by Charles and Elizabeth (Perkins) Prothro and did not involve any additional fund-raising by the University. It has already been described in the chapter covering the construction of the chapel and its subsequent history (see Chapter XVIII).

Ruter Hall, constructed in 1955, was twenty-six years old in 1981. No major changes had been made to it since that time, and it was in need of renovation. It was not air-conditioned and contrasted badly with the newer men's residence halls built in 1966. Because of this need, Fleming and the Board decided in the spring of 1981 to renovate it. Having already been turned down by three sources for grants to cover the cost, they felt they had no choice but to recur to what had been done in the funding of Mood Hall and the Fondren-Jones Science Building. They would use creative financing by selling endowment resources from one fund to another and using the gain for construction purposes. Once again W-K-M quasi-endowment funds were used. In the case of Ruter, $650,000 was transferred.[139]

When Shilling arrived as new President on July 1, 1981, the renovation of the Fondren-Jones Science Hall, the Lois

President Durwood Fleming and Lois Perkins. Mrs. Perkins left a moving testament to be opened at her death that now appears on a bronze plaque in the vestibule of the Chapel. Southwestern University, Special Collections.

Perkins Chapel, and Ruter Hall were all in the process of being completed. Just as Cameron Fairchild had been the University architect for all the buildings constructed from 1939 to 1961, George Page had been the architect for all the buildings during the twenty years of the Fleming era. Though some of Page's work has stood the test of time, two of his major projects, the circular University Commons and the glass-fronted addition to the library, were removed in later years. During the period from 1981 to 2000, a Buildings and Grounds Master Plan designed by new architects guided the construction agenda, resulting in the campus that exists today.

Inflation, the Stock Market, and the Endowment during the Fleming Period

Inflation at the national level caused major problems for Fleming during his tenure, much more so than for Finch or Shilling. That, along with a slowing economy, produced "stagflation," an economic phenomenon still described today by the nickname coined during the 1970s. During the Finch years, the annual compounded average rate of inflation was exactly 2.0 percent. Later, during the Shilling years, it was 3.8 percent. From Fleming's first year to his last, the total increase in inflation was 178.7 percent, for a compounded average rate of 5.3 percent per year over his two decades. This figure means that Southwestern theoretically needed 5.3 percent more disposable income each year than the previous year just to keep operating the same program with the same number of teachers for the same number of students at the same level. Dealing with this situation was painful for Trustees and administrators and accounts for much of the Trustee "anguish," as it is described in Board minutes, in trying to establish a balanced operating budget.[140]

Inflation was hardly noticeable in Fleming's first five years, never in any year amounting to as much as 2.0 percent, about the same average as during the Finch years. Then it began an erratic trend upward for the next fifteen years. For three years it was in the 2.0 percent to 3.9 percent range; for seven years it was 4.0 percent to 6.9 percent; for two years it was 7.0 percent to 9.9 percent; and for three years it was above 10.0 percent, attaining a high of 13.5 percent in Fleming's last year. Increases in student charges for room, board, and tuition were difficult to decide on for fear of driving present students away and of frightening off prospective students. Though significant increases in student charges were enacted in spite of this fear, they were always more a matter of playing catch-up for inflationary surges already experienced than of getting ahead of the inflationary curve.

Neither was the stock market as kind to Fleming as it was to Finch and Shilling. When Finch was made permanent President in early 1950, the Dow-Jones Industrial Average was 209. At the end of his tenure it was 684, an increase of 227.1 percent over the eleven years. The annual compounded average increase in security values was 11.4 percent. With the market booming, Southwestern even borrowed money to invest in stocks, such as Transcontinental and Texas Eastern, which its Trustees correctly predicted would gain significantly in value. Its W-K-M holdings gained 40 percent during the five-and-a-half years from the time they were turned over to Southwestern until they were sold. These transactions went far toward breaking the economic straitjacket Southwestern had worn for so long.

When Shilling took over as President in 1981 the Dow-Jones Industrial Average was 977. Toward the end of the 1980s it began its remarkable climb to close at 10,448 on June 30, 2000, when he retired. The total increase during Shilling's nineteen years was 969.4 percent, for an annual compounded average increase of 13.3 percent. The extraordinary sums of new money raised by him were often multiplied by the stock market gains they experienced as a part of the endowment.

For Fleming, however, the stock market was not so cooperative. The Dow-Jones Industrial Average was 690 on July 1, 1961, when he assumed the presidency. It was only 977 twenty years later. The total increase over the two decades was a meager 41.6 percent. The annual compounded average increase was 1.8 percent. Trustee A. Frank Smith, Jr., remarked in the January Board meeting of 1972 that the performance of the stock market in 1971 was the worst since the Depression.[141] The almost imperceptible advance in stock market values means that Southwestern's money managers could not count on the appreciation of its securities to increase the value of the endowment. Endowment increase would come almost exclusively from new money attracted to the University, not from investment gains in equities.

Though we do not have an audited market value endowment figure for 1961, when Fleming took over, we do have a figure of $6,598,026 reported in the audit for the following year.[142] Nineteen years later, at the end of the Fleming period, the market value of the endowment was $37,914,778, an increase of 474.6 percent since 1962, for an average compounded annual increase of 9.6 percent. This figure is remarkable given the fact that the stock market was so anemic and that Fleming's administration experienced only five years of income from the Brown Challenge program that began in 1976, none of which enjoyed significant gain in the stock market during his tenure. The stock market did not begin to boom until five or six years after Fleming's retirement. It was during the Finch and Shilling years that stock market advance was a major factor in Southwestern's endowment growth.

National economic forces were not kind to Fleming. This fact must be remembered when one studies the budgetary, endowment, and development picture of the Fleming years. The overall rather stagnant economic picture of the times needs to be kept in mind when considering some of the financial operations engaged in during those years. In comparison with the Finch and Shilling administrations, Fleming engaged in a high-risk financial operation, especially in terms of constructing buildings that were underfinanced when begun and in terms of operational budgets that only came into balance during the year rather than, as will be seen in the next chapter, being balanced at the outset. The buildings ended up being paid for, and most of the budgets ended up being balanced, but the means used to achieve these ends were, in some instances, reminiscent of the financing engaged in during the Great Depression.

The fact that Southwestern did as well as it did over the two decades was due to Fleming's continuing insistence on advancing the University in spite of negative economic circumstances and to his development of the Houston connection consisting of the Browns, the Cullens, and other longtime friends of the University. Though the Trustees who had provided the connections with other persons so useful to Southwestern through the 1930s, '40s, and '50s gradually disappeared, others, such as Charles Prothro, A. Frank Smith, Jr., Roy Cullen, and Ed Clark, arose to take their place. They supported Fleming strongly.

Internal Change and the Brown Challenge (1961–1981)

Academic and Faculty Change

Dean Wicke had adumbrated new directions in academics during his tenure as dean during the latter Finch years. Many on the faculty eyed his changes with suspicion, and he had difficulty putting them into practice. The resistance he encountered changed completely during the Fleming years, and academic change became the order of the day. This change began slowly during the early 1960s, with the replacement of the numerical grading system by the letter system in 1962.[1] It gathered force during the middle '60s and became full-blown during the late '60s. By the middle '70s it had pretty well spent its force. The Humanities in Practice Program, initiated in 1976, was the last major curricular change during the Fleming administration. By the late '70s the educational program of the University had settled into a regular pattern once again, albeit a pattern with a different ethos in which regular reexamination of the curriculum and a search for creative ways of providing it became an expected part of the educational process. It would become a regular feature of the master planning process during the Shilling years.

More academic change occurred more quickly at Southwestern during the eleven years from 1965 to 1976 than at any other period in its history. The overall background for this change was the turmoil in American higher education caused by the social and political situation in the country described in Chapter XX. Very important also was the fact that the University had a President and two academic deans who were not afraid of change. In the years immediately after his coming to Southwestern, Professor Clifford had received a commendation from Dean Wicke for his "extraordinarily creative work" in two special English courses. Later, as dean, Clifford continued to put a premium on creativity. In 1964 he critiqued the University curriculum to the Trustees by telling them that it was "good and solid but totally unimaginative, extremely weak in its appeal to students."[2] Consequently, he supported the efforts of the faculty to instigate more exciting ways of performing the educational function of the institution even when he sometimes disagreed with what they did. He tried to guide the faculty rather than prescribe to it.

The support of major administrators for curricular change, however, would not have been effective without faculty members who were energized to make changes. This third ingredient, an energized faculty, became a part of the Southwestern educational landscape as the faculty was reconstituted during the Fleming years. This remaking of the faculty occurred as older faculty members retired and were replaced by younger ones and as the faculty was enlarged by the addition of new positions. Both Fleming and Clifford insisted that Southwestern must eliminate all one-person departments.[3] That objective was accomplished in 1971, when the Home Economics Department was abolished with the retirement of its last chairperson.

The faculty inherited by Fleming from Finch, including part-time persons and administrators with faculty rank, numbered fifty-seven. The comparable faculty he passed on to Shilling numbered eighty-seven, an increase of 53 percent. Of the fifty-seven teachers inherited from Finch, forty-five retired, resigned, or died during Fleming's twenty years. By 1979–1980 some 81 percent of the faculty had been employed by him. Though lack of comparable records makes it impossible to ascertain the average age of the faculty for earlier administrations, the faculty in 1979–1980 was the youngest in the judgment of this author of any that Southwestern had had for many years. At that time not a single full-time faculty member was more than sixty-five years old. With a mandatory retirement age of seventy, there would be no retirements for five years except for those that might occur for voluntary or health reasons. The average age of full-time faculty members in the fall of 1979 was a small fraction over forty-five.[4] These younger persons brought a new dynamic to the faculty that, in many cases, infected the older faculty members, a number of whom became change advocates themselves. A year earlier, in the fall of 1978, 69 percent of the full-time teachers, all of whom had doctorates, were tenured. Twenty-nine percent of the part-time teachers had doctorates.[5]

The new faculty employed by Fleming formed a fairly stable group. Of the ones employed during the twenty years from 1962–1963 through 1981–1982, sixty-one would serve for more than ten years. They are listed in continuation with the year of initial appointment:

1962	Jefferson H. Campbell (English), Edwin M. Lansford (Biochemistry)
1963	None
1964	Robert L. Soulen (Chemistry)
1965	Francisco Betancourt (Foreign Languages), Tibb Burnett (Physical Education/Drama), William B. Jones (History), Claude L. Kennard (Art History), William L. Merritt (Men's Basketball Coach/ Physical Education), F. Ellsworth Peterson (Music), William D. Swift (Dean of Students, V.P., Sociology)
1966	Jim L. Bridges (Business Administration), John B. Chapman (Mathematics)*, Lois W. Parker (English)
1967	Fred R. Hilgeman (Chemistry)*, Horace S. Jacob (Biology), Suk-soon Suh (Political Science)
1968	Virginia Carwell (English), Leonard F. Giesecke (Economics), Raymond L. Schroeder (Music)
1969	Charlaine Eicher (Library), Jack T. Harris (English), Tex Leo Kassen (Athletic Director/Physical Education), Regine Reynolds (French)
1970	B. Joe Colwell (Economics), Guss D. Farmer, Jr. (Art), Fred R. Goodson (Drama and Speech), James L. Mallon (Baseball Coach/Physical Education)
1971	None
1972	Harold D. Eidson, Jr. (Mathematics/Computer Science), Billie G. Fullingim (Education), Farley W. Snell (Chaplain/Religion)
1973	Gerhild Rogers (German)
1974	Edward G. Golla (Chemistry), Dan C. Hilliard (Sociology)*, Bruce W. Mossman (Education), Kenny Mac Sheppard (Music)*, W. Nick Sikes (Education)
1975	T. Walter Herbert (English)*, Glada C. Munt (Volleyball Coach/Physical Education/Athletic Director)*, Francis W. O'Brien (Political Science)
1976	Weldon S. Crowley (History), Theodore D. Lucas (Dean Fine Arts/Music), Henry W. Wolgemuth (Library)
1977	Jan C. Dawson (History), Sharon C. Johnson (Education)*, G. Benjamin Oliver (Dean Arts and Sciences/Philosophy), Gary H. Richter (Mathematics)*
1978	George A. Brightwell, Jr. (Business Administration/Registrar), Paul D. Peak (Men's Basketball Coach/ Physical Education), Jesse E. Purdy (Psychology)*, Jon D. Swartz (Psychology/Head Librarian)
1979	Richard J. Hossalla (Theater), Gwen K. Neville (Anthropology), Pamela G. Rossman (Music)*, Suzanne Schulz-Widmar (Music)
1980	Robert A. Morgan (Biology), Mary Ann Visser (Art)*
1981	Reda F. Clay (Women's Basketball Coach/Physical Education), Richard T. Denman (Mathematics/ Computer Science)*, Norma S. Hart (Library), Robert C. Reinehr (Psychology), Kenneth D. Roberts (Economics)*

*Still active at Southwestern as a teacher in 2005–2006.

The Endowed Chair Concept

An important factor in understanding the large number of new faculty members who were recruited for Southwestern and for the endowment corpus created during the Fleming years was use of the endowed chair concept. The endowed chair idea had first been introduced to Southwestern in 1952 under President Finch, when Herman and George Brown established an endowment for a chair in honor of their mother, Lucy King Brown. Dr. George C. Hester was appointed to that chair in 1960 just before Finch retired. By the time Fleming retired in 1981 Southwestern had twelve additional chair endowments and several additional professorships at lesser amounts.

The endowed chair was not a new concept in American higher education when Southwestern began to use it extensively, but it was primarily a concept used at large graduate universities to fund research positions. Though other undergraduate institutions also possessed endowed chairs, Fleming employed the concept on a larger scale, so far as I know, than any other similar institution. It became an important arrow in his development quiver. Encouraging potential donors to endow chairs became as productive in raising funds as encouraging them to donate money for named buildings. It is impossible to know exactly how much the chairs added to the endowment because the endowment associated with chairs was always invested in securities, bonds, real estate, and other assets that had an ever-changing value, and new chairs were being added at a rate of more than one every other year. Nevertheless, using figures from 1978 for the eleven chairs then funded, when the average value of the chairs was $531,250, a total figure for the thirteen chairs in 1981 would have been $6.9 million.[6] Since this figure represents the book value, the market value would have been somewhat higher. The average book value for the five additional professorships at this point was $103,003. This endowment money for chairs and professorships was particularly significant because it, unlike similar money put into buildings, improved the quality of the faculty directly and immediately.

Though the specifications established for each chair differed somewhat, the chairs instituted by The Brown Foundation in 1964 were intended to bring in new faculty blood from the outside. This was so much the case that when President Fleming chose to nominate an outstanding young faculty member, Dr. Jeff H. Campbell, who was already on the faculty, to the Herman Brown Chair in English in 1966, he did not make the appointment until he had cleared it with George Brown. After reviewing the facts in the case, Brown approved.[7]

In order not to create a potentially divisive situation by bringing in new chairholders whose rank and salaries would outstrip those of the old-line professors who had gained their status as a result of many years of service, the salaries of chairholders were kept within the full professor range already established. In the case of most of the new chairholders the benefit was that of receiving high professorial rank and salary at an earlier stage in their careers than might have ordinarily been the case. These new chairholders became important elements in promoting the academic changes that were soon enacted at the University.

The establishment of the Hugh Roy and Lillie Cullen Chair in Economics in 1968 was particularly important for the University.[8] A special Convocation was held for the inauguration of the chair, and members of the Cullen family and other trustees of the Cullen Foundation attended.[9] Mr. A. Frank Smith, Jr., lawyer for the Foundation, was especially instrumental in obtaining the grant. The gift of the Cullen Chair initiated what became a long-standing connection between the Foundation and Southwestern University. Mr. Roy H. Cullen became a member of the Board in 1973 and is still active in 2005. The Cullen Foundation, which followed up its gift of the chair in 1968 with funds for the restoration of the Administration Building in 1975–1976, has continued to support the University through the years. At the center of the campus today is the Roy H. Cullen Academic Mall. Completed in 1993 through a grant from the Cullen Foundation in honor of Roy Cullen's longtime service as a Trustee, it is emblematic of the Foundation's longtime support of the University.

The full list of the thirteen chairs instituted by the end of the Fleming administration with the names of the initial and subsequent chairholders until 2000 is as follows:

Lucy King Brown Chair
- Established: 1952.
- First holder: George C. Hester, 1960–1965.
- Second holder: William B. Jones, 1965–1976.
- Third holder: Weldon S. Crowley, 1976–1997.
- Fourth holder: Andrew J. Senchack, Jr., 1998–.

Lillian Nelson Pratt Chair
- First holder: Robert L. Soulen, 1964–1996.
- Second holder: Vicente Villa, 1996–2000.

Herman Brown Chair
First holder: Thomas A. Perry, 1964–1965.
Second holder: Jefferson H. Campbell, 1966–1974.
Third holder: T. Walter Herbert, 1975–2006.
Margarett Root Brown Chair
First holder: F. Ellsworth Peterson, 1965–2004 .
Hugh Roy and Lillie Cullen Chair
First holder: B. Joe Colwell, 1970–1992.
Second holder: Kenneth D. Roberts, 1996–.
Elizabeth Root Paden Chair
First holder: Edmund G. McCurtain, 1974–1979.
Second holder: Gwen K. Neville, 1979–1998.
Third holder: Laura Hobgood-Oster, 2000–.
Brown Visiting Professorship
First holder: Jim L. Bridges, 1977–1978.
Second holder: Jon D. Swartz, 1978–1982.
Third holder: Naomi S. Baron, 1984–1987.
Carolyn and Fred McManis Chair
Established: 1972.
First holder: David C. Blumenfeld, 1978–1986.
Tower-Hester Chair
First holder: Francis W. O'Brien, 1975–1987.
Second holder: Timothy J. O'Neill, 1987–.
John Shearn Chair
First holder: Eldred C. Speck, 1978–1983.
Second holder: Frank J. Imke, 1983–1985.
Third holder: Jerome L. Valentine, 1988–1993.
Fourth holder: Don M. Parks, 1996–.
Wilson-Craven Chair
First holder: Roy C. Amore, 1978–1979.
Second holder: Robert Lee, 1980–1983.
Third holder: Winston B. Davis, 1983–1992.
Fourth holder: Farley W. Snell, 1995–1999.
Robert Sherman Lazenby Chair
First holder: Bob M. Brown, 1980–1981.
Second holder: Robert C. Roeder, 1983–2003.
Herbert and Kate Dishman Chair
Established: 1980.
First holder: Vicente D. Villa, 1985–1996.
Second holder: Frank S. Guziec, Jr., 1996–.

Making Academic Changes by Changing the Academic Calendar

The desire to make the academic program more exciting for students began with a renewed emphasis on new-student orientation. Though for many years new students had begun their careers at Southwestern with some sort of orientation, sometimes quite elaborate, this event took a new turn in 1965. In that year students were expected to come to campus having read during the summer selected works previously designated by the faculty. Student groups discussed these works and heard lectures on them by teachers and outside guests after they came to the campus before the beginning of formal fall semester classes. The readings for fall 1966 were Loren Eisley's *The Immense Journey*, George Bernard Shaw's *Man and Superman*, Eric Fromm's *The Art of Loving*, and James Baldwin's *The Fire Next Time*. In addition, students listened to Bela Bartok's *Concerto for Orchestra* and studied Leonardo Da Vinci's *Adoration of the Magi*.[10] One of the lecturers for fall 1968 was Willie Morris, editor of *Harper's* and author of *North Toward Home*, a book that was used during orientation. Though the focus of the orientation period gradually changed over the years, its attempt to initiate the academic career of the new student with an exciting intellectual adventure before the beginning of classes continued.[11]

The most time-consuming activity of the faculty in curriculum revision was its attempt to develop a new academic calendar. The effort began when the faculty approved a motion in early 1966 to "institute a thorough study of the academic calendar with an end of substituting a more flexible system for the present two-semester plan."[12] The result was a decision to divide the fall semester into a fifteen-week portion where four courses would be normal for the student, with examinations before Christmas, and a three-week period during January where each student would take one course. The spring semester continued as one eighteen-week period with five courses for each student.[13] The purpose of the change was to give the student an opportunity to delve deeply into one subject in a restricted period of time in January without the distraction of other courses. This change was also calculated to force teachers to introduce new courses and to devise new teaching techniques, particularly to break up the purely lecture format followed by some in all their classes. Three hours of lecture for each of the five days during the three-week session would have been impractical, and teachers would be forced to redesign old courses even if they did not introduce new ones.

The faculty wrestled with some form of alternate calendar schedule for six years, changing it somewhat almost every year. Faculty meetings were long and contentious each year over the issues that arose. In order to put the matter to rest, Dean Clifford sent a memo to the faculty on

January 30, 1969, with six calendar options for the faculty to vote on at the next meeting. They were:

1. The Traditional Semester System
2. The Semester System with Early Start
3. Two-Semester System plus Inter-term Option
4. Two-hour January Plan, with fifteen-hour ceiling for Fall Semester
5. Four-One-Five System
6. The Four-One-Four System (using the unit system rather than semester hours to describe courses)

The faculty voted at its next meeting to adopt the 4-1-4 calendar.[14]

Since the 4-1-4 calendar would abandon the semester-hour system for the unit system, it was the most radical of all the calendars. It would force a redesign of all majors, minors, and degrees and, because of the time involved in this process, could not be implemented for the following 1969 fall semester. It would have to be delayed for a full year. To prepare for the changeover, Dean Clifford and Dr. Edwin Lansford attended a conference on 4-1-4 calendars at Florida Presbyterian College during the summer after the new calendar was voted. They reported back to the faculty in September on model 4-1-4 calendars and stressed the various combinations of particular calendars, winter terms, and credit systems available.[15] Faced with the realistic prospect of going through another round of decision-making that would include the restructuring of all the courses in the catalog, the faculty rescinded the previous 4-1-4 calendar action by a vote of 44 to 15.[16] The two-semester calendar was then adopted for the next few years with an optional January term. By now, however, the faculty was tired of the continual struggle to modify the calendar in a more desirable direction. Every new calendar presented its own set of problems.

Though the optional January session was abolished in May 1973 and a regular two-semester system reinstituted,[17] a three-weeks May session was soon added for the period immediately following Commencement for students wanting an opportunity to gain three additional semester hours of academic credit before beginning the summer vacation.[18] With the inauguration of a regular summer school once again in 1975–1976, this three-week session became a part of that program. Along with the reintroduction of summer school, two other calendar changes remained permanently as a result of the decade-long process of modifying the calendar. The ending of the fall semester before Christmas, which had become normal after it was instituted in 1966, was continued. The five-and-a-half day weekly class schedule of earlier years that had been changed to a five-day week in 1968 was maintained as well.[19] Another calendar change voted by the faculty in 1975 was the holding of a December Commencement for fall semester graduates.[20] This practice continued through 1987, when it was discontinued.

Academic Internships, Scholars Program, and CLEP Program

Though academic calendar revision did not have the favorable results hoped, other academic actions and programs initiated in 1966 had more successful outcomes. One of the most important and long-lasting was the academic internship program. In it students handpicked by professors in their major fields worked with top management in business, industry, and the professions, thereby receiving insights and experiences in direct participation venues that they might have never gained in a purely academic setting. The workplace became a classroom. The academic internship was an educational and not a vocational program, and the major professor strictly supervised each intern.[21] Twenty-six students were engaged in the program by the fall of 1967.[22]

A Scholars Program was established in 1967 that allowed specially designed degree programs for students who showed promise of being outstanding. About thirty freshmen were selected each year to participate in seminars and special courses, ending with a Senior Scholars Project and a Scholars Oral. The graduate was awarded a degree marked "Southwestern Scholar in [blank]," with the name of the major filling in the blank.[23] Interdisciplinary teaching, independent study, and an honors program also added excitement and value to mainstream teaching.[24]

The pace of academic change was so rapid in 1965–1966 that the faculty voted to hold a once-a-month non-legislative faculty meeting to ensure that important items would receive substantial debate before faculty action was taken on them.[25] In spite of the doubtful results from some of the academic experiments that were attempted, Dean Clifford was generally satisfied with what was occurring. He told the Trustees that "one of the most important results of the new academic programs is intangible—an openness to innovations and a desire to try new programs and new approaches."[26]

The apogee of the first wave of academic changes during the decade came with the work of a special Curriculum and Student Life Committee that met during the summer of 1967. The seven faculty members chosen for the task were Jones (History and chairperson), Custer (Education), Girvin (Biology), Hummel (French), Osborn (Voice), Peterson (Music), and Score (Religion/Philosophy), with the two academic deans and the Dean of Students as *ex officio* members without vote. The committee was charged with surveying "the existing situation at Southwestern, consider[ing] the underlying philosophy and goals of the institution, and prepar[ing] a report making proposals for a revised program implementing this philosophy and these goals."[27] The committee worked for several hours each day over a period of seven weeks. Meetings were open to all faculty members, with twenty-two persons in addition to the committee members attending from time to time. The President called its report "exciting," and the faculty adopted it with few changes early the following fall.[28] After also being approved by a Board Committee, the general recommendations in the report were enacted into specific operational provisions by the various councils and committees of the University over a period of several years.[29]

The single most important academic change that came about as a result of the Curriculum and Student Life Report was the adoption of a method whereby students might meet the general education requirements of the University. This method was use of the College-Level Examination Program (CLEP) developed in 1965 by the College Entrance Examination Board (CEEB). This program consisted of General Examinations and Subject Examinations.[30] Southwestern modified its general education requirements to match the General Examinations of the CLEP program and used them to test for the general education knowledge of students. The examinations consisted of English Composition, Humanities (with subscores in Fine Arts and Literature), Mathematics (with subscores in Basic Skills and Course Content), Natural Sciences (with subscores in Biological Science and Physical Sciences), and Social Sciences–History (with subscores in Social Sciences and History). These examinations were obligatory for all new students, who, with specified scores on the examinations, could be exempted from or gain credit for appropriate general education requirements. Special examinations were developed on campus for the Religion and Foreign Language requirements, for which there were no equivalent CLEP examinations. Four hours of Physical Education courses and one additional course in Religion continued to be required. Dean Clifford stated in the fall of 1968 that the CLEP program was proving very satisfactory. He reported that "students were granted exemption for 787 courses, giving them 787 more elective courses. Credit was also granted for 273 courses. 107 students received credit in one or more courses, and 26 received credit in 4 or more courses."[31]

Taking the CLEP tests continued as a requirement for all new students through the 1972–1973 academic year. At that point there was general agreement that exemption from or credit for general education courses on the basis of a test, however well designed, could not make up for the intangible knowledge gained from classroom experience, and the requirement that all new students take the test was dropped. The CLEP tests were made optional and folded into the advanced placement regulations. Though the CLEP tests did not continue to function after 1973 as originally adopted by the faculty in 1967, Southwestern was the first school in the country to use the College-Level Examination Program and other similar tests as a way of giving students an opportunity to exempt or to gain credit for all the general degree requirements of the University.[32] This fact underscores the bold character of the faculty in academic matters during the decade after 1965.

International Studies, Humanities in Practice, and University Studies Programs

One of the new programs that began during the late 1960s and has continued with a strong emphasis until today is the International Studies Program. It began when Southwestern joined the Association of Colleges and Universities for International-Intercultural Study (ACUIIS) in 1969.[33] ACUIIS was an organization operated out of the Methodist Board of Higher Education in Nashville and was composed of about thirty-five member institutions. Dr. William B. Jones was appointed the Southwestern University faculty representative to ACUIIS and began working with an International Studies Committee to develop a coherent plan for international studies in 1970. This program became a minor field of study the following year and was expanded into a major field in 1973.[34] Students and faculty members from Southwestern began to attend ACUIIS programs in various European, Asian, and Latin American countries, and Southwestern sent a group of students almost every summer to study at the ACUIIS center in Graz, Austria. A program in fine arts, begun in 1977, also sent students to England in the summer. When the ACUIIS organization ceased operation, Southwestern inaugurated its own Summer Abroad Program in London and Vienna in 1980.[35] An International House was established on campus in 1973 in the old President's home. About a dozen students interested in international culture and affairs lived in it each semester and regularly hosted students from across the campus at its programs.[36] It was the most successful living-learning situation established on campus and continued until the house was moved from the site in 1986. In addition, Southwestern began to participate in some cooperative projects such as the Washington International Semester offered each semester on the campus of American University in Washington, D.C.

The last experimental academic program of the type begun around 1965 was the Humanities in Practice Program, begun in the fall of 1976. The Humanities Division under the chairmanship of Dr. Martha Allen presented a proposal for this program to the National Endowment for the Humanities in 1975–1976.[37] When it was not funded, Dr. Allen went to Washington to talk with the NEH persons involved in making the funding determination. When they learned that she had traveled to Washington on her own initiative and at her own expense without reimbursement from the University, they reconsidered the program and funded it. The idea of the proposal was to develop an alternative humanities core program. Five teachers from the Departments of English, Philosophy, Fine Arts, Religion, and History taught the approximately sixty first-year students.[38] They presented their material as part of a unified curricular design that was divided into topics rather than disciplines. The two first-year courses were entitled "Humanities in Praxis." Each carried six semester hours of credit. The second-year courses of three semester hours each built on the work of the first year. The first-semester course was entitled the "Nature of Man" and examined the major traditional answers to the question "What is man?" as expressed in the humanities, fine arts, science, and social science. The second-semester course was entitled "The Creative Impulse." It was described as "a study of man's impulse to create order and beauty out of his environment, his social contacts and his experiences."[39]

The Humanities in Practice Program was experimental and as such was not continued beyond the first two years, but its emphasis on interdisciplinary teaching over topics not generally included in a major field continued in a University Studies Program begun in 1978. A six-hour, one-semester humanities course gave three hours' credit in English and three in philosophy. Biology and mathematics professors taught a new course entitled "You Bet Your Life," emphasizing the use of probability statistics with regard to common diseases. A six-hour course entitled "Chicago 1893–1933" gave three hours' credit each in American history and sociology, as well as involving the entire class in a week's trip to Chicago. A course entitled "Darwin, Marx, and Wagner," studying the nineteenth-century intellectual ferment in science, politics, and music initiated by the persons whose names appear in the title, involved professors at Southwestern from biochemistry, political science, and music.

In the fall of 1979 Professor Martha Allen developed a course in Black History taught by her and Professor Lamar Kiraven of Huston-Tillotson College in Austin. Half of the evening classes were taught on the Huston-Tillotson campus and half on the Southwestern campus.[40]

Programmatic Initiatives in the School of Fine Arts

A new Music–Christian Education program was set up in Fine Arts in the fall of 1980. It was designed to produce either a B.A. in Christian Education through the Religion Department or a B.Mus.Ed., with an emphasis in Christian Education, through the Music Department.[41] The program had only moderate success and was dropped in 1986 when the Religion and Philosophy Department abolished its Christian Education Program.

A new program in summer theater for adults and children, called "Southwestern Summer Stage," inaugurated its first season in June 1980. It provided family entertainment at minimal cost while giving students some semi-professional acting experience. *The Fantasticks* and *Godspell* were presented for two weeks each, while *Hansel and Gretel*, which was produced especially for children, ran for six days.[42] With a few exceptions, the Summer Stage program has operated annually since that time.

Special Studies and Computing

Just as the Shilling administration would become known for its emphasis on master planning, the Fleming administration became known for its many special studies. During the first decade of Fleming's tenure at least a dozen studies of different aspects of the University, including studies of academic departments, campus organizations, and the internal organization of the University, were made.[43] The number of these studies did not diminish during the next ten years.

Though these studies came about individually and were not part of an overall institutional plan, they nevertheless show that new initiatives were generally the product of considerable deliberation. One of Dean Clifford's most useful functions was to serve as the special advisor to the President with regard to these studies and to critique them for him. An important example of what was a regular procedure during the fifteen years of Clifford's deanship is the Seeger Report on Science and Mathematics in 1966.

Raymond J. Seeger, of the National Science Foundation in Washington, came to the campus in December 1965 to do an in-depth study and to make suggestions as to what was needed to "bring the Science Division into a truly first-class position."[44] The first two parts of his report were shared with all the members of the division. The final section was confidential and directed only to the President.[45] Fleming sent the twenty-page report to Clifford for comment. Reading today Seeger's direct but carefully phrased report and Clifford's insightful response to it, one is struck by the high quality of advice Fleming received from the two men.

Among many other things the report contained, it made the first mention of computing at Southwestern in a planning document. One of Seeger's recommendations was the establishment in the near future of a University Computing Center. He suggested renting an IBM 1620 at an educational discount cost of fifteen thousand to eighteen thousand dollars per year.[46] The University at this point could not afford the machine, and it was not until 1969 that Southwestern could do more than offer a few theoretical computer courses in the mathematics department. In that year the National Science Foundation provided funds that allowed the University to tie into a nine-school network coordinated by the University of Texas computer center through teletype terminals on a time-sharing basis. Two years later the first on-site system, an IBM 1130, was leased.[47] In 1972–1973 the position of Coordinator of Data Processing was established with the appointment of Harold Eidson.[48] The evolution of computing from that point on is another story, but Eidson played a prominent role in it. He retired in 2002 after thirty years. A major in computer science was introduced into the curriculum in fall 1981.[49]

SACS Self-Studies and Other Major Studies as Planning Documents

In his January report to the Board of Trustees in 1975, President Fleming said: "We have had three major studies and revisions of the curriculum over the past seven years."[50] He was referring to the Curriculum and Student Life Study of 1967, the President's Planning Committee Report of 1972–1973, and the Academic Program Survey Report of 1975 that was still underway when he made his statement. There would be two other major studies as well. They would be the Program and Governance Study of 1977–1979 and the Excellence in the Eighties report in 1980. In addition, during Fleming's two decades at Southwestern there were three SACS Self-Studies with their Visiting Committee Responses, that of 1961, which Finch left for him, that of 1971, and that of 1981, which he left almost completed for Shilling.

Looking at these five major internal studies and the three SACS Self-Studies together as one process is the best way of understanding Fleming's overall planning procedure. President Fleming looked on each of these studies as a master plan, or a significant component thereof, and looked on the general process by which they were produced as his planning process. The clearest example of this process comes from the years 1969 through 1973.

In his January 1969 report to the Board of Trustees Fleming speaks of the need for a long-range "master plan." He then lays out six items that should appear in it.[51] This list was increased to twelve by the time of the April report. He says that the master plan should deal with: (1) the aims and objectives of the University; (2) Board of Trustee operation; (3) administrative operation; (4) faculty work and program; (5) the curriculum; (6) the library; (7) educational facilities; (8) the student body; (9) the physical plant; (10) business operations; (11) development; and (12) relationships with the various publics.[52] With this background in mind, one would expect a master plan document to be produced. Instead of a master plan, however, a plan for producing the impending SACS Self-Study was instituted. While it was being produced, Fleming told the Trustees that he expected "to press for the implementation of the major recommendations" coming out of it. He said: "The ultimate recommendations that will result from the [1971] Self-Study will be considered an 'institutional road map.'"[53] After receiving the report of the SACS Visiting Committee a few months later, he formed an elaborate President's Planning Committee that folded the recommendations of the Self-Study and the report of the Visiting Committee into a report for faculty consideration. This PPC report, he said, "will become the directional device for the institution over the next five years, at least."[54]

This procedure of promoting interplay between SACS

Self-Studies and major internal studies as a part of one continual planning process can be seen with regard to the 1961 and 1981 SACS Self-Studies as well. Though the 1961 SACS Self-Study was generated during Finch's tenure, the Visiting Team came to the campus shortly after Fleming arrived as new President. He used its visit and the subsequent report as a plan for action. Ten years later there was hardly a recommendation made by the 1961 Visiting Team that had not been addressed. The report by the Visiting Team in 1971 was quite different from the one in 1961. It highly praised what the University had done during the last decade and based its recommendations on those proposed by the University in the Self-Study Report itself. The report has few recommendations not made in the Self-Study by the faculty and administrative personnel that prepared it. It is apparent that there has been a decided change in the perception of the University by the Visiting SACS Committee from that of the equivalent committee a decade earlier. The Visiting Team does not say, as did the 1961 team, that "the central problem of the faculty is its apparent complacency with itself," or that "there is a general need for improving the quality of instruction," or that "good new professors are more important than new buildings."[55] If there was anything that the academic activity of the 1960s showed, it was that the faculty was not complacent, that significant attempts were being made to improve the quality of instruction, and that procuring good new professors was receiving as high a priority as putting up new buildings.

Each of the major internal studies made during the 1970s was a stage on the way to the Self-Study of 1981, not that it was planned that way, but that is how it worked out. Each was produced by a representative committee or council composed of faculty members, students, and administrators; each required significant amounts of time to complete; each dealt with what were considered to be the essential problems of the University; each was presented to the President, who in turn presented it to the faculty for approval; and each, after modification and approval by the faculty, was selectively implemented.

The PPC, the Academic Program Survey Committee, and the Provost Appointment

After nine months of study, the President's Planning Committee (PPC), chaired by Dr. Ellsworth Peterson, presented its report to the faculty. After another three-and-a-half months of debate, the faculty approved the seven chapters of the report in May 1973. Though it replaced the old three-council system with a two-council system and returned the school to the old two-semester academic calendar, its most controversial recommendation was its call for a new three-school structure and a new Faculty Senate-Council structure. The new school would be a School of Professional Studies.[56]

Each of the three schools would be led by a dean, with one of the three deans also serving as provost in addition to acting as dean for his own school. The function of the provost would be "to coordinate the academic program of the university in such areas as academic planning, student recruitment, registration procedures, academic testing and counseling, and publication of the catalogue."[57] A three-person committee of consultants that had visited the campus in February 1970 had earlier recommended the appointment of "a vice president and Provost (an on-campus president) to whom all deans would report. This," the committee said, "would free the president for more off-campus activities in development and secure financial and denominational support." This committee consisted of Dr. Stewart Allen, Executive Director, Association of Texas Colleges and Universities; Mr. Douglas MacLean, Vice President for Staff Services, University of Houston; and Dr. Marshall Steel, former president of Hendrix College. The SACS Visiting team endorsed this earlier committee recommendation in its 1971 report.[58] Neither the three-school recommendation nor the provost recommendation was implemented at the time.

By the early 1970s inflation was becoming serious, and the President was forced to report to the Trustees that he would have to recommend the same budget for 1975–1976 as for 1974–1975. He said: "It is a real economic enigma we face at Southwestern University. On the one hand, we are in the strongest financial position in the history of the school, for which we are very grateful; and, on the other hand, our cash flow for the annual budget is in the shortest supply, percentage-wise, at any time during my administration."[59] As a result, he set up a committee, called the Academic Program Survey Committee, to design a way of meeting the financial crisis. He charged the committee to "examine all aspects of the academic program and to make recommendations for improving efficiency of operation. No presupposition regarding the present program," he said, " should be exempt from examination, and plans should be drawn up for various contingencies. Academic organization and financial matters should be studied, but administrative organization and student life should not form part of the study, except insofar as they affect the former." He stated that he would institute on his own all those aspects of the report not requiring faculty action but would submit to the entire faculty all those matters calling for their consideration. The committee, appointed on April 28, 1975, was composed of six faculty members and four administrators. Jones was named chair, with Clifford, Adams, Custer, Phillips, Carwell, Colwell, Whitmore, Girvin, and Farmer as the other members.[60]

The committee completed its work during the summer and presented its report to the President on August 25. The Report consisted of two major sections. Section I contained recommendations regarding ways of achieving economy in the regular academic program of the University. Section II contained a series of six contingency plans to be considered if worse came to worst, with a listing of the advantages and disadvantages of each plan. Most of the recommendations were administrative in nature. After the faculty received the report, those items of a legislative nature were submitted to the appropriate bodies for action. A person or committee was delegated to implement each recommendation.[61]

Sometime in late September, President Fleming approached Jones and offered him a new position, about to be created, that of Administrative Vice President and Provost. Effectively uniting the PPC's academic rationale for recommending its creation in 1973 with the SACS Visiting Committee's administrative rationale for it in 1971, the position would "free the president for more off-campus activities in development." Fleming had lost three persons, Drs. Roy B. Shilling, Jr., Jerald Walker, and John Van Valkenburg, in the last few years from vice presidential positions in development when the first two accepted presidencies at other institutions and the third had wanted to secure a position in his home state. Fleming now felt that his best course of action would be, in effect, to become his own vice president for development without the title. In order to do so, he would choose someone on the inside to share some of his presidential responsibilities. After the successful conclusion of the Academic Program Survey Report, he chose the chair of the committee that produced the report to fulfill that role. In describing the functions of the position to the faculty he said:

> This new position, Administrative Vice President and Provost, has two sides as the title clearly describes. As Administrative Vice President, Dr. Jones and I will divide the supervisory responsibilities of administering the institution between us as occasion and experience shall dictate. He will assume direct responsibility for the institution when I am away, referring to me such issues as he feels should be decided by the President. In the legislative process of the University he will serve as an ex-officio member in all committees, councils and divisions, with right to voice but not of vote. He will review all legislation and call for delay in the implementation of any act or action which he feels I should review. Some University personnel and functions which do not pertain clearly to any other office may be attached to his. As Provost, Dr. Jones will assume responsibility for the coordination of regular University planning, communication, and implementation procedures.[62]

The Board of Trustees approved Jones for the position on October 24, 1975. Ironically, the financial exigency that occasioned the Academic Program Survey Report disappeared within a year when The Brown Foundation of Houston announced a ten-year challenge grant for the institution. As all efforts turned toward meeting the annual goals of the challenge, the contingency plans for economic exigency disappeared from consideration. Within two years after the appointment of Jones, two other new academic administrators would come to head the College of Arts and Sciences and the School of Fine Arts.

Three Deans of the College of Arts and Sciences

Though Dean Ullrich had been scheduled to retire as dean when he reached sixty-five in 1956, he was asked to stay on after the proposed Greenlee appointment did not work out. He served two years in that capacity until Wicke was appointed in 1958, at which point he gave up his administrative duties and became a full-time classroom teacher. When Wicke left in 1961, Finch, who was also leaving, asked Ullrich once again to serve as dean until Fleming could make his own appointment. He did so until 1962, when Fleming appointed Clifford.

By the time of his final retirement under Fleming, Ullrich had served as dean since 1926 under six Presidents—Barcus, Vivion, Bergin, Score, Finch, and Fleming. His ability to work effectively under persons with personalities as different as these six Presidents is remarkable. The highlight of his career may have been the Vivion, Bergin, and Score years, when he was the stabilizing force behind the academic program in a time of economic poverty and worldwide armed conflict. He also penned during the Bergin years the model followed by both Bergin and Score in their buildup of the institution after the Wiess gift turned the fortunes of the University in a positive direction. Fleming said of him at the time of his retirement in 1962 that he could never repay his debt of gratitude to him for his fine help and support during the first year of his administration.[63]

Born on August 29, 1891, at New Baden, Texas, Ullrich died on February 16, 1974, at the age of eighty-two. A Second Lieutenant during World War I, he came to Southwestern in 1920. His major hobby was woodcarving, an art he had picked up from his father, who was a cabinetmaker. During his career and during his retirement he carved dozens of gifts for his friends.[64]

Clifford served as dean of the College of Arts and Sciences until the end of the 1976–1977 academic year, when he was appointed Professor of Humanities. His primary teaching fields were Greek and Latin, with occasional courses in English, history, and religion. He was one of the most erudite persons in Southwestern's long history.

On Clifford's retirement from the deanship in 1977, Dr. G. Benjamin Oliver succeeded him. Though a native of Texas, he was Associate Professor and Chairman of the Department of Philosophy at Hobart and William Smith Colleges in New York when contracted. He received his B.A. in Philosophy from the University of Texas in 1960, an M.Div. in Philosophy of Religion from Union Theological Seminary in 1963, and an M.A. and Ph.D. from Northwestern University in 1966 and 1967, respectively. He had traveled widely and been the holder of a Rockefeller Brothers Fellowship.[65] He was made Provost in 1986 and was elected President of Hiram College in 1989. His influence on the academic program of the University was quite strong and would increase under Shilling.

Three Deans of the School of Fine Arts

Dean John D. Richards came to Southwestern immediately after World War II in 1946 as a teacher of choral music. He was voted tenure in 1949 and made dean of the School of Fine Arts in 1955 on the retirement of Dean Meyer. He was a superb musician and developed choirs known for the technical excellence of their performances. Even after he was appointed dean, he considered himself first and foremost a conductor of choral music and took a low-key approach to his responsibilities as dean.

Nelson F. Adams, Richards's successor in 1974, was as forthright in his exercise of the deanship as Richards was reserved. He was especially vigilant in advocating the cause of the School of Fine Arts in budget considerations. He came to the University with superb credentials. In addition to his A.B. in Music Theory and Composition and his M.Rel.Ed. from Duke University, he had a M.Sac. Mus. and a D.Sac.Mus. from Union Theological Seminary in New York. His doctorate was in Organ and Musicology.[66] After a promising beginning of one-and-a-half years at Southwestern, he was killed in a tragic automobile accident over the Christmas holidays near Asheville, North Carolina.[67] Jones, who had been in his new position as Administrative Vice President and Provost only two months at the time, assumed the role of Acting Dean of the School of Fine Arts and served as chairman of the Search Committee for a new dean.[68]

Theodore D. Lucas was appointed to replace Adams as dean, coming to the position on June 1, 1976. With an A.B. and an M.A. from San Diego State University in 1963 and 1964, respectively, he had a D.M.A. obtained in 1970 from the University of Illinois. His strength was in Music Theory. He came from Beloit College to his post.[69] He remained at Southwestern until 1989, when he left to become chair of the Department of Music at San Jose State University.

The Program and Governance Study and the Excellence in the Eighties Report

In the chapter on Planning and Projections for the Future in the 1971 Self-Study, Professors Jones and Lansford had stated that "the University does not presently seem to be organized in a way that ensures its engagement most effectively in the planning process, that is, in planning carried out continuously and routinely as a normal function. It is important that planning as a major part of University operation be accepted by all its components. It is strongly recommended that this planning function be centered in some regularly constituted part of the University structure."[70] After the assumption of his new position in 1975, Jones began to act on this belief. In describing the rationale for Fleming's call for a new Program and Governance Study in 1978, he wrote about it as follows:

> One of the great lacks we have experienced in our planning over the years is a long-range view of where we are going. Most of our planning has been sporadic and occasional. We have seldom paused to establish goals and the procedures for achieving them. Often we gear up to plan for specific projects that are not integrated into the total University program. To remedy this defect, President Fleming stated in his last report to the Board of Trustees that he intended to set in motion a long-range planning process for the faculty and administration. He would like for us not only to study our organization, but also to formulate a long-range program for the University. This would involve the academic, student life, financial, and governance structure of the University. We would want the faculty, working with the administration and students, to devise and adopt plans in these areas.... We need to think about the future and to plan systematically for the achievement of those goals that we adopt. We need to be in a continual posture of planning, action, and evaluation.[71]

The result of the Program and Governance Study was to place the planning function in a new council. It proposed a four-council system of governance that was adopted by the faculty. It set up an Academic Affairs Council, a Faculty Affairs Council, a Student Life Council, and a University Council. Whereas the first three bodies dealt with specific functions related to their titles, the University Council was designed to serve as an overall coordination and planning body for the whole University working under the chairmanship of the President and Provost.[72] It was in place to take charge of the master planning process inaugurated by Shilling when he arrived.

Before this new structure had really begun to function, President Fleming announced in January 1980 the formation of a task force of twelve persons, including the two academic deans, two students, and eight faculty members, to work through the spring semester and into the summer to define overall University goals. The number of faculty members was later increased to ten. Fleming said that the committee was being asked to define what true excellence would mean for Southwestern in "a long-range plan to move Southwestern ahead."[73] It would, he said, follow the lines of a paper produced earlier by Dr. T. Walter Herbert, a member of the committee. Dr. Douglas Hooker was named chair. Though the title of the report submitted by the committee in the summer was "The Quest for Excellence at Southwestern University," the work of the committee is usually referred to as the "Excellence in the Eighties" study. The emphasis on the word "excellence" came from the influence of John W. Gardner's book, *Excellence: Can We Be Equal and Excellent Too?*, published in 1961.

The word "excellence" was used in several contexts around the University during the time the committee was at work. The William Carrington Finch Excellence in Teaching Award was announced in April 1980, and the Pauline and J. C. Fleming Endowment for Excellence was established in May 1981.[74] J. C. Fleming was Durwood's uncle in Lubbock. When "Uncle Carl" died in early 1971, he left a considerable portion of his estate, amounting to almost $250,000, to the University headed by his nephew. His gift was listed in the catalogs from 1973–1974 to 1980–1981 as having the purpose of "establish[ing] a visiting professorship." In 1981–1982 its purpose was changed to that of providing "an endowment for excellence 'to strengthen the academic program.'" This change was made possible by a stipulation regarding use of the endowment dating from 1967, when it was first worked out with "Uncle Carl," that the President in consultation with the chief academic officer should use it "for a purpose which shall be deemed to promote the achievement of excellence by the University."[75]

The Excellence in the Eighties Study was completed during the summer of 1980 and reviewed by the faculty, the Executive Committee of the Board, and the Board of Trustees during the fall. The faculty approved it, and specifics for action were sent to the four councils for implementation.[76]

The Quest for Excellence Report came nearer to being a master plan than any other study or report made during the Fleming administration. Following an introduction, the report made a statement of policies and principles, set out a series of recommendations for the immediate and long-term future of the academic program, and concluded with a section entitled "The Cost of Excellence." In a table provided as a part of the report, the program was calculated to require an expenditure of $36.9 million from the operational budget over a theoretical ten-year period. The Vice President for Fiscal Affairs, Mr. Kirk Treible, who produced the table, calculated that it would require an additional endowment of $56.1 million and a plant fund expenditure of $5.5 million. The total market value of the endowment at the time (1981) was $37.9 million.

The Quest for Excellence is perhaps the best written of all of the reports produced over the two decades of Fleming's tenure. One of its strongest features was that it dealt principally with programmatic rather than with organizational issues. It did not mention the council structure, a topic to which earlier studies had devoted a great deal of attention. Its main topics were the student body, the faculty, and the academic program. It discussed the latter topic under four headings: maintaining high standards of rigor and accomplishment; enriching the learning environment; strengthening departmental major programs, and improving educational support facilities. It defined the "central mission" of the University as that of being "an undergraduate educational institution known for the high quality of its academic program and the superior achievement of its graduates." It emphasized the need "to develop a student body that represents the diversity of American society," the need to develop levels of financial aid that will make it possible for low-income students to attend, and the development of a strong resource base for faculty enrichment. It mentioned in particular the need to "develop a systematic program for increasing faculty and staff salaries." It recommended implementing a budgeting system "wherein salary rates apply from September 1 to August 31 of each academic year" rather than continuing "the present system of establishing salary rates according to the calendar year [January 1–December 31]." The current system, it said, was predicated upon using faculty salary as a "'balancing item,' something to be determined after enrollment is known."

The Excellence in the Eighties report was produced at precisely the moment between the exit of one President and the election of another. As a result, with the introduction of a new planning style by the succeeding administration, it lost its thrust as an independent, freestanding document. The Shilling administration immediately moved to an institutional master-planning concept that made planning a regular, annual part of the institutional process. Nevertheless, the recommendations of the committee in the report were not lost. Many of them were included in the first master plan that was developed under Shilling in 1982. For example, the recommendation about using the academic year rather than the calendar year for establishing salary rates was put into place by the new President almost immediately.

One of the most interesting parts of the report is the appendix, entitled "Model for a Paracollege at Southwestern University," written by the committee chair, Dr. Douglas Hooker. Though it did not become a part of the main report, perhaps because it was considered too radical and/or too expensive at the time, it has many similarities to the Paideia program instituted recently by the Schrum administration as a result of an $8.5 million grant by the Priddy Foundation of Wichita Falls in 2002.

Fleming's Educational and Leadership Principles

In spite of the fact that Fleming never articulated an overall philosophy of education, he did adhere to some basic principles during the course of his administration. Perhaps his most succinct overall statement of principles, including his feeling about the relationship of institutions of higher education to the federal government, was as follows:

> One of the temptations of the sixties and early seventies for institutions of higher education was to go to the federal government for loans and grants to finance the construction of buildings, the inauguration of programs, and the maintenance of research activities. This direction for Southwestern would have saved many heartaches, but it would have created a situation of dependence. Southwestern does not on principle avoid contact with the state and federal government. Indeed, all financial institutions are inextricably involved with them at many levels in a financial manner, but Southwestern has avoided those relationships insofar as possible that compromise its independence.
>
> These financial principles have been tied to a similar set of academic and student life principles. These principles are: 1) maintaining a strong undergraduate program; 2) engaging in a slow, steady growth of the student body; 3) strengthening the residential character of the institution; 4) focusing the academic program on the liberal arts and selected pre-professional programs; and, 5) balancing tradition and change. These educational principles are based on three undergirding commitments: 1) to serve society; 2) to serve the Church; and, 3) to foster the moral and social development of the student.[77]

Fleming also felt that a President should "make reasonable progress each year" even in the presence of "unknowns," "warnings," and "discouragements." He based some of his less than completely funded building initiatives and some of his less than balanced budgets on this precept.

> I, therefore, prefer for us to adopt a basic attitude of optimism, refuse to set the fundamental direction of our program from what we read each day in the newspapers and watch on TV, and do the best possible job to advance Southwestern amid the strident voices that otherwise would discourage us. If all of us were work-

ing at the highest pitch possible and exploiting our full potential, we could rationally pause, adopt a "wait and see" stance. . . . [But we are not exploiting our full potential] and [to wait and see in such a circumstance] generally [would], thereby, create a greater frustration than we are already experiencing.[78]

Bad times, Fleming felt, called for greater exertion and involved taking greater risks than would ordinarily be prudent, but, knowing his Trustees and feeling that the risks were not excessive, his general course of action was always to move forward.

Student Life: Participation in Campus Activities and in the Surrounding World

While faculty members and Trustees were dealing with the academic side of the institution from 1961 to 1981, another form of educational endeavor—the participation of students in campus activities and in the world around them—was also occurring. Some of the events they witnessed or participated in were the following (listed by the date the event was mentioned in the yearbook):

Mid-1960s

- Charter Day (February 5) celebrated in 1963, 1964, 1965, 1966, and 1967.

1965

- A guest speaker discusses the Vietnam situation.
- Gov. Connally proclaims February 5, 1965 [Charter Day], SU day in Texas.

1966

- Seniors attend their last required chapel.
- Mask and Wig productions: *Tartuffe*, by Molière; *Hippolytus*, by Euripides; and *Teahouse of the August Moon*, by John Patrick.
- Artist Series presentations: Preservation Hall Jazz Band from New Orleans; Dallas Symphony; and *La Traviata*, by the Turnau Opera Players.

1968

- Lady Bird Johnson receives honorary degree.
- Mask and Wig productions: *The Royal Hunt of the Sun*, by Peter Shafer; "A Night of One-Act Plays" directed by senior drama majors; *The Diary of Anne Frank*, by Goodrich and Hackett; and *Stop the World! I Want to Get Off*, by Newley and Bricusse.

1969

- The *Sou'wester* of 1969 and 1970 contains pictures of student activists protesting the Vietnam War and the Nixon Administration.
- Required assembly abolished.
- Women's dress rules abolished.

1970

- Yearbook dedicated to the hope and construction of peace.
- Moratorium Day and student march through town.
- Earth Day.

1971

- Programs on birth control and transplant surgery.
- Barbara Jordan speaks on campus.
- Madelyn Murray O'Hair speaks on campus.

1972

- Arthur Rubenstein plays concert and receives honorary degree before packed audience.

1973

- Students listed in yearbook by dorm rather than by class.

1974

- In Memoriam—Bob Lancaster (sculptor; self-inflicted death).
- Streakers.
- Ku Klux Klan and John Birch Society persons speak on campus.
- Student-run Coffee House.
- B.O.S.S. (Black Organization for Social Survival) formed.
- Twenty-one different summer conferences, seminars, and camps are held on campus, with an attendance of 2,695 persons.

1975

- In Memoriam—Mrs. Gervasi, Head Librarian (death from heart attack).
- Southwestern fields its first women's volleyball team.

1976

- In Memoriam—Dean Adams (death in automobile accident).
- Social and Academic Internships.
- Texas Politics internship in Austin inaugurated.
- Coed dorm established.
- Salvage archaeology done by students in area to be flooded by dam forming Lake Georgetown.
- Barbara Jordan given honorary degree.
- "Mood Man" appears as a regular feature in *The Megaphone* as students try to keep the original architecture of Mood Hall.
- Men participating in intramural tackle football required to sign a liability release by the University for any injury that might occur. Intramural tackle football lasts only a few more years.
- William Seale, well-known historian of the White House, receives the Distinguished Alumnus Award and speaks at luncheon program.

1977

- In Memoriam—Janice Bickham (sophomore student murdered on San Gabriel bridge).
- The tradition of electing a Miss Southwestern ends in 1977.
- Southwestern fields its first women's basketball team since the 1920s.

1978

- Presentation of a University Mace as a gift from Mrs. J. N. R. Score and Dr. John Score in memory of President J. N. R. Score. The Mace, designed by a special SU Committee, was the work of the noted artist-craftsman, Mr. David Moore, of Galveston.

1980

- Jerry Rubin speaks on campus.

1981

- *Sou'wester* dedicated to Dr. Fleming for twenty years of devotion to the University.
- The choir, under the direction of Kenny Sheppard, performs at the International Bach Festival in Santa Fe, New Mexico. During the trip the choir sings at a number of Methodist churches, colleges, and high schools.

One of the pleasures of residence life at Southwestern from the beginning until 1976 was the food service. Contrary to the usual student complaints about institutional food in most places, references to it throughout Southwestern history up to this point were generally favorable, even during the Great Depression. The person that upheld this tradition through the last two decades of Southwestern's private food service was Edith Elizabeth Williams. Dietitian and supervisor from 1957 through 1975, she was popularly known as "Sarge." Sarge was an ample and bluff woman with a hearty laugh who took no guff from students. They loved her. When she retired in December 1975, the University employed the Shamrock System, its first professional food service. For three years Shamrock struggled valiantly to meet student expectations of "Sarge"-type meals while making a modest profit on its contract. It finally gave up the struggle and was replaced in 1979 by the Saga Food Service. By that time most of the students who had known "Sarge" were gone and a contracted food service became the norm. The last vestige of the old ways in food service ended with the retirement of Mr. and Mrs. Carl Langennegger in 1981.[79] They ran the Snack Bar in the University Commons, where Carl's rolls earned a community-wide reputation. With their retirement, the professional food service inherited control of the Snack Bar to go with its operation of the University Commons.

Bill Swift and Change in the Student Life System

During its almost a century of existence in Georgetown prior to 1965, Southwestern's student life program was run by the President, the academic deans, the deans of women and of men, and the faculty as a whole. They employed a bevy of proctors, housemothers, and other such persons to help them with their task.[80] But the student life program was not considered to be a major arm of the University in the same sense as the academic program, with its own professional staff. When Fleming assumed the presidency in 1961, one of the recommendations he found waiting for him from the SACS Visiting Team was that "a professionally trained dean of students be appointed." The committee said that "the fact that nine officers of the university and ten faculty committee chairmen now report directly to the President on student personnel matters indicates the need for coordination. In chart form, the President is now serving as Dean of Students."[81] Fleming took the recommendation to heart and almost every year thereafter until 1965, when the first Dean of Students was appointed, he called the need for such a position to the attention of the Trustees.[82] He was aided in his ability to make the hire by the student turmoil throughout the country during the 1960s, the hippie movement, and the involvement of U.S. troops in Vietnam. Expertise on the proper conduct of student affairs by untrained teachers and administrators in the face of this tumult could no longer be assumed to be adequate for the times. Special persons trained in the field were deemed necessary.

William D. Swift was the first person employed at the senior staff level to handle student affairs. He, more than any other person, was responsible for the development of a professional student life program with an underlying philosophy that continues to the present. A major premise of that philosophy was to involve young people in the decisions that govern their community life as students. He believed that persons of student age who were being sent to Vietnam in the armed forces and eighteen-year-olds who had been granted the right to vote by the Congress should be treated as persons having some right to determine their own lifestyle on campus.[83] In 1977 Swift reported to the Trustees that "over the past twelve years we have systematically moved to gradually increase student participation in the governance of the institution. . . . I am convinced we did the right thing."[84]

Swift came to Southwestern from SMU, where he had served as Director of the Methodist Student Movement, Associate Dean of Students, and Dean of Men during his eleven years there. He had a B.S. in Naval Sciences from the University of South Carolina and served in the navy from 1942 to 1946. He later took a B.A. in Sociology from the same institution and an M.Div. from Emory University. During his academic career he was awarded a Phi Beta Kappa key and elected to the Omicron Delta Kappa and Blue Key leadership societies. Over the years his student life functions were somewhat modified and his titles were appropriately changed to reflect his added responsibilities. He was also the Affirmative Action officer and drew up the first affirmative action plan for the University in 1974.[85]

Fleming met regularly with a Student Advisory Council made up of twenty campus leaders as a way of keeping the lines of communication open and supported Swift strongly in his general principle of providing greater opportunities for student involvement in campus governance and activities.[86] Fleming stated his belief about student involvement in campus affairs as follows:

> As opposed to the militant student, we feel that the active and aggressive student is desirable. Benign and apathetic students leave much to be desired. . . . With the burning issues of this world on the agenda of mankind, it is hardly logical to suggest to students that they should not concern themselves or get involved. They are disturbed over the institution of war in a day of so-called civilization; they are concerned over the problems of poverty and pollution; and they are understandably upset over the obvious faults and evils in adult society, particularly at the exhibitions of hypocrisy in private thinking and in public duty. They want to get involved as their way of saying that they think they can improve the lot of man. Why not? . . . The principal reason we have a minimum of student tensions and unrest at Southwestern is traced to our having recognized the need of students to be respected, heard, and involved.[87]

Swift believed that student participation involved student responsibility. Though, as he said, students were less willing to accept the role of the university as "a substitute parent" than in earlier years, this did not mean that all rules for community life should be abandoned. There were rules and regulations appropriate for campus life that should be observed. He felt that it was incumbent upon university officials and students "to make incisive distinctions between what is a legitimate requirement for an institution to achieve its educational goals and what is a carry over from the old 'in loco parentis' day."

Among the generally accepted norms from the past that would not be accepted by students of the 1960s and '70s, Swift felt, was the double standard. "We are going to find it increasingly hard to enforce a double standard with regard to such things as women's curfew hours, or sign out procedures, and the complete freedom which has been accorded to the men for so long."[88] He also believed that the day of student mass gatherings was gone, whether for chapel, assembly, or dance. Big band–style dances were no longer in fashion. There was no longer an audience for the type of all-campus dances for which the main ballroom in the Bishops' Memorial Union had been constructed. The new fashion was for smaller, more intimate gatherings. In response, Swift said that his staff was "seeking ways of creating opportunities for students to experience the challenge and support of a community even if for a short time. This calls for new forms of programming—a working with the students where they are, as best we can."[89] Though it was not his doing, required chapel and required assembly disappeared in 1967 and 1968.

Accepting the consequences of some of his beliefs when put into practice was sometimes difficult for Swift. He watched with dismay as the gathering of groups in the parlors of the residence halls vanished with the advent of a room visitation program in which persons of the opposite sex were allowed in student rooms. He said: "Small groups gather in the rooms to talk, watch TV, listen to music, and sometimes study. . . . Given the fact that approximately 50% of the students are oriented to different Greek groups we are left with an inescapable conclusion that campus social life will never be on a community basis anymore. Atomization of the campus is virtually complete."[90] Personally, he was uncomfortable with what he felt was the individualistic orientation of students and their desire "to be able to move in and out of situations with few claims being made on them or their time." He was also uncomfortable with what he felt was their almost exclusive pursuit of professional preparation rather than of the broad knowledge that comes from a liberal arts preparation.[91]

The year 1973 was, Swift remarks, one of the most difficult of his career.[92] It was the year that the President and faculty accepted the recommendation of the President's Planning Committee that the direction of student life be removed from the hands of the faculty as a whole and placed in the hands of a council made up of student, faculty, and administrative representatives. Fleming reported to the Trustees that the faculty had voted a Community Life Council, knowing "that they were historically removing themselves from the decision-making process as related to student governance and activities outside the classroom."[93] It was also the year of the new room visitation rules and when students beyond the first year could choose to live off campus. Major administrators experienced considerable relief when only forty-one chose to do so.[94] The general issue of "student desire to determine their own life-style" as represented by off-campus housing and visitation in the residence halls was not settled until Charles Prothro and A. Frank Smith, Jr., chair and vice chair of the Board, respectively, came to campus and held interviews with twelve students and eight faculty and administrative persons.[95]

Reorganization of Student Life Administration

By 1975 the new student life program had been in place for a decade, and most of the changes that would be made during the Fleming administration were in place. A staff of persons schooled in the new techniques of student life affairs had been employed to take care of the operational functions. Swift's title was changed from Dean of Students to Vice President for Student Development and Services, and the athletic program was placed under his supervision.[96] Associate Dean of Students Suzanne Gordon became Dean of Student Development and was made responsible for student housing.[97]

Within three years another major change involving Swift was made. For some time Fleming had been dissatisfied with what he felt was the lack of satisfactory results in the admissions area. Since 1963 the admissions function had been attached to the registrar's office so that the registrar, first Howard Long (1963), then Grady Anderson (1970), were in charge of the operation. Two admissions consultants in January 1978 recommended the addition of a "marketing" effort to the recruiting effort.[98]

Because of his success in all his other posts, Swift was tapped to become responsible for admissions. This could be done, it was felt, because of the strength of his staff. Dr. Barbara H. Brightwell had just been employed as Dean for Student Development and Assistant Professor of Psychology. She came with a B.B.A., and an M.Ed. from the University of Houston, and a D.Min. from the San Francisco Theological Seminary. She was a seasoned teacher and administrator, having been voted the Outstanding Faculty Member at Houston Baptist University in 1969. She had won many honors in her college career, was a member of many professional organizations, and had done extensive work in church organizations. She came to Southwestern from a position as Principal of St. Agnes Academy in Houston.[99]

As Vice President for Admissions and Student Development, Swift would maintain responsibility for student affairs. While he focused his attention on admissions, he would leave most of the work in student affairs to his staff, headed by Dr. Brightwell. The most notable single step promoting the "marketing" effort recommended by the consultants was the placement of a special multipage advertising insert about Southwestern in major newspapers throughout the state in late summer 1979, at a cost of about seventy thousand dollars. The insert was placed in six major metropolitan newspapers and supposedly reached 1.25 million homes.[100] The Trustees, who voted the expenditure, expressed the feeling in their September meeting "that it was already proving its worth in public relations and reaching student prospects and their families."[101] Swift would maintain direction of the admissions function along with his student life responsibilities until admissions was set up as a separate function of its own in 1982 with Mr. John Lind as vice president.

Drug and Alcohol Policy

Though the consumption of alcohol was prohibited on campus, the use of beverage alcohol, particularly the perennial practice of drinking beer, continued as it had in the past in some student rooms. Out of respect for student privacy, rooms were not searched to enforce the stated policy.[102]

Beginning around 1970 some evidence began to surface of drug use. University policy prohibiting drug possession and/or use was well publicized. At the outset Swift felt that there was fair acceptance of this policy, and no one seemed to take up the cause of students who were disciplined for violations.[103] Within a year he felt that the situation had become more serious. He stated:

> Again, out of a real sense of frustration I have to speak of the drug situation. All evidence points to the fact that we are reflecting the general youth culture with an increased use of marijuana. We have no evidence of any commercial pushers on our campus or who come to our campus, but there are so many sources in Austin that it is all too simple to purchase the substance. There are a number of our students who have been in counseling with our University Counselor and many of these have had or do have drug problems.[104]

Drug usage crested in the early 1970s. In 1977 Swift could say that though its usage did exist in small "pockets" of students, his information indicated that marijuana was not in general usage in the student body as a whole.[105]

The Greek System and Deferred Rush

During the early 1960s the Greek system was strong and was a major factor in campus social life. Out of a class of 269 first-year students that enrolled at Southwestern in the fall of 1968, 184 (68.4 percent) pledged a fraternity or sorority within the first few weeks of school.[106] Many in the faculty, however, were less than pleased with this "success," particularly the way it overlapped and weakened the academic and student life orientation program that was being promoted with so much effort. Fraternities and sororities obtained during the summer the names of the new students who had been admitted for the fall semester and contacted them with literature and often with pre-enrollment parties before they ever matriculated at the University. Formal fraternity and sorority rush was conducted during the first few weeks of the semester, making it difficult for new students to focus on the real meaning of their new college careers.

In the fall of 1969 the Student Life Council began to consider instituting deferred rush for the Greek system on campus.[107] Finally, at a meeting of the Council on November 24, with seventeen of the twenty Council members present, and with four fraternity, five sorority, and four independent students as invited guests, the Council approved deferring Greek rush until the beginning of the second semester. The Council recommendation then went to the faculty, where a spirited discussion on the matter ensued at its meetings in December and January. Various motions and substitute motions were presented. The crucial motion on January 26 to set deferred rush for the beginning of the second semester passed by a vote of 32 to 26. The other two parts of the full motion approved by the faculty were that freshmen on probation would not be eligible for rush and that the program of deferred rush would be subject to review after a year.[108]

Two weeks later President Fleming announced that the Board of Trustees at its January 29 meeting had indicated interest in the deferred rush issue and that the Trustees wished to have an opportunity to discuss it with the faculty. Therefore, he set up a President's Committee on Deferred Rush. The committee consisted of three professors, three students, and three Trustees. The Trustees were Charles Prothro, A. Frank Smith, Jr., and Senator John Tower. The teachers were Professors Brown, Peterson, and Anderson. The three students were Ron Underwood, Paul Bell, and Mandy Weaver. He stated that the Board had committed itself to accept as final the decision reached by the committee.[109] The President's committee met and unanimously accepted the faculty decision that formal rush be deferred until the beginning of the spring semester, prior to the beginning of classes, and to review the matter again after a year. It did, however, add one statement to the faculty action. It affirmed "strongly . . . its belief that the fraternity system is and should continue to be an essential part of campus life at Southwestern University."[110] A year later the ad hoc Committee to Evaluate Deferred Rush recommended that the new system be continued.[111]

In the interview conducted by Dr. Martha Allen with Dr. Fleming in 1993, Fleming commented on the deferred rush matter. He said: "If we ever got the attention of the alumni, we always got it over that issue. You just had to touch it—just touch it—and you would get letters and phone calls." The most serious student protest he ever had, he affirmed, was in 1977, toward the end of his administration, when the fraternities made an attempt to overturn deferred rush. A group of fraternity men came to his house one evening at about nine or ten. Though there was "a lot of commotion," he stood on his front porch, listened, and talked it out with them.[112] The men retired to their fraternity houses and caused no more trouble.

One of the reasons Fleming was so careful in his handling of the deferred rush issue, in addition to his knowledge about how sensitive it was to certain alumni, was that he was not a fraternity man and did not want to be accused of being partial. He felt he had to preserve his posture of impartiality. This author, however, learned what his real sentiments were just prior to the faculty meeting on April 14, 1970, when the President invited him to be the Commencement speaker on May 31.[113] This invitation was Fleming's way of validating his actions as chair of the Student Life Council, in which he had shepherded the deferred rush issue through to success. Southwestern still practices deferred rush today.

International Faculty Members

Though Southwestern had occasionally had faculty members from abroad prior to World War II, the internationalism occasioned by the war and President Score's personal interest in persons that had suffered from Nazi racial policies caused the influx of a significant contingent of foreign-born faculty members. Professors Frederick W. Lenz and Mali G. Lenz were the first to arrive in 1946. Eleven others taught on the faculty at one time or another during the Score and Finch years. The peak year was 1950, when ten were on the faculty at one time, with nine in both 1949 and 1951. Seven were Germans, with one each from Czechoslovakia, China, Austria, Turkey, Lebanon, and Pakistan. Except for the Lenzes, Gaupp, and Merzbach, none stayed longer than four years. They tended to use their few years at Southwestern as a staging point for other employments.

Six foreign-born persons joined the faculty during the Fleming years. Each was from a different country—Cuba, Korea, Uruguay, India, Germany, and France. Of the six, three stayed long enough to achieve tenure. They were Suk-soon Suh (Political Science), Horace S. Jacob (Biology), and Regine Reynolds (French). Jacob died of cancer after serving twenty-six years on the faculty, Reynolds left after seventeen years to accept a position at Agnes Scott College, and Suh retired as chair of the Political Science Department.

Suh's career was unusual, almost melodramatic, and he left a strong imprint on students both in his Korean and in his Texan teaching careers. Scion of a prominent Korean family, Suh was educated in both Korea and Japan before coming to the United States, where he completed his Ph.D. in political science at the University of Nebraska in 1953. In 1959 he returned to the United States on a Rockefeller Foundation research grant for studies at the University of California (Berkeley) and at Harvard. Upon his return to South Korea in 1960, he was tapped to serve as Minister of Public Information in the fledgling democracy being established. A military coup ousted the government, and Suh, after some harrowing experiences, became a professor at Yonsei University. While at Yonsei he served as an editorial writer for South Korea's largest newspaper and was a prominent radio commentator. His open prodemocracy stance put him on the government's enemy list, and he was in considerable danger of being imprisoned or worse. In the meantime, some of his friends in the State Department in the United States arranged for him to receive a Fulbright Teaching Fellowship that brought him and his family to the United States, where he taught at Earlham College, Richmond, Indiana.[114] When this writer learned that Suh might stay in the United States because of the danger he faced if he returned to South Korea, he, with the cooperation of President Fleming and Dean Clifford, invited him to teach in the Department of History and Government at Southwestern. Suh became chair of the Department of Political Science when it was set up as a department separate from history in 1976. He also became chair of the International Studies Program and Director of the Summer School. He retired in 1990.

Gender and Ethnic Distribution of the Faculty

Though the size of the faculty, including nonteaching and part-time faculty, increased from fifty-four to eighty-two between 1960–1961 and 1980–1981, the proportion of women on the faculty declined during those twenty years, from 29.6 percent in the former year to 24.4 percent in the latter year. In addition, only 18.6 percent of persons with full-time positions in 1980–1981 were women. This shortage of women in full-time positions was also found in other positions of relatively high distinction. Of fourteen department chairpersons on the faculty, only two were women, and only one of Southwestern's endowed chairholders was a woman. The *Self-Study Report 1981* describes the situation as being one of long standing.[115]

In one area, however, some gains had been made toward gender equity. Using a multiple regression formula that permits the calculation of an "equitable salary" and that takes into account factors judged to be relevant to the equitable determination of salary, a table in the *Self-Study Report 1981* showed that no bias could be detected in comparing the total equitable salary calculated for women with that for men.[116] This finding is not surprising. Southwestern had begun to use the formula some years earlier to attack bias in the distribution of salaries. The same formula was also used to eliminate bias among the academic divisions of the University and among the professorial ranks.

Though there were no black or Hispanic professors at Southwestern in 1980–1981, three Hispanic professors had taught on the faculty during the Fleming years. The first was Dr. Sarah S. Zajicek, a Professor of Education from 1954 to 1967. She resigned in 1967 to accept a position at a college in San Antonio, where she lived. The second was Dr. Francisco Betancourt, a professor of Spanish. Coming to Southwestern in 1965, he resigned in 1978 to accept a university position in his native Puerto Rico. The third was Dr. J. Manuel Sánchez de Bustamente. Coming to Southwestern in 1966 as an exile from Cuba, he taught Spanish for three years.

Steps toward Library Modernization

Though four professors—Cody, Hyer, Shands, and Carroll—had maintained the library since 1880 as a part of their teaching responsibilities, the appointment of Margaret Mood McKennon as librarian in 1903 marked the real beginning of a library oriented to standard college library techniques. She cataloged the holdings she found at the outset according to the Dewey Decimal System. That system is still in use today more than one hundred years later, and one today may occasionally come across a volume with the accession data done in her hand. Located on the east side of the third floor of the Administration Building, the library remained there, with some auxiliary space on the first floor, until the construction of the Cody Memorial Library building in 1939. The library holdings that were transferred to that building from the old Administration Building were mostly books donated by friends and patrons, with the addition of a small number of books and periodicals that had been purchased from the meager budgets allocated to the library during Southwestern's years of penury. Many of them were maintained over the years by being rebound from time to time in the bindery by student workers. The library was always critiqued for its limited holdings by outside examiners during the McKennon years, but it was praised for the care with which it was maintained given its limited budget and space.

After the retirement of Mrs. McKennon in 1944, the library suffered not only from limited budgetary resources, but also from a lack of consistent leadership. In the thirteen years between 1944 and 1957, there were seven library directors. The only noteworthy advances made during those years were the move to the new Cody Memorial Library building in 1939 and the many special gifts, such as the Blake collection, made to it by Margarett and Alice Brown.

The second long-term director of the library was Mrs. Mildred Gervasi. She served from 1957 until 1975, when she died from a heart attack. Though she seemed to many people to be more interested in protecting her books than in lending them, she was efficient and supervised the move to the new building when it was completed in 1966. She also supervised the accession in 1970 of the Isabel Gaddis Collection of J. Frank Dobie, purchased for the University by Mr. and Mrs. Charles N. Prothro,[117] and the procurement in 1973 of the Ruth and Will W. Jackson Collection, which included the Granbery papers.[118] The most important change in the library during Gervasi's tenure was the decision of Fleming and Clifford to increase the library budget. When he arrived, Fleming found a recommendation from the 1961 SACS Visiting Team that "a significant increase in the book budget be given a high priority."[119] He took the recommendation to heart and increased the annual median library budget as a percentage of the education and general budget over the next nine years to 6.5 percent, never going below 5.4 percent in any year and once going as high as 7.3 percent.[120] The comment of the 1971 SACS Visiting Team was that the library had "received strong financial support in recent years."[121]

After the death of Mrs. Gervasi, Dr. B. F. Jackson, Jr., was appointed Head Librarian. He is the same Jackson whom Score had brought to Southwestern from First Methodist Church in Fort Worth in the 1940s and who was one of the persons involved in initiating the Negro

Fine Arts School (see Chapter XVII). After leaving Southwestern in 1951 and working with Scarritt College and the Methodist Board of Education in Nashville, Jackson moved to Denver, where he became Director of the Taylor Educational Resources Library at the Iliff School of Theology. In addition to his extensive experience in producing motion pictures and other forms of audiovisuals, he was a trained librarian. Both he and his two sons were graduates of Southwestern, and he decided to spend the last two years of his active career at his alma mater.[122]

Jackson's impact on the library program was immediate and profound. He was appreciated by his colleagues in the library, popular with students and faculty, and looked on by administrative officials of the University as being a marvelous administrator. Under him the library joined the computer-based cataloging system AMIGOS, became connected with the Ohio College Library Consortium (OCLC),[123] and established a special collections cataloging project that after two years had completed the cataloging of about 80 percent of the fifteen thousand volumes in special collections.[124] One of his most important contributions was changing the image of the library. In summing up Jackson's contributions, Fleming said: "He inspired and motivated faculty and students to use our excellent library resources more frequently for their personal benefit and in support of our instructional program."[125] The announcement by Dean Clifford at the October 1977 meeting of the Board of Trustees that the cataloging project had almost been completed was one of the inducements that caused Senator John Tower to make his "surprise announcement" at the same meeting that he planned give all of his official papers to Southwestern University.[126]

Revision of the Bylaws

The changes that had occurred in both the University and the country during the quarter century since the last revision of the Bylaws in 1941 made a new revision desirable. One change in the number of Board members had already been made in 1964 when the category of "at large" members was expanded to eleven, making a total membership of nineteen Annual Conference members and eleven at-large members.[127] Additional *ex officio* members were the President of the University and the bishops of the sponsoring Annual Conferences, making a maximum total of thirty-five if all positions were filled. Another change occurred in 1969 when the New Mexico Conference discontinued its connection with Southwestern because of its heavy responsibility in supporting McMurry College.[128]

In that same year a Trustee-faculty committee was appointed to work on a complete revision of the Bylaws. The original committee was composed of Chairman Prothro, Vice Chairman Smith, and Professors Score and Davis, assisted by Dr. Jud Custer. Mr. John Robinson, a Houston lawyer and alumnus, served as legal counsel throughout the two-year process.[129] He later became a member of the Board. When the committee proposed the possibility of adding two faculty members and two students to the Board, the current Board expressed opposition because of the conflict of interest that would have them voting on items that affected their own interests.[130] It did, however, approve a proposal to add two recent graduates to membership. Each graduating senior class would nominate by election one of its members to a two-year term. This nominee, upon election by the entire Board, would become a member of the Board.[131] It also agreed to invite the Rio Grande Conference to become a sponsoring conference, with both a ministerial and a lay delegate.[132] The President of the Alumni Association was added as an *ex officio* member, and the number of at-large members was raised to sixteen. With the President and bishops also as *ex officio* members, the Board of Trustees was constituted as a body "comprised of not more than fifty (50) members, three-fifths (3/5) of whom must be members of The United Methodist Church."[133] Though some of the unique privileges of faculty members in their relationship to the Board in the 1941 document were not continued in the 1971 document, it did include a strong section on tenure based on the academic freedom statement of the American Association of University Professors. The 1971 document as modified over the years is still the operative set of Bylaws under which the University operates.

Easy Relations among Trustees and Their Friends

The connections among Southwestern Trustees and other persons of influence in the state that had been so important to the well-being of the University in the mid-1930s continued through the Bergin, Score, Finch, and Fleming administrations. As some Trustees retired from the scene, others came on stage. Charles N. Prothro joined the Board in 1952 as a part of the Perkins connection with the University. Married to Elizabeth, the only daughter of Joe and Lois Perkins, Charles became like a son to them. Joe, the son of Elizabeth and Charles, succeeded Charles on the Board in 1982. The Perkins-Prothro connection continued into the Shilling and Schrum administrations with a gift of $3.5 million from the Perkins-Prothro Foundation in 2005 to construct a building that will serve as the headquarters for the academic administration of the University and house the Paideia program. Elizabeth was an artist with the camera and presented the University with large photographs, measuring approximately 5' x 7½', of campus scenes taken by her that were placed in conspicuous places in the Cullen Building. Charles became chair of the Board in 1966 upon the retirement of John D. Wheeler. A. Frank Smith, Jr., replaced his father, Bishop A. Frank Smith, Sr., on the Board in 1961, only a year before the bishop's death. He became chair in 1977. "Charles Prothro and Frank Smith just idolized John Wheeler," says Fleming, because "he was the old rock. He had a frame of reference. . . . Frank Smith was as natural to follow Charles Prothro as Charles was natural to follow John Wheeler."

Roy Cullen became a part of the influential fraternity of friends interested in Southwestern in the early 1970s. Whenever he came to the campus, he felt at home and showed it by the easy relations he established with students, faculty, and other Trustees. He impressed everyone by never trying to impress anyone. He tried not to cause trouble for anyone. On one occasion when he did not have a ride back to his private plane at the Georgetown airport to return to Houston, he hiked the four or five miles from the campus to the Georgetown airport to reach it. Roy Shilling was mortified when he later found out about it and chided him for not letting someone know he needed a ride. Roy Cullen told him not to worry about it, that he needed the exercise. His wife was an amateur distance runner. His aunt, Wilhelmina Robertson, was the featured speaker at the rededication of the Administration Building as the Cullen Building in 1977. Though she had earlier disclaimed her ability to serve in that capacity and a script had been prepared for her, she abandoned the script in the emotion of the moment and spoke from her heart. A bronze plaque was placed in one of the hallways on the first floor of the Cullen Building commemorating a speech made by an early Cullen ancestor, Ezekiel W. Cullen, a member of the third Congress of the Republic of Texas, on January 4, 1839. It reads:

> Intelligence is the only aristocracy in a government like ours; and the improved and educated mind has and will ever triumph over the ignorant and uneducated mind. . . .

The Cullen Foundation has continued to support Southwestern until the present, most recently providing gifts for restoration of the Cullen Building.

Ed Clark was an intimate friend of John Tower. Tower became a Trustee in 1968 and is presently commemorated by two large flagpoles bearing American and Texas flags in the center of the campus in front of the Charline and Red McCombs Campus Center presented by his daughters. Clark had helped Tower become the first Republican Senator from Texas in the twentieth century and later raised the almost half million dollars needed to endow the Tower-Hester Chair in Political Science (1973–1975). Clark was also a strong supporter of Lyndon Johnson, and Johnson as President had named him Ambassador to Australia. Political party was not as important to the persons who formed the fellowship of Southwestern Trustees as a feeling of partnership in Texas culture, a desire to improve Texas society, and mutual trust.

Clark, says Fleming, was "one of the greatest individual types I ever met. He was not a scholar, but he was a man of books and libraries and he was an omnivorous reader, and especially in his heyday, he knew what was going on in politics, yes, even in religion, that is his Episcopal side." He was a great book collector and gave his fine Texana and Australian collections to Southwestern. He felt it would be "obscene" to sell them. On one occasion he phoned me from Austin and asked me to meet him an hour later at the Southwestern library. At the scheduled time Clark and Chancellor Ransom of the University of Texas arrived, and Ransom presented to Southwestern some fine books from his personal collection that Clark had urged him to give. Clark had also become a close friend of both George and Herman Brown when Herman lived in Austin. He would tell George Brown from time to time what a good job Durwood was doing.

While Prothro was chair of the Board, Fleming says he seldom called him except for something big or for an emergency. When he did, Prothro would often end up flying down in his plane from Wichita Falls for a couple of hours to talk, then fly back. For Frank Smith it was different. Though Smith was managing partner of the Vinson, Elkins, Connally, and Smith law firm in Houston, he was never too busy to see Fleming for lunch there. When Smith came to the campus for meetings, he would sometimes arrive a bit rumpled, having chosen to drive from Houston in a Jeep. Though not a graduate of Southwestern, he was devoted to the school. Once when he was present at a budget meeting in the President's conference room, he learned that the University could not fund all of the sabbaticals due to faculty members for the forthcoming year. He asked how much it was, took out his checkbook, and wrote a check, as I remember it, for something like four or five thousand dollars to fund them. A touching incident involving Smith was an ascent to the tower of the Cullen Building just after he became Board chair in the late 1970s. He said that his father, Bishop Smith, had told him that he and his future wife, Bess Crutchfield, had written their names in the tower while they were students. He asked if it would be possible to see if the names were still there. My records describe the resultant climb to the tower and search for the names as follows:

> We ascended the circular metal stairwell with a student to the little room inside the tower at its highest point and looked for the names of Frank and Bess among the many written on the stone walls and wooden beams. The student remarked that he didn't find Bess Crutchfield but that he did find a Hallie, to which Smith called out exultantly, "That's Aunt Hallie!" A little more searching in the same area yielded his parents' names as well—A. Frank Smith and Bess Crutchfield. He was overcome with joy.[134]

The coming on the Board of A. Frank Smith, Jr., said Durwood Fleming, "influenced, I think, more money to Southwestern than any other one that's out there. I think the Trustees would say that there was no doubt about it. He was the lawyer for the Cullens. People trusted him."[135] The A. Frank Smith, Jr., Library Center, dedicated in the fall of 1988, was named for him.

One of the strengths of the last five Presidents of Southwestern, from Score to Schrum, is that each has walked easily among the network of Texans represented by the persons mentioned above, many of whom have had a major hand in shaping the Texas of today. They have maintained many connections begun in earlier generations and established new ones as well. The confluence of circumstances that brought these important persons in Texas history to take an interest in Southwestern is one of its greatest success stories.

George Brown Continues Herman's Interest in Southwestern

When assessing the contributions of The Brown Foundation to Southwestern University, one must begin with the work of Herman Brown on the Board of Trustees from 1949 until his death in 1962. Bill Finch was "dear and close" to the Browns, says Fleming, and the contribution that Herman and Margarett made to Southwestern during the Finch years was more than a little based on their apprecia-

George and Alice Brown being presented with the plaque naming the Brown College of Arts and Sciences after The Brown Foundation and all the Browns. Southwestern University, Special Collections.

tion for him.[136] When Herman learned in 1961 that Finch was going to Vanderbilt, he wrote him: "In my gratitude to you for your invaluable devotion to the school, I want to pay these expenses [of moving to Nashville] if you will be good enough to have the transfer people send me the bill." Finch replied, expressing great appreciation, but informing him that Vanderbilt was paying for the move. Failing in this, Herman offered to pay the expenses of Bill and Lucy to attend the Ecumenical Conference of the Methodist Church in Oslo. Once again Finch had to refuse. He said that he simply couldn't leave Vanderbilt for such an extended time so shortly after having taken up his responsibility there.[137]

The interest of Herman and Margarett in Southwestern was manifested in so many ways other than monetary that to measure it by a dollar sign would be to do an injustice to the high level of their personal involvement. It was surely a serendipitous event that Herman died in the evening after returning from a meeting on the Southwestern campus and that the new President of Southwestern, Durwood Fleming, who had known the Browns in Houston, would be asked by George to do Herman's funeral.[138] Less than three months later he did Margarett's funeral as well in the chapel of St. Paul's Methodist Church.[139]

After Herman's death, George Brown and Herbert Frensley, their right-hand man and president of the Brown shipbuilding operation, continued Herman's interest in Southwestern just as if Herman were still alive. Not only were the Frensleys members of Fleming's church in Houston, but the two families were also neighbors.[140] Fleming says that he talked to Herb Frensley more than he did to George Brown so as not to bother George.[141] George and Alice would occasionally come to the campus. They were present when the Brown College of Arts and Sciences was named to honor all the Browns and The Brown Foundation in 1975 and for the first Brown Symposium in 1978. Rather than being a foundation like any other distributing its largesse to worthy recipients on the basis of meritorious proposals, The Brown Foundation was part of a family connection with Southwestern that started when the Brown brothers began their construction business in Central Texas, when they courted and married two Southwestern alumnae, and when Herman Brown became a member of the Southwestern Board of Trustees. After Herman's and Margarett's deaths, George and Alice simply did what they felt Herman and Margarett would have wanted done for Southwestern. George's loyalty to the commitment he and Herman had lived by, that they would share everything equally, is a remarkable testimony to the fidelity of their relationship.

The Brown Foundation Matching Gift Proposal and Three New Chairs (1963–1964)

The first major expression of George's interest in Southwestern after Herman's death was The Brown Foundation's Matching Gift proposal in 1963. The Foundation's gift of $500,000 would be matched by $1,000,000 raised by Southwestern for permanent improvements. The Foundation also announced that it would be contributing $750,000 to establish three additional professorships, later raised to chairs, at $250,000 each to join the already established Lucy King Brown Chair in History.[142] The campaign by Southwestern to meet its matching grant component got underway immediately, with William A. Smith leading the Houston solicitation effort. Within a little more than a year the campaign there soon reached $700,000, with the expectation of another $100,000 to come in. Fleming praised Smith for his work and stated that $200,000 or more was expected from Austin, Dallas, San Antonio, and Fort Worth. When the question arose in the Board as to why Smith, a Catholic, would support a Protestant college so strongly, David Searls explained that Bill Smith was one of those men who always sought the public good and was a close personal friend of several Board members.[143] He was particularly close to Herman Brown. The University awarded Smith an honorary degree on October 13, 1982, for two decades of interest in Southwestern.[144]

The Brown Challenge: Phase I (1968–1970)

One of Fleming's first surprises in dealing with the budget after his arrival in 1961 was that faculty raises the past year had been so meager that the Trustees voted a Christmas bonus amounting to about $9,000 to be divided among them. McCook expressed the hope that salary raises in the future might be of sufficient import to avoid the necessity of making bonus payments.[145] For the next five years Fleming raised salaries 5 percent each year, amounting to approximately 30 percent.[146] In spite of this increase, Dean Clifford told the Trustees in 1964 that he was having difficulty recruiting competent teachers because Southwestern's salaries were not competitive. He stated that the whole faculty recruiting program was "fast approaching an acute stage."[147] Three years later Clifford said that the situation was "critical." Southwestern's D rating on the A.A.U.P. faculty rating scale was "no secret" in higher education circles.[148]

Developments from 1966 to 1968 brought the burgeoning financial problem to a head. The four new buildings and assorted other small projects were completed in the former year, and the Advancement Campaign already described was initiated to pay the $1,700,000 that was needed to complete their funding. With the failure of the campaign, the entire amount had to be borrowed from the Southwestern Life Insurance Company. Repayment would cover a ten-year period and be repaid at a rate of $54,900 per quarter beginning June 1, 1967. Whereas University budgets had been balanced prior to this time and even produced a slight surplus each year, all surpluses and unspecified gifts now had to go to service the debt.[149] These extra monies only lasted about a year and forced Fleming to present an initial budget for 1968–1969 with a planned deficit of $110,000.[150]

During his years at Southwestern up to this point, Fleming had been in conversation with George Brown and Herbert Frensley on a regular basis. He informed them from time to time of the exact situation of Southwestern so that they would feel that they had insider knowledge about the institution. In an earlier visit with Herbert Frensley on April 9, 1965, Fleming had told him of the plan to build the two dormitories, the University Commons, and the library addition, one of the dormitories to bear Herman's name. Herbert's grin had let him know that George would be pleased.[151]

In April 1967 Fleming and Prothro paid a formal visit to George in Houston and talked with him about Southwestern's mounting financial problems. They left the conversation feeling that The Brown Foundation would offer further support.[152] They followed up their visit by presenting a detailed explanation in written form of university needs. In it they explained that $15 million, at a minimum, would be needed over the next ten years to bring the institution to a truly first-class position.[153] George Brown felt that Southwestern was not yet ready to do what would be required of it for a matching grant of that magnitude and suggested that Fleming come up with a more realistic alternative.[154] In a subsequent proposal, Fleming suggested a 3:2 match, with Southwestern raising $750,000 a year for three years, to be matched by $500,000 annually from the Foundation. The Foundation responded favorably, and in the spring of 1968 Fleming was able to announce that The Brown Foundation had offered a "challenge grant" to Southwestern of $1.5 million in return for Southwestern's raising $2.25 million over the next three years. The Foundation had called it a "matching grant" in its statement to Fleming. Writing his announcement for the public, Fleming scratched out the word "matching" and wrote in the word "challenge."[155] Much the same thing occurred in 1976 when the Foundation made its next "matching grant" to the University. Fleming wrote Merritt Warner, Executive Administrator, asking for permission to use the term "challenge" instead of "matching." Warner replied that the Executive Committee had no objection to the change.[156]

The Foundation, however, added an unexpected element of its own that was very unusual. It committed $300,000 to be paid in three annual installments to support the operational budget. Requesting gifts for the operational budget was not a common practice in fund-raising, and Fleming had not suggested these annual gifts in his proposal. Brown and Frensley added them because they knew that Fleming had just proposed a budget to the Southwestern Trustees with a potential deficit of $110,000. Following his policy of keeping Brown and Frensley precisely informed about Southwestern's situation, he had mentioned the potential deficit in one of his intimate conversations with them. The receipt of the first $100,000 virtually wiped out, as was intended, the projected $110,000 potential deficit, and subsequent payments by the Foundation kept the University budget balanced for several more years.[157]

Changing of the Guard in Fiscal Affairs and Development

During the same year that the first Brown Challenge was announced, several changes occurred in the fiscal affairs and development staffs of the University. Mr. Basil Phillips replaced I. J. McCook upon the retirement of the latter, Fayez Sarofim & Company was selected to service the University's portfolio, and Dr. Roy B. Shilling, Jr., became Executive Vice President, responsible for coordinating development efforts. He would be in charge of planning and supervising the program to match the first Brown Challenge.

McCook, who had served as chief financial officer since 1929, was elected at the time of his retirement in 1968 as a lifetime Honorary Trustee. His title—Vice President, Finance—was retired to be always held in the future as a memorial to him, and he was voted "a permanent relationship with the University in terms of privileges, courtesies, and considerations."[158] His successor, Basil Phillips, was an alumnus who had graduated with a B.B.A. in 1949 and served as the University Auditor from 1959 to 1962. In the latter year, he had moved to Nashville, where he served as Administrator of the Medical Center Programs at Vanderbilt University. He and his wife, Alyce, had met at Southwestern, where they had lived in the barracks after World War II. She was the daughter of the Reverend Otto Moerner, an early Southwestern graduate.

At the same time, Fayez Sarofim & Company of Houston was selected to manage the University's investments, with Sarofim to manage the account personally.[159] He has served in that capacity ever since, to the great satisfaction of the University. President Shilling was able to announce at his community-wide retirement function in 1999 that Fayez Sarofim had pledged $8 million to the University, to be paid over several years, for the renovation of the Alma Thomas Fine Arts Center. The School of Fine Arts was renamed the Sarofim School of Fine Arts in his honor.

Also in 1968, Roy B. Shilling, Jr., was named Executive Vice President. He was a graduate of McMurry College (1951), held a B.D. from the Perkins School of Theology (1957), and an M.A. and a Ph.D. (1966, 1967) from Indiana University. He came to Southwestern from Baldwin-Wallace College, Cleveland, where he was Director of Planning and Research.[160] His role was to advise and coordinate the activities and programs administered by the Vice President for Fiscal Affairs, the Dean of the School of Arts and Sciences, the Dean of the School of Fine Arts, the Dean of Students, and the Directors of Public Relations and the Annual Fund.[161] With Grogan Lord as General Chairman, Ed Clark as Honorary Chairman, and Senator Tower as Alumni Chairman, the Challenge Campaign proceeded vigorously, and Shilling predicted that its goal would be met on schedule.

Unfortunately for Southwestern but fortunately for Shilling, he was elected President of Hendrix College, Conway, Arkansas, within less than a year after his coming. President Fleming said about Shilling's departure in addressing the Trustees: "He simply could not afford to refuse such an offer. . . . Roy Shilling has brought a quality of excellence and expertise to our total program in one short year the like of which has not been experienced here in years. He is expert in diagnosing problems, in developing plans, in restructuring organization, in bringing off results, and in working with people."[162] Grogan Lord "accorded high praise to Dr. Shilling's commitment and unceasing efforts on behalf of Southwestern and the current Challenge Campaign."[163] Shilling would return to Southwestern to succeed Fleming as President in 1981. No replacement was secured immediately for Shilling, but Mr. Dick Dini of Houston was secured to give two days a month for working with staff member Jim Reid to complete the campaign. It was completed successfully in early 1970. Dini would later be employed by Fleming to work with the development staff in the Brown Challenge of 1976, because his firm, Richard F. Dini Associates, had been used by The Brown Foundation to help prepare the grant.[164]

"A Critical but Marvelous Period"

Though the three annual $100,000 gifts from The Brown Foundation for use in balancing the budget had indeed kept it balanced through 1970, they were a one-time fix and only deferred the real problem. The problem was that no new money had been generated to pay the debt service of $219,600 per year on the $1,700,000 borrowed in 1967 from the Southwestern Life Insurance Company. Beginning in 1970 the debt service was shown as an operating expense and paid out of the current fund. This meant that what had been a slight operating surplus through 1970 became an operating deficit after that date. The budget surplus or deficit figures are as follows:[165]

Fiscal Year	Surplus/deficit w/o debt service	Surplus/deficit with debt service
1970–71	$12,464	($207,136)
1971–72	85,266	(134,334)
1972–73	12,330	(207,270)
1973–74	1,279	(218,321)
1974–75	(30,859)	(250,459)
1975–76	(383,255)	
1976–77	(274,390)	

By 1975 the Southwestern Life Insurance Company debt was down to the $300,000+ range, and the Trustees agreed to use some W-K-M quasi-endowment monies to pay out the note. The balance of $317,537 was paid on October 31, 1975.[166]

In addition to the debt, the expenditure causing the greatest difficulty was salaries, wages, and benefits. In 1975 they consumed 63 percent of the University budget.[167] Even a small percentage increase had considerable effect on the total budget. Yet there was a need to raise faculty and staff salaries each year. Inflation was quite strong, and without equally strong salary increments the standard of living of University personnel would decline. Until 1972–1973 salary raises had been included in the regular budget when it was presented to the Trustees for adoption. For 1972–1973 Fleming announced that there would be no salary increases. Student fees had been significantly increased, and the University might lose many of its present students and not achieve the desired freshman class enrollment. He did hold out the hope that a good enrollment figure for the fall might make it possible to give increases.[168] In spite of this hope, the necessary enrollment figure did not materialize. Fall semester enrollment dropped from 862 in 1971 to 819 in 1972, and salaries remained at the level of the previous year. Though salaries were increased for 1973–1974, money had to be taken from surplus to accomplish it, and the salary adjustments did not take effect until November 1, 1973, after the fall semester enrollment of 900 had been ascertained. From 1974 through 1976 salary changes were announced in October and made retroactive to September. In 1977–1978 new salaries became effective on January 1, 1978, and successively on January 1, 1979, 1980, and 1981.[169] Fleming felt that he had no choice but to delay the salary increases one semester each year. The University had run deficit budgets for seven years, from 1970–1971 through 1976–1977, inflation was increasing steadily, and student enrollment was unpredictable from year to year.

In order to allay the suspicions of the faculty that he and his staff were not doing everything they could with regard to salaries, he included three faculty members in the group that put together the budget for 1974–1975.[170] He also formed the Academic Program Survey Committee referred to earlier to provide suggestions about how to achieve economies in the regular academic program and to come up with various contingency plans for worst-case scenarios. It was at this point that he also appointed an Administrative Vice President and Provost so that, having lost three chief development officers, he could, in effect, become his own Vice President for Development. He described to the Trustees the financial situation of the University in October 1975 as follows:

> To summarize, our total income has reached an all time high; Southwestern[,] asset-wise, is in the best financial condition it has ever been in. The book value of the endowment portfolio has passed the $16.0 million mark; the plant value continues to increase. The annual budget is now more than $4.0 million. Had we been able to continue the development stride we set for ourselves five years ago, we would have been at this time in solid, sound financial condition. But the specter of inflation interrupted and has upended our plans. . . . The expense side of our operations has, like yours, gone "out of sight." Costs have risen and soared. The erratic stock market, in which our investments have suffered, has troubled us. . . . Added to this is our reticence to continue to raise student costs lest we upset the source of new student recruits and cause our present students to transfer because "it costs too much to attend Southwestern." . . . With all the negatives affecting annual income, we do very well indeed excepting our ability to generate sufficient sums to service the principal and interest on our loan. . . . We are involved in a very critical but marvelous period.[171]

The reason for Fleming's reference to being "involved in a very critical but marvelous period" is that the University had just completed successfully Phase II of the Brown Challenge, now to be described. For having raised $8 million in the five years from 1971 to 1975, it received $2 from The Brown Foundation.

The Brown Challenge: Phase II—"The Program for Progress" (1971–1975)

As a result of the successful completion of the Brown Challenge of 1968 to 1970, later called Phase I of the three-phase Brown Challenge, Fleming, Charles Prothro, Grogan Lord, David Searls, and Director of Development Jim Reid visited George Brown in Houston. In a two-and-a-half-hour conference, they discussed the possibility of moving toward a Phase II campaign effort. They presented, in chart form, statistical information that documented the growth and development of Southwestern over the previous five years.

The second section of the presentation outlined a tentative program for the development of SU over the next five years. The five men projected needs of $7,450,000. Their outline called for increasing the Phase I annual contribution of The Brown Foundation to the budget from $100,000 to $150,000 for three years. Four million dollars would be added to the endowment by raising the endowment level of current professorships and chairs and adding new ones. The Administration Building and the Alma Thomas Fine Arts Center would be renovated for $3 million and become an Academic Center. The total program would last five years and be concluded during the 1974–1975 academic year. It would be highlighted in 1973 by the Centennial Celebration of Southwestern in Georgetown. Brown was interested but made no commitment. He concluded the meeting by telling them to come back to see him after they had refined their plans with the Trustees and decided definitively on what they wanted to accomplish.[172]

When Fleming presented the "refined" proposal to George Brown and Herbert Frensley in the fall, it was substantially the same as that presented earlier, only with its price raised from $7.45 million to $10 million. The annual contribution of $150,000 to the budget was extended from three years to four, the endowment for professorships and chairs was raised from $4 million to $5, $750,000 was included for the work of the library, and $150,000 was included to cover the costs of temporary housing during the construction period.[173] The proposal specified a 4:1 match, with Southwestern raising $8 million to qualify for $2 from The Brown Foundation. Though the Board had voted to rename the College of Arts and Sciences in honor of the Browns, George asked that this not be done. He did state that the Foundation would look with favor upon the naming of the proposed Academic Center in honor of Herman Brown.[174]

On November 23 The Brown Foundation responded to the refined proposal. It accepted the $10 million goal but did not mention further contributions to the operating budget. The Foundation would give $2 million, to be divided between endowment and physical plant, if the University would raise $8 million over a five-year period. It accepted the notion that the new Academic Center would be named for Herman Brown.[175] This new commitment by the Foundation for a Phase II Brown Challenge gave the University a launching pad for a major campaign.

The Program for Progress and Its Leaders

Grogan Lord was made General Chairman of the new "Challenge Campaign, Phase II," shortly thereafter renamed "The $10 Million Program for Progress."[176] Dr. Jerald C. Walker, the Vice President for University Relations since October 1970, was the administrative officer in charge of the campaign. Walker had a B.A. from Oklahoma City University, a B.D. from the Divinity School of the University of Chicago, and a Rel.D. from the School of Theology at Claremont. He came to Southwestern from Beatrice, Nebraska, where he served as President of John J. Pershing College during 1969–1970.[177] Serving under him as coordinator of the campaign was Norman J. Peters, previously a staff member of Stephens College, Columbia, Missouri.[178] Walker served through four of the five years of the campaign before being elected President of Baker University in Baldwin City, Kansas.[179] He had served very acceptably and left with the good wishes of the President and the chair of the Board.[180] Succeeding Walker was Dr. John Van Valkenburg, who came from Huntingdon College, Montgomery, Alabama. He had a B.S. from Adrian College, an M.A. from Michigan State University, and an L.H.D. from Adrian.[181] He resigned almost exactly a year later to accept a post with the University of Montevallo in Alabama, his home state.[182] His leaving did not affect the campaign, however, since it was completed by the time he left.

In the fall of 1973, the firm of Richard F. Dini Associates of Houston was employed to work on the Program for Progress there. The Brown Foundation furnished office space at no cost. [183] Dini's work was highly satisfactory, and hopes began to rise that the campaign would be completed successfully.[184] Fleming was confident enough that he suggested to the Board that because of the $6 million given by The Brown Foundation to the University since 1962,[185] the College of Arts and Sciences should be renamed in honor of Mr. and Mrs. George R. Brown, Mr. and Mrs. Herman Brown, and The Brown Foundation, Inc., of Houston.[186] The Board voted the honor as requested, and a special event was held on April 18, 1975.[187] By then $8 had been raised by Southwestern toward the $10 Million Program for Progress, making possible the receipt of the entire $2 million from the Foundation.[188]

Unhappiness of the Board with University Financial Management

At the meeting of the Board in January 1971, Chairman Charles Prothro made a point of complimenting President Fleming, Vice President Phillips, and previous financial officers for "keeping us in the black" and for presenting a balanced budget.[189] In the next few years, however, Prothro became more and more apprehensive about the amount of interfund borrowing that was occurring to keep the budget balanced.[190] By 1975 the total interfund borrowing debt on the books accumulated over the last six years was $836,957. The large amount of the debt was such that the Board finally agreed to clear it by using some of the market gain from the W-K-M unrestricted endowment fund.[191] It also agreed to Fleming's recommendation to pay off the remaining debt of $317,537 owed to the Southwestern Life Insurance Company from the same source at the same time.[192]

Unfortunately, the deficit for 1975–1976 was $383,255 even without having to make the once familiar debt payment. This large a deficit made everyone recognize that the problem was acute, and steps were taken by the Business Office to stanch the hemorrhage of funds. Nevertheless, the deficit for the following year was still $274,390.[193] These deficits caused the Board to believe that the Business Office was not doing enough to control expenditures. Feeling that he had lost the confidence of the Board, Phillips resigned prior to the January 1977 Board meeting.[194] The Board immediately put into place new regulations governing interfund borrowing. It limited interfund borrowing for operational purposes to $50,000 (aggregate), stated that such borrowing must be cleared quarterly, and required that the Executive Committee must specifically approve any amount above $50,000.[195]

Righting the Financial Ship

The person chosen to bring the financial ship to even keel as Vice President for Fiscal Affairs was Mr. Kirk Treible. Treible, who had an M.B.A. from the University of West Virginia, came to Southwestern from West Virginia Wesleyan College, where he was Acting Treasurer. He had held other positions previously and had been a captain in the U.S. Air Force.[196]

Treible immediately carried out several measures that brought relief to the budget, but not all of his success can be attributed to actions initiated by him. He took over as chief fiscal officer precisely at the time when the first returns from the new Brown Challenge initiated in 1976 began to accrue to the operating budget of the University. Gifts to the operating budget from 1976 to 1980 increased annually from $852,826 in the former year to $1,718,845 in the latter year. The Brown Foundation matched these gifts with contributions to the endowment in amounts ranging from $1,012,817 in 1976 to $1,718,845 in 1980, with amounts in between for the middle years.[197] At the same time, it must also be recognized that both Treible and Phillips had to contend with rampant inflation from 1975 to 1981. It ran at the following rates during those years: 1975, 11.0 percent; 1976, 9.1 percent; 1977, 5.8 percent; 1978, 6.5 percent; 1979, 7.6 percent, 1980, 11.5 percent; and 1981, 13.5 percent.

But Treible did adopt a firmer attitude in financial matters and took some actions that were important for the University. His first action was to request that the Executive Committee rescind its recent action that had changed the fiscal year from its traditional July 1–June 30 dates to January 1–December 31. The action had been taken to bring the University's fiscal year into compliance with the Brown Challenge reporting year. Treible felt that it was more important to keep the fiscal year consonant with the academic year and with past practice than to change it to facilitate fund reporting. The Executive Committee granted his request.[198]

He also presented in his first meeting with the Board of Trustees "A Proposed Five Year Projection of Current Fund Operations 1977–1978 to 1982–1983."[199] It was, so far as I know, the first long-term budget projection *based on specified income and expense assumptions* made by any fiscal officer of the University. Such projections are commonplace today.

Perhaps the action taken that produced the most dramatic cost-cutting results was in the area of energy. From 1972 to 1977, during the energy crisis experienced by the country because of Middle Eastern developments, energy expenditures at Southwestern increased from $99,667 to $569,376, or from 3.2 percent of the operational budget to 10.6 percent.[200] With the installation of an IBM System 7 Energy Control Computer in the heating and cooling plant, a dramatic conservation of energy occurred that brought with it substantial savings.[201] By 1981 the IBM System 7 had brought utility costs down to 6.4 percent of the operational budget.[202]

As a result of these and other practices, the four budgets presided over by Treible from 1977–1978 through 1980–1981 were all balanced, with surpluses each year of $22,891, $62,470, $480,354, and $43,648, respectively. The Board of Trustees was pleased and commended Treible in 1978 when the Deloitte, Haskins & Sells auditing firm presented "a clean opinion," the first in a number of years.[203] It commended Treible for making such an opinion possible. Other compliments followed for the Business Office in 1979 and 1980.[204]

Durwood Fleming, president; Ambassador Edward A. Clark, campaign director; and A. Frank Smith, Jr., Chair of the Board of Trustees, celebrate the successful conclusion of the 1979 Brown Challenge goal. Southwestern University Publications Department.

The Brown Challenge Grant: Phase III (1976–1995)

Phase III of the Brown Challenge Program that ran from 1976 to 1995 was so remarkable in its conception and so successful in its execution that most people now think of it alone when the phrase "Brown Challenge" is mentioned. Indeed, however, three other Brown programs preceded it, two of them bearing the "Brown Challenge" name. They were all called "matching" programs by The Brown Foundation, and the Matching Gift Program of 1963–1964 was run by Southwestern under that name. The second and third programs in 1968–1970 and 1971–1975 were also called "matching" programs by the Foundation but were renamed by Fleming for publicity purposes. He coined the term "Brown Challenge" for the 1968–1970 campaign and used it also for the 1971–1975 campaign until it was renamed the Program for Progress.

Fleming first learned that The Brown Foundation might be thinking about another matching program for Southwestern sometime during the year prior to the announcement of the program in late April 1976. On that occasion Herbert Frensley and George Brown sat down with him and talked several hours about some new ideas they had about using grants. The grant program they had in mind would stimulate, they hoped, the three recipient institutions that would benefit from it to devise ways of getting their alumni and authentic supporters to meet the challenges specified in the awards, thereby doubling the gifts. The Foundation voted the program into existence on April 23, 1976, naming the Houston Museum of Fine Arts, Rice, and Southwestern as the recipients.[205] George Brown used the same technique five years later. Fleming says that in his last conversation with George Brown, "just before I finished up my tenure," Brown told him that the Foundation was going to renew the plan for ten more years beyond 1985. Knowing that Fleming would leave the presidency on July 1, Brown slipped the prospect of the extension to him before trustees of the Foundation formally voted it on November 23, 1981.[206] This author, who had been appointed Administrative Vice President and Provost only six months earlier, was present with the President in his office when two emissaries of The Brown Foundation initially unveiled its program either on or just after April 23, 1976. Since the Administration Building was being renovated at the time, Fleming's temporary office, where he received the emissaries, was in the little Field House back of the big parking lot.

Describing the origin of the Brown Challenge for the Southwestern Trustees in his Board report six months later, Fleming said that George R. Brown and Herbert J. Frensley and other trustees of The Brown Foundation set about the task "a year ago" of evolving a plan for Southwestern, Rice, and the Houston Museum of Fine Arts. The plan called for using 65 percent of the income of the Foundation for ten years as a challenge or as matching grant funds for those three institutions. Southwestern would be required to raise $575,000 for 1976 in order to be eligible for $770,000 from the Foundation. Gifts raised by the University would go to the operational budget. The program was designed to help Southwestern balance its current operations budget each year and to build up endowment support for the University after the conclusion of the Brown Challenge. All matching funds received from the Foundation would go into restricted endowment. Only the earnings could be used for operational purposes.[207]

Two things are clear from the record. First, the Phase III program of 1976 proceeded from George Brown as a direct result of his and, it should be added, Alice's desire and not as a result of any proposal that had been made by Southwestern, as in the cases of Phase I and Phase II. Secondly, though the program outlined by The Brown Foundation was larger by far than those proposed by Southwestern earlier that George Brown had gently turned down, he avoided the trap of making the program impossibly large by breaking it down into incremental annual goals that would be met by donations from a wide network of persons who would be enticed into giving.

The Challenge program provided an inducement to giving for everybody. Repeat gifts would be matched on a 1:1 basis. New gifts or new money above a past gift amount would be matched on a 2:1 basis. Gifts from alumni in the last five classes would be matched on a 4:1 basis. In addition to the matching awards, there were also incentive awards for specified levels of participation by the various classes. For 1976, more than 50 percent of the current students participated, and twenty-four alumni classes were organized to contact each other. Six early classes had 50 percent participation or more.[208] The final total of participants in 1976 was exactly 1,800, with a total of $852,826 being raised to match the goal of $575,000 set by The Brown Foundation.[209] Successive years yielded even better results. Ambassador Clark served as the annual campaign chairman for 1979 and thereafter through the Fleming years and continued into the Shilling period.

The Development Office was organized for the campaign around three young development officers, all of whom later had outstanding careers at Southwestern and elsewhere. The first was Marcus C. Raney. Raney came to Southwestern in 1975 as Director of Alumni Relations and Coordinator of University Relations. He was appointed Director of Development in 1977. He left in 1980 for a position at Trinity University, where he was the chief development officer for many years. Marilyn Mock Parrott succeeded him as Acting Director. With a B.A. in English from North Texas State University and an M.A. in Management from Goddard College, Plainfield, Vermont, she had come to Southwestern in 1978 as Director of Alumni Relations and Annual Giving. Richard B. Eason, a graduate of Southwestern, had worked as an Admissions Counselor and Director of Southwestern's Houston Office from 1973 to 1977. He was invited back to Southwestern in 1980 and worked with Marilyn Mock Parrott in development. Both Marilyn Parrott and Rick Eason would play important roles in the Shilling administration.

The earliest fundamental decision made by the Foundation as a consequence of the magnificent results soon achieved by Southwestern was whether it would match the excess raised beyond the Foundation's announced goal for the University or limit its match precisely to the goal. Its decision to match all funds raised had the result over the years of adding a great deal of money to Southwestern's endowment that a more narrow interpretation would not have allowed. At every point during the next twenty years The Brown Foundation exhibited its desire for Southwestern to succeed and to take full advantage of the campaign. George Brown and Herbert Frensley seemed to delight in Southwestern's success and enjoyed enhancing the campaign as it went along. The most important enhancement, of course, was the decision in 1981 to extend the campaign to twenty years. The results of the Brown Challenge during the five years of the Fleming administration appear in the following table.[210]

Year	Brown Foundation Goal	Total Raised by SU	Matching Funds from Foundation
1976	$575,000	$852,826	$1,012,187
1977	650,000	995,864	1,131,388
1978	730,000	962,790	1,182,055
1979	825,000	1,354,729	1,624,153
1980	930,000*	1,718,845	1,992,319
Total	$3,710,000	$5,885,054	$6,942,102

*The goal remained at $930,000 for the remaining five years of the ten-year campaign.

The Brown Symposium and the Brown Scholars Program

While the Brown Challenge was being pursued, the restricted endowments already provided by The Brown Foundation for the support of the Brown Chairs had begun to build up a surplus beyond what was being paid out in Brown Chair salaries and for the normal research activities associated with each chair. In order to use the excess for an academic activity that would enhance the disciplines associated with the chairs, the University presented The Brown Foundation with a proposal to use some of these surplus funds to establish a Brown Symposium Series. Each chairholder in rotation would be responsible for presenting a two- or three-day symposium, to take place yearly, that would bring to campus persons of national and international repute in areas represented by their chairs. Distinct from the traditional lecture series, these symposia would be integrated into the regular curricular design of the University. The Foundation approved the request with enthusiasm.

The first symposium on October 25–27, 1978, sponsored by Dr. Robert L. Soulen (chemistry), featured John A. Wheeler, Kip S. Thorn, and Harlan J. Smith, all world-renowned physical scientists. Wheeler was Professor of Physics at the University of Texas and had been one of Ein-

Brown Chairholders at the first Brown Symposium with George and Alice Brown. Left to right: T. Walter Herbert, Jon D. Swartz, Weldon Crowley, Alice Brown, George Brown, Edmund G. McCurtain, and Robert A. Soulen. Southwestern University, Special Collections.

stein's collaborators. Thorn was Professor of Theoretical Physics at the California Institute of Technology. Smith was Director of the McDonald Observatory and former Chairman of the Department of Astronomy at the University of Texas. They spoke on the topic "Cosmology: the Changing Philosophies of Science."[211] The event was an outstanding success and was attended by George and Alice Brown. It established the series on the national scene as a major academic event. The Brown Symposium Series has continued every year since then, bringing to campus speakers, musicians, artists, and writers of distinction. It has attracted visitors from all over the United States to hear them. Some of the topics of these symposia have been "Benjamin Britten and the Ceremony of Innocence," "Punctuated Evolution: The Slender Thread of Life," "Macrohistory: New Visions of the World," "Global Climates: Past, Present & Future," "Communities," "Drawing and Crossing Boundaries: The Roots of Texas Music," "The Human Genome Project: Advances, Repercussions, and Challenges," and "España y América: Cultural Encounter—Enduring Legacy."

As the Brown Symposium was being initiated, President Fleming recommended the establishment of a Brown Scholars Program. It would be funded by the yield from a $615,350 endowment corpus that would be created by transferring a portion of the surplus that investment appreciation had generated in the endowment for the several Brown Chairs.[212] The program was designed to attract about twelve students of the highest caliber and to be Southwestern's premier scholarship award. The Brown Foundation approved this program as well.

Two of Fleming's Major Achievements

Though the Fleming administration was continually buffeted by contrary winds, it made good progress against them. Two developments were most critical—first, the building up of the endowment and the setting up of a regular annual fund-raising program and, second, an improvement in the quality of the faculty and major administrators. The former proceeded primarily from Fleming's successful relationship with Herman and George Brown, which he brought with him from Houston and continued over the course of twenty years as President, finally resulting in the Brown Challenge of 1976 that would last through 1995.

The latter can be measured only indirectly. A rough measure of the improvement of the faculty can be obtained by comparing the honors received and the books published by faculty members in the first four years of his administration and in the last four years. Between 1961 and 1965 no major honors were received and no books were published by any faculty member. From 1977 to 1981 various teachers won honors and published books.

In 1977 Dr. Ellsworth Peterson was presented a Minnie Stevens Piper Foundation Award, one of ten persons chosen from across the state as an outstanding professor by the San Antonio–based foundation. Both Regine Reynolds and Douglas Hooker published books that same year. Hers was entitled *Les Devisants de l'Heptameron: Dix personnages en quete d'audience*, and his was entitled *The Healthy Personality and the Christian Life*. Two books appeared in 1979, one by Francis O'Brien entitled *Two Peacemakers in Paris* and the other by Norman Spellmann entitled *Growing a Soul: The Story of A. Frank Smith*. T. Walter Herbert produced *Moby-Dick and Calvinism* in 1977 and *Marquesan Encounters* in 1980. As a result of his work, Herbert was awarded a Guggenheim Fellowship for 1981–1982. Though he was approached by search by several institutions of note, he chose to stay at Southwestern as the first person to be named University Scholar.

The quality of Fleming's major administrators can be adduced from the fact that four of them eventually left Southwestern to become college presidents. The first was Roy B. Shilling, Jr., who, as already mentioned, went in 1969 to Hendrix College, Conway, Arkansas, then came back to Southwestern as President in 1981. Jerald C. Walker went as President to Baker University, Baldwin City, Kansas, in 1974, then later to Oklahoma City University in the same role. G. Benjamin Oliver went as President to Hiram College, Hiram, Ohio, in 1989. Kirk Treible also left Southwestern in 1989 to become President of Andrew College in Cuthbert, Georgia. Andrew College is a Methodist-related two-year liberal arts college founded in 1854.

The Resignation of Durwood Fleming and the Election of Roy B. Shilling, Jr.

Fleming began staging toward retirement about three years before it actually occurred.[213] He planned it with A. Frank Smith, Jr., after which he informed the Executive Committee that the date would be August 31, 1982. Later reflection, however, led him to believe that he should move the date up a year.[214] Actually, he did not move up the date so much as he determined that the retirement should occur in two stages. The final retirement date remained August 31, 1982, but he proposed retiring from the presidency on July 1, 1981, to become chancellor for his final year. At a called session of the Board of Trustees on June 13, 1980, he read a statement to that effect. The Trustees complied by amending the Bylaws to create the position of chancellor. Fleming was named Chancellor-elect, to become effective at the time his successor was named and in office.[215] The resolution describing the work of the chancellor specified that he would carry out such activities as he, the new President, and the chairman of the Board of Trustees might agree upon. He would be "particularly instrumental in working with the president in continuing the cultivation of friends and institutions in support of the University."[216]

At the same meeting of the Board where the Bylaws were amended to create the position of chancellor, the Trustees established two criteria in regard to the qualifications for the new President. First, they "assumed that the new president would be most effective if he/she were a member of the supporting denomination." Therefore, preference would be given to a Methodist. Secondly, they wanted a person with strong enough academic credentials "to provide leadership of the institution, normally meaning an earned Ph.D.," but equivalent credentials would be acceptable.[217]

The Executive Committee named a Presidential Search Committee composed of Charles N. Prothro, Chairman; A. Frank Smith, Jr., *ex officio;* Students, James Shaw and Casey Triggs; Faculty, Robert L. Soulen and Ellsworth Peterson; Trustees, Roy H. Cullen, Charles L. Giesler, W. Grogan Lord, Robert T. Rork, Mrs. Jack Stauffer Wilkes, and Kelly Williams. Dr. F. Burr Clifford, now retired from the deanship, was asked to serve as Secretary.[218] The committee met only twice, on November 19 and December 3, whereupon "it became obvious they had found the candidate for the presidency who met all requirements—Dr. Roy B. Shilling,

Jr." A special session of the Board was called for December 12, 1980. At the meeting Chairman Prothro announced that the committee recommended Shilling as the thirteenth President and distributed his credentials. The two faculty members and two students on the committee made statements in support of the recommendation. After a unanimous vote by the Trustees in behalf of the recommendation, the Shillings and Dr. Fleming were invited to the meeting. Fleming praised the work of the Search Committee, and Shilling responded appropriately.[219]

Durwood and Lurlyn Fleming built a house at 1400 Vine Street in Georgetown during the spring of 1981 and moved into it so that the new President might occupy the President's home immediately.[220] He established the chancellor's office in the Field House, with Marjorie Beech as his secretary. Miss Beech, as she was known, had served three Presidents—Score for two years and Finch and Fleming for twenty-eight years. She retired with Fleming on August 31, 1982.

Fleming was restless in his role as chancellor. Reflecting on it later, he recognized that "once the last meeting [as President] is over, it's over. There's no question about it. There's nobody asks you or tells you [what to do] anymore. . . . I was cut off from the land of the living. I was just wandering around a good deal of the time. Oh, we began to enjoy our privacy and enjoy our new home. . . . It's just that I had to go through this period of time."[221] The University awarded him an honorary degree at the next Commencement. Shortly after his retirement from the chancellorship, he and Lurlyn moved to Dallas to be closer to their early roots and to their relatives, especially their three children and their families.

Master Plans and Financial Stability (1981–1990)

From Agrarian Backwater to Supersuburb

In 1961, the year in which Durwood Fleming became President of Southwestern, Georgetown was still the rural backwater that it had been fifty years earlier. This backwater status was the main reason for the "removal controversy" of 1910–1911 that resulted in the establishment of Southern Methodist University in Dallas, with the loss for Southwestern of its role as the Central University. During the ensuing half century, Southwestern led a perilous existence, barely escaping bankruptcy and several further attempts to move it elsewhere. Georgetown retained its position as county seat of Williamson County, but the town had little else to recommend it as a growing community. Its population did not change significantly over the fifty-year period, and most of the wealth of the county was in the agrarian east surrounding Taylor. The main railroad connecting Austin with Dallas to the north and Houston to the east ran through Taylor, and the north-south highway between Dallas and Austin through Georgetown was of the stop-and-go variety, passing through many small towns between those two points.

Southwestern emerged from its long night of insolvency in 1937 as a result of a marvelous matching gift from an alumna, Mrs. Louisa Carothers Wiess, just in time to face into World War II. Lyndon Johnson provided the political help needed to supply the school with naval and marine students during that worldwide conflict, and it received a second major infusion of endowment money from Fred McManis, a Houston friend of President Score, during the immediate postwar years. These and related developments, along with the resolute decision of President Finch to begin the process of shedding the big university educational model in favor of a liberal arts model, meant that Southwestern entered the 1960s with a limited but balanced budget, a new campus design, important friends, and a clarified conception of its role as an educational institution. Among its Trustees was Herman Brown, who, with his wife, Margarett, manifested in many ways a special interest in the school.

Durwood Fleming built on these foundations during his twenty-year tenure as President. Especially important was his support for deepening the liberal arts orientation of the institution, successfully conducting several major financial campaigns to meet matching goals established through the generosity of George Brown and The Brown Foundation, and improving the quality of the faculty. It was during his administration as well that Georgetown and Williamson County began to change in remarkable ways.

The agents of change for the city and the county were the construction by the federal government of a north-south interregional highway from Dallas to Austin through Georgetown and Round Rock in the mid-1960s and of two dams on the San Gabriel River during the late '70s. The highway was Interstate 35. The two dams were the North Fork Dam west of Georgetown and the Granger Dam in the eastern part of the county. The highway brought Williamson County into the national network of interstate highways, and the dams created lakes that furnished sufficient water for large-scale industrial growth in the county. As the interstate highway gradually superseded the railroad as the principal mode for freight and passenger transportation in Central Texas, Round Rock and Georgetown gradually superseded Taylor as the major population centers in the county.

In *Road, River, and Ol' Boy Politics: A Texas County's Path from Farm to Supersuburb*, Linda Scarbrough says that these two forces, the road and the river, changed Williamson County "from an agrarian backwater" to a "suburban juggernaut."

> An agricultural center for a century, Williamson County became a suburban phenomenon in the late 1980s—one

of the fastest-growing counties in the United States. Between 1970 and 1980, its population went from thirty-seven thousand (where it had remained essentially frozen since 1900) to seventy-seven thousand. By 1990 it had doubled again to 140,000. At century's end, the county housed a quarter of a million people and the world's top-grossing personal computer manufacturer [Dell]. Fifteen years into the twenty-first century, Williamson County's population is expected to approach a million. It is an Edge City in the making.[1]

These changes, so profound in their consequences for Southwestern and so obvious today, were not widely discerned in 1981 when Roy B. Shilling, Jr., became President of the University. One of those who did understand early on the meaning of these changes was Dr. George C. Hester, Professor of Government and holder of the Lucy King Brown Chair of History at Southwestern, former mayor of Georgetown, and confidant of Senator John Tower. Speaking in 1992 about Hester, Grogan Lord, philanthropist, Georgetown resident, and one of the longest-serving Trustees in Southwestern history, said, "I used to pick him up and we'd go park under a shade tree. He'd talk for hours about what was going to occur economically along the I-35 corridor from San Antonio, up through Austin, to here. It's unreal how it's played out. He was so right. That was more than 30 years ago."[2]

Roy Shilling's Background for the Presidency at Southwestern

No more appropriate person than Roy B. Shilling, Jr., could have been picked to assume the role of President of Southwestern in these circumstances of change. He was a man on the move coming to an area on the move. Illustrative of his lifelong penchant for reaching out after the novel and, what might be to others, impossible, is his reaction to an article that appeared in the *Dallas Morning News* in 1983. Responding to its report that NASA was "working out arrangements to fly journalists, educators, scientists and other private citizens on future shuttle flights," he immediately wrote a letter to the space center expressing a desire "to be among the first college and university presidents, if not the first to volunteer for assignment" on one of the flights. In his letter to NASA he referred to his military service during the Korean War period and to his "excellent" health. He said he had been jogging since 1965, doing three to five miles most days. When a year later he had received no response, he reaffirmed to NASA in another letter his previously expressed interest "in flying in a shuttle when it should be possible."[3]

Shilling was born on April 7, 1931, in the tiny southern Oklahoma town of Enville, population 60. His father was a school superintendent who later became an itinerant Methodist minister. The family moved frequently, and he graduated from high school in the West Texas town of Mertzon, where he played football as a lineman on the high school team. Though he seriously considered attending Southwestern, he finally ended up at McMurry College, where he graduated in 1951. He and his wife, Margaret Riddle of Ovalo, Texas, met when both were students at McMurry in the fall of 1952, after he returned for additional studies. They met in September and were married the next month. He was drafted in November. Their son was born in 1954 while he was in the military service, and their daughter was born in 1957 after the Shillings returned to Texas.[4]

While serving with the 101st Airborne in Kentucky, he was hospitalized with pneumonia and lost forty pounds during his illness. Following his return to duty in the 101st Airborne, and with his unit already having shipped out, he was reassigned to the Third Infantry at Fort McNair in Washington, D.C. Speaking in later years about his military experience, he said: "The experience in the military was very painful for me, though I was fortunate to be in this country and not overseas. But it helped me focus on what was important." He seriously considered entering the ministry, but changed his mind even though he earned a Bachelor of Divinity degree from the Perkins School of Theology at Southern Methodist University in 1957. When asked by Linda Scarbrough years later in an interview why he decided against the ministry, he remarked: "It wasn't so much that I decided against anything, but I suddenly had the opportunity to go back to McMurry College to work for the president there, and it seemed to be very satisfying to be working in that line. There was something terribly attractive to me about being part of a college or university community. I never thought about being president."[5]

He received the M.S. and the Ph.D. degrees from Indiana University, completing his work in 1967. Prior to his becoming President of Hendrix College, he was assistant to the president at McMurry College and Tennessee Wesleyan College, an assistant in development at Ball State University (Indiana), a research associate at Indiana

University, a director of planning and research at Baldwin-Wallace College (Ohio), and executive vice president of Southwestern University. He was a conspicuous success wherever he went.

During those years of service at other institutions, Shilling gained many types of experience, experience that would be useful as he dealt later with his responsibilities at Hendrix and Southwestern. One such experience, expressive of his lifelong determination to press ahead to seek results where others might have given up, is recorded in a letter he received, after his election to the presidency at Southwestern, from the Reverend James E. Whedbee, a member of the Holston Conference of The Methodist Church in Johnson City, Tennessee. Whedbee wrote:

> In June, 1962, I had just graduated from high school in Knoxville, Tennessee, and had been accepted at the University of Tennessee for September. . . . I'm not sure why—maybe it was because I was to be a pre-ministerial student—but you and T[ennessee] W[esleyan] C[ollege] showed an interest in me and began recruiting me. I vividly remember the hot summer day when you visited in my home even though I think I had "warned" you that I was not interested and, furthermore, could not afford the college. After you left, I was interested; and you had helped me begin to see that maybe my family and I could afford it. After a visit to the campus and further conversation with you and others at the college, I was "on my way" to TWC. Through scholarships and the student work program, I was able to graduate with no college debts!! This letter is to say "THANK YOU!"[6]

When Shilling came to Southwestern in 1981, he brought with him a national reputation as a major college administrator. Hendrix College in Conway, Arkansas, the Methodist liberal arts college in that state, had thrived under his guidance since 1969. Major buildings had been built, faculty salaries had been significantly increased, the budget was balanced every year, the endowment had more than doubled, the faculty had been improved, and student enrollment had been stabilized. The College was also one of the early recipients of a Lilly Endowment grant for interdisciplinary program development and faculty renewal and had received a Ford Foundation Venture Fund grant in the early 1970s for faculty development and curricular reform.

While at Hendrix, Shilling had been recognized at the state level through membership on the boards of many prominent private and state organizations. At the national level he had served on the Board of Directors of the National Council of Independent Colleges and Universities from 1972 to 1976, completed two terms on the Executive Committee of the Southern University Conference (1974–78, 1979–1983), was a consultant to the U.S. Office of Education from 1968 to 1974 for reviewing proposals submitted under provisions of the Education Professions Development Act, and had been chairman of the Rhodes scholarship selection Committee for Arkansas in 1973 and 1974. He was one of the incorporators and had served as President of the National Association of Schools and Colleges of the United Methodist Church and had served on the Church's General Board of Higher Education and Ministry from 1972 to 1980. He presented papers regularly on the financing, management, and governance of colleges and universities at institutes and workshops across the nation.[7]

Shilling was the first President to come to Southwestern with formal educational preparation for administration in institutions of higher education and with significant previous experience as a college president. His Ph.D. at Indiana University in higher education administration gave him an academic background in educational philosophy and practice, his year at Southwestern in 1968–1969 (see Chapter XXI) acquainted him with the University itself, and his twelve years at Hendrix gave him the opportunity to experience the reality of the presidential office, both its possibilities and its limitations. There should have been little surprise among students, faculty, administrators, and Trustees that when he came to Southwestern he would come with well-formed ideas about what he wanted to do and that he would immediately begin to speak and act in terms of those ideas.

The Shilling Themes

Reading the speeches delivered by Shilling during his two decades at Southwestern, one is struck by the degree to which he always stayed "on message." He introduced many of the themes and phrases that would become staples of his rhetoric in his first talk to the faculty delivered on December 12, 1980, six months before he formally assumed the office of President. He introduced other comparable ideas and amplified the earlier ones in a speech to the faculty nine months later at the beginning of his first academic year. His basic theme in both speeches had to do with the nature of the Church-related University and his understanding of its function in society. The University is, he said,

> an expression of The United Methodist Church's concern for higher education, which is *value-centered* and focused on the *full development of the whole person.* [It offers] an education which is *cosmopolitan and ecumenical* in nature, which is *open to every person* who might benefit from a rigorous educational experience, and one which calls persons *to free themselves from ignorance* and parochialism, and from the limitations of a particular age, upbringing, or circumstance. . . .
>
> [T]he University is *both a learning and a faith community.* As a learning community it should *reflect the highest traditions of the academy,* and as a faith community it should *reflect a broad central core of commonly shared values rooted in the Judeo-Christian ethic.*[8] [Italics added.]

The words italicized in these two paragraphs continued to appear in Shilling's speeches and writings during the entirety of his nineteen-year administration. In addition to these fundamentals, he referred time and again to other related ideas. He said that in order to move Southwestern University into a position of prominence, the "creative energies" of the faculty must be freed to make it possible for them to make the contribution of which they were capable. As for himself, the sole criterion for his decision-making would be to do "what is in the university's long-term best interest and welfare." In going about its business, the University must particularly avoid the bane of narrowness. There must be within the University "a healthy respect for diversity and for pluralism."[9]

Important for the Southwestern of today, he said, was its "rugged sense of identity" rooted in its origin during the Republic of Texas. It should never lose that sense of identity as it gained prominence on the national scene. Critical to the success of that enterprise would be the setting up of a planning process that focused the self-image of the institution "in distinct and clear-cut fashion." Though Southwestern University had become an undergraduate institution through historical circumstance, he asserted that that mission was appropriate for it today. It would "continue to be a baccalaureate, degree-granting institution, or essentially so," moving to a position of "national maturity" by enhancing what it was already doing well and by modifying those aspects of its life and work that needed to be realigned in response to changing needs and conditions. Shilling concluded his speech to the faculty in August 1981 by stating that "the end of learning is serving. Knowledge without compassion and perspective fails to achieve its full potential and is misdirected in its goals."[10]

"National Maturity" and the Master Plan

The element in Shilling's early talks drawing most attention from both the faculty and outsiders was the phrase "national maturity." It was not common in educational parlance and had been chosen expressly by Shilling to signify the goal toward which he felt Southwestern should strive. He used it over and over again in his writings, conversations, and talks in his first eighteen months as the appropriate phrase for what Southwestern should achieve as an educational institution.

The phrase "national maturity" sprang from Shilling's recognition that Southwestern's success had not placed it among the distinguished liberal arts institutions found in the north central and northeastern parts of the country, but that by resolute effort it could achieve that status in the foreseeable future. The idea was very clear in his mind, and he had difficulty understanding why it did not gain immediate traction with the faculty. Some of the faculty treated the matter humorously and said that Southwestern must first achieve "national puberty" before it could move on to "national maturity." This may have resulted from their lack of belief in the concept of a master plan, which was being advanced rapidly during these months. After their experience of many years in which Southwestern had operated with only a vague sense of direction, there was little faith that all aspects of university planning could be encompassed in a single process that would result in a precise planning document that would be adhered to by everyone. This concept of a master plan, so dubious in the minds of some people, proved to be a powerful mechanism for achieving the results for which the Shilling administration came to be noted.

Shilling took the teasing about "national puberty" with good grace and, with a laconic smile, joined in the humor by referring to it on several occasions in joking fashion. In mid-1982 a reporter tried to define precisely the meaning of "national maturity" during a long interview with him. The *Dallas Morning News,* said the reporter, had defined it as "national prominence" or as "a national caliber program." These interpretations were partially accurate but were not broad enough to encompass all that Shilling thought the term should mean.[11] He defined it clearly in the first Master Plan in 1982, where it appeared as the overall goal for the University.

> The goal of Southwestern University as it moves toward its sesquicentennial celebration in 1990 is to become an institution of national maturity. National maturity for Southwestern is understood to mean the achievement of a level of performance in every area of University life and work equivalent to that generally recognized on the national scene as appropriate for the very best institutions which are committed to undergraduate education as their central mission, to maintaining a strong liberal arts tradition, and are known for the high quality of their academic programs and the superior achievements of their graduates.[12]

However much or little the faculty may have accepted the term, it remained central to Shilling's thinking, as defined in the first Master Plan. In a report to the Trustees in 1991, he said that "it is evident that we have achieved national maturity in the 1980s."[13] When in 1994 the Carnegie Foundation for the Advancement of Teaching moved Southwestern from the category of "regional" to "national" in the first comprehensive reclassification of American institutions of higher education in some years, he said that the change was "a matter of great importance in our rise to national maturity."[14]

The SACS Reaffirmation Committee Report and the Master Plan

The faculty under the leadership of Dr. Judson S. Custer had almost completed the decennial SACS Self-Study for 1981–1982 when Shilling assumed the presidency. Though he entered into the process almost at the point of its completion, he had the development of a comprehensive Master Plan for the University included prominently among its recommendations.[15] The University had fared well in the Self-Study of 1971, and there was no reason to believe that it would not do so this time. The University had made evident gains during the last decade.

Nevertheless, the report of the visiting team disappointed the campus community, just as the team did not make a strong impression on campus members during its visit. Some of the team members were not considered to be up to the task to which they had been assigned, some of the recommendations of the team were considered to be gratuitous, and the factual information on which some of their recommendations were based was faulty. Shilling was annoyed by the fact that the Reaffirmation Committee stated that the University "is beginning to formulate several master plans," as if the master plan concept was a hit-or-miss effort in its first stages rather than an almost completed document available for the team at the time of its visit. He was also perturbed by the fact that the person responsible for an examination of the fiscal affairs section of the Self-Study presumed to instruct him and his fiscal officer about how to improve the financial operation of the institution. Southwestern had balanced its budget for the last five years, and he, as the chief executive officer of two colleges, had never run a deficit budget.

Southwestern's response to the Reaffirmation Committee report covered eight pages.[16] It was very detailed and, though worded respectfully, can only be taken as a statement by the University that the visiting team did not, as Shilling reported to the Board of Trustees, do its "homework" adequately.[17] The changes made by the Reaffirmation Committee from the rough draft to the final copy of the report were minor. Only a few of the most glaring misstatements and errors of fact were corrected.[18] The procedure of the Reaffirmation Committee and its response to Southwestern's objections were such that Shilling considered the process flawed.

Shilling was well acquainted with the self-study process. At the time of his election to the presidency of Southwestern, he was vice chairman and chairman-elect of the Executive Board of the Commission on Institutions of Higher Education in the North Central Association of Schools and Colleges. He felt that the Southern Association process as represented by the example he had just experienced was unhelpful. Though he was entreated to become a Reaffirmation Committee leader from time to time, he did not become involved until the last year of his presidency. At that time he was called to lead a SACS team to visit Lambuth University in Jackson, Tennessee. After the visit was over, E. Ellis Arnold III, President of the institution, sent a letter of appreciation to him thanking him for his leadership. He said: "The recommendations by the committee will be extremely beneficial to us in our quest for continued improvement. Everyone was extremely complimentary of your thoroughness in guiding us through the SACS visit. Your words of encouragement will continue to inspire our efforts, and we are grateful for your interest in the future of Lambuth."[19]

The Master Planning Process: 1981–1986

One of Shilling's first acts as President was to send a memo to the University community stating his desire to enter actively into the planning process. He said that he would chair the University Council, the council responsible for the process, when his presence on campus allowed, but that Dr. William B. Jones would preside at meetings of both the faculty and the University Council when he was away.[20] As Administrative Vice President and Provost with a leadership role in the Council, Jones took over responsibility for the process and led it as its "scribe" until he stepped down from his position in 1986, though he still remained as a contributing member of the Council after that time. As scribe, he worked in concert with the faculty member chosen each year to chair the Master Plan Subcommittee to develop the agenda, to take minutes, and to prepare the interim drafts of emerging plans.

The planning process followed the same general pattern each year, though it changed slightly as time and experience dictated. The University Council completed its first plan in the spring of 1982, and modified the document annually thereafter. The Council was composed of representative faculty, student, and administrative members. Meetings of the Council were open to all faculty members, and open meetings of the Master Plan Subcommittee were held regularly, at which faculty members made suggestions for the annual plans as they were developed. Each year the University Council forwarded the finished Master Plan to the full faculty for modification and/or approval at its regular meetings. After its approval, the faculty sent the Master Plan to the Board of Trustees, upon whose approval it became the official university planning document. The Board selected from among the priorities suggested in the Master Plan those that would become the major University priorities for the year.

The first product of the Master Plan Subcommittee in the fall of 1981 was a substantial document entitled "Material for a Master Plan for Southwestern University."[21] It was composed of all the material from the past that might be useful, such as "The Quest for Excellence at Southwestern University," produced in the year before Shilling came, suggestions made by faculty members at open meetings held from time to time, and speeches made by the President. This material formed the basis for the first, forty-seven-page Master Plan adopted by the faculty and the Board in April 1982.

The first Plan included an Introduction, an Overall Master Plan Goal (see above), and ten chapters devoted to individual topics. Each chapter was divided into three sections: Background, Goal, and Objectives and Activities. Illustrative of the organization of all the chapters is the first chapter, Mission and Church Relatedness. It had its own goal and nine objectives, with each objective having from one to four specific activities to be engaged in for its accomplishment. The objectives and activities were very specific. Chapter III, Physical Plant and Grounds, estimated that $35,196,000 would be needed to take care of deferred maintenance for the four years 1981–1982 to 1984–1985.[22] Corresponding narrative and numerical goals were set for many other objectives.

By 1985–1986 the ten chapters had expanded to twelve and were as follows:

One.	Mission and Church Relatedness
Two.	The Academic Program
Three.	Physical Plant and Grounds
Four.	Faculty and Staff
Five.	Student Affairs
Six.	Enrollment and Student Aid
Seven.	Development
Eight.	Institutional Management
Nine.	Public Relations/Constituency
Ten.	Fiscal Affairs
Eleven.	Intercollegiate Athletics
Twelve.	Special Opportunities

The "Special Opportunities" chapter authorized the President to secure an unforeseen advantage when overriding reasons for pursuing that advantage did not allow for regular procedures to be followed. In such cases the President would "then inform the University Council of his action and the reasons therefore."[23]

The second Master Plan, for 1982–1983, produced a description of what the University should look like in 1990. In that year:

- the average SAT score for entering students should be 1050;
- the average faculty salary should be at the 95 percent level of equivalent schools as measured on the A.A.U.P. scale;
- the student body should number 1,250;
- the market value of the endowment should be $90 to $105 million;

- a reconfigured campus should be integrated around a central academic mall according to a Skidmore, Owings & Merrill plan;
- the library should be twice its present size, with 250,000 volumes and with a budget comprising 7.4 percent of E&G expenditures;
- the University would have modernized its management by using the latest advances in technology;
- it would have a quality residence hall system in both facilities and program, with three of its residence halls having been renovated and a new one built;
- it would have an integrated academic/student life educational environment emphasizing the development of the whole person as a responsible and mature change agent in society;
- it would have an integrated liberal arts curriculum with educational objectives clearly articulated and related to students developing as effective leaders;
- it would have a faculty operating as teacher-scholars with active professional lives complementing and reinforcing their educational activity in behalf of students;
- it would have a student body whose graduates entered into business and professional life easily and successfully and who competed for (and succeeded in obtaining) nationally based graduate and professional school scholarships;
- it would present an image in the public domain as a school known for the excellence of its educational program and the high achievement of its graduates;
- it would be an institution that takes its Church-relatedness seriously and tries to translate that relationship into effective ways of implementing the essence of the Judeo-Christian heritage;
- it would have a strong alumni program based on the appreciation of the graduate for the quality and humanizing dimension of his/her educational program at Southwestern; and
- it would have a smoothly functioning public relations and development program whose effectiveness makes it possible to draw a high level of support from contributions made by alumni, friends, foundations, and corporations.[24]

Only once before in its history had any Southwestern President begun his administration with such a clear-cut statement of what he hoped to achieve. President J. W. Bergin had begun his tenure in 1935 with an almost off-the-cuff statement of five major goals for his presidency (see Chapter XV). Though he achieved those goals, their achievement was not so much a matter of planning as it was of the logic of development, of moving in linear fashion from one goal to another without an overall development program. There never was in his case a recognized strategy from the outset for the achievement of his goals, particularly one that encompassed the entirety of university operation, as in the case of the Master Plan of 1983. The observation made by President Finch in 1992 about his administration is probably true for all Southwestern Presidents until the time of Shilling. He said: "We were running for one year at a time, or one day or one week at a time."[25] In the case of Shilling, the goals outlined in the 1983 Master Plan were those established by the faculty and Trustees with his encouragement. They were set in the context of a Master Plan framework that envisioned an entire development process. Each goal was framed in terms of major objectives to be achieved and accompanied by specific activities to be carried out in procuring it.

The Trustees adopted a formal resolution in October 1982 affirming the master planning process, accepting the current document as the basis for future planning, requiring that it be modified and approved annually by the Board, and stating that "the President [should] organize the development program of the University so as to achieve Master Plan goals."[26]

Several years passed after the adoption of the first Master Plan in 1982 before the University community fully understood that the day of adding, during the year, budget items that did not appear in the Master Plan was over. Shilling referred to this fact when he told the Board "that some stress has been felt within the University community as we have moved toward funding Master Plan priorities in preference to more traditional funding patterns, but that this stress should disappear over the years as the budget comes more and more to reflect the Plan priorities."[27]

The Facilities and Grounds Master Plan

Though the term Master Plan is generally taken to refer to the programmatic plan described above, there were in fact two master plans that ran concurrently. The second was the Facilities and Grounds Master Plan, some-

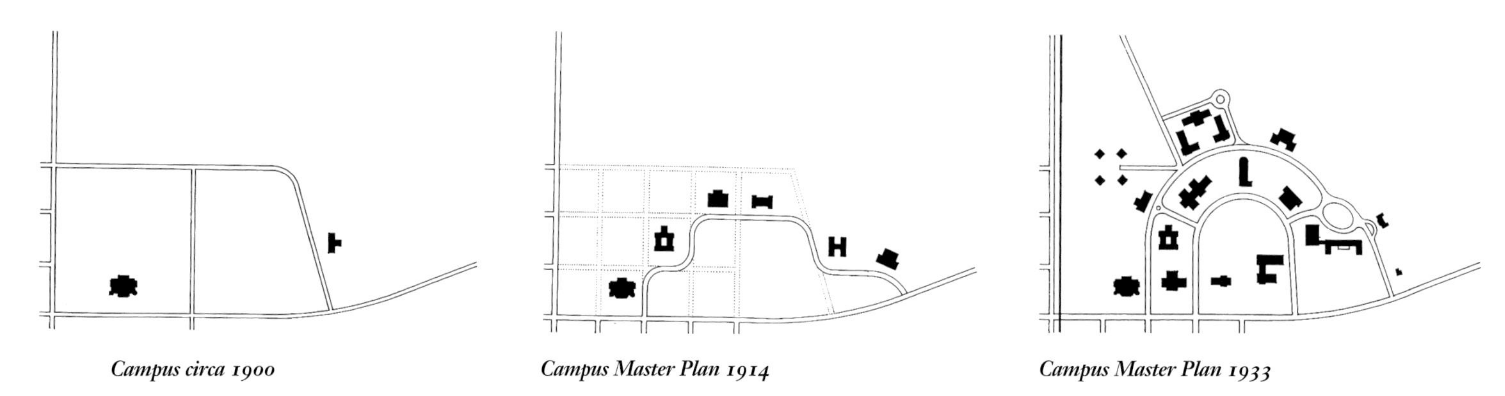

Campus circa 1900 *Campus Master Plan 1914* *Campus Master Plan 1933*

Facilities and grounds designs and/or master plans, 1914–1999. Southwestern University Publications Department.

times called the Campus Master Plan. The process for producing it began simultaneously with the one already described, though it was very different in operation. Due to the technical nature of the task involved in its creation, the planning committee for it was made up exclusively of Trustees who worked with the President and other selected administrators. Its first major accomplishment was to choose an architectural firm to design a "physical plan" for the University, after which it and the chosen firm engaged in a series of discussions with a broad cross section of Southwestern constituents.[28]

The firm chosen in December 1981 to draw up the Facilities and Grounds Master Plan was Skidmore, Owings & Merrill (SOM), one of the largest architectural firms in the country. It had designed the U.S. Air Force Academy campus in 1958, the 100-story John Hancock Tower in Chicago in 1965–1970, the one-million-square-foot Bank of America World Headquarters in San Francisco in 1969, and the 109-story Sears Tower in Chicago in 1973.

Craig W. Hartman, the architect responsible for the Southwestern plan, headed the SOM Houston office in 1981. Still active today, during his career Hartman has received over fifty special recognitions for design, including five National American Institute of Architects Honor Awards. In 2001 he received a special award from the California Chapter of AIA in recognition of his "lifetime achievement in architectural design."[29] One of his most successful creations was his visionary plan for the facilities and grounds of Southwestern University. Though Southwestern and SOM severed their relationship amicably in 1991, when SOM's Houston branch relocated away from that city, the fundamental concepts of the Hartman plan have guided the physical development of the University ever since.[30] Hartman wrote a chapter describing the development of the plan for the volume published in 1999 commemorating the nineteen-year tenure of Shilling at Southwestern. The volume was entitled *Southwestern: A University's Transformation.*[31]

After a careful examination of the interaction of students and teachers as they pursued their daily round of activities on campus, Hartman and his study team validated President Shilling's observation that "the campus seemed mysteriously vacant, even during the peak of the academic year with the entire student body present." The reason for this apparent lack of activity became clear when he and his team recognized that the main student campus destinations were located on the periphery rather than focused toward the center. The center of the campus was an area to be navigated to reach other places rather than the place where the most significant campus activities occurred. The fundamental concept of the SOM plan thus came to be the creation of a clear focus for the University at the heart of the campus. The major obstacle to creating this new space, says Hartman, was the crescent-shaped drive built during the mid-1950s. The cars parked end-to-end the length of the drive created a wall. Difficult to penetrate, it

> had essentially broken the heart of the campus away, like an island, from the rest of the University. The new plan called for a tree-lined pedestrian promenade replacing this drive, with parking moved to smaller, localized lots on the campus perimeter. This promenade [today] links all the principal buildings surrounding the academic mall and also clearly defines the edges of the central space at the heart of the campus.[32]

The plan minimized the use of the car and favored a walking campus instead as a means of increasing inter-

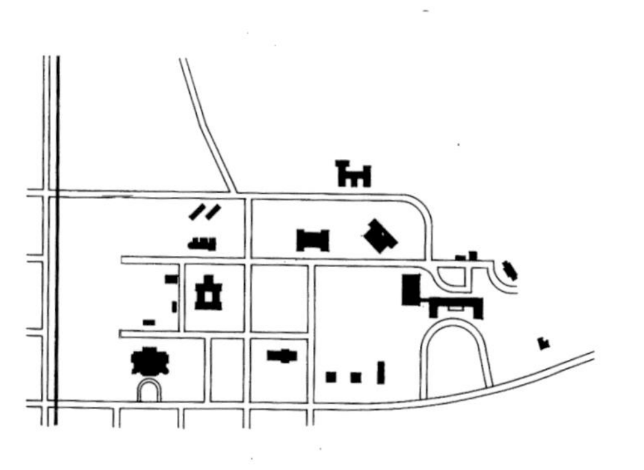

Campus circa 1950

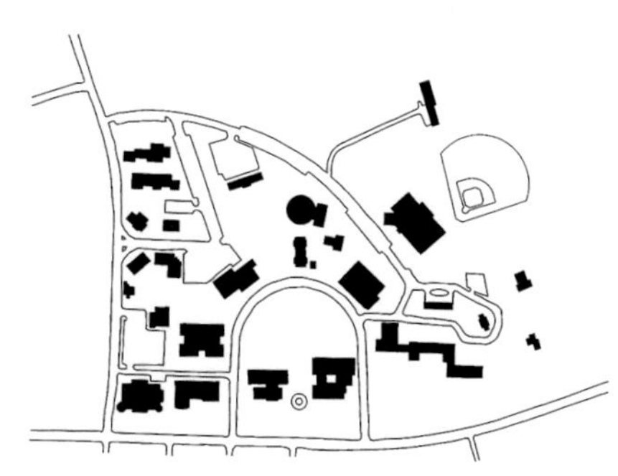

Campus circa 1982

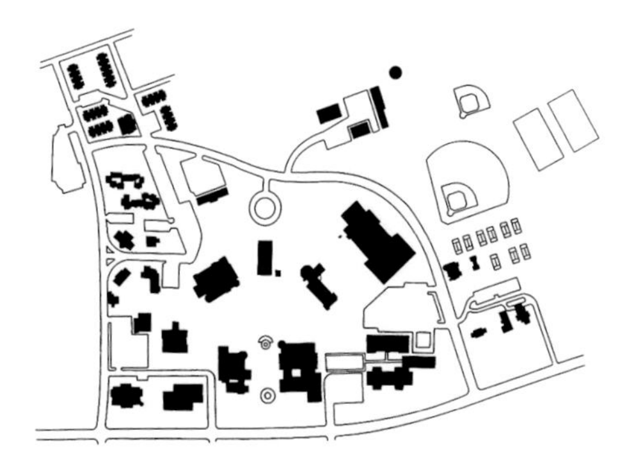

Campus circa 1999

action among students. Informal places of gathering were created for coincidental encounters with fellow students and faculty. The plan also called for gradually phasing academic space away from campus buildings on the periphery and centralizing it in buildings on the mall.

Looking at the configuration of the campus in 1999 in preparation for writing his chapter for the Shilling commemorative book, Hartman said that "it is extraordinary how much has been accomplished. The plan largely has been realized and the campus transformed."[33] A major reason for the success of the plan has been the fact that "it did not rely upon the imposition of a single major new structure to redefine the campus character." Rather, it relied upon "gently building" upon what existed. Because the plan was developed at the outset of the Shilling administration, the more than twenty-five principal construction projects carried out during his administration were all placed where they would achieve maximum advantage in accomplishing the objective of the plan. The plan received a design excellence award from *Progressive Architecture* in 1983.[34] The campus today is often hailed by outsiders as one of the most beautiful and functionally efficient liberal arts campuses in the United States.

By 1986 the master planning process had become a normal feature of University operation. Shilling was very pleased with its success. He remarked to the Board that "the master planning process which we established five years ago has been directly responsible for helping us define clearly our highest priorities. By suggesting additions and changes each year, the Master Plan has been updated annually as a vital, living document, reflecting mission, goals, and our highest priorities in light of changing conditions."[35]

Herbert E. Dishman Helps Get the Plan Underway

When one looks at the initiation of the master planning process from a distance of twenty-five years, the resulting master plans seem so rational as to have been almost inevitable. Both the Programmatic and the Facilities and Grounds Master Plans were in place by the end of Shilling's first year. Yet one thing was missing—the money needed to finance the many background tasks that needed to be performed to begin turning the Programmatic Master Plan into reality. Since the regular budget had been instituted without providing sufficient funds for this purpose, the plan suffered the prospect of being underfunded. At that point, on June 16, 1982, a longtime supporter of the institution, Herbert E. Dishman, wrote Shilling that he wanted to give $100,000 to be used by the President where most needed. Shilling responded immediately, stating that it would be used for the "most urgent institutional priorities" related to the Master Plan. These priorities consisted of necessary but unexciting infrastructure expenditures needed to get the program off the ground, particularly in the university relations and admissions areas. Among other things, these included a communications audit and publications assistance. When asked by me to list for this book the names of some of those Trustees who had influenced the institution most strongly during his administration, Shilling placed the name of Herb Dishman high on his list. Dishman's gift of $100,000 to "stake the new president," as Dishman put it, was critical to the early success of the Master Plan. In a subsequent letter that summer to Dishman, Shilling said: "I don't know if you really can appreciate how much of an impact your gift of $100,000 will have on the life of this institution."[36]

Dishman, a strong Methodist layman in Beaumont, had become interested in Southwestern when his daughter, Mary, became a student there in 1957, during the Finch administration. A victim of polio, she had to leave after a year for surgery. Eleven years later, in 1968, Dishman made a gift of $50,000 to the first three-year Brown Challenge campaign of 1968–1970 under President Fleming.[37] Southwestern conferred an honorary degree on him in 1970, and he was made a Trustee in 1973. Two granddaughters graduated from Southwestern, one, Kristen, in 1985 and the other, Rhonda, in 1987.

Dishman's first big money came from his formation of the Prudential Drilling Co. of Houston. He later served on the board of the First Security National Bank of Beaumont. He was also at one time chair of the Board of Trustees at Trinity Methodist Church in that city and was a Trustee of Lon Morris College, of the Texas Methodist Foundation, and of the Moody House in Galveston. He and his wife, Kate Kuhn, whom he had married in 1933, had similar beliefs regarding the use of their money. As of this writing, Kate lives in Kerrville at the age of ninety-five next to her daughter, Mary Sherlock.

Dishman's beliefs about the proper use of money caught the attention of the *Beaumont Enterprise* in 1983, and he was featured in an article. Born in Port Arthur, Texas, on September 18, 1901, Dishman grew up poor but not hungry. He worked hard to earn his first $100,000 but, according to the reporter, couldn't wait to give it away.

> To have kept all of the money, Dishman says, would have enslaved him, cowed him, beaten him. He kept some for himself and for his wife, just enough. He never stopped earning money and he never stopped giving it away. . . . "My daddy was a rice farmer, and we spent the day out in the cold drying rice one time. On the way home we spotted this German boy without a coat on, standing up against a shed," Dishman says. "Papa stopped and gave him what was left of our lunch and took off his coat and gave it to the boy and walked home in his shirtsleeves." . . . His uncle offered him [Herbert] a real estate job that led him into the oil business and great wealth. . . . Never having gone to college himself, Dishman valued education as his father had. After earning his first large sum, $112,000, he donated it in parts to Lon Morris College, the Methodist Children's School in Waco and Southwestern University in Georgetown. While he maintained ties with all of them, it is with Southwestern that he reserves a special feeling.[38]

As mentioned by the reporter, Dishman's feeling for Southwestern was special. Particularly notable in his correspondence with Presidents Fleming and Shilling was his wish that his money should serve the best interests of the institution as defined by its Presidents, not himself. Also notable in his correspondence with them was his assurance that his commitments to Southwestern were always the first of his philanthropic donations to be paid each year. He was thus in character when he sent Shilling the unsolicited $100,000 in 1982 that was used to jump-start the Master Plan. Today there are a Herbert and Kate Dishman Chair in Science and a Herbert and Kate Dishman Professorship. Dr. Vicente Villa, Professor of Biology, was appointed as the first holder of the chair in 1985. Dr. Leonard Giesecke, Professor of Economics, held the professorship at the time of his untimely death from a heart attack in 1994. Dishman left in his will instructions for his trustees to complete his commitments to Southwestern after his death. They did so and over half a million dollars came to the University from them in accordance with his wishes.

It was to attend the graduation of his granddaughter Rhonda, in May 1987, that Dishman and his wife made their last visit to the campus. Shilling visited him on October 31, 1988, scarcely a month and a half before his death. He and Rick Eason subsequently attended Dishman's funeral service in Beaumont on December 13. Though it would be rash to try to select all the Trustees whose service and giving pattern over the years have been exemplary, certainly the name of Herbert E. Dishman would be on everyone's list as being worthy of that honor.

The Brown Challenge Threshold Campaign and the Death of George Brown

The most promising element for the future of Southwestern at the time of Shilling's assumption of the presidency was the recent informal notification by George R. Brown that the Brown Challenge would be extended another ten years until December 31, 1995. Edward A. Clark referred to it in his remarks on July 1, 1981, the day that Shilling took office.[39] Since the Foundation would not officially vote the extension until November 23, the impending extension of the campaign was not publicized immediately. In addition, The Brown Foundation had opened the prospect of negotiations with the three institutions in the program for improving some of the features of the grant. These negotiations were completed speedily, and a new Matching Funds Program Agreement was signed by the Foundation on December 9, 1981, and by Southwestern a week later.[40] The most conspicuous changes were an improvement in the incentive awards and a new pattern of direct awards. From the eighth through the twentieth years the direct awards would remain constant. By raising $930,000 each year, Southwestern could qualify for $1,375,000.[41]

Once the new Brown Challenge Agreement had been signed, Shilling moved to stabilize the fund-raising program by placing it on a multiple-year basis. His suggestion that the Brown Challenge campaign be moved to a three-year plan was approved by the Foundation and began with the years 1982–1984. It would be called the Brown Challenge Threshold Campaign and would set an aggregate goal of $6 million for the three years. Shilling explained it to alumni and friends as follows:

> To increase the flow of operating gifts and grants, to encourage larger gifts of appreciated property, and stocks as well as cash, to enable the University to be more precise and systematic in planning its revenues and expenditures on a continuing basis, to offer donors tax economies achieved in making a three-year gift in any one or more of the three years, to free staff and trustees to solicit building and endowment gifts, the University is inviting its alumni and friends to give indication of their support patterns on a multiple-year basis rather than one year at a time as has been the practice.[42]

The Threshold Campaign had the effect Shilling sought, especially increasing the flow of big gifts to the Brown Challenge and building projects through its use of various techniques whereby big givers could maximize their gifts to advantage for tax and other purposes. By April 15, 1982, over $2.5 million had been given or pledged. By December 27, 1982, the amount had risen to $4,222,766, and by April 22, 1983, it was $5,022,364.[43]

The unique aspect of this success was that most of it had been achieved before a public announcement of the extension of the Brown Challenge was made, a delay from mid-December 1982 until early November 1983. Around November 5, the *Chronicle of Higher Education* and newspapers throughout the state ran articles announcing that a $27.9 million challenge grant had been made by The Brown Foundation, Inc., to be paid over twenty years. Shilling stated in news releases that the $27.9 million from the Foundation would be added to the $20.9 million that Southwestern would raise, making a total of $48.8 million as a minimum over the twenty years. It was touted as "the largest challenge gift ever made to a small college in the United States."[44] The announcement of the extension had been delayed purposely as a matter of timing to enhance the Threshold Campaign and to help bring it to completion. The timing of the publicity was validated by the fact that the *Texas Magazine*, the magazine included each week in the Sunday *Houston Chronicle*, featured Southwestern as its cover story, with a long narrative and picture layout on May 13, 1984.[45]

While Southwestern was chalking up these successes for the Brown Challenge, it lost the person responsible for the Brown Challenge itself—George R. Brown. He died on January 22, 1983. He had visited the campus twice in 1982—for the inauguration of Roy Shilling in May and on the occasion when his wife, Alice Pratt Brown, received an honorary degree in October.[46] In his Board Report after Brown's death, Shilling said about him: "It was he, perhaps, more than any other person, who made it possible for the University community to believe that Southwestern could become one of the best small universities in the country."[47] At the same Board meeting, the Trustees adopted a resolution expressing "its recognition of gratitude for his unparalleled beneficence to the University, which has given birth to a new institutional self-concept."[48] A year later Alice died, and her funeral was held on April 14, 1984. To honor her, the Board adopted a resolution to the family extolling her "wise, constructive philanthropy" that "influenced the growth of the arts and higher education in Texas and continue[s] to benefit Southwestern University."[49]

In a letter to John H. Duncan, a later Board chair, Jake Schrum, Vice President for University Relations, included a report of the financial contributions from The Brown Foundation to Southwestern University during the period of George and Alice's trusteeship in the Foundation. It was as follows:

Contributions from The Brown Foundation to Southwestern University 1954–1984.[50]

Summary

Contributions on matching fund pledges	$15,688,781.86
Contributions for Chairs/Professorships	895,675.00
Contributions for buildings	164,176.64
Contributions for scholarships	83,633.38
Contributions matching individual gifts	16,060.84
Grants to current operations, memorials, fine arts, etc.	310,625.00
Total contributions	**$17,158,952.72**

The feeling of Alice and George Brown for Southwestern is perhaps most evident in their leading The Brown Foundation in 1981 to extend the Brown Challenge for ten years beyond the original grant period of 1985. Recognizing that the prospects of their own mortality would probably not outlast Southwestern's need for the Brown Challenge, they extended it to 1995. George lived for only a little more than a year after the extension agreement was signed in 1981; Alice lived less than two-and-a-half years after the signing.

Financial Results of Shilling's First Year; Jake Schrum Comes on Board

The financial results of Shilling's first year at Southwestern were astounding. From the date of his assumption of the presidency on July 1, 1981, to his Board Report of October 13, 1982, Southwestern received a total of $13,409,300 in gifts or pledges for all purposes. This amount was itemized in the Board Report as follows:

$5,000,000, Houston Endowment Inc. (residence halls);
$4,000,000, pledges (Threshold Campaign);
$1,732,800, Brown Foundation, Inc. (endowment);
$1,000,000, Cullen Foundation (faculty development);
$1,000,000, Mabee Foundation (residence halls);
$250,000, Moody Foundation (residence halls);
$200,000, Pew Memorial Trust (computerize library holdings);
$100,000, Dr. and Mrs. Herbert Dishman (President's discretionary fund);
$100,000, Miss Eula Ione Clay (bequest-endowment);
$26,500, Davidson Family Foundation (scholarships).[51]

When asked by a reporter for the *Austin American-Statesman* how the school could raise so much with such a small development staff, Vice President Schrum replied that it was due to the work of that staff and the volunteer efforts of the Board of Trustees. He emphasized that the University did not hire professional fund-raisers. "We work very hard—there's no getting around it," Schrum said.[52]

Schrum's comment about not using professional fund-raisers highlighted a primary feature of Shilling's fund-raising practice. He often used outside professional help to provide the University with the best information possible on whatever issue was at hand, but he always depended on himself, his staff, Trustees, and friends to do any fund-raising. If he had had reason to employ anyone to help with fund-raising, it would have been the Richard F. Dini & Associates firm. Dini had worked for the University as "fund-raising counsel" during almost the entire decade of the 1970s, first with the Program for Progress after 1971 and later after 1975–1976 with the Brown Challenge, which he had helped design for George R. Brown.

Though Dini offered his services to Shilling soon after he took office in 1981, Shilling employed him only one time, in 1983, to conduct a feasibility study for the fund-raising campaign then being contemplated. After conducting the study, he reported that the desired campaign goal of $30–35 million was reasonable "in an intensive, well organized effort over a two to three-year period." He suggested that the campaign should "be operated as a quiet, systematic effort aimed primarily at some 300 major gift prospects." This assessment became the basis for Board approval on October 28, 1983, of what was designed to be a two-and-a-half- to three-year Campaign for Southwestern to raise the $30–35 million.[53] Shilling did not subsequently accept Dini's contract to supply a person to do professional fund-raising and counseling services on the scene, preferring to do it himself with his own staff, now headed by Vice President Schrum.[54]

Jake Schrum was the first major administrative person employed by Shilling after he came to the University. Shilling presented him to the Board of Trustees as the new Vice President for University Relations on January 22, 1982.[55] Whereas President Fleming had largely operated as his own Vice President for Development, Shilling filled the position with a person he considered to be an up-and-coming development officer on the national scene. Schrum was at the time Vice President at Texas Wesleyan College in Fort Worth.

Born February 9, 1946, Schrum was a native of Sugar Land. He attended Southwestern from 1964 to 1968, where he was a member of Blue Key and President of the Student Association. He met his wife, Jane Woodman, while a student there. After graduating from Southwestern with a B.A. in Psychology in 1968, he attended the Perkins School of Theology for two years. He returned to Southwestern in 1970 as an Administrative Intern, working with Chaplain Charles Neal.[56] He was also Director of Herman Brown Residence Hall, where he and his wife lived. He completed his M.Div. degree at Yale University. Before assuming his position at Texas Wesleyan, he served on the staff at Wesleyan University in Connecticut, Yale University, and Muhlenberg College in increasingly important positions.

He would remain at Southwestern for three-and-a-half years until he left for Emory University, where he became Vice President for Development and Planning in the summer of 1985.

The Endowment and the Economic Situation in Texas during the 1980s

Given the extraordinary financial results achieved by Southwestern during the first year of Shilling's tenure and the increasing success that occurred during the decade of the 1980s, one might be tempted to attribute that success simply by the increase in the endowment. It increased from $37,914,778 in 1981 to $126,672,522 in 1990, a 334 percent gain, truly a significant increase. That increase can be explained almost entirely by the 12.0 percent annual gain experienced from the rise in the Dow-Jones Industrial Average from July 1, 1981, to July 1, 1990, and from the annual gifts by The Brown Foundation to the endowment during that time that also experienced the same annual market gain.[57] That explanation, however, is too simple. The endowment gain, for all its importance, does not measure the full range of factors that were at work during the '80s, particularly the tense economic climate of the decade. A true understanding of Southwestern's success during the '80s must take into account a number of factors that cannot be measured by the endowment increase alone.

The economic improvement in the country during the 1980s was not one that created much confidence, especially in Texas. James Michener describes the climate of the '80s in his foreword to Red McCombs's autobiography, *The Red Zone*. Michener says that when he came to Texas in 1981 "the state was then at the crest of the oil and real estate boom, and everyone seemed to be rolling in money. By the time I had finished my novel, the boom was over and the crash had wiped out countless oil companies and land developers and ranchers. There were six or seven massive office buildings in Austin and Houston, newly finished, with no tenants. They were referred to as 'see-throughs.'"[58] One of the major reasons for the crash of the oil market was that OPEC abandoned its fixed price for oil on December 8, 1986.[59]

Another factor disturbing the economic situation was the savings and loan debacle. It roiled the economic waters of the nation for about a decade, from October 1979 until Congress enacted the Financial Institutions Reform, Recovery, and Enforcement Act (FIRREA) of 1989. "Disaster struck," says one account, "after Paul Volcker, then chairman of the Federal Reserve board, decided in October 1979 to restrict the growth of the money supply, which, in turn, caused interest rates to skyrocket. Between June 1979 and March 1980 short-term interest rates rose by over six percentage points, from 9.06 percent to 15.2 percent. In 1981 and 1982 combined, the S&L industry collectively reported almost $9 billion in losses. Worse, in mid-1982 all S&Ls combined had a negative net worth . . . of $100 billion, an amount equal to 15 percent of the industry's liabilities."[60] Savings and loan institutions failed all across the country, nowhere more than in Texas.

In addition to these problems, the stock market, in spite of its general advance, was erratic. It declined during the academic years 1981–1982, 1983–1984, and 1987–1988. On Monday, October 19, 1988, the stock market plunged 508 points, 22.6 percent, a larger percentage decline in one day than on Black Thursday of 1929. These gyrations of the stock market, combined with the other factors mentioned above, made people nervous. Red McCombs felt the effects of the situation keenly. "At the time," he said, "I had my own cash shortage, the result of what was referred to in Texas as the financial holocaust. Oil prices had crashed, the real estate market collapsed, banks and savings and loans had gone belly up. I had plenty of assets, but not much that was liquid."[61] He called the late 1980s and early 1990s "scary financial times."[62]

In 1983 Shilling also called attention to the fact that the financial nervousness in the country was exacerbated among institutions of independent higher education by special circumstances. Independent institutions were experiencing declining enrollments because the pool of traditional college-age students was shrinking, a steady-state personnel situation had developed, energy costs were spiraling upward, and state institutions were beginning to compete strongly with independent institutions for the philanthropic dollar. "The process of translating institutional priorities into budgetary decisions," said Shilling, "is most painful."[63] By 1986 Southwestern was having to cut back on its goals for the annual Brown Challenge and the Campaign for Southwestern.[64]

Nevertheless, through all these problems the development of Southwestern continued unabated, though not at the pace first hoped for. Southwestern weathered the countervailing winds better than most institutions. By 1992, Shilling could say: "We are one of the relatively small number of institutions which has improved itself significantly during the last decade. General economic decline has, in our case, been counteracted by developing an increased base of public support."[65] Though Shilling could point to the increased base of public support as the reason for Southwestern's success, much of it must be attributed to his leadership. He was uncompromising in his pursuit of the goals set out in the Master Plan in spite of bad economic times. In some of his written statements he said that Southwestern was "swimming against the tide."

Illustrating his will to succeed was his bout with shingles during 1985 and 1986. Though he was forced to enter the Methodist Hospital in Houston for diagnosis and treatment on November 26, 1985, he continued to function normally on campus once he was dismissed. He came to the office every day, made his regular round of calls, and conducted cabinet meetings. Those who participated in the cabinet meetings suffered with him from knowing how much he was hurting. A friend wrote him from Arkansas in early 1987: "I trust your health problems are under control."[66] He kept his condition as quiet as possible, and many people on campus did not even know he had shingles.

The Campaign for Southwestern

Once the Master Plan process had been put in place and the multiple-year pledge program for meeting the Brown Challenge had been established, Shilling initiated a third major program—the Campaign for Southwestern. The Master Plan had set a need of $35,196,000 to take care of deferred maintenance for the four years 1981–1982 to 1984–1985. Money must be raised for it. In addition to the building repairs included in deferred maintenance, several new buildings were needed and certain academic priorities needed to be addressed. Consequently, Shilling and Schrum presented the need for a multi-million-dollar fund-raising campaign to the Board.

They said that the University might need $20–30 million for operations, $20 million for capital improvements, and $40–50 million for endowment, totaling $100 million over the next decade. They recommended that the Board support the appointment of Mr. Dick Dini to do a sixty-to-ninety-day feasibility study for such a campaign. The Board approved, and Dini conducted the feasibility study already referred to.[67] Shilling also contracted with Dublin and Associates of San Antonio to do a study regarding the initiation of an enhanced public relations program to raise the profile of the University. Both Dini and Dublin reported back that Southwestern was in a position to raise about $35 million over three years. Meanwhile, the Academic Affairs Council had specified the academic priorities that might fit within a $35 million campaign. The Board voted on October 28, 1983, to authorize the President and the Board Chair to initiate such a campaign.[68] The idea of conducting the campaign to take care of deferred maintenance and construct new buildings was dropped.

As in most campaigns, a private solicitation of expected big donors was conducted prior to the announcement of the public campaign. Commitments came in slowly. Eighteen months later only $4.5 million had been raised or pledged. The campaign was kicked off officially at the Houston Country Club on November 21, 1985. John H. Duncan was the chair. A five-year, $30 million campaign was announced on that occasion. The $30 million would be used as follows:

$5 million to provide funds for the operation of an expanded library.
$12 million for teaching positions.
$5 million for fifty endowed scholarships.
$5 million for renovation and expansion of the Fine Arts Center.
$3 million endowment for fine arts program.[69]

Pledges continued to come in slowly. Shilling tried to spur them on by saying that "our vision . . . must not be allowed to blur or fade as we face the forthcoming period of economic uncertainty,"[70] but only a little less than $12 million had come in by April 22, 1988, the last date on which a report on the campaign was made.[71] The campaign faded away, and one might have thought that the day of big campaigns was over. Such, however, was not the case. It was soon succeeded by another campaign in the 1990s for $75 million that was conspicuously successful and would raise $91 million.

Deferred Maintenance and Small Campus Projects in the 1980s

The Campaign for Southwestern was designed to further the principal aim of the 1980s Master Plan, which was to improve the academic program. The $30 million to be raised was designated for the five priorities listed above related to that aim. All the money was to go to academic programs, teaching positions, student scholarships, or construction directly connected to the academic enterprise. Nevertheless, deferred maintenance remained a major campus problem, and the addition of adequate residence hall space for students could not be ignored. Both were addressed outside the Southwestern Campaign.

Roy Shilling believed that campus design and appearance were extremely important. Visitors to the campus often judged the institution, he felt, by what they saw on the outside. He wanted them to see the campus like a as jewel, polished and shining. The overall campus design produced by SOM was, in a sense, a reflection of his sense of order. Everything had its place and should be in its proper place, like the way he kept his office, always orderly. He believed in keeping a clean desk and seldom left the office without clearing off his desk and putting all stray papers in their proper drawers. As he jogged around campus each morning he noticed the things that needed to be tended to. One of the first things his secretaries often did after he came in was to phone the maintenance crew and tell them what he had observed. On one occasion he listed in a memo for the grounds supervisor eighteen conditions that needed correcting.[72]

Deferred maintenance, he felt, suggested inattention to detail. It came about because the campus and/or its buildings had not been tended with due diligence. For example, he insisted that cracked sidewalks be replaced in timely fashion and that a sweep of the campus be made by someone each morning to pick up unsightly trash. Of a more serious nature was the deferred maintenance that had built up over the years from inability to take care of problems as they arose because of finances. One of the first pieces of information he requested from the Vice President for Fiscal Affairs after he assumed the presidency was an estimate for dealing completely with deferred maintenance. The amount listed in the first Master Plan was more than $35 million. The gradual clearing away of the deferred maintenance problem during his first decade at Southwestern, while not as exciting as the construction of the many buildings that sprang up during his second decade, was in some ways just as important. After nineteen years at the helm of the institution, he left a campus that was in good condition and was always spic and span.

Some small projects dealt with during this period were of longer standing. Shilling convinced the Board in 1983 that Odds and Ends Hall, the last auxiliary building remaining from World War II, should be removed.[73] The old President's home, the last wooden structure on campus, serving at the time as the International House, was removed in 1986 and donated to the Williamson County Crisis Center.[74] A life safety program was completed in 1990 that included a fire alarm system upgrade, emergency exit signage, smoke detectors in dormitories, and campus security lights, at a cost of $400,000. The most difficult and frustrating project of the 1980s was the asbestos abatement project. Practically all of the buildings constructed after World War II had some asbestos in flooring, ceiling tiles, or insulation. With the discovery that the inhalation of asbestos over a long period of time was harmful and with courts awarding large sums to persons who could prove that they had been so harmed, the liability associated with doing nothing became exorbitant. Consequently, Southwestern engaged in a widespread program of asbestos removal that spread over two summers, 1989 and 1990, costing $3.1 million.[75]

Mabee Hall, the Library Addition, and a Bond Issue

The most pressing construction needs during the 1980s were to upgrade the residence hall facilities and to bring the library up to acceptable standards in both space and operation. To take care of the renovation of the residence building it had funded early in the Fleming administration, the Moody Foundation of Galveston gave $250,000 in 1982. The Mabee Foundation of Tulsa also made a challenge grant of $1 million for residence facilities in the same year, contingent upon the University's raising a $1.5 match by December 15. The Houston Endowment also made a $5 million grant for the improvement of the physical plant.[76] These grants made possible the renovation of the Moody-Shearn, Herman Brown, and Kurth residence halls during 1983.[77] Also contemplated was the construction of a new women's residence hall, to be named the J. E. and L. E. Mabee Residence Hall. Connected to Kurth Hall, it would provide spaces for approximately 170 students.

With the amount of money being poured into the renovation of the three residence halls, the potential renovation of Laura Kuykendall Hall, and the 170 additional spaces soon to be available, Shilling felt that the residence requirements for students should be changed from one year to three years. Not only were the financial implications of empty rooms under the current requirement serious, but the new requirement would also strengthen the residential nature of the campus. Consequently, he informed the Executive Committee that the residency requirements for new students would be changed to three years.[78] Much to his chagrin, the faculty disagreed and voted to maintain the present requirement.

Shilling was so hesitant to begin the construction of Mabee Hall in the face of this rebuff that he had to be dissuaded by the cabinet not to tell Board Chairman Frank Smith to cancel the building.[79] Construction of the new building by Graeber, Simmons & Cowan proceeded and was completed under budget in 1985.[80] Upon its completion the residence hall complex on the east side of the campus was named the Jesse H. and Mary Gibbs Jones Center in honor of the founder of the Houston Endowment.[81]

While these projects were being completed, Skidmore, Owings & Merrill had been retained to develop plans for the renovation or replacement of Laura Kuykendall Hall, the building of a new library, and a design for the eastern quadrant of the campus.[82] It did so, recommending that LK Hall be replaced by other buildings. Though the financial resources available at the time did not permit the replacement of LK, the building was renovated, a major addition to the library was made, and the eastern quadrant of the campus was landscaped. The funding for all of these projects was carried through by the issuance of $17.8 million of tax-exempt bonds. The "interest and principal payments on the bonds would be met with income earned from gifts to the endowment that might normally be solicited and expended for the construction projects." The bonds made the construction immediate and the gifts to endowment moved the money from an "expiring resource" to "perpetual service" through an endowment gift rather than a construction gift.[83] The Board congratulated Kirk Treible for conducting the bond operation with the Chemical Bank of New York and the InterFirst Bank, Wichita Falls. Charles Prothro of Wichita Falls, former chair of the Board, helped greatly in the transaction.[84]

The Cullen Trust issued a challenge grant of $1.25 million in early 1987 to help with the library project.[85] An equal matching amount raised by the University met the challenge. Built at a cost of $6,850,000, the library was completed and dedicated in 1988. It was named the A. Frank Smith, Jr., Library Center in honor of Smith, the lawyer for the Cullen Foundation, who had served as a Trustee since 1961 and as chair of the Board for many years. In its new configuration it housed the library, the academic computing center, language and graphics laboratories, and a wing of five classrooms.[86] In addition to doubling the size of the library, the building also added a distinctive architectural feature to the campus with its conspicuous Renaissance-style octagonal entryway. This feature was replicated in 1993 by a new thrust stage theater facility built immediately to the west of the library as a part of the Alma Thomas Fine Arts Center.

Faculty Salary Increases

Though the progress made on the development and construction fronts was pleasing to the faculty, the most attractive feature of Shilling's program to them was his belief in paying the faculty well. Every presidential administration from that of Mood to Fleming had agonized over the problem of providing adequate compensation for the faculty. The extreme poverty of the University through most of its history prevented them from doing much about it in comparison with peer institutions in the rest of academe. The first glimmer of hope that Southwestern might someday outgrow its reputation for low faculty salaries came during the administration of William C. Finch, when Southwestern for the first time developed a respectable endowment. Evidence of an interest in improving faculty compensation can be seen in a salary augmentation program instituted by Finch that was aided by a Ford Foundation grant of $171,000 in 1956. The grant specified that the money must be kept in the endowment for ten years.[87] Finch reported that the faculty salary schedules for 1956–1957 included increases averaging approximately twice the minimum set by the terms of the Ford grant.[88]

Average faculty salary increased steadily in terms of purchasing power from 1958 through 1972, when inflation began to outpace the rate of salary increase.[89] Whereas the average salary for the twenty-four faculty members continuing from 1969 through 1978 increased 54 percent, the consumer price index increased 76 percent.[90] In addition, the date for salary changes had been pushed back from September 1 to January 1 of each academic year. A new faculty member beginning on September 1 of a given year would not receive an increase for sixteen months.

This pushing back of the date for salary changes had another effect. It meant that Southwestern had to report its salary scale to the American Association of University Professors, the recognized arbiter in the field, using the salaries of the previous year that were still in effect in September rather than new September salaries as reported by all other institutions. Consequently, Southwestern's salaries always ranked low in comparison with the faculty salaries at peer institutions published each year in the A.A.U.P. magazine *Academe*, because the figures were a year behind all the others. Whatever may have been the argument of an earlier administration for using January 1 as the date for salary increases each academic year, the faculty read *Academe* carefully and could hardly be convinced that it was being paid better in relation to salaries at other institutions than *Aca-*

deme reported. Whereas Southwestern ranked at the 46th, 52nd, 56th, and 60th percentiles, respectively, for the years 1978–1979 through 1981–1982, it jumped to the 82nd percentile in 1982–1983.[91] Though some of the jump in rank of 22 percentile points was due to the healthy increase in actual salary given in 1982–1983, a good portion was due to the fact that Shilling pushed the date for salary increases back to September 1. The effect was that Southwestern salaries jumped two years on the A.A.U.P. scale.

Roy Shilling believed in paying faculty members well, and he started doing so at the outset of his administration as far as resources allowed. By 1984–1985 the faculty was being paid at the 90th percentile level of equivalent institutions in the country. He tried with good success to hold at least to that level thereafter. When I served on an examination team for the Methodist Board of Higher Education at a college in Pennsylvania in the mid-1980s, the leader of the team, a president from a similar institution, asked me why Roy paid such high faculty salaries when he could get faculty members for much less. Shilling's philosophy was that higher salaries were a part of a circle of factors important for building a quality institution. Higher salaries attracted better teachers, who in turn attracted better students, who together made a more attractive institution, which attracted more development dollars, et cetera. The effect might not always be immediate, but it was predictable.

New Cabinet Officers

Until the end of the Shilling administration, the officers chosen by the President to head up the principal work areas of the University were called his cabinet. How far back this custom goes in Southwestern history cannot be identified with certainty. Most of the early officers of the University, even its Presidents, were faculty members that held certain administrative responsibilities as well. They were not thought of as being essentially different from other faculty members. The notion of a president with a team of officers exercising primarily administrative rather than faculty responsibilities only began to develop gradually in the twentieth century. When the President and the group around him in charge of the major units of the university began to be recognized as a unique part of the institutional structure, the term "cabinet" was the most convenient one at hand to describe the phenomenon. It went back in its nomenclature to the English political system headed by a prime minister with his cabinet. The United States government followed the English system in this regard, as did the Methodist Church in America. The American president and the bishops of the Methodist Church still have their cabinets today. Recently the term "senior staff" has replaced the term "cabinet" with reference to the principal officers of the University. That term is military and corporate rather than political and ecclesiastical in its background, though that is not the intent of its use at Southwestern.

The cabinet inherited by Shilling consisted of: William B. Jones, Administrative Vice President and Provost; G. Benjamin Oliver, Dean, the Brown College of Arts and Sciences; Theodore D. Lucas, Dean, the School of Fine Arts; Barbara Hinson Brightwell, Dean for Student Development; William D. Swift, Vice President for Admissions and Student Development; Judson S. Custer, Vice President for Educational Services; and Kirk Treible, Vice President for Fiscal Affairs. By 1990 all of them had either retired, resigned to return to teaching, or accepted positions elsewhere—Custer in 1982, Brightwell in 1984, Jones in 1986, Swift in 1988, and Oliver, Lucas, and Treible in 1989.

The first new officer in the Shilling cabinet was Jakie B. Schrum, who came in early 1982 to assume the position of Vice President for University Relations.[92] That job also included financial development. John W. Lind was employed for the new position of Vice President for Admissions in late 1982. The position of Vice President for Educational Services was phased out the same year. The two student life positions in the cabinet were scaled down to one in 1984, with Barbara Brightwell taking a private position in her field and Swift's becoming Dean of Students again. He held that position until his retirement in 1988, when Roger A. Ballou replaced him. Michael R. Rosenthal replaced Oliver as Provost and Dean of the Faculty, and Carole A. Lee replaced Lucas in Fine Arts after a vacancy of a year. The Dean of Fine Arts, however, was removed as a member of the cabinet. Replacing Treible as Vice President for Fiscal Affairs in 1989 was Daniel C. Bryant. Bryant was formerly business manager and treasurer of Rockhurst College in Kansas City, Missouri. Besides his service to Rockhurst, Bryant had held administrative positions at Gallaudet College in Washington, D.C.

John W. Lind, the new Vice President for Admissions, came to Southwestern from his position at Beloit College, where he had served in admissions for nine years, the last five as Director of Admissions and Financial Aid. He held a B.A. in economics from Beloit and an M.A. in sociology from Roosevelt University. After completing his M.A., he had taught sociology at Lakeland College in Wisconsin. He accepted the position in admissions at Beloit after six-and-a-half years at Lakeland.[93] During his twenty-one-year tenure at Southwestern, he instituted one of the most successful admissions programs at any college in the United States. He met almost every goal either he or the University set and was in large part responsible for the high quality of the student body in the 1990s. He was an excellent leader for his assistants, diligent in his work habits, and meticulous in his attention to detail. Roy Shilling said about him: "John Lind rewrote the book on admissions and financial aid as a result of his dramatic and continuing success at SU."[94]

After Schrum's departure from Southwestern in 1985 to accept the role of Vice President for Development and Planning at Emory University, Roy Shilling was faced with the task of choosing someone to replace him. His choice lay between Rick Eason, Director of Development, and Marilyn Mock, Director of University Relations. Though Shilling was a "small cabinet" man, the work of Eason and Mock was so exceptional that he decided to go against his predisposition and to set up two cabinet positions to avail himself of both persons in major leadership positions. Eason became Vice President for Development, and Mock became Vice President for University Relations. Each worked with him throughout his entire administration.

Eason possessed outstanding talents for development work. He was a big thinker, smooth, bold, positive, and aggressive without being domineering. He eventually became Vice President for Development at the University of Texas. Mock ran a highly successful public relations program for the University. She was able to capitalize on Southwestern's successes to maximum advantage year after year in public relations. She was also often the "truth in the room" person for Shilling. In cabinet meetings she would cut away the vagaries in discussions and boil issues down to their nub. Eason and Mock often accompanied Shilling on his important development calls. One cartoon sent to him has a secretary at her desk informing her boss by phone: "A couple of suits and a skirt to see you." The two "suits" pictured are labeled in ink as "Rick" and "Roy," while the person wearing the skirt is labeled "Marilyn."[95] In commenting on the work of the two, Shilling said that their "professional fundraising and positioning efforts combined to make the transformation [of the University] possible from a staff standpoint."[96]

Provosts and Academic Deans

Though Jones possessed the title of Administrative Vice President and Provost, during the administration of President Fleming, he had exercised the former role much more extensively than the latter. Fleming had created the office of Administrative Vice President to free himself to do fundraising, and Jones acted under him primarily as an internal president. He carried the title of Provost as well but left most of the academic work to Dean Ben Oliver, whom he had personally recruited from Hobart and William Smith Colleges in 1976. Oliver was an excellent academician.

When Shilling came to Southwestern in 1981, the rationale for the Administrative Vice President position disappeared. He employed Schrum as his development officer and managed the institution effectively without any need for an internal president. Jones compensated for this change in scenario by investing himself in the development of the Master Plan, which went along successfully every year. He also became adept in the use of the computer and developed the first institutional database to assist principally in decision-making at the administrative level. He worked with the mathematics department in developing the computer science major and employed Robert A. Horick, the first computer science person in support of Harold Eidson. Shilling was always interested in what the numbers had to say about Southwestern, both internally and in comparison with peer institutions, and was pleased with these efforts.

At the end of the 1983–1984 academic year, the position of Provost was dropped, and no one held it during the 1984–1985 and 1985–1986 academic years.[97] It was reinstituted for the 1986–1987 academic year, with the new position of associate provost also being established. Oliver occupied the former position, Lucas the latter.[98] Jones remained Administrative Vice President. By now, however, he had already indicated that he wanted to go back to teaching rather than continue in his administrative position. When he broached the subject of his return to teaching in the History Department, Shilling was surprised and indicated that he could continue as Administrative Vice President with his current responsibilities as long as he chose. When Jones continued to reiterate his desire to return to teaching, they worked out a compromise. Jones would return to teaching half-time and do institutional research with the other half of his time. By now the Southern Association of Colleges and Schools had established a requirement that institutions of higher education should have an institutional research officer, and Jones became that officer. The institutional research officer was added as one of the persons holding *ex officio* membership on the University Council, allowing him to continue making contributions to the master plan. He also continued to perform various special services for the President when called upon from time to time.

To balance out the appointment of the Dean of the School of Fine Arts as Associate Provost, an Associate Provost was named for the Brown College of Arts and Sciences as well. This person was Dr. Jeanie Watson. She came for the 1986–1987 academic year as Associate Provost and Associate Professor of English. She held a B.A. from Baylor, an M.A. from Midwestern State University, and a Ph.D. from Ohio University. She had taught at Marshall University, Gustavus Adolphus College, Stonehill College, and the University of Nebraska. She came to Southwestern from Rhodes College, where she had taught since 1983.[99]

The provost-with-two-associate-provosts arrangement did not last long. When Oliver was elected President of Hiram College in the spring of 1989, both Lucas and Watson left, he to San Jose State University as chair of the Music Department and she to Hamline University as dean of the College of Liberal Arts. She subsequently went to Tulane University as dean of the H. Sophie Newcomb Memorial College and became president of Nebraska Wesleyan University in 1997. A search for a new Provost and Dean of the Faculty was instituted during the spring of 1989. Dr. Michael R. Rosenthal, B.A., Case Western Reserve University, M.S. and Ph.D., University of Illinois at Urbana-Champaign, was chosen. He was a chemist and formerly vice president and dean of St. Mary's College of Maryland. He began service on August 1, 1989.[100] With Lucas and Watson gone, the two associate provost positions were scrapped.

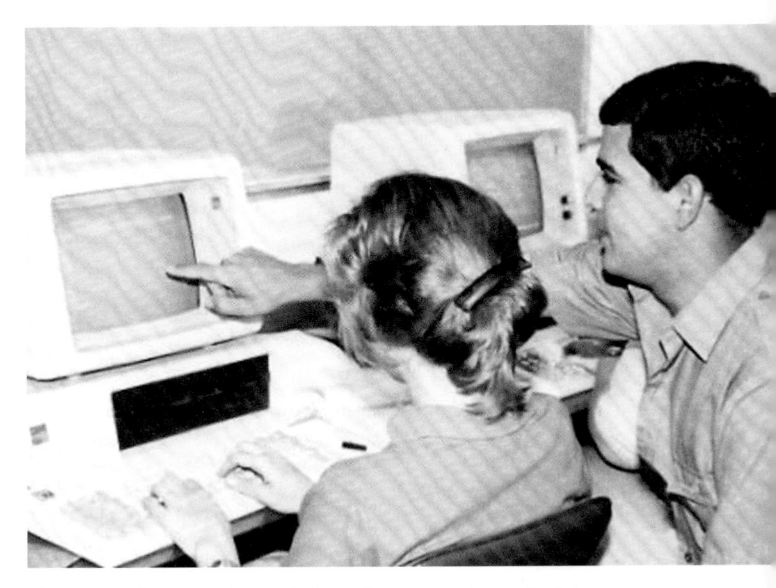

The computer literacy requirement in the curriculum was unique at the time it was approved. The *Dallas Times Herald* reported on December 1, 1985, that Southwestern was one of the few liberal arts colleges in the country, and the only one in Texas, that was requiring all students to become computer literate. Southwestern University, Special Collections.

A New General Education Program

In contrast to the 1961–1981 period, when experimentalism was the dominating characteristic of academic change at Southwestern and little remained permanently fixed for the long-term future, the academic changes that occurred during the 1981–1989 period have, by and large, remained on the books and, with some fine-tuning, are still in place today. The principal achievements were the development of a new general education (core curriculum) program, a reduction in the number of degrees, a reduction in teacher course loads, and the establishment of departmental program reviews. Inasmuch as they involved the teaching faculty, the establishment of the Cullen Faculty Endowment and Southwestern's participation in the Exxon/Kettering Public Leadership Project also fit into a discussion of academics.

When commenting in 1997 about the major changes that took place during the 1980s, President Shilling said: "The heart of the plan for the 1980s was the reframing of the University as a liberal arts institution with a curriculum consistent with the finest traditions of liberal arts education, which, among other things, meant shrinking our nine degrees to four and putting a meaningful and coherent comprehensive general education program in place."[101] Shilling had called for these changes from the beginning of his administration and considered them to be among his most important legacies for the University. They are also important legacies left by Dean G. Benjamin Oliver, who, as dean and later as Provost, played a strong role in bringing them about.

Having been encouraged by Shilling to study the University's "core curriculum and distribution requirements," the Academic Affairs Council set about the task of doing so in the spring of 1982. It secured faculty approval for its work in early fall 1984. The new program took effect in the fall of 1985. The major change in the general education program was to replace a distribution requirements program based upon selection by the students of courses offered by departments from the four divisions/School of the University with courses referred to as "Perspectives on Knowledge" (POK) courses, according to the pattern described below. The main difference between the POK program and the one it replaced was basing requirements on acquiring knowledge of the way the world works rather than specifying the disciplines used to study it. The Academic Affairs Council was delegated to approve courses from the different departments of the University that would serve to fulfill POK requirements. In addition to the POK courses, there were certain Foundation courses and several other General Education Requirements. The total number of credit hours required for completion of the core curriculum was forty-one. In addition, the student was obligated to show competence and/or knowledge in three other types of experience. The requirements were as follows:

Area One: Foundation Courses	
English Composition	3 hours
Freshman Symposium	3 hours
Mathematics	3 hours
Total	9 hours
Area Two: Perspectives on Knowledge	
American and Western Cultural Heritage	3 hours
Other Cultures and Civilizations	3 hours
The Religious Perspective	3 hours
Values Analysis	3 hours
The Natural World	6 hours
Aesthetic Experience	6 hours
Social Analysis	6 hours
Total	30 hours
Area Three: Other General Education Requirements	
Successful completion of Computer Literacy	0 hours
Continued Writing Experience	0 hours
Integrative or Capstone Experience related to Major Field	0 hours
Fitness and Recreational Activity	2 hours
Total	2 hours
Grand Total	**41 hours**[102]

The computer literacy requirement was unique at the time it was approved. The *Dallas Times Herald* reported on December 1, 1985, that Southwestern was one of the few liberal arts colleges in the country, and the only one in Texas, that was requiring all students to become computer literate. "'This is unique in the annals of computer literacy,' said Naomi Baron, a visiting professor from Brown University who is guiding development of computer requirements at Southwestern University.... Baron, who taught at Brown University for 14 years before coming to Southwestern for a two-year period [as a Guggenheim Fellow], said the school is breaking new ground in computer literacy."[103]

The most contentious part of the core curriculum over the years has been the Freshman Symposium, now transformed into a First-Year Seminar. The intention in its development was to give the first-year class a common educational experience in its first semester on campus by studying together some different, important topic each fall. The entire entering class, averaging perhaps 320 persons each year, met one time a week for a lecture by an expert on the topic being studied, then met a second time during the week in fifteen to seventeen small discussion groups of no more than twenty students each led by teachers serving as discussion leaders. A great deal of reading and writing was required of the students on the topic being studied. One of the main arguments against the symposium was that it required fifteen to twenty teachers each year to give up a regular course in their discipline to lead a symposium group over a topic in which they had little expertise. Nevertheless, the idea persisted over the years in spite of several close faculty votes.[104] Eventually the symposium mutated into a seminar-type experience attended by the student every day during orientation week and completed during the semester before the termination of the regular semester-long courses. The same number of groups and teachers was required for the seminars as for the symposium, but teachers taught special topics chosen by them and students selected the courses they wanted to take.

Reduction in the Number of Degrees

One of Southwestern's inheritances from the past, when it tried to follow the big university model, was a proliferation in the number of degrees it offered. Even after Finch and Fleming began to espouse the liberal arts and sciences model, many persons in the faculty supported the idea of promoting professional degrees alongside the basic B.A. and B.S. in spite of a suggestion in 1981 from the Southern Association of Colleges and Secondary Schools that eight different degrees were too many for a small school. Shilling and many others on the faculty agreed. Consequently, the faculty, led by the dean and the Academic Affairs Council, began a steady plan to reduce that number.

Though the Bachelor of Music Education degree had already been eliminated in 1980, the reason for the elimination was more a strategic internal decision by the School of Fine Arts than an attempt to move the University more in a liberal arts direction. The real initiation of a calculated reduction process began on January 15, 1985, when the faculty eliminated the Bachelor of Business Administration degree. The Board of Trustees looked on this action as a serious matter and voted three days later to set up a committee to consider it. Chairman A. Frank Smith, Jr., appointed a joint Trustee/faculty committee of nine persons to consider it. Dean Oliver and Dr. Leonard Giesecke, chair of the Department of Economics and Business, led the five faculty members on the committee. When they offered to the four Trustees a number of documents showing that the best schools offered business and accounting majors within the B.A., as Southwestern proposed to do, the committee approved a resolution, subsequently ratified by the entire Board, confirming the prior legislation of the faculty eliminating the B.B.A.[105]

Following the elimination of the B.B.A. in 1985, the elimination of three other degrees followed at intervals of a year each, the Bachelor of Applied Science in 1986, the Bachelor of Science in Social Science in 1987, and the Bachelor of Science in Secondary Education in 1988.[106] Students already enrolled for those degrees when they were abolished were allowed to complete them, but no new students were admitted for them after those dates. Southwestern was left with only four degrees. They were the Bachelor of Arts and the Bachelor of Science offered in the Brown College of Arts and Sciences and the Bachelor of Arts and the Bachelor of Music in the School of Fine Arts. This action in reducing the number of degrees offered by eliminating those that were basically professional was of vital importance in helping Southwestern secure a chapter of Phi Beta Kappa in 1994.

Other Academic Actions

Paralleling Shilling's arrival at Southwestern, the Academic Affairs Council put into place a systematic procedure wherein every academic major and program offered by the University began to be reviewed at least once every ten years, in addition to and at a time different from that of the self-study for SACS. Required participants in the review were three persons from outside the department, a consultant in the field from another university, and a person from outside the division.[107] At the same time that this and other enactments raised expectations for faculty performance, the dean and the President acted to improve the faculty workload. In September 1983 Shilling asked the department chairs to look at the issue of reducing the four-course-per-semester teaching load to a three-course load.[108] Action on this issue was slow in coming, but in April 1987 he announced to the Board of Trustees that that the teaching load in most departments was seven courses per year, three in one semester and four in the other.[109]

This reduction in teaching load was part of a general effort to improve the faculty development program at the University. It had begun in late 1981, when the Cullen Foundation announced a $1 million grant to establish a Cullen Faculty Endowment for faculty enrichment and development.[110] The enrichment and development program was set up in such a way that individual faculty members or faculty groups could propose growth plans that would be submitted to a Growth Plan Advisor Committee. Faculty members were not required to submit such plans, but those that did participate received emoluments corresponding to the approved needs they projected in their plans.[111] During the period from 1983–1984 to 1990–1991, a total of 192 individual projects and 10 group projects were supported, for a total of $491,707. These totals do not include the 15 faculty members sent to the People's Republic of China and Thailand, at a cost of $62,056, by the Cullen Faculty Development Fund in preparation for the Freshman Symposium in the fall of 1988. During those same eight years, an average of four faculty members per year went on sabbatical, and an average of thirty-five per year received faculty travel funds from other university budgets.[112]

During the mid-1980s, Southwestern gained recognition for leadership in teaching when it was chosen as one of the eighteen colleges and universities nationally to participate in a leadership and public service project funded by the Kettering and Exxon Foundations. Moreover, Southwestern was chosen to coordinate the activities of the five Texas universities participating in the project.[113] As a part of that project, Dr. Martha Allen organized an American Studies/history seminar in 1988 involving fifteen students and persons in Georgetown's leadership structure.[114]

International Programs in the 1980s

The promising development of an international studies program during the Fleming administration, with both an academic major and minor and overseas travel for students, was continued and enlarged during the decade of the 1980s. The formation of a Global Citizens' Fund in 1982, established by an endowment grant given by Mr. and Mrs.

Everett DuPuy of Austin, permitted students to enjoy study trips to the United Nations in New York and to engage in other forms of international activity on campus.[115]

The Music Department established a unique relationship with the prestigious Aldeburgh [Music] Festival in England. With the assistance of a grant of $10,000 from the King Foundation of Fort Worth, several music majors and two faculty members were able to participate in the festival in June 1983, having been invited by Donald Mitchell, a director of the festival. Mitchell had come to know Southwestern during 1982, when Ellsworth Peterson invited him as one of the featured speakers at the Brown Symposium, entitled "Gustav Mahler and His Vienna."[116]

A permanent arrangement was made for student study in England in 1985 with the establishment in the regular budget of money for taking around thirty students to England each fall for a semester of work at no additional charge to them beyond regular tuition. The first group went for the fall semester of 1985, and the program has continued through the years.[117] Though there have been slight alterations, the program still operates today very much as it did when it began. Two teachers from Southwestern in different academic disciplines accompany the students, with the students taking a British Life and Culture course from visiting British lecturers and courses in the disciplines represented by the two Southwestern teachers. Students also take regular field trips in London and the United Kingdom.

The United Kingdom was not the only country in which Southwestern students studied. They also engaged regularly in study-travel opportunities to other countries. Representative of their travels was 1987, in which they studied in Greece, England, various central European countries, and Mexico. Six of them studied at the Catholic University of the West in Angers, France, under a special sister relationship agreement established with that University.[118]

Perhaps the most remarkable academic program of an international nature during the Shilling years was the two-year Focus on Asia program during 1988–1990. Special financial backing for the program was secured by the procurement of a $200,000 grant from the National Endowment for the Humanities and a $52,000 grant from the Pew Memorial Trust.[119] The principal writer of the applications was Dr. Kenneth D. Roberts, Associate Professor of Economics and Business Administration.[120] Roberts, with a B.B.A. from the University of Texas, an M.B.A. from the Wharton School at the University of Pennsylvania, and a Ph.D. from the University of Wisconsin, specializes in Mexican and Chinese economic development. He became the holder of the Hugh Roy and Lillie Cullen Chair in Economics in 1996. He has traveled to China a number of times to do research and to deliver papers at academic meetings. His specialty is the nature and effect of the migration of Chinese peasants to the cities.

Highlighting the Focus on Asia program during 1988–1989 was the development of the fall semester Freshman Symposium around the topic "China and the Chinese." The spring semester Brown Symposium focused on Asia, with related course development projects incorporating Asian perspectives. In preparation for the Freshman Symposium, fifteen faculty members from Southwestern participated in a five-week study tour in China and Thailand during the summer of 1988. The trip was planned as a "total immersion" experience for the participants.[121] Toward the conclusion of the two-year Focus on Asia program in 1990, the Arthur Vining Davis Foundation of Florida gave $100,000 to support the permanent addition of Asian elements into the curriculum of the University.[122] The conclusion of the Focus on Asia program coincided with the 150th anniversary of the University, eliciting a news article in the *Austin American-Statesman*, which called Southwestern a "small school with [a] future."[123]

The person most responsible for furthering the Asian emphasis at the University since 1988 has been Professor Steven C. Davidson. With a B.A. from the University of Virginia, an M.A. from the University of Chicago, and a Ph.D. from the University of Wisconsin, he came to Southwestern just in time to participate in the faculty trip to China before he had even taught a class on campus. A specialist in East Asia, he has consistently promoted Asian interests in the curriculum. It is largely due to him that Southwestern includes Chinese as one of its regular languages for study today. Students majoring in International Studies may choose any one of three areas of emphasis for their work—Europe, East Asia, or Latin America.

Honors for Southwestern in the 1980s

Southwestern's advance during the 1980s soon began to receive national attention. The attention was of two kinds—that related to President Shilling as the leader in the University's rise to prominence and that related to the rapid progress of the University per se. Shilling brought attention with him when he came to Southwestern and garnered it increasingly over the years. The most tangible proof of his immediate impact was the invitation for

Southwestern to join the Southern University Conference simultaneously with his assumption of office. Former President Finch wrote him on July 11, 1988, saying that he was "delighted to know that Southwestern is at last a member of the Southern University Conference. . . . I am sure that your relationship with the group [as President of Hendrix] had much to do with its coming as it did."[124] The Southern University Conference was formed in 1935 to provide a forum for college and university presidents in the southeast to discuss the major academic and intellectual issues of the day. Only presidents of schools with standing were invited to become members.

In 1985 Shilling was elected President of the University Senate of the United Methodist Church.[125] He served for four years, handling during his tenure complex and thorny situations involving Morristown College, Boston University, and SMU. Though an alumnus of SMU, he conducted the University Senate investigation of the athletic affair plaguing that institution with an even hand. The Perkins School of Theology awarded him the Distinguished Alumnus Award during that time.[126]

The following year, 1986, Shilling was chosen as one of the top one hundred college and university leaders in the nation in a two-year study, funded by the Exxon Foundation, that was completed at Bowling Green State University.[127] James Fisher, President Emeritus of the Council for Advancement and Support of Education, one of the two directors of the study, said that the study demonstrated "that effective presidents are different. They are strong, risk-taking leaders with a dream."[128]

Three years later Shilling was elected to a three-year term on the Board of Directors of the American Council on Education, the major organization representing the nation's colleges, universities, and higher education associations.[129] During the same year, he was one of thirteen American university presidents invited to participate in the second Japan-U.S. Conference of University Presidents, held in Kyoto, Japan. He had earlier participated in the first such conference in 1985, sponsored by Drew University.[130] With each recognition accorded him, Shilling brought increasing recognition to the institution he headed.

The most helpful recognition for the University at the national level came from its appearance as one of the best regional institutions in the country in the special higher education edition of the *U.S. News & World Report* each year beginning in 1983. Notable is the fact that Southwestern was categorized in 1983 as a comprehensive university because it offered professional degree programs, such as business administration, along with its liberal arts program.[131] As a result of its elimination of professional degrees, Southwestern was soon reclassified as a liberal arts institution. In 1988 it was ranked as the #1 regional liberal arts school in the country among the more than four hundred in that category. The October 10, 1988, issue of the magazine had the following to say about Southwestern.

> When economic disaster rocked the Texas oil patch a few years ago, sending promising but newly poor high-school students scrambling for places in less costly public colleges, Southwestern University in Georgetown, Tex., was ready for the slump. The top-ranked regional liberal-arts school had a powerful antidote on its side: Money, and lots of it. With an endowment of more than $80,000 for each of its 1,100 students—comparable with such national universities as Emory and Columbia—the private Southwestern, located north of Austin, could survive and even thrive during the crunch.
>
> Southwestern, however, was more than lucky—it was smart. The school recruited a top-notch faculty—more than 90 percent have doctorates—doubled the size of its library with a $6.5 million addition, and recruited a higher caliber of students. It awarded merit scholarships ranging from $1,000 to $7,000 to almost a fifth of the student body, helping Southwestern to raise the average SAT scores of this year's freshman class to 1,102, a 122-point increase over 1980.
>
> The school's large resources have been used to diversify the student body as well. Southwestern awards need-based scholarships averaging $5,400—helping to nearly triple minority enrollment to 13 percent since 1982.[132]

In 1985 Southwestern was included for the first time in the *New York Times Selective Guide to Colleges* and also in *The Best Buys in College Education.*[133] From that time on it was included regularly in a highly laudatory way in most of the important college guidebooks.[134] In 1987 it was cited in *Money* magazine as being one of the ten best buys in American higher education. Reporting on the *Money* magazine article, the *Houston Post* said that "simply put . . . Southwestern University is a bargain." Its endowment of over $101 million, continued the *Post*, places it among the top thirty schools across the nation in endowment per student. Two-thirds of its students receive financial aid. In the past ten years more than 70 percent of SU applicants who have applied to medical school have been accepted and 90 percent have made it into law school.[135]

In 1987 Southwestern was invited by the Tufts Educom Data Sharing Project to join a consortium of seventy-five of the most prestigious independent colleges and universities in the country that regularly share data on a confidential basis and hold national meetings twice a year to discuss ways of improving their work.[136]

National Visibility and Special Events

Though some of the publicity that came to the University during the 1980s was a natural function of its increasing prominence on the national scene, Marilyn Mock, Vice President for University Relations, promoted it assiduously. Operating on the basis of Shilling's belief that Southwestern, with a plain name and a previously undistinguished record, must tout itself if its accomplishments were to become known, Mock directed an impressive Visibility Campaign for almost twenty years.[137] The interest in Southwestern manifested by the *New York Times* and other media outlets did not always happen without human intervention. She wrote and visited them regularly, informing them of what was happening at Southwestern, why it was important, and why they should be interested.

Fortunately, Mock had a great deal to work with, not only with respect to the academic and financial progress of the University, but also in terms of special events that occurred from time to time. The *Houston Chronicle* wrote about some of these events in an article on May 13, 1984. Its reporter wrote while on campus:

> As part of its profile-raising, Southwestern has been drawing big names in the world of arts and science to the small campus. One of the best-known, playwright Edward Albee, spent a month-long residency here last summer doing workshops and producing one of his plays *[Who's Afraid of Virginia Woolf?]*. Shelly Berman appeared recently, playing Tevye in Fiddler on the Roof for four sold-out performances. This spring, Nobel Prize winner Dr. Paul Berg, the "father of recombi-

Scene from the Brown Symposium production of *Curlew River* in 1985. The Public Broadcasting System broadcast it on February 20, 1985, and subsequently re-broadcast it over 125 television stations across the country. Southwestern University, Special Collections.

nant DNA technology," and Dr. Michael S. Brown, professor of genetics and director for the Center for Genetic Study at the University of Texas Health Science Center at Dallas, met here in a two-day [Brown] symposium on molecular cloning that drew representatives from some 40 high schools, 17 universities and 10 medical centers.[138]

One of the most striking events was a production of Benjamin Britten's *Curlew River*, filmed in the Lois Perkins Chapel during the 1985 Brown Symposium sponsored by Ellsworth Peterson.[139] The Public Broadcasting System broadcast it on February 20, 1985, and subsequently rebroadcast it over 125 television stations across the country.[140]

During the spring of 1988, Southwestern hosted between 7,000 and 8,000 visitors on campus for approximately thirty university events ranging from a record-setting Parents' Weekend (750 people) to a lecture by Alex Haley (1,100 people) to a chorale/symphony performance of *Carmina Burana* (600 people). Haley, the author of *Roots*, was the principal speaker at the Brown Symposium sponsored by Weldon Crowley.[141] Another speaker of note on campus was Professor Ehud Sprinzak of Hebrew University in Jerusalem. He spoke on religious fundamentalism and terrorism in the Near East.[142]

In addition to using special events for publicity purposes, Mock encouraged President Shilling to write op-ed pieces and essays from time to time for publication in newspapers and magazines. After delivering the keynote address at the annual meeting of the Texas Independent College Fund, he was invited by the *Texas Business* magazine to write an essay for its October 1983 issue on the relationship of business and the free enterprise system to independent higher education. After the appearance of the article, Shilling contributed editorial page essays to several Texas newspapers. His *Texas Business* article was the basis for an editorial page column in *The Dallas Times Herald*.

Student Life—Alcohol Policy during the 1980s

Perhaps the most persistent, almost intractable student problem at Southwestern over the years has been student use of alcohol in the face of university rules to the contrary. Even in its early years, when abstinence from alcohol by all students was the accepted norm, the most prevalent student offense, aside, perhaps, from prohibited contact between men and women, was drinking or drunkenness. In the face of the increasing pressures for social drinking that developed during the twentieth century, university rules for nonuse of alcohol on campus became more and more difficult to enforce. Individuals and groups practiced all sorts of stratagems to get around the rules. By the time of the Fleming era the policy of allowing no alcohol at all on campus had become practically impossible to enforce except in the broadest sense. Shilling inherited an alcohol policy that in effect did not allow alcohol openly on campus but also did not seek it out in dormitory rooms.

At the same time, the stance of the United Methodist Church on alcohol use had changed subtly over the years. It had become not so much one requiring abstinence as of supporting abstinence as the historic stand of the Church while emphasizing the detrimental effects of alcohol *abuse*. Shilling, in his Inaugural Dinner Speech in 1982, gave emphasis to an attack on alcohol and drug abuse along with other prevalent student problems.[143]

An opportunity to attack the problem from a new angle and to adopt a more viable policy occurred when Congress passed the National Drinking Age Act in 1984. It required all states to raise their minimum purchase and public possession of alcohol age to twenty-one. States that did not comply faced a reduction in highway funds under the Federal Highway Aid Act.[144] What these mandates did was to make the federal government a possible partner with the University in not allowing drinking on campus for students less than twenty-one years of age.

Included in the 1985 Master Plan was a new alcohol statement intended to bring Southwestern's policy into line with United Methodist belief and practice and the new federal law. The statement was a set of recommendations reflecting a special Student Life Study made during the year by a blue-ribbon committee and approved by the faculty. It was presented to the Board of Trustees as "A Possible Alcohol Statement" and was issued by the administration after refinement and review by legal counsel.[145] The essence of the statement, as far as campus practice was concerned, was to ban all student use of alcohol for persons below the age of twenty-one, with the imposition of strict guidelines for the use of alcohol for persons twenty-one years of age or older.

Because of the new alcohol policy, a successful Greek Rush was developed in 1987 without alcoholic beverages, even for those of legal age. An Alcohol Awareness Week was held at the end of February and was well attended.[146] The grand finale of Alcohol Awareness Week was an evening called Casino Night, where "everything was set up to look like and convey the ambiance of a real gambling hall including bank windows where folks cashed in many chips for cash vouchers. . . . Upon arrival each student received $10,000 worth of chips and was let loose. With their winnings at the end of the night they could bid for prizes during the auction."[147] The University became increasingly active in the fight against alcohol and drug abuse, and Alcohol Awareness programs were sponsored each year. Southwestern became an active member of the Central Texas Consortium for Alcohol Abuse and Prevention.[148]

Student Life—The Regular and the Unique

Ronald Reagan, who served as President of the United States from 1981 to 1989, dominated the decade of the 1980s politically. Though a majority of the student body always formed a moderate center in the political orientation of the campus during the decade, as revealed in questionnaires administered each year, that center became gradually smaller, with a somewhat larger conservative right wing during the mid-'80s. The conservative movement reached its apex around the time of Reagan's summit meeting with USSR General Secretary Gorbachev in Geneva (November 19–20, 1986). After that event the political attitude began to swing in a more liberal direction. By late 1985 some students had already formed a Student Coalition for an Organized Peace (S.C.O.P.E.) effort that portended a growing liberal sentiment. Toward the end of Reagan's administration, with the congressional Iran-Contra hearings in 1988, the liberal momentum gained strength, and the balance between conservative and liberal students to the right and left of the moderates was restored.

National Alumni Phonathon conducted by students in connection with a Halloween Costume Party in the mid '80s. Southwestern University, Special Collections.

Whatever may have been student feeling with regard to international politics, the two events that shocked them most were the explosion of the space shuttle *Challenger* on January 28, 1986, killing seven crew members, including Christa McAuliffe, a schoolteacher, and the nuclear accident at Chernobyl in the USSR on April 24, 1987, reinforcing awareness of the danger of nuclear catastrophe. Sally Ride, the first woman to orbit the earth, had come to the campus as a speaker on April 29, 1985. Her appearance only nine months before the explosion of the *Challenger* brought the accident home to students in a particularly poignant way.

Closer to home, the suicide of one student, the attempted suicide of another, the abduction of a female student at gunpoint on campus, who escaped by jumping from the moving automobile of the kidnapper, and several burglaries caused tension to rise on campus during 1982. By adding two additional security officers, the University brought the number up to five and began maintaining twenty-four-hour coverage of the campus. In spite of the increased security, a low level of crime continued. President Shilling reported on January 10, 1983, that a faculty office was burglarized, basketball players' wallets were rifled in the locker room, women's wallets were stolen, and a stereo set was taken from a student's room. The Bishops' Memorial Union building was also broken into over the Christmas holidays, though few items of value were taken. In spite of these incidents, the report required by the federal government of the incidence of crime on campus revealed a rate very low in comparison with those of most other colleges and universities.

In addition to increasing the number of police officers on campus, Shilling and Dean Barbara Brightwell announced on October 13, 1982, that a Student Development Center had been instituted to provide counseling and help to students. Because of its uniqueness, the Hogg Foundation gave it a demonstration grant of $5,850. This center utilized the holistic approach to health and emphasized the wellness concept. New to the panoply of illnesses with which the center had to deal was AIDS. The death of actor Rock Hudson, who died of acquired immune deficiency syndrome (AIDS) in 1986, had a sobering effect on many students. They also began to have serious discussions about abortion. A debate on abortion was held in the Cullen Auditorium on November 7, 1986.

On another note, students continued to engage in a wide range of extra-curricular activities. The Union sponsored many of them, one of which in 1982 was rappelling. "Sing," an annual contest in the Theatre during Homecoming among campus organizations to produce the most hilarious or interesting skit, was perhaps the most widely attended purely student event each year. By 1984 faculty members had adopted the custom of serving a midnight breakfast in the Commons to students during examination week. The Campus Crusade for Christ established a group at Southwestern and, during 1987, met on Tuesday nights in the faculty lounge of the Student Union Building. Professors Villa and Jones served as the advisors to the Hispanic Awareness Society organized during the Fleming years.

Many students engaged in efforts to help the University in its fund drives and to recruit new students. Each year a phone bank was set up in the Cullen Building for students to make calls to SU alumni soliciting gifts from them to the annual fund as a part of the Brown Challenge. At the eighth annual Alumni Phonothon sponsored by the Student Foundation in 1984, a total of $63,420 was raised. A new record was established only three years later when $101,000 was raised. The Admissions Office established its own student organization called Students Helping the Admissions Recruitment Process (SHARP). Students working for SHARP gave campus tours to student prospects and their families and did other things helpful to the recruitment effort.

Unique or colorful events occurred from time to time. In 1984 the editor of *The Megaphone* tried to change the name of the campus newspaper to the *Townsman*. A student vote restored the old name. Two years later the beginning-of-the-year freshman retreat was held at the Greene Family Camp north of Temple. The entire entering class was loaded into buses and taken to the camp for several days as a part of freshman orientation. The old International House (previously the President's home) was destroyed by fire on February 19, 1988, two years after having been moved off campus.

The winter weather became a topic for conversation and play in 1982 and 1986. On January 13 of the former year snow covered the campus, and students played Frisbee in the snow. In the latter year it snowed during the Christmas holidays and again during January. Sledding down the golf course hills on old Commons trays and riding on inner tubes pulled by trucks on the football field were popular.

The Achievement of Financial Stability

The decade of the 1980s was the first in which Southwestern achieved real financial stability. It ran up healthy operational surpluses each year beginning in 1983–1984 in spite of the continually rising cost of financial aid, the generous salary increases each year, and the relatively small proportion that tuition revenues formed of the total income budget. Tuition revenue never ranged above 50 percent of total income in any year during the decade and was as low as 37 percent in 1983–1984. Of course, this low percentage was due to the happy circumstance that the Brown Challenge brought in substantial resources to the operational budget each year. In order to raise the percentage that tuition revenues formed of total revenues, annual tuition increases were substantial. Because of the high inflation rate during Shilling's first year, tuition was raised 16 percent and room and board was increased 18 percent.[149]

Since the University was committed to meeting 100 percent of the demonstrated financial need of applicants, the rise in student charges made it necessary to increase student aid each year to help those students that had difficulty handling the new charges.[150] Institutional financial aid was finally capped at 16 percent of the educational and general budget to keep it from cutting further into other budget priorities.[151] A Parent Loan Fund was established to extend loan aid to students on more favorable terms than might be obtainable from an ordinary bank loan. Loans were made to parents of SU students at a preferred interest rate, with the loans going into collection status when the student left Southwestern. The balance of the loan was to be repaid within five years.[152] The University also entered into the federal work-study program as well, thus providing another income source for needy students.[153] In 1983–1984 about half of the aid funds dispensed came from Southwestern's own funds and half from federal and state funds.[154]

By 1985–1986 tuition income had increased 138 percent since 1980–1981, gift revenue from the Brown Challenge in support of the operating budget had increased 60 percent, and endowment income had increased 104 percent. Instructional expense, including faculty salaries and academic support, had increased 77 percent. Scholarship/grant awards had increased more than 146 percent.[155]

By that year Shilling could say that budget performance was "exceptional." Revenues exceeded expenses by nearly $500,000, with about $300,000 of the 1985–1986 gift revenue rolled forward as "Revenue Received in Advance." This gift revenue became a buffer for subsequent years when economic circumstances might slow the flow of philanthropic dollars to the institution, as was in fact the case.[156] This money rolled forward became insurance against a deficit budget. Advance gifts of more than $600,000 were rolled forward for the 1988–1989 financial year.[157]

Supplementing increased revenues, a program of budget containment was practiced. Shilling was a "hands on" budget maker and held long and careful budget meetings in which every aspect of the budget was examined. Though he was not a "zero budget" exponent, i.e., forcing every department to draw up a budget from zero every year, he went over each line item with the major officers, who had to justify the expenditures they presented for approval. A budget assumption model by the Business Office that predicted with a high level of certainty the anticipated revenues resulting from changes in rates of return on endowment, short-term investments, and increases in tuition and room and board rates was established.[158] In 1986–1987 a decentralization of the heating system with the elimination of the central boiler plant enabled the University to save more than $100,000 annually, a reduction of from 7.2 percent of the 1980–1981 operating budget to 4.7 percent.[159] In 1984 Shilling determined that the golf course could not be subsidized any longer by the operating budget, and the elimination of the golf course became a real possibility. Facing this prospect, Vice President Rick Eason developed a successful plan to open the course to the general public on a fee basis. Within a year the golf course was paying its own way.

On October 4, 1985, Shilling felt that he could say what no earlier President had been able to say since the establishment of Southwestern in Georgetown in 1873, that "the financial stability of the University has been firmly established."[160] During the forty-eight years from the time in 1937 when the gift of Louisa Carothers Wiess had saved the school from bankruptcy to Shilling's pronouncement in 1985, Southwestern had become one of the stronger liberal arts schools financially on the national scene. Its future course would now be a matter of how it used its financial stability.

Trustee leaders in the Brown Challenge Program, c. 1987. Left to right: A. Frank Smith, Jr., Roy Cullen, President Roy B. Shilling, Ambassador Edward A. Clark, John H. Duncan, and Admiral B. R. Inman. Southwestern University, Special Collections.

Becoming a National Liberal Arts Institution (1990–2000)

Overview

Though the financial situation of the University was quite different in the 1980s from that in the 1950s, some of the actions of the Shilling and Finch administrations during those two decades were quite similar. In order to put the institution on a sound financial basis and to promote a liberal arts emphasis, President Finch reduced faculty numbers, dropped the intercollegiate football program, abandoned the graduate program, and gave up summer school (see Chapter XVIII). In the selection of Dean Wicke, he also began a practice of selecting deans with strong liberal arts beliefs, a course of action followed by his successors. Under Shilling, the number of University degrees was reduced from eight to four between 1985 and 1988, and the program of scholarship athletics was eliminated in 1990 in favor of a nonscholarship program. In a sense, Shilling completed what Finch had begun. He also chose deans committed to a strong liberal arts program to build up the curriculum in that direction. The core curriculum established in the mid-1980s under Dean Oliver was a part of that program and is still in operation in 2005.

Shilling's action in reducing the number of degrees carefully removed professional degree studies and the big university model as an option for the University once and for all, and this was an important element in an invitation to join the Associated Colleges of the South in 1993–1994. The action with regard to athletics resulted in an invitation to join the Southern Collegiate Athletic Conference. Both associations were composed of a small number of the better liberal arts institutions in the South, and these invitations marked their recognition of Southwestern's emergence as a peer institution. These administrative moves, along with the procurement of a magnificent Olin Foundation grant that came at about the same time, cinched 1993–1994 as a climactic year in the life of the University. It marked the definitive achievement by the University of the kind of institution its Presidents had been moving toward for almost half a century. Southwestern would no longer seek to *become* a respected national liberal arts institution, but to improve its quality as a recognized institution of that kind.

The actions of Finch and Shilling aroused considerable opposition at the time from a substantial minority of students, faculty, and Trustees. Nevertheless, they were carried through and became a normal part of the University structure that exists today. Membership in ACS and SCAC was complemented by the establishment of a Phi Beta Kappa chapter and reclassification as a national liberal arts institution by the Carnegie Foundation for the Advancement of Teaching. These events together, all taking place in 1993–1994, marked the end of the long trajectory after World War II in establishing the character of the Southwestern that exists today.

Vision 2000—From High Achievement to Unquestioned Excellence

As the decade of the 1980s began to come to an end with most of the goals of the first Master Plan realized in either their original or in a revised form, Shilling began to think about a new master plan for the '90s. Working with the staff, primarily with Provost Oliver, he prepared "A Statement of Affirmation and Direction" that, after having been modified and approved by the faculty, he presented to the Trustees. He said that the document would become a starting point for a revamped planning process that would focus "on moving from high quality to unquestioned excellence within the educational program." The University's "definition" is no longer in question, he continued. "Southwestern University is an undergraduate liberal arts institution committed to a broad-based, value-centered education focused on the full development of each student. The overall goal of the Master Plan," Shilling asserted, "has been to achieve a position of national maturity in which the quality of a Southwestern University education would be recognized nationally. In a very real sense, Southwestern has arrived on the national scene. This, however, is not an occasion for complacency. We now face a present and exciting challenge: *we must move from a plateau of high achievement to unquestioned excellence* [italics added]."[1]

The forward movement in the development of a new master plan for the 1990s was halted when Provost Oliver accepted the presidency of Hiram College in early 1989. In the face of Oliver's impending departure, the University Council developed a Transitional Master Plan for 1989–1990 that contained most of the work and major ideas to date for the new master plan.[2]

When Provost Rosenthal arrived in the fall to replace Oliver, he found that he was in charge of producing three major documents—the Southern Association Self-Study that was underway, the application for a chapter of Phi Beta Kappa, and a new master plan. Rosenthal asked Bill Jones to assume a leadership role in the preparation of the new master plan because of his role in the development of the first master plan and because of his input into the Transitional Master Plan. Together they formulated a procedure approved by the faculty to break up the planning process into three stages, those of composing a Basic Master Plan, an Expanded Master Plan, and a Detailed Master Plan.

In order to begin this process, a Master Plan Steering Committee was appointed to work intensively on writing the Basic Master Plan. The committee was composed of persons selected by the President in consultation with the University Council and ratified by the faculty. The fifteen persons appointed worked with Farley Snell (Religion) as Presider and Bill Jones (History) as Agenda Formulator and Scribe. Snell and Jones served as co-coordinators for the master plan, just as Glen McClish (Communication) and Debbie Ellis (English) were doing for the Phi Beta Kappa application document and as George Brightwell (Registrar) was doing for the SACS Self-Study. Rosenthal served as an *ex officio* member of all three groups and was responsible for the overall process with regard to all three documents.

The Basic Master Plan published in 1989–1990 was relatively brief and suitable for independent publication. It consisted of a series of overarching goals and major objectives. The document was subsequently amended every other year in odd-numbered years. An Expanded Master Plan was published the following year with changes being made in even-numbered years. Separate Detailed Master Plans could be written by departments, divisions, or schools of the University to further elaborate their own development needs and aspirations.[3] The Basic and Expanded Master Plans were comprehensive in scope and spoke to operations across the entire University. Detailed Master Plans were not one plan but referred to possible plans that could be drawn up during the 1990s related to various components of University work, such as the International Studies Program and the program for the School of Fine Arts. Detailed Master Plans would not be drafted for every area of the University but only for those where a special effort was to be made.[4]

At the initiation of the new master planning process in 1987, Shilling reported that of the sixty-six objectives listed in the first Master Plan approved in 1982, only three remained to be achieved prior to the target date of 1990.[5] Four years later in 1991 he could report that the new academic mall and the theater project were underway and that the accomplishment of those two projects would bring to conclusion the construction projects set out in the Master Plan of the 1980s. It would be, he said, "the final establishment of the over-arching concept originally envisioned by Skidmore, Owings and Merrill, our Master Plan Architects during the 80s."[6] After a final update by SOM of the Campus Master Plan, the working relationship with that firm was severed "amicably" in 1991 because of its relocation away from Houston. The firm of Sasaki Associates of Dallas was chosen to replace it.[7]

Development of the Athletic Program under Fleming

If the issue of deferred rush was the great campus struggle during the Fleming administration, the issue of scholarship versus nonscholarship athletics was the great campus struggle during the Shilling era. Both controversies involved strong feelings among students, faculty, and Trustees. The major difference between the two struggles, aside from their subject, was that the former was long-running and not definitively settled in the minds of some people for many years after its onset, while the latter, though contentious, was settled relatively quickly. Once it was done, the decision was accepted, and a new structure emerged to support it.

The intercollegiate athletic program was quite different in 1981, when Shilling inherited it, from the one bequeathed to Fleming by Finch. In 1961 the athletic program was still recovering from the abandonment of intercollegiate football in 1951 and from the small 3.6 percent of the E&G budget accorded to athletics in 1960–1961 in comparison with the 13.7 percent of the budget it received in 1950–1951. In 1960–1961 women's athletics was restricted almost entirely to intramural events when the Board of Trustees voted "to permit women students to participate in intercollegiate sports on a tournament basis only, to be sponsored as part of the program of Physical Training for Women, and not to be or become a part of an inter-collegiate athletic program for women in [any] manner, shape or form."[8]

The athletic program gradually gained momentum during the Fleming era so that by 1981 Southwestern had a respectable intercollegiate athletic program in NAIA Division II for both men and women. It offered four scholarship sports in men's and women's basketball, women's volleyball, and men's baseball as a part of the Big State Conference. Some prominent coaches and teachers employed were Tex L. Kassen in 1969 as Athletic Director, James L. Mallon in 1970 as baseball coach, Glada Munt in 1975 as volleyball coach, and Paul Peak in 1978 as men's basketball coach. Kassen served fifteen years until his retirement in 1984, Mallon served thirty-one years until his retirement in 2001, Munt is still active after thirty years, and Peak resigned in 1991 after thirteen years to take a position elsewhere. His decision was triggered by the Trustee decision to discontinue the scholarship athletic program.

Kassen was a beloved figure on campus and, after his retirement, continued to work regularly without remuneration for twenty years in the physical education center until his death in 2004. He was a well-known figure even at ninety years of age at track and field events and working the sidelines as an official at University of Texas football games.

Mallon's career was especially notable. While at Southwestern he became one of the leading college baseball coaches in America, his teams winning 1,197 college games during his career, all at Southwestern, an average of over 35 games per year. By 1999 he had sent twenty-five players to the pros, including four to the majors, including Mike Timlin, star pitcher for several teams, including the 2004 World Champion Boston Red Sox. Mallon was also named in 1999 as SCAC Coach of the Year for the third consecutive season after his baseball teams had won three championships in a row.[9]

Particularly important in building up the athletic program was Title IX of the Educational Amendments of 1972, which banned sex discrimination in schools, whether in academics or athletics. As a part of his responsibility, Dean Swift produced an affirmative action program for the University that was submitted to the federal authorities in Dallas. He also completed a Self-Evaluation for the Title IX equality in women's athletics program required by federal legislation. In compliance with the federal mandates, Southwestern built up the women's side of its athletic program. When Kassen retired as Athletic Director in 1984, Shilling appointed Dr. Carla Lowry to the position. Dr. Glada Munt, the current director, was appointed in 1994.

During the 1980s, the coaches in the four scholarship sports regularly produced winning teams. In 1981–1982, Shilling's first year, the volleyball team was the runner-up at the NAIA national tournament and completed the year with 45 wins and 11 losses. The baseball team had 41 wins and 19 losses. Only 4 of the losses were in the Big State Conference. In 1984 Southwestern completed one hundred years of baseball by playing a double-header against the University of Texas, whose team it had also played a century earlier in 1884. Though it lost both games by scores of 5-2 and 9-1, it showed that it could compete strongly against one of the premier powers in college baseball. The volleyball team was fourth in the NAIA national playoffs in 1988. In 1986 and 1987 the men's basketball team competed in the NAIA tournaments in Kansas City. Bobby Deaton was accorded NAIA All-American honors. In 1990 the basketball team won the NAIA District IV title and traveled to Kansas City to contend for the national championship for the third time in seven years. Senior guard Ray Baranco was named first-team NAIA All-American and became SU's all-time leading scorer with 2,327 points.[10] Whatever the reasons behind the movement leading to the scholarship versus nonscholarship controversy, the inability of the school to produce winning teams was not one of them.

Not all of the intercollegiate athletics programs were of the scholarship variety. Nonscholarship teams were produced regularly in men's and women's tennis and in golf for competition in the Big State Conference. Lacrosse became a Southwestern sport in 1982. At the lacrosse banquet in the spring, Travis Mathis, son of Isabel Brown Wilson, was named most valuable player. A soccer team was first pictured in the 1990 *Sou'wester*.

Events Leading Up to the Scholarship/Nonscholarship Controversy

Dissatisfaction with Southwestern's membership in the Big State Conference had been growing for some time among the faculty. At a faculty meeting shortly after Shilling's arrival, Dr. Douglas Hooker, faculty athletic representative, presented several arguments for Southwestern's withdrawal from that conference. Shilling spoke in agreement, and the faculty voted to support Hooker's recommendation.[11] Two days later Shilling reported this action to the Board and supported it by saying that "as we have improved our academic standing and athletic program, the Conference has failed to grow correspondingly."[12] He said that Southwestern should become an "independent" until such time as it could secure a more satisfactory conference alignment.[13] Southwestern withdrew from the conference as of fall 1982.[14]

The issue of conference alignment broadened into a full study of the athletic program by a faculty Athletic Study Committee. The committee was charged to make recommendations about the sports to be offered at Southwestern, whether they should be offered on an intramural or intercollegiate basis, and to what extent the University should provide grants-in-aid for those participating.[15] The committee report, approved by the faculty in early 1984, recommended removing the four-hour physical education activity degree requirement so as to release faculty members to teach other substantive courses, to do other coaching and intramural work, and to give students more choices within an enhanced physical education program.[16] Emphasis was placed on enhancing intramural and lifetime sports.[17] None of these faculty actions addressed directly the issue of scholarship athletics, but the fact that the issue had been mentioned as a matter worth discussing suggests that there was some latent sentiment in the direction of discontinuing scholarship support offered by the athletic department to attract athletic talent.

The Faculty Votes on Scholarship versus Nonscholarship Athletics

After the conclusion of the faculty action in 1984, nothing of significance was done to alter the athletic stance of the University until 1989, when the issue of scholarship versus nonscholarship athletics was raised in the course of considering whether to join the new Heart of Texas athletic conference that had been formed when the Big State Conference disbanded in 1987. The Heart of Texas was a scholarship conference, and membership in it by Southwestern would commit it to scholarship athletics. The policy implications of joining the conference became a subject for discussion in drawing up the Basic Master Plan.

The Master Plan Steering Committee, with Snell as chair and Jones as scribe, addressed the scholarship/nonscholarship matter but felt that it could not make a specific recommendation regarding it in the Basic Master Plan given the widespread difference of opinion about it in the faculty. Consequently, it presented the proposed master plan to the faculty with the alternative of continuing scholarship athletics or of moving to a nonscholarship program. Snell, Hilliard, and Lansford were constituted as a subcommittee to compile information and to seek objective data. A decision about joining the Heart of Texas Conference was postponed until a decision had been made about scholarship athletics.[18]

In order to discuss these matters thoroughly before having to vote on them, the faculty met on December 12, 1989, as a nonlegislative committee-of-the-whole. In that meeting both the philosophical and practical aspects of scholarship aid were discussed. Provost Rosenthal stated that he was "skeptical of scholarship athletics," and President Shilling added that it would be impossible to approach the question solely on a philosophical basis. It also had to be looked at, he said, from the standpoint of institutional priorities, whether Southwestern could "buy" all its goals. This latter statement referred to the fact that HOT conference membership would cost more than the program then in place. "We can't have a 12 to 1 student load," he continued, "a 3-3 course load, salaries at 90%+, add 3 faculty members per year, meet 100% of financial need, offer academic scholarships, and have additional athletic expenses."[19]

A second nonlegislative committee-of-the-whole meeting was held on January 16, 1990, to discuss the Basic Master Plan. Shilling said that he assumed a "quality" athletic program either way the faculty decided the scholarship issue. Dean Rosenthal said that he did not believe that moving from scholarship athletics meant that Southwestern would cease to have quality or winning teams. Coupled with SU's strong academic reputation, he said, "we can attract, by other kinds of scholarship programs, scholar-athletes of first rank, as other quality liberal-arts colleges have done." The meeting adjourned with the expectation of deciding the issue at the regular faculty meeting the following week.[20]

At that meeting, on January 23, 1990, President Shilling took his strongest stand yet on the issue, emphasizing the economics of the matter. He said that financial aid had risen this year to 17–18 percent of the total operational budget even with the 16 percent cap and that the University had to rein in expenses somewhere. He said that SU wanted an educational program of excellence, and believed that the school "should have a student intercollegiate non-scholarship athletic program, on a level playing field, with as many students as possible involved in it." In answer to a question from Professor Allen, asking whether there was "any evidence that the schools we would come to resemble have actually saved $0.5 million per year," Shilling answered "no." He added that Southwestern simply didn't "have the dollars to continue athletic scholarships as in the past, and that a non-scholarship athletic program is most appropriate for us at this time." The total of athletic scholarships at the time amounted to $220,500.

At the conclusion of the discussion, the faculty voted on the two options presented in the proposed Basic Master Plan regarding intercollegiate athletics. Option A was for a program with scholarship aid; it received 44 votes. Option B was for no scholarship aid; it received 42 votes. With the scholarship issue having been decided, the vote for the Basic Master Plan as amended to include scholarship athletics was 84 for and 0 against.[21]

The Board of Trustees Decides the Athletic Scholarship Issue

Two days later the Executive Committee of the Board considered the issue. In order to give those who opposed his position an opportunity to express their point of view, Shilling invited three faculty members representing the scholarship position to speak at the meeting. They were Dr. Carla D. Lowry, Athletic Director, Dr. W. Nick Sikes, faculty representative on the Athletic Committee, and Dr. Richard T. Denman, Chair of the Athletic Committee. Provost Rosenthal and Vice Presidents Lind, Eason, Mock, and Bryant also made brief reports. After considerable discussion, the Executive Committee voted to recommend to the Board of Trustees that the University move toward a nonscholarship intercollegiate athletic program beginning the next academic year. It also recommended that the University expand and enrich its intramural and club sport programs to involve as many students as possible.[22]

At the full Board meeting two weeks later, President Shilling presented the original Basic Master Plan, including both Options A and B, to the Trustees for action. He emphasized that the only serious disagreement within the University concerning the Master Plan for the 1990s was the option whether to continue a scholarship intercollegiate athletic program or to move to a nonscholarship program.[23] He informed them that the faculty had endorsed Option A for scholarship athletics by a vote of 44 to 42 but that the Executive Committee had recommended Option B for nonscholarship athletics. Because the President's position for nonscholarship athletics was well known, the Board Chair, Mr. John Duncan, asked Shilling to leave the room for the discussion and vote. No other administrative officers from the University were present for any part of the discussion. The Board accepted the recommendation of the Executive Committee, then prepared a statement, the first two paragraphs of which read:

> The Southwestern University Board of Trustees has voted to adopt the Master Plan, *Vision 2000*, with the provision that the University move toward a strong non-scholarship athletic program by the year 2000.
>
> We are asking President Shilling to appoint and convene, this spring, a steering committee composed of faculty, administrators, and students to recommend to the Board, by its fall, 1990 meeting, a plan for the transition to a strong non-scholarship athletic program. We expect the University to give exemplary leadership in the development of a prominent non-scholarship athletic program which engages the broadest possible participation of students and which will serve as a model of success for universities of our size and character in our region and nation.[24]

The Board meeting and the action it might take had been widely advertised on campus, in town, and in the region. The next day the *Austin American-Statesman* provided a description of the student demonstration that greeted the meeting of the assembled Trustees and how the students received it on campus.

> Southwestern University trustees voted Friday to eliminate $220,500 in athletic scholarships as about 100 students protested with signs and chants of "Save our scholarships." . . . The trustees' decision came in a closed-door session. . . . When the trustees gathered in the A. Frank Smith Jr. Library Center on the campus of Southwestern . . . they were met by students demonstrating loudly but peaceably in favor of retaining athletic scholarships. As some Pirate coaches and athletic officials watched from a distance, the students carried signs reading "A model to be emulated, not eliminated," "What's next?" and "Why change a good thing?" [Admiral B. R.] Inman [a Trustee] met briefly

with the students after the meeting ended and told them that the athletic program "has been flat in funding the last three years." Students were both angry and disappointed at the decision. "They didn't listen to a word we said," one student said.[25]

One Trustee did hear them and made a promise that he remembered almost a decade later. When Red McCombs made a $1 million gift to construct new athletic fields on the east side of the campus in 1999, a reporter from the *San Antonio Express-News* asked why he did so. He answered that it was to help fulfill a promise he made to the students when he was chair of the Executive Committee of the Board of Trustees that recommended giving up scholarship athletics and going for NCAA Division III nonscholarship status. He said, "I promised the student body we'd rebuild all the athletic facilities."[26]

The New Intercollegiate Athletic Program

As a result of the Board action, Shilling announced on February 27, 1990, the formation of an Athletic Transition Steering Committee consisting of five students, four faculty members, and three administrators.[27] Roger Ballou, Dean of Students, served as chair. For three years Southwestern athletic teams continued to participate in NAIA Division II while the University phased in additional men's and women's intercollegiate sports programs to qualify for full NCAA Division III membership and the student athletes holding scholarships graduated year by year. By the fall of 1993 Southwestern was a fully participating member of the NCAA and dropped its NAIA affiliation.[28] Ironically, in the fall of 1992 the volleyball team made its sixth consecutive appearance in the NAIA national championship tournament, and baseball Coach Jim Mallon was inducted into the NAIA Hall of Fame.[29] During the 1993–1994 academic year, Southwestern joined the Southern Collegiate Athletic Conference, composed of Trinity in Texas, Hendrix in Arkansas, Rhodes in Tennessee, the University of the South in Tennessee, Centre in Kentucky, Millsaps in Mississippi, and Oglethorpe in Georgia.[30]

The action by Southwestern in joining the NCAA was part of a trend by smaller colleges and universities across the country. Division III of the NCAA had been formed in 1972–1973 with 232 schools. By 1996 it had 401 schools, most of which had migrated from the NAIA. One of the major differences between the two associations was that NAIA schools tended to put most of their money into a few sports, such as football or basketball, while NCAA Division III schools supported broad-based programming for different sports.[31] Southwestern had to bring the number of its intercollegiate sports up to twelve in order to qualify. By the time it did so, it competed in six men's and six women's sports: women's volleyball, men's baseball, and men's/women's soccer, cross-country, basketball, tennis, and golf.[32]

The controversy leading to a nonscholarship athletic program was perhaps the most divisive issue Shilling faced during his years at Southwestern. He had run a scholarship athletic program at Hendrix, and he did not try to introduce a nonscholarship program at Southwestern when he came. Neither did he introduce it into the discussions being held by the Master Plan Steering Committee that brought the issue to the faculty in 1989. Though Shilling believed in the nonscholarship position, he only began to speak in its behalf when it came to the faculty as an option in the Basic Master Plan. Once it was under discussion in faculty meetings, he supported it strongly. Over the years many, but not all, of the opponents who had originally opposed the move to nonscholarship athletics came to accept it, either grudgingly or willingly, as the advantages gained by its adoption became more evident.

Addressing in 1997 the move to NCAA Division III nonscholarship athletics, Shilling said that the most important gain was the increase in the number of students participating in intercollegiate athletics. Whereas a total of 124 student athletes were certified for eligibility in 1992–1993, in 1996–1997 there were 201, an increase of 62 percent. Men increased from 75 to 120, while women increased from 49 to 81.[33] Important to him also was the introduction in 1989 of a formal intramural program. Until that time, coaches and/or student activities personnel handled intramurals informally. By 1998, 80 percent of Southwestern's students and over 100 staff and faculty members participated. An outdoor recreation component was added in 1993 that provided life skills and experience in hiking, camping, rafting, canoeing, and rock climbing.[34] In spite of entreaties from some of the other Presidents in the SCAC, Shilling, a high school football lineman, refused to add intercollegiate football to the athletic program at Southwestern.

Refusal to Allow a Fifth Fraternity

The tension that had existed since the time of the Heidt administration in the 1880s between the conduct of fraternity/sorority members and University student life rules surfaced briefly again in 1990. A Fraternity Task Force of fourteen persons led by Dean Ballou made an in-depth study of the quality of life in the fraternity houses. It examined fraternity rush, hazing, alcohol abuse, sexism, racism, and degree of support for the academic experience.[35] When, in the midst of the study, the Student Affairs Council admitted a fifth fraternity to be organized on campus, the faculty insisted on discussing the matter thoroughly. It did so because there had not been any faculty discussion of the Greek system for twenty years, and not a single faculty member on the SAC had voted to admit the new fraternity when it came up for vote. The five students on the SAC had outvoted the three faculty members 5-3.[36] Dean Ballou also reported that the four fraternities were still in debt for loans they had received several years before.[37]

The faculty arrived at no formal decision, but in early 1991, Dean Ballou reported that the fifth fraternity had been dissolved, apparently because of widespread faculty opposition to it.[38] The Fraternity Task Force held a series of meetings with fraternity alums in early 1992 and concluded its work when the alums agreed to support certain goals sought by the University in their local chapters. No opposition was voiced by the faculty to the admittance of a new sorority, Alpha Xi Delta, to replace the Delta Zeta sorority that had been closed by its national office because of low membership.[39]

Fraternity Housing Problems

During the fall semester of 1995, the Kappa Alpha Order requested a loan from the University to make housing repairs. A cursory examination of the house convinced the President that repairs were needed, and he recommended that a Trustee committee be formed to look into the matter. Accordingly, a task force of Dr. Turner M. Caldwell III (Phi Delta), Dr. J. Charles Merrill (Kappa Sigma), Mr. Joe S. Mundy (Pike), and Mr. Douglas A. Paisley (Kappa Alpha) was set up to report in the spring.[40] A more detailed examination of the Kappa Alpha house over the Christmas break by engineers revealed that problems in the house involving the electrical system, plumbing, and fire safety were so fundamental that they recommended immediate closure of the house. Consequently, the house was closed on January 12 for health and safety reasons, and the members living in the house were moved to the new Grogan and Betty Lord Residential Center.[41] In light of the poor conditions found in the KA house, the Trustee committee asked that the other fraternity houses be examined as well. Though the problems found in those houses were not as serious as those in the KA house, they prompted the Board to adopt the Trustee task force recommendation that a fraternity housing study be authorized and that a plan be formulated to maintain and rehabilitate the fraternity houses.[42]

The fraternity housing study determined that the amount of money required to restore all the houses would be about $1.3 million if rolled into existing loans and would have to be advanced to the fraternities and then repaid. This procedure called into question the long-standing issue of whether the fraternities or the University owned the houses. Both the University and the fraternities had certain legitimate historical ownership rights. But one thing was certain. If the fraternities owned the houses, their alumni could not claim tax deductions for money contributed to repay direct restoration costs or restoration loans. Only if Southwestern was certified as the owner could alumni money donated for house improvements be claimed as an income tax deduction. If the houses belonged to Southwestern, the University, as a tax-exempt institution, could likely receive a private-letter ruling allowing donors to make their contributions tax-deductible. They would be contributing to the University, not to the fraternities.[43]

To resolve this problem, the Trustee Fraternity Housing Committee presented a report that was unanimously approved by the Board. It had three sections. Section A, titled Fire and Life Safety Standards, required each fraternity to meet all current fire and safety codes within one year, that is, by August 15, 1997, or to present an alternative plan to renovate or rebuild its house. After having been brought up to code, each house would be inspected monthly to assure continuing compliance. Section B applied to the renovation project of the Kappa Alpha fraternity house. Canceling its present ninety-nine-year lease and executing documents conveying all interests in the KA house and grounds to the University, the fraternity would sign a new lease agreement to meet the expected private-letter I.R.S. ruling. After this was done, the University would lend $600,000 for the restoration project and repayment of the present unpaid loan of $119,000, with KA alumni representatives agreeing to raise at least $400,000 over a period of five years for that purpose. Section C allowed the other fraternities to be "participating" or "non-participating" parties to the agreement, that is, choosing the path used by the KA's or not. The Kappa Sigma and Phi Delta Theta fraternities chose not to participate.[44] Nevertheless, since they were required to fulfill all the health and safety provisions of the Trustee resolution, they were granted the right to borrow up to $100,000 to be used solely for fire and safety improvement projects at 7 percent APR, with principal and interest to be paid in full at the end of a term not to exceed five years from the loan origination date.[45]

The renovation of the KA house proceeded with dispatch, and the members were able to move in at the beginning of the spring semester 1997, with a ribbon-cutting on January 18. Chapter members were enthusiastic and alumni members were very supportive.[46] The Kappa Alpha example was so powerful that the Pi Kappa Alphas elected to become a "participating" fraternity and to rewrite their deed as the KA's had done. The old Pike house was razed in the summer of 1997, and a new house costing over $1 million was ready by the fall semester of 1998.[47]

The Alcohol Raid on the Kappa Sigma House

Between 1996 and 1999, six Southwestern students died. In all but one of those cases, alcohol was involved. One of the last was that of a student on April 26, 1998, at Blue Hole on the San Gabriel River. The autopsy of the twenty-one-year-old student revealed that he had a blood-alcohol level of .10, the legal limit needed to declare intoxication under Texas law. Four of the other five students that died were under the legal drinking age of twenty-one.

This incident and a change in Texas law in September 1997, putting in place a "zero-tolerance" provision, led Texas Alcohol and Beverage Commission officials to warn that the new provision would be strictly enforced. During the summer, the TABC agent for Williamson County visited Southwestern and other schools to explain that his commission would specifically target underage drinking among college students, "with particular concern about those providing alcohol to minors."

In line with this warning, a raid was conducted on the Kappa Sigma fraternity in late September by TABC officers and the Southwestern Police. They raided a house party that had not been registered with the Office of Student Life, as was required when alcohol is involved. The officials issued forty-nine minor-in-possession (MIP) citations, though, admittedly, some of those receiving them may not have been drinking alcohol. Ten open cases of beer were found during the raid. One student, a Kappa Sigma officer, was arrested for providing alcohol to minors.

A campus-wide town meeting was held a few days later where students contested "the crack-down and [the] ambiguity" of the MIP law.[48] They were particularly incensed that Southwestern police had been a part of the raid and accused the administration of having known about it beforehand. Though Southwestern officials denied the charge, they supported the action of the Southwestern officers in participating in the raid. They explained that the Southwestern Police were licensed by the State of Texas, were obligated to uphold Texas law, and must support other State officers in the exercise of their duty.

Shilling reported to the Board of Trustees a few weeks later that the situation had quieted down, and, he hoped, would "ultimately have the effect of letting everyone know that Southwestern intends to uphold state and federal law in relation to alcohol use and possession."[49] The incident was reported on national news broadcasts and generated quite a bit of publicity for Southwestern.

Student Life in the 1990s

During the 1990s the membership of students in Greek letter organizations declined as a percentage of campus enrollment. In 1991, Dean Ballou reported that 47 percent of campus males were fraternity members and that 38 percent of the women were members of sororities.[50] By 1998 the total membership of both sexes in Greek letter organizations had dropped to about 35 percent of the student body. Clearly, the influence of the fraternities and sororities had declined over the decade. One of the reasons that can be adduced for this declining influence was the increasingly aberrant behavior of those organizations, as noted above. Another reason was the increasing strength of the student life program. The *Sou'wester* for 1998 listed eighty-five student organizations, including athletic teams, recognized by the Dean of Students. Their breadth of activities was such that most student interests could be accommodated. These activities were very important because 80 percent of the student body lived in campus housing by 1998. Even though only first-year students were required to live on campus, residence halls were filled to 98.5 percent of capacity.[51] A campus full to capacity needed activities beyond the classroom to help fill the lives of its students. Even though a large majority of them now brought automobiles to college and could get away when they chose, most of the students' time was spent on campus.

Particularly memorable to the students in 1992 was

an effort to help the victims of Hurricane Andrew. The hurricane first struck Florida on August 24, then continued through the Gulf and, finally, hit the coastline of Louisiana. Alpha Phi Omega, the Southwestern student service fraternity, organized student volunteers to work in Louisiana two weekends during the fall helping in relief efforts. Forty-eight students made the five-hundred-mile trip to Franklin, Louisiana, the first weekend and another fifty went two weeks later to Dulac, Louisiana. Senior Jon Porter, APO cofounder, came up with the idea after watching the television news show *Nightline*. The first group of students left the Bishops' Memorial Union on a Friday afternoon on a chartered bus loaded with saws, ropes, shovels, crowbars, and water donated by Georgetown businesses and campus personnel. They arrived at 2:00 A.M. at their destination just in time to sleep a little at a community center before going to work Saturday morning. Most of their work involved clearing away the wreckage of the hurricane. The second group worked at rehabilitating some of what had been damaged.[52]

Another form of social work for students came from the establishment on campus of the new position of Director of Student Religious Activities in 1994. Funded by the Moody Memorial Methodist Church of Galveston, the person employed for the position was Dr. Beverly Jones, B.A., Texas A&M, M.Div., Princeton, and Ph.D., Claremont Theological Seminary.[53] In 1996 she initiated an alternative spring break called "Destination: Service." It involved thirty-five students who went to Albuquerque, New Mexico, with the Cooperative Ministries program. Students repaired homes, helped improve a day care center building, and worked in child care.[54] In 1998 the alternative spring break program attracted seventy applications for its activities.[55] Destination: Service in 1999, so its report states, was spent by sixty-five SU students building and repairing houses, working with inner-city children, improving trails and conditions in a national park, and assisting with dental work in Central America."[56] About seventy students traveled to six locations nationally to do service work during spring 2000.[57]

Student life activities during the 1990s were led by Sherri Babcock, appointed Dean of Student Life in July 1992. She was made Vice President in 1994. After her graduation from Southwestern with a B.A., she earned an M.B.A. from the Edwin L. Cox School of Business at Southern Methodist University. Her thirteen years of volunteer work for Southwestern after graduation included serving four years as President of the Alumni Association, being a member of the Board of Trustees, and acting as chair of the Board's Student Life Subcommittee.[58] It was as a result of her impressive work on the Student Life Subcommittee that President Shilling brought her to work on the staff after the resignation of Dean Roger Ballou. She was particularly involved in helping with design elements of the Red and Charline McCombs Campus Center and in setting up a professional staff in the Student Life area to do counseling.

Special Events

The Sesquicentennial Year in 1990 was celebrated during the entire month of February with a series of special events, especially on February 8, the day before the annual Board meeting. Celebrating February as Black History Month, *Ebony* magazine sponsored a reception honoring Mr. Ernest Clark, the first African American graduate of Southwestern. Founders' Day celebrated 150 years of Methodist higher education in Texas with a sermon by Bishop Sharon A. Christopher (1966). Former Presidents Fleming and Finch participated during the day with the dedication of an historic marker. The Brown Symposium featured Stephen J. Gould on the topic "Punctuated Evolution: The Slender Thread of Life," and Martin Marty spoke to large audiences of church and campus persons during the Willson Lectures.[59]

Brown Symposium XXI, February 4–5, 1999, attracted the largest audience in the history of the event. Because of the fame of its participants, it attracted nationwide attendance and was featured in newspapers as far away as Lima, Peru. The principal participants were Rigoberta Menchú, a Guatemalan Mayan woman who had received the 1992 Nobel Peace Prize; Carlos Fuentes, internationally known novelist and diplomat; and Joaquín Achúcarro, the leading pianist in the Hispanic world. Several other fine speakers and musical groups filled out the two-day program. Attendance at the event was so great that it was simulcast to two auditoriums on campus to take care of the overflow crowd. Special measures had to be taken to ensure that Southwestern students would be able to have seats in the main auditorium.[60]

Conversations on Southwestern's Role as a Church-related School

At a faculty meeting on January 18, 1994, President Shilling shared with the faculty some of his thoughts regarding the place of Southwestern as a Church-related institution in contemporary society. Speaking extemporaneously without notes, he said that it was becoming increasingly difficult to understand what the term "church related university" means today. Officially, during the last ten to fifteen years, the Methodist Church had given responsibility to the University Senate for determining what institutions are Church-related and for setting standards for being recognized as such. However effective this action might be formally, he continued, it cannot belie the fact that a greater gap has been developing between the institutions of the Church and the Church itself than existed in years past. Because of this widening gap, he said, he was increasingly concerned about the character of the University and the messages it was sending on the eve of the twenty-first century. He often wondered, he admitted, how best to perpetuate the distinctive nature of Southwestern University. In conclusion, he said that for him it came down finally to the fact that "unless we all work together and have that caring, inclusive approach, we will lose our character as and the essence of being a church related institution."[61]

Sharing his innermost thoughts on the nature of a Church-related institution was an expression of Shilling's increasing desire to establish a more precise understanding of what Southwestern should be doing as a Methodist institution. He carried this interest a step further in 1997, when he appointed a President's Task Force for Religious Life. It was designed to feed into but be separate from the master plan process then underway. Under the leadership of Dr. Beverly Jones, the Task Force was composed of twenty-two persons—ministers, administrators, Trustees, staff, teachers, and students—and met at a special retreat away from the campus on November 7–8.[62] Though never presented anywhere for adoption, Shilling presented the final formulation of the Task Force to the Board with his commendation. Its nine-point statement probably comes as near to being a consensus understanding of Southwestern's mission as a Methodist institution as any formed during the Shilling era. It reads as follows:

> For Southwestern University, connection to The United Methodist Church means:
>
> 1. inclusion over exclusion of persons and thought;
> 2. providing a safe/sacred place for discussion in the classroom, in groups, and campus wide;
> 3. educating persons so that they are thoughtful, reflective, and responsible to the commitments they make to their present and future communities;
> 4. contributing to the formation of character through learning;
> 5. continuing the tradition of open dialogue and discovery between and among students, staff, and faculty;
> 6. fostering an environment that makes spiritual development possible;
> 7. maintaining religious studies in the curriculum;
> 8. seeking opportunities to engage the church in dialogue about a vision for society;
> 9. promoting the well being of humanity, the environment and all that is.[63]

Chaplain Farley Snell had produced in 1976 a statement that had spoken to the meaning of church-relatedness in his early years (see Chapter XX). Now, twenty-two years later, the new chaplain-designate had worked with a group to produce another such statement. She became chaplain on Snell's retirement in 1999.

Chaplain Snell preached in the chapel for over twenty-seven years. Because for much of that time he also served as chair of the Department of Religion and Philosophy, he was more a chapel preacher and teacher than a standard chaplain. As coordinator of the Religion Lecture Series, he brought scores of internationally recognized scholars and theologians to campus. A native Floridian, he held the A.B. degree from Florida Southern College and an M.Div. and Th.D. from Union Theological Seminary in New York. A person of independent mind who refused to be forced to do what he did not believe in, he was a splendid preacher, always preaching from the lectionary. At the time of his retirement, the University published a book of his sermons entitled *Sometimes a Surprising Word*.[64] The Wilson-Craven Chair he held, designated by the donor to be held by the chaplain, passed to Dr. Beverly Jones.[65]

The Academic Program in the 1990s

After the thorough overhaul of the core curriculum in the late 1980s, no major changes were made in academics through the remainder of the Shilling administration. When Provost Dale Knobel came to the campus in the fall of 1996, he began to take an intensive look at the curriculum, which he called "very traditional," making Southwestern "look like a little University."[66] His statement surprised some faculty members, since they were under the impression that a "university model" was precisely the thing they had escaped by the academic changes made during the 1980s. As it worked out, Knobel's two-year tenure was too short for the campus to experience much in the way of change under him, and he was kept busy directing the formation of the new master plan for 2010.

Nevertheless, Knobel did several things that suggest what he might have done on a larger scale had he remained at Southwestern longer. He worked with the science faculty during his first year at Southwestern to design a program to "propel science education at S.U. to a new level of excellence." The program was tentatively dubbed "Science for the 21st Century." Its purpose was to enhance student research opportunities, bring new computer technology into science labs, introduce state-of-the art "microscale" laboratory techniques in chemistry, and upgrade instructional equipment. Funded by the Fleming Fund for Excellence, the program would provide for an enhancement of science instruction to match laboratory upgrades that would accompany the forthcoming addition to the Fondren-Jones Science Hall. The allocation of Fleming Lecture resources to this initiative for three or four years would allow SU to plan for a major interdisciplinary speaker series that would focus upon the philosophical, religious, legal, and moral implications of scientific developments.[67] The biology department ran a successful summer undergraduate research fellows program in line with this design in 1997, while the mathematics, physics, and chemistry departments each had exciting summers as well in line with the program.[68]

Apart from Knobel's Science for the 21st Century program, most of the other academic changes in the 1990s were occasional rather than part of a pattern of development. The long-standing argument among faculty members about course evaluations that had gone on since the time of Dean Wicke in the late 1950s was finally settled when a system of anonymous course evaluations by students was instituted. The faculty also implemented a plus/minus grading system in the fall of 1996 after a delay of eight years from the time it was first proposed.[69] A First-Year Seminar was voted in the spring of 1998 to replace the current First Year Colloquium that had in turn earlier replaced the Freshman Symposium.[70] Certain changes were made in the decennial departmental review regulations that called for more intensive reviews to be done more frequently.[71] The "continued writing experience" requirement in general education was fortified on October 18, 1999, when the Deborah S. Ellis Writing Center was opened in Mood-Bridwell Hall, with a full-time teacher trained in the field to help students.[72] Ellis, a scholar in medieval literature and a popular teacher in the English Department, had recently died unexpectedly.

The University also began a regular observance of Martin Luther King Day on January 20, 1997, with special classes and other appropriate events on campus.[73] Professor Maria Lowe (Sociology) and Tanya Williams (Director of Diversity Education) conducted a Civil Rights Seminar and Tour during the May term of 1999. During the course, the class made a one-week bus tour across the South to visit places associated with the Civil Rights movement to experience them firsthand.[74]

After the departure of Dr. Theodore Lucas as dean from the School of Fine Arts in 1989, Dr. Carole Lee was appointed associate dean in 1990 and dean in 1991. Her academic credentials were strong. She held a B.A. from the University of California at Berkeley, an M.A. from San Francisco State University, and a D.M.A. from the School for the Arts at Boston University (1978). Educated in musicology and theory, piano performance, and art history, she came to the University after nearly two decades at Eastern Connecticut State College, where she served as Professor of Music and Chairman of the Department of Music. She visited China with her husband, a music director, on several occasions while dean, serving as a visiting professor in Beijing and Shanghai, as well as in Taiwan.[75] The strength of the School of Fine Arts during her tenure was the fine performing faculty she assembled. A significant accomplishment was the organization of the Southwestern Chamber Soloists, composed of four highly accomplished faculty members. They performed in the Weill Recital Hall of Carnegie Hall in New York on January 27, 1996.[76] She resigned in 2002.

The Brown Chair Endowment

The endowment corpus of the original Brown Chair Program, dating from 1952 and added to in the 1960s, had appreciated enough in value over the years that a second program, the Brown Symposium, was established to operate out of it in 1978. A Brown Scholars Program was established in the same year to serve as the premier student scholarship at Southwestern for funding the brightest and best student applicants for enrollment (see Chapter XXI). A sixth permanent Brown Chair, named the John H. Duncan Chair, was established in 1997 and conferred upon Dr. William B. Jones, who had given up his Lucy King Brown Chair to assume administrative duties in 1975.[77]

A fourth use of Brown Chair endowment income occurred in 1989 with the establishment of the Brown Fellows Program. The program was designed to support the scholarly activities of promising junior faculty members. The grants would provide support for a specific period so that they might have the necessary time, by giving them a reduced teaching load, and resources to undertake and bring to completion substantial scholarship and research within their disciplines. The two persons designated at any one time as Brown Fellows would win the award in competitive applications and review.[78]

The corpus of the Brown Chair endowment continued to rise during the precipitous stock market ascent of the 1990s, providing increased income beyond the needs of the programs already in existence. By this time many excellent faculty members had joined the University. Consequently, Brown Distinguished Teaching Professorships were established in 1998 to reward them and to make it possible for them to undertake special study and travel opportunities.[79] Persons appointed to these professorships would hold the position for a period of three years, with a special discretionary expense budget of fifteen thousand dollars and a one-month additional salary emolument each year.[80] A comparable Brown Distinguished Research Professor Program was established the following year to help faculty members whose expertise was in research. Professor Walt Herbert was responsible for much of the language creating the Research Professorship Program.[81]

The first three persons appointed to the Brown Distinguished Teaching Professorships were Dr. Suzanne Chamier (French), Dr. Jan Dawson (History), and Dr. Ed Kain (Sociology).[82] Dr. Chamier's specialty was Francophone Africa. Dr. Dawson was recognized as one of the outstanding teachers on campus and a leader in establishing the major in Women's Studies. Dr. Kain was prominent in national sociological circles and had published widely, having recently completed a book entitled *The Myth of Family Decline*. He was also an expert on HIV and AIDS and lectured widely on those subjects. He was appointed in the year 2000 to join Dr. Herbert as one of the two University Scholars. They received certain special privileges to facilitate their research and writing.[83]

The first persons selected to Brown Distinguished Research Professorships were Dr. Jesse Purdy (Psychology) and Dr. Eric Selbin (Political Science).[84] Purdy was one of the few psychological researchers who performed experiments using fish as research animals. A special laboratory for this work was included in the Olin Building design during its construction. He published the results of many of the research projects done by him and his students in scholarly journals. President Schrum appointed him to the John H. Duncan Chair in 2004. Selbin was a specialist in Latin America. He published *Modern Latin American Revolutions* in 1993 and authored a number of articles in scholarly journals. Both Purdy and Selbin were popular teachers as well.

The Roy and Margaret Shilling Lectureship Program, initiated as the University's premier lectureship in 2000 in honor of the retiring presidential couple, completed the uses to which the Brown Chair endowment money was being employed forty years after Herman and George Brown established the first Brown Chair. The excellent investment experience enjoyed by the endowment made it possible that by the year 2000 it supported seven separate Brown programs that have been of immense benefit to the University.[85]

Finch Professors

The Finch Professorship Award, established by the family of President Finch in 1979–1980, became over the years the outstanding honor given to faculty members for their service. Possible recipients are nominated every other year by a panel of five persons composed of the two most recent Finch Award winners, two students, and the Provost from the names of teachers submitted by faculty members and students. The President makes the selection from among the nominees presented to him by the committee. The persons on the following page have been honored as award winners through the year 2000.

Though each of these teachers deserves special mention, most of them have already been referred to in other contexts. The person that has received the most national attention is Vicente Villa. Born in Laredo, Texas, Villa came to Southwestern in 1985 from New Mexico State University. When it appeared in the recruiting process that he might not come, President Shilling and Dean Oliver made a special plane trip to visit him on site and persuaded him to accept an appointment as the first holder of the Herbert and Kate Dishman Chair in Science. Once at Southwestern, he rapidly became a favorite of students and worked in his quiet, unassuming way to encourage Hispanic and other students to believe they could succeed at college and in life.

In the spring of 1988, he won a Minnie Stevens Piper State of Texas Award for general excellence.[86] In September 1993 he was chosen from among 389 nominees across the

1980	T. Walter Herbert (English). Holder of the Herman Brown Chair; University Scholar. B.A., Harvard University; M.Div., Union Theological Seminary; Ph.D., Princeton University.
1982	Weldon S. Crowley (History). Retired 1997. Holder of the Lucy King Brown Chair in History. B.A., McMurry College; M.Div., Drew University; M.A., Ph.D., University of Iowa.
1984	F. Ellsworth Peterson (Music). Retired 2002. Holder of the Margarett Root Brown Chair. B.M., Southwestern University; S.M.M., Union Theological Seminary; M.A., Ph.D., Harvard University.
1986	Leonard F. Giesecke (Economics). Died 1994. Holder of the Herbert and Kate Dishman Professorship. B.A., M.A., Ph.D., University of Texas at Austin.
1988	Martha M. Allen (History). Retired 1997. B.A., M.A., Southern Methodist University; Ph.D., University of Texas at Austin.
1990	Jan C. Dawson (History). Retired 2004. Brown Distinguished Teaching Professor (1998–2001). A.B., University of California at Berkeley; M.A., Ph.D., University of Washington.
1992	Robert L. Soulen (Chemistry). Retired 1996. Holder of the Lillian Nelson Pratt Chair in Science. B.A., Baker University; Ph.D., Kansas State University.
1994	Gwen K. Neville (Sociology and Anthropology). Retired 1998. Holder of the Elizabeth Root Paden Chair in Sociology. B.A., Mary Baldwin College; M.A., Ph.D., University of Florida.
1996	W. Douglas Hooker (Psychology). Retired 2004. A.B., Wofford College; M.A., Wayne State University; Ph.D., University of Texas at Austin.
1998	Edward L. Kain (Sociology). University Scholar; Brown Distinguished Teaching Professor (1998–2000). B.A., Alma College; Ph.D., University of North Carolina at Chapel Hill.
2000	Vicente D. Villa (Biology). Retired 2003. Holder of the Herbert and Kate Dishman Chair in Science, later the John H. Duncan Chair. B.A., University of Texas at Austin; Ph.D., Rice University.

nation as the U.S. Professor of the Year by the Council for Advancement and Support of Education (CASE). He went to Washington, D.C., the next spring where he delivered a lecture at the Smithsonian Institution and received a ten-thousand-dollar cash prize contributed by the Carnegie Foundation for the Advancement of Teaching. His selection was recognized by the Associated Press, *USA Today*, and the *Chronicle of Higher Education*, was featured on a Spanish-speaking television network with approximately five hundred outlets, and was carried by television stations and newspapers all over the state.[87] Three years later the Carski Foundation awarded him the Distinguished Teaching Award funded by the American Society of Microbiology. It carried a two-thousand-dollar cash prize and a certificate.[88]

An article published in the *Southwestern Quarterly* in the fall of 1993 explained who Villa was in the following words.

> A Mexican American who grew up in Laredo and [who] worked as a shoeshine boy along the banks of the Rio Grande River, Villa was encouraged by his parents, whom he calls "pro-education," and teachers who pushed him to excel. He says, "The bottom line is perseverance. Don't give up. Be a fighter. Those expectations really saved me." After Laredo Junior College, Villa completed a B.S. in biology at UT-Austin and a Ph.D. in microbiology at Rice University. An animated lecturer and deeply spiritual man, Villa exudes a passion for science. . . .
>
> SU President Roy B. Shilling, Jr. is proud to have recruited Villa eight years ago from New Mexico State University, where Villa won nine teaching excellence awards during the thirteen years he worked there. . . .
>
> A Mexican American student [at Southwestern] frequently lingered outside his classroom, listening to his lectures. He followed Villa onto the elevator one day and said, "You know, you're a pretty good lecturer for a Mexican American." Villa did not hesitate. He punched the elevator's stop button, abruptly halting it

between floors of the science building. Villa responded, "Let me talk to you. Your statement reveals a lot. Don't buy into the idea that if you're Mexican American, you can't do it. It's a myth. It's not so. Don't set limits on yourself. I'm telling you, you must run with your talents!" Lecture over, Villa took his finger off the button and the pair descended together.[89]

Quality Teachers and Approach to Gender Equity

With a competitive salary scale and the buyer's market for college teachers that came to prevail across the nation during the Shilling years, Southwestern was able to recruit and retain more and more good teachers, some of them outstanding. Whereas in earlier years there was a scattering of high-quality teachers around the University, during the decades of the 1980s and '90s many were of that grade. Some departments were stronger than others, but there were no weak departments. A student attending Southwestern could expect to receive an education appropriate for enrolling in graduate school or entering a profession in every major offered.

Federal legislation prohibiting the enforced retirement of teachers because of age took effect in 1994. The last person to be retired under the previous age provisions of the University was Dr. Edwin M. Lansford, Jr., Professor of Biochemistry, who retired after thirty-one years in 1993. He held a B.A. in chemistry from Rice, a B.A. in meteorology from UCLA, and an M.A. and a Ph.D. from the University of Texas. He was a member of Phi Beta Kappa and came to Southwestern in 1962 from the Clayton Foundation Biochemical Institute at the University of Texas. He served as secretary of the faculty for many years and coordinated 452 Faculty Forums beginning in 1978. The Faculty Forum was a voluntary meeting of faculty members for lunch every Monday, with one of its members or an invited guest providing a program.[90]

The following persons were employed during the Shilling years and had remained for at least ten years by 2005.

Name	Discipline	Employed
Roeder, Robert C.	Physics	1983
Veerkamp, Patrick B.	Art	1983
Gaines, David J.	English	1984
Haskell, Halford W.	Classics	1984
Lowry, Carla d'Estelle	Kinesiology	1984
Howe, Thomas N.	Art and Art History	1985
Rawji, Gulnar H.	Chemistry	1985
Riquelme, Sonia	Spanish	1985
Varner, Victoria Star	Art	1985
Villa, Vicente D.	Biology	1985
Gould, Florence C.	Political Science	1986
Kain, Edward L.	Sociology	1986
Molitorisz, Joseph	German and French	1986
O'Brien, William D.	Physics	1986
Parks, Joan G.	Librarian	1986
Thompson-Price, Judy	Theatre and Communication	1986
Juhl, Kathleen	Theatre	1987
O'Neill, Timothy J.	Political Science	1987
Sellers, Fred Evans	Business	1987
Shelton, Therese N.	Mathematics	1987

continued on following page

continued from preceding page

Name	Discipline	Employed
Shen, Hsueh-Yung	Music	1987
Carl, Glenda Warren	French	1988
Davidson, Steven Craig	History	1988
Delaney, John Edward	Business	1988
Fabritius, Stephanie L. Brown	Biology	1988
Hunt, James W.	Education	1988
Potter, Walter M.	Math and Computer Science	1988
Chamier, Suzanne	French	1989
Olson, Therese E.	Library	1989
Pursley, Roy D.	Economics and Business	1989
Brody, Lynne	Library	1990
Muir-Broaddus, Jacqueline E.	Psychology and Education	1990
Young, Mary E.	Economics	1990
Anderson, Amy Fuge	Library	1990
Hendrix, Dana	Library	1991
Lowe, Maria R.	Sociology	1991
Meyers, Helene	English	1991
Richards, Kendall C.	Mathematics	1991
Smith, Jimmy C.	Kinesiology	1991
Benavides, Miguel Angel	Athletic Training Education	1992
Kilfoyle, James A.	English	1992
Olson, David	Communication	1992
Ore, John	Theatre	1992
Seagraves, Rhonda S.	Intercollegiate Athletics	1992
Selbin, Eric A.	Political Science	1992
Snyder, Robert S.	Political Science	1992
Stallard, Kathryn E.	Library	1992
Tamagawa, Kiyoshi	Music	1992
Adrian, Sherry E.	Education	1993
Bruns, Kerry A.	Chemistry	1993
Ferrari, Lois	Music	1993
Asbury, David	Music	1993
Bednar, Robert M.	Communication	1994
Craddock, N. Elaine	Religion	1994
Early, Dirk W.	Economics	1994
Fonken, Carol	Library	1994
Giuliano, Traci Ann	Psychology	1994
Northrop, Emily M.	Economics	1994
Parks, Don M.	Business	1994
Sheller, Rebecca Ann	Biology	1994

continued on following page

continued from preceding page

Name	Discipline	Employed
Winnubst, Shannon M.	Philosophy	1994
Cain, Bruce A.	Music	1996
Castro, Daniel, Jr.	History	1996
Guziec, Frank S.	Chemistry	1996

During the two decades from 1980–1981 through 1999–2000, Southwestern began to approach gender balance in its teaching faculty. Of the 305 full-time and part-time teachers that taught during those years, 143 (43.6 percent) were women. Of the 92 that taught only one or two years, 43.5 percent were women. Of those that taught three to five years, 42.3 percent were women. Of those that taught six to nine years, 43.3 percent were women. Of those that taught ten or more years, 46.4 percent were women.

Salary equity between the sexes was practiced inflexibly. President Shilling was scrupulous in making sure that the multiple regression salary equation provided by the American Association of University Professors and used to calculate bias resulted in a deviation of less than 1 percent between what total women's salaries were predicted to be, using the agreed upon variables, and what they were actually paid.

Achieving a Phi Beta Kappa Chapter

One of Ambassador Clark's constant refrains whenever he was on campus was that Southwestern must gain a Phi Beta Kappa chapter. Since charters are granted to the Phi Beta Kappa members on a faculty rather than to an institution, it was not until the end of the Fleming administration that the Phi Beta Kappa members on the faculty felt that they could make an application that would have a reasonable possibility of success. The current rule (2005) is that 10 percent of the full-time arts and sciences teaching faculty must be members, but in no instance may there be fewer than ten full-time faculty members.[91]

When the first Southwestern application to gain a chapter was made is uncertain, but it was probably around 1979 or 1980, since Professor David Blumenfeld (Philosophy) announced "with regret" to the faculty on April 15, 1986, that Southwestern's third consecutive triennial application for the establishment of a Phi Beta Kappa chapter had been turned down.[92] The next self-study application document was completed in late 1989, and two professors representing the national organization visited the campus in the spring of 1990. Though their report was favorable, the Phi Beta Kappa Council once again turned down the application the following year. Another application was accordingly submitted for the next triennial application period, and a three-person Phi Beta Kappa Committee on Qualifications visited Southwestern in 1993. In its final session with university officials, the committee "enthusiastically praised all aspects of the University and offered its unqualified support during the remainder of the process."[93]

Provost Rosenthal was particularly helpful in working with the Phi Beta Kappa committee when it came to campus and announced to the faculty in December that Southwestern had been approved by the Phi Beta Kappa Senate "without reservations" and that Southwestern would have advocates at the upcoming meeting of the Council in San Francisco during the summer.[94] The vote there was favorable, and the Theta of Texas chapter was installed at Southwestern on March 25, 1995, with thirty students, twenty Charter Members from the faculty and staff, and six Foundation members.[95]

With the addition of a Phi Beta Kappa chapter, Southwestern students now had two opportunities for recognition by a national scholastic honorary society. The nation's first chapter of Alpha Chi had been established at Southwestern beginning with President Bishop's setting up a Scholarship Society in 1915. The Scholarship Society idea spread, and the Southwestern chapter became the nucleus for the Scholarship Societies of Texas. It became the Alpha chapter of Alpha Chi in 1934 when the organization became national in scope (see Chapter XII). There were 298 chapters of Alpha Chi throughout the country in 1995.[96]

Becoming a National Liberal Arts Institution

As described earlier (see Chapter XXII), Southwestern began to be included in the rankings of colleges and universities by the *U.S. News & World Report* in 1983. Though the magazine first included Southwestern as a comprehensive institution, it soon placed Southwestern in the regional liberal arts category. It was listed as the top institution in the country among the more than 400 that comprised that type.[97] Because of the large number of regional institutions, the magazine subsequently partitioned the category into four U.S. geographical regions, with Southwestern becoming the top school in the West. The other type of liberal arts institution, besides the regional, was the national liberal arts school. There were 164 of them in 1995, and they included prestigious schools with a national reach and reputation.[98]

The *U.S. News and World Report* used the classification made by the Carnegie Commission on Higher Education to prepare its rankings each year. That Commission developed its system in 1970–1971 to support its program of research and policy analysis. By 1994 the classification had been updated twice, in 1976 and 1987, and had become the leading framework for describing institutional diversity in U.S. higher education.[99] When Shilling heard that it would be updated again in 1994, he kept close tabs on the process. By then he, as well as others on campus, felt that Southwestern's progress since 1987 would automatically cause it to be moved into the national liberal arts category.[100] When he learned from private sources that Southwestern was provisionally scheduled to be retained as a regional institution, he spoke to Marilyn Mock and Michael Rosenthal about it. They in turn worked with Bill Jones to write a letter to the Carnegie Commission making a case for placing Southwestern in the national category.[101] Shilling received a letter in return from Dr. Ernest Boyer of the Carnegie Commission that was most complimentary of Southwestern and suggested that the classification might be changed. It was, indeed, classified as a national liberal arts institution when the definitive rankings were announced in 1994.[102]

For some people the idea of going from #1 among the regional colleges to about #50 in the national liberal arts category was a dubious promotion. Jones explained it by saying that it was like going from being the best Triple-A baseball club to the major leagues. The competition would be tougher but the quality of play would be better. "Every school in our classification," he said, "is a quality institution, therefore ranking slightly higher or lower does not make that much difference. Southwestern has jumped through a hoop to join institutions where fiftieth is good."[103] Speaking about the reclassification in later years, Shilling said that Red McCombs, whose work as chair of the Board had helped make possible the transformation of Southwestern, was somewhat doubtful of pushing for the change. "It was difficult for him to give up being #1 in the region in the early years and starting all over in the rankings."[104]

Red and Charline McCombs

Dr. David Medley, a chemist, graduate of Southwestern during the Score years, and son of Coach R. M. Medley, said in an interview with this author that the best thing his father did for Southwestern was to give Red McCombs a scholarship. The Baylor coach called Coach Medley and asked if he could send a young man down from Waco who wanted to play football. Coach Medley said to send him on down.[105] This incident became the foundation for the relationship of Red McCombs with Southwestern, a relationship of momentous consequence for the University. McCombs himself referred to the story of how he came to enroll at Southwestern at the dedication of the Red and Charline McCombs Campus Center in 1998. He recounts it in his autobiography as follows.

> After finishing high school at seventeen, I hitchhiked across the state in the summer of 1945, trying to find a college that would give me a scholarship. I made a tour of six or seven campuses and was rejected by most of the coaches on sight. Then, to my delight, I thought I had made the squad at Baylor which didn't have a team at the time but planned to renew the sport since World War II was ending. I had made it through two weeks of a training camp, big and willing and naïve, raw as a crate of turnips.
>
> After the last day's workout, Bill Henderson, the athletic director and acting football coach, called me in with another ragged candidate. We were the last players to be cut. "You two kids can't help us," he said, as gently as he could, "but I've fixed it for you to go to school if you want."
>
> He said we had a choice of scholarships at Southwestern or Tyler Junior College. I asked him if Southwestern was a four-year school. He said, yes. I asked

where it was. He said, "Just down the road at Georgetown." I said, "I'll go there." I will always be grateful for Bill Henderson's help and kindness. That was the start of my education. I was the first member of my family, on either side, to attend college.

I will always be grateful to Southwestern for giving a scholarship to a mediocre athlete. I'm *not* being modest when I say that. I played both ways in the line, then enlisted in the army in 1946. For eighteen months, part of it served in Korea, I sent half my pay home and when I returned had enough for a new car. I enrolled at Del Mar Junior College in Corpus Christi, and played one more season of football. Then I exercised my veteran's option to attend the University of Texas.[106]

Because Red attended Southwestern in 1945–1946 and Charline during 1946–1947, they did not meet on campus. They found each other later at home in Corpus Christi and were married in 1950. As they prospered in business, they began to make gifts to the school. By the time of his Commencement address in 1997, when he and Charline were awarded honorary degrees, the McCombs Family Foundation had enabled more than one hundred students to earn Southwestern degrees with resources provided from an endowed scholarship fund established by Red and Charline in 1983. He said in his Commencement speech in 1997, "I have very fond memories of almost this same time of the year 52 years ago when, as a 17-year-old, I came to this campus for the first time."[107]

Red and Charline were "hands on" people, and they appeared on campus from time to time. On those occasions they often mixed with students and faculty without any pretense. Once when he attended an Academic Affairs Council meeting in the Trustee room upstairs in the old, circular University Commons, he began by saying that he was attending as a listener. He hoped that the members of the Council would go right on with business and ignore his presence, as he did not pretend to be knowledgeable about the subject being discussed.

He also remembered little things and insisted on carrying through his commitments even after eight or ten years, as he did in the case of his commitment to the students at the time of the scholarship athletic controversy in 1989–1990. At a Trustee meeting on one occasion, Rock Houston congratulated me for a paper I had recently written that had been distributed by mail to all the Trustees prior to the meeting. Red said nothing at the time but made a mental note of the comments about the paper. Several weeks later, I received a handwritten note from McCombs in Minneapolis, where, as owner of the Minnesota Vikings football team, he was at that time. In the note he said that he had just read the paper referred to at the meeting and that he, too, wanted to express his appreciation for it.

Charline was always bright, gracious, and sensitive. On the occasion of the large luncheon on October 17, 1998, celebrating the success of the Leadership 2000 financial campaign, she made an unexpected announcement in celebration of her seventieth birthday. A few days later Roy Shilling wrote her a thank-you letter that said: "It was a stunning moment Saturday when you announced a $70,000 gift to fund scholarships for minority women. You stirred the emotions of all of us, and you especially touched the lives of the women on our faculty who are thrilled at your sensitive direction of this gift."[108]

Charline was a regular participant in the McCombs philanthropies. An exception to this rule occurred when the Executive Committee approved the construction of a ninety-six-bed apartment complex on October 1, 1999, for a cost of $4.65 million. Shortly after the meeting Red informed Shilling that he wanted to make a $1 million gift in honor of Charline in connection with the apartment complex and wished it to be kept secret. The gift allowed the setting up of a different financial plan for the buildings than had been contemplated by making it possible to amortize a loan for the buildings from the endowment over eighteen years at 7 percent interest. The resulting residential complex was named the Charline Hamblin McCombs Residential Center.[109] The total McCombs gift at the time was $2 million, $1 million for the new athletic fields already mentioned and $1 million for the two-building residential center built behind Martin Ruter Hall and, with it, forming a three-building quadrangle.

Red McCombs became a member of the Board of Trustees in 1987 and was appointed soon thereafter as a member of its Executive Committee. He was elected chair of the Board in 1992. His work in that capacity and the gifts made by him and Charline to the University were crucial in helping it achieve its goals during the 1990s. He and Shilling worked in tandem to achieve the results that were brought about during the '90s. Though McCombs and Shilling were both strong-minded men and sometimes had their differences, they respected one another and worked closely together. Their achievements at Southwestern working as a team were remarkable.

The Olin Building

The third major event in the 1993–1994 academic year, in addition to getting the Phi Beta Kappa chapter and being named a national liberal arts institution, was the procurement of a $6.5 million grant from the F. W. Olin Foundation of New York for the construction of an academic building. Born in 1860, Olin graduated with a degree in engineering from Cornell, after which he entered the gunpowder and ammunition business. He founded the Equitable Powder Manufacturing Company in 1892 and the Western Cartridge Company in 1902. In 1938 he established a foundation to help independent colleges and universities construct buildings, primarily for engineering and science but also for other facilities in information technology, business, the humanities, and the arts. He died in 1951.[110] As of 1993, the F. W. Olin Foundation had a net worth of $300 million and had paid for the construction of sixty-three buildings at fifty colleges and universities.[111]

Roy Shilling and Rick Eason began to cultivate the Olin Foundation in 1990 about constructing a 39,000 square foot academic building to house electronic classrooms, a language learning center, an experimental psychology laboratory, faculty offices, and two large lecture halls.[112] Their grant request was turned back each year from 1990 through 1992, but they were encouraged to reapply each following year. Marilyn Mock and Isabel Brown Wilson joined Shilling and Eason in their 1993 visit to Mr. Lawrence W. Milas, President of the Foundation, and Southwestern was selected as one of the four finalists from over ninety applicants to receive a site visit by Foundation trustees during the spring of 1994 to determine the winners of the two Olin grants for the year.[113]

Milas phoned Shilling and McCombs during a retreat of the Executive Committee and the Campaign Steering Committee on June 13, 1994, to announce that Southwestern had been selected to receive $6.5 million to construct and equip the academic building proposed in the application.[114] In fact, the grant eventually topped out at $6.8 million by an additional grant of $300,000 to provide equipment.[115]

Lawrence W. Milas made the public announcement of the grant on September 7–8 in Dallas, Austin, Houston, and Georgetown. He said: "I cannot recall another college

On the occasion of the dedication of the Olin Building in 1996, Board Chair Red McCombs presented Larry Milas of the Olin Foundation with two steers from his ranch. One was named "Larry Milas" and the other "Olin." Southwestern University, Special Collections.

among the many that I have been involved with over the last 20 years that has made as much improvement in its quality and standing in so short a time. It is a remarkable story and one that should be a required case study for all other colleges." Milas continued by enumerating some of the things he said the Foundation had learned about Southwestern. "First, there has been strong institutional planning which has enabled Southwestern to identify its quality goals.... Second, with the support of its Board, Southwestern has taken strong and decisive action to achieve its goals.... [Third,] in particular, there has been outstanding administrative and financial management.... [Fourth,] Southwestern's success is also due to the essential financial support of its Board, its alumni, and its friends.... And, [fifth,] you are not standing still." Milas compared the Olin grants to the Nobel Prize. The process of winning an award "has caused many to describe our grants" he said, "as a kind of Nobel prize for colleges. But unlike the Nobel prize, our grants bring recognition not only for what you have already accomplished, but also for what we expect you will accomplish in the years ahead."[116]

Shilling stated at the time that, when completed in 1996, the outside of the new Olin academic building would look like all the other classic, solid limestone structures on campus but that inside the building would be a strictly twenty-first-century structure, with computerized classrooms and labs for the psychology, communications, and modern and classical language departments. "With the new building," said Shilling, "Southwestern will join the technological revolution that is sweeping colleges across the country and changing the nature of the classroom. In the electronic classrooms, professors will control video players, laser disc players and a variety of sound and image equipment by touching the screens on their electronic lecterns."[117] While the Olin Building was under construction, a prototype classroom was opened in Mood-Bridwell Hall. It was Southwestern's first electronic classroom.[118]

On the occasion of the Olin Building dedication, Red McCombs had brought two steers and a Stetson hat from his ranch to give to Larry Milas. The steers were placed in a temporary pen in front of the Olin Building and given to Milas by Red during the ceremony. One was named "Larry Milas" (LM) and the other "Olin" (O). The occasion was hilarious. One could tell that Milas, though pleased, had some difficulty dealing with the event, the like of which he had probably never experienced. Unable to care for the animals himself, he asked Red to keep the steers for him on his ranch. Red wrote him that "LM" and "O" were "running and romping at the RM Ranch in Johnson City."[119] Roy Shilling later sent Milas a photo album of the dedication. Milas wrote back, thanking him for the album, and adding: "The Building looks great and so do Red, my steers and the Stetson. It was a great time!"[120] After Red received his honorary doctorate from Southwestern, Milas wrote him: "Now that you have a doctorate and you are officially entitled to all the privileges and respect which this honor requires, I am more confident than ever that my two prize steers, 'Olin' and 'L[,]' are in the right hands—and that's no bull."[121]

Honorary Degrees and Other Awards over the Years

One of the rights of colleges and universities has traditionally been that of awarding honorary degrees to persons of merit. Southwestern and its root colleges have practiced this right since 1840. During the first eighty-two years of its history, from the time of Rutersville College in 1840 to the end of the Bishop administration in 1922, that right was exercised very seldom. Only 51 honorary degrees were awarded during that period, a rate of only 3 every five years.

The big change came with the Golden Anniversary Celebration of Southwestern in Georgetown in 1923. On that occasion President Horn awarded 9 honorary degrees, 5 D.D.'s to ministers and 4 LL.D.'s to laymen. This gesture started a new trend. Without much else in the way of honor to offer donors and other important persons, the Presidents from Horn to Fleming, from 1923 to 1981, offered 279 honorary degrees in fifty-nine years, a rate of 4.7 per year. Aside from Horn's one-year Golden Anniversary gesture of 9, the President offering the greatest number of honorary degrees was Score, with an average of 6.6 per year over his seven years. Presidents Vivion, Bergin, Finch, and Fleming all offered an average of between 4.0 and 4.7 per year. President Fleming had a regular schedule by which he prorated doctorates of divinity among Southwestern's supporting Annual Conferences. He hardly ever celebrated a major event on campus without awarding an honorary degree to some luminary.

President Shilling dropped back in his awarding of honorary degrees to the rate of earlier years. During his nineteen years, he awarded only 27 degrees, an average of 1.4 per year. Of these, 21 were given in his first ten years. Only 6 were given in his last nine years. They were to Jake B. Schrum, Kenneth Wayne Day, Wilhelmina Cullen Robertson, Isabel Brown Wilson, Red McCombs, and Charline McCombs. There were several reasons for this change during his administration. On the one hand, the D.D. degree became less important for pastors as seminaries developed the D.Min. degree and more and more ministers sought this earned degree. Second, the Distinguished Alumnus Award given by the Alumni Association was ratcheted upward to honor graduates of distinction. Lois Perkins felt this award was perhaps the greatest of her career. Third, the Southwestern Medal was created in 1997 to be given upon the approval of the President and the Board of Trustees to select members of the Southwestern University extended family who had distinguished themselves through service. It was given to Genevieve and Red Caldwell in 1998. Hardly anyone can be said to have been more loyal and to have done more for the University and its students than she and her family. The Caldwell-Carvey foyer in the Fine Arts Center also marks this contribution. Fourth, faculty members, wishing to reserve them for persons of exceptional merit, became increasingly reluctant about awarding honorary degrees to persons for purposes of stoking development. Nevertheless, Southwestern, along with practically all the other major universities, continues to award honorary degrees in appropriate circumstances from time to time.

Red McCombs and Dan Rather. For the kickoff of the Leadership 2000 Campaign on January 14, 1995, Red McCombs secured Dan Rather, his friend, fellow Texan, and CBS news anchor, to deliver the keynote address to several hundred volunteers. Southwestern University, Special Collections.

Many of the persons that received honorary degrees in the past, though they were well known in their own time, are hardly known today. The names of others who have received those degrees are still an honor to Southwestern. Some of them awarded during the career of this author are, ordered by date of conferral, John Goodwin Tower, Mrs. Lyndon Baines Johnson, John Taylor King, Ima Hogg, Arthur Rubenstein, Albert C. Outler, Barbara Jordan, Michale E. DeBakey, James Jarrell Pickle, Charles Aubrey LeMaistre, Alice Pratt Brown, B. R. Inman, Wilhelmina Ruth Delco, Elspeth Rostow, Henry Gabriel Cisneros, and Sarah R. Weddington.

The Leadership 2000 Campaign for $75 Million

In his telephone conversation with Shilling and McCombs to inform them of the Olin grant, Larry Milas had mentioned only one condition beyond fulfilling the pledges already made as being absolutely necessary for Southwestern to receive the grant—that the current Leadership 2000 campaign goal be set at not less than $75 million.[122] Milas was referring to a capital campaign that had been initiated in December 1991. The two men made the pledge without hesitation.

During 1991, the Institutional Advancement Committee of the Board had engaged Marts & Lundy, Inc., a national counseling service for fund-raising by nonprofit organizations, to conduct a feasibility study for a major campaign. In December Marts & Lundy reported that a "comprehensive fund-raising campaign in the magnitude of $75 million" could be sought over a period of five years but that a leadership committee of about ten persons should be set up during 1992. After the leadership group had been identified, a quiet campaign should be conducted with no public announcement until some "critical solicitations" had been made. The Board, accepting the report, voted that a $75 million campaign should be engaged in, subject to the successful formation of a Campaign Committee to be constructed and chaired by Red McCombs.[123] McCombs was not only elected chair of the Campaign Committee, but was also elected in 1992 as chair of the Board of Trustees. Of the $75 million to be raised, $23 million was to go to endowment, $10 million to current operations, and $42 million to facilities.[124] The total goal was later adjusted to $75.5 million, and the distribution among the three categories was altered slightly.

After the naming of the Campaign Committee, the quiet campaign began. Though no precise date was set for beginning the public portion of the campaign, it was agreed that it should not begin until sufficient financial commitments had been made by key donors and foundations to guarantee a good possibility of success. With 50 percent of the total goal having been raised by the end of 1994, the public campaign was initiated on January 14, 1995, at a major event on campus.[125] For that event, Red McCombs secured Dan Rather, his friend, fellow Texan, and CBS News anchor, to deliver the keynote address to several hundred volunteers, and, as a gesture of thanks and a symbol of the campaign momentum, McCombs announced that he and his spouse, Charline, were contributing $100,000 to fund a scholarship at SU in Rather's name. He also indicated that a room in the proposed campus center would be named for the news anchor.[126]

Though the campaign lasted seven years instead of the originally contemplated five, three for the quiet and four for the public phases, it was the most successful campaign ever run in Southwestern history. The following percentages of the total $75 million goal were reached in successive years: 1992—10 percent; 1993—27 percent; 1994—50 percent; 1995—74 percent; 1996—78 percent; 1997—89 percent; 1998—100+ percent. When Eason reported the reckoning on October 15, 1998, a total of $76,123,318 had been raised.[127]

The Library

Dr. Jon D. Swartz assumed leadership of the library from 1981 to 1990. He did not have library training but was a bibliophile and a prolific author in his field. He came to the position from a three-year stint as the Brown Visiting Professor of Education and Psychology.[128] Lynne Brody came to the library as Director in 1990 and is still serving. She earned her A.B. in Sociology and Art History from Douglass College, Rutgers University, and her M.L.S. from Simmons College. Before her appointment at Southwestern, she served as Head Librarian, Undergraduate Library, at the University of Texas at Austin.[129]

Within a year of her coming, the President cited Brody to the Board of Trustees for exemplary leadership in the library.[130] When Southwestern joined the Associated Colleges of the South consortium in 1994, she became a very important member of its committee seeking a $1.2 Mellon Foundation Library Grant.[131] At that time ACS was composed of Trinity, Sewanee, Rhodes, Hendrix, Centenary, Centre, Millsaps, Birmingham-Southern, Rollins, Morehouse, Furman, and Richmond in addition to Southwestern. When the grant was received, Southwestern became a part of the Palladian Alliance, the electronic library consortium of the ACS schools. The grant from the Mellon Foundation allowed students at member schools to tap into thousands of periodical titles, abstracting and indexing services, and information databases and not only read information online, but also download full-text versions of journal articles for hard-copy printout. Southwestern ranked third among the thirteen colleges and universities in usage volume.[132]

Another leap forward in library and information technology occurred when Southwestern was chosen in 1999 to be the center for the ACS Technology Center in a competition among all fifteen member institutions of the consortium (the number had increased since 1994). It was funded by a grant of $1,250,000 from the Andrew W. Mellon Foundation.[133] The new Technology Center, containing training labs, a multimedia and video conferencing center, and staff offices, was established in the A. Frank Smith, Jr., Library Center at the suggestion of Library Director Brody. Dr. Suzanne Boniface came from ACS headquarters in Atlanta, Georgia, to serve as the center's director. Once established, the center began serving as the site for extensive training programs for faculty of the member institutions and for a new "virtual department" in classics with a complementary program in archaeology. Regular workshops were held during the summer for all fifteen participating institutions, several Mellon Faculty Fellows were generally in residence on campus during each academic year, and up to fifteen student interns from the different institutions did their work at the center.[134]

Shilling commented to the faculty that the awarding of the Technology Center "was the most significant thing that has happened to us in a while," and that it reminded him of how far SU had come since it began trying to join the ACS. He said that in his view, "We will remember this as a transforming event in our lives." Jones praised Lynne Brody's help in "conceptualizing the participation of the library" and in determining how use of library offices and facilities would help create the center. Jones announced that she would receive a new title, Dean of Library Services, for her many accomplishments since coming to SU in 1990.[135] With the intention of making the library a center of intellectual life, she had recruited an exemplary staff, expanded the special collections area, and—with grants from the

Vaughan Foundation—created five well-furnished study alcoves. In the year 2000, Dean Brody and her staff created a lecture series entitled "The Writer's Voice." Under that program a prominent writer is brought to campus each year to talk with students, faculty, and community about the writer's craft, using the body of his or her works as the focus. To date the following writers have been featured: Joyce Carol Oates, Russell Banks, Michael Chabon, Margaret Atwood, Tony Kushner, and Carlos Fuentes.

Technological Developments

Until 1991 the work of two people, Harold Eidson and Barbara Bielss, encompassed most of the work in administrative computing. Computer Science had been established as a field of study in a combined department of Mathematics and Computer Science largely due to the influence of the mathematics chair, Ralph Whitmore, and a staff of persons with expertise in computer science began to be built into the department. Robert A. Horick was employed as the first person to provide expertise for the faculty in its use of computers. Joining Southwestern in 1983, he said in an interview: "We bought five of our first microcomputers from a young man in a white Cadillac. His name was Michael Dell."[136] Born in Tyler, Texas, Horick held a B.A. in mathematics and music from respectively the University of Rochester and the Eastman School of Music, an M.S. in management from Purdue University, and a Ph.D. in Slavic language and literature from the University of Chicago. He was a Renaissance man. His computer expertise came from private study. In 1991 he was made Executive Director of University Information Systems, and later he became Director of Networked Systems.

The construction of the new A. Frank Smith, Jr., Library Center in 1988 included the automation of the library system at the cutting edge of library technology then prevalent. The system was funded from the proceeds of the Thatcher Atkin estate and completed in the spring of 1990 at a cost of approximately $350,000.[137] In the same year the University purchased personal computers for all faculty members.[138]

The current organization of Information Technology was established in 1994, when Dan Bryant, Vice President for Fiscal Affairs, assembled a group of twenty-three persons, including especially mathematics professor Walt Potter, to outline a new structure. As a result, Robert C. Paver was employed in 1995 as Associate Vice President for Information Technology Services. Paver, B.A., M.A., came with ten years of experience at Microelectronics and Computer Technology Corporation (MCC) in Austin and has served in the leadership role since that time.[139]

The construction of an Internet "home page" for the University in 1995 and the construction of the Olin Building in 1996 with the latest technological equipment further pushed the University in the direction of full computerization. During the latter year a $2 million project networked all faculty/staff offices, classrooms, residence halls, and common areas. The upgrading of desktop computers for faculty and staff, the upgrading of the voice mail system, the bringing in of cable TV and video, and the replacing of the major administrative computer were all accomplished as a part of the project.[140] Each student was provided with one port per pillow in dorm rooms, video services were added to residence halls, and more computerized classrooms were built around campus. The most aggressive part of the plan was bringing some five hundred rooms, with eight to nine hundred students, up to the proper standard.[141] The entire project was completed in 1998.[142]

The Building Boom

Whereas the Master Plan of the 1980s focused on program initiatives, the Master Plan of the '90s focused on building priorities.[143] Shilling said that Southwestern must now build a campus worthy of the educational program it had put in place. The Leadership 2000 Campaign was calculated to secure that end. The University constructed and/or renovated the equivalent of 50 percent of the total square footage of the campus during the campaign, spending $60 million for new facilities, renovations, and deferred maintenance.[144] Of the thirty-one projects listed below, 3 were completed prior to the beginning of the campaign in 1991, twenty were completed during the campaign, and eight were completed in 1999 and 2000 after its official conclusion. Except for the renovation of the President's home, the last eight came from the momentum established during the campaign.

- Mabee Residence Hall, 1985.
- A. Frank Smith, Jr., Library Center, 1988.
- Snyder Athletic Field, 1990.
- Life safety improvement changes, 1991.
- Jesse H. and Mary Gibbs Jones Theater, 1992.

- Physical Plant Building, 1993.
- Rufus Franklin Edwards Studio Art Building, 1993.
- Roy H. Cullen Academic Mall, 1993.
- Corbin J. Robertson Physical Education Center, 1995.
- Mood-Bridwell Hall electronic classroom, 1995.
- Grogan and Betty Lord Residential Center (seven buildings), 1995.
- McCook-Crain Building relocation, 1995.
- Campus infrastructure project, Phases I and II, 1995, 1996.
- F. W. Olin Academic Building, 1996.
- Julie Puett Howry [Golf, Tennis, and Baseball] Center, 1996.
- Fountainwood Observatory, 1997.
- Rockwell Baseball Field lighting, 1997.
- Robert K. Moses, Jr., Soccer Field, 1997.
- Brown-Cody Residence Hall, 1997.
- Kappa Alpha fraternity house, 1997.
- Information Technology Services enhancements, 1998.
- Red and Charline McCombs Campus Center, 1998.
- Pi Kappa Alpha fraternity house, 1998.
- Fondren-Jones Science Hall expansion, 1999.
- $1 million in NMR (Nuclear Magnetic Resonance Spectroscope) and other new science building equipment, 1999.
- Fine Arts Gallery, 1999.
- Kyle E. White Religious Activities Center relocation, 1999.
- A softball field and two soccer fields on east side of campus, 2000.
- Charline Hamblin McCombs Residential Center, 2000.
- Modest makeover of Martin Ruter Hall, 2000.
- Renovation of the President's home (Turner-Fleming House), 2000.

Money to construct these projects was donated by many foundations and scores of people. Because income from the pledges would be coming in at different rates over different periods of time, different financial models were used to accelerate the construction of buildings. These were all consolidated into one financial plan that called for all the obligations to be retired in 2014.[145] Every building and project was dedicated free of debt, and none of the building funds was taken from operating revenues.[146]

In addition to the construction of buildings, some key land purchases were made during the closing years of the Shilling administration. When it appeared that a Houston land developer might build a modular housing subdivision adjacent to University property on the east side of the campus, the University worked with the city to stop the development.[147] The Executive Committee then worked out an arrangement to purchase some of the land from the developer, who gave up his project to build modular housing. The University now owns slightly more than seven hundred contiguous acres of land stretching east from the railroad tracks bordering the campus on the west.

Development of the Core Campus

From the time of its construction in 1898–1900, the Main Building, or the Administration Building, or the Cullen Building, all names by which that building was known by succeeding generations, became when built the symbol of the campus. It *was* the University. Its majestic hallways today still cast their spell and re-create a time when that was literally true. The Ladies' Annex, built in the 1880s, carried the symbolism of education for women in its time, but it burned down in 1925. Its replacement, the Woman's Building, or, later, Laura Kuykendall Hall, was a large, fine building in its own way, and was an essential part of campus work. In addition to housing women, it was attached to an adjoining building that included the main dining hall and the School of Fine Arts. But its increasingly antiquated housing arrangements and brick construction brought about its inevitable removal in 1997 in favor of women's residence halls more in keeping with the times and the general stone architecture of the campus. Mood Hall was a part of the core campus in location and style but was not so in terms of its function. No thrilling extracurricular events such as Christmas candlelight services, magnificent pageants, or Dinners of the Golden Bowl became a part of its tradition, as in the case of the Woman's Building. It was simply a residence hall and, at times, a dining hall as well. It became a part of the core campus in function only in the late 1970s, when it lost its residence hall status in favor of becoming a major faculty office and classroom building. After its construction in 1950, the Lois Perkins Chapel, standing at the apex of the crescent drive, came to be the keystone around which other buildings joined these to comprise the modern core campus.

The core campus today is composed of buildings standing at the heart of the campus dedicated to the principal educational work of Southwestern, both curricular and extracurricular. Architect Craig Hartman was right in 1982 when he identified as one of the major problems of the campus a lack of unity in the location of the buildings devoted to its main educational functions. The major campus buildings were constructed on peripheral sites originally to prevent unity. The Main Building and the Annex had been built at a considerable distance from one another precisely to keep the men and women separate. The women lived, studied, and played basketball on their part of the campus. The men did the same on their part of the campus. Separation rather than unity was sought. This tradition of separation maintained some of its force in campus design even after the academic program had been unified for many years.

Building placement to promote the unified educational function of the institution gradually began to appear after 1939 as the library, the Alma Thomas Fine Arts Center, the Fondren Science Hall, and the Bishops' Memorial Union were constructed around the crescent drive, but the idea of placing buildings specifically to promote campus unity was not strong. The circular University Commons, constructed in the mid-1960s, was built on the periphery and required students to walk away from the heart of the campus. The Facilities and Grounds Master Plan of the early '80s turned what had been a rather haphazard architectural movement toward unity into a rational, purposeful movement. The razing of West Gymnasium in order to build the F. W. Olin Building on its site and the razing of the Bishops' Memorial Union and the circular University Commons to build the Red and Charline McCombs Campus Center on the site of the former Union solidified the Skidmore, Owings & Merrill plan of bringing the primary educational functions to the heart of the campus. The impending construction of a major new academic building today between the Olin Building and the Alma Thomas Fine Arts Center will complete the campus core, the circle of educational buildings at the heart of the campus.

One of the major developments in campus design during the last quarter century has been the formation of a separate physical education complex angling off northeast from the campus core. The construction of the Sid W. Richardson Physical Education Center in 1976 and its subsequent enlargement and transformation into the Corbin W. Robertson Physical Education Center in 1995 inaugurated the concept by establishing a locus for indoor athletic activities adjacent to associated fields for outdoor activities. The major athletic fields, once dominating the west side of the campus, were moved to the east side of the campus as a part of the athletic complex. Though new fields and courts for tennis, soccer, softball, and baseball usurped part of the golf course on the east side of the campus and reduced it to a six-hole course, present plans call for eventually amplifying it to either a nine-hole or an eighteen-hole course. The Fountainwood Observatory, with its two large, electronically controlled telescopes, sits at one corner of the athletic fields shielded from campus and town lights as it searches the sky.

The Red and Charline McCombs Campus Center

Due to limitations in the facilities of the Bishops' Memorial Union, plans began to be made in 1990 for renovation and expansion of that building. A seventeen-member committee, chaired by Dean Ballou, later succeeded by Dean Babcock, reviewed campus needs and a subgroup visited Carleton College, Macalester College, Colorado College, and SMU to examine similar facilities there.[148] During the planning process, an examination of the foundation of the Union building revealed that the strength of the concrete was problematical and that the present building could not be expanded with assurance that its foundation would be adequate for the proposed expansion. Consequently, the idea began to take hold that the current building should be removed and a new one built in its place. Shilling reported in 1994 that the expected cost of a new building would be $10.2 million.[149]

Though Hastings & Chivetta of St. Louis, Missouri, who were at the time also doing the architectural work for the $7.425 million Corbin J. Robinson Physical Education Center, were the design architects for the building, Robin Bruno, AIA, of Group Two Architecture of Austin served as the representative of Southwestern with Hastings & Chivetta to achieve maximum design benefits for the funds available.[150] For the decade of the 1990s Bruno served in that role for most University projects when he was not the design architect for the project himself. His work and that of his firm were so satisfactory over the years that officials at the University almost felt that he was one of them.

Construction of the building was not begun, however,

until early 1997, after Red and Charline McCombs pledged a gift of $5 million, subsequently raised to $6 million to meet the goals of Leadership 2000. It was the largest gift ever received by the University from an alumnus or alumni couple. The gift was also certified for matching funds under the terms of a $3 million Mabee Challenge Grant.[151] In addition to the McCombs and Mabee gifts, additional funding for what had become an $11.2 million building was secured from the Perkins-Prothro Foundation and the Vivian L. Smith Foundation.[152]

One of the main features of the new building was its foyer on the first floor. It duplicated to the extent possible many of the main features of the old Bishops' Memorial Union, including the large fireplace and terrazzo floor map of Central Texas in pioneer times. The main floor concourse of the Center recognized persons and foundations that had made gifts of $1 million or more to the University over the years and persons who had made deferred gifts in excess of $1 million.[153] When completed, the 63,000-square-foot center included campus dining facilities, a ballroom, the Post Office, the University Bookstore, Snack Bar, and displays of the McCombs Americana Collection. It also included offices for student organizations, the Gender Awareness Center, student development personnel, Student Activities, Diversity Education, and Religious Life. After a decade of use, it has proved to be perhaps the most popular building on campus, with something for everyone.[154]

The Garey Announcement and Summary of the Leadership 2000 Campaign

The day of October 17, 1998, the day of the dedication of the new Campus Center, was one of the most dramatic in the history of Southwestern. Though it was accompanied by one of the heaviest rainstorms Central Texas had experienced for many years, the event was carried out with style. It also served to conclude the Leadership 2000 financial campaign with the announcement that its goal of $75.5 million had been achieved. For that purpose Dan Rather, who had delivered the speech opening the public phase of the campaign in January 1995, came once again and highlighted its conclusion.[155]

The most startling event of the day, however, was an announcement by Jack and Camille (Cammy) Garey of a $15 million bequest for student scholarships. It was the single largest pledge ever made to the University. It was estimated that when the gift eventually accrued to the University it would underwrite 120 scholarships a year—10 percent of the student body. Since the Garey gift came within the time frame of the Leadership 2000 Campaign, it pushed the final campaign total to $91,952,261.[156] Some 5,872 Southwestern alumni participated at some level during the campaign. The total contributed by the campus community was just under $1,950,000, including the bequest of almost $1 million from the estate of the late Professor John Score.[157]

The Gareys had lived in the Georgetown area for about two decades and had noted Southwestern's progress over the years. Cammy, who was reared in Georgetown, said: "The gift was Jack's idea and I agreed wholeheartedly because Southwestern enriched my life as I was growing up in Georgetown. A church-related, liberal arts university makes a huge impact on a small town. Many of my public school teachers, Sunday school teachers, Girl Scout leaders, synchronized swimming instructors and friends were from Southwestern families." Though both are graduates of the University of Texas, he with B.B.A. and J.D. degrees from U.T. Austin and she with a B.S. in physical therapy from the U.T. Medical Branch in Galveston, they chose Southwestern to be the recipient of their gift because, they said, "we wanted to support quality education in our local community with the assurance that it would be well-managed and with the hope that it will make a significant difference." Working to put themselves through college had shown them the value of scholarships and made their decision to provide funds for student scholarships an understandable choice.

Jack Garey was born in Brady, Texas. After serving in the United States Navy and attending the University of Texas, he practiced law in Austin from 1957 until 1978, specializing in personal injury and workers' compensation. In the latter year, he established the Garey Construction Company, Inc., which did road and highway construction. He was appointed by Governor Clements to a six-year term on the Texas Workers' Compensation Commission in 1990 and served as chair of that Commission for two years. Though Cammy was born in Austin, she grew up in Georgetown, where she graduated from high school. After completing her college and postgraduate education, she practiced physical therapy in Texas and several other states from 1964 until 1986. In 1983 she became manager of the Garey ranch. She has served as an elected officer in a number of community organizations and is a member of the First United Methodist Church in Georgetown.

In September 2005 the Gareys followed up on their gift to Southwestern by announcing that they were donating through their wills the 525-acre ranch west of Georgetown, where they live, to the City of Georgetown. It will eventually be developed by the City as Garey Park. Including the cash donation they made to the City with the gift of the ranch, the total value of their gift was approximately $15 million.

In commenting on the gift to Southwestern, Jack Garey said: "By good fortune and the grace of God, we had accumulated resources far in excess of the needs of ourselves and our family. . . . Hopefully, we can inspire other similar gifts to make this University truly competitive with others in this country." Both he and she have served on the Southwestern Board of Trustees since making their gift.[158]

George and Herman Brown. "The wonder is that . . . [the money] . . . was all given without anyone from The Brown Foundation ever asking anything of a quid pro quo nature except that Southwestern become the best small University it could possibly become." Used by permission of Isabel Brown Wilson, daughter of George Brown.

Conclusion of the Brown Challenge Program

The twenty-year Brown Challenge Program came to an end on December 31, 1995. One might have thought that the ending of this magnificent program would have depressed the morale of University leaders, but such was not the case. Of course, the annual infusion of funds into the endowment from The Brown Foundation was missed, but the ending occurred at the midpoint in the Leadership 2000 Campaign, which picked up the fund-raising momentum without skipping a beat. Success in achieving the purpose for which George Brown had instituted the Brown Challenge was proved by the quiet way it ended. It ended, as he would have hoped, with Southwestern's having built a strong fund-raising program into its annual operational plan. By the end of 1998 the Leadership 2000 program had raised $92 million in a seven-year campaign, and the annual fund-raising program was strong and vigorous. In noting the conclusion of the Brown Challenge, Shilling said that it was more responsible than anything else in making it possible for Southwestern to become a National Liberal Arts College.[159] A landscaped fountain and marker were established in a conspicuous place on the central mall to commemorate what the Brown Challenge had done for the University.[160]

During the twenty years of its operation, Southwestern raised a total of $31,841,735 in operational funds to achieve matching grants of $28,206,802 from The Brown Foundation for the endowment.[161] Southwestern's endowment grew from $18.5 million in 1975 to $197 million in 1995. Alumni participation in the annual fund grew from 6 percent to 34.9 percent over the same years.[162] The Brown Challenge endowment money, combined with the Foundation's other contributions to Southwestern's endowment, represented approximately $104 million—or nearly half—of the University's more than $213 million permanent endowment in 1996.[163]

The Brown Foundation also made a number of gifts to the Leadership 2000 Campaign in addition to its annual challenge grants made to the endowment. In 1993 it made a $5 million grant to construct a new residence hall to replace Laura Kuykendall Hall. It was named the Brown-Cody Residence Hall in memory of Margarett Root Brown, Alice Pratt Brown, and Florence Root Cody. The building incorporated several of the architectural features of the old LK Hall, including the original veranda on the south façade.[164] Two years later The Brown Foundation authorized "an anonymous contingent grant" of $500,000 to "assist in meeting the conditions of a special challenge grant awarded by the Mabee Foundation of Tulsa, Oklahoma."[165] In 1997, the same year that Brown-Cody Hall was dedicated, The Brown Foundation made a $1 million grant to meet the conditions of the McCombs Challenge.[166] A year later it made a grant of $100,000 for faculty development to help Southwestern qualify for a $750,000 Kresge Challenge grant that had been offered to complete work on the science building expansion.[167] In 1996 Mrs. Isabel Brown Wilson made unrestricted gifts to the campaign totaling $200,000.[168] She was also responsible for a $50,000 grant from the Foundation to underwrite a new book by William B. Jones "chronicling the history of Southwestern University over the first 160 years or so."[169]

Pratt and Castaneda have provided the following data regarding the total contributions of The Brown Foundation to Southwestern University as of March 15, 1998: "Southwestern University. Grant No. 76-083. Total Paid in Matching Funds: $28,206,802.00. Total Paid to Date: $40,637,901.00."[170]

This latter figure may be close to the actual amount of money given by the Foundation since its inception in 1951, but it is, when looked at more broadly, considerably less than what has actually been given by the Brown family over the years. It likely does not include the cost of the many valuable books donated by Margarett Brown to the library, or the cost of the swimming pool built by Herman Brown with his own crew, or the cost of the architect from St. Louis who drew up the plan for landscaping the campus, or the cost of the crew sent by Margarett to do landscaping, or the cost of Umlauf's statue of the Madonna and Child, or the cost of the art exhibits arranged by Margarett for the Fine Arts Center, or the scholarships donated by her to foreign students, or any of a number of other personal but long since forgotten contributions. It does not include the money generated for Southwestern by Herman from his confrontation with the I.R.S. over the McManis estate or paid out by him to his lawyers for their contesting the issue. It does not include the money made by the University from his advice about purchasing Transcontinental stock with money that he lent to make the purchase. Above all, it does not include the untold amount of credibility that accrued to the University as a result of its connection with The Brown Foundation for over half a century. The wonder is that it was all given without anyone from The Brown Foundation ever asking anything of a quid pro quo nature except that Southwestern become the best small University it could possibly become. Not many institutions have such an opportunity.

Total Student Enrollment and Faculty Numbers

The total fall semester student enrollment for Southwestern topped 1,000 for the first time in 1979, after which it hovered around the 1,000 level for six years.[171] From 1985 through 1989 it moved ahead steadily each year, reaching a total of 1,219 in 1989. From that point on through the decade of the 1990s the fall semester headcount enrollment remained at between 1,200 and 1,300 each year. First-year students came from thirty-five states and twelve foreign countries in the fall of 1999.[172]

Though enrollment stabilized during the 1990s, the retention rate of students improved, and the full-time-equivalent enrollment increased. The retention rate improved from an average of 50 percent for the years 1977–1982 to the low 60s for 1980s.[173] During the 1990s it moved into the low 70s, where it has remained.[174] The result of this improvement in the retention of students to graduation meant that the full-time-equivalent enrollment during the '90s generally averaged around 1,200. Even the spring semester headcount enrollment had reached 1,200 by the spring of 2000, when 1,232 students matriculated.[175]

A part of the reason for the retention increase was an improvement in the quality of the student body. For ten consecutive years beginning in 1982 a new record was set for freshman applications, providing a larger pool from which to select students.[176] In 1993 the President reported that the average SAT score of entering students was above 1100 for the sixth consecutive year. For the first time in 1990, 50 percent of the first-year entering students were in the top 10 percent of their high school graduating class. In 1997, 1998, and 1999 the numbers in the top 10 percent were 52 percent, 55 percent, and 58 percent, respectively.[177]

The movement toward a 3-3 teaching load or its equivalent for all teachers that was begun in the 1980s was continued and achieved in the '90s. In addition, the student-to-teacher ratio was lowered consistently until an 11 to 1 ratio was achieved in 1999.[178] With a more intensive use of sabbaticals by the faculty, release time from teaching for Brown Fellows, and a reduced teaching load for University Scholars, the number of full-time-equivalent faculty members increased from 69 to 108 between 1983 and 1996 (56 percent).

Minority Student Enrollment

Vision 2000, the Basic Master Plan for the decade of the 1990s, called for Southwestern to achieve a 12:1 student-to-faculty ratio, to establish six courses per year as the normal faculty load, to maintain a student enrollment of 1,200 (FTE) students, and "to include within the diversity of the student body at least 5% African-American students, 15% Hispanic students, and as large a contingent as possible of international students." As has already been seen, Southwestern did achieve the first three of those goals. Though it pursued the fourth goal vigorously, it did not succeed in bringing the percentage of African American students to 5 percent of the student body.

In 1981, when Shilling first came to Southwestern, there were twenty-four African American students on campus. They formed 2.4 percent of the student body. That percentage remained about the same during the 1980s and '90s, sometimes up a little, sometimes down a little. Nothing the University did seemed to be effective in improving the number of African Americans on campus. Neither the making of special recruitment visits to high schools with high concentrations of African American students, the granting of generous scholarships, or the use of special programs seemed to affect their application rate significantly. Southwestern's Minority Presence Committee designed one program in 1988 called Passport to the Future to help with the problem.

Run by Felecia M. Johnson, an African American instructor of music, Passport to the Future was designed to bring fifty to a hundred African American students in the ninth grade to campus for a weekend to give them an understanding of what college was like and to encourage them to start thinking at that early grade level about going to college. During the weekend on campus, they participated in specially designed mini-classes on everything from AIDS to hip-hop algebra. They also gained useful information in sessions on applying to college, preparing for SAT's, choosing a career, and understanding financial aid.[179] Though the program was helpful to those in attendance, it did not make an impact on the established African American enrollment pattern.

The enrollment of Hispanic students was another matter. From 1989 until 1996, at least 15 percent of every entering first-year class was Hispanic. In the case of Hispanic students Southwestern had two advantages. The first was that Southwestern had the Spanish-speaking Rio Grande Annual Conference as one of its sponsoring Conferences. That Conference often met on campus during the summer, providing an opportunity for its pastors and lay delegates to get to know Southwestern.

The second advantage was the annual meeting of the Lorenzo de Zavala Youth Legislative Session on campus. The LDZ program is an eight-day mock legislative session on Latino issues where around two hundred Hispanic sophomores and juniors learn how to network and build constituencies. Ernesto Nieto, a Southwestern alumnus of 1964 who came to Southwestern on a basketball scholarship, developed the National Hispanic Institute, the sponsor of LDZ, in 1979. He began to hold LDZ on campus in 1985. It still meets at Southwestern today. More important than dealing with issues, networks, and constituencies, Nieto works to build up a sense of pride in being Hispanic, involving the students in lectures and exercises to show that Hispanic culture is an advantage to those who know how to capitalize on its assets. By 1994 Nieto had trained over ten thousand young people since his founding of the National Hispanic Institute fifteen years earlier.[180]

In 1988, Univision, the national Spanish-language television network, filmed a segment on the Institute featuring Dr. Vicente Villa, Professor of Biology, talking about the recruitment of Hispanics into colleges.[181] Over the years the LDZ program has been the first introduction to Southwestern for hundreds of Hispanic students. In 1991 alone, thirty-seven alumni of the Lorenzo de Zavala Youth Legislative Session were enrolled at Southwestern.[182] Nieto was honored as a Distinguished Alumnus in 1994 and delivered the Commencement speech to the graduating seniors in 2004. The National Hispanic Institute sponsors a number of programs besides LDZ and operates in several states. Nieto has narrated the development of his idea in a fascinating book entitled *Third Reality: Crafting a 21st Century Latino Agenda* (2001).

Foreign and Non-Anglo Faculty

When Shilling became President in 1981, there were three foreign-born full-time, tenured, or tenure track persons on the faculty—one from Korea, one from India, and one from France. There was one Asian American and one Jew. There were no African or Hispanic Americans. The total from these categories was five. There were no visiting teachers.

Ten years later in 1991 the number of foreign-born full-time, tenured, or tenure track persons had increased to five—one from India, one from Tanzania, one from Chile, one from Hungary, and one from Spain. There were four non–Anglo Americans—one Hispanic, two Asian Americans, and one African American. The number of Jews had increased to four. The total from these categories was thirteen. There was one additional full-time visiting person, making a total of fourteen.

In Shilling's last year there were five foreign-born full-time, tenured, or tenure track persons—one from Tanzania, one from Chile, one from Hungary, one from Mexico, and one from Peru. The number of non–Anglo Americans had increased to eight—four Hispanics, three Asian Americans, and one African American. The number of Jews was four. The total from these categories was seventeen. There were three additional full-time visiting persons, making a total of twenty.

Along with the increased percentage of women on the faculty already discussed in this chapter, the faculty became more diverse over the nineteen years of Shilling's tenure. The major exception to this increasing diversity was in the number of African Americans on the faculty or in major administrative positions. There was only one two-year period, 1987–1989, when there were as many as two African Americans on the faculty, and they did not remain. This lack of African Americans on the teaching faculty of the University did not come about from lack of effort on the part of Shilling to attract and keep them.

One person employed by Shilling was Dr. Gregory Washington, who came as an Administrative Intern on January 15, 1987. Washington, with a Ph.D. in philosophy from Stanford University, came to Southwestern from his previous position as dean at Morristown College, a two-year school in northeast Tennessee. At one time or another at Southwestern, he taught philosophy, directed the Office of Multicultural Affairs, and led the Operation Achievement program. He left Southwestern on January 1, 1992, to become Associate Vice President for Multicultural Affairs at Oklahoma State University. His tenure at Southwestern was almost exactly five years.[183]

Another was Dr. Sybil Hampton. She was appointed Special Assistant to the President on September 1, 1993. With a B.A. from Earlham College, an M.S.T. from the University of Chicago, and a M.Ed. and an Ed.D. from Columbia University, Dr. Hampton came with experience of more than twenty-five years in higher education. She was on a year's leave of absence from the University of Wisconsin at Madison at the time she came to Southwestern.[184] She worked closely with Shilling and was made a member of the cabinet after one year on campus.[185] Two years later she was elected President of the Winthrop Rockefeller Foundation in Arkansas, her home state.[186] Her tenure at Southwestern was almost exactly three years.

Recognizing the difficulty of recruiting minority faculty members to come to an institution such as Southwestern in a nonurban area with only a small population of other minority persons, Dr. Jones made a proposal to the Board of Higher Education and Ministry of The United Methodist Church. The proposal called for the establishment of a National Minority Faculty Registry to serve the 100+ institutions of the United Methodist Church. Southwestern would maintain the registry and make it available to those institutions wishing to pay a small fee for its use. It was financed initially by a five-thousand-dollar grant that was matched by Southwestern.[187] It subsequently became self-supporting. Eighty-eight institutions joined the first year. Advertisements were published regularly in *The Chronicle of Higher Education* informing readers about the existence of the registry and inviting minority persons seeking positions to send their vitae to the office for distribution to institutions requesting the names of persons with their qualifications. At the request of other non-Methodist and State institutions, the registry was opened to all colleges and universities. By 1990 over two hundred schools used the services of the registry, over six hundred applicants were registered in the database, and over a thousand requests for vitae were received from member institutions each year.[188] The registry is now in its twentieth year of existence and may be accessed over the Internet by member institutions.

Effect of the Hopwood Decision on Minority Scholarships

Since the *Bakke* decision of 1978, when the U.S. Supreme Court ruled that universities may consider race in admissions to maintain diverse enrollment or to remedy past discrimination, colleges and universities throughout the country regularly awarded scholarships to members of minority groups in the name of affirmative action goals. Southwestern, like other schools, used scholarships as incentives to help it achieve its minority enrollment goals. By means of such scholarships and other inducements, Southwestern moved from a low of 7.0 percent minority enrollment in 1983 to a high of 21.0 percent in 1992. The figure averaged around 20 percent for the next five years until 1996. It then dropped precipitously to 12.0 percent in the two years between 1996 and 1998.

The reason for the drop was a decision in the Cheryl Hopwood case by the Fifth U.S. Circuit Count of Appeals in 1996 in behalf of Hopwood and her co-applicants against the State of Texas. It specified that any consideration of race, even as one factor among many, in making admissions decisions, is unconstitutional. The U.S. Supreme Court declined to review the decision.[189] Though it had legal force only in the states of Mississippi, Louisiana, and Texas, the decision sent a tremor through institutions of higher education all across the country and affected directly the colleges and universities in the three states presided over by the Fifth Circuit Court of Appeals in New Orleans. It meant that minority students in those states would be forced to go to educational institutions in other states if they were to obtain the kind of scholarships they needed to continue their education. When its own legal counsel informed Southwestern that the Circuit Court opinion in all likelihood included private as well as public institutions, Southwestern was forced to cancel the distribution of any new scholarships to persons based on minority group status. This action caused a drop in Southwestern's minority enrollment from 20.4 percent in 1996 to 12.0 percent in 1998, with a further drop likely unless some remedy could be found to ameliorate the situation.

Because of the seriousness of the matter, Roy Shilling, Rick Eason, and Richard Anderson began to work with the Texas Methodist Foundation to see if a way could be found out of the impasse. Though tied to the Annual Conferences of the United Methodist Church in Texas, the Texas Methodist Foundation was an independent entity as far as Southwestern was concerned and had no legal connection to the University. The three men worked out an agreement with officials of the Foundation whereby it would initiate a scholarship program benefiting African American, Hispanic, and Native Americans attending Southwestern. It would provide scholarships of from five thousand dollars to full tuition based on specified criteria. A target of at least twenty awards of five thousand dollars per year would be given each entering class and five awards of full tuition. At least two of the full tuition awards would go to African American students and two to Hispanic students. The awards would be renewable. A selection committee of three to five persons chosen by the Foundation in consultation with Southwestern would distribute the awards annually.[190] The awards would be called Dixon Scholarships in honor of the recently deceased Bishop Ernest T. Dixon, the first African American bishop to preside over the Southwest Texas and the Rio Grande Annual Conferences.

Funds for the program would be provided by the transfer of endowment money currently held by Southwestern for minority scholarships to the Texas Methodist Foundation. This money consisted primarily of $1 million (1989 book value) in the Jesse H. and Mary Gibbs Jones Minority Scholars Program and $70,000 donated by Charline McCombs for minority women scholarships.[191] Other donations were also secured, and the corpus in the hands of the Foundation in late 1999 had grown to almost $3 million. Seventeen Dixon scholars matriculated at Southwestern in the fall of 1999, and the percentage of minority students jumped to 18.4 percent. Twenty-one new Dixon scholars were scheduled to enroll in the fall of 2000.[192]

Shilling's Personality

Because Shilling was so conspicuously resolute in going by the book, he gained a reputation in some quarters of having ice water in his veins and being unfeeling. Some persons in town felt that he was not as personable or interested in the town as Finch or Fleming had been. Unlike Bill Finch, he had not lived in Georgetown for long years before he

Presidents Shilling, Finch, and Fleming, representing 50 years of leadership at Southwestern University. Southwestern University, Special Collections.

became President and created a large circle of friends for himself. Unlike Durwood Fleming, he had not started a Rotary Club whose meetings he attended every Friday noon. Finch said about Fleming that toward the end of his administration, "[Y]ou couldn't have a funeral without Durwood conducting the funeral service."[193] Linda Scarbrough depicted Shilling correctly when she wrote about him following an interview: "His natural reserve, too, makes the intensely public president's job difficult. At both Hendrix and Southwestern, Shilling and his wife, Margaret, purchased private homes away from campus. . . . 'I think I'm a very private person [said Shilling]. The most difficult thing for me is to function in a public role.'"[194]

This picture of Shilling as a "very private" person who was not at ease functioning in a public role contrasts with that of the calm and collected, urbane man whom most people saw in those situations. After a luncheon on campus sponsored by Shilling for Richard Oppel, editor of the *Austin American-Statesman*, Oppel wrote him a letter of thanks. He said, "I've known a lot of people who are good at conducting meetings, but none better than you. Your warmth and openness makes people feel important and free to talk candidly."[195] That warmth showed through especially when members of the Southwestern community experienced illness or sorrow. Shilling was conscientious in contacting the aggrieved persons, expressing his condolences, and offering to help in any way he could. If he was at times very direct in pointing out the mistakes made by people in the performance of their duties, he was also very generous in his award of praise to them for jobs well done.

As quoted in Chapter XXII, Shilling concluded his first official speech to the faculty in August 1981 by stating that "the end of learning is serving. Knowledge without compassion and perspective fails to achieve its full potential and is misdirected in its goals."[196] Ten years later, precisely at the point where Southwestern was gaining a Phi Beta Kappa chapter and being recognized as a National Liberal Arts institution, he emphasized in one of his reports to the Trustees that "quality alone is not enough."

> Quality alone is not enough. For us, it must be a quality that inculcates those shared values, which we believe are at the heart of the Judeo-Christian tradition—the foundation of which is our unyielding faith in, and unshakable commitment to, the sacred worth and dignity of every member of this community. These values compel us to be a nurturing, caring, inclusive community. We cherish diversity, globalism, ethnicity, ecumenicity, and knowledge, and we deplore and seek to eradicate vestiges of racism, parochialism, sectarianism, and ignorance. We place the common good above personal gain, and we hold that a loving, caring concern for others is by no means outdated. As a church-related university, we understand and embrace such concepts as love, grace, mercy, justice, and forgiveness.[197]

Shilling, Southwestern, and the Georgetown Community

Because of his private personality, it is not surprising that one of the least-well-known facets of the Shilling administration is the attention he and his administration paid to community interests. Not all of the things that were done by Southwestern for the community were done directly by him or at his instigation. Faculty members often initiated them and carried them out, but they were acting with an implicit understanding that Southwestern supported and encouraged such actions. In 1983 Martha Allen organized Handcrafts Unlimited as an outlet for arts and crafts produced by Georgetown-area residents age fifty and older. Their creations were sold at a store on the town square. This activity was picked up by *The New York Times* and publicized. The *Times* said that "last year more than 400 artisans contributed while 50 volunteers from the university and town ran the store."[198] Allen won the Citizen of the Year Award from the Chamber of Commerce for her work in this venture. The store still operates today. Another teacher, Dan C. Hilliard, Professor of Sociology, played a strong role in bringing Meals on Wheels to Georgetown.

At the same ceremony at which Martha Allen received the Citizen of the Year Award, Roy Shilling received the Owen W. Sherrill Award for Economic Development. He had been on the team of volunteers who worked to recruit Vista Chemical Company, Incorporated, to locate in Georgetown. When the $525 million a year company announced that it might not come, Shilling did everything he could to retain Vista's interest in Georgetown. He offered to turn some land east of the campus between Highway 29 and the San Gabriel River into a University research park, subject to approval by Southwestern's Board of Trustees.[199] Though the project did not materialize, Shilling had impressed members of the Chamber by his extraordinary efforts to bring it about. He and Eason followed up by subsequently playing major roles in a yearlong effort to establish a nonprofit Georgetown Industrial Foundation. The

GIF was set up to offer incentives, including cheap land and low-interest loans, to business prospects. Mayor Tim Kennedy praised them for their efforts.[200]

Begun in 1988, Operation Achievement was conceived of by the Minority Presence Committee. It was a program, operated in cooperation with the Georgetown Independent School District, in which Southwestern University personnel and students worked with "at risk" seventh graders who were struggling with math and English. Operated originally out of the office of Dr. Jones, his secretary, Beth Williams, led a group of student volunteers who mentored forty students.[201] A decade later it had become a program sponsored by the Education Department for all levels of junior high school and high school "at risk" students. Fifteen paid Southwestern students worked as staff mentors and forty students served as volunteer mentors. Mentors worked one-on-one with students, providing friendship, helping with schoolwork, and participating in enrichment activities designed to broaden the students' visions of the world. In 1998 Director La Vonne Neal secured a two-year, $30,000 GTE Focus Grant for work with parents and in math/science enrichment activities, including summer camps for 1998 and 1999.[202]

In the course of these efforts, recognition was given to the fact that junior high and high school teachers often had Hispanic students in their classes who needed special attention because of their struggle to cope with two cultures. Southwestern inaugurated a program in the fall of 1989 in which seventeen teachers enrolled to take special Spanish courses in after-school classes designed to give them a greater appreciation for Spanish culture. Each teacher volunteering for the project agreed to monitor five Hispanic students, helping to raise their self-esteem and boost their achievements.[203]

After reading an article in 1988 about the University of Rochester's forming a partnership with its host city, Roy Shilling picked up the phone and called new Georgetown school superintendent Jim Gunn. He proposed a similar partnership between GISD and Southwestern. After twenty community leaders met nine times in as many months during 1988 and 1989, the two institutions decided to focus their efforts on literacy.[204] Thus was born the Partners in Literacy Program, reaching from kindergarten years to adulthood. Grants totaling almost half a million dollars in support of the project from the Meadows Foundation of Dallas ($140,000), the Hewlett Foundation of Menlo Park, California ($150,000), and the Hearst Foundation of San Francisco ($25,000) led to the purchase of IBM computers and other equipment for the program. The equipment was used to attack the illiteracy of grade-schoolers and junior high students during the day and that of adults at night.

Widespread attention was given to the program in the *Philanthropic Digest*, in several major metropolitan newspapers, and on Austin television. The American Association of Higher Education invited Southwestern to make a presentation about the program at its national conference in Chicago in 1990.[205] The Association of Texas Colleges and Universities recognized Southwestern that same year with its Excellence in Higher Education Award for the University's role in community outreach programs. Dr. Jim Gunn said about the GISD/Southwestern linkage: "Southwestern has done an outstanding job in all of these programs. . . . And to think, the task force came about one evening when Roy Shilling called me at home and simply said, 'We have a lot of potential here.'"[206]

In 1999 Southwestern was awarded a U.S. Department of Education grant totaling up to $2.4 million over four years for an Upward Bound project. The program targets fifty-plus Williamson County ninth- to eleventh-grade students each year, from families sending their first generation of children to college and other economically disadvantaged populations, to advance their chances of achieving a college education.[207] Operating out of the old Pirate Tavern, now owned by Southwestern and located across from the Cullen Building, the program is still in operation.

On June 4, 2003, three years after Shilling's retirement, the Georgetown Area Community Foundation honored him with its Lifetime Achievement Award at a gala held at the home of Jack and Cammy Garey. The first paragraph of the citation accurately describes the person and his relationship to Georgetown.

> Basically an undemonstrative person, most of Roy Shilling's actions with regard to Georgetown have been basic and fundamental rather than demonstrative and striking. One thing is sure. He has believed that Southwestern was good for Georgetown and that Georgetown was good for Southwestern.

Medical Help to Kosovo

Most people in the United States knew little about Kosovo when Serbia began to practice ethnic cleansing there after the breakup of the old Yugoslavia. They soon learned about it when reports of widespread atrocities against its population began to be a regular feature of news articles and broadcasts in February 1998. The population of Kosovo, though a traditional area of Serbia bordering on Albania, was 90 percent Albanian, and the Serbian strongman, Slobodan Milosevic, a hard-line Serbian nationalist, wanted to reconstitute its Serb population majority by forcibly removing the Albanians. During the summer of 1998, a quarter of a million Kosovar Albanians were forced from their homes as their houses, villages, and crops were destroyed. Evidence of the massacre of entire villages in Kosovo, Croatia, and Bosnia came to light, as the Milosevic government in Belgrade encouraged the ethnic Serbs in Bosnia to fight Muslims and Croats in those two republics as well. The war claimed hundreds of thousands of lives, and by the end of May 1999, over 230,000 refugees had arrived in the former Yugoslav Republic of Macedonia, over 430,000 had fled to Albania, and some 64,000 had gone to Montenegro. An estimated 1.5 million people, constituting 90 percent of the population of Kosovo, were expelled from their homes. Some 225,000 Kosovar men were believed to be missing, the result of "ethnic cleansing" carried out by Serbian paramilitary forces loyal to Milosevic. The NATO nations took a hard line against the Serbian venture and carried out a seventy-eight-day bombing campaign against Serbia that finally brought the conflict to a halt.

Roy Shilling was horrified by what he heard and felt he had to do something to help the refugees displaced to Albania and Macedonia. Rick Eason would later say: "[I]t was Dr. Shilling's passion for the idea of providing relief to the people in need in the Balkans that began the program."[208] Shilling began his effort by voicing his concern to a number of people in telephone calls, out of which was born the Southwestern University Global Leadership Initiative in April. He visited Red McCombs personally about the matter. McCombs was so struck by Shilling's anguish that he agreed to commit $250,000 to support a medical relief effort. An office was set up on campus, and a project coordinator, Susan Harper, was employed to manage the effort.

In an announcement to the campus about this action, Shilling stated that Southwestern would be working with the International Medical Corps (IMC) of Los Angeles to deploy medical personnel. He said he hoped students, faculty, and staff would help to locate medical service volunteers and enlist other persons to perform tasks helpful to the effort.[209] Rick Eason carried the message to the faculty.[210] An Advisory Committee of fifteen persons was set up that included faculty members, staff, students, and alumni, including two alumni physicians, Dr. Douglas Benold (1944) and Dr. Bill Engvall (1955).[211] Students took up collections of money in support of the effort and made up one hundred health kits that were sent to the refugees.[212] Shilling also wrote to all the National Liberal Arts College presidents. He explained that Southwestern's role in the effort would be to provide a pool of medical personnel that would be drawn upon by the IMC, the organization that would do the actual scheduling and deployment of medical workers. Expenses for those chosen to go abroad would be paid for from the McCombs money. He said he was writing to enlist their aid in locating medical service volunteers.[213]

By June 19, 162 medical persons from across the country had volunteered through Southwestern to go to the stricken area in the Balkans. Of these, 8 physicians and 3 nurses were chosen by IMC to go and to serve in refugee camps in Macedonia and Albania. Four of them served about two weeks each, 5 served about three weeks, and 2 served about four weeks.[214] The first to leave for the Balkans was Dr. Barney Davis, an alumnus of 1966, who lived in Eastland, Maryland.[215] He went to Albania. The last to return was Jacqueline Switzer, RN, who came back from Macedonia on September 4. Deployment of medical personnel lasted over a period of four months.

The effect on campus of the Global Leadership Initiative, as the Kosovo effort came to be called, was very intense. The Commencement speaker in May 1999 was Ann Alloway Stingle, a graduate of Southwestern, past spokesperson for the American Red Cross and currently the Executive Director of the Victims of War project in Albania. So that it might reach a larger audience, her speech was simulcast to other spaces on campus beyond the site of the Commencement itself.[216] Early in the fall semester Dr. James Kliewer of Temple, Texas, gave a talk to the campus community on his experiences as a medical volunteer in Macedonia.[217] He had already been on campus during the summer to share his slides with the Advisory Committee.[218] His daughter, Ingrid, was a student member of the Advisory Committee.

After Serbia agreed to withdraw its forces from Kosovo on June 9, peace of a sort gradually descended on the Balkan region, and the European Union, the United States, and other countries undertook a massive relief effort. In light of this development, the need to send more medical personnel to the region through private sources became less important, and the effort at Southwestern was gradually phased out. Though the Global Leadership Initiative Advisory Committee continued its work into the 1999–2000 academic year, its efforts became more and more integrated into the regular international program effort of the University.

Just as the Georgetown Partners in Literacy Campaign had begun with a contact by Shilling with Superintendent Jim Gunn after he had been animated by an article he was reading, the Global Leadership Initiative had been initiated by a visit to Red McCombs by him when he decided that he could no longer sit on the sidelines without doing something. In both cases Shilling's idea was problematical. There was no guarantee of a positive result. In both cases his conviction and enthusiasm brought a positive response from the ones that received the calls. Roy Shilling was a man of big ideas. They did not always work out. But he was never afraid to propound them. During his entire career, he had been practicing the ideas of Jim Collins and Jerry Porras, to be discussed later, before he ever read their book.

Some Ideas That Didn't Work Out

Because so many of Shilling's unusual ideas worked out splendidly, one might be tempted to think that he succeeded in every venture. Such is not the case. Like any other person, he had his disappointments. The disappointments, however, never deterred him from propounding another idea, oftentimes more ambitious than the one that failed. One of his great disappointments in the 1980s has already been referred to, the failure of the $35 million Campaign for Southwestern (1983 to 1988) to achieve more than one-third of its goal. He followed it up in the 1990s with the even more ambitious Leadership 2000 Campaign (1982–1998), when its $92 million final total exceeded the goal of $75.5 million by $16.5 million.

One of his last major unfulfilled ideas was that of attracting a gift from a major foundation that would endow the full tuition cost of a Southwestern education, leaving students responsible only for room, board, and auxiliary expenses. This idea came out of his relationship with Mr. Lawrence W. Milas, President of the F. W. Olin Foundation, Inc., who had become his friend at the time Southwestern received the $6.8 million Olin grant in 1994. On September 12, 1997, he sent a letter to Milas outlining his proposal.

In the letter he proposes a breathtaking concept. He says that he has been struck by "the similarities of purpose and core values" of the Olin Foundation and of Southwestern University. These could, he feels, be best perpetuated "in the vision and implementation of a merger of the major assets of our two organizations which would have the most profound and lasting impact on American higher education imaginable. It would, forever, change the face of higher education in this country." It would be operated through an Olin Scholars Program. Olin Scholars would have the best value in American higher education.

"Every student would enroll in the University as an Olin Scholar and sign a contract indicating his/her concurrence with and acceptance of the core values of the University." This education would be offered tuition-free, according to "*your dream*" [italics added]. The Olin Scholars would become the undergraduate equivalents to Rhodes, Fulbright, and Marshall scholars. The Olin Foundation "could make the ultimate 'leverage grant' by endowing in perpetuity the Olin Scholars Program at Southwestern University. A gift of approximately $300+ million would enable the University to offer one of the finest undergraduate educational experiences possible to every enrolling student, whose entire tuition would be funded by the Olin Scholars Program Endowment. As a condition of such a gift, we would agree to raise an additional $100 million." This $100 million would provide the facilities, faculty, and student services necessary. After outlining how the University would look with 220 additional students and with $73 million in new and renovated buildings, he concludes by saying that he and Red McCombs would like to visit him about this concept.[219]

That this concept was not merely an idle pipe dream in Shilling's mind without any expectation that it might be achieved is disproved by the fact that he included his letter to Milas in the records of the Executive Committee and that Red McCombs referred to it at the Board meeting of November 14, 1997. McCombs said that "a gift of $300 million would endow every student's tuition and would require [only] a $7,500–8,000 room and board fee [from the student]."[220] The faculty was also aware of the proposal, since Shilling told them on November 18 that the Olin Foundation had turned it down. The principal reason for the turndown was that the Olin Foundation had decided to establish an Olin College, which would prepare future leaders through an innovative engineering education. Located in Needham, Massachusetts, it opened in 2002.[221]

McCombs hints in a letter to Milas of January 6, 1998, that the idea of a tuition-free education may have come from Milas himself. McCombs says in it: "I am trying to accomplish your vision of a tuition-free Southwestern and will keep you posted as to our progress."[222] It is quite possible that Milas had discussed his "tuition-free" idea with either or both of the two men and that Shilling was trying to turn the concept in Southwestern's direction. Shilling never gave up on the idea of creating a "tuition-free" institution. He told the Board of Trustees on January 30, 1998, that he, according to Board Minutes, "was not backing away from the concept of endowing tuition and that he felt that it would position the University for the 21st Century."[223]

After the Olin turndown, Shilling was still trying to promote the central idea contained in the proposal as late as January 12, 1999. The presidential files contain the draft of a proposal to Michael Dell on that date written for Red McCombs to send to Dell following up on a personal visit he and Shilling had made to Dell in April 1998. It introduces the concept of a Dell Scholars Program Endowment, asking for an outright gift of $300 million, or a gift commitment of $350 million to be paid over four years.[224] Though Shilling today does not recall whether he and McCombs handed Dell a copy of the proposal, he says he vividly remembers the visit he and McCombs made to Dell. "Red led the conversation and rolled out the tuition endowment concept. . . . Michael certainly got the message from Red."[225]

Changes in Administrative Leadership during the 1990s

One of the most significant changes that occurred in 1995 was the resignation of Daniel C. Bryant as Vice President for Fiscal Affairs. Upon his departure, Richard L. Anderson, B.B.A., C.P.A., who had been employed as comptroller in January 1984 and later made Associate Vice President for Finance, was promoted to the position of Acting Vice President for Business and Finance (1996).[226] His performance was so strong that he was made Vice President for Fiscal Affairs in 1997. He has continued in that office under President Schrum.

Toward the end of November 1995, Provost Michael Rosenthal resigned his position to assume the position of Deputy Secretary of Higher Education with the Maryland Higher Education Commission. In light of his departure, Shilling announced that a full search would be made during the spring and that Dr. William B. Jones would serve as Interim Provost and Dean of the Faculty until another appointment could be made.[227]

The national search resulted in the appointment of Dale T. Knobel, who assumed office in August 1996. Knobel was a professor of American history at Texas A&M University, where he won an achievement award and led an honors liberal arts program. His bachelor's degree was from Yale and his doctorate from Northwestern University. He was also the author or coauthor of three books. After a two-year stint at Southwestern as Provost and Dean of the Faculty, he left in 1998 to become President of Denison University in Granville, Ohio. Jones was once again appointed Interim Provost in August 1998 and served until May 1999.

With the failure of the search for a new Provost in the spring of 1999, Dr. James W. Hunt, Professor and Chair of the Department of Education and Chair of the Division of Social Sciences, was named as Acting Provost and Dean of the Faculty. He assumed that role on May 24, the same date Jones became Executive Vice President. At the same time, President Shilling stepped down from exercising day-to-day responsibility for University operation and passed that task to Jones. Shilling moved to his house in south Austin and worked during the summer and fall of 1999 to close out his major projects and to complete other unfinished business prior to taking a sabbatical in the spring of 2000. He retired on July 1, 2000, as did Jones. New President Jake Schrum assumed responsibility on that date. Red McCombs also gave up his position as chair of the Board of Trustees in favor of Jim Walzel, who had served as chair of the Presidential Search Committee.

This narration of multiple leadership changes might lead the uninformed observer to suspect that leadership was fragile and that little was done that had a lasting impact during the period from 1995 to 2000. Such, however, was not the case. The mantle of responsibility passed easily from one person to another as each player worked to assure the success of his replacement. During this time, a third major master plan was begun and completed, one that amended the aims of the University, that defined its core purpose, and that identified its core values. Indeed, the construction of the new master plan focused the administrative direction of the University during this period and provided the major link that unified the efforts of students, faculty, and staff during the period of leadership transition.

Collins and Porras: *Built to Last*

In early March 1995 Red McCombs alerted Roy Shilling to a lecture to be given in Austin by James C. Collins, one of the two authors of the book *Built to Last: Successful Habits of Visionary Companies* (New York: HarperBusiness, 1994).[228]

His attendance at the lecture on March 9 was a defining experience.

Shilling was at the time considering his report for the April Board meeting and thinking about the many good things that had happened to Southwestern in the last few years. The lecture by Collins and the *Built to Last* book confirmed his thinking about the reasons for Southwestern's recent success, reasons he had sensed and now found articulated with precision in the book. As he said later, "To me, the book *was* the story of Southwestern." Though Collins and Porras listed six reasons for the success of visionary companies, Shilling focused on two in his report to the Trustees in April.

The single most important element related to success, according to Collins and Porras, is having and preserving a set of core values. "A visionary company," they wrote, "almost religiously preserves its core ideology—changing it seldom, if ever. Core values in a visionary company form a rock-solid foundation and do not drift with the trends and fashions of the day; in some cases, the core values have remained intact for well over one hundred years. . . . Yet, while keeping their core ideologies tightly fixed, visionary companies display a powerful drive for progress that enables them to change and adapt without compromising their cherished core ideals." Southwestern, observed Shilling, was an educational institution like that. It was over a hundred years old and had preserved its core ideology intact.

In addition to preserving its core values, the visionary company, said Collins and Porras, also has "Big Hairy Audacious Goals." Visionary companies may appear strait-laced and conservative to outsiders, but they are not afraid to make bold commitments to "Big Hairy Audacious Goals" [BHAGs]. Visionary companies have judiciously used BHAGs to stimulate progress and "blast past comparison companies at crucial points in history." Once again, in Shilling's mind, Southwestern met the standard. Its rise to prominence among liberal arts colleges and universities in the country has been partly due, he wrote, to the fact that in the past it has chosen BHAGs for itself. The goal of becoming a National Liberal Arts Institution was a BHAG. Securing a Phi Beta Kappa chapter was a BHAG. Competing with dozens of other institutions for an Olin Foundation grant was a BHAG. And initiating a "Leadership 2000" campaign for $75 million was a BHAG. "We have worked," wrote Shilling, "for Big Hairy Audacious Goals ever since we established the first master plan back in the early 1980s."

Shilling also agreed with the conclusion of the book. Collins and Porras said that "there is no ultimate finish line for a highly visionary company. There is no 'having made it.' . . . Comfort is not the objective in a visionary company. Indeed, visionary companies install powerful mechanisms to create discomfort—to obliterate complacency—and thereby stimulate change and improvement before the external world demands it."[229]

The New Master Plan

With Knobel in place as the new Provost in 1996–1997 and with most of the goals of the previous master plan having been accomplished, Shilling encouraged him to begin development of the master plan for 2010.[230] Taking advantage of the enthusiasm for the ideas in *Built to Last*, six faculty and staff members went to the management laboratory of Jim Collins in Boulder, Colorado, where they picked his brain about how to identify core values.[231] They came back with a new design for developing the master plan that was discussed with academic departments and divisions. It called for widespread participation in the process by all members of the campus community, including alumni and Trustees.

In order to achieve full participation, classes were dismissed for one day in the fall (November 6) and one day in the spring (February 18) for all participants. A dozen groups of about thirty persons each met on the designated days for a four-hour period, half of the groups meeting in the morning and half in the afternoon. Each group in the fall came up with its understanding of the core purpose of the University and its list of core values.[232] A smaller, elected group later refined these into a single, final list for presentation to the faculty. Each group in the spring came up with several very large goals for the future (BHAGs) that were refined into a final list in the same way. One hundred copies of *Built to Last* were purchased and distributed around the campus for reading. Participants in the November 6 meetings included approximately one hundred faculty members, one hundred staff persons, twenty Trustees and alumni, and two hundred students.[233] Over three hundred persons met on February 18.[234]

The core purpose as finally adopted by the faculty in March 1998, and subsequently adopted by the Board of Trustees, was:

Fostering a liberal arts community whose values and actions encourage contributions toward the well-being of humanity.

The core values were:

Promoting lifelong learning and a passion for intellectual and personal growth.
Fostering diverse perspectives.
Being true to one's self and others.
Respecting the worth and dignity of persons.
Encouraging activism in the pursuit of justice and the common good.[235]

The Aims of the University, as adopted by the Board of Trustees in 1972, were officially amended in 2001 to include the Core Purpose and the Core Values of the University. After final modification by the faculty in early February 1999, the overall goal for the "envisioned future" read as follows:

We believe that we should strive for no less than making Southwestern University "an inspiration to other preeminent undergraduate colleges because its innovative programs are transforming liberal arts education."[236]

After Provost Knobel left Southwestern for the presidency of Denison University in the summer of 1998, Jones became Interim Provost for the academic year 1998–1999. He and Shilling appointed Dr. James Hunt to serve as coordinator of the master planning process and to bring it to its conclusion by working with the faculty to draw up the list of specific objectives and activities for implementing the goals of the plan.[237] Hunt was one of the six persons who had visited Jim Collins in Boulder and had been a key person in the master plan work to date. The faculty completed "The Southwestern University 2010 Strategic Plan" and approved it on February 22, 2000, subject to approval by the Board of Trustees.[238] The Board adopted it as a "work-in-progress" for further consideration and completion during the 2000–2001 academic year and authorized President-elect Jake B. Schrum to appoint a Board committee to develop an additional section of the plan covering management issues, facilities, resource development, and institutional planning, as well as to give final review to the entire document. SOM and Group Two Architecture were appointed as an architectural team to develop a Facilities Master Plan for 2010.[239]

Shilling Retirement and Search

At the Board meeting on March 26, 1999, Roy Shilling announced that effective June 30, 2000, he wished to step down as Southwestern University's thirteenth President. He asked that Dr. William B. Jones, currently Interim Provost and Dean of the Faculty, be named Executive Vice President to serve as Chief Operating Officer within the University. He in turn would focus his work in the fall semester off campus on fund-raising and increasing the University's visibility. He commented that he would still be involved in the fall with the cabinet, construction, and budget meetings. He requested a presidential sabbatical during the spring semester through his retirement date of June 30, 2000. The Board granted his request and named Mr. James V. Walzel as Chair of the Presidential Search Committee.[240]

Walzel, a member of the Board of Trustees since 1994, had a B.A. and a Bachelor of Science in Chemical Engineering from Rice University. He was chair of the HNG Storage Company in Houston and a member of St. Paul's United Methodist Church. He also served on the Board of Directors of the Institute for Religion and Health at the Texas Medical Center and on the Board of Directors of the Texas Methodist Foundation. One of his children, Sunday Walzel Coffman, was a Southwestern graduate of 1983. He and his family had made a gift to the University during 1995 for the renovation and refurbishing of the former Sid Richardson gymnasium, incorporated as a part of the new Corbin W. Robertson Physical Education Center. On Shilling's recommendation, the former center was renamed the Walzel Courts and Natatorium.[241]

The Search Committee consisted of ten members, six Trustees, three faculty members, and one student. They were: Trustees, Nettie Ruth Bratton (1948), Roy H. Cullen, Larry J. Haynes (1972), Merriman Morton (1963), James Walzel, Bishop Joe A. Wilson, (1959); Faculty, Florence Gould, Walt Herbert, Vicente Villa; Student, Misty McLaughlin (2002). Walzel told the faculty that the committee hoped to have a nomination by the March 2000 Board meeting.[242]

The faculty displayed keen interest in the presidential election process. That interest centered primarily around two issues: first, having the finalists appear on campus so that the faculty could hear them speak and talk to them, and, second, learning whether the candidates would support adding a "sexual orientation" phrase to the University's antidiscrimination statement. The Presidential Search Committee did not accommodate the first interest in spite of strong faculty pressure to bring it about. Most of the viable candidates were sitting college presidents, it stated, many of whom would likely withdraw should information about their candidacies get back to their home campuses, which would be the case if they came to Southwestern for campus interviews.[243]

Sexual Orientation Statement as an Issue in the Search Process

The faculty interest in learning the position of the presidential candidates about adding a "sexual orientation" phrase to the University's antidiscrimination statement had a history of more than ten years in faculty meetings. The faculty had adopted a "Policy and Procedure on Sexual Harassment" on April 1, 1986, followed by subsequent refinements accepted by both the faculty and the Board of Trustees in April 1987.[244] This new policy was tested in 1988 when allegations of sexual harassment and assault were brought to the President's attention by a group of women, both faculty and students. He spoke to the faculty off the record about the nature of the problems and "condemned sexism and its reprehensible practices, which," he said, "will not be accepted."[245]

Though the approval of a Women's Studies major and minor on March 28, 1989, was not precisely related to the issue of sexual harassment, this approval did occur in the climate of opinion prevalent during the sexual harassment discussion.[246] Written largely by Dr. Jan Dawson, the proposal related to this approval, like the Jessie Daniel Ames Lecture Series established in 1985, established an academic focus for women's issues. Three new women's organizations—a Women's Soccer Club, Women in Communication, and Equal Voice for Women—came into existence, and two more—a Women's Softball Club and a Gay-Lesbian Student Union—waited in the wings for approval. Dean Ballou said that he was "delighted" at the student move to form a gay support group. It would need, he said, a strong faculty member representative as a critical component of the group's success.[247] The Sexual Harassment document was amended in 1990 to provide for a Sexual Harassment Officer and a Sexual Harassment Advisory Staff.[248] Equal Voice for Women sponsored a "Rape Education Week" the first week in April 1990.[249] In the summer of the same year the Women's Studies and Gender Awareness Programs received a fifty-thousand-dollar challenge grant from the RGK Foundation. Dr. George and Ronya Kozmetsky had established the RGK Foundation in 1966. Kozmetsky was an almost legendary figure as Dean of the University of Texas at Austin and the Graduate School of Business (1966–1982). He was a successful businessman and a cofounder of Teledyne (1960) before he was tapped as dean.[250]

The first request that sexual orientation be added to the University's list of nondiscrimination categories came from the Student Affairs Council in March 1991.[251] The faculty passed it the following year by a margin of 56 to 15 (79 percent to 21 percent).[252] The Board of Trustees considered the matter at its meeting the following fall but did not choose to amend the current statement. It "affirmed the university's historic and continuing commitment to the sacred worth and dignity of every person, regardless of any factor, and the importance of our being an inclusive, caring community." In other words, it suggested that it did not need to affirm for the record what it already practiced.[253]

Another attempt was made in March 1993 to add "sexual orientation" to the statement by asking the Board to reconsider its previous decision. The motion was approved 59 to 16 (79 percent to 21 percent) by the faculty.[254] This time the Board appointed five of its members to meet with a group composed of five students, five faculty members, and four staff members to discuss the matter, but with the same result.[255] The issue of domestic partners surfaced in 1995 when a consideration of fringe benefits was being made. The matter was discussed in the faculty meeting but no vote was taken.[256] Further discussion of the matter occurred occasionally during various faculty meetings from 1996 through 1998, but an impasse seemed to have been reached between the Board and the faculty by that point. Neither side was willing to compromise its position.

The issue was opened again in late 1999, when Southern Methodist University was reported to have added "sexual orientation" to its nondiscrimination statement. A motion requesting the Board to add the words "sexual orientation" to the University Statement of Non-Discrimination passed by a vote of 69 to 11 (80 percent to 13 percent), with 6 (7 percent) abstaining. The faculty secretary, Kiyoshi Tamagawa, "noted that subsequent research revealed that the SMU statement is NOT an exact equivalent for SU's Federally mandated non-discrimination statement published in the front of the Faculty Handbook."[257] Though Dr. Jones reported to the Board on December 10 that the faculty and Student Congress had voted to ask the Board of Trustees to include the words "sexual orientation" in the University's nondiscrimination statement and that he had just recently received a petition with 757 signatures requesting the same action, the Board decided to take no action.[258] By that time it was bidding farewell to Roy Shilling in a series of celebrations and getting ready to welcome the new President.

The sexual orientation issue came up in three more faculty meetings before the end of the 1999–2000 academic year. On the first two occasions a decision to take action was thwarted by caution concerning the supposed position of the President-elect, Jake Schrum. On March 7 the statement was made in the meeting that "reports from several quarters suggest that he is in favor of inclusion." On April 4 a more precise statement of his views was offered. "President-elect Jake Schrum," the speaker reported, "has expressed a willingness to take up the non-discrimination clause with the Board when he takes office." Therefore, cautioned the speaker, it is "not clear whether pressing forward with this initiative at this time would be of any benefit to his efforts."[259] On April 25 a resolution of support was made for President-elect Schrum "in any petition he might make to the Board of Trustees to include sexual orientation in the University's non-discrimination clause." A paper ballot was held, and the resolution was adopted, with 90 in favor, 3 against (91 percent to 3 percent), and 6 (6 percent) abstentions.[260]

Reporting on the fall meeting of the Board of Trustees, *The Megaphone* announced that President Schrum had reported to the Board that Southwestern would be adding a new statement to its existing policies, namely, a Statement of Nondiscrimination and Domestic Partner Benefits Policy. The statement would be added to the Faculty, Staff and Student Handbooks as well as to the University Catalog. Schrum said: "I made the decision and simply informed the Board of my decision on November 10, 2000." He did not ask for a vote from the Board.[261]

Retirement Events and the Sarofim School of Fine Arts

On January 14, 1999, Roy Shilling and Rick Eason visited Mr. Fayez Sarofim in Houston and presented him a naming proposal for the School of Fine Arts.[262] Sarofim said that he would think about it and get back to them. On March 29 Red McCombs sent Sarofim a letter asking that he contribute $8 million to make the Fine Arts facilities truly first-class.[263] The three men, Shilling, Eason, and McCombs, continued to discuss the matter. Eason sent McCombs a detailed letter on May 13 outlining Shilling's concept of naming the Fine Arts Center for Fayez Sarofim on the basis of his performance in managing the University's endowment since the early 1970s (actually 1968). The naming would be conditional on his pledging $8 million for the building to be paid over five years. The gift would remain anonymous and the naming would recognize Sarofim's role in making Southwestern's endowment performance among the top ten nationally.[264]

Dr. Jake B. Schrum, fourteenth president of Southwestern University, and Dr. Ron Swain, senior adviser to the president, enjoying a conversation with an unidentified person. Southwestern University, Special Collections.

The gala event at the Fine Arts Center on December 10, 1999, in honor of Shilling's retirement was highlighted by his announcement that Fayez Sarofim earlier in the week had agreed to make an $8 million gift for the School of Fine Arts. In appreciation for the gift, the Board of Trustees voted to name the school "The Fayez Sarofim School of Fine Arts." Group Two Architecture was appointed as the architect of record for the renovation and expansion of the Alma Thomas Fine Arts Center.[265] The gift came after an anonymous $3.5 million donation in 1995 by Sarofim to fund a new visual arts wing and brought his total contributions to almost $13 million. The son of a wealthy Egyptian family, Sarofim came to the United States in 1946. After attending Harvard Business School, he founded his Houston-based investment firm, Fayez Sarofim & Company, in 1958.[266]

At the Board meeting prior to the gala on December 10, Chairman Red McCombs read a letter from Mrs. Isabel Brown Wilson on behalf of The Brown Foundation, Inc., suggesting that the recently funded lectures on public ethics and community service be named the Roy and Margaret Shilling Lecture Series in recognition of their extraordinary service to Southwestern University. The Board unanimously approved a resolution so naming the lectures.[267] Over nine hundred students, faculty, staff, donors, alumni, and area residents attended the inaugural Roy and Margaret Shilling Lecture two months later on February 16. Mr. Bill Moyers spoke on the "Soul of Democracy," followed by questions from four students who were members of the Student Leadership Steering Committee.[268]

The Presidential Search Committee acted with dispatch. As secretary of the committee, Marilyn Mock had sent out introductory letters and a small brochure to 877 persons. President Shilling was also asked to publicize the search among his fellow college presidents. By October 1 he had talked by phone with 85 presidents of national liberal arts colleges and selected United Methodist colleges. From all these contacts, Chairman Walzel was able to tell the Board of Trustees on December 10 that 153 nominations had been received, from which there were 91 applications.[269] The slate was narrowed to 10, then to 6. Various members of the Search Committee made visits to those 6 individuals and narrowed the group down to 3 finalists. The entire committee interviewed those 3, who were all sitting college presidents, in four-hour interviews. Dr. Jake Schrum was chosen from among those 3 and recommended for election as the fourteenth President of Southwestern University on January 10, 2000. The Board elected him unanimously.[270] Schrum was introduced to the Board and made a brief presentation. He assumed office on July 1, 2000.

Bibliographical Note

Most of the major sources cited in this book can be found at Southwestern University. The five main places where they reside are in the General Collection and Special Collections sections of the A. Frank Smith, Jr., Library Center, the Presidential Archives stored in Austin but obtainable through the President's Office, the main vault in the Business Office, the Information Research Office, and the Office of University Relations.

The four indispensable sources are the Minutes of the Board of Trustees, the Minutes of the Executive Committee, the Faculty Minutes, and, from about 1934 on, the individual volumes prepared by the administration for each Board meeting. From earliest times until the late 1940s, the first three of these sources were all kept in large journals. They were handwritten until shortly after the beginning of the twentieth century, when some of them began to be typewritten. The typewritten pages were then placed in journals with secure systems locking the pages in place to prevent loss. The pages were numbered sequentially in each volume. The most important features of these journals were that the secretaries kept the records in meticulous fashion and that none of the volumes was lost. The Board Minutes and Executive Committee Minutes were kept in separate journals until midway into the twentieth century, when they began to be kept in the same volume. Though the Faculty Minutes were kept with the same formality as the others at the outset, they gradually became more informal and less comprehensive in explaining faculty actions. Faculty secretaries corrected both these faults during the Fleming and Shilling years.

Beginning with President Vivion in the mid-1930s, some of the Presidents occasionally began to publish all the material for each annual Board meeting in 8½" x 11" volumes bound in flexible covers. This system became standard in the 1950s for all Board meetings. Nevertheless, the journal system for recording Board and Executive Committee actions continued until 1985, when the Board Minutes for the last Board meeting began to be published as a part of the preparatory material for the next Board meeting.

The oldest journals of minutes are found today in the Special Collections section of the library. The most recent journals are to be found in the Business Office vault. The many individual, flexible-backed volumes holding the Board Minutes, the Executive Committee Minutes, preparatory materials for Board meetings, and the Faculty Minutes since the 1950s must now be searched out in the Presidential Archives or in other administrative offices where copies may have been kept. Fortunately, a beautifully organized index in the President's Office is available for the Presidential Archives.

Abbreviations and Short Titles for Notes and Bibliography

BOV = Business Office Vault
CC = Cody Collection
CCSB = Cody Collection Scrapbook
CWL = Charles Wright Letters
GC = Giddings Collection
GCM = Georgetown College Minutes
GL = Granbery Letters
HBTO = Handbook of Texas Online
LC = Love Collection
MHHS = Mood-Heritage Museum Hall of Honor Historical Sketches
MKSB = McKennon Scrapbook
MSB = Mood Scrapbooks
PANC = Pearl A. Neas Collection
RBSSB = Roy B. Shilling Scrapbooks
SC = Special Collections
SLC =Smith Library Center
SU = Southwestern University
SU Curators 1870–79 = Records of the Texas University Faculty [Curator Section 1870–79]
SU Curators-Trustees 1869–1912 = Minutes of the Board of Curators 1869–1906, Trustees 1906–1912
SU Ex Com 1907–23 = Minutes of the Executive Committee of the Board of Trustees 1907–1923
SU Ex Com 1923–36 = Minutes of Executive Committee of Board of Trustees 1923–1936
SU Ex Com 1936–40 = Minutes of the Executive Committee of Southwestern University 1936–1940
SU Ex Com 1940–41 = Minutes of the Executive Committee 1940–1941
SU Ex Com 1942–52 = Minutes of the Executive Committee 1942–1952
SU Faculty 1879–90 = Records of the Texas University Faculty 1879–90
SU Faculty 1890–1904 = Faculty Minutes 1890–1904
SU Faculty = Faculty Minutes
SU Faculty 1912–13 = Faculty Minutes 1912–1913
SU Faculty 1913–34 = Faculty Minutes 1913–1934
SU Faculty 1934–44 = Faculty Minutes 1934–1944
SU Faculty 1945–46 = Faculty Minutes 1945–1946
SU Trustees 1871–93 = Texas University Company 1871–93
SU Trustees 1894–1907 = Board of Trustee Minutes 1894–1907
SU Trustees 1913–25 = Minutes of the Board of Trustees 1913–1925
SU Trustees 1925–34 = Minutes of the Board of Trustees 1925–1934
SU Trustees 1935–47 = Minutes of the Board of Trustees 1935–1947
SU Trustees 1947–53 = Minutes of the Board of Trustees 1947–1953
SU Trustees 1953–57 = Minutes of Meetings of Board of Trustees 1953–1957
SU Trustees 1957–60 = Minutes of Meetings of Board of Trustees 1957–1960
SU Trustees 1960–66 = Minutes of the Board of Trustees 1960–1966
SU Trustees 1967–78 = Minutes of the Board of Trustees and Exec. Com. 1967–1978
SU Trustees 1978–85 = Minutes of the Board of Trustees and Exec. Com. 1978–1985
SUPA = Southwestern University Presidential Archives
WC Sun = *Williamson County Sun*

The location listed by Ralph Jones for material used by him from the Cody Collection has been changed since his time. Consequently, the footnote references in his *Southwestern University: 1840–1961* to information in that collection are not useful for locating that material today.

Bibliography

Primary Sources for the Early Years

Ayres, David. "Early Methodism in Texas." *The Texas Christian Advocate*, August 13, 1857, 1 p.

Bell, Thomas W. *A Narrative of the Capture and Subsequent Sufferings of the Mier Prisoners in Mexico, Captured in the Cause of Texas, Dec. 26th, 1842 and Liberated Sept. 16th, 1844*. Orig. 1845; Waco: Texian Press, 1964.

Bentley, F. Edward. "Documents Regarding the Minutes of the Board of Trustees of Soule University." SU, SLC, SC.

Eby, Frederick, ed. *Education in Texas: Source Materials*. University of Texas Bulletin, Vol. No. 1824. Austin: University of Texas, 1918.

Fisher, Rebecca Jane Gilleland. "Response by Mrs. Rebecca J. Fisher." *Proceedings of Texas Veteran Association*, 1905: 10–16.

Fowler, Littleton M. "Letters of Rev. Littleton M. Fowler, Methodist Missionary." Austin, private transcription, June 24, 1953. SU, SLC, SC.

Friend, Llerena, ed. "Thomas Bell Letters." *The Southwestern Historical Quarterly* 63, no. 1 (1959): 99–109; no. 2 (1959): 299–310; no. 3 (1960): 457–468; no. 4 (1960): 589–599.

Giddings, Wallace Matthews. Letters and Information on Jabez Demming Giddings and Family. 2 vols. SU, SLC, SC.

Lee, Mrs. A. J. "Some Recollections of Two Texas Pioneer Women." *The Methodist Historical Quarterly* 1, no. 2 (1909): 207–213.

Matthews, Henry. "The Henry Matthews Diaries." Handwritten manuscript. ca. 1840. SU, SLC, SC.

Muir, Andrew Forest, ed. *Texas in 1837: An Anonymous, Contemporary Narrative*. Austin: University of Texas Press, 1958.

Olmsted, Frederick Law. *A Journey Through Texas; or, A Saddle-trip on the Southwestern Frontier: with a statistical appendix*. New York: Dix, Edwards & Co., 1857.

Southwestern. Assorted Printed Material on the Opening of Texas University. 1873. SU, SLC, SC.

Tanner, Finch, and Fleming. "Tanner-Finch Letters on William H. Seat." SUPA. File entitled "Dr. Ralph W. Jones 69 back."

Texas-Gammel. "An Act to Establish and Incorporate the Wesleyan Male and Female College of San Augustine (1844)." In *The Laws of Texas: 1822–1897*, ed. H. P. N. Gammell, pp. 2:931–934. Austin: The Gammell Book Company, 1898.

———. "An Act to Incorporate the McKenzie Institute in Red River County [1854]." In *The Laws of Texas: 1822–1897*, ed. H. P. N. Gammell, pp. 4:107–108. Austin: The Gammell Book Company, 1898.

———. "An Act to Incorporate the McKenzie Male and Female College (1860)."In *The Laws of Texas: 1822–1897*, ed. H. P. N. Gammell, pp. 4:111–113. Austin: The Gammell Book Company, 1898.

———. "An Act to Incorporate Soule University (1856)." In *The Laws of Texas: 1822–1897*, ed. H. P. N. Gammell, pp. 4:353–354. Austin: The Gammell Book Company, 1898.

———. "An Act to Incorporate the South Western University (1875)." In *The Laws of Texas: 1822–1897*, ed. H. P. N. Gammell, pp. 617–619. Houston: The Gammell Book Company, 1898.

Wallis, Jonnie Lockhart. *The Life and Letters of Dr. John Washington Lockhart, 1824–1900*. New York: Arno Press, 1930.

"[Wesleyan College Report]." *Western Christian Advocate*, , May 9, 1845.

Wilson, Francis. *Memoirs of a Methodist Circuit Rider—Francis Wilson*. Edited by William E. Smith. Austin: William E. Smith, 1983.

Wright, Charles. Charles Wright Letters. Connecticut State Library, copies at SU, SLC, SC.

Writings by Martin Ruter and F. A. Mood

Gregory, G., D.D. *An History of the Christian Church, from the Earliest Periods to the Present Time*. A new edition, corrected and enlarged. 2 vols. London: Printed for C. and G. Kearsley, Fleet Street, 1795. [See Ruter's *Concise History of the Christian Church*.]

Mood, Francis Asbury. *For God and Texas: Autobiography of Francis Asbury Mood, 1830–1884*. Edited by Mary Katherine Metcalfe Earney. Dallas: Listo Publications, 2001. Mood's 3-vol. autographed original in the SLC, SC.

———. "Letter of F. A. Mood to D. W. Snyder." Georgetown, March 26, 1875. SU, SLC, SC, Small Collections, Box 2, Folder 8.

———. *Methodism in Charleston: a narrative of the chief events relating to the rise and progress of the Methodist Episcopal church in Charleston, S.C., with brief notices of the early ministers who labored in that city*. 1st ed. Nashville: E. Stevenson and J. E. Evans, for the Methodist Episcopal Church, South, 1856.

———. *A Narrative of the Facts Relating the Founding and Progress of Southwestern University from 1840 to 1882*. Galveston: Shaw & Blaylock, Printers, 1882.

Ruter, Martin. *A Concise History of the Christian Church, from Its First Establishment to the Present Time; Containing a General View of Missions, and Exhibiting the State of Religion in Different Parts of the World, Compiled from the Works of Dr. G. Gregory, with Numerous Additions and Improvements*. New York: B. Waugh and T. Mason, for the Methodist Episcopal Church, J. Collord, Printer, 1834.

———. *An Easy Entrance into the Sacred Language; Being a Concise Hebrew Grammar, without Points. Compiled for the Use and Encouragement of Learners, and Adapted to Such as Have not the Aid of a Teacher*. Cincinnati: Published by Martin Ruter, for the Methodist Episcopal Church, Morgan and Lodge, Printers, 1824.

———. *The Juvenile Arithmetick and Scholar's Guide; Wherein Theory and Practice Are Combined and Adapted to the Capacities of Young Beginners; Containing a Due Proportion of Examples in Federal Money; and the Whole Being Illustrated by Numerous Questions Similar to Those of Pestalozzi*. Cincinnati: Published and sold by N. and G. Guilford, W. M. and O. Farnsworth, Jr., Printers, 1828.

———. *A Sketch of the Life and Doctrine of the Celebrated John Calvin, Including Some Facts Relative to the Burning of Servetus*. Portland: Printed by A. & J. Shirley, 1814.

Books—Biography and Autobiography

Barcus, Joseph Garland. *Barcus-Barkhurst Family*. Waco: Texian Press, 1996.

Brown, Ray Hyer. *Robert Stewart Hyer: The Man I Knew*. Salado, Tex.: The Anson Jones Press, 1957.

Burleson, Rufus C. *The Life and Writings of Rufus C. Burleson, D.D., LL.D., Containing a Biography of Dr. Burleson by Hon. Harry Haynes*. Compiled and published by Mrs. Georgia J. Burleson, 1901.

Campbell, Mrs. S. R. "Martin Ruter." In *Biographical Sketches of Eminent Itinerant Ministers Distinguished, for the Most Part, as Pioneers of Methodism within the Bounds of the Methodist Episcopal Church, South*, ed. T. O. Summers. Nashville: Southern Methodist Publishing House, 1859.

Caro, Robert A. *The Years of Lyndon Johnson: The Path to Power*. New York: Alfred A. Knopf, 1982.

Cody, Claude Carr. *The Life and Labors of Francis Asbury Mood, D.D.* Chicago: F. H. Revell, 1886.

Custer, Judson S., and Jeff H. Campbell. *Dobie at Southwestern University: The Beginnings of His Literary Career, 1906–1911*, ed. J. S. Custer. Austin: Jenkins Publishing Company, 1981.

Du Bose, Horace M. *The History of Methodism.* Nashville: Publishing House of the Methodist Episcopal Church, South, 1916.

———. *Life of Joshua Soule.* Nashville and Dallas: Publishing House of the M. E. Church, South, 1911.

Gross, John O. *Martin Ruter: Pioneer in Methodist Education.* [Nashville]: Board of Education of The Methodist Church, 1956.

Hall, Jacquelyn Dowd. *Revolt against Chivalry: Jessie Daniel Ames and the Women's Campaign against Lynching.* New York: Columbia University Press, 1979.

McEnteer, James. *Fighting Words: Independent Journalists in Texas.* Austin: University of Texas Press, 1992.

McLean, John H. *Reminiscences.* Nashville: Publishing House of the M. E. Church, South, 1918.

Masterson, Ralph. *Sketches from the Life of Dr. Horace Bishop.* n.p.: n.p., [ca. 1933].

Pickrell, Annie Doom. *Pioneer Women in Texas.* Austin: The E. L. Steck Company, 1929.

Pratt, Joseph A., and Christopher J. Castaneda. *Builders: Herman and George R. Brown.* College Station: Texas A&M Press, 1999.

Smith, Ernest Ashton. *Martin Ruter.* New York and Cincinnati: The Methodist Book Concern, 1915.

Spellmann, Norman W. *Growing a Soul: The Story of A. Frank Smith.* Dallas: SMU Press, 1979.

Stubbs, Thomas McAlpin. *Family Album: An Account of the Moods of Charleston, South Carolina, and Connected Families.* Atlanta: Curtiss Printing Company, Inc., 1943.

Woolworth, Laura Fowler, ed. *Littleton Fowler, 1803–1846: A Missionary to the Republic of Texas, 1837–1846.* [Shreveport]: Printed privately, 1936.

General Books

Allen, Martha Mitten. *The Gracious Gift: The Negro Fine Arts School, 1946–66.* Georgetown: Georgetown Heritage Society, 1998.

Crocket, George L. *Two Centuries in East Texas: A History of San Augustine County and Surrounding Territory.* Dallas: The Southwest Press, 1932.

Eby, Frederick. *The Development of Education in Texas.* New York: The Macmillan Company, 1925.

Flexner, Abraham. *Medical Education in the United States and Canada: A Report to the Carnegie Foundation for the Advancement of Teaching.* Bulletin Number Four (1910). New York: Carnegie Foundation for the Advancement of Education, 1910. 1960.

Fountain-Schroeder, Joanna, ed. *Jessie Daniel Ames' Book Collection.* Southwestern University Bibliographic Series. Georgetown: SU, 1986.

Garber, Paul Neff. *The Methodists of Continental Europe.* New York: Board of Missions and Church Extension of The Methodist Church, 1949.

Jones, Ralph Wood. *Southwestern University 1840–1961.* Austin: Jenkins Publishing Co., 1973.

McCombs, Red. *The Red Zone, Cars, Cows, and Coaches: The Life and Good Times of a Texas Dealmaker.* Austin: Eakin Press, 2002.

Machann, Clinton, and James W. Mendl. *Krasna Amerika: A Study of the Texas Czechs, 1851–1939.* Austin: Eakin Press, 1983.

Moore, John M., and John R. Nelson, eds. *Texas Methodist Educational Convention: Proceedings and Addresses.* [Dallas]: Blaylock Publishing Company, [1906].

Nail, Olin W. *History of Texas Methodism 1900–1960.* Austin: Capital Printing Company, 1961.

———, ed. *Texas Methodist Centennial Yearbook.* Elgin, Tex.: 1934. 799 pp.

Náñez, Alfredo. *History of the Rio Grande Conference of the United Methodist Church.* Dallas: Bridwell Library, Southern Methodist University, 1980.

Phelan, Macum. *A History of Early Methodism in Texas, 1817–1866.* Nashville, Richmond [etc.]: Cokesbury Press, 1924.

———. *A History of the Expansion of Methodism in Texas: 1867–1902.* Dallas: Mathis, Van Nort & Co., 1937.

Prochazkova, Schneeberger, et al. *Osmdesat Let Milosti (Eighty Years of Grace).* Prague: Evangelical Methodist Church, 2000.

Scarbrough, Clara Stearns. *Land of Good Water: A Williamson County, Texas, History.* Georgetown: Williamson County Sun Publishers, 1973.

Scarbrough, Linda. *Road, River, and Ol' Boy Politics: A Texas County's Path from Farm to Supersuburb.* Austin: Texas State Historical Association, 2005.

Schmidt, Charles Frank. *History of Blinn Memorial College (1883–1934).* San Antonio: Lodovic Printing Company, 1935.

———. *History of Washington County.* San Antonio: The Naylor Company, 1949.

Southwestern. *Southwestern: A University's Transformation.* Georgetown: Southwestern University, 1999.

Springer, Angus. *Exits and Entrances.* Austin: Whitley Company, 1982.

Thrall, Homer S. *A Brief History of Methodism in Texas.* Nashville: Publishing House of the M. E. Church, South, 1894.

Vernon, Walter N., et al. *The Methodist Excitement in Texas.* Dallas: The Texas United Methodist Historical Society, 1984.

Wright, Marcus J. *Texas in the War 1861–1865.* Edited by H. B. Simpson. Hillsboro, Tex.: The Hill Junior College Press, 1965.

Newspaper, Magazine, and Journal Articles

Anonymous. "Dr. and Mrs. Suh become Naturalized U.S. Citizens." *Williamson County Sun,* Georgetown, May 25, 1975.

———. "Heated Words Used in the Conference." *The Constitution* (Atlanta), November 24, 1900. p. 5.

———. "Locating Southwestern University Proved Difficult Task." *The Megaphone,* Georgetown, April 9, 1940. 1–40. SU, SLC.

———. "Pioneer Resident of Georgetown Dies at 105." *San Antonio Express,* January 5, 1957. SU, SLC, SC. Pasted on the inside back page of Soule University Catalogue for 1859–60.

———. "Second Day of the Methodists." *The Constitution* (Atlanta), December 1, 1899. p. 2.

———. "They're More Than Just Old Rocks to Southwestern." *Williamson County Sun?,* no date. SU, SLC, SC.

Arthur, Dora Fowler. "The Reverend Littleton Fowler: Missionary to the Republic of Texas." *The Methodist Historical Quarterly* 1, no. 2 (1909): 117–138.

Carlyon, J. T. "Changes and Trends in Theological Thought." In *The History of Texas Methodism 1900–1960,* ed. O. W. Nail, pp. 449–470. Austin: Capital Printing Company, 1961.

Cody, Claude Carr. "The Old Southwestern College Building." *Williamson County Sun,* Georgetown, January 19, 1923.

———. "Rev. Martin Ruter, A. M., D. D." *The Methodist Historical Quarterly* 1, no. 1 (1909): 7–38.

———. "Soule University," *The Methodist Historical Quarterly* 2, no. 3 (1911): 221–234.

Granbery, John C. "Dr. Granbery in France." *The Megaphone,* October 9, 1917. SU, SLC, Microfilm collection.

Jones, R. L. "Folk Life in Early Texas: The Autobiography of Andrew Davis." *Southwestern Historical Quarterly* (1939–1940): 43.

Lee, Mrs. A. J. "Rev. J. W. Kenney." *The Methodist Historical Quarterly* 1, no. 1 (1909): 45–55.

McLean, John H. "Chauncey Richardson." *The Methodist Historical Quarterly* 2, no. 2 (1910): 149–157.

———. "Our Early Schools." *The Methodist Historical Quarterly* 2, no. 1 (1910): 62–70.

———. "Rev. John W. P. McKenzie, D. D." *The Methodist Historical Quarterly* 1, no. 1 (1910): 61–66.

Osburn, John D. "McKenzie College." *The Southwestern Historical Quarterly* 63, no. 4 (1960): 533–553.

Sinks, Julia Lee. "Rutersville College." *The Quarterly of the Texas State Historical Association* 2, no. 2 (1898): 124–133.

Vivion, Harriet Winton. "King Vivion, The Eighth President of Southwestern." *Southwestern Magazine* 48 (June 1930).

West, Donald J. "Heidt, John Wesley." In *The Encyclopedia of World Methodism*, vol. 1, p. 1105. [Nashville]: The United Methodist Publishing House, c. 1974.

Pamphlets

Anonymous. *The Lois Perkins Chapel, 1943–1981: The Culmination of a Dream.* Georgetown, 1981.

Brown, Bob Marion. *Robert Stewart Hyer.* Georgetown: In Cody, Hyer, McLean, Sanders, Young tract of the MHHS, 1982.

Cody, Claude Carr, John M. Barcus, and Laura Kuykendall, eds. *The Book of Southwestern.* Georgetown: Von Boeckmann Jones Co., 1923.

College Entrance Examination Board. *College-Level Examination Program: Description and Uses, 1967.* CEEB, 1967.

Custer, Judson S. *Charles Wright (1811–1885).* Georgetown: MHHS, 1985.

———. *Reverend Robert Alexander (1811–1882) and Eliza Perkins Ayers Alexander (1821–1878).* Georgetown: MHHS, 1994.

Duncan, Sharon. *Ann Catherine (Goodwin) Haynie.* Georgetown: MHHS, 1984.

Evans, Mary Jane. *D. H. Snyder and J. W. Snyder.* Georgetown: MHHS, ca. 1984–1994.

Institute of Texan Cultures, University of Texas. *The Czech Texans.* 1972. 2nd. ed.

Geiser, Samuel Wood. *Medical Education in Dallas 1900–1910.* Dallas, 1952.

McCook, Jane Brown. *Claude Carr Cody.* Georgetown: In Cody, Hyer, McLean, Sanders, Young tract of the MHHS, [1984–1994].

———. *Laura Kuykendall.* Georgetown: MHHS, 1989.

Swartz, Jon D. *J. Frank Dobie.* Georgetown: MHHS, 1988.

———. *John Howell McLean.* Georgetown: In Cody, Hyer, McLean, Sanders, Young tract of the MHHS, 1984–1994?

———, ed. *Jessie Daniel Ames: An Exhibition at Southwestern University.* Mood-Heritage Museum. Georgetown, 1986.

Young, Paul P. *Ryland Fletcher Young.* Georgetown: In the Cody, Hyer, McLean, Sanders, Young tract of the MHHS, 1982.

Yoxall, Dan. *Lois Craddock Perkins (1887–1983).* Georgetown: MHHS, 1992.

Individual Letters

Anonymous. "Letter That Refers to the Honor Council." Handwritten. Georgetown, October 17, 1913. SU, SLC, SC.

Bunting, Dorothy Shell. "Dorothy Bunting Letter to Nancy Porsche." Handwritten. Supplied by President's Office to author.

Finch, William C. "Finch Letter to Wm. B. Jones." Typewritten. March 11, 2005. Author's personal files.

Gambrell, Herbert. "Herbert Gambrell Letter to Ralph Jones." June 18, 1974. SUPA.

Howard, Claud. "Letter to Alpha Chi's." Georgetown, March 16, 1940. SU, SLC, SC, Centennial Celebration, Neas Box 2, Folder: Miscellaneous.

Malac, Marian Bartak. "Letters of Marian Bartak Malac." Typed letters. Blairsville, Georgia, October 6, 2000, and February 19, 2001.

Neas, Pearl A. "Letter from Pearl A. Neas to R. G. Perryman, President American Association of Collegiate Registrars and Admissions Officers." March 28, 1962. Pearl A. Neas Collection, Box ?, Folder ?, Fleming Inaugural Committee Papers. SU, SLC, SC, PANC.

Rollins, Hyder E. "Letter Donating Recommendations from Former Southwestern Professors." Handwritten letter. Georgetown, April 22, 1958. SU, SLC, SC, Small Collections, Hyder E. Rollins Gift, Box 3, Folder 2.

Shilling, Roy B., Jr. "Random Thoughts." Email to Jones. Georgetown, January 5, 2005.

Stanford, Rosemond, and C. C. Cody, Jr. Stanford-Cody Letters. 1938. BOV.

Thomas, Joseph D. "Two Letters from J. D. Thomas." Typewritten. Dallas, September 10 and October 22, 1970. Author's personal files.

Towner, Walter. "Walter Towner Welcoming Letter." Typed letter. Dallas, July 24, 1925. SU, SLC, SC, Box entitled President; Folder: Southwestern University: Presidents. Charles McTyeire Bishop.

Ullrich, Oscar A. "Assessment of Financial Situation." Typed letter. Georgetown, May 14, 1935. SU, SLC, SC, Box entitled President; Folder: Faculty Letter to President Vivion, May 14, 1935.

Vaughn, Gerald F. "Gerald F. Vaughn to Kathryn Stallard" about John R. Allen. Newark, Delaware, May 22, 2005. SU, SLC, SC.

Electronic Sources

Ames, Jessie Daniel. "Jessie Daniel Ames Papers: Inventory." University of North Carolina at Chapel Hill. http://www.lib.unc.edu/mss/inv/a/Ames, Jessie_Daniel.html.

Anderson, H. Allen. "Cawthon, Peter Willis." HBTO. July 23, 2002.

Anonymous. "Fisher, Rebecca Jane Gilleland." HBTO. July 23, 2002.

———. "Giddings-Stone Mansion." http://www.brenham-mansion.com. Internet. July 22, 2002.

———. "Trustees of Dartmouth College v. Woodward." http://www.dartmouth. edu/~govdocs/case/dartmouthcase.htm. June 10, 2003.

———. "Westminster Junior College and Bible Institute." HBTO. July 23, 2002.

Bailey, Anne J. "Carter, George Washington." HBTO. July 23, 2002.

Batchelder, P. M. "McDonald, William Johnson." HBTO. July 23, 2002.

Benham, Priscilla Myers. "Moore, Francis, Jr." HBTO. July 23, 2002.

Blanton, Joseph E. "Hill, John Christopher Columbus." HBTO. July 23, 2002.

Brandenstein, Sherilyn. "Fondren, Ella Florence." HBTO. July 23, 2002.

Carnegie Foundation for the Advancement of Teaching, The. "The Carnegie Classification of Institutions of Higher Education." http://www.carnegie foundation.org.

Chance, Joseph E. "Moore, John Creed." HBTO. July 23, 2002.

Charleston Daily Mail. January 20, 1935. http//:Ancestry.com.

Christian, Carole E. "Chappell Hill Female College." HBTO. July 23, 2002.

———. "Giddings, Jabez Demming." HBTO. July 23, 2002.

———. "Soule University." HBTO. July 23, 2002.

Cutrer, Thomas W. "Sexton, Franklin Barlow." HBTO. July 23, 2002.

Dixon, Ford. "Granbery, John Cowper, Jr." HBTO. July 23, 2002.

Ely, Bert. "Savings and Loan Crisis." ©1993, 2002 David R. Henderson. All rights reserved. http://www.econlib.org.

Fleming, Richard T. "Daniel James Moody, Jr." HBTO. July 23, 2002.

———. "Rollins, Hyder Edward (1889–1958)." HBTO. July 23, 2002.

Friedman, S. Morgan. "The Inflation Calculator." http://www.westegg.com/inflation/infl.cgi.

Griggs, William Clark. "McMullan, Francis." HBTO. July 23, 2002.

Hairston, Maxine. "Perry, George Sessions." HBTO. July 23, 2002.

Haynes, Charlie C., Jr. "Veal, William G." HBTO. July 23, 2002.

Hazlewood, Claudia. "West, James Marion." HBTO. July 23, 2002.

Hiett, Norris A. "Shelby, Thomas Hall." HBTO. July 23, 2002.

Hyman, Carolyn. "Hughes, Thomas Proctor." HBTO. July 23, 2002.

Jakobi, Patricia L. "Cody, Claude Carr, Jr." HBTO. July 23, 2002.

Johnston, Sheila Weems. "Internet reference to *The Blue and Gray from Hawkins County, Tennessee 1861–1865.*" Internet page created September 1, 1999.

Keeton, W. Page. "Sweatt v. Painter." HBTO. July 23, 2002.

Kliener, Diana J. "Fondren, Walter William." HBTO. July 23, 2002.

———. "Germany, Eugene Benjamin." HBTO. July 23, 2002.

Kolodziejski, Thomas J., Jr., "Why 21?" http://www.geocities.com/omniscientpunk/story14.html?200527.

Laycock, Doug. "*Hopwood v. Texas:* Timeline of Events." http://www.law.utexas.edu/hopwood.

Leatherwood, Art. "Fondren Foundation." HBTO. July 23, 2002.
Long, Christopher. "Ku Klux Klan." HBTO. July 23, 2002.
Masters, B. E. "McKenzie College." HBTO. July 23, 2002.
Maxwell, Robert S. "Kurth, Ernest Lynn." HBTO. July 23, 2002.
Minor, David. "Weatherford College." HBTO. July 23, 2002.
———. "Westminster College." HBTO. July 23, 2002.
Patenaude, Lionel V. "Jones, Jesse Holman." HBTO. December 4, 2002.
Phi Beta Kappa. "The Phi Beta Kappa Society: How to Apply for a Chapter." http://www.pbk.org/affiliate/chapterform.htm.
Sneed, Edgar P. "Knickerbocker, Hubert Renfro." HBTO. July 23, 2002.
Standifer, Mary M. "Barcus, John M." HBTO. July 23, 2002.
Stevens Point Daily Journal. October 13, October 18, 1933. http://Ancestry.com.
Swartz, Jon D. "McLean, John Howell." HBTO. July 23, 2002.
Temple, Louann Atkins. "Daniel Baker College." HBTO. July 23, 2002.
Vernon, Walter N. "Náñez, Alfredo." HBTO. July 23, 2002.
Walker, Dionne. "Who is F. W. Olin?" prism online: exploring the future of engineering education. http;//www.prism-magazine.org/septoo/html/olin 2.cfm.
Ward, Forrest E. "Score, John Nelson Russell." HBTO. July 23, 2002.
Wilson, Robert L. "Methodism and Foreign Policy Since World War II." http://www.cmpage.org/biases/chapter2.html.

Trustee, Executive Committee, and Faculty Minutes

Georgetown. Minutes of Georgetown College. Handwritten. January 29, 1870, to September 13, 1873. SU, SLC, SC.
Southwestern. Records of Texas University Faculty [Curator Section 1870–79]. Handwritten minutes. October 4, 1869, through June 11, 1890. SU, SLC, SC.
———. Texas University Company 1871–1893 [Trustees]. Handwritten minutes. December 11, 1871, through September 8, 1893. SU, SLC, SC.
———. Minutes of the Board of Curators 1873–1906, Trustees 1906–1912. Handwritten. SU, SLC, SC.
———. Board of Trustee Minutes 1894–1907. Handwritten minutes. June 1, 1894, to April 17, 1907. SU, SLC, SC.
———. Minutes of the Board of Trustees 1913–1925. June 13, 1913, to February 11, 1925. SU, BOV.
———. Minutes of the Board of Trustees 1925–1934. June 15, 1925, to June 1, 1934. SU, BOV.
———. Minutes of the Board of Trustees 1935–1947. May 23, 1935, to April 30, 1947. SU, BOV.
———. Minutes of the Board of Trustees 1947–1953. November 12, 1947, to April 17, 1953. SU, BOV.
———. Minutes of Meetings of Board of Trustees 1953–1957. November 12, 1957, to November 13, 1957 (part one). SU, BOV.
———. Minutes of the Board of Trustees 1957–1960. November 13, 1957 (part 2) to November 11, 1960 (part 1). SU, BOV.
———. Minutes of the Board of Trustees 1960–1966. November 11, 1960 (part 2) to October 24, 1966. SU, BOV.
———. Minutes of the Board of Trustees 1967 1978, including Executive Committee Minutes. February 3, 1967–April 28, 1978, with Ex. Com. February 2, 1967–June 23, 1978. SU, BOV.
———. Minutes of the Board of Trustees 1978–1985. September 20, 1978, to January 18, 1985. SU, BOV.
(To access the Trustee Minutes since 1985, see the Bibliographical Note above.)
———. Minutes of the Executive Committee of the Board of Trustees 1907–1923. May 27, 1907, to September 24, 1923. SU, BOV.
———. Minutes of Executive Committee of Board of Trustees 1923–1936. October 11, 1923, to April 8, 1936. SU, BOV.
———. Minutes of the Executive Committee of Southwestern University 1936–1940. July 17, 1936, to January 9, 1940. SU, BOV
———. Minutes of the Executive Committee of Southwestern University 1940–1941. February 16, 1940, to October 15, 1941. SU, BOV.
———. Minutes of the Executive Committee of Southwestern University 1942–1952. February 25, 1942, to February 20, 1952. SU, BOV.
(To access the Executive Committee Minutes since 1952, see the Bibliographical Note above.)
———. Records of Texas University Faculty 1879–90. Handwritten minutes. October 4, 1869, through June 11, 1890. SU, SLC, SC.
———. Faculty Minutes 1890–1904. Handwritten minutes. September 16, 1890, to May 3, 1904. SU, SLC, SC.
———. Faculty Minutes 1904–1912. Handwritten minutes. March 9, 1891, to June 12, 1912. SU, SLC, SC.
———. Faculty Minutes 1912–13. Handwritten. 1912–1913. SU, BOV.
———. Faculty Minutes 1913–34. Typewritten. September 5, 1913, to July 31, 1934. SU, BOV.
———. Faculty Minutes 1934–1944. September 14, 1934, to December 15, 1944. SU, BOV.
———. Faculty Minutes 1945–1946. January 2, 1945, to November 30, 1946. SU, BOV.
(To access the Faculty Minutes since 1947, see the Bibliographical Note above.)

Catalogs—University Catalogs and Annual Conference Minutes

Annual Conference Journal. *Minutes Seventy-first Annual Session of the North Texas Annual Conference.* 1937.
———. *West Texas Conference Journal, Sixty-Eighth Annual Session.* Report of the Special Committee. SU, SLC, SC.
———. *South Georgia Conference Journal.* "Joseph King Vivion" [Memoir]. 1969. SU, SLC, SC, Box entitled President; Folder: Vivion Inauguration.
McKenzie. *Annual Catalogue of the Students and Faculty of McKenzie College for 1860–61.* Nashville: Southern Methodist Publishing House, 1861.
Rutersville. *Second Annual Catalogue of Rutersville College, 1841.* Austin: S. Whiting, Public Printer, 1842.
Soule. *Catalogue of Soule University: 1858–9.* Galveston: Christian Advocate Office, 1859.
———. *Catalogue of Soule University, Chappell Hill Texas, 1859–60.* Galveston: Texas Christian Advocate Book Press, 1860.
Southwestern. *Texas University 1874* [Catalogue]. Georgetown: Strickland & Clarke, Stationers and Printers, Galveston, 1874.
———. *Register and Announcement of Southwestern University . . . 1878–9.* Galveston: Shaw & Blaylock, Steam Printers, 1878–79.
———. *Register of Southwestern University . . . 1881–82.* Galveston: Place of Shaw & Blaylock, [1882].
———. *Register of Southwestern University . . . 1883–1884.* Georgetown: "Sun" Job Printing Office, 1884.
———. *Register of Southwestern University and the Ladies' Annex* [for 1892–93]. Georgetown, 1892–93.
———. *Register of Southwestern University and Ladies' Annex* [for 1897–98]. Georgetown, 1897–98.
———. *Catalogue Southwestern University 1898–'99.* Georgetown: News Print, 1898 99.
———. *Bulletin of Southwestern University* [for 1903–1904]. Georgetown, 1903–1904.
———. *Register for . . . 1932–1933; Announcements for . . . 1933–1934.* Georgetown: Southwestern University, 1933.
———. *Register for . . . 1935–1936; Announcements for . . . 1936–1937.* Georgetown: Southwestern University, 1936.
———. *Register for . . . 1938–1939; Announcements for . . . 1939–1940.* Georgetown: Southwestern University, 1939.
———. *Announcements for the Session 1947–1948; Register for the Session 1946–1947.* Georgetown: Southwestern University, 1947.
———. *Southwestern University Bulletin 1964–65.* Georgetown, 1964–1965.

———. *Southwestern University Bulletin 70–71*. Georgetown, 1970–71.
———. *Southwestern University Catalogue 1978–1979*. Georgetown, 1978–79.
———. *Southwestern University Catalogue 1977–1978*. Georgetown, 1977–78.

Presidential Archives

Fleming, Durwood. "Highlights of Southwestern University 1961–1972." 1972. Pres. Archives.
Southwestern. Alma Thomas Estate Files. Archives. President's Office. Box C4, #70262 (123946487).
———. Bishop A. Frank Smith Files. Archives. President's Office. Box T4, #070288.
———. Bron J. Marion West, Jr., Files. Archives. President's Office. Box T5, #070289.
———. Brown Foundation 1963 File. Archives. President's Office. Box B3, #070235.
———. Brown Foundation 64–68 File. Archives. President's Office. Box B3, #070235.
———. Brown Foundation, Inc., 1970–84, File. Archives. President's Office. Box #72044168.
———. Brown Foundation, Inc., 1985–89, File. Archives. President's Office. Box #72044168.
———. Brown Foundation, Inc., 1993–94, File. Archives. President's Office. Box #72044168.
———. Brown Foundation, Inc., 1995–96, File. Archives. President's Office. Box #72044168.
———. Brown Foundation, Inc., 1997–99, File. Archives. President's Office. Box #72044168.
———. The Brown Foundation Grant '76 File. Archives. President's Office. Box B1, #070233.
———. Brown Foundation, Inc., File [untitled]. Archives. President's Office. Box B1, #070233.
———. Charles T. Thrift File #1. Archives. President's Office. Box H2, #070230.
———. Claud Howard Files. Archives. President's Office. Box F12, #070211.
———. Dini, R. F., & Associates, Inc., File. Archives. President's Office. Box #070259.
———. Doering, Anne Marie, File. Archives. President's Office. Box #070259.
———. E. B. Germany Files. Archives. President's Office. Box T2, #070286.
———. F. and M. Lenz Files. Archives. President's Office. Box F15, #070214.
———. Fondren Science Building Files. Archives. President's Office. Box U5, #070241.
———. Frederick Gaupp Files. Archives. President's Office. Box F10, #070209 (72043963).
———. George C. Hester Files. Archives. President's Office. Box F12, #070211.
———. Global Leadership and Kosovo Files. Archives. President's Office. Box #72043959.
———. Gregory Washington File. Archives. President's Office. Box #070227.
———. Herbert E. and Kate Dishman Files. Archives. President's Office. Box #72044169.
———. Herman Brown File [1946–1959]. Archives. President's Office. Box B1, #070233.
———. Herman Brown File [1959–1962]. Archives. President's Office. Box B1, #070233
———. Howard S. Greenlee Files. Archives. President's Office. Box F11, #0070210.
———. I. J. McCook Files. Archives. President's Office. Box F17, #070216.
———. Integration File. Archives. President's Office. Box U6, #070242.
———. J. C. Godbey Files. Archives. President's Office. Box F11, #070210.
———. J. Frank Dobie Files. Archives. President's Office. Box C19, #070277.
———. J. N. R. Score Files. Archives. President's Office. Box 23, #070222 (7022270222).
———. Jesse H. Jones Files. Archives. President's Office. Box C21, #070279.
———. Jesse H. Jones Scholarships Files. Archives. President's Office. Box U9, #070245.
———. Jessie D. Ames Files. Archives. President's Office. Box C4, #70262 (123946487).
———. Kirk Treible File. Archives. President's Office. Box #070225.
———. Kirk Treible 2 File. Archives. President's Office. Box #72044171.
———. Ludwig Herman Merzbach Files. Archives. President's Office. Box #72043964.
———. Lyndon B. Johnson Files. Archives. President's Office. Box C20, #070278.
———. M. Howard Knox Files. Archives. President's Office. Box F14, #070213.
———. McCombs Files. Archives. President's Office. Box #344537, Box #72044170.
———. Mary Moody Northen Files. Archives. President's Office. Box C22, #070280.
———. Memorandum: My Resignation (W. Graves Blanton). Archives. President's Office. Box #070202.
———. Mr. J. C. Fleming Estate File. Archives. President's Office. Box C19, #070277.
———. Mrs. Alma Thomas Files. Archives. President's Office. Box T5, #070289.
———. Mrs. Carolyn McManis Files. Archives. President's Office. Box C21, #070279.
———. Mrs. Herman Brown 1956–58 File. Archives. President's Office. Box B1, #070233.
———. Mrs. Herman Brown 1959–63 File. Archives. President's Office. Box B1, #070233.
———. Mrs. J. J. Perkins Files. Archives. President's Office. Box C6, #070264.
———. Myron F. Wicke Files. Archives. President's Office. Box F29, #070228.
———. Oscar A. Ullrich Files. Archives. President's Office. Box F27, #070226.
———. Pearl A. Neas Files. Archives. President's Office. Box F18, #070217.
———. Seth Ward Bible Chair. Archives. President's Office. Box C14, #070272.
———. Threshold Campaign File. Archives. President's Office. Box B3, #070235.
———. William B. Jones Files. Archives. President's Office. Box F13, #070212.
———. W-K-M Company Files. Archives. President's Office. Box C4, #70262 (123946487).
———. Wm. C. Finch Files. Archives. President's Office. Box F9, #070208.

Reports during the Fleming Period (Author's Copies)

Seeger, Raymond J. "Science and Mathematics Program of Southwestern University." January 6, 1966. Personal Files.
Southwestern. "Articles of Incorporation and Bylaws with Restated Articles of Incorporation, Southwestern University." Mimeograph. January 29. 1971, with corrections as of February 19, 1971.
———. Report of the President's Committee on Religion and Religious Life. 1970.
———. Report on the Department of Religion and Philosophy. 1977.

Scrapbooks and Collections

Allen, Martha M. Martha M. Allen Collection. SU, SLC, SC.
Baker, Sarah. F. D. Love Collection. 1998. SU, SLC, SC.
Barcus, J. Samuel. J. Samuel Barcus Family Papers. SU, SLC, SC.
Cody, Claude Carr. Cody Collection, Incoming Correspondence. SU, SLC, SC.
———. Cody Collection Scrapbook #3, #4, #5, #6, #7, #8, #9, #11, #12, #13, #14, #15, #16, #17. SU, SLC, SC.
Giddings, Jabez D. Giddings Collection. 1871–1905. SU, SLC, SC.
Granbery, John C., and Mary Catt Granbery. Granbery Letters. 1970. SU, SLC, SC.
McKennon, Margaret Mood. McKennon Scrapbooks #20, #21, #22, #23, #28, #29, #30, #31, #34, #35, #36, #37, #38. SU, SLC, SC.
McMinn, Reba U. "McMinn Letters." Handwritten. Georgetown, Dallas, and New York, September 25, 1913, to February 13, 1917. SU, SLC, SC, McMinn Letters, Small Collections, Box 2, Folder 14.
Mood, F. A. F. A. Mood Scrapbooks. 3 vols. SU, SLC, SC.
Neas, Pearl Alma. Pearl A. Neas Collection, Boxes 1, 5, 7, 9, 10. SU, SLC, SC.
Score, President J. N. R. John Nelson Russell Score, Correspondence 1947–1949. SU, SLC, SC.
Shilling, Roy B., Jr. Shilling Scrapbook 1981–1982. Shilling Personal.
———. Shilling Scrapbook 1982–1992. Shilling Personal.
———. Shilling Scrapbook 1992–1999. Shilling Personal.
Southwestern. "John C. Granbery Letters," in *Special Collections in Methodism: William C. Finch, John C. Granbery, Henry E. Meyer,* ed. N. S. Assadourian, pp. 25–29. Georgetown, 1990. SU, SLC.
———. "Small Collections Finding Aids." SU, SLC, SC.
Ullrich, Oscar. Oscar A. Ullrich Papers. SU, SLC, SC.
Utley, Dan K. "Information on W. C. Vaden House." Typescript. SU, SLC, SC, Small Collections: Non-Southwestern, Box 2, Folder 4.
Various. "Alum Letters about Southwestern." Author's library.
Vivion, King. Miscellaneous Vivion Papers. 1928–1935.

Southern Association of Colleges and Schools

Southern Association of Colleges and Secondary Schools. "A Special Study of Southwestern University, 1934." 1934. SU, SLC, SC.
———. Report of the Visiting Committee. 1961.
———. Report of the Visiting Committee. 1971.
———. Report of the Reaffirmation Committee. 1982. SU, SLC, SC.
SU. Self-Study Report [1971]. 1971. SU, SLC, SC.
———. Self-Study Report [1981]. 1981. SU, SLC, SC.
———. Self-Study Report 1992. 1991.

Publications (General)

Marquis. *Who Was Who in America with World Notables.* 4 vols. Chicago: Marquis–Who's Who, Inc., 1968.
Southwestern. *Southwestern Magazine.* 1898–2000.
———. *The Sou'wester.* 1904–2000.
———. *The Megaphone.* 1907–2000.
———. *Southwestern Bulletin.* Southwestern University. April 1914.
———. *Ex-Students' Newsmagazine.* 1961.
———. *Southwestern Reports.* 1962.
———. *The Bulletin of Southwestern University.* 1978.
———. *Southwestern Quarterly.* 1989–.
———. *Southwestern University Generations.* Spring 2005.
Williamson County Sun Publishers. *Williamson County Sun.* 1918–2000. SU, SLC, Microfilm.

Government Publications

Census, U.S. 1850 United States Federal Census, Fayette County, Texas. 1850.
———. 1860 Federal Census of Red River County Texas. 1978 (copied and indexed mimeograph volume).
———. 1880 United States Federal Census, Williamson County, Texas. 1880.
Census, Bureau of the. Decennial Census Documents from 1850 to 1920.
Red River County. 1838–1881 Tax Rolls for Red River County, Texas. Microfilm Reel 1194-01.

Interviews

Barbour, Mary Ann. "Interviews by WBJ." 2004.
Benold, Douglas M., M.D. "Interview by WBJ." Written response to questions. Sept. 30, 2004.
Finch, William C. "Conversation comment to WBJ." Nov. 9, 2000.
———. "Interviews by Martha Allen." August 1992. SU, SLC, SC.
Fleming, Durwood. "Interviews by Martha Allen." 1993. SU, SLC, SC.
———. "Oral History of George and Herman Brown by Chris Castaneda." SU, SLC, SC. 1990.
Gaddy, Hal, M.D. "Interview by WBJ." Telephone conversation. Sept. 19, 2004.
Lord, Grogan. "Oral History of George and Herman Brown by Chris Castaneda." 1991. SU, SLC, SC.
Medley, David. "Interview by WBJ." Office interview. Sept. 23, 2004.
Score, John Nelson Russell, II. "Interview by Martha Allen." Tapes and typescript. Ca. 1994. SU, SLC, SC.

Theses and Dissertations

Barnet, Elva Marshall. "Paul Whitfield Horn, 1870–1932." Master's thesis. Texas Technological College, 1938.
Etheridge, Truman Harrison. "Education in the Republic of Texas." Doctoral dissertation. University of Texas, 1942.
Jones, Ralph Wood. "A History of Southwestern University, 1873–1949." Doctoral dissertation. University of Texas, 1960.
Kuykendall, Laura. "The Dean of Women and Her Problems as Found on a Small University Campus." Master's thesis. Southwestern University, 1926.
Massengale, Robert Glenn. "Collegiate Education in the Methodist Episcopal Church, South 1902–1939." Doctoral dissertation. Yale University, 1950.
Sudo-Shimamura, Takako. "John C. Granbery: Three Academic Freedom Controversies in the Life of a Social Gospeler in Texas (1920–1938)." Master's thesis. University of Texas at Austin, 1971.
Willbern, Glen DeWitt. "A History of Southwestern University Georgetown Texas." Master's thesis. University of Texas, 1928.

Manuscripts

Benold, Nell Barnes. "Memories of Laura Kuykendall Hall." Handwritten. Georgetown, November 29, 2000.
Cox, Jackson B. "History and Genealogy of Jackson Berry Cox and Wife Julia Barcus." Typescript. September 1, 1937. SU, SLC, SC, Small Collections, Box 2, Folder 4.
Eidson, Harold. "Computing at Southwestern University." Author's personal files.
Gray, Herbert Lee. "The God Within." Typed manuscript. May 1941. SU, SLC, SC.
Jones, L. D., Jr. "Memories of Southwestern University, 1943." Typed manuscript. August 23, 2004.

Jones, William B. "The First Year of the Flemings at Southwestern." November 8, 2002.

Katsurinis, Stephen Avery. "In His Own Words: Dr. Durwood Fleming on His Early Years at Southwestern University 1961–1962." Typed. November 15, 1987.

Lockett, Mellville Beveridge. "Autobiography of M. B. Lockett." Manuscript. 1916. SU, SLC, SC.

McReynolds, John O., et al. "Report to Board of Trustees." Typewritten. Georgetown, May 28, 1908. SU, SLC, SC, found loose in the index to the Minutes of the Board of Curators 1869–1906, Trustees 1906–1912, inside the back cover.

Mooney, Booth. "A University with an Individuality." Typescript. June 20, 1936. SU, SLC, SC, Centennial Celebration, Neas Box 2, Folder: Various Papers and Essays.

Sensabaugh, Oscar Fitzgerald. "Recollections." Handwritten. July 10, 1951.

Southwestern. "A Presentation of the Facilities of Southwestern University, Georgetown, Texas. Available for Use by the Federal Government in the War Emergency, 1942–43." Mimeographed document with hard covers. January 1943. SU, SLC, SC.

Spellmann, Norman W. "The Role of Southwestern University Faculty in the Desegregation of Georgetown's Public Schools: 1962–65." Typescript. January 20, 1997. SU, , SC.

———. "Rutersville College: The Beginnings of Methodist Higher Education in Texas." Paper presented at the 1984 Annual Meeting of the Southwest Region of the American Academy of Religion. March 17, 1984.

Steelman, Edmund H. "Symbolism of the Lois Perkins Chapel." Typescript. Ca. 1981.

Williams, Randall. "Literary & Debating Societies: A Brief History." Manuscript. 2000. SU, SLC, SC.

Woodcock, David G. "Our Buildings Shape Us." Typescript. September 8, 1998. SU, SLC, SC.

Notes

CHAPTER I
Martin Ruter's Vision for Texas

1. Mrs. S. R. Campbell, "Martin Ruter," *Biographical Sketches of Eminent Itinerant Ministers Distinguished, for the Most Part, as Pioneers of Methodism within the Bounds of the Methodist Episcopal Church, South*, Thomas O. Summers (Nashville: Southern Methodist Publishing House, 1859), p. 328.
2. Andrew Forest Muir, *Texas in 1837: An Anonymous, Contemporary Narrative* (Austin: University of Texas Press, 1958), pp. 79–85.
3. Campbell, "Martin Ruter," p. 342.
4. John O. Gross, *Martin Ruter: Pioneer in Methodist Education* ([Nashville]: Board of Education of The Methodist Church, 1956), p. 39.
5. Muir, *Texas in 1837*, pp. 27, 29.
6. Ibid., p. 34.
7. Ibid., pp. 36–37, 193. Morrell was born in Tennessee in 1803 and came to Texas in 1835. He was important in Texas Baptist history for the next thirty-five years.
8. Campbell, "Martin Ruter," pp. 340–341.
9. Archives, Wm. C. Finch Files, p. 19.
10. Gross, *Martin Ruter: Pioneer*, p. 8.
11. Macum Phelan, *A History of Early Methodism in Texas, 1817–1866* (Nashville, Richmond [etc.]: Cokesbury Press, 1924), p. 89. Phelan cites Ernest Ashton Smith, *Martin Ruter* (New York, Cincinnati: The Methodist Book Concern, 1915), p. 35, for this surmise.
12. Finch Files. p. 26.
13. Claude Carr Cody, "Rev. Martin Ruter, A. M., D. D.," *The Methodist Historical Quarterly* 1 (1): 16–17. Cody states that the edition was twenty-four pages, duodecimo.
14. Martin Ruter, *An Easy Entrance into the Sacred Language; Being a Concise Hebrew Grammar, without Points. Compiled for the Use and Encouragement of Learners, and Adapted to Such as Have not the Aid of a Teacher.* (Cincinnati: Published by Martin Ruter, for the Methodist Episcopal Church, Morgan and Lodge, Printers, 1824).
15. Gross, *Martin Ruter: Pioneer*, pp. 23, 26.
16. Ibid., p. 30.
17. Ibid., p. 19.
18. Martin Ruter, *The Juvenile Arithmetick and Scholar's Guide; Wherein Theory and Practice Are Combined and Adapted to the Capacities of Young Beginners; Containing a Due Proportion of Examples in Federal Money; and the Whole Being Illustrated by Numerous Questions Similar to Those of Pestalozzi* (Cincinnati: Published and sold by N. and G. Guilford, W. M. and O. Farnsworth, Jr., Printers, 1828).
19. Cody, "Martin Ruter," pp. 16–17. The bibliographical information furnished by Cody for the latter book is: *The New American Spelling Book, and Juvenile Preceptor; Adapted to Walker's Principles of English Orthography and Pronunciation*, published at Cincinnati in 1831.
20. Martin Ruter, *A Sketch of the Life and Doctrine of the Celebrated John Calvin, Including Some Facts Relative to the Burning of Servetus* (Portland: Printed by A. & J. Shirley, 1814).
21. Cody, "Martin Ruter," pp. 16–17.
22. Anonymous, "Trustees of Dartmouth College v. Woodward," http://www.dartmouth.edu/~govdocs/case/dartmouthcase.htm June 10, 2003.
23. Martin Ruter, *A Concise History of the Christian Church, from Its First Establishment to the Present Time; Containing a General View of Missions, and Exhibiting the State of Religion in Different Parts of the World, Compiled from the Works of Dr. G. Gregory, with Numerous Additions and Improvements* (New York: B. Waugh and T. Mason, for the Methodist Episcopal Church, J. Collord, Printer, 1834).
24. G. Gregory, D.D., *An History of the Christian Church, from the Earliest Periods to the Present Time*, 2 vols. (London: Printed for C. and G. Kearsley, Fleet Street, 1795).
25. Cody, "Martin Ruter," pp. 16–17.
26. See Olin W. Nail, *Texas Methodist Centennial Yearbook* (Elgin, Tex.: 1934), p. 36, for a copy of the letter dated August 17, 1835, sent by Travis to the *New York Christian Advocate and Journal.* Travis's "little son" was at the time attending a small school taught by Lydia McHenry in the home of David Ayres. This information comes from Mrs. A. J. Lee, "Some Recollections of Two Texas Pioneer Women," *The Methodist Historical Quarterly* 1, no. 2 (1909): 207–213. An announcement in the November 14, 1835, edition of the *Telegraph and Texas Register* says that "Miss McHenry respectfully announces to the public her intention of opening a Boarding-school for young ladies and misses, on the first of February next [1836], at Montville. The scholars will be boarded in the family of David Ayres, where the best of care will be taken of their health and morals." Those in San Felipe wishing more information were referred to "W. B. Travis." See Truman Harrison Etheridge, "Education in the Republic of Texas" (doctoral dissertation, University of Texas), 1942, p. 46.
27. Gross, *Ruter: Pioneer*, p. 35.
28. Letter of Alexander to Fowler, November 23, 1837, in Vol. 1 of Littleton M. Fowler, "Letters of Rev. Littleton M. Fowler, Methodist Missionary," Austin, June 24, 1953.
29. Homer S. Thrall, *A Brief History of Methodism in Texas* (Nashville: Publishing House of the M. E. Church, South, 1894), p. 51.
30. Gross, *Martin Ruter: Pioneer*, p. 39.
31. Campbell, "Martin Ruter," pp. 340–341.
32. Cody, "Martin Ruter," p. 20. The statement by David Ayres ("Early Methodism in Texas," *The Texas Christian Advocate*, August 13, 1857) that "he preached, by invitation, before both Houses of Congress, then in session there" is unlikely. Campbell and Cody are more likely right.
33. Henry Matthews, "The Henry Matthews Diaries," ca. 1840, 5 MS vols.
34. David Ayres, "Early Methodism in Texas," *The Texas Christian Advocate*, August 13, 1857, p. 1. Early in its history, the name of the town was spelled both "Rutersville" and, as in this piece, "Ruterville."
35. Campbell, "Martin Ruter," p. 358.
36. Ibid., pp. 357–358.
37. Walter N. Vernon, Robert W. Sledge, Robert C. Monk, and Norman W. Spellmann, *The Methodist Excitement in Texas* (Dallas: The Texas United Methodist Historical Society, 1984), p. 33.

38. Cody, "Martin Ruter," p. 23.
39. Campbell, "Martin Ruter," pp. 343–344.
40. Ibid., p. 348.
41. Ibid., pp. 342–343.
42. Campbell, "Martin Ruter," pp. 346–347.
43. Thrall, *History of Methodism in Texas*, p. 52.
44. Campbell, "Martin Ruter," pp. 346–347.
45. Ibid., 353–354.
46. Ibid., p. 352.
47. Letter of Fowler to Mrs. M. M. Porter, May 22, 1838, and letter of Alexander to Fowler, May 23, 1838, both in Vol. 1 of "Fowler Letters."
48. Letter of Alexander to Fowler, May 23, 1838, "Fowler Letters," Vol. 1.
49. Cody ("Martin Ruter," pp. 33–37) states that Ruter's remains were disinterred twice, finally being removed to Navasota a few miles from Washington, where they now rest with an appropriate monument of Vermont marble commemorating his life. He cites an article in the *Texas Advocate* of November 14, 1901, which gives a full description of all the nineteenth-century activities related to these matters.
50. Laura Fowler Woolworth, *Littleton Fowler, 1803–1846: A Missionary to the Republic of Texas, 1837–1846* ([Shreveport]: Printed privately, 1936), pp. 26–27.
51. Letter of Ruter to Fowler, April 17, 1838, in Vol. 1 of "Fowler Letters."

CHAPTER II
Pursuing the Vision: Rutersville College

1. Frederick Eby lists Washington College as having been granted a charter in 1837, Manhattan College in 1838, and DeKalb College in 1839. According to him none of these ever developed. Thus, says Eby, Rutersville College "has the honor of being the first college to materialize in Texas." Frederick Eby, *The Development of Education in Texas* (New York: The Macmillan Company, 1925), p. 94.
2. Ralph Wood Jones, *Southwestern University 1840–1961* (Austin: Jenkins Publishing Co., 1973), pp. 38–39, 335. A copy of the Articles of Agreement and Constitution of the Rutersville Company is located in the MSS Files in the Archives of the Texas History Center, University of Texas, Austin, Texas.
3. Judson S. Custer, *Reverend Robert Alexander (1811–1882) and Eliza Perkins Ayers Alexander (1821–1878)* (Georgetown: MHHS, 1994). Also see Alexander's letter of August 24, 1838, in Littleton M. Fowler, "Letters of Rev. Littleton M. Fowler, Methodist Missionary," Austin, June 24, 1953.
4. Jonnie Lockhart Wallis, *The Life and Letters of Dr. John Washington Lockhart, 1824–1900* (New York: Arno Press, 1930), as cited by Custer, *Robert and Eliza Alexander*.
5. Custer, *Robert and Eliza Alexander*. Custer's information is taken from J. K. Holland, "Reminiscences of Austin and Old Washington," *Texas State Historical Association Quarterly* 1 (October 1897): 94–95.
6. Claude Carr Cody, *The Life and Labors of Francis Asbury Mood, D.D.* (Chicago: F. H. Revell, 1886), p. 297.
7. Julia Lee Sinks, "Rutersville College," *The Quarterly of the Texas State Historical Association* 2, no. 2 (1898): 124. Mrs. Sinks says that her information about the beginning of Rutersville College came from a document written by John Rabb, one of the original Proprietors, given to her by Mrs. Martha Richardson, wife of the first President.
8. Mrs. A. J. Lee, "Some Recollections of Two Texas Pioneer Women," *The Methodist Historical Quarterly* 1, no. 2 (1909): 207–213. Mrs. A. J. Lee, the author, was the daughter of the Rev. J. W. Kenney and the niece of Lydia A. McHenry.
9. Mrs. A. J. Lee, "Rev. J. W. Kenney," *The Methodist Historical Quarterly* 1, no. 1 (1909): 47–51.
10. Norman W. Spellmann, "Rutersville College: The Beginnings of Methodist Higher Education in Texas," unpublished manuscript, March 17, 1984, p. 4.
11. Fowler, "Fowler Letters," Letter of Alexander to Fowler, August 28, 1838. Also, Sinks, "Rutersville College," p. 124.
12. Fowler, "Fowler Letters," Letter of Alexander to Fowler, August 28, 1838.
13. Spellmann, "Rutersville Beginnings," p. 4. Spellmann's information is from Alexander's letter of April 10, 1839, and Fowler's letter of April 26, 1839, found in the *Western Christian Advocate* of July 19, 1839.
14. Sharon Duncan, *Ann Catherine (Goodwin) Haynie* (Georgetown: MHHS, 1984).
15. Spellmann, "Rutersville Beginnings," p. 4, with information from Fowler's letters as above.
16. John H. McLean, "Chauncey Richardson," *The Methodist Historical Quarterly* 2, no. 2 (1910): 149–150. In some sources the college is simply called Tuscumbia College.
17. Ibid., pp. 155–156.
18. Priscilla Myers Benham, "Moore, Francis, Jr.," HBTO, July 23, 2002.
19. The charter is reproduced in Frederick Eby, *Education in Texas: Source Materials* (Austin: University of Texas, 1918), pp. 189–193.
20. Henry Matthews, "The Henry Matthews Diaries," ca. 1840, Vol. V (MS).
21. Rutersville Board of Trustees, "Report of the Board of Trustees," *Christian Advocate and Journal*, February 14, 1844, as quoted by R. Jones, *SU 1840–1961*, p. 43.
22. Sinks, "Rutersville College," p. 127.
23. Rutersville, *The First Annual Catalogue of Rutersville College, 1840*, n.d. [1841]. Catalogs were published at the end of each year and carried the names of the students and teachers who participated. The academic year was divided into two "terms." The academic year began in late July and continued until Commencement on the Thursday preceding the 28th of June of the succeeding year. There was a week's vacation during the last week of January and a summer break of nine weeks from Commencement until late July, when the next academic year began. Because the first classes began on February 1, it is unclear just exactly what terms were covered by the catalogs for "1840" and "1841," the calendar year or the academic year terms.
24. Truman Harrison Etheridge, "Education in the Republic of Texas" (doctoral dissertation, University of Texas, 1942), pp. 253–254.
25. Ibid., p. 255. The incident is taken from Dudley G. Wooten, *Comprehensive History of Texas, 1685–1897*, 2 vols. (Dallas: W. G. Scarff, 1897), 1:656.
26. Rutersville, *Second Annual Catalogue of Rutersville College, 1841* (Austin: S. Whiting, Public Printer, 1842).
27. Natalie Ornish, *Pioneer Jewish Texans: Their Impact on Texas and American History for Four Hundred Years, 1590–1990* (Dallas: Texas Heritage Press, c. 1989), p. 43. Though she is wrong in saying that his "gift is likely, the first major endowment by an individual to a Texas University," it is nevertheless another ecumenical building block in the turbulent life of that hero of the Texas Revolution and testimony to the fact that additional gifts continued to accrue to the College after the initial listing.
28. Summers is quoted by Spellmann, "Rutersville Beginnings," p. 6.
29. Spellmann, "Rutersville Beginnings," p. 7. Spellmann's information is from a letter by Summers of November 17, 1840, in the *Western Christian Advocate*, January 8, 1841, p. 50.
30. Spellmann, "Rutersville Beginnings," p. 8. Spellmann's information is from a letter by Summers of October 29, 1841, in the *Texas Methodist Historical Quarterly* 1, no. 3 (January 1910): 244–245.
31. William C. Finch, "Annual Report [of President and Officers]," 1953–1961, November 12, 1953, President's Report, p. 1-9. Finch says: "Since this report was written, we have had official confirmation that the old college bell of Ruterville [sic] College has been given to Southwestern University by the Airline Baptist Church of Houston, Texas, whose minister had spent one year at Southwestern. It is a very happy circumstance that the Ruterville College bell will be brought to the campus and provision made for placing properly as a memorial somewhere on the campus."

32. Etheridge, "Education in the Republic of Texas," p. 253.
33. CCSB #6. From two articles by C. C. Cody of January 20 and 27, 1921, entitled "Rutersville College," printed in an unnamed newspaper.
34. CWL, Letter of May 5, 1845.
35. CCSB #6.
36. CWL, Letter of July 30, 1845.
37. CWL, Letter of July 1, 1846.
38. Eby (Eby, *Source Materials*, pp. 198–199) prints an extract of it from the *National Register*, Washington, Texas, June 26, 1845.
39. Matthews, "The Henry Matthews Diaries," Vol. 5 (MS.).
40. Duncan, *Ann Catherine (Goodwin) Haynie*.
41. Judson S. Custer, *Charles Wright (1811–1885)* (Georgetown: MHHS, 1985). Most of Professor Custer's information came from fifteen letters penned by Wright to his sister and brother during his two years at Rutersville. The originals are in the Connecticut State Library, with copies at Southwestern. See the Bibliography entry for the CWL.
42. CWL, Letter of July 30, 1845.
43. Eby, *Source Materials*, p. 196.
44. CWL, Letters of November 21 and December 8, 1846, and May 17, 1847.
45. Custer, *Charles Wright*.
46. Llerena Friend, ed., "Thomas Bell Letters," *The Southwestern Historical Quarterly* 63 (1959–1960): 300.
47. Ibid., p. 307.
48. Ibid., p. 308.
49. Ibid., 457–458.
50. Ibid., p. 463.
51. Ibid., 462–464.
52. Ibid., pp. 466–468.
53. Thomas W. Bell, *A Narrative of the Capture and Subsequent Sufferings of the Mier Prisoners in Mexico, Captured in the Cause of Texas, Dec. 26th, 1842 and Liberated Sept. 16th, 1844* (Waco: Texian Press, 1964), pp. iv–v.
54. Ibid., pp. v–vi.
55. Sinks, "Rutersville College," pp. 125–126. All other sources also record him as one of the victims.
56. Joseph E. Blanton, "Hill, John Christopher Columbus," HBTO, July 23, 2002.
57. Annie Doom Pickrell, *Pioneer Women in Texas* (Austin: The E. L. Steck Company, 1929), pp. 32–37. The author mistakenly has her attending McKenzie College rather than Rutersville College.
58. Rebecca Jane Gilleland Fisher, "Response by Mrs. Rebecca J. Fisher," *Proceedings of Texas Veteran Association*, 1905, p. 12.
59. Anonymous, "Fisher, Rebecca Jane Gilleland," HBTO, July 23, 2002. Also, MKSB #20, p. 8. "Mrs. Rebecca Fisher's Address at University," *Georgetown Commercial*, May 17, 1912.
60. Eby, *Source Materials*, pp. 196–198.
61. Spellmann, "Rutersville Beginnings," p. 14.
62. Macum Phelan, *A History of Early Methodism in Texas, 1817–1866* (Nashville, Richmond [etc.]: Cokesbury Press, 1924), pp. 300–301.
63. Eby, *Development of Texas Education*, p. 141.
64. Jones, *SU 1840–1961*, pp. 46–47. His information comes from the *Christian Advocate and Journal*, March 19, 1845, typed copy of the report to the Texas Conference, San Augustine, Texas, January 8, 1845, located in the Cody Collection of the Southwestern University Library.
65. Jones, *SU 1840–1961*, p. 48. His information comes from Fowler, "Fowler Letters," Vol. 5.
66. The quotation appears in Ralph Wood Jones, "A History of Southwestern University, 1873–1949" (doctoral dissertation, University of Texas, 1960), pp. 50–51, fn. 60.
67. Homer S. Thrall, *A Brief History of Methodism in Texas* (Nashville: Publishing House of the M. E. Church, South, 1894), p. 266. Thrall taught at Rutersville College on two occasions during his early ministry in connection with his pastorates in that area.
68. CWL, Letter of November 21, 1846.
69. Phelan, *Early Methodism in Texas*, p. 301.
70. Sinks, "Rutersville College," p. 130.
71. Jones, *SU 1840–1961*, pp. 59–60. His information comes from Mood's "History of Southwestern University," p. 2, typed copy located in the TU Files, Archives, Texas History Center, University of Texas, Austin, Texas.
72. Phelan, *Early Methodism in Texas*, pp. 331–332.
73. U.S. Census, 1850 United States Federal Census, Fayette County, Texas. For some reason, Mrs. Richardson is listed as "Margaret." She was born in Massachusetts and is without doubt Chauncey's wife, known everywhere else as Martha.
74. Jones, *SU 1840–1961*, pp. 57–58. His information comes from an untitled letter of November 22, 1851, located in the Cody Collection of the Southwestern University Library.
75. Jones, *SU 1840–1961*, p. 49.
76. McLean, "Chauncey Richardson," pp. 150–152.
77. Phelan, *Early Methodism in Texas*, pp. 331–332.
78. Ibid., p. 336.
79. Jones, "History of SU" (dissertation), p. 57, fn. 69. His information comes from the June 2, 1853, Minutes of the Board of Trustees of Rutersville College, 1853–1867, located in the MSS Files, Archives, Texas History Center, University of Texas, Austin, Texas.
80. Jones, *SU 1840–1961*, pp. 51–52.
81. Jones, "History of SU" (dissertation), p. 58. Taken from Rutersville College Correspondence, 1835–1885, MSS Files, Archives of the Texas History Center, University of Texas, Austin, Texas.
82. Jones, "History of SU" (dissertation), pp. 58–60. Taken from Arthur August Grusendorf, "The Social and Philosophical Determinants of Education in Washington County, Texas, from 1835 to 1937" (Ph.D. thesis, University of Texas, Austin, Texas, June 1938), pp. 139, 141.
83. Jones, "History of SU" (dissertation), pp. 60–61. Taken from Rutersville Board Minutes of May 24, 1856.
84. Sinks, "Rutersville College," pp. 130–131.
85. Jones, "History of SU" (dissertation), p. 62. Taken from Rutersville Board Minutes, June 30, 1856.
86. Jones, "History of SU" (dissertation), p. 63. Taken from William F. Ledlow, "History of Protestant Education, A Study of the Origin, Growth, and Development of Educational Endeavors in Texas," (unpublished Ph.D. dissertation, University of Texas, 1926), pp. 141–142.
87. Jones, "History of SU" (dissertation), pp. 64–65. Taken from the Proceedings Relative to Monument and Military Institute, pp. 1–2, located in the MSS Files, Archives of the Texas History Center, University of Texas, Austin, Texas.
88. Jones, "History of SU" (dissertation), p. 73. Taken from Rutersville Board Minutes, April 29, 1861.

CHAPTER III
Competition in the Piney Woods: Wesleyan College

1. Frederick Law Olmsted, *A Journey Through Texas; or, A Saddle-trip on the Southwestern Frontier: with a statistical appendix* (New York: Dix, Edwards & Co., 1857), pp. 43, 55.
2. George L. Crocket, *Two Centuries in East Texas: A History of San Augustine County and Surrounding Territory* (Dallas: The Southwest Press, 1932), p. 307.
3. Walter N. Vernon, Robert W. Sledge, Robert C. Monk, and Norman W. Spellmann, *The Methodist Excitement in Texas* (Dallas: The Texas United Methodist Historical Society, 1984), p. 45. Their information is taken from Dora Fowler Arthur, "Jottings . . . of Littleton Fowler," *Texas Historical Association Quarterly* 2 (July 1898–April 1899): 78.
4. Homer S. Thrall, *A Brief History of Methodism in Texas* (Nashville: Publishing House of the M. E. Church, South, 1894), pp. 76–77.
5. Crocket, *Two Centuries in East Texas*, p. 109.
6. Francis Wilson, *Memoirs of a Methodist Circuit Rider—Francis Wilson, As Edited by William E. Smith* (Austin: William E. Smith, 1983), p.

102. Much of the material in this chapter on Francis Wilson comes from his *Memoirs*, as edited by Smith, and from Crocket's *Two Centuries in Eastern Texas.* Smith says that Wilson left about a thousand pages of handwritten notes that were difficult to read and decipher. Smith edited the grammar of the selections in the book for consistency. Crocket used the manuscripts of Wilson's "Autobiography" and "Memoirs."

7. Crocket, *Two Centuries in East Texas*, p. 301.
8. Truman Harrison Etheridge reports ("Education in the Republic of Texas" [Austin, University of Texas, 1942], p. 244) that since the purchase of the building by the Trustees, the Reverend J. M. Rankin, a Presbyterian preacher, had rented the building and taught there for two years, from 1840 to 1842.
9. Crocket, *Two Centuries in East Texas*, p. 302. Crocket, who supplies many of the details of this chapter, consulted many local records, which he carefully identifies, for his information. Particularly useful to him were issues of *The Red Lander*, the San Augustine county newspaper.
10. Crocket, *Two Centuries in East Texas*, p. 303.
11. Truman Harrison Etheridge, "Education in the Republic of Texas" (doctoral dissertation, University of Texas, 1942), p. 245.
12. Ralph Wood Jones, *Southwestern University 1840–1961* (Austin: Jenkins Publishing Co., 1973), p. 62. R. Jones includes accounts of the debate from two different sources.
13. Macum Phelan, *A History of Early Methodism in Texas, 1817–1866* (Nashville, Richmond [etc.]: Cokesbury Press, 1924), pp. 217–218. The HBTO says that the *Soda Lake Herald* was issued weekly in Marshall between November 1845 and sometime in 1846.
14. Etheridge, "Education in the Republic of Texas," p. 425.
15. Phelan, *Early Methodism in Texas*, pp. 217–218.
16. Etheridge, "Education in the Republic of Texas," pp. 259–264.
17. Wilson, *Memoirs*, pp. 170–172.
18. Texas-Gammel, "An Act to Establish and Incorporate the Wesleyan Male and Female College of San Augustine (1844)," *The Laws of Texas: 1822–1897*, Gammell (Austin: The Gammell Book Company, 1898), 2:931–934.
19. Different sources give March 1, 1844, March 2, 1844, and the first Monday in March 1844 as dates for the opening of the first session. I have chosen the date published in the newspaper announcement, which is also the date given by Wilson in his *Memoirs.*
20. Phelan, *Early Methodism in Texas*, pp. 232–234. Poe's brother came to Texas in December 1844 and took the three children back to Ohio with him.
21. Crocket, *Two Centuries in East Texas*, p. 307.
22. John H. McLean, "Our Early Schools," *The Methodist Historical Quarterly* 2, no. 1 (1910): 64.
23. Wilson, *Memoirs*, pp. 64–65.
24. Crocket, *Two Centuries in East Texas*, p. 279.
25. Thrall, *History of Methodism in Texas*, pp. 86–87.
26. Wilson, *Memoirs*, pp. 121–124.
27. Ibid., pp. 134–136.
28. Crocket, *Two Centuries in East Texas*, p. 307.
29. Francis Wilson, "[Wesleyan College Report]," *Western Christian Advocate*, May 9, 1845, p. 15.
30. Wilson, *Memoirs*, p. 119.
31. Frederick Eby, *Education in Texas: Source Materials* (Austin: University of Texas, 1918), pp. 388–390.
32. Frederick Eby, *The Development of Education in Texas* (New York: The Macmillan Company, 1925), p. 97.
33. Crocket, *Two Centuries in East Texas*, pp. 305–306.
34. Jones, *SU 1840–1961*, pp. 66–67. Kendal's name is spelled variously as "Kendal" and "Kendall" in different sources. I have chosen the former spelling. The newspaper is variously given as *Red Lander*, *Red-Lander*, and *Redlander*. I have chosen the first option.
35. Etheridge, "Education in the Republic of Texas," p. 261. In his "notes," held in the Archives of the Texas State Library and consulted by Etheridge, Crocket is much more explicit about his belief in Russell's poor character. He says, "he was not a minister" but "a fighting man" and had already been in two shooting scrapes. He says Russell designated Miss Kendal as "a woman of loose virtue" and that after the homicide her brother fled to Mexico, where he lived for the rest of his life. Etheridge provides evidence that in his mind rebuts Crocket's notion that Russell was not a minister. For his part, he says that the allegation that Kendal fled and lived in Mexico for the rest of his life is "scarcely plausible. There has never been a time in Texas," he says, "that one had to run away for defending the name and reputation of his women folks" (p. 265). My judgment about these facts is reflected in the main text.
36. Crocket, *Two Centuries in East Texas*, p. 305.
37. Ibid., p. 308.
38. Thomas W. Cutrer, "Sexton, Franklin Barlow," HBTO, July 23, 2002.
39. Wilson, *Memoirs*, pp. 153–154.
40. Vernon, Sledge, Monk, and Spellmann, *Methodist Excitement in Texas*, p. 100. The authors of this book take their quotation from Macum Phelan, *A History of the Expansion of Methodism in Texas: 1867–1902* (Dallas: Mathis, Van Nort & Co., 1937), p. 44.
41. Crocket, *Two Centuries in East Texas*, p. 309.
42. Eby, *Source Materials*, pp. 369–370. Eby quotes Rankin, *Texas in 1850*, pp. 101–104.
43. Crocket, *Two Centuries in East Texas*, pp. 310–313.
44. Olmsted, *A Journey Through Texas*, pp. 69–70.
45. Dora Fowler Arthur, "The Reverend Littleton Fowler: Missionary to the Republic of Texas," *The Methodist Historical Quarterly* 1, no. 2 (1909): 122.

CHAPTER IV
Education and Plantation Economics: McKenzie College

1. Frederick Eby, *The Development of Education in Texas* (New York: The Macmillan Company, 1925), p. 132. Though John McLean first made the statement about the importance of McKenzie College, I have quoted Eby, who accepts McLean's judgment, because of his stature in the field of education.
2. Macum Phelan, *A History of Early Methodism in Texas, 1817–1866* (Nashville, Richmond [etc.]: Cokesbury Press, 1924), p. 187.
3. Ibid. Phelan says that he took his facts about McKenzie's education from a Memoir contained in the *Journal of the North Texas Conference, 1881.*
4. Ralph Wood Jones, *Southwestern University 1840–1961* (Austin: Jenkins Publishing Co., 1973), p. 70.
5. John D. Osburn, "McKenzie College," *The Southwestern Historical Quarterly* 63, no. 4 (1960): 533.
6. Ibid.
7. John H. McLean, "Rev. John W. P. McKenzie, D. D.," *The Methodist Historical Quarterly* 1, no. 1 (1909): 62.
8. Ibid., pp. 61–63.
9. Phelan, *Early Methodism in Texas*, p. 188. McLean says forty-two appointments ("Rev. John W. P. McKenzie, D.D., p. 63"). Inasmuch as Phelan cites McKenzie himself from the Introduction he wrote for *North Texas Pulpit*, a book of sermons published by J. W. Hill in 1880, his figure of thirty-two is to be preferred.
10. McLean, "John W. P. McKenzie," p. 63.
11. Osburn, "McKenzie College," p. 534.
12. Ibid., p. 535.
13. Phelan, *Early Methodism in Texas*, pp. 19–21, 173–178, 181–185, 189–193. He says he got it directly from Davis's daughter, Mrs. A. Laswell of Waxahachie, Texas. The autobiography was later published as R. L. Jones, "Folk Life in Early Texas: The Autobiography of Andrew Davis," *Southwestern Historical Quarterly* 43 (1939–1940). I have used Phelan's transcription.
14. U.S. Census, 1860 Federal Census of Red River County Texas, pp. 4–5. At the time of this incident, Abner was about thirty-seven and

John about thirty-four years old. In the 1860 census Abner is listed as "collecting clerk," which probably means financial manager.

15. Census, 1860 Census of Red River County, pp. 4–5. In the summer of 1860, the census taker lists twenty-three free white persons living at McKenzie College. He lists them in one category, not as inhabiting separate living units, just as he lists persons elsewhere living in boardinghouses. Some of them certainly lived in the big women's building where the McKenzie family lived. All of them lived close enough around to be considered part of the McKenzie unit. There were three nuclear families: McKenzie, his wife, and four children; a farmer and his wife, who doubled as a teacher, with their two children; and a housekeeper, probably for the entire institution, and her daughter, who was also a student. Abner McKenzie, the minister/publisher of the school newspaper, the overseer, and three teachers are listed as singles. There were also five other students, four boys and one girl, Martha McKenzie, age sixteen, listed under Abner's name and perhaps his daughter. Abner, at fifty-seven, was the oldest of the twenty-three residents, while the farmer and his wife had a baby of nine months.
16. The data furnished by Frederick Eby, *Education in Texas: Source Materials* (Austin: University of Texas, 1918), p. 141, as to the precise number of degrees awarded each year between 1844 and 1861, differ slightly in some instances from the numbers carried later in Southwestern University catalogs for those same years. Both, however, agree that the total number awarded during that time period was sixty-seven. The degree awarded to Davis in 1844 was given as an honor to an especially precocious student before the regular collegiate program had been instituted.
17. Osburn, "McKenzie College," p. 536. Osborn quotes the June 2, 1849, edition of the paper.
18. Ibid., pp. 536–537.
19. McLean, "John W. P. McKenzie," p. 66.
20. B. E. Masters, "McKenzie College," HBTO, July 23, 2002.
21. Osburn, "McKenzie College," pp. 548–549.
22. Ibid., pp. 544–545.
23. John H. McLean, *Reminiscences* (Nashville: Publishing House M. E. Church, South, 1918), p. 48.
24. Texas-Gammel, "An Act to Incorporate the McKenzie Institute in Red River County [1854]," *Laws of Texas: 1822–1897*, Gammel (Austin: The Gammel Book Company, 1898), 4:107–108. Ralph Jones and B. E. Masters list the first charter date as 1848. They were probably following early Southwestern University catalogs that carried the 1848 date erroneously.
25. Catalog, *Annual Catalogue of the Students and Faculty of McKenzie College for 1860–61* (Nashville: Southern Methodist Publishing House, 1861), pp. 14–15.
26. Masters, "McKenzie College."
27. Ralph Wood Jones, "A History of Southwestern University, 1873–1949" (doctoral dissertation, University of Texas, 1960), pp. 94–95. Jones incorporates the text of the deed, taken from B. E. Masters, "A History of Early Education in Northeast Texas," (Master's thesis, University of Texas, 1929), pp. 52–54. Masters took it from the Clarksville Red River County Clerk Record, Book M, 455, dated March 16, 1860.
28. Osburn, "McKenzie College," pp. 537–538. A copy of the charter can be found in Texas-Gammel, "An Act to Incorporate the McKenzie Male and Female College (1860)," *The Laws of Texas: 1822–1897*, Gammel (Austin: The Gammel Book Company, 1898), 4:111–113.
29. Jones, *SU 1840–1961*, p. 75.
30. Osburn, "McKenzie College," p. 538.
31. McKenzie, *Annual Catalogue of the Students and Faculty of McKenzie College for 1860–61* (Nashville: Southern Methodist Publishing House, 1861).
32. Osburn, "McKenzie College," pp. 539–540.
33. Ibid., pp. 542–543.
34. Mellville Beveridge Lockett, "Autobiography of M. B. Lockett," 1916, p. 44.
35. McLean, *Reminiscences*, p. 46.
36. Jones, *SU 1840–1961*, p. 83.
37. Osburn, "McKenzie College," p. 550.
38. McLean, *Reminiscences*, p. 45.
39. Osburn, "McKenzie College," p. 542.
40. McKenzie, *McKenzie Catalogue 1860–61*, p. 13.
41. Ibid., p. 19.
42. McLean, *Reminiscences*, p. 49.
43. Osburn, "McKenzie College," pp. 551–552.
44. McLean, *Reminiscences*, pp. 64–65.
45. Ibid., p. 39.
46. Jones, *SU 1840–1961*, pp. 77, 80.
47. McLean, *Reminiscences*, pp. 61, 65.
48. Jones, *SU 1840–1961*, p. 80.
49. McLean, *Reminiscences*, p. 45.
50. Lockett, "Lockett Autobiography," pp. 40–43.
51. McLean, "John W. P. McKenzie," pp. 64–67.
52. Osburn, "McKenzie College," p. 546.
53. McLean, "John W. P. McKenzie," pp. 63–64.
54. Osburn, "McKenzie College," p. 544.
55. McLean, *Reminiscences*, p. 48.
56. Osburn, "McKenzie College," p. 544.
57. McLean, *Reminiscences*, pp. 81, 93.
58. Jones, *SU 1840–1961*, p. 76. R. Jones quotes B. W. Martin, "Some Educational Institutions of East Texas" (Master's thesis, University of Texas, Austin, Texas, June 1924), pp. 16–17, whose information came from McKenzie's daughter, Mrs. Smith Ragsdale. Southwestern acquired the grinding stone from the McKenzie Plantation gristmill sometime prior to 1941 from a donor through the instrumentality of Dean Ruth Ferguson. It was mounted on a pedestal on the lawn between the Cody Memorial Library and University Avenue in mid-1941. The concrete bench next to it is supported on stones taken from Rutersville College, Wesleyan College, Soule University, and the Woman's Annex at Southwestern. See "The Centennial Celebration" in Chapter XV.
59. Red River County, 1838–1881 Tax Rolls for Red River County, Texas, Microfilm Reel 1194-01.
60. Phelan, *Early Methodism in Texas*, pp. 463–464. The visitor was the Rev. John W. Fields, secretary of the Board of Trustees.
61. Osburn, "McKenzie College," p. 541.
62. Ibid., p. 539.
63. Ibid., pp. 544–545.
64. Lockett, "Lockett Autobiography," p. 46.
65. McLean, *Reminiscences*, pp. 53–79.
66. Marcus J. Wright, *Texas in the War 1861–1865* (Hillsboro, Tex.: The Hill Junior College Press, 1965), pp. 97–98.
67. William Clark Griggs, "McMullan, Francis," HBTO, July 23, 2002.
68. SU Curators 1870–79, Minutes of Apr. 20, 1870 and Apr. 6, 1871.
69. Macum Phelan, *A History of the Expansion of Methodism in Texas: 1867–1902* (Dallas: Mathis, Van Nort & Co., 1937), p. 167. Phelan takes his material from a pamphlet entitled "History of Marvin College," by Berry B. Cobb, a member of the Dallas Bar. Debt problems persisted and the mortgage on the building was foreclosed in 1879. Thereafter the school had no official church connection. It continued operation until the close of the 1883–1884 session, "piling up debt" in the meantime, when it was taken over by the City of Waxahachie and made a part of the public school system.
70. Jones, *SU 1840–1961*, p. 84. R. Jones says that the six McKenzie graduates "constituted a third of the Board of Curators who met on that day." They actually constituted a fifth of the total of thirty Curators.
71. SU Curators 1870–79, Minutes of July 10, 1877.
72. McLean, "John W. P. McKenzie," p. 66.
73. McLean, *Reminiscences*, p. 52.
74. Osburn, "McKenzie College," p. 553.

75. Jones, *SU 1840–1961*, p. 84.
76. P. M. Batchelder, "McDonald, William Johnson," HBTO,. July 23, 2002.
77. Osburn, "McKenzie College," pp. 533–534.

CHAPTER V
Occasion for Dismay: Soule University

1. Francis Asbury Mood, *For God and Texas: Autobiography of Francis Asbury Mood, 1830–1884* (Dallas: Listo Publications, 2001), p. 154.
2. Claude Carr Cody, "Soule University," *The Methodist Historical Quarterly* 2, no. 3 (1911): 227.
3. Mood, *For God and Texas*, pp. 12–13.
4. Ibid., pp. 33–34.
5. Ibid., pp. 41–42.
6. Francis Asbury Mood, *Methodism in Charleston: a narrative of the chief events relating to the rise and progress of the Methodist Episcopal church in Charleston, S.C., with brief notices of the early ministers who labored in that city* (Nashville: E. Stevenson and J. E. Evans, for the Methodist Episcopal Church, South, 1856). The book is composed of thirty-seven articles published by Mood in the *Southern Christian Advocate*. They can be found in MSB, Vol. 1, pp. 5–25, 96.
7. Mood, *For God and Texas*, p. 90.
8. Ibid. Her information is taken from Thomas McAlpin Stubbs, *Family Album: An Account of the Moods of Charleston, South Carolina, and Connected Families* (Atlanta: Curtiss Printing Company, Inc., 1943), pp. 65, 66, 68.
9. Mood, *For God and Texas*, p. 92.
10. Ibid., pp. 175–176.
11. Ibid., p. 123.
12. Ibid., pp. 119–122.
13. Ibid., pp. 134–135.
14. Ibid., pp. 140–141.
15. Ibid., p. 141, fn. 17. This incident, reported by Mrs. Earney in the footnote, is also recorded in Cody's biography of Mood.
16. Mood, *For God and Texas*, pp. 142–143.
17. MSB. Mood includes copies of the *Weekly Record* in his scrapbooks beginning December 16, 1865. These are found in Vol. 2, pp. 16–41.
18. Cody, "Soule University," p. 229.
19. Mood, *For God and Texas*, pp. 144–145.
20. Ibid., pp. 145–146.
21. Carole E. Christian, "Chappell Hill Female College," HBTO, July 23, 2002.
22. Ralph Wood Jones, *Southwestern University 1840–1961* (Austin: Jenkins Publishing Co., 1973), p. 86.
23. Cody, "Soule University," p. 221.
24. Jones, *SU 1840–1961*, p. 52.
25. Ibid.
26. Ibid., pp. 86–87.
27. Macum Phelan, *A History of Early Methodism in Texas, 1817–1866* (Nashville, Richmond [etc.]: Cokesbury Press, 1924), p. 366.
28. Jones, *SU 1840–1961*, pp. 87–90. Using the same facts, Ralph Jones and I come to very different conclusions about the motives involved in the selection process. He states that "the members of the Texas Conference, at this time all ministers, came upon a new method, at least for them, of extracting money from Methodist brethren for the purpose of endowing educational institutions. The plan was simply to announce the organization of a new school and grant the location to the community offering the highest bid" (p. 89). I find his conclusion unwarranted. My reading of letters and documents from the time reveals Methodist laymen who were careful in their financial dealings and not persons who were manipulated by a cabal of ministers. Though the Annual Conference was indeed made up only of ministers, laymen were fully cognizant of what was happening and held the purse strings. Ministers recognized this fact, as revealed by their correspondence with some of their more affluent "brethren," witness the Jabez Giddings correspondence in the Southwestern University library relating to both Soule and Southwestern. Manipulation of these brethren by their ministers would have put at risk any endeavor where it might have been tried. I look upon the process of requiring competitive bids as being the proper exercise of fiduciary responsibility. WBJ.
29. Horace M. Du Bose, *Life of Joshua Soule* (Nashville, Dallas: Publishing House of the M. E. Church, South, 1911), p. 189.
30. Ibid., p. 237. Since 1816 the Methodist Episcopal Church had prohibited slaveholders from holding any official position if they resided in states where emancipation was legally possible and where liberated slaves might enjoy freedom. By a second marriage, Bishop James O. Andrew inherited slaves through his wife. Some of the slaves were too old to work and some were children, too young to be put out on their own. Andrew and his wife were willing to free them but felt that such a course would be casting them off. In addition, Georgia, where he lived, did not allow emancipation with subsequent freedom. The 1844 General Conference passed the famous "Finley Resolution" asking Bishop Andrew to "desist" from exercising the office of Bishop as long as he was a slaveholder. Southerners were incensed at the action. It appeared to them to violate the Church law of 1816. Soule agreed with them.
31. Ibid., pp. 268–269.
32. F. Edward Bentley, "Documents Regarding the Minutes of the Board of Trustees of Soule University," document entitled "Whatever Happened to Rev. William J. Sasnett, First Elected President of Soule University?" From 1858 until 1860, reports Bentley, Sasnett served as President of the LaGrange (Georgia) Female College and from 1860 until 1865 left Georgia briefly to be the President of the East Alabama Male College. He died on November 3, 1865, at the age of forty-five.
33. Homer S. Thrall, *A Brief History of Methodism in Texas* (Nashville: Publishing House of the M. E. Church, South, 1894), p. 269.
34. Phelan, *Early Methodism in Texas*, pp. 402–404.
35. Texas-Gammel, "An Act to Incorporate Soule University (1856)," *The Laws of Texas: 1822–1897*, Gammel (Austin: The Gammel Book Company, 1898), 4:353–354.
36. Thrall, *History of Methodism in Texas*, p. 270.
37. Christian, "Chappell Hill Female College."
38. Thrall, *History of Methodism in Texas*, p. 269.
39. Soule, *Catalogue of Soule University: 1858–59* (Galveston: Christian Advocate Office, 1859).
40. Ibid. The General Conference of 1844 authorized the division of Texas into two Conferences.
41. Phelan, *Early Methodism in Texas*, pp. 403–404.
42. Ralph Wood Jones, "A History of Southwestern University, 1873–1949" (doctoral dissertation, University of Texas, 1960), p. 143 (taken from Soule Board Minutes of February 19, 1857), and CCSB #5, Letter of November 6, 1873, from B. D. Dashiell, Chappell Hill, to F. A. Mood.
43. Soule, *Soule Catalogue 1858–59*, pp. 21–22.
44. Cody, "Soule University," p. 227.
45. Soule, *Soule Catalogue 1858–59*, pp. 21–22.
46. In a document of November 6, 1873, sent by B. D. Dashiell to F. A. Mood, Dashiell says that the land was donated (CCSB #5). Ralph Jones says (Jones, *SU 1840–1961*, p. 94) that it was purchased.
47. Cody, "Soule University," p. 224.
48. Ibid., p. 225.
49. Soule, *Soule Catalogue 1858–59*, p. 5.
50. Ibid., p. 13.
51. Ibid., p. 20.
52. Soule, *Catalogue of Soule University, Chappell Hill Texas, 1859–60* (Galveston: Texas Christian Advocate Book Press, 1860).
53. Bentley, "Documents on Soule Minutes," document entitled "Presidents of Soule University or Soule College."
54. Anne J. Bailey, "Carter, George Washington," HBTO, July 23, 2002.
55. Phelan, *Early Methodism in Texas*, p. 466.

56. Cody, "Soule University," p. 227.
57. Ibid., pp. 226–227.
58. Jones, *SU 1840–1961*, pp. 97–99.
59. Jones, "History of SU" (dissertation), pp. 148–150.
60. Jones, *SU 1840–1961*, p. 99.
61. Bailey, "Carter."
62. Carole E. Christian, "Soule University,." HBTO,. July 23, 2002.
63. Cody, "Soule University," pp. 227–228.
64. Thrall, *History of Methodism in Texas*, p. 269.
65. CC, Incoming Correspondence, undated statement entitled "Soule University," Box 1, Folder 4.
66. Bailey, "Carter."
67. John H. McLean, "Our Early Schools," *The Methodist Historical Quarterly* 2, no. 1 (1910): 64.
68. Cody, "Soule University," pp. 227–228. He takes this statement from Francis Asbury Mood, *A Narrative of the Facts Relating the Founding and Progress of Southwestern University from 1840 to 1882* (Galveston: Shaw & Blaylock, Printers, 1882), p. 6.
69. Jones, "History of SU" (dissertation), p. 25, fn. 24, reports that the Soule University minutes are located in the Bridwell Library, Perkins School of Theology, Southern Methodist University.
70. Jones, *SU 1840–1961*, p. 92.
71. CC, Incoming Correspondence, undated statement entitled "Soule University," Box 1, Folder 4.
72. Bentley, "Documents on Soule Minutes," document entitled "Soule University from 1872 to 1887."
73. Phelan, *Early Methodism in Texas*, p. 466.
74. Frederick Eby, *The Development of Education in Texas* (New York: The Macmillan Company, 1925), p. 141.
75. Thrall, *History of Methodism in Texas*, p. 269.
76. Jones, *SU 1840–1961*, p. 100.
77. Bentley, "Documents on Soule Minutes," document entitled "Presidents of Soule University or Soule College."
78. CCSB #5, Letters to F. A. Mood from B. D. Kavanaugh of August 17, 1867, and from B. D. Dashiell of December 6, 1873. The only O. H. McOmber located by the author in an extensive search was a Civil War soldier from Carlton, New York, named Otis H. McOmber. He was born about 1833 and died in 1897. He was twenty-eight years old when he joined the Union army as a private in the Seventieth New York Infantry, Company B. He was captured at the Battle of the Wilderness. He and his wife had two children, a daughter born in 1861 and a son in 1863. He would have been thirty-four years old in 1867. The likelihood that he is the McOmber connected with Soule, however, cannot be reasonably inferred unless further evidence turns up strengthening that surmise.
79. Jones, *SU 1840–1961*, p. 99. Bentley does not record Peter Alexander Stewart among his list of persons invited to assume the presidency.
80. Sheila Weems Johnston, "Internet reference to *The Blue and Gray from Hawkins County, Tennessee 1861–1865*." Internet page created September 1, 1999.
81. Phelan, *Early Methodism in Texas*, p. 464.
82. CCSB #5, Letter to F. A. Mood from B. T. Kavanaugh, July 25, 1867.
83. Jones, *SU 1840–1961*, pp. 90, 100–101.
84. Eby, *Development of Texas Education*, pp. 181–187.
85. Jones, *SU 1840–1961*, p. 102.
86. Cody, "Soule University," p. 229.
87. Thrall, *History of Methodism in Texas*, p. 172.
88. CCSB #5. Letter to F. A. Mood from B. T. Kavanaugh, December 24, 1867.
89. CCSB #5, Letter to F. A. Mood from B. D. Dashiell, November 6, 1873.
90. Joseph E. Chance, "Moore, John Creed," HBTO, July 23, 2002.
91. CCSB #5, Letter to F. A. Mood from R. W. Kennon, September 8, 1868.
92. CCSB #5, Letter to F. A. Mood from H. N. McTyeire, October 12, 1868.
93. CCSB #5, Letter to F. A. Mood from W. G. Connor, September 9, 1868.
94. CCSB #5, Letter to F. A. Mood from John H. Stone, October 28, 1868.
95. Mood, *For God and Texas*, p. 147.
96. Ibid., pp. 147–148.

CHAPTER VI
Fulfillment of the Vision: Southwestern University (1868–1873)

1. John H. McLean, *Reminiscences* (Nashville: Publishing House M. E. Church, South, 1918), pp. 151–152.
2. Francis Asbury Mood, *For God and Texas: Autobiography of Francis Asbury Mood, 1830–1884* (Dallas: Listo Publications, 2001), p. 156.
3. Claude Carr Cody, *The Life and Labors of Francis Asbury Mood, D.D.* (Chicago: F. H. Revell, 1886), p. 280.
4. Mood, *For God and Texas*, pp. 156–157. B. T. Kavanaugh had written Mood on October 10, 1868, telling him that Judge Felder, before his recent death, had held a debt of some fifteen or seventeen thousand dollars, which the Judge had said he would donate to the University. Twelve thousand dollars of that amount was what he subscribed to the school as an endowment for a Chair. "Misfortune overtook him in his last illness," says Kavanaugh, "and he added a codicil to his will which made the donation void, and he died." Nevertheless, continues Kavanaugh, Col. Giddings of Brenham is the attorney for both the estate of Judge Felder and of the University. "He says he believes he can relieve the U[niversity] from the whole debt. *How* I don't know. This matter and all the questions growing out of it will soon be settled, and then it will be known what the debts are. There are not many of any amnt outside of this." Mood's surprise is not a question of his having been unacquainted with the seventeen-thousand-dollar debt but of his apparent assumption, as Kavanaugh had intimated, that it would be taken care of by Giddings. See CCSB #5, Letter to F. A. Mood from B. T. Kavanaugh, October 10, 1868.
5. Mood, *For God and Texas*, p. 156. Chrietzberg later went with him to Southwestern and became one of the first three faculty members there.
6. Tanner, Finch, and Fleming, "Tanner-Finch Letters on William H. Seat,." Letter of July 5, 1958, from Eloise Tanner, granddaughter of William H. Seat, to President Finch. Found in the Ralph Jones files (President's Office Archives). Mrs. Tanner states in her letter that she has the Andrew Johnson letter and Seat's diary in her possession. She says that the diary "is most interesting because it has the autographs of many famous people stating what they would present to the University. Thomas Carlyle, under the date of November 22, 1870, said he would give the Oliver Cromwell Letters; Samuel F. B. Morse, November 9, 1871, a set of telegraphic instruments for the illustration of Telegraphy. Some of the other names are: Gladstone, William Cullen Bryant, etc. I remember my mother telling us that the things donated to the University during the four years my grandfather was abroad, were sent to Galveston, and as I understand it, never reached the University. I am not sure if some of the things did reach the University or whether all of them were felt [sic; read "left"] in the ship. It is my recollection that there was not enough money to transport them to Georgetown. My grandfather paid all his expenses during the four years he was in Europe on this mission." In a letter of February 4, 1968, to President Fleming, Mrs. Tanner says that the diary has gotten away from her. Macum Phelan (Macum Phelan, *A History of the Expansion of Methodism in Texas: 1867–1902* [Dallas: Mathis, Van Nort & Co., 1937], p. 226) says that the material was shipped in boxes to Galveston, where "it lay on the wharves and rotted."
7. Mood, *For God and Texas*, p. 157.
8. Ibid., pp. 157–159.
9. Ralph Wood Jones, *Southwestern University 1840–1961* (Austin: Jenkins Publishing Co., 1973), Appendix A, pp. 347–349. After the October 4 document adopted by the Soule University Board of Trustees became the operating document for the Educational Convention in

Galveston, Mood, as secretary of the Convention, copied an extract of the Soule Trustees meeting back into Southwestern University Curator Minutes at a later date to provide a starting point for the origin of Southwestern. When he did so, he omitted the two concluding paragraphs in which the Soule Trustees expressed their view that Soule itself might become the Central Methodist University.

10. Mood, *For God and Texas*, pp. 157–159.
11. Ibid., pp. 159–160.
12. Ibid.
13. SU Curators 1870–79. Curator minutes from October 4, 1869 through the annual meeting in June 1879 are found today in two versions. The first is the original set of minutes covering the dates indicated in a handwritten volume by Mood, who served as secretary. The volume was abandoned in 1879, when he decided to start a new volume for curator minutes. He recopied all the minutes of the first ten years into a new, much larger, more substantial, and more handsome volume. The new volume, beginning with the old, recopied minutes, became the repository for subsequent minutes of meetings held from 1879 to 1912. When the faculty began to keep minutes for itself in 1879, it did so in the unused portion of the old Curator Minutes book. The last set of curator minutes is succeeded by the first set of faculty minutes dated June 21, 1879. Inasmuch as Mood took some liberties in recopying the old minutes in the new book, expanding or contracting them at points from the original, I have used the original, unrevised version as being closer to the actions reported and less subject to the "improvement" often found in events when looked at in retrospect. I have used the later version at a few points, however, where it is helpful in clarifying events.
14. Mood, *For God and Texas*, pp. 160–161.
15. Ibid., p. 161.
16. Cody, Francis Asbury Mood, p. 165.
17. SU Trustees 1871–92, printed report dated October 29, 1884, fastened to inside cover of volume.
18. SU Curators 1870–79, April 20–22, 1870. All the material in the preceding paragraphs related to the Galveston Convention is taken from these minutes.
19. Mood, For God and Texas, p. 161.
20. Ibid., p. 162.
21. SU Curators 1870–79. April 6, 1871.
22. Mood, For God and Texas, p. 162.
23. Ibid., pp. 162–164.
24. SU Curators 1870–79, April 6–8, 1871.
25. Mood, *For God and Texas*, pp. 164–165. Though he says in the autobiography that the two seniors graduated in 1871, they are listed in the Southwestern University catalog of 1877 as having graduated in 1872. He was more likely accurate in compiling the numbers of all the alumni of the root colleges for the catalog than in remembering the data for one year when writing the autobiography.
26. GC, Letter of February 26, 1872, from P. C. Carnes to J. D. Giddings.
27. Mood, *For God and Texas*, pp. 164–165. J. D. Giddings may have been involved. See footnote 4.
28. From an article on J. D. Giddings by John Henry Brown in *Indian Wars and Pioneers of Texas* printed on pp. 228–229 of Letters on Jabez Giddings and Family.
29. Letters on Jabez Giddings and Family. Article of June 29, 1878, from *The Texas Sentinel*, pp. 224–225.
30. Carole E. Christian, "Giddings, Jabez Demming," HBTO, July 23, 2002.
31. GC, Letter of September 13, 1871. The description by Ralph Jones of the events connected with the establishment of the Texas University Company and the motives of its founders is quite different from that portrayed by me. The reason is that he did not have access to Mood's letter of September 13, 1871, and, therefore, had no idea that Mood was the originator of the joint stock company plan. Had he possessed that letter, his narrative would likely have been quite different. WBJ.
32. SU Curators-Trustees 1869–1912, November 1–3, 1871, pp. 23–25.
33. SU Curators 1870–79, Nov. 2–3, 1871. Also, MKSB #34, pp. 51–55, Letter of early June 1910 from J. C. S. Morrow to Capt. D. H. & J. W. Snyder.
34. SU Curators-Trustees 1869–1912, November 3, 1870, p. 26.
35. Francis Asbury Mood, *A Narrative of the Facts Relating the Founding and Progress of Southwestern University from 1840 to 1882* (Galveston: Shaw & Blaylock, Printers, 1882), pp. 12–13.
36. The letter was among a collection presented to Southwestern University a few years ago by Wallace Giddings, a Georgetown businessman and descendant of J. D. Giddings.
37. SU Curators-Trustees 1869–1912, December 9–11, 1871, pp. 27–31.
38. Ibid.
39. SU Curators 1870–79, December 9–11, 1871.
40. SU Curators 1870–79, December 11, 1871.
41. MSB, Vol. 2, p. 68.
42. SU Curators-Trustees 1869–1912, from "Appointment of Agent," p. 32. Though the Texas University Company was legally dissolved for not having met within six months the capitalization terms specified in its organizational plan, the men comprising it continued to act together in support of the university project. The name, "The Texas University Company," often continued to be used with reference to them even though it was no longer technically valid.
43. F. Edward Bentley, "Documents Regarding the Minutes of the Board of Trustees of Soule University," document entitled "When Did Dr. Mood Resign as President of Soule University?"
44. Mood, For God and Texas, p. 165.
45. Clara Stearns Scarbrough, *Land of Good Water: A Williamson County, Texas, History* (Georgetown: Williamson County Sun Publishers, 1973), p. 157.
46. Ibid., p. 184.
47. Frederick Eby, *The Development of Education in Texas* (New York: The Macmillan Company, 1925), p. 151.
48. Georgetown College Minutes, Meetings of January 29, 1870, through September 13, 1873. The land had been donated by John J. Dimmitt and George W. Glasscock, Jr., the latter acting in the name of his late father, George W. Glasscock, Sr., for whom Georgetown was named. The deeds for the property were executed on March 5, 1870. The land is located today on the north side of University Avenue between Ash and College Streets. The old high school now used as the Williams Elementary School is located on it.
49. Scarbrough, *Williamson County History*, pp. 242–243.
50. SU Trustees 1871–92, Meeting of September 20, 1872. The minutes state that the visit took place "about" April 25 rather than "on" April 25. It had definitely occurred before May 20, for the Trustees of Georgetown College approved a motion on that date to reimburse J. C. S. Morrow $20 for the "hire of [a] hack for use of members of University Company."
51. Scarbrough, Williamson County History, p. 244.
52. Georgetown College Minutes, Meetings of October 7 and October 23, 1871.
53. SU Curators 1870–79, November 3, 1871.
54. Mood, *For God and Texas*, pp. 165–166.
55. Georgetown College Minutes, Meeting of February 7, 1872.
56. SU Trustees 1871–92, April 23, 1872.
57. SU Trustees 1871–92, September 20, 1872.
58. SU Trustees 1871–92, March 8, 1873.
59. Eby, *Development of Texas Education*, pp. 157–162.
60. Georgetown College Minutes, Meeting of November 30, 1872.
61. Mood, *For God and Texas*, p. 166.
62. Cody, *Francis Asbury Mood*, p. 309, footnote.
63. Mood, *For God and Texas*, p. 166. Bishop Keener served as a proxy for one of the curators, who was absent at the meeting on December 31, 1872, where Mood was elected Regent. He voted for Mood. Subsequently, Mood's appointment each year at the Texas Annual Conference was as Regent.
64. SU Curators-Trustees 1869–1912, December 31, 1872, pp. 35–36. Mood kept the notes made in pencil by the person who recorded the

actions taken by the curators at the meeting. These notes were then transferred in ink onto two pages in an improved narrative style. Both the pencil and the ink versions are on the stationery of Alford, Miller, and Veal, Galveston, Tx. At the bottom of the page is the following statement: "I hereby confirm the election of Rev. F. A. Mood DD as regent of the Texas University. J. C. Keener 31 Dec 1872." See CCSB #5.

65. Jones, *SU 1840–1961*, p. 146. Cody's biography of Mood gives the date for his resignation as January 1873. The date given by R. Jones comes from Soule Trustee minutes and is to be preferred. B. D. Dashiell says that, as of the date of his letter, November 6, 1873, Mood "is still nominal Pres. his resignation having never been accepted." CCSB #5.
66. Mood, *For God and Texas*, pp. 167–168.
67. Ibid., pp. 168–172.
68. Georgetown College Minutes, Meeting of June 3, 1873.
69. MKSB #34, pp. 51–55, undated letter from J. C. S. Morrow to Capt. D. H. & J. W. Snyder, Georgetown, Texas, during the first week in June 1910.
70. MSB, Vol. 2, p. 97.
71. SU Curators 1870–79, August 21, 1873.
72. Mood, *Founding and Progress of Southwestern*, p. 14.
73. Georgetown College Minutes, Meeting of Sept. 13, 1873.
74. Mood, *For God and Texas*, p. 173.

CHAPTER VII
Francis Asbury Mood as Regent (1873–1884)

1. Southwestern, Assorted Printed Material on the Opening of Texas University.
2. MSB, Vol. 2, p. 98.
3. F. Edward Bentley, "Documents Regarding the Minutes of the Board of Trustees of Soule University," document entitled "Notes on Soule University."
4. Southwestern, Assorted Material on Opening.
5. Francis Asbury Mood, *A Narrative of the Facts Relating the Founding and Progress of Southwestern University from 1840 to 1882* (Galveston: Shaw & Blaylock, Printers, 1882), p. 15.
6. SU Curators-Trustees 1869–1912, October 6, 1873, p. 38.
7. SU Curators 1870–79, Minutes of December 13, 1873.
8. MSB. Mood pasted the first small catalog into his scrapbook page by page. It is dated in his own handwriting as January 1874.
9. MSB, Vol. 2, p. 93. He died of typhoid fever in Austin on September 18, 1873.
10. SU Curators 1870–79, December 13, 1873.
11. Anonymous, "Pioneer Resident of Georgetown Dies at 105," *San Antonio Express*, January 5, 1957.
12. Southwestern, *Texas University 1874* [catalogue] (Georgetown: Strickland & Clarke, Stationers and Printers, Galveston, 1874).
13. Clara Stearns Scarbrough, *Land of Good Water: A Williamson County, Texas, History* (Georgetown: Williamson County Sun Publishers, 1973), p. 245. Scarbrough's information came from an interview with Mrs. Henry E. Meyer, wife of the former Dean of the School of Fine Arts at Southwestern University. Mrs. Meyer knew Margaret Mood McKennon for more than twenty years. Scarbrough's other source was a letter of October 24, 1972, from Fletcher Metcalfe Croom, granddaughter of F. A. Mood, quoting her mother, the same Margaret Mood McKennon.
14. Scarbrough, *Williamson County History*, pp. 192–194.
15. U.S. Census, 1880 United States Federal Census, Williamson County, Texas.
16. Scarbrough, *Williamson County History*, p. 244.
17. Francis Asbury Mood, *For God and Texas: Autobiography of Francis Asbury Mood, 1830–1884* (Dallas: Listo Publications, 2001), p. 173.
18. Ibid. This observation by Mary Katherine Metcalfe Earney, editor of Mood's *Autobiography*, came from conversations with her grandmother, Margaret Mood McKennon.
19. Ibid., p. 174.
20. SU Curators 1870–79, December 13, 1873.
21. Claude Carr Cody, *The Life and Labors of Francis Asbury Mood, D.D.* (Chicago: F. H. Revell, 1886), pp. 316–318.
22. SU Trustees 1871–92, Minutes of February 10, 1875.
23. Charlie C. Haynes, Jr., "Veal, William G," HBTO, July 23, 2002.
24. SU Trustees 1871–92, February 25, 1875.
25. Macum Phelan, *A History of the Expansion of Methodism in Texas: 1867–1902* (Dallas: Mathis, Van Nort & Co., 1937), p. 167.
26. SU Trustees 1871–92, July 14, 1880.
27. Phelan, *Expansion of Methodism in Texas*, pp. 91–92.
28. MSB, Vol. 2, p. 98.
29. SU Curators 1870–79, July 23, 1874.
30. Rufus C. Burleson, *The Life and Writings of Rufus C. Burleson, D.D., LL.D., Containing a Biography of Dr. Burleson by Hon. Harry Haynes* (compiled and published by Mrs. Georgia J. Burleson, 1901), p. 343.
31. Frederick Eby, *The Development of Education in Texas* (New York: The Macmillan Company, 1925), pp. 157–159.
32. Ibid.
33. Ibid., pp. 159–163.
34. Ibid., pp. 163–166.
35. Ibid., p. 168.
36. Ibid., pp. 169–170.
37. Burleson, *Life of Burleson*, p. 343.
38. MSB, Vol. 3, p. 15.
39. Phelan, *Expansion of Methodism in Texas*, p. 161.
40. Gerald F. Vaughn, "Gerald F. Vaughn to Kathryn Stallard," Newark, Delaware, May 22, 2005. Allen's memoir appears in the *Minutes Seventy-first Annual Session of the North Texas Annual Conference*, 1937.
41. MSB, Vol. 3, p. 49. Mood's son, R. Gibbs Mood, who became the inheritor of the scrapbooks, must have been the one who put the materials relative to Mood's death into the scrapbooks.
42. See MSB, Vol. 3, p. 87, for a newspaper reprint of the original charter presented to the Legislature for ratification. It is exactly the same as that later approved except for the change in name.
43. *The Megaphone*, October 30, 1934, p. 1. Margaret Mood McKennon received a letter from the State Archivist, Harriet Smither, dated October 29, 1934, in which she states that she is including "a very fine letter written by your father to Governor Davis." That letter is the one sent by Mood to Davis on June 5, 1873. Mrs. McKennon turned them over to *The Megaphone*, which printed them both in full.
44. MSB, Vol. 2, p. 122. R. W. Kennon, President Board of Curators, W. B. Norris, President Board of Trustees, and Geo. F. Alford, Secretary, signed the newspaper article articulating this information. This information also appeared in a Centennial edition of *The Megaphone* in 1940. See Anonymous, "Locating Southwestern University Proved Difficult Task," *The Megaphone*, April 9, 1940.
45. SU Trustees 1871–92, February 11, 1875.
46. There was, however, some ambivalence about the way the name should be written until the final change to Southwestern in 1906. Almost from the beginning, it was written three different ways: "South Western," "SouthWestern," and "Southwestern."
47. Texas-Gammel, "An Act to Incorporate the South Western University (1875)," *The Laws of Texas: 1822–1897*, Gammell (Houston: The Gammell Book Company, 1898), pp. 617–619.
48. MSB, Vol. 2, p. 154. The present seal of the University appears in a June 26, 1879, article from the *Williamson County Sun* included by Mood in his scrapbook. The Board of Trustees officially approved it on December 13, 1879. See SU Trustees 1871–92.
49. SU Trustees 1871–92, June 22, 1880.
50. SU Curators-Trustees 1869–1912, July 17, 1875, p. 41.
51. SU Curators 1870–79, July 17, 1875. R. W. Kennon sent Mood a copy of the resolutions passed by the Texas Annual Conference in a letter of March 27, 1874. It is found in CCSB #5.
52. SU Trustees 1871–92, December 14, 1875.

53. SU Curators 1870–79, July 10, 1877.
54. GC, Letter of September 11, 1877.
55. Carole E. Christian, "Soule University," HBTO, July 23, 2002.
56. SU Faculty 1879–90, Minutes of October 3 and October 5, 1887.
57. SU Curators 1870–79, July 19, 1875.
58. Ralph Masterson, *Sketches from the Life of Dr. Horace Bishop* (n.p.: n.p., [ca. 1933]), p. 35.
59. SU Trustees 1871–92, December 9, 1875.
60. GC, Letters of January 31, 1876; February 12, 1876; February 19, 1876.
61. Thomas Proctor Hughes was an unusual person. Elected by a large majority to represent Williamson County at the Secession Convention in 1861, he was the first delegate to vote against secession. He worked zealously in the popular referendum that followed to persuade Williamson County residents to vote against secession. Nevertheless, he joined the Confederate army when Texas seceded and fought through the war. He became rich through real estate holdings after the war and made many contributions to Southwestern University. He was also a strong prohibitionist. See Carolyn Hyman, "Hughes, Thomas Proctor," HBTO, July 23, 2002.
62. GC, Letter of February 19, 1876.
63. GC, Letter of December 27, 1876.
64. GC, Letter of September 28, 1877.
65. SU Curators 1870–79, June 15, 1879.
66. GC, Letters of October 24 and November 2, 1877. Horace Bishop explains the purpose of the proposed sale of the five hundred acres in these two letters.
67. SU Trustees 1871–92, December 21, 1877.
68. SU Curators 1870–79, June 15, 1879. Trustee minutes report that the draft for $1,911.00 was made to him on May 27, 1879, by which time Mood was already living in the house.
69. Article of June 29, 1878, from *The Texas Sentinel*, found on pp. 224–225 of Letters on Jabez Giddings and Family.
70. SU Trustees 1871–92, June 22, 1880.
71. CCSB #4, Letter to C. C. Cody from F. A. Mood, August 3, 1883.
72. Mood, *For God and Texas*, p. 174.
73. The technical term adopted in the nineteenth century for the Annual Conferences that sponsored Southwestern University was "patronizing Annual Conferences." Though that term is still the official term appearing in legal documents, the words "supporting" and "sponsoring" will be used in its stead in this book, since they express what it really means in modern parlance.
74. SU Curators 1870–79, July 7 and July 9, 1877.
75. Mood, *Founding and Progress of Southwestern*, pp. 17–18.
76. SU Trustees 1871–92. June 17, 1879.
77. SU Trustees 1871–92. December 24, 1883.
78. Francis Asbury Mood, "Letter of F. A. Mood to D. W. Snyder," Georgetown, March 26, 1875. Photo copy of the original found by R. Jones in the D. H. Snyder envelope, MSS Files, Archives, Texas History Center, University of Texas, Austin, Texas.
79. Ralph Wood Jones, *Southwestern University 1840–1961* (Austin: Jenkins Publishing Co., 1973), p. 177. See also SU Trustees 1871–92, Minutes of December 13, 1879, and June 7, 1885.
80. Mood, *Founding and Progress of Southwestern*, p. 21.
81. MKSB #34, p. 1. Letter from J. C. S. Morrow to Capt. D. H. & J. W. Snyder, Georgetown, Texas, first week of June 1910.
82. Mood, *Founding and Progress of Southwestern*, pp. 16–19.
83. Southwestern, *Register of Southwestern University . . . 1881–82* (Galveston: Place of Shaw & Blaylock, [1882]).
84. Mood, *Founding and Progress of Southwestern*, pp. 18–19, for 1882. For 1888–1889 see SU Trustees 1871–92, June 11, 1889.
85. Mood, *Founding and Progress of Southwestern*, pp. 18–19.
86. Eby, *Development of Texas Education*, p. 139.
87. GC, Letter of October 1, 1872.
88. Scarbrough, *Williamson County History*, p. 251.
89. SU Curators 1870–79, December 22, 1877. SU Trustees 1871–92, December 22, 1878, and April 12, 1879.
90. Mood, *Founding and Progress of Southwestern*, p. 17.
91. Scarbrough, *Williamson County History*, p. 246. Since no denomination making such an announcement (Mood) or causing such a rumor (Scarbrough) has been identified, it is quite possible that it was the offer by the Masons in Round Rock that caused the consternation.
92. SU Curators 1870–79, June 18, 1878.
93. Cody, *Francis Asbury Mood*, pp. 321–322.
94. Southwestern, *Register and Announcement of Southwestern University . . . 1878–9* (Galveston: Shaw & Blaylock, Steam Printers, 1878–79).
95. SU Faculty 1879–90, March 19, 1884.
96. Southwestern, *Register for 1881–82*, p. 7.
97. SU Faculty 1879–90, December 13, 1879, and September 18, 1880.
98. SU Faculty 1879–90, October 26 and October 30, 1880, September 16, 1881, and April, 1882.
99. SU Curators 1870–79, July 7–10, 1877.
100. MKSB #31, p. 59, "Incidents in Early Days of Southwestern University's History Recounted by Ex," *WC Sun*, July 23, 1937.
101. Claude Carr Cody, "The Old Southwestern College Building," *Williamson County Sun*, January 19, 1923. Cody recounts the history of the two bells in the original college building as follows. "The original bell of the Georgetown College was secured by Mr. James Harris through the Band of Hope. The second bell was bought with much effort when after use for years it [the original bell] became cracked and the last bell [the second bell] was cast [in 1887] for Southwestern University under the good offices of Capt. D. H. Snyder. The money for its purchase was raised by him from one of the big cattlemen's association. When the building was sold to the city of Georgetown [see Chapter XII] the bell was not included in the sale. It is now resting on the Southwest corner of the Methodist Church building." From its temporary resting place at the Methodist Church, it was brought to the campus, where Miss Kuykendall had it placed on top of the new Woman's Building when it was built in 1926. See Chapter XIII.
102. Cody, *Francis Asbury Mood*, pp. 331–332.
103. Ibid., pp. 330–334. For the number expelled, see SU Trustees 1871–92, Minutes of June 19, 1880.
104. SU Faculty 1879–90, May 27, 1880, and April 25, 1884.
105. SU Faculty 1879–90, February 11 and May 19, 1884.
106. SU Faculty 1879–90, December 26, 1883, and October 1–2, 1884.
107. SU Faculty 1879–90, April 10, 14, 15, and 28, 1884.
108. Southwestern, *Register of Southwestern University . . . 1883–1884* (Georgetown: "Sun" Job Printing Office, 1884), pp. 11–12.
109. Mood, *Founding and Progress of Southwestern*, p. 18.
110. Ibid.
111. Scarbrough, *Williamson County History*, p. 246. Also, MKSB #31, p. 59, "Incidents in Early Days of Southwestern University's History Recounted by Ex," *WC Sun*, July 23, 1937.
112. Cody, *Francis Asbury Mood*, p. 322. Also, *Southwestern Bulletin*, Apr., 1914, p. 1.
113. Cody, *Francis Asbury Mood*, p. 329.
114. SU Curators 1870–79, June 15, 1878. Apparently he spelled his name with one "l," whereas his father spelled his name with two—Dashiel and Dashiell.
115. SU Curators-Trustees 1869–1912, June 19–22, 1880, p. 82.
116. SU Trustees 1871–92, June 23, 1883, and May 31, 1884.
117. Oscar Fitzgerald Sensabaugh, "Recollections," July 10, 1951, with a three-page autobiography of Daisy Lane at the end of the manuscript.
118. SU Trustees 1871–92, June 7 and June 9, 1889.
119. SU Curators-Trustees 1869–1912, June 6–9, 1890, p. 235.
120. SU Curators 1870–79, June 15, 1878.
121. Cody, *Francis Asbury Mood*, pp. 336–337.
122. SU Faculty 1879–90, April 18, 1884.
123. SU Faculty 1879–90, September 1 and September 8, 1884.
124. SU Trustees 1871–92, September 11, 1884.
125. Cody, *Francis Asbury Mood*, pp. 344–351.
126. SU Faculty 1879–90, November 12, 1884.

CHAPTER VIII
Townspeople, Trustees, and Teachers to the Fore (1884–1890)

1. Mellville Beveridge Lockett, "Autobiography of M. B. Lockett," 1916, p. 172.
2. CCSB #6, C. C. Cody, "Forty Years Ago," probably *Williamson County Sun*, 1919.
3. Clara Stearns Scarbrough, *Land of Good Water: A Williamson County, Texas, History* (Georgetown: Williamson County Sun Publishers, 1973), pp. 196–200.
4. Ibid., p. 210. Scarbrough's quotation is taken from a letter by Snyder published in the *Williamson County Sun*, February 11, 1909.
5. Scarbrough, *Williamson County History*, pp. 218–219.
6. Lockett, "Lockett Autobiography," p. 162.
7. CCSB #13, "Improving Our Texas Horse," by Capt. D. H. Snyder, read before the Williamson County Farmers' Institute September 6, 1890, printed in an unnamed newspaper, probably the *Williamson County Sun*, on September 6, 1890.
8. Scarbrough, *Williamson County History*, pp. 206–207.
9. Mary Jane Evans, *D. H. Snyder and J. W. Snyder* (Georgetown: MHHS, ca. 1984–1994).
10. Scarbrough, *Williamson County History*, pp. 207–209.
11. Ibid., p. 209.
12. Evans, *D. H. and J. W. Snyder*. Mary Jane Evans was the granddaughter of John Wesley Snyder.
13. William C. Finch, Interviews by Martha Allen,. August 1992, Tape 2, p. 23.
14. SU Faculty 1879–90, November 15, 1884, pp. 66–77.
15. GC, Letter to Hon. Heber Stone from W. A. Shaw of Dallas, May 14, 1897. Shaw says that "the error in selection of Regent No. 2 was natural, resulting as it did from following the bad advice of one or more good bishops."
16. In a newspaper article appearing in the Atlanta *Constitution* reporting on the annual session of the North Georgia Conference meeting in La Grange, Georgia, the reporter wrote as follows: "Dr. John W. Heidt, secretary, called the roll, which consists of several hundred names. The doctor's magnificent voice can be heard by all and no amount of confusion bothers him." Anonymous, "Second Day of the Methodists," *The Constitution*, Friday, December 1, 1899.
17. SU Curators-Trustees 1869–1912, June 6–9, 1885, pp. 135–139.
18. Anonymous, "Heidt, John Wesley," *The Encyclopedia of World Methodism* ([Nashville]: The United Methodist Publishing House, c. 1974).
19. CCSB #11, "Rev. John W. Heidt, D.D.," *Atlanta Constitution*, December 24, 1893.
20. Ibid.
21. SU Faculty 1879–90, May 24, 1886, pp. 110–112.
22. SU Curators-Trustees 1869–1912, June 5–8, 1886, pp. 132–133.
23. SU Curators-Trustees 1869–1912. June 3–6, 1887, pp. 172–175.
24. Ibid.
25. Ibid., pp. 161–165.
26. SU Faculty 1879–90, June 7 and 16, 1887, pp. 141–143.
27. SU Faculty 1879–90, June 1–6, 1888, pp. 182–183, 188–190.
28. CCSB #4, Letter to Cody of November 12, 1886.
29. Anonymous, "Heated Words Used in the Conference," *The Constitution*, Saturday, November 24, 1900. In an article about a heated argument that broke out on the floor of the North Georgia Annual Conference, there is a section entitled "Dr. Heidt Asks for Peace," in which the reporter cites his words for three paragraphs.
30. MKSB #31, p. 59, "Incidents in Early Days of Southwestern University's History Recounted by Ex," *WC Sun*, July 23, 1937.
31. GC, Letter of December 27, 1876, from F. A. Mood to J. D. Giddings.
32. SU Curators-Trustees 1869–1912, June 1–6, 1888, pp. 184–185.
33. Southwestern, *Register of Southwestern University and the Ladies' Annex* [for 1892–93] (Georgetown: 1892–93).
34. SU Faculty 1879–90, June 5–8, 1886, p. 126.
35. In his report to the Curators in June 1887, Heidt says that "setting the boarding arrangement in place [during 1886–1887] for young ladies has caused the enrollment to almost double [over 1885–1886]." His statement is at variance with the figures. Though the enrollment for men increased 23 percent, that for women increased only 2 percent. See SU Curators-Trustees 1869–1912.
36. See SU Curators-Trustees 1869–1912, Minutes of annual meetings of 1886 through 1892.
37. Ralph Wood Jones, *Southwestern University 1840–1961* (Austin: Jenkins Publishing Co., 1973), p. 192. I have been unable to find the source for Jones's statement about Mood's receiving the plans just before his death but have no doubt that he had one. Mood made a report to the faculty in April 1884 about a trip to Nashville. This trip would have been the occasion for contracting a Vanderbilt architect. The subsequent actions of the Board of Curators several years later presume that they have the plans in their hands that are referred to as having been drawn up by a Vanderbilt architect. WBJ.
38. Jones, *SU 1840–1961*, p. 192. Once again, I have been unable to locate a source for this reference, but it appears to be accurate. WBJ.
39. SU Trustees 1871–92, Minutes of June 4–7, 1887, pp. 95–96. Today it would be close to the eastern entry to the campus off of Highway 29.
40. Francis Asbury Mood, *For God and Texas: Autobiography of Francis Asbury Mood, 1830–1884* (Dallas: Listo Publications, 2001), p. 176.
41. SU Curators-Trustees 1869–1912, June 3–6, 1887, p. 143.
42. Ibid., p. 155.
43. Jones, *SU 1840–1961*, p. 193.
44. GC, Letter of July 31, 1897.
45. SU Trustees 1894–1907, June 18, 1897, p. 85.
46. Jones, *SU 1840–1961*, p. 194.
47. CCSB #9. The exact figures are written in pencil on a small piece of paper by Mood on October 28, 1883, only fifteen days before his death. The paper contains the names of the twelve Georgetown persons who pledged $25,000 of the $35,150 "subscribed" at the November 1883 Educational Convention in Georgetown for the new Ladies' building. Cody gives this same list in an article in the *Southwestern Bulletin*, April 1914, p. 1. Mood also lists all major donations made by Georgetown persons since 1873. He lists the value of the original gift of building and grounds as $65,000, the gifts for the construction of the original Annex building as $2,000, and the gifts for the third-story addition and the mansard roof (1881) as $4,000. These amounts, plus the $35,150 pledged by Georgetown residents in the campaign for the new Ladies' building, bring total Georgetown contributions over the eleven years to $106,150.
48. Jones, *SU 1840–1961*, p. 205.
49. Mood, *For God and Texas*, pp. 178–179.
50. GC, Letter of unknown month and day of 1898.
51. SU Trustees 1871–92, June 8 and December 29, 1887, pp. 97–98, 129.
52. Anonymous, "Giddings-Stone Mansion" (http://www.brenham-mansion.com), July 22, 2002.
53. GC, Letter of March 27, 1895.
54. GC, Letter of December 31, 1897.
55. GC, Letter of August 17, 1897.
56. Ray Hyer Brown, *Robert Stewart Hyer: The Man I Knew* (Salado, Tex.: The Anson Jones Press, 1957), pp. 54, 58. Mrs. Brown has an entire chapter called "Mexico." Hyer accompanied both the Snyders and Heber Stone to their gold mining operations in Mexico. From Stone's letters and internal evidence in the book, he went with the Snyders in 1895 and with Heber Stone in 1897.
57. GC, Letter of May 31, 1900.
58. SU Faculty 1890–1904, January 23 and January 28, 1896, p. 118. He was fifteen years old.
59. SU Trustees 1871–92, November 2, 1888, p. 129.
60. SU Trustees 1894–1907, May 26, 1899, pp. 113–114.
61. Olin W. Nail, *Texas Methodist Centennial Yearbook* (Elgin, Tex.: 1934), pp. 208–214. Article by Chas. C. Selecman.
62. SU Trustees 1871–92, June 2–4, 1888, pp. 119–123.

63. Frederick Eby, *The Development of Education in Texas* (New York: The Macmillan Company, 1925), pp. 187–189.
64. SU Curators-Trustees 1869–1912, June 1–6, 1888, pp. 180–181.
65. SU Curators-Trustees 1869–1912, May 30–June 2, 1895, p. 292.
66. SU Faculty 1879–90, October 19, 1897, pp. 153–154.
67. SU Curators-Trustees 1869–1912, Curators report to the Conferences of 1887, pp. 148–152.
68. SU Trustees 1871–92, June 4, 1887, pp. 95–96.
69. SU Faculty 1890–1904, Various minutes from October 3, 1887, through October 28, 1889, pp. 144–204.
70. SU Faculty 1890–1904, September 6, 1897, pp. 149–150. Its head, Wesley Peacock, was still corresponding with Dean Cody as late as 1914 about the success of its students at Southwestern, some of whom, he says, have been "signal failures with you, yet others have been eminently successful." Cody Incoming Correspondence, Letter of April 28, 1914, from Wesley Peacock to Dean Cody, Box 1, Folder 4.
71. SU Curators-Trustees 1869–1912, May 27–30, 1898, pp. 343–344.
72. CCSB #12. The "Address" is printed in an unnamed newspaper, probably The Texas Christian Advocate.
73. Jones, *SU 1840–1961*, p. 198.
74. SU Trustees 1871–92, June 11, 1889, pp. 143–145.
75. SU Faculty 1879–90, June 4, 1888, pp. 172–174.
76. SU Curators-Trustees 1869–1912, June 1–6, 1888, p. 195.
77. Ibid., p. 197.
78. SU Trustees 1871–92, June 10, 1889, pp. 141–142.
79. Evans, *D. H. and J. W. Snyder.*
80. Jones, *SU 1840–1961*, p. 194.
81. Scarbrough, *Williamson County History*, page undetermined.
82. SU Curators-Trustees 1869–1912, June 7–9, 1889, p. 214.
83. SU Curators-Trustees 1869–1912, January 15, 1890, pp. 215–216.
84. Ibid., pp. 216–219.
85. Donald J. West, "Heidt, John Wesley," *The Encyclopedia of World Methodism* ([Nashville]: The United Methodist Publishing House, c. 1974).
86. SU Faculty 1879–90, January 27, 1890, pp. 212–213.
87. CCSB #13, C. C. Cody, "Southwestern University," January 1890.
88. CCSB #4, Letters of February 12, 1890, October 14, 1892, and February 19, 1896.
89. CCSB #12, brief note in unnamed newspaper, probably the *Williamson County Sun.*
90. CCSB #6, Letter from John V. Heidt of January 29, 1909.

CHAPTER IX
Leadership Problems and Campus Culture (1890–1898)

1. Jackson's paper can be found in practically any anthology of major American historical writings.
2. Horace Du Bose reports (Horace M. Du Bose, *The History of Methodism* [Nashville: Publishing House of the Methodist Episcopal Church, South, 1916], p. 309) that Chappell was one of the Trustees of Vanderbilt University in 1910, when the Board of Trust took its first definitive action to separate Vanderbilt from the Methodist Church. Chappell voted against the action.
3. SU Curators-Trustees 1869–1912, June 6–9, 1890, pp. 220–231.
4. SU Curators-Trustees 1869–1912, June 6–9, 1890, pp. 220–231, and of June 5–6, 1891, pp. 245–246.
5. John H. McLean, *Reminiscences* (Nashville: Publishing House M. E. Church, South, 1918), p. 180.
6. Jon D. Swartz, *John Howell McLean* (Georgetown: In Cody, Hyer, McLean, Sanders, Young tract of the Mood-Heritage Museum Hall of Honor Historical Sketches, 1984–1994?).
7. Ralph Wood Jones, *Southwestern University 1840–1961* (Austin: Jenkins Publishing Co., 1973), p. 208.
8. Herbert Gambrell, "Herbert Gambrell Letter to Ralph Jones," June 18, 1974. Presidential Archives, Ralph Jones file.
9. Jones, *SU 1840–1961*, p. 209. The quotation is taken by R. Jones from Lulu Daniel Hardy, "College Days at Southwestern," pp. 47–48, from an unpublished manuscript, "Whose Leaf Does Not Wither." He says in a footnote that "Mrs. Hardy, wife of James C. Hardy, A. M., Southwestern University, 1896, paints a vivid picture of life at Southwestern about 1900."
10. Jon D. Swartz, "McLean, John Howell," HBTO, July 23, 2002.
11. Mellville Beveridge Lockett, "Autobiography of M. B. Lockett," 1916, pp. 189–190.
12. SU Faculty 1879–90, Minutes of May 17, 1886, p. 110.
13. SU Faculty 1879–90, September 9, 1886, p. 117.
14. SU Faculty 1879–90, November 22, 1886, pp. 120–121.
15. SU Faculty 1879–90, December 9, 1889, pp. 207–208.
16. McLean, *Reminiscences*, pp. 131–132.
17. Ibid., p. 129.
18. Ibid., pp. 119–120.
19. Ibid., pp. 131–135.
20. SU Faculty 1890–1904, September 25, 1893, p. 72.
21. Bob Marion Brown, *Robert Stewart Hyer* (Georgetown: In Cody, Hyer, McLean, Sanders, Young tract of the MHHS, 1982).
22. Ray Hyer Brown, *Robert Stewart Hyer: The Man I Knew* (Salado, Tex.: The Anson Jones Press, 1957), p. 156. Since SMU did not open until 1915, he taught physics at the medical college.
23. SU Curators-Trustees 1869–1912, June 2–5, 1893, pp. 269–274.
24. SU Curators-Trustees 1869–1912, June 5–8, 1886, p. 129.
25. SU Curators-Trustees 1869–1912, June 9, 1885, p. 120.
26. SU Curators-Trustees 1869–1912, June 1–6, 1888, pp. 188–190.
27. SU Curators-Trustees 1869–1912, June 3–7, 1892, p. 262.
28. In his annual report to the Curators for 1886–1887, the Regent informed them that four students had died during the academic year, three from typhoid fever. SU Curators-Trustees 1869–1912, June 3–6, 1887, pp. 167–177. Sanders left seven children—Samuel, Nannie, Albert, Shipp, Martha, Mary, and John Randolph. All of them graduated from Southwestern. John Randolph, the youngest, came back to Southwestern at the age of 100 in 1992 to give several of his father's books to Southwestern. *Southwestern Quarterly* 4, no. 1 (Fall 1992): 7.
29. CCSB #6, Article of 1919 in *The Megaphone.*
30. Claude Carr Cody, John M. Barcus, and Laura Kuykendall, *The Book of Southwestern* (Georgetown: Von Boeckmann Jones Co., 1923), p. 8.
31. Dan K. Utley, "Information on W. C. Vaden House," Small Collections, Box 2, Folder 4.
32. Southwestern, *Register of Southwestern University and Ladies' Annex* [for 1897–98] (Georgetown: 1897–98).
33. SU Trustees 1871–92, Minutes for the Executive Committee of July 16, 1892, pp. 179–180.
34. SU Curators-Trustees 1869–1912, May 30–June 2, 1895, p. 292.
35. SU Faculty 1879–90, May 24, 1887, p. 137.
36. CCSB #4.
37. CCSB #4, Letter to C. C. Cody from H. C. Pritchett, State Superintendent of Public Instruction, July 18, 1891.
38. SU Curators-Trustees 1869–1912, June 3–7, 1892, p. 264.
39. CC, Incoming Correspondence. James S. Giddings (Cody Collection, Box 1, Folder 4) says that he belonged to the Adelphi Society.
40. Randall Williams, "Literary & Debating Societies: A Brief History," 2000. SU, SLC, SC.Mr. Williams, a student at Southwestern in the class of 2000, has written a fine, succinct description of the literary societies at Southwestern during their half century of existence. I am grateful for his work and am dependent on him for much of what I say in this section.
41. SU Faculty 1890–1904, January 8, 1895, February 26, 1895, March 26, 1895, and September 22, 1896, mention the Grady Literary Society. An article entitled "Exercises of the Helion Literary Society" is found in CCSB #8.
42. Jones, *SU 1840–1961*, p. 162.
43. SU Curators-Trustees 1869–1912, June 3–7, 1892, pp. 254–259, and June 2–5, 1893, p. 271.
44. Williams, "Literary & Debating Societies," pp. 1–2.

45. Ibid., p. 2.
46. Many of these records can be found in the Special Collections section of the Smith Library Center at Southwestern University.
47. Jones, *SU 1840–1961*, pp. 159–160, citing "The Critic's Book of the Alamo Society."
48. Williams, "Literary & Debating Societies," p. 2.
49. Ibid.
50. Ibid.
51. CC, Incoming Correspondence, Letter of August 1, 1914, from C. M. Bishop to C. C. Cody, Box 1, Folder 8.
52. SU Faculty 1879–90, April 2, 1885, p. 79.
53. SU Faculty 1879–90, May 5, 1890, p. 222.
54. SU Faculty 1890–1904, November 23, 1891, pp. 30–31, and April 4, 1892, p. 41.
55. SU Faculty 1890–1904, November 19, 1895, p. 114.
56. SU Faculty 1890–1904, February 8, 1898, p. 161.
57. Faculty minutes of various dates from 1885 through 1897.
58. SU Faculty 1879–90, May 8, 1889, p. 192.
59. SU Faculty 1890–1904, October 29, 1895, p. 106.
60. SU Curators-Trustees 1869–1912, May 30–June 2, 1895, pp. 296–299.
61. SU Faculty 1879–90, October 17, 1887, January 30, 1888, and February 6, 1888, pp. 147, 156–158.
62. SU Curators-Trustees 1869–1912, June 5–8, 1886, p. 131.
63. SU Curators-Trustees 1869–1912, June 3–6, 1887, p. 160.
64. SU Faculty 1879–90, October 3, 1887, pp. 144–145.
65. SU Faculty 1879–90, December 19, 1887, pp. 152–153.
66. SU Faculty 1879–90, June 5, 1890, pp. 227–228.
67. SU Faculty 1879–90, May 28, 1889, p. 195.
68. SU Faculty 1890–1904, November 17, 1896, p. 132.
69. SU Curators-Trustees 1869–1912, June 5–8, 1886, pp. 124–125.
70. SU Faculty 1879–90, November 9, 1885, pp. 92–94.
71. SU Faculty 1879–90, November 7, 1887, p. 150.
72. Clara Stearns Scarbrough, *Land of Good Water: A Williamson County, Texas, History* (Georgetown: Williamson County Sun Publishers, 1973), p. 249.
73. SU Faculty 1879–90, December 9, 1884, p. 71, and December 18, 1885, p. 98.
74. SU Faculty 1879–90, May 25, 1887, p. 137.
75. SU Curators-Trustees 1869–1912, June 1–6, 1888, p. 199.
76. SU Curators-Trustees 1869–1912, June 7–11, 1889, p. 206.
77. Lockett, "Lockett Autobiography," pp. 29–48.
78. Ibid., p. 251.
79. Ibid., pp. 154–213.
80. Ibid., p. 175.
81. Brown, *Hyer: The Man I Knew*, p. 45. The Mood house was on the northwest corner and the church parsonage was to be on the southeast corner.
82. CCSB #8, news article entitled "Church Dedicated," 1896. In her biography of her father, Ray Hyer Brown (see bibliography) states that Hyer, though not an architect, designed the building. Mrs. Brown wrote her biography, as she says, largely from memory and, writing half a century later, probably confused Hyer's role in the construction process. Hyer's love for the building is undoubted. She says he made the communion table and carved the words "In Remembrance of Me" by hand. She says that though in later years he became a member of other churches, "in his heart this, I think, remained his church home" (p. 46).
83. Scarbrough, *Williamson County History*, p. 248.
84. Lockett, "Lockett Autobiography," pp. 188–189. The catalogs do not begin listing the chair until 1903.
85. SU Trustees 1871–92, June 6, 1891, pp. 162–163.
86. SU Curators-Trustees 1869–1912, May 30–June 2, 1895, p. 292.
87. SU Faculty 1890–1904, March 3, 1896, p. 119.
88. SU Trustees 1894–1907, May 29–June 1, 1896, pp. 43–45.
89. CCSB #3, Letter to the Curators on the state of the building fund campaign. Mimeographed sheet of June 17, 1897, attached to the front inside cover.
90. CCSB #12.
91. SU Trustees 1894–1907, May 27–30, 1898, pp. 91–111.
92. Ibid., p. 107.
93. SU Curators-Trustees 1869–1912, Report to the Annual Conferences, in minutes of May 27–30, 1898, pp. 342–344.
94. Scarbrough, *Williamson County History*, p. 248.
95. CCSB #8, "Southwestern University," article in undesignated newspaper.
96. Scarbrough, *Williamson County History*, p. 248.
97. SU Curators-Trustees 1869–1912, June 2–5, 1893, p. 272.
98. GC, Letter to Hon. Heber Stone from W. A. Shaw, Dallas, May 14, 1897.
99. SU Curators-Trustees 1869–1912, May 29–30, 1897, pp. 315–316.
100. Lockett, "Lockett Autobiography," pp. 189–190.
101. SU Faculty 1890–1904, June 1, 1897, pp. 146–147.
102. SU Curators-Trustees 1869–1912, May 30, 1897, p. 317.
103. CCSB #4, Letters of July 3, 1890, July 18, 1891, and May 7. 1894. SU Curators-Trustees 1869–1912, May 28–June 1, 1897, pp. 319, 327–328. At the time of Pritchett's death in May 1908, the faculty adopted a resolution stating that "no man in Texas has had a greater influence upon the education of our state, and that influence has been uniformly good. We, as an institution, have lost one of our best friends." SU Faculty 1891–1912, May 12, 1908, p. 104.
104. Jones, *SU 1840–1961*, p. 211.
105. Brown, *Hyer: The Man I Knew*, pp. 36–37.
106. Ibid., pp. 38–41. The Special Collections section of the SLC possesses an X-ray picture made by Hyer in the summer of 1899. Presidents, Score Correspondence 1947–49.
107. SU Curators-Trustees 1869–1912, May 28–June 1, 1897, pp. 326–328.
108. SU Curators-Trustees 1869–1912, July 6, 1897, pp. 330–333.
109. SU Curators-Trustees 1869–1912, May 27–30, 1898, pp. 338–339.
110. SU Faculty 1890–1904, May 30, 1898, p. 169.

CHAPTER X
Expansion during the Hyer Years (1898–1911)

1. Census figures for 1870 show that of these 1,573 people, 1,327 (84.4 percent) were white, 246 (15.6 percent) were black.
2. M. B. Lockett says that when he came to Georgetown in 1886 its population was about 1,500, certainly not above 2,000 (see the section on Lockett in Chapter IX). Clara Scarbrough reports the following population figures: 1870, 500 people or less; 1878, 1,500 people; 1890, 2,447 people; 1900, 2,790 people. See Clara Stearns Scarbrough, *Land of Good Water: A Williamson County, Texas, History* (Georgetown: Williamson County Sun Publishers, 1973), pp. 244, 345–346.
3. Ray Hyer Brown, *Robert Stewart Hyer: The Man I Knew* (Salado, Tex.: The Anson Jones Press, 1957), p. 24.
4. Ibid., pp. 179–180.
5. Ibid., p. 94. Mrs. Brown, working from memory rather than records, dates this incident to 1903. Records do not indicate such a trip in 1903, and it must have occurred after their return from the trip to the Ecumenical Conference in London, as indicated by Ralph Wood Jones, *Southwestern University 1840–1961* (Austin: Jenkins Publishing Co., 1973), p. 218.
6. Brown, *Hyer: The Man I Knew*, pp. 65, 89.
7. Ibid., p. 18.
8. Ibid., p. 44.
9. Ibid., pp. 19–21.
10. Ibid., pp. 22–24.
11. Ibid., pp. 42–43. Ray Hyer Brown, Regent Hyer's daughter, received a Diploma in Expression from Southwestern in 1910.
12. SU Curators-Trustees 1869–1912, May 25–28, 1900, p. 358.
13. Brown, *Hyer: The Man I Knew*, p. 43.
14. Ibid., p. 28.
15. Ibid., pp. 28–29.
16. Ibid., pp. 29–30.

17. Ibid., pp. 30–31.
18. Ibid., p. 30.
19. Ibid., p. 113.
20. Ibid., pp. 54–58.
21. Ibid., p. 74.
22. Mellville Beveridge Lockett, "Autobiography of M. B. Lockett," 1916, p. 226.
23. Southwestern, *Catalogue Southwestern University 1898–99* (Georgetown: News Print, 1898–99), pp. 13–14. Description probably written by Hyer.
24. David G. Woodcock, "Our Buildings Shape Us," typescript, September 8, 1998.
25. SU Trustees 1894–1907, May 27, 1899, p. 146.
26. SU Trustees 1894–1907, June 30–August, 1899, pp. 157–161, 176–178.
27. SU Trustees 1894–1907, May 26, 1900, p. 232.
28. Three of the original pews are now located on the first floor of the building to provide seating for visitors. Their length, however, has been cut down from the original dimensions.
29. SU Trustees 1894–1907, May 26, 1900, pp. 228–236.
30. SU Trustees 1894–1907, May 23, 1902, pp. 331–354. The Endowment fund also had a cash balance of $114.15, making a total of $650.80 in the Endowment fund.
31. CCSB #12, article entitled "Endowment for Southwestern University."
32. SU Curators-Trustees 1869–1912, May 26–29, 1899, p. 350; May 25–28, 1900, p. 361; May 24–25, 1901, p. 373.
33. CCSB #15, Harrison's article is dated August 14, 1902.
34. SU Curators-Trustees 1869–1912, October 1, 1902, pp. 385–389.
35. SU Curators-Trustees 1869–1912, June 4–6, 1904, p. 419, and June 2–5, 1905, pp. 435–453.
36. SU Curators-Trustees 1869–1912, June 4–6, 1904, pp. 419–423. Also, CCSB #15. Hyer and Harrison published their exchange of letters in the *Texas Christian Advocate* in June, 1904.
37. CCSB #15, W. Wiess, Beaumont, "Endowment for Southwestern University," *Texas Christian Advocate*, [October or November 1907].
38. SU Curators-Trustees 1869–1912, May 29–30, 1908, p. 535.
39. Brown, *Hyer: The Man I Knew*, p. 65.
40. Southwestern, *Catalogue for 1898–99*. Also, SU Curators-Trustees 1869–1912, May 26–29, 1899, p. 350.
41. SU Curators-Trustees 1869–1912, May 29–June 1, 1903, pp. 395–403.
42. SU Curators-Trustees 1869–1912, June 4–6, 1904, p. 417.
43. SU Curators-Trustees 1869–1912, May 29–30, 1908, p. 532.
44. CCSB #4, Letter to C. C. Cody from the chairman of the Committee on Summer School at Harvard University, responding to Cody's inquiry of November 20.
45. SU Faculty 1890–1904, May 19, 1896, p. 125, and May 18, 1897, pp. 144–145.
46. SU Faculty 1890–1904, January 27, 1903.
47. SU Curators-Trustees 1869–1912, May 24–25, 1901, p. 367.
48. SU Curators-Trustees 1869–1912, Trustees, June 1–4, 1908, p. 535.
49. SU Faculty 1879–90, June 5, 1890, pp. 227–228.
50. SU Faculty 1890–1904, May 31, 1892, p. 47.
51. SU Curators-Trustees 1869–1912, May 26–29, 1899, p. 351.
52. Southwestern, *Bulletin of Southwestern University* [for 1903–04] (Georgetown: 1903–04), p. 107.
53. SU Trustees 1894–1907, May 29–30, 1903, p. 361.
54. SU Trustees 1894–1907, October 29, 1904, p. 400.
55. SU Trustees 1894–1907, June 2–3, 1905, p. 406.
56. SU Trustees 1894–1907, May 24–27, 1907, pp. 467–510.
57. CCSB #12, R. S. Hyer, "Address to the Annual Conferences," *Texas Christian Advocate*, Fall 1898. Hyer did not include Texas A&M in its list. Its numbers have been supplied from another source.
58. CCSB #6, presumably C. C. Cody, "Southwestern University," September 24, 1908.
59. SU Trustees 1894–1907, May 29–30, 1903, pp. 358–359.
60. Samuel Wood Geiser, *Medical Education in Dallas 1900–1910* (Dallas: Southern Methodist University Press, 1952). See footnote 27, p. 15.
61. Geiser, *Medical Education in Dallas*.
62. Lockett, "Lockett Autobiography," pp. 225–226.
63. SU Trustees 1894–1907, June 24, 1903, p. 368.
64. Abraham Flexner, *Medical Education in the United States and Canada: A Report to the Carnegie Foundation for the Advancement of Teaching* (New York: Carnegie Foundation for the Advancement of Education, 1910), p. 310.
65. Geiser, *Medical Education in Dallas*. Geiser says that he tried to find a charter for the Texas College of Physicians and Surgeons in the office of the Secretary of State in Austin but could find none. He surmises that the medical college operated under the general charter of Southwestern University. A more likely explanation for his not finding the charter is that the school took over the name and charter of the Dallas Medical College, as revealed in the letter to the joint committee, and did not seek a new charter.
66. SU Curators-Trustees 1869–1912, June 4–6, 1904, p. 427.
67. *The Sou'wester*, 1909.
68. SU Curators-Trustees 1869–1912, June 4–6, 1904, pp. 425–426.
69. Brown, *Hyer: The Man I Knew*, p. 117.
70. Geiser, *Medical Education in Dallas*.
71. CCSB #5, "Big Dual Affair," probably *Dallas News*, April 4, 1905.
72. SU Trustees 1894–1907, June 2–3, 1905, pp. 410–411.
73. SU Faculty 1891–1912, September 14, October 4, and October 17, 1905, pp. 37–40.
74. SU Trustees 1894–1907, June 1–2, 1906, typed insert between pp. 452–453.
75. SU Curators-Trustees 1869–1912, June 9–11, 1910, Liabilities, p. 647.
76. John O. McReynolds et al., "Report to Board of Trustees," Georgetown, May 28, 1908.
77. Flexner, *Report on Medical Education*, p. 310.
78. SU Curators-Trustees 1869–1912, June 9–12, 1911, pp. 675–676.
79. Geiser, *Medical Education in Dallas*. SU Trustees 1913–25, June 12–13, 1919, p. 310.
80. Flexner, *Report on Medical Education*, pp. 309–312.
81. Geiser, *Medical Education in Dallas*. The current Southwestern Medical School of the University of Texas dates from 1943. It has no relationship to the previous Southwestern University Medical College.
82. CCSB #12. Article in an unnamed but probably Georgetown newspaper of May 22, 1902.
83. SU Curators-Trustees 1869–1912, May 23–24, 1902, pp. 378–379.
84. CCSB #12, "Dr. Hyer Will Remain," unnamed newspaper, June, 1902.
85. SU Curators-Trustees 1869–1912, June 2–5, 1905, pp. 439–444.
86. CCSB #15, Letter to the editor from A. P. Smith of Valley Mills entitled "Attack Upon the S.W.U. and Georgetown," *Texas Christian Advocate*, 1903.
87. John M. Moore and John R. Nelson, *Texas Methodist Educational Convention: Proceedings and Addresses* ([Dallas]: Blaylock Publishing Company, [1906]), p. 223.
88. Moore and Nelson, *Educational Convention 1906*, pp. 225–226.
89. CCSB #15, "Texas Educational Commission," editorial of April 26, 1906.
90. Jon D. Swartz, *J. Frank Dobie* (Georgetown: MHHS, 1988).
91. SU Faculty 1890–1904, April 23, 1900.
92. Brown, *Hyer: The Man I Knew*, pp. 101–102.
93. *Sou'wester*, issues of 1904–1911.
94. SU Curators-Trustees 1869–1912, June 11–14, 1909, p. 563.
95. SU Curators-Trustees 1869–1912, May 25–28, 1900, pp. 360–361.
96. SU Trustees 1894–1907, February 13, 1905, p. 402.
97. *Sou'wester*, issues of 1904–1911.
98. SU Faculty 1891–1912, May 2 and May 9, 1911, pp. 202–203.
99. Jones, *SU 1840–1961*, p. 237.
100. SU Faculty 1891–1912, May 30, 1909, pp. 130–131.

101. SU Faculty 1891–1912, December 8, 1906, and January 15, 1907, pp. 63–65.
102. PANC, Box 9. Folder 8, p. 139. "Pirates' Football 'Squad' (12 Men) of 1897 Recalled," *Austin Statesman*, November 5, 1943.
103. SU Faculty 1891–1912, May 5 and May 12, 1908, pp. 103, 105.
104. *Sou'wester*, issues of 1909–1911.
105. SU Curators-Trustees 1869–1912, May 29–30, 1908, p. 542. Albert G. Sanders was born in 1885. As a student in 1946–1950, the author knew Sanders, who was a professor of Spanish at Millsaps College. T. J. Mosley taught physics at Southwestern after his return from England. He left Southwestern in 1916 for Washington, D.C., where he was associated with the National Bureau of Standards. In 1918 he was with the Navy Department, where he stayed until 1923, when he took a position at the Forest Products laboratory. He also wrote extensively for technical publications. In 1924 he was awarded first place by *The Forum* magazine for a story entitled "The Secret of the Crossroads." It was a sociological study of the race problem. *The Megaphone*, "Former S. U. Student Wins Honors as Writer. T. J. Mosley, S. U. Student, Professor and Rhodes Scholar, Gets $1000 as First Prize," October 7, 1924. McDugald K. McLean was born on July 16, 1884. He died at the age of thirty-six on September 8, 1922. His given name is sometimes carried in Southwestern records as "McDougal," but it was properly McDugald Keener McLean. The "McDugald" was his mother's maiden name.
106. Anonymous, "Letter That Refers to the Honor Council," Georgetown. October 17, 1913. SU, SLC, SC. At the bottom of the October 17, 1913, letter, is a statement by someone who must have been studying the subject: "Algebra exam by May Munge 1882, is signed at bottom: 'I received no assistance.'"
107. SU Faculty 1891–1912, April 7, 1903, and October 24, 1905, p. 41.
108. CCSB #16, "The Ward Memorial Building," unnamed newspaper, probably 1910.
109. Allen Collection, Box 2, Laura B. Riggs, "Southwestern University's Self-Perception 1876–1986: A Study of Its Catalogs and Yearbooks."
110. Norman W. Spellmann, *Growing a Soul: The Story of A. Frank Smith* (Dallas: SMU Press, 1979), p. 24. His quotation is from an article found in the Cody Scrapbooks.
111. SU Faculty 1891–1912, March 2, 1909, pp. 124–125.
112. SU Faculty 1891–1912, April 27, 1909, p. 133.
113. SU Curators-Trustees 1869–1912, June 11–14, 1909, pp. 576–577.
114. CCSB #6, presumably C. C. Cody, "Southwestern University," probably *Texas Christian Advocate*, September 24, 1908.
115. All of the material on the Barcus family comes from the following two sources unless otherwise indicated. Joseph Garland Barcus, *Barcus-Barkhurst Family* (Waco: Texian Press, 1996), and Jackson B. Cox, "History and Genealogy of Jackson Berry Cox and Wife Julia Barcus," typescript, September 1, 1937.
116. Barcus Family Papers, Scrapbook 4.1, handwritten letter headed "Stanford Chapel," no date.
117. Mary M. Standifer, "Barcus, John M.," HBTO, July 23, 2002.
118. Claude Carr Cody, John M. Barcus, and Laura Kuykendall, *The Book of Southwestern* (Georgetown: Von Boeckmann Jones Co., 1923), p. 17.
119. SU Faculty 1913–34, April 4, 1922, p. 244.
120. Spellmann, *Growing a Soul*, p. 27.
121. CCSB #12, "S. W. U. Commencement," unnamed newspaper, about May 27–June 1, 1903.
122. CCSB #12.
123. Jacquelyn Dowd Hall, *Revolt against Chivalry: Jessie Daniel Ames and the Women's Campaign against Lynching* (New York: Columbia University Press, 1979), p. 6. Most of the Ames material, except for that related to Southwestern, comes from Hall's book.
124. Ibid., p. 8.
125. Presidential Archives, Jessie D. Ames Files, "Mrs. Jessie D. Ames dies Monday in Austin," *WC Sun*, February 24, 1972, Sec. 2, p. 5.
126. Hall, *Revolt against Chivalry*, p. 28. Mrs. J. M. Daniel was not only devoted to her church but also to Southwestern University. She contributed $1,000 to the Cody Foundation in 1914 and challenged the Woman's Missionary Society of the local Methodist Church to match her $1,000 gift to the $300,000 campaign with an equal $1,000 gift, which it did. See *Southwestern Bulletin*, April 1914, p. 2.
127. SU Ex Com 1923–36, October 11, 1923.
128. *Megaphone*, "Ex-student Delivers Address at Chapel. Mrs. Ames gives Interesting Talk on Constitution of U. S.," November 18, 1924.
129. SU Trustees 1925–34, June 14, 1926, p. 48.
130. Essay entitled "Jessie Daniel Ames" by Martha Mitten Allen, in Jon D. Swartz, ed., *Jessie Daniel Ames: An Exhibition at Southwestern University* (Georgetown: Mood-Heritage Museum, 1986).
131. "Mrs. Ames Speaks Here on Race Problem," *Megaphone*, November 19, 1929, p. 1.
132. Joanna Fountain-Schroeder, *Jessie Daniel Ames' Book Collection* (Georgetown: SU, 1986), pp. vii–x.
133. Jessie Daniel Ames, "Jessie Daniel Ames Papers: Inventory," University of North Carolina at Chapel Hill.
134. The western part of the present Czech Republic was called Bohemia prior to the end of World War I. The word "Czech" was not commonly used with reference to the land, the language, or the people prior to that time.
135. Schneeberger Prochazkova et al., *Osmdesat Let Milosti (Eighty Years of Grace)* (Prague: Evangelical Methodist Church, 2000), p. 12.
136. University of Texas Institute of Texan Cultures, *The Czech Texans* (1972), p. 6.
137. SU Curators-Trustees 1869–1912, May 29–30, 1908, pp. 539–540.
138. Joseph D. Thomas, "Two Letters from J. D. Thomas," Dallas, September 10 and October 22, 1970. From the author's personal files.
139. Bess and Hallie Crutchfield were nieces of Dr. & Mrs. John R. Allen. The Allens took them in as daughters after the death of their mother, Mrs. Allen's sister. The two girls lived with them while attending Southwestern. After his superannuation in 1921 and the death of his wife in 1923, Allen lived with Hallie (Mrs. George F. Pierce) in Dallas until his death in 1937. Since Allen served in effect as the father of Bess, he was Bishop A. Frank Smith's father-in-law.
140. SU Trustees 1913–25, June 13–14, 1913, p. 8.
141. "James Fred Rippy," *Southwestern Magazine* 48 (June 1930): 25.
142. SU Trustees 1957–60, November 11, 1960, p. 297.
143. Clinton Machann and James W. Mendl, *Krasna Amerika: A Study of the Texas Czechs, 1851–1939* (Austin: Eakin Press, 1983), p. 184.
144. Institute of Texan Cultures, *Czech Texans*, p. 13.
145. SU Curators-Trustees 1869–1912, June 9–11, 1910, pp. 600–603.
146. Paul Neff Garber, *The Methodists of Continental Europe* (New York: Board of Missions and Church Extension of the Methodist Church, 1949), pp. 26–27, 85–86.
147. Ibid., p. 94.
148. Marian Bartak Malac, "Letters of Marian Bartak Malac," Blairsville, Georgia, October 6, 2000, and February 19, 2001. From the author's personal files. Mrs. Malac, Bartak's daughter, was kind enough to furnish the author with two letters and various other materials about the life of her father. She attended Southwestern in 1945–1946 for her freshman year but returned to Prague with the family in the summer of 1946. She attended Charles University there until she met her husband, whom she married in April 1949. They were forced to flee the Communist government and arrived in the United States in October 1949. She was able to complete her degree at Duke University, and her husband obtained a Master of Forestry degree. Her sister, Helen Bartak Trimarchi, also attended Southwestern from 1949 to 1951, completing her degree at Duke in 1952. The author met Dr. Bartak during World War II in Nashville, where he was a high school student.
149. Malac, "Bartak Malac Letters," October 6, 2000. Also, MKSB #36, "Jos. P. Bartak, S. U. Alumnus, Arrives from Prison Camp," *WC Sun*, June 12, 1942.
150. The description of Rollins comes from Dr. T. Walter Herbert, Professor of English, Holder of the Herman Brown Chair, and University Scholar at Southwestern, whose undergraduate study at Harvard overlapped the last two years of Rollins's life, and who met Rollins there. Rollins had already been diagnosed with cancer.

151. Judson S. Custer and Jeff H. Campbell, *Dobie at Southwestern University: The Beginnings of His Literary Career, 1906–1911* (Austin: Jenkins Publishing Company, 1981), p. 16. Taken by Jeff H. Campbell from J. Frank Dobie, "Some Things Kept from College," *Southwestern University Ex-Students' Newsmagazine,* May 1957, p. 3.
152. Richard T. Fleming, "Rollins, Hyder Edward (1889–1958)," HBTO, July 23, 2002.
153. Custer and Campbell, *Dobie at Southwestern,* p. 15.
154. Ibid., pp. 71, 79.
155. Fleming, "Rollins."
156. Swartz, *J. Frank Dobie.*
157. Fleming, "Rollins."
158. Hyder E. Rollins, "Letter Donating Recommendations from Former Southwestern Professors," Georgetown, April 22, 1958. SU, SLC, SC, Small Collections, Hyder E. Rollins Gift, Box 3, Folder 2.

CHAPTER XI
The Removal Controversy: Hyer versus Cody (1907–1911)

1. SU Curators-Trustees 1869–1912, June 7–11, 1889, pp. 204, 207.
2. SU Curators-Trustees 1869–1912, May 29–June 1, 1896, pp. 302–304, and May 28–June 1, 1897, p. 311.
3. SU Curators-Trustees 1869–1912, June 1–4, 1906, pp. 458–459.
4. SU Faculty 1891–1912, December 17, 1907, p. 90.
5. Mellville Beveridge Lockett, "Autobiography of M. B. Lockett," 1916, pp. 225–226.
6. SU Curators-Trustees 1869–1912, May 28–30, 1908, pp. 524, 528.
7. Jane Brown McCook, *Claude Carr Cody* (Georgetown: In Cody, Hyer, McLean, Sanders, Young tract of the Mood-Heritage Museum Hall of Honor Historical Sketches, [1984–1994]). Also, article entitled "T. H. Cody Weds Miss Lockett," of unknown date in unnamed newspaper in CCSB #14.
8. CCSB #7, assorted materials on Cody.
9. CCSB #4, eleven grade reports from fall 1871 to May 1, 1875.
10. CCSB #7, copy of a letter from Haygood.
11. Ralph Wood Jones, *Southwestern University 1840–1961* (Austin: Jenkins Publishing Co., 1973), pp. 167–168.
12. The four original letters of Alexander H. Stevens of November 9 and December 25, 1860, of November 16, 1861, and of November 7, 1873, are found in CCSB #4. The three letters reprinted in the newspaper are found in CCSB #8. The newspaper article referring to Cody's lecture on Stephens is found in CCSB #7.
13. CCSB #4.
14. CCSB #7.
15. Many different items of material from CCSB #4, CCSB #7, CCSB #14, and CCSB #17.
16. SU Curators-Trustees 1869–1912, May 23–24, 1902, p. 384.
17. SU Curators-Trustees 1869–1912, June 4–6, 1904, pp. 415–419, 427.
18. SU Trustees 1894–1907, June 4–6, 1904, p. 382.
19. SU Trustees 1894–1907, February 7, 1906, p. 424; April 4, 1906, pp. 425–426; April 27, 1906, p. 428. Lockett, "Lockett Autobiography," p. 227, reports that add-ons finally brought the cost of the building up to $60,000.
20. SU Curators-Trustees 1869–1912, June 1–4, 1906, pp. 454–466.
21. CCSB #15, Letter of July 5, 1906, by John R. Allen to the *Texas Christian Advocate,* entitled "Notes from Southwestern University."
22. SU Trustees 1894–1907, May 24–27, 1907, p. 483.
23. SU Curators-Trustees 1869–1912, December 27, 1907, pp. 511–513.
24. SU Curators-Trustees 1869–1912, June 1–4, 1906, pp. 454–466.
25. Ibid.
26. SU Curators-Trustees 1869–1912, May 24–27, 1907, p. 484.
27. SU Curators-Trustees 1869–1912, June 9–12, 1911, p. 681.
28. SU Curators-Trustees 1869–1912, May 29–30, 1908, p. 540.
29. Ibid., pp. 519–543. Lockett's figure of $64,059.94 for 1907 presumably includes the actions taken by the Trustees in December 1907. It is roughly equivalent to the Trustee figure of "about $60,000" in 1908.
30. Lockett, "Lockett Autobiography," p. 227.
31. Robert Glenn Massengale, "Collegiate Education in the Methodist Episcopal Church, South 1902–1939" (doctoral dissertation, Yale University, 1950), p. 114.
32. Jones, *SU 1840–1961,* pp. 221–222.
33. SU Curators-Trustees 1869–1912, May 29–30, 1908, p. 525. A Biblical Bond form seen by the author denoting that the donor was a member of the "500 Club" was for $300.00. The 1925 figures come from an audit by Ernst and Ernst reported in Board minutes for December 17, 1931, p. 335. The 1978 figure comes from the October 20, 1978, Trustee minutes, p. 12. See SU Trustees 1978–85.
34. SU Trustees 1925–34. The 1925 figures come from the Ernst and Ernst audit reported in Board minutes for December 17, 1931, p. 335.
35. Presidential Archives, Jesse H. Jones Files, Letter from Jesse H. Jones to Dee Simpson, February 26, 1947, congratulating him on being awarded an honorary degree by Southwestern.
36. Lionel V. Patenaude, "Jones, Jesse Holman," HBTO, December 4, 2002.
37. Jesse Jones Files, "Jesse H. Jones Dies Friday in Houston," *Austin Statesman,* June 2, 1956.
38. Presidential Archives, Jesse H. Jones Scholarships Files, "Jesse H. Jones Has Been A&M's Most Consistent Backer for Three Decades," *The Texas Aggie,* May 10, 1950.
39. Presidential Archives, Mrs. Alma Thomas Files, copy of a document to the Board of Trustees from Jesse H. Jones, April 24, 1937. According to the terms of the agreement, Jones would have given Southwestern $1,000 a year between 1913 and 1937, either $24,000 or $25,000 by 1937. From 1937 until he fulfilled the total $32,500 amount he pledged in that year, he paid the University $1,300 each year.
40. Presidential Archives, Seth Ward Bible Chair, July 23, 1970.
41. SU Curators-Trustees 1869–1912, May 24–27, 1907, p. 473.
42. SU Curators-Trustees 1869–1912, June 9–11, 1910, p. 609.
43. John H. McLean, *Reminiscences* (Nashville: Publishing House M. E. Church, South, 1918), p. 83.
44. CCSB #12, article of April 7, 1898, by Holt entitled "Educational Policy of Texas Methodism," in unnamed newspaper or Church paper.
45. CCSB #15, Article of October 2, 1902, entitled "Some Timely Corrections."
46. SU Ex Com 1907–23, three-page insert between pp. 16 and 17.
47. CCSB #16, undated article entitled "The Ward Memorial Building" from unnamed newspaper.
48. SU Curators-Trustees 1869–1912, June 9–11, 1910, pp. 603–604. Also, Jones, *SU 1840–1961,* pp. 225–226.
49. Jones, *SU 1840–1961,* p. 240.
50. CCSB #16, Article of March 15, 1910, entitled "Would Have S.W.U. Move to Ft. Worth," in *The News.*
51. SU Curators-Trustees 1869–1912, May 26–29, 1899, p. 346.
52. Jones, *SU 1840–1961,* p. 241.
53. Ibid.
54. CCSB #3, Letters of October 20 and November 6, 1909.
55. Judson S. Custer and Jeff H. Campbell, *Dobie at Southwestern University: The Beginnings of His Literary Career, 1906–1911* (Austin: Jenkins Publishing Company, 1981), p. 80.
56. CCSB #3, Letter of March 15, 1910, from R. S. Hyer to H. A. Boaz.
57. SU Faculty 1891–1912, March 22 and March 29, 1910.
58. Lockett, "Lockett Autobiography," pp. 170–172.
59. Ibid., pp. 228, 231.
60. Article of March 24, 1910, in the *Texas Christian Advocate,* and of March 25, 1910, in the Dallas *News,* reported by Glen DeWitt Willbern, "A History of Southwestern University Georgetown Texas," master's thesis, University of Texas, p. 152.
61. CCSB #16, Article of March 31, 1910, in [*The News*?], entitled "Dr. Hyer in Answer to Dr. Boaz."
62. CCSB #16.
63. CCSB #16, article of April 12, 1910, by J. R. Mood in unnamed newspaper, entitled "Founder's Son Writes," and article of April 23, 1910,

by R. G. Mood in unnamed newspaper, entitled "Calls Dr. Boaz to Strict Account."
64. CCSB #16, article of April 9, 1910, in *The News*, entitled "Discusses Plan to Move Southwestern University."
65. CCSB #16, article of April 21, 1910, in the *Texas Christian Advocate*, "Dr. H. A. Boaz Replies to Dr. R. S. Hyer."
66. CCSB #16, copy of questionnaire of April 18, 1910, to "Dear Friend."
67. MKSB #20, p. 8, "Real Beginning of S. M. U.," taken from the Dallas *News* of April 27, 1911.
68. Ray Hyer Brown, *Robert Stewart Hyer: The Man I Knew* (Salado, Tex.: The Anson Jones Press, 1957), p. 124.
69. CCSB #5, Letter of April 20, 1910.
70. CCSB #5, Letter of April 23, 1910.
71. Lockett, "Lockett Autobiography," p. 228.
72. Brown, *Hyer: The Man I Knew*, pp. 122, 124.
73. MKSB #20, p. 8, "Real Beginning of S. M. U.," taken from the Dallas *News* of April 27, 1911.
74. Brown, *Hyer: The Man I Knew*, p. 124.
75. Lockett, "Lockett Autobiography," p. 230.
76. Jones, *SU 1840–1961*, p. 243, fn. 13. Letter of April 20, 1906, contained in the SLC, Special Collections, Cody Collection, Removal File.
77. MKSB #20, "Real Beginning of S. M. U.," *Dallas News*, April 27, 1911.
78. Lockett, "Lockett Autobiography," p. 230.
79. CCSB #16, article of June 10, 1910, in *The News*, entitled "Board of Trustees Opposed to Removal: Vote Against Changing Location of Southwestern."
80. CCSB #5, Letter of J. M. Richardson, Sherman, Texas, of April 25, 1910, to Cody.
81. CCSB #16, article of April 22, 1910, in *The News*, entitled "Polytechnic College's Offer to Southwestern."
82. CCSB #16, article dated April 30, 1910, in *The News*, entitled "H. A. Boaz's Statement: Defines His Attitude in Regard to Southwestern University Removal Proposition."
83. CCSB #16, Letter from Buttrick to Barcus of May 20, 1910, contained in article of May 25, 1910, in the Dallas *News*, entitled "Southwestern University: Citizens' Club of Georgetown and University Committee Present Statistical Statement."
84. CCSB #16, article of May 1, 1910, in the Dallas *News* containing the Boaz statements.
85. CCSB #16, article of May 4, 1910, in *The News*, entitled "Southwestern University: Some Historical Facts Are Related About This Church Institution."
86. CCSB #16, article of May 14, 1910, entitled "Dallas to Work for University."
87. CCSB #16, article of May 19, 1910, in unnamed newspaper, entitled "Dallas After Southwestern."
88. CCSB #16, article entitled "To Move Southwestern," in unnamed newspaper quoting the *Houston Post* of May 10, 1910.
89. CCSB #5, Letter of May 17, 1910 to C. C. Cody.
90. Jones, *SU 1840–1961*, pp. 242–243.
91. CCSB #16, articles of about May 18, 1910, in *The News*, entitled "Call Mass Meeting to Get University" and "Mass Meeting to Be Held Tonight."
92. CCSB #16, night letter of May 25, 1910, to Bishop W. A. Candler, Atlanta, Georgia, from John O. Daniel, President of Chamber of Commerce, John O. McReynolds, Vice Chairman of University Committee, and Robt. S. Hyer, President S. W. U.
93. CCSB #16, Letter of June 6, 1910, from Bishop W. A. Candler to "Dear Friend" [C. C. Cody].
94. CCSB #5, Letter of May 30, 1910.
95. Lockett, "Lockett Autobiography," pp. 230–231.
96. CCSB #16, article of May 26, 1910, in *The News*, entitled "Delegation to Dallas: Number of Prominent Citizens and Business Men Depart from Georgetown."
97. CCSB #16, article of May 27, 1910, in the Dallas *News*, entitled "University Officials Invite City's Offer." Also article entitled "Brooks' Invitation to Dallas."
98. CCSB #16, Article of May 25, 1910, in the Dallas *News*, entitled "Georgetown Ideal Place: Citizens Suggest That Dallas Build New School and Cease Efforts for Southwestern University."
99. CCSB #16, Article of June 10, 1910, in the Dallas *News*, entitled "$400,000 Raised to Offer Southwestern: Success Crowns Campaign to Secure Fund for Big Methodist Institution."
100. SU Curators-Trustees 1869–1912, June 9–11, 1910, pp. 579–654.
101. Ibid.
102. CCSB #16, article of June 11, 1910, in *The News*, entitled "Think Conferences May Act: Rev. J. M. Peterson Telephones Statement After Action Is Taken."
103. CCSB #16, article of June 17, 1910, in *The News*, entitled "Mr. Bishop Favors Removal."
104. CCSB #5, Letter of June 24, 1910, from Robert A. John, Attorney at Law, to C. C. Cody.
105. CCSB #3, Letter of August 16, 1910, from Robert Gibbs Mood to C. C. Cody.
106. Oscar Fitzgerald Sensabaugh, "Recollections," July 10, 1951. Sensabaugh's manuscript was kindly provided by Gerald R. Sensabaugh, Jr., of Georgetown, his grandson.
107. CCSB #16, article of August 7, 1910, probably in *The News*, entitled "Dallas' Attitude Given Expression . . . Chamber Commerce Announces Proposition for University Without Regard to Southwestern University."
108. CCSB #16, article of Sept. 13, 1910, in *The News*, entitled "Southwestern University Removal Is Opposed."
109. Willbern, "History of Southwestern," pp. 168–170. Minutes of the West Texas Conference, October, 1910.
110. Willbern, "History of Southwestern," p. 171. Minutes of the West Texas and Texas Conferences.
111. CCSB #16, article of November 11, 1910, in *The News*, entitled "Highly Compliments Baylor University: Endowment of $200,000."
112. CCSB #3, Letter of January 12, 1911, from A. K. Ragsdale, San Antonio, to C. C. Cody.
113. CCSB #3, Letter of January 20, 1911, from John M. Barcus, Weatherford, to C. C. Cody.
114. CCSB #3, Letters of January 26 and February 3, 1911, from J. Sam Barcus, Cisco, to C. C. Cody.
115. CCSB #3, Letter of March 9, 1911, from E. Hightower, State Sunday School Conference, Waco, to C. C. Cody.
116. MKSB #20, p. 7, "Dr. Hyer Elected President of Southern Methodist University," from the Dallas *News*, April 14, 1911.
117. SU Curators-Trustees 1869–1912, June 9–12, 1911, pp. 660–669.
118. Ibid., pp. 670–673.
119. Ibid., pp. 674–675.
120. Ibid., p. 678.
121. Ibid., pp. 679–680.
122. Brown, *Hyer: The Man I Knew*, p. 126.
123. Jones, *SU 1840–1961*, p. 245, n. 14. Ralph Jones took the quotation from an undated article from an unnamed newspaper found in Scrapbook #9, p. 26, in SLC, Special Collections.
124. Brown, *Hyer: The Man I Knew*, p. 127.
125. Ibid., p. 145.
126. Ibid., p. 142.
127. Ibid., p. 163.
128. Herbert Gambrell, "Herbert Gambrell Letter to Ralph Jones," June 18, 1974. SUPA.
129. LC. Box 2, Folder 9, Letter of July 23, 1921, from Mellie in Dallas to F. D. Love in Georgetown.
130. LC. Box 2, Folder 10, Letter from Pearl to F. D. Love, on July 30, August 6, August 13, or August 20, 1921.
131. "Pegues, Albert Shipp," in *Who Was Who in America with World Notables* (Chicago: Marquis–Who's Who, Inc., 1968), Vol. IV.

132. Lockett, "Lockett Autobiography," p. 235.
133. Ibid.
134. Gambrell, "Gambrell Letter," June 18, 1974.
135. Brown, *Hyer: The Man I Knew*, p. 201.
136. SU Trustees 1925–34, June 3, 1929, p. 214.
137. William C. Finch, conversation comment to WBJ, SU campus, November 9, 2000.
138. William C. Finch, Interviews by Martha Allen, August 1992, four tapes (transcribed), Tape 1, p. 36.
139. William C. Finch, "Annual Report [of President and Officers]," 1953–1961, November 15, 1955, p. 1-6.

CHAPTER XII
A New Mission (1911–1922)

1. Walter Towner, "Walter Towner Welcoming Letter," Dallas, July 24, 1925. SU, SLC, SC, President Folder: Southwestern University: President Charles McTyeire Bishop.
2. MKSB #20, p. 15, "Southwestern University's New President," Houston *Post.*
3. MKSB #36, p. 66, "Dr. & Mrs. C. M. Bishop Make Georgetown Their Home," *WC Sun*, November 22, 1940.
4. Ibid.
5. Herbert Gambrell, "Herbert Gambrell Letter to Ralph Jones," June 18, 1974. SUPA, Ralph Jones File.
6. SU Faculty 1891–1912, September 11, 1911, p. 213.
7. MKSB #20, "Southwestern Notes," September 28, 1912, no page number.
8. MKSB #20, pp. 25–26, "Houston Interested in Homecoming," *WC Sun*, and "Prof. Dobie Promoted," *Georgetown Commercial.*
9. SU Faculty 1891–1912, October 24, 1911, p. 221.
10. SU Curators-Trustees 1869–1912, December 9, 1911, p. 684.
11. Ralph Wood Jones, *Southwestern University 1840–1961* (Austin: Jenkins Publishing Co., 1973), p. 252. Jones cites a newspaper article from the *Georgetown Commercial* of October 6, 1911.
12. MKSB #20, p. 28, "Mrs. Rebecca Fisher's Address at University," *Georgetown Commercial*, May 17, 1912.
13. MKSB #20, p. 27, "Dr. Cody Cannot Forget," *WC Sun.*
14. MKSB #20, p. 21, "Southwestern Song,"
15. MKSB #20, p. 24, "Notice to Automobile Owners," unnamed newspaper.
16. Cody Collection, Incoming Correspondence, Letter of C. M. Bishop to Cody, Aug. 1, 1914. Box 1, Folder 8.
17. SU Ex Com 1907–23, December 10, 1912, p. 36.
18. SU Trustees 1925–34, December 17, 1931, pp. 329–349.
19. SU Curators-Trustees 1869–1912, June 7–8, 1912, pp. 691–713.
20. SU Faculty 1912–13, June 13 14, 1913, pp. 10–11.
21. SU Trustees 1913–25, June 12–13, 1914, pp. 47–48.
22. SU Trustees 1913–25, June 11–12, 1915, pp. 87–89.
23. SU Trustees 1913–25, June 16–17, 1916, pp. 91–111.
24. SU Ex Com 1907–23, August 31, 1917, pp. 78–79.
25. SU Faculty 1913–34, December 11, 1918, p. 148.
26. SU Trustees 1913–25, January 18, 1918, pp. 176–177.
27. SU Ex Com 1907–23, October 12, 1918, pp. 88–89.
28. SU Ex Com 1907–23, February 18, 1919, pp. 89–90.
29. SU Trustees 1913–25, June 12–13, 1919, pp. 294–297.
30. SU Trustees 1913–25, June 14–15, 1918, p. 219.
31. S. Morgan Friedman, "The Inflation Calculator" (http://www.westegg.com/inflation/infl.cgi).
32. SU Trustees 1913–25, June 14–16, 1917, p. 139.
33. SU Ex Com 1907–23, December 16, 1912, pp. 36–37.
34. SU Ex Com 1907–23, January 3 and February 6, 1913, pp. 37–38.
35. SU Ex Com 1907–23, June 13–14, 1913, pp. 13–15, 26.
36. SU Faculty 1913–34, December 15, 1913, p. 14.
37. MKSB #21, p. 11, E. Curtis Vinson, "Endowment for Southwestern University," *Georgetown Commercial*, December 19, 1913.
38. SU Ex Com 1907–23, January 3, 1914, p. 47.
39. SU Trustees 1913–25, January 6, 1914, pp. 26–31.
40. MKSB #22, p. 1, "Southwestern's Great Campaign Launched," *Georgetown Commercial*, February 27, 1914.
41. *Southwestern Bulletin*, April 1914, pp. 2–3.
42. SU Ex Com 1907–23, March 16, 1914. p. 49.
43. SU Ex Com 1907–23, June 4, 1914. pp. 50–51.
44. SU Trustees 1913–25, June 12–13, 1914, p. 43.
45. SU Trustees 1913–25, June 12–13, 1914, p. 46–47.
46. Ibid., pp. 50–66.
47. SU Ex Com 1907–23, July 1, 1914, p. 51.
48. SU Trustees 1913–25, June 11–12, 1915, p. 72.
49. Ibid., p. 88.
50. MKSB #23, p. 52, December 23, 1915.
51. SU Trustees 1925–34, June 16–17, 1916, pp. 95–96.
52. SU Ex Com 1907–23, February 12, April 5–6, May 30, 1916, pp. 62–64.
53. SU Trustees 1913–25, June 16–17, 1916, p. 107.
54. SU Trustees 1913–25, June 14–16, 1917, pp. 126–127.
55. SU Trustees 1913–25, June 16–17, 1916, pp. 103–106.
56. SU Ex Com 1907–23, June 14–16, 1917, pp. 64–65.
57. SU Trustees 1913–25, June 14–16, 1917, p. 127.
58. Ibid., pp. 140–143.
59. SU Ex Com 1907–23, February 23, 1917, pp. 69–70.
60. SU Trustees 1913–25, June 14–16, 1917, pp. 127–128.
61. SU Ex Com 1907–23, September 18, 1917, pp. 80–81.
62. CCSB #6, C. C. Cody, "Texas Methodism and Southwestern University," probably *Texas Christian Advocate*, November 15, 1917.
63. SU Ex Com 1907–23, January 10, 1918, p. 84.
64. SU Trustees 1913–25, June 14–15, 1918, p. 247.
65. SU Ex Com 1907–23, March 20, 1918, p. 85.
66. Southern Association of Colleges and Secondary Schools, A Special Study of Southwestern University, 1934, p. 20.
67. SU Ex Com 1940–41, April 12, 1940, p. 73.
68. SU Trustees 1913–25, June 14–15, 1918, p. 193.
69. SU Faculty 1912–13, February 5, 1913, pp. 22–23.
70. Robert Glenn Massengale, "Collegiate Education in the Methodist Episcopal Church, South 1902–1939" (doctoral dissertation, Yale University), p. 134.
71. SU Trustees 1913–25, June 13–14, 1913, p. 7.
72. SU Faculty 1912–13, October 22, 1912, p. 9.
73. SU Faculty 1912–13, February 5, 1913, p. 23.
74. MKSB #23, p. 36, "S. U. Admitted as Member of Southern States Ass'n," *WC Sun*, November 11, 1915.
75. MKSB #23, p. 76, "Dr. Nichols President of College Ass'n," *Georgetown Commercial*, January 5, 1917.
76. SU Trustees 1913–25, June 14–16, 1917, pp. 126–127.
77. SU Ex Com 1907–23, October 7, 1920, and January 23, 1921, pp. 106–108.
78. *The Megaphone*, "Mrs. McKennon First Woman to Receive B.A. from University," by Ruth Ferguson. Actually the article is from *The Southwestern Magazine* section of *The Megaphone* of December 19, 1933. The three issues of the magazine were printed in the student paper during the 1933–1934 academic year. Also, *Megaphone*, "Legend of the Bell Staged Tomorrow. 8,000 Expected to Witness Pageant," June 3, 1927.
79. *Megaphone*, January 23, 1923, p. 1.
80. Anonymous, "They're More Than Just Old Rocks to Southwestern," *Williamson County Sun[?]*, no date.
81. SU Trustees 1913–25, June 12–13, 1919, p. 309.
82. SU Ex Com 1907–23, May 6, 1919, pp. 90–91.
83. SU Trustees 1913–25, June 9–10, 1920, p. 322.
84. SU Trustees 1913–25, June 7–8, 1922, p. 426.
85. SU Trustees 1925–34, January 8, 1931, p. 282.
86. Paul P. Young, *Ryland Fletcher Young* (Georgetown: In the Cody, Hyer, McLean, Sanders, Young tract of the MHHS, 1982). Most of the facts about Young in this portrayal come from this tract written by his son.
87. SU Trustees 1935–47, May 19, 1943.
88. SU Ex Com 1907–23, November 13, 1916, p. 67.

89. SU Trustees 1913–25, June 14–16, 1917, pp. 133–134.
90. CCSB #6, "Dr. Francis Asbury Mood's Body Removed Last Saturday," *WC Sun*, November 27, 1917.
91. SU Ex Com 1907–23, November 27, 1917, p. 83.
92. SU Ex Com 1907–23, April 26, 1921, pp. 108–110. It was moved once again to its present site a bit closer to Mood Hall in the late 1990s.
93. MKSB #23, p. 52, "The Degree of Bachelor of Music Offered at Southwestern University," *Texas Christian Advocate.*
94. SU Faculty 1913–34, September 19, 1913, pp. 3–6.
95. SU Trustees 1913–25, June 12–13, 1914, p. 36.
96. SU Faculty 1913–34, April 7 and April 15, 1915, p. 41–44.
97. Jones, *SU 1840–1961*, pp. 251, 281. Also, "Scholarship Society National Body Now . . . ; Convention Votes to Rename Body Alpha Chi," *Megaphone*, February 27, 1934. p. 1.
98. SU Trustees 1913–25, June 8–9, 1921, p. 380.
99. Barcus Family Papers, Box 4.
100. MKSB #21, pp. 5, 7, printed flyer June 7, 1913.
101. MKSB #21, p. 42, "The May Festival," *Georgetown Commercial*, February 26, 1915.
102. MKSB #23, p. 11, "Miss Kuykendall Receives High Praise for Her Leadership: The Event Is the Beginning of An Annual Celebration. Will Perhaps Be Merged into a Homecoming," *Megaphone*, May 7, 1915.
103. Alma Barrett was the sister of Vera Barrett, also a student at Southwestern and mother of Genevieve Britt Caldwell (Trustee 1981–1992) and the grandmother of Turner M. Caldwell (Trustee 1993 to present), both strong supporters of Southwestern.
104. SU Faculty 1913–34, March 5, 1918, p. 132.
105. MKSB #20, p. 20, "University Christmas Entertainment," *Georgetown Commercial*, December 23, 1912.
106. MKSB #23, p. 44, "Christmas Service at Woman's Building," *Georgetown Commercial*, December 10, 1915. The following description of the event is taken from this article.
107. "Carol Services," *Southwestern Magazine* 48 (December 1929): 9.
108. William C. Finch, "Annual Report [of President and Officers]," 1953–1961, November 12, 1953.
109. "Carol Services," *Southwestern Magazine* 48 (December 1929): 9.
110. Jane Brown McCook, *Laura Kuykendall* (Georgetown: MHHS, 1989).
111. Claude Carr Cody, John M. Barcus, and Laura Kuykendall, *The Book of Southwestern* (Georgetown: Von Boeckmann Jones Co., 1923), pp. 18–19.
112. Ralph Wood Jones, "A History of Southwestern University, 1873–1949" (doctoral dissertation, University of Texas, 1960),p. 502, fn. 41.
113. Barcus Family Papers, "University Centennial Praised," *Dallas Morning News*, October 26, 1939.
114. SU Trustees 1913–25, June 5–6, 1923, p. 485.
115. SU Trustees 1913–25, June 4–5, 1924, pp. 531–532.
116. Ibid., p. 566.
117. Laura Kuykendall, "The Dean of Women and Her Problems as Found on a Small University Campus" (master's thesis, Southwestern University, 1926), p. 58.
118. Ibid., pp. 59–60.
119. Ibid., pp. 75–79.
120. Ibid., pp. 97–99.
121. Ibid., p. 128.
122. MKSB #21, p. 1, "The Barbarian."
123. SU Faculty 1912–13, January 14, 1913, p. 18.
124. MKSB #21, p. 12, "Anti-Frat Men Hold Meeting," *WC Sun*, January 30, 1913.
125. SU Faculty 1912–13, May 27, 1913, pp. 42–43.
126. SU Trustees 1913–25, June 12–13, 1914, p. 40.
127. Reba U. McMinn, "McMinn Letters," Georgetown, Dallas, and New York, September 25, 1913, to February 13, 1917. "Collection Description and Inventory" compiled by Cory W. Williams.
128. McMinn, "McMinn Letters," September 25, 1913.
129. Ibid., October 9, 1913.
130. Ibid., October 17, 1913.
131. MKSB #21, p. 13, "Riis Speaks in Georgetown," *WC Sun*, February 27, 1913.
132. McMinn, "McMinn Letters," May 27, 1914.
133. SU Trustees 1913–25, June 12–13, 1914, pp. 37–38.
134. SU Trustees 1913–25, June 12–13, 1919, p. 278.
135. SU Trustees 1913–25, June 13–14, 1913, p. 3.
136. SU Faculty 1912–13, May 20 and 27, 1913, pp. 39–42.
137. MKSB #21, p. 43, H. Bascom Simpson, "Southwestern's Prohibition Association," *Georgetown Commercial*, March 5, 1915.
138. SU Faculty 1913–34, February 17, March 15, September 21, and December 13, 1921, pp. 200–203, 215, 229.
139. SU Faculty 1913–34, April 7, 1915 and December 11, 1916, pp. 43 and 85.
140. SU Faculty 1913–34, May 4, 1918, p. 135.
141. SU Faculty 1913–34, October 14, 1921, p. 114.
142. SU Faculty 1913–34, October 3, 1915, p. 55.
143. SU Trustees 1913–25, June 14–16, 1917, p. 168.
144. SU Trustees 1913–25, June 9–10, 1920, pp. 325–326.
145. Ibid., pp. 326–327.
146. SU Faculty 1913–34, February 9, 1921, p. 198.
147. SU Faculty 1913–34, September 14, 1914, pp. 27–28.
148. SU Faculty 1913–34, November 6, 1916, p. 82.
149. SU Faculty 1913–34, June 5, 1917, pp. 112–113.
150. SU Trustees 1913–25, June 12–13, 1919, pp. 283–284.
151. SU Faculty 1891–1912, October 10 and November 21, 1911, pp. 219 and 223.
152. MKSB #20, p. 23, "White Sox vs. S. U.," *Georgetown Commercial*, March 28, 1912.
153. Jones, *SU 1840–1961*, p. 260.
154. *Megaphone*, articles of January 16 and 23, 1923.
155. H. Allen Anderson, "Cawthon, Peter Willis," HBTO, July 23, 2002.
156. SU Trustees 1913–25, June 12–13, 1919, p. 282.
157. SU Trustees 1913–25, June 9–10, 1920, p. 321.
158. SU Trustees 1913–25, June 8–9, 1921, p. 368.
159. SU Faculty 1912–13, May 27, 1913, p. 43.
160. SU Faculty 1913–34, September 14, 1914, pp. 28–29.
161. SU Faculty 1913–34, January 11, February 15, 1915, pp. 33–35; May 1, 1916, p. 67; March 12, 1917, p. 99.
162. SU Faculty 1913–34, September 27, 1915, pp. 53–54.
163. McMinn, "McMinn Letters," February 13, 1917.
164. SU Faculty 1913–34, March 31, 1917.
165. MKSB #23, p. 86, "Grand Patriotic Rally Held Tuesday Afternoon," *WC Sun*, April 12, 1917.
166. SU Faculty 1913–34, May 8, 1917.
167. SU Trustees 1913–25, June 14–16, 1917, pp. 131–132.
168. Ibid., p. 161.
169. SU Trustees 1913–25, June 14–15, 1918, p. 209.
170. John C. Granbery, "Dr. Granbery in France," *Megaphone*, October 9, 1917. Letter of Granbery published by *Megaphone*.
171. GL, Letter to May Catt Granbery, Staunton, Virginia, written by John C. Granbery, Jr., from Soufli, Greece, June 22–23, 1920. The Granbery Letters are part of the Jackson-Greenwood Collection donated to Southwestern by Mrs. Ruth G. Jackson of San Antonio in 1975. W. W. Jackson and his wife, Ruth Jackson, were friends of the Granberys. He invited Granbery to teach in San Antonio after he was dismissed from Southwestern. Apparently May Granbery gave the letters to Ruth, who in turn donated them to Southwestern. This letter currently resides in Packet 8.5 of Box 8.
172. SU Ex Com 1907–23, October 12, 1917, pp. 81–82.
173. SU Trustees 1913–25, June 14–15, 1918, pp. 198–199, 209.
174. CCSB #14, "Dr. C. C. Cody, Jr., Organizes Ambulance Company," *Houston Post*, June 16, 1917.
175. SU Trustees 1913–25, June 14–15, 1918, p. 201.

176. Ibid., pp. 213–215.
177. Ibid., p. 219.
178. SU Faculty 1913–34, June 30, 1918, pp. 142–143.
179. SU Trustees 1913–25, June 12–13, 1919, pp. 294–297.
180. Ibid., pp. 279–280.
181. SU Faculty 1913–34, June 12–13, 1919, pp. 170–171.
182. SU Trustees 1913–25, June 12–13, 1919, pp. 286–287.
183. SU Faculty 1913–34, February 5, 1917, pp. 93–94.
184. SU Faculty 1913–34, December 4, 1917, pp. 126–127.
185. Ibid.
186. SU Faculty 1913–34, January 8, 1919, pp. 149–150.
187. SU Faculty 1913–34, June 12–13, 1919, p. 285.
188. MKSB #23, p. 52, *Texas Christian Advocate*, February 24, 1916.
189. MKSB #23, p. 56, "Dr. Bishop Preaches Sermons in Houston," *Georgetown Commercial*, March 10, 1916, reprinted from the *Houston Post* of March 5, 1916.
190. SU Faculty 1913–34, June 5, 1917, p. 111.
191. MKSB #23, p. 36, "Anti-mob Association," *WC Sun*, November 11, 1915, taken from the *Texas Christian Advocate*.
192. MKSB #23, p. 37, "College Presidents' Anti-Mob Organization," *Georgetown Commercial*, November 12, 1915. The date in the heading of the article is November 6, 1915.
193. MKSB #23, p. 52, "Lynching and Mob Law Again," *Texas Christian Advocate*, February 23, 1916.
194. MKSB #23, p. 57, "Colleges of South Formally Organize to Fight Lynching," unnamed newspaper of Birmingham, Alabama, just prior to April 13, 1916.
195. MKSB #23, p. 58, "Dr. Bishop's Address on Mob Violence," *WC Sun*, April 20, 1916 (article dated April 15, 1916). Also, MKSB #23, p. 59, "Lynching, The Great American Sport," unnamed newspaper, [ca. April 15, 1916].
196. James McEnteer, *Fighting Words: Independent Journalists in Texas* (Austin: University of Texas Press, 1992), p. 69.
197. Takako Sudo-Shimamura, "John C. Granbery: Three Academic Freedom Controversies in the Life of a Social Gospeler in Texas (1920–1938)" (master's thesis, University of Texas at Austin, 1971), pp. 3–15. Most of the description of Granbery's early life given below comes from these pages.
198. Southwestern, "John C. Granbery Letters," *Special Collections in Methodism: William C. Finch, John C. Granbery, Henry E. Meyer*, (Georgetown: SU, SLC, 1990), pp. 25–28.
199. MKSB #21, p. 15, "Dr. John C. Granbery Addresses Review Club," *Georgetown Commercial*, October 13, 1913.
200. Sudo-Shimamura, "Granbery: Three Controversies," p. 18. He quotes "An Address to the Social Service Commission," taken from the *Texas Christian Advocate*, April 19, 1914.
201. MKSB #22, p. ?, "Dr. Granbery Predicts Great Labor War," *San Antonio Express*, November 16, 1914.
202. MKSB #22, p. 29, "Another Deliverance from Dr. Granbery," *Texas Christian Advocate*, after November 29, 1914.
203. Cody Collection, Incoming Correspondence, Box 1, Folder 9, Letter to Dr. C. C. Cody from Jno. H. Griffith, Griffith Lumber Company, Bertram, December 27, 1914.
204. MKSB #21, p. 38, "Social Problems of Interest to Women," *Georgetown Commercial*, December 4, 1914.
205. MKSB #22, p. ?, "What Is Socialism," address of Dr. J. C. Granbery, in one of the Georgetown newspapers, January 6, 1915.
206. MKSB #23, p. 15, "Dr. Granbery at Thorndale," *Georgetown Commercial*, June 4, 1915.
207. MKSB #23, p. 28, "Dr. Granbery in Bryan," *WC Sun*, August 26, 1915.
208. MKSB #23, p. 80, "Dr. Granbery at San Antonio," *Megaphone*, May 30, 1916.
209. MKSB #23, p. 64, "Dr. Granbery Writes on McDonald Address," *Georgetown Commercial*, June 30, 1916.
210. MKSB #23, p. 67, "Dr. Granbery Addresses Baylor University," published in the *Waco Morning News*, reprinted in the *Georgetown Commercial*, September 8, 1916.
211. SU Faculty 1913–34, November 6, 1916, p. 82.
212. MKSB #23, p. 83, "Men's Suffrage League," *WC Sun*, February 15, 1917.
213. SU Faculty 1913–34, June 5, 1917, p. 116.
214. SU Trustees 1913–25, June 14–16, 1917, pp. 149–150.
215. Ibid., pp. 151–152.
216. SU Ex Com 1907–23, January 10, 1918, p. 84.
217. SU Trustees 1913–25, January 18, 1918, pp. 179–182.
218. Ibid.
219. Presidential Archives, Claud Howard Files, undated, unattributed article entitled "Dr. C. A. Nichols, 81, Dies Following Heart Attack."
220. Gambrell, "Gambrell Letter." However, in his 1919 Board report, Bishop merely says that "late in the summer vacation, Professor S. H. Moore tendered his resignation of the chair of history," June 12–13, 1919, p. 297.
221. SU Trustees 1913–25, June 14–15, 1918, p. 271.
222. Cody Collection, Incoming Correspondence, Letter of July 25, 1919, from John C. Granbery, writing while on a boat going to Smyrna, Greece, to Cody, Box 1, Folder 5.
223. GL, Letter to May Catt Granbery, Georgetown, from C. M. Bishop, Houston, April 23, 1940.
224. SU Faculty 1913–34, October 14, 1920, pp. 190–191.
225. SU Faculty 1913–34, October 1, 1921, p. 221.
226. SU Trustees 1913–25, June 7–8, 1922, pp. 413, 435.
227. SU Faculty 1913–34, December 13, 1920, pp. 195–196.
228. SU Faculty 1913–34, June 3, 1919, p. 157.
229. SU Faculty 1913–34, May 6, 1921, p. 205.
230. SU Faculty 1913–34, June 7 and December 6, 1921, pp. 201–202, 207.
231. SU Faculty 1913–34, March 9, 1922, p. 243.
232. SU Faculty 1913–34, March 7, 1922, pp. 239–242.
233. SU Trustees 1913–25, June 14–15, 1918, pp. 231–233, 255.
234. SU Trustees 1913–25, June 9–10, 1920, pp. 357–358.
235. SU Trustees 1913–25, June 12–13, 1919, p. 307.
236. SU Trustees 1913–25, June 9–10, 1920, p. 335.
237. Massengale, "Methodist Collegiate Education," pp. 366–367.
238. SU Ex Com 1907–23, October 3, 1919, pp. 94–95.
239. The Lois Perkins name would later be enshrined in the Lois Perkins Chapel, completed in 1950. Her son-in-law, Charles N. Prothro, served as either treasurer, vice chair, or chair of the Board for twenty of the thirty years he was a member from 1952 to 1981. Her grandson, Joe N. Prothro, served as a member of the Board from 1982 to 1998.
240. SU Trustees 1913–25, June 8–9, 1921, pp. 384–387.
241. Ibid., pp. 392–393.
242. Ibid., p. 402.
243. SU Trustees 1913–25, June 7–8, 1922, p. 425.
244. SU Trustees 1913–25, June 8–9, 1921, p. 401.
245. SU Trustees 1913–25, June 7–8, 1922, p. 421. He served as pastor of St. Paul's in Houston for three years before going to St. Paul's Methodist Church in Muskogee, Oklahoma, where he served one year. He was there when Southern Methodist University invited him to become Professor of New Testament in 1925. See the newspaper article, probably from the *Dallas News*, dated July 24, 1925, entitled "SMU Elects Bible Teacher," included among the materials associated in the Walter Towner welcoming letter referenced in endnote #1.
246. SU Faculty 1913–34, November 30, 1921.
247. SU Ex Com 1907–23, December 1, 1921, p. 115.
248. *Megaphone*, articles of May 25, 1926, December 13, 1927, and June 1, 1928.
249. MKSB #36, p. 66, "Dr. & Mrs. C. M. Bishop Make Georgetown Their Home," *WC Sun*, November 22, 1940.
250. Claud Howard, "Letter to Alpha Chi's," Georgetown, March 16, 1940. SU, SLC, SC, Centennial Celebration, Neas Box 2, Folder: Miscellaneous.

CHAPTER XIII
"Crippled . . . But Worth Saving" (1922–1928)

1. Elva Marshall Barnet, "Paul Whitfield Horn, 1870–1932" (master's thesis, Texas Technological College, 1938), pp. 23–25.
2. Ibid., pp. 10–23.
3. Ibid., pp. 1–9.
4. *The Megaphone*, "S. U. Sunday School Shows Steady Growth," December 12, 1922.
5. Barnet, "Horn," p. 76.
6. Ibid., pp. 69–79.
7. Barnet, "Horn," p. 29.
8. Ibid., pp. 49–52.
9. Ibid., pp. 58–59.
10. Ibid., pp. 49–52.
11. *Megaphone*, "Dr. Horn Makes Short Visit to University," February 26, 1924.
12. Barnet, "Horn," pp. 81–82. Barnet quotes the *Southwestern Magazine* of May 1930.
13. SU Faculty 1913–34, October 3, 1922, p. 255.
14. SU Trustees 1913–25, June 7–8, 1922, p. 438.
15. SU Faculty 1913–34, May 1, 1923.
16. *Megaphone*, "Frank Dobie Reviews Early School Days," February 27, 1923. Typographical errors in the original corrected.
17. *Megaphone*, "Active May Fete Work Begins Tuesday," March 6, 1923.
18. Claude Carr Cody, John M. Barcus, and Laura Kuykendall, *The Book of Southwestern* (Georgetown: Von Boeckmann Jones Co., 1923), pp. 20–25. The unknown alumna who wrote *The Spirit of Southwestern* may have been Margaret Mood McKennon. She was notably reluctant to associate her name with her writings. Her authorship of "The Legend of the Bell" for the 1927 pageant would not have been known had not Ruth Morgan Ferguson included it in an article she wrote about Mrs. McKennon in 1933. Mrs. McKennon also wrote poetry, which, in spite of the urgings of her friends, she never published. *Southwestern University Generations*, p. 3. Sue Mood McMichael died on July 14, 2000. A longtime SU benefactor, she provided, in her estate, for the creation of a McMichael Student Enrichment Fund that makes awards to students to participate in experiences that will encourage their development as bright, moral, and courageous leaders concerned with the betterment of society.
19. Cody, Barcus, and Kuykendall, *Book of Southwestern*, pp. 12–13.
20. SU Trustees 1913–25, June 7–8, 1922, p. 441, and June 5–6, 1923, pp. 500, 506.
21. *Megaphone*, "New Rules for Church Colleges of Methodism," January 9, 1923. Also, see Robert Glenn Massengale, "Collegiate Education in the Methodist Episcopal Church, South 1902–1939" (doctoral dissertation, Yale University, 1950), p. 286.
22. SU Trustees 1913–25, June 5–6, 1923, pp. 477–483.
23. SU Ex Com 1907–23, July 18, 1923, pp. 142–143.
24. SU Trustees 1913–25, September 19, 1923, p. 547.
25. SU Ex Com 1923–36, May 27, 1924.
26. The $55,000 figure is only approximate. Since the gift involved insurance and Southwestern agreed to pay some of the premiums, the amount of the premiums would have to be deducted from the $55,000 to get a precise figure.
27. SU Ex Com 1923–36, May 3, 1924.
28. SU Trustees 1913–25, June 5–6, 1923, p. 502.
29. Ibid., pp. 454, 471, 475–476.
30. Ibid., pp. 462–464, 469.
31. Takako Sudo-Shimamura, "John C. Granbery: Three Academic Freedom Controversies in the Life of a Social Gospeler in Texas (1920–1938)" (master's thesis, University of Texas at Austin, 1971), p. 23.
32. CCSB #14, "Sixty-eighth Birthday Anniversary," November 5, 1922. Also, *Megaphone*, November 28, 1922.
33. *Megaphone*, "Granberry [sic] Sails Soon for European Tour," May 22, 1923.
34. Christopher Long, "Ku Klux Klan," HBTO, July 23, 2002.
35. Walter N. Vernon, Robert W. Sledge, Robert C. Monk, and Norman W. Spellmann, *The Methodist Excitement in Texas* (Dallas: The Texas United Methodist Historical Society, 1984), pp. 264–265.
36. Norman W. Spellmann, *Growing a Soul: The Story of A. Frank Smith* (Dallas: SMU Press, 1979), p. 110.
37. *Megaphone*, June 5, 1923.
38. *Megaphone*, "Notice to University Knights Ku Klux Klan," October 16, 1923.
39. Sudo-Shimamura, "Granbery: Three Controversies," pp. 24–27.
40. Ibid., pp. 27–29.
41. Ibid., p. 30.
42. Ibid., pp. 31–32.
43. Richard T. Fleming, "Daniel James Moody, Jr.," HBTO, July 23, 2002.
44. *Megaphone*, "Dr. J. C. Granbery Leaves Southwestern," March 10, 1925.
45. *Megaphone*, First Summer School Edition, July 1925.
46. *Megaphone*, "Granbery Says Man in Process with Universe. Fills Pulpit at Evening Hour at Local Methodist Church," May 22, 1928.
47. Sudo-Shimamura, "Granbery: Three Controversies," pp. 32–40.
48. Ibid., pp. 38–42.
49. SU Trustees 1913–25, June 4–5, 1924, pp. 549–551.
50. *Megaphone*, "Paul Whitfield Horn," November 27, 1923. Also, SU Faculty 1913–34, December 14, 1923.
51. Norris A. Hiett, "Shelby, Thomas Hall," HBTO, July 23, 2002.
52. SU Ex Com 1923–36, December 25, 1923.
53. SU Faculty 1913–34, January 8, 1924, p. 286.
54. SU Ex Com 1923–36, January 14, 1924.
55. SU Trustees 1913–25, March 26, 1924, pp. 511–516.
56. *Megaphone*, "New President for Southwestern. Dr. J. Sam Barcus Elected by Board in Special Session to Fill Place of Dr. Horn," April 10, 1924, pp. 1, 6.
57. CCSB #3, Letter from J. Sam Barcus, Cisco District Presiding Elder, to Prof. Cody, January 26, 1911.
58. MKSB #28, p. 30, "Barcus Ends Term at Southwestern: Retiring President Recalls His Predecessors," *Austin American*, Georgetown, August 4, [1928].
59. Ralph Wood Jones, *Southwestern University 1840–1961* (Austin: Jenkins Publishing Co., 1973), p. 266.
60. SU Trustees 1913–25, June 4–5, 1924, pp. 519–572.
61. *Megaphone*, "The Greater Southwestern Movement," April 27, 1926, p. 6.
62. SU Ex Com 1923–36, October 1, 1924.
63. SU Trustees 1925–34, June 15, 1925, pp. 1–36.
64. SU Ex Com 1923–36, November 23, 1927.
65. CCSB #16, copy of letter from R. S. Hyer to "Dear Friend," April 18, 1910.
66. MKSB #22, p. ?, "Southwestern's Great Campaign Launched," *Georgetown Commercial*, February 27, 1914, p. 1.
67. *Megaphone*, November 28, 1922.
68. The description of the fire and associated events is taken from various articles in *The Megaphone* of January 13, 1925, and an article entitled "Eyewitness Recalls Memorable Morning When Old Annex Was Burned to the Ground" in *The Megaphone* of January 10, 1928, p. 4. No attempt has been made to footnote the quotations from the articles. They may all be found in these two issues of *The Megaphone*. There are conflicting accounts as to when the fire began. The "Eyewitness" article states that its author was asleep and that he was awakened "at about the hour of 2:30" by "boys scrambling through the hall outside" his door in response to the cry "Everybody out! The Annex is on fire!" The article was written three years after the event, however, and mistakes the day of its occurrence as Sunday rather than Thursday, when it actually occurred. One article of January 13, 1925, states that the general alarm was sounded at four o'clock, while a third says that the tragedy occurred between "mid-night and dawn."
69. SU Trustees 1913–25, February 11, 1925, p. 579.

70. *Megaphone*, "President's Home to Be Made of Griffith Place," April 27, 1926, p. 8. It was listed as 1305 E. University. Ave. in the census of 1930.
71. *Megaphone*, "Laura Kuykendall—Dean of Women," by Charley, April 27, 1926, p. 4.
72. *Megaphone*, "Georgetown Approaches Mark with Total Subscription of $37,450.00," January 27, 1925.
73. SU Ex Com 1923–36, February 11, 1925.
74. *Megaphone*, "Review of the Greater Southwestern Movement," June 9, 1925, p. 8.
75. SU Trustees 1925–34, June 15, 1925, pp. 25–26.
76. Folder describing the new Woman's building, April 17, 1925, p. 7. Also, "The Annex as It Will Soon Look," *The Megaphone*, Dec. 8, 1925.
77. SU Trustees 1925–34, June 14, 1926, pp. 31–35, 59.
78. *Megaphone*, "Contract for Annex Goes to Johnson Construction Company. J. E. Johnson of Waco Gets Dormitory Contract for $183,000," June 2, 1925. Also, *WC Sun*, June 5, 1925.
79. *Megaphone*, "The Annex as It Will Soon Look," December 8, 1925.
80. SU Trustees 1925–34, June 14, 1926, pp. 49–50.
81. *Megaphone*, "Southwestern's New Home for Girls," June 3, 1927.
82. MKSB #38, p. 38, "The Bell Atop Elevator Shaft at Kuykendall Hall," *WC Sun*, March 3, 1944, reprint of a *Megaphone* article. "When Kuykendall Hall was built, Dean Laura Kuykendall . . . remembered the old bell and succeeded in making for it a place at the top of the elevator tower to preserve it and the memories for future generations. . . . [Originally, the bell] was lashed in the tower rising above the roof of what was known as the old three-story Prep building. . . . But the Prep Building was sold to the city soon after World War I, and was torn down. . . . When the tower was taken down the bell was thrown to one side. In recent years the bell has been rung by students after an athletic victory or a celebration of sorts."
83. *Megaphone*, "Legend of the Bell Staged Tomorrow. 8,000 Expected to Witness Pageant," June 3, 1927.
84. SU Trustees 1913–25, June 5–6, 1923, p. 479.
85. SU Trustees 1925–34, June 4–5, 1928, p. 165.
86. SU Trustees 1913–25, June 15, 1925, p. 12.
87. SU Trustees 1925–34, June 6, 1927, pp. 88–89.
88. SU Trustees 1925–34, June 14, 1926, p. 56.
89. Ibid., pp. 55–56.
90. SU Trustees 1925–34, June 6, 1927, p. 85.
91. SU Ex Com 1923–36, March 30, 1925.
92. SU Trustees 1925–34, June 6, 1927, p. 101.
93. Ibid., pp. 100–101.
94. SU Trustees 1925–34, June 4–5, 1928, pp. 149–151.
95. Ibid., p. 143.
96. SU Trustees 1925–34, June 6, 1927, pp. 104–105.
97. *Megaphone*, "Dr. Bishop Denies Merger Report. 'Absolutely No Foundation for Report of Merger of S. M. U. and S. U.,'" February 17, 1920, p. 1.
98. *WC Sun*, articles of April 6 and May 4, 1928, the latter entitled "Committee Recommends Baylor Removal. Future of Great Educational Institution Will Be Determined at General Convention."
99. *WC Sun*, "First Baptist Church Opposes Baylor Removal. Church Conference Votes Almost Unanimously Against Proposed Removal," April 27, 1928, p. 1.
100. SU Trustees 1925–34, June 6, 1927, pp. 86–87.
101. SU Ex Com 1923–36, May 6, 1927.
102. Anonymous, "Locating Southwestern University Proved Difficult Task," *The Megaphone*, April 9, 1940. "Southwestern Not to Be Moved to San Antonio. Statement Made by Texas Papers Denied by Dean Ullrich in Chapel," *The Megaphone*, May 10, 1927.
103. *Megaphone*, "Southwestern Not to Be Moved Says President," May 24, 1927.
104. SU Ex Com 1923–36, June 18 and August 14, 1928.
105. MKSB #29, p. 60, "Dr. John R. Allen Is Honor Guest of Southwestern Commencement," unattributed, newspaper article, ca. June 1933. Allen's memoir (North Texas Annual Conference Journal, *Minutes Seventy-first Annual Session of the North Texas Annual Conference* 1937), says that he was at Southwestern twenty years, 1892 to 1912. Though Bishop A. Frank Smith, his son-in-law, says specifically that he resigned in 1912 at the age of sixty, University catalogs list him for twenty-two years. Smith says in his memoir of Allen that for a time after his retirement, "he was publisher and editor of the *Williamson County Sun*, published at Georgetown."
106. Dorothy Shell Bunting, "Dorothy Bunting Letter to Nancy Porsche." From the author's personal files.
107. Clara Stearns Scarbrough, *Land of Good Water: A Williamson County, Texas, History* (Georgetown: Williamson County Sun Publishers, 1973), pp. 390–391. Also, *Megaphone*, "Professor Hester Wins Election," September 20, 1932, p. 4, and "Hester Leaves for Washington for Service," September 18, 1934, p. 3.
108. *Megaphone*, April 9, 1946, p. 1.
109. I was invited to Southwestern to succeed him in the Lucy King Brown Chair in 1965 and would occasionally sit in Hester's classroom to enjoy his lectures on Texas and United States history. He had a gift for using the apt anecdote to illustrate his points.
110. *Megaphone*, "New Book By S. U. Professor Now Off Press. Dr. Claud Howard Releases New Book, 'Coleridge's Idealism,'" December 16, 1924.
111. *Megaphone*, October 29, 1935, p. 1.
112. *Megaphone*, September 25, 1928, June 3, 1930, December 8, 1931.
113. John Nelson Russell Score, II, Interview by Martha Allen, Georgetown, Southwestern University, Tape 2, p. 39.
114. Presidential Archives, J. C. Godbey Files. See "Dr. Godbey, Retired S. U. Bandleader, Stages Come-Back on Local Podium," *Megaphone*, February 18, 1947.
115. SU Ex Com 1923–36, August 23, 1926.
116. *Megaphone*, February 12, 1929, p. 3.
117. MKSB #29, p. 50, October 21, 1932. Also, MKSB #30, p. 56, "Scholia Club Meets at Southwestern," *Progressive Citizen*, April 23, 1936.
118. MKSB #30, p. 20, "Southwestern U. Prof Named as Scientists' Leader," *Austin American*, [Fall 1934]. Also, MKSB #30, p. 33, "Godbey Announces Topics for State Teachers," *WC Sun*, November 23, 1934.
119. *Megaphone*, February 12, 1929, p. 3.
120. SU Trustees 1925–34, June 9, 1930, p. 263.
121. SU Trustees 1925–34, June 4–5, 1928, pp. 127, 137–138.
122. SU Trustees 1913–25, March 26, 1924, pp. 511–516.
123. *Megaphone*, May 27, 1924.
124. SU Trustees 1925–34, June 4–5, 1928, pp. 146–149.
125. Ibid., p. 128.
126. Massengale, "Methodist Collegiate Education," pp. 271, 305–307.
127. SU Trustees 1925–34, Minutes of June 14, 1926, pp. 40–41.
128. SU Faculty 1913–34, October 4, 1927.
129. MKSB #28, p. 17, "Firing Line: Will Durant Unappreciated," *Daily Texan*, [Spring] 1928.
130. SU Trustees 1925–34, June 6, 1927, p. 77.
131. *Megaphone*, May 13, 1930.
132. *Megaphone*, "Blue Key Society to Organize Friday," December 8, 1925.
133. SU Trustees 1925–34, June 4–5, 1928, p. 127.
134. Jones, *SU 1840–1961*, p. 537, n. 93, quoting the *Williamson County Sun*, April 30, 1926.
135. SU Trustees 1925–34, June 4–5, 1928, p. 119.
136. *Megaphone*, "Lefty Edens to Succeed Gardner as Head Coach. 'Lefty' is Ex-student of S. U. and Coach of North Texas Agricultural College," April 21, 1925, p. 2.
137. MKSB #34, pp. 51–52, "Colorado River Takes Life of Coach C. M. Edens," *WC Sun*, August 4, 1939.
138. SU Trustees 1925–34, June 4–5, 1928, pp. 124–125.
139. SU Faculty 1913–34, May 4, 1928, p. 398.
140. SU Faculty 1913–34, June 4–5, 1928, p. 130.
141. Ibid., p. 158.
142. Barcus Family Papers, Scrapbook 3.3, "1920–1947, Twenty-sev-

enth Birthday Party of the J. C. Godbey Sunday School Class, First Methodist Church, Georgetown, Texas, Honoring Its Membership, Monday Night, March 10, 1947," unattributed, undated article.
143. SU Trustees 1925–34, June 6, 1927, p. 77.
144. Vernon, Sledge, Monk, and Spellmann, *Methodist Excitement in Texas*, p. 213.
145. Massengale, "Methodist Collegiate Education," pp. 489–490.
146. J. T. Carlyon, "Changes and Trends in Theological Thought," in *The History of Texas Methodism 1900–1960*, ed. Olin W. Nail (Austin: Capital Printing Company, 1961), pp. 459–460.
147. Massengale, "Methodist Collegiate Education," p. 489.
148. *WC Sun*, "M. E. Conference at San Antonio in Uproar," November 6, 1925, p. 3, in article dated October 30.
149. Jones, *SU 1840–1961*, p. 272.
150. Olin W. Nail, *History of Texas Methodism 1900–1960* (Austin: Capital Printing Company, 1961), p. 125.
151. Vernon, Sledge, Monk, and Spellmann, *Methodist Excitement in Texas*, p. 216.
152. Carlyon, "Theological Thought," p. 461.
153. West Texas Special Committee, pp. 70–73.
154. *The Sou'wester*, 1914, p. 18.
155. MKSB #23, p. 67, "Dr. Gray Addresses Equal Suffrage League," *Williamson County Sun*, September 21, 1916.
156. SU Trustees 1913–25, January 18, 1918, pp. 173–183.
157. SU Faculty 1913–34, December 13, 1920, pp. 195–196.
158. SU Ex Com 1907–23, December 1, 1921, p. 115.
159. *Megaphone*, "Southwestern Faculty Family Honored," October 7, 1924.
160. *Megaphone*, "Students Send Dr. Gray to Canada," December 14, 1926.
161. *Megaphone*, "To the Students and Faculty of Southwestern University," January 11, 1927.
162. Carlyon, "Theological Thought," p. 461.
163. *Southwestern Magazine*, "A Statement of Personal Faith," November 1926, pp. 7–8.
164. Herbert Lee Gray, "The God Within," May 1941, p. 5.
165. Jones, *SU 1840–1961*, Appendix "M," pp. 371–372. Barcus's full statement before the Annual Conference on the Gray controversy is found in J. Sam Barcus, "A Chapter in the History of Heresy in Colleges," *The Methodist Quarterly Review* (October 1927), pp. 697–699.
166. Nail, *Texas Methodism 1900–1960*, p. 126.
167. SU Trustees 1925–34, June 6, 1927, p. 78. On the effect of Barcus's stand, also see the *Williamson County Sun* for November 5, 1926.
168. SU Faculty 1913–34, July 27, 1928.
169. SU Trustees 1925–34, September 20, 1928, p. 167.
170. SU Faculty 1913–34, September 14, 1928, p. 401.

CHAPTER XIV
Holding On during the Great Depression (1928–1935)

1. *The Megaphone*, "Reminiscences of Early College Pranks Recited by President Vivion to Interviewer," by Gill H. DeWitt, January 19, 1932.
2. Harriet Winton Vivion, "King Vivion, the Eighth President of Southwestern," *Southwestern Magazine*, June 1930, p. 16.
3. PANC, Box 7,. Scrapbook #3, Lorraine Barnes, "Dr. Vivion Outlines His Idea of School of Higher Learning," *Austin American*, October 4, 1933. Ms. Barnes commented that in her interview with him "the Scottish burr in Dr. King Vivion's voice grows thicker as he discussed small colleges versus large universities."
4. SU Ex Com 1923–36, August 27, 1935. Vivion's gesture in setting up King's Palace for the boys gave them something like the Snyder Hall situation for girls, where especially needy girls could do their own housework and cooking in exchange for a much reduced rate.
5. MKSB #28, p. 28, "Considering Head for Southwestern," unnamed newspaper, Dallas, Texas, July 20, 1928.
6. MKSB #28, p. 27, "S.U. Board of Trustees Names Prexy," unnamed newspaper, August 24, 1928.
7. *South Georgia Conference Journal*, "Joseph King Vivion" [Memoir], 1969.
8. Three articles from the *WC Sun*, June–August 1933.
9. *Megaphone*, "New President Well Received by Students," September 25, 1928, p. 1.
10. "King Vivion Inaugurated," *Southwestern Magazine* 48 (November 1929): 35, 41. The information about Vivion's being tapped by Bishop Hay for the position is found in Hay's remarks made at the inauguration ceremony on June 3, 1929.
11. Robert Glenn Massengale, "Collegiate Education in the Methodist Episcopal Church, South 1902–1939" (doctoral dissertation, Yale University, 1950), p. 199.
12. *Megaphone*, "Dr. King Vivion at Church Meet in Nashville; Is President of College Section of Methodist Episcopal Church," March 19, 1935, p. 1.
13. Massengale, "Methodist Collegiate Education," p. 194, fn. 33.
14. *WC Sun*, "Church Seeks College Unity in Texas," June 5, 1928, p. 6.
15. *Ibid.*
16. *WC Sun*, "Methodists to Unify Control in Education," January 4, 1929, p. 31, taken from unnamed Dallas newspaper of December 30, 1928.
17. MKSB #28, p. 26, "Georgetown Little Troubled by Rumor of Southwestern University Removal," *Austin American*, January 14, 1929.
18. MKSB #28, p. 28, "Georgetown May Lose Methodist School to Dallas," Associated Press article in unnamed newspaper, Dallas, January 12, 1929.
19. SU Faculty 1913–34, January 15, 1929, p. 417.
20. *Megaphone*, "University Officials Deny Reports of S.U. Moving," January 15, 1929, p. 1.
21. MKSB #28, p. 31, "Deny Reports Southwestern to Be Moved: Officials of University Say Institution in Good Shape," *Dallas News*, January 15, 1929.
22. *Megaphone*, "H. W. Brown Makes Talk in Chapel," January 29, 1929, p. 1.
23. SU Trustees 1925–34, June 3, 1929, p. 175.
24. *Megaphone*, "Rumor of Southwestern Removal and Unification with S. M. U. Branded as Unauthorized by President Selecman," January 22, 1929, p. 4.
25. MKSB #28, p. 32, "Bishop Moore Talks of Church Schools," *WC Sun*, January 25, 1929.
26. MKSB #28, p. 33, "Plans Formed to Perpetuate Southwestern," *Dallas News*, April 22, 1929, reprint from *WC Sun*, April 21.
27. MKSB #28, p. 15, "Educational Group of Texas Southern Methodists Meet," *WC Sun*, October 25, 1929.
28. Ralph Wood Jones, *Southwestern University 1840–1961* (Austin: Jenkins Publishing Co., 1973), pp. 282–283.
29. The Brown report, found in Nashville, contains a series of recommendations based on the survey made by Warren Brown in 1928–1929. It suggests that the five Annual Conferences should "set up a system of colleges of liberal arts that would have the assurance of permanence." This system should be based on institutions located at three strategic points—Dallas, San Antonio, and Abilene. Southern Methodist would anchor the northern section, with Texas Woman's College (old Polytechnic, future Texas Wesleyan) continuing to serve women. Abilene would anchor the northwestern section, with the new McMurry College being the liberal arts institution there. *San Antonio would anchor the south. Southwestern would be moved there, where Westmoorland College would be merged with it* [italics added]. Wesley College in Greenville and Weatherford College in Weatherford, which were being operated as self-help schools, would be replaced by one institution of the same type (Massengale, "Methodist Collegiate Education," pp. 217–218). One possible way of understanding the fate of the Brown report is that, sometime during his stay in Texas, Warren Brown discussed the nature of what his recommendations might be with Bishop Moore and President Vivion. He found them so opposed to his proposals that he did not issue a formal report while in Texas. It could have been Vivion's knowledge of what such a report might contain if it should be issued that caused him to

organize the highly publicized meeting of influential Southwestern supporters on April 20 to set up a defense against it. Sensing that his report was dead in the water, Brown returned to Nashville and filed it, while Moore held a pro forma final meeting of the Educational Commission on October 22 in Dallas, effectively ending its work.

30. SU Trustees 1925–34, June 3, 1929, p. 201
31. *Megaphone*, "Southwestern U. Launches Firm Financial Program," May 27, 1929, p. 4.
32. MKSB #29, p. 23, "Southwestern to Begin Expansion Campaign at Once," *WC Sun*, April 18, 1930.
33. SU Trustees 1925–34, June 3, 1929, p. 211.
34. Ibid. Also, Ralph Wood Jones, "A History of Southwestern University, 1873–1949" (doctoral dissertation, University of Texas, 1960), p. 545, fn. 103. It references I. J. McCook, "Investments," p. 4.
35. SU Trustees 1925–34, Minutes of June 9, 1930, p. 259. The correct totals for columns 1 and 3 are $553,950.49 and $67,077.69 respectively.
36. SU Trustees 1925–34, January 9, 1930, pp. 245, 260.
37. Grogan Lord, "Oral History of George and Herman Brown by Chris Castaneda," Houston, Southwestern SU, SLC, SC, Small Collections, Oral Histories, February 12, 1991. Also, MKSB #28, p. 36, "Business Manager for Southwestern U," *Dallas News*, dated Georgetown, September 14, 1929.
38. *Megaphone*, "Seniors Take-off Faculty Tuesday," April 9, 1932.
39. GL, Box 8, Packet 8.4, Letter of August 10, 1939.
40. Presidential Archives, Mrs. Alma Thomas Files, Letter of Thomas to McCook, February 22, 1967.
41. Southern Association of Colleges and Secondary Schools, "A Special Study of Southwestern University, 1934," p. 7.
42. Jones, "History of SU" (dissertation), p. 541. R. Jones attributes this quotation to "I. J. McCook, 'Investments,' 3–4."
43. Jones, "History of SU" (dissertation), p. 545.
44. SU Trustees 1935–47, May 23, 1935, pp. 12–13. The removal of the two faculty members from the Executive Committee came as the result of a recommendation by the S.A.C.S.S. examination team that visited the campus on March 2–3, 1934. See endnote #41. It said that it doubted that "good administrative procedure would permit of such an arrangement as just noted, whereby two faculty members are members of the executive committee of the board of trustees" (p. 8).
45. The category entitled "Interfund Advancements" was borrowing by one university fund needing money from another university fund showing a surplus. The fund borrowing the money would provide a note to the lending fund providing for repayment under specified terms with a designated rate of interest.
46. Jones, "History of SU" (dissertation), pp. 545–546, taken from "I. J. McCook, 'Investments,' p. 4." The total for the first column below is only 99.6 percent.
47. Jones, "History of SU" (dissertation), p. 547.
48. Charles Frank Schmidt, *History of Blinn Memorial College (1883–1934)* (San Antonio: Lodovic Printing Company, 1935), pp. 15–16.
49. Charles Frank Schmidt, *History of Washington County* (San Antonio: The Naylor Company, 1949), p. 108. Also, Schmidt, *Blinn College*, pp. 95–96.
50. SU Trustees 1925–34, January 8, 1931, pp. 285–287.
51. Ibid.
52. MKSB #29, p. 31, "College Merger Is Approved by Board," *Houston Chronicle*, January 10, 1931.
53. MKSB #29, p. 32, "King Vivion Inaugurated Pres. of Blinn College," *WC Sun*, January 30, 1931.
54. MKSB #29, p. 36, "Plans for Merger of S. U.-Blinn Memorial College Approved," *WC Sun*, December 18, 1931.
55. Southwestern, *Register for . . . 1932–1933; Announcements for . . . 1933–1934* (Georgetown: Southwestern University, 1933), pp. 9–10.
56. SU Trustees 1925–34, June 2, 1933, p. 403.
57. SU Trustees 1925–34, April 20, 1932, pp. 374–375.
58. SU Trustees 1925–34, June 2, 1933, p. 407.
59. SU Trustees 1925–34, October 24, 1933, pp. 428–429.
60. SU Ex Com 1923–36, February 8, 1934.
61. Schmidt, *Blinn College*, pp. 98–99.
62. SU Trustees 1925–34, May 31, 1934, pp. 456–457.
63. SU Ex Com 1923–36, July 26, 1935.
64. Southwestern, *Register for . . . 1938–1939; Announcements for . . . 1939–1940* (Georgetown: Southwestern University, 1939), p. 35.
65. SU Trustees 1925–34, January 9, 1930, pp. 215–248.
66. Walter N. Vernon, "Náñez, Alfredo," HBTO, July 23, 2002.
67. Alfredo Náñez, *History of the Rio Grande Conference of the United Methodist Church* (Dallas: Bridwell Library, Southern Methodist University, 1980), pp. 49–54.
68. CCSB #6, C. C. Cody, "Does Southwestern University Pay?," April, 1907, from unnamed newspaper.
69. Náñez, *Rio Grande Conference*, pp. 66–69.
70. SU Faculty 1913–34, March 12, 1929.
71. SU Trustees 1925–34, June 3, 1929, p. 176.
72. *Megaphone*, April 9, 1932, p. 1.
73. SU Faculty 1913–34, March 3, 1931.
74. SU Faculty 1913–34, January 27–28, 1932.
75. SU Trustees 1925–34, May 31, 1934, p. 439.
76. Southwestern, *Register for . . . 1935–1936; Announcements for . . . 1936–1937* (Georgetown: Southwestern University, 1936,. pp. 156–157.
77. PANC, Box 7, Scrapbook #1, extract from Bishop's report to the Board of Trustees of June 8, 1921.
78. PANC, Box 7, Scrapbook #1, telegraphic letter of May 29, 1924.
79. PANC, Box 7, Scrapbook #1, editorial page of *Texas Christian Advocate*, June 19, 1924.
80. Bureau of the Census, Decennial Census Documents from 1850 to 1920, Thirteenth Census of the United States: 1910—Population, Williamson County, Justice of the Peace, Precinct #1.
81. PANC, Box 7, Scrapbook #1, "Death of Former Citizen," probably from *WC Sun*, June 27, 1919. Both graves have marble markers with their names, Hester and Isaac.
82. MKSB #36, p. 10, "Pearl Neas, Southwestern U.'s Registrar, in Texas Who's Who," *Austin American*, May 3, 1941.
83. PANC, Box 7, Scrapbook #1, Letter of recommendation dated March 26, 1918.
84. PANC, Box 7, Scrapbook #1, Letter of recommendation dated June 21, 1918.
85. PANC, Box 7, Scrapbook #1, "Miss Pearl A. Neas, Assistant Registrar of Southwestern," *The Megaphone*, May, 1, 1919.
86. PANC, Box 7, Scrapbook #1, "To Whom It May Concern," undated letter of recommendation, probably written before December 1, 1921, when he left the institution.
87. Pearl A. Neas, "Letter from Pearl A. Neas to R. G. Perryman, President, American Association of Collegiate Registrars and Admissions Officers," March 28, 1962.
88. PANC, Box 7, Scrapbook #1, "Registrar Leader," probably from *WC Sun*, May 18, [1928?]. Also, PANC, Box 7, Scrapbook #1, "Pearl Alma Neas, Registrar," probably *WC Sun*, ca. 1933.
89. Ullrich Papers, Folder entitled Correspondence: Board of Trustees, Letter from Dean Ullrich to "Members of The Board of Trustees," March 10, 1938.
90. PANC, Box 7, Scrapbook #2, "Miss Neas Back from Valley Trip," *Megaphone*, November 15, 1932.
91. MKSB #29, p. 56, "Miss Neas Back from Long Trip for University," probably *The Megaphone*, March 11, 1933.
92. Southern Association, "Special Study," p. 7.
93. Barcus Family Papers, Scrapbook 4.3, "Tribute Will Be Paid Friday to Late Miss Pearl A. Neas," *WC Sun*, February 21, 1963.
94. Ibid.
95. SU Trustees 1935–47, May 23, 1935, p. 5.
96. Jones, "History of SU" (dissertation), pp. 562–563.
97. *Megaphone*, "Norman Thomas on Campus Today; Noted Socialist Leader of U. S. and One of the Greatest Thinkers," December 10, 1929, p. 1.

98. MKSB #29, p. 41, April 20, 1932.
99. MKSB #30, p. 19, "Methodist Stude[nt]s Predominate in Southwestern," *WC Sun*, October 19, 1934.
100. MKSB #29, p. 38, "Rev. Heinsohn, First M.E. Pastor Returned 5th Time," *WC Sun*, November 20, 1931.
101. SU Trustees 1925–34, May 31, 1934, p. 441.
102. *Megaphone*, "S. U. Students Favor Hoover," October 9, 1928, p. 1.
103. *Megaphone*, "Roosevelt, Bullington Lead Megaphone Vote; Students Divided on 18th Amendment," November 1, 1932, p. 1.
104. SU Trustees 1925–34, January 9, 1930, pp. 226–227.
105. *Megaphone*, "Southwestern to Get Federal Relief Fund for Many Students; List of Students to Receive Work Is Twenty-eight," February 20, 1934, p. 1.
106. *Megaphone*, "The Pirate Tavern Formally Opened Tuesday Night; New Structure a Beautiful Addition to the Campus," February 18, 1930, p. 1. Also, "How 'Tavern' Came to Be Called That Name Told by Ex-Southwestern Student," October 2, 1945, reprinting original *Megaphone* article of February 12, 1938.
107. *Megaphone*, "What Four Years at Southwestern Has Meant to Me," May 19, 1937.
108. Ullrich Papers, Folder entitled Correspondence: Board of Trustees, undated letter shortly after May 19, 1931. The letter is unsigned, but the content identifies Gibbons almost certainly as the author.
109. SU Trustees 1925–34, June 2, 1933, p. 409.
110. SU Faculty 1913–34, March 15, 1932, p. 509.
111. SU Trustees 1925–34, June 3, 1929, p. 188.
112. Ibid., p. 200.
113. SU Trustees 1925–34, January 9, 1930, p. 230. The comment of the neighbor came from a conversation of the author with Mrs. Mary Ann Barbour, daughter of Dean Ullrich, on May 26, 2004.
114. SU Trustees 1925–34, January 9, 1930, p. 253.
115. SU Ex Com 1923–36, April 29, 1932.
116. MKSB #30, p. 12, "Southwestern U. Announces Big Slash in Tuition," *WC Sun*, February 6, 1934.
117. SU Trustees 1925–34, April 20, 1932, pp. 361–362.
118. SU Trustees 1925–34, June 3, 1929, pp. 195–197.
119. SU Trustees 1935–47, May 23, 1935, p. 18.
120. SU Trustees 1925–34, October 24, 1933, p. 425.
121. SU Trustees 1925–34, June 2, 1933, p. 408.
122. *Megaphone*, "Davidson to Direct Educational Work; Assumes Duties with the Civilian Corps at Denison," February 27, 1934, p. 1.
123. *The Megaphone*, "Quebedeaux and Davidson Are Awarded; Dorothy Davidson Gets Dictionary for Highest Average," September 18, 1934, p. 4.
124. MKSB #31, p. 25, "Magna Cum Laude Seniors, Woodrow Wyatt and Dorothy Davidson Active in Many Fields," *Megaphone*, May 14, 1937.
125. MKSB #31, p. 6, Peal A. Neas, "Randolph Wood Tinsley, A Personal Appreciation," *WC Sun*, 1936.
126. MKSB #29, p. 59, "Honored by McMurry," unattributed, undated news article of ca. June 1, 1933.
127. MKSB #29, p. 5, "'Capt.' Kidd to Assist Edens," unattributed, undated news article of ca. Sept., 1929.
128. MKSB #31, p. 48, "Kidd Leaves Southwestern," *WC Sun*, February 11, 1938.
129. MKSB #31, p. 68, "Ex-Southwestern Man Will Succeed Roy B. Henderson," *Austin American*, February 22, 1938.
130. MKSB #30, p. 17, "Returns to Southwestern," *WC Sun*, August 31, 1934.
131. Takako Sudo-Shimamura, "John C. Granbery: Three Academic Freedom Controversies in the Life of a Social Gospeler in Texas (1920–1938)" (master's thesis, The University of Texas at Austin, 1971), pp. 40–41.
132. MKSB #28, p. 31, "Southwestern Revisited," *WC Sun*, June 8, 1928.
133. MKSB #28, p. 33, "What Is to Become of Our Church Schools?," reprint in *WC Sun* on April 19, 1929, of article by Dr. John C. Granbery in *Texas Christian Advocate*.
134. MKSB #30, p. 20, "Annual Dinner of Golden Bowl Is Held Friday, Mrs. John C. Granbery Named Honor Guest by Dean," *WC Sun*, October 26, 1934.
135. MKSB #30, p. 32, "Faculty Club to Meet Monday, Mrs. McKennon and Dr. Granbery Are on Program," *WC Sun*, November 23, 1934.
136. SU Faculty 1934–44, January 8, 1935, p. 581.
137. MKSB #30, p. 46, "Supervisor of Women Announced by Bergin," *Austin Statesman*, September 1, 1935.
138. SU Ex Com 1923–36, October 22, 1935.
139. SU Trustees 1925–34, January 9, 1930, p. 238.
140. Southern Association, "Special Study."
141. SU Faculty 1913–34, April 3, April 10, 1934, pp. 562–563.
142. SU Faculty 1913–34, December 17, 1934, p. 580. Also, SU Ex Com 1923–36, December 18, 1934.
143. SU Faculty 1934–44, March 18, 1935.
144. SU Ex Com 1923–36, July 26, 1935.
145. SU Trustees 1935–47, May 23, 1935, p. 3.
146. SU Ex Com 1923–36, December 22, 1931.
147. MKSB #29, p. 40, "Southwestern University Starts Drive to Secure $100,000 to Pay Its Debts," *Austin American*, April 22, 1932.
148. MKSB #29, p. 48, "Southwestern University Will Carry On in Great Work," *WC Sun*, May 27, 1932.
149. *Megaphone*, "Tapp Estate Leaves $150,000 for School," February 24, 1933, p. 4.
150. *Megaphone*, "Harrells Give $30,000 to Endowment," December 19, 1933, p. 1.
151. SU Trustees 1935–47, May 23, 1935, p. 14.
152. SU Trustees 1925–34, June 2, 1933, p. 400.
153. SU Faculty 1913–34, February 20, 1933.
154. SU Trustees 1935–47, May 23, 1935, p. 13.
155. SU Trustees 1925–34, January 8, 1931, pp. 292–293.
156. SU Ex Com 1923–36, September 17, 1931. Ralph Jones states—Jones, "History of SU" (dissertation), pp. 542–543—that "the faculty had already taken a 10% salary cut in 1931. It agreed to another 25% reduction on Apr. 20, 1932." Ralph Jones, who is usually very accurate in reporting his facts when he has adequate data, is simply mistaken in this regard. He probably did not see the statement in the Executive Committee minutes that "no action was taken" after the Executive Committee discussed the possibility of a 10 percent cut. This writer verified the amount of the cut in faculty salaries during the Depression by comparing the salaries in 1929–1930, 1932–1933, and 1935–1936. All seventeen salaries in 1932–1933, except for that of Vaden, were exactly 25 percent lower than they had been in 1929–1930. For some reason Vaden's was only 21.2 percent less. There was no change in assigned salaries between 1932–1933 and 1935–1936. Pearl A. Neas confirms that there was only one across-the-board salary reduction of 25 percent in a letter of April 29, 1942, from her to President-elect Score. She says: "You may not know that all staff salaries were reduced 25% during the depression." See Presidential Archives, Pearl A. Neas Files, Box F18, #070217.
157. SU Trustees 1925–34, April 20, 1932, pp. 358–359.
158. Ibid., pp. 351–355.
159. SU Ex Com 1923–36, October 6, 1932.
160. SU Faculty 1913–34, October 19, 1932, p. 520.
161. SU Faculty 1913–34, February 20, 1933, p. 528.
162. SU Trustees 1925–34, June 2, 1933, pp. 401, 408.
163. SU Ex Com 1923–36, June 15, 1933. SU Faculty 1913–34, June 20, 1933.
164. Southern Association, "Special Study," p. 18.
165. SU Ex Com 1923–36, July 13, 1933.
166. Southern Association, "Special Study," p. 32.
167. SU Trustees 1925–34, May 31, 1934, p. 451.
168. Ibid., pp. 442–444.
169. Ibid., p. 453.
170. SU Ex Com 1923–36, December 18, 1934.
171. Oscar A. Ullrich, "Assessment of Financial Situation," Georgetown, May 14, 1935.
172. SU Trustees 1935–47, May 23, 1935, pp. 18, 27. SU Ex Com 1923–36, May 24, 1935.

173. SU Ex Com 1923–36, July 26, 1935.
174. *Megaphone*, "Southwestern Will Not Be Moved; Commissioners Decide That University Will Remain in Present Location," February 27, 1934, p. 1.
175. MKSB #29, p. 47, "Methodists Urge Unified School Plan," *Houston Chronicle*, October 31, 1932.
176. Jones, "History of SU" (dissertation), pp. 551–552.
177. Massengale, "Methodist Collegiate Education," pp. 219–220.
178. The $432,414 in obligations was reported as follows: $271,650, Missouri State Life Insurance Company; $15,000, Farmers State Bank of Georgetown; $7,500, National Bank of Commerce, Houston; $45,094, unpaid teachers' salaries; $52,609, owed to the endowment fund; $40,561, other notes and open accounts.
179. Jones, "History of SU" (dissertation), pp. 551–552.
180. Massengale, "Methodist Collegiate Education," pp. 219–220.
181. MKSB #30, p. 3, "Move Southwestern to San Antonio Plan of Methodist Board," *Austin American*, September 28, 1933.
182. Ibid.
183. MKSB #30, p. 2, "Vivion Declares Southwestern to Stay Where It Is," *Austin American*, September 28, [1933].
184. MKSB #30, p. ?, Lorraine Barnes, "Southwestern U. Proud of Financial Status So Scoffs at Rumor of Its Removal," *Austin Statesman*, October 2, 1933.
185. *Megaphone*, "Vivion Denies Southwestern Will Move; Southwestern Will Stay in Georgetown President Declares in Formal Statement; Here Permanently: Church Does Not Intend to Sell Christian Education," October 4, 1933.
186. SU Trustees 1925–34, October 24, 1933, pp. 427, 434–435.
187. MKSB #30, p. 6, "North Texas M. E. Compromises on College Mergers, Reorganization Entrusted to Committee of 30 by Conference," *Austin Statesman*, October 29, 1933.
188. *Megaphone*, "Conferences Plan New Joint Commission; Trustees to Have Complete Power for Final Action," p. 1.
189. PANC, Box 7, Scrapbook #3, "West Texas M.E. Conference Ends at San Antonio; Conference Accepts North Texas Plan for Educational Commission; Victory for S.U.," *Williamson County Sun*, November 3, 1933.
190. PANC, Box 7, Scrapbook #3, "President Vivion Leads Fight to Organize New Education Commission; Board of Trustees Back University President in Efforts to Stabilize School," October 31, 1933.
191. PANC, Box 7, Scrapbook #3, "School Union Step Nearer," unknown San Antonio newspaper, January 22, 1934.
192. PANC, Box 7, Scrapbook #3, Minutes of the "Joint Commissions—Southwestern System of Colleges," February 20, 1934. Most of the material in this section is taken from these minutes.
193. SU Trustees 1935–47, May 23, 1935, pp. 20–21.
194. Southern Association, "Special Study," p. 6.
195. Vivion Collection. The thirty-seven persons include all the persons that signed the two petitions and/or wrote personal letters to the administration.
196. MKSB #35, p. 28, "Women's Building Named in Honor of Dean Kuykendall," *WC Sun*, May 24, 1940. Also, SU Ex Com 1940–41, August 2, 1940, p. 100.
197. SU Ex Com 1923–36, July 26, 1935.
198. MKSB #30, p. 45, "Vivion Resigns as S. U. Prexy," *WC Sun*, August 2, 1935.
199. MKSB #30, p. 39, "President Vivion to Be in Nashville," *WC Sun*, March 29, 1935.
200. MKSB #30, pp. 51–55, "Goes to McKendree M.E. Church, Nashville," *WC Sun*, November 8, 1935.
201. MKSB #30, p. 56, "Grady Timmons Baccalaureate Speaker June 8," *Progressive Citizen*, May 23, 1936.
202. SU Ex Com 1923–36, August 27, 1935.
203. SU Trustees 1935–47, August 27, 1935, pp. 37–39.
204. MKSB #30, p. 46, "Dr. Score to Head Southwestern, Fort Worth Pastor Elected to Succeed Dr. King Vivion," *San Antonio Express*, August 28, 1935.
205. MKSB #30, p. 47, "Dr. Score in Conference Here Wednesday," *WC Sun*, ca. August 23, 1935.
206. MKSB #30, p. 46, "Dr. J. N. R. Score Refuses Offer, Presidency of Southwestern Is Declined by Pastor," *Houston Post*, August 29, 1935.
207. SU Trustees 1935–47, October 22, 1935, p. 38.
208. Norman W. Spellmann, *Growing a Soul: The Story of A. Frank Smith* (Dallas: SMU Press, 1979), p. 295.
209. MKSB #30, p. 49, "Southwestern Prexy Greeted," *Houston Post*, October 31, 1935.

CHAPTER XV
Toward Financial Stability (1935–1942)

1. SU Trustees 1935–47, June 4, 1936, pp. 53–54.
2. MKSB #31, p. 26, Don Scarbrough, "Bergin Piloted Southwestern U. out of the Red and into Black," *Austin Statesman*, May 2, 1937.
3. MKSB #34, p. 35, Will H. Mayes, "College President John W. Bergin Cut Business Teeth as Post Newsboy," *Houston Post*, May 21, 1939.
4. MKSB #30, p. 48, "Dr. Bergin Heads Southwestern, Announces Six-Ply Program of Building and Expansion," *San Antonio Express*, October 23, 1935. In his 1937 Board Report he clarified the goal of seven hundred students by saying that "the number 700 does not literally mean 700 but such an approximation of that number whereat it was believed Southwestern could do her most outstanding work [p.72]."
5. SU Trustees 1935–47, June 4, 1936, p. 54.
6. Mary Ann Barbour, Interviews by WBJ, Georgetown, 2004 (interview of June 30, 2004). Her source was Grant Scoggins, first chair trumpet in the band during the Bergin years.
7. MKSB #30, p. 50, "Acting President Made Permanent by Board of Trustees Action Tues.," *WC Sun*, October 25, 1935.
8. MKSB #31, p. 64, "Russian Princess Famous Musician in Central Texas; Will Conduct Tour of Russian Chorus in Late Spring," *WC Sun*, April 16, 1937.
9. *Stevens Point Daily Journal*, Stevens Point, Wisconsin, October 13 and October 18, 1933, and June 15, 1934. Also, *Charleston Daily Mail*, January 20, 1935.
10. MKSB #31, p. 23, "Mme. Slaviansky Selected as S.U. Voice Professor," *WC Sun*, March 27, 1936.
11. MKSB #30, p. 56, "The Southwestern University Chorus," *WC Sun*, April 26, 1936.
12. MKSB #30, p. 61. "The Southwestern Chorus," *Bulletin of Southwestern University* 5 (May 1936): 2.
13. SU Trustees 1935–47, June 4, 1936, pp. 48, 55.
14. MKSB #34, p. 73, "Views of Southwestern University," April 1937.
15. MKSB #31, p. 24, "Russian Chorus Returns Intact; Discouraged Packards Make Trip in Good Style; Travels to Chicago and Back," *Megaphone*, May 14, 1937.
16. SU Trustees 1935–47, June 7, 1937. p. 80.
17. MKSB #34, p. 37, "Chorus Departure Set for Sunday; Will Make Trip to Baltimore by Bus," *WC Sun*, May 12, 1939.
18. MKSB #34, p. 49, July 14, 1939.
19. MKSB #34, p. 55, "Mme. Slaviansky to Direct Methodist Church Choir," September 15, [1939].
20. MKSB #34, p. 33, "Program of the Faculty Club," March 18, 1940.
21. SU Trustees 1935–47, May 8, 1941, pp. 231–254.
22. SU Ex Com 1940–41, November 22, 1940, p. 110.
23. MKSB #35, p. 85, "Miss Slaviansky and Mr. Gross Are Presented in Chicago Concert," *WC Sun*, January 24, 1941.
24. MKSB #36, p. 18, "Mme. Slaviansky Heads Chicago Russian Chorus," *Austin American*, March 14, 1941.
25. MKSB #36, p. 25, "Slaviansky Conducts Great Festival," *Musical News*, April 3, 1941.
26. MKSB #36, p. 85, "Miss Slaviansky and Mr. Gross Are Presented in Chicago Concert," *WC Sun*, January 24, 1941.
27. SU Trustees 1935–47, June 4, 1936, p. 48.
28. MKSB #31, p. 4, "Famed Band Leader Comes to Southwestern," *WC Sun*, June 12, 1936.

29. Barbour, Barbour Interviews by WBJ, June 30, 2004. Her source was Grant Scoggins, first chair trumpet in the band during the Bergin years.
30. MKSB #31, p. 5, "Southwestern's 'Swing Band,'" *WC Sun*, August 21, 1936.
31. Ibid.
32. MKSB #31, p. 4, "Famed Band Leader Comes to Southwestern," *WC Sun*, June 12, 1936.
33. MKSB #34, p. 73, "Views of Southwestern University," April 1937.
34. SU Trustees 1935–47, June 7, 1937, p. 75.
35. MKSB #31, p. 4, "Southwestern U. Solicitors Seek Students: University Is Putting On Campaign for Increase in Enrollment," *WC Sun*, July [1936].
36. MKSB #31, p. 30, "SU Pageant Is Set Saturday in Georgetown," *Austin American-Statesman*, April 3, 1937.
37. SU Trustees 1935–47, June 7, 1937, pp. 79–80.
38. *The Megaphone*, "SU 'Swing Band' Does Swinging at Five Texas Towns," November 3, 1936, p. 1.
39. SU Trustees 1935–47, May 19, 1938, p. 141.
40. SU Ex Com 1936–40, February 21, 1939, p. 129.
41. SU Trustees 1935–47, May 18, 1939, p. 154.
42. Barbour, Barbour Interviews by WBJ, June 30, 2004, Her source was Grant Scoggins, first chair trumpet in the band during the Bergin years.
43. *Megaphone*, p. 1, articles of November 10, 1936, and October 26, 1937.
44. MKSB #35, p. 88, "Long Hours Spent in Producing Southwestern U. 'Pigskin Prevue,'" *Austin Daily Tribune*, February 11, 1941.
45. Norman W. Spellmann, *Growing a Soul: The Story of A. Frank Smith* (Dallas: SMU Press, 1979), p. 312. Most of the material related to the life of A. Frank Smith in Chapters XV–XVIII comes from this carefully researched and well-written biography. Spellmann obtained most of his information from source materials carefully referenced in the book. Persons wishing to access these source materials should consult Spellmann's book for the relevant information as to their location, particularly Chapter 2 (entitled "Study to Show Thyself Approved," pp. 19–44, endnotes, pp. 433–437) and Chapter 14 (entitled "Southwestern University," pp. 287–314, endnotes, pp. 477–484).
46. Spellmann, *Growing a Soul*, p. 314.
47. Ibid., p. 289.
48. Ibid., p. 292.
49. Ibid., p. 288.
50. Ibid.
51. MKSB #31, p. 30, "Southwestern U. Freed of Debt; Endowment Hiked by $200,000 Due to Gifts of Houston Woman," *Dallas Morning News*, March ?, 1937, from Georgetown, Texas, March 15, 1937.
52. Spellmann, *Growing a Soul*, p. 289.
53. *Megaphone*, "Frank Andrews, Distinguished S. U. Ex, Dies," December 15, 1936, p. 1.
54. Presidential Archives, Mrs. J. J. Perkins Files, Score to J. J. Perkins, August 25, 1948.
55. MKSB #36, p. 1, "Mrs. William Wiess," *The Southwestern Advocate*, October 12, 1939, p. 24.
56. MKSB #36, p. 1, "William Wiess," *The Southwestern Advocate*, October 12, 1939, p. 24.
57. SU Trustees 1935–47, January 19, 1937, pp. 67–69.
58. Ibid.
59. SU Faculty 1934–44, February 27, 1937, pp. 616–617.
60. *Megaphone*, "Southwestern Clears Debts; Adds Endowment," March 16, 1937, p. 1.
61. *Megaphone*, "Report Made by Trustees," March 16, 1937, p. 2.
62. Ullrich Papers, Correspondence, Wiess Gift, Letter of March 17, 1937, from Oscar A. Ullrich to Dr. C. C. Cody.
63. William C. Finch, Interviews by Martha Allen, August 1992, four tapes (transcribed). Finch referred to it in his interviews with Dr. Allen in 1992 as follows: "Dr. McCook, I think, Lucy [Mrs. Finch] was just reading somewhere recently about his wild ride from Georgetown to Houston, to bring the figures to show that we had on the last day, a matter of hours before the deadline, that we had managed" (tape 1, p. 25). I believe that I first learned about the trip directly from Dr. McCook, with whom I discussed these and many other matters. More than thirty years, however, have dimmed my memory of the particulars of some of these conversations, and I cannot vouch for the details of the trip.
64. *The Sou'wester*, 1937. A photocopy of the actual dated, notarized document appears in the volume.
65. SU Trustees 1935–47, June 7, 1937, pp. 71–114.
66. SU Ex Com 1940–41. This amount is $1,125 more than the $615,295.35 reported at the Executive Committee meeting on April 21, 1937 (p. 22). The amount reported there is without detail except for the $44,004.23 in notes and pledges, which is the same in both reckonings.
67. SU Trustees 1935–47, June 7, 1937, p. 104.
68. *Megaphone*, "Bergin for Bishop!," November 2, 1937, p. 2.
69. SU Trustees 1935–47, June 7, 1937, pp. 112–113.
70. Ullrich Papers, Correspondence, Board of Trustees, Letter of March 10, 1938, from Oscar A. Ullrich to the Board of Trustees.
71. SU Ex Com 1923–36, July 26, 1935.
72. Lucy Belle Morgan was the sister of Ruth Morgan Ferguson, soon to be named Dean of Women.
73. MKSB #29, p. 5, "Waggoner to Head Work in Religious Education Here," unnamed, undated Georgetown newspaper, 1929.
74. *Megaphone*, "Seniors Take-off Is Huge Success," p. 1.
75. *Megaphone*, "Tribute Paid to Luther Waggoner," October 20, 1936, p. 2.
76. Ullrich Papers, Correspondence, Board of Trustees, Letter of March 10, 1938, from Oscar A. Ullrich to the Board of Trustees.
77. MKSB #36, p. 32, John C. Granbery, "Honoring Luther J. Waggoner," *WC Sun*, June 6, 1941.
78. SU Trustees 1935–47, May 18, 1939, p. 190.
79. GL, Packet 9.5, Letter from Ella Tucker Granbery to John C. Granbery, January 27, 1937.
80. SU Ex Com 1936–40, January 19, 1937, p. 31.
81. MKSB #31, p. 57, Pearl Alma Neas, "Mrs. Granbery Resigns as Supervisor of Women at Southwestern Univ., An Appreciation," unnamed, undated newspaper.
82. Stanford-Cody Letters, Stanford to Cody, May 29, 1938.
83. MKSB #31, p. 80, "So'western Swastika Laid to Prof Ouster," *Austin American-Statesman*, May 22, 1938.
84. SU Ex Com 1936–40, February 11, 1938, pp. 47–48.
85. Ibid., p. 48.
86. In his account of Granbery's appearances before the Executive Committee and the full Board, Takako Sudo-Shimamura (Takako Sudo-Shimamura, "John C. Granbery: Three Academic Freedom Controversies in the Life of a Social Gospeler in Texas [1920–1938]" [master's thesis, University of Texas at Austin, 1976], pp. 43–47) seems not to have had a precise record of what occurred at his disposal. His account is close to what actually happened but is in error on a number of fundamental issues and minor points. Illustrations are his dating of the Executive Committee and Board meetings and his statement that Granbery was given only thirty minutes to make his case at the Board meeting. He dates the two meetings as February 5 and May 9 rather than February 11 and May 19, respectively. At the Board meeting a motion was indeed made to limit Granbery to thirty minutes, as Sudo-Shimamura alleges, but it was laid on the table, and he got as much time as he needed. Sudo-Shimamura appears to have had access to the memories of one or another of the persons who attended the meeting but not to an actual copy of the minutes.
87. SU Ex Com 1936–40, January 19, 1937, p. 31.
88. Patricia L. Jakobi, "Cody, Claude Carr, Jr.," HBTO, July 23, 2002.
89. Ullrich Papers, Correspondence, Board of Trustees, Letter of March 10, 1938, from Oscar A. Ullrich to the Board of Trustees.
90. Ibid.
91. SU Trustees 1935–47, May 19, 1938, pp. 117.
92. Stanford-Cody Letters, Stanford to Cody, May 29, 1938.

93. Ullrich Papers, Faculty, Correspondence, Wiess Gift, Letter dated March 5, 1938, by Bergin to the Board.
94. Ibid.
95. Stanford-Cody Letters, Cody to Stanford, May 27, 1938.
96. SU Trustees 1935–47, May 19, 1938, p 136.
97. Ibid., p. 143.
98. MKSB #31, p. 80, "So'western Swastika Laid to Prof Ouster," *Austin American-Statesman*, May 22, 1938.
99. MKSB #35, p. 83, announcement in unspecified Austin newspaper.
100. MKSB #31, p. 96, "Dr. Grandbery [sic] Is Named Member of Society," *WC Sun*, July 15, 1938.
101. Stanford-Cody Letters, Stanford to Cody, May 23, 1938.
102. Stanford-Cody Letters, Stanford to Cody, May 29, 1938.
103. Ullrich Papers. Faculty, Correspondence, Wiess Gift, Letter dated March 5, 1938, by Bergin to the Board.
104. *Megaphone*, articles in issues of April 18, 1936, April 16, 1937, and April 26, 1938.
105. Sudo-Shimamura, "Granbery: Three Controversies," pp. 43–47.
106. *Megaphone*, "Young Men Patriots Sanction Defensive War," May 5, 1936, p. 3.
107. *Megaphone*, "Ed Stanford Is A.S.U. President," September 28, 1937.
108. Sudo-Shimamura, "Granbery: Three Controversies," p. 68.
109. Ibid., p. 79.
110. Ford Dixon, "Granbery, John Cowper, Jr.," HBTO, July 23, 2002.
111. James McEnteer, *Fighting Words: Independent Journalists in Texas* (Austin: University of Texas Press, 1992), pp. 67-68.
112. Ibid., p. 78.
113. MKSB #31, p. 1, "Dr. C. T. Thrift Named Head of Religious Activity at S. U.," unnamed newspaper, prior to September 14, 1936.
114. Ullrich Papers, Letter of March 10, 1938, from Dean Ullrich to "Members of the Board of Trustees"; Letter from Dean Ullrich to C. C. Cody, Jr., June 3, 1938.
115. SU Trustees 1935–47, June 7, 1937, pp. 71–114.
116. SU Trustees 1935–47, May 19, 1938, p. 141.
117. Ibid., p. 137.
118. SU Ex Com 1936–40, June 17, 1938, p. 55.
119. SU Ex Com 1936–40, February 21, 1939, p. 97.
120. SU Trustees 1935–47, May 19, 1939, pp. 159–164.
121. Ibid., p. 173.
122. MKSB #34, p. 93, "Abstract of the Minutes of the Executive Committee Meeting Held on June 13, 1939." Also, Presidential Archives, Charles T. Thrift File #1, "University in Texas Honors Dr. Thrift," *Lakeland Ledger*, February 11, 1965.
123. MKSB #29, p. 20, "Plans Being Made to Start on New Building: Noted Architect on Campus Monday to Draw Up Plans" and "Memorial Library Building Total Is Now in Sight," *WC Sun*, May 8, 1930. Also, SU Trustees 1925–34, June 1, 1931, p. 311.
124. SU Trustees 1935–47, Minutes of Called Meeting of the Finance Committee of the Board of Trustees, Houston, Texas, August 18, 1938, pp. 145–146.
125. SU Ex Com 1936–40, October 14, l938, pp. 67–68.
126. Spellmann, *Growing a Soul*, p. 293.
127. Ibid., pp. 293–294.
128. MKSB #34, p. 19, probably *WC Sun*, after December 22, before December 30, 1938.
129. SU Ex Com 1936–40, February 21, 1939, p. 94.
130. MKSB #34, p. 3, "Work Is Started on S.U. Library," *Austin American-Statesman*, January 2, 1939.
131. MKSB #34, p. 59, "Formal Opening Cody Memorial Library Building," November 26, 1939.
132. SU Trustees 1935–47, May 18, 1939, pp. 147–198.
133. MKSB #35, p. 31, "Jesse Jones Will Be One of Main Speakers at Fete," *WC Sun*, March 15, 1940.
134. SU Ex Com 1936–40, October 13, 1939, p. 185.
135. SU Trustees 1935–47, July 10, 1941, p. 256.
136. SU Trustees 1935–47, May 18, 1939, pp. 160–161.
137. MKSB #34, pp. 21, 45, "Georgetown Requested To Give $5,000 on Gymnasium Project" and "Council Presented with a Petition Containing Names of 259 Voters," two undated articles, probably in the *WC Sun*, probably January 1939.
138. SU Trustees 1935–47, May 18, 1939, pp. 169, 171–172.
139. SU Ex Com 1936–40, December 22, 1939, p. 217.
140. SU Ex Com 1940–41, February 16, 1940, pp. 5–6.
141. Ibid., pp. 6–7.
142. MKSB #35, p. 70, article from unnamed newspaper of September 28, 1940.
143. Spellmann, *Growing a Soul*, p. 290.
144. MKSB #36, p. 38, "Benefactor of Southwestern U. Dies in K. C.; Heart Attack Is Fatal to J. M. West, Austin Tribune Publisher," *WC Sun*, August 29, 1941.
145. Claudia Hazlewood, "West, James Marion," HBTO, July 23, 2002.
146. SU Ex Com 1940–41, July 10, 1941, p. 228.
147. Presidential Archives, Bron J. Marion West, Jr., Files, "Eccentric Millionaire, Silver Dollar West, Dies," *Dallas Morning News*, December 18, 1957, Part I-21.
148. SU Ex Com 1940–41, February 21, 1941, pp. 171–172, and April 18, 1941, p. 203. Also, SU Ex Com 1942–52, July 31, 1942, pp. 57, 61, 72.
149. SU Ex Com 1940–41, April 12, 1940, pp. 42–87.
150. MKSB #34, p. 73, "Views of Southwestern University," April 1937.
151. Booth Mooney, "A University with an Individuality," June 20, 1936, probably taken from Pearl Neas, who uses the same figure.
152. SU Trustees 1935–47, May 18, 1939. p. 172.
153. SU Trustees 1935–47, June 7, 1937, pp. 71–114.
154. SU Ex Com 1940–41, February 16, 1940, pp. 1–41.
155. SU Trustees 1935–47, May 16, 1940, p. 219.
156. SU Ex Com 1940–41, February 21, 1941, pp. 150–193.
157. SU Trustees 1935–47, June 7, 1937, p. 74.
158. SU Ex Com 1936–40, June 17, 1938, p. 55.
159. SU Trustees 1935–47, May 16, 1940, pp. 209–210, 221–222.
160. SU Trustees 1935–47, May 8, 1941, pp. 231–254.
161. SU Trustees 1935–47, May 18, 1939, pp. 184–190.
162. SU Trustees 1935–47, May 8, 1942, p. 304.
163. *Megaphone*, "Southern Ass'n. Lifts Probation on Southwestern," March 29, 1938, p. 1.
164. SU Trustees 1935–47, May 19, 1938, pp. 120–121.
165. Ibid., pp. 115–116.
166. MKSB #34, p. 79, "Abstract of Minutes of Meeting of the Executive Committee," February 21, 1939.
167. SU Trustees 1935–47, May 18, 1939, p. 155.
168. SU Ex Com 1936–40, February 16, 1940, p. 4.
169. SU Ex Com 1936–40, April 12, 1940, p. 50.
170. SU Ex Com 1936–40, February 21, 1939, p. 96.
171. SU Trustees 1935–47, May 16, 1940, p. 200.
172. *Megaphone*, Pearl A. Neas, "Over Fifty Percent of Student Body Is Preceeded [sic] at S.U. by Relatives" and "Forty-Five S.U. Students from Parsonage Homes," Nov. 2, 1937, pp. 3–4.
173. MKSB #31, p. 35, "Majority of S.U. Students Belong to the Methodist Church," *WC Sun*, October 29, 1937.
174. SU Trustees 1935–47, May 16, 1940, p. 200.
175. SU Trustees 1935–47, May 19, 1938, pp. 122–123.
176. SU Trustees 1935–47, November 25, 1941, p. 262.
177. SU Ex Com 1936–40, October 13, 1939, pp. 211–213. Figures furnished by the Registrar's Office.
178. MKSB #31, p. 52, "Mrs. Ferguson Is Named New Dean of Women," *WC Sun*, August 13, 1937.
179. *Megaphone*, "Mrs. Ruth Ferguson Assumes New Duties in Girls Dormitory as Dean of Women," September 14, 1937, p. 1.
180. *The Megaphone*, May 4, 1948, p. 3, has a number of articles covering the May Day celebration. It is called the May Fête in each instance where it is identified.
181. Ralph Wood Jones, "A History of Southwestern University, 1873–1949" (doctoral dissertation, University of Texas, 1960), p. 502, endnote 41. The last May Fête occurred in 1950. It "came to a tragic

close," says Ralph Jones, "when a stray dog investigated the May pole for his own natural purposes in the midst of the circle of dancing girls. The source is the writer's eye-witness account."

182. Nell Barnes Benold, "Memories of Laura Kuykendall Hall," Georgetown, November 29, 2000. Barbour. Barbour Interviews by WBJ.
183. SU Trustees 1935–47, June 7, 1937, p. 78.
184. SU Trustees 1935–47, November 25, 1941, p. 261.
185. SU Trustees 1935–47, May 8, 1941, p. 234.
186. SU Trustees 1935–47, May 16, 1940, p. 201. Also, SU Trustees 1957–60, April 16, 1958, p. 51.
187. MKSB #34, p. 53, "McMurry Mentor Chosen to Succeed Edens as S. U. Coach," *WC Sun*, August 11, 1939.
188. SU Trustees 1947–53, April 21, 1948, p. 36.
189. Coach Medley approached me on the golf course one afternoon several years after I came to Southwestern in 1965. He said, "Young man, I see you're playing with only three clubs." I said, "Yes, sir, my wife and I have four young children, and I can't afford a full set." He said in response: "You're the person I've been looking for. Neely Landrum [a major Southwestern donor] has just given me a new set of the best clubs money can buy. Though I would rather continue using my old set, I must use the ones Landrum gave me. I haven't wanted to sell my clubs to just anyone, so I've been looking for someone to give them to, someone who needs them and will appreciate them." With that, he took the bag off his shoulders and gave it to me. On examining the set later, I could see why he was so partial to it. It was made up of clubs calculated to enhance his particular golf style. One of the clubs was a 2½ driver to accommodate his wood shots that were not particularly long but very accurate. WBJ.
190. SU Trustees 1935–47, June 7, 1937, p. 82.
191. SU Ex Com 1940–41, February 16, 1940, p. 36.
192. SU Trustees 1935–47, June 7, 1937, p. 80.
193. SU Trustees 1935–47, May 19, 1938, p. 124.
194. SU Trustees 1935–47, June 4, 1936, p. 49.
195. SU Trustees 1935–47, May 19, 1938, p. 118.
196. *Sou'wester*, 1941, p. 121. Ralph Jones is mistaken in placing it on September 27, 1941. See Jones, "History of SU" (dissertation), p. 584.
197. SU Trustees 1935–47. May 16, 1940, p. 224.
198. SU Ex Com 1940–41, Feb. 21, 1946, p. 157.
199. SU Trustees 1935–47, May 8, 1941, p. 249.
200. MKSB #35, p. 85, "Birthday Picnic Ends in Tragedy for S.U. Student," *WC Sun*, January 17, 1941.
201. Barbour, Barbour Interviews by WBJ.
202. *Megaphone*, "Godbey Speaks on War Problems," November 9, 1937, p. 1.
203. MKSB #34, p. 30, "Dr. J. P. Bartak in Georgetown," *WC Sun*, April 14, 1939.
204. MKSB #36, p. 21, "Knickerbocker to Speak Here for Theta Sigs," *Austin Tribune*, April 2, 1941.
205. Edgar P. Sneed, "Knickerbocker, Hubert Renfro," HBTO, July 23, 2002.
206. MKSB #36, pp. 25–26, "Knickerbocker Looks to Britain," *Austin American*, April 23, 1941, and "'All Aid to Britain Short of Nothing' Knickerbocker Urges," *WC Sun*, April 25, 1941.
207. SU Ex Com 1940–41, August 2, 1940, pp. 89, 91, 125.
208. SU Trustees 1935–47, May 8, 1941, p. 235.
209. SU Trustees 1935–47, November 25, 1941, p. 262.
210. SU Ex Com 1940–41, February 21, 1941, p. 151.
211. SU Ex Com 1940–41, November 22, 1940, pp. 110–125.
212. MKSB #36, p. 14, "Civilian Pilot Training Course at S. U. Expands Consistently," *WC Sun*, May 16, 1941.
213. SU Ex Com 1940–41, Condensed Financial Report, October 15, 1941, pp. 1–14.
214. MKSB #35, p. 74, "Flying School Opens This Week," *WC Sun*, October 11, 1940.
215. MKSB #35, p. 88, "20 S'western Students Fly," *Austin Daily Tribune*, February 11, 1941.
216. MKSB #36, p. 31, "Southwestern Aviation Course Is Successful; Training for Airmen May Be Broadened in Near Future to 100," *WC Sun*, May 20, 1941.
217. MKSB #36, p. 38, "Southwestern Arranges Courses for Air Men; New Requirements Allow Students to Become Cadets with Thirty Hours Work," *WC Sun*, August 29, 1941.
218. SU Trustees 1935–47, November 25, 1941, p. 268.
219. SU Trustees 1935–47, May 8, 1941, p. 251.
220. Ibid., p. 254.
221. SU Trustees 1935–47, July 10, 1941, pp. 256–258.
222. SU Trustees 1935–47, November 25, 1941, pp. 272–273.
223. Ibid., p. 277.
224. Spellmann, *Growing a Soul*, p. 479, endnotes 42–45. Their letters to each other on this issue are dated from December 2 to December 17, 1941.
225. Ibid., pp. 295–296.
226. SU Trustees 1935–47, February 11, 1942, p. 283.
227. Ibid., p. 284.
228. Spellmann, *Growing a Soul*, p. 296.
229. Presidential Archives, Bishop A. Frank Smith Files, Score to AFS, March 11, 1943,
230. Perkins Files, Finch to Mrs. Perkins, January 21, 1960.
231. SU Trustees 1935–47, February 11, 1942, pp. 284–287.
232. PANC, Box 9, Folder 6, p. 90, "Southwestern Gets Holiday after Prexy Is Grid Hero," *WC Sun*, November 21, 1941.
233. SU Faculty 1934–44, February 25, 1942, unnumbered page between pp. 688–689.
234. SU Trustees 1935–47, May 8, 1942, pp. 289–291.

CHAPTER XVI
World War II Expansion (1942–1945)

1. Ralph Wood Jones, *Southwestern University 1840–1961* (Austin: Jenkins Publishing Co., 1973), p. 302.
2. Norman W. Spellmann, *Growing a Soul: The Story of A. Frank Smith* (Dallas: SMU Press, 1979), p. 303.
3. Ralph Wood Jones, "A History of Southwestern University, 1873–1949" (doctoral dissertation, University of Texas, 1960), p. 591.
4. MKSB #36, p. 78, "Plans for Southwestern U. Outlined by Rev. Mr. Score, *Fort Worth Star-Telegram*, February 12, 1942.
5. Presidential Archives, Oscar A. Ullrich Files, memos of July 16, 1943, August 5, 1943, and August 7, 1944.
6. John Nelson Russell Score II, Interviews by Martha Allen, Georgetown, Southwestern University, Tape 3, pp. 86–87.
7. Various, "Alum Letters about Southwestern."
8. Ullrich Files, January 24, 1944.
9. Ullrich Files, February 4 and September 12, 1944.
10. Ullrich Files, April 18, 1942.
11. Forrest E. Ward, "Score, John Nelson Russell," HBTO, July 23, 2002.
12. Presidential Archives, Lyndon B. Johnson Files, Score to LBJ, December 16, 1943.
13. Angus Springer, *Exits and Entrances* (Austin: Whitley Company, 1982), pp. 11, 15.
14. Jones, "History of SU" (dissertation), p. 592.
15. SU Ex Com 1942–52, April 21, 1942, p. 31. Also, Spellmann, *Growing a Soul*, p. 297.
16. SU Trustees 1935–47, February 11, 1942, pp. 284–285.
17. Jones, "History of SU" (dissertation), p. 610.
18. SU Trustees 1935–47, April 30, 1947, pp. 477–481. The brochure is printed as an appendix in these Board minutes.
19. David Minor, "Westminster College," HBTO, July 23, 2002.
20. SU Ex Com 1942–52, February 25, April 21, July 31, 1942, and March 5, 1943, pp. 5–6, 34, 63, 93.
21. SU Trustees 1935–47, May 17, 1944, p. 390.
22. SU Ex Com 1942–52, August 24, 1943, pp. 129–130.
23. SU Trustees 1935–47, November 19, 1942, pp. 331–334.
24. SU Ex Com 1942–52, March 5, 1943, p. 88.

25. SU Trustees 1935–47, November 16, 1943, pp. 374–375.
26. SU Ex Com 1942–52, March 21, 1944, p. 156.
27. MKSB #38, p. 41, "Southwestern to Pursue Plan for Expansion; President Score Announces 3½ Million Goal Next Two Years," *WC Sun*, May 26, 1944.
28. SU Trustees 1935–47, May 16, 1945, p. 423.
29. SU Faculty 1945–46, January 25, 1946, p. 27.
30. SU Trustees 1935–47, May 15, 1946, pp. 451–452.
31. Presidential Archives, Mrs. J. J. Perkins Files, Score to Mrs. Perkins, May 19, 1947.
32. SU Trustees 1947–53, April 21, 1948, p. 33.
33. SU Ex Com 1942–52, April 26, 1949, p. 201.
34. SU Ex Com 1942–52, October 14, 1949, p. 223.
35. SU Trustees 1947–53, November 15, 1949, p. 93.
36. LBJ Files, Score to Johnson, April 21, 1944.
37. Perkins Files, Mrs. Perkins to Score, January 9, 1948.
38. Robert A. Caro, *The Years of Lyndon Johnson: The Path to Power* (New York: Alfred A. Knopf, 1982), p. 261.
39. Ibid., p. 413.
40. Ibid., pp. 409, 413, 425.
41. Ibid., p. 448.
42. Joseph A. Pratt and Christopher J. Castaneda, *Builders: Herman and George R. Brown* (College Station: Texas A&M Press, 1999), p. 50.
43. Ibid., pp. 63–64.
44. I am presuming that Pearl Neas herself contributed the collection to the Cody Memorial Library. All of the LBJ letters come from files that she would have kept in the Registrar's office and have been carefully sorted out from the other types of correspondence and work related to the office. All of the letters are typed, and those in the collection are carbon paper copies of the originals. Pearl typed them herself. She was an excellent typist, having come to Southwestern as a stenographer in 1913. The letters on the part of Johnson are so personal and refer so often to events and conversations between him and Neas of which his secretaries would have been unaware that they must be attributed to him rather than to someone writing for him. Whenever an occasional letter comes to Neas from a secretary in the office, it is expressly indicated as such. Johnson dictated all his letters but often added handwritten comments when he signed them.
45. PANC, Box 1, Folder 3, January 1, 1943.
46. PANC, Box 1, Folder 4, April 18, 1944.
47. PANC, Box 5, Folder 5, May 2, 1944.
48. MKSB #37, p. 68, "Broadcast Series at Southwestern Begins August 20," *WC Sun*, August 6, 1943.
49. PANC, Box 1, Folder 3, May 1, 1943.
50. PANC, Box 1, Folder 7, April 19 and 23, 1947.
51. PANC, Box 1, Folder 7, April 28, 1947.
52. PANC, Box 1, Folder 6, March 27 and 28, 1945.
53. PANC, Box 1, Folders 3, 5, 6, on May 1, 1943, December 16, 1944, February 21, 1945, and October 18, 1945.
54. PANC, Box 1, Folder 5, August 1, 1944.
55. PANC, Box 1, Folder 6, April 17, 1945.
56. PANC, Box 1, Folder 7, October 16, 1947.
57. PANC, Box 1, Folder 8, June 2 and July 26, 1948.
58. PANC, Box 1, Folder 8, October 25, 1948.
59. PANC, Box 1, Folder 8, telegram of January 3, and letter of January 6, 1949.
60. LBJ Files, March 22, 1943. He closes a letter to LBJ on May 8, 1944: "With Love and appreciation."
61. LBJ Files, March 24, 1944.
62. LBJ Files, March 17, 1948.
63. LBJ Files, Score to LBJ, April 19, 1946.
64. LBJ Files, May 17, 1948.
65. LBJ Files, Walter Jenkins to Score, July 23, 1948.
66. LBJ Files, Score statement on Johnson, July 13, 1948.
67. LBJ Files, Score to Johnson, August 2, 1948, Johnson to Score, December 2, 1948.
68. LBJ Files, December 7, 1948.
69. MKSB #37, p. 17, "Southwestern Participating in Training Program," *WC Sun*, May 1, 1942.
70. LBJ Files, July 6, 1943.
71. SU Trustees 1935–47, May 19, 1943, p. 348.
72. LBJ Files, December 16, 1943.
73. Southwestern, "A Presentation of the Facilities of Southwestern University, Georgetown, Texas. Available for Use by the Federal Government in the War Emergency, 1942–43," January 1943.
74. SU Trustees 1935–47, May 19, 1943, p. 348.
75. SU Ex Com 1942–52, March 5, 1943, pp. 91–92.
76. LBJ Files, Score telegram to Johnson, January 8, 1943.
77. LBJ Files, Score letter to Johnson, January 9, 1943.
78. LBJ Files, January 18, 1943.
79. PANC, Box 1, Folder 3, February 18, 1943.
80. LBJ Files, February 27, 1943.
81. PANC, Box 1, Folder 6, March 1, 1943.
82. PANC, Box 1, Folder 3, March 4, 1943.
83. PANC, Box 1, Folder 6, February 24, 1945.
84. PANC, Box 1, Folder 6, April 23, 1945.
85. SU Ex Com 1942–52, August 24, 1943, pp. 128–129.
86. SU Ex Com 1942–52, March 5, 1943, pp. 91–92.
87. Ibid., p. 87.
88. LBJ Files, March 17, 1943.
89. LBJ Files, March 24, 1943.
90. LBJ Files, January 17, 1944.
91. SU Trustees 1935–47, May 19, 1943, p. 348.
92. LBJ Files, LBJ to Score, March 24, 1943, Score to LBJ, March 29, 1943.
93. LBJ Files, April 24, 1943.
94. MKSB #37, p. 43, "Johnson's Address to Seniors Of Southwestern to Be on Air," *Austin American*, May 25, 1943.
95. MKSB #37, p. 63, "Cong. Johnson to Deliver S. U. Address; 103rd Commencement Speaker Announced as Pres. Score Departs for Eastern Conference," *WC Sun*, May 19, 1943.
96. MKSB #37, p. 59, March 5, 1943.
97. MKSB #37, p. 63, "Educators Plan with Navy Vast Program; New York Meeting Lays Ground Work for Supplying Navy with Trained Personnel," *WC Sun*, May 14, 1943.
98. SU Trustees 1935–47, November 19, 1942, p. 320.
99. SU Trustees 1935–47, May 8, 1942, p. 309.
100. SU Ex Com 1942–52, April 21, 1942, p. 34.
101. SU Ex Com 1942–52, July 31, 1942, pp. 62, 72.
102. SU Ex Com 1942–52, March 5, 1943, p. 84.
103. SU Ex Com 1942–52, April 21, 1942, p. 35.
104. SU Trustees 1935–47, November 19, 1942, p. 321.
105. SU Ex Com 1942–52, March 5, 1943, pp. 89–90, 112.
106. SU Ex Com 1942–52, March 21, 1944, p. 155.
107. PANC, Box 9, Folder 10, p. 156, "Southwestern Pasteurizing Plant in Service," *WC Sun*, March 2, 1945.
108. Report of Business Manager, November 12, 1953.
109. Exec. Com. Report of August 15, 1956.
110. President's Report, Nov. 14, 1956, pp. 3–10.
111. SU Ex Com 1942–52, March 21, 1944, p. 158.
112. SU Trustees 1935–47, April 30, 1947, p. 477.
113. SU Faculty 1934–44, January 6, 1942, p. 287.
114. SU Faculty 1934–44, April 7, 1942, p. 690.
115. SU Trustees 1935–47, February 11, 1942, p. 282.
116. SU Trustees 1935–47, May 29, 1943, pp. 365–366.
117. LBJ Files. LBJ called it "The Ship" in a telegram to Score on January 17, 1944.
118. SU Ex Com 1942–52, August 24, 1943, pp. 128–129.
119. MKSB #37, p. 72, "Mood Hall Repairs Progress Rapidly," *WC Sun*, September 10, 1943. John Score says that the roof was put over the atrium at Mood so that it could serve as a parlor for the girls to receive the boys on dates, have parties, and entertain. Score, Interviews by Allen, Tape 2, p. 45.

120. L. D. Jones, Jr., "Memories of Southwestern University, 1943," August 23, 2004.
121. SU Ex Com 1942–52, August 24, 1943, p. 131.
122. Ibid., pp. 127–129.
123. SU Trustees 1935–47. November 21, 1945, p. 435.
124. MKSB #37, p. 78, "Kappa Alpha Fraternity Buys Dr. Gray Home," *WC Sun*, August 20, 1943.
125. SU Trustees 1935–47, November 21, 1945, pp. 433–435.
126. SU Ex Com 1942–52, August 24, 1943, pp. 128–129.
127. SU Ex Com 1942–52, September 19, 1944, p. 163.
128. "Fire Destroys Sneed House," *oHThe Bulletin of Southwestern University*, November 1978, p. 1.
129. SU Ex Com 1942–52, August 24, 1943, pp. 131–134.
130. MKSB #37, p. 106, "'Woodie' McCook Reported Missing in Asiatic Zone," *WC Sun*, August 20, 1943.
131. SU Trustees 1935–47, November 16, 1943, p. 381, May 16, 1945, p. 421.
132. PANC, Box 9, Folder 9, p. 150, "McCook Memorial Infirmary Now in Service," *WC Sun*, September 1, 1944.
133. MKSB #37, p. 14, "Ross Wilder Is One of Army Fliers Raiding Tokio," *WC Sun*, May 22, 1942.
134. MKSB #37, p. 54, "Georgetown Woman Who Lived in Asia Joins WAACs to Avenge Cruel Treatment of Friends," *WC Sun*, February 19, 1943.
135. PANC, Box 9, Folder 10, p. 159, "Capt. Anne Marie Doering Stationed at MacArthur's Headquarters in Manila," September 7, 1945.
136. Presidential Archives, Doering, Anne Marie, File.
137. MKSB #37, p. 78, "Patriotic Spirit Hovers over the Assembly; President Score and Naval Officers Speak at Convention," unnamed newspaper, July 9, 1943.
138. Presidential Archives, M. Howard Knox Files, "Reported Killed in Action," Late 1944 and November 28, 1945.
139. MKSB #37, p. 92, "Commander of Navy V-12 Unit Arrived on Southwestern Campus," unnamed newspaper, shortly after June 1, 1943.
140. PANC, Box 1, Folder 3, June 30, 1943.
141. Jones, "Marine Memories."
142. SU Ex Com 1942–52, August 24, 1943, p. 127.
143. MKSB #37, p. 78, "Patriotic Spirit Hovers over the Assembly; President Score and Naval Officers Speak at Convention," unnamed newspaper, July 9, 1943.
144. SU Trustees 1935–47, May 17, 1944, p. 393.
145. LBJ Files, January 5, 1944.
146. LBJ Files, February 9, 1944.
147. PANC, Box 9, Folder 10, p. 155, "SS S'western Is Launched," *Austin American*, May 1, 1945.
148. Jones, "Marine Memories."
149. MKSB #37, p. 79, "Johnson Will Inspect Naval Unit Here," *WC Sun*, August 27, 1943.
150. PANC, Box 1, Folder 6, PAN to LBJ, November 28, 1945.
151. LBJ Files, March 1, 1948.
152. LBJ Files, March 12, 1948.
153. SU Trustees 1935–47, January 14, 1944, pp. 384–385.
154. David Minor, "Weatherford College," HBTO, July 23, 2002.
155. SU Trustees 1935–47, May 17, 1944, p. 390.
156. SU Ex Com 1942–52, September 19, 1944, p. 163.
157. SU Trustees 1935–47, May 16, 1945, p. 421.
158. SU Ex Com 1942–52, September 12, 1945, p. 171.
159. SU Trustees 1935–47, November 21, 1945, p. 435, and May 15, 1946, p. 451.
160. SU Trustees 1935–47, November 21, 1945, p. 435.
161. SU Trustees 1935–47, May 15, 1946, pp. 442, 450–451.
162. MKSB #37, p. 93, "Southwestern Can Be Accused of Hoarding," *Houston Chronicle*, July 17, 1943.
163. MKSB #38, pp. 40–41, "Pirates Carry Off Game by 14-4 Count" and "Layne Holds Southwestern to Three Hits," *Austin American*, March 25–26, 1944.
164. MKSB #37, p. 37, June 29, 1943.
165. MKSB #37, p. 100, October 3, 1943.
166. MKSB #37, p. 98, Harold V. Ratliff, "Star-Studded Grid Squad Brings Plenty of Worries for Southwestern's Coach," unnamed newspaper, September 11, 1943.
167. MKSB #37, p. 93, "All That's Troubling Southwestern Coach Now Is Schedule," unnamed newspaper, Associated Press, July 3, 1943.
168. David Medley, Interview by WBJ, Georgetown, September 23, 2004.
169. MKSB #37, p. 105, "Southwestern and Tulsa Battle to 6-6 Tie," *Austin American*, October 31, 1943.
170. MKSB #38, p. 19, "SWU Pirates Resume Sun Bowl Drills Next Week," *San Antonio Express*, December 2, 1943.
171. MKSB #38, p. 27, "Pirates Rally to Score in Last Minutes; 18,000 Fans Brave Chilly Weather to See Sun Bowl Tilt," *Austin American Statesman*, January 2, 1944.
172. MKSB #38, p. 28, "Spot Collins Standout Star in Sun Bowl," *San Antonio Express*, January 4, 1944.
173. SU Trustees 1935–47, May 17, 1944, p. 394.
174. PANC, Box 9, Folder 9, p. 152, "Mexicans, Pirates Promise Razzle-Dazzle Bowl Tilt," and Folder 10, p. 153, "Pirates Win Second Bowl," *Austin Statesman*, December 29, 1944, and January 2, 1945.
175. PANC, Box 9, Folder 10, p. 162, "Williamson Lists Texas' Foes Ahead," *Austin Statesman*, September 25, 1945.
176. PANC, Box 9, Folder 10, p. 163, "Navy Transfers Five Pirate Starters to UT," *Austin American*, October 23, 1945.
177. All these numbers are taken from a catalog count.
178. SU Trustees 1947–53, November 15, 1949, p. 77.

CHAPTER XVII
From War to Peace (1945–1949)

1. Presidential Archives. Lyndon B. Johnson Files, exchange of letters and telegrams of September 14, 1943, and January 17, March 3, and March 7, 1944.
2. SU Trustees 1935–47, May 17, 1944, pp. 392, 397, 408.
3. PANC, Box 1, Folder 6, March 21, 1945.
4. SU Trustees 1935–47, November 21, 1945, p. 433.
5. SU Trustees 1935–47, May 15, 1946, p. 447.
6. Southwestern, *Announcements for the Session 1947–1948; Register for the Session 1946–1947* (Georgetown: Southwestern University, 1947).
7. SU Trustees 1947–53, November 12, 1947, pp. 12–13.
8. SU Trustees 1947–53, April 17, 1953, p. 248.
9. Angus Springer, *Exits and Entrances* (Austin: Whitley Company, 1982), pp. 3–12.
10. Ibid., pp. 3–5.
11. Ibid., pp. 13–14.
12. Ibid., p. 13.
13. Maxine Hairston, "Perry, George Sessions," HBTO, July 23, 2002.
14. John Nelson Russell Score II, Interviews by Martha Allen, Georgetown, Southwestern University, Tape 1, p. 34.
15. Presidential Archives, F. and M. Lenz Files, Roland H. Bainton to Score, October 28, 1944.
16. Lenz Files, correspondence of November 3, 1944, and October 13 and October 18, 1945.
17. PANC, Box 9, Folder 10, p. 161, "Dr. Frederick W. Lenz Assumes Duties at S.U.," *WC Sun*, October 5, 1945.
18. Lenz Files, "'Dead' Languages Come to Life for Dr. Lenz," *The Daily Texan*, April 30, 1954, p. 6.
19. Lenz Files, Finch to Lenz, January 18, 1950.
20. Lenz Files, Lenz to Finch, August 15, 1953.
21. Lenz Files, Finch to Lenz, April 20, 1954.
22. Lenz Files, Finch to Lenz, December 11, 1954.
23. President's Report, November 15, 1955.
24. Lenz Files, September 21, 1955, and April 23, 1957.
25. Lenz Files, Finch to Lenz, May 1, 1958.
26. Lenz Files, November 17, 1959. Also, Ullrich to Lenz, June 14, 1961.

27. Lenz Files, Undated document.
28. Presidential Archives, Frederick Gaupp Files, F. E. Gaupp, "Twenty Years Ago," November 1959.
29. The author, as chair of the Department of History and Political Science, knew both Fred Gaupp and Ludwig Merzbach during their last three years as teachers before their retirement and as personal friends thereafter.
30. Presidential Archives, Claud Howard Files. A copy of the *Southwestern University Ex-Students Newsmagazine*, April 1958, appears in the Howard files. It is listed as the SU Bulletin, Series 58, April 1958, Number 4. Much of the information about the Gaupps comes from an article in it entitled "Dr. F. E. Gaupp Wins S. U. 1957 Best Teacher Award."
31. SU Faculty 1945–46, November 30, 1946, p. 61.
32. Presidential Archives, Oscar A. Ullrich Files, Score to Ullrich, December 27, 1946.
33. Gaupp Files, Score to W. L. Clayton, Department of State, Washington, D.C., April 10, 1947.
34. Presidential Archives, Ludwig Herman Merzbach Files. I heard the story independently from its presence in Clifford's eulogy soon after it happened.
35. Merzbach Files. Translation from German.
36. Merzbach Files. I have slightly modified the wording in this "Certificate" at two points to smooth out the English in which it was originally written.
37. Louann Atkins Temple, "Daniel Baker College," HBTO, July 23, 2002.
38. SU Trustees 1935–47, April 30, 1947, Appendix: A University of Small Colleges, pp. 477–481.
39. SU Ex Com 1942–52, August 9, 1946, pp. 175–180.
40. SU Trustees 1935–47, November 20, 1946, p. 458.
41. SU Trustees 1935–47, April 30, 1947, Appendix: A University of Small Colleges, pp. 477–481.
42. SU Trustees 1935–47, April 30, 1947, p. 466.
43. SU Trustees 1947–53, November 12, 1947, p. 10.
44. SU Trustees 1947–53, April 21, 1948, pp. 34–35.
45. SU Trustees 1935–47, April 30, 1947, Appendix: A University of Small Colleges, pp. 477–481.
46. Ullrich Files, Score to Ullrich, December 27, 1946.
47. SU Trustees 1935–47, April 30, 1947, pp. 465, 471–472.
48. Ibid., pp. 471–472.
49. SU Trustees 1947–53, November 12, 1947, p. 9.
50. SU Ex Com 1942–52, April 26, 1949, p. 210.
51. Ibid., pp. 211–212.
52. SU Trustees 1947–53, April 27, 1949, p. 66.
53. SU Ex Com 1942–52, April 26, 1949, pp. 210–211.
54. SU Ex Com 1942–52, May 30, 1949, p. 214.
55. SU Trustees 1947–53, November 15, 1949, p. 80.
56. David Minor, "Weatherford College," HBTO, July 23, 2002.
57. SU Trustees 1947–53, April 27, 1949, p. 69.
58. SU Trustees 1947–53, November 15, 1949, p. 80.
59. Anonymous, "Westminster Junior College and Bible Institute," HBTO, July 23, 2002.
60. SU Ex Com 1942–52, May 30 and July 1, 1949, pp. 214, 220–221. SU Trustees 1947–53, November 15, 1949, pp. 81–82.
61. SU Trustees 1947–53, April 14, 1950, pp. 111–112.
62. Temple, "Daniel Baker."
63. SU Trustees 1947–53, November 12, 1952, p. 240.
64. SU Trustees 1935–47, May 17, 1944, pp. 390–392. Also, SU Ex Com 1942–52, August 24, 1943, pp. 131–133.
65. Ralph Wood Jones, "A History of Southwestern University, 1873–1949" (doctoral dissertation, University of Texas, 1960), p. 603.
66. Ibid., pp. 603–604.
67. Ibid., p. 604. Ralph Jones says that his information on the formation of the Association came from a copy of "An Incomplete History of Texas Methodist Association," contained in a copy of the Minutes of the Annual Meeting of June 30, 1958, available to him in the Texas Methodist College Association file found in the President's office at Southwestern.
68. Jones, "History of SU" (dissertation), p. 605.
69. SU Faculty 1934–44, January 6, 1942, p. 687.
70. SU Trustees 1935–47, May 8, 1942, p. 302.
71. SU Ex Com 1942–52, July 31, 1942, pp. 70–71.
72. SU Faculty 1945–46, November 30, 1946.
73. SU Trustees 1947–53, November 12, 1947, p. 7.
74. SU Faculty 1945–46, January 2, 1945, p. 1.
75. SU Trustees 1957–60, April 17, 1959, p. 143.
76. Ullrich Files, October 12, 1943.
77. Ullrich Files, April 23, 1948.
78. Ullrich Files, April 12 and April 23, 1947.
79. Presidents, Score Correspondence 1947–49, Memo of Score to Berglund, November 24, 1947.
80. Southwestern, "Small Collections Finding Aids," the Glamazons Collection, compiled by Mandy Brown, April 26, 2001.
81. Ullrich Files, September 24, 1948.
82. MKSB #38, loose clipping, "W. Angie Smith Elected Bishop by Methodists," *WC Sun*, June 16, 1944.
83. SU Trustees 1935–47, May 15, 1946, p. 442.
84. Presidential Archives, Mrs. J. J. Perkins Files, December 1, 1947.
85. Martha Mitten Allen, *The Gracious Gift: The Negro Fine Arts School, 1946–66* (Georgetown: Georgetown Heritage Society, 1998), p. 14.
86. Ibid., pp. 14–15.
87. Ibid., p. 24.
88. Ibid., pp. 23–25.
89. Ibid.
90. Ibid., p. 2.
91. Ibid., p. 81.
92. Ibid., pp. 27–30.
93. Ibid., pp. 30–34.
94. Ibid., p. 23.
95. Ibid., p. 19.
96. Ibid., p. 13.
97. Ibid., pp. 9–10.
98. Ibid., pp. 37–38.
99. Ibid., pp. 43–44.
100. Ibid., pp. 53–55.
101. Ibid., pp. 56–57.
102. Ibid., p. 56.
103. Southwestern, *Southwestern University Bulletin 70–71* (Georgetown: 1970–71), p. 108.
104. Norman W. Spellmann, *Growing a Soul: The Story of A. Frank Smith* (Dallas: SMU Press, 1979), p. 309.
105. SU Trustees 1935–47, November 16, 1943, p. 371.
106. Mary Ann Barbour, Interviews by WBJ, Georgetown, 2004.
107. PANC, Box 1, Folder 6, PAN to LBJ, January 18, 1945.
108. PANC, Box 9, Folder 10, p. 153, January 19, 1945.
109. Sherilyn Brandenstein, "Fondren, Ella Florence," HBTO, July 23, 2002. Diana J. Kliener, "Fondren, Walter William," HBTO, July 23, 2002. Art Leatherwood, "Fondren Foundation," HBTO, July 23, 2002.
110. SU Trustees 1947–53, November 5, 1948, pp. 47–49.
111. Spellmann, *Growing a Soul*, p. 309.
112. Jones, "History of SU" (dissertation), pp. 599–600. The name of the company is variously written as W-K-M, W.K.M., and WKM in the sources. Since W-K-M valves are still some of the finest industrial valves produced today, that name will be used in this document except in quotations, where whatever the company is called in the quotation will be maintained.
113. Jones, "History of SU" (dissertation), pp. 599–600. The name of the donor is written Fred McManis in all the Southwestern records, though the original Irish spelling of McManus was used in the announcement of the gift in the *WC Sun* of October 7, 1949. Wheaton College in Illinois, the other college sharing with Southwestern the W-K-M money, named a residence hall in his honor. It is McMa-

nis-Evans Hall. Its professorship set up in honor of the couple is called the Carolyn and Fred McManis Professorship of Christian Thought. Rice University also has a McManis Professor of Philosophy.

114. Presidential Archives, Bishop A. Frank Smith Files, Letters of July 18 and 21, 1948, between AFS and Score.
115. A. F. Smith Files, September 19, 1949.
116. "Southwestern University Is Given Half Interest in 5 Million Dollar Firm," *WC Sun*, October 7, 1949.
117. Presidential Archives, W-K-M Company Files, "W-K-M's First Half Century Ends," *pipe lines* [sic], ACF Industries, Inc., W-K-M Valve Division, August 1969.
118. SU Ex Com 1942–52, May 30, 1949, p. 214.
119. Spellmann, *Growing a Soul*, p. 308.
120. SU Trustees 1947–53, November 15, 1949, pp. 93–94. Ralph Jones is mistaken in stating that the date on which Score accepted the offer was September 23, 1949.
121. SU Trustees 1947–53, November 15, 1949, p. 94.
122. Jones, "History of SU" (dissertation), p. 600.
123. Perkins Files, "Remarks by Lois Perkins on the Presentation to Her of the Ex-Students' Outstanding Alumna Award," Southwestern University, May 1, 1970.
124. Spellmann, *Growing a Soul*, p. 297.
125. Ibid., p. 299.
126. Ibid., pp. 298–299.
127. SU Trustees 1935–47, May 19, 1943, pp. 345–346.
128. SU Trustees 1947–53, November 15, 1949, p. 78.
129. SU Trustees 1947–53, March 5, 1943, p. 85.
130. Perkins Files, Score to Mr. & Mrs. Perkins, May 17, 1948.
131. SU Ex Com 1942–52, September 9, 1948, p. 196.
132. Perkins Files, Score to Mr. & Mrs. Perkins, November 18, 1948.
133. Perkins Files, Score to Mr. & Mrs. Perkins, May 16, 1949.
134. Perkins Files, Score to J. J. Perkins, July 7, 1949.
135. SU Ex Com 1942–52, May 30, 1949, pp. 213–214.
136. Perkins Files, Score to J. J. Perkins, September 8, 1949.
137. Perkins Files, Score to J. J. Perkins, September 13, 1949.
138. Perkins Files, Score to J. J. Perkins, September 8, 1949.
139. Presidential Archives, I. J. McCook Files, September 20, 1949.
140. Perkins Files, Score to J. J. Perkins, September 22, 1949.
141. SU Trustees 1947–53, November 15, 1949, p. 93.
142. SU Trustees 1947–53, April 21, 1948, p. 33.
143. LBJ Files, May 26, 1949.
144. SU Ex Com 1942–52, May 30, 1949, p. 215.
145. SU Ex Com 1942–52, June 16, 1949.
146. Score, Interviews by Allen, Tape 3, p. 8.
147. Ibid., Tape 1, p. 22.
148. Durwood Fleming, Interviews by Martha Allen, June 21–23, 1993, Tape 2, p. 15.
149. A. F. Smith Files, June 20, 1949, Score to AFS, quotation.
150. SU Ex Com 1942–52, July 1, 1949, p. 218.
151. Presidential Archives, E. B. Germany Files, July 13, 1949.
152. A. F. Smith Files, AFS to Score and Score to AFS, July 29 and August 1, 1949.
153. A. F. Smith Files, August 2, 1949.
154. A. F. Smith Files, August 9, 1949.
155. A. F. Smith Files, September 12, 1949.
156. A. F. Smith Files, September 17, 1949.
157. A. F. Smith Files, September 19, 1949.
158. Spellmann, *Growing a Soul*, p. 306.
159. Score, Interviews by Allen, Tape 1, p. 18.
160. Hal Gaddy, M.D., Interview by WBJ, Georgetown, September 19, 2004.
161. Douglas M. Benold, M.D., Interview by WBJ, Georgetown, September 30, 2004.
162. SU Trustees 1947–53, November 15, 1949, p. 91.
163. SU Trustees 1947–53, October 14, 1949, p. 226.
164. SU Ex Com 1942–52, from Mrs. Score's letter of October 11, 1949, quoted on p. 242.
165. SU Trustees 1947–53, November 15, 1949, p. 88.
166. William C. Finch, Interviews by Martha Allen, August 1992, Tape 1, p. 10.
167. SU Trustees 1947–53, September 27, 1949, p. 75.
168. SU Ex Com 1942–52, October 14, 1949, pp. 227–228.
169. SU Trustees 1947–53, November 15, 1949, pp. 81, 90.
170. SU Trustees 1947–53, September 27, 1949, pp. 75–76.
171. SU Trustees 1947–53, November 15, 1949, pp. 84–85.
172. Presidential Archives, J. N. R. Score Files, Mrs. Score in Dallas to Finch, September 10, 1951.

CHAPTER XVIII
Emergence of a New Campus (1949–1961)

1. Presidential Archives, Wm. C. Finch Files, April 1, 1949.
2. Finch Files, May 23, 1949.
3. Finch Files, Letter from Raymond E. Dewey, Acting President, Southwestern College, September 1, 1949.
4. Finch Files, Letter from Score to Raymond E. Dewey at Southwestern College, September 7, 1949.
5. Finch Files, February 17 and February 20, 1942.
6. MKSB #37, p. 84, "Finch Will Leave for Columbia U. to Study for Navy," *Austin American*, August 31, 1943.
7. Finch Files, November 26, 1943.
8. SU Trustees 1935–47, January 14, 1944, p. 386.
9. Finch Files, January 14, 1944.
10. Finch Files, January 27, 1944.
11. Finch Files, December 2, 1944.
12. Finch Files, January 25, 1945. Finch does not indicate what kind of ship it was.
13. Finch Files, April 19, 1945.
14. Finch Files, June 5, 1945.
15. Finch Files, August 21, 1945.
16. Finch Files, October 10, 1945.
17. Finch Files, September 26, 1945.
18. Finch Files, October 19, 1945.
19. SU Trustees 1935–47, November 20, 1946, p. 460.
20. SU Trustees 1947–53, April 14, 1950, p. 97.
21. Exec. Com. Report, August 15, 1956, p. 2-1.
22. Finch affirmed to me in a private conversation that he was not following a preconceived strategy in giving up football and eliminating the graduate program but was doing what had to be done at the time to make Southwestern a viable institution financially.
23. William C. Finch, Interviews by Martha Allen, August 1992, Tape 3, pp. 11–12.
24. SU Trustees 1947–53, April 17, 1951, pp. 164–165.
25. Ibid., pp. 157–158.
26. Figures compiled from the salary schedules included in the Board reports of April 14, 1950 (pp. 117–122) and April 17, 1951 (pp. 169–173).
27. SU Trustees 1947–53, April 17, 1951, p. 153.
28. SU Trustees 1947–53, April 17, 1952, p. 210.
29. SU Trustees 1947–53, November 14, 1950, p. 133.
30. SU Trustees 1947–53, April 17, 1951, pp. 162–163.
31. Ibid., p. 149.
32. Figures taken from official audits of the years indicated.
33. SU Trustees 1953–57, April 2, 1954, p. 42.
34. President's Report, November 5, 1954.
35. Ibid., and Dean's Report of April 1, 1955.
36. President's Report, April 1, 1955, pp. 1-14.
37. Finch, Interviews by Allen, Tape 3, pp. 20–21. Finch says in the 1992 interview that because of the pressure of the Southern Association, he and Ullrich agreed to close up the graduate program. He adds that Dr. Cody "was very unhappy" when he reported this agreement to the Board of Trustees. "He literally, publicly ate me out in the Board of Trustees. I was embarrassed. Dean Ullrich, too. We were both sitting there. We didn't reply to him."

38. President's Report, November 5, 1954, p. 1-8.
39. Report of Exec. Com., September 13, 1954, p. 2-4.
40. President's Report, April 23, 1957. Also, Faculty Minutes, April 5, 1955.
41. President's Report, February 17, 1956, and July 29, 1957.
42. SU Trustees 1953–57, April 13, 1956, p. 179.
43. Presidential Archives, Bishop A. Frank Smith Files, January 1, 1952.
44. Finch, Interviews by Allen. "I never ran campaigns, and that was a mistake. I never had had the experience of running a campaign.... What fundraising we did in the ... eleven years I was college president, we did out of my office. We never employed an outside company to make a survey. We never employed an outside company to set up our fundraising for us. We played with the idea, but never did it" (Tape 3, p. 13).
45. SU Trustees 1957–60, November 13, 1959, p. 208.
46. A. F. Smith Files, January 4, 1952.
47. Presidential Archives, Mrs. J. J. Perkins Files, undated letter of Mrs. Perkins to Finch before October 26, 1950.
48. SU Trustees 1947–53, November 14, 1950, p. 135.
49. Anonymous, *The Lois Perkins Chapel, 1943–1981: The Culmination of a Dream* (Georgetown: 1981). Also, SU Ex Com 1942–52, September 26, 1950, p. 249.
50. SU Trustees 1947–53, April 14, 1950, p. 111.
51. SU Ex Com 1942–52, September 26, 1950, p. 249.
52. Presidential Archives, J. Frank Dobie Files, Letter of Finch to Tom Lee, November 8, 1952.
53. Edmund H. Steelman, "Symbolism of the Lois Perkins Chapel," ca. 1981, p. 6.
54. Anonymous, Lois Perkins Chapel, 1943–1981.
55. SU Ex Com 1942–52, November 13, 1951, p. 266.
56. SU Trustees 1947–53, April 17, 1952, p. 205.
57. SU Ex Com 1942–52, February 20, 1952, p. 273.
58. SU Trustees 1947–53, April 7, 1952, p. 213.
59. SU Trustees 1947–53, November 12, 1952, p. 240.
60. SU Trustees 1947–53, April 17, 1953, p. 263.
61. Dobie Files, J. Frank Dobie, "Nobody Knows What His Memory Will Do," *Austin American-Statesman*, November 2, 1952.
62. SU Ex Com 1942–52, November 13, 1951, p. 266.
63. Presidential Archives, Mrs. Alma Thomas Files, April 25, 1957.
64. Dan Yoxall, *Lois Craddock Perkins (1887–1983)* (Georgetown: MHHS, 1992).
65. Joseph A. Pratt and Christopher J. Castaneda, *Builders: Herman and George R. Brown* (College Station: Texas A&M Press, 1999), p. 197.
66. Ibid., p. 192. Quotation from a letter of July 11, 1939.
67. Though Pratt and Castaneda hypothesize that "Representative Johnson came through" by helping procure the W.P.A. funds that constructed the new Cody Memorial Library and "a portion of the new gymnasium," such is not the case. As described in Chapter XV, Jesse Jones and Senator Morris Sheppard were the two persons who made it possible to get the funds for the library. The West Gymnasium did not use any federal funds. It was funded by Jim West and other private donors.
68. MKSB #37, p. 80, "Heroes and Stars on Bond Rally Program Accompany Johnson on Inspection at S. U. Navy-Marine Training Center," *WC Sun*, September 3, 1943.
69. Presidential Archives, Herman Brown File [1946–1959], Score to Herman Brown, April 6, 1946.
70. Herman Brown 1946–59, Score to Herman Brown, December 3, 1947, and January 16, 1948.
71. SU Trustees 1947–53, November 5, 1948, pp. 49–50.
72. Herman Brown 1946–59, Herman Brown to Score, December 1, 1948.
73. Herman Brown 1946–59, Letter of Ullrich to Finch, April 18, 1958.
74. Though Pratt and Castaneda state that the meeting he attended was a Board meeting, it must have been some other kind of undetermined meeting if Herman was indeed in Georgetown on November 15. The fall Board meeting was held at 10:00 A.M. on October 31, 1962, with a meeting of the Executive Committee the day before at 7:30 P.M. Herman Brown is recorded as being present at both meetings.
75. Durwood Fleming, "Oral History of George and Herman Brown by Chris Castaneda," Dallas, July 12, 1990, pp. 15–16. Though Brown was an Episcopalian, he was not active. He liked both Freeman, pastor of St. Paul's Methodist, and Fleming, to whom he had made a donation of land for the establishment of St. Luke's.
76. Presidential Archives, William B. Jones Files, Letter of Fleming to Finch, December 10, 1962.
77. Report of Exec. Com., August 30, 1955.
78. *The Megaphone*, "S.U. Now Has Largest William Blake Exhibit of Art in Southwest," December 4, 1945.
79. SU Trustees 1947–53, April 17, 1951.
80. SU Trustees 1960–66, April 14, 1961, p. 36.
81. Presidential Archives, Mrs. Herman Brown 1956–58 File, October 5, 1957.
82. President's Report, November 14, 1956, and November 13, 1957.
83. Finch, Interviews by Allen, Tape 2, p. 23.
84. SU Ex Com 1942–52, February 20, 1952.
85. SU Trustees 1947–53, April 17, 1952, p. 213.
86. President's Report, November 12, 1953, and April 2, 1954.
87. Presidential Archives, Mrs. Herman Brown 1959–63 File, undated but received by President's Office on April 12, 1962.
88. Presidential Archives, Brown Foundation 1963 File, "Resume of Gifts to Southwestern University from Mr. and Mrs. Herman Brown and from The Brown Foundation, 1950–1963."
89. Herman Brown 1946–59, Letter to Finch from Herman Brown's secretary.
90. Presidential Archives, Lyndon B. Johnson Files, correspondence of January 14, 19, and 26, 1949.
91. SU Trustees 1947–53, November 14, 1950.
92. President's Report, April 2, 1954.
93. SU Trustees 1953–57, April 2, 1954, p. 40.
94. President's Report, November 5, 1954.
95. President's Report, April 14, 1956.
96. SU Ex Com 1942–52, April 16, 1951, pp. 259–265.
97. SU Trustees 1947–53, April 17, 1951.
98. SU Trustees 1947–53, November 14, 1951, pp. 178, 193.
99. President's Report, April 23, 1957.
100. Finch, Interviews by Allen, Tape 3, p. 14.
101. SU Ex Com 1942–52, September 26, 1950, pp. 249–258.
102. SU Trustees 1947–53, November 14, 1950.
103. SU Trustees 1947–53, April 17, 1952.
104. Pratt and Castaneda, *Builders*, p. 101.
105. Ibid., p. 130.
106. Ibid., pp. 255–257.
107. SU Ex Com 1942–52, February 20, 1952, p. 275.
108. SU Trustees 1947–53, November 12, 1952, p. 238.
109. In the President's Report of November 15, 1955, Finch calls Dr. Fred Gaupp an Associate Professor "of the Lucy King Brown Department of History."
110. SU Trustees 1947–53. President's Report, April 23, 1957.
111. SU Ex Com 1942–52, November 13, 1951, pp. 266–271.
112. Presidential Archives, W-K-M Company Files, Letter from I. J. McCook to John D. Wheeler, November 5, 1954.
113. SU Trustees 1947–53, November 14, 1951, p. 175.
114. SU Ex Com 1942–52, February 20, 1952, pp. 272–277.
115. SU Ex Com 1942–52, November 13, 1951, pp. 266–271.
116. A. F. Smith Files, Finch to AFS, February 7, 1952.
117. W-K-M Files, typescript document entitled "The W-K-M Company," of about March 30, 1954.
118. President's Report, November 5, 1954.
119. W-K-M Files, Memorandum of Agreement between the Proprietors and the American Car and Foundry Company, April 10, 1954.
120. SU Trustees 1953–57, November 5, 1954, p. 73. Though Finch was later to view as very wise the placement of this money into the endowment by the Trustees, he was initially opposed to it because there were so many immediate building needs at the University. See Finch, Interviews by Allen, Tape 2, p. 4.

121. Report of Exec. Com., May 31, 1954.
122. SU Trustees 1953–57, Report of Exec. Com. for meeting of August 15, 1956, contained in Board Minutes of November 14, 1956, pp. 222–224.
123. SU Trustees 1960–66, April 14, 1961, pp. 55–56.
124. W-K-M Files, IRS "Notice of Adjustment," October 17, 1963.
125. W-K-M Files, Document of ca. March 30, 1979.
126. W-K-M Files, Letter of Fleming to Robert K. Jewett, January 6, 1975.
127. W-K-M Files, Fleming to H. Malcolm Lovett, May 29, 1979.
128. Presidential Archives, Mrs. Carolyn McManis Files, Letter from Carolyn McManis to Finch. Undated.
129. Carolyn McManis Files, Finch to Carolyn McManis, May 13, 1954.
130. Carolyn McManis Files, Carolyn McManis to Finch, July 26, 1954, and March 11, 1958.
131. SU Trustees 1947–53, Report of the Exec. Com. of April 16, 1951, pp. 143, 145.
132. SU Ex Com 1942–52, February 20, 1952, p. 274.
133. SU Trustees 1947–53, November 12, 1952, p. 238.
134. Finch, Interviews by Allen, Tape 2, pp. 29–31.
135. SU Trustees 1947–53, November 12, 1952, p. 232.
136. Ibid., pp. 227, 229.
137. Presidential Archives, Fondren Science Building Files.
138. SU Trustees 1947–53, April 17, 1953, p. 247.
139. President's Report, November 12, 1953. The Clinic was moved slightly southwest of its original location to its current location in 1995–1996. It now serves as the offices for Career Services.
140. A. F. Smith Files, AFS to Finch, April 26, 1954.
141. A. F. Smith Files, Finch to AFS, April 30, 1954.
142. A. F. Smith Files, AFS to Finch, May 19, 1954.
143. Finch, Interviews by Allen, Tape 2, pp. 29–31.
144. Fondren Science Building, dedication program brochure.
145. Report of Exec. Com., September 13, 1954, pp. 2-5 and 2-6.
146. A. F. Smith Files, March 13, 1950.
147. A. F. Smith Files, March 21, 1950.
148. Thomas Files, February 11, 1954.
149. SU Trustees 1947–53, April 17, 1951, p. 159.
150. Thomas Files, "Great-Grandmother Says 'I've Done a Lot of Living,'" *Austin American-Statesman*, May 23, 1971.
151. Thomas Files, "Travelers Visit Taj Mahal," *Austin Statesman*, March 2, 1955.
152. Presidential Archives, Claud Howard Files, found in a copy of the *Southwestern University Ex-Students Newsmagazine*, April 1958, located in the file.
153. Thomas Files, "Great-Grandmother Says 'I've Done a Lot of Living,'" *Austin American-Statesman*, May 23, 1971.
154. SU Trustees 1947–53, November 14, 1951, pp. 180–181, and April 17, 1953, p. 249.
155. Thomas Files, Letter of Finch to Wayman Adams, artist, January 4, 1956. Adams was a leading portrait artist, who agreed to do the portrait for $2,500. If either Mrs. Thomas or the Southwestern committee was displeased with it, they would not be obligated to accept it.
156. Thomas Files, "Great-Grandmother Says 'I've Done a Lot of Living,'" *Austin American-Statesman*, May 23, 1971.
157. Thomas Files, February 22, 1967.
158. Thomas Files, December 9, 1970.
159. Thomas Files, February 16, 1972.
160. Thomas Files, September 8, 1976.
161. Thomas Files, February 25, 1954.
162. Thomas Files, March 11, 1954.
163. Finch, Interviews by Allen, Tape 2, p. 27.
164. President's Report, November 5, 1954, p. 1-3.
165. Thomas Files, mimeographed report of the Exec. Com., November 1, 1954.
166. Norman W. Spellmann, *Growing a Soul: The Story of A. Frank Smith* (Dallas: SMU Press, 1979), p. 311, fn. 139, Finch to AFS, December 19, 1950, Presidential Papers, Southwestern University.
167. SU Trustees 1947–53, April 17, 1952, p. 214.
168. SU Trustees 1947–53, November 12, 1952, p. 239. Also, Finch, Interviews by Allen, Tape 3, p. 10.
169. President's Report, November 5, 1954, p. 1-5.
170. Finch, Interviews by Allen, Tape 2, p. 31.
171. A. F. Smith Files, December 20, 1954.
172. Report of Exec. Com., February 17, 1955.
173. President's Report, November 15, 1955, p. 1-7.
174. President's Report, April 14, 1956, p. 1-5
175. Thomas Files, J. Fisher Simpson, "Alma Thomas Theatre and Fine Arts Center Dedicated," *Texas Christian Advocate*, April 20, 1956.
176. Thomas Files, December 30, 1954.
177. Thomas Files, December 31, 1954.
178. Thomas Files, Report from McCook to Thomas, January 31, 1958.
179. Thomas Files, McCook to Thomas, January 2, 1959.
180. Thomas Files, Phillips to Fleming, March 29, 1974.
181. Thomas Files, Letters of acknowledgement dated November 23, 1965, April 13, 1966, January 9, 1967, November 26, 1968, and November 18, 1972.
182. Thomas Files, April 21, 1968, May 25, 1968.
183. SU Trustees 1953–57, November 13, 1957, p. 282.
184. Thomas Files, April 25, 1957.
185. Thomas Files, May 2, 1957.
186. SU Trustees 1957–60, Exec. Com. meeting of April 15, 1958, p. 34.
187. Presidential Archives, Alma Thomas Estate Files, Letter from W. Grogan Lord to Mr. Tack Thomas, grandson of Mrs. Thomas, February 15, 1979.
188. Finch, Interviews by Allen, Tape 2, pp. 25–26.
189. President's Report, April 14, 1956, p. 1-5.
190. Report of Exec. Com., February 17, 1956, p. 2-2.
191. President's Report, November 14, 1956, p. 1-7.
192. Report of Exec. Com., July 29, 1957, p. 2-1.
193. SU Trustees 1957–60, Exec. Com. meeting of February 18, 1959, p. 142.
194. Finch, Interviews by Allen, Tape 2, p. 27.
195. SU Trustees 1953–57, November 14, 1956, pp. 211–212.
196. SU Trustees 1957–60, April 17, 1959, p. 131.
197. President's Report, November 5, 1954, p. 1-3. At the time of McCook's retirement in 1968, the Board ordered the title "Vice-President, Finance" to be retired and to be always held in the future as a memorial to Dr. McCook. He was voted a permanent relationship with the University in terms of privileges, courtesies, and considerations. See SU Trustees 1967–78, May 10, 1968, p. 248.
198. Business and Fiscal Affairs Report, April 14, 1961, pp. 4-6, 4-7.
199. Business and Fiscal Affairs Report, November 13, 1959, p. 3-20.
200. SU Trustees 1957–60, November 13, 1959, pp. 192–193.
201. Business and Fiscal Affairs Report. April 14, 1961, pp. 4-6, 4-7.
202. SU Trustees 1960–66, April 14, 1961, p. 38.
203. SU Trustees 1957–60, November 13, 1959, p. 212.
204. MKSB #38, p. 20, "Union Bl'dg. for S.U.; Homecomers Pledge Series F, G Bonds," *WC Sun*, November 12, 1943.
205. SU Trustees 1947–53, April 27, 1949, p. 57.
206. SU Trustees 1947–53, April 17, 1953, pp. 248, 262–263.
207. SU Trustees 1953–57, April 13, 1956, p. 177.
208. President's Report, November 14, 1956, p. 1-8.
209. SU Trustees 1953–57, April 23, 1957, p. 245.
210. President's Report, April 23, 1957.
211. SU Trustees 1957–60, Exec. Com. meeting of April 15, 1958, p. 28.
212. SU Trustees 1957–60, November 7, 1958, p. 104.
213. SU Trustees 1957–60, April 16, 1958, p. 53.
214. Spellmann, *Growing a Soul*, p. 312.
215. SU Trustees 1953–57, November 5, 1954, p. 74.
216. Exec. Com., September 13, 1954, p. 2-8.
217. SU Trustees 1953–57, November 15, 1955, p. 134.
218. President's Report, April 14, 1956, p. 1-6.
219. Ibid.

220. President's Report, November 14, 1956, 1-7.
221. SU Trustees 1953–57, Report of Exec. Com. meeting of April 13, 1956, p. 176.
222. SU Trustees 1960–66, April 14, 1961, p. 38.
223. President's Report, November 14, 1956, p. 1-8.
224. SU Trustees 1953–57, April 23, 1957. Report of Exec. Com., February 8, 1957, pp. 241–244.
225. President's Report, April 2, 1954, p. 1-5, November 5, 1954, p. 1-5, and November 15, 1955, p. 1-18.
226. President's Report, November 11, 1960, p. 14-1.
227. Finch, Interviews by Allen. President's Report, November 11, 1960, p. 14-1. Peterson to WBJ in personal conversation.
228. Finch, Interviews by Allen, Tape 2, p. 16.
229. Presidential Archives, Howard S. Greenlee Files, Finch to Greenlee, April 30, 1957.
230. A. F. Smith Files, AFS to Finch, September 16, 1952.
231. SU Trustees 1957–60, April 16, 1958, p. 56.
232. SU Trustees 1957–60, April 16, 1958. Exec. Com. Report, April 15, 1958, p. 29.
233. SU Trustees 1957–60, April 17, 1959. Exec. Com. Report, February 18, 1959, p. 145.
234. SU Trustees 1957–60, November 13, 1959, p. 205.
235. *Megaphone*, "Oh, What a Week!," October 16, 1959, p. 2.
236. Fiscal Report, October 31, 1961, pp. 3-7 and 3-8.
237. Southwestern, *Southwestern University Bulletin 1964–65* (Georgetown: 1964–1965), p. 10. Also, SU Trustees 1960–66, September 11, 1963. Exec. Com. Report of August 7, 1963, p. 147.

CHAPTER XIX
Emergence of a New Institutional Model (1949–1961)

1. Faculty Minutes, October 16, 1956.
2. President's Report, November 15, 1955, pp. 1-4 and 1-5.
3. SU Trustees 1947–53, November 14, 1951, p. 192.
4. President's Report, April 2, 1954, p. 1-1.
5. President's Report, November 14, 1956, p. 1-9.
6. President's Report, November 13, 1957, p. 1-3.
7. President's Report, April 23, 1957, p. 1-3.
8. SU Trustees 1957–60, April 16, 1958, pp. 49–50.
9. Presidential Archives, Herman Brown File [1946–1959], January 28, 1957.
10. SU Trustees 1957–60, April 1, 1959, p. 150.
11. SU Trustees 1957–60, April 1, 1960, p. 258.
12. SU Trustees 1957–60, April 16, 1958, p. 59.
13. President's Report, November 15, 1955, p. 1-3.
14. Ibid., pp. 1-10 thru 1-12.
15. SU Trustees 1953–57, November 15, 1955, p. 132.
16. Presidential Archives, Myron F. Wicke Files, Finch to Wicke, November 15, 1956.
17. William C. Finch, Interviews by Martha Allen, August 1992, Tape 3, p. 11.
18. Ibid., Tape 2, p. 5.
19. President's Report, April 2, 1954, p. 1-4. Also, SU Trustees 1953–57, April 2, 1954, p. 40.
20. Finch, Interviews by Allen, Tape 1, p. 12.
21. Faculty Minutes, September 15, 1956.
22. Finch, Interviews by Allen, Tape 3, p. 24.
23. Faculty Minutes, September 12, 1958.
24. SU Trustees 1957–60, November 13, 1959, p. 203.
25. Finch, Interviews by Allen, Tape 3, p. 7.
26. President's Report, November 5, 1954, p. 1-7.
27. SU Trustees 1953–57, November 5, 1954, p. 76.
28. Faculty Minutes, November 15, 1954.
29. Faculty Minutes, April 5, 1955.
30. President's Report, April 23, 1957, p. 1-3.
31. SU Trustees 1957–60, April 17, 1959, p. 143.
32. SU Trustees 1957–60, November 10, 1960, p. 9.
33. SU Trustees 1960–66, April 14, 1961, p. 39.
34. *Ex-Students' Newsmagazine*, June 1961.
35. SU Trustees 1957–60, April 16, 1958, p. 53.
36. President's Report, April 2, 1954, pp. 1-4 and 1-5.
37. SU Trustees 1957–60, April 1, 1959, p. 155.
38. Report of VP Fiscal, November 13, 1959, p. 3-5.
39. SU Trustees 1960–66, April 14, 1961, p. 39.
40. President's Report, November 12, 1953, pp. 1-5 and 1-6.
41. SU Trustees 1957–60, November 13, 1959, p. 192.
42. SU Trustees 1957–60, November 7, 1958, p. 102.
43. Personal observation of Finch to the author.
44. Registrar's Report, April 14, 1961, p. 8-5.
45. Ibid.
46. President's Report, April 14, 1956, pp. 1-3 and 1-4.
47. SU Trustees 1960–66, Exec. Com., February 14, 1961, p. 29.
48. President's Report, November 13, 1957, p. 1-3.
49. Faculty Minutes, May 20 and July 20, 1953, and May 18, 1956.
50. SU Trustees 1935–47, June 7, 1937, p. 78.
51. Dean of Men's Report, August 15, 1956, p. 9-1.
52. Faculty Minutes, May 18, 1956.
53. Dean of Men's Report, April 17, 1959, p. 10-1.
54. Dean of Men's Report, November 11, 1960, p. 10-1.
55. Finch, Interviews by Allen, Tape 3, pp. 15–16.
56. SU Trustees 1960–66, April 14, 1961, p. 41.
57. SU Trustees 1953–57, April 1, 1955, p. 97.
58. President's Report, April 1, 1955, p. 1-9.
59. SU Trustees 1953–57, April 1, 1955, insert into minutes between pp. 100 and 101.
60. President's Report, November 1, 1960.
61. SU Trustees 1957–60, November 13, 1959, p. 203.
62. SU Trustees 1957–60, November 7, 1958, p. 90.
63. SU Trustees 1957–60, November 7, 1958. Ex. Com., November 6, 1958, p. 89.
64. SU Trustees 1947–53, April 17, 1952, p. 200.
65. SU Trustees 1953–57, April 1, 1955, p. 98.
66. Ibid., p. 97.
67. President's Report, April 1, 1955, pp. 1-4 and 1-5.
68. SU Trustees 1957–60, Ex. Com., April 15, 1958, p. 35.
69. SU Trustees 1957–60, November 7, 1958, p. 88.
70. SU Trustees 1957–60, April 17, 1959, pp. 130–131.
71. Finch, Interviews by Allen, Tape 2, pp. 32ff.
72. President's Report, April 1, 1955, three-page "Addendum" in Greenlee files.
73. Ibid.
74. SU Trustees 1953–57, April 1, 1955, p. 99.
75. Presidential Archives, Howard S. Greenlee Files, Finch to Coons, Occidental College.
76. Greenlee Files, Finch to Gross, February 22, 1956.
77. Report of Dean A&S, April 16, 1958, p. 5-7.
78. Wicke Files, December 30, 1949.
79. Faculty Minutes, October 29, 1952.
80. Wicke Files, Wicke to Finch, November 21, 1952.
81. Faculty Minutes, December 12, 1952.
82. Wicke Files, February 22, 1957.
83. Faculty Minutes, October 2, 1956.
84. Wicke Files, Finch to Wicke, March 19, 1957.
85. Wicke Files, Wicke to Finch, August 22, 1957.
86. Faculty Minutes, September 13, 1957.
87. Wicke Files, Wicke to Finch, September 5, 1957.
88. SU Trustees 1953–57, November 13, 1957, pp. 292–293.
89. Wicke Files, Wicke (handwritten) to Finch, November 18, 1957.
90. Wicke Files, December 16, 1957, January 17 and February 4, 1958.
91. Wicke Files, Wicke to Finch, February 4, 1958.
92. Wicke Files, Wicke (handwritten) to Finch, February 7, 1958.
93. Wicke Files, Finch to Wicke, February 14, 1958.
94. Wicke Files, Wicke (handwritten) to Finch, February 17, 1958.
95. SU Trustees 1957–60, April 16, 1958, p. 52.

96. SU Trustees 1957–60, April 1, 1960, p. 259.
97. SU Trustees 1960–66, April 14, 1961, p. 33.
98. *The Megaphone*, "Dr. M. F. Wicke to Succeed Dean Ullrich in September," March 14, 1958, p. 1.
99. SU Trustees 1957–60, April 16, 1958, p. 51.
100. Wicke Files, Publicity Department, Southwestern, June 1958.
101. Presidential Archives, Integration File, Walter J. Ligon, 2802 Pacific St., Bellmore, L.I., N.Y., September 17, 1963, to Miss Mary Elizabeth Fox, Director of Publicity, Director of Ex-Students' Association, Georgetown, Tex..
102. W. Page Keeton, "Sweatt v. Painter," HBTO, July 23, 2002.
103. SU Trustees 1947–53, President's Report, April 17, 1951, p. 156.
104. Integration File, document signed by 121 students. Undated, but refers to the *Brown v. Board of Education of Topeka* decision of May 17, 1954.
105. Integration File, Finch to Mr. Pete Cawthon, 5 Pinehurst Drive, Tuscaloosa, Alabama, April 23, 1959.
106. Integration File, Finch to Mr. and Mrs. W. W. Powell, Houston, Texas, May 8, 1959.
107. Integration File, Finch to Mr. and Mrs. Harry Peacock, Scarritt College, Nashville, Tenn., March 11, 1960.
108. Integration File, document signed by 121 students. Undated, but refers to the *Brown v. Board of Education of Topeka* decision of May 17, 1954.
109. SU Trustees 1953–57, November 5, 1954, p. 72.
110. Presidential Archives, J. Frank Dobie Files, June 8, 1955.
111. Dobie Files, July 8, 1955.
112. *Megaphone*, "Segregation Issue Upheld by Senate," November 7, 1958, p. 2.
113. *Megaphone*, "Integration Report Considered by Senate," March 13, 1959.
114. Robert S. Maxwell, "Kurth, Ernest Lynn," HBTO, July 23, 2002.
115. SU Trustees 1960–66, November 10, 1960, p. 9.
116. Integration File, Finch to Kurth, April 15, 1959.
117. Integration File, Wheeler to Kurth, June 23, 1959.
118. Presidential Archives, E. B. Germany Files, Southwestern news release, June 1, 1959. Also, Diana J. Kliener, "Germany, Eugene Benjamin," HBTO, July 23, 2002.
119. Integration File, E. B. Germany to Kurth, April 7, 1960.
120. Integration File, Finch to Germany, April 9, 1960.
121. Integration File, Finch to Wheeler, April 9, 1960.
122. Integration File, J. D. Wheeler to Ernest Kurth, April 5, 1960.
123. Integration File, Finch to Kurth, October 13, 1960.
124. William C. Finch, "Finch Letter to Wm. B. Jones." March 11, 2005.
125. SU Trustees 1957–60, November 10, 1960, p. 291.
126. Integration File, Pete Cawthon, Tuscaloosa, Ala., to Pearl Neas, April 18, 1959.
127. Integration File, Finch to Pete Cawthon, 5 Pinehurst Drive, Tuscaloosa, Alabama, April 23, 1959.
128. Integration File. The cards are in a separate envelope related to the correspondence on this issue.
129. Integration File, Finch to Lil Dimmitt, 1405 East 16th Street, Georgetown, Texas, April 23, 1959.
130. Integration File, Cawthon to Finch, April 27, 1959
131. Integration File, Finch to Mr. and Mrs. W. W. Powell, May 8, 1959.
132. Integration File, Mrs. Willard Powell (handwritten) to Finch, May 13, 1959.
133. Integration File, Finch to Medley, May 1, 1959.
134. SU Trustees 1957–60, Ex. Com., August 11, 1959, p. 200.
135. Integration File, "Survey of Student Opinion on Segregation," May 4, 1959.
136. Integration File, results of segregation questionnaire, May 12, 1959.
137. *Megaphone*, "Finch Tells Senate about Sit-In Policy," February 24, 1961.
138. Integration File, Finch to President S. Walter Martin, Emory University, Atlanta, Ga., March 9, 1961.
139 Integration File, "Southwestern's Current Policy Concerning Integration," April 1, 1960.
140. SU Trustees 1957–60, November 10, 1960, p. 289.
141. SU Trustees 1957–60, November 13, 1959, p. 204.
142. SU Trustees 1957–60, April 1, 1960, p. 258.
143. SU Trustees 1957–60, November 10, 1960, p. 296.
144. SU Trustees 1960–66, Ex. Com., February 14, 1961, pp. 28–29.
145. *Southwestern Reports*, "Construction Continues," February 1962, p. 1.
146. SU Trustees 1960–66, April 14, 1961, p. 38.
147. President's Report, October 19, 1970, p. 1-4.
148. Presidential Archives, Mary Moody Northen Files, September 29, 1959.
149. Northen Files, June 23, 1958.
150. Northen Files, November 24, 1958.
151. Northen Files, Finch to Moody Foundation, January 4, 1959.
152. Northen Files, February 17, 1959.
153. Northen Files, April 10, 1959.
154. Northen Files, October 2, 1959.
155. Northen Files, October 27, 1959.
156. Northen Files, October 31, 1959.
157. Northen Files, December 4, 1959.
158. Northen Files, December 13, 1959.
159. Northen Files, December 21, 1959.
160. Finch, Interviews by Allen, Tape 3, pp. 10–11.
161. SU Trustees 1957–60, November 13, 1959, p. 192.
162. SU Trustees 1957–60, December 12, 1959.
163. Northen Files, December 22, 1959.
164. Northen Files, Finch to Dan Moody, December 18, 1959.
165. Northen Files, November 16, 1960.
166. Northen Files, May 31, 1961.
167. Finch, Interviews by Allen, Tape 3, pp. 10–11.
168. Northen Files, June 30, 1961.
169. Wicke Files, Marjorie Beech to Wicke, November 13, 1958.
170. Wicke Files, April 1, 1959.
171. Wicke Files, Report of the Dean of the College of Arts and Sciences, April 1, 1959.
172. SU Trustees 1957–60, November 13, 1959. Ex. Com., August 11, 1959.
173. Finch, Interviews by Allen, Tape 3, p. 23.
174. SU Trustees 1957–60, November 13, 1959, p. 196.
175. Finch, Interviews by Allen, Tape 2, pp. 6–7.
176. Dean A&S Report, April 1, 1960, p. 6-3.
177. Ibid., p. 6-5.
178. SU Trustees 1957–60, April 1, 1960, p. 261.
179. SU Trustees 1960–66, November 10, 1960, p. 7.
180. Dean A&S Report, April 1, 1960, p. 6-4.
181. SU Trustees 1957–60, April 1, 1960, pp. 245–246.
182. Ibid., p. 244.
183. Dean A&S Report, April 1, 1960, p. 6-5.
184. Wicke Files, Southwestern Publicity Department announcement, June 16, 1960.
185. Faculty Minutes, May 12, 1960.
186. Faculty Minutes, November 8, 1960.
187. Wicke Files, Memorandum to the faculty on Curricular Revisions made by Committee on Academic Policy, November 14, 1960.
188. Wicke Files, Memo to the Faculty, January 7, 1961. Also, document from the Commission on Public Relations and Methodist Information, January 9, 1961.
189. Wicke Files, Publicity Dept., Southwestern, September 28, 1964.
190. Finch, Interviews by Allen, Tape 2, pp. 5–6.
191. Dean A&S Report, April 14, 1961, p. 6-3.
192. SU Trustees 1960–66, April 14, 1961, p. 35.
193. Ibid., p. 36.
194. Wicke Files, September 11, 1961.
195. RBSSB 1992–99.
196. Presidential Archives, Wm. C. Finch Files, September 11, 1961.
197. Norman W. Spellmann, *Growing a Soul: The Story of A. Frank Smith* (Dallas: SMU Press, 1979), p. 312.
198. Finch Files, Letter from Finch to John Berglund, February 3, 1961.
199. Faculty Minutes, February 3, 1961.

200. Finch Files, Finch memo to the faculty, February 15, 1961.
201. Finch Files, Letter to John D. Wheeler from Finch, February 15, 1961.
202. Dean of Men's Report, April 14, 1961, p. 11-1.
203. SU Trustees 1960–66, April 14, 1961, p. 36.
204. Spellmann, *Growing a Soul*, p. 313.
205. Ibid., pp. 313–314.
206. SU Trustees 1960–66, April 14, 1961, pp. 19–21.
207. Presidential Archives, Mrs. Alma Thomas Files, May 29, 1961.
208. Finch Files, telegram from Fleming to Finch, October 12, 1964.

CHAPTER XX
Southwestern during an Age of Social Unrest (1961–1981)

1. President's Report, October 10, 1969, p. 1-12.
2. William B. Jones, personal experience. Gene Jacob, owner of Gus's Pharmacy in Georgetown, states that Fleming bought sausage on more than one occasion. When Gene asked his father, Ben, why Fleming bought so much sausage, his father stated that it was to give to wealthy women in Houston.
3. Southwestern, Self-Study Report [1981], Appendix 4-e. Visit to Mrs. O'Hara narrated by Fleming to the author.
4. Presidential Archives, Jessie D. Ames Files, Fleming to Jessie D. Ames, September 1, 1964.
5. Ames Files, Jessie D. Ames to Fleming from Tryon, N.C., September 20, 1964.
6. Ames Files, Jessie D. Ames to "My dear Dr. Fleming," June 17, 1967.
7. Ames Files, Article, *Austin American-Statesman*, September 21, 1969.
8. PANC, Box 10, Folder 4, Letters of Neas to Lulu D. Ames of March 28 and April 4, 1962, Letters of Ames to Neas of April 2 and April 4.
9. Ames Files, Lulu Ames to "Dear Durwood," October 27, 1969.
10. Ames Files, Lulu Ames to "Dear Durwood," July 7, 1971.
11. Ames Files. Lulu Ames prepared a special printed brochure on February 24, 1973, in honor of her mother on the first anniversary of her death. She prefaced it with a short letter to the reader, followed by a copy of the service of worship from the church bulletin of February 24, 1972, with the full texts of the statements made by Durwood Fleming and Bob Breihan at the service.
12. Durwood Fleming, Interviews by Martha Allen, June 21–23, 1993, Tape 1, pp. 1–12.
13. *Ex-Students' Newsmagazine*, "Fleming Becomes Twelfth President of Southwestern University in Georgetown," June 1961, and Fleming, Interviews by Allen.
14. Fleming, Interviews by Allen, Tape 1, p. 17.
15. Ibid., Tape 1, p. 38.
16. Stephen Avery Katsurinis, "In His Own Words: Dr. Durwood Fleming on His Early Years at Southwestern University 1961–1962," November 15, 1987, no pagination.
17. Fleming, Interviews by Allen, Tape 1, p. 18.
18. Katsurinis, "In His Own Words," no pagination.
19. William B. Jones, "The First Year of the Flemings at Southwestern," November 8, 2002, no pagination.
20. Fleming, Interviews by Allen, Tape 4, pp. 20–21.
21. Katsurinis, "In His Own Words," no pagination.
22. Fleming, Interviews by Allen, Tape 1, p. 37.
23. Ibid.
24. Katsurinis, "In His Own Words," no pagination.
25. Fleming, Interviews by Allen, Tape 2, p. 23.
26. Ibid., Tape 1, pp. 25–26.
27. *The Megaphone*, Editorial Policy, October 6, 1976.
28. President's Report, October 10, 1969, p. 1-12.
29. President's Report, October 20, 1976, pp. 1-1/2.
30. Southwestern, 1981 Self-Study Report, p. 179.
31. Reported in personal conversation with author by Norman Peters. Confirmed by Farley Snell.
32. *Ex-Students' Newsmagazine*, "Fleming becomes twelfth president of Southwestern University in Georgetown," June 1961.
33. Walter N. Vernon, Robert W. Sledge, Robert C. Monk, and Norman W. Spellmann, *The Methodist Excitement in Texas* (Dallas: The Texas United Methodist Historical Society, 1984), p. 346. Quoted from *The Dallas Journal*, June 2, 1937.
34. Norman W. Spellmann, *Growing a Soul: The Story of A. Frank Smith* (Dallas: SMU Press, 1979), p. 360.
35. James McEnteer, *Fighting Words: Independent Journalists in Texas* (Austin: University of Texas Press, 1992), pp. 92–94.
36. Robert L. Wilson, "Methodism and Foreign Policy Since World War II."
37. Fleming, Interviews by Allen, Tape 1, p. 25.
38. Norman W. Spellmann, "The Role of Southwestern University Faculty in the Desegregation of Georgetown's Public Schools: 1962–65," January 20, 1997, p. 3.
39. Ibid.
40. Ibid., pp. 5–6.
41. Ibid., p. 7.
42. Ibid., pp. 7–8.
43. Ibid., pp. 9–10.
44. Ibid., p. 10.
45. Ibid., pp. 11–12.
46. The controversy and its tortuous path through the courts is documented in newspaper articles of the time.
47. Spellmann, "Faculty in Georgetown Desegregation," p. 14.
48. Report of Admin VP & Provost, "The Administration of President Durwood Fleming 1961–1981: A Summary," April 23, 1981, pp. 2-1 thru 2-8.
49. Presidential Archives, Integration File, before July 6, 1961.
50. Integration File, Renick to Wheeler, July 6, 1961.
51. Integration File, Wheeler to Renick, September 22, 1961.
52. Integration File, Renick to Fleming, October 25, 1961.
53. SU Trustees 1960–66, April 6, 1962, pp. 80–84.
54. Ibid.
55. Integration File, Letter of committee, April 3, 1962, Letter of Fleming in reply, April 12, 1962.
56. Integration File, Wray Weddell, Jr., "SU Chief Balks at Integration Query," *The Austin American*, ca. June 1, 1962.
57. Integration File, Wray Weddell, Jr., "No Segregation Policy at Southwestern," *The Austin American*, June 1, 1962, p. 29.
58. Integration File, Summary by I. J. McCook of discussion by the Special Committee to consider the integration question to be presented at the fall meeting of the Board, June 29, 1962.
59. Integration File, Report of the Special Committee to the Board of Trustees, October 31, 1962. Also, SU Trustees 1960–66, Special Committee on Integration, Appendix, p. 99, October 31, 1962.
60. Integration File, Response of the President to the Committee Report, October 31, 1962.
61. Integration File, September 17, 1963, Letter of Walter J. Ligon to Mary E. Fox given to Fleming November 6, 1963, Letter of Fleming to Walter J. Ligon.
62. Integration File, Letter of Fleming to Sharon Vance, September 20, 1963.
63. Integration File, Letter of Fleming to Wilton Woods and Lamar Hankins, January 20, 1964.
64. SU Trustees 1960–66, March 31, 1964, p. 164.
65. Integration File, Memorandum from Marjorie Beech to Fleming, July 23, 1964.
66. Integration File, personal and confidential to Dean F. Burr Clifford, August 10, 1964 (dictated August 7).
67. President's Report, October 18, 1965, p. 1-10.
68. Integration File, Letter from Mrs. Suzanne Barton Fisk, Dallas, Tex., to Fleming, April 25, 1966, Fleming reply to Mrs. Suzanne Barton Fisk, May 4, 1966.
69. Integration File, Letter from Clarence A. Laws, Deputy Regional Director, Office for Civil Rights, Dallas, Tex., April 16, 1969, Fleming's reply to Laws, May 23, 1969.
70. SU Trustees 1967–78, May 1, 1970, pp. 283–284; October 27, 1972, p. 32; October 26, 1973, p. 48.

71. President's Report, October 18, 1972, pp. 1-10/11.
72. President's Report, April 24, 1974, p. 1-11/12.
73. Report of Dean A&S, October 16, 1975, p. 3-3.
74. Report of VP Student Dev., October 20, 1976, p. 7-3.
75. Dean of Students' Report, January 23, 1975, p. 7-2.
76. Report of Dean A&S, April 2, 1954, p. 5-5. Chaplain's Report, April 15, 1976, pp. 8-1/2.
77. Chaplain's Report, April 22, 1967, p. 7-2.
78. Fleming, Interviews by Allen, Tape 4, pp. 26–27.
79. Faculty Minutes, February 16, 1965.
80. Chaplain's Report, October 12, 1967, p. 6-1.
81. Southwestern, Report of the President's Committee on Religion and Religious Life.
82. President's Report, April 28, 1971, p. 1-6. The Academic Program Survey Report recommended in 1975 that two positions, that of the Director of Social Internships and one in history, be eliminated. Blanton objected to his termination and claimed that he was protected under faculty tenure provisions. The Trustees voted to oppose his suit against the University for damages but ended up settling out of court because the likely cost of pursuing the matter would be much greater than a reasonable settlement would be.
83. Chaplain's Report, October 20, 1976, p. 8-1/2.
84. Southwestern, Report on the Department of Religion and Philosophy, p. 2.
85. Report of Dean A&S, April 20, 1978, p. 4-2.
86. SU Trustees 1960–66, January 31, 1963. Exec. Com. meeting, January 30, 1963, p. 127.
87. SU Trustees 1960–66, September 11, 1963. Exec. Com. meeting, August 7, 1963, p. 147.
88. Presidential Archives, Mary Moody Northen Files, Fleming to Northen, February 15, 1963.
89. Northen Files, Fleming to Northen, April 17, 1964.
90. Northen Files, Northen to Fleming, October 9, 1964.
91. Northen Files, Fleming to John Rose, September 6, 1966.
92. SU Trustees 1960–66, October 29, 1964, containing Annual Report [of President and Officers], p. 1-12.
93. SU Trustees 1960–66, November 9, 1961, p. 62.
94. President's Report, October 12, 1967, p. 1-9.
95. Report of VP Fiscal, October 12, 1967, p. 2-6.
96. President's Report, April 22, 1967, p. 1-10.
97. President's Report, January 24, 1968, p. 1-14.
98. Report of VP Fiscal, April 22, 1967, p. 2-2.
99. SU Trustees 1960–66, November 10, 1960, p. 8.
100. SU Trustees 1960–66, April 14, 1961, p. 38.
101. SU Trustees 1960–66, October 31, 1962, p. 105.
102. SU Trustees 1960–66, March 29, 1963, pp. 133–134.
103. President's Report, January 25, 1967, p. 1-4.
104. SU Trustees 1960–66, October 28, 1965, p. 202.
105. President's Report, May 3, 1967, Insert.
106. Ibid.
107. SU Trustees 1967–78, February 3, 1967, pp. 214–215.
108. President's Report, January 25, 1967, p. 1-9.
109. Presidential Archives, Memorandum: My Resignation (W. Graves Blanton).
110. SU Trustees 1967–78, May 10, 1968, p. 244.
111. SU Trustees 1967–78, February 3, 1967, p. 215.
112. SU Trustees 1960–66, President's Report, October 30, 1964, p. 1-12.
113. President's Report, October 20, 1976, p. 1-17.
114. Southwestern, *Southwestern University Catalogue 1978–1979* (Georgetown: 1978–79), p. 10.
115. SU Trustees 1935–47, November 25, 1941, p. 261.
116. President's Report, January 23, 1975, p. 1-9.
117. From personal experience of the author, who had an office and taught in the building.
118. Report of VP Fiscal, October 16, 1975, p. 2-4.
119. President's Report, January 20, 1977, p. 1-11.
120. President's Report, October 6, 1977, pp. 1-17/18.
121. SU Trustees 1967–78, Ex. Com. meeting, June 24, 1977, p. 112.
122. VP Fiscal Report, January 19, 1978, pp. 2-7/8.
123. SU Trustees 1967–78, January 28, 1977, p. 101, and Ex. Com. meeting, March 9, 1978, p. 203.
124. President's Report, April 20, 1978, p. 1-12.
125. VP Ed Services Report, April 20, 1978, p. 4-2.
126. President's Report, January 15, 1981, p. 1-6.
127. President's Report, January 19, 1979, p. 1-8.
128. Presidential Archives, George C. Hester Files, "Fire Destroys Sneed House," *The Bulletin of Southwestern University*, November 1978, p. 1.
129. S.A.C.S., Report of the Visiting Committee. "Two frame buildings, Sneed and guest house, which are used as residence halls for women students, are, contrary to the assertion on p. 181 of the Self-Study Report considered by a number of people not to be suitable for continued use. Fire hazard was felt to be a real problem with these structures" (p. 45).
130. SU Trustees 1978–85, Ex. Com. meeting, November 15, 1978, p. 18.
131. Presidential Archives, Kirk Treible 2 File, memo from KT to residents of Sneed House, October 30, 1978.
132. Report of VP Fiscal, April 19, 1979, p. 2-1.
133. SU Trustees 1978–85, January 26, 1979, pp. 26–27.
134. SU Trustees 1978–85, President's Report, January 19, 1979, p. 1-10.
135. SU Trustees 1978–85, Exec. Com. meeting, June 13, 1980, p. 121.
136. President's Report, October 10, 1980, p. 1-13.
137. Ibid.
138. SU Trustees 1978–85, Ex. Com. meeting, April 15, 1981, p. 151.
139. SU Trustees 1978–85, May 1, 1981, p. 155.
140. SU Trustees 1967–78, October 27, 1969, p. 270.
141. SU Trustees 1967–78, January 29, 1972, p. 14.
142. Even though the national Accounting Board did not mandate that annual audits report the market value of the endowment until 1996, Southwestern audits reported that figure in 1962 and every year thereafter. Earlier comparative records are unavailable, though the market value is often reported for dates that do not correspond with the time of the audit.

CHAPTER XXI
Internal Change and the Brown Challenge (1961–1981)

1. Faculty Minutes, December 4, 1962.
2. SU Trustees 1960–66, March 31, 1964, p. 162.
3. President's Report, January 24, 1968, p. 1-6.
4. Report of Admin VP & Provost, April 20, 1978, 3-5.
5. Report of Admin VP & Provost, January 19, 1978, p. 9-8.
6. President's Report, April 20, 1978, unnumbered page after 1-16. The average is actually for ten chairs, since the funds for the eleventh chair were held in trust by a bank. Its income was paid out each year to the University.
7. President's Report, October 18, 1966, 1-9/10.
8. President's Report, May 2, 1968, p. 1-13.
9. President's Report, October 10, 1969, p. 1-2.
10. Report of Dean A&S, October 18, 1966, pp. 4-1/2.
11. President's Report, October 15, 1968, p. 1-8.
12. Faculty Minutes, January 4, 1966.
13. SU Trustees 1960–66, February 3–4, 1966, pp. 194h–194i.
14. Faculty Minutes, February 4, 1969.
15. Faculty Minutes, September 9, 1969.
16. Faculty Minutes, September 16, 1969.
17. Report of Dean A&S, May 11, 1973, p. 5-3.
18. Report of Admin VP & Provost, October 20, 1976, pp. 2-5/6.
19. Faculty Minutes, January 16, 1968.
20. Faculty Minutes, August 30, 1975.
21. SU Trustees 1960–66, February 3–4, 1966, pp. 194i–194j.
22. Report of Dean A&S, October 12, 1967, p. 3-4.
23. Faculty Minutes, April 2, 1968.

24. President's Report, March 19, 1966, p. 1-7.
25. Faculty Minutes, March 1, 1966.
26. Report of Dean A&S, May 2, 1968, p. 3-2.
27. Faculty Minutes, May 9, 1967.
28. President's Report, October 12, 1967, pp. 1-9/10.
29. President's Report, January 24, 1968, p. 1-7.
30. College Entrance Examination Board, *College-Level Examination Program: Description and Uses, 1967* (1967).
31. Report of Dean A&S, October 15, 1968, p. 5-1.
32. Report of Admin VP & Provost, October 20, 1976, pp. 2-5/6.
33. SU Trustees 1967–78, October 27, 1969, p. 271.
34. Report of Dean A&S, October 19, 1973, pp. 5-3/4.
35. Report of Dean A&S, April 10, 1980, p. 2-1.
36. President's Report, October 17, 1974, p. 1-9.
37. Report of Dean A&S, April 15, 1976, p. 4-3.
38. President's Report, October 6, 1977, p. 1-13.
39. Southwestern, *Southwestern University Catalogue 1977–1978* (Georgetown: 1977–78), p. 47.
40. Report of Dean A&S, April 19, 1979, p. 3-2.
41. President's Report, January 19, 1979, p. 1-7.
42. President's Report, October 10, 1980, p. 1-16.
43. Southwestern, Self-Study Report (1971), p. 220.
44. President's Report, October 18, 1965, p. 1-6.
45. Raymond J. Seeger, "Science and Mathematics Program of Southwestern University," January 6, 1966, two public and one confidential parts. Clifford's response of four pages is attached to the original copy.
46. Seeger Report, January 26, 1966, p. 1-c.
47. Report of VP Fiscal, April 23, 1969, p. 2-2.
48. Harold Eidson, "Computing at Southwestern University," p. 1.
49. President's Report, January 15, 1981, p. 1-4.
50. President's Report, January 23, 1975, p. 1-6.
51. President's Report, January 24, 1969, pp. 1-6 thru 1-10.
52. President's Report, April 23, 1969, p. 1-11.
53. President's Report, October 19, 1970, p. 1-14.
54. Durwood Fleming, "Highlights of Southwestern University 1961–1972," 1972, Point #19.
55. S.A.C.S.S., Report of the Visiting Committee.
56. Faculty Minutes, April 3, 1973.
57. Southwestern, Report of the President's Planning Committee, pp. 9–10.
58. SACS, Report of the Visiting Committee, p. 8.
59. President's Report, January 23, 1975, pp. 1-8 thru 1-10.
60. Southwestern, Report to the President: Academic Program Survey Committee, Introduction.
61. Southwestern, Academic Program Survey Committee Report, Progress Report to faculty, March 1, 1976.
62. President's Report, October 16, 1975, separate four-page statement dated October 14, 1975, inserted after the President's Report.
63. SU Trustees 1960–66, April 6, 1962, p. 76.
64. President's Report, April 24, 1974, p. 1-5.
65. President's Report, October 6, 1977, p. 1-9.
66. President's Report, April 24, 1974, p. 1-8.
67. President's Report, January 23, 1976, pp. 1-3/4.
68. Ibid., pp. 1-4/5.
69. President's Report, April 15, 1976, p. 1-4.
70. Southwestern, 1971 Self-Study Report, p. 239.
71. Report of Admin VP & Provost, January 19, 1978, p. 2-5.
72. President's Report, April 17, 1979, p. 1-8.
73. President's Report, January 10, 1980, p. 1-11.
74. SU Trustees 1978–85, May 1, 1981, p. 155.
75. Presidential Archives, Mr. J. C. Fleming Estate File, February 24, 1967.
76. President's Report, January 15, 1981, p. 1-6.
77. President's Report, October 11, 1979, pp. 1-7 thru 1-14.
78. President's Report, October 19, 1973, p. 1-9.
79. SU Trustees 1978–85, May 1, 1981, p. 154.
80. President's Report, October 6, 1977, p. 1-15.
81. SACSS, 1961 Visiting Committee Report, p. 11.
82. President's Report, October 18, 1965, p. 1-10.
83. Dean of Students' Report, October 18, 1972, p. 7-2.
84. Report of VP Student Dev., April 21, 1977, p. 7-3.
85. President's Report, October 17, 1974, p. 1-10.
86. President's Report, September 16, 1971, p. 1-11.
87. President's Report, October 10, 1969, pp. 1-11/12.
88. Dean of Students' Report, April 28, 1971, p. 7-3.
89. Dean of Students' Report, May 5, 1972, p. 7-1.
90. Dean of Students' Report, April 24, 1974, p. 7-1/2.
91. Ibid.
92. Dean of Students' Report, May 11, 1973, p. 7-2.
93. SU Trustees 1967–78, April 12, 1973, p. 39.
94. President's Report, October 19, 1973, p. 1-5.
95. SU Trustees 1967–78, April 12, 1973, p. 39.
96. President's Report, October 16, 1975, p. 1-14.
97. President's Report, March 14, 1975, p. 1-8.
98. President's Report, January 19, 1979, p. 1-5.
99. Southwestern, Self-Study Report (1981), Appendix VII-k.
100. President's Report, January 19, 1979, p. 1-5.
101. SU Trustees 1978–85, September 28, 1979, p. 53.
102. President's Report, April 24, 1974, p. 1-13.
103. Dean of Students' Report, October 19, 1970, p. 7-3.
104. Dean of Students' Report, April 28, 1971, p. 7-2.
105. Report of VP Student Dev., April 21, 1977, p. 7-2.
106. Dean of Students' Report, October 15, 1968, p. 7-2.
107. Dean of Students' Report, October 10, 1969, p. 6-2.
108. Faculty Minutes, December 9, 1969, and January 26, 1970.
109. Faculty Minutes, February 9, 1970.
110. Dean of Students' Report, April 22, 1970, p. 6-2.
111. President's Report, April 28, 1971, p. 1-7.
112. Durwood Fleming, Interviews by Martha Allen, June 21–23, 1993, Tape 3, p. 7.
113. President's Report, April 28, 1971, p. 1-7.
114. Anonymous, "Dr. and Mrs. Suh Become Naturalized U.S. Citizens," *Williamson County Sun*, May 25, 1975.
115. Southwestern, 1981 Self-Study Report, Appendix V-i.
116. Ibid., Appendix V-I, Chart 5.4.
117. President's Report, October 19, 1970, pp. 1-2/3.
118. President's Report, October 19, 1973, p. 1-5.
119. SACSS, 1961 Visiting Committee Report, p. 10.
120. Southwestern, 1971 Self-Study Report, Appendix VI-c.
121. SACS, 1971 Visiting Committee Report, p. 33.
122. President's Report, October 16, 1975, pp. 1-7/8.
123. Report of Dean A&S, April 15, 1976, p. 4-2.
124. Report of Dean A&S, October 6, 1977, p. 4-2.
125. President's Report, January 19, 1978, p. 1-3.
126. SU Trustees 1967–78, October 14, 1977, p. 120.
127. SU Trustees 1960–66, March 31, 1964, p. 163.
128. President's Report, April 23, 1969, p. 1-4.
129. President's Report, January 20, 1971, p. 1-4.
130. SU Trustees 1967–78, January 30, 1970, p. 279.
131. SU Trustees 1967–78, May 1, 1970, p. 287.
132. Ibid., p. 280.
133. Southwestern, "Articles of Incorporation and Bylaws with Restated Articles of Incorporation, Southwestern University," January 29, 1971, with corrections as of February 19, 1971.
134. Personal experience of author.
135. Fleming, Interviews by Allen, Tape 1, p. 29.
136. Ibid., Tape 1, p. 32. Herman Brown to Finch, May 15, 1961.
137. Presidential Archives, Mr. Herman Brown File [1959–1962], Herman Brown to Finch, May 15 and May 31, 1961.
138. Fleming, Interviews by Allen. Fleming says that he was in New York when George called him and told him that Herman had died. He

came back immediately and held the funeral in St. Paul's Church with Al Freeman. Tape 1, p. 32.

139. Presidential Archives, Mrs. Herman Brown 1959–63 File, January 26, 1963.
140. Fleming, Interviews by Allen, Tape 3, pp. 10–11.
141. Ibid., Tape 3, p. 12.
142. SU Trustees 1960–66, September 11, 1963, pp. 145–146.
143. SU Trustees 1960–66, March 31, 1964, pp. 159–161.
144. President's Report, October 13, 1982, p. 1.
145. SU Trustees 1960–66, November 9, 1961, p. 61.
146. President's Report, January 26, 1966, pp. 1-3/4.
147. SU Trustees 1960–66, January 28, 1964, p. 153.
148. Report of Dean A&S, April 22, 1967, p. 4-2.
149. President's Report, January 24, 1969, pp. 1-10/11.
150. SU Trustees 1967–78, February 2, 1968, p. 237.
151. Fleming, Interviews by Allen, Tape 3, pp. 12–13.
152. SU Trustees 1967–78, May 3, 1967, p. 221.
153. President's Report, October 12, 1967, p. 1-12.
154. Presidential Archives, Brown Foundation 64-68 File, November 2, 1967.
155. Brown Foundation 64–68, April 4, 1968, draft of an announcement by Durwood Fleming.
156. Presidential Archives, Untitled Brown Foundation, Inc., File, June 15, 1976.
157. Report of VP Fiscal, May 2, 1968, p. 2-4.
158. SU Trustees 1967–78, May 10, 1968, p. 248.
159. SU Trustees 1967–78, July 17, 1968, p. 253.
160. President's Report, May 2, 1968, p. 1-7.
161. Report of Exec. VP, October 15, 1968, p. 4-1.
162. President's Report, April 23, 1969, p. 1-8.
163. SU Trustees 1967–78, May 2, 1969, p. 260.
164. Fleming referred to the use of the Dini & Associates firm by The Brown Foundation to construct the terms of the grant at a meeting on May 4, 1976 (see Presidential Archives, The Brown Foundation Grant '76 File), and William F. Murphy, Jr., Vice-President of Dini & Associates referred to it on May 5, 1976, in a letter to Fleming (see Presidential Archives, Dini, R. F., & Associates, Inc., File).
165. Southwestern, Special Report for the President: Office of Vice President for Fiscal Affairs, September 12, 1975, Schedule 1-5. Also, Southwestern, 1981 Self-Study Report, Appendix IV-d.
166. Report of VP Fiscal, January 23, 1976, p. 2-2.
167. Southwestern, Fiscal Affairs Report 1975, p. 10.
168. President's Report, January 20, 1972, p. 1-9.
169. President's Report, October 6, 1977, p. 1-20.
170. President's Report, January 18, 1974, p. 1-9.
171. President's Report, October 16, 1975, pp. 1-17/18.
172. President's Report, April 22, 1970, pp. 1-14/15.
173. President's Report, October 19, 1970, pp. 1-15/16.
174. SU Trustees 1967–78, October 27, 1970, p. 297.
175. President's Report, January 20, 1971, pp. 1-9/10.
176. SU Trustees 1967–78, May 6, 1971, pp. 1, 4.
177. President's Report, October 19, 1970, p. 1-9.
178. SU Trustees 1967–78, May 6, 1971, p. 4. An incident that temporarily caused a stir on campus occurred on October 25, 1973. On that date William T. P. Zader, a twenty-six-year-old development officer working under Mr. Peters, delivered a blistering five-page indictment of President Fleming's development work at a meeting of the Development Council and resigned his position. The next day Grogan Lord reported on the event to the Board of Trustees. Zader had already engaged in a newspaper tiff with Don Scarbrough, editor of the *WC Sun*, taking him to task for not including the lower-echelon administrative personnel when the *Sun* published pictures of the faculty and major administrative leaders of the University. The Trustees gave President Fleming a full vote of confidence after the report by Grogan Lord.
179. President's Report, April 24, 1974, p. 1-15.
180. SU Trustees 1967–78, May 3, 1974, p. 57. He later became President of his alma mater, Oklahoma City University.
181. President's Report, April 24, 1974, p. 1-10.
182. SU Trustees 1967–78, March 21, 1975, p. 71.
183. President's Report, October 19, 1973, p. 1-6.
184. SU Trustees 1967–78, January 25, 1974, p. 53.
185. President's Report, April 24, 1974, p. 1-16.
186. SU Trustees 1967–78, May 3, 1974, p. 58.
187. President's Report, March 14, 1975, p. 1-11.
188. President's Report, January 23, 1975, p. 1-8.
189. SU Trustees 1967–78, January 29, 1971, p. 299.
190. Report of Admin VP & Provost, October 20, 1976, pp. 2-5/6.
191. SU Trustees 1967–78, Exec. Com. meeting, October 10, 1975, p. 76.
192. SU Trustees 1967–78, October 24, 1975, p. 78.
193. Southwestern, 1981 Self-Study Report, Appendix IV-d.
194. President's Report, January 20, 1977, pp. 1–5.
195. SU Trustees 1967–78, Exec. Com. meeting, February 25, 1977, p. 104.
196. President's Report, October 6, 1977, p. 1-9.
197. Southwestern, 1981 Self-Study Report, p. 83.
198. SU Trustees 1967–78, Exec. Com. meeting of October 13, 1977, p. 115.
199. SU Trustees 1967–78, October 14, 1977, pp. 131–136.
200. President's Report, October 6, 1977, p. 1-18.
201. SU Trustees 1967–78, January 13, 1978, pp. 161–163.
202. Presidential Archives, Kirk Treible File, "Cost of Utilities" Schedule.
203. SU Trustees 1978–85, Exec. Com. meeting, September 29, 1978, pp. 1–2.
204. SU Trustees 1978–85, September 28, 1979, p. 53, and Exec. Com. meeting, October 3, 1980, p. 125.
205. Fleming, Interviews by Allen, Tape 3, pp. 12–15.
206. Joseph A. Pratt and Christopher J. Castaneda, *Builders: Herman and George R. Brown* (College Station: Texas A&M Press, 1999), p. 266.
207. President's Report, October 20, 1976, p. 1-15.
208. President's Report, January 20, 1977, pp. 1-6/7.
209. Southwestern, 1981 Self-Study Report, Appendix IV-c.
210. Ibid., p. 83, Table 4.1.
211. Presidential Archives, George C. Hester Files, "First Brown Symposium Great Success," *The Bulletin of Southwestern University*, November 1978, pp. 4–5.
212. SU Trustees 1967–78, January 13, 1978, Resolution 1, pp. 147–149.
213. Fleming, Interviews by Allen, Tape 4, p. 12.
214. President's Report, January 15, 1981, p. 1-7.
215. SU Trustees 1978–85, June 13, 1980, p. 124.
216. SU Trustees 1978–85, October 17, 1980, p. 132.
217. SU Trustees 1978–85, June 13, 1980, p. 124.
218. SU Trustees 1978–85, October 17, 1980, p. 129.
219. SU Trustees 1978–85, December 12, 1980, p. 142.
220. President's Report, April 23, 1981, p. 1-2.
221. Fleming, Interviews by Allen, Tape 4, pp. 12–13.

CHAPTER XXII

Master Plans and Financial Stability (1981–1990)

1. Linda Scarbrough, *Road, River, and Ol' Boy Politics: A Texas County's Path from Farm to Supersuburb* (Austin: Texas State Historical Association, 2005), p. 1.
2. *Southwestern Quarterly* 5, no. 2 (Winter 1994).
3. RBSSB 1982–92, September 3, 1983, and August 31, 1984.
4. RBSSB 1981–82, Tom Buckner, "Introducing SU's President," *The Sunday Sun*, July 26, 1981.
5. RBSSB 1982–92, Linda Scarbrough, "View from the Top," *WC Sun*, Sec. 2, p. 6, June 24, 1992.
6. RBSSB 1981–82, March 30, 1982.
7. SU Trustees 1978–85, Report of the Exec. Com., December 12, 1980, pp. 140–141.

8. RBSSB 1981–82, *Southwestern: The Bulletin of Southwestern University* 6, no. 1 (September 1981).
9. RBSSB 1981–82, original handwritten copy, also typescript, also published in *Southwestern: The Bulletin of Southwestern University* 5, no. 3 (February 1981).
10. RBSSB 1981–82, *Southwestern: The Bulletin of Southwestern University* 6, no. 1 (September 1981).
11. RBSSB 1981–82, "Interview with President Shilling," transcript of an interview conducted by "F", a non-SU reporter who refers to Shilling in the transcript as "S."
12. President's Report, April 5, 1991.
13. Ibid.
14. President's Report, April 15, 1994.
15. President's Report, October 8, 1981.
16. SACS, Report of the Reaffirmation Committee. Southwestern's response is attached at the end.
17. President's Report, April 15, 1982, p. 18.
18. SACS, 1982 Visiting Committee Report, pp. 1–47.
19. RBSSB 1992–99, February 1, 1999.
20. RBSSB 1981–82, July 20, 1981.
21. President's Report, January 14, 1982.
22. RBSSB 1981–82, "The Master Plan of Southwestern University: Adopted by the Faculty on April 6, 1982; Adopted by the Board of Trustees on April 23, 1982."
23. President's Report, April 19, 1986, pp. 15–47.
24. SU Trustees 1978–85, October 28, 1983, pp. 314–320.
25. William C. Finch, Interviews by Martha Allen, August 1992, Tape 3, pp. 11–12.
26. SU Trustees 1978–85, October 21, 1982, pp. 210–244.
27. SU Trustees 1978–85, Exec. Com. meeting, April 21, 1983, pp. 260–262.
28. SU Trustees 1978–85, October 16, 1981, p. 177.
29. Information culled from several Internet articles covering Skidmore, Owings & Merrill and Craig Hartman.
30. President's Report, September 20, 1991.
31. Craig W. Hartman, "A Sense of Place," in *Southwestern: A University's Transformation*, pp. 30–36.
32. Ibid., p. 35.
33. Ibid., p. 36.
34. Southwestern, Self-Study Report 1992, p. 157.
35. Board Minutes, January 17, 1986, p. 19.
36. Presidential Archives, Herbert E. and Kate Dishman Files, Letters of June 16, July 14, and August 19, 1982.
37. Dishman Files, thanked by Fleming on July 10, 1968.
38. Dishman Files, Mask Lisheron, "Man Discovers Inner Wealth Giving Can Give," *Beaumont Enterprise*, December 8, 1983.
39. RBSSB 1981–82, Remarks of Edward A. Clark, July 1, 1981.
40. President's Report, January 14, 1982.
41. Presidential Archives, Brown Foundation, Inc., 1970–84, File, Katherine Dobelman to RBS, December 9, 1981.
42. Presidential Archives, Threshold Campaign File, rough draft of explanation.
43. President's Report, April 22, 1983, p. 4.
44. Brown Foundation 1970–84, many articles from newspapers over the state.
45. Brown Foundation 1970–84, May 10, 1984, Letter of Jake Schrum to ten persons enclosing an advance copy of "this Sunday's *Texas Magazine* in *The Houston Chronicle* which features Southwestern University as the cover story."
46. RBSSB 1982–92, "Last Days at SU," *The Megaphone*, January 27, 1983, photograph of George Brown with Shilling in May, 1982.
47. President's Report, April 22, 1983.
48. SU Trustees 1978–85, April 22, 1983, p. 267.
49. Brown Foundation 1970–84, April 27, 1984.
50. Brown Foundation 1970–84, Letters from John Duncan (September 12, 1984) to Jake Schrum and from Schrum (September 17, 1984) back to Duncan.
51. President's Report, October 13, 1982, p. 21.
52. RBSSB 1982–92, Terry Goodrich, "Southwestern Raises Money at Good Price," *Austin American-Statesman*, December 31, 1981, p. B3.
53. President's Report, October 28, 1983, pp. 1–2.
54. Presidential Archives, Dini, R. F., & Associates, Inc., File, October 19, 1983, Dini letter to Shilling.
55. SU Trustees 1978–85, January 22, 1982, pp. 182–187.
56. President's Report, October 19, 1970, pp. 1-9 and 8-1.
57. A model making this calculation, beginning with the $37,914,778 endowment in 1981 and incremented annually by 12 percent, plus the annual gifts from The Brown Foundation also incremented by 12 percent annually, resulted in a final theoretical endowment of $126,105,949, a difference of only $566,573 from the actual endowment of $126,672,522 in 1990.
58. Red McCombs, *The Red Zone, Cars, Cows, and Coaches: The Life and Good Times of a Texas Dealmaker* (Austin: Eakin Press, 2002), p. viii.
59. *The Sou'wester,* 1986, p. 30.
60. Bert Ely, "Savings and Loan Crisis," ©1993, 2002 David R. Henderson, all rights reserved.
61. McCombs, *Red Zone*, p. 71.
62. Ibid., p. 172.
63. President's Report, April 22, 1983.
64. President's Report, October 17, 1986.
65. Board Exec. Com. Minutes, September 25, 1992, p. 13.
66. RBSSB 1982–92, Letter from Ruth B. King, Conway, Ark., to RBS, February 7, 1987.
67. SU Trustees 1978–85, Exec. Com., April 21, 1983, pp. 260–262.
68. SU Trustees 1978–85, October 28, 1983, pp. 293–322.
69. RBSSB 1982–92, Southwestern [Bulletin], November 21, 1985.
70. Board Minutes, January 17, 1986, pp. 17–18.
71. President's Report, April 22, 1988, p. 15.
72. RBSSB 1981–82, RBS memo to Treible entitled "Condition of the Campus," July 12, 1982.
73. SU Trustees 1978–85, April 22, 1983, p. 265.
74. Board Minutes, January 17, 1986.
75. Board Minutes, October 25, 1989.
76. RBSSB 1982–92, "SU Granted $5 Million," *The Megaphone*, September 2, 1982.
77. President's Report, October 28, 1983.
78. SU Trustees 1978–85, Minutes, January 21, 1983, pp. 245–259.
79. Personal recollection by Francie Schroeder and Wm. B. Jones.
80. SU Trustees 1978–85, Minutes Exec. Com., August 11, 1983, pp. 290–292.
81. Board Exec. Com. Minutes, August 26, 1985.
82. SU Trustees 1978–85, Minutes, October 28, 1983, pp. 293–322.
83. SU Trustees 1978–85, Minutes Exec. Com., March 14, 1984, p. 326.
84. Board Minutes, January 18, 1985, p. 4.
85. President's Report, January 16, 1987, p. 15.
86. Southwestern, 1992 Self-Study Report, p. 81.
87. President's Report, February 17, 1956, and July 29, 1957.
88. SU Trustees 1953–57, April 13, 1956, p. 179.
89. President's Report, January 19, 1978, p. 1-7.
90. Southwestern, Self-Study Report [1981], Appendix IV-n.
91. Southwestern, 1992 Self-Study Report, p. 59.
92. Though often shortened to "Jake," Schrum's legal name is "Jakie."
93. SU Trustees 1978–85, October 21, 1982, p. 221.
94. Roy B. Shilling, Jr., "Random Thoughts," Georgetown, January 5, 2005.
95. RBSSB 1982–92, cartoon from "The Far Side" for Saturday, January 14, 1986.
96. RBSSB 1982–92.
97. SU Trustees 1978–85, Minutes, April 27, 1984, p. 331.
98. Board Minutes, January 17, 1986, pp. 19, 24.
99. President's Report, October 17, 1986, p. 21.
100. *Southwestern Quarterly* 1, no. 1 (Fall 1989): 17.
101. President's Report, April 10, 1997.
102. Southwestern, 1992 Self-Study Report, pp. 37–40.
103. RBSSB 1982–92, "Finding the Keys to Success; University Stresses

Computer Literacy in Learning," *Dallas Times Herald*, December 1, 1985, p. 41.
104. Faculty Minutes, April 4, 18, and 25, 1989.
105. President's Report, with "A Report on the Business Program at Southwestern University," prepared by the joint Trustee/faculty committee, April 19, 1985.
106. Southwestern, 1992 Self-Study Report, Appendix 7.
107. President's Report, January 14, 1982, p. 7.
108. Faculty Minutes, September 27, 1983.
109. President's Report, April 22, 1988, p. 13.
110. President's Report, January 14, 1982, p. 3.
111. President's Report, January 10, 1983, p. 10.
112. Southwestern, 1992 Self-Study Report, Appendix 10, p. 225.
113. RBSSB 1982–92, Anne Friou, "Dr. Roy B. Shilling, Jr."
114. RBSSB 1982–92, President's Report, January 29, 1988, p. 32.
115. President's Report, January 14, 1982, p. 8.
116. President's Report, January 10, 1983, p. 9.
117. President's Report, January 17, 1986, p. 11.
118. President's Report, January 16, 1987, p. 13.
119. President's Report, April 22, 1988, p. 9.
120. President's Report, October 13, 1988, p. 18.
121. Ibid., p. 17.
122. President's Report, February 9, 1990, p. 19.
123. RBSSB 1982–92, Shilling Scrapbook 1982–1992, Sive Vaidhyanathan, "Less = More: Southwestern Marks 150th as Small School with Future," *Austin American-Statesman*, February 5, 1990.
124. RBSSB 1981–82, Finch to RBS, July 11, 1981.
125. SU Trustees 1978–85, Minutes, January 18, 1985, p. 384.
126. RBSSB 1982–92, Letter of James E. Kirby, Dean, Perkins School of Theology, SMU, to RBS, December 18, 1986.
127. Shilling Scrapbook 1982–1992, Monty Jones, "UT's Flawn Listed as Top Leader with Shilling of Southwestern," *Austin American-Statesman*, October 28, 1986, p. B3.
128. RBSSB 1982–92, "Survey Includes Southwestern's President Shilling among Top 100 Presidents," *Southwestern University News*, November 3, 1986.
129. RBSSB 1982–92, Monty Jones, "Southwestern President May Help Shape Education," *Austin American-Statesman*, February 19, 1989.
130. RBSSB 1982–92, Anne Friou, "Dr. Roy B. Shilling, Jr.," Fall 1989.
131. RBSSB 1982–92, "Southwestern Ranked as Top-Notch University," *Austin American-Statesman*, December 5, 1983, p. B3.
132. RBSSB 1982–92, "Marks of Distinction," *U.S. News & World Report*, October 10, 1988, pp. C22 ff.
133. SU Trustees 1978–85, January 18, 1985, pp. 382–444.
134. President's Report, October 4, 1985.
135. RBSSB 1982–92, Raquel Roberts, "Southwestern University: Texas' Best-Kept Secret: State's Oldest College Gains Recognition with Outstanding Academic Credentials, Aggressive Recruiting," *The Houston Post*, October 25, 1987, Section G.
136. President's Report, January 29, 1988.
137. Board Minutes, January 17, 1986, p. 5.
138. RBSSB 1982–92, Ken Hammond, "Small School, Big Bucks," *Texas: Houston Chronicle Magazine*, May 13, 1984.
139. President's Report, October 4, 1985, p. 13.
140. Board Minutes, January 16, 1987, p. 5.
141. President's Report, April 22, 1988, p. 14.
142. Faculty Minutes, September 22, 1987.
143. RBSSB 1981–82, "Inaugural Dinner Speech," April 22, 1982.
144. Thomas J. Kolodziejski, Jr., "Why 21?"
145. Board Minutes, April 19, 1985, p. 4.
146. President's Report, April 21, 1987, p. 9.
147. *Sou'wester*, 1987. About p. 44.
148. President's Report, February 1, 1991, p. 22.
149. SU Trustees 1978–85, October 16, 1981, p. 175.
150. President's Report, April 27, 1984, p. 4.
151. Faculty Minutes, March 15, 1988.
152. SU Trustees 1978–85, Exec. Com. meeting, April 13, 1982, p. 189.
153. SU Trustees 1978–85, Exec. Com. Minutes, December 7, 1981, p. 181.
154. President's Report, January 10, 1983, pp. 14–15.
155. President's Report, January 17, 1986, p. 12.
156. Board Minutes, January 17, 1986, p. 21.
157. President's Report, October 13, 1988, p. 13.
158. President's Report, April 21, 1987, p. 11.
159. President's Report, January 16, 1987, p. 16, and October, 1987, p. 15.
160. President's Report, October 4, 1985, p. 11.

CHAPTER XXIII
Becoming a National Liberal Arts Institution (1990–2000)

1. President's Report, January 29, 1988, Attachment A, pp. 11, 17.
2. President's Report, April 5–6, 1989, p. 13.
3. Faculty Minutes, October 3, 1989.
4. President's Report, September 20, 1991, pp. 34–35.
5. President's Report, October, 1987, p. 16.
6. President's Report, September 20, 1991, p. 36.
7. Ibid., p. 37.
8. SU Trustees 1960–66, Exec. Com., February 14, 1961, p. 29.
9. "Mallon: 1,000 Wins!," *Southwestern Quarterly* 10, no. 1 (1999): 41.
10. *Southwestern Quarterly* 1, no. 3 (Spring 1990): 12.
11. Faculty Minutes, January 12, 1982.
12. President's Report, January 14, 1982, p. 11.
13. SU Trustees 1978–85, January 22, 1982, pp. 182–187.
14. President's Report, April 15, 1982, p. 19.
15. President's Report, October 28, 1983, pp. 4–5.
16. Faculty Minutes, December 13, 1983.
17. Faculty Minutes, January 23, 1984.
18. Faculty Minutes, November 28, 1989.
19. Faculty Minutes, December 12, 1989.
20. Faculty Minutes, January 16, 1990.
21. Faculty Minutes, January 23, 1990.
22. Board Exec. Com. Minutes, January 25, 1990, pp. 21–22.
23. President's Report, February 9, 1990, p. 11.
24. Board Minutes, February 9, 1990, pp. 5–6.
25. RBSSB 1982–92, Randy Riggs, "Southwestern Drops Athletic Scholarships," *Austin American-Statesman*, February 10, 1990.
26. Presidential Archives, McCombs Files, Dan Calderon, "McCombses Give $2 Million," *San Antonio Express-News*, October 27, 1999, p. 11B.
27. Faculty Minutes, February 27, 1990.
28. President's Report, November 4, 1993, p. 17.
29. Faculty Minutes, October 20, 1992.
30. Faculty Minutes, November 16, 1993.
31. RBSSB 1992–99, Letter from Joe Seeber, August 23, 1996, enclosing article from *USA Today*, August 21, 1996, entitled "Money at the Heart of the Matter: Expenses Prompt Schools' Defections to NCAA Division III."
32. President's Report, April 15, 1994, p. 28.
33. President's Report, April 10, 1997, pp. 75–76.
34. President's Report, October 16, 1998, p. 53.
35. President's Report, February 9, 1990, p. 17.
36. Faculty Minutes, April 5, 1990.
37. Board Minutes, April 6, 1990, p. 9.
38. Faculty Minutes, February 19, 1991.
39. President's Report, April 2–3, 1992, p. 24.
40. Board Minutes, November 2, 1995, p. 9.
41. Board Minutes, January 18, 1996, pp. 19, 42.
42. Board Minutes, March 28, 1996, p. 15.
43. Faculty Minutes, April 23, 1996.
44. Board Minutes, August 15, 1996, pp. 21–31.
45. Board Minutes, November 8, 1996, p. 9.
46. Faculty Minutes, January 21, 1997.

47. Board Minutes, September 12, 1997, p. 33.
48. Eric Van Danen, "Campus Alcohol Policy, Arrest Stir Debate," *Southwestern Quarterly* 10, no. 1 (1999): 30–31.
49. President's Report, Oct. 16, 1998, pp. 53-54.
50. Faculty Minutes, October 15, 1991.
51. President's Report, October 16, 1998, p. 54.
52. *Southwestern Quarterly* 4, no. 1 (Fall 1992): 2–3.
53. President's Report, November 10, 1994, p. 43.
54. Board Minutes, January 18, 1996, p. 42.
55. President's Report, March 27, 1998, p. 70.
56. *The Sou'wester,* Year 2000, p. 25.
57. Report of Exec. VP, March 31, 2000, pp. 42–43.
58. Board Minutes, September 25, 1992, p. 68.
59. President's Report, April 5–6, 1990, pp. 14–16.
60. President's Report, March 26, 1999, pp. 55–56.
61. Faculty Minutes, January 18, 1994.
62. Board Minutes, September 12, 1997, pp. 28, 39–41.
63. President's Report, March 27, 1998, p. 84.
64. *Southwestern Quarterly* 10, no. 2 (1999): 33.
65. Faculty Minutes, September 21, 1999.
66. Faculty Minutes, January 21, 1997.
67. President's Report, April 10, 1997, p. 51.
68. President's Report, November 14, 1997, p. 69.
69. Faculty Minutes, November 28, 1995.
70. Faculty Minutes, April 21, 1998.
71. Faculty Minutes, September 16, 1997.
72. Report of Exec. VP, March 31, 2000.
73. Faculty Minutes, November 19, 1996.
74. *Southwestern Quarterly* 10, no. 1 (1999): 32–33.
75. President's Report, October 5, 1990, and September 20, 1991, pp. 21, 39.
76. Board Minutes, January 18, 1996, p. 41.
77. Faculty Minutes, September 16, 1997.
78. Presidential Archives, Brown Foundation, Inc., 1985–89, File, RBS to Dobelman, May 12, 1989.
79. President's Report, October 16, 1998, p. 50.
80. Faculty Minutes, August 21, 1998.
81. Faculty Minutes, April 29, 1999.
82. President's Report, October 16, 1998, p. 50.
83. Faculty Minutes, April 25, 2000.
84. Report of Exec. VP and COO, December 10, 1999, p. 52.
85. President's Report, March 26, 1999, pp. 72–75.
86. President's Report, October 13, 1988.
87. President's Report, November 4, 1993, p. 13.
88. Ibid., p. 41.
89. *Southwestern Quarterly* 5, no. 1 (Fall 1993): 2–4.
90. *Southwestern Quarterly* 4, no. 3 (Spring 1993): 13.
91. Phi Beta Kappa, "The Phi Beta Kappa Society: How to Apply for a Chapter."
92. Faculty Minutes, April 15, 1986.
93. President's Report, April 1, 1993.
94. Faculty Minutes, December 7, 1993.
95. President's Report, April 28, 1995.
96. *Southwestern Quarterly* 6, no. 1 (Fall 1994): 3.
97. President's Report, April 15, 1994, p. 19.
98. President's Report, April 28, 1995, p. 6.
99. The Carnegie Foundation for the Advancement of Teaching, "The Carnegie Classification of Institutions of Higher Education."
100. President's Report, February 1, 1991.
101. Faculty Minutes, November 16, 1993.
102. Faculty Minutes, December 7, 1993.
103. *Southwestern Quarterly* 5, no. 3 (Spring 1994): 3.
104. Roy B. Shilling, Jr., "Random Thoughts," Georgetown, January 5, 2005.
105. David Medley, Interview by WBJ, Georgetown, September 23, 2004.
106. Red McCombs, *The Red Zone, Cars, Cows, and Coaches: The Life and Good Times of a Texas Dealmaker* (Austin: Eakin Press, 2002), pp. 213–214.
107. "Leadership with a Passion and a Purpose," *Southwestern Quarterly* 8, no. 4 (Summer 1997): 6.
108. McCombs Files, RBS to Charline McCombs, October 22, 1998.
109. McCombs Files, Memo to Exec. Com., October 11, 1999.
110. Dionne Walker, "Who Is F. W. Olin?," prism online: exploring the future of engineering education.
111. RBSSB 1992–99, Starita Smith, "Southwestern Gets $6.5 Million Grant," *Austin American-Statesman,* September 7, 1994, Sec. B.
112. Board Minutes, October 5, 1990, p. 9.
113. President's Report, November 4, 1993.
114. Minutes of the Exec. Com. and Campaign Steering Com., June 13, 1994, p. 14.
115. Faculty Minutes, March 19, 1996.
116. President's Report, November 10, 1994, pp. 37–39.
117. RBSSB 1992–99, Smith, "Southwestern Gets $6.5 Million Grant."
118. President's Report, April 28, 1995, p. 21.
119. McCombs Files, Letter from Red to Larry Milas, November 15, 1996.
120. RBSSB 1992–99, handwritten letter from Larry Milas to RBS, March 10, 1997.
121. McCombs Files, Letter to McCombs from Larry Milas, December 30, 1997.
122. Minutes of the Exec. Com. and Campaign Steering Com., June 13, 1994, p. 14.
123. Board Minutes, December 6, 1991, pp. 9–10.
124. Board Minutes, January 18, 1996, p. 38.
125. Board Minutes, October 18, 1994.
126. *Southwestern Quarterly* 6, no. 3 (Spring 1995): 2.
127. Board Minutes, October 16, 1998, p. 9.
128. Board Minutes, May 1, 1981, p. 155.
129. President's Report, October 5, 1990, p. 31.
130. President's Report, February 1, 1991, p. 21.
131. Faculty Minutes, February 27, 1996.
132. President's Report, April 10, 1997, p. 52.
133. Faculty Minutes, February 2, 1999.
134. Board Minutes, February 5, 1999, p. 20, and President's Report, March 26, 1999, p. 52.
135. Faculty Minutes, March 23, 1999.
136. *Southwestern Quarterly* 10, no. 2 (1999): 31.
137. President's Report, October 13, 1988, p. 12.
138. President's Report, October 5, 1990, p. 21.
139. Faculty Minutes, December 20, 1994.
140. Board Minutes, January 24, 1997, p. 23.
141. Faculty Minutes, March 25, 1997.
142. President's Report, March 27, 1998, pp. 76–77.
143. President's Report, April 1, 1993, p. 34.
144. President's Report, February 5, 1999, p. 45.
145. Board Minutes, September 12, 1997, pp. 30–31.
146. President's Report, March 27, 1998, pp. 61–62.
147. Board Minutes, September 16, 1998, p. 19.
148. President's Report, October 5, 1990, p. 22, and February 1, 1991, p. 22.
149. President's Report, April 15, 1994, p. 36.
150. President's Report, November 4, 1993, p. 26.
151. Board Minutes, January 18, 1996, p. 71.
152. Dan Yoxall, "McCombs Campus Center Dedicated," *Southwestern Quarterly* 10, no. 1 (1999): 18.
153. Board Minutes, September 16, 1998, p. 16.
154. Yoxall, "McCombs Campus Center Dedicated," *Southwestern Quarterly* 10, no. 1 (1999): 18.
155. "Alumni and Friends Make Historic Campaign a Reality," *Southwestern Quarterly* 10, no. 1 (1999): 6.
156. Board Minutes, February 5, 1999, p. 20.

157. Ibid., pp. 44–45.
158. Dan Yoxall, "Philanthropy: Surprise! $15 Million for Scholarships," *Southwestern Quarterly* 10, no. 1 (1999): 17.
159. President's Report, April 28, 1995, p. 28.
160. Board Minutes, August 15, 1996, p. 22.
161. Joseph A. Pratt and Christopher J. Castaneda, *Builders: Herman and George R. Brown* (College Station: Texas A&M Press, 1999), p. 166. Richard Anderson supplies the Southwestern figure. Pratt and Castaneda supply the Brown contribution. Their figure is slightly lower that than of Anderson, who carries a figure of $28,209,623 for the Brown contribution.
162. Board Minutes, January 18, 1996, p. 35.
163. President's Report, November 8, 1996, p. 40.
164. Presidential Archives, Brown Foundation, Inc., 1993–94, File, Louisa Stude Sarofim letter to RBS, September 20, 1993.
165. Presidential Archives, Brown Foundation, Inc., 1995–96, File, Louisa Stude Sarofim letter to RBS, June 12, 1995.
166. Presidential Archives, Brown Foundation, Inc., 1997–99, File, RBS to Dobelman, May 30, 1997.
167. Brown Foundation 1997–99, M. S. Stude to Eason, June 17, 1998.
168. Brown Foundation 1995–96, Shilling to Dobelman, February 15, 1996.
169. Brown Foundation 1997–99, RBS to Mrs. Isabel Brown Wilson, April 27, 1999, and Maconda Brown O'Connor, Ph.D., to RBS, May 19, 1999.
170. Pratt and Castaneda, *Builders*, p. 266.
171. President's Report, November 4, 1993, p. 15.
172. Faculty Minutes, September 21, 1999.
173. President's Report, January 29, 1988, p. 33.
174. President's Report, September 20, 1991.
175. Report of Exec. VP and COO, March 31, 2000, p. 46.
176. President's Report, April 5, 1991, p. 13.
177. Report of Exec. VP and COO, December 10, 1999.
178. Faculty Minutes, September 21, 1999.
179. *Southwestern Quarterly* 4, no. 3 (Spring 1993): 7.
180. Nancy Pagliarini, "Scraping Down to the Original Paint," *Southwestern Quarterly* 5, no. 3 (Spring 1994): 4–5.
181. President's Report, October 13, 1988, p. 20.
182. *Southwestern Quarterly* 2, no. 3 (Spring 1991): 3.
183. Presidential Archives, Gregory Washington File.
184. President's Report, November 4, 1993, p. 17.
185. Faculty Minutes, August 26, 1994.
186. President's Report, November 8, 1996, pp. 46–48.
187. President's Report, October 4, 1985, p. 12.
188. RBSSB 1982–92, "Roy Shilling," *Austin Business Journal*, March 26–April 1, 1990.
189. Doug Laycock, "*Hopwood v. Texas:* Timeline of Events" (http://www.law.utexas.edu/hopwood).
190. McCombs Files, memorandum from Richard Anderson to nine persons with attachment entitled "Agreement Establishing the Texas Methodist Foundation Scholarship Program for Minority Students Enrolling in Southwestern University," December 18, 1998.
191. President's Report, March 26, 1999, p. 11.
192. Board Minutes, March 31, 2000.
193. William C. Finch, Interviews by Martha Allen, August 1992, Tape 2, p. 2.
194. RBSSB 1982–92, Linda Scarbrough, "View from the Top," *WC Sun*, June 24, 1992, Sec. 2, p. 6.
195. RBSSB 1992–99, Letter from Richard Oppel, editor of the *Austin American-Statesman*, to RBS, March 11, 1997. The author remembers this meeting clearly, as he was in attendance.
196. RBSSB 1981–82, *Southwestern: The Bulletin of Southwestern University* 6, no. 1 (September 1981).
197. President's Report, November 4, 1993, p. 14.
198. Robin Suro, "Separation Anxiety," *Southwestern Quarterly* 3, no. 3 (Spring 1992), reprint from *The New York Times*, April 5, 1992.
199. RBSSB 1982–92, "Sharon Hogan, "Shilling Gives Industry Hunt New Twist," *The Sunday Sun*, February 7, 1988.
200. RBSSB 1982–92, Ken Martin, "Education: Southwestern's New Face," *The Sunday Sun*, June 25, 1989, Sec. 2, p. 7.
201. Ibid.
202. Carrie Johnson, "A Decade of Enrichment: Operation Achievement Turns 10," *Southwestern Quarterly* 9, no. 2 (1998): 10–11.
203. RBSSB 1982–92, *The Sunday Sun*, June 25, 1989, Sec. 2, p. 7.
204. RBSSB 1982–92, Linda Scarbrough, "View from the Top," *WC Sun*, June 24, 1992, Sec. 2, p. 6.
205. President's Report, February 9, 1990, p. 18.
206. Dan Yoxall and Ken Williams, "Reaching Out Together," *Southwestern Quarterly* 1, no. 4 (Summer 1990): 2–5.
207. McCombs Files, RBS to Red McCombs, June 2, 1999.
208. Presidential Archives, Global Leadership and Kosovo Files, notes of WBJ on Global Leadership Initiative meeting, August 23, 1999.
209. Kosovo Files, email from Eric Van Danen to faculty, staff, and students, April 16, 1999.
210. Faculty Minutes, April 29, 1999.
211. Kosovo Files, email from Susan Harper to members of the Advisory Committee, April 27, 1999.
212. Kosovo Files, email from Beverly Jones to students, staff, and faculty, May 4, 1999.
213. Kosovo Files, memorandum from RBS to National Liberal Arts College Presidents advising them of the Global Leadership Initiative, April 19, 1999.
214. Kosovo Files, "Global Leadership Initiative: Report on Kosovo Project and Plans for the Future," November 30, 1999.
215. Dan Yoxall, "Alumnus First to Volunteer in SU Balkan Relief Effort," *Southwestern Quarterly* 10, no. 2 (1999): 5.
216. Faculty Minutes, April 29, 1999.
217. Kosovo Files, email announcement to faculty, students, and staff from Molitorisz, September 21, 1999.
218. Kosovo Files, Global Leadership Initiative Update, July 5, 1999.
219. Board Minutes, September 12, 1997, pp. 55–59.
220. Board Minutes, November 14, 1997, p. 9.
221. Faculty Minutes, November 18, 1997.
222. McCombs Files, Letter from Red to Larry Milas, January 6, 1998.
223. Board Minutes, January 30, 1998, p. 19.
224. McCombs Files, draft of a proposal to Michael Dell written for Red McCombs to send him, January 12, 1999.
225. Personal communication from RBS to WBJ.
226. Faculty Minutes, April 23, 1996.
227. Board Minutes, January 18, 1996, p. 40.
228. McCombs Files, March 9, 1995, information from Francie Schroeder, Admin. Asst. to the President.
229. President's Report, April 28, 1995, p. 16–18.
230. President's Report, April 10, 1997, p. 47.
231. President's Report, November 14, 1997, p. 64.
232. Faculty Minutes, September 16, 1997.
233. Faculty Minutes, November 18, 1997.
234. President's Report, March 27, 1998, p. 63.
235. Board Minutes, March 27, 1998, p. 6.
236. Carrie Johnson, "What Does Southwestern Stand For?" *Southwestern Quarterly* 10, No. 1 (1999): 20–21.
237. Board Minutes, September 16, 1998, p. 15.
238. Faculty Minutes, February 22, 2000.
239. Board Minutes, March 31, 2000, pp. 12, 17.
240. President's Report, March 26, 1999, p. 16.
241. Board Minutes, November 2, 1995, p. 9.
242. Faculty Minutes, April 29, 1999.
243 Faculty Minutes, October 19, 1999.
244. Faculty Minutes, April 1, 1986. Also, Board Minutes, April, 1987, p. 6.
245. Faculty Minutes, April 19, 1988.
246. Faculty Minutes, "Proposal for a Women's Studies Major and Minor," March 28, 1989.

247. Faculty Minutes, December 1, 1989.
248. Faculty Minutes, February 27, 1990.
249. President's Report, April 5–6, 1990, p. 15.
250. *Southwestern Quarterly* 1, no. 4 (Summer 1990): 41.
251. Faculty Minutes, March 19, 1991.
252. Faculty Minutes, March 17, 1992.
253. Board Minutes, September 25 and October 30, 1992, pp. 8 and 11.
254. Faculty Minutes, March 16, 1993.
255. Board Minutes, November 4, 1993, p. 11.
256. Faculty Minutes, March 21, 1995.
257. Faculty Minutes, October 26, 1999.
258. Board Minutes, December 10, 1999, p. 9.
259. Faculty Minutes, March 7 and April 4, 2000.
260. Faculty Minutes, April 25, 2000.
261. Lacy Klosterman, "Nondiscrimination Policy Passed by Schrum," *The Megaphone*, December 7, 2000, p. 1.
262. McCombs Files, RBS to McCombs, February 16, 1999.
263. McCombs Files, McCombs letter to Sarofim, March 29, 1999.
264. McCombs Files, Letter to McCombs from Eason, May 13, 1999.
265. Board Minutes, December 10, 1999, p. 8.
266. RBSSB 1992–99, David Hafetz, "Donor Adds $8 Million to Long List of Gifts to Southwestern," *Austin American-Statesman*, December 11, 1999.
267. Board Minutes, December 10, 1999, p. 13.
268. Report of Exec. VP, March 31, 2000, p. 47.
269. Board Minutes, December 10, 1999, p. 9.
270. Board Minutes, January 10, 2000, p. 24.

Page numbers followed by f indicate figures

About the Author

Photo by Taylor Jones

WILLIAM BURWELL JONES came to Southwestern University in 1965 as the Lucy King Brown Professor of History. He retired in 2000 as Executive Vice President and Chief Operating Officer of the University after having served at various times as Chair of the History Department, Director of the International Studies Program, Director of Institutional Research, Administrative Vice President, and Provost. His honors include the Outstanding Professor Award bestowed by the Southwestern University Students' Association.

Dr. Jones received a B.A. from Millsaps College, a B.D. from Emory University, and a Ph.D. from Vanderbilt University. He is the former director of the Sweet Memorial Training School for Christian Workers in Santiago, Chile, where he and his wife, Carol, taught for five years. He has lectured at a number of professional meetings, and his articles and book reviews have appeared in scholarly journals in the United States, Canada, Spain, and Argentina. He also has translated into English a 1529 work by Juan de Valdés that completes the corpus of that important Reformation figure.

In spite of his training as a European and Latin American historian, Jones has always enjoyed exploring the history around him. In *To Survive and Excel: The Story of Southwestern University, 1840–2000* he has turned his attention to the history of the institution where he worked for 35 years.